RULERS OF BABYLONIA FROM THE SECOND DYNASTY OF ISIN TO THE END OF ASSYRIAN DOMINATION

(1157–612 BC)

THE ROYAL INSCRIPTIONS OF MESOPOTAMIA

Volumes Published

ASSYRIAN PERIODS

1 Assyrian Rulers of the Third and Second Millennia BC (TO 1115 BC)
A. KIRK GRAYSON

2 Assyrian Rulers of the Early First Millennium BC I (1114–859 BC)
A. KIRK GRAYSON

3 Assyrian Rulers of the Early First Millennium BC II (858–745 BC)
A. KIRK GRAYSON

BABYLONIAN PERIODS

2 Rulers of Babylonia: From the Second Dynasty of Isin to the End of Assyrian Control (1157–612 BC)
GRANT FRAME

EARLY PERIODS

2 Sargonic and Gutian Periods (2334–2113 BC)
DOUGLAS FRAYNE

3/1 Gudea and His Dynasty
DIETZ OTTO EDZARD

3/2 Ur III Period (2112–2004 BC)
DOUGLAS FRAYNE

4 Old Babylonian Period (2003–1595 BC)
DOUGLAS FRAYNE

SUPPLEMENTS

1 Royal Inscriptions on Clay Cones from Ashur Now in Istanbul
V. DONBAZ and A. KIRK GRAYSON

THE ROYAL INSCRIPTIONS OF MESOPOTAMIA

BABYLONIAN PERIODS / VOLUME 2

Rulers of Babylonia

From the Second Dynasty of Isin to the End of Assyrian Domination

(1157–612 BC)

GRANT FRAME

UNIVERSITY OF TORONTO PRESS

Toronto Buffalo London

University of Toronto Press 1995
Toronto Buffalo London

Reprinted 2002
Reprinted in paperback 2014

ISBN 978-0-8020-0724-7 (cloth)
ISBN 978-1-4426-2374-3 (paper)

Printed on acid-free paper

Canadian Cataloguing in Publication Data

Frame, Grant

Rulers of Babylonia : from the second dynasty of Isin
to the end of Assyrian domination
(1157–612 BC)

(The royal inscriptions of Mesopotamia. Babylonian Periods ; v. 2)
Includes bibliographical references.
ISBN 978-0-8020-0724-7 (bound) ISBN 978-1-4426-2374-3 (pbk.)

1. Babylonia – Kings and rulers. 2. Babylonia – History – Sources.
3. Cuneiform inscriptions, Akkadian. 4. Akkadian language – Texts.
I. Title. II. Series.

PJ3831.F73 1995 935 C94-932817-0

The research and publication of this volume
have been supported by
the Social Sciences and Humanities Research Council of Canada
and the University of Toronto.

To

Frances Redshaw and Jean Marshall Dawes

Contents

Preface

In the course of the preparation of this volume, I have been aided by numerous individuals and institutions; I would like to express by sincere appreciation to all of them.

My greatest thanks must be extended to A.K. Grayson, the director of the Royal Inscriptions of Mesopotamia Project, who conceived the concept of the project and has dedicated himself to its continuation and success. His constant support and advice have been much appreciated and are gratefully acknowledged.

R.D. Biggs, J.N. Postgate, and W.G. Lambert kindly served as readers for the volume and made numerous valuable comments on the preliminary manuscript. In addition, A.K. Grayson and D.R. Frayne collated a number of inscriptions for me, read the preliminary manuscript, and offered helpful suggestions. As Editor-in-Chief, R.F.G. Sweet provided valuable assistance in connection with the preparation of the volume. Their time and care is greatly appreciated.

Thanks must be expressed to the various museums and museum authorities who have allowed me to collate documents in their collections, provided me with information, and facilitated me in my research. In particular, L. Jakob-Rost, E. Klengel-Brandt, and J. Marzahn at the Vorderasiatisches Museum (Berlin), J.A. Brinkman and R.D. Tindel at the Oriental Institute (Chicago), V. Donbaz at the Archaeological Museums (Istanbul), D. Collon, J. Curtis, I. Finkel, J.E. Reade, and C.B.F. Walker at the British Museum (London), W.W. Hallo at Yale University (New Haven), P.R.S. Moorey at the Ashmolean Museum (Oxford), B. André-Salvini at the Musée du Louvre (Paris), H. Behrens and E. Leichty at the University Museum (Philadelphia), S.M. Goldstein at the St. Louis Art Museum (St. Louis), and B. Bohen at the World Heritage Museum (Urbana). I would also like to thank R.M. Boehmer of the Deutsches Archäologisches Institut, Abteilung Baghdad (Berlin), for access to the records and photographs of the Uruk-Warka expedition.

Numerous individuals kindly collated texts for me, provided information on particular pieces, or aided my research in some way. These include J.A. Armstrong, P.-A. Beaulieu, R.D. Biggs, P. Calmeyer, B. Cifola, P.E. Dion, B.R. Foster, D.A. Foxvog, H.D. Galter, A.R. George, M. Gibson, P. Gerardi, A. Harrak, C.E. Jones, U. Kasten, O.W. Muscarella, J. Oelsner, M.A. Powell, K. Reiter, F. Rochberg, W.H. van Soldt, E. von Dassow, J.W. Wevers, C. Wilcke, T.C. Young, Jr., and R.L. Zettler. Special thanks must be given to A. Cavigneaux for help with the texts from Sūḫu.

Here in Toronto, several individuals contributed to the technical preparation of the volume: K. Glaser, H. Grau, J. Ruby, T. Sagrillo, R. Westerby, and L. Wilding. My deepest gratitude is offered to them.

Finally, my appreciation must go to the Social Sciences and Humanities Research Council of Canada and the University of Toronto, without whose support the Royal Inscriptions of Mesopotamia Project would not be able to continue its research and publish its results.

Toronto
May 1994

G.F.

Editorial Notes

As in the four previous volumes published in the Royal Inscriptions of Mesopotamia series (RIMA 1 [1987], RIME 4 [1990], RIMA 2 [1991], and RIME 2 [1993]), the editorial principles followed in the preparation of this volume are those of the Royal Inscriptions of Mesopotamia Project's Editorial Manual (2nd ed., Toronto, 1990).

The present volume is the first to appear in the sub-series allotted to the periods designated the Babylonian Periods by the RIM project. These begin with the Kassite Period, since the period of the First Dynasty of Babylon has been assigned to the Early Periods (its inscriptions are published in RIME 4). The first Babylonian dynasty in the RIM system is therefore the Kassite Dynasty, not the First Dynasty of Babylon. Although the first to appear, the present volume, dealing with the period from the end of Kassite rule to the end of the Assyrian domination of Babylonia, is the second planned for the Babylonian sub-series; hence it will be referred to by the abbreviation RIMB 2.

Readers new to the RIM series should note the system used to designate the texts. Most of the texts edited in this volume are identified by a four-element designator of the type B.2.4.5. The B identifies the sub-series to which the text is assigned as Babylonian; the second element in this example (2) identifies the dynasty as the second treated in the subseries, following the sequence given in the list of Contents (pp. vii–viii); the third element (4) identifies the ruler to whom the text is ascribed as the fourth of his dynasty; and the fourth element (5) identifies the text as the fifth inscription of that ruler in the sequence used in this edition. The principle that has determined the sequence of the texts is explained in the Introduction. However, the texts presented in the section that begins on p. 275 all have S.0 as the first two elements of their four-element designator. The abbreviation S as the first element of a text designator appears here for the first time in RIM publications. It identifies the texts as coming from the land of Sūḫu. The 0 of the second element indicates that, as far as we know, the question of dynasty number is inapplicable with reference to the rulers of Sūḫu (zero is also used to denote the dynasty in the RIM volumes devoted to the Assyrian Periods, since the Assyrians officially had only one dynasty). A zero is also used for the third element if the king to whose reign a text should be assigned cannot be identified (see pp. 68–69, 84–86, 271–74, 324–31). Numbers in the 1000 range, beginning with 1001, have been used to indicate uncertain identifications. The two known rulers of Sūḫu have therefore been numbered 1001 and 1002, since their order within the dynasty cannot be determined. The justification for giving them consecutive numbers is that they stand in a father-son relationship (see pp. 278–323). Numbers in the 1000 range have also been used as the fourth element for texts that cannot be assigned with certainty to a particular reign. Some of these have nevertheless been placed within a certain reign when there is some basis for an informed guess (see pp. 35, 62–63, 81–82, 192–93, 286–87, 322–23). In other cases, the impossibility of identifying the reign has been acknowledged by designating the reign (third element) as zero (see pp. 68–69, 324–31). Numbers in the 2000 range, beginning with 2001, have been used for the fourth element in the case of texts written for persons other than the king (see pp. 43–44, 48–49, 84–86, 93–97, 107–108, 112–13, 123–29, 141–42, 230–47, 258–59, 271–74). Texts of this class, which have been thought eligible for inclusion in a volume of royal inscriptions if they attest the existence of a ruler or of someone closely connected with a ruler (e.g., a family member or a high official), are always placed after the inscriptions for the relevant reign that are more typically royal in nature. The understanding of what constitutes a royal inscription has been extended to include texts of the genre commonly called historical-literary, and in one instance even an excerpt from a kudurru inscription has been included (B.2.4.11). A fifth element is added to the text designator if a particular exemplar needs to be identified.

Royal names are transcribed as in J.A. Brinkman's Appendix in Oppenheim, Ancient Mesopotamia pp. 335–48, except that vowel quantity is marked (thus Marduk-kabit-aḫḫēšu [e in the penultimate syllable, not i, after Brinkman]). Another exception is that Marduk-apla-iddina is used instead of Brinkman's Merodach-Baladan.

The abbreviations c, p, and n found in the catalogues of exemplars for texts attested in more than one copy indicate, respectively, whether an exemplar has been collated by autopsy, collated from a photograph, or not collated. The political conditions that prevailed during the preparation of this volume unfortunately made it impossible for the author to collate all the texts he had hoped to examine.

In the case of texts with multiple exemplars, the text is given as a master text reconstructed from the combined evidence of the witnesses. Transliterations of all multiple exemplars, other than bricks, are given in the style of musical scores on the microfiches found in a pocket inside the back cover. Major variants, defined essentially as non-orthographic variants and variants in the spelling of proper names, are given at the bottom of the page below the text. Minor orthographic variants are given at the end of the book on pp. 333–38.

The manuscript was prepared on an Apple Macintosh IIsi computer, using MicroSoft Word 5.1 with CuneiformOriental font, and the camera-ready copy submitted to the publisher was printed on a Linotronic 300 PostScript typesetter.

Toronto
June 1994

R.F.G. Sweet
Editor-in-Chief

Bibliographical Abbreviations

AASF	Annales Academiae Scientiarum Fennicae, Series B. Helsinki, 1909–
AB	Assyriologische Bibliothek. Leipzig, 1881–
Abel and Winckler, KGV	L. Abel and H. Winckler, Keilschrifttexte zum Gebrauch bei Vorlesungen. Berlin, 1890
ADFU	Ausgrabungen der Deutschen Forschungsgemeinschaft in Uruk-Warka. Berlin and Leipzig, 1936–
AfK	Archiv für Keilschriftforschung, vols. 1–2. Berlin, 1923–25
AfO	Archiv für Orientforschung, vol. 3– (vol. 1–2 = AfK). Berlin, Graz, and Horn, 1926–
AHw	W. von Soden, Akkadisches Handwörterbuch, 3 vols. Wiesbaden, 1965–81
AJ	The Antiquaries Journal, Being the Journal of the Society of Antiquaries of London. London, 1921–
AJSL	American Journal of Semitic Languages and Literatures. Chicago, 1884–1941
Amiet, Luristan	P. Amiet, Les antiquités du Luristan. Paris, 1976
An = *Anum*	R.L. Litke, A Reconstruction of the Assyro-Babylonian God Lists, ^{d}An: *A-nu-um* and An: *Anu šá amēli*. Yale University Ph.D. Dissertation, 1958
ANEP^{2}	J.B. Pritchard (ed.), The Ancient Near East in Pictures Relating to the Old Testament, 2nd edition. Princeton, 1969
ANET^{3}	J.B. Pritchard (ed.), Ancient Near Eastern Texts Relating to the Old Testament, 3rd edition. Princeton, 1969
AnOr	Analecta Orientalia. Rome, 1931–
AO	Der Alte Orient. Leipzig, 1901–45
AOAT	Alter Orient und Altes Testament. Neukirchen-Vluyn, 1968–
AOS	American Oriental Studies. New Haven, 1935–
ARRIM	Annual Review of the Royal Inscriptions of Mesopotamia Project. Toronto, 1983–91
AS	Assyriological Studies. Chicago, 1931
ASJ	Acta Sumerologica. Hiroshima, 1979–
AUWE	Ausgrabungen in Uruk-Warka Endberichte. Mainz am Rhein, 1987–
BA	Beiträge der Assyriologie und semitischen Sprachwissenschaft, vols. 1–10. Leipzig, 1890–1927
Babelon, Manual	E. Babelon, Manual of Oriental Antiquities Including the Architecture, Sculpture, and Industrial Arts of Chaldæa, Assyria, Persia, Syria, Judæa, Phoenicia, and Carthage, new edition. London, 1906
Bagh. For.	Baghdader Forschungen. Mainz am Rhein, 1979–
Bagh. Mitt.	Baghdader Mitteilungen. Berlin, 1960–
Ball, Light	C.J. Ball, Light from the East, or the Witness of the Monuments. London, 1899
Barnett, Ivories^{2}	R.D. Barnett, A Catalogue of the Nimrud Ivories with Other Examples of Ancient Near Eastern Ivories in the British Museum, 2nd edition. London, 1975
Basmachi, Treasures	F. Basmachi, Treasures of the Iraq Museum. Baghdad, 1976
BASOR	Bulletin of the American Schools of Oriental Research. New Haven, 1919–
Bauer, Asb.	T. Bauer, Das Inschriftenwerk Assurbanipals (=AB, Neue Folge 1–2). Leipzig, 1933
BE	Babylonian Expedition of the University of Pennsylvania, Series A: Cuneiform Texts, vols. 1–14. Philadelphia, 1893–1914
BE Res	Babylonian Expedition of the University of Pennsylvania, Series D: Researches and Treatises, vols. 1, 3–5. Philadelphia, 1904–10
Becker, AUWE 6	A. Becker, Uruk: Kleinfunde I: Stein. Mainz am Rhein, 1993
Beek, Atlas	M.A. Beek, Atlas of Mesopotamia. A Survey of the History and Civilisation of Mesopotamia from the Stone Age to the Fall of Babylon. Trans. by D.R. Welsh; H.H. Rowley (ed.). London and Edinburgh, 1962
Bernhardt, TMH NF 5	I. Bernhardt, Sozialökonomische Texte und Rechtsurkunden aus Nippur zur Kassitenzeit. Berlin, 1976
Berytus	Berytus, Archaeological Studies. Beirut, 1934–
Bezold, Cat.	C. Bezold, Catalogue of the Cuneiform Tablets in the Kouyunjik Collection of the British Museum, 5 vols. London, 1889–99
Bezold, Literatur	C. Bezold, Babylonisch-Assyriche Literatur. Leipzig, 1886
Bezold, Ninive und Babylon^{4}	C. Bezold, Ninive und Babylon, 4th edition (=Monographien zur Weltgeschichte 18). Bielefeld and Leipzig, 1926

BibMes	Bibliotheca Mesopotamica. Malibu, 1975–
BIN	Babylonian Inscriptions in the Collection of J.B. Nies. New Haven, 1917–
BiOr	Bibliotheca Orientalis. Leiden, 1943–
BJVF	Berliner Jahrbuch für Vor- und Frühgeschichte. Berlin, 1961–
Block, Gods	D.I. Block, The Gods of the Nations. Studies in Ancient Near Eastern National Theology (=Evangelical Theological Society Monograph Series 2). Jackson, Mississippi, 1988
BM Guide	British Museum. A Guide to the Babylonian and Assyrian Antiquities, 3rd edition. London, 1922
BMQ	British Museum Quarterly, vols. 1–37. London, 1926–73
Börker-Klähn, Bildstelen	Börker-Klähn, Altvorderasiatische Bildstelen und Vergleichbare Felsreliefs (=Bagh. For. 4). Mainz am Rhein, 1982
Borger, Asarh.	R. Borger, Die Inschriften Asarhaddons, Königs von Assyrien (=AfO Beih. 9). Graz, 1956
Borger, Brief Sîn-idinnams	R. Borger, Ein Brief Sîn-idinnams von Larsa an den Sonnengott sowie Bemerkungen über "Joins" und das "Joinen". Göttingen, 1991
Borger, HKL	R. Borger, Handbuch der Keilschriftliteratur, 3 vols. Berlin, 1967–75
Borger, WAO^2	R. Borger, et al., Die Welt des Alten Orients. Keilschrift – Grabungen – Gelehrte, 2nd edition. Göttingen, 1975
Brandis, Münz	J. Brandis, Das Münz-, Mass- und Gewichtswesen in Vorderasien bis auf Alexander den Grossen. Berlin, 1866; repr. Amsterdam, 1966
Brinkman, PKB	J.A. Brinkman, A Political History of Post-Kassite Babylonia 1158–722 B.C. (=AnOr 43). Rome, 1968
Brinkman, Prelude	J.A. Brinkman, Prelude to Empire: Babylonian Society and Politics, 747–626 BC (=Occasional Publications of the Babylonian Fund 7). Philadelphia, 1984
BRM	Babylonian Records in the Library of J. Pierpont Morgan, 4 vols. New Haven and New York, 1912–23
BSA	Bulletin on Sumerian Agriculture. Cambridge, 1984–
BSMS	Bulletin of the (Canadian) Society for Mesopotamian Studies. Toronto, 1981–
BSOAS	Bulletin of the School of Oriental and African Studies, University of London. London, 1917–
CAD	The Assyrian Dictionary of the Oriental Institute of the University of Chicago. Chicago, 1956–
Cagni, Erra	L. Cagni, L'épopea di Erra (=Studia Semitici 34). Rome, 1969
CAH	I.E.S. Edwards, C.J. Gadd, N.G.L. Hammond, et al. (eds.), The Cambridge Ancient History, 2nd and 3rd editions. Cambridge, 1970–
Calmeyer, Datierbare Bronzen	P. Calmeyer, Datierbare Bronzen aus Luristan und Kirmanshah. Berlin, 1969
Calmeyer, Reliefbronzen	P. Calmeyer, Reliefbronzen in babylonischem Stil: Eine westiranische Werkstatt des 10. Jahrhunderts v. Chr. Munich, 1973
Canfora, Trattati	L. Canfora, M. Liverani, and C. Zaccagnini, I trattati nel mondo antico forma ideologia funzione (=Saggi di Storia Antica 2). Rome, 1990
Champdor, Babylon	A. Champdor, Babylon. Translated from the French by Elsa Coult. London and New York, 1958
Clay, BE 8/1	A.T. Clay, Legal and Commercial Transactions Dated in the Assyrian, Neo-Babylonian and Persian Periods Chiefly from Nippur. Philadelphia, 1908
Clay, BRM 1	A.T. Clay, Babylonian Business Transactions of the First Millennium B.C. New York, 1912
Clay, YOS 1	A.T. Clay, Miscellaneous Inscriptions in the Yale Babylonian Collection. New Haven, 1915
de Clercq, Collection	H.F.X̣. de Clercq and J. Ménant, Collection de Clercq, catalogue méthodique et raisonné, antiquités assyriennes, cylindres orientaux, cachets, briques, bronzes, bas-reliefs etc., 2 vols. Paris, 1888/1903
Collon, First Impressions	D. Collon, First Impressions: Cylinder Seals in the Ancient Near East. London, 1987
Contenau, Manuel	G. Contenau, Manuel d'archéologie orientale, 4 vols. Paris, 1927–47
Contenau, TCL 12	G. Contenau, Contrats néo-babyloniens, I: de Téglath-phalasar III à Nabonide. Paris, 1927
CRRA	Compte Rendu de la Rencontre Assyriologique Internationale. [various locations], 1950–
CRRA 19	P. Garelli (ed.), Le palais et la royauté (archéologie et civilisation). Paris, 1974
CT	Cuneiform Texts from Babylonian Tablets in the British Museum. London, 1896–
Dalley, Mari and Karana	S. Dalley, Mari and Karana: Two Old Babylonian Cities. London and New York, 1984
Deimel Festschrift	Miscellanea Orientalia Dedicata A. Deimel Annos LXX Complenti (=AnOr 12). Rome, 1935
Delitzsch, AW	F. Delitzsch, Assyrisches Wörterbuch zur gesamten bisher veröffentlichten Keilschriftliteratur under Berücksichtigung zahlreicher unveroffentlichter Texte (=AB 7). Leipzig, 1887–90

van Dijk, VAS 24	J. van Dijk, Literarische Texte aus Babylon. Berlin, 1987
Donbaz, NTA	V. Donbaz, Ninurta-tukulti-Aššur. Zamanına ait orta Asur idarî begeleri (=Türk Tarih Kurumu Yayinlari 6/19). Ankara, 1976
Donbaz and Grayson, RICCA	V. Donbaz and A.K. Grayson, Royal Inscriptions on Clay Cones from Ashur Now in Istanbul (=The Royal Inscriptions of Mesopotamia, Supplements 1). Toronto, 1984
Durand, Doc. Cun. 1	J.-M. Durand, Documents Cunéiformes de la IVe Section de l'École pratique des Hautes Études, tome I: Catalogue et copies cunéiformes. Paris, 1982
Ebeling, KAR	E. Ebeling, Keilschrifttexte aus Assur religiösen Inhalts, 2 vols. (=WVDOG 28 and 34). Leipzig, 1919/23
Ellis, Foundation Deposits	R.S. Ellis, Foundation Deposits in Ancient Mesopotamia (=YNER 2). New Haven and London, 1968
Essays Finkelstein	M. de Jong Ellis (ed.), Essays on the Ancient Near East in Memory of J.J. Finkelstein. Hamden, 1977
Essays Meek	W.S. McCullough (ed.), The Seed of Wisdom: Essays in Honour of T.J. Meek. Toronto, 1964
Fales, Alfabeto	F.M. Fales (ed.), Prima dell'Alfabeto. Venice, 1989
Fales, ARIN	F.M. Fales (ed.), Assyrian Royal Inscriptions: New Horizons in Literary, Ideological, and Historical Analysis. Rome, 1981
Falkenstein, LKU	A. Falkenstein, Literarische Keilschrifttexte aus Uruk. Berlin, 1931
Figulla, UET 4	H.H. Figulla, Business Documents of the New-Babylonian Period. London, 1949
Finkbeiner, AUWE 4	U. Finkbeiner, Uruk: Kampagne 35–37, 1982–1984; die archäologische Oberflächenuntersuchung (Survey), 2 vols. Mainz am Rhein, 1991
Foster, Before the Muses	B.R. Foster, Before the Muses: An Anthology of Akkadian Literature, 2 vols. Bethesda, Maryland, 1993
Frame, Babylonia	G. Frame, Babylonia 689–627 B.C.: A Political History. Leiden, 1992
Frayne, Early Dynastic List	D.R. Frayne, The Early Dynastic List of Geographical Names (=AOS 74). New Haven, 1992
Frayne, RIME 4	D. Frayne, Old Babylonian Period (2003–1595 BC). Toronto, 1990
FuB	Forschungen und Berichte. Berlin, 1957–
Gadd, UET 1	C.J. Gadd, L. Legrain, and S. Smith, Royal Inscriptions. London, 1928
Galter, Ea/Enki	H.D. Galter, Der Gott Ea/Enki in der akkadischen Überlieferung: eine Bestandsaufnahme des vorhandenen Materials. Graz, 1983
de Genouillac, Kich	H. de Genouillac, Premières recherches archéologique à Kich (Fouilles françaises d'El-'Akhymer, mission d'Henri de Genouillac, 1911–12), 2 vols. Paris, 1924/25
George, House Most High	A.R. George, House Most High: The Temples of Ancient Mesopotamia (=Mesopotamian Civilizations 5). Winona Lake, Indiana, 1993
George, Topographical Texts	A.R. George, Babylonian Topographical Texts (=Orientalia Lovaniensia Analecta 40). Leuven, 1992
Ghirshman, Kunstschätze	R. Ghirshman, et al., Kunstschätze aus Iran. Kunstschätze von der prähistorischen bis zur islamischen Zeit. Zurich, 1962
Ghirshman, Perse	R. Ghirshman, Perse: Proto-Iraniens, Médes, Achéménides. Paris, 1963
Ghirshman, Sept mille	R. Ghirshman, et al., Sept mille ans d'art en Iran. Paris, 1961
Gibson and Biggs, Seals	M. Gibson and R.D. Biggs, Seals and Sealing in the Ancient Near East (=BibMes 6). Malibu, 1977
Glassner, Chroniques	J.-J. Glassner, Chroniques mésopotamiennes. Paris, 1993
Gnoli and Vernant, La mort	G. Gnoli and J.-P. Vernant (eds.), La mort, les morts dans les sociétés anciennes. Cambridge and Paris, 1982
Goetze, YOS 10	A. Goetze, Old Babylonian Omen Texts. New Haven and London, 1947
Grayson, BHLT	A.K. Grayson, Babylonian Historical-Literary Texts (=TSTS 3). Toronto and Buffalo, 1975
Grayson, Chronicles	A.K. Grayson, Assyrian and Babylonian Chronicles (=TCS 5). Locust Valley, 1975
Grayson, RIMA 2	A.K. Grayson, Assyrian Rulers of the Early First Millennium BC I (1114–859 BC). Toronto, 1991
Grayson, RIMA 3	A.K. Grayson, Assyrian Rulers of the Early First Millennium BC II (858–745 BC). In press
Gressmann, ABAT[2]	H. Gressmann, Altorientalische Bilder zum Alten Testament. Berlin and Leipzig, 1927
Gurney, UET 7	O.R. Gurney, Middle Babylonian Legal Documents and Other Texts. London, 1974
Halévy, Documents religieux	J. Halévy, Documents religieux de l'Assyrie et de l'Assyrie et de la Babylonie. Paris, 1882
Hall, Sculpture	H.R. Hall, Babylonian and Assyrian Sculpture in the British Museum. Paris and Brussels, 1928
Haller, Gräber	A. Haller, Die Gräber und Grüfte von Assur (=WVDOG 65). Berlin, 1954
Hama 2/2	P.J. Riis and M.-L. Buhl, Hama: fouilles et recherches 1931–1938. II 2: Les objets de la période dite Syro-Hittite (Âge du Fer). Copenhagen, 1990
Harper, Literature	R.F. Harper, Assyrian and Babylonian Literature: Selected Translations. New York, 1904
Herzfeld, Iran	E.E. Herzfeld, Iran in the Ancient East. London and New York, 1941; repr. London, 1976

Herzfeld, Persian Empire	E. Herzfeld, The Persian Empire: Studies in Geography and Ethnography of the Ancient Near East. Wiesbaden, 1968
Hilprecht, BE 1	H.V. Hilprecht, Old Babylonian Inscriptions Chiefly from Nippur, 2 vols. Philadelphia, 1893/96
Hilprecht, Excavations	H.V. Hilprecht, The Excavations in Assyria and Babylonia (=BE Res 1). Philadelphia, 1904
Hilprecht, Explorations	H.V. Hilprecht, Explorations in Bible Lands during the 19th Century. Philadelphia, 1903
Hilprecht, Freibrief	H. Hilprecht, Freibrief Nebukadnezar's I, Königs von Babylonien c. 1130 v. Chr. Leipzig, 1883
Hrouda, Isin 1	B. Hrouda (ed.), Isin-Išān Bahrīyāt I. Die Ergebnisse der Ausgrabungen 1973–1974 (=Bayerische Akademie der Wissenschaften philosophisch-historische Klasse NF 79). Munich, 1977
Hrouda, Isin 2	B. Hrouda (ed.), Isin-Išān Bahrīyāt II. Die Ergebnisse der Ausgrabungen 1975–1978 (=Bayerische Akademie der Wissenschaften philosophisch-historische Klasse NF 87). Munich, 1981
Hrouda, Isin 3	B. Hrouda (ed.), Isin-Išān Bahrīyāt III. Die Ergebnisse der Ausgrabungen 1983–1984 (=Bayerische Akademie der Wissenschaften philosophisch-historische Klasse NF 94). Munich, 1987
Hunger, Kolophone	H. Hunger, Babylonische und assyrische Kolophone (=AOAT 2). Neukirchen-Vluyn, 1968
Huot, Larsa 1985	J.-L. Huot, Larsa: Travaux de 1985 (=Éditions Recherche sur les Civilisations, 'Mémoire' no 83). Paris, 1989
Huot, Larsa et 'Oueili 1978–1981	J.-L. Huot (ed.), Larsa (8eme et 9eme campagnes, 1978 et 1981) et 'Oueilli (2eme et 3eme campagnes, 1978 et 1981): Rapport Préliminaire (=Éditions Recherche sur les Civilisations, 'Mémoire' no 26). Paris, 1983
IAR	Iraq Archaeological Reports. Series of the British School of Archaeology in Iraq and the Directorate of Antiquities, Baghdad. Warminster, 1988–
IEJ	Israel Exploration Journal. Jerusalem, 1951–
ILN	The Illustrated London News. London, 1842–
IrAnt	Iranica Antiqua. Ghent, 1961–
JAOS	Journal of the American Oriental Society. New Haven, 1893–
Jastrow, Religion	Morris Jastrow, Jr., Die Religion Babyloniens und Assyriens. Giessen, 1905
JCS	Journal of Cuneiform Studies. New Haven and Cambridge, Mass., 1947–
Jean, Littérature	C.-F. Jean, La littérature des babyloniens et des assyriens. Paris, 1924
Jean, Milieu biblique 2	C.-F. Jean, Le milieu biblique avant Jésus-Christ II: La littérature. Paris, 1923
JEOL	Jaarbericht van het Vooraziatisch-Egyptisch Genootschap 'Ex Oriente Lux'. Leiden, 1933–
Jeremias, HAOG^2	A. Jeremias, Handbuch der altorientalischen Geisteskultur, 2nd edition. Leipzig, 1929
JNES	Journal of Near Eastern Studies. Chicago, 1942–
Johns, ADD	C.H.W. Johns, Assyrian Deeds and Documents, Recording the Transfer of Property, Including the So-called Private Contracts, Legal Decisions and Proclamations, Preserved in the Kouyunjik Collections of the British Museum, Chiefly of the Seventh Century B.C., 4 vols. Cambridge, 1898–1923
Jordan, Uruk-Warka	J. Jordan, Uruk-Warka nach den Ausgrabungen durch die Deutsche Orient-Gesellschaft (=WVDOG 51). Leipzig, 1928
JRAS	Journal of the Royal Asiatic Society. London, 1834–
Keiser, BIN 2	C. Keiser and J.B. Nies, Historical Religious and Economic Texts and Antiquities. New Haven, 1920
King, BBSt	L.W. King, Babylonian Boundary-Stones and Memorial-Tablets in the British Museum, 2 vols. London, 1912
King, First Steps	L.W. King, First Steps in Assyrian: A Book for Beginners. London, 1898
King, History	L.W. King, A History of Babylon from the Foundation of the Monarchy to the Persian Conquest. London, 1915
King, LIH	L.W. King, The Letters and Inscriptions of Hammurabi, King of Babylon, about 2000 B.C. to Which Are Added a Series of Letters of Other Kings of the First Dynasty of Babylon, 3 vols. (=Luzac's Semitic Text and Translation Series vols. 2–3 and 8). London, 1898–1900
Klengel-Brandt, Reise	E. Klengel-Brandt, Reise in das alte Babylon. Leipzig, 1970
Koldewey, Königsburgen	R. Koldewey, Die Königsburgen von Babylon, 2 vols. (=WVDOG 54–55). Leipzig, 1931–32
Koldewey, Pflastersteine	R. Koldewey, Die Pflastersteine von Aiburschabu in Babylon (=WVDOG 2). Leipzig, 1901
Koldewey, Tempel	R. Koldewey, Die Tempel von Babylon und Borsippa (=WVDOG 15). Leipzig, 1911
Koldewey, WEB^4	R. Koldewey, Das wieder erstehende Babylon: die bisherigen Ergebnisse der deutschen Ausgrabungen, 4th edition. Leipzig, 1925

8. Kongress 2/1B	Actes du huitième Congrès International des Orientalistes, tenu en 1899 à Stockholm et à Christiania, deuxième partie, section 1, B. Leiden, 1891
Kramer Anniversary	B. Eichler (ed.), Kramer Anniversary Volume: Cuneiform Studies in Honor of Samuel Noah Kramer (=AOAT 25). Neukirchen-Vluyn, 1976
Kraus Festschrift	G. van Driel, Th.J.H. Krispijn, M. Stol, and K.R. Veenhof (eds.), Zikir Šumim. Assyriological Studies Presented to F.R. Kraus on the Occasion of His Seventieth Birthday. Leiden, 1982
Kugler, SSB	F.X. Kugler, Sternkunde und Sterndienst in Babel, 2 vols. + 3 addenda (in 2 parts). Münster, 1907–35
Lambert, Cat.	W.G. Lambert, Catalogue of the Cuneiform Tablets in the Kouyunjik Collection of the British Museum, 3rd Supplement. London, 1992
Land Between Two Rivers	The Land Between Two Rivers. Twenty years of Italian archaeology in the Middle East. The treasures of Mesopotamia. Turin, 1985
Landsberger, Brief	B. Landsberger, Brief des Bischofs von Esagila an König Asarhaddon (=Mededelingen der Koninklijke Nederlandse Akademie van Wetenschappen, Afd. Letterkunde, NR 28/6). Amsterdam, 1965
Langdon, Kish	S. Langdon and L. Watelin, Excavations at Kish, the Hebert Weld and Field Museum of Natural History Expedition to Mesopotamia, 4 vols. Paris, 1924–34
Langdon, NBK	S. Langdon, Die neubabylonischen Königsinschriften (=VAB 4). Leipzig, 1912
Langdon, OECT 1	S. Langdon, The H. Weld-Blundell Collection in the Ashmolean Museum, vol. 1: Sumerian and Semitic Religious and Historical Texts. Oxford, 1923
Layard, Discoveries	A.H. Layard, Discoveries among the Ruins of Nineveh and Babylon, with Travels in Armenia, Kurdistan and the Desert. London, 1853
Layard, ICC	A.H. Layard, Inscriptions in the Cuneiform Character from Assyrian Monuments. London, 1851
Layard, Monuments 1	A.H. Layard, The Monuments of Nineveh. London, 1849
Layard, Nineveh	A.H. Layard, Nineveh and Its Remains, 2 vols. London, 1849
Legrain, PBS 13	L. Legrain, Historical Fragments. Philadelphia, 1922
Legrain, PBS 15	L. Legrain, Royal Inscriptions and Fragments from Nippur and Babylon. Philadelphia, 1926
Lehmann-Haupt, Šamaššumukîn	C.F. Lehmann[-Haupt], Šamaššumukîn, König von Babylonien 668–648 v. Chr. (=AB 8). Leipzig, 1892
Leichty, Sippar	E. Leichty, Tablets from Sippar, 3 vols. (=Catalogue of the Babylonian Tablets in the British Museum 6–8). London, 1986–88
Lenormant, Choix	F. Lenormant, Choix de textes cunéiformes inédits ou incomplètement publiés. Paris, 1873–75
Lenormant, Études accadiennes	F. Lenormant, Études accadiennes, 3 vols. (=Lettres assyriologiques, seconde série). Paris, 1873–80
Levey, Chemistry	M. Levey, Chemistry and Chemical Technology in Ancient Mesopotamia. Amsterdam, London, New York, and Princeton, 1959
Levine and Young, Mountains and Lowlands	L.D. Levine and T.C. Young, Mountains and Lowlands: Essays in the Archaeology of Greater Mesopotamia (=BibMes 7). Malibu, 1977
Longman, Autobiography	T. Longman, Fictional Akkadian Autobiography: A Generic and Comparative Study. Winona Lake, Indiana, 1991
Lotz, Tigl.	W. Lotz, Die Inschriften Tiglathpileser's I. Leipzig, 1880
LSS	Leipziger semitistische Studien. Leipzig, 1903–
Luckenbill, ARAB	D.D. Luckenbill, Ancient Records of Assyria and Babylonia, 2 vols. Chicago, 1926–27
Luckenbill, Senn.	D.D. Luckenbill, The Annals of Sennacherib (=OIP 2). Chicago, 1924
Lyon, Manual	D.G. Lyon, An Assyrian Manual for the Use of Beginners in the Study of the Assyrian Language. Chicago, 1886
LZB	Literarisches Zentralblatt für Deutschland. Leipzig, 1924–43
MAIB	Mémoires de l'institut national de France, académie des inscriptions et belles-lettres. Paris, 1899–
Mallowan, Nimrud	M.E.L. Mallowan, Nimrud and Its Remains, 2 vols. London, 1966
Man in the Ancient World	Man in the Ancient World: An Exhibition of Pre-Christian Objects from the Regions of the Near East, Egypt and the Mediterranean, February 10 – March 7, 1958. Flushing, New York, 1958
MAOG	Mitteilungen der Altorientalischen Gesellschaft. Leipzig, 1925–43
Margueron, Mesopotamia	J.-C. Margueron, Mesopotamia. Trans. by H.S.B. Harrison. London, 1965
McCown, Nippur 1	D.E. McCown, R.C. Haines, and D. Hansen, Nippur I: Temple of Enlil, Scribal Quarter, and Soundings (=OIP 78). Chicago, 1967
MDOG	Mitteilungen der Deutschen Orient-Gesellschaft. Berlin, 1898–
Meissner, BuA	B. Meissner, Babylonien und Assyrien, 2 vols. Heidelberg, 1920/25
Meissner, Chrestomathie	B. Meissner, Assyrisch-babylonische Chrestomathie für Anfänger. Leiden, 1895
Meissner, Literatur	B. Meissner, Die babylonisch-assyrische Literatur. Wildpark-Potsdam, 1927
Ménant, Annales	J. Ménant, Annales des rois d'assyrie. Paris, 1874

Ménant, Babylone	J. Ménant, Babylone et la chaldée. Paris, 1875
Meyer, Jahrtausende	G.R. Meyer, Durch vier Jahrtausende altvorderasiatischer Kultur, 2. Auflage. Berlin, 1962
de Meyer (ed.), Tell ed-Dēr 3	L. de Meyer (ed.), Tell ed-Dēr: Soundings at Abū Habbah (Sippar). Louvain, 1980
MJ	Museum Journal of the University Museum, University of Pennsylvania, vols. 1–24. Philadelphia, 1910–35
Moore, NBAD	E.W. Moore, Neo-Babylonian Business and Administrative Documents: Ann Arbor, 1935
Moorey, Adam Collection	P.R.S. Moorey, Ancient Persian Bronzes in the Adam Collection. London, 1974
Moorey, Ancient Bronzes	P.R.S. Moorey, E.C. Bunker, E. Porada, and G. Markoe, Ancient Bronzes, Ceramics, and Seals: The Nasli M. Heeramanek Collection of Ancient Near Eastern, Central Asiatic, and European Art. Los Angeles, 1981
Moorey, Catalogue Ashmolean	P.R.S. Moorey, Catalogue of the Ancient Persian Bronzes in the Ashmolean Museum. Oxford, 1971
Moorey, Kish	P.R.S. Moorey, Kish Excavations 1923–33 with a Microfiche Catalogue of the Objects in Oxford Excavated by the Oxford-Field Museum, Chicago Expedition to Kish in Iraq. Oxford, 1978
Moortgat, Kunst	A. Moortgat, Die Kunst der alten Mesopotamien. Die klassische Kunst Vorderasiens. Cologne, 1967
Muscarella, Bronze and Iron	O.W. Muscarella, Bronze and Iron: Ancient Near Eastern Artifacts in The Metropolitan Museum of Art. New York, 1988
MVAG	Mitteilungen der Vorderasiatisch-Aegyptischen Gesellschaft, vols. 1–44. Berlin and Leipzig, 1896–1939
Myres, Handbook	J.L. Myres, Handbook of the Cesnola Collection of Antiquities from Cyprus. New York, 1914
NABU	Nouvelles assyriologiques bréves et utilitaires. Paris, 1987–
Nashef, Rép. Géogr. 5	K. Nashef, Die Orts- und Gewässernamen der mittelbabylonischen und mittelassyrischen Zeit. Wiesbaden, 1982
Northedge, IAR 1	A. Northedge, A. Bamber, and M. Roaf, Excavations at ʿĀna, Qalʿa Island. Warminster, 1988
J. Oates, Babylon	J. Oates, Babylon (=Ancient Peoples and Places 94). London, 1979
OECT	Oxford Editions of Cuneiform Texts. Oxford, London, and Paris, 1923–
OIC	Oriental Institute Communications. Chicago, 1922–
OIP	Oriental Institute Publications. Chicago, 1924–
OLZ	Orientalistische Literaturzeitung. Berlin and Leipzig, 1898–
Oppenheim, Ancient Mesopotamia	A.L. Oppenheim, Ancient Mesopotamia: Portrait of a Dead Civilization. Revised edition completed by E. Reiner. Chicago and London, 1964
Oppert, Dour-Sarkayan	J. Oppert, Les inscriptions de Dour-Sarkayan (Khorsabad). Paris, 1870
Oppert, EM 1	J. Oppert, Expédition scientifique en Mésopotamie exécutée par ordre du gouvernement de 1851 à 1854 par Mm. Fulgence Fresnel, et al. Tome 1: Relation du voyage et résultats de l'expédition. Paris, 1863
OrAnt	Oriens Antiquus, Rivista del Centro per le Antichità e la Storia dell'Arte del Vicino Oriente. Rome, 1962–
Orthmann, Der alte Orient	W. Orthmann (ed.), Der alte Orient (= Propyläen Kunstgeschichte 14). Berlin, 1975
PAOS	Proceedings of the American Oriental Society
Parpola, LAS	S. Parpola, Letters from Assyrian Scholars to the Kings Esarhaddon and Assurbanipal, 2 vols. (=AOAT 5/1–2). Kevelaer and Neukirchen-Vluyn, 1970 and 1983
Parpola and Watanabe, SAA 2	S. Parpola and K. Watanabe, Neo-Assyrian Treaties and Loyalty Oaths. Helsinki, 1988
Parrot, Assyria	A. Parrot, The Arts of Assyria (=The Arts of Mankind 2). Trans. by S. Gilbert and J. Emmons. New York, 1961
PBS	Publications of the Babylonian Section, University Museum, University of Pennsylvania, 15 vols. Philadelphia, 1911–26
Peters, Nippur	J.P. Peters, Nippur, or Explorations and Adventures on the Euphrates. The Narrative of the University of Pennsylvania Expedition to Babylonia in the Years 1888–1890, 2 vols. New York and London, 1897
Pinckert, Nebo	J. Pinckert, Hymnen und Gebete an Nebo (LSS 3/4). Leipzig, 1920
Place, Ninive et l'Assyrie	V. Place, Ninive et l'Assyrie, 3 vols. Paris, 1867
Pognon, Bavian	H. Pognon, L'inscription de Bavian, 2 vols. (=Bibliothèque de l'École des Hautes Études, IVe section, 39 and 42). Paris, 1879–80
Pomponio, Nabû	F. Pomponio, Nabû. Il culto e la figura di un dio del Pantheon babilonese ed assiro (=Studi Semitici 51). Rome, 1978
Pope, Survey	A.U. Pope, A Survey of Persian Art from Prehistoric Times to the Present, 6 vols. and index. New York and London, 1938–58
Porada, 7000 Years of Iranian Art	E. Porada, et al., 7000 Years of Iranian Art. Catalogue of the Exhibition Circulated by the Smithsonian Institution, Washington, D.C., 1964
Porter, Travels	R.Ker Porter, Travels in Georgia, Persia, Armenia, Ancient Babylonia, etc. etc. during the years 1817, 1818, 1819, and 1820, 2 vols. London, 1821–22

Postgate, Royal Grants	J.N. Postgate, Neo-Assyrian Royal Grants and Decrees (=Studia Pohl, Series Maior 1). Rome, 1969
PSBA	Proceedings of the Society of Biblical Archaeology, vols. 1–40. London, 1878–1918
PSD	Å.W. Sjöberg (ed.), The Sumerian Dictionary of the University Museum of the University of Pennsylvania. Philadelphia, 1992–
1 R	H.C. Rawlinson and E. Norris, The Cuneiform Inscriptions of Western Asia, vol. 1: A Selection from the Historical Inscriptions of Chaldaea, Assyria, and Babylonia. London, 1861
3 R	H.C. Rawlinson and G. Smith, The Cuneiform Inscriptions of Western Asia, vol. 3: A Selection from the Miscellaneous Inscriptions of Assyria. London, 1870
4 R	H.C. Rawlinson and G. Smith, The Cuneiform Inscriptions of Western Asia, vol. 4: A Selection from the Miscellaneous Inscriptions of Assyria. London, 1875
4 R^2	H.C. Rawlinson and T.G. Pinches, The Cuneiform Inscriptions of Western Asia, vol. 4: A Selection from the Miscellaneous Inscriptions of Assyria, 2nd edition. London, 1891
5 R	H.C. Rawlinson and T.G. Pinches, The Cuneiform Inscriptions of Western Asia, vol. 5: A Selection from the Miscellaneous Inscriptions of Assyria and Babylonia. London, 1884
RA	Revue d'assyriologie et d'archéologie orientale. Paris, 1886–
Ratton, Bronzes antiques	C. Ratton, Bronzes antiques de la Perse du IIIe millénaire à l'époque romaine ... Collection de Son Excellence le Dr. Ing. Franz-Josef Bach ancien ambassadeur d'Allemagne en Iran. Paris, 1973
RB	Revue biblique. Paris, 1892–
Rép. Géogr.	W. Röllig (ed.), Beihefte zum Tübinger Atlas des vorderen Orients, Reihe B, Nr. 7: Répertoire géographique des texts cunéiformes. Wiesbaden, 1974–
Reuther, Merkes	O. Reuther, Die Innenstadt von Babylon (Merkes) (=WVDOG 47). Leipzig, 1926
Revue du Louvre	La revue du Louvre et des musées de France, Paris, 1951–
Revue sémitique	Revue sémitique d'épigraphie et d'histoire ancienne. Paris, 1893–1919
RIM	The Royal Inscriptions of Mesopotamia Project. Toronto
RIMA	The Royal Inscriptions of Mesopotamia, Assyrian Periods. Toronto, 1987–
RIMA 2	A.K. Grayson, Assyrian Rulers of the Early First Millennium BC I (1114–859 BC). Toronto, 1991
RIMA 3	A.K. Grayson, Assyrian Rulers of the Early First Millennium BC II (858–745 BC). In press
RIME	The Royal Inscriptions of Mesopotamia, Early Periods. Toronto, 1990
RIME 4	D. Frayne, Old Babylonian Period (2003–1595 BC). Toronto, 1990
RLA	Reallexikon der Assyriologie. Berlin, 1932–
RLV	Reallexikon der Vorgeschichte, vols. 1–15. Berlin, 1924–32
Rost, Tigl.	P. Rost, Die Keilschrifttexte Tiglat-Pilesers III. nach den Papierabklatschen und Originalen des Britischen Museums. Leipzig, 1893
Rost, Vorderasiatisches Museum	L. Jakob Rost, Das Vorderasiatische Museum. Berlin, 1987
Rost and Marzahn, Babylon	L. Jakob-Rost and J. Marzahn, Babylon (=Vorderasiatisches Museum, Kleine Schriften 4). Berlin, 1983
RP	Records of the Past, Being English Translations of the Assyrian and Egyptian Monuments, 12 vols. London, 1873–81
RT	Receuil de travaux relatifs à la philologie et à l'archéologie égyptiennes et assyriennes, vols. 1–40. Paris, 1870–1923
SAA	State Archives of Assyria. Helsinki, 1987–
SAAB	State Archives of Assyria Bulletin. Padua, 1987–
Saggs, Assyria	H.W.F. Saggs, The Might That Was Assyria. London, 1984
Salonen, Landfahrzeuge	A. Salonen, Die Landfahrzeuge des alten Mesopotamien (=AASF B 72/3). Helsinki, 1951
Salonen, Ziegeleien	A. Salonen, Die Ziegeleien im alten Mesopotamien (=AASF B 171). Helsinki, 1972
Sayce, Religion	A.H. Sayce, Lectures on the Origin and Growth of Religion as Illustrated by the Religion of the Ancient Babylonians, 2nd edition. London, 1888; repr. New York, 1980
Scheil, Sippar	V. Scheil, Une saison de fouilles à Sippar (=Mémoires publiés par les membres de l'Institut Français d'Archéologie Orientale du Caire 1/1). Cairo, 1902
Schmidt, Persepolis	E.F. Schmidt, Persepolis I: Structures, Reliefs, Inscriptions (=OIP 68); Persepolis II: Contents of the Treasury and Other Discoveries (=OIP 69); Persepolis III: The Royal Tombs and Other Monuments (=OIP 70). Chicago, 1953, 1957, and 1970
Schrader, KB	Keilinschriftliche Bibliothek, Sammlung von assyrischen und babylonischen Texten in Umschrift und Übersetzung, vols. 1–6. Berlin, 1889–1915
Seidl, Kudurru-Reliefs	U. Seidl, Die babylonischen Kudurru-Reliefs: Symbole mesopotamischer Gottheiten. Freiburg, Switzerland, and Göttingen, 1989
Seux, ERAS	M.-J. Seux, Épithètes royales akkadiennes et sumériennes. Paris, 1967
Šilwa, Cracow and Jena	J. Šilwa and E. Kluwe, From the Archaeological Collections of Cracow and Jena. Warsaw and Cracow, 1988

Sjöberg, Temple Hymns	A.W. Sjöberg and E. Bergmann, The Collection of the Sumerian Temple Hymns (=TCS 3). Locust Valley, 1969
SMEA	Studi Micenei ed Egeo-Anatolici
G. Smith, Assyrian Disc.	G. Smith, Assyrian Discoveries. New York, 1875
Sollberger, UET 8	E. Sollberger, Royal Inscriptions Part 2. London, 1965
Sommerfeld, Aufstieg Marduks	W. Sommerfeld, Der Aufstieg Marduks: die Stellung Marduks in der babylonischen Religion des zweiten Jahrtausends v. Chr. (=AOAT 213). Neukirchen-Vluyn, 1982
Southesk, Catalogue	J. Southesk, Catalogue of the Collection of Antique Gems Formed by James Ninth Earl of Southesk K.T. Edited by his daughter Lady Helena Carnegie in two volumes. London, 1908
Starr, SAA 4	I. Starr, Queries to the Sungod: Divination and Politics in Sargonid Assyria. Helsinki, 1990
Steible, NSBW	H. Steible, Die neusumerischen Bau- und Weihinschriften, 2 vols. (=Freiburger Altorientalische Studien 9:1–2) Stuttgart, 1991
Steinmetzer, Kudurru	F.X. Steinmetzer, Die babylonischen Kudurru (Grenzsteine) als Urkundenform. Paderborn, 1922
Stephens, YOS 9	F.J. Stephens, Votive and Historical Texts from Babylonia and Assyria. New Haven, 1937
StOr	Studia Orientalia (Societas Orientalis Fennica). Helsinki, 1925–
Strassmaier, AV	J.N. Strassmaier, Alphabetisches Verzeichniss der assyrischen und akkadischen Wörter der Cuneiform Inscriptions of Western Asia vol. II (=AB 4). Leipzig, 1886
Streck, Asb.	M. Streck, Assurbanipal und die letzten assyrischen Könige bis zum Untergang Nineveh's, 3 vols. (=VAB 7). Leipzig, 1916
Strommenger and Hirmer, Mesopotamien	E. Strommenger and M. Hirmer, Fünf Jahrtausende Mesopotamien: Die Kunst von den Anfängen um 5000 v. Chr. bis zu Alexander dem Grossen. Munich, 1962
Studies Hallo	M.E. Cohen, D.C. Snell, and D.B. Weisberg (eds.), The Tablet and the Scroll: Near Eastern Studies in Honor of William W. Hallo. Bethesda, Maryland, 1993
Studies Mikasa	M. Mori (jt. ed.), Near Eastern Studies Dedicated to H.I.H. Prince Takahito Mikasa on the Occasion of His Seventy-fifth Birthday (=Bulletin of the Middle Eastern Culture Center in Japan 5). Wiesbaden, 1991
Studies Oppenheim	R.D. Biggs and J.A. Brinkman (eds.), Studies Presented to A.L. Oppenheim, June 7, 1964. Chicago, 1964
Studies Reiner	F. Rochberg-Halton (ed.), Language, Literature, and History: Philological and Historical Studies Presented to Erica Reiner (=AOS 67). New Haven, 1987
Studies Sjöberg	H. Behrens, et al. (eds.), Dumu-e_2-dub-ba-a: Studies in Honor of Ake W. Sjöberg (=Occasional Publications of the Samuel Noah Kramer Fund 11). Philadelphia, 1989
Studies Smith	E. Robbins and S. Sandahl (eds.), Corolla Torontonensis: Studies in Honour of Ronald Morton Smith. Toronto, 1994
Studies Tadmor	M. Cogan and I. Eph'al (eds.), *Ah, Assyria ...* Studies in Assyrian History and Ancient Near Eastern Historiography Presented to Hayim Tadmor (=Scripta Hierosolymitana, Publications of the Hebrew University of Jerusalem, vol. 33). Jerusalem, 1991
Tallqvist, Götterepitheta	K.L. Tallqvist, Akkadische Götterepitheta (=StOr 7). Helsinki, 1938
TCL	Textes cunéiformes du Musée du Louvre, Département des Antiquités Orientales. Paris, 1910–
TCS	Texts from Cuneiform Sources. Locust Valley, 1966–
Thompson, Esarh.	R.C. Thompson, The Prisms of Esarhaddon and Ashurbanipal found at Nineveh, 1927–8. London, 1931
TMH	Texte und Materialien der Frau Professor Hilprecht Collection of Babylonian Antiquities in Eigentum der Universität Jena
TSBA	Transactions of the Society of Biblical Archaeology. London, 1872–93
TSTS	Toronto Semitic Texts and Studies. Toronto, 1970–
TUAT	O. Kaiser (ed.), Texte aus der Umwelt des Alten Testaments. Gütersloh, 1982–
UCP	University of California Publications in Semitic Philology, vols. 1–24. Berkeley, 1907–63
UE	Ur Excavations. Oxford, London, and Philadelphia, 1926–
UET	Ur Excavations, Texts. London, 1928–
UF	Ugarit-Forschungen, Internationales Jahrbuch für die Altertumskunde Syrien-Palästinas. Neukirchen-Vluyn, 1969–
Unger, Babylon	E. Unger, Babylon: die heilige Stadt nach der Beschreibung der Babylonier. Berlin and Leipzig, 1931
UVB	Vorläufiger Bericht über die von (dem Deutschen Archäologischen Institut und der Deutschen Orient-Gesellschaft aus Mitteln) der Deutschen Forschungsgemeinschaft unternommenen Ausgrabungen in Uruk-Warka. Berlin, 1930–
VAB	Vorderasiatische Bibliothek. Leipzig, 1907–16
Van Buren, Found.	E.D. Van Buren, Foundation Figurines and Offerings. Berlin, 1931

VAS	Vorderasiatische Schriftdenkmäler der Königlichen Museen zu Berlin. Leipzig and Berlin, 1907–
Walker, CBI	C.B.F. Walker, Cuneiform Brick Inscriptions in the British Museum, the Ashmolean Museum, Oxford, the City of Birmingham Museums and Art Gallery, the City of Bristol Museum and Art Gallery. London, 1981
Walker, CT 51	C.B.F. Walker, Miscellaneous Texts. London, 1972
Waterman, Tel Umar 2	L. Waterman, Second Preliminary Report upon the Excavations at Tel Umar, Iraq, conducted by the University of Michigan, the Toledo Museum of Art, and the Cleveland Museum of Art. Ann Arbor, 1933
von Weiher, AUWE 12	E. von Weiher, Uruk: Spätbabylonische Texte aus dem Planquadrat U 18. Mainz am Rhein, 1993
von Weiher, SbTU 3	E. von Weiher, Spätbabylonische Texte aus Uruk, vol. 3 (=ADFU 12). Berlin, 1988
Weissbach, Miscellen	F.H. Weissbach, Babylonische Miscellen (=WVDOG 4). Leipzig, 1903
Wetzel, Spätzeit	F. Wetzel, E. Schmidt, and A. Mallwitz, Das Babylon der Spätzeit (=WVDOG 62). Berlin, 1957
Wetzel, Stadtmauern	F. Wetzel, Die Stadtmauern von Babylon (=WVDOG 48). Leipzig, 1930
Wetzel and Weissbach, Hauptheiligtum	F. Wetzel and F.H. Weissbach, Das Hauptheiligtum des Marduk in Babylon, Esagila und Etemenanki (=WVDOG 59). Leipzig, 1938
Winckler, AOF	H. Winckler, Altorientalische Forschungen, 3 vols. Leipzig, 1893–1905
Winckler, Sammlung	H. Winckler, Sammlung von Keilschrifttexten, 3 vols. Leipzig, 1893–95
Winckler, Untersuchungen	H. Winckler, Untersuchungen zur altorientalischen Geschichte. Leipzig, 1889
WO	Die Welt des Orients. Wuppertal, Stuttgart, and Göttingen, 1947–
Woolley, UE 5	C.L. Woolley, The Ziggurat and Its Surroundings. London and Philadelphia, 1939
Woolley, UE 6	C.L. Woolley, The Buildings of the Third Dynasty. London and Philadelphia, 1974
Woolley, UE 8	C.L. Woolley, The Kassite Period and the Period of the Assyrian Kings. London, 1965
Woolley, UE 9	C.L. Woolley, The Neo-Babylonian and Persian Periods. London, 1962
Woolley and Moorey, Ur	C.L. Woolley, Ur "of the Chaldees," rev. and updated by P.R.S. Moorey. London, 1982
WVDOG	Wissenschaftliche Veröffentlichungen der Deutschen Orient-Gesellschaft. Leipzig and Berlin, 1901–
WZJ	Wissenschaftliche Zeitschrift der Friedrich Schiller Universität Jena. Jena, 1951–
YNER	Yale Near Eastern Researches. New Haven and London, 1967–
YOS	Yale Oriental Series, Babylonian Texts. New Haven, 1915–
ZA	Zeitschrift für Assyriologie und verwandte Gebiete. Berlin, 1886–
Zadok, Rép. Géogr. 8	R. Zadok, Geographical Names According to New- and Late-Babylonian Texts. Wiesbaden, 1985
ZAW	Zeitschrift für die alttestamentliche Wissenschaft. Giessen, Berlin, etc., 1881–
Zawadzki, Fall of Assyria	S. Zawadzki, The Fall of Assyria and Median-Babylonian Relations in Light of the Nabopolassar Chronicle. Poznan, 1988
ZDMG	Zeitschrift der Deutschen Morgenländischen Gesellschaft. Leipzig and Wiesbaden, 1879–
Zettler, Inanna Temple	R.L. Zettler, The Ur III Temple of Inanna at Nippur: The Operation and Organization of Urban Religious Institutions in Mesopotamia in the Late Third Millennium B.C. (=Berliner Beiträge zum Vorderen Orient 11). Berlin, 1992
Ziegler, Terrakotten	C. Ziegler, Die Terrakotten von Warka (=ADFU 6). Berlin, 1962
ZK	Zeitschrift für Keilschriftforschung und verwandte Gebiete, vols. 1–2. Leipzig, 1884–85

Other Abbreviations

c	collated
c.	circa
cm	centimetre(s)
col(s).	column(s)
dia.	diameter
DN	divine name
dupl.	duplicate
E	east
ed(s).	editor(s)
ex(s).	exemplar(s)
fig(s).	figure(s)
frgm(s).	fragment(s)
GN	geographical name
MB	Middle Babylonian
n	not collated
N	north
NA	Neo-Assyrian
n(n).	note(s)
NB	Neo-Babylonian
no(s).	number(s)
NS	New Series
OAkk.	Old Akkadian
OB	Old Babylonian
obv.	obverse
p	collated from photo
p(p).	page(s)
pl(s).	plate(s)
PN	personal name
reg.	registration
rev.	reverse
RN	royal name
S	south
W	west
var(s).	variant(s)
vol(s).	volume(s)

+	Between object numbers indicates physical join
(+)	Indicates fragments from same object but no physical join

Object Signatures

A	Asiatic collection of the Oriental Institute, Chicago
A Babylon	Collection of the Nebuchadnezzar Museum, Babylon
AH	Abu Habba collection of the British Museum, London
AO	Collection of Antiquités Orientales of the Musée du Louvre, Paris
Ash	Collection of the Ashmolean Museum, Oxford
B	1) Signature of objects in the Babylon collection of the Arkeoloji Müzeleri, Istanbul 2) Siglum (infix) for excavation numbers from the Iraqi excavations at Babylon
BE	Prefix of excavation numbers from the German excavations at Babylon
BM	British Museum, London
Bu	E.A.W. Budge collection in the British Museum, London
CBS	Babylonian Section of the University Museum, Philadelphia
D	Signature for Mesopotamian materials in the Royal Ontario Museum, Toronto
DT	Daily Telegraph collection of the British Museum, London
EŞ	Eşki Şark Eserleri Müzesi of the Arkeoloji Müzeleri, Istanbul
FMNH	Signature of objects in the collections of the Field Museum of Natural History, Chicago
H	Signature of objects in the collections of the City of Bristol Museum and Art Gallery
HE	Signature of objects in the collection of the École Pratique des Hautes Études, IVe Section, Paris
HMR	Excavation numbers for objects found at Uhaimir by the Oxford-Field Museum expedition to Kish
HS	Hilprecht collection of Babylonian Antiquities of Fr. Schiller University, Jena
IB	Excavation numbers of the Munich expedition to Isin-Išān Bahrīyāt
IM	Iraq Museum, Baghdad
JS	J. Shemtob collection of the University Museum, Philadelphia
K	Kuyunjik collection of the British Museum, London
Ki	L.W. King collection in the British Museum, London
L	Excavation numbers of the French expedition to Larsa
LA	Los Angeles County Museum of Art
LB	Tablets in the Liagre Böhl collection, Leiden
ML	Signature of cuneiform materials in the McLennan Library belonging to the McGill University Ethnological collections, Montreal
MMA	Metropolitan Museum of Art, New York
N	Siglum (infix) for excavation numbers from the American excavations at Nippur
ND	Prefix of excavation numbers from the British excavations at Nimrud, Iraq
NBC	James B. Nies collection of the Yale University Library, New Haven
NT	Siglum (infix) for excavation numbers of inscribed objects from the American excavations at Nippur
PMA	Philadelphia Museum of Art
PT	Excavation numbers for objects found on the Persepolis terrace by the Oriental Institute expedition
PTS	Princeton Theological Seminary
Rm	H. Rassam collection of the British Museum, London
ROM	Royal Ontario Museum, Toronto
Sm	G. Smith collection of the British Museum, London
Sp	Spartoli collection of the British Museum, London
U	Prefix of excavation numbers from the British-American excavations at Ur, Iraq
UCBC	University of California Babylonian collection
UCLM	Lowie Museum of Anthropology, University of California, Berkeley
UIOM	University of Illinois Oriental Museum, Urbana
UM	University Museum, Philadelphia
UM L-	Signature of objects on loan to the University Museum, Philadelphia
VA	Vorderasiatisches Museum, Berlin
VA Bab	Babylon collection of the Vorderasiatisches Museum, Berlin
VAG	Casts in the collection of the Vorderasiatisches Museum, Berlin
VAT	Tablets in the collection of the Vorderasiatisches Museum, Berlin
W	Excavation numbers of the German excavations at Uruk/Warka
WHM	World Heritage Museum, Urbana
YBC	Babylonian collection of the Yale University Library, New Haven

RULERS OF BABYLONIA
FROM THE SECOND DYNASTY OF ISIN
TO THE END OF ASSYRIAN DOMINATION

(1157–612 BC)

Introduction

The Babylonian royal inscriptions edited in this volume come from the period from the fall of the Kassite dynasty in the middle of the twelfth century to the collapse of Assyrian power towards the close of the seventh century BC. In 626 the Babylonian Nabopolassar ascended the throne of Babylon and began the process which led to the final ejection of the Assyrians from Babylonia and the firm foundation of the Neo-Babylonian dynasty. The inscriptions of Nabopolassar and his successors (B.7) will be presented in the next two volumes of this series (RIMB 3–4). During the approximate five centuries covered by this volume there were a number of short-lived dynasties in Babylonia of varying backgrounds and for a time the land was controlled by its northern neighbour Assyria.[1]

Several Assyrian rulers, beginning with Tiglath-pileser III in 728 BC, controlled Babylonia and some of these were included in the canonical lists of rulers of Babylonia. Votive and building inscriptions which were composed in the names of Assyrian rulers and which come from Babylonia and/or deal with Babylonia have been included in this volume whether these rulers ever specifically claimed the title "king of Babylon" or not. Inscriptions which are clearly Assyrian in nature (e.g., those on prisms) will not be presented here. In particular, the lengthy inscription of Esarhaddon which describes his restoration of Babylon is not included in this volume; that inscription has several major recensions — some of which are known only from Assyrian exemplars and some of which are found only upon prisms. For the convenience of the users of the RIM series, it is planned that the inscriptions of the Assyrian rulers presented in this volume will also be included in the Assyrian volumes (RIMA). While this will result in a certain amount of duplication, it will allow all the inscriptions of an Assyrian ruler to be presented in one volume.

For the most part, the relative order and basic chronology of the rulers of Babylonia during this time are reasonably well established by various king lists and chronicles. The absolute chronology for their reigns from the end of the tenth through to the middle of the eighth centuries (rulers B.6.3–14), however, remains uncertain.[2]

There are comparatively few Babylonian royal inscriptions from this period, and indeed the first part of it has sometimes been termed a "Dark Age." The royal inscriptions that do exist concentrate on building projects and the dedication of various objects to gods. They thus provide relatively little information on the political events of the time. The order in which the inscriptions are presented for any one ruler is basically geographical, commencing with inscriptions from or dealing with Babylon and then proceeding north to south for the major centres within the heartland of Babylonia. Although they are not strictly speaking royal inscriptions and may well have been composed considerably later than the events they purport to describe, a number of historical-literary texts are presented in this volume (primarily among the texts of Nebuchadnezzar I, B.2.4) since they provide information of historical value. These are presented after any inscriptions which can be associated with particular sites. In addition, a number of short possession or dedicatory inscriptions of Babylonian officials whose dates cannot be determined with any degree of certainty have been included; these are presented with the "Unidentified" texts (B.4.0 and B.6.0).

Among the texts presented in this volume are a number of inscriptions which are found incised on bronze objects (especially arrow heads and daggers). These pieces are frequently stated in the scholarly literature to have come from Luristan or to be similar to Luristan bronzes. O.W. Muscarella has noted that very few bronzes have been scientifically excavated in Luristan, that not a single inscribed bronze attributed to Luristan comes from scientific excavations either in Luristan or elsewhere, and that numerous so-called Luristan bronzes are forgeries. He suggests that at least some of the inscribed pieces may actually have been found in Iraq and later

---

[1] For the history of the period, see Brinkman, PKB; Brinkman, Prelude; Brinkman, CAH[2] 3/1 pp. 282–313 and CAH[2] 3/2 pp. 1–70; Frame, Babylonia; and Wiseman, CAH[3] 2/2 pp. 443–81.

[2] The dates of the kings' reigns cited in this volume follow those set forth by J.A. Brinkman in Oppenheim, Ancient Mesopotamia pp. 335–48.

been smuggled into Iran.[3] Published statements as to the provenance of these pieces having been Luristan generally appear to go back to statements by antiquities dealers and thus must be treated with suspicion. The presence of Babylonian royal inscriptions on numerous objects supposedly from a region outside Babylonian control is also disquieting, though W.G. Lambert has suggested that some of these inscriptions may have been copied from Babylonian votive objects which had found their way to Luristan.[4] Thus, the provenances of the inscribed "Luristan bronzes" included in this volume are not known and some of the inscriptions may date after the time of the king they mention.

The present locations of the various items described in this volume as being in the Foroughi collection are not known. I am informed that a large part of this collection was given to the Iranian government and is possibly now in the Iran Bastan Museum, Teheran. The remainder of the collection is still in the possession of the Foroughi family and found in Paris.

A number of inscriptions of the rulers of the Middle Euphrates state of Sūḫu in the eighth century were discovered during salvage work in the Ḥadītha area in the 1980s and these, together with two other inscriptions from this region which have been known for some time, are presented at the end of this volume (dynasty S.0). Unlike conventional Babylonian royal inscriptions, these provide information on the military encounters of the rulers. In particular, a number describe in lively prose the defeat of two thousand Arameans who had come to plunder the neighbouring state of Laqû.

The texts in this volume have not previously been edited together in a systematic manner, but most of the material dating down to 722 BC was described by J.A. Brinkman in his thorough study of the political history of the years 1158–722 BC (PKB).[5]

The editorial procedures of the RIM series are outlined in the Editorial Notes by R.F.G. Sweet. It should be noted that following the practice in RIME 4, the name of the god Enlil and the goddess Ninlil are transliterated ^{d}*en-líl* and ^{d}*nin-líl* respectively, not ^{d}EN.LÍL and ^{d}NIN.LÍL. However, it is not clear in all cases if these are what the ancient scribes would have actually pronounced. The aim of the bibliographies is to provide complete references to works directly relevant to the inscriptions. No attempt has been made, however, to cite all the histories and related studies of the material.

[3] See Muscarella, Bronze and Iron p. 120 n. 6, and in Levine and Young, Mountains and Lowlands p. 171.
[4] W.G. Lambert, AfO 22 (1968–69) p. 11.
[5] Note in particular his introductory comments on pp. 4–12 and his catalogue of written sources on pp. 319–64.

SECOND DYNASTY OF ISIN

B.2

The manner in which the Kassite dynasty was succeeded by the Second Dynasty of Isin is not clear since almost nothing is known of the reign of the first ruler of the new dynasy, Marduk-kabit-aḫḫēšu, beyond his name, the length of his reign, and the fact that he was succeeded by his son, Itti-Marduk-balāṭu. According to King List A, the Second Dynasty of Isin (BALA PA.ŠE) comprised eleven kings who reigned for a total of one hundred and thirty-two years and six months (1157–1026 BC). From the name of the dynasty, it is generally assumed that the initial capital of the dynasty was located at Isin, but there is no proof of this. The first and second rulers of this dynasty (Marduk-kabit-aḫḫēšu and Itti-Marduk-balāṭu) were father and son, and the third through seventh (Ninurta-nādin-šumi, Nebuchadnezzar I, Enlil-nādin-apli, Marduk-nādin-aḫḫē, and Marduk-šāpik-zēri) were also related to one another. However, there is no clear evidence that any of the other rulers of this dynasty were related to one another in any way. See Brinkman, PKB pp. 90–92 and RLA 5/3–4 (1977) pp. 183–89, and Grayson in RLA 6/1–2 (1980) p. 92 iii 5′.

Marduk-kabit-aḫḫēšu

B.2.1

According to Babylonian King List A, Marduk-kabit-aḫḫēšu was the first ruler of the Second Dynasty of Isin. The length of his reign in that king list is damaged and has been read as both seventeen and eighteen years; however, the older and better preserved King List C clearly states that he reigned for eighteen years (1157–1140 BC). He was the father of Itti-Marduk-balāṭu, his successor. No royal inscriptions of this king and no documents dated by his regnal years are attested. For details of reign, see Brinkman, PKB pp. 40, 93, and 323–24 no. 1.

Itti-Marduk-balāṭu

B.2.2

Itti-Marduk-balāṭu, the second ruler of the Second Dynasty of Isin, succeeded his father Marduk-kabit-aḫḫēšu on the throne of Babylon and, according to King List C, reigned for eight years (1139–1132 BC). One royal inscription of the king is known, but only the beginning of the inscription — recording the king's genealogy, titles, and epithets — is preserved (B.2.2.1). In addition, one fragmentary kudurru recording a private land-sale (King, BBSt no. 30) and five economic tablets (see Böhl, AfK 2 [1924–25] pp. 49–64) come from his reign. For details of the reign of Itti-Marduk-balāṭu, see Brinkman, PKB pp. 41, 94–98, and 324 no. 2.

1

A piece of limestone in the Vorderasiatisches Museum (Berlin) preserves part of the introductory section of an Akkadian inscription of Itti-Marduk-balāṭu.

COMMENTARY

The stone bears the number VA 2577 in the Vorderasiatisches Museum and was purchased from a private collection. The piece measures 24×14 cm. The inscription, written in Babylonian script, has been collated.

In line 8, there is a trace of the head of a vertical wedge after the divine determinative and it would fit with a reading ⸢*a*⸣. The restoration of the titles in lines 12 and 13 is uncertain; with regard to line 13, see in particular Brinkman, PKB p. 96. There is a small raised winkelhaken after KI in line 13 and this could suggest the beginning of an IN sign and the proposed "king of *Su*[*mer* (*and*) *Akkad*]." In general, an epithet mentioning a city precedes one mentioning a wider area and one might then think of "king [of Babylon]" in line 12, even though this city is already mentioned in the title in line 7. The restoration tentatively proposed (LUGAL [*dan*(?)-*num*(?)], "[*mighty*] king") is based on an inscription of the slightly earlier king Marduk-apla-iddina I where "mighty king" does precede "king of Sumer and Akkad" (Messerschmidt and Ungnad, VAS 1 no. 34 lines 16–18). For a study of the titles used by Itti-Marduk-balāṭu in this inscription, see Brinkman, PKB pp. 95–96.

BIBLIOGRAPHY

1889 Winckler, Untersuchungen pp. 139–40 (edition)
1907 Messerschmidt and Ungnad, VAS 1 no. 112 (copy)
1924–25 Böhl, AfK 2 pp. 49–50 (partial translation)
1968 Brinkman, PKB pp. 5, 94–96 and 324 no. 2.2.1 (translation, study)

TEXT

1) KI-^{d}AMAR.UTU-TI.L[A]
2) LUGAL *šar-r*[*i*]
3) *mi-gir* DINGIR.M[EŠ]
4) DUMU ^{d}AMAR.UTU-DUGUD-ŠEŠ.M[EŠ-*šú*/*šu*]
5) NUN *na-*ʾ-[*du*]
6) *gít-ma-*[*lu*]
7) GÌR.NÍTA TIN.T[IR.KI]
8) *ni-bi-it* ^{d}⸢*a*(?)⸣-[*nim*(?)]
9) *ù* ^{d}*d*[*a-gan*]
10) ÉNSI ^{d}[*en-líl*]
11) *ù* ^{d}*nin*-[*líl*]
12) LUGAL [*dan*(?)-*num*(?)]
13) LUGAL KI.I[N(?).GI(?) URI(?).KI(?)]
14) *a-na* ⸢^{d}⸣[...]
15) ⸢AN(?)⸣ x [...]
Lacuna

1–15) Itti-Marduk-balāṭu, king of kings, favourite of the gods, son of Marduk-kabit-aḫḫē[šu], (5) pio[us] (and) perf[ect] prince, viceroy of Baby[lon], who was chosen by the gods *A*[*nu*] and D[agan], (10) vice-regent for the god [Enlil] and the goddess Nin[lil, *mighty*] king, king of *Su*[*mer* (*and*) *Akkad*], for the god/goddess [...] ... [...]
Lacuna

Ninurta-nādin-šumi

B.2.3

Ninurta-nādin-šumi, the third king of the Second Dynasty of Isin, ruled for six years (1131–26 BC). It is not known if he was related to the previous king, Itti-Marduk-balāṭu, or not; however, he himself was followed by at least four descendants: Nebuchadnezzar I, Enlil-nādin-apli, Marduk-nādin-aḫḫē, and Marduk-šāpik-zēri (B.2.4–7). According to a poorly preserved Assyrian chronicle (Grayson, Chronicles p. 188 col. iv?), Ninurta-nādin-šumi appears to have invaded Assyria at one point and to have been opposed at that time by the Assyrian ruler Aššur-rēša-iši I (1132–1115 BC).

A label found on two bronze daggers (B.2.3.1) is the only royal inscription attested for this king. For a fragmentary kudurru possibly dating to this king's reign, see Borger, AfO 23 (1970) p. 26. For details of the reign of Ninurta-nādin-šumi, see Brinkman, PKB pp. 41, 98–104, and 324–25 no. 3.

1

Two bronze daggers have a short inscription written in Akkadian indicating that they belonged to Ninurta-nādin-šumi.

CATALOGUE

Ex.	Museum number	Lines preserved	cpn
1	Foroughi collection, number unknown	1–4	p
2	Foroughi collection, number unknown	1–4	p

COMMENTARY

With regard to the present location of pieces in the "Foroughi collection," see the introduction to this volume. The original provenances of the daggers are not known. They are similar to other pieces commonly stated to have come from Luristan, but on this matter, see the introduction to this volume. One of the two exemplars is presumably the dagger with an inscription of this ruler seen by Contenau in Iran in 1931 (RA 29 [1932] p. 29) and reported to be on the market in Teheran in 1932 by Herzfeld (Persian Empire p. 29 no. 2). If not, this could be a third exemplar of this inscription. For this "third" piece, see also Langdon in Pope, Survey 1 pp. 279 and 283 no. 6; Nagel, AfO 19 (1959–60) p. 95 no. 5; Calmeyer, Datierbare Bronzen p. 60 no. 31C; and Moorey, Catalogue Ashmolean p. 31 no. 2. One of the two daggers in the Foroughi collection measured 42.5×4 cm in size. The inscriptions on the two daggers are identical and no score is provided in the microfiche.

BIBLIOGRAPHY

1961 Ghirshman, Sept mille no. 274 (study)
1962 Dossin, IrAnt 2 pp. 151–52 and pls. XV–XVI no. 3 (exs. 1–2, photo, edition)
1964 Porada, 7000 Years of Iranian Art no. 140 (study)
1968 Brinkman, PKB p. 100 and p. 325 no. 3.2.1 (exs. 1–2, translation, study)
1969 Calmeyer, Datierbare Bronzen p. 60 nos. 31D and E, fig. 57, and p. 163 nos. 25–26 (exs. 1–2, transliteration, study; drawing)
1971 Moorey, Catalogue Ashmolean p. 31 no. 1 (exs. 1–2, study)

TEXT

Obverse
1) *ša* ^{d}*nin-urta*-SUM-MU
2) LUGAL ŠÁR
Reverse
3) LUGAL KÁ.DINGIR.RA.KI
4) LUGAL KI.IN.GI URI.KI

1–4) (Property) of Ninurta-nādin-šumi, king of the world, king of Babylon, king of Sumer (and) Akkad.

Nebuchadnezzar I

B.2.4

Upon the death of Ninurta-nādin-šumi, his son Nebuchadnezzar I ascended the throne. Babylonian King List C indicates that he reigned for twenty-two years (1125–1104 BC). According to the Synchronistic History, Nebuchadnezzar attempted to capture Assyrian fortresses on two occasions. On the first occasion, the Babylonian forces retreated when the Assyrian king Aššur-rēša-iši I sent troops against them, and on the second, the Babylonian army was defeated (see Grayson, Chronicles pp. 162–64 no. 21 ii 1′–13′). Despite these setbacks, Nebuchadnezzar I was considered a great king in Babylonian eyes because he punished Elam for its recent devastating invasions of Babylonia and for its removal of the cult statue of the god Marduk from Esagila. The details of his campaigns into Elam are not always clear, but Elamite forces suffered a defeat on at least one occasion and the statue of Marduk was recovered. As suggested by Lambert, it may have been at the time of the celebrations connected with the reinstallation of Marduk in his temple in Babylon that that god was raised to the position of head of the Babylonian pantheon (Essays Meek pp. 3–13; see also Sommerfeld, Aufstieg Marduks pp. 182–89).

A bilingual inscription records Nebuchadnezzar's renovation of the shrine Ekitušḫegaltila at Babylon for the god Adad (B.2.4.1) and a Sumerian brick inscription describes his work in the Ekur at Nippur (B.2.4.2). Several bronze daggers bear a label mentioning the king (B.2.4.3) and a bronze hatchet with an inscription indicating that it belonged to him also has a prayer to the god Marduk (B.2.4.4). A few historical-literary works describe the king's campaigns against Elam and the recovery of the statue of Marduk. These have been included here although they are not strictly speaking royal inscriptions (B.2.4.5–10), as has a passage from a boundary stone (kudurru) from the king's reign which describes part of a campaign into Elam (B.2.4.11). Although the name of the king is not preserved in B.2.4.6–7 and 9–10, they can be assigned to this king in view of their content. B.2.4.1 and B.2.4.8–10 are bilingual inscriptions, written in Sumerian and Akkadian; B.2.4.2 is written in Sumerian, and the remainder are in Akkadian. Inscription B.2.4.1 is written on a stone tablet; B.2.4.5–9 and B.2.4.1001 are found upon clay tablets; B.2.4.2 is on bricks; B.6.2.4.3 is on bronze daggers; B.6.2.4 is on bronze hatchet(s); B.2.4.10 is on a clay cylinder; and B.2.4.11 is on a stone stela.

According to a later inscription of the Babylonian king Simbar-Šipak (B.3.1.1), a throne had been made during the reign of Nebuchadnezzar for the god Enlil in Ekurigigal at Nippur. The Neo-Babylonian king Nabonidus stated that he had found a stela which had been set up in the Gipāru at Ur by "Nebuchadnezzar, son of Ninurta-nādin-šumi," and which depicted the *entu*-priestess (Clay, YOS 1 no. 45 i 29–33). The stela may have been set up to mark the installation of Nebuchadnezzar's daughter as *entu*-priestess. Nebuchadnezzar is also included among a number of other royal donors of precious objects to a temple in a Neo-Babylonian inventory from Ur (Figulla, UET 4 no. 143:11 and 13).

At least three stone kudurrus come from the king's reign and each describes an action by Nebuchadnezzar I. The first (King, BBSt no. 6) records the grant of special privileges to several villages because of the bravery of their chief during a campaign to Elam. The initial part of the text describes that campaign and, as already mentioned, it is presented below as B.2.4.11. The second kudurru was composed in the king's sixteenth year and describes the grant of an estate to the *nešakku*-priest of Enlil at Nippur (Hinke, Boundary Stone pp. 142–87). The third kudurru records the grant of land to a god and his priests (King, BBSt no. 24). For a possible fourth kudurru, see Seidl, Bagh. Mitt. 4 (1968) p. 43 no. 69. Two economic texts also date to the king's reign (Clay, BRM 1 nos. 1 and 1a).

A literary text which is commonly called the Marduk Prophecy and which may have been composed to praise Nebuchadnezzar I for his recovery of the statue of the god Marduk is translated in Foster, Before the Muses 1 pp. 304–307 (with further bibliography). A further historical-literary text which might be assigned to Nebuchadnezzar is DT 71, published by J. Hehn in BA 5 (1906) pp. 326–29 and 386–88 no. 4. M. Weippert, however, has argued that this text describes Ashurbanipal's conflict with Elam, not Nebuchadnezzar's; see ZAW 84 (1972) pp. 482–83.

For details of the reign of Nebuchadnezzar I, see Brinkman, PKB pp. 41–42, 104–16, and 325–29 no. 4.

1

A bilingual inscription on two fragments of what is probably the same limestone tablet describes work by Nebuchadnezzar I on Ekitušḫegaltila ("House, Abode of Life-Giving Abundance"), a sanctuary of the god Adad at Babylon.

CATALOGUE

Ex.	Museum number	Babylon photo number	Dimensions (cm)	Lines preserved	cpn
1	LB 1530	715	11×13.3×2	Sumerian i 1–12, iv 1–13; Akkadian i 1–12, iv 1–13	c
2	Chicago A 3647	715	—	Sumerian ii 1–7; Akkadian ii 1–6	p

COMMENTARY

The two fragments were originally purchased by R. Koldewey in 1905 for the Deutsche Orient-Gesellschaft. Since he added the notation "Aus Birs?" for them in the expedition photo register, the seller may have claimed that they had come from Borsippa (Birs Nimrud). The pieces were later stolen from the excavation house at Babylon and found their way onto the antiquities market. Ex. 1 was purchased by Böhl from an antiquities dealer in Paris. It was kindly collated by W.H. van Soldt. Ex. 2 now belongs to the Oriental Institute (Chicago), but has been missing for a number of years. The publication rights to this exemplar are held by J.A. Brinkman, who will re-edit the piece from museum photographs (which were unavailable to the present writer) in a forthcoming publication. The exemplar is edited here from the excavation photograph, which shows only one side of the fragment; thus, it is not known if there is anything on the other side of the piece or not.

Assuming that the two pieces come from the same tablet, the exact spatial relationship between the two remains uncertain and it has been thought best to list the two pieces separately in the catalogue. Because LB 1530 is still increasing in thickness at the point at which it breaks off on the lower right of the obverse, Weidner notes that either the lines were extemely long or each side had more than one column. He suggests that ex. 1 may have parts of cols. i and iv and ex. 2 parts of cols. ii and iii (AfO 16 [1952–53] p. 72). Weidner's suggestion has been accepted here, but it must be remembered that this arrangement is not proven. It is possible that ex. 2 comes from a different tablet and inscription than ex. 1 and that what is given below as iv 1ff. comes immediately after i 12. It is also possible that the identification of the obverse and reverse of ex. 2 is incorrect and what is shown on the excavation photograph is the first few lines of col. iii instead of col. ii.

The Sumerian and Akkadian versions of the inscription are on alternate lines, with the Akkadian lines indented and a line ruling separating each pair of lines from the next pair. Each pair of lines is given one line number in the edition; the Akkadian version of a line follows the Sumerian version. The two pieces are written in contemporary Babylonian script; for comments on the script, see Böhl, BiOr 7 (1950) p. 43.

In view of the damaged nature of the inscription, a line-by-line translation is provided. As noted by Böhl (BiOr 7 [1950] p. 44), the text of ex. 1 has four basic parts: (1) mention of the king (i 1–6), (2) dedication to the god (i 7–12), (3) description of a battle (iv 1–7), and (4) renovation of a temple (iv 8ff.).

Ekitušḫegaltila was likely part of Enamḫe, the temple of the god Adad located in the western part of Babylon.

BIBLIOGRAPHY

1939 Böhl, JEOL 6 p. 263 no. 3 (ex. 1, study)

1950 Böhl, BiOr 7 pp. 42–46 and pls. I–III (ex. 1, photo, copy, edition, study)

1952–53 Weidner, AfO 16 pp. 71–73 no. 3 (exs. 1–2, study; ex. 2, copy of obverse [col. ii])

1968 Brinkman, PKB pp. 5, 106, 109, 112–13, and 325–26 no. 4.2.1 (exs. 1–2, study)

1982 Sommerfeld, Aufstieg Marduks pp. 183–84 (study)

TEXT

Col. i

1)	^{d}AG-*ku-dúr-ri*-ÙRU nu[n ní-tuku(?) (...)] NUN [*na*ʾ*du*(?) (...)]	i 1) Nebuchadnezzar, [*pious*] prince, [(...) *for whom*]
2)	^{d}AMAR.UTU ur-sag dingir-re-e-[ne-ke$_4$ ...] *ši-mat la šá-n*[*a-an išīmušu*(*m*)]	i 2) the god Marduk, hero among the gods, ⸤decreed⸥ a fate without equ[al],
3)	sun$_5$-na zé-tuku dingir gal-gal-⸢e⸣-[ne (...)] *aš-ru pa-liḫ* [*ilāni rabûti* (...)]	i 3) humble, who reveres the great gods [(...)],
4)	gú-ki-gál ní bí-in-tur-[tur (...)] *kan-šu mut-nen-nu*-[*ú* (...))]	i 4) submissive, prayerful, [(...)],
5)	sipa gi-na ú-a ki-š[u-peš$_5$/peš$_6$ (...)] *re-e-ú ki-nu za*-[*ni-in māḫāzī*(?)]	i 5) true shepherd, who provides for the cul[t centres],
6)	lugal níg-si-sá lugal KÁ.DINGIR.[RA.KI (...)] [...]	i 6) king of justice, king of Babyl[on (...)]:
7)	^{d}iškur en-e nè-ḫu[š ...] *a-na* ^{d}IŠKUR EN *mug*-[*dáš-ri* ...]	i 7) for the god Adad, the powerful lord [...],
8)	nam-kal-kal-la gú-gal nir-gá[l (...)] *dan-dan-ni a-šá-ri-di* [...]	i 8) almighty, foremost, sovereign [(...)],
9)	en-e gù-šu-nigin-na níg-alim-a-bi [...] *be-lí šá i-na ta-nu-qa-ti-š*[*u kabtāti*(?) ...]	i 9) my lord at whose *mighty* battle-cry [...],
10)	ur$_5$-ša$_4$ za-pa-ág du$_{10}$-ga an-ta bi x [...] *ṭa-bu ri-gim ra-mi-mi-š*[*u eliš* ...]	i 10) the sound of whose roar on high is pleasant ... [...],
11)	lugal é-nam-ḫé é-ki-tuš-ḫé-gál-ti-l[a (...)] *be-el é-nam-hé a-šib é-ki-tuš-ḫé*-[*gál-ti-la* (...)]	i 11) lord of Enamḫe ("House of Plenty"), who dwells in Ekitušḫegaltila [(...)],
12)	ù-ma al-sá-sá-mu bàd-gal-mu [(...)] *mu-šak-ši-id ir-ni-it-ti-ia* [*tukultīia* (...)]	i 12) who makes me triumph, my helper [(...)]

i 1 The Akkadian version omits the king's name.
i 2 The Akkadian version omits the god's name.
i 7 nè-ḫuš for ní-ḫuš, which stands for Akkadian *mugdašru*.
i 9 šu-nigin likely for tal$_5$, which can stand for *tanūqātu* (see AHw p. 1320a).
i 10 Possibly *ina šamê*, "in the sky/heavens," instead of *eliš*, "on high," for the Sumerian an-ta (suggestion by W.G. Lambert).

Col. ii

1) [...] x mi-ni(*)-in-x-kúr
[...] x (x) TU *ga-ri-i* [(x)]
2) [...] (x)-x-ra BAL/GÌR(?) x-ga-a
[...] *am-ḫaṣ-ma*
3) [...] ba-e-⸢da⸣-an-gar
[...] x TA *aš-ku-un*
4) [... k]i-in-gi uri.KI-ta ba-ni(*)-in-TAR
[... *ina*] KUR *šu-me-ri ù ak-ka-di-i ap-ru-us*
5) [...] x e-ne
[...]*-i i-ru-ni*(*)
6) [... a]l-ma-⸢az⸣-za
[...] *lìb-bi-i*[*a*]
7) [...] ⸢IN(?)⸣ mi-ni(*)-in-[x x (x)]
[...]

Lacuna (approximately 5 double-lines)

Col. iii

Lacuna (approximately 13 double-lines, the last few lines of which may be preserved in part on ex. 2)

Col. iv

1) ki ti-saḫ$_4$ šen-šen-na giš-lá-ka-nam [(...)]
aš-šum a-šar a-na-an-ti šá-aš-me tu-[*qu-un-ti* (...)]
2) GIŠ.tukul sìg-ga šu-nir silig-silig-ga dingir gal è-a x [(...)]
i-na ti-iṣ-bu-ut kak-ki pe-te(?)*-e šu-ri-*⸢*in*⸣-[*ni* ...]
3) gá-e á-taḫ-mu ak-a-ab zag(-)tab-mu gin-a NA x [...]
ru-ṣa-am-ma ia-a-ti ⸢*i*(?)*-du*(?)⸣*-ú-a al-ka*[*m* ...]
4) na-⸢nam⸣ gi-na-⸢bi⸣ [...]
i-na an-⸢*ni-šu*⸣ [*kīni* ...]
5) GIŠ.gibil x [...]
A LU ŠU Ú x [...]
6) GIŠ.tukul-bi GIŠ E x [...]
kak-ka x (x) [...]
7) ù x (x) ki x (x) [...]
ù x [...] A [...]
8) ^{d}AG-*ku-dúr-r*[*i*-ÙRU ...]
[...]
9) ki mè-⸢ka⸣ x [...]
AL LA x x [...]
10) nam-bi-⸢šè⸣ x [...]
a-na šat-t[*i* ...]
11) é-ki-tuš-ḫé-g[ál-ti]-l[a ...]
É *šu-bat*(?) I(?) [...]
12) ⸢zálag⸣ GA/BI x [...]
[(x)] x x x x (x) [...]
13) x x (x) x [x] x [...]
[(x)] x [...]

ii 1) [...] ... enemy.

ii 2) [...] I smote and

ii 3) [...] ... I established.

ii 4) [(...)] I cut off [...] from the land of Sumer and Akkad.

ii 5) [...] ...

ii 6) [...] my heart.

ii 7) [...] ...

Lacuna

Lacuna

iv 1) because in the place of battle, strife, (and) fighting [(...)]

iv 2) at the clash of arms and the *revealing* of the standard, the great god going forth [(...)].

iv 3) Help me! Come *to* my *side*! ... [...]

iv 4) By his reliable positive answer [...]

iv 5) fire [...]

iv 6) his weapon ... [...]

iv 7) ... [...]

iv 8) Nebuchadne[zzar ...]

iv 9) in the place of fighting [...]

iv 10) On account of this [...]

iv 11) Ekitušḫeg[alti]l[a ...]

iv 12) ... [...]

iv 13) ... [...]

---

ii 1 For the Akkadian "enemy," the Sumerian appears to have "became hostile."

ii 1, 4, and **7** (Sumerian version) and **ii 5** and **iv 4** (Akkadian version). In each case, it is not clear whether there are two vertical wedges in the NI sign or just one.

ii 6 For the Akkadian "my heart," the Sumerian has "rejoiced."

iv 4 The phrase "reliable positive answer" usually refers to the gods Šamaš and Adad giving a reply by means of extispicy.

iv 11 The Akkadian version may have a translation of the Sumerian name of the temple if one assumes that what appears to be an I is actually a ḪÉ and thus part of the word *ḫegallu*, "abundance."

2

Several bricks found at Nippur are reported to be stamped with a Sumerian inscription of Nebuchadnezzar I recording work on the Unumaḫ. The text of only one of these is known.

COMMENTARY

The brick (2 NT 483) was found in 1950 in room EN-13 of the Enlil Temple, level III, and is currently in the University Museum (Philadelphia). It measures 28×28×7 cm and has been collated.

Bricks with this inscription were found in the pavement or as part of a sump pit in room EN-13 and in a socle in street 20. For the findspots, see McCown, Nippur 1 pp. 13–14 and 17.

The term unu-maḫ can be translated literally "Great Abode." It is possible that unu is used here for únu/unu$_6$ and that the term stands for "Great Dining Hall." For a possible connection of room EN-13 with food preparation or offerings, see McCown, Nippur 1 pp. 30–31.

BIBLIOGRAPHY

1968 Brinkman, PKB pp. 5, 113 n. 624 and 326 no. 4.2.3 (edition, study)
1985 Behrens, JCS 37 p. 239 no. 51 (study)

TEXT

1) ^{d}en-líl-lá
2) umun kur-kur-ra
3) lugal-a-ni-ir
4) ^{d}AG-*ku-dúr-ri*-ÙRU
5) nun ní-te-na
6) sig$_4$-al-ùr-ra
7) mi-ni-in-du$_8$-àm
8) ki-gar ⌜unu-maḫ⌝-a
9) mi-ni-in-dù-dù

1–9) For the god Enlil, lord of lands, his lord: Nebuchadnezzar, (5) prayerful prince, made baked bricks and built the base of the Unu-maḫ (with them).

3

An Akkadian inscription on four bronze daggers states that each was the property of the king Nebuchadnezzar.

CATALOGUE

Ex.	Museum number	Dimensions (cm)	Lines preserved	cpn
1	Foroughi collection, number unknown	—	1–4	p
2	Foroughi collection, number unknown	45×4.3	1–4?	n
3	Foroughi collection, number unknown	42.5×2.7	1–4	n
4	Iran Bastan Museum (Teheran), number unknown	Length: 42	1–4	n

COMMENTARY

With regard to the present locations of the pieces in the Foroughi collection, see the introduction to this volume. The published photo of one side of ex. 2 (Datierbare Bronzen pl. 2 no. 3) shows traces which would appear to duplicate lines 3–4. However, Calmeyer identifies this piece as having been no. 272 in the Paris catalogue Sept mille ans d'art en Iran and Ghirshman's entry for that piece (ibid. p. 48 [followed in Kunstschätze and Porada, 7000 Years of Iranian Art]) states that the inscription is visible on only one side and is in the name of the king Nebuchadnezzar I. This would suggest that the inscription on the obverse (lines 1–2) is preserved. Thus there may be some confusion with regard to the identification of the piece in the catalogue with our ex. 2. The Foroughi collection is known to have had several daggers on which the inscription is only partially preserved (see below).

Since it has not been possible to collate exs. 2–4, no score is given for this text in the microfiche and the edition is based upon the photographs of ex. 1. The only variant known is found on ex. 4, which has *šá* ᵈAG-NÍG.DU-ÙRU in line 1. According to the published copy of that exemplar, the form of the KÁ in line 3 is somewhat unusual.

The published literature indicates that these bronze pieces come from Luristan, but note the cautionary statements in the introduction to this volume.

Dossin states that there are three further daggers which probably have this inscription; however, only the titulary of the reverse is preserved on each (IrAnt 2 [1962] p. 152). In view of similar titulary on bronze daggers of other kings from about this time (B.2.3.1, B.2.5.1, and B.2.6.4), their ascription to this king must remain uncertain. They are listed below as B.2.0.1002.

Neither this inscription nor inscription B.2.4.4, which is found on a bronze hatchet, gives the name of the king's father. They are assigned to this king instead of to the Neo-Babylonian monarch by this name because most inscribed bronzes come from c. 1215–940 BC and because no bronzes with inscriptions of Neo-Babylonian monarchs are otherwise attested.

BIBLIOGRAPHY

1931 Contenau, RA 28 p. 107 (ex. 4, transliteration)
1938 Langdon in Pope, Survey 1 pp. 279 and 283 no. 7 (ex. 4, copy in type, study)
1941 Herzfeld, Iran p. 134 (ex. 4?, transcription)
1959–60 Nagel, AfO 19 p. 95 no. 2 and p. 97 fig. 2 (ex. 4, drawing, study)
1961 Ghirshman, Sept mille nos. 272 and 275 (exs. 2–3, study)
1962 Dossin, IrAnt 2 p. 152 and pl. XVII no. 4 (ex. 1, photo; exs. 1–3, edition)
1962 Ghirshman, Kunstschätze no. 126 (ex. 2, study)
1964 Porada, 7000 Years of Iranian Art nos. 138 and 141 (exs. 2–3, study)
1968 Brinkman, PKB p. 326 nos. 4.2.2 (ex. 4, study) and 4.2.5 (exs. 1–3, study)
1969 Calmeyer, Datierbare Bronzen p. 60 no. 31F and p. 164 no. 30 (ex. 4, transliteration, study) and p. 60 nos. 31G–I, fig. 58, p. 164 nos. 31–33, and pl. 2 no. 3 (ex. 2, photo; ex. 3, drawing; exs. 1–3, transliteration, study)
1971 Moorey, Catalogue Ashmolean p. 31 nos. 3–4 (study)

TEXT

Obverse
1) *ša* ᵈAG-*ku-dúr-ri*-ÙRU
2) LUGAL ŠÁR
Reverse
3) LUGAL KÁ.DINGIR.RA.KI
4) LUGAL KI.IN.GI URI.KI

1–4) (Property) of Nebuchadnezzar, king of the world, king of Babylon, king of Sumer (and) Akkad.

4

An inscription written in Akkadian which records a prayer to the god Marduk and states that the object belonged to the king Nebuchadnezzar is found upon (apparently) two bronze hatchets in the Foroughi collection. The hatchets are said to come from Luristan, but there is no proof that this reported provenance is correct.

COMMENTARY

As noted by Calmeyer (Datierbare Bronzen p. 67), there appear to be two hatchets in the Foroughi collection with this inscription. Photographs of the obverse of two exemplars have been published: ex. 1 = Dossin, IrAnt 2 (1962) pl. XXIV top and middle; and ex. 2 = Calmeyer, Datierbare Bronzen pl. 4 no. 1. A photograph of the reverse of (apparently only) one exemplar has been published: ex. 2 = Calmeyer, Datierbare Bronzen pl. 4 no. 2; Dossin, IrAnt 2 (1962) pl. XXIV bottom; and Amiet, Luristan p. 30 fig. 26. The photo of the obverse published by Calmeyer (ex. 2) is not always clear, but appears to be an exact duplicate of what is found on ex. 1 (including having NA for *ru* in line 2). No score is provided for the inscription in the microfiche, and the edition presented below is based upon the photos published by Dossin — obverse from ex. 1 and reverse from (apparently) ex. 2.

The inscription reads like a Kassite period seal inscription and W.G. Lambert suggests that it may have been copied off of another item, or items, in Luristan. One hatchet measures 16 cm in length.

BIBLIOGRAPHY

1961 Ghirshman, Sept mille no. 269 (study)
1962 Dossin, IrAnt 2 p. 158 and pl. XXIV no. 14 (photo, edition)
1962 Ghirshman, Kunstschätze no. 124 (study)
1964 Porada, 7000 Years of Iranian Art no. 135 (photo, study)
1968 Brinkman, PKB pp. 106 n. 575 and 326 no. 4.2.4 (edition, study)
1968–69 Lambert, AfO 22 p. 11 (edition)
1969 Calmeyer, Datierbare Bronzen pp. 67 nos. 33B′–C′ and 164 nos. 28–29, and pl. 4 nos. 1–2 (photo, transliteration, study),
1971 Moorey, Catalogue Ashmolean p. 33 no. 1 (study)
1975 Borger, HKL 2 p. 47 (study)
1976 Amiet, Luristan pp. 29–30 and fig. 26 (photo of reverse, study)
1982 Sommerfeld, Aufstieg Marduks p. 184 (edition)
1993 Foster, Before the Muses 1 p. 303 (translation)

TEXT

Obverse
1) *te-le-ʾ-e* ᵈAMAR.UTU
2) *mut-nen-na-a e-ṭe₄-ra*(*)
3) *muš-te-ʾ-ú aš-ra-ti-ka*
4) UGU *na-ki-ri šu-zu-uz-za*
5) ⸢*i*⸣*-zi-qa ša-ra-ka a-se-ʾ na-ak-*⸢*ri*⸣*-ia*

Reverse
6) *du-un-ni-in kak-ki-ia-ma*
7) *lu-šam-*⸢*qí*⸣*-ta ge-ri-ia*
8) *ša* ᵈAG*-ku-dúr-ri-*ÙRU LUGAL ŠÁR

1–4) O god Marduk, you are able to rescue the prayerful man (and) to make the one who is assiduous toward your sanctuaries stand (in victory) over (his) enemies.
5) Your breeze wafted to me; I am able to throw down my enemies.

6–7) Strengthen my weapons so that I may overthrow my foes!
8) (Property) of Nebuchadnezzar, king of the world.

5

A partially preserved Neo-Assyrian copy of a historical-literary text written in Akkadian describes how the god Marduk had listened to the prayers of Nebuchadnezzar and commanded him to take him back to Babylon from Elam.

---

2 *ra*(*): text has NA.

COMMENTARY

The fragmentary tablet is in the Kuyunjik collection of the British Museum (K 3426). It was copied for an Assyrian king (probably Ashurbanipal) from another copy of the inscription in Babylon (see the colophon, rev. 2′–3′). The tablet measures 7.3×10.1×2.5 cm. The inscription is written in Neo-Assyrian script and has been collated. There is a gap between rev. 1′ and 2′; rev. 3′ is written in signs larger than those of the remainder of the inscription.

BIBLIOGRAPHY

1887–90 Delitzsch, AW pp. 306 and 308 (study)
1891 Bezold, Cat. 2 p. 532 (study)
1893 Winckler, Sammlung 2 p. 72 (copy)
1894 Boissier, Revue sémitique 2 pp. 76–78 (partial edition, study)
1897 Winckler, AOF 1/6 pp. 542–43 (edition)
1901 King, CT 13 pl. 48 (copy)
1968 Brinkman, PKB p. 328 no. 4.3.8 (study)
1975 Grayson, BHLT pp. 42–43 and 45 (study)
1977 Roberts, Essays Finkelstein pp. 183–87, especially nn. 23 and 45–47 (study)
1982 Sommerfeld, Aufstieg Marduks pp. 187–88 (study)
1993 Foster, Before the Muses 1 p. 301 (translation)

TEXT

Obverse

1) *a-šib i-na* KÁ.DINGIR.RA.KI ^{d}AG-NÍG.DU-ÙRU [*šarru*(?)]
2) *il-tam-mir ki-i* UR.MAḪ *ki-i* ^{d}IŠKUR *i-šag-*[*gum*]
3) LÚ.GAL.MEŠ-*šú e-du-ú-tu ki-ma la-ab-bu ú-šag-*[*lat*(?)]
4) *a-na* ^{d}AMAR.UTU EN TIN.TIR.KI *il-la-ku su-pu-ú-*[*šú*]

1–4) In Babylon dwells Nebuchadnezzar, [*the king*]. He rages like a lion (and) thun[ders] like the god Adad. Like a lion, he *frigh*[*tens*] his distinguished nobles. [His] supplications go to the god Marduk, lord of Babylon:

5) *a-ḫu-lap at-*⸢*tu*⸣*-ú-a šu-ta-nu-ḫu ù ú-tu-l*[*u*(?)]
6) *a-ḫu-lap i-na* KUR-*ia šá ba-ke-e ù sa-pa-a-d*[*u*]
7) ⸢*a*⸣*-ḫu-lap i-na* UN.MEŠ-*ia šá nu-um-bé-e ù ba-ke-*⸢*e*⸣
8) [*a*]*-di ma-ti* EN TIN.TIR.KI *ina* KUR *na-ki-ri áš-ba-a-ti*
9) [*li*]*b*(?)*-bal-*⸢*kit*⸣ *i-na lìb-bi-ka* TIN.TIR.KI *ba-nu-um-ma*
10) [*a-n*]*a* ⸢*é*⸣*-*[*s*]*ag-íl šá ta-ram-mu šu-us-ḫi-ra pa-ni-ka*

5–10) "Have pity on me, one who is dejected and *prost*[*rate*]! Have pity on my land, which weeps and mourns! Have pity on my people, who wail and weep! O lord of Babylon, how long will you dwell in the land of the enemy? May beautiful Babylon be remembered by you! Turn your face back to Esagila ("House Whose Top Is High"), which you love!"

11) [*suppê*(?)] ^{d}AG-NÍG.DU-ÙRU EN KÁ.DINGIR.RA.KI *iš-mé-e-ma*
12) [x x x *u*]*l-tu* AN-*e in-da-naq-qu-ta-áš-ši*
13) [x x x (x) *i*(?)]*-na pi-i* ⸢*aq*⸣*-bak-ka a-na-ku*
14) [x x x x] x *šá du-un-*⸢*qa*⸣ *al-ta-tap-pa-rak-ka*
15) [x x x x x (x)]-⸢*ia te*(?)⸣*-ba-a-ṭa a-na* KUR MAR.TU.KI
16) [... *ši*(?)]*-kìn ṭè-mì-ka ši-me*
17) [x x x x (x) ELA]M.⸢MA⸣.KI *a-na* KÁ.DINGIR.RA.[K]I *li-qa-an-nu*
18) [x x x *bēl*(?) KÁ.D]INGIR.RA.KI ELAM.MA.KI [*l*]*ud-din-ak-ka*
19) [...] x-⸢*ka*⸣ *e-li-ti* ⸢*ù šá*⸣*-pil-ti*

11–12) The lord of Babylon listened to [*the supplication*(*s*) *of*] Nebuchadnezzar and [*his command*] comes down *to him* from heaven:
13–19) "[... *b*]*y* (my own) mouth I spoke to you. [*Instructions* (*promising*)] good fortune, I have sent to you. [*With*] my [*support*] you *are to attack* the land of Amurru. [...] listen to [*the iss*]*uing* of your instructions! [...] take me [*from* E]lam to Babylon! Let me, [... *the lord of* Ba]bylon, give Elam to you! [...] above and below."

---

obv. 9 Or "May the (re)building of Babylon occur to you!"
obv. 16 Possibly [... *a*(?)]*-mat*, "[*the wor*]*ding*," instead of [... *ši*(?)]*-kìn*, "[*the iss*]*uing*." *ṭè-mi-ka*, "your instructions," is presumably an error for *ṭè-mi-ia*, "my instructions."
obv. 19 Foster, Before the Muses 1 p. 301 suggests "[I will exalt] your [kingship] everywhere."

20) [...] x *iṣ-ṣa-bat* [(x x)] DINGIR.MEŠ-*šú*
21) [...] x [(x)]
Lacuna
Reverse
Lacuna

1′) [...] x [...] x ⸢ŠE(?)⸣

Colophon
2′) [...] URI.KI GABA.RI KÁ.DINGIR.RA.KI *šaṭ-ṭir ba-ri*
3′) [...] MAN ŠÚ MAN KUR AN.[Š]ÁR.⸢KI⸣

20–21) [...] has seized [(...)] his gods [...]
Lacuna

Lacuna

rev. 1′) [...]

Colophon
rev. 2′) [...] Akkad, written (and) collated (from) a copy (*in*) Babylon.
rev. 3′) [...] king of the world, king of Assyria.

6

A description of battles between Babylonia and Elam is found on a partially preserved tablet in the British Museum. The first part of the text records earlier conflict in the time of the last two kings of the Kassite dynasty (Zababa-šuma-iddina and Enlil-nādin-aḫi), but the name of the king mentioned in the main body of the text is not preserved. In view of similar texts clearly dealing with the time of Nebuchadnezzar I, the inscription is generally assigned to him, but this assignment must be considered unproven. This historical-literary inscription is written in Akkadian.

COMMENTARY

The damaged tablet comes from the Kuyunjik collection of the British Museum (K 2660). It measures 9.5×8.5 cm. The inscription is written in Neo-Assyrian script and has been collated. An examination of the tablet by the author and S. Parpola shows that it is almost certain that there is nothing missing on the reverse before the line given as 1 here.

Tadmor points out that there are a number of hapax legomena in the text (JNES 17 [1958] p. 137).

BIBLIOGRAPHY

1870 3 R pl. 38 no. 2 (copy in type)
1889 Winckler, Untersuchungen p. 46 (partial edition)
1891 Bezold, Cat. 2 p. 463 (study)
1897 Winckler, AOF 1/6 pp. 534–38 (edition)
1958 Tadmor, JNES 17 pp. 137–39 (edition)
1968 Brinkman, PKB pp. 79–80, 88–90, 106, and 328 no. 4.3.9 (study)
1977 Roberts, Essays Finkelstein pp. 183–87, especially nn. 24, 32, 38, and 48 (study)
1991 Longman, Autobiography pp. 194–95 and 243 (translation, study)
1993 Foster, Before the Muses 1 pp. 294–96 (translation)

TEXT

Obverse
Lacuna
1′) [...] x x x [...] x x x x KUR x (x)
2′) [(x) ^{d}*za-ba$_4$-ba$_4$*]-⸢MU⸣-SUM.NA LUGAL *iṭ-⸢ru⸣-da* BALA-*šú i-kiš*
3′) [x x x (x)]-ŠI *ku-dúr-na-an-ḫu-un-di bu-uk-ra-šu*

Lacuna
1′) [...] ... [...] ...
2′) He (Šutruk-nanḫundi) drove away the king [Zababa]-šuma-iddina (and) *did away with* his reign.
3′) [...] his son Kudur-nanḫundi.

B.2.4.6 obv. 3′ Tadmor suggests [... *ú-šat*]-*lim*, "[handed] over [the reign] to" (JNES 17 [1958] pp. 137–38), but one would then expect *ana* before Kudur-nanḫundi.

4′) [x x (x) *ša i*]*na*(?) UGU AD.MEŠ-*šú ár-na*-<*šu*> *šu-tu-ru šur-bu-u ḫi-ṭu-šú kab-tu*
5′) [(x) *lem-né*]-⸢*e*⸣-*ti ú-kap-pi-da ana* KUR URI.KI *ib-ta-ni te-ki-tu*
6′) [x x (x)] x ^{d}BAD-MU-⸢ŠEŠ⸣ LUGAL *pa-na maḫ-ri-ia*
7′) [*ša*(?) x x x] *nu-kur-ti iš-ku-nu ḫa-lu-gi i-ta-mu*-<*u*>
8′) [x x x x-*m*]*a* UN.MEŠ KUR URI.KI *kul-lat-si-na a-bu-biš* ⸢*is*⸣-*p*[*u-un*]
9′) [(x) *ma-ḫa-z*]*i ṣi-ru-ti ṇa-gab-šú-nu ú-še-me* [*kar-miš* (...)]
10′) [^{d}AMAR.UTU E]N(?) *ra*-⸢*ba*⸣-*a id-de-ki ina šu-bat* [...]
11′) [x x x x x (x)] *šu-me-ri u* URI.KI *iš*-⸢*lu*(?)⸣-[*la* x x x]
12′) [x x x x] ⸢^{d}⸣BAD-MU-ŠEŠ *i-b*[*u-ka* x x x]
13′) [...-*s*]*u*(?) *uk-ki-šá* BALA-[*šú*]
14′) [x x x (x)] ⸢*la*⸣ *nab-nit ba-bi*-⸢*li ge-re-e*⸣ [x x x]
15′) [x x x x] x-*šú* x [...] x [...]
16′) [...] x *en-ni-ti* x [...]
17′) [...] x x (x) [...]
18′) [...] x [...]
Lacuna (approximately three lines missing)
Reverse
(Lacuna)
1) [...] (x) x [...]
2) [...-*m*]*u*(?)-*ú*-⸢*ni*⸣ [...]
3) [... *gi*]-⸢*tal*⸣-*lu-tú im-qu-tu iṣ*-⸢*ṣa*⸣-*bat* KUR-⸢*e*(?)⸣ (x)
4) [...] x ⸢EGIR⸣ *ú-dal-li-ba* LÚ.KÚR-[*š*]*ú*(?)
5) [x x x (x)] x-⸢*šu*(?)⸣ *iṭ-ṭu-lu iš-te-ni-ʾ-ú di-in* ^{d}AM[AR.UTU]
6) [x (x) *mar*(?)-*ṣ*]*i*(?)-*iš dal-biš uš-šu-ši-iš a-ta-me-m*[*a*]
7) [x x (x)] x-*ia šá ina e-lam-ti uš-šu-bu lu-mut* u_4-*ma-ma*
8) [x x x] x-*ma* MÈ-*šú a-a a-tur a-na ar-ki-ia*
9) [x x (x) K]I *si-ta-at* UN.MEŠ *ina* SAG *uq-né-e ú-qí-šu-ma*
10) [*ul*(?) *a-tu*(?)-*r*]*am-ma ki-i la lìb-bi* DINGIR.MEŠ ^{d}*èr-ra gaš*-⸢*ri*⸣ DINGIR.MEŠ
11) [*qu-r*]*a*(?)-*di-ia ú-nap-pi-iṣ*
12) [...] x *mu-un-ni-šu i-bir ṣi-in-di-ia*
13) [(x) x] x x x *mu-ur-ni-is-qí-ia ina-ár kàt-til-lu*
14) [(x) *a*]-*dur-ma mu-tú ana* MÈ *ul a-ir a-tu-ra ar-kiš*
15) [x x] ⸢*kab-ta*⸣-*ma ana* URU.KAR-BÀD-*a-pil*-^{d}30 *at-ta-šab šu-ḫar-riš*
16) [...] x x-*ma e-la-mu-ú pa-nu-uš-šú at-ta-ṣi*
17) [x x x x *ina*] *ma-a-a-li šá ni-is-sa-ti ta-ni-ḫi*

4′–5′) [*This king*, whose] offence exceeded those of his (fore)fathers (and) [whose] grievous crime was greater than (theirs), plotted [ev]il against the land of Akkad (and) fabricated evil reports.
6′–8′) [...] Enlil-nādin-aḫi, a king who preceded me, [*who* ...] established enmity [...] (and) spoke of ... [...] and he (Kudur-nanḫundi) over[whelmed] all the people of the land of Akkad like a flood.
9′) He turned all their august [cult ce]ntres [into ruins].
10′) He made [the god Marduk], the great [lo]rd, rise from [*his* ...] seat.
11′) He took [*to Elam*] as booty [the ...] of Sumer and Akkad.
12′–13′) [...] he led Enlil-nādin-aḫi [away *to Elam*, ... *h*]*im*, (and) did away with [his] reign.
14′) [...] not a native of Babylon, (but rather) a foe [...]
15′) [...] his [...]
16′) [...] (divine) punishment [...]
17′) [...] ... [...]
18′) [...]
Lacuna
(Lacuna)
rev. 1) [...] ... [...]
rev. 2) [...] ... [...]
rev. 3) [... who was] terror-stricken, took to the mountains.
rev. 4) [...] ... harassed *his* enemy.
rev. 5) They observed [*the omens concerning*] *him* (and) sought the judgment of the god Ma[rduk].
rev. 6) [... *worr*]*ied*, harassed, (and) perturbed, I said (to myself):
rev. 7–8) "[*Unlike*] my [*predecessor*] who *flourished* in Elam, let me die this very day! [...] (*from*) battle with him, let me not turn back!"
rev. 9–10a) [... wi]th the remainder of (my) people I waited for him at the head of the Uqnû (River) and [*did not tu*]*rn* (*back*).
rev. 10b–11) Against the will of the gods, the god Erra, (most) powerful of the gods, smote my [*war*]*riors*.
rev. 12) The enfeebling [...] *bound* my team (of horses).
rev. 13) [...] ... the *kattillu*-demon was killing my thoroughbred horses.
rev. 14) [I] was afraid of death. I did not advance into battle (but rather) turned back.
rev. 15) [...] were heavy and I sat benumbed *at* the town Kār-Dūr-Apil-Sîn.
rev. 16) The Elamite [*advanced*] and I withdrew before him.
rev. 17) [*I lay* on] a bed of depression (and) sighs, (praying):

obv. 7′ Possibly *ḫa-lu-qì*-<*i*> *i-ta-mu*-<*u*>, "spoke of *destruction*"? For *ḫu/aluqqāʾum*, see AHw p. 355a.
rev. 7 The translation is based upon that proposed by Foster in Before the Muses 1 p. 295.

18) [...] x ⸢ʾ(?)-*in*(?)⸣-*ni-ma pa-nu-uš-šú a-tak*-ZU
19) [...] x-⸢*ia*(?)⸣ *la tu-paṭ-ṭa-ra rík-sat*(*) KÁ.MEŠ
20) [...] x *nak-ra-šu li-ter-ba*
21) [...] x *šá-di-du lim-né-e-ti*
22) [...] *ina sè-qar šap-ti-ia*
23) [...-*t*]*a*(?)*-am-ma li-nu-uḫ lìb-bi* ^{d}BAD
24) [...] ⸢*kab*⸣*-ta-tuš liš-tap-šiḫ*
25) [...] ⸢*saḫ*(?)⸣*-maš-ti*
26) [... *t*]*a*(?)*-me*-⸢*ia*(?)⸣ (x)
Lacuna

rev. 18) "[...] me *that* I ... before him!
rev. 19) [...] do not release the bonds of the gates!
rev. 20) [...] may his enemy enter!
rev. 21) [...] one who *endures* evil.
rev. 22) [...] by the word(s) of my lips.
rev. 23) [...] ... and may the heart of the god Enlil be appeased!
rev. 24) [...] may his emotions be soothed!"
rev. 25) [...] turmoil
rev. 26) [...] ...
Lacuna

7

A partially preserved historical-literary text which was written in Akkadian was found at Babylon. The inscription describes a campaign into Elam and purports to be a report sent to the people of Babylon by the victorious Babylonian king while he was still in Elam. The inscription is tentatively assigned to Nebuchadnezzar I because of similarities between it and other inscriptions of that king describing his campaigns into Elam (in particular B.2.4.11 i 12–43).

COMMENTARY

The inscription is found on two fragments of a clay tablet which appear on Babylon excavation photographs 2955–2956 and which bear the excavation number BE 46154. The larger of the two fragments is in the Vorderasiatiches Museum, Berlin (VAT 15584), while the present location of the smaller fragment is not known. The smaller fragment is the lower left corner of the tablet. It is uncertain exactly how much space there was between it and the larger fragment, which forms the right side of the piece. VAT 15584 measures 9.5×9.5×2.2 cm. The copy of the inscription published by J.J.A. van Dijk was made by him utilizing VAT 15584, the excavation photographs, and a partial copy made by A. Falkenstein. VAT 15584 has been collated; however, it has suffered damage (particularly in the upper right corner) since it was found and photographed. The smaller fragment is no longer available for collation. Thus, the excavation photographs have also been used to provide the edition presented below. Restorations generally follow those proposed by A.R. George. The script and orthography indicate that the text was copied around the Neo-Babylonian period.

BIBLIOGRAPHY

1986 van Dijk, Orientalia NS 55 p. 170 (partial edition)
1987 van Dijk, VAS 24 no. 87 (copy)
1989 George, BiOr 46 382–83 (partial edition, study)
1992 Hurowitz, ZA 82 p. 52 n. 17 (study)
1993 Foster, Before the Muses 1 p. 302 (translation)

---

rev. 19 *sat*(*): text has BE.
rev. 21 Possibly "the one who perpetrates evil."

TEXT

Obverse

1) [*ana*(?) *bābilāīi*(?) *ṣāb*(?)] *ki-di-ni lit-ti mas-*⸢*se*⸣*-e mu-de-e a-ma-ti ra-áš ṭè-*⸢*e*⸣*-*[*mi*]

2) [... GA]L(?).LA *na-áš ki-su* LÚ.ŠAGAN.LÁ.MEŠ *šu-ut* TIN.TIR.KI TUR *u* GAL*-i qí-*[*bi*(?)]*-*⸢*ma*(?)⸣

3) [*umma*(?) *nabû-kudurrī-uṣur*(?) G]ÌR.NÍTA ^{d}*en-líl* NUMUN TIN.TIR.KI LUGAL *be-el-ku-nu-ma*

4) [*umma*(?)] ⸢*a*⸣*-na na-re-e-ma*

5) [(...) *bēlu*(?) *rabû*(?) *marduk ša ul*]*-tu* u_4*-me ma-ʾ-*⸢*du*⸣*-ti* KI *kul-lat ma-ḫa-zi šab-su*

6) [... *l*]*u*(?) *ti-*⸢*da*⸣*-a*

7) [*itūrma*(?) *re-e-m*]*a*(?) *a-na* TIN.TIR.KI *ir-ši-ma*

8) [*ana*(?) *é-sag-í*]*l*(?) *pa-rak-ku ra-áš-ba*

9) [... *u*]*r*(?)*-ta ra-biš ú-ma-ʾi-ra-an-ni-ma ur-ḫa pa-da-ni*

10) [*ḫarrān*(?) KUR E]LAM.MA.KI *a-la-ka iq-ba-*⸢*a*⸣

11) [*ana*(?) *amat*(?) *bēli*(?) *rabî*(?) ^{d}AMAR.UT]U(?) *áš-ḫu-ut ak-kud-ma* ÉRIN*-ni* ^{d}*en-líl* ^{d}UTU *u* ^{d}AMAR.UTU *ú-paḫ-*⸢*ḫir-ma*⸣

12) [... *ana* KUR E]LAM.MA.KI *ú-šá-aṣ-bi-tu ḫar-ra-n*[*i* (x x)]

13) [... *pa-da-n*]*i né-su-tu ḫar-ra-ni la* A.MEŠ *e-te-et-ti-qu* GI$_6$ *u*[*r*(?)*-ra*(?)]

14) [... ÍD(?) *ú*(?)*-l*]*a*(?)*-a-a* LÚ.KÚR *ṣe-e-ni e-la-mu-ú maš-qa-a-ti iṣ-*⸢*ṣúr*(?)⸣ [(...)]

15) [...] *um-man-*[*ni*(?)]

16) x [...]*-et-ti-qu* A.⸢MEŠ⸣ *la áš-qí-ma la ú-pa-áš-ši-ḫa an-ḫu-u*[*s*]*-*⸢*su*⸣*-un*

17) UK ⸢KI⸣ [...] *ur-ri-ḫa ú-*⸢*ṣi*⸣*-šú*

18) GIŠ.TUKUL.MEŠ *š*[*a* ...] *a-na* ⸢KÚR⸣*-tu*$_4$

19) *ina e-muq* ^{d}*en-l*[*íl*(?) ...]*-ri la i-šá-a* LUGAL KUR ELAM.MA.KI [*u*]*ḫ*(?)*-ḫur*

20) *ma-ḫi-iṣ* BAD$_5$.BAD$_5$*-šú* x [... *s*]*u*(?)*-*⸢*up*⸣*-pu-ḫa pu-ḫur-šú pur-ru-ur* ⸢ÉRIN⸣.MEŠ*-šú* ⸢*i*⸣*-zib-ma* ÍD.MEŠ*-*⸢*šú*⸣ [BAL(?)]

21) *šu-ḫar-ru-ra* [...] *ú-qat-tu* KUR*-su*

22) URU.MEŠ*-šú dan-nu-*[*ti* (...) *u*]*m*(?)*-taš-ši-ra šá-da-a-šú i-te-li*

1–2) [*To the people of Babylon*], privileged [*people*], members of the expert professions, those who are knowledgeable (and) wise, [...] ... merchants (lit. "those who carry money-bags") (and) commercial agents, (all) those of Babylon, (both) great and small, *say* (the following):

3) "[*Thus* (*says*) *Nebuchadnezzar*], viceroy for the god Enlil, a descendant of (a native family of) Babylon, the king your lord:

4) '[*The following*] (*is to be used*) for the stela:

5–10) [(...) With regard to *the great lord,* the god Marduk, who] has been angry with all the cult centres for a long time, [...] you *should* know (that) he [*has relented and*] taken [pity] on Babylon. [He *summoned me to Esagila*], the awe-inspiring sanctuary, [and] he gave me a magnificent commission. He told me to go by road (and) path [*on campaign to* the land of] Elam.

11–13) Anxiously, I concerned myself [*with the command of the great lord, the god Marduk*]. I assembled the troops of the gods Enlil, Šamaš, and Marduk and [...] had them take the road [to the land of] Elam. They [*travelled*] distant [paths] (and) traversed waterless routes by night (and) *d*[*ay*].

14–22) [... *at the Ul*]*āia* [*River*], the wicked enemy, the Elamite, *kept guard over* the watering places. [...] *troo*[*ps* ... trav]ersed. I did not give (them) water to drink or allow them (time) to recover from their fatigue. ... [...] I hastened to go forth against him. The weapons [...] for *war*. By the strength (granted me) by the god *Enl*[*il* ...] could not have [...]; the king of the land of Elam *held back.* (20) His defeat was accomplished; [his ...] were scattered; (and) his assembled (forces) were dispersed. He abandoned his troops and [*crossed*] his rivers. *He was* benumbed [...] I destroyed his country. [He] abandoned his strong cities [(...)] (and) disappeared.

---

obv. 1 *Kidinnu*-status (translated here "privileged") indicated that the individual or city was under divine protection. In at least the first millennium it could indicate the possession of such privileges as freedom from certain taxes and from the expropriation of land by civil authorities, exemption from military service and corvée duty, and the right of appeal to the king in court cases (see Frame, Babylonia pp. 35–36).

obv. 4 The restoration was suggested by A.R. George (private communication) and is based upon the opening of another royal letter copied in the first millennium (Gurney, UET 7 no. 155 rev. v 7–8, restored from an unpublished duplicate).

obv. 14 The restoration [... ÍD *ú-l*]*a-a-a*, "[... the Ul]āia [River]," (proposed by A.R. George) is based upon the fact that the boundary stone BM 90858 (King, BBSt no. 6; see B.2.4.11) describes a battle there between the forces of Nebuchadnezzar I and those of the Elamite king (i 28–29).

obv. 14 A preferable reading to *iṣ-*⸢*ṣúr*(?)⸣ [(...)], "*kept guard over,*" might be *is-t*[*e*(?)*-kir*(?)], "*bloc*[*ked up*]" (Hurowitz, ZA 82 [1992] p. 52 n. 17). Foster (Before the Muses 1 p. 302) translates "[blocked] the watering place in the gr[oves]," presumably reading GIŠ.KI[RI$_6$.MEŠ ...]. The traces of the final sign appear to be:

obv. 19 Foster (Before the Muses 1 p. 302) suggests "Through the might of Enlil, [Shamash, and Marduk, which] has no [equ]al, I overwhelmed(?) the king of Elam."

23) *ur-ri-iḫ-ma* x [...] ⸢^{d}⸣AMAR.UTU *qar-rad* DINGIR.MEŠ *šá-qa-a a-ta-mar*
24) *ù* DINGIR.MEŠ *šá* KUR x [...]-*ma iq-bu-ú it-tan-ma-ru it-ti-šú*
25) *áš-ši-ma ṣur-ru* (x) [... *pal*(?)]-*ḫa-ku ú-šá-áš-*⸢*mi*⸣-*ra bi-ki-ti*
26) *qa-at* EN GA[L-*i* (*marduk*) *aṣbatma ú-š*]*á-aṣ-bi-tu ú-ru-uḫ* KUR-*šú*

23–26) I hastened on and [...] saw the god Marduk, the exalted hero of the gods. Moreover, the gods of the land [... *who*] had ordered [...], were seen with him. I *took heart* [...] *I was* [*awe-str*]*uck*. I *let forth uncontrolled wailing*. [I grasped] the hand of the great lord, [the god Marduk, and] caused him to take the road towards his (own) country.

Reverse
1) ⸢NÍG.GA É *šub-ti*⸣ [...] x [(...)] *šad-lu-ti*
2) ⸢*ù*⸣ x x [(x)] ⸢GAR RA(?)⸣ [...] x [(...)] *a-ta-mar*
3) ⸢DIŠ(?) AQ(?) QA(?) TI(?)⸣ [...] x *la ni-*⸢*bi*⸣ [*lū*(?)] *ka-bit-ma*
4) ⸢*lu*(?)-*ú*(?) *zu*(?)-*uk*(?)-*ki*(?)⸣ [...] *ḫar-ra-ni*
5) x ⸢MEŠ(?) GAL Ú(?)⸣ x [...] *i-ram-*⸢*ma*(?)⸣ x [(x)] x *pa-nu-šú*
6) x x x x [...] NÍG.GA-*šú*
7) ⸢UD(?) MU(?) UM(?)⸣ x [...] x ^{d}EN *šá* TE ⸢KUR GEŠTU(?).II(?) PA A MA⸣ [(x)] x RA *ki-i ṣi-iḫ-ti*
8) x ⸢I KI/DI⸣ [...] x UB 4.ÀM KÙ.⸢GI NÍG.GA TIN.TIR.KI⸣ *šu-ut* TI LA MA/BA [(x)].
9) x [...] ⸢*a-na*⸣ [(x x)] ⸢*é*⸣-*sag-íl* [(x x)]
10) [...] x-*ma i-ta-*⸢*ri*⸣ x x x ⸢NI MA NI⸣ x *zi-bi aḫ-ra-*⸢*taš*⸣
11) [...] RI *tu-tar-ra* [(...)] *áš-*[*r*]*u-uš-šú*
12) [...] ⸢DA⸣ A [(x)] ⸢*ka*(?)-*am*(?)-*ma*(?)⸣ *šuk-na*
13) [... *l*]*a*(?) *tu-ḫal-la-qa* ⸢RA⸣ x [(x)]-⸢*šú*⸣-*un*
14) [... *p*]*i-it-la-ḫa maš-*[*kán*(?)]-*šú-un*
15) [... B]AL(?) NU *ḫi-it-mu-ṭiš* ⸢Ú(?)⸣-[(x x)] (x)-⸢*ma*(?)⸣
16) [...] x-*du-ú* ⸢*a*⸣-*la-ka pa-*⸢AS⸣-[x]
17) [...] x *li-ḫal*(*)-*liq nap-šat-*⸢*su*⸣

rev. 1–17) The property of the temple, the dwelling [...] extensive. Moreover, ... [...] I saw. ... [...] countless [...] was [*indeed*] weighty and ... [...] road (rev. 5) ... [...] ... his face ... [...] his property ... [...] the god Bēl ... as delight ... gold, the property of Babylon, ... [...] to [(...)] Esagila (rev. 10) [...] ... *food-offerings* in the future. [...] you should return (it) to its place. [...] ... set up a (*commemorative*) *tablet*! [...] *do not* destroy their ...! [...] revere their *pos*[*ition*]! (rev. 15) [...] ... quickly ... [...] ... to go ... [...] may he put an end to his life!'"

18) [...] *šu-bi-lu šá* TA KUR ELAM.MA.KI *ana* LÚ.TIN.TIR.KI.MEŠ *iš-pu-ra*

rev. 18) [...] *message* which he sent from the land of Elam to the people of Babylon.

8

This partially preserved inscription comes from the first tablet of a historical-literary text of Nebuchadnezzar I. The bilingual (Sumerian-Akkadian) text describes how the god Marduk had become angry with Babylonia in the past and how the Elamites had devastated that land. The inscription is continued on B.2.4.9. One exemplar has a colophon which indicates that it was copied in the time of Ashurbanipal.

---

obv. 23 van Dijk (Orientalia NS 55 [1986] p. 170) suggests *ur-ri-iḫ-ma a*[*r-ki-šú i-na āl* ...] ("I hurried af[ter him and in the city Susa ...]"). The traces after the *-ma* would be compatible with the start of an AR sign.
obv. 24 van Dijk suggests ... *māt* U[RI.KI *šá* ... *a-lik*]-*ma iq-bu-ú* ("... the gods of the land of A[kkad who] had commanded (me): ['Go to ...!']"). The head of only one horizontal wedge is discernible following KUR; thus, while the restoration URI.KI makes good sense in the context, it must remain uncertain. Possibly [... *a-la-kam*]-*ma*, i.e., "the gods of the land [... who] had ordered [the going ...]"?
obv. 25 van Dijk tentatively proposes a meaning "Ich geriet in Aufregung(?)" ("I *became excited*") for *áš-ši-ma* and suggests we then read *ṣur-ru-*[*up lìb-bi* ...] ("[my heart] bur[ned ...]").
rev. 17 *ḫal*(*): text has ⸢AN⸣.

CATALOGUE

Ex.	Museum number	Excavation number	Registration number	Dimensions (cm)	Lines preserved	cpn
1	K 4874 (+) Rm 255 (+) K 6088	—	—	10.1×7.5×2.4; 6.6×4.6×2.4; 5.3×3.1×2	Sumerian 1–35; Akkadian 1–35	c
2	K 2211 + 3649 + 6189 + 8636 + 9168 (+) 10739	—	—	10×13.2×1.1; K 10739: 3.3×4.7×.8	Sumerian 1–2, 4–5, 7, 9–14, 17–26, 28; Akkadian 1–27	c
3	VAT 17051	BE 33135	—	7.7×7.3×2.8	Sumerian 1–14; Akkadian 4–18; rev. 1′–11′	c
4	BM 47805 + 48032 + 48035 + 48037 + 48046	—	81-11-3,512 + 741 + 744 + 746 + 755	4.5×7.9×3.1	Sumerian 13–30; Akkadian 14–31	c

COMMENTARY

All four exemplars are fragments of clay tablets. Exs. 1 and 2 come from the Kuyunjik collection of the British Museum. Ex. 3 was found at Babylon. Ex. 4 comes from Rassam's excavations; pieces in the 81-11-3 collection come mainly from Dilbat, Borsippa, and Babylon. Part of a colophon is preserved on ex. 1 and it indicates that the tablet was the first tablet of a longer composition and that it was from the collection of Ashurbanipal. Lambert has kindly informed me that unpublished pieces of this inscription identified by him and I.L. Finkel confirm his earlier suggestion (JCS 21 [1967] p. 127) that the inscription continues with our B.2.4.9. These new pieces will be published by Finkel. An unpublished copy of this inscription has also been found in the "library" of the temple of the god Šamaš at Sippar (see Al-Rawi and George, Iraq 52 [1990] p. 149 n. 1).

Exs. 1–2 are in Assyrian script and exs. 3–4 are in Babylonian script. Exs. 1 and 2 have the Sumerian and Akkadian versions on alternate lines, except in the case of short lines, where the Akkadian follows the Sumerian on one line (ex. 1 lines 6, 10, 13, 15–17, and 22; ex. 2 lines 3, 6, 8, 10, 13, 15–17, 19, 22, and 27). In all cases where the beginning of a separate Akkadian line is preserved, it is indented. Ex. 3 has the Sumerian and Akkadian in separate columns, the Sumerian in the left column and the Akkadian in the right column. The lines are arranged so that the Akkadian line is beside its Sumerian equivalent. For most of ex. 4, the Sumerian and Akkadian versions are on the same lines, with the Akkadian placed in the middle of the Sumerian (which is thus split into two parts). In the case of long lines, however, the Akkadian version was placed after the Sumerian one on a separate, indented line (lines 18 and 20–21). Thus, no two exemplars have exactly the same line arrangement. The arrangement of lines in the edition gives each pair of passages (one Sumerian passage and one Akkadian passage) one line number; thus, the line numbering follows that used by Lambert in his edition of the inscription. The translation is an amalgam of the Sumerian and Akkadian versions. The edition basically follows that of Lambert in JCS 21 (with additions by him in CRRA 19). Lines 1, 4, and 31–35 (both versions), lines 3 and 7 (Sumerian version), and line 5 (Akkadian version) follow ex. 1; the remaining lines are a conflation of two or more exemplars, always including ex. 1.

The exact placement of the text on the reverse of ex. 3 is not certain, although it may represent a later part of the inscription. Since its relation to B.2.4.8 and B.2.4.9 is not clear, it is presented separately here, at the end of B.2.4.8.

BIBLIOGRAPHY

1880 Delitzsch in Lotz, Tigl. pp. 149 and 181 (ex. 1 [K 4874], study)

1885 Haupt, ZK 2 p. 269 (ex. 1 [K 4874], study)

1887–90 Delitzsch, AW pp. 286 and 369 (ex. 1 [K 4874], study)

1888 Sayce, Religion pp. 169 n. 1, 454 nn. 3–4, and 511–12 (ex. 1 [K 4874], translation, study)

1891 Bezold, Cat. 2 pp. 422, 551, 671, 762, and 769 (exs. 1 [K 4874, 6088], 2 [K 2211, 3649, 6189], study)

1893 Bezold, Cat. 3 pp. 947, 990, and 1111 (ex. 2 [K 8636, 9168, 10739], study)

1896 Bezold, Cat. 4 p. 1598 (ex. 1 [Rm 255], study)

1932 Langdon, JRAS pp. 33–41 (ex. 1 [K 4874], copy, edition)

1944 Falkenstein, ZA 48 p. 74 (exs. 1 [K 4874], 2 [K 2211], study)

1956 Borger, Asarh. p. 117 §87a (ex. 1 [K 4874], study)

1957–58 Borger, AfO 18 p. 118 §87a (exs. 1 [K 4874], 2 [K 2211], study)

1967 Lambert, JCS 21 pp. 126–38 (exs. 1 [K 4874(+)Rm 255], 2 [K 2211+8636+9168], 3–4, copy, edition)

1974 Lambert, CRRA 19 pp. 432–40 (exs. 1–4, transliteration, study; exs. 1 [K 6088], 2 [K 3469, 6189, and 10739], copy)

1977 Roberts, Essays Finkelstein pp. 183–87, especially pp. 185–86 (study)

1982 Sommerfeld, Aufstieg Marduks p. 187 (exs. 1–4, study)

1988 Block, Gods pp. 136 and 147–48 (ex. 1, partial translation, study)

1993 Foster, Before the Muses 1 pp. 290–93 (exs. 1–4, translation)

TEXT

1) zà-mí x [...] nam-kala ki-šár-ra u$_4$-ul-dù-a-a-ni-šè
ta-nit-[ti ... dan-n]u-us-su šá kiš-šá-ti ana u$_4$-mi ṣa-a-ti

1) The praise of [... *who*]*se* (the god Marduk's) might (is) over the world forever,

2) KÁM(?)-ri-a-bi [...]-⸢bi(?)⸣ lá-lá ka-tar zi du$_{11}$-ga
*uz-zu-u[š(?) ...]-*ḪAR-*šú ṭa-a-bu šu-pa-a a-na da-la-li*

2) [*Who*]*se anger* [*is grievous, but who*]*se* [*rele*]*nting* is sweet, glorious for praise.

3) ki dúru ki šub [...] ba-ab-lá-e giskim-bi ì-ma-al-la
šá šu-ud-d[u]-u šu-šu-bu ba-šu-ú it-ti-šú aḫ-ra-taš UN.MEŠ *kul-lu-mu na-ṣa-ar it-ti-šú*

3) (He is the one) in whose power it is to make (a region) desolate and to resettle (it), (and who) *shows* future people how to watch for his sign.

4) ^{d}*na-bi-um-k[u$_7$-dur-ri-ú-ṣur* lugal KÁ.DINGIR.RA.KI a]l-si-sá ki-šu-peš$_6$ da-gan-bi sá-dug$_4$ bí-in-gi$_4$-gi$_4$
^{d}MIN *ša[r ba-ab-i-lí muš-te-ší]r kul-lat ma-ḫa-zi mu-kin sat-tuk-ki*

4) (With regard to) Nebuc[hadnezzar], king [of Babylon], who administers correctly all the cult centres (and) confirms the regular offerings,

5) nam-kù-zu x [...] x á-na ár mu-un-da-i-i sag-bi-šè íb-ta-an-è
ú-šar-ri-[ḫa ...] is-su ú-še-ṣa-a a-na re-še-e-ti

5) He (Marduk) made [his] wisdom splendid, extolled his power and made him supreme;

6) maḫ-bi íl-l[a ... nam-gu-l]a-bi
ú-šar-ba-a [...] ul-la-a pa-ra-aṣ nar-bi-šú

6) He made [his ...] great [(...)] and exalted his destined greatness.

7) ^{d}*na-bi-um-ku$_7$-d[ur(?)-ri-ú-ṣur* lugal KÁ.DINGIR.RA.KI al-s]i-sá ki-šu-peš$_6$ da-gan-bi sá-dug$_4$ bí-in-gi$_4$-gi$_4$
^{d}MIN *šar ba-ab-i-⸢lí⸣ mu[š-te-šír ku]l-lat ma-ḫa-zi mu-kin sat-tuk-ki*

7) Nebucha[dnezzar], king of Babylon, who administers correctly all the cult centres (and) confirms the regular offerings,

8) nu-nus(NUNUZ) bala sù [...] a-má-ru$_{10}$ na-an-na-ke$_4$
li-i-pu ru-u-qu šá šar-ru-ú-⸢ti ze⸣-ru na-aṣ-ru šá la-am a-bu-bi

8) Distant descendant of kingship, seed preserved since before the flood,

9) ⸢^{d}en⸣-me-dur-a[n-ki lugal zimbir.KI-r]a-ta è DUG.bur-zi-gal kù-ga al-gub-ba GIŠ.erin-na-ta gùr-ru
ṣi-it ^{d}en-[me-dur-an-ki] šar si-ip-par mu-kin ma-k[al]-ti KÙ-*ti na-šu-ú e-ri-ni*

9) Offspring of Enmedura[nki], king of Sippar, who set up the pure bowl (and) took up the cedar-wood,

10) [x x (x)] x (x) [... ba-a]b-su-uš-me
a-šib ma-ḫar ^{d}UTU *u* ^{d}IŠKUR DINGIR.MEŠ *da-a-a-ni*

10) Who sat in the presence of the gods Šamaš and Adad, the divine judges,

11) [... lugal níg-si-s]á sipa zi-da suḫuš kalam-ma bí-in-gi-na-ta
ap-lu a-šá-ri-du [šá ^{d}nin-urta-na-din]-⸢šu⸣-me LUGAL *mì-šá-ri re-ʾ-u ki-i-nu mu-kin iš-di ma-a-ti*

11) Foremost son [of Ninurta-nādin]-šumi, the just king (and) true shepherd, who makes the foundations of the land firm,

12) [...] x-bi bíl dur-an-ki-ke$_4$ u$_4$-ul-dù-a u$_4$-ul-dù-a-ke$_4$
um-mat ^{d}IŠKUR *u* ^{d}*gu-la* DINGIR.MEŠ *šur-bu-ti pir-ʾi ni-ip-pu-ru ki-si-it-ti ṣa-a-ti*

12) ... of the god Adad and the goddess Gula, the supreme gods, scion of Nippur, one of ancient stock,

---

2 The translation basically follows that of Foster in Before the Muses 1 p. 291.
4 Akkadian version has "ditto" for Sumerian "Nebuc[hadnezzar]."
7 Akkadian version has "ditto" for Sumerian "Nebucha[dnezzar]."
8 Following Foster (Before the Muses 1 p. 291), possibly "watched for" instead of "preserved."
9.3 MIN (Text: A), "ditto," for ^{d}*en-[me-dur-an-ki]*, "En[meduranki]," of the Akkadian version.
9 The bowl and cedar were used in divination.
11.3 MIN, "ditto" for [*šá* ^{d}*nin-urta-na-din*]-⸢*šu*⸣-*me*, "[of Ninurta-nādin]-šumi," of the Akkadian version.
12 Sumerian version uses the name of a temple, dur-an-ki, as a designation for the city Nippur; with regard to dur-an-ki, see George, Topographical Texts p. 261.

13) [...] x ⸢^{d}šu-zi⸣-an-na-ke$_{4}$ na[m-... a]n-šár gal-la
an-gub-bu-u reš-tu-u šá ^{d}šu-zi-an-na ta-li-mat an-šár

13) First attendant of the goddess Šuzianna, favourite sister of (the god) Anšar,

14) [an ^{d}en-lí]l-⸢bi⸣-da mu-ni-in-sa$_{4}$-a dingir gal-gal-e-ne šà-ge-pà-da-me-en
ni-bit ^{d}a-nim ù ^{d}da-gan i-tu-ut ku-un lìb-bi DINGIR.[MEŠ G]AL.MEŠ *a-na-ku-ma*

14) The one chosen by the gods Anu and Dagan, (and) selected by the steadfast hearts of the great gods, I —

15) ⸢u$_{4}$⸣-bi-a bala lugal sag-gá-ke$_{4}$ giskim-bi a[b-...]
i-nu-šú ina pa-le-e šar-ri maḫ-ri-i iš-na-a i-da-a-tu

15) At that time, in the reign of a previous king, the portents changed.

16) níg-sig$_{5}$-ga ab-te-ri-a [n]am-ḫul-la ba-ab-x [...]
da-mì-iq-tu is-si-ma le-mut-tu sad-rat

16) Good departed and evil was constant.

17) en-e lipiš-bi na-an-bal-la [šà]-dib-ba in-[...]
be-lu$_{4}$ i-gug-ma ki-mil-ta ir-ši

17) The lord (Marduk) became angry and (full of) wrath.

18) kur-ra al-mu-un-da-ab-bé dingir-re-e-ne m[u-un-š]ub-ba al-bal šu sag-gá-na níg-lul-la ab-zi-zi-e-a
iq-bi-⸢ma ma-a⸣-ta id-du-ši DINGIR.MEŠ-*š[á] iš-ni ṭè-em* UN.MEŠ-*šá šu-ḫu-za sur-ra-a-ti*

18) He commanded and the land was abandoned by its gods. The thinking of its people changed; they were incited to treachery.

19) sag-é/líl x [x] x (x) ⸢gú⸣-šub-ba-meš ul-ḫé ⸢ši-in⸣-[e$_{11}$ (...)] x ^{d}lamma níg-si-sá ki-bar-ra al-gub-bu
⸢iz⸣-nu-⸢ú ra-bi⸣-[ṣu] šul-me e-lu-⸢u⸣ [ana šu-puk AN-*e la-mas-si] mi-šá-ri it-ta-ziz a-ḫi-ta*

19) The guardians of peace became angry and went up to the dome of heaven; the protective spirit of justice stood aside.

20) ^{d}x [x zi-a]l-la-aš nam-lú-u$_{18}$-lu ba-an-šub-ba dingir ma-ra-ab-tuku-a gú-sag-KAL-ir sì-ga
[^{d}x] x *na-ṣir nap-šá-a-ti ni-ši i-te-ez-ba ki-ma [la r]aš(?)* DINGIR-*ma e-ma-a gim-rat-si-in*

20) The god ..., who guards living creatures, abandoned the people; they all became like those who have no god.

21) udug-ḫul-didli šà-ba kalam-ma e-ra nam-tar sag nam-BAD-e-ne <<⸢la⸣>> [ú]ru-šu-peš$_{6}$ al-sun$_{5}$-ne-eš
ú-tuk-[k]u lem-nu-ti im-lu-u qé-reb ma-a-ti nam-ta-ru la [p]a-du-u ma-ḫa-zi-iš i-ter-bu

21) Evil demons filled the land; merciless *namtaru*-demons entered the cult centres.

22) ma-da ab-tur-ra-àm [m]a-al-gi-bi ši-in-kúr-ru-da
iṣ-ḫir-ma ma-a-tu$_{4}$ mi-lik-šá iš-ni

22) The land diminished; its thinking changed.

23) níg-zi elam-ma.KI ḫé-⸢li⸣-bi nu-mu-un-da-ab-kal-la [... m]è gìr-íl-la-a-ni ši-in-sar-re
ṣe-e-nu e-la-mu-u la mu-šá-qir AN [... *ta]-ḫa-za-šú ti-bu-šú iḫ-tam-ṭù*

23) (With regard to) the wicked Elamite, who did not esteem its *treasures,* [...] his battle (and) his attack were swift.

24) úru-didli íb-ta-an-gi ir-ra-šè ba-an-si dingir-re-e-ne ši-in-bi-ra-ka zag líl-lá ba-ni-in-ri
ú-šá-aḫ-rib da-ád-me na-mu-iš um-me [DINGIR.MEŠ *iš-t]a-lal ú-nam-me eš-re-e-ti*

24) He laid waste the settlements (and) turned (the land) into a desert. He carried off the gods (and) turned the sanctuaries into ruins.

25) ^{d}⸢šà⸣-zu lugal dingir-re-⸢e⸣-[ne n]am tar-tar-e-dè [...] x ši-in-zi gi$_{4}$-gi$_{4}$ ba-an-è
^{d}AMAR.UTU *šár-ri* DINGIR.⸢MEŠ *mu⸣-šim ši-ma-a-t[i* ...] x KUR.KUR *i-ḫaṭ gim-re-e-ti*

25) The god Marduk, king of the gods, who determines the fates, [...] the lands, observed everything.

26) [x-šà-í]b-bi-me-a ^{d}nu[n]-gal-e-ne an-na-ke$_{4}$ [...] x nu-mu-un-da-ab-íl-íl
ag-ga-gi-ma be-lu$_{4}$ ^{d}í-gì-gì ina [AN-*e ul*] ⸢*i*⸣-*na-áš-šu-ú ka-dàr-šu*

26) When the lord (Marduk) is angry, the Igīgū gods in heaven cannot endure his arrogance.

27) [su-zi-bi ḫ]u-[l]uḫ-ḫa igi-túl-bi šúr-ra [(x)] lú na-me nu-gub-ba
gal-ta-at-ma na-mur-rat-su a-na né-kel-[mi-šu a-me-l]u ma-na-ma ul iz-ziz

27) His fearsome splendour is terrifying; at his angry look no man can stand.

13.3 ^{d}M[IN], "the goddess di[tto]" for ^{d}*šu-zi-an-na*, "the goddess Šuzianna," of the Akkadian version.
13 Sumerian version has "great Anšar."
19 The x before ^{d}lamma could be the end of e$_{11}$ ([DU$_{6}$.D]U), thus indicating that there is nothing missing between e$_{11}$ and ^{d}lamma.

28) [ki-gal(?)] gìr-ús-bi á-šu-uš nu-un-gál-la [(x x) dum-d]am-a-ni-ta ab-didli ur$_4$-ur$_4$-re-e-dè
ul ip-tin ki-gal-lu ki-bi-is-su ul i-x [... *a-na ú-t*]*a-zu-me-šú i-ár-ru-ra ta-ma-a-ti*

28) The earth did not support his tread nor [...]; at his roaring the seas are agitated.

29) [... nu-mu-u]n-da-ab-ḫa-za gá-gá-bi dingir-ki-šár-ra-e-ne [e]-ne-šè bí-in-gúr-ru-uš
ul uk-til ú-ḫu-me ši-kin še-pi-[*šu* DINGIR.MEŠ *šá k*]*iš-šá-ti šá-a-šú kan-šu-uš*

29) The rocky mountains did not sustain his footstep; the gods of the universe are submissive to him.

30) [... n]am-gu-la šu-bé ši-⸢in-šid-da⸣ [(...) mir-r]a a-ba ši-in-šed$_7$-dè
⸢*bu-uš kul-lat*⸣ *mim-ma-ma qa-tu*[*š-šu pa-qid* ...] x *i-gu-gu li-ni-iḫ-šú man-nu*

30) Things of every kind are entrusted to his control. [(...) When] he has become angry, who can appease him?

31) [... a]l-zu-zu-e-d[è ...] x-bi níg-galam-ma-bi igi in-è
[...] x *šá il-ma-du* [...] x-*šu-ma i-bar-ru-u ník-lat-su*

31) [...] who learned [...] him and see his skilful work

32) [... n]í-te-a-ni [... k]ur-kur-ra mu-lu ḪI-du$_{11}$-ga
[...] x *ra-ma-*[*an-šu* ...] ^{d}*en-líl* DINGIR.MEŠ *te-le-ʾu*

32) [...] himself [...] the Enlil of the gods, the capable,

33) [... ^{d}nun-gal]-e-n[e ... id]im bí-tar-ri-in
[...] ^{d}⸢*í*⸣-[*gì-gì* ...] *ru-bu-u muš-tal-lu$_4$*

33) [...] the I[gīgū gods ...], judicious prince,

34) [...] tar-r[a(?) ...] x da-ra-aḫ ní-te bí-íb-ri-a
x [...] *šá ina* x [...] *me-lam-me zu-ʾu-nu ra-mu-u pul-ḫa-a-ti*

34) [...] who in [...] adorned with awe-inspiring radiance, seated in awesome splendour,

35) kala-g[a(?) ...] x [...] nam-en-bi sag-rib-bé
dan-n[*u*(?) ...] *šu-tu-qat be-lu-us-su*

35) *The migh*[*ty one* ... who]se lordship excels.

Catch-line on ex. 1 (line 64 of exemplar)
1) ní-galam [... ár mu-u]n-da-i-i gír-gal-nin-ma-ke$_4$

Catch-line on ex. 1
1) (His) skilfulness [... let me pra]ise ...

Colophon on ex. 1 (lines 65–68 of exemplar)
1) DUB1.KÁM [(...) *ekal aššur-bāni-apli šar kiššati šar māt aššur ša* ^{d}*na-bi-u*]*m*(?) *u* ^{d}*taš-me-tu$_4$ uz-nu ra-pa-áš-tu iš-ru-ku-uš*
2) *i-ḫu-u*[*z-zu īna namirtu nisiq tupšarrūti ša ina šarrāni ālik maḫ*]*-ri-ia mám-ma šip-ru šu-a-tu la i-ḫu-uz-zu*
3) *né-me-e*[*q nabû tikip santakki mala bašmu ina* DUB.ME]Š(?) *áš-ṭur as-niq ab-re-e-ma*
4) *a-na t*[*a-mar-ti šitassīia q*]*é-reb* É.GAL-*ia ú-kin*

Colophon on ex. 1
1–4) First tablet [(...) Palace of Ashurbanipal, king of the world, king of Assyria, the one] on whom [the god Nabû] and the goddess Tašmētu bestowed broad understanding, [who] has [sharp eyes (and who learned) the highest level of scribal art], that skill [which] no one [among the kings who had prec]eded me had learned. I have written [on tablets], checked (and) collated [everything pertaining to cuneiform signs], the art [of the god Nabû]. I set (them) up in my palace so that [they might be seen and read to me].

Reverse of ex. 3
Lacuna

1′) [...]
[...] x [...]

rev. 1′) [...]

2′) [...]
[...] ⸢^{d}⸣*í-gì-gì* x [...]

rev. 2′) [...] the Igīgū gods [...]

3′) [...]
[...] *i-ra-piš* x [...]

rev. 3′) [...] is broad [...]

4′) [...]
[...] x *maḫ-ri* x [...]

rev. 4′) [...] front [...]

5′) [...]
[x x] x-*ú šá ṭa-bat ḫi-i*[*s-sat-su* ...]

rev. 5′) ... men[tion] of [whom] is pleasant [...]

6′) [...]
[(x)] x x *šá ana pa-aṭ* AN-*e u* K[I-*tim* ...]

rev. 6′) ... who to the limit(s) of heaven and nether[world ...]

7′) [...]
sa-niq mit-ḫur-ti ri-HI [...]

rev. 7′) Who makes opposing forces agree, ... [...]

Colophon The restoration is based upon Hunger, Kolophone no. 319 type d.

8′) [...] x
DINGIR *el-lu šá e-diš-ši-šu šur-r*[*u-ḫu* ...]
9′) [...] x GA
gam-ma-lu-ú mu-še-zib en-ši [...]

Space
10′) [... SA]R(?) ba-an-è DUB AŠ [d]*na-bi-u*[*m*(?)-...]
11′) [...] (x) x x [...]
Lacuna

rev. 8′) The holy god, who alone is splen[did ...]

rev. 9′) The merciful, who preserves the weak [...]

rev. 10′–11′) No translation warranted.

9

As noted earlier, inscriptions 8 and 9 are actually parts of the same bilingual inscription, with inscription 8 being the first part of the text and inscription 9 a later portion of it. Inscription 9 describes the return of the statue of the god Marduk from Elam — including the end of the events leading up to it and the celebrations to mark it.

CATALOGUE

Ex.	Museum number	Registration number	Dimensions (cm)	Lines preserved	cpn
1	K 3444 + BM 99067	K 3444 + Ki 1904-10-9,96	8.9×17.1	1–43	c
2	K 3317 + 3319	—	8×16.4	15–39	c
3	K 5191	—	4.7×4.3	2–10, 12–13	c
4	BM 35000	Sp 2,524	5.6×6.5	1–6	c

COMMENTARY

All exemplars are found upon clay tablets or tablet fragments. Exs. 1–3 are part of the Kuyunjik collection of the British Museum. Ex. 4 was acquired by the British Museum from Messrs Spartali & Co. and entered in the museum registry in 1879. B. Foster has informed me that his statement in Before the Muses 1 p. 300 that the tiny fragment K 8319 belongs to the same tablet as K 3317 + 3319 (ex. 2) was incorrect. Exs. 1 and 2 each preserve part of a colophon indicating that it was from the palace of Ashurbanipal. Exs. 1–3 are in Neo-Assyrian script and ex. 4 in late Babylonian script.

Rather than following the line numbering practice employed with inscription 8, in which each pair of passages (one Sumerian passage and one Akkadian passage) was given only one line number, the line numbering for this text follows the line arrangement of ex. 1. This has been done in order to facilitate the use of earlier scholarship on the text which employs that line numbering. Where the beginning of the line is preserved and the Akkadian version starts a new line, both exs. 1 and 2 indent the Akkadian version. As far as they are preserved, exs. 2–3 have the same arrangement of lines as ex. 1, except that ex. 2 puts the Sumerian and Akkadian versions of line 25 on separate lines. Ex. 4 has each of lines 1–5 on two lines; line 6 is insufficiently preserved to determine if it was on two lines or one. There are traces of line rulings on ex. 4 after the exemplar's second and fifth lines (after line 1 and part way through line 3 of the master line).

The master line for lines 6–7, 9–11, 13–14, and 18–21 comes from ex. 1; the master line for lines 24–27 and 35 comes from ex. 2. The remaining lines are a conflation of two or more exemplars. The translation is for the most part based upon the Akkadian version of the inscription.

A study of some of the peculiarities of the Sumerian version (lines 1–11) is presented by T. Jacobsen in Studies Tadmor.

BIBLIOGRAPHY

1873 Talbot, TSBA 2 p. 65 (exs. 1 [K 3444], partial copy in type, partial edition)
1875 4 R pl. 20 no. 1 (exs. 1 [K 3444], 2, composite copy in type)
1882 Halévy, Documents religieux pls. 99–101 (exs. 1 [K 3444], 2, transliteration into Hebrew characters)
1891 4 R[2] pl. 20 no. 1 (exs. 1 [K 3444], 2, composite copy in type)

1891 Bezold, Cat. 2 pp. 522, 534, and 697 (exs. 1 [K 3444], 2, 3, study)
1897 Winckler, AOF 1/6 pp. 538–40 (exs. 1 [K 3444], 2, edition of Akkadian lines)
1902 Martin, RT 24 pp. 96–99 (exs. 1 [K 3444], 2, edition)
1906 Hehn, BA 5 pp. 339–44 (exs. 1 [K 3444], 2, edition)
1918–19 Meek, AJSL 35 pp. 134 and 139 (ex. 1 [BM 99067], copy)
1927 Thureau-Dangin, RA 24 p. 185 (study)
1958 Jestin, RA 52 pp. 193–202 (exs. 1–2, edition of Sumerian lines)
1964 Lambert, Essays Meek pp. 9–10 (exs. 1–4, study)
1967 Lambert, JCS 21 pp. 126–27 (study)
1968 Brinkman, PKB pp. 112–13 and 329 no. 4.3.10 (exs. 1–4, study)
1977 Roberts, Essays Finkelstein pp. 183–87, especially nn. 10 and 52 (study)
1987 Mayer and Sommerfeld, Orientalia NS 56 pp. 209 and 217 (exs. 1–2, study)
1991 Jacobsen, Studies Tadmor pp. 288–91 (exs. 1–2, partial transliteration, study)
1992 George, Topographical Texts p. 402 (exs. 1–2, study)
1993 Foster, Before the Muses 1 pp. 299–300 (exs. 1–2, translation)

TEXT

1) [...] (x) in-šub-bé-e-ne-⸢šè⸣ ní-bi-⸢ta⸣ nam-kur-re-e-ne ug$_5$-⸢ga-gin$_7$(?)⸣ im-šèg GIŠ.tukul á-bi lál-e adda-a-ni sal-la-ke$_4$

2) [x x *i*]*p*(?)*-par-ši-du ma-la ik-šu-du-uš kak-ku ina ra-ma-ni-šú-nu* ⸢*ki*⸣*-ma mi-*⸢*tu-ut ḫal-pe*⸣*-e i-di-šú-nu uk-tas-sa-ma mu-uṣ-ṣu-u šal-mat-su-un*

1–2) [...] fled, the arms of all those whom the weapon(s) touched became stiff of their own accord, like (the arms of) those who died of cold; their bodies lay sprawled out.

3) [x x] an-ta ki-ta á-zi-da á-gùb-bu igi egir a-má-ru$_{10}$ mu-un-dib-eš-àm uru šà-ba uru bar-ra edin edin-na sìg-sìg bí-in-si a-ri-a mu-un-DU-DU

4) [x] x AN *e-liš u šap-liš im-na ù šu-me-la pa-ni ù ar-ku uš-bi-ʾ a-bu-ba-niš-ma* ŠÀ URU *a-ḫat* URU *ṣi-i-ru ba-ma-a-ti šá-qu-um-ma-tu ú-šam-li-ma ú-šá-li-ka na-mu-iš*

3–4) He (the god Marduk) caused [...] to pass above and below (the land), to the right and the left, in front and behind, like the (very) flood. He filled the inner city, the suburbs, the steppe, (and) the plain with deathly silence and turned it into a desert.

5) [(x) lú(?)-s]ag ní-te-a-ni ù-⸢gul⸣-gá-gá še-še-ga lú igi-du$_8$-a-bi sag-ús ab-ta-bu-bu-lu en-e šà-ba-a-ni na-me mu-un-BU-i šà-ne-ša$_4$ nam-mi-in-gub

6) [(x) *r*]*e-e-ši pa-li-iḫ-šu mut-nen-nu-ú mu-un-dag-ri šá ana ta mar ti šú kak da a pu tuq qu ma a di ú-šam-ṣu-šú ma-la lib-bu-uš la ik-la-a un-nen-ni*

5–6) [(...)], the servant who reveres him, prayerful, obedient, who is constantly attentive for his (Marduk's) appearance, did not cease praying until he (Marduk) had made him obtain his heart's desire.

7) [en]-⸢e⸣ i-bí-bar-ra alam sukud-da-a-ni u$_4$-šú-uš-e múš nu-túm-ma su-GAM-ma su-mu nu-ku$_5$-da úr-ra-a-ni gi$_6$ du$_{10}$-ga-bi nu-til-la-e-da-ni ù-sá na-nam

8) [(x)] ⸢*a*⸣*-di at-tap-la-su la-an-šu e-la-a u*$_4$*-mi-šam la na-par-ka-a ṣur-ri qid-da-a-ti ina zu-um-ri-ia la ip-par-su-ú-ma ina ut-lu mu-ši ṭa-a-bu la ú-qat-ta-a šit-ti*

7–8) Until I had regarded his lofty figure, so long as dejectedness of heart — (which afflicted me) daily without end — had not left my body, I did not get enough sleep in the sweet lap of night.

9) [šà (x)] mu-un-gig-ga-mu šùd-dè kúš-ù-mu šu-íl-la-mu u$_4$-šú-uš-e kir$_4$ šu mar-ra-mu sískur-ra-a-ni ù-gul-gá-gá šà-bi dagal-la arḫuš tuk-a gú-bi nigin šà-bi-ta uru kù-ga

10) [*ina u*]*n-nen-ni-ia šum-ru-ṣu-ti ik-ri-bi-ia šu-nu-ḫu-ti ni-iš qa-ti-ia ù la-ban ap-pi-ia šá u*$_4$*-mi-šam a-bal-lu-uš ut-nen-nu-šú*

11) [*ṣu*]*r-ru-uš šad-lim re-e-mu ir-ši-ma ki-šad-su ú-saḫ-ḫi-ra ana qé-reb* URU KÙ.GA

9–11) Upon my piteous entreaties, my ardent prayers, my supplication(s), and my expression(s) of humility by which I daily besought him (and) prayed to him, in his generous heart he had pity and turned back unto the holy city.

12) [x (x) š]à-bi túm-ma-a-ra uru edin mu-un-DU-a-ni šà-bi-ta níg-ḫul elam-ma.KI-ke$_4$ kaskal a-li-ri ḫar-ra-an asila$_4$ ḫé-en-da-še-še-ga šà šu-an-na-ta mu-un-dib

13) [x] *šá ub-la lìb-ba-šú a-lak* URU EDIN *ki i-ku-*

12–14) Having made up his mind, when he went out from the wickness in Elam, going by (way of) city (and) steppe, he took a road of jubilation, a path of rejoicing, a route (*indicating his*) attention (*to*) and acceptance (*of my prayers*), unto Šuanna (Babylon).

šam-ma iš-tu qé-reb lem-né-ti e-lam-ti ḫar-ra-an šu-lu-lu(*) *ú-ru-uḫ ri-šá-a-ti*

14) [*ṭ*]*u-da-at taš-me-e ù ma-ga-ri iṣ-ba-ta ana qé-reb šu-an-na*.KI

15) un ma-da igi-kár-kár-ra-ab é-gar$_8$-bi ⸢sukud⸣-da ḫé-du$_7$ še-er-ma-al šu-li-le-eš bar-dagal-la da-gan-bi ir$_5$-ra-ag-a-e-dè

16) *ib-tar-ra-a ni-iš ma-a-ti la-an-šú e-la-a šu-su-mu e-tel-la na-par-da-a šu-lu-la kul-lat-si-na pu-tuq-qa-šu*

15–16) The people of the land regarded his lofty, fitting, majestic, bright (and) joyful appearance; all of them paid attention to him.

17) nam-ba-ni-íb-sun$_5$-na ù-mu-un ba-ni-in-ri dul-mar-ra-bi ní-dúb-dúb-bu

18) *i-ru-um-ma be-lu$_4$ ir-*⸢*ta*⸣*-me šu-bat-su ni-iḫ-ta*

17–18) The lord entered and took up his peaceful abode.

19) ká-su-lim nam-lugal-la-bi-šè é-šà-sìg-ga pirig-gá ba-ni-íb-si-sá-e me-li ár-i-i

20) *ká-su-lim pa-paḫ be-lu-ti-šú im-me-ra ma-li ri-šá-a-ti*

19–20) Kasulim ("Gate of Radiance"), his lordly shrine, became bright, filled with rejoicing.

21) an-ki-bi-ta du$_8$-du$_8$-bé-e-ne a-ab-ba za-ba-lam-a-ni si ba-ni-íb-sá ḫur-sag máš mu-un-da-ri-bi

22) *šá-mu-ú ḫé-en-gál-la-šú-nu er-ṣe-tu$_4$ ḫi-ṣib-šá tam-tu$_4$ mi-šìr-ta-šá šá-du-ú i-rib-šú*

21–22) The heavens (brought him) their abundance, the earth its yield, the sea its wealth, (and) the mountain its gift.

23) sískur-bi-ne-ne èm i-bí nu-mu-un-bar-ra níg a-na eme gù-bal-bal-e

24) *kit-ru-ba-áš-šú šu-ut la maḫ-ra ma-la šu-un-na-a li-šá-a-nu*

23–24) (People) of all different languages bless him who has no rival.

25) mu-un-dugud-da-bi mu-un-ši-in-íl-íl-eš ù-mu-un lugal-la-šè : *ka-bit-ti bi-lat-su-nu na-šu-ú a-na be-el be-lu$_4$*

25) They brought their weighty tribute to the lord of lords.

26) ^{e}UDU bí-in-šum-mu-dè-eš gud-gal-⸢gal⸣-la bí-in-šár-šár-ra níg-KU-DU ul mu-un-ši-in-gál-le-eš na-NE bí-in-si-si

27) *as-lu ṭu-ub-bu-ḫu du-*⸢*uš*⸣*-šu-ú* GU$_4$.MAḪ*-e zi-i-bu šur-ru-ḫu ṣe-e-lí qut-rin-na*

26–27) Fine sheep were slaughtered (and) prime bulls (provided) in abundance. Food offerings were lavish (and) incense was burnt.

28) ir-si-im mi-ni-in-⸢è⸣ ir-sim bí-in-du$_{10}$(*)-[ga]

29) *ar-man-nu uš-te-eṣ-*⸢*ṣa*⸣*-*[*ni*]*m*(?) *i-ri-*⸢*še*⸣ *ṭa-bu-*⸢*ú*(?)⸣

28–29) The *armannu*-aromatic gave off a sweet fragrance.

30) sískur-didli [...]-in-du$_8$-du$_8$ me-⸢li⸣-gal si ba-ni-íb-si

31) *ni-qé-e* [...] x-*ti na-qí* [*m*]*a*(?)*-li ri-šá-a-ti*

30–31) A sacrifice [...] was made; (*the place*) was full of rejoicing.

32) x [(x)] x [...] x dag gir$_{17}$-zal nam-mu-un-ši-in-gá-gá

33) [...] x DU U *ta-*⸢*šil*⸣*-ta šak-na-at*

32–33) [...] ... *a celebration* took place.

34) [...] x zú-NE-NE-ra-bi igi-⸢du$_8$ gu$_4$⸣-ud ^{d}asar-ri-ke$_4$

35) [DINGIR.MEŠ *ša-m*]*a-me u qaq-qa-ri ṣi-ḫi-*⸢*iš i*⸣*-*[*n*]*a*(?)*-ṭa-lu* ^{d}AMAR.UTU *qar-du*

34–35) [The gods of hea]ven and earth were looking at the valiant god Marduk with joyful pleasure.

36) [...] x z[à]-mí an-ti

37) [...] *t*[*a*]*-nit-tu$_4$ qur-di*

36–37) [...] the praise of (his) valour.

---

15 The Sumerian version has "... joyful (and) bright appearance ..."

19–20 A.R. George (Topographical texts pp. 390 and 402–3) states that Kasulim(ma) ("Gate of Radiance") is a variant form of Kasilimma ("Gate of Well-Being"), the gate of Marduk's cella in the temple Esagila. The Sumerian version has "rejoicing (and) praise" (me-li ár-i-i).

21 The Sumerian version has "The heavens and the earth (brought him) their abundance ..."

23–24 The translation is based upon the Akkadian; the Sumerian indicates something somewhat different. CAD 17/1 [Š] p. 403 suggests "those who were not seen before(?), (people) of different languages, bring their offerings" (reading *qitrubaššu* instead of *kitrubaššu*).

27 The reading *ṣe-e-lí* (*ṣelû*, "to burn") instead of *ṣe-e-ni* (*ṣênu*, "to heap up") follows a suggestion by W.G. Lambert (private communication).

29 The copy by Pinches in 4 R^2 has *-ú* as the final sign of the line, but only a tiny trace of this sign is preserved on ex. 1, the only ex. preserving any part of it. The trace might suggest *-t*[*u*] rather than *-ú* and thus indicate the plural "sweet fragrances."

38) [... še]n(?)-šen-na ⸢šen-(erasure)-ḫur⸣-[s]ag-gá a-lá-e

39) [...] *ú-nam-ma-ru a-⸢lu⸣-ú ⸢u⸣ [l]i-li-si*

38–39) [...] *makes brilliant* the *alû*-drum and the *lilissu*-drum.

Colophon on ex. 1

40) [(DUB x.KÁM ...) *ekal aššur-bāni-apli šar kiššati* LUGA]L KUR *aš-šur*.KI

41) [*ša nabû u tašmētu uznu rapaštu išrukūš īḫuzu īna namirtu nisiq*] *ṭup-šar-ru-ti*

42) [*ša ina šarrāni ālik maḫrīia mamma šipru šuʾātu lā īḫuzu nēmeq nabû tikip sa-an-tak-k*]*i*(?) *ma-la ba-áš-mu*

43) [*ina ṭuppāni ašṭur asniq abrēma ana tāmarti šitassīia qereb* É.GAL]-*ia ú-kin*

Colophon on ex. 1

40–43) [(... tablet ...) Palace of Ashurbanipal, king of the world, kin]g of Assyria, [the one on whom the god Nabû and the goddess Tašmētu bestowed broad understanding, who has sharp eyes (and who learned) the highest level] of scribal art, [that skill which no one among the kings who had preceded me had learned. I have written on tablets, checked, (and) collated] everything pertaining to [cuneiform signs, the art of the god Nabû]. I set (them) up [in] my [palace so that they might be seen and read to me].

Colophon on ex. 2 (rev. 17–18 of exemplar)

1) [...] I x x [...]

2) [(*ekal*) *aššur-bāni-apli*] MAN ŠÚ MAN KUR [*aš-šur*.KI]

Colophon on ex. 2

1) [...] ... [...]

2) [(Palace of) Ashurbanipal], king of the world, king of [Assyria].

10

A cylinder fragment preserves part of a bilingual historical-literary text which describes how the sun-god appointed the king of Babylonia and commanded him to plunder Elam. The name of the king is not preserved and the inscription is tentatively assigned to Nebuchadnezzar I because similar inscriptions record events in his reign.

COMMENTARY

The fragment BM 51255 (82-3-23,2251) is part of the right end of a clay cylinder. The piece comes from Rassam's excavations and is part of a collection made up of pieces from Sippar, Babylon, Borsippa, Dilbat, and Nineveh (see Reade in Leichty, Sippar 1 p. xxxii). The fragment measures 10.7 cm in length; the diameter of the right end is 5.7 cm. The script exhibits archaizing features. The inscription was edited from the original, with some additional collations being made by W.G. Lambert.

The inscription is written in two columns. The Sumerian version of the inscription is in the left column and the Akkadian version in the right column, with the Akkadian version of a line placed opposite the Sumerian version. In the edition, the two versions are given one line number, with the Akkadian line being given immediately after the Sumerian line. The Akkadian version of lines 1 and 8 is indented. The translation basically follows the Akkadian version, with help from the Sumerian version in lines 11 and 16.

BIBLIOGRAPHY

1994 Frame, Studies Smith pp. 59–72 (copy, edition, study)

Colophons The colophon of ex. 1 is preceded by two line rulings, while that of ex. 2 is preceded by a single line ruling. The restoration of the colophon of ex. 1 is based upon Hunger, Kolophone no. 319 type d, as was the restoration of the colophon of ex. 1 of B.2.4.8. Line 2 of the colophon of ex. 2 is written with larger sign forms than line 1 of that exemplar.

TEXT

1)	[...] *muš-te-ši-ru kib-ra-a-ti* [(...)]	1) The one who administers correctly (all) regions (of the world) [(...)],
2)	[...] x *la a-ni-ḫu šá ki-iš-šat* AN *ù* KI *i-ḫi-iṭ-ṭù* N[U(?) (x)]	2) The tireless one, who watches over all of heaven and netherworld ...
3)	[... šú]-šú *be-lu ša saḫ-pu bir-bir-ru-šu* KUR-*i ù tam-ta* [(x)]	3) The lord, whose shining light covers mountain and sea,
4)	[...] x pàr-ra-bi *ù nam-ri-ir-<ru> be-lu-ti-šu kàt-mu kiš-šá-tú šu-par-r*[*u*(?)-*ur*(?)-*tú*(?)]	4) And whose awe-inspiring sheen covers the *wide[spread]* world,
5)	[... mu-u]n-da-ab-lá-a *mu-tál-lu šá a-na a-mat ṣi-it pi-šu ú-paq-qu* ⸢^{d}⸣[*í-gì-gì*]	5) The noble one at whose utterance the [Igīgū] gods pay attention,
6)	[... ur$_4$-u]r$_4$(?) x [... gub]-bé-eš *ù a-na na-dan ur-ti-šu* ^{d}*a-nun-na-ku i-ár-ru-ru* x [(...)] *na-zu-uz-zu kam-si-iš*	6) And at the issuing of whose command the Anunnakū gods take fright [(...)], presenting themselves on their knees (lit. "stand kneeling"),
7)	[...]-an-da-ab-si-sá-e *da-a-a-nu ṣi-ru pa-ri-is pu-ru-us-se-e šá* DINGIR ⸢*ù* ^{d}⸣I[NANNA(?)]	7) The august judge, who makes decisions for god and *go[ddess]*,
8)	[...] a-a-bi-e-ne *a-šib é-babbar-ra tukul*(*)-*ti ab-bé-e-šu*	8) The one who dwells in Ebabbar ("Shining House"), *the one on whom* his fathers *rely* —
9)	[u$_4$-bi-a ...] x URU eridu.KI-ga-ke$_4$ [...] (x)-⸢bi(?)⸣ *i-nu-šu li-ip* LUGAL-*ti* NUMUN *da-ra-a bi-nu-ut šu-an-na*	9) At that time, a royal descendant, one of an enduring lineage, scion of Šuanna (Babylon),
10)	[... šà(?) (...)] x in-du$_{10}$-du$_{10}$ ⸢*šak-kan*⸣-*ka er-šá pal-ḫa mut-né-en-na-a mu-*⸢*ṭib lìb-bi*⸣-*šu*	10) Wise viceroy, reverent, prayerful, one who makes his (the Sun-god's) heart glad,
11)	[... dingir(?)-re(?)]-⸢e(?)⸣-ne [...] x lugal sag-ús-⸢sa⸣ *ki-*⸢*i*(?)⸣ [*i*(?)-*n*]*a*(?) *ut-ni-ni ù tes-pí-ti* ^{d}UTU-*šá nu-ur* DINGIR.MEŠ ⸢*i*⸣-*bal-lu sà-an-tak*	11) *Because* the king constantly besought the Sun-god, the light of the gods, *with* supplication(s) and prayer(s),
12)	[...u]n(?)-šár-ra-ke$_4$ [... dù]-a-ba e-da-an-sum *ḫa-diš ip-pa-lis-ma id-din-šu šar-ru-ut kiš-šat ni-ši gi-mir kib-ra-a-ti*	12) He (the Sun-god) looked happily (upon him) and gave him the kingship of all people (and) of every region (of the world).
13)	[...] x-bi [...] na-nam *ú-šat-lim-šum-ma ḫaṭ-ṭa i-šar-ta ku-us-si du-ur* UD.⸢MEŠ⸣ *pa-le-e la-ba-ri*	13) He granted him a just sceptre, an eternal throne, (and) a reign of long duration.
14)	[...] mi-ni-íb-sù-sù-ú-a *ú-ma-ʾ-ir-šu-ma a-na šá-lal* KUR *e-lam-ti ú-šá-ʾ(-)i(-)*x [...]	14) He gave orders to him to plunder the land of Elam and *he* ...
15)	[... m]i-ni-íb-tu-lu [...]-sìg-sìg-ge *ib-ba-bíl-ma a-na* KUR *e-lam-ti ú-saḫ-ḫir-*[*ši*(?)] *im-ḫa-ṣa dab-da-a-š*[*a*(?)]	15) He had been brought to the land of Elam; he turned [*it*] back (and) inflicted a defeat upon *i*[*t*].
16)	[...] x šà gú elam-ma.KI-ke$_4$ [...]-eš DINGIR.MEŠ GAL.MEŠ *šá it-ti* KUR *ak-ka-di-i is-b*[*u*(?)-*su*(?)] *i-ru-ú a-na qé-reb* ⸢*ma*(?)-*a*(?)-*tì*(?) *e*(?)⸣-[*lam-ti*]	16) The great gods who had become *an*[*gry*] with the land of Akkad (and) *had gone* to the land of Elam
17)	[...] [...] x [(x)] x x [...]	17) [...] ... [...]
Lacuna		Lacuna
1′)	[...] [...] x [... x (x)] x *el kib-*⸢*ra-a*⸣-[*ti* ...]	1′) ... over the regions (of the world) [...]

8 *tukul*(*): text has ŠU.

9 The Sumerian version has "Eridu" for the Akkadian "Šuanna." These terms are both clearly attested as names for Babylon for the first time during the Second Dynasty of Isin; see George, Topographical Texts pp. 241 and 251.

2′) [...]
[*liš*(?)-*t*]*ar-ba pa-la-šu-ma i-na* KUR *šu-me-ri ù* ⌈*ak*⌉-*k*[*a-di-*(*i*) *l*]*i-ku-un a-na ṣa-a-ti*

2′) [*May*] his reign [*be made*] *great* and may it be securely established forever in the land of Sumer and Akk[ad]!

11

A stone kudurru (boundary stone) from Sippar records the fact that Nebuchadnezzar I granted an exemption from taxation and from the jurisdiction of the province Namar to the villages of Bīt-Karziabku as a reward for the bravery of its chief Šitti-Marduk during a campaign into Elam. Such royal grants are not normally included in the RIM volumes; however, a portion of this particular kudurru is edited here because it provides useful historical information on that campaign.

COMMENTARY

The kudurru was found in room 50 of the temple of the god Šamaš at Sippar by Abd-al-Ahad Thoma in 1882 and is now in the British Museum (BM 90858; 82-5-22,1800). It measures 65 cm in height and is 21.5 cm wide and 17 cm thick. Divine symbols are carved on one face of the monument. The inscription is written in two columns, each of sixty lines; the script is contemporary Babylonian. Only the first 43 lines are presented here. The remainder of the text records the issuing of the special privileges to the villages of Bīt-Karziabku, the names of the witnesses to the royal grant (including the governors of Isin, Babylon, and Namar), and the curse formulae. The inscription does not bear a specific date or place of issue. It has been collated from the published photographs.

A detailed literary study of this passage is presented by V. Hurowitz in ZA 82 (1992) pp. 39–59.

Bīt-Karziabku (i 25 and 35) was the name of both a Kassite clan and a district located in or near the province of Namar (often located in the Ḫamrīn basin); see Nashef, Rép. Géogr. 5 pp. 62 and 202.

BIBLIOGRAPHY

1883 Hilprecht, Freibrief (copy, edition)
1883–84 Pinches and Budge, PSBA 6 pp. 144–70 (copy in type, edition)
1884 5 R pls. 55–59 (copy in type)
1886 Bezold, Literatur p. 60 §32 (study)
1892 Peiser in Schrader, KB 3/1 pp. 164–74 (edition)
1904 Gray in Harper, Literature pp. 8–11 (translation)
1907 Hinke, Boundary Stone p. 131 fig. 49 (photo of relief)
1912 King, BBSt no. 6 (photo, edition)
1913 Thureau-Dangin, RA 10 pp. 97–98 (i 40–43, study)
1922 BM Guide pp. 66–67 no. 192 and pl. XXV (photo of relief, study)
1922 Steinmetzer, Kudurru pp. 12–14 no. 6 (study; additional bibliography)
1935 von Soden, OLZ 38 345–46 (i 27 and 37, study)
1947 Oppenheim, JNES 6 p. 127 (i 24, study)
1952–53 Weidner, AfO 16 p. 18 n. 134 (i 9–10, study)
1962 Strommenger and Hirmer, Mesopotamien pl. 272 (photo of relief)
1968 Brinkman, PKB pp. 106–16 and 327 no. 4.2.9 (study)
1968 Seidl, Bagh. Mitt. 4 p. 43 and pl. 23a no. 67, and passim in article (photo of relief, study)
1970 Seux, RA 64 p. 188 (i 5, study)
1980 Walker and Collon in de Meyer, Tell ed-Dēr 3 p. 101 no. 50 (study)
1985 George, RA 79 pp. 70–71 (i 16–18, study)
1987 Mayer and Sommerfeld, Orientalia NS 56 pp. 200 and 212 (i 17–18, 27, and 37, study)
1987 Reade, ARRIM 5 p. 48 (study)
1987 von Soden, RA 81 p. 190 (i 17–18, study)
1989 George, BiOr 46 382–83 (i 12–13 and 18, study)
1989 Seidl, Kudurru-Reliefs p. 43 and pl. 23a, and passim (photo of relief, study)
1992 Hurowitz, ZA 82 pp. 39–59 (edition, study)
1993 Foster, Before the Muses 1 pp. 297–98 (translation)

TEXT

Col. i
1) *e-nu-ma* ᵈAG-*ku-dúr-ri*-ÙRU NUN *na-a-du*
2) *na-as-qu ṣi-it* TIN.TIR.KI *e-tel* LUGAL.MEŠ

i 1–13) When, (with regard to) Nebuchadnezzar — the pious (and) pre-eminent prince, offspring of

3) ÉNSI *qar-du* GÌR.NÍTA URU.DÙG
4) ^{d}UTU KUR-*šu mu-šam-mi-ḫu ni-ši-šu*
5) *na-ṣir ku-dúr-re-ti mu-kin-nu* AB-*le-e*
6) LUGAL *ki-na-a-ti ša di-in mi-šá-ri i-din-nu*
7) *zi-ik-ru qar-du šá a-na e-peš* MÈ *kit-pu-da e-mu-qa-šú*
8) *na-áš* GIŠ.BAN *ez-zi-ti la a-di-ru* MÈ
9) *ša dan-na* KUR *lul-lu-bi-i ú-šam-qí-tu i-na* GIŠ.TUKUL
10) *ka-šid* KUR *a-mur-ri-i ša-li-lu kaš-ši-i*
11) *na-siq* LUGAL.MEŠ NUN *na-ra-am* ^{d}AMAR.UTU
12) *ú-ta-ʾ-ir-šu-ma* LUGAL DINGIR.MEŠ ^{d}AMAR.UTU
13) *a-na tur-ri gi-mil-li* KUR URI.KI *ú-šat-ba-a* GIŠ.TUKUL.MEŠ-*šu*

Babylon, sovereign of kings, valiant vice-regent, viceroy of Babylon, the sun-god of his land, who makes his people flourish, (i 5) who protects the boundaries, who confirms *the border lines*, just king who renders righteous decisions, valiant male whose strength is directed towards doing battle, who bears a terrible bow, who does not fear battle, who overpowered the mighty Lullubû land with (his) weapon(s), (i 10) defeated the Amorite land (and) plundered the Kassites, pre-eminent among kings, prince beloved of the god Marduk — the king of the gods, the god Marduk, commissioned him (Nebuchadnezzar), he raised his weapons in order to avenge the land of Akkad.

14) *iš-tu* URU *de-e-er ma-ḫa-az* ^{d}*a-nim*
15) *ši-iḫ-ṭa iš-ta-ka-an a-na* 30 DANNA
16) *i-na* ITI.<<ITI>>.ŠU.NUMUN.NA *iṣ-ṣa-bat ḫar-ra-a-na*
17) TA *kal* R[I] *aq-qu-ul-lu i-kab-ba-bu ki-i i-šá-ti*
18) *ù ṭú-d*[*u*(?)] *šá gir-re-è-ti i-ḫa-am-ma-ṭu ki nab-li*
19) *ia-ʾ-nu* A.MEŠ *saḫ-ḫi ù bu-ut-tu-qu maš-qu-ú*
20) *ni-is-qu šá* GAL.MEŠ ANŠE.KUR.RA.MEŠ *it*(*)-*ta-ši-iz-zu*
21) *ù šá eṭ-li qar-di pu-ri-da-šu it-tu-ra*
22) *il-lak* LUGAL *na-as-qu* DINGIR.MEŠ *na-šu-šu*
23) *i-red-di* ^{d}AG-*ku-dúr-ri*-ÙRU GABA.RI NU TUK
24) *ul id-dar dan-na-at* A.ŠÀ *iš-ka-ra-a-ti ul-lap*

i 14–24) From the city Dēr, the cult centre of the god Anum, he made an incursion to (a distance of) thirty leagues. In the month of Duʾūzu he set out on campaign. During the whole ti[me] (of the campaign) *the blistering heat* burnt like fire and the (very) roadways scorched like flames. There was no water in the places which were (normally) waterlogged and the drinking places were cut off. (i 20) The best of the great horses gave out (lit. "stood") and the legs of the strong warrior sought for a respite (lit. "turned"). (Yet) the king, the pre-eminent one, goes on, the gods supporting him. Nebuchadnezzar proceeds on; he has no equal. He does not fear the difficult terrain; *he* (*even*) *increases the daily march*.

25) ^{m}*šit-ti*-^{d}AMAR.UTU EN É *ša* É-^{m}*kar-zi-ia-ab-ku*
26) *ša* GIŠ *ma-gar-ra-šu* É *i-mit-ti*
27) LUGAL EN-*šú la im-mir-ku-ma ma-gar-ra-šú uk-til-la*
28) *ur-ri-iḫ-ma* LUGAL *dan-nu ik-ta-šad a-na* GÚ ÍD *ú-la-a*
29) *in-nin-du-ma* LUGAL.MEŠ *ki-lal-la-an ip-pu-šu* MÈ
30) *i-na bi-ri-šu-nu in-na-pi-iḫ i-šá-tu*
31) *i-na tur-bu-ʾ-ti-šu-nu na-ʾ-du-ru* IGI ^{d}UTU-*ši*
32) *a-šam-šá-tu iṣ-ṣa-nun-da i-sa-ar me-ḫu-ú*
33) *i-na mi-ḫe-e ta-ḫa-zi-šu-nu*
34) *eṭ-lu* EN GIŠ.GIGIR *ul ip-pal-la-sa šá-na-a šá it-ti-šú*

i 25–34) Šitti-Marduk, the head of the house of Bīt-Karziabku, whose chariot was (stationed) on the right flank of the king, his lord, did not lag far behind, but (rather) kept his chariot ready. The mighty king hastened on and came to the bank of the Ulāia River. The two kings came together, engaging in battle. (i 30) Fire flared up between them. The face of the sun was darkened by the dust (they raised up). Dust storms whirled; the storm whipped around. In the storm of their battle, the warrior in (his) chariot could not see the second man (in the chariot) with him.

35) ^{m}*šit-ti*-^{d}AMAR.UTU EN É *šá* É-^{m}*kar-zi-ia-ab-ku*
36) *ša* GIŠ *ma-gar*-<*ma*>-*ra-šu* É *i-mit-ti*
37) LUGAL EN-*šú la im-mir-ku-ma* GIŠ *ma-gar-ra-šú uk-til-la*
38) *la i-dur-ma* MÈ *it-ta-rad a-na* LÚ.KÚR
39) *ù a-na* <LÚ>.KÚR EN-*šu i-te-ru-ub a-tar-ta*

i 35–43) Šitti-Marduk, the head of the house of Bīt-Karziabku, whose chariot was (stationed) on the right flank of the king, his lord, did not lag far behind, but (rather) kept his chariot ready. He did not fear the battle, but (rather) went down against the enemy. Moreover, he penetrated deep into (the

i 5 AB-*le-e* is to be connected to *eblu*, "border rope, border line" (see CAD 1/2 [A] p. 177), *ašlu* (*èš-le-e*), "measuring rope" (see Foster, Before the Muses 1 p. 298), or *aplu*, "heir" (see Seux, RA 64 [1970] p. 188 and Hurowitz, ZA 82 [1992] p. 44).
i 20 *it*(*): text has DA.
i 24 The meaning of *iš-ka-ra-a-ti ul-lap* is not clear. CAD 7 [I/J] p. 250 translates "gives (the horses) rein (lit. lengthens the reins)." Hurowitz (ZA 82 [1992] pp. 43 and 45) proposes a translation "he slips through(?) the *iškaru*-fields(?)."
i 25 For the reading of the name Šitti-Marduk, see Borger, AfO 23 (1970) p. 8.
i 39 In view of the omission of LÚ before KÚR, we might read *ana* PAB EN-*šu*, "in order to protect his lord," instead of "into (the midst of) the enemy of his lord" (suggestion of J.N. Postgate).

40) *i-na* INIM ᵈ*iš-tar ù* ᵈIŠKUR DINGIR.MEŠ EN.MEŠ MÈ
41) *ul-te-es-ḫi-ir ḫul-te-lu-diš* LUGAL KUR ELAM.MA.KI *i-te-mid* KUR-*šú*
42) *ù* LUGAL ᵈAG-*ku-dúr-ri*-ÙRU *it-ta-ši-iz i-na li-ti*
43) *iṣ-ṣa-bat* KUR ELAM.MA.KI *i-iš-ta-lal* NÍG.GA-*ša*

(The issuing of the royal grant follows.)

midst of) the enemy of his lord. (i 40) By the command of the goddess Ištar and the god Adad, the gods (who are) the lords of battle, he put Ḫulteludiš, the king of Elam, to flight (and) he (Ḫulteludiš) disappeared. Thus, king Nebuchadnezzar stood in triumph; he seized the land of Elam (and) plundered its property.

1001

A badly damaged fragment of a tablet in the British Museum (BM 34637, Sp 2,120) has traces of what may be a historical-literary text written in Akkadian. A copy of the text made by T.G. Pinches has been published by C.B.F. Walker (Walker, CT 51 no. 73). R. Borger (HKL 2 p. 310) notes that the text mentions Elamite(s) (line 12′) and suggests that the inscription may deal with Nebuchadnezzar I. A late date of composition for the text would be suggested by the use of the term *bīt qašāti* (É GIŠ.BAN.MEŠ), "bow fiefs" in line 4′. So little of the text is readable that any identification remains problematic and no edition is presented here. The fragment was purchased by the British Museum from Messrs Spartoli & Co. and was entered in the museum registry in 1879. Most of the pieces in the second Spartoli collection are believed to come from Babylon (so Barnett in Walker, CT 51 p. 3). The fragment measures 10.4×11.2 cm.

Enlil-nādin-apli

B.2.5

Enlil-nādin-apli succeeded his father Nebuchadnezzar I and, according to Babylonian King List C, ruled Babylonia for four years (1103–1100 BC). In addition to one short royal inscription on a bronze dagger (B.2.5.1), at least one kudurru dates to the king's reign (Hilprecht, BE 1/1 no. 83). That kudurru comes from Enlil-nādin-apli's fourth year and describes the king's settlement of a dispute between the governor of the province of Bīt-Sîn-māgir and a temple over the ownership of a plot of land located along the Tigris in southern Babylonia. Another kudurru (King, BBSt no. 11) describes the grant of a plot of land to a subordinate of the governor of the Sealand and must date from around the time of Enlil-nādin-apli's reign, since the governor, Eanna-šuma-iddina, is also mentioned in the first kudurru. A partially preserved passage in a Babylonian chronicle appears to state that while the king of Babylon was on a campaign against Assyria there was a rebellion led by Nebuchadnezzar, or a relative of Nebuchadnezzar's, and that someone, presumably the king of Babylon, returned and was killed (see Walker, Kraus Festschrift pp. 400–402 and 410–12 lines 19–21). C.B.F. Walker argues cogently that it is most likely that the chronicle refers to events in the reign of Enlil-nādin-apli and records a successful rebellion led by his uncle Marduk-nādin-aḫḫē (a brother of Nebuchadnezzar I), who succeeded him on the throne of Babylon (see B.2.6); it is also possible, however, that the passage describes a rebellion led by Nebuchadnezzar I against his father Ninurta-nādin-šumi or one led by Enlil-nādin-šumi against Nebuchadnezzar I. For details of the reign of Enlil-nādin-apli, see Brinkman, PKB pp. 116–18 and 329–30 no. 5.

1

A label mentioning Enlil-nādin-apli and written in Akkadian is found incised on a bronze dagger in the Foroughi collection. The current location of the piece is not known. It is said to come from Luristan — though this may simply go back to a statement from an antiquities dealer — and is similar to other so-called Luristan bronzes. The inscription has been collated from the published photographs.

BIBLIOGRAPHY

1962 Dossin, IrAnt 2 p. 153 and pl. XIX no. 6 (photo, edition)

1968 Brinkman, PKB pp. 117 and 329 no. 5.2.1 (transliteration, study)

1969 Calmeyer, Datierbare Bronzen pp. 60 no. 31K and 164 no. 34 (transliteration, study)

1971 Moorey, Catalogue Ashmolean p. 31 no. 5 (study)

TEXT

Obverse
1) ⌜*šá* ᵈ*en-líl*-SUM⌝-IBILA
2) ⌜LUGAL⌝ ŠÁR
Reverse
3) LUGAL KÁ.DINGIR.RA.KI
4) LUGAL KI.IN.GI URI.⌜KI⌝

1–4) (Property) of Enlil-nādin-apli, king of the world, king of Babylon, king of Sumer (and) Akkad.

Marduk-nādin-aḫḫē

B.2.6

Marduk-nādin-aḫḫē, who succeeded Enlil-nādin-apli on the throne of Babylonia, ruled for eighteen years (1099–1082 BC). He was a son of Ninurta-nādin-šumi and thus a brother of Nebuchadnezzar I and an uncle of Enlil-nādin-aḫḫē. A fragment of a chronicle covering the period may indicate that Marduk-nādin-aḫḫē took the throne after leading a rebellion against his nephew when the latter set out to conquer Aššur (see introduction to B.2.5).

According to the Bavian inscription of Sennacherib (Luckenbill, Senn. p. 83 lines 48–49), Marduk-nādin-aḫḫē had raided the Assyrian city of Ekallāte and carried off the statues of the gods Adad and Šala. However, any advantage gained over Assyria was short-lived. Tiglath-pileser I of Assyria was able to invade Babylonia, capture Babylon, Dūr-Kurigalzu, Sippar, and Opis, and burn Marduk-nādin-aḫḫē's palaces at Babylon (see RIMA 2 A.0.87.4 lines 44–51 and A.0.87.10 lines 45–53, and Grayson, Chronicles pp. 164–65 no. 21 ii 14′–24′). Towards the end of Marduk-nādin-aḫḫē's reign, Arameans migrated onto the alluvial plain of Mesopotamia in increasing numbers because of famine in their own areas. Marduk-nādin-aḫḫē disappears from the scene during the disruptions caused by their movements (see Grayson, Chronicles p. 189 Assyrian Chronicle Fragment 4 lines 2′–9′).

In addition to two labels mentioning Marduk-nādin-aḫḫē which are engraved on bronze daggers (B.2.6.3–4), two other royal inscriptions are preserved from the king's reign: a description of the restoration of the Eganunmaḫ temple at Ur found on four stone door sockets (B.2.6.1) and a description of work on the oven of the shrine of the moon-god at Ur found on a large copper cylinder (B.2.6.2). These latter two inscriptions are written in Sumerian. A label mentioning an official found on a bronze dagger may date from around this time and it is presented here also (B.2.6.2001). In addition, several kudurrus, stelae, and economic texts date to the reign of Marduk-nādin-aḫḫē (see Brinkman, PKB pp. 331–33 nos. 6.2.6–13 and RLA 7/5–6 [1989] p. 377, to which add the kudurru composed at Opis in the king's thirteenth year, which has been published by K. Al-Adami in Sumer 38 [1982] pp. 121–33). For details of the reign of Marduk-nādin-aḫḫē, see Brinkman, PKB pp. 42–43, 119–30, and 330–33 no. 6; note also the mention of the king in a magical text (von Weiher, AUWE 12 no. 129 ii 17).

1

A Sumerian inscription recording the restoration of the Eganunmaḫ ("House, Exalted Storehouse") by Marduk-nādin-aḫḫē for the god Nanna (Sîn) is found on four stone door sockets from Ur.

CATALOGUE

Ex.	Museum number	Registration number	Excavation number	Measurements (cm)	Lines preserved	cpn
1	CBS 17244	—	U 7818	—	1–15	c
2	BM 120518	1928-10-9,1	U 7818	71.5×50.5×41.5	1–15	c
3	—	—	U 7818	—	—	n
4	—	—	U 7818	—	—	n

COMMENTARY

The four limestone door sockets were found *in situ* at the entrance to the sanctuary and at the entrances to the three southwesterly rooms of the Enunmaḫ/Eganunmaḫ temple at Ur. Ex. 1 was accessioned in the University Museum (Philadelphia) on March 21, 1929. Exs. 3–4 are presumably in Iraq, but their present museum numbers are not known. The master exemplar is ex. 1; the arrangement of lines is the same on both ex. 1 and ex. 2.

According to the copy in UET 1, the end of line 12 reads bí-in-gi-a, but exs. 1 and 2 clearly have bí-in-gi$_4$-a. Since exs. 3–4 could not be collated it is not known if they had -gi- or -gi$_4$-. According to UET 1 p. 95, the inscription measures 7.0×5.8 cm.

BIBLIOGRAPHY

1927 Woolley, AJ 7 pp. 406 and 409–10 (provenance)
1928 Gadd, UET 1 no. 306 (exs. 1–4, composite copy, edition)
1968 Brinkman, PKB pp. 5, 121 n. 694 and 330 no. 6.2.1 (study)
1969 Brinkman, Orientalia NS 38 p. 334 (exs. 1–4, study)
1974 Woolley, UE 6 p. 50 (provenance)

TEXT

1) ^{d}nanna lugal-a-ni-ir
2) ^{d}AMAR.UTU-SUM-ŠEŠ.MEŠ
3) lugal kiš
4) lugal úri.KI-ma
5) lugal KÁ.DINGIR.RA
6) lugal ki-in-gi uri.KI
7) ú-a úri.KI-ma
8) mú-mú é-kiš-nu-gál
9) é-gá-nun-maḫ
10) é libir-ra diri-ga
11) mu-na-an-dù
12) ki-bi-šè bí-in-gi$_4$-a
13) KU GIŠ.ig
14) na$_4$ mu-bi šuba$_4$-a
15) a mu-un-na-ru

1–15) For the god Nanna, his lord: Marduk-nādin-aḫḫē, king of the world, king of Ur, (5) king of Babylon, king of Sumer (and) Akkad, who provides for Ur, restorer of Ekišnugal, (re)built (and) restored Eganunmaḫ, (10) the temple which had collapsed due to old age, (and) dedicated to him (this) *door socket*, the name of whose stone is "*It shines.*"

10 The translation assumes that diri stands for the Akkadian verb *qâpu*, "to collapse" ("the temple which had collapsed due to old age" rather than "the very old temple"); note in particular B.2.7.2 line 14 and B.2.8.1001 ii 9, where we have sumun-bi ì-diri-ga, "which had collapsed due to old age," and zag-mu-ta sumun-bé-eš diri-ga, "which had collapsed at the beginning of the year due to old age," respectively.
13 KU GIŠ.ig stands for *b/purṣimtu* (GIŠ.KU-ig), which is generally taken to refer to a box under a door's pivot stone (see CAD 2 [B] p. 333 and AHw p. 140).
14 The translation "*It shines*" assumes that šuba$_4$(MÙŠ) stands for šuba(ZA.MÙŠ)/šúba(ZA.MÙŠ); see also Kutscher, Kramer Anniversary p. 309.

2

A large copper cylinder from Ur bears a poorly preserved Sumerian inscription stating that Marduk-nādin-aḫḫē had rebuilt the oven of the sanctuary of the moon-god Nanna (Sîn).

COMMENTARY

The object bears the Ur excavation number U 17627a and is currently in the British Museum (BM 123124; 1932-10-8,8). It was found in the tenth season of excavations at Ur in a brick box cut into the brickwork of the Ur III level under the Larsa-period sanctuary at the southern corner of room 3 of the so-called kitchen block, which is located in the northwestern section of the ziqqurat terrace. In the same box was found a copper cylinder of Nūr-Adad (RIME 4 E4.2.8.3 ex. 12). Two further copper cylinders of Nūr-Adad were discovered in a similar box in room 6 (RIME 4 E4.2.8.3 exs. 10–11). The Nūr-Adad text describes the construction of an oven and a du$_{8}$-maḫ (possibly a cauldron) for the god Nanna. Presumably Marduk-nādin-aḫḫē discovered the cylinder of Nūr-Adad while restoring the building and had a similar cylinder made and placed in the old Larsa period foundation deposit. The piece is solid and measures 33.0 cm in length and 6.5 cm in diameter. The inscription has been collated and W.G. Lambert kindly made available to the author an unfinished copy of the text which he had prepared a number of years ago. However, the inscription is poorly preserved and many parts of the text are difficult to read and understand.

BIBLIOGRAPHY

1932–33 Gadd, BMQ 7 pp. 43–44 (study)
1932 Woolley, AJ 12 p. 375 (provenance)
1933 Woolley, MJ 23 p. 220 (provenance)
1939 Woolley, UE 5 pp. 38 and 47 (provenance)
1965 Sollberger, UET 8 no. 101 (copy)
1965 Woolley, UE 8 p. 69 (study)
1967 Seux, ERAS pp. 391, 397, 405, 423, 431, and 433 (study)
1968 Brinkman, PKB pp. 5, 121 n. 695, and 331 no. 6.2.5 (study)
1968 Ellis, Foundation Deposits pp. 114–15 (study)
1969 Brinkman, Orientalia NS 38 p. 334 (study)

TEXT

Col. i
1) d⸢nanna⸣
2) en temen ⸢an-ki⸣-[(x x)]-a
3) ⸢nir⸣-gál x ⸢ZI⸣ x [x (x)]
4) giš-nu$_{11}$ [(x)] ⸢gal⸣
5) ⸢SAG⸣ x x x x
6) šà x x x [...]
7) maḫ x [...] x
8) NI ⸢KIN(?)⸣ [...] x
9) ⸢lugal⸣ x [(x)] x ⸢KI⸣ [(x)]
10) x x [...] ⸢TI(?)⸣ [(x)]
11) lugal-a-⸢ni-ir(?)⸣

1–11) For the god Nanna, lord of the foundation of heaven (and) netherworld, noble ..., great light, (5) ..., king ..., his lord:

12) ⸢dAMAR.UTU⸣-SUM-⸢ŠEŠ⸣.[ME]Š
13) ⸢nun ní-tuku⸣
14) x x x [...] ⸢en(?)⸣
15) sipa ⸢ní bí⸣-⸢in(?)⸣-[t]ur-⸢tur⸣-d[è]
16) ŠU IR [(x x)] NI/IR
17) en <me>-te dEN.DIŠ.DIŠ-ke$_{4}$
18) en GÍD/SÙ/MU[Š] [(x)] uri$_{5}$.KI-ma

12–33) Marduk-nādin-aḫḫē, pious prince, ..., (15) shepherd ..., the lord fitted for the god EN.DIŠ.DIŠ, lord ... of Ur, ..., (20) king [...], king [...], king of Sumer (and) Akkad, king of the [four] quarters (of the world), whose deeds are pleasing (25) to the god Sîn (and) the great gods, ... (30) [*Su*]*me*[*r (and)*] Akkad, ...

19) KI/DI/ŠÀ(?) ŠA(?) NE(?) x x x [(x x)] LU É x x [...]
20) lugal [x x x] x
21) lugal [(x)] x x x
Col. ii
22) ⌈lugal ki⌉-èn-gi ⌈uri.KI⌉
23) ⌈lugal an-ub-da⌉ [límmu]-⌈ba⌉
24) ⌈níg-kì⌉-kìd-da-ni
25) s[u ^{d}]⌈EN.ZU-na⌉
26) ⌈dingir gal⌉-gal-⌈la⌉ du$_{10}$-du$_{10}$-ge-eš
27) [(x)] NE [x] GAR ⌈INANNA⌉ ZI
28) [(x)] bí-⌈in(?)⌉-x-⌈im(?)⌉-ma
29) x x GA [(x)]
30) [ki]-èn-g[i(?) (x)] uri.KI-ke$_4$
31) x [x] (x) BI [(x)]
32) [...] x [x]
33) x [x (x)] (x) KU RU NE
34) u$_4$-⌈bi⌉-a
35) ⌈gir$_4$(?)⌉ maḫ
36) ⌈èš⌉ x ^{d}EN.ZU(?)-ke$_4$
37) ki-kin-nim-kin-sig(*)
38) gú-si-a dingir-re-e-ne-ke$_4$
39) làl(?) íl-⌈íl⌉-šè
40) gir$_4$(?) maḫ
41) te-èš gal-bi
42) ⌈šà(?)⌉-bi-ta [(x)]
43) x AN diri-ga x x
44) GIBIL [(x)] x [(x)]
45) [(x)] x [x x] AN x x
46) [x (x)] GAR [x] x TA [(...)] TUM(?)
47) [x x] diri-ga

34–47) At that time, the great *oven* of the shrine of the god *Sîn*, *where all the morning and evening meals of* the gods ... (40) the great *oven*, its great *roaring* inside it ...

Col. iii
48) nam-bi-⌈šè(?)⌉ [x (x)]
49) ^{d}EN.⌈ZU⌉ [...]
50) en KA(?) [...]
51) nam-⌈lugal-la⌉ x [(x)] x A x [x (x)]
52) ^{d}[A]MAR.UTU-
53) SUM-⌈ŠEŠ⌉.MEŠ
54) nun ⌈še-ga-a-ni-ir⌉
55) sipa šu-gibi[l(?)-a]k(?) x
56) nam-ti-[la(?) (x)]
57) u$_4$ sù(?)-rá [x] x
58) bala(?) x [x (x)]
59) x x [x (x)]
60) MU [(x)] x [x x]
61) [(x)] GAR SI [...] (x)
62) sag(?)-⌈sag⌉-[e(?)]-⌈eš⌉ x [(x) ḫé]-en-rig$_7$

48–62) On account of this, [... may] the god Sîn, [...] lord [...] kingship ... grant to Marduk-nādin-aḫḫē, his obedient prince, (55) the shepherd *who restores* ... a *long* life-span (and) a *reign* ...!

34–47 At this point the Nūr-Adad inscription has u$_4$-bi-a gir$_4$-maḫ ú-sù-sù-^{d}EN.ZU-na-ka ninda íl-e kìlib-dingir-re-e-ne-er du$_8$-maḫ-únu-gal-ba mí zi-dè-eš du$_{11}$-ga kin-sig kin-nim-ma gù-nun-bi di-dam nam-ti-la-ni-šè mu-na-dù šu-luḫ-u$_4$-ul-lí-a-ka-ni ki-bé mu-na-gi$_4$, "at that time, a great oven for the meals of the god Suen which provides bread for all the gods (and) a great *cauldron* cared for in the (dining) hall, roaring loudly at the morning and evening meals, he made for him (the god Nanna) and for his own life. He restored the traditional cleansing rites" (RIME 4 E4.2.8.3 lines 37–50).

37 -sig(*), text has -ma. The signs MA and SIG would, however, not be very different in form in this script.

58 The Nūr-Adad text has here bala-nam-ḫé, "a reign of abundance" (RIME 4 E4.2.8.3 line 54) but the sign following bala(?) in our text is clearly not nam.

3

A bronze dagger in the Louvre (AO 14055) bears a short Akkadian inscription indicating that it belonged to the king Marduk-nādin-aḫḫē. The object measures 36.0×3.2 cm. According to G. Contenau, the piece was one of several inscribed daggers which had appeared on the antiquities market and which, according to the statements of the sellers, came from the region of Nihavand. The inscription has been collated.

BIBLIOGRAPHY

1931 Contenau, RA 28 pp. 105–106 (photo, copy, edition)
1932 Pope, ILN October 29 pp. 666–67 and fig. 3 (photo; translation by Langdon)
1938 Langdon in Pope, Survey 1 pp. 279 and p. 284 no. 10 (copy in type, edition) and 4 pl. 55B (photo)
1947 Contenau, Manuel 4 p. 2162 fig. 1200 (photo)
1959–60 Nagel, AfO 19 pp. 95–96 no. 1 and p. 97 fig. 1 (drawing, study)
1968 Brinkman, PKB p. 331 no. 6.2.3 (study)
1968 Herzfeld, Persian Empire p. 30 no. 4 (study)
1969 Calmeyer, Datierbare Bronzen p. 60 no. 31L, fig. 59, and p. 164 no. 37 (transliteration, drawing, study)
1971 Moorey, Catalogue Ashmolean p. 32 no. 8 (study)

TEXT

Obverse
1) *šá* ᵈAMAR.UTU-SUM-ŠEŠ.MEŠ
2) LUGAL ŠÁR
Reverse
3) DUMU ᵈ*nin-urta*-SUM-MU
4) LUGAL KÁ.DINGIR.RA.KI

1–4) (Property) of Marduk-nādin-aḫḫē, king of the world, son of Ninurta-nādin-šumi, king of Babylon.

4

Three bronze daggers bear short Akkadian inscriptions stating that the pieces belonged to the king Marduk-nādin-aḫḫē. The daggers are similar to so-called Luristan bronzes and published reports refer to them as such.

CATALOGUE

Ex.	Museum number	Registration number	Dimensions (cm)	Lines preserved	cpn
1	LA M.76.97.498	—	Length of blade: 28.7; length of hilt: 13	1–4	c
2	BM 123061	1932-5-14,2	36.8×5.2	1–4	c
3	Foroughi collection, number unknown	—	—	1–4	p

COMMENTARY

Ex. 1 was formerly in the collection of Mrs. Christian R. Holmes (New York). It is now part of the Nasli M. Heeramaneck Collection of Ancient Near Eastern Art in the Los Angeles County Museum of Art and was collated by B. Cifola. Ex. 2, which was purchased by the British Museum, is reported to have been found in a cave not far from Kermanshah together with another inscribed bronze dagger (B.2.6.2001) and a bronze bowl; however, there is no proof of the accuracy of this provenance, which likely goes back to a statement by an antiquities dealer.

In view of the fact that ex. 3 omits several signs, Dossin has raised the possibility that the inscription on this dagger may be a modern addition (IrAnt 2 [1962] p. 153).

The master line follows ex. 1. The line arrangement is the same for both exs. 1 and 2 and that of ex. 3 only varies in that it puts ŠEŠ.MEŠ of line 1 at the beginning of line 2.

BIBLIOGRAPHY

1931 Contenau, RA 28 p. 107 (study)
1932–33 Gadd, BMQ 7 pp. 44–45 and pl. XVIII (ex. 2, photo, translation, study)
1932 Pope, ILN October 29 pp. 666–67 and figs. 4–5 (ex. 1, photo; translation by Langdon does not fit this dagger, but rather only B.2.6.3)
1932–33 Weidner, AfO 8 pp. 258–59 and fig. 6d (ex. 1, copy, edition)
1938 Langdon in Pope, Survey 1 pp. 279 and 283 nos. 8 and 9, and 4 pl. 55C [not A as stated in vol. 1] and D–E (exs. 1–2, photo, study; ex. 1, copy in type, edition)
1939 Meek, BASOR 74 p. 9 (ex. 2, translation)
1946 Maxwell-Hyslop, Iraq 8 p. 45 (ex. 2, translation, study)
1959–60 Nagel, AfO 19 pp. 95–96 nos. 3 and 6 and p. 97 figs. 3 and 5 (exs. 1–2, study; ex. 1, photo; ex. 2, drawing)
1962 Dossin, IrAnt 2 pp. 152–53 and pl. XVIII no. 5 (ex. 3, photo, edition)
1963 Ghirshman, Perse p. 282 fig. 343 (left) and p. 283 (ex. 2, photo, study)
1964 Maxwell-Hyslop and Hodges, Iraq 26 p. 52 and pl. XII no. 5 (ex. 2, photo, study)
1968 Brinkman, PKB pp. 330–31 no. 6.2.2 (exs. 1–2, study) and no. 6.2.4 (ex. 3 study)
1968 Herzfeld, Persian Empire p. 30 nos. 5–6 (exs. 1–2, study)
1969 Calmeyer, Datierbare Bronzen pp. 60–61 nos. 31M–O and fig. 60, and p. 164 nos. 35–36 and 38 (exs. 1–3, transliteration, study; ex. 2, drawing)
1971 Moorey, Catalogue Ashmolean pp. 31–32 nos. 6, 7, and 9 (exs. 1–3, study)
1974 Moorey, Ancient Bronzes from Luristan (London) p. 46 and pl. IIB (ex. 2, photo, study)
1981 Moorey, Ancient Bronzes no. 76 (ex. 1, photo, translation, study)

TEXT

Obverse
1) *šá* [d]AMAR.UTU-SUM-ŠEŠ.MEŠ
2) LUGAL ŠÁR
Reverse
3) LUGAL KÁ.DINGIR.RA.KI
4) LUGAL KI.IN.GI URI.KI

1–4) (Property) of Marduk-nādin-aḫḫē, king of the world, king of Babylon, king of Sumer (and) Akkad.

2001

A bronze dagger bears a label indicating that it belonged to Šamaš-killanni, the *ša rēši* of the king. The date of this particular inscription is not known, but most inscribed daggers which can be dated come from the Second Dynasty of Isin (see Sass, UF 21 [1989] p. 353). Since the dagger is reported to have been found in the same cave near Kermanshah as B.2.6.4 ex. 2, its inscription is arbitrarily presented here. As noted above, there is no proof as to the accuracy of the statement about the provenance.

COMMENTARY

According to Maxwell-Hyslop, the piece, BM 123060 (1932-5-14,1), measures 45 cm in length, while Nagel (AfO 19 p. 96 n. 10) states that it is 36.8 cm long. The piece was not available in the museum for collation. The inscription has been collated from the published photographs; however, the first half of line 1 is not clear on any of them.

The *ša rēš šarri* ("*ša rēši* of the king") is attested in Babylonia as a royal official from the Kassite period down to the Persian period. The term *ša rēši* is often translated as "eunuch." While it seems likely that it has that meaning in Assyrian contexts, its meaning in Babylonian contexts is disputed. With regard to the *ša rēši and ša rēš šarri*, see Brinkman, PKB pp. 309–11 and Brinkman and Dalley, ZA 78 (1988) pp. 85–86.

BIBLIOGRAPHY

1931 Contenau, RA 28 pp. 107–108 (translation)
1932–33 Gadd, BMQ 7 pp. 44–45 and pl. XVIII (photo, translation, study)
1938 Langdon in Pope, Survey 1 pp. 279 and 284 no. 11 and 4 pl. 55A [not C as stated in vol. 1] (photo, edition)
1939 Meek, BASOR 74 pp. 9–10 (translation, study)
1946 Maxwell-Hyslop, Iraq 8 p. 45 (translation, study)
1959–60 Nagel, AfO 19 pp. 95–98 no. 4 and fig. 4 (drawing, study)
1963 Ghirshman, Perse p. 282 fig. 343 (right) and p. 283 (photo, study)
1968 Brinkman, PKB pp. 11 no. 3 and 362 no. i (study)
1968 Herzfeld, Persian Empire p. 30 no. 7 (study)
1969 Calmeyer, Datierbare Bronzen pp. 61 no. 31A' and fig. 62 and p. 164 no. 41 (drawing, transliteration, study)
1971 Moorey, Catalogue Ashmolean p. 32 no. 15 (study)
1974 Moorey, Ancient Bronzes from Luristan (London) p. 46 and pl. IIA (photo, study)

TEXT

1) *šá* [d]UTU-*kil-la-an-ni*
2) LÚ.SAG LUGAL

1–2) (Property) of Šamaš-killanni, the *ša rēši* of the king.

Marduk-šāpik-zēri

B.2.7

Marduk-šāpik-zēri succeeded his father, Marduk-nādin-aḫḫē, on the throne of Babylonia and ruled for thirteen years (1081–1069 BC). His reign was described as a time of abundance and prosperity for the people of Babylonia; towards its end, he concluded a peace treaty with Aššur-bēl-kala of Assyria. See Walker in Kraus Festschrift pp. 399–402 and 414 lines 27–28 and p. 416 lines 4–7, and Grayson, Chronicles p. 165 no. 21 ii 25′–30′.

Inscriptions of the king record the rebuilding of the fortifications of Babylon (B.2.7.1) and the restoration of the Ezida temple at Borsippa (B.2.7.2). The former inscription is written in Akkadian upon a clay cylinder, while the latter is written in Sumerian and is only known via a late copy on a clay tablet. A bronze dagger has a label of the king written in Akkadian (B.2.7.3) and a stone weight from Nippur bears a Sumerian inscription of an official of the king (B.2.7.2001). A Neo-Babylonian inventory from Ur includes Marduk-šāpik-zēri among a number of other royal donors of precious objects to a temple (Figulla, UET 4 no. 143:15). A few kudurru and economic texts also come from his reign. For details on the reign of Marduk-šāpik-zēri, see Brinkman, PKB pp. 43, 130–35, and 334–35 no. 7 and RLA 7/5–6 (1989) p. 378; note also Arnaud, Syria 53 (1976) p. 79 no. 182 and p. 81.

1

The restoration of the fortifications of the city of Babylon appears to be recorded in a fragmentary Akkadian inscription of Marduk-šāpik-zēri.

COMMENTARY

The inscription is found on a fragment of the left end of a clay cylinder. The piece was once in the possession of Mr. Talcott Williams (Philadelphia); its original provenance and present location are not known. The fragment is 7.98 cm in length; its original diameter at the left end would have been about 5.3 cm and at the centre about 7.8 cm. Parts of two columns are preserved; the piece would have had originally three (Jastrow) or four (Hilprecht) columns. According to Jastrow's estimation, each column would have had 30–32 lines when complete. The inscription is edited from the copy published by Hilprecht (BE 1/2 no. 148).

The rebuilding of the city wall of Babylon may also be mentioned in two chronicles (see Walker in Kraus Festschrift pp. 399–402 and 414 line 27 and p. 416 line 4), but this remains uncertain since the key word "wall" is restored in both texts.

BIBLIOGRAPHY

1889 Jastrow, ZA 4 pp. 301–23 (copy in type, edition, study)
1891 Knudtzon, ZA 6 pp. 163–65 (study)
1892 Peiser in Schrader, KB 3/1 pp. 162–63 (partial edition)
1893 Hilprecht, BE 1/1 p. 44 n. 4 (study)
1893 Hilprecht, ZA 8 pp. 116–20 (partial copy in type, study)
1893 Jastrow, ZA 8 pp. 214–19 (study)
1896 Hilprecht, BE 1/2 no. 148 (copy)
1955 Poebel, AS 15 pp. 15–16 (study)
1968 Brinkman, PKB pp. 5, 131, 135 n. 801, and 334 no. 7.2.2 (partial transliteration, study)
1992 George, Topographical Texts pp. 343–44 (study)

TEXT

Col. i
1) ⸢^{d}⸣[A]MAR.UTU-*ša-pí-ik-*
2) *ze-ri-im*
3) LUGAL KÁ.DINGIR.RA.KI
4) LUGAL *da-núm*
5) LUGAL *kiš-ša-ti*
6) [L]UGAL *kib-ra-at*
7) [(x)] *ar-ba-um*
8) [x] x ⸢PI(?)⸣ IR
9) [x x x (x)] x
Lacuna

i 1–9) Marduk-šāpik-zēri, king of Babylon, mighty king, (i 5) king of the world, king of the four quarters (of the world), ... [...]
Lacuna

1′) [(x) KÁ].⸢DINGIR.RA⸣.KI
2′) x E x Ú UM
3′) *ú-sí-im*
4′) *ša* ^{d}*iš-tar*
5′) *ù*
6′) ⸢^{d}⸣*in-ni-na*
7′) ⸢*aš/áš*⸣*-ru ša-aḫ-ṭú*
Col. ii
1) A[N ...]
2) A[N ...]
3) AB x [...]
4) ŠA A[N ...]
5) ⸢*ù*(?)⸣ [(x)]
6) LUGAL K[Á.DINGIR.RA.KI (...)]
7) KA x [...]
8) KI KUD KUD A[N(?) ...]
9) [...]
10) ZU x [...]
11) PI x [...]
12) *i-nu-um* [...]
13) *be-*⸢*lum*⸣ x [...]
14) [x] x [...]
Lacuna

i 1′–ii 14) [Ba]bylon, ... *I/he made suitable for* the goddess Ištar and the goddess Innina — humble, respectful, (ii 1′)... *and* king of B[abylon] ... (ii 10′) ... when [...] lord [...]
Lacuna

1′) x [...]
2′) ÍD.B[URANUN(?).KI(?)]
3′) *in qé-r*[*e-eb*]
4′) KÁ.DINGI[R.RA.KI]
5′) *ba-*⸢*ba*⸣*-*[*ni/ti*(?)]
6′) *ú-dan-n*[*in-ma*(?)]
7′) BÀD *im-gur-*[^{d}*en-líl*]
8′) BÀD x [...]
9′) KI x [...]
Lacuna

ii 1′–9′) [...] *Eu*[*phrates*] river insi[de] Baby[lon], I/he strength[ened] the gat[es *and* ...] the (city) wall Imgur-[Enlil], the wall ...
Lacuna

Margin
1) DAM x [...]

Margin
1) ... [...]

---

i 2′ Possibly [*r*]*e-e-*⸢ʾ(?)⸣*-ú-um*, "shepherd."

2

In the fifteenth year of the reign of the Babylonian king Kandalānu (633 BC), a scribe copied an inscription of Marduk-šāpik-zēri which described the restoration of the Ezida temple ("True House") at Borsippa for the god Nabû, who is called by the name Mudugasâ.

COMMENTARY

The tablet BM 26295 (98-5-14,113) is written in a pseudo-archaic script and measures 4.7×7.9 cm. It was purchased by the British Museum from S.A. Turabian (Istanbul). There are single line rulings after lines 1–16 and a double ruling after line 17 (i.e., before the colophon). The inscription of Marduk-šāpik-zēri is written in Sumerian and the colophon is in Akkadian. The inscription has been collated. The readings in the first parts of lines 1 and 4 were proposed by Sommerfeld (Aufstieg Marduks p. 186 n. 1).

As noted by Brinkman (PKB p. 134 n. 793), the family to which the scribe belonged (the family Ḫuṣābu, line 21) is well attested at Borsippa in the seventh century.

BIBLIOGRAPHY

1898–1900 King, LIH no. 70 (copy, edition)
1968 Brinkman, PKB pp. 5, 131 n. 780, 134 n. 793, and 334 no. 7.2.1 (partial transliteration, study)
1978 Pomponio, Nabû pp. 63–64 (study)
1982 Sommerfeld, Aufstieg Marduks p. 186 (study)

TEXT

Obverse
1) [^{d}mu-du$_{10}$-ga-s]a$_{4}$(?)-a
2) [...] ⌈GU⌉-e
3) [...] x dingir-e-ne-ke$_{4}$
4) ⌈a⌉-s[a]g(?) ⌈^{d}lugal⌉-dim$_{11}$-<me>-er-an-ki-a
5) ur-maḫ é-<sag>-íl-la
6) é-zi-da-bi
7) ù-mu-un bar-zi-pà.KI
8) du$_{10}$-gál é-zi-da
9) lugal-a-ni-ir
10) ^{d}AMAR.UTU-*ša-pí-ik-ze-ri-im*
11) me-a-am(*) gù-dé-a-ni
12) nun šu-dù-dù-a-ni
13) ki-gar é-zi-da
Reverse
14) sumun-bi ì-diri-ga
15) ši-in-ne(*)-ba-dím-ma
16) ki-bi-šè
17) mu-un-na-gi

Colophon
18) *ki-ma la-bi-ri-šú*(*)
19) *šá-ṭi-ir-ma ba-ar-im*
20) IM.GÍD.DA ^{md}AG-MU-SI.SÁ
21) *bu-kúr* ^{m}*ḫu-ṣa-bi*

1–9) For [the god *Mudugas*]*â*, ... of the gods, *heir* of the god Lugaldimmeranki, (5) lion of Esagila and Ezida, lord of Borsippa, *who dwells in* Ezida, his lord:

10–17) Marduk-šāpik-zēri, *I*, the one called by him (the god), the prince *to whom he stretched out his hand*, (re)constructed and restored the base of Ezida, which had collapsed due to old age.

Colophon
18–19) Written and collated according to its original.

20–21) Tablet of Nabû-šumu-līšir, descendant of Ḫuṣābu.

8 The translation "*who dwells in*" assumes that du$_{10}$-gál is a variant for du$_{10}$-gar.

22) ITI.BÁR MU 15.KAM
23) *kan-da-la-an*(*) LUGAL
24) KÁ.DINGIR.RA.KI

22–24) Month of Nisannu, fifteenth year of Kandalānu, king of Babylon.

3

A bronze dagger in the Royal Ontario Museum (Toronto) has an Akkadian inscription stating that it belonged to the king Marduk-šāpik-zēri.

COMMENTARY

The dagger (ROM 938.35, formerly D 1513) was purchased from the Kelekian collection in New York in 1938. It is similar to other so-called Luristan bronze daggers; however, nothing is known about the original provenance of the piece. It measures 43.7×5.2×1.3 cm in size. The inscription has been collated and a copy of it appears on the cover of this volume.

BIBLIOGRAPHY

1939 Meek, BASOR 74 p. 1 fig. 1 and pp. 8–9 (photo, edition)
1946 Maxwell-Hyslop, Iraq 8 p. 45 (edition, study)
1959–60 Nagel, AfO 19 pp. 95–96 no. 7 and p. 97 fig. 6 (drawing, study)
1968 Brinkman, PKB pp. 131 and 334 no. 7.2.3 (edition, study)
1968 Herzfeld, Persian Empire p. 29 no. 1 (study)
1969 Calmeyer, Datierbare Bronzen p. 61 no. 31P and p. 164 no. 39 (transliteration, study)
1971 Moorey, Catalogue Ashmolean p. 32 no. 10 (study)

TEXT

Obverse
1) *ša* ᵈAMAR.UTU-*ša-pí-ik*-NUMUN
Reverse
2) ⌜LUGAL⌝ ŠÁR

1–2) (Property) of Marduk-šāpik-zēri, king of the world.

2001

A stone weight in the shape of a duck, which was found at Nippur, has a Sumerian inscription indicating that it weighed ten minas and belonged to Napsamenni, a servant of the king Marduk-šāpik-zēri.

COMMENTARY

The duck weight (IM 71204) bears the excavation number 9 N 99. It was found at Nippur in December 1964 to the southeast of the expedition house site in a mud mortar pit within a thick and extensive ash layer. It is made of black stone and measures 13×18×13 cm. The inscription was collated from a cast of the inscription in the Oriental Institute, Chicago.

Napsamenni also appears in an administrative document from Nippur (Bernhardt, TMH NF 5 no. 44 iv 14 [104]) as diviner and *nešakku*-priest of the god Enlil. That document lists garments brought from Babylon to Nippur by Napsamenni on the occasion of a marriage in the second year of the previous king, Marduk-nādin-aḫḫē.

BIBLIOGRAPHY

1968 Brinkman, PKB pp. 122 n. 709, 134, and 335 no. 7.2.7 (study)
1969 Buccellati and Biggs, AS 17 no. 56 (copy, transliteration)

TEXT

1) na_4 10 ma
2) m(*)*nap-sa-me-ni*
3) ugula azu nu-èš d50-lá
4) ìr dAMAR.UTU-*ša-pí-ik*-NUMUN
5) lugal KÁ.DINGIR.RA.KI-ke_4

1) Stone weight, (weighing) ten minas.
2–5) Napsamenni, overseer of the diviners, *nešakku*-official of the god Enlil, servant of Marduk-šāpik-zēri, king of Babylon.

2 The inscription has a horizontal wedge instead of a vertical wedge for the masculine determinative.

Adad-apla-iddina

B.2.8

Adad-apla-iddina succeeded Marduk-šāpik-zēri as ruler of Babylonia and reigned for twenty-two years (1068–1047 BC). Although scholars once thought that he was an Aramean usurper, this has recently been shown not to have been the case (see Walker in Kraus Festschrift pp. 414–15). The Assyrian Synchronistic History states that the Assyrian king Aššur-bēl-kala appointed "Adad-apla-iddina, descendant (son) of Esagil-šadûni, descendant (son) of a nobody," as Marduk-šāpik-zēri's successor; Aššur-bēl-kala then married the daughter of the new ruler of Babylonia, thus joining the people of the two lands (Grayson, Chronicles p. 165 no. 21 ii 31′–37′). The two Babylonian chronicles describing the reign of Adad-apla-iddina do not mention Aššur-bēl-kala, and Adad-apla-iddina is described as "a descendant (son) of Itti-Marduk-balāṭu." We are told that Arameans and a usurper rebelled against him, desecrated all the sanctuaries of the land, and demolished the cities of Agade, Dēr, Duranki (Nippur), Sippar, and Parsa (Dūr-Kurigalzu); Suteans also plundered the land of Sumer and Akkad. Adad-apla-iddina is reported to have frequented the shrines of the god Marduk, appeased both him and the god Nabû, and restored their rites. (See Walker in Kraus Festschrift pp. 399–402 lines 29–34 and p. 416 lines 8–11.) The Assyrian and Babylonian accounts thus record Adad-apla-iddina's genealogy in different ways, but neither indicates that he was a relative of the previous king, Marduk-šāpik-zēri. Possibly the Itti-Marduk-balāṭu who is stated to be his ancestor in the Babylonian sources was the second king of the dynasty by that name; Adad-apla-iddina may have been related to that ruler through a younger son named Esagil-šadûni, who is mentioned as his ancestor in the Synchronistic History. In only two of his own inscriptions does Adad-apla-iddina record his parentage. In one he states that he was the son of the goddess Ninisina (B.2.8.10 line 3) and in the other the reading is uncertain (B.2.8.7 line 9).

According to current opinion, it was during the time of Adad-apla-iddina that the Assyrian campaign recorded in the Broken Obelisk against two cities in the Babylonian province of Dūr-Kurigalzu took place (see RIMA 2 A.0.89.7 iii 4–8). Kadašman-Buriaš, the Babylonian governor of the province, was captured by the Assyrians. In retaliation, after the death of Aššur-bēl-kala in 1056, the Babylonians may have aided in the ouster of the new Assyrian king, Erība-Adad II, by Aššur-bēl-kala's brother Šamšī-Adad IV, since the Assyrian King List tells us that Šamšī-Adad went up to Assyria from Babylonia (Karduniaš) to depose Erība-Adad.

Two inscriptions may state that Adad-apla-iddina rebuilt the city wall of Babylon (B.2.8.1 and B.2.8.1001) and two other inscriptions of his may come from Babylon or be connected with that city (B.2.8.2–3). Inscriptions of Adad-apla-iddina record the making of a gold belt decorated with precious stones for the statue of the god Nabû at Borsippa (B.2.8.5) and the restoration of the city wall of Nippur (B.2.8.6) and of temples at Kish (B.2.8.4), Isin (B.2.8.7), Larsa (B.2.8.9), and Ur (B.2.8.10–11). One inscription of the king comes from Uruk (B.2.8.8) and another is found on a bronze dagger of unknown provenance (B.2.8.12). Inscription B.2.8.5 is a bilingual one, written in Sumerian and Akkadian; inscriptions B.2.8.3–4, B.2.8.7–10, and B.2.8.1001 are written in Sumerian; and B.2.8.2, B.2.8.6, and B.2.8.11–12 are in Akkadian. Too little of B.2.8.1 is preserved to be certain of its language. The inscriptions are found upon bricks (B.2.8.1, B.2.8.4, B.2.8.7, and B.2.8.9–11), clay tablets (B.2.8.5 and B.2.8.8), clay cylinders (B.2.8.2 and B.2.8.1001), a truncated clay cone (B.2.8.6), a bead (B.2.8.3), and a dagger (B.2.8.12). Two economic texts and at least three kudurrus — including one from Opis — were also composed during the king's reign (see Brinkman, PKB p. 337 nos. 8.2.8–11; Frame, AOF 13 [1986] pp. 206–211; and Arnaud, Syria 53 [1976] p. 79 no. 183 and p. 81). For details of the reign of Adad-apla-iddina, see Brinkman, PKB pp. 43–44, 135–44, and 335–38 no. 8.

1

A fragment of a brick from Babylon has a partially illegible inscription stamped on its edge which mentions the king Adad-apla-iddina and possibly Imgur-Enlil ("The God Enlil Showed Favour"), the name of Babylon's inner city wall.

COMMENTARY

The current location of the brick fragment is not known. It bears the Babylon excavation number BE 59431 and appears on Babylon excavation photo 3455. The piece was found among refuse near the southeast gate on the east side of the inner city wall (the Zababa Gate) in the 1913–14 season of excavations. The inscription has been collated from the excavation photograph. While the name of Babylon's inner city wall Imgur-Enlil may appear in line 3, only the dingir sign is clear on the photograph. Wetzel, who saw the original, stated that the line had ... *im-(gur)-*^{ilu}*EN-LIL*, that is *im-*[*gur*]*-*^{d}*en-líl*.

BIBLIOGRAPHY

1914 Wetzel, MDOG 53 p. 28 (transliteration)

1930 Wetzel, Stadtmauern pp. 64 and 79, and pl. 37 (provenance, study by Unger)

1968 Brinkman, PKB pp. 5, 140 n. 843 and 336 no. 8.2.1 (translation, study)

1992 George, Topographical Texts p. 344 (transliteration)

TEXT

1) ^{d}IŠKUR-IB[I]LA-*i-din-nam*
2) LUGAL ⸢KÁ⸣.DINGIR.RA.⸢KI⸣
3) [BÀD(?)] (x) ⸢*im*(?)⸣-[*gur*(?)]-^{d}⸢*en*(?)-*líl*(?)⸣
4) (traces)

1–4) Adad-apla-iddina, king of Babylon, [... *the* (*city*) *wall*] *Im*[*gur*]-*Enlil*.

2

A fragment of a clay cylinder in the Babylon collection of the Eski Şark Eserleri Müzesi in Istanbul has part of an Akkadian inscription of Adad-apla-iddina.

COMMENTARY

The cylinder fragment (B 230a) is in the Babylon collection in the Tablet Archives of the Eski Şark Museum in Istanbul and measures approximately 3.5×7.5 cm. The inscription has not been collated.

As noted by Brinkman and Donbaz, the writing ŠÀ.TÙR before the name of the city Babylon in line 2 is unexpected. One would expect *šar* (LUGAL or MAN). They point out that "ŠÀ.TÙR usually stands for *šasurru*, which has a phonetic similarity to *šarru*; but this seems a rather slim coincidence on which to construct a hypothesis." (*Šasurru* regularly means "womb, uterus, larva.")

Brinkman and Donbaz point out that line 4 may have had either the name of a god or of an individual (with the masculine personal determinative omitted). In view of the fact that line 5 is indented, it is likely either to complete a word or a name begun in the previous line or to have simply *ù*, "and." In the latter case, the king may be described as the "legitimate heir of the gods [... and] Nin[...]" (lines 3–6); however, the traces in the published copy would not appear to support a reading ⸢*ù*⸣. In B.2.8.10, Adad-apla-iddina calls himself "son of the goddess Ninisina" and "son-in-law of the divine (moon) crescent."

BIBLIOGRAPHY

1974 Brinkman and Donbaz, JCS 26 p. 157 (copy, transliteration)

TEXT

1) ⸢^{d}IŠKUR⸣-*ap-lam-i-din-*[*nam*]
2) ŠÀ.TÙR KÁ.DINGIR.RA.[KI]
3) IBILA *ki-i-n*[*u-um*]
4) *ša* ^{d}[...]
5) x [...]
6) ^{d}NIN x [...]
7) ⸢NI(?)⸣ PI(?) x [...]
8) RU BI x [...]
9) AN x [...]
10) DA [...]
11) x x [...]

1–4) Adad-apla-iddina, *king* of Babylon, legitimate heir of/who(m) [...]

5–11) (Not sufficiently preserved to allow translation.)

3

A bead in the Iraq Museum has a Sumerian inscription of the king Adad-apla-iddina stating that he had given the object to the god Marduk.

COMMENTARY

The disk-shaped bead (IM 76765) is made of agate and is milky white with brown veins. It measures 3.8 cm in diameter and 1 cm in thickness. The inscribed side is slightly convex and the other side is concave. It is pierced lengthwise and is missing the lower right edge. The piece entered the Iraq Museum in 1971 through confiscation and thus its original provenance is not known. However, since the inscription refers to the god as the "king of Babylon" and appears to connect him with a temple at that city, the bead may have come from Babylon. The inscription was collated from the published photograph, which is not always clear (in particular, line 1 is basically not visible).

NUN×NUN-an-ni-gal (line 1) is an esoteric writing of Marduk (information courtesy of W.G. Lambert). With regard to èš-gú-zi (line 3), an esoteric writing for Esagila (èš-gú-zi being parallel to é-sag-íl), see George, Topographical Texts p. 295.

BIBLIOGRAPHY

1981 Bahija Ismail, Sumer 37 pp. 114–15 (copy, edition)
1985 Bahija Ismail, Land Between Two Rivers pp. 320 and 387–88 no. 151 (photo, edition)

TEXT

1) NUN×NUN-an-ni-gal
2) lugal TIN.TIR.KI
3) [umun(?)] èš-gú-zi-da
4) bàd-gal maḫ-a-ni
5) lugal-a-ni-ir
6) ^{d}IŠKUR-IBILA$_{x}$(DUMU.DIŠ)-*i-din-nam*
7) lugal KÁ.DINGIR.R[A.KI]
8) nám-tí-lá-ni-šè ⸢ì(?)⸣-[na-ba(?)]

1–8) To Marduk, lord of Babylon, [*lord*] of Esagila, his august helper, (5) his lord: Adad-apla-iddina, king of Babylon, [*presented*] (this object) for the sake of his life.

4

A stamped brick inscription of Adad-apla-iddina written in the Sumerian language and dealing with Emeteursaga, the temple of the god Zababa at Kish, is known from several exemplars.

CATALOGUE

Ex.	Museum number	Excavation number	Registration number	Dimensions (cm)	Lines preserved	cpn
1	BM 90286	—	1821-1-20,13	35.5×33×5	1–9	n
2	Ash 1924.634	HMR 342	—	10×8.5×6	7–9	c
3	Ash 1930.39	—	—	37×33×6	1–9	c
4	FMNH 156011	—	—	—	—	n

COMMENTARY

Ex. 1 was found by R. Ker Porter at al-Uḥaimir (Kish) in 1818 and presented to the British Museum in 1821. According the C.B.F. Walker, the inscription is now "completely illegible" (CBI p. 63). The copy published by Porter was made by C. Bellino from fifteen exemplars with the same inscription found at the site. Exs. 2–4 were found by the Oxford-Field Museum expedition to Kish; ex. 3 is currently on display in the Ashmolean Museum. According to Walker, exs. 1–3 are stamped on the face with a stamp measuring 16/15.6×8.5 cm. The master line follows ex. 3. There are no known variants and no score is presented in the microfiche.

BIBLIOGRAPHY

1822 Porter, Travels 2 p. 394 and pl. 77a (provenance, copy in type)
1861 1 R pl. 5 no. 22 (ex. 1, copy in type)
1872 G. Smith, TSBA 1 p. 72 no. 52 (ex. 1, translation)
1875 Ménant, Babylone p. 125 (ex. 1, translation)
1875 G. Smith, RP 5 p. 86 no. 50 (ex. 1, translation)
1886 Bezold, Literatur p. 123 §68.2 (ex. 1, study)
1922 BM Guide p. 69 no. 206 (ex. 1, study)
1924 Langdon, Kish 1 pp. 16–17 and 65 (ex. 1, edition)
1968 Brinkman, PKB pp. 5, 140 and 336 no. 8.2.3 (exs. 1, 4, study)
1974 Walker, Iraq 36 p. 27 no. 8 (ex. 1, study)
1981 Walker, CBI no. 72 (exs. 1–3, transliteration [Ash. 1924.634, instead of Ash. 1930.39, said to be complete])

TEXT

1) ^{d}IŠKUR-IBILA-
2) *i-din-nam*
3) lugal KÁ.DINGIR.RA.KI-ma
4) é-me-te-ur-sag-gá
5) a-PI-in-zálag-ga
6) ^{d}za-ba$_4$-ba$_4$
7) Ì KAL RA
8) DÙ TI RA
9) UD MA A NI ŠÈ

1–9) Adad-apla-iddina, king of Babylon, *made* Emeteursaga ("House Worthy of the Hero") *shine*. The god Zababa ...

5

A bilingual inscription of Adad-apla-iddina records the presentation of a belt to the statue of the god Nabû at Borsippa. The inscription is known from two Neo-Assyrian copies on clay tablets.

CATALOGUE

Ex.	Museum number	Registration number	Dimensions (cm)	Lines preserved	cpn
1	BM 79503	89-10-14,51	10.9×6.2×1.9	Sumerian 1–11; Akkadian 1–17	c
2	—	Sm 397	3.0×2.5×2.0	Sumerian 6–10; Akkadian 5–9	c

COMMENTARY

Ex. 1, a damaged clay tablet, was purchased for the British Museum in 1889 from Selim Homsey and Company. Ex. 2, the lower left-hand corner of a clay tablet, is part of the Kuyunjik collection in that museum and thus likely comes from Nineveh. It was identified by R. Borger as having this inscription. The inscription is written in Neo-Assyrian script on both exemplars.

The inscription of Adad-apla-iddina is written with the Sumerian and Akkadian versions on alternate lines and with a line ruling following each pair of lines. Each pair of lines is given one line number in the edition presented below; the Akkadian line is given after the Sumerian one. On ex. 2, the Akkadian lines are clearly indented. The colophon on ex. 1 is from the time of Esarhaddon, is written in Akkadian, and is separated from the preceding section by a double line ruling.

The scribe of ex. 1 copied the inscription from a damaged copy of the text and wrote *ḫi-pí eš-šú*, "new break," where his model was damaged (lines 5 and 8 of the Sumerian version; 7 and 8 of the Akkadian version). These notations have not been included in the translation. Ex. 2 has an unidentifiable sign (⸢KI(?)⸣) on the left edge and situated a little below the level of the igi of line 10.

Contrary to normal RIM practice, both exemplars are presented in full in the edition below; lines 1–4 and

5 A similar verbal form, a-PI-in-gibil-la, appears in a brick inscription from Isin (B.2.8.7 lines 13–14).
9 Possibly u$_4$-ma-a-ni-šè, "for his victory" (suggestion of W.G. Lambert).

11–17 are found only on ex. 1. Thus, no score for this inscription is presented in the microfiche. The translation is a conflation, using both the Sumerian and the Akkadian versions.

The careers of Urad-Gula (the owner of ex. 1), his father Adad-šuma-uṣur, and some of their relations are discussed in Parpola, LAS 2 pp. XV–XIX. Urad-Gula was deputy chief physician under Sennacherib and exorcist under Esarhaddon; several letters from him to the Assyrian king have been preserved.

BIBLIOGRAPHY

1925 Gadd, StOr 1 pp. 28–33 (ex. 1, copy [by S. Smith], edition)
1931 Langdon, RA 28 p. 136 (ex. 2, copy)
1937 Meissner, MAOG 11/1–2 pp. 46–47 (ex. 1, study)
1941–44 Weidner, AfO 14 p. 314 n. 133a (ex. 1, study)
1953 Falkenstein, MDOG 85 pp. 4–5 (ex. 1, study)
1968 Hunger, Kolophone no. 498 (ex. 1, edition of colophon)
1968 Brinkman, PKB pp. 5, 140, and 336 no. 8.2.2 (ex. 1, study)
1982 Sommerfeld, Aufstieg Marduks p. 186 n. 1 (ex. 1, study)
1983 Parpola, LAS 2 pp. 452–53 no. 14 (ex. 1, edition of colophon)
1991 Borger, Brief Sîn-idinnams pp. 63–66 [27–30] (exs. 1–2, transliteration, study)

TEXT

1) la-bar bùlug-gá ušumgal sag-gi$_4$-a x [x (x) ní-g]ùr-gùr-ru GAL ŠE x [x (x)]
ana suk-kal-li šur-bi-i ú-šum-gal la ma-ḫar [...]
x *mut-le-*⸢*li*⸣*-i* ⸢*e*⸣-[x x (x)] x [(x)]

1) For the supreme vizier, dragon without equal, ... sublime ...

2) nam-⸢áb-ba⸣ ^{d}dumu-du$_6$-kù a-sag šà-AŠ-DU dumu zu[r-zur-ri ^{d}]⸢e$_4$⸣-ru$_6$ ù-tu-ud-⸢da⸣
bi-⸢*en*⸣ *bi-in-du$_6$-kù ap-li gít-ma-li ma-*[*r*]*i* ⸢*kun*⸣*-ni-i i-lit-ti* ^{d}*e$_4$-ru$_6$-u$_8$-a*

2) Offspring of the god Dumu-duku, perfect heir, honoured son, offspring of the goddess Erua,

3) lú(*)-ur$_4$-ra sag-ki ág-gá-bi mu-lu gi aš-te MA GIŠ.ù-luḫ sag-zi-bi
ḫa-mi-im sak-⸢*ke*⸣*-e u te-re-e-ti mu-šar-šid ku-us-se-e ù-luḫ-ḫi ú-ma-ni*

3) The one who has gathered to himself (all) rites and ordinances, who makes secure the throne, the sceptre, and the crown,

4) níg-bal[a(?) x na]m-lugal sa$_4$ <ù>-mu-un bàd-si-ab-ba.KI é-zì-da dúr-ma[r]-ra
⸢*mu*⸣*-k*[*in*(?) *pa-le*(?)]-⸢*e*⸣ *na-bu-u šar-ru-ti be-el bár-sipa.*⸢KI⸣ *a-šib é-*⸢*zi*⸣*-da*

4) *Who esta*[*blishes*] *a reign*, who decrees kingship, the lord of Borsippa who dwells in Ezida,

5) ex. 1 x x BA giskim-ti maḫ-a-ni ù-ma $^{bi\text{-}pí\ eš\text{-}šú}$ en-sá-sá lugal-a-ni-ir
ex. 2 [...]
ex. 1 ⸢*a*⸣-[*l*]*ik i-di-šu tu-kul-ti-šú* GAL*-ti mu-šak-šid ir-nit-ti-šú be-lí-šu*
ex. 2 ⸢*a*(?)*-lik*(?) *i*(?)⸣-[...]

5) His helper, his august protector, who makes him triumph, his lord:

6) ex. 1 [^{m}]^{d}IŠKUR-IBILA*-i-di-nam* lugal KÁ.DINGIR.RA.KI a-gi$_7$$^{e\text{-}gu}$ ní-tuku-bi
ex. 2 ⸢^{m}(*)⸣^{d}IŠKUR-IBIL[A-...]
ex. 1 [MI]N *šar ba-ab-i-lí ru-bu-ú pa-liḫ-šu*
ex. 2 MIN ⸢*šar*⸣ *b*[*a-*...]

6) Adad-apla-iddina, king of Babylon, prince who reveres him,

7) ex. 1 [K]A-sì-s[ì x x (x)] x gú mi-ni-íb-dub-ba šà-ge-túm lal-e-a-ni-ir níg-zi-gál si-si-[(a)]
ex. 2 KA-sa$_6$-sa$_6$-k[e ...]
ex. 1 [*ana*] ⸢*ṣu*⸣-[*mi-ra-t*]*i-šú ṣi-bi-* $^{bi\text{-}pí\ eš\text{-}šú}$ ŠÀ*-šú a-ma-ri še-bé-e lit-tu-t*[*i*]
ex. 2 *ana ṣu-mi-ra-ti-*[...]

7) To (obtain) what he strives for, ... his desire, to experience the fullness of old age,

---

2 The tablet appears to have nam-⸢áb-ba⸣ and *bi-*⸢*en*⸣, not nam-⸢dím⸣ and *bi-*⸢*nit*⸣ (against CAD 2 [B] p. 243); reading confirmed by A.R. George and W.G. Lambert. Dumu-duku is one of the fifty names of Marduk in the Babylonian Epic of Creation. The Sumerian ^{d}dumu-du$_6$-kù may have been read Mār-duku rather than Dumu-duku (see M. Krebernik, RLA 7/5–6 [1989] p. 378); the Akkadian version has Bin-duku (*bi-in-du$_6$-kù*).

3 The translation "crown" is based upon the Sumerian sag-zi; the meaning of the Akkadian *ú-ma-ni* is not clear.

5 Possibly ⸢á(?)-su$_8$(?)⸣-ba in Sumerian version to match Akkadian ⸢*a*⸣-[*l*]*ik i-di-šu*; see Borger, Brief Sîn-idinnams p. 65 [29].

6 For "Adad-apla-iddina" of the Sumerian version, the Akkadian version has "ditto" (MIN).

8)	ex. 1 [á-ta]ḫ ⸢mar⸣-ra KA GAR $^{\text{ḫi-pí eš-šú}}$ DA SAG$^{\text{ú-e}}$ U^{ú} U x [x (x)] ex. 2 á-taḫ mar-r[a ...] ex. 1 *[re-ṣ]u-us-* $^{\text{ḫi-pí eš-šú}}$ *e-peš a-bu-⸢ti*(?)⸣ x [x (x)] ex. 2 *re-ṣu-us-su* [...]	8) ... his aid ... *to intercede* ...
9)	ex. 1 TÚG.ÍB-lá kù(*)-GI ḫuš-a na$_4$ ⸢kal-la⸣ mí-zi-dè-eš ⸢du$_{11}$⸣-[ga] ex. 2 TÚG.ÍB-lá kù-[...] ex. 1 *né-bé-eḫ ḫu-ra-ṣi ru-uš-ši-i šá ina ab-⸢ni⸣ a-qar-t*[*i* x x (x)] ex. 2 *né-bé-eḫ* ⸢*ḫu*⸣-[...]	9) A belt of red gold which is duly adorned with valuable stone(s)
10)	ex. 1 igi gìr-peš-bal-a am ù-na-gub-bu ugu-bi ma-⸢an(?)-gub(?)⸣ ex. 2 ⸢igi⸣ g[ìr(?)-...] ex. 1 *ù ana* IM 4-*ti ri-mu kàd-ru-tu e-liš na-zu-uz-⸢zu⸣* ex. 2 [...]	10) And (decorated with depictions of) rampant bulls standing upon it facing the four directions
11)	me-te íb-lá kéš-da-a-ni mu-un-na-ni-⸢íb⸣-dí[m]-⸢ma⸣ a mu-un-⸢na⸣-ru ⸢*a*⸣*-na si-mat šib-bi-šú ki-iṣ-ṣu-ra-a-ti ú-še-piš-ma iš-⸢ruk⸣*	11) He had made and presented (to the god) to be an ornament for his *braided* belt.
Colophon		
12)	11.ÀM MU.ŠID.BI.IM *šá* UGU *né-bé-ḫi šá* EN *bár-sipa*.⸢KI⸣	12) Eleven are its lines. That which is (written) upon the belt of the lord of Borsippa.
13)	LIBIR.RA.BI.GIM AB.SAR BA.AN.È	13) Written (and) collated according to its original.
14)	*i-na* KA *ṭup-pi* GAZ.MEŠ *šà-ṭir a-me-ru la i-ṭa-pil ḫi-pa-a* ⸢*li*⸣*-šal-lim*	14) Written according to the wording of damaged tablets. Anyone who sees (this) should not damage (it)! (Instead), let him restore the break(s)!
15)	⸢DUB⸣ ^{m}ÌR-^{d}*gu-la* LÚ.MAŠ.MAŠ.ME.EN	15–17) Tablet of Urad-Gula, the exorcist, [so]n of Adad-šuma-uṣur, chief exorcist of Es[ar]haddon, king of Assyria.
16)	[DUM]U ^{md}IŠKUR-MU-*ú-ṣur* ⸢LÚ⸣ *šá-an-gam-ma-*⸢*ḫu*⸣	
17)	*ša* ⸢^{m}⸣[A]N.Š[ÁR]-⸢PAP-AŠ⸣ MAN [K]UR *aš-šur*.KI	

6

A small truncated cone found at Khorsabad has an Akkadian inscription of Adad-apla-iddina recording the restoration of Nēmet-Marduk, the outer wall of Nippur, for the god Enlil.

COMMENTARY

The current location of the object is not known. Winckler states that it is in the Louvre (Untersuchungen p. 28 n. 2), but there is no record of it in that museum. He may have simply assumed that it was there because many of the pieces found at Khorsabad by Place were sent to the Louvre. According to Oppert the piece is 5.5 cm in length. The cone may have been taken to Khorsabad from Nippur after an Assyrian campaign into Babylonia. The edition presented below follows the copy by Oppert for lines 1–6 and the heliograph facsimile for lines 7–10.

It is uncertain if the word for "king" is preserved in line 3, and if it is preserved, whether it is written LUGAL or MAN. Oppert leaves a blank space for the sign in his

9 Restore *kīniš kunnû* (or similar) at the end of the Akkadian line to match the Sumerian mí-zi-dè-eš ⸢du$_{11}$⸣-[ga].
11 PSD 1/1 [A] p. 158 reads mu-un-na-dù íb-dím-ma in the Sumerian line, but collation shows that the sign after NA is NI not DÙ.

printed copy, but transliterates *sar* (which can stand for LUGAL and MAN) underneath the blank space. The line is not shown on the heliograph. The copy by Oppert indicates that only *šul* is found on line 7 and that *ḫi* BÀD NIBRU.KI is on line 8; but the heliograph shows that *šul-ḫi* BÀD is on one line.

BIBLIOGRAPHY

1867–70 Oppert in Place, Ninive et l'Assyrie 2 p. 308 (copy in type, edition) and 3 pl. 78 no. 4 (heliograph facsimile)
1870 Oppert, Dour-Sarkayan p. 28 (copy in type, edition)
1872 G. Smith, TSBA 1 p. 72 no. 52 (translation)
1875 G. Smith, RP 5 p. 86 no. 50 (translation)
1875 Ménant, Babylone p. 125 (translation)
1886 Bezold, Literatur p. 123 §68.1 (study)
1889 Winckler, Untersuchungen p. 28 n. 2 (edition)
1968 Brinkman, PKB pp. 5, 140 n. 846, and 336 no. 8.2.4 (translation, study)
1992 George, Topographical Texts p. 350 (edition)

TEXT

1) ᵈIŠKUR-IBILA-
2) *i-di-na-am*
3) [LUGAL] KÁ.DINGIR.RA.KI
4) *e-pí-iš*
5) *né-met*-ᵈAMAR.UTU
6) BÀD
7) *šul-ḫi* BÀD
8) NIBRU.KI
9) *a-na* ᵈ*en-líl*
10) *be-lí-šu*

1–10) Adad-apla-iddina, [king] of Babylon, builder of (5) Nēmet-Marduk ("Bulwark of the God Marduk"), the outer wall of the (city) wall of Nippur, for the god Enlil, his lord.

7

An inscription written in Sumerian and recording the renovation of the temple Egalmaḫ by the king Adad-apla-iddina for the goddess Ninisina is stamped on several bricks at Isin.

CATALOGUE

Ex	Museum number	Excavation number	Lines preserved	cpn
1	IM 76547	IB 148a	1–10	n
2	—	IB 148b	1–14	n

COMMENTARY

In their first season of work at Isin (1973), German excavators found eight paving bricks with this inscription in the street in their northern area I; the bricks measured 38×34/33×6.5/6 cm. Exs. 1 and 2 are from among these; the inscription stamped on them measures 9×15/15.5 cm. More bricks stamped with this inscription were later found in rooms IV and XIII and court B of the Gula temple. The transliteration is based upon a composite copy of the inscription made by C. Wilcke. Detailed information on the exemplars was also kindly supplied by Wilcke.

Lines 6, 8, 12, and 14 are indented, but separated from the previous line by a line ruling.

BIBLIOGRAPHY

1973 Edzard, Sumer 29 p. 43 no. 1 (study)
1973 Hrouda, Sumer 29 pp. 38–39 (provenance)
1977 Edzard and Wilcke in Hrouda, Isin 1 pp. 89–90 (exs. 1–2, edition)
1981 Hrouda, Isin 2 pp. 13 and 20 (provenance)
1987 Wilcke in Hrouda, Isin 3 p. 120 and pl. 2 fig. 1 (provenance)

TEXT

1) ^{d}nin-EZEN-na
2) gašam(NUN.ME.TAG)
3) dingir-re-e-ne
4) nin-a-ni-ir
5) ^{d}IŠKUR-IBILA-
6) *i-din-nam*
7) lugal ⌈KÁ⌉.DINGIR.RA.
8) KI-ke$_4$
9) dumu x (x) LÁ(?) BI
10) é-gal-máḫ(AL)
11) èš ki-⌈ág⌉-gá-
12) a(*)-ni
13) a-PI-in-
14) gibil-la

1–14) For the goddess Ninisina, wisest of the gods, his lady: (5) Adad-apla-iddina, king of Babylon, son of ..., renovated (10) Egalmaḫ ("Exalted Palace"), her beloved shrine.

8

A poorly preserved tablet from Uruk bears a copy of an inscription of Adad-apla-iddina. The inscription of Adad-apla-iddina is written in Sumerian and the later colophon in Akkadian.

COMMENTARY

The unbaked tablet IM 78551 bears the Uruk excavation number W 23556. It was found during the thirty-second season of excavations at Warka by the German Archaeological Institute (1973–74) in Ob XV 3, R. 38, in debris. The piece measures 8.2×c.5.0×2.5 cm. The inscription has not been collated and is edited from the published copy.

There are line rulings after each of lines 1–11, but, as far as one can tell, none after the lines of the colophon. Lines 2, 4, and 8 are indented. A small, detached fragment of the tablet which cannot be placed has traces of a few signs:

Lacuna
1′) [...] x x x [...]
2′) [...] ⌈NE(?)⌉ [...]
Lacuna

Since there is no line ruling between the two lines, it is likely that this fragment comes from the colophon.

BIBLIOGRAPHY

1979 Cavigneaux, Bagh. Mitt. 10 pp. 123–24 no. 8 (copy, partial transliteration)
1983 Cavigneaux, UVB 31–32 pp. 55–56 (study)

12 a(*): text has MIN.

TEXT

Obverse
1) ⸢^{d}⸣IŠKUR-[I]BILA-
2) *i-din-nam*
3) lugal KÁ.⸢DINGIR⸣.RA.
4) ⸢KI⸣-ma
5) AB-a
6) èš gal-bi
7) PI-i-in-ba
8) sù-ud-da
9) [(...)]
Reverse
10) [... ^{d}]⸢inanna(?)⸣
11) [x (x)] x TA
Colophon
12) *šá* U[GU ...]
13) x [...]
14) AŠ KAL [...]
15) x [...]
16) x [...]
Lacuna

1–11) Adad-apla-iddina, king of Babylon, *presented* ... its great shrine; *for the future* [...] ...

Colophon
12–16) That which is (written) up[on ...] ... [...]
Lacuna

9

Numerous bricks have been found at Larsa stamped with a Sumerian inscription describing the building of the enclosure wall of the Ebabbar temple by the king Adad-apla-iddina for the god Utu (Šamaš).

COMMENTARY

Only one excavation number is known for these bricks (L 7084) and this number actually refers to numerous exemplars left in situ in the pavement of the interior court of the Ebabbar temple (see Arnaud, Syria 48 [1971] p. 291). The only other clearly stated findspot is at the beginning of the corridor northeast of room 8 of the temple; see Arnaud, Syria 53 [1976] p. 49 no. 22 (=Sumer 34 [1978] p. 165 no. 22, where it is said to be northwest, not northeast of the corridor). According to Birot (Syria 45 [1968] p. 246), the brick(s) (or more likely the area of the stamped inscription on them) known by him measured 13.5×8 cm. Complete bricks with inscriptions of Adad-apla-iddina from Larsa are stated to measure 29.0×29.0×5.5 cm (see Huot, Larsa 1985 p. 32). The bricks mentioned by Arnaud in Syria 48 (1971) p. 291 were stamped on their face. None of the exemplars could be collated and the edition presented below follows the copy published by Arnaud in Syria 58 (1981) p. 99 (=Sumer 41 [1985] p. 143 [Arabic section]). Lines 2 and 4 are indented, but found within separate line rulings.

Note the use of the eme-sal form iz-zi for bàd (Akkadian *igāru*) in line 7.

BIBLIOGRAPHY

1968 Birot, Syria 45 pp. 242–43 and 246–47 no. 6 (copy, edition)
1971 Arnaud, Syria 48 p. 291 (study)
1976 Arnaud, Syria 53 pp. 48–49 nos. 7 and 22–23 (study)
1978 Arnaud, Sumer 34 p. 165 nos. 7 and 22–23 (study)
1981 Arnaud, Syria 58 p. 42 no. 1, and pp. 82 and 99 (copy, edition)
1983 Arnaud in Huot, Larsa et ʾOueili 1978–1981 p. 229 no. 1 (study)
1985 [Arnaud], Sumer 41 p. 143 [Arabic section] (copy)
1989 Huot, Larsa 1985 p. 32 (study)

TEXT

1) ^{d}IŠKUR-IBILA-
2) *i-din-nam*
3) lugal KÁ.DINGIR.RA.
4) KI-ma
5) sag-gal
6) ^{d}utu-ke$_4$
7) iz-zi é-a
8) é-babbar-ra
9) dúr šu-íl
10) ba-ni-in-ak

1–10) Adad-apla-iddina, king of Babylon, (5) ... of the god Šamaš, built the (enclosure) wall of the temple Ebabbar ("Shining House"), *the abode of prayer.*

10

A brick inscription from Ur, written in Sumerian and stamped on the brick, records that Adad-apla-iddina renovated Egišnugal for the god AŠimbabbar (a name of the moon-god). An Akkadian version of this text is B.2.8.11.

CATALOGUE

Ex.	Museum number	Excavation number	Registration number	Dimensions (cm)	Lines preserved	cpn
1	BM 116989	U 3130	1924-9-20,252	27×21.5×5	1–11	c
2	IM 1038	U 3130	—	—	—	n

COMMENTARY

Both exs. 1 and 2 bear the same Ur excavation number, U 3130, which is reported to come from the great court of Nanna. Presumably several bricks were found at the same spot (see Woolley, UE 8 p. 69) and were given the same excavation number. Woolley reports that fragments of brick pavement which can be assigned to Adad-apla-iddina were found against the northeast face of the ziqqurat, as well as in the great court of Nanna (Woolley, UE 8 p. 4 and AJ 5 [1925] pp. 7 and 15). It is not noted if the bricks from the ziqqurat façade bore the same inscription as those from the court of Nanna. Gadd states that he used an imperfect exemplar for his edition of this inscription in StOr 1. Since this is not the exemplar in London which is published in UET 1 (our ex. 1), could it be ex. 2, about which we have no detailed information? Ex. 1 is stamped on the face of the brick with a stamp measuring 17.5×9.3 cm. Line 2 is indented, but is separated from line 1 by a line ruling. Since it has not been possible to examine ex. 2 and since no details about it are known, the edition follows ex. 1.

BIBLIOGRAPHY

1925 Gadd, StOr 1 pp. 27–28 (edition)
1928 Gadd, UET 1 no. 166 (ex. 1, photo, copy, edition)
1928–29 Poebel, AfO 5 pp. 103–104 (edition)
1965 Woolley, UE 8 pp. 4, 69, and 103 (provenance; ex. 2, study)
1968 Brinkman, PKB pp. 5, 140–41, and 336–37 no. 8.2.5 (exs. 1–2, study)
1969 Brinkman, Orientalia NS 38 p. 335 (study)
1981 Walker, CBI no. 73 (ex. 1, transliteration)

5 The understanding of sag-gal is not clear. It might stand for sag-kal (Akkadian *ašarēdu*), "foremost," but, as noted by Arnaud, Syria 58 [1981] p. 82, this term is not normally followed by a divine name. If the first sign could be KA (against the published copies), one might have gù-gal, for Akkadian *gugallu*, "canal-inspector," or *gukallu*, "exorcist" (suggestion of W.G. Lambert).

TEXT

1) ^{d}IŠKU[R]-IBILA-
2) *i-din-*⸢*nam*⸣
3) dumu ^{d}nin-EZEN.KI-na
4) lugal KÁ.DINGIR.RA.⸢KI⸣
5) mu$_{10}$-ús-sá
6) ^{d}u$_{4}$-sakar-ra-ke$_{4}$
7) ú-a uri$_{5}$.KI
8) é-⸢giš⸣-nu$_{11}$-gal
9) al-gibil-⸢la⸣
10) ^{d}AŠ-ím-babbar-ra
11) lugal-a-ni-ir

1–11) Adad-apla-iddina, son of the goddess Ninisina, king of Babylon, (5) son-in-law of the divine (moon) crescent, the one who provides for Ur, renovated Egišnugal (10) for the god AŠimbabbar, his lord.

11

An Akkadian version of the previous, Sumerian, text recording Adad-apla-iddina's restoration of the Egišnugal temple for the god AŠimbabbar (divine name only partially preserved) is stamped on one brick from Ur.

COMMENTARY

The brick fragment (CBS 16482) bears the Ur excavation number U 2877 and was found loose at the site during the 1925–26 season of excavations. It measures 32.5×33×7.5 cm. The inscription is stamped on the face of the brick; line 2 is indented, but separated from line 1 by a line ruling. The edition presented here follows the published copy since the inscription appears to have have been better preserved when copied by Gadd than it is now. The inscription is faint and collation shows that in particular less of EZEN (line 3), *nin* (line 7), *un*, and *iš* (line 9) are now preserved than was seen by Gadd (and his copy already shows the EZEN, *un*, and *iš* as damaged).

BIBLIOGRAPHY

1928 Gadd, UET 1 no. 167 (copy, edition)
1968 Brinkman, PKB pp. 5, 140–41, and 337 no. 8.2.6 (study)
1969 Brinkman, Orientalia NS 38 p. 335 (study)
1985 Behrens, JCS 37 p. 239 no. 52 (study)

TEXT

1) ^{d}IŠKUR-IBILA-
2) *i-din-nam*
3) DUMU ^{d}NIN.⸢EZEN⸣.KI.NA
4) LUGAL KÁ.DINGIR.RA.KI
5) *e-mu*
6) ^{d}*nanna-ri*
7) *za-nin*
8) URI$_{5}$.KI
9) *mu-u*[*n*(?)-*di*(?)-*i*]*š*(?)
10) *é-giš-*[*nu*$_{11}$]*-gal*
11) *a-na* ^{d}A[Š.ÍM.BABBAR.RA(?)]
12) *be-lí-*[*šu*]

1–12) Adad-apla-iddina, son of the goddess Ninisina, king of Babylon, (5) son-in-law of the god Nanna, the one who provides for Ur (and) *re*[*nov*]*ated* (10) Egiš[nu]gal for the god A[Šimbabbar, his] lord.

12

A bronze dagger in the St. Louis Art Museum bears an Akkadian inscription stating that it belonged to the king Adad-apla-iddina.

COMMENTARY

The object was donated to the St. Louis Art Museum by J. Ternbach in 1964 and bears the museum accession number 11:64. The piece had once been in the possession of E. Herzfeld and at one point had been loaned by J. Ternbach to the Queens College Art collection in Flushing, New York. The original provenance of the dagger is not known; the piece is similar to daggers reported to come from Luristan. It measures 42.3×4.9 cm. The inscription has been collated from a photograph provided by the St. Louis Art Museum.

BIBLIOGRAPHY

1941 Herzfeld, Iran p. 134 and pl. XXVIII no. 3 (photo, transcription)
1958 Porada in Man in the Ancient World p. 15 no. 45 (study)
1959–60 Nagel, AfO 19 pp. 95–96 no. 8 and p. 99 fig. 7 (drawing, study)
1968 Brinkman, PKB p. 337 no. 8.2.7 (study)
1968 Herzfeld, Persian Empire p. 30 no. 8 (copy, transcription)
1969 Calmeyer, Datierbare Bronzen p. 61 no. 31Q and fig. 61, and p. 164 no. 40 (drawing, transliteration, study)
1971 Moorey, Catalogue Ashmolean p. 32 no. 11 (study)

TEXT

1) *ša* ᵈIŠKUR-IBILA-SUM.NA
2) LUGAL ŠÁR

1–2) (Property) of Adad-apla-iddina, king of the world.

1001

The restoration of Imgur-Enlil, the inner city wall of Babylon, by Adad-apla-iddina (reading of RN not absolutely certain) is recorded on a fragment of a clay cylinder from Babylon. The inscription is written in Sumerian.

COMMENTARY

The fragment 79-B-13 was found at Babylon near the southeastern corner of the inner fortification wall, between the two fortification walls, not far from the Zababa gate. The inscription has been edited from the published copy, with help from the published photographs. The language of the inscription is unusual in several places and the corresponding translation is thus tentative.

The inscription was assigned by Al-Rawi to Adad-apla-iddina for the following reasons: (1) The name of the king often appears in the first line of an inscription and the traces of the last sign in i 1 appear to be those of a NAM sign. The names of only a few rulers of Babylonia, including Adad-apla-iddina, end with this sign. (2) A brick with an inscription of this king mentioning Imgur-Enlil was found in the same area (B.2.8.1). (3) The language of the inscription, a "hypersophisticated classroom Sumerian," is reminiscent of other inscriptions of this period (e.g., B.2.8.5 and B.2.8.8). His assignment is followed here, but must not be taken as certain.

BIBLIOGRAPHY

1981 Al-Rawi, Sumer 37 pp. 116–17 (photo, copy, edition)
1985 Al-Rawi, Sumer 41 pp. 25–26 no. 5 (photo, copy, study)
1992 George, Topographical Texts p. 344 (partial edition)

TEXT

Col. i
1) [*Adad-apla-i-din-na*]*m*(?)
Lacuna (space for 4 or 5 lines)
1′) [...] x
2′) [...] A
3′) [...] x
4′) [...] x
5′) [...] x [...] x
6′) [...] x
7′) [...] x
Lacuna
Col. ii
1) éš-kìri un-šár-ra
2) šu-gá al-dab-bé-da
3) me-en-gá u$_4$-bi-a
4) ^{d}asari igi ús-sa DU
5) su-zi-eš kur-ku-bi
6) mu-un-da$_5$(?)-ús-ús-e
7) bàd *im-gur-*^{d}*en-líl*
8) bàd KÁ.DINGIR.RA.KI-ke$_4$
9) zag-mu-ta sumun-bé-eš diri-ga
10) ši-in-da-ab-zi-zi-da
11) temen-bi libir-ra
12) sá bí-in-du$_{11}$-ga-e-a
13) gaba ki-gal-la(*)
14) uš$_8$-bi al-tag-ga-bi
15) [n]íg-u$_4$-bi-da-gin$_7$
16) [k]i-bi-šè al-gi-gi-da
17) [x] x (x) x ⌜lugal(?)⌝-e
18) [x x x x]-a-gá
19) [x x x] x dím-ma
20) [x x x-u]n-du$_8$-ru(?)-na
21) [x (x) n]am-ba-kúr-ra
22) x (x) alam-mu
23) [m]u-un-da$_5$(?)-gi-na

i 1) [*Adad-apla-iddin*]*a*
Lacuna
i 1′–7′) (Too poorly preserved to allow translation.)
Lacuna

ii 1–3a) I am the one who takes in his (lit. "my") hand the lead rope of all the people.

ii 3b–6) At that time, with regard to the god Asari, *the one who goes at the fore*, I respectfully followed his desires.

ii 7–21) In order to re-erect the wall Imgur-Enlil ("The God Enlil Showed Favour"), the (city) wall of Babylon, which had collapsed at the beginning of the year due to old age, to reach its ancient foundation, to lay its foundation on the breast of the netherworld, and to restore it (ii 15) as it had been in the past, ... *the king* ... may he not *change*.

ii 22–23) ... my statue I put *with it*.

---

ii 3-4 The meaning of these lines is uncertain. Al-Rawi suggests "the august norms of antique times the god Asari let me observe" (taking me-EN-gá to be me-uru$_{16}$-gá), and Cavigneaux (apud Al-Rawi) "I am the one whom (Asari) let follow ..." (taking igi ús-sa DU to be ši-ús-sa-mèn).
ii 4 With regard to Asari (Asarre) as a name for Marduk, see George, Topographical Texts pp. 248–49.
ii 13 la(*): text appears to have UŠ.

Marduk-aḫḫē-erība

B.2.9

According to Babylonian King List A, the ninth ruler of this dynasty reigned for a total of six months (1046 BC). His name is damaged in the king list, but he is generally identified with the Marduk-aḫḫē-erība who left a kudurru composed about this time (Hilprecht, BE 1/2 no. 149). The kudurru states that the king had ordered officials to measure a tract of land in the province of Bīt-Piriʾ-Amurru in northern Babylonia and give the land to Kudurru, a Ḫapiru. No other inscriptions of the king are attested and it is not known if he was related to either his predecessor or his successor. For details of the reign of Marduk-aḫḫē-erība, see Brinkman, PKB pp. 44, 144–46, and 338–39 no. 9.

Marduk-zēr?-[x]

B.2.10

Babylonian King List A is the only source which preserves at least part of the name of the penultimate ruler of the Second Dynasty of Isin. The final element of the name is not preserved and the identification of the middle element (NUMUN?) not certain. The king list states that he reigned for twelve years (1045–1034 BC). It is not known if he was related to his predecessor or his successor and there are no further sources for his reign. For details about this king, see Brinkman, PKB pp. 44–45, 146–47, and 339 no. 10.

Nabû-šumu-libūr

B.2.11

Nabû-šumu-libūr, the last king of the dynasty, ruled for eight years according to Babylonian King List A (1033–1026 BC). Little is known about his reign, although his name appears in a broken passage in the Religious Chronicle (Grayson, Chronicles p. 133 no. 17 i 16).

In addition to a brief royal inscription found on a stone weight (B.2.11.1), only one other text is known which comes from the reign of Nabû-šumu-libūr: an economic document recording the purchase of a plot of land in the king's first regnal year (see Lackenbacher, RA 77 [1983] pp. 143–54; and Brinkman and Walker, RA 79 [1985] pp. 72–74). For details of his reign, see Brinkman, PKB pp. 45, 147–48, and 339–40 no. 11.

1

A duck weight from Nimrud has an Akkadian inscription stating that it weighed thirty minas and belonged to the king Nabû-šumu-libūr.

COMMENTARY

The duck weight (BM 91432, 48-11-4,128) was found at Nimrud in rubble covering the Northwest Palace. This piece and a stone duck weight from the time of Erība-Marduk (B.6.13.1) which was also found at Nimrud had likely been taken to that city by some Assyrian ruler after a victorious campaign or raid into Babylonia. The duck weight is made of fine-grained white marble and weighs 39 pounds 1 ounce 1 dwt. 6 grains. Since the head of the duck is damaged, the object would have weighed originally a little more than it does now. The inscription has been collated.

BIBLIOGRAPHY

1849 Layard, Monuments 1 pl. 95a no. 11 (drawing)
1849 Layard, Nineveh 2 p. 316 (provenance)
1851 Layard, ICC pl. 83 F (copy in type)
1853 Layard, Discoveries pp. 600–601 (study)
1856 Norris, JRAS 16 pp. 218–19 and no. 2 on the plate following p. 222 (copy in type, study)
1866 Brandis, Münz pp. 46–47 (study)
1889 Winckler, Untersuchungen p. 46 (transliteration)
1901 Johns, ADD 2 p. 264 (study)
1907 King, PSBA 29 p. 221 (copy in type, edition)
1907 Weissbach, ZDMG 61 pp. 394–95 and 948 no. 6 (translation, study)
1922 BM Guide p. 213 no. 255 (study)
1955 Poebel, AS 15 p. 23 (transliteration)
1968 Brinkman, PKB pp. 6, 147–48 and 339–40 no. 11.2.1 (transliteration, study)
1975 Barnett, Ivories[2] p. 4 (study)

TEXT

1)	30 MA GI.NA	1) Thirty minas, correct (weight).
2)	*šá* ^{d}AG-MU-*li-bur* LUGAL ŠÁR	2) (Property) of Nabû-šumu-libūr, king of the world.

Unidentified

B.2.0

1001

A tiny fragment of a clay tablet in the Kuyunjik collection of the British Museum (K 18603) has been identified by W.G. Lambert as preserving part of a bilingual royal inscription which may possibly be assigned to either a Kassite ruler or a ruler of the Second Dynasty of Isin (Lambert, Cat. p. 25). The inscription is arbitrarily presented here. The piece measures 3.4×3.2 cm and the inscription is written in Neo-Assyrian script. It was collated by A.K. Grayson.

TEXT

Side 1
Lacuna
1′) [...] x x [...]
2′) [...] x ᵈiškur [...]
3′) [...] AN [...]
4′) [...] x ub-da límmu-ba [...]
5′) [...] SA(?) mu-um u_4-bi [...]
6′) [...] x ḪI IR [...]
7′) [...] x BI AN [...]
8′) [...] x MIR MEŠ M[È ...]
9′) [...] x [....]
Lacuna

Side 2
Lacuna
1′) [...] x (x) [...]
2′) [...] x ᵐᵈ[...]
3′) [...] EN x [...]
4′) [...] x ⸢KI(?)⸣ x [...]
5′) [...] x [...]
Lacuna

Side 1
Lacuna
1′–9′) No translation warrranted.
Lacuna

Side 2
Lacuna
1′–5′) No translation warranted.
Lacuna

1002

According to G. Dossin, three bronze daggers in the Foroughi collection which are said to come from Luristan no longer preserve the text on their obverse (the side which gave the ruler's name) but only the royal titulary on their reverse. He suggests that they may belong to Nebuchadnezzar I and are duplicates of our inscription B.2.4.3, which has the following on the reverse: LUGAL KÁ.DINGIR.RA.KI LUGAL KI.IN.GI URI.KI, "king of Babylon, king of Sumer (and) Akkad" (lines 3–4 of the inscription). As Brinkman notes, however, similar titulary is also found on daggers from the reigns of Ninurta-nādin-šumi (B.2.3.1), Enlil-nādin-apli (B.2.5.1), and Marduk-nādin-aḫḫē (B.2.6.4). See Dossin, IrAnt 2 (1962) p. 152; Brinkman, PKB pp. 10-11; and Calmeyer, Datierbare Bronzen p. 61.

SECOND DYNASTY OF THE SEALAND

B.3

According to Babylonian King List A, the Second Dynasty of the Sealand comprised three kings who reigned for a total of twenty-one years and five months (1025–1005 BC); the Dynastic Chronicle, however, gives them a total of twenty-three years. Both sources state that these kings formed a dynasty of the Sealand (BALA KUR *tam-tim*/A.AB.BA). The second ruler of this dynasty (Ea-mukīn-zēri) is known to have been a usurper, but the third (Kaššû-nādin-aḫḫē) may have been the son of the first (Simbar-Šipak). See Brinkman, PKB pp. 149–50 and RLA 8/1–2 (1993) p. 8; and Grayson, Chronicles p. 143 no. 18 v 8′ and RLA 6/1–2 (1980) p. 92 iii 9′.

Simbar-Šipak

B.3.1

According to King List A, Simbar-Šipak, the next ruler of Babylonia and founder of the Second Sealand Dynasty, reigned for eighteen years (1025–1008 BC), although the Dynastic Chronicle allots him a reign of only seventeen years. (The pronunciation of the Kassite god's name employed as part of the ruler's name is not clear, the final sign ḪU being read either *-ḫu* or *-pak*; on this matter, see most recently Sommerfeld, AfO 32 [1985] p. 17.) Simbar-Šipak was the son of one Erība-Sîn and the Dynastic Chronicle states that Simbar-Šipak was a resident of the Sealand and had been a soldier "of the dynasty of Damiq-ilīšu," which presumably indicates some connection with the First Dynasty of the Sealand since the third king of that dynasty had borne the name Damiq-ilīšu. A second chronicle also states that he had been a soldier — possibly a soldier of the Sealand, although the passage is damaged at this point. If Simbar-Šipak is to be identified with the Babylonian ruler Sibir, whom Ashurnasirpal II states had captured the city of Atlila in the land of Zamua (see RIMA 2 A.0.101.1 ii 84), this would indicate that Simbar-Šipak had ruled, or at least campaigned, as far as the region of Kifri in the northeast. The Dynastic Chronicle states that Simbar-Šipak "was slain by the sword" and buried in the palace. Since his successor was a usurper, Simbar-Šipak may well have been killed during a rebellion against his rule. For details of the reign of Simbar-Šipak, see Brinkman, PKB pp. 45–46, 150–55, and 340 no. 12, and Grayson, Chronicles p. 142 no. 18 v 2′–4′ and p. 181 no. 24 lines 12′–13′.

Two royal inscriptions of this king are known and both are written in Akkadian. One records that Simbar-Šipak had a throne made for the statue of the god Enlil in the Ekurigigal shrine at Nippur (B.3.1.1) and the other is a simple label on a bronze arrow head (B.3.1.2). One kudurru is preserved from this king's reign (King, BBSt no. 27). It was composed at the town of Saḫrītu and records both the private sale of a plot of land and the apprenticing of three brothers in the king's twelfth year. A kudurru from the reign of Nabû-apla-iddina refers to attempts by Simbar-Šipak to restore the cult of the god Šamaš at Sippar after it had been thrown into disorder by Aramean and Sutian invaders (King, BBSt no. 36).

1

Two late copies of an Akkadian inscription of Simbar-Šipak recording the making of a throne for the god Enlil in the Ekurigigal at Nippur are known. According to the inscription, the throne had been made by Nebuchadnezzar I, but had been carried off, along with other property of the god, by Arameans when they and the Sutians had ravaged the land during the reign of Adad-apla-iddina. By some means, the Assyrians (Subartu) had acquired this property from the Arameans and eventually returned it to Duranki (Nippur) via Baltil (Aššur). The construction of this throne is also mentioned in a Babylonian chronicle (Grayson, Chronicles p. 181 no. 24 lines 12′–13′).

CATALOGUE

Ex.	Museum number	Registration number	Dimensions (cm)	Lines preserved	cpn
1	WHM 13.14.1729 (formerly UIOM 2499)	—	7.2×13×3.2	1–33	c
2	BM 82953	83-1-21,116	4.3×5×2.1	1–5, 21–28	c

COMMENTARY

Ex. 1 is a clay tablet which is broken into several pieces. A few tiny fragments, some with traces of one or two signs, are preserved with this exemplar; none can be read or assigned to any particular part of the inscription with any degree of confidence. Lines 1–18 are on the obverse of the tablet and 19–33 on the reverse. Ex. 2, a tablet fragment, was identified as a duplicate of this inscription by W.G. Lambert and its existence was then communicated by him to the author. The colophon on ex. 2 indicates that the text had originally been found upon the throne itself. The master line follows ex. 1, with some help from ex. 2 in lines 25–26.

The script of both exemplars is Babylonian. According to Brinkman, PKB p. 340, the script of ex. 1 indicates that it was copied sometime between the late seventh and early fifth centuries. Goetze suggests that it might come from the early years of the reign of Nebuchadnezzar II (JCS 19 [1965] p. 125). The script of ex. 2 suggests a date around the second quarter of the first millennium.

Ekurigigal was a shrine within the storehouse of the Ekur temple (see George, House Most High p. 117 no. 683).

BIBLIOGRAPHY

1965 Goetze, JCS 19 pp. 121–35 (ex. 1, copy, edition, study)
1966 Hallo, IEJ 16 p. 239 (ex. 1, study)
1968 Brinkman, PKB pp. 5, 152–53, and 340 no. 12.2.1 (ex. 1, study)
1982 Sommerfeld, Aufstieg Marduks pp. 190–92 (partial edition)
1985 Sommerfeld, AfO 32 p. 15 (ex. 1, edition of lines 4–5)
1991 Brinkman, NABU pp. 18–19 no. 21 (ex. 2, copy, transliteration; ex. 1, study)

TEXT

1) *a-na* ^{d}*en-líl* EN *šur-bi-i šá-qí-i* LUGAL *gim-r*[*i*]
2) MAS.SÙ-*ú ṣi-i-ri e-tel* AN-*e u* KI-*tim mu-šim* NAM.MEŠ
3) *kab-ti šit-ra-ḫu šá i-na* ⸢*gim*⸣-*ri* DINGIR.MEŠ *la iš-šá-an-na-nu* EN-*us-su*
4) LUGAL DINGIR.MEŠ EN *si-ḫi-ip* ⸢*šá*⸣-*ma-mi šá a-na ṣi-it* KA-*šú* ^{d}*í-gì-gì kul-lat-su-nu i-nu-qu pal-ḫiš*
5) *ù a-na na-da-nu ur-*⸢*ti*⸣-*šú* ^{d}*a-nun-na-ki kiš-šat-su-nu i-šu-bu a-*⸢*pi*⸣-*šam*
6) EN *é-kur u* NIBRU.KI *a-šib é-kur-igi-gál* EN-*šú*
7) ^{m}*sim-bar-*^{d}*ši-i-pak* LUGAL *mi-šá-ru re-e-šú šaḫ-ṭi*
8) *muš-te-šir al-ka-ka-a-ti* ^{d}*a-nim ù* ^{d}*da-gan mu-šal-li-mu me-si-šú-un*
9) GIŠ.GU.ZA ^{d}*en-líl šá é-kur-igi-gál šá* ^{md}AG-NÍG.DU-ÙRU LUGAL *maḫ-ri i-pu-uš*

1–6) For the god Enlil, supreme lord, exalted, king of the universe, august leader, sovereign of heaven and netherworld, who decides the fates, venerable, splendid, whose rulership cannot be equalled among all the gods, king of the gods, lord of the whole expanse of the heavens, at whose utterance all the Igīgū gods moan in fear (5) and at the giving of whose order(s) all the Anunnakū gods shake like reeds, lord of Ekur and Nippur, who dwells in Ekurigigal, his lord:

7–8) Simbar-Šipak, just king, (his) respectful servant, who administers correctly the rites of the gods Anu and Dagan (and) duly performs their cultic rites,

9–19) (With regard to) the throne of the god Enlil in Ekurigigal which Nebuchadnezzar (I), a previous

10) *i-na* BALA-*e* ^{md}IŠKUR-IBILA-MU LUGAL TIN.TIR.KI LÚ.KÚR *a-ra-mu ù su-tu-ú*
11) *a-a-bi é-kur ù* NIBRU.KI *mu-šal-pít dur-an-ki*
12) *šá* ZIMBIR.KI URU *ṣa-a-ti šu-bat* DI.KUD.GAL.LA DINGIR.MEŠ *ú-šaḫ-bit me-si-šú-un*
13) *iš-lul-ú-ma* KUR *šu-me-ri u ak-ka-di-i ú-šam-qí-tu gi-mir* É.KUR.MEŠ
14) *bu-šá-a* NÍG.GA ^{d}*en-líl šá a-ra-mu it-ba-lu-ma i-ki-*⸢*mu*⸣ *su-bar-ti*
15) *ina qí-bit* ^{d}*en-líl ma-lik* DINGIR.MEŠ *šá-qí-i* E[N] EN.EN
16) ^{d}AMAR.UTU LUGAL *gim-ri šá šu-ud-du-ú ù šu-šu-*⸢*bu*⸣ *ba-šu-ú* KI-*šú*
17) ^{d}*ut-*u_{18}*-lu ḫur-ba-šú a-a-bi* ⸢*sa-*ʾ*-i*⸣*-di ga-re-*⸢*e*⸣
18) *bu-šá-a* NÍG.GA ^{d}*en-líl aš-šur*.KI-*ú i-du-ú-ma ú-še-ri-ib qé-reb bal-til*.[KI]
19) *ul-tu qé-reb bal-til*.KI *a-na dur-an-ki i-tu-ru áš-ru-uš-š*[*ú*(?)]
20) ^{m}*sim-bar-*^{d}*ši-i-pak* GÌR.NÍTA ^{d}*en-líl* ⸢*it-pe-šú*⸣ *na-ram* ^{d}[x]
21) *re-*ʾ *pal-ḫu šá áš-rat* ^{d}*en-líl ši-te-*⸢ʾ⸣*-a mu-du-*[*ú*]
22) *a-na ud-du-uš é-kur ù* NIBRU.KI *ik-kud it-*⸢*ta*⸣*-*ʾ*-id* [x]
23) GIŠ.GU.ZA GIŠ.MES GIŠ *da-ru-ú šá iḫ-zi-šú ṣa-ri-ri-um-ma šu-tu-ru nab-nit-*[*su*]
24) *a-na si-ma-a-ti* ^{d}EN.LÍL-*ú-ti-šú ṣir-ti ú-še-piš-ma iš-*[*kun*]

25) *a-na šat-ti* ^{d}AMAR.UTU EN GAL-*ú* ^{d}*en-líl* DINGIR.MEŠ *š*[*ur*(?)]-*b*[*u*(?)-*ú*(?)]
26) *i-na* GIŠ.GU.ZA *šu-*⸢*a-šú*⸣ *ina a-šá-bi-šú ši-mat* ^{m}*sim-bar* ⸢^{d}⸣*ši i p*[*ak*]
27) LUGAL *mi-šá-ru re-*ʾ *bi-bil lìb-bi-šú ana* MUNUS.SIG$_5$ ⸢*li-iš*⸣*-ša-k*[*ín*(?)]

Colophon on ex. 1
28) *ki-ma* SUMUN-*šú šá-ṭir-ma* IGI.TAB ŠU.II ^{md}AMAR.UTU-LUGAL-⸢*a*⸣*-ni* A-*šú šá* ^{m}*ri-mu-ut-*^{d}AG
29) A ^{m}*lu-*È*-a-na-*ZÁLAG-^{d}*ìr-ra* ŠÀ.BAL.⸢BAL ^{m}⸣^{d}EN.ZU-TI-⸢A.RA⸣.ZU LÚ.⸢GALA⸣
30) ^{d}INANNA UNUG.KI *u* ^{d}*na-na-a* LÚ.KU$_4$.É ^{d}⸢*ka*⸣*-ni-sur-*⸢*ra*⸣ [DUB.SA]R(?) *é-an-na*
31) *ṭup-pi* (erasure) ^{m}*ri-mu-ut-*^{d}AG ŠÀ.BAL.BAL^{md}EN.ZU-TI-A.RA.ZU
32) LÚ.GALA ^{d}INANNA UNUG.KI *u* ^{d}*na-na-a* LÚ.KU$_4$.É ^{d}*ka-ni-sur-ra* (erasure)
33) ITI.GAN.GAN.NA UD 1.KÁM *šá-ṭir*

Colophon on ex. 2 (rev. 8′ of exemplar)
1) [*ša ina muḫḫi* GIŠ.G]U.ZA *šá* NIBRU.KI [(...)]

king, had made — during the reign of Adad-apla-iddina, king of Babylon, hostile Arameans and Sutians, enemies of Ekur and Nippur, who desecrated Duranki, upset in Sippar — the ancient city (and) abode of the great judge of the gods — their cultic rites, plundered the land of Sumer and Akkad, (and) overthrew all the temples. The goods (and) property of the god Enlil which the Arameans had carried off and (which) the Subartu had (subsequently) taken (from them), (15) at the command of the god Enlil — exalted ruler of the gods, lord of lords — the god Marduk — king of the universe, who has the power to make (a region) desolate and to resettle (it) — (and) the god Utulu — terror of (his) enemies, slayer of (his) foes — an Assyrian recognized the goods (and) property of the god Enlil and brought (them) into Baltil (Aššur). It returned from Baltil to *i*[*ts*] place in Duranki.

20–24) Simbar-Šipak, viceroy for the god Enlil, wise, beloved of the god [...], reverent shepherd, who is assiduous toward the sanctuaries of the god Enlil, the knowledgeable one, was exceedingly concerned about the renovation of Ekur and Nippur. He had constructed and set [up] a throne (made) of *mēsu*-wood — the durable wood — whose mountings were made of *ṣāriru*-gold and [whose] form was extra large, (in sum, a throne) suitable for his (Enlil's) august position as supreme god.
25–27) On account of this, when the god Marduk — the great lord, Enlil of the gods, *s*[*up*]*r*[*eme*] (deity) — sits upon this throne, may the fate of Simbar-Šip[ak] — just king, shepherd, (and) his (the god Marduk's) favourite — be *esta*[*blished*] favourably.

Colophon on ex. 1
28–30) Written and collated according to its original. (By) the hand of Marduk-šarrani, son of Rīmūt-Nabû, son of Lūṣi-ana-nūr-Irra, descendant of Sîn-leqe-unnēnī, the lamentation-priest of the goddesses Ištar of Uruk and Nanāia, one privileged to enter the temple of the goddess Kanisurra, [*scribe*] of Eanna.

31–32) Tablet of Rīmūt-Nabû, descendant of Sîn-leqe-unnēnī, the lamentation-priest of the goddesses Ištar of Uruk and Nanāia, one privileged to enter the temple of the goddess Kanisurra.
33) Written in the month Kislīmu, on the first day.

Colophon on ex. 2
1) [That which is (written) upon the thr]one at Nippur [(...)].

17 Relying upon a similar passage in an inscription of Esarhaddon (Messerschmidt and Ungnad, VAS 1 no. 78 rev. 24), Goetze read the end of the line as *múš-ḫar-mi-ṭi ga-re-e*, "who annihilates (his) adversaries," although he noted in his commentary that the shape of the first sign was not exactly what one would expect. Goetze's copy suggests the reading ⸢*sa-*ʾ*-i*⸣*-di ga-re-*⸢*e*⸣, "slayer of (his) foes" (see also Sommerfeld, Aufstieg Marduks p. 191), and collation confirms the accuracy of the copy. Collation of the three relevant signs showed:
27.2 [*bi-bil*] *lìb-bi-ka*, "your [favo]urite," for *bi-bil lìb-bi-šú*, "his favourite."

2

A bronze arrow head has an Akkadian inscription indicating that the piece belonged to Simbar-Šipak. The arrow head was formerly no. 225A in the collection of Mr. Peter Adam (London) and had been purchased in Iran. It is similar to several inscribed arrowheads said to come from Luristan, though none of these was found by controlled excavation. The piece measures 6.5 cm in length. The inscription has been collated from the published photographs.

BIBLIOGRAPHY

1971 Moorey, Catalogue Ashmolean p. 33 no. 1 (study)
1974 Moorey, Adam Collection pp. 51–52 and 196 no. 20 (photo of obverse, study; copy, edition by Sollberger)
1975 Sotheby's (London) auction catalogue November 10 no. 43 (photo, study; copy, edition by Sollberger)
1989 Sass, UF 21 pp. 349–50 no. 1 (edition)
1991 Sotheby's (London) auction catalogue July 8 no. 132 (photo, translation, study)

TEXT

Obverse
1) *šá si-im-bar-ši-pak*
Reverse
2) DUMU [m]*eri-ba-*[d]30

1–2) (Pṛoperty) of Simbar-Šipak, son of Erība-Sîn.

Ea-mukīn-zēri

B.3.2

According to Babylonian King List A, Ea-mukīn-zēri (abbreviated to Ea-mukīn) reigned for only five months (1008 BC), which was not sufficient to credit him with an official regnal year. The Dynastic Chronicle states that he was a usurper, that he reigned for only three months, and that he was buried in the swamp of Bīt-Ḫašmar. He is possibly to be identified with a priest at Eridu by this name who appears in the witness list of a kudurru dated to the twelfth year of Simbar-Šipak (1014 BC); see King, BBSt no. 27 bottom edge 1. No royal inscriptions of the king are attested, nor are any documents dated by his regnal years. For details of the reign of this king, see Brinkman, PKB pp. 46, 155–56, and 341 no. 13; and Grayson, Chronicles p. 143 no. 18 v 5′–6′.

Kaššû-nādin-aḫḫē

B.3.3

Only one short inscription is preserved from the three-year reign of the third and last king of the Second Dynasty of the Sealand, Kaššû-nādin-aḫḫē (1007–1005 BC), a short possession inscription on a bronze arrow head (B.3.3.1). The Dynastic Chronicle states Kaššû-nādin-aḫḫe was the son of ᵐSAP-*pa-a-a* (Grayson, Chronicles p. 143 no. 18 v 7′) and Brinkman has tentatively suggested that this might be a hypocoristic for Simbar-Šipak, the first king of the dynasty (PKB pp. 156–57 n. 944). According to a kudurru from the time of Nabû-apla-iddina (ninth century), regular food offerings to the Ebabbar temple at Sippar had been discontinued during the reign of Kaššû-nādin-aḫḫē because of famine in the land (King, BBSt no. 36 i 24–28). The entry for this king in the Dynastic Chronicle ends with the statement "in the palace." By analogy with an entry for Simbar-Šipak, this may indicate that Kaššû-nādin-aḫḫē had been buried in the palace. For details of the reign of Kaššû-nādin-aḫḫē, see Brinkman, PKB pp. 156–57, 341 no. 14, and 395.

1

A bronze arrow head has a short Akkadian inscription indicating that the object belonged to Kaššû-nādin-aḫḫē.

COMMENTARY

The arrow head was once in the collection of Dr. F. Bach (Aachen), a former German ambassador to Iran. It was sold at auction in Paris in 1973 and its current location is not known. Nothing is known of its original provenance, though it is similar to various inscribed bronze arrow heads that are said to come from Luristan. Additional information on the piece was kindly supplied by P. Calmeyer. The piece is 7.9 cm in length and 1.6 cm in width. The inscription has been collated from the published photographs.

BIBLIOGRAPHY

1968 Brinkman, PKB p. 395 (transliteration, study)

1969 Calmeyer, Datierbare Bronzen pp. 74 and 165 no. 49, and pl. 5 nos. 4 and 5 (photo, transliteration, study)

1971 Moorey, Catalogue Ashmolean p. 33 no. 2 (study)

1973 Ratton, Bronzes antiques no. 58 (photo, study)

1989 Sass, UF 21 p. 350 no. 2 (edition)

TEXT

Obverse
1) *šá* *[d]kaš-šú-ú*-SUM-ŠEŠ.MEŠ
Reverse
2) LUGAL ŠÁR

1–2) (Property) of Kaššû-nādin-aḫḫē, king of the world.

BAZI DYNASTY

B.4

Upon the death of Kaššû-nādin-aḫḫē, a new dynasty came to power in Babylonia and its three kings reigned for a total of twenty years and three months (1004–985 BC). Babylonian King List A states that these kings came from the dynasty of *ba-s*[*a*(?)], while the Dynastic Chronicle states that they came from the dynasty of Bīt-Bazi (or Bīt-Bāzi, É-m*ba-zi*). The location of Bīt-Bazi is not clear, but it may have lain near the juncture of the Diyala and Tigris rivers (see Frayne, Early Dynastic List p. 45; and Nashef, Rép. Géogr. 5 pp. 54–55). The term also referred to a Kassite tribe or clan and thus indicates that the dynasty probably had a Kassite origin. There is no clear family relationship between the three rulers, although it is likely that the second (Ninurta-kudurrī-uṣur I) and third (Širikti-Šuqamuna) were brothers. See Brinkman, PKB pp. 157–60; and Grayson, Chronicles p. 143 no. 18 v 12′ and RLA 6/1–2 (1980) p. 92 iii 13′.

Eulmaš-šākin-šumi

B.4.1

Eulmaš-šākin-šumi was the first of the three kings of the Bazi dynasty. King List A accords him a reign of seventeen years (1004–988 BC); the Dynastic Chronicle, however, allots him a reign of only fourteen years before his apparent burial in the palace at Kār-Marduk (Grayson, Chronicles p. 143 no. 18 v 9′).

A large number of bronze arrow heads (B.4.1.1) and a bronze dagger (B.4.1.2) bear labels mentioning this king. In addition, a kudurru from the time of Nabû-apla-iddina states that Eulmaš-šākin-šumi had restored food offerings to the god Šamaš at Sippar, which had been discontinued during the reign of Kaššû-nādin-aḫḫē, and that he had also given to the god a garden located in the city of Babylon (King, BBSt no. 36 i 24–ii 17). For details of the reign of this king, see Brinkman, PKB pp. 46–47, 160–62, and 341–42 no. 15.

1

A large number of bronze arrow heads have a short Akkadian inscription of Eulmaš-šākin-šumi recording that they were the property of that king.

CATALOGUE

Ex.	Museum number	Dimensions (cm)	Lines preserved	cpn
1	Chappée collection, number unknown	Length: 7	1–2	n
2	Foroughi collection, number unknown	—	1–2	p
3–14	Foroughi collection, numbers unknown	—	—	n
15	formerly Adam collection 225B	Length: 6.4	1–2	p
16	AO 25212	7.2×1.3	1–2	c
17	AO 26245	7.3×1.4	1–2	c

COMMENTARY

The arrow heads are said to come from Luristan, but none were found by controlled excavation; the provenance may simply go back to statements by antiquities dealers. Ex. 15 was purchased by Mr. Peter Adam in Iran. Exs. 16–17 were donated to the Louvre by M. Foroughi and are likely to be identified with two of the exemplars earlier mentioned by Dossin as being in the Foroughi collection in Teheran (exs. 2–14). An arrow head with this inscription was sold at Sotheby's (New York) in 1991 and it is possible that it is to be identified with one of our exemplars. Since it has not been possible to collate most of the exemplars and since none are known to have any variants, no score is provided in the microfiche for this inscription. In every known case, the exemplar divides the inscription between the two sides of the arrow head as indicated below.

BIBLIOGRAPHY

1932 Contenau, RA 29 p. 29 (ex. 1, copy, edition)
1938 Langdon in Pope, Survey 1 pp. 279 and 284 no. 12 (ex. 1, edition)
1962 Dossin, IrAnt 2 p. 160 and pl. XXVI no. 17 (ex. 2, photo; exs. 2–14, edition)
1968 Brinkman, PKB pp. 161 and 342 no. 15.2.1 (exs. 1–14, study)
1968 Herzfeld, Persian Empire p. 30 no. 10 (ex. 1, study)
1969 Calmeyer, Datierbare Bronzen pp. 74 and 165 nos. 50–63 (exs. 1–14, transliteration, study)
1971 Moorey, Catalogue Ashmolean p. 33 nos. 3–4 (exs. 1–14, study)
1974 Moorey, Adam Collection pp. 52 and 196 no. 21 (ex. 15, photo of obverse, study; copy, edition by Sollberger)
1975 Sotheby's (London) auction catalogue November 10 no. 44 (ex. 15, photo, study; copy, edition by Sollberger)
1989 Sass, UF 21 p. 350 no. 3 (exs. 1–15, edition)
1991 Sotheby's (New York) auction catalogue December 12–13 no. 158 (photo, translation, study)

TEXT

Obverse
1) *šá é-ul-maš*-GAR-MU
Reverse
2) LUGAL ŠÁR

1–2) (Property) of Eulmaš-šākin-šumi, king of the world.

2

A bronze dagger has an Akkadian inscription indicating that it was the property of Eulmaš-šākin-šumi. The inscription may be a duplicate of the previous inscription (B.4.1.1).

COMMENTARY

The dagger is in the collection of Dr. G. Ligabue (Venice). Published reports state that it came from Luristan, but this may be based upon the statement of an antiquities dealer or upon the similarity of the piece to other inscribed daggers said to come from that region. The piece measures 51.5 cm in length and the blade 3.5 cm in width. The inscription runs down the rib of the blade, not across or around the blade immediately below the handle as is the usual case. The inscription has been edited from the published photographs. As edited, the inscription is a duplicate of the previous inscription; however, the reading of the second line is not certain. Lambert does not indicate that there is anything after the ruler's name and Fales states only that the traces are not sufficient to postulate the expected restoration.

A dagger with a duplicate inscription may be found in the Foroughi collection; see Calmeyer, Datierbare Bronzen p. 64.

BIBLIOGRAPHY

1968–69 Lambert, AfO 22 pp. 9–10 no. 2 and figs. 2–3 (photo, edition)
1969 Calmeyer, Datierbare Bronzen p. 64 (study)
1971 Moorey, Catalogue Ashmolean p. 32 no. 12 (study)
1989 Fales, Alfabeto p. 245 no. 76 (photo, edition, study)

TEXT

1) *šá é-ul-maš*-GAR-MU
2) ⸢LUGAL(?)⸣ [ŠÁR(?)]

1–2) (Property) of Eulmaš-šākin-šumi, *king* [*of the world*].

Ninurta-kudurrī-uṣur I

B.4.2

Ninurta-kudurrī-uṣur, who succeeded Eulmaš-šākin-šumi as ruler of Babylonia, ruled for three years (987–985 BC) according to King List A; the Dynastic Chronicle, however, gives him a reign of only two years (Grayson, Chronicles p. 143 no. 18 v 10′). Although he is listed as being part of the same dynasty as Eulmaš-šākin-šumi, there is no evidence to indicate whether or not he was related to that ruler.

It is not certain if the labels on two bronze arrow heads presented here (B.4.2.1001) refer to this king or to the similarly named king who ruled for eight months about forty years later (B.6.2). A kudurru from the time of Nabû-mukīn-apli refers to a lawsuit which took place in the second year of the reign of Ninurta-kudurrī-uṣur I (King, BBSt no. 9). For details of the reign of this king, see Brinkman, PKB pp. 47, 162–63, and 342–43 no. 16.

1001

A short Akkadian inscription on two bronze arrow heads from the Foroughi collection records that they belonged to the king Ninurta-kudurrī-uṣur. Following Brinkman in PKB p. 163, the inscription is tentatively assigned to Ninurta-kudurrī-uṣur I, instead of to Ninurta-kudurrī-uṣur II (B.6.2), since the latter only reigned for a few months. Borger (HKL 3 p. 31), however, prefers to assign this inscription to Ninurta-kudurrī-uṣur II.

CATALOGUE

Ex.	Museum number	Lines preserved	cpn
1	Foroughi collection, number unknown	1–2	p
2	Foroughi collection, number unknown	1–2	n

COMMENTARY

The pieces are said to come from Luristan, but no evidence for this — beyond the fact that they are similar to other inscribed arrow heads also said to come from Luristan — is presented in the literature. On this matter, see the introduction to this volume. The exemplar which is mentioned in the exhibition catalogues from Paris, Zurich, and Washington measures 6 cm in length. Since ex. 2 is not reported to have any variants and has not been collated, the transliteration presented below follows ex. 1 and no score for this inscription is found in the microfiche.

BIBLIOGRAPHY

1961 Ghirshman, Sept mille no. 279 (study)
1962 Dossin, IrAnt 2 p. 160 and pl. XXVII no. 18 (ex. 1, photo; exs. 1–2, edition)
1962 Ghirshman, Kunstschätze no. 129 (study)
1964 Porada, 7000 Years of Iranian Art no. 145 (study)
1968 Brinkman, PKB pp. 163 and 342–43 no. 16.2.1 (exs. 1–2, translation, study)
1969 Calmeyer, Datierbare Bronzen pp. 74 and 165 nos. 64–65 (exs. 1–2, transliteration, study)
1971 Moorey, Catalogue Ashmolean p. 33 no. 5 (exs. 1–2, study)
1989 Sass, UF 21 p. 350 no. 4 (exs. 1–2, edition)

TEXT

Obverse
1) *šá* ^{d}MAŠ-NÍG.DU-PAB
Reverse
2) LUGAL ŠÁR

1–2) (Property) of Ninurta-kudurrī-uṣur, king of the world.

Širikti-Šuqamuna

B.4.3

Širikti-Šuqamuna, the last ruler of the Bazi dynasty, reigned for only three months (985 BC). He was probably killed or deposed since his successor is said to have come from a different dynasty. According to the Šamaš-šuma-ukīn Chronicle (Grayson, Chronicles p. 130 no. 15 lines 20–21), Širikti-Šuqamuna was the brother of Nebuchadnezzar (Nabû-kudurrī-uṣur), which is probably an error for Ninurta-kudurrī-uṣur, the second king of the Bazi dynasty. No contemporary inscriptions are attested for the reign of Širikti-Šuqamuna. For details of his reign, see Brinkman, PKB pp. 47, 164, and 343 no. 17.

Unidentified

B.4.0

2001

An Akkadian inscription records the dedication of a field to the goddess Uṣur-amāssu of Uruk by Kaššû-bēl-zēri, a governor of the Sealand. The exact date of the inscription is not known; although a king is mentioned in line 10, his name is not given. However, other individuals with names including the divine name Kaššû are attested only during the years c. 1008–955 BC (see Brinkman, PKB p. 257). Thus, the inscription should date from sometime around this dynasty.

COMMENTARY

The provenance of the tablet (AO 7038) is not known; however, since the inscription was dedicated to a goddess of Uruk (line 11), it may have come from that much-robbed site. The tablet measures 8.3×4.5 cm. The inscription is written in Neo-Babylonian script and has been collated.

With regard to the reading of the end of line 7, see Nashef, Rép. Géogr. 5 p. 308.

BIBLIOGRAPHY

1922 Thureau-Dangin, RA 19 pp. 86–87 (copy, edition)

1956 Borger, Asarh. p. 118, commentary to rev. 3 (line 13, study)

1968 Brinkman, PKB pp. 250, 257, and 297 (study)

TEXT

Obverse

1) 12 ⸢ŠE.NUMUN(?)⸣ 1 ⸢IKU⸣ 3 (BÁN) 1 KÙŠ GAL-*tu*
2) ⸢A.GÀR(?)⸣ x-⸢ŠI(?)⸣-^{d}IŠKUR UNUG.KI
3) ⸢GÚ ÍD⸣ LUGAL NAM A.AB.BA
4) UŠ AN.TA IM.SI.SÁ ÚS.SA.DU ÍD LUGAL
5) UŠ <<AN>> KI.<TA> IM.U_{18}.LU ÚS.SA.DU ⸢*a*⸣-*šìr-tu*
6) SAG.KI AN.TA IM.MAR.⸢TU⸣ ÚS.SA.DU ÍD ^{d}*gu-la*
7) SAG.KI KI.TA IM.KUR.RA ÚS.SA.DU ÍD ^{d}⸢*é*(?)⸣-[*a*(?)]

1–7) (A field of) twelve (*kurru*) at the ratio of three *sūtu* of seed per *iku* (measured by) the large cubit, in *the cultivable area of* ...-Adad, (in the region of) Uruk, on the bank of the royal canal, in the province of the Sea(land): upper length, to the north, next to the royal canal; (5) lower length, to the south, next to the sanctuary; upper width, to the west, next to the canal of the goddess Gula; (and) lower width, to the east, next to the canal of the god *E*[*a*] —

1 Assuming a *kurru* of 300 *qû* and a *sūtu* of 10 *qû*, the field would have measured 120 iku (ca. 97.2 hectares); see M. Powell, RLA 7/7–8 (1990) pp. 480–82 §§II.11 and IIA and p. 498 §IV.6.

8) ^{md}*kaš-šú-ú*-EN-NUMUN DUMU ^{m}ŠEŠ-DÙ LÚ.GAR KUR A.AB.[BA]
Reverse
9) *a-na ur-ru-uk* UD.MEŠ-*šú šá-lam* NUMUN-*šú*
10) *ù šal-meš* DU.MEŠ *ma-ḫar* LUGAL-*šú*
11) *a-na* ^{d}ÙRU-INIM-*sa a-ši-bat* UNUG.KI
12) *be-el-ti-šú i-qí-iš*(*)
Colophon
13) *šá ina* UGU NA$_4$.KIŠIB *šá i-na* NA$_4$ GÚ *šá* ^{d}ÙRU-*a-mat-su*

8–12) Kaššû-bēl-zēri, son of Aḫu-bani, the governor of the Sealand, presented (this land) to the goddess Uṣur-amāssu, who dwells in Uruk, his lady, in order to prolong his days, to ensure the well-being of his offspring, and so that he might live in safety in the presence of his king.

Colophon
13) That which is (written) upon a seal which is on the necklace of the goddess Uṣur-amāssu.

2002

A bronze arrow head in the Foroughi collection has an inscription of one Ninurta-ušallim. Calmeyer has suggested that the inscription may give him the title governor of Babylon, but the inscription is not clear on the published photograph and the writing of the word for governor would be unique. Arrow heads with inscriptions of Babylonian rulers come from the late eleventh and tenth centuries: from the reigns of Simbar-Šipak (B.3.1.2), Kaššû-nādin-aḫḫē (B.3.3.1), Eulmaš-šākin-šumi (B.4.1.1), Ninurta-kudurrī-uṣur I (or less likely Ninurta-kudurrī-uṣur II; B.4.2.1001), Mār-bīti-apla-uṣur (B.5.1.1), and Nabû-mukīn-apli (B.6.1.1). The date of this particular inscription is not known, and it is arbitrarily placed here.

COMMENTARY

The arrow head is said to come from Luristan, but on this matter, see the introduction to this volume. The inscription has been edited from the published photograph, but the exact meaning of the inscription remains unclear.

Instead of reading *ušallim* for SILIM-*im*, one might follow Calmeyer and read *mušallim*. Babylon seems to be mentioned in line 2 and we might expect a word for governor to precede it. The normal writing for governor, however, is LÚ.GAR.UŠ$_4$ and thus the presence of IM instead of LÚ would be unexpected.

BIBLIOGRAPHY

1962 Dossin, IrAnt 2 p. 161 and pl. XXIX no. 24 (photo, edition)
1968 Brinkman, PKB pp. 11 no. 9 and 363 no. m (study)
1969 Calmeyer, Datierbare Bronzen p. 166 no. 77 (transliteration)
1971 Moorey, Catalogue Ashmolean p. 33 no. 9 (study)
1989 Sass, UF 21 p. 351 no. 9 (edition)

TEXT

Obverse
1) ^{d}MAŠ-SILIM(?)-*im* A(?) ⸢É⸣.BAR
Reverse
2) IM GAR(?).UŠ$_4$(?) TIN.⸢TIR.KI⸣

1–2) Ninurta-ušallim, *a šangû*-priest ... Babylon.

8 Or Aḫu-bānī; this was the name of a Kassite tribe (see Brinkman, PKB pp. 249–51 and n. 1597).
12 *iš*(*): text has KA.

2003

A bronze arrow head in the Foroughi collection has an inscription which may belong to a governor. As noted under the previous inscription, arrow heads with inscriptions that can be dated come from the late eleventh and tenth centuries. The date of this particular inscription is not known, and it is arbitrarily placed here. The piece is said to come from Luristan but no evidence for this — beyond the fact that it is similar to other inscribed arrow heads also said to come from Luristan — is provided in the literature. The inscription is edited from the published copy.

BIBLIOGRAPHY

1962 Dossin, IrAnt 2 p. 162 no. 25 (copy, edition)
1968 Brinkman, PKB pp. 11 no. 8, 304, and 363 no. n (study)
1969 Calmeyer, Datierbare Bronzen p. 166 no. 78 (transliteration)
1971 Moorey, Catalogue Ashmolean p. 33 no. 9 (study)
1989 Sass, UF 21 p. 351 no. 12 (edition)

TEXT

Obverse
1) x x (x)-ŠI-^{d}MES
Reverse
2) EN(?).NAM

1–2) ...-Marduk, *the provincial governor.*

ELAMITE DYNASTY

B.5

King List A gives the name of only one ruler (Mār-bīti-apla-uṣur, name mostly restored), for the next dynasty and does not assign him to any particular place or group. The Dynastic Chronicle, however, states that he was a descendant of Elam and may refer to the new dynasty as "dynasty of [*Ela*]*m*" (BALA [ELAM.M]A.KI). Thus this dynasty is generally referred to as the "Elamite Dynasty." See Grayson, Chronicles p. 143 no. 18 v 13′–15′ and RLA 6/1–2 (1980) p. 92 iii 14′.

Mār-bīti-apla-uṣur

B.5.1

Mār-bīti-apla-uṣur, who succeeded Širikti-Šuqamuna on the throne of Babylon, reigned for six years (984–979 BC). Although his name is an Akkadian one, meaning "O God Mār-Bīti Protect the Heir," a chronicle states that he was a "*remote* descendant of Elam" (ŠÀ.BAL.BAL ⌈LIBIR(?) ELAM⌉.MA.KI), which might indicate that one of his ancestors was an Elamite, possibly even an Elamite king. Upon his death, he was buried in the palace. Several bronze arrow heads bear inscriptions mentioning him (B.5.1.1). For details of his reign, see Brinkman, PKB pp. 47, 165–66, and 343–44 no. 18, and Grayson, Chronicles p. 143 no. 18 v 13′–15′.

1

An Akkadian inscription is found on several bronze arrow heads stating that they were the property of Mār-bīti-apla-uṣur.

CATALOGUE

Ex.	Museum number	Dimensions (cm)	Lines preserved	cpn
1	Foroughi collection, number unknown	—	1–2	p
2	Foroughi collection, number unknown	—	1–2	p
3	Foroughi collection, number unknown	—	—	n
4	Foroughi collection, number unknown	—	—	n
5	AO 25213	7.8×1.3	1–2	c
6	AO 25276	5.1×1.4	1–2	c
7	AO 26247	7.2×1.4	1–2	c

COMMENTARY

The arrow heads are said to come from Luristan, but on this matter, see the introduction to this volume. Exs. 5–7 were donated to the Louvre by M. Foroughi and some of them may also be listed among exs. 1–4, which were part of the Foroughi collection in Teheran; however, neither ex. 5 nor ex. 7 can be either ex. 1 or ex. 2. Those exemplars which were collated all have the complete inscription and divide it in the same manner. As noted by Brinkman (PKB p. 165 n. 1002), the photograph of the obverse of ex. 2 is not clear and would not preclude a reading A for DUMU in line 1. If that exemplar does have A, it would be the only variant known for the inscription. Thus, no score is presented for this inscription in the microfiche.

BIBLIOGRAPHY

1962 Dossin, IrAnt 2 p. 160 no. 19 (exs. 1–4, edition) and pl. XXVII no. 19a (ex. 1, photo) and no. 19b (ex. 2, photo)
1968 Brinkman, PKB pp. 165 and 344 no. 18.2.1 (exs. 1–4, study)
1969 Calmeyer, Datierbare Bronzen pp. 74 and 165 nos. 66–69 (exs. 1–4, transliteration, study)
1971 Moorey, Catalogue Ashmolean p. 33 no. 6 (exs. 1–4, study)
1989 Sass, UF 21 p. 350 no. 5 (exs. 1–4, edition)

TEXT

Obverse
1) *šá* ᵈDUMU-É-A-PAB
Reverse
2) LUGAL ŠÁR

1–2) (Property) of Mār-bīti-apla-uṣur, king of the world.

UNCERTAIN DYNASTIES

B.6

Following the death of Mār-bīti-apla-uṣur in 979 BC, a period began during which there were numerous, frequently brief, reigns by individuals whose dynastic and/or family affiliation is often unknown or uncertain. This period lasted for about three and a half centuries, until Nabopolassar gained control over all of Babylonia, founded a new dynasty, and created the Neo-Babylonian empire in the last quarter of the seventh century. During a large portion of this time, Babylonia did not exist as an independent kingdom. Several Assyrian kings, beginning with Tiglath-pileser III in 728 (B.6.19), ruled Babylonia directly, sometimes taking the title "king of Babylon" and sometimes not, sometimes being listed in the canonical lists of rulers of Babylonia and sometimes not. In addition, a number of other rulers were actually vassals of Assyria, some being Babylonians appointed by the Assyrian king and others being relatives of the Assyrian king.

The longest continuous sequence of rulers coming from one family occurred in the ninth century, when Nabû-šuma-ukīn I was succeeded, in turn, by his son Nabû-apla-iddina, grandson Marduk-zākir-šumi I, and great-grandson Marduk-balāssu-iqbi (B.6.5–8), for a total of approximately eighty years. Although no Arameans are known to have been recognized as rulers of Babylonia, at least six Chaldeans were: Erība-Marduk and Marduk-apla-iddina II of the tribe of Bīt Iakīn (B.6.13 and B.6.21 [and B.6.25]), Nabû-šuma-iškun and Mušēzib-Marduk of the tribe of Bīt-Dakkūri (B.6.14 and B.6.29), Nabû-mukīn-zēri of the tribe of Bīt-Amukāni (B.6.18), and Marduk-apla-uṣur, whose tribal affiliation is not known (B.6.12).

Babylonian King List A provides the dynastic affiliation for a number of the rulers during this time but the information is often unclear or difficult to reconcile with other known information. At least seven rulers — Erība-Marduk, Nabû-šuma-iškun, Nabû-nāṣir, Nabû-nādin-zēri, Nabû-šuma-ukīn II, Bēl-ibni, and Mušēzib-Marduk (B.6.13–17, B.6.26, and B.6.29), and possibly several rulers immediately preceding Erība-Marduk — are stated to belong to the E dynasty (BALA E), Nabû-mukīn-zēri (B.6.18) to the dynasty of *šá-pi-i*, Shalmaneser V (B.6.20) to the dynasty of *bal-til*, Marduk-apla-iddina II (B.6.21) to the dynasty of KUR *tam* (presumably KUR *tam-<tim>*, "Sealand"), and Sennacherib and his son Aššur-nādin-šumi (B.6.23 and B.6.27) to a dynasty of *ḫa-bi-gal*. The dynasties of *šá-pi-i* and *bal-til* probably refer to the cities of Šapīia and Aššur respectively and Brinkman has argued cogently that E, in BALA E, probably refers to the city of Babylon. In addition, *ḫa-bi-gal* probably refers to Ḫanigalbat, an area in northern Mesopotamia controlled by Assyria. One wonders, however, what the difference in the use of the two terms *bal-til* and *ḫa-bi-gal* was meant to imply, since both were applied to Assyrian kings, and why the other Assyrian kings mentioned in this king list — Tiglath-pileser III, Sargon II, and Esarhaddon (B.6.19, B.6.22, and B.6.31) — were not also described as being members of one or the other dynasties. Tiglath-pileser III was, after all, the father of Shalmaneser V, who was assigned to the dynasty of Baltil, while Sargon and Esarhaddon were, respectively, the father and son of

Sennacherib, who was assigned to the dynasty of Ḫanigalbat (Ḫabigal). It is worth noting that when mentioning the first regnal period of Marduk-apla-iddina II (B.6.21), King List A describes him as being from a Sealand dynasty, but when mentioning his second regnal period (B.6.25), it describes him as ÉRIN *ḫa-bi*, which presumably means "a soldier of Ḫani(galbat)." In addition, while King List A states that Erība-Marduk (B.6.13) was a member of the E dynasty, the Dynastic Chronicle states that he was the sole member of a dynasty of the Sealand. In sum, the information on the dynastic affiliation of the rulers of Babylonia during this time is frequently not clear and, following currently common practice, this period will be treated as "one dynasty" here. See Brinkman, PKB pp. 52–59 and 166–71; and Grayson, Chronicles p. 144 no. 18 vi 1′–13′ and RLA 6/1–2 (1980) pp. 92–93 iii 15′–iv 23′.

Nabû-mukīn-apli

B.6.1

Nabû-mukīn-apli, who succeeded Mār-bīti-apla-uṣur as ruler of Babylonia, founded a new dynasty and reigned for thirty-six years (978–943 BC). Although the king enjoyed a long reign, conditions in the land were not peaceful. Some years the New Year's festival was not celebrated and the Religious Chronicle explicitly states that it was actions by hostile Arameans that had made it impossible to celebrate it on a number of these occasions. A kudurru composed at the town of Ālu-ša-mamīti (King, BBSt no. 9) records the settlement of a dispute over the ownership of an estate and the payment of back taxes which were owed on the land up until the twenty-fifth year of the king's reign (954 BC); it is possible that it was the unsettled conditions in the land which had made the collection of the taxes difficult. After the death of Nabû-mukīn-apli, the throne passed to his son Ninurta-kudurrī-uṣur II (B.6.2) and soon thereafter to another of his sons, Mār-bīti-aḫḫē-iddina (B.6.3).

The only royal inscription of this king is found on several bronze arrow heads and a bronze sword (B.6.1.1). Labels mentioning two of his sons appear on bronze situlae and arrow heads (B.6.1.2001–2003) and inscriptions of two officials who likely date to this time are found on a bronze arrow head and an iron dagger (B.6.1.2004–2005). In addition to the kudurru mentioned above (King, BBSt no. 9), a tiny kudurru fragment (see J.A. and M.E. Brinkman, ZA 62 [1972] pp. 91–98) and possibly an unpublished economic text in Geneva (see Sollberger, JCS 5 [1951] p. 19 no. 2.9) date to the king's reign. For details of the reign of Nabû-mukīn-apli, see Brinkman, PKB pp. 48, 171–74, and 344–45 no. 19. For the possibility that Nabû-mukīn-apli (or more accurately his son Ninurta-kudurrī-uṣur II) was related to the second king of the Bazi dynasty, Ninurta-kudurrī-uṣur I (B.4.2), see ibid. p. 175.

1

A number of bronze arrow heads and a bronze sword bear a short Akkadian inscription stating that they were the property of Nabû-mukīn-apli.

CATALOGUE

Ex.	Museum number	Dimensions (cm)	Lines preserved	cpn
1	Foroughi collection, number unknown	—	1–2	p
2	Foroughi collection, number unknown	—	1–2	p
3	Foroughi collection, number unknown	—	1–2	p
4	Foroughi collection, number unknown	—	—	n
5	Ligabue collection, number unknown	6.7×1.4	1–2	(p)
6	Ligabue collection, number unknown	6.55×4.95×0.3	1–2	p
7	Ligabue collection, number unknown	8.3×1.6×0.5	1–2	p
8	AO 25214	6×1.5	1–2	c
9	AO 26246	6.7×1.4	1–2	c
10	AO 26249	7.1×1.6	1–2	c
11	AO 26250	7.6×1.7	1–2	c
12	AO 26248	5.6×1.3	1–2	c
13	—	51 cm long	1–2	n

COMMENTARY

Exs. 1–12 are bronze arrow heads and are said to come from Luristan, though none were found by controlled excavation. Ex. 13 is a bronze sword. The obverse of ex. 5 has been collated from the published photograph; the reverse is edited from the published copy. Exs. 9–12 were presented to the Louvre by M. Foroughi; thus it is possible that some of them are to be identified with exs. 1–4. It is not clear that ex. 12 has this inscription since all that is preserved of the ruler's name is ᵈ⸢AG(?)⸣-[...]. Ex. 13 was seen by W.G. Lambert on the antiquities market in 1988; a transliteration of the inscription was kindly provided by him. Calmeyer, Reliefbronzen p. 149 n. 162 refers to an unpublished arrow head with an inscription of Nabû-mukīn-apli in the Adam collection. No piece with an inscription of this king was subsequently published in Moorey's catalogue of that collection (Moorey, Adam Collection).

BIBLIOGRAPHY

1962 Dossin, IrAnt 2 p. 161 and pl. XXVIII no. 21 (exs. 1–3, photo; exs. 1–4, edition)
1968 Brinkman, PKB p. 173 and p. 344 no. 19.2.1 (exs. 1–4, study)
1968–69 Lambert, AfO 22 p. 9 no. 3 and fig. 4 (ex. 5, copy, edition)
1969 Calmeyer, Datierbare Bronzen pp. 74 and 165 nos. 70–73 (exs. 1–4, transliteration, study)
1971 Moorey, Catalogue Ashmolean p. 33 nos. 7–8 (exs. 1–5, study)
1972 J.A. Brinkman and M.E. Brinkman, ZA 62 p. 93 n. 11 (exs. 2, 5, study)
1980 Salvini, SMEA 22 pp. 315–17 and pls. I–II (exs. 6–7, photo, copy, transliteration; ex. 6, translation)
1989 Fales, Alfabeto p. 246 nos. 77 [93 of bibliography] (ex. 7), 78 [92] (ex. 5), and 79 [94] (ex. 6) (exs. 5–7, photo, composite edition, study)
1989 Sass, UF 21 p. 351 no. 6 (exs. 1–5, edition)

TEXT

Obverse
1) *šá* ᵈPA-GIN-A
Reverse
2) LUGAL ŠÁR

1–2) (Property) of Nabû-mukīn-apli, king of the world.

2001

A bronze situla has an Akkadian inscription stating that the object belonged to the prince Ninurta-kudurrī-uṣur. This individual is most probably the son of Nabû-mukīn-apli, who later succeeded to the throne (B.6.2).

COMMENTARY

Only two fragments of the situla are preserved. Their maximum height is 6.5 cm and they do not join. The original provenance of the piece is not known, but it has been compared to bronze situlae said to have come from Luristan. They are in a private collection and the inscription has been collated from the published photographs.

Following previous scholars, it is tentatively assumed here that the text refers to the son and eventual successor of Nabû-mukīn-apli (Ninurta-kudurrī-uṣur II) since there is at present no evidence to indicate that Ninurtu-kudurrī-uṣur I (B.4:2) was the son of his predecessor (although this is not impossible). The assignment to the son of Nabû-mukīn-apli is supported by the existence of bronze arrow heads with an inscription of a prince by the name of Rīmūt-ilī (B.6.1.2003) and a bronze situla with an inscription of a Rīmūt-ilī, who was apparently described as the "chief administrator of the temples" (B.6.1.2002), since a kudurru dating to the reign of Nabû-mukīn-apli mentions in successive lines a prince by the name of Ninurta-kudurrī-uṣur and a prince by the name of Rīmūt-ilī, who held the office of "chief administrator of the temples" (King, BBSt no. 9 iv A 30–31). The assignment of this inscription, however, remains unproven. It is not necessary to assume that the owner of the situla actually later succeeded to the throne; it could have been the property of an otherwise unattested son of some other monarch.

BIBLIOGRAPHY

1966 Amandry, Antike Kunst 9/2 p. 59 no. 3 and fig. 3, pp. 66–67, and pl. 13 nos. 3a–b (photo, copy, translation, study)
1966 Calmeyer, BJVF 6 pp. 69–70 (transliteration, study)
1968 Brinkman, PKB pp. 163 and 344–45 no. 19.2.4 (study)
1969 Calmeyer, Datierbare Bronzen p. 166 no. 79 (transliteration)
1971 Moorey, Catalogue Ashmolean p. 33 no. 2 (study)
1973 Calmeyer, Reliefbronzen pp. 24–25 and 148 and pl. 6 fig. 2 no. A 12 (photo, copy, transliteration, study)

TEXT

1) *šá* [md]MAŠ-NÍG.DU-PAB A LUGAL

1) (Property) of Ninurta-kudurrī-uṣur, son of the king.

2002

A bronze situla has an Akkadian inscription stating that it belonged to Rīmūt-ilī, the chief administrator of the temples (reading of title not absolutely certain). Since a son of Nabû-mukīn-ilī by that name bore that title (King, BBSt no. 9 iv A 31) and since some bronze arrow heads bear labels referring to "Rīmūt-ilī, son of the king" (B.6.1.2003), this inscription is tentatively assigned to the son of Nabû-mukīn-apli.

COMMENTARY

The situla was once in the collection of Mrs. William H. Moore; its current location is not known. The original provenance of the piece is not known, although it is said to come from Luristan. The piece measured 15.3 cm in height. Only a few signs are visible on the published photo and the transliteration presented below is based upon the published copy. The name of the individual was initially read Rīḫu-ša-ilī, but is now thought to be read Rīmūt-ilī (see Brinkman, PKB p. 174 n. 1067).

BIBLIOGRAPHY

1932 Pope, ILN October 22 p. 614 fig. 5 (photo)
1938 Contenau, Revue des arts asiatiques 12 p. 36 and fig. 9 (drawing of object)
1938 Dussaud in Pope, Survey 1 p. 272 (study of object)
1938 Langdon in Pope, Survey 1 pp. 280 and 284 no. 13, and 4 pl. 70A (photo, copy in type, edition)
1947 Contenau, Manuel 4 p. 2174 fig. 1210 right (drawing of object)
1965 Calmeyer, BJVF 5 pp. 42–43 no. N1 (drawing of object, study)
1966 Amandry, Antike Kunst 9/2 p. 66 (study)
1966 Calmeyer, BJVF 6 p. 69 no. N1 (study)
1967 Borger, HKL 1 p. 415 (study)
1968 Brinkman, PKB pp. 174 and 345 no. 19.2.5 (study)
1968 Herzfeld, Persian Empire pp. 27 and 31 no. 16 (study)
1969 Calmeyer, Datierbare Bronzen p. 166 no. 80 (transliteration)
1971 Moorey, Catalogue Ashmolean p. 33 no. 1 (study)
1973 Calmeyer, Reliefbronzen pp. 80–81 and 147 no. N 1 (drawing of object, study)

TEXT

1) *šá* ^{m}*ri-mut*-DINGIR.MEŠ ⌜ŠÀ(?)⌝.TAM É.⌜KUR(?)⌝.MEŠ x x [(...)]

1) (Property) of Rīmūt-ilī, *chief administrator of the temples* ...

2003

Three bronze arrow heads bear a possession inscription of the prince Rīmūt-ilī. Since a son of Nabû-mukīn-apli bore that name (King, BBSt no. 9 iv A 31), the inscription is assigned to him. For a bronze situla which may also have an inscription of this individual, see B.6.1.2002.

CATALOGUE

Ex.	Museum number	Dimensions (cm)	Lines preserved	cpn
1	A. Mazda collection (Teheran), number unknown	—	1–2	n
2	AO 25552	6.9×1.9×.6	1–2	n
3	Private collection	—	1–2	n

COMMENTARY

No information on the provenances of the pieces is available, though they have been compared to other inscribed arrow heads said to come from Luristan. Information on ex. 2 was kindly supplied by B. André-Salvini from museum records. Ex. 3 is inscribed in mirror writing and R. Borger has suggested that it may be a modern forgery (HKL 2 p. 210). The forms of two of the signs on that exemplar (*mut* in line 1 and LUGAL in line 2) are abnormal. The master line follows ex. 1.

BIBLIOGRAPHY

1969 Calmeyer, Datierbare Bronzen p. 75 fig. 75 and p. 166 no. 81 (ex. 1, copy, transliteration)
1971 Nougayrol, RA 65 p. 179 (ex. 3, copy, edition)
1989 Sass, UF 21 p. 351 no. 7 (ex. 1, edition)

TEXT

Obverse
1) ^{m}*ri-mut*-DINGIR.MEŠ
Reverse
2) A LUGAL

1–2) Rīmūt-ilī, son of the king.

2004

An Akkadian inscription on a bronze arrow head states that the object was the property of Mār-bīti-šuma-ibni, the *sakrumaš*-official. The only other occurrence of an individual with this name is on a kudurru from the reign of Nabû-mukīn-apli (King, BBSt no. 9 i 19, 25, passim). Since similar arrow heads were made during the time of that king, the inscription is tentatively dated to this king's reign.

COMMENTARY

The arrow head is in the Foroughi collection. It is said to have come from Luristan, but no real evidence as to its original provenance is available. The inscription was collated from the published photographs. With regard to the position of *sakrumaš* (a military title), see Brinkman, PKB pp. 305–307.

BIBLIOGRAPHY

1962 Dossin, IrAnt 2 p. 161 and pl. XXVIII no. 20 (photo, edition)
1968 Brinkman, PKB pp. 11–12 no. 7 and p. 345 no. 19.2.6 (study)
1969 Calmeyer, Datierbare Bronzen p. 165 no. 74 (transliteration)
1989 Sass, UF 21 p. 351 no. 8 (edition)

TEXT

Obverse
1) *šá* ^{d}DUMU-É-MU-DÙ
Reverse
2) *sak-ru-maš*

1–2) (Property) of Mār-bīti-šuma-ibni, the *sakrumaš*-official.

2005

An iron dagger has an Akkadian inscription engraved upon it stating that it belonged to Ninurta-nādin-šumi, son of Šerik, the *sakrumaš*-official. As noted by Calmeyer, an individual with this name and title appears in a kudurru from the time of Nabû-mukīn-apli (King, BBSt no. 9 iv A 35–36). Thus this inscription is tentatively assigned to the reign of Nabû-mukīn-apli.

COMMENTARY

The iron dagger-blade was once in the collection of Dr. F. Bach (Aachen) but was sold at auction in Paris in 1973. The current location of the object is not known, but additional information on the dagger was kindly furnished by P. Calmeyer. The original provenance of the piece is not known, but Calmeyer mentions it in his study of datable bronzes from Luristan and Kermanshah. The piece is 24.05 cm in length. The inscription was not chiselled onto the piece but was already impressed into the wax mould from which the dagger-blade was made. As a result the inscription is unclear in spots. The inscription has not been collated and the edition presented here follows that provided by Calmeyer.

BIBLIOGRAPHY

1969 Calmeyer, Datierbare Bronzen p. 166 no. 82 (transliteration)
1973 Ratton, Bronzes antiques no. 53 (study)

TEXT

1) *šá* ^{md}MAŠ-SUM-M[U]
2) DUMU ^{m}*še*-⸢*rik* LÚ(?) *sak*⸣-*ru-maš*

1–2) (Property) of Ninurta-nādin-šumi, son of Šerik, the *sakrumaš*-official.

Ninurta-kudurrī-uṣur II

B.6.2

Nabû-mukīn-apli was succeeded by his son Ninurta-kudurrī-uṣur II, who reigned for a total of eight months and twelve days (943 BC). No inscriptions are clearly attested from his short reign; however, two Luristan bronze arrow heads with possession inscriptions of a king by the name of Ninurta-kudurrī-uṣur which have been tentatively attributed to Ninurta-kudurrī-uṣur I (B.4.2.1001) could conceivably belong to the second king by that name. A bronze situla mentioning a prince by this name probably refers to him and dates to the reign of his father (see B.6.1.2001). He was also mentioned in first place in the witness list of a kudurru from the time of Nabû-mukīn-apli, preceding two of his brothers (King, BBSt no. 9 iv A 30). For details of the reign of this king, see Brinkman, PKB pp. 48, 175, and 345 no. 20.

Mār-bīti-aḫḫē-iddina

B.6.3

Following the brief reign of Ninurta-kudurrī-uṣur II, a second son of Nabû-mukīn-apli, Mār-bīti-aḫḫē-iddina, ascended the throne. It is not known how long he reigned (942–? BC) and no inscriptions are attested for his reign. Just as Ninurta-kudurrī-uṣur II, he had been mentioned in the witness list of a kudurru from the reign of his father, Nabû-mukīn-apli (King, BBSt no. 9 iv A 32). For details of the reign of Mār-bīti-aḫḫē-iddina, see Brinkman, PKB pp. 49, 175–76, and 346 no. 21.

Šamaš-mudammiq

B.6.4

It is not known if Šamaš-mudammiq was related to his predecessor, Mār-bīti-aḫḫē-iddina, or not. No king list preserves the length of his reign, but the Synchronistic King List gives as his contemporaries the Assyrian kings Aššur-dān II (934–912 BC) and Adad-nārārī II (911–891 BC). Several battles were fought between the forces of Šamaš-mudammiq and Adad-nārārī II and as far as we know the Babylonians always lost. The Assyrian king claims to have conquered the entire land of Karduniaš (Babylonia) and to have annexed various cities in its northeastern and northwestern parts (e.g., Laḫīru, Arrapḫa, and Īdu [Ḫīt]); see RIMA 2 A.0.99.2 lines 26–29 and 34–35. No Babylonian inscriptions are attested from the time of Šamaš-mudammiq. For details of his reign, see Brinkman, PKB pp. 49, 177–80, and 346–47 no. 22.

Nabû-šuma-ukīn I

B.6.5

Nabû-šuma-ukīn I may have been the son of Šamaš-mudammiq but the passage in the Synchronistic History which would suggest this is damaged and would require an emendation (Nabû-šuma-iškun to Nabû-šuma-ukīn). It is not known how long he reigned but he was a contemporary of Adad-nārārī II (911–891 BC) and Tukultī-Ninurta II (890–884 BC) of Assyria. According to the Synchronistic History, Adad-nārārī II defeated Nabû-šuma-ukīn in battle and took a great amount of booty back to Assyria. The two kings then exchanged daughters in marriage, established friendly relations, and fixed the border between the two countries (see Grayson, Chronicles pp. 166–67 no. 21 iii 9–21). However, the new border meant that some areas previously annexed to Assyria by Adad-nārārī II were returned to Babylonia and the exchange of daughters implies that Babylonia was on an equal footing with Assyria. Thus, the Assyrians may actually have lost the battle despite the statements of the Synchronistic History, which was after all an Assyrian document. A period of basically amicable relations between Babylonia and Assyria began and lasted for about eighty years. Nabû-šuma-ukīn established a dynasty which was to hold the throne of Babylonia for most of the ninth century. No inscriptions of this king and no Babylonian documents dated to his reign are attested. For details of his reign, see Brinkman, PKB pp. 49–50, 180–82, and 347 no. 23.

Nabû-apla-iddina

B.6.6

Nabû-apla-iddina, the son and successor of Nabû-šuma-ukīn, reigned for at least thirty-three years. The earliest possible date for his first regnal year is 890 and the latest possible date for his death is 851, with his reign overlapping all or parts of those of the Assyrian kings Tukultī-Ninurta II (890–884 BC), Ashurnasirpal II (883–859 BC), and Shalmaneser III (858–824 BC). Relations between Babylonia and Assyria remained good for the most part. On one occasion, either early in the reign of Nabû-apla-iddina or late in that of his father Nabû-šuma-ukīn, Tukultī-Ninurta II and his army peacefully passed through Babylonian territory. Ashurnasirpal II claims to have captured two Babylonian fortresses east of the Tigris, and Babylonia is known to have supported a rebellion against that Assyrian king in the land of Sūḫu (on the middle Euphrates) in 878 BC, but Nabû-apla-iddina later concluded a treaty with Shalmaneser III. Although no royal inscriptions of this king are attested, several kudurrus date to his reign. Two of these record the king's granting of land to individuals (King, BBSt nos. 28 and 29) and one his endowment of the Ebabbar temple at Sippar (King, BBSt no. 36). In the latter kudurru, Nabû-apla-iddina claimed to have overthrown the Sutians (Assyrians). A document dating to his reign or shortly thereafter establishes the distribution of regular food offerings in the Eanna temple at Uruk (see McEwan, Iraq 45 [1983] pp. 187–98 and figs. 1–2). For details of the reign of Nabû-apla-iddina, see Brinkman, PKB pp. 50, 182–92, and 347–49 no. 24.

Marduk-zākir-šumi I

B.6.7

Nabû-apla-iddina was succeeded by his son Marduk-zākir-šumi I. It is not known exactly how long Marduk-zākir-šumi reigned, but the latest possible date for his accession is 851 BC and the earliest possible date for his death is 824 BC. Soon after he ascended the throne his brother Marduk-bēl-usāti led a major rebellion against him and Marduk-zākir-šumi had to turn to Assyria for aid. The Assyrian king Shalmaneser III conducted two campaigns in Babylonia (in 851 and 850 BC), helped to put down the rebellion against the Babylonian king, visited Babylon, Borsippa, and Cutha, and received tribute from the leaders of some of the Chaldean tribes. To mark the friendship between the two monarchs, they are depicted clasping hands on the central panel of the throne base in Fort Shalmaneser at Nimrud. Later, when rebellion broke out in Assyria towards the end of the reign of Shalmaneser, Marduk-zākir-šumi probably sent aid to help Šamšī-Adad V defeat his brother Aššur-dannin-apla. The Babylonian king then appears to have imposed a humiliating treaty upon Šamšī-Adad, one in which Babylonia and the Babylonian king were the dominant parties.

A cylinder seal from Babylon bears a dedicatory inscription of the king to the god Marduk (B.6.7.1) and a badly damaged tablet records the granting of privileges to the citizens of Borsippa by the king (B.6.7.2); both inscriptions are written in Akkadian. In addition, it is reported that the name of Marduk-zākir šumi I is inscribed on a piece of jewellery — apparently a carnelian amulet set in gold — found in one of the royal graves at Nimrud (see Damerji, Studies Mikasa p. 13, and George, Minerva 1/1 [1990] p. 29), but nothing further is known about the piece or its inscription. A brief inscription of an official of Adinu, the head of the Chaldean tribe of Bīt-Dakkūri, which is found on a bronze bowl is also presented here (B.6.7.2001), even though it is not strictly speaking a royal inscription or even an inscription of a royal official. A kudurru from the king's second year records that Marduk-zākir-šumi I granted land, a house, and a regular supply of food to a temple official at Uruk (Thureau-Dangin, RA 16 [1919] pp. 117–41) and one from the king's eleventh year records the private sale of some land located near Dilbat (Messerschmidt and Ungnad, VAS 1 no. 35). For details of the reign of Marduk-zākir-šumi I, see Brinkman, PKB pp. 50–51, 192–205, and 349–51 no. 25, and Brinkman, RLA 7/5–6 (1989) pp. 378–79. The treaty between Marduk-zākir-šumi I and Šamšī-Adad V has recently been re-edited by Parpola and Watanabe (SAA 2 no. 1) and Brinkman (Canfora, Trattati pp. 107–12).

1

An extremely large lapis lazuli cylinder seal which was to be worn on a cord or chain around the neck of the cult statue was presented to the god Marduk in Esagila by Marduk-zākir-šumi I. The inscription on the seal is written in Akkadian.

COMMENTARY

This seal (VA Bab 646) bears the excavation numer BE 6404; an impression of the inscription is shown on the Babylon excavation photo no. 700. It was found in a basket filled with various kinds of stones in room E of a Parthian building in Amran-ibn-Ali on April 18, 1900. See Wetzel, Spätzeit pl. 14 Dd8IV and pl. 15 for the location of the room. The seal is made of lapis lazuli and is pierced. It measures 19×3.5 cm, making it the largest cylinder seal known to the author. It would originally have had gold fittings at either end. The statue of the god Marduk is depicted on the seal. The inscription has been collated. The piece is now chipped and parts of lines 1–3 cannot be verified on the original; however, they can be read from the published photos (which are followed at these parts in the transliteration presented below).

It is not impossible that this inscription is to be assigned to Marduk-zākir-šumi II (B.6.24); however, since Marduk-zākir-šumi I reigned for a considerable period of time (at least 27 years), while Marduk-zākir-šumi II reigned for only part of one year, it seems more likely that the inscription is to be assigned to the former than to the latter.

BIBLIOGRAPHY

1900 Delitzsch, MDOG 5 pp. 13–15 and fig. 3 (drawing of figure on seal, translation)
1900 Koldewey, MDOG 5 pp. 3–5 (provenance, study)
1903 Weissbach, Miscellen no. 6 (copy, drawing of figure on seal, edition)
1911 Koldewey, Tempel pp. 46–48 and fig. 74 (photo [inscription not visible], study)
1956 Borger, Asarh. p. 120 commentary to 80-7-19,44 rev. 15 (study)
1957 Schmidt, Persepolis 2 p. 57 (study)
1957 Wetzel, Spätzeit pp. 32, 37–38 no. 15 and pls. 43e–h and 44b (provenance, photo, copy, study)
1962 Meyer, Jahrtausende pp. 102–104 (translation, study)
1968 Brinkman, PKB pp. 5, 203, and 349–50 no. 25.2.1 (study)
1971 Opificius, RLA 3/8 p. 578 (study)
1975 Boehmer in Orthmann, Der alte Orient pp. 361–62 and fig. 108a (drawing of relief, study)
1977 Gelb in Gibson and Biggs, Seals pp. 109, 112, and 121 sub no. XX (study)
1983 Rost and Marzahn, Babylon p. 27 (translation)
1987 Collon, First Impressions no. 785 (drawing of relief, study)
1992 Wittmann, Bagh. Mitt. 23 p. 262 no. 61 (edition, study)
1994 Watanabe, ASJ 16 p. 243 no. 3.1 (edition)

TEXT

1) *a-na* ^{d}AMAR.UTU EN GAL-*i da-pi-ni ti-*⌈*iz*⌉*-qa-*<*ri*> *šá-qí-i* ⌈EN⌉ *gim-ri*

2) *be-el be-lí* DI.KUD *ṣi-ri pa-ri-su* EŠ.BAR *da-ád-me*

3) EN KUR.MEŠ EN KÁ.DINGIR.⌈RA.KI *a*⌉*-šib* ⌈*é*⌉*-sag-íl be-lí-šu*

4) ^{d}AMAR.UTU-MU-MU LUGAL ŠÚ NUN *pa-liḫ-šu*

5) *ana* TIN ZI.MEŠ-*šu* SILIM NUMUN-*šú* GÍD.DA UD.MEŠ-*šú* GIN BALA-*šú*

6) *sà-kap* LÚ.KÚR-*šú ù* ⌈*šal*⌉*-meš* DU.⌈MEŠ⌉ *ma-ḫar-šu da-riš*

1–3) For the god Marduk, great lord, heroic, eminent, exalted, lord of everything, lord of lords, august judge who makes decisions for (all) the inhabited world, lord of (all) lands, lord of Babylon, the one who dwells in Esagila, his lord:

4–8) Marduk-zākir-šumi, king of the world, prince who reveres him, in order to ensure his good health (and) the well-being of his descendant(s), to prolong his days, to confirm his reign, to defeat his enemy, and to live in safety in his (the god Marduk's) presence forever, had made and presented (to

7) NA$_4$.KIŠIB NA$_4$.ZA.GÌN *eb-bi šá ina* KÙ.GI ḪUŠ.A *ki-niš kun-nu-ú*
8) *si-mat* GÚ-*šu* KÙ *ú-še-piš-ma* BA

Marduk this) seal of shining lapis lazuli, which is duly (and) carefully manufactured with red gold, (as an item) fitting for his holy neck.

2

A poorly preserved inscription which is written in Akkadian and which describes the granting of privileges (in particular *zakûtu*, the exemption from certain taxes) to the people of Borsippa by Marduk-zākir-šumi I is found on a tablet fragment in the British Museum. The inscription appears to indicate that while the city of Babylon had been granted *zakûtu* in the king's accession year, unrest in the land (the rebellion of Marduk-bēl-usāte?) prevented the granting of similar privileges to Borsippa at that time and that it was only in the king's sixteenth year that these privileges were granted to Borsippa.

COMMENTARY

The tablet fragment (BM 62908; 82-9-18,2877) measures c. 10×7.5 cm. The piece is part of a collection of objects from H. Rassam's excavations in Babylonia. Most objects in the 82-9-18 collection come from Sippar, but some do come from other sites, including Babylon, Dilbat, and Borsippa (see Reade in Leichty, Sippar 1 p. xxxiii). In view of the contents of the inscription, this fragment may also have come from the last-mentioned city. The inscription has been collated. Because of the poor state of preservation of the tablet, the inscription is frequently difficult to understand and the edition must be considered tentative.

BIBLIOGRAPHY

1982 Brinkman, CAH² 3/1 p. 307 (study)
1988 Frame and Grayson, ARRIM 6 pp. 15–21 (photo, copy, edition, study)

TEXT

Obverse
Lacuna
1′) [...] x-⸢*šú*(?)⸣-*nu i*-x [...]
2′) [... KÁ.DINGIR.RA.K]I *u bár-sip*[*a*.KI ...]
3′) [... LUG]AL TIN.TIR.KI RI x x [...]
4′) [...] x *qé-reb šá-ma-mi-i le-u$_5$ za-ku-ut* KÁ.DINGIR.R[A.KI ...]
5′) [... *id*(?)-*b*]*u-bu it-ti-šú* Ì SA[G.DU]-*su* ŠÉŠ TU MA ⸢A(?)⸣ x [...]
6′) [... *it*]-*ta-aṭ-ṭa-lu ur-d*[*am*(?)-*m*]*a*(?) *a-na qaq-qa-ri* MU NA x [...]
7′) [...] ⸢NUN(?)⸣-*ma na-ra-a*[*r*] *za-ku-*[*u*]*t* KÁ.DINGIR.RA.KI *u bár-sipa*.KI *ú-rak*(?)-*k*[*is*(?) ...]
8′) [... KÙ.G]I(?) *ṣa-ri-ri ú-šeš-ṭir-ma i-na* KÁ SILIM.MA *pa-paḫ* ᵈEN ⸢*ú*⸣-[*kin*(?) ...]
9′) [...] x *i-na e-ša*(*)-*a-ti u dal-ḫa-a-ti* I[M ...]
10′) [... K]Á.DINGIR.RA.KI *an-du-ra-ra u ki-din*(*)-*nu* KÁ.DINGIR.R[A.KI ...]

Obverse
Lacuna
1′) [...] their [...] ... [...]
2′) [... Babylon] and Borsippa [...]
3′) [... ki]ng of Babylon ... [...]
4′) [...] within the heavens *the writing board* (recording) the exemption of Babylon [...]
5′) [... *they sp*]*eak* with him; *they* anoint his head with oil ... [...]
6′) [... while] they watched, he *desc*[*ended*] to the earth ... [...]
7′) [...] *the prince commissioned auxiliary troops* (*to protect*) the exemption of Babylon and Borsippa [...]
8′) [...] he had (it) inscribed [upon *a canopy*] of *ṣāriru*-gold and [*set* (*it*) *up*] in the "Gate-of-Well-being," the cella of the god Bēl [...]
9′) [...] in the disorder and trouble [...]
10′) [...] Babylon, the freedom and privileged status of Babylon [...]

11′) [... *ú*(?)]-*kin*(?) *i-na* ⌈UGU⌉ AN-*e* KÙ.GI *šá* ^{d}EN *iš-ṭur-ma a-na* *u*$_{4}$*-um ṣ*[*a-a-ti* ...]	11′) [... *he*] *established.* He inscribed (it) upon the gold canopy of the god Bēl and for the fut[ure ...]
12′) [...-*p*]*i*(?)-*ma i-na* MU SAG ⌈NAM⌉.LUGAL.[LA] ^{d}AMAR.UTU-MU-⌈MU⌉ L[UGAL TIN.TIR.KI (...)]	12′) [...] and in the accession year of Marduk-zākir-šumi, k[ing of Babylon ...]
13′) [... LU]GAL ŠÁR NUN *pa-liḫ* DINGIR-*ti-šu-nu* GAL-*ti za-ku-ut* KÁ.DINGIR.R[A.KI ...]	13′) [... ki]ng of the world, prince who reveres their great divinity, [...] the exemption of Babylon [...]
14′) [...] *u saḫ-maš-ti šá* KUR.URI.⌈KI⌉ *im-m*[*a*(?)-*šu*(?)-*ú*(?) ...]	14′) [... *on account of the rebellion*] and unrest in the land of Akkad *were* [*forgotten* ...]
15′) [... *bá*]*r-sipa*.KI *la iš-šá-ki-in nu-uk-*[*k*]*u*(?)-*r*[*u* x] x UN *ar-ka-nu* [...]	15′) [... *the exemption of* Bo]rsippa was not established; to change ... afterwards [...]
16′) [... D]I.KUD(*) ⌈*sa*⌉-*ni-iq* ⌈*mit*⌉-*ḫur-tu*$_{4}$ *i-na* ITI.BÁR UD 11.KÁM KÁ x [...]	16′) [the god Nabû ...], *the judge* who makes opposing sides agree, in the month of Nisan, on the eleventh day, the gate [...]
17′) [...] ⌈^{d}*zar*⌉-*pa-ni-tu*$_{4}$ *i-ru-um-ma a-na* MAN-*ti* ^{d}AMAR.UTU-MU-MU LU[GAL ...]	17′) [...] the goddess Zarpanītu entered and for the kingship *of* Marduk-zākir-šumi, ki[ng ...]
18′) [...] ⌈*ki-am*(?)⌉ *iš-al a-a-um-ma la iq-bi-šú ina* MU 16.K[ÁM ...]	18′) [...] *thus he asked* but no one answered him. In the sixteenth year [...]
19′) [...] x-⌈*di*(?)⌉-*šú gu-um-mu-ru te-re-e-ti* [...]	19′) [...] ... *to complete*, the omens [...]
20′) [...] x ⌈BU⌉ *áš-šú za-*[*ku*(?)-*ut*(?) ...]	20′) [...] ... because of *the exe*[*mption* ...]
21′) [...] x *áš-šú* ⌈*an*⌉-*d*[*u*(?)-*ra*(?)-*ar*(?) ...]	21′) [...] ... because of *the fre*[*edom* ...]
22′) [...] x [...]	22′) [...] ... [...]
Lacuna	Lacuna
Reverse	Reverse
Lacuna	Lacuna
1′) [...] ⌈É(?)⌉ x MU(?) ⌈IŠ(?)⌉ x [...]	1′) [...] ... [...]
2′) [...]-*ma gi-né-e* LÚ.Ì.SUR.GI.NA L[Ú ...]	2′) [...] regular offerings, the oil presser of the regular offerings, [...]
3′) [...] LÚ.AZLAG.MEŠ *e-piš šip-ri šá* ⌈É(?)⌉ [...]	3′) [...] the fullers, those who do the work of *the temple* [...]
4′) [... *ina ilki u tup*]-⌈*šik*⌉-*ku ma-la ba-šu-ú ú-zak-ki-šú-nu-ti-m*[*a* ...]	4′) [...] he released them [from feudal obligations and corvée]-labour of every kind and [...]
5′) [... *ú-z*]*ak-ki-šú-nu-ti* LÚ *ḫal-qu* LÚ *mun-nab-t*[*u* ...]	5′) [... he] released them. The runaway, the fugitive [...]
6′) [*ša*(?) ... *lu*(?)]-⌈*ú*(?)⌉ TA KUR *a*-⌈*ra*(?)⌉-*mi lu-ú* TA ⌈URU⌉ x [...]	6′) [who ... *whe*]*ther* from the land of *Aramu* or from the city of [...]
7′) [... *in-n*]*ab-bi-tu-ú-nu* ⌈LÚ⌉.EN.NAM L[Ú.ŠÀ.TAM LÚ.GAR.UŠ$_{4}$ LÚ.GAR LUGAL ...]	7′) [... fl]ed, a provinical governor, a [chief administrator (of a temple), a governor, a royal official ...]
8′) [... L]Ú.GAR LÚ.EN.⌈NAM⌉ L[Ú.Š]À.TAM LÚ.GAR.UŠ$_{4}$ LÚ.[GAR] ⌈LUGAL *ù*(?)⌉ L[Ú(?) ...]	8′) [... *an*] *official*, a provincial governor, a chief administrator (of a temple), a governor, a royal [official], *and* a [...]
9′) [...] x ⌈DUMU⌉ [x x x] *la e-re-bi* L[Ú(?) ...]	9′) [...] the citizen[s ...] is not to enter [...]
10′) [...] x x U ⌈*la* ŠÉŠ⌉ *la pa-*$^{!}$*ṭár*(?) *a-na a-*⌈*šar šá*(?)⌉-[*nim*(?)-*ma*(?) ...]	10′) [...] ... is not to anoint, not to *release*, to *an*[*other*] place [...]
11′) [... *p*]*a-ni* DUMU.MEŠ *bár-sipa*.⌈KI *ú*⌉-*šad-gi*[*l* x] x [*b*]*il-ti* DUM[U.MEŠ ...]	11′) [...] he entrusted to the citizens of Borsippa; ... tax of the citizen[s ...]
12′) [...] x x x x [x x T]I *a-n*[*a* x x] DI RAM x [...]	12′) [...] ... [...]
13′) [...] x x ⌈AD Ú(?)⌉ x x [...]	13′) [...] ... [...]
14′) [...] x x x x x [...]	14′) [...] ... [...]
15′) [... R]U(?) LÚ *ḫa-za-an-nu* LÚ.NÍMGIR [...]	15′) [...] a mayor, a herald [...]
16′) [...]-*ú pa-ni-šú ú-šad-gil* NÍG.GA-*šú* x [...]	16′) [...] he entrusted to him; his property [...]
17′) [...] x L[Ú.E]N.NAM LÚ.ŠÀ.TAM LÚ.GAR.UŠ$_{4}$ L[Ú.GAR LUGAL ...]	17′) [...] a provincial governor, a chief administrator (of a temple), a governor, a [royal official ...]
18′) [...] x ⌈*a-na*⌉ [*b*]*ár-sipa*.⌈KI⌉ *im-mi-da i-na* 1 GUR 1 (BÁN) ⌈A(?)⌉.Š[À(?) ...]	18′) [...] he imposes [...] *for* Borsippa. In one *kurru*, one *sūtu of field* [...]

rev. 18′ Possibly *i-na* UKKIN x [...], "in the assembly ...," instead of "in one *kurru*, one *sūtu of field* (suggestion J.A. Brinkman).

19′) [...] x x *la be-lí iš-pu-*⸢*ra*⸣ *a-na* A ⸢BU⸣ x (x) NI 4 GADA Ú x [...]
20′) [... *ub*(?)*-b*]*i*(?)*-*⸢*ib*⸣ *šum-ma* LÚ.EN.NAM LÚ.⸢ŠÀ.TAM⸣ LÚ.GAR.UŠ$_4$ LÚ.GAR LUGAL [...]
21′) [...] x *bár-sipa*.KI UL KA(?) x KU *la i-du-ú ḫi-ṭa šá-a-šú ina muḫ-ḫ*[*i* ...]
22′) [...] x *u* É-*ia be-lí lu* [...]
23′) [... DUM]U.MEŠ *bár-sipa*.KI *šá* ^{d}AMAR.UTU-MU-MU LUGAL TIN.TIR.KI *a-na a-mat* ^{d}AG *be-l*[*í-šú* ...]
24′) [...] x *šá* ^{d}AG *a-na* ^{d}AG *be-lí-*⸢*šú*⸣ *ub-bi-ib ina bár-sipa*.KI ⸢URU(?)⸣ UD x [...]
25′) [...] *a*[*n*(?)]*-na-a is-su-ḫ*[*u*]*-ma* SUḪUŠ UN.MEŠ *bár-sipa*.⸢KI⸣ [...]
26′) [... *l*]*u-ú* NUN ⸢*lu*⸣*-ú* GÌR.NÍTA *lu-ú* LÚ *ak-lu*$_4$ *lu-ú* L[Ú.NU.BÀNDA(?) ...]
27′) [...] KI ÌR.⸢MEŠ⸣ *šá* ^{d}⸢AG⸣ EN-*ia* Š[U] x x [...]
28′) [...] x x ⸢DI(?)⸣ x LA ŠÁ ŠI TI [...]
29′) [...] x [x] x BU PA x x Ú [...]
30′) [...] x AN ⸢AR(?)⸣ x [...]
Lacuna

19′) [...] my lord wrote ... [...]
20′) [... *he puri*]*fied*. If a provincial governor, a chief administrator (of a temple), a governor, a royal official [...]
21′) [...] Borsippa ... unknowingly a sin to him against [...]
22′) [...] ... and of my house, my lord ... [...]
23′) [... the citi]zens of Borsippa whom Marduk-zākir-šumi, the king of Babylon, at the command of the god Nabû, [his] lord [...]
24′) [...] he purified [...] ... of the god Nabû for the god Nabû, his lord, (and) in Borsippa, *the city* ... [...]
25′) [Anyone who ...] removes this [...] and [...] the foundation of the people of Borsippa [...]
26′) [...] whether prince, or viceroy, or overseer, or [*lieutenant* ...]
27′) [...] the servants of the god Nabû, my lord, ... [...]
28′) [...] ... [...]
29′) [...] ... [...]
30′) [...] ... [...]
Lacuna

2001

A label mentioning an official of Adinu, the chief of the Chaldean tribe of Bīt-Dakkūri, is found on a bronze bowl. Adinu is known to have submitted to Shalmaneser III in 850 BC and to have presented him with tribute. This action is recorded and depicted on the bronze gates of Balawat; see Michel, WO 4 (1967–68) p. 34 vi 6–7 and p. 36 no. 15. Thus this inscription is likely to date around the middle of the ninth century. Since Marduk-zākir-šumi I was on the throne of Babylon in 850 BC, this inscription is presented with those of that king; however, it could instead come from the reign of Marduk-zākir-šumi's predecessor, Nabû-apla-iddina (B.6.6).

COMMENTARY

According to Godard, the bowl was found near Zalū Āb (a village located about 30 km northeast of Kermanshah). The piece is now in the Los Angeles County Museum of Art (LA M.76.97.361). It was once in the collection of Mrs. Christian R. Holmes and later in that of Nasli M. Heeramaneck. The bowl measures 8.1 cm in height and 11.2 cm in diameter. The inscription has been edited from the published photographs.

The title *šaknu* could be used for both provincial governors and officials subordinate to higher officials, including those subordinate to provincial governors; see CAD 17/1 [Š] pp. 191–92.

---

rev. 24′ Possibly ⸢URU(?)⸣.ZI[MBIR.KI ...], "Si[ppar ...]" (suggestion J.A. Brinkman).
rev. 28′ Possibly *ina e-ši-ti*, "in the disorder" (suggestion J.A. Brinkman).

BIBLIOGRAPHY

1933 Godard, Gazette des Beaux-Arts 10 (6th series) pp. 132–33, 135, and 137 fig. 17 (photo, study)
1938 Pope, Survey 1 pp. 280 and 285 no. 14, and 4 pl. 68A (photo, copy in type, edition)
1968 Brinkman, PKB pp. 11–12 no. 13, 198, 244 n. 1567, 266, and 363 no. p (edition, study)
1968 Herzfeld, Persian Empire p. 31 no. 18 (transliteration, study)
1969 Calmeyer, Datierbare Bronzen pp. 78–79 no. 40A and fig. 80 and p. 166 no. 87 (drawing, transliteration, study)
1971 Moorey, Catalogue Ashmolean p. 34 no. 1 (study)
1981 Moorey, Ancient Bronzes no. 417 (photo, translation, study)

TEXT

1) *šá* ᵐ*ab-di*-DINGIR LÚ.GAR-*nu šá* ᵐ*a-di-ni* A ᵐ*da-ku-ri*

1) (Property) of Abdi-il, *šaknu*-official of Adinu, the Dakkurian.

Marduk-balāssu-iqbi

B.6.8

Marduk-zākir-šumi I was succeeded by his son Marduk-balāssu-iqbi. The length of his reign is unknown, but it cannot have begun before 823 BC and it ended about 813 BC, when he was taken captive to Assyria by Šamšī-Adad V (king of Assyria 823–811 BC) after the latter's second campaign into Babylonia. It had probably been in the previous year that Šamšī-Adad had first invaded Babylonian territory; at that time, after initial devastating successes, the Assyrian forces appear to have been turned back by Marduk-balāssu-iqbi with the aid of Chaldeans, Elamites, Kassites, and Arameans. (See RIMA 3 A.0.103.1 iii 70–iv 45 and A.0.103.2 iii 17′–iv 10′; and Grayson, Chronicles p. 168 no. 21 iii 6′–9′.)

No inscriptions of the king are known. A stamped brick inscription from Tell ʿUmar has often been assigned to this king (see Waterman, Tel Umar 2 p. 78 and pl. XXV fig. 2; and Brinkman, PKB pp. 206 and 351 no. 26.2.1). The object cannot be located for collation, but the inscription is likely to be assigned to Nabonidus rather than Marduk-balāssu-iqbi (see Pettinato, Mesopotamia 5–6 [1970–71] p. 54 n. 20). Only two documents dating to his reign are known: a school tablet found at Uruk from his first regnal year (Cavigneaux, Bagh. Mitt. 10 [1979] pp. 111–17) and a Neo-Babylonian copy of an economic text dating to his second regnal year found at Nippur (A 33600 = 4 NT 3, unpublished). For details of the reign of Marduk-balāssu-iqbi, see Brinkman, PKB pp. 51, 205–10, and 351–52 no. 26 and RLA 7/5–6 (1989) p. 376.

Baba-aḫa-iddina

B.6.9

It is not clear whether the new king of Babylonia, Baba-aḫa-iddina, was related to his predecessor, Marduk-balāssu-iqbi, or not. It is not impossible that he is to be identified with an official (*paqid mātāti*), who was a son of Lidanu, in a text from the reign of Marduk-balāssu-iqbi. It is likely that 812 BC was the king's sole regnal year. Šamšī-Adad V (king of Assyria 823–811 BC) campaigned for a third time against Babylonia in 812 and claims to have taken the Babylonian king, his family, Babylonian gods, and extensive booty back to Assyria. Several cities to the east of the Tigris were looted by the Assyrian king, who then visited Cutha, Babylon, and Borsippa, where he made offerings to the gods, and southern Babylonia, where he received tribute from the Chaldean leaders. At some point before he died in 811 BC, Šamšī-Adad was credited with the title "king of Sumer (and) Akkad" in Assyrian inscriptions. (See RIMA 3 A.0.103.2 iv 11′–29′ and A.0.103.9 line 2; and Grayson, Chronicles pp. 168–69 no. 21 iv 1–14.)

No royal inscriptions or economic documents are attested from the reign of Baba-aḫa-iddina. For details of his reign, see Brinkman, PKB pp. 51, 210–13, and 352 no. 27.

Ninurta?-apl?-[...]
Marduk-bēl-[zēri]
Marduk-apla-uṣur

B.6.10–12

As a result of the aforementioned three campaigns by Šamšī-Adad V into Babylonia, and a fourth one by the same king in 811 BC, Babylonia appears to have fallen into a state of anarchy. Little is known about events in Babylonia in the thirty or forty years following the death of Baba-aḫa-iddina. There appears to have been a period during which there was no acknowledged king of the land before Ninurta?-apl?-[...] ascended the throne. There is no known connection between this individual and the next two rulers — Marduk-bēl-zēri and Marduk-apla-uṣur — or between any of them and any previous or later rulers of Babylonia. The first of these three kings is only known from an entry in a fragment of a synchronistic king list; the first two elements of his name cannot be read with certainty and the final element is not preserved. The last element of the name of the second king is not preserved in the king list; however, an economic text composed at the town Udannu dated by the accession year of a Marduk-bēl-zēri (Clay, JAOS 41 [1921] p. 313; see also Brinkman, PKB p. 214 n. 1334, and Brinkman and Kennedy, JCS 35 [1983] p. 63 no. AB.1) is presumably to be assigned to this king, thus suggesting the restoration in the king list. The final element of the name of the third king is not preserved in the king list, but he is also mentioned in the Dynastic Chronicle, which notes that he was a Chaldean and the sole ruler of his dynasty (Grayson, Chronicles p. 144 no. 18 vi 3′–5′). The lengths of the reigns of these kings are not known.

During this period of time, Adad-nārārī III (king of Assyria 810–783 BC) defeated a Babylonian army on one occasion, imposed tribute on Chaldean leaders, and visited the temples of Babylon, Borsippa, and Cutha. As already noted, at some point before he died, he claimed the title "king of Sumer (and) Akkad." According to an Assyrian eponym chronicle, campaigns were conducted against the city of Dēr in 795 BC and 794 BC; in 785 BC the statue of the patron deity of that city which had been carried off to Assyria by Šamšī-Adad V in 813 BC was returned to the city. (See Grayson, Chronicles p. 169 no. 21 iv 15–22 and p. 182 no. 24 rev. 8; Ungnad, RLA 2/5 [1938] pp. 429–30; and RIMA 3 A.0.104.8 lines 22–24.)

No royal inscriptions are attested for these kings, but Marduk-apla-uṣur may be mentioned in an inscription assigned to the later ruler Nabû-šuma-iškun (B.6.14.1 i 1). In addition, there are inscriptions of two Chaldean leaders which could conceivably date to this time: one of Nabû-šumu-līšir of Bīt-Dakkūri and the other of Marduk-šākin-šumi of Bīt-Iakīn. These two inscriptions are arbitrarily presented here and given the numbers B.6.10.2001 and 2002 respectively. For details about this period, see Brinkman, PKB pp. 52–59, 213–20, and 353–54 nos. 28–30, and RLA 7/5–6 (1989) pp. 375–76.

2001

A stone weight in the Metropolitan Museum of Art bears a short Akkadian inscription stating that it belonged to the palace of Nabû-šumu-līšir of the Dakkūru tribe. As noted by Brinkman, the "formula 'Palace of PN' is usually reserved for royal property, but there is no other indication that Nabu-shumu-lishir was ever king. He bears no royal title in the inscription; and his name is preceded by a masculine personal determinative, which hardly ever occurs in Babylonian inscriptions of this period before the names of reigning monarchs" (PKB p. 215). Brinkman suggests that Nabû-šumu-līšir may have been a minor Chaldean prince between 811 BC and 770 BC and possibly one of the "kings" of Chaldea who paid tribute to Adad-nārārī III. (See RIMA 3 A.0.104.8 lines 22–23 and Brinkman, PKB p. 216.)

COMMENTARY

The stone weight (MMA 74.51.4426) is made of jadeite. It measures 10.7 cm in length and 2.7 cm in thickness at the middle; it weighs 164.3 grams. Although Ward states that the piece was brought from Babylonia by the Wolfe Expedition (1884–85), it was actually acquired by di Cesnola in Cyprus in 1874, presumably from an antiquities dealer. Collation of line 4 and information on the type of stone were kindly provided by E. von Dassow.

Calmeyer (Reliefbronzen p. 148) notes that a Nabû-šumu-līšir who was the son of one Šumu-libši is mentioned as governor of Babylon and *šatammu*-official of Esagila on a bronze situla (B.6.0.2002). While it is not impossible that both texts refer to one individual, it seems more likely that they refer to different individuals.

BIBLIOGRAPHY

1885 Ward, PAOS [=JAOS 13 (1889)] pp. lvi–lvii (copy, edition)

1891 Lehmann-Haupt, 8. Kongress 2/1B pp. 173–74 (copy, edition)

1892 Lehmann–Haupt, Šamaššumukîn 1 pp. 95–96 (edition)

1907 Weissbach, ZDMG 61 pp. 395–96 no. 8 (edition, study)

1914 J.L. Myres, Handbook of the Cesnola Collection of Antiquities from Cyprus (New York) pp. 445, 450, and 556 no. 4426 (photo, study)

1968 Brinkman, PKB pp. 215–16, 262, and 363–64 no. s (edition, study)

TEXT

1) 1/3 GÍN GI.NA
2) É.GAL [md]PA-MU-SI.SÁ
3) A [m]*da-kur*
4) LÚ PA TE PA SI [d]AMAR.UTU

1) One-third mina, correct (weight).
2–4) Palace of Nabû-šumu-līšir, the Dakkurian, the ... of the god Marduk.

1 Literally "One-third (mina in) shekel(s)"; for the use of 1/3 GÍN to mean one-third mina, see Weissbach, ZDMG 61 (1907) p. 380.
4 The reading of the line is obscure. Past suggestions include LÚ.PA.TE.IS.SI [d]AMAR.UTU, "vice-regent for the god Marduk" (LÚ.PA.TE.IS.SI for PA.TE.SI; following Ward and Lehmann-Haupt) and LÚ.PA.ŠE *pa-liḫ* [d]AMAR.UTU, "man from Isin, one who reveres the god Marduk" (following Weissbach). The PA and TE immediately following LÚ could conceivably be one single sign (Brinkman, PKB p. 215 n. 1338); the end of the upper horizontal wedge of the PA touches the first winkelhaken of the TE.

2002

A cylinder seal in the British Museum bears an inscription of Marduk-šākin-šumi, descendant of Iakīnu, who is quite possibly to be identified with the father of Erība-Marduk (B.6.13). If so, he may have been one of the "kings of Chaldea" who send tribute to Adad-nārārī III. (See RIMA 3 A.0.104.8 lines 22–23 and Brinkman, PKB p. 216.)

COMMENTARY

The seal (BM 129532; 1945-10-13,76) measures 3.35×1.4 cm and is made of black and white speckled diorite. It was formerly in the Tyszkiewicz and Southesk collections. The relief on the seal depicts a male figure with a long curved staff in his hand facing the inscription. The inscription is written to be read from the seal; an impression has the inscription written in reverse (mirror-writing). Pinches states that the "characters on the original are very scratchy and difficult to read on account of their shallowness. Apparently the engraver had some difficulty in producing them" (Southesk, Catalogue 2 p. 83). The inscription has been collated.

BIBLIOGRAPHY

1908 Southesk, Catalogue 2 pp. 82–83 and pl. VI no. Qβ39 (photo of impression, copy, edition, study [by Pinches])
1945–48 Leemans, JEOL 10 p. 438 (edition)
1964 Brinkman, Studies Oppenheim pp. 28–30, especially nn. 159 and 174 (study)
1968 Brinkman, PKB pp. 215–16, 262, and 364 t (study)
1987 Collon, First Impressions no. 553 (photo of impression, study)

TEXT

1) *šá* ^{md}AMAR.UTU-GAR-⸢MU⸣
2) A ^{md}AMAR.UTU-⸢NUMUN(?)-TIN(?)⸣
3) ŠÀ.BAL.BAL
4) ^{m}*ia*-⸢*ki*⸣-*na*
5) NÍG.BA <^{m}>*u*-⸢*ṣur*(?)⸣-^{d}AMAR.⸢UTU⸣
6) IN.RA(?).RU(?)

1–6) (Property) of Marduk-šākin-šumi, son of Marduk-*zēra-uballiṭ*, descendant of Iakīnu. Gift *presented by Uṣur*-Marduk.

Erība-Marduk

B.6.13

The circumstances under which the next ruler of Babylonia, Erība-Marduk, came to the throne are not known, nor is the exact length of his reign. He was king for at least nine years, with his reign ending at some point before 760 BC. He was the son of Marduk-šākin-šumi and a member of the Chaldean tribe of Bīt-Iakīn in the Sealand. A seal in the British Museum bears an inscription of one Marduk-šākin-šumi of the same Chaldean tribe (B.6.10.2002) and it is quite likely that he is to be identified as the father of Erība-Marduk. The Dynastic Chronicle describes him as being the sole member of a Sealand dynasty (Grayson, Chronicles p. 144 no. 18 vi 6′–8′). A later ruler of Babylonia, Marduk-apla-iddina II, traced his ancestry back to Erība-Marduk and described his ancestor as one "who has made firm the foundation(s) of the land" (B.6.21.1 lines 12–14), in other words the one who had reorganized or reunified Babylonia after a period of unrest and uncertainty.

A chronicle indicates that Erība-Marduk did not take the hand of the god Bēl (Marduk) in the New Year's festival until his second year. This could suggest that he did not control the city of Babylon early in his first year when that ceremony should have taken place. The chronicle states that he slew Arameans who had seized fields belonging to the inhabitants of Babylon and Borsippa and had returned the fields to their original owners. He is also said to have set up some object/objects (possibly thrones) in the Esagila and Ezida temples (see Grayson, Chronicles pp. 182–83 no. 24 rev. 9–15). Esarhaddon later stated that Erība-Marduk had restored Eḫiliana, the shrine of the goddess Nanāia inside the Eanna complex at Uruk (B.6.31.18 lines 11–13). According to an inscription of the Neo-Babylonian ruler Nabonidus, the people of Uruk had replaced the old statue of the goddess Ištar in Eanna with a new, less appropriate one during the reign of Erība-Marduk (Langdon, NBK Nbn. 8 iii 11–29). The Uruk Prophecy, which may have been composed in the Seleucid period, is likely referring to Erība-Marduk when it describes a ruler as follows: "[Aft]er him a king will arise, but he will not provide justice for the land. He will not make (correct) decisions for the land. He will take away from Uruk the ancient protective goddess of Uruk and make (her) dwell in Babylon. He will make one who is not the protective goddess of Uruk dwell in her sanctuary (and) he will dedicate to her people who do not (rightly) belong to her. He will impose a heavy tribute upon the people of Uruk. He will lay Uruk waste, allow the canals to fill with silt, (and) abandon the cultivated fields" (rev. 3–7). For a recent study of the Uruk Prophecy, see Beaulieu, Studies Hallo pp. 41–52.

The Assyrian king Aššur-dān III (772–755 BC) conducted three campaigns into Babylonia, two against the town Gannanāti (771 BC and 767 BC), and one against the city of Marad (770 BC); see Ungnad, RLA 2/5 (1938) pp. 430 and 432. At least one of these campaigns (767 BC), and quite possibly the other two as well, took place while Erība-Marduk was on the throne of Babylon.

Two stone duck weights with short inscriptions of Erība-Marduk have been preserved (B.6.13.1–2), as has one private economic text recording a sale of land which was composed at Babylon in the ninth year of the king's reign (Brinkman, Studies Sjöberg pp. 37–47). For details of his reign, see Brinkman, PKB pp. 59, 221–24, and 354–55 no. 31.

1

A stone duck weight found at Nimrud has a brief inscription stating that it weighed thirty minas and that it was from the palace of Erība-Marduk.

COMMENTARY

The duck weight (BM 91433, 40-4-4,4) was found in the Northwest Palace at Nimrud by Austen Henry Layard. It is made of a green stone, which is said to be either syenite or basalt. The duck weight is appoximately 32 cm long and, according to museum records, weighs 15.061 kilograms. The inscription has been collated.

This stone weight, as well as one of Nabû-šumu-libūr (B.2.11.1), may have been taken to Nimrud as booty by an Assyrian ruler after a raid into Babylonia.

BIBLIOGRAPHY

1853 Layard, Discoveries pp. 600–601 (copy in type)
1856 Norris, JRAS 16 pp. 217–18 and pl. facing p. 222 no. 1 (copy in type, translation, study)
1866 Brandis, Münz p. 46 (translation)
1872 G. Smith, TSBA 1 p. 75 no. 59 (translation)
1875 Ménant, Babylone p. 130 (translation)
1875 G. Smith, RP 5 p. 91 no. 57 (translation)
1889 Winckler, Untersuchungen p. 32 (edition)
1907 Weissbach, ZDMG 61 p. 395 no. 7 (translation, study)
1915 Weidner, MVAG 20/4 p. 103 (translation)
1922 BM Guide p. 213 no. 253 (translation, study)
1938 Weissbach, RLA 2/5 pp. 463–64 (translation)
1968 Brinkman, PKB pp. 6, 223 n. 1399, and 354 no. 31.2.1 (study)
1969 Pritchard, ANEP[2] no. 120 (photo, study)

TEXT

1) 30 MA.NA GI.NA
2) É.GAL *eri-ba*-[d]AMAR.UTU
3) LUGAL TIN.TIR.KI

1) Thirty minas, correct (weight).
2–3) Palace of Erība-Marduk, king of Babylon.

2

A fragment of a stone duck weight which was found at Uruk bears a partially preserved inscription indicating that it belonged to Erība-Marduk.

COMMENTARY

The fragment (W 23428) was found in 1973 on the surface at Uruk in Qa XXV 3 (area of the Gareus temple) and is shown on the excavation photo 14121. It is now in the Iraq Museum (museum number not known). The piece is made of black basalt and measures 14.1×c.11 cm. The inscription is restored from the previous inscription and has been collated from the published photograph.

BIBLIOGRAPHY

1983 Wilcke, UVB 31–32 p. 54 and pl. 28f–g (photo, copy, edition)
1993 Becker, AUWE 6 no. 555 (photo, copy, edition, study)

TEXT

1) [x MA.NA] ⸢GI⸣.NA
2) [É.GAL *eri*]-*ba*-^{d}⸢AMAR⸣.UTU
3) [LUGAL TIN.TIR].⸢KI⸣

1) [x mina(s)], correct (weight).
2–3) [Palace of Erī]ba-Marduk, [king of Babylon].

Nabû-šuma-iškun

B.6.14

The exact date and manner in which Nabû-šuma-iškun succeeded Erība-Marduk and came to the throne is not known. Although he was also a Chaldean, he was not a descendant of Erība-Marduk, but rather a member of the Bīt-Dakkūri tribe. Since his reign ended in 748 BC and since he is known to have ruled for at least thirteen years, it is clear that he had become king by 760 BC at the latest. There appears to have been discontent and unrest in Babylonia during the reign of this king. According to one chronicle, the statue of the god Nabû did not leave its sanctuary to attend the procession of the statue of the god Bēl (Marduk) during the New Year's festival at Babylon in the king's fifth and sixth years (Grayson, Chronicles p. 130 no. 15 line 22). This would suggest that conditions in the land were so unsettled as to make it unsafe for Nabû's statue to travel even the short distance from Borsippa to Babylon. Although no royal inscriptions of Nabû-šuma-iškun are attested, we do have an Akkadian historical-literary text which attributes a large number of crimes to his account (B.6.14.1) and which clearly reflects discontent with his reign. In addition, an Akkadian inscription of a governor of Borsippa, Nabû-šuma-imbi, has been preserved on a clay cylinder (B.6.14.2001). While recording work on a storehouse of the Ezida temple, the document also describes disorder at Borsippa during the king's reign. One kudurru dated at Borsippa in the king's eighth year (Messerschmidt and Ungnad, VAS 1 no. 36) and three economic texts, composed in his tenth and thirteenth years, also attest to the reign of this king. For details on the reign of Nabû-šuma-iškun, see Brinkman, PKB pp. 60, 224–26, and 355–56 no. 32, and Brinkman and Kennedy, JCS 35 (1983) p. 63 no. AE.

1

A historical-literary text from Uruk mentions the Dakkurian Nabû-šuma-iškun and describes various criminal and impious acts which he had committed. Among other matters, he is said to have plundered the Esagila temple at Babylon and introduced gods of the Sealand and of Chaldeans and Arameans into that temple. He broke treaties and oaths sworn by the gods and committed heinous crimes against the people of his cities. It is stated that he seized private individuals and their property without just cause and burned alive sixteen Cuthians. The inscription was likely composed sometime after the reign of Nabû-šuma-iškun and intended to demonstrate that he, a Chaldean of the tribe of Bīt-Dakkūri, had shown favour to the Chaldeans and Arameans at the expense of the older population of the land. It is worthy of note that in no part of the text as it is currently preserved is Nabû-šuma-iškun called "king." Regrettably the tablet is badly damaged and the ancient scribe had copied the text from an already-damaged original. Thus the edition presented here must often be considered most tentative.

COMMENTARY

The four-column clay tablet bears the inventory number W 22660/0 and measures 17.6×13.5×3 cm. The piece was found in the 1970/71 season of excavations at Uruk in a private house in Ue XVIII1 level II, near level I. The text is written in Late Babylonian script and in the Akkadian language. Every second line is followed by a line ruling and these divisions have been followed in the translation. The scribe copied the inscription from a damaged original and noted where the original was damaged by writing *ḫi-pí*, "broken" (ii 3 and 29; iii 4′, 5′, 6′, 7′, 17′, and 18′; and iv 55′) or *ḫi-pí eš-šú* "new break" (iii 18′). In the translation presented below, these notations have not been included and the passages are simply marked "..." The inscription has been collated against the published photographs; however, large portions of the text are poorly preserved (especially columns i and ii) and are not clear on the available photographs. Thus, it has been necessary to rely upon the published copy in numerous places.

BIBLIOGRAPHY

1979 von Weiher, UVB 29–30 p. 98 (provenance, study)

1984 von Weiher, Bagh. Mitt. 15 pp. 197–224 and pls. 22–23 (photo, edition, study)

1986 Hunger, AfO 33 p. 367 (iii 30–31, 44 and 56, study)

1988 von Weiher, SbTU 3 no. 58 (copy, edition)

1993 Glassner, Chroniques pp. 235–40 no. 51 (translation)

TEXT

Obverse

Col. i

1) [... ^{m}]⸢^{d}AMAR.UTU⸣-IBILA-ÙRU 2) [...] ⸢LÚ⸣ *kal-di*	i 1–2) [...] Marduk-apla-uṣur [...] the Chaldean.
3) [...] ⸢ÍD *i*⸣*-diq-lat* 4) [...] x-⸢*ši*⸣*-ma*	i 3–4) [...] Tigris River [...] ...
5) [...] x ⸢*šip*(?)*-ri*⸣ 6) [...] ⸢*i*⸣-[*du*]-⸢*uk*(?)⸣*-ma*	i 5–6) [...] ... [...] *he k*[*il*]*led;*
7) [...] (x) x x UŠ 8) [...] x x [...]-⸢*e*(?)⸣*-ti*	i 7–8) [...] ... [...] ...
9) [...] x ⸢KI(?)⸣ x [x (x)] x-*ma* 10) [...] x x x [(x)] x LÚ-*tú*	i 9–10) [...] ... [...] ... people
11) [...] x *šá* UD [(+)]⸢5(?)⸣.KÁM 12) [...] x x [x (x)] x	i 11–12) [...] ... [...] the *fifth* day [...] ...
13) [...] x [x x] A GIŠ x [x (x)] 14) [...] *ana* ⸢*é*(?)*-sag*(?)⸣*-íl*	i 13–14) [...] ... [...] *to Esagila.*
15) [...] ⸢DU⸣ [...] UL 16) [...] x IB	i 15–16) [...] ...
17) [...] DI 18) [...] x x	i 17–18) [...] ...
19) [...] x 20) [...]	i 19–20) [...]
21) [...] x	i 21) [...]
Lacuna	Lacuna

Col. ii

1) *ina* u_4-⸢*me*(*)*-šú*(*)⸣*-ma* ^{d}AG-MU-GAR-⸢*un*⸣ TA *qé-reb* 2) TIN.⸢TIR.KI⸣ *a-na* KUR-*šú pa-ni-*⸢*šú*⸣ *iš-kun-ma*	ii 1–2) *At that time* Nabû-šuma-iškun directed his attention from Babylon to his (own) land.

---

i 1 Marduk-apla-uṣur may well be the king by that name who reigned shortly before Nabû-šuma-iškun (B.6.12).

ii 1 *ina* u_4-⸢*me*(*)*-šú*(*)⸣*-ma* ("At that time"); von Weiher (SbTU 3 p. 16) states that the signs are closer to *ina* UD *šal-ši-ma* ("on the third day").

3) *ina* ⸢*a-mat*⸣ ^{d}AG *u* ^{d}AMAR.UTU EN.MEŠ $^{\text{ḫi-pí}}$

4) *ina* x [(x)] ⸢RI⸣ *ana qé-reb* É-*šú i-ru-um-ma*

5) *la* ⸢*i*⸣*-tur-ma a-na* ⸢*e*⸣*-peš ta-ḫa-zi*

6) *ù a-lak* KASKAL x x-*šú la* ⸢*ú*⸣*-ṣi*

7) *iš-ni-ma ina* MU 3.KÁM ^{d}*na-na-a é-zi-da*

8) *ra-ʾi-*⸢*mat*(?)⸣ ^{d}AG *a-na* É *mu-um-mu ú-še-rib-ma*

9) ^{d}AG ⸢*ina*⸣ TIN.TIR.KI *ik-le-e-ma nu-bat-tu*$_4$

10) *ù* UD.È[Š.È]Š *a-na* 1-*en* ⸢*u*$_4$(?)⸣*-mì ú-ter*

11) *it-*⸢*ti*⸣ TÚ[G S]IG$_5$ ^{d}EN *šá* ITI.ZÍZ.ÀM

12) TÚG SIG$_5$ ^{d}[A]G x x-*ti-in*

13) *šá-nu-*⸢*ú*⸣ (x) *šá* x *áš-*(x)-⸢*ri*(?)⸣ *šá* ^{d}EN

14) *a-na* ^{d}[*t*]*aš-me-t*[*u*$_4$] *ú-šat-ri-iṣ*

15) *pe-er-tú* ŠÁ KIN ŠAB TUR x (x) *ú-*⸢*ṭaḫ*(?)⸣-*ḫ*[*i*(?)-*i*]*d*(?) x x KÙ.GI

16) ŠÁ KIN *ù ana pa-paḫ* ^{d}EN *i-ru-um-ma* x x *ú-qar-rab*

17) GA.RAŠ.SAR *ik-kib é-zi-da* ⸢ŠÁ(?) KIN(?)⸣ ^{d}AG

18) *ú-*[*qa*]*r-rib u* <LÚ>.KU$_4$.É.MEŠ ⸢*ul*⸣*-ta-kil*

19) ⸢^{d}*é*⸣*-a* EN *né-me-qí* ⸢*šá*⸣ *šu-bat-su*

20) ⸢*ṣir*(?)⸣*-ti* AN Ú ZA(?) U(?) KI IN x ŠU ⸢DA(?)⸣ TU

21) ⸢*ina šu*⸣*-bat si-mat* DINGIR-*ti-šú* GAL-*ti*

22) ⸢*ú-šat-bi-ma*⸣ *ina* ⸢KÁ⸣ x (x) x *ú-šeš-*⸢*šeb*⸣

23) ⸢^{d}DI⸣.KUD x ⸢TIN.TIR.KI⸣ (x) x BI ⸢KA(?)⸣

24) x-⸢BI-*šú i-de-ek-ki*⸣*-ma* ⸢*ú-šá*⸣*-lak*(?)

25) [x (x)] A KUR x x (x) x x-*an-*⸢*ni*⸣*-ma*

26) x [(x)] ⸢BI NE *di-ik-šú*⸣ [(x)] x-⸢*pu*⸣*-uš*

27) ⸢*šá*⸣ [(x)] x RI RA(?) x x [...] x [(x)] x x

28) *šá* x x (x) [...] ⸢IT⸣ [(x)] x U

29) x (x) x [(x)] ŠÁ x KI [...] ⸢Ù(?)⸣ UD x x LÁ $^{\text{ḫi-pí}}$

30) x ⸢MU(?)⸣ [...] x [...] x-*zu-uz*(?)

31) [(x)] x [...] ⸢*a*⸣*-ši-bat* GIŠ.GU.ZA

32) x [...] ⸢7⸣ *la-ab-bi*

33) [...] x-*dur-ma*

34) [...] ⸢*ú*⸣*-šak-bi-is*

35) x x x [...] x *mi-iḫ-ši*

36) ⸢*ù*(?)⸣ x ⸢UR(?)⸣ [... *ú-š*]*á*(?)*-aṣ-mi-is-si*

37) ⸢*šá*(?)⸣ ^{d}INAN[NA ...] x ^{d}INANNA x [(x)]

38) x [(x)] x [...] x *ú-šap-ṭir*

39) [(x)] x NI ⸢KÚ(?)⸣ x x (x) ŠI ⸢*ù*(?)⸣ IM.SAḪAR.RA

40) [...] x *ú-šat-ri-iṣ*

41) [...] ^{d}*nin-*UG$_5$

42) [...] x ⸢*uq*⸣*-tar-rib*

43) [...] ^{d}AG *ina* TIN.⸢TIR⸣.KI *pu-ud-ma*

44) [...]-⸢*ma ina*⸣ [I]M(?).⸢GI(?)⸣.MEŠ *ú-šib*

45) [...] (x) ⸢TIN(?).TIR(?)⸣.KI x ⸢ID/DA(?)⸣ MAR(?) ṢA

ii 3–4) At the command of the gods Nabû and Marduk, <his> lords, he entered ... into his house;

ii 5–6) He did not go out again either to do battle or to go on a journey ...

ii 7–8) Further, in the third year he brought (the statue of) the goddess Nanāia of Ezida, the beloved of the god Nabû, into the temple's sacred workshop.

ii 9–10) He held back (the statue of) the god Nabû in Babylon and turned the eve of the (*eššēšu*)-festival and the *eššēšu*-festival day (itself) into (*a festival of only*) one *day*.

ii 11–12) With the good gar[ment] of the god Bēl (Marduk) *in* the month of Šabaṭu, the good garment of the god [Na]bû ...

ii 13–14) ... of the god Bēl he *extended to* the goddess Tašmētu.

15–16) *Hair ... he made abundant* ... gold ... he entered the sanctuary of the god Bēl, introducing ...

ii 17–18) He introduced the leek, which is taboo to Ezida ... the god Nabû, and made those privileged to enter the temple eat (it).

ii 19–20) The god Ea, the lord of wisdom, whose *exalted* dwelling ...

ii 21–22) He made (him) get up from (his) dwelling, (a place) befitting his great divinity, making (him) sit in the gate ...

ii 23–24) The god Madānu ... Babylon ... he removes his ... and *makes* (*him*) *go* (*away*).

ii 25–36) ... and ...

ii 27–28) ... [...] ... [...] ...

ii 29–30) ... [...] ... [...] ...

ii 31–32) [...] she who sits on the throne [...] seven lions.

ii 33–34) [...] ... and [...] he trampled.

ii 35–36) ... [...] ... *and* [... he ha]rnessed it.

ii 37–38) *That which* the goddess Iš[tar ...] the goddess Ištar ... [...] he had released.

ii 39–40) ... [...] he extended.

ii 41–42) [...] the god *Ninpirig* [...] he brought near.

ii 43–44) [...] the god Nabû was detained in Babylon and [...] and dwelt among *the rebels*.

ii 45–46) [...] *Babylon* ... [...] he burned with fire.

---

ii 3 The translation assumes that the end of the line originally had EN.MEŠ-*šú*.

ii 6 von Weiher (SbTU 3 pp. 7 and 16) suggests ... <<KASKAL>> *ge*[*r*?-*r*]*i*?-*šú* or KASKAL *ša*[*r*?!-*r*]*i*?-*šú*. Possibly KASKAL ⸢*it-ti*⸣-*šú* as in iii 51′?

ii 41 It is assumed here that UG$_5$ is used for UG (=PÌRIG). The god Ninpirig was the vizier of the sun-god Šamaš; see Finkelstein, RA 67 (1973) pp. 115–18.

46) [...] x x *ina* IZI *iq-lu*$_4$

47) [... *š*]*á*(?)-⌜*a*⌝-*šú* E[N] GAL ^{d}AMAR.UTU
48) [...] x x ⌜^{d}AMAR.UTU⌝ [x (x)] MU(?) LUGAL DU-*ma*

ii 47–48) [...] *him*, the great lord, the god Marduk, [...] the god Marduk ... the king *went*.

49) [...] x [...] ḪI *iq-bi*
50) [...] x-*ma* GAR-*an*

ii 49–50) [...] ... he said [...] and sets.

51) [...] x ŠAL ŠI-*ma*
52) [...] x MAḪ

ii 51–52) [...] ... [...] ...

53) [..] ⌜EN⌝ *kám-su*
54) [...] UD AS MIR

ii 53–54) [...] ... [...] ...

55) [... K]A(?) x [(x)]

ii 55) [...] ...

Lacuna

Reverse

Col. iii

Lacuna

1′) [x x (x)] x [...]

iii 1′) [...]

2′) [x x] x [(x)] x [...]
3′) [x x] x ^{d}⌜NIN⌝ x x x [...]

iii 2′–3′) [...] ... [...] ... [...]

4′) *i-nu* EN *šit-ra-ḫu za-kut* TIN ⌜$^{\text{ḫi-pí}}$⌝
5′) *bár-sipa*.KI ⌜*ù*(*)⌝ $^{\text{ḫi-pí}}$

iii 4′–5′) When the splendid lord ... the exemption of Bab<ylon>, Borsippa and ...

6′) *ù a-de-e šá* ^{md}50-AŠ-KUR DUMU ^{m}*ku-* $^{\text{ḫi-pí}}$
7′) LÚ.GAR.KUR URU *la-rak ina muḫ-ḫi-ši-na ú-šeṣ-* $^{\text{ḫi-pí}}$

iii 6′–7′) And the oath which Enlil-AŠ-KUR, son of Ku-... the governor of the city Larak, had *caused them* (the people) <*to take*>,

8′) *ina* TIN.TIR.KI *bár-sipa*.KI *u* GÚ.DU$_8$.A.KI
9′) *ina ma-ḫar* ^{d}EN ^{d}AG *u* ^{d}U.GUR *ú-šat-ri-iṣ*

iii 8′–9′) In Babylon, Borsippa, and Kutha, he extended in the presence of the gods Bēl, Nabû, and Nergal .

10′) *šat-ti-šam-ma da-ku ḫa-ba-lu šá-ga-šú*
11′) *ṣa-ba-ti il-ki u tup-šik-ki* UGU-*šú-nu ú-šá-tir*

iii 10′–11′) Yearly he increased against them (the level of) killing, robbing, murdering, (and) performance of feudal obligations and corvée-labour.

12′) *ina* <1>-*en u*$_4$-*mi* 16 *ku-ta-a-a ina* KÁ.GAL ^{d}*za-ba*$_4$-*ba*$_4$
13′) *šá qé-reb* TIN.TIR.KI *ina* IZI *iq-lu*$_4$

iii 12′–13′) On a <single> day he burned (alive) sixteen Cuthians with fire in the gate of the god Zababa, which is inside Babylon.

14′) DUMU.MEŠ TIN.TIR.KI *ana* KUR *ḫat-ti u* KUR ELAM.MA.KI
15′) *a-na šul-ma-nu-ti ú-bil*

iii 14′–15′) He carried off citizens of Babylon to the lands of Ḫatti and Elam as *greeting-gifts*.

16′) DUMU.MEŠ TIN.TIR.KI [D]AM.MEŠ-*šú-nu* DUMU.MEŠ-*šú-nu*
17′) *ù áš-ta-pi-ri*(*)-*šú-nu* È-*ma ina* EDIN *ú-* $^{\text{ḫi-pí}}$

iii 16′–17′) He expelled the citizens of Babylon, their wives, children and servants, and he <*settled them*> in the steppe.

18′) ⌜É(?)⌝ DUMU.MEŠ TIN.TIR.KI $^{\text{ḫi-pí eš-šú}}$ -*šú* SAG $^{\text{ḫi-pí}}$
19′) *ana* DU$_6$ *u kar-mu iš-pu-uk-ma ana* UGU É.GAL *ú-ter*

iii 18′–19′) *The house*(*s*) of the citizens of Babylon ... he piled up into heaps of ruins and *turned* (*them*) *over to* his palace.

20′) SILA.DAGAL.LA *mu-taq* ^{d}*šár-ur*$_4$ *na-ram* EN-*šú*
21′) *šá* ITI ⌜3(?)-*šú*(?)⌝ SILA URU-*šú i-ba-ʾ-ú*

iii 20′-21′) (With regard to) the public square, the route of the god Šarʾur, beloved of his lord, who goes along the street(s) of his city in *the third* month,

22′) SILA *mu-ta-qí-šú is-kir-ma ana* UGU É.GAL-*šú* GUR-*ma*
23′) *su-*⌜*qí*(?)⌝ *la mu-ta-qí-šú ú-šá-bi-ʾ-šú*

iii 22′–23′) He blocked off the roadway of his (Šarʾur's) route and *turned* (*it*) *over to* his palace; he had him (Šarʾur) go along a road which was not part of his route.

24′) ^{m}SIG$_5$-*iq*-^{d}IŠKUR DUMU ^{md}IŠKUR-MU-KÁM EN SILIM-*šú*
25′) *ba-lu ḫi-ṭi u bar-tu*$_4$ *iṣ-bat-su-ma*

iii 24′–25′) He seized Mudammiq-Adad, the son of Adad-šuma-ēreš, his ally, without (Mudammiq-Adad having committed) any transgression or rebellion;

---

iii 4′ Following von Weiher (SbTU 3 p. 17), the translation "Bab<ylon>" assumes an original TIN.TIR.KI at the end of the line.
iii 5′ ⌜*ù*(*)⌝: copy has ŠI-MA. Possibly GÚ.DU$_8$.A.KI was originally found at the end of the line (cf. iii 8′).
iii 7′ Following von Weiher (SbTU 3 p. 17), the translation "*caused* ... <*to take*>" assumes an original *ú-šeṣ-bi-tu* at the end of the line.
iii 17′ *ri*(*): copy has ḪU. The translation "he <*settled them*>" assumes that the end of the line originally had *ú-še-šib-šú-nu-ti* (compare iv 41′); suggestion of R.D. Biggs.

26′) UN.MEŠ-*šú ma-la ba-šu-u a-na kal-di* 27′) *ù* LÚ *a-ra-mu a-na šul-ma-nu-ti ú-bil*	iii 26′–27′) He carried off his (Mudammiq-Adad's) people, as many as there were, to the Chaldeans and Arameans as *greeting-gifts*.
28′) URU.MEŠ-*šú* A.ŠÀ.MEŠ-*šú* É.MEŠ-*šú* GIŠ.KIRI$_6$.MEŠ-*šú* 29′) *ù mim-ma-a-šú ma-la ba-šú-ú pa-ni-šú ú-šad-gil*	iii 28′–29′) He put at his own disposal his (Mudammiq-Adad's) villages, fields, houses, orchards, and possessions, as many as there were.
30′) ^{m}*il-ta-gab*-DINGIR *šá* URU.BÀD *šá ana* KAR-*bi šá* GÚ ÍD *pu-rat-ti* 31′) *ina a-de-e u ma-mit ana pa-ni-šú ú-ṣa-am-ma*	iii 30′–31′) (With regard to) Śagab-il of the city Dūru, who in order to save (himself) had come out *from* the bank of the Euphrates (and gone) before him (Nabû-šuma-iškun) with a treaty and oath,
32′) *ik-kib ru-bé-e pa-ru-ti pi-šat la qa-bé-e* 33′) DÙ-*su ù* URU-*šú ana šá-la-li im-ni*	iii 32′–33′) He (Nabû-šuma-iškun) committed against him that which is taboo to princes, (namely) insults (and) unspeakable abuse, and he counted his city as booty.
34′) *ina* MU 6.KÁM *a-na é-sag-íl* É.GAL ^{d}50 DINGIR.MEŠ 35′) *a-na ud-*⸢*du*(?)⸣*-ši-šu* IGI.II(*) *iš-*⸢*kun*⸣*-ma*	iii 34′–35′) In the sixth year, he directed his attention to *renovating* Esagila, the palace of the Enlil of the gods (Marduk).
36′) *šá é-sag-gíl ma-la ba-šu-ú šá* LUGAL.MEŠ 37′) *a-lik maḫ-ri-šú ú-še-ri-bu qé-*⸢*reb*⸣*-šú*	iii 36′–37′) The property of Esagila, as much as previous kings had brought into it,
38′) *ú-še-ṣa-am-ma ina qé-reb* É.GAL-*šú ik-mis-*⸢*ma*⸣ 39′) *a-na i-di rama-ni-šú ú-ter-*⸢*ma*⸣	iii 38′–39′) He brought out and collected inside his (own) palace; he appropriated (it) for himself:
40′) KÙ.BABBAR KÙ.GI NA$_4$.MEŠ *ni-siq-ti šu-qu-ru-ti* 41′) *ù mim-ma si-mat* DINGIR-*ú-ti ma-la ba-šú-u*	iii 40′–41′) (Namely) silver, gold, precious, valuable stones and everything befitting a divinity, as much as there was.
42′) DINGIR.MEŠ KUR *tam-tim* LÚ *kal-du u* LÚ *a-ra-*⸢*mu*⸣ 43′) GIM *bi-bil lìb-bi-šú ú-šat-ri-ṣa ina lìb-*⸢*bi*⸣	iii 42′–43′) In accordance with his (own) desire, he installed there the gods of the Sealand, the Chaldeans, and Arameans.
44′) MUNUS.ŠÀ.É.GAL-*šú ú-za-an a-na šul-ma-nu-*⸢*ti*⸣ 45′) *a-na* KUR *ḫat-ti u* KUR ELAM.MA.KI *i-šar-ra[k]*	iii 44′–45′) He adorned his palace women (and) presented (them) as *greeting-gifts* to the lands of Ḫatti and Elam.
46′) 7-*tu*$_4$ MU.AN.NA *i-na ka-šá-di a-na qé-*⸢*reb*⸣ 47′) É-^{m}*da-ku-ri ana* ḪUL-*tim il lik* ⸢*ma*⸣	iii 46′–47′) When the seventh year arrived, he went to Bīt-Dakkūri with evil intent;
48′) *ár-ka-nu* ^{md}PA-MU-GAR-*un* DUMU ^{m}*da-ku-*⸢*ri*⸣ 49′) <*ina*> *a-*⸢*de*⸣*-e u ma-mit* DINGIR.MEŠ GAL.MEŠ	iii 48′–49′) Afterwards, Nabû-šuma-iškun, the Dakkurian, <in accordance with> the treaty and the oath (sworn by the names) of the great gods,
50′) ANŠE.KUR.RA.MEŠ ÉRIN.MEŠ *u* GIŠ.GIGIR.MEŠ È-*ma* 51′) *a-na a-lak* ⸢KASKAL⸣ *it-ti-šú iš-pur*	iii 50′–51′) Brought out horses, soldiers, and chariots and ordered (them) on a campaign with him.
52′) NINDA.ḪI.A KAŠ.SAG *ù* ŠE.BAL.LA 53′) *a-na kal ma-dak-ti-šú id-din*	iii 52′–53′) He gave bread, fine beer, and *ḫirigalû*-flour to his entire camp.
54′) *ina* ITI.ŠE UD 20.KÁM *ina*(?) *u*$_4$*-me* x-*ti šá* ^{d}UTU *u* ^{d}AMAR.UTU 55′) *a-na a-de*(*)*-e u ma-mit la ip-làḫ-ma*	iii 54′–55′) On the twentieth day of the month of Addaru, the day ... to the gods Šamaš and Marduk, he did not respect (his sworn) treaty and oath;
56′) UN.MEŠ *ma-la ina* EDIN *par-*⸢*ga*⸣*-niš rab-ṣa* 57′) *i[p*(?)*]-pu-šá* ⸢*ḫi*(?)⸣*-du-*⸢*tú*⸣ *u* ⸢*i*⸣*-sin-ni*	iii 56′–57′) The people, as many as were encamped in green pastures, *held* joyful celebrations.

Col. iv

Lacuna	Lacuna
1′) [...] x	iv 1′) [...]
2′) [...] ⸢IK/TUK(?) TI(?)⸣ 3′) [...]-⸢*ma*(?)⸣	iv 2′–3′) [...] ... [...]
4′) [...] ⸢^{d}EN⸣ 5′) [... *ú*]*-še-šib*	iv 4′–5′) [...] the god Bēl [... he] settled.

---

iii 30′ With regard to the reading Śagab (or possibly Śagib?), for *il-ta-gab*, see Fales, Orientalia NS 47 (1978) pp. 91–98 (reference courtesy P.-A. Beaulieu). Instead of URU.BÀD(EZEN×BAD), "Dūru," possibly URU.UBARA(EZEN×KASKAL), "Udannu" (photo not clear); with regard to the two towns, see Beaulieu, Orientalia NS 61 (1992) pp. 400–24.

iii 35′ IGI.II(*): text has URU.

iii 54′ von Weiher (SbTU 3 p. 10) tentatively suggests UD *me-lul*$^{?!}$*-ti* ("the festival day of cultic games").

iii 55′ *de*(*): text has KE.

6′) [...] ^{d}30
7′) [...]-⸢*ki*⸣-*ma*
8′) [... *ina*(?)] ⸢*at*(?)-*ma*⸣-*ni*
9′) [...]-*ma*
10′) [...]-*ti-šá*
11′) [...] x-*ma*
12′) [... TI]N.TIR.KI
13′) [... *ú*(?)-*ki*(?)]-*in-šu-nu-ti*
14′) [...]-*lu-ti*
15′) [...] TIN.TIR.KI
16′) [...] x ⸢LUL⸣ AM MA
17′) [...] ⸢*ik*⸣-*mi-su*
18′) [...] ⸢*ul*⸣-*te-eb*
19′) [...] x ⸢*lu*⸣-*uš-pur*
20′) [...] EN GAL-*ú* ^{d}AMAR.UTU
21′) [...] ⸢ZI(?) KA(?)⸣ *ik-kel-mu-ma*
22′) [...]-⸢*nu*(?) *ú*⸣-*šat-bu-niš-šum-ma*
23′) [...] ⸢É(?)-*ti*⸣-*šú iš-lul*
24′) [...] x ⸢DI(?) *mul*⸣-*taḫ-ṭi-šú*
25′) [...] *in-né-sír-ma*
26′) [...] *mun-nab-tu*
27′) [...] *i-tu-*⸢*ram*(?)⸣-*ma*
28′) [...] KUR *ak-ka-di-i*
29′) [... -*m*]*a*(?) *iq-li*
30′) [...].⸢KI⸣ x [(x)].⸢KI⸣ [(x)] *bár-sipa*.KI
31′) [...] (x) x ⸢KI(?)⸣ *dil-bat*.KI *ù* GÚ.DA.KI
32′) [...]-⸢*šu* UGU(?)⸣-*šú ana a-lik pa-na*
33′) [...]-⸢*di*(?)⸣-*šu-un i-maš-šá-ʾ bu-šá-šú-un*
34′) [...] x-*ak-ki il-lik-ma*
35′) [...] x x DÙ LÚ.GAR.KUR *la-rak*
36′) [... *a-de*]-⸢*e*(?) *u ma*⸣-*mit-šú ina* DINGIR.MEŠ GAL.MEŠ EN 7-*šú*
37′) [...] x-*ma iṣ-ba-tu it-ti-šú*
38′) [...] x ⸢LÚ.MEŠ UR$_5$(?).MEŠ⸣ *ina ba-lu ḫi-ṭi*
39′) [...] x-⸢*ri*⸣-*ia ú-ṣa-bit*(?)-*ma*
40′) [...] x x x *ú-bil-šú-nu-ti-ma*
41′) [... *ina*(?) *ṣ*]*e*(?)-⸢*e*(?)⸣-*ri ú-še-šib-šú-nu-ti*
42′) [...] ⸢A⸣ x *a-na me-e mar-ru-ti*
43′) [...] x *šu-nu-ti*
44′) [...] x *ik-šu-dam-ma* ^{d}AG *šá ana pa-an*
45′) [...] x *ina* TIN.TIR.KI *ik-la*
46′) [...] x x MA IR SI(?) KUR LA
47′) [x (x)] ⸢ŠI⸣ x x [x x (x)] x BU *ú-še-piš-ma*
48′) [x (x)] x [...] *u* ^{d}AG ⸢IBILA⸣ *ṣi-ra*
49′) [...] ⸢*iš*(?)⸣-*lul-šú iq-bu-ú*
50′) [...] x
51′) [...]
52′) [...]-*ki-šú*
53′) [...]
54′) [...]
55′) [...] ⸢*ḫi-pí*⸣
Edge
1) [... M]U(?).MEŠ ḪI

iv 6′–7′) [...] the god Sîn [...]
iv 8′–9′) [... *in*] *the shrine* [...]
iv 10′–11′) [...] ... [...] ...
iv 12′–13′) [... Bab]ylon [... *he estab*]*lished* them.
iv 14′–15′) [...] ... [...] Babylon
iv 16′–17′) [...] ... [... *that*] he had gathered
iv 18′–19′) [...] ... [...] let me send.
iv 20′–21′) [...] the great lord, the god Marduk [...] ... glared;
iv 22′–23′) [...] ... they removed him and [...] he plundered [...] *of* his *house*.
iv 24′–25′) [...] ... his/its survivor(s) [...] he was confined;
iv 26′–27′) [...] the fugitive [...] he turned back;
iv 28′–29′) [...] the land of Akkad [...] he burned.
iv 30′–31′) [...] ... Borsippa [...] ... Dilbat and *Cutha*.
iv 32′–33′) [...] *against him for a leader* [...] their [...] he plunders their possessions.
iv 34′–35′) [...] ... he went and [...] ... the governor of Larak.
iv 36′–37′) [... *the treat*]*y* and oath (sworn by the names of) the great gods, seven times [...] ... and they seized with him.
iv 38′–39′) [...] *these* men ... without (any) transgression [...] ... he *seized*;
iv 40′–41′) [...] ... he took them and [...] settled them [*in the ste*]*ppe*.
iv 42′–43′) [...] ... *to* the bitter water [...] them.
iv 44′–45′) [...] he reached and the god Nabû, who before [...] he held back in Babylon.
iv 46′–47′) [...] ... [...] ... he had made;
iv 48′–49′) [...] and the god Nabû, the august heir [...] *he plundered it, they said*.
iv 50′–51′) [...]
iv 52′–53′) [...] ... [...]
iv 54′–55′) [...] ...
Edge
1) [...] ...

Edge 1 Possibly *ḫi*-<*pí*>.

2001

An Akkadian inscription of Nabû-šuma-imbi, a governor of Borsippa, is found on a damaged clay cylinder. The inscription records the restoration of a storehouse in the Ezida complex at Borsippa by the governor for the god Nabû and describes turmoil in the city during the reign of Nabû-šuma-iškun.

COMMENTARY

The cylinder (BM 33428; Rm 3,105) measures 18×6.7 cm. The main piece comes from a shipment of material from Rassam's excavations in Babylonia sent to the British Museum in 1879. A cylinder fragment from a shipment sent by Rassam in 1880 (registration lot 80-11-12) was apparently joined to the main piece before they were registered. One of the pieces, presumably the one received later, is marked as having come from Birs Nimrud (Borsippa); it may have been found in the Nabû temple there (see Reade, Iraq 48 [1986] p. 109). The cylinder is solid and inscribed in two columns. The inscription has been collated and the edition presented here basically follows that of Lambert in JAOS 88.

The inscription was likely composed during the reign of Nabû-šuma-iškun or shortly thereafter since it refers to events "during the reign of king Nabû-šuma-iškun" (i 17′). However, since the text ends with the statement that it was an "inscription dealing with the storehouse, from the enclosure wall of Ezida," it is possible that the cylinder was "copied from the wall by some one with antiquarian interest under the Late Babylonian empire," as noted by Lambert in JAOS 88 (1968) p. 125. The frequent use of *-mi* for *-ma* (e.g., ii 7) points to a late date for the copy. The author of the inscription, Nabû-šuma-imbi, son of Ēda-ēṭir, is also mentioned as governor of Borsippa in a kudurru from the eighth year of the king's reign (Messerschmidt and Ungnad, VAS 1 no. 36 iii 6–7).

BIBLIOGRAPHY

1892 Strong, JRAS pp. 350–68 (copy in type, edition)
1895 Winckler, AOF 1/3 pp. 254–63 (edition)
1915 Weidner, MVAG 20/4 pp. 103–105 (study)
1918 Meissner, OLZ 21 220–21 (study)
1965 Landsberger, Brief p. 58 n. 110 (study)
1968 Brinkman, PKB pp. 225–26 and 356 no. 32.2.3 (study)
1968 Lambert, JAOS 88 pp. 123–30 (edition)
1986 Reade, Iraq 48 pp. 108–109 (provenance)
1986 Reade in Leichty, Sippar 1 p. xxix (provenance)

TEXT

Col. i

1) [...] (x)-*ni-šu* IDIM *šar-ḫi* ^{d}*mu-du*$_{10}$*-ga-sa*$_{4}$*-a šá-qí-i e-tel-*⸢*li*⸣
2) [x x] ^{d}*nin-sig*$_{5}$*-ga ka-nu-ut* ^{d}INANNA.MEŠ *be-let da-ad-mi šá-ga-pu-ur-ti i-lat* [*p*]*aṭ gim-ri*
3) [^{d}*ut*]-*u*$_{18}$*-lu* EN *gaš-ri šá i-na ma-ḫar* DINGIR.MEŠ *kal-šú-nu il-la-ka ḫar-*⸢*ra*⸣*-ni*
4) [x x] DINGIR.MEŠ *gít-ma-*⸢*li*⸣ *šu-pu-ú na-ram* ^{d}*nin-ši-kù*
5) [x x *n*]*é-me-qí ù ši-tul-ti muš-ta-bi-li te-re-e-ti*
6) [x x (x)] x LUGAL-*ú-ti mu-ma-ʾ-ir gim-ri na-din* GIŠ.GIDRU GIŠ.GU.ZA *u* BALA-*e a-ge-e* ⸢LUGAL⸣-*ú-ti*
7) [x x (x)] x ^{d}*nu-nam-nir gít-ma-li* DUMU *kun-nu-ú i-lit-ti ru-bat* DINGIR.MEŠ ^{d}*e-ru-u*$_{8}$*-ú-a*
8) [x x (x)] x *é-sag-íl* EN *gim-ri šit-lu-ṭu na-ram* ^{d}AMAR.UTU

i 1–20) [For the god ...] ... venerable, splendid, the god Mudugasâ, exalted, sovereign, [*spouse of*] the goddess Ninsiga — (most) honoured of (all) goddesses, mistress of (all) the inhabited world, majestic, goddess of absolutely everything — the god [Ut]ulu, the powerful lord who marches in front of all the gods, perfect [...] of the gods, resplendent, beloved of the god Ninšiku (Ea), (i 5) [*endowed with*] wisdom and insight, who evaluates omens, [...] of kingship, the one who directs everything, who grants sceptre, throne, reign, (and) royal crown, perfect [*offspring*] of the god Nunamnir, honoured son, offspring of the princess of the gods, the goddess Erua, [...] of Esagila, lord of everything, victorious, beloved of the god Marduk, [... of the god As]ari, eldest son, foremost, the one who goes in

9) [x x ^{d}*as*]*ar-ri* IBILA *reš-tu-ú a-šá-rid a-lik maḫ-ri šá it-ti a-bi a-li-di-š*[*ú* ...] x x x x-*ti*
10) [x x x D]I.KUD DINGIR.MEŠ LUGAL DINGIR.MEŠ GAL.MEŠ *šá i-na ṣi-taš u šil-la-an šu-*[*pu-ú*(?) ...]
11) [x x DIN]GIR.MEŠ *ma-lik rama-ni-šú le-qu-ú un-né-ni še-mu-ú tés-li-ti rap-šú uz-*[*ni* ...]
12) [*ša a-na u*]*r-ti-šú ka-bit-ti* ^{d}*í-gì-gì ap-pi i-lab-bi-nu-šú* ^{d}*a-nun-na-ki* x [...]
13) [...] ME.⸢LÁM⸣ KÙ.MEŠ *ḫa-lip na-mur-ra-ti šá pul-ḫa-a-ti ma-lu-*[*ú* ...]
14) [...-*š*]*u*(?) *i-šak-ka-nu šip-ṭu u* ^{d}IMIN.BI *la i-šak-*[...]
15) [... *mu*(?)-*šal*(?)-*s*]*u-ú a-la-li ina qar-ba-a-ti mu-al-lid* AN x [...]
16) [...] x-*ti šá-ki-nu* ḪÉ.NUN *ṭuḫ-da u meš-re-e a-*[*na* ...]
17) [...] x x [x] x x DINGIR.MEŠ GAL.ME[Š ...]
18) [...] (x) *ú-šam-mi-ḫi ú-*[...]
19) [...] x *la iš-šá-an-na-*⸢*ni*⸣ x [...]
20) [...] TI MA x x x [...]

front, the one who [...] with the father who begat him ... (i 10) [...] judge of the gods, king of the great gods, the one who *is res*[*plendent*] in the east and in the west, [... of the go]ds, his own counsellor, the one who accepts entreaties (and) hearkens to supplications, one who has broad under[standing, ..., the one to whose] venerable command the Igīgū gods submit themselves humbly (and) the Anunnakū gods [... *clad in*] a holy awe-inspiring sheen, garbed in terrifying splendour, filled with fearfulness, [...] established judgment and the Sibitti gods do not [... (i 15) ..., *the one who has*] work songs [*su*]*ng* in the land, the one who begot ... [...] ... who establishes plenty, abundance, and wealth for [...]... the great gods [...] who makes prosper [...] is not equalled [...] ... [...]

Lacuna (about 20 lines missing)

1′) x x x [...]
2′) ⸢*šu*⸣-*te-šur ni-š*[*e*(?) ...]
3′) *a-na* BÀD.SI.AB.B[A ...]
4′) *i-šad-di-ḫi ú-ru-u*[*ḫ* ...]
5′) [*á*]*š-ruk-ka-ti šu-a-ti* x(*) [...]
6′) *ú-raš ta-na-da-a-ti* SI/ḪAB(*) MA(*) [...]
7′) *šá áš-ruk-ka-ti šu-a-ti*(*) *i*(*)-*na*(*) x(*) [...]
8′) ⸢*i*⸣-*qu-pu-ú-mi i-ni-šu* ⸢*il*⸣-[...] EN [...]
9′) *šá ul-tu* u_4-*mi pa-ni ul-tu ul-la-nu-*⸢*ú*(?)⸣-*a* LÚ.GAR.UŠ$_4$ LÚ *qí-pi* B[ÀD(?).SI.AB.BA]
10′) *la i-pu-šu šip-ri šu-a-ti ia-a-ši* ^{md}AG-MU-*im-bi* DUMU ^{m}AŠ-⸢SUR⸣
11′) LÚ *né-šak-ki* LU.KU$_4$.É ^{d}AG LÚ.GAR.UŠ$_4$ *bár-sipa*.KI *du-uš-mu-ú pa-liḫ* DINGIR-*ú-ti-šú*
12′) *ra-bi-ti na-an-za-az maḫ-ri-šu re-du-ú mut-nen-nu-ú*
13′) ⸢*šá*⸣ *a-na pa-ra-aṣ* ^{d}AG EN KUR.KUR EN *i-lì pu-tuq-qu sa-an-tak*
14′) *šip-ri šá-a-ši ú-qa-a-a-an-ni-mi ú-šad-gil pa-ni-ia*

Lacuna

i 1′–15′a) ... [...] to administer the people correctly [...] to Borsippa [...] he proceeds along the road [...] (i 5′) this storehouse [...] a praiseworthy *structure* ... [...] of this storehouse in [... which] had buckled and become weak [...] ... [...] which from time immemorial, from long before me, no governor (or) commissioner of B[orsippa] (i 10′) had done, he charged me with this work and entrusted (it) to me — me, Nabû-šuma-imbi, son of Ēda-ē[ṭir], *nešakku*-official, one privileged to enter the temple of the god Nabû, governor of Borsippa, slave who reveres his great godhead (and) stands in service before him, prayerful soldier who constantly pays attention to the cult of the god Nabû, lord of the lands (and) lord of the gods. I began that work and ordered that it be done.

15′) *šip-ri šá-a-ši ú-šar-ri-i-mi e-pe-šú aq-bi iš-šá-ak-na-a-mi*
16′) *i-na bár-sipa*.KI URU *kit-ti ù mi-šá-ri e-šá-a-ti dal-ḫa-a-ti si-ḫi*
17′) *ù saḫ-ma-šá-a-ti i-na* BALA-*e* ^{d}AG-MU-*iš-kun* LUGAL DUMU ^{m}*da-ku-ri*
18′) LÚ.TIN.TIR.KI.MEŠ LÚ.BÁRA.SIPA.KI.MEŠ URU *du-te-e-ti* GÚ ÍD.BURANUN.KI
19′) *gab-bi* URU *kal-di* LÚ *a-ra-mi* LÚ.DIL.BAD.KI.MEŠ UD.MEŠ *ma-ʾ-du-ú-ti*
20′) *a-na lìb-bi a-ḫa-meš* GIŠ.TUKUL-*šú-nu i-še-el-li a-ḫa-meš ú-ra-sa-a-pu*
21′) ⸢*ù*⸣ *it-ti* LÚ.BÁRA.SIPA.⸢KI⸣.MEŠ *i-na* UGU A.ŠÀ.MEŠ-*šú-nu ip-pu-šú ṣu-la-a-ti*

i 15′b–21′) Disorders, disturbances, revolt, and turmoil occurred in Borsippa, the city of truth and justice. During the reign of king Nabû-šuma-iškun, the Dakkurian, the Babylonians, the Borsippians, (the people of) the town Dutēti (which is on) the bank of the Euphrates, all the Chaldeans, Arameans, (and) the people of Dilbat *sharpened* their weapons for many days (to fight) with one another (and) slew one another. Moreover, they fought with the Borsippians over their fields.

i 5′–7′ The signs marked with an asterisk were copied by Strong but are no longer preserved.

22′) [x (x)] x x x ^{md}AG-MU-SUM.NA DUMU ^{m}KAL-^{d}AG LÚ.KU$_4$.É ^{d}AG LÚ.ŠÀ.TAM *é-zi-da*

23′) [x x x] x x x ⸢*i*⸣-*na* ⸢*rama*⸣-*ni-šú i-na* UGU ^{md}AG-MU-*im-bi* DUMU ^{m}AŠ-SUR LÚ.GAR.UŠ$_4$ *bár-sipa*.KI *iš-kun*

Col. ii

1) *i-na šat mu-ši ki-ma šar-ra-qí-iš nak-ri a-ḫa* LÚ *ḫa-*[*al-qu-ti*(?) ...]

2) *za-ma-nu-ú lem-nu-ú-ti su-ku-ku-ú-ti la še-mi-ia-ma eg-*[*ru-ti*(?) ...]

3) *a-na é-zi-da ú-tir-mi é-zi-da ù bár-sipa*.K[I ...]

4) *iṣ-ba-tu-mi* UGU URU *ù é-kur ri-ig-mi ù ši-s*[*i-ti*]

5) *iš-kun-ú-mi ip-pu-šú ṣu-la-a-ti ù* É ^{md}AG-MU-[*im-bi* DUMU ^{m}AŠ-SUR]

6) LÚ.GAR.UŠ$_4$ *bár-sipa*.KI *i-na mu-ši-šú-mi* LÚ.BÁR.SIPA.KI.MEŠ *u* LÚ.(x) [...]

7) *šá a-na re-ṣu-ut a-ḫa-meš iz-zi-zu il-mu-ú-mi ina til-pa-na u* ⸢GIŠ⸣ (x) [... *ul-tu li-la-a-ti*]

8) *a-di na-pa-ḫi* ^{d}UTU-*ši ip-pu-šú ta-nu-qa-a-ti ul-tu li-l*[*a-a-ti*]

9) *a-di na-pa-ḫi* ^{d}UTU-*ši* ^{md}AG-MU-*im-bi* DUMU ^{m}AŠ-SUR LÚ.GAR.UŠ$_4$ *bár-s*[*ipa*.KI ...]

10) [...] x-*ti ú-ṣal-li* ^{d}AG x x x-*ú-a ia-ʾ-nu* [...]

11) [...] x x x ⸢BA⸣ x [x x] x [...]

Lacuna (about 30 lines missing)

1′) [...] x-*šú-nu* x [...]

2′) [...]

3′) [...] x x x [x x] x *iṣ-ru-pu* x x [...]

4′) [...] x-*si nu-uḫ-ši* ⸢*ù a-na*⸣ x [...]

5′) [...] x Ú x-*ra-a-nu áš-ruk-k*[*a-ti* ...]

6′) [... ^{m}]^{d}AG-MU-*im*-⸢*bi*⸣ DUMU ^{m}AŠ-SUR LÚ.GAR.UŠ$_4$ [*bár-sipa*.KI]

7′) [... *p*]*a-li-ḫi-šú* ⸢*na*⸣-*an-za-az ma*[*ḫ-ri-šú* ...]

8′) [... DINGIR-*ú*]-*ti-šú ra-bi-ti liq-bu*-⸢*ú*⸣ [...]

9′) [...] x *lim-gur sa-li-mi* SIG$_5$ x [...]

10′) [*a-na ši-rik-ti liš*]-*ruk-šú ù a-na qiš-ti* [*li-qis-su* ...]

11′) [...] x MEŠ ^{d}*be-let* ^{d}IŠ.TAR.MEŠ [...]

12′) [...] AN *il-ti reme-né-ti ba-na-*[*at* ...]

13′) [...] x *mit-gu-rat a-mat-si ṣi-i*[*t pi-i-šá*]

14′) [*la ut-tak-ka-ru l*]*a in-nen-nu-ú qí-bi*[*t-si* ...]

15′) ⸢*i-na ma-ḫar*⸣ [x x x] x *pa-ri-is* EŠ.BAR AN-*e* ⸢*ù*⸣ [KI-*tim* ...]

16′) DUMU ^{d}*en-lí*[*l* DINGIR.MEŠ] ⸢*u$_4$*⸣-*mi-šam lit-tas-qar a-bu-*[*ti* ...]

17′) *lu-ú-uṣ-ṣib* [x x x x] ⸢*u$_4$*(?)-*mi*(?)⸣.MEŠ SÙ.MEŠ MU.[MEŠ ...]

18′) *ba-laṭ na-mar* [...] ⸢*a-na ši-rik*⸣-*t*[*i* ...]

19′) NUNUZ *lu-ú* [x x x (x) *na-a*]*n*-⸢*na-bu*⸣ x [...]

20′) *i-na* É.GAL [x x x (x)] x *lu mit-gu*-⸢*rat a-mat*⸣-*si* x [...]

21′) *it-ti é-z*[*i-da*] ⸢*ù*⸣ *bár-sipa*.KI *li-ku-un re*-⸢*é*⸣-[*us-su* ...]

22′) *li-ṭi-ib* [*at-m*]*u-šú* UGU LUGAL DINGIR.MEŠ EN EN.EN *tal-lak-t*[*i* ... *é-zi-da*]

23′) *ù bár-sip*[*a*.KI *i*]-*na ma-ḫar* ^{d}AG *u* ^{d}*na-na-a* DINGIR.MEŠ *šur-bu-t*[*i* ...]

i 22′–ii 11) [...] ... Nabû-šuma-iddin, son of Aqar-Nabû, one privileged to enter the temple of the god Nabû, the chief administrator of Ezida [...]... by himself he set *against/concerning* Nabû-šuma-imbi, son of Ēda-ēṭir, governor of Borsippa. (ii i) By night, like thieves, the enemy, the foreigner, *fug*[*itives*, ...], wicked enemies, with stopped ears, who would not listen to me, *per*[*verse*, (...)] I returned [...] to Ezida, and Ezida and Borsippa [...] they seized and set up a hue and cr[y] over the city and temple, (ii 5) as they fought. On this night, the Borsippians and the people of [...], who were present to help one another, surrounded the house of Nabû-šuma-[imbi, son of Ēda-ēṭir], governor of Borsippa and with arrows and [... From evening] until sunrise they raised battle-crys. From eve[ning] until sunrise Nabû-šuma-imbi, son of Ēda-ēṭir, governor of Bors[ippa ...]... prayed, "Nabû, my ... are no more!" [...] ... [...]

Lacuna

ii 1′–10′a) [...] their [...] ... [...] burnt [...] plenty, and to [... (ii 5′) ...] ... the storehouse [...] Nabû-šuma-imbi, son of Ēda-ēṭir, governor [of Borsippa ...] who reveres him (and) stands in service bef[ore him ...] his great [godhead], let them speak [...] let him agree! [Let him be]stow on him [as a gift] and [grant him] as a present peace (and) good [...]!

ii 10′b–20′) [May the goddess Nanāia], ... mistress of (all) the goddesses [...], the compassionate goddess, creat[or of ...], whose word is favourable, [whose] utte[rance cannot be changed, whose] command cannot be altered [...], intercede [for me] daily (ii 15′) in the presence of [the god Nabû] ... who makes decisions for heaven and [netherworld ...], the son of the Enlil [of the gods (Marduk)]! May I increase [(*my*) *good fortune*]! [...] distant days, year[s ...], life of shining [...] as a gift [...] offspring, may [...] progeny [...] in the palace [...] may her word be favourable! [...]

ii 21′–32′) May [his position as] shepherd be confirmed with (regard to) Ez[ida and] Borsippa! [...] May his [words] be pleasing unto the king of the gods, the lord of lords! [...] way [... Ezida] and Borsippa in the presence of the god Nabû and the goddess Nanāia, the supreme gods [...] May he

ii 17′ For the tentative restoration "(*my*) *good fortune*," see B.6.22.3 ii 21.

24′) *liš-ba-a lit-t[u-tu] i-na šá-áš-mi qab-li* MÈ *dan-nu ù a-lak* [EDIN ...]

25′) *šá-a-ši* NUNUZ-*š*[*ú* x (x)] x x-*šú re-ṣu-us-si a-la-ki šum-qut* x [...]

26′) ḪÉ.NUN MA x [x (x)] ⌈ḪÉ⌉.GÁL *ma-ʾ-da li-ma-al-la-a* ŠU.II-*šú i-n*[*a* ...]

27′) *ù i-na* [x] x ⌈^{d}⌉*èr-ra šal-ba-bi* DUMU ^{d}*en-líl ra-a-mi ga-á*[*š*(?)-*ru*(?) ...]

28′) *pat-ri* ⌈*šib*⌉-[*ṭi*] *la* TE-*šú šá-lim-ti lu šá-ak-na-si a-a-bi-šú lem-nu-*⌈*ú*⌉-[*ti* ...]

29′) *bul-l*[*a-šu*]*n*(?) *ki-ma la-ʾ-mi* DINGIR-*ú-ti-ku-nu ù nar-bi-k*[*u-nu lid-lul*]

30′) *a-na* [U]N.MEŠ *dar-ka-a-ti at-ta-mi* EN *lu tuk-la-šu* NAB [...]

31′) *i-bi šu-uš-šú a-na* u_4*-mi da-ru-ú-ti ta-nit-ti-*[*ku-nu* ...]

32′) *ik-ri-bi u ṣu-le-e šá* ^{md}AG-MU-*im-bi* LÚ.GAR.UŠ$_4$ *bár-sipa*.KI ^{d}A[G ...]

33′) MU.SAR *šá áš-ruk-ka-ti šá du-ru é-zi-da*

experience the fullness of old [age]! In strife, war, fierce battle, and camp[aigning, ...] (ii 25′) he, [his] offspring, his [...] to go to his aid, to overthrow [...] may he fill his hands with plenty [... (and)] great abundance! At [...] and at ... of the god Erra, the raging one, beloved son of the god Enlil, *the pow*[*erful* ...] May dagger (and) pla[gue] never draw near him! May peace be established for *him*! [...] to extinguish his wicked enemies like embers! [May he praise] your (Nabû and Nanāia's) godhead and [your] greatness (ii 30′) for (all) future generations! May you, lord, be his help [...] Call him [*so that he may sing* of your] fame for future days! O god Na[bû *accept*] the prayers and supplications of Nabû-šuma-imbi, governor of Borsippa!

ii 33′) Inscription dealing with the storehouse, from the enclosure wall of Ezida.

Nabû-nāṣir

B.6.15

There is no evidence to indicate if Nabû-nāṣir (often referred to as Nabonassar after the Greek form of the name) was or was not related to the previous king, Nabû-šuma-iškun. His reign lasted for fourteen years (747–734 BC) and with it a new era commenced in Babylonia. He is the first person mentioned in the list of kings of Babylonia generally attributed to Claudius Ptolemaeus (the "Ptolemaic Canon") and the Babylonian Chronicle begins with him. Economic documents start to increase in number with his reign and, according to a Hellenistic tradition, the accurate recording of the movement of the stars began in the time of this king. His reign, however, was overshadowed by that of Tiglath-pileser III, who ascended the throne of Assyria in 745 BC and reigned until 727 BC. In 745 BC Tiglath-pileser campaigned extensively in Babylonia, but his actions seem to have been directed mainly against the Aramean and Chaldean tribes rather than against the Babylonian government itself. Although there is no evidence that the Assyrian king tried to depose Nabû-nāṣir, he did at one point claim sovereignty over Babylonia by taking the title "king of Sumer and Akkad." In the following years, Tiglath-pileser made several campaigns into border regions which had earlier belonged to Babylonia. Around 745 BC there were hostilities between the cities of Babylon and Borsippa, and Nabû-nāṣir is reported to have campaigned against Borsippa. In 734 the Babylonian king took ill and died in his palace. He was succeeded by his son Nabû-nādin-zēri. (See Grayson, Chronicles pp. 70–72 no. 1 i 1–13.)

No inscriptions of Nabû-nāṣir himself are attested, but three copies of an Akkadian inscription of two individuals from Uruk recording their restoration of the Akītu temple in the king's fifth year are known (B.6.15.2001). At least 22 economic texts have also been preserved which are dated by the regnal years of Nabû-nāṣir (see Brinkman and Kennedy, JCS 35 [1983] pp. 63–66 no. AF); this is the largest number known from any reign since that of Kaštiliašu IV in the thirteenth century. For details of the reign of Nabû-nāṣir, see Brinkman, PKB pp. 60, 226–34, and 356–57 no. 33.

2001

An Akkadian inscription on three clay cylinders describes the restoration of the temple for the New Year's festival at Uruk for the goddess Uṣur-amāssu by two individuals, namely Bēl-ibni and Nabû-zēra-ušabši, sons of Bulluṭu. The text was composed in the fifth year of Nabû-nāṣir (743 BC).

CATALOGUE

Ex.	Museum number	Registration number	Dimensions (cm)	Lines preserved	cpn
1	NBC 2502	—	Length: 8.3; Dia. at end: 2.3; Dia. at centre: 4.1	1–25	c
2	YBC 2170	—	Length: 7.8; Dia. at end: 2.3; Dia. at centre: 4.0	1–8, 12–25	c
3	BM 113205	1915-4-10,3	Length: 9.9; Dia. at ends: 2.2	1–24	c

COMMENTARY

All three exemplars were purchased (ex. 3 from J.E. Gejou of Paris) and thus their original provenance is not known. However, since the inscription deals with a temple at Uruk, it is probable that they come from that site. The colophon (lines 21–25) is found on the left edge of all exemplars. The script is contemporary Babylonian and the line arrangement is the same for all exemplars. The master line follows ex. 1, with help from ex. 3 in lines 1–10 and 20.

BIBLIOGRAPHY

1920 Keiser, BIN 2 no. 31 (ex. 1, copy; exs. 1–2, edition)

1922 Ungnad, OLZ 25 70 (exs. 1–2, study)

1937 Stephens, YOS 9 no. 74 (ex. 2, copy)

1940 Oppenheim, Orientalia NS 9 pp. 27–28 (ex. 1, study to line 3)

1968 Brinkman, PKB pp. 233 and 356–57 no. 33.2.3 (exs. 1–3, study)

1969–70 Brinkman, WO 5 pp. 39–50 (exs. 1–3, edition, study)

TEXT

1) *a-na* ^{d}ÙRU-*a-mat-su* GAŠAN *ṣir-ti da-i-na-at di-ni ma-a-ti*
2) *pa-ri-sa-at* EŠ.BAR AN-*e ù er-ṣe-ti bu-uk-rat* ^{d}IŠKUR
3) *na-ár-mat* ^{d}AMAR.UTU *šá la in*$_{5}$(NIN)-*né-nu-ú qí-bi-is-su*

1–3) For the goddess Uṣur-amāssu, august lady, who renders judgment for the land, who makes decision(s) for heaven and netherworld, daughter of the god Adad, beloved of the god Marduk, the one whose command cannot be revoked:

4) *a-ki-ti šá ul-tu u*$_{4}$-*mu ru-qu-tu la-ba-riš il-lik-ma*
5) *šu-uš-šu im-ma-šu-ma sa-ra-ḫi-iš uš-bu*
6) *i-ga-ru-šú i-qu-pu-ma qup-pu-ʾ uš-šá-šu-un*
7) *ú-ṣu-ra-tu-šú im-ma-šá-a-ma iš-nu-ú ši-kin-ši-in*
8) LUGAL LÚ *qí-pu* LÚ *ru-bu-ú ù* LÚ.EN URU
9) *a-na e-peš šip-ru šu-a-ti ù ud-dúš a-ki-ti ú-zu-šú la iš-kun-nu-ma*

4–9) With regard to the Akītu (temple), which long ago had become old, whose name had been forgotten, and which (now) stood in ruins, its walls had buckled and their foundations collapsed. Its ground-plan had been forgotten and its (the ground-plan's) shape had changed. No king (or) commissioner (or) prince or city ruler had turned his attention to do this work and to renovate the Akītu (temple).

10) *ár-ka-na* ^{md}EN-*ib-ni ù* ^{md}AG-NUMUN-GÁL-*ši* DUMU.MEŠ *šá* ^{m}*bul-lu-ṭu* UNU[G].⌈KI-*ú*⌉
11) *a-na e-peš šip-ru šu-a-ti ù ud-dúš a-ki-ti ú-zu-šú-nu iš-kun-nu-ma*
12) *al-la ù tup-šik-ki ina gi-mir lìb-bi-šú-nu in-na-šu-ma*
13) *maš-tak la-le-e el-lu-tu a-na* ^{d}*iš-tar ú-še-pi-iš*

10–13) Finally, Bēl-ibni and Nabû-zēra-ušabši, sons of Bulluṭu of Uruk, turned their attention to do this work and to renovate the Akītu (temple). Hoe and basket were taken up by them wholeheartedly and *they* had an abode of pure riches built for the goddess.

14) *ina šat-ti* ^{d}ÙRU-*a-mat-su* GAŠAN *ṣir-ti a-na a-ki-ti* É-*šá ḫa-diš ina e-re-bi-šá*
15) *ù ina šu-bat* DINGIR-*ti-šá* GAL-*ti šá-qí-iš i-na a-šá-bi-šá*

14–17a) On account of this, when the goddess Uṣur-amāssu, the august lady, enters with pleasure into her Akītu (temple) and when she sits on high in the abode of her great divinity, may she duly turn her

16) UGU ^{md}EN-*ib-ni ù* ^{md}AG-NUMUN-GÁL-*ši bu-ni-šá nam-ru-tú ki-niš lit-ru-uṣ-ma*
17) *li-ir-ri-ki* u_4*-mi-šú-nu a-na* GÍD.DA u_4*-mi-šú-nu* TI.LA *nap-šá-ti-šú-nu*
18) *šá-la-ma* NUMUN-*šú-nu la ba-še-e* GIG-*šú-nu a-ki-ti eš-šiš ú-še-piš*
19) MU 5.KAM ^{d}AG-ÙRU-*ir* LUGAL KÁ.DINGIR.RA.KI
20) *ina* GUB *šá* ^{md}AG-GIN-NUMUN DUMU ^{md}AG-NUN.ME-DINGIR.MEŠ GÌR.NÍTA KUR.UG.UD.KI

Colophon on exs. 1–2
21) GIŠ ^{md}AG-*na-ʾ-id*
22) DUMU ^{m}*nad-na-a*
23) LÚ.GALA
24) ^{d}INANNA UNUG.KI
25) *ú-šá-bal-kit*

Colophon on ex. 3
21) *šá* ^{m}ÌR-^{d}*na-na-a*
22) DUMU ^{m}AN.NAM(?)-*ú-a*
23) LÚ.É.BAR UNUG.KI
24) *ú-šá-pu-ú*

shining countenance upon Bēl-ibni and Nabû-zēra-ušabši and may she lengthen their days!
17b–18) They had the Akītu (temple) built anew in order to prolong their days, to ensure their good health (and) the well-being of their offspring, (and) to ensure they not become ill.
19) Fifth year of Nabû-nāṣir, king of Babylon.

20) In the presence of Nabû-mukīn-zēri, son of Nabû-apkal-ilī, viceroy of ...

Colophon on exs. 1–2
21-25) The hand of Nabû-naʾid, son of Nadnāia, lamentation-priest of the goddess Ištar of Uruk, copied (this).

Colophon on ex. 3
21-24) (Document) which Arad-Nanāia, son of *Annamua*, the *šangû*-priest of Uruk, *made public*.

22.3 The reading of the name ^{m}AN.NAM(?)-*ú-a* is uncertain. As noted by Brinkman (WO 5 [1969–70] p. 47), one might expect ^{md}DN-KUR-*ú-a* ("DN is My Mountain"). Could it be MEŠ instead of NAM, with the additional traces being striations in the clay? The resulting name Ilūʾā would mean "My god"; with regard to DINGIR.MEŠ being used to refer to a singular deity, see Beaulieu, JNES 52 (1993) p. 254 n. 38.
24.3 The verb *ú-šá-pu-ú* basically means "he made appear/made visible/proclaimed."

Nabû-nādin-zēri

B.6.16

Nabû-nādin-zēri, whose name was sometimes abbreviated to Nādin(u), was the son and successor of Nabû-nāṣir. Basically nothing is known of his reign except that it lasted for two years (733–732 BC) and that it ended when he was deposed in a rebellion led by a provincial official (*bēl pīḫati*) by the name of Nabû-šuma-ukīn, who himself seized the throne. No inscriptions are known from the reign of Nabû-nādin-zēri. With regard to his reign, see Brinkman, PKB pp. 60, 234–35, and 357 no. 34.

Nabû-šuma-ukīn II

B.6.17

According to Babylonian King List A, Nabû-šuma-ukīn II was the son of Nabû-nādin-zēri; however, the Babylonian Chronicle does not mention this although it regularly noted such matters. Since Nabû-šuma-ukīn assumed the throne by deposing Nabû-nādin-zēri in a rebellion, it is unlikely that the two were father and son. The new king reigned for a little over one month, in 732 BC, before he was deposed by Nabû-mukīn-zēri. No texts from the reign of Nabû-šuma-ukīn II are attested. With regard to his reign, see Brinkman, PKB pp. 60, 235, and 357–58 no. 35.

Nabû-mukīn-zēri

B.6.18

Nabû-šuma-ukīn II was soon deposed by Nabû-mukīn-zēri, the leader of the Chaldean tribe of Bīt-Amukāni. Nabû-mukīn-zēri (whose name was generally abbreviated to Mukīn-zēri) was credited with a reign of three years (731–729 BC) and, according to Babylonian King List A, came from the dynasty of *šá-pi-i*, which probably refers to his tribal capital of Šapīia. Nabû-mukīn-zēri was deposed by the Assyrian king Tiglath-pileser III in 729 BC, but he seems to have maintained some control over parts of southern Babylonia for another one or two years. The Assyrian king had campaigned against Šapīia in 731 BC, but it was only in 729 BC that he defeated Nabû-mukīn-zēri's forces, devastated the area of the Bīt-Amukāni, and ascended the throne of Babylonia. Not all Babylonians had supported Nabû-mukīn-zēri in opposing the Assyrians; some in fact appear to have actively aided the latter. No inscriptions of Nabû-mukīn-zēri are attested; the one economic text (Clay, BRM 1 no. 22) dated by the king's regnal years comes from his fourth year, thus probably from a part of the country which had not yet fallen to the Assyrians. Information on this reign comes primarily from the inscriptions of Tiglath-pileser III and various letters found at Nimrud and Nippur. For details on the reign of Nabû-mukīn-zēri, see Brinkman, PKB pp. 61, 235–40, and 358–59 no. 36, and S.W. Cole, Nippur in Late Assyrian Times, 750–612 B.C. (unpublished University of Chicago doctoral dissertation, 1990).

Tiglath-pileser III

B.6.19

Tiglath-pileser III (Tukultī-apil-Ešarra, also referred to as Pūlu, Phulos, etc.), who was king of Assyria for eighteen years (744–727 BC), reigned over Babylonia for the last two years of his life (728–727 BC). After defeating Nabû-mukīn-zēri, and various Chaldean and Aramean tribes, Tiglath-pileser took the hand of the god Marduk at the New Year's festival in 728 BC. He was the first Assyrian ruler to be acknowledged in Babylonian tradition as a king of Babylonia, although Tukultī-Ninurta I had earlier claimed the rulership of that land. Babylonian King List A and the Ptolemaic Canon include him in their rulers of Babylonia and a Babylonian chronicle states that after defeating Nabû-mukīn-zēri, he ascended the throne of Babylon and ruled in Akkad (Babylonia) for two years. (See Grayson, Chronicles, pp. 72–73 no. 1 i 19–26 and RLA 6/1–2 [1980] p. 93 iv 8′ and p. 101). No royal inscriptions of Tiglath-pileser are attested from Babylonia. Five economic texts are dated by his regnal years over Babylonia (three from his first year and two from his second year), including two composed at Babylon; not one of these, however, gives him the title "king of Babylon." For details on the reign of Tiglath-pileser III, see in particular Brinkman, PKB pp. 61–62, 240–43, and 359–60 no. 37; Brinkman and Kennedy, JCS 35 (1983) p. 65 no. AJ; and Leichty in Studies Reiner pp. 227–29.

Shalmaneser V

B.6.20

Shalmaneser V (Šulmānu-ašared, also referred to as Ulūlāia), the son and successor of Tiglath-pileser III, reigned over both Assyria and Babylonia for five years (726–722 BC). He was included by Babylonian King List A and the Ptolemaic Canon in their lists of rulers of Babylonia and a Babylonian chronicle states that he had ruled Akkad (Babylonia) for five years. (See Grayson, Chronicles p. 73 no. 1 i 27–30 and RLA 6/1–2 [1980] p. 93 iv 9′ and p. 101.) Almost nothing is known about events in Babylonia during his reign, although the later Assur Ostracon refers to the deportation of individuals from Bīt-Adini (located in southern Babylonia), likely part of the Chaldean Bīt-Dakkūri tribe. No inscriptions of the king are attested from Babylonia, but one economic text from Babylon is dated by his third year as "king." With regard to the reign of Shalmaneser V, see Brinkman, PKB pp. 62–63, 243–45, and 360 no. 38; and Brinkman and Kennedy, JCS 35 (1983) pp. 65–66 no. AK.

Marduk-apla-iddina II

B.6.21

Marduk-apla-iddina II (Merodach-baladan of the Bible) was leader of the Chaldean tribe of Bīt-Iakīn and a descendant of an earlier king of Babylonia, Erība-Marduk (B.6.13). King List A credits Marduk-apla-iddina with two separate reigns, one of twelve years (721–710 BC) and one of nine months (703). Around 729, he had paid tribute to the Assyrian king Tiglath-pileser III, who was besieging the town of Šāpīia in Bīt-Amūkāni. At that time, Assyrian texts described him as the "King of the Sealand." When there was trouble in Assyria at the death of Shalmaneser V, Marduk-apla-iddina II seized control of Babylonia from the Assyrian king and commenced his first reign over Babylonia as a whole. After an unsuccessful military attempt to deal with Babylonia and its Elamite allies in 720, Sargon II (king of Assyria 721–705 BC) occupied himself with matters elsewhere in his realm until 710 BC, when he again invaded Babylonia. Assyrian forces drove Marduk-apla-iddina from Babylon and back to Dūr-Iakīn, his tribal capital, which they besieged from 709 to 707 BC. Dūr-Iakīn fell and Marduk-apla-iddina fled to Elam. Sargon claimed the rulership of Babylonia for the remainder of his life (B.6.22). Soon after his successor Sennacherib (king of Assyria 704–681 BC) ascended the thrones of Assyria and Babylonia, there was a rebellion in Babylonia and Marduk-zākir-šumi II seized the throne (B.6.24). His reign was short-lived and he was replaced by Marduk-apla-iddina after only one month. Marduk-apla-iddina's second reign then commenced (B.6.25) and lasted for nine months before Sennacherib marched south and forced him to flee once more, this time to the marshes of the Sealand. In 700 BC, the Assyrian king sent forces to deal with him there and he fled to the town Nagītu, which was situated on an island, probably in the marshes in Elam. Nothing more is heard of Marduk-apla-iddina after this.

Inscriptions of Marduk-apla-iddina II record his restoration of the Eanna temple at Uruk (B.6.21.1–3). A cylinder seal bearing a votive inscription of a Marduk-apla-iddina is also likely to be assigned to him (B.6.21.4). In addition, an inscription of the governor of Kish mentions work by the king on the bridge over the Nār-Bānītu canal (B.6.21.2001). B.6.21.3 apparently comes from Marduk-apla-iddina's second reign and B.6.21.4 may have been composed before he became king, but they are presented here in order to keep all the inscriptions of this ruler in one place. Of these inscriptions three are written in Akkadian (B.6.21.1, B.6.21.4, and B.6.21.2001) and two in Sumerian (B.6.21.2–3). B.6.21.1 is found on a clay cylinder, B.6.21.4 is on a cylinder seal, and the remainder are on bricks.

In addition to the inscriptions listed above, note the existence of a stela from Uruk with a badly damaged inscription which has sometimes been attributed to Marduk-apla-iddina II; see Börker-Klähn, Bildstelen no. 258 and Becker, AUWE 6 no. 794. For a terracotta lion from Uruk which has an inscription mentioning an individual whose name ends in -apla-iddina, see Ziegler, Terrakotten no. 384; Ellis, RA 61 (1967) p. 51 n. 3; and Becker, AUWE 6 no. 1057. Both of these pieces are in Baghdad and neither inscription has ever been published.

Two kudurrus are preserved from the king's reign. One kudurru, dating to Marduk-apla-iddina's seventh year and composed at Babylon, records the king's grant of land to the governor of Babylon (Messerschmidt and Ungnad, VAS 1 no. 37), and the other, which is badly damaged, records the king's endowment of a temple (King, BBSt no. 35). Approximately thirty-five other legal and administrative texts also date to his reigns; see Brinkman and Kennedy, JCS 35 (1983) pp. 8–13 no. A, and Fales, SAAB 2 (1988) pp. 41–57. For details of the reign(s) of Marduk-apla-iddina II, see Brinkman, Studies Oppenheim pp. 6–53 and RLA 7/5–6 (1989) p. 375.

1

An Akkadian inscription written upon a clay cylinder found at Nimrud records the restoration of part of Eanna ("House of Heaven"), the temple of the goddess Ištar at Uruk, and in particular the restoration of the shrine of Ningizzida (a god of the netherworld) in that temple by Marduk-apla-iddina II. The inscription also describes how the god Marduk had become reconciled with his land after allowing it to remain under Assyrian (Subarian) control for a number of years and how he had chosen Marduk-apla-iddina to become ruler of Babylonia and to re-establish the independence of that land.

COMMENTARY

The cylinder ND 2090, now in the Iraq Museum (Baghdad), was found in 1952 at Nimrud in the rubbish fill in room ZT4 of the Northwest Palace. It is made up of three pieces and measures 15.7×7.6 cm. It has not been possible to examine the cylinder and the inscription is edited from the published copy, with some help from the published photograph (which shows only part of the inscription, c. lines 12–26).

Sargon II has left an inscription stating that he had work done on the Eanna temple at Uruk (B.6.22.3), which has a number of phrases also found in this text. Possibly the cylinder of Marduk-apla-iddina was found while work was being carried out for Sargon and it was taken to Assyria to serve as a model for Sargon's inscription.

As noted by K.R. Veenhof (apud Brinkman, Prelude p. 49 n. 230), line 34 contains a passage identical with Erra Epic v 35 (*bilassunu kabittu lišdudū ana qereb šuanna*, "May they drag their weighty tribute into Šuanna"); see Cagni, Erra p. 124.

BIBLIOGRAPHY

1952 Mallowan, ILN August 23 pp. 294–96 and fig. 4 (photo of one side, study)
1953 Gadd, Iraq 15 pp. 123–34 (copy, edition, study)
1954 Follet, Biblica 35 pp. 413–28 (edition, study)
1957 Lenzen, Iraq 19 pp. 146–50 (provenance, study)
1957 von Soden, Orientalia NS 26 pp. 136–37 (study)
1964 Brinkman, Studies Oppenheim pp. 14 and 41 no. 44.2.1 (partial translation, study)
1966 Mallowan, Nimrud 1 p. 175 and fig. 107 (photo of one side)

TEXT

1) *a-na* ^{d}*iš-tar be-*⸢*let*⸣ KUR.KUR *šur-bu-*[*t*]*i* DINGIR.MEŠ *qa-rit-ti*
2) ^{d}*nin-é-an-na a-šib-*⸢*ti*(*)⸣ [U]NUG.KI *šá kul-lat* [*pá*]*r-ṣi ḫa-am-mat*

1–2) For the goddess Ištar, mistress of the lands, supreme (among) the gods, valiant, the goddess Nineanna ("Lady of Eanna"), who dwells in Uruk, who has gathered to herself all the divine offices:

2 -⸢*ti*(*)⸣: Gadd (Iraq 15 [1953] p. 123) reads *-ti ina* and his copy would suggest *-t*[*i*] *ina*, but one expects the participle *āšibti* to be followed by a noun and not a preposition. Possibly what Gadd took to be a new horizontal wedge (*ina*) was the end of the TI.

3) *é-an-na šá* [d]*šul-gi* LUG[AL] *maḫ-ri ú-še-pi-šú-[m]a il-li-ku la-ba-riš*
4) *ù* É [d]*nin-giz-zi-da šá an-àm* LUGAL *pa-*⸢*ni*⸣ *ú-še-pi-šú qé-reb-šú*
5) ⸢É *šu-a*⸣*-ti* É.GAR$_8$.MEŠ-*šú i-qu-pu-ma up-[t]a-aṭ-ṭi-ru rik-su-šú*
6) *[sa]-mit-su iḫ-ḫar-mi-mu-*⸢*ma*⸣ *i-tu-[r]u up-pu-uš-šú*
7) *[ina*(?) *lìb*(?)*-b]i*(?) LUGAL.MEŠ *a-lik maḫ-ri la ib-bal-ki-[t]u e-peš šip-ri-šú*
8) *[i-n]u-šú* EN GAL-*ú* [d]AMAR.UTU *it-ti* [K]UR.[U]RI.KI *k[i-m]il-tuš is-bu-us-ma*
9) [MU x+]1.KÁM-*ma* LÚ.KÚR *lem-nu* LÚ *su-bar-ú ina* KUR.URI.K[I] *ip-pu-uš be-lu-tú*
10) *[a*(?)*-d]i*(?) *u$_4$-me im-lu-*⸢*ú*⸣ *ik-šú-[d]a a-dan-na*
11) [EN] GAL-*ú* [d]AMAR.UTU *a-na* ⸢KUR⸣.URI.KI *šá ik-mi-lu ir-[š]u-ú sa-li-ma*

12) *[ip]-pa-lis-ma* [d]AMAR.UTU-IB[I]LA-SUM.NA LUGAL KÁ.DINGIR.RA.KI NUN *p[a]-liḫ-šú ti-ri-iṣ qa-ti-šú*
13) [IBI]LA GI.NA *reš-tu-*⸢*ú*⸣ *šá eri-ba-*[d]AMAR.UTU LUGAL KÁ.DING[IR.R]A.KI *mu-kin* SUḪUŠ KUR
14) *[ana]* SIPA-*ut* KUR *šu-me-*⸢*rim*⸣ *u* URI.KI MU-*šú ki-niš it-ta-b[i* L]UGAL DINGIR.MEŠ [d]*asar-ri*
15) *[iq-b]i i-na ṣi-it pi-šú an-nu-um-ma lu-ú* SIPA ⸢*mu*⸣*-pa-aḫ-ḫir* BIR.MEŠ
16) *[ina] e-muq* EN GAL-*i* ⸢d⸣AMAR.UTU *ù* UR.SAG DINGIR.[M]EŠ [d]*ut-u$_{18}$-lu*
17) ⸢BAD$_5$⸣.BAD$_5$ ÉRIN-*ni* SU.BIR$_4$.KI [DA]GAL-*tim* ⸢*im*⸣*-ḫaṣ-ma ú-ša[b]-bir kak-ki-šú-un*
18) ⸢*su*⸣*-kup-*⸢*ta*⸣*-šú-nu iš-kun-*⸢*ma*⸣ *ina qaq-qar* KUR.⸢URI.KI⸣ *ú-šap-*⸢*ri*⸣*-sa kib-si-šú-un*
19) *i-na uz-na ṣir-ti šá* ⸢d⸣*é-a mu-*⸢*um*⸣*-mu ba-an* ⸢*ka*⸣*-la i-qí-[šú]-*⸢*šú*⸣
20) *ḫa-si-sa pal-ka ú-šat-li-mu-uš* d⸢*nin*⸣*-ši-[kù]*
21) *a-na šul-*⸢*lum*⸣ *par-ṣi áš-ru* ⸢*ki*⸣*-du-de-e ud-du-*⸢*šú*⸣ *ma-ḫa-[zi]*
22) *ù eš-ret* GI$_6$.PÀR DINGIR.MEŠ ⸢GAL⸣.MEŠ *šá* KUR.URI.KI *ú-zu-[u]n-šú ib-ši-[ma]*

23) *áš-rat é-an-na šu-bat* d⸢*iš*⸣*-tar be-let* KUR.KUR GAŠAN-*šú [i]š-te-ʾ-*⸢*e*(?)⸣*-[ma]*
24) É.GAR$_8$ *é-an-na ki-di-a-*⸢*ni*⸣ *šá* KISAL *[š]ap-li-[i]*

3–7) (With regard to) Eanna, which Šulgi, a previous king, had had built and which had become old, and (with regard to) the shrine of the god Ningizzida, which Anam, an earlier king, had had constructed inside it, (5) (with regard to) this temple, whose walls had buckled and whose bondings had disintegrated, whose [para]pet had collapsed and which had become *unrecognizable*, (and) whose reconstruction had not [occ]urred to the kings, (his) predecessors,
8–11) [At that] time, the great lord, the god Marduk, had turned away in divine wrath from the land of Akkad, and the evil enemy, the Subarian, exercised the rule over the land of Akkad for *[seve]n* [years, (10) *unt]il* the days had elapsed, the appointed time had arrived, (and) the great [lord], the god Marduk, became reconciled with the land of Akkad, with which he had become angry.
12–15) He (the god Marduk) looked (with favour) upon Marduk-apla-iddina (II), king of Babylon, prince who reveres him, to whom he (the god Marduk) stretched out his hand, legitimate eldest son of Erība-Marduk, king of Babylon, who has made firm the foundation(s) of the land. The king of the gods, the god Asari, duly named him [to] the shepherdship of the land of Sumer and Akkad (and) personally [sa]id: "This is indeed the shepherd who will gather the scattered (people)."

16–18) [With] the power of the great lord, the god Marduk, and of the hero of the gods, the god Utulu, he defeated the widespread army of Subartu and shattered their weapons. He brought about their overthrow and prevented them from treading on the territory of the land of Akkad.
19–22) With the excellent understanding which the god Ea, the creator, maker of all things, had bestowed upon him, (20) (and with) the extensive knowledge which the god Ninši[ku] had granted him, he directed his attention to performing the rites, *to administering correctly* the rituals, and to renovating the cult centres and the sanctuaries of the divine residences of the great gods of the land of Akkad.
23–26) He was assiduous toward the sanctuaries of Eanna, the abode of the goddess Ištar, mistress of the lands, his lady. (With regard to) the outer enclosure wall of Eanna in the lower courtyard (25)

---

4 Or *dingir-àm*, "Dingiram," instead of *an-àm*, "Anam." For the inscriptions of this early ruler of Uruk, see RIME 4 E.4.4.6.
6 The reading *up-pu-uš-šú*, "*unrecognizable*" follows von Soden (Orientalia NS 26 [1957] p. 137 and AHw p. 1424b); cf. *ár-bu-uš-šú*, "ruin" (Gadd, Iraq 15 [1953] p. 123 and CAD 11/1 [N] p. 126 sub *naḫarmumu*).
7 The restoration is based upon B.6.22.3 i 24; however, from the copy there does not appear to be enough room for this. Gadd reads: *[man-ma] šá*.
9 The restoration "*[seve]n*" is based upon the fact that Tiglath-pileser III and Shalmaneser V — two Assyrian monarchs — were considered to have ruled Babylonia for a total of seven years immediately preceding the accession of Marduk-apla-iddina II (B.6.19–20). Gadd prefers to restore "eight," thus including the accession year of Tiglath-pileser to the throne of Babylonia in the total (Iraq 15 [1953] p. 127).
10 von Soden suggests *[ki-m]a* or *[ul-t]u*, "when" or "after" instead of *[a*(?)*-d]i*(?), "*[unt]il*" (Orientalia NS 26 [1957] p. 137).
23 Gadd reads *-ú-[ma]* at the end of the line (Iraq 15 [1953] p. 123), but -⸢*e*⸣*-[ma]* seems equally possible or better from the copy and published photograph. B.6.22.3 i 33 has *-e-ma* at this point and this would be preferable grammatically.

25) *ù* É ᵈ*nin-giz-zi-da šá qer-bé-ni šu-pu-š*[*u*] ⸢*i*⸣*-du-u*[*š-šú*]

26) *sa-mit-su is-suḫ-ma ú-nam-*[*m*]*ir te-me-e*[*n-šú*]

27) URU$_4$.MEŠ-*šú ina te-me-qí ik-ri-bi u la-ban ap-pi id-di-*⸢*ma*⸣ GIM *kin-né-e ú-kin-m*[*a*]

28) *i-na* SIG$_4$.ḪI.A *el-le-ti r*[*e*]*-ši-šú ul-li-ma ú-*⸢*nam*⸣*-me-ra* GIM *u$_4$-*[*mi*]

29) UGU *šá pa-ni ú-šá-tir-ma ú-nak-ki-la* ⸢*bi*⸣*-na-a-*[*ti*]

30) *a-na šat-ti ši-pir šu-a-ti* ⸢ᵈ⸣*iš-tar be-let* KUR.K[UR *ḫ*]*a-diš ina* IGI.BAR-[(*šá*)]

31) ⸢*a*⸣*-na* ᵈAMAR.UTU-IBILA-SUM.NA ⸢LUGAL KÁ⸣.DIN[GIR.R]A.KI *liš-ruk* TIN MU.A[N.NA]-*šú li-iṣ-ṣib-ma liš-ba-a lit-ut-t*[*ú*]

32) [*i*]*-na qí-bi-ti-šú ṣir-ti šá la n*[*a-k*]*a-ri kul-lat na-k*[*i-r*]*i-šú a-na* GÌR.II-*šú li-šak-niš-ma*

33) [(x) LUG]AL.⸢LUGAL⸣.MEŠ *na-ki-ri-šú nu-*⸢*ḫuš*⸣ *kib-rat* ⸢*ár*⸣*-ba-ʾ-i* [*ḫi*]*-ṣib* KUR-*i ù tam-tim*

34) [GU]N-⸢*su*⸣*-nu* ⸢DUGUD⸣*-ta liš-du-*⸢*du*⸣ *a-*[*n*]*a qé-reb šu-an-*⸢*na*⸣.KI

35) [*qí*(?)*-š*]*a*(?)*-at-*⸢*su*⸣*-*[*n*]*u lim-ḫur-ma a-na é-sag-íl* [*l*]*i-še-rib ma-ḫar* EN ⸢EN⸣.EN

36) BAL[A]-*šú i-*⸢*na*⸣ [TI]N.TIR.KI [*l*]*i-kun a-na* ⸢*ṣa-a*⸣*-ti*

37) ⸢MU.SAR-*e*⸣ LUGAL *a-lik maḫ-ri-ia e-*[*p*]*iš* É *šu-a-ti a-mur-ma* MU.S[AR]-⸢*šú*⸣ *la ú-nak-kìr-ma it-ti* M[U].SAR-*e-a* GIN

38) *man-nu ár-ku-ú lu-ú* LUGAL *lu-ú* DUM[U] LUGAL *lu* LÚ ⸢*qí*⸣*-pu lu* LÚ.[GAR-*n*]*u lu* LÚ *šá-tam lu* LÚ *ḫa-*[*z*]*a-an-nu*

39) *šá* E[N] GAL-*ú* ᵈAMAR.UTU MU-*šú i-na*[*m-b*]*u-ma* ⸢*a-na*⸣ *e-peš* ⸢*é*⸣*-an-na* GEŠTU-*šú i-ša*[*k-k*]*a-nu*

40) MU.[S]AR *šu-a-tu li-mu-*[*u*]*r-ma i*[*t-t*]*i* MU.SAR-*šú-ma lu-*⸢*kin*⸣ *a*[*ḫ-r*]*a-taš*

and (with regard to) the temple of the god Ningizzida, which had been constructed inside it *to one side*, he tore down its parapet and laid bare [its] foundation.

27–29) With fervent entreaties, prayers, and expression(s) of humility, he laid its foundations (anew) and made (them) as firm as a mountain. He raised its top with (ritually) pure bricks and made (it) as bright as daylight. He made (it) larger than before and fashioned (its) *structure* artfully.

30–36) On account of this, when the goddess Ištar, mistress of the lands, looks upon this work with pleasure, may she bestow a (long) life on Marduk-apla-iddina (II), king of Babylon! May she increase his years and may he experience the fullness of old age! By her august command, which cannot be changed, may he subjugate at his feet all of his enemies and may the kings, his enemies, drag their weighty [trib]ute — the [abun]dance of the four quarters (of the world), the yield of mountain and sea — into Šuanna (Babylon)! (35) May he receive their [*pres*]*ent* and may he bring (them) into Esagila, before the lord of lords! May his reign be established in Babylon for all time!

37–40) I saw the royal inscription of a king who had preceded me (and) who had built that temple. I did not alter his royal inscription, but (rather) I placed (it) with my own royal inscription. Anyone in the future — whether king, or son of a king, or commissioner, or [govern]or, or chief administrator (of a temple), or mayor — who, appointed by the great lord, the god Marduk, decides to (re)build Eanna, let him see this royal inscription and let him place (it) with his own royal inscription for the future!

2

Numerous bricks from Uruk have been found which are stamped with a Sumerian inscription recording the renovation of the Eanna temple by Marduk-apla-iddina II for the goddess Inanna (Ištar).

---

31 Gadd reads MU.AN.NA.MEŠ (Iraq 15 [1953] p. 124), but the copy would suggest there is room for only MU.A[N.NA].

35 The reading [*qí*(?)*-š*]*a*(?)*-at-*⸢*su*⸣*-*[*n*]*u*, "their [*pres*]*ents*," is based upon a suggestion by von Soden (Orientalia NS 26 [1957] p. 137).

CATALOGUE

Ex.	Museum number	Excavation number	Registration number	Warka photo number	Warka provenance	Dimensions (cm)	Lines preserved	cpn
1	—	W 1700a	—	818	Od XV 4, by the niche in the asphalt pavement of the late period	35×35×8	1–10	p
2	—	W 1700b	—	817	As ex. 1	As ex. 1	1–10	p
3	—	W 1701a	—	818	As ex. 1	As ex. 1	1–10	p
4	—	W 69	—	31	Eanna area, surface of mound	34×34	1–10	p
5	—	W 1253d	—	—	As ex. 4	51×33×10.5	1–10	n
6	—	W 4767	—	820	—	—	1–8	p
7	BM 90269	—	51-1-1,282	—	Pavement at base of the "Bowarieh Mound" on SW side	51×32.5	1–10	n
8	BM 90270 + 90740	—	51-1-1,276	—	As ex. 7	35×35×8.5	1–10	n
9	BM 90271	—	51-1-1,277	—	As ex. 7	42×36×7	1–10	n
10	—	W number unknown	—	Number unknown	—	—	1–9	n

COMMENTARY

Exs. 1–6 and 10 come from the excavations of the Deutsche Orient-Gesellschaft at Uruk. The excavation photograph of ex. 6 is basically illegible. As far as the present author has been able to tell, the brick copied on Jordan, Uruk-Warka pl. 107d (our ex. 10), does not appear to be one of exs. 1–6. Exs. 7–9 come from the excavations at Warka by W.K. Loftus. According to C.B.F. Walker, copies of exs. 8 and 9 are found in W.K. Loftus and H.A. Churchill, Drawings in Babylonia pl. XIX nos. 1–2 (manuscript volume in the Department of Western Asiatic Antiquities of the British Museum); a smaller copy of ex. 7, with the inscription totally distorted, is given ibid., pl. V no. 9. Details on exs. 7–9 come from Walker, CBI (which also states that these exemplars are stamped with a double-edged stamp) and from preliminary work-notes kindly supplied by Walker. As far as one can tell, all bricks are stamped on the face.

Exs. 4, 5, 7, and 9 have the same variants to the master text:

9) insertion of -a- between -gá- and -ni
10) mu-na-dù for mu-un-na-dím.

No score of this inscription is provided in the microfiche.

Two bricks with inscriptions of Marduk-apla-iddina II were found during a surface survey at Uruk in the 35th to 37th seasons (1982–84). The inventory numbers for these pieces are not known, but one was found in F 24 c4 and the other in N 8 a3; see Kessler in Finkbeiner, AUWE 4 p. 183 nos. 25a–b. Kessler notes that the first can be compared to this inscription. No further information on these two bricks and their inscriptions is available.

A similar inscription of the king (B.6.21.3) states that work on Eanna took place in the king's second reign (703 BC). Although this text does not mention this, it is possible that it also comes from the king's second reign.

BIBLIOGRAPHY

1861 1 R pl. 5 no. 17 (exs. 7, 9, composite copy in type)
1872 G. Smith, TSBA 1 p. 76 no. 60 (exs. 7, 9, translation)
1873 Lenormant, Choix no. 8 (exs. 7, 9, composite copy)
1874 Lenormant, Études accadiennes 2 pp. 367–68 (exs. 7, 9, composite copy, edition)
1875 Ménant, Babylone p. 131 (exs. 7, 9, translation)
1875 G. Smith, RP 5 p. 91 no. 58 (exs. 7, 9, translation)
1886 Bezold, Literatur p. 59 §31 (exs. 7, 9, study)
1889 Winckler, Untersuchungen p. 32 (exs. 7, 9, edition)
1892 Peiser and Winckler, ZA 7 p. 184 (exs. 7, 9, edition)
1922 BM Guide p. 65 nos. 187–89 (exs. 7–9, study)
1928 Jordan, Uruk-Warka pp. 42–43 and 50 no. 5 and pls. 101c and 107d (provenance; ex. 4, photo, edition [by Schroeder]; ex. 10, copy)
1930 Langdon, Kish 3 p. 17 (exs. 7, 9, edition)
1930 Schott, UVB 1 p. 55 and pl. 27 no. 18 (exs. 1–5, composite copy, edition)
1964 Brinkman, Studies Oppenheim p. 42 no. 44.2.2a (exs. 1–5, 7, 9–10, study)
1981 Walker, CBI no. 74 (exs. 7–9, transliteration)

TEXT

1) nin ^{d}inanna
2) nin kur-kur-ra
3) nin-a-ni-ir

1–10) For the lady, goddess Inanna, mistress of the lands, his lady: Marduk-apla-iddina (II), (5) king of Babylon, descendant of Erība-Marduk, king of

4) ^{d}AMAR.UTU-EDURU-SUM.NA
5) lugal KÁ.DINGIR.RA.KI
6) numun(*) SU-^{d}AMAR.UTU
7) lugal ki-in-gi uri.KI
8) é-an-na
9) é ki-ág-gá-ni
10) mu-un-na-dím

Sumer (and) Akkad, (re)constructed Eanna, her beloved temple.

3

A Sumerian inscription is found stamped on several bricks from Uruk. It also records the restoration of the Eanna temple by Marduk-apla-iddina II for the goddess Inanna (Ištar), but adds that this took place in his second reign.

CATALOGUE

Ex.	Excavation number	Warka photo number	Warka provenance	Lines preserved	cpn
1	W 3283	824	Qc XV 3 debris	8–12	p
2	W 4089	820	Eanna area	7–12	p
3	W 4382	817	Eanna area	1–12	p
4	W 4431	819	Court with drain, north, building J, 50 cm above upper edge of drain	2–12	p
5	W 4556	819	—	1–9	p
6	W number unknown	—	SW brick wall of the filtration plant (room 12)	1–12	n

COMMENTARY

With regard to exs. 1–4, Schott indicates that complete bricks with this inscription would measure 34×34×7–7.5 cm and that the inscription itself measures 7.9×13.5 cm. It appears from the photographs that exs. 1–5 are found stamped on the face; ex. 6 is reported to be stamped on the side. Although ex. 6 is said to have the same line arrangement as the other exemplars, the inscription is stated to be in three columns, each column having four lines. No exemplar is known to have any variants and no score for this inscription is provided on the microfiche.

BIBLIOGRAPHY

1930 Jordan, UVB 1 pp. 17–18 (ex. 6, provenance)
1930 Schott, UVB 1 pp. 54–55 nos. 16–17 (exs. 1–4 and 6, edition) and pl. 27 no. 16 (exs. 1–4, composite copy)
1964 Brinkman, Studies Oppenheim pp. 26 and 42 no. 44.2.2b (exs. 1–4, study)

TEXT

1) nin ^{d}inanna
2) nin kur-kur-ra
3) nin-a-ni-ir
4) ^{d}AMAR.UTU-IBILA-SUM.NA

1–12) For the lady, goddess Inanna, mistress of the lands, his lady: Marduk-apla-iddina (II), (5) king of Babylon, king of Sumer (and) Akkad, king with clean hands, in (his) second kingship (re)constructed

B.6.21.2 line 6 numun(*): the form of the sign is unusual and resembles BAL to a certain extent.

5) lugal KÁ.DINGIR.RA.KI
6) lugal ki-in-gi uri.KI
7) lugal šu-luḫ-ḫa
8) nam-lugal-la-ta min-kam
9) é-an-na
10) é ki-ág-gá-ni
11) nam-ti-la-ni-šè
12) mu-na-dím

Eanna, (10) her beloved temple, for the sake of his life.

4

A cylinder seal bears a short votive inscription of Marduk-apla-iddina, son of Iakīn, who is likely to be identified with the Babylonian king by that name who was the also a member of the Bīt-Iakīn tribe. Since Marduk-apla-iddina II is given no title, it is possible that this inscription was composed before he became king.

COMMENTARY

The cylinder seal (IM 67920) is made of chalcedony and measures 4.2×1.8 cm. It was acquired through the antiquities market and thus its original provenance is not known. The relief depicts an individual fighting a lion. The inscription, when seen on an impression, appears reversed. The inscription has been collated from the published photograph (which is not always clear).

BIBLIOGRAPHY

1987 Collon, First Impressions no. 369 (photo of impression, study)
1992 Wittmann, Bagh. Mitt. 23 p. 263 no. 66 (edition, study)
1994 Watanabe, ASJ 16 pp. 243–44 no. 3.2 (edition)

TEXT

1) ⸢*a-na*⸣ UMUN-*šú* ^{md}MES-A-⸢MU⸣
2) ⸢A⸣ ^{m}*ia*$_4$-⸢*kin*$_7$⸣ BA

1–2) To his lord, Marduk-apla-iddina (II), son of Iakīn, presented (this object).

2001

A brick found at Kish has an Akkadian inscription on it describing the building of a bridge across the Nār-Bānītu canal by Marduk-apla-iddina II for the goddess Ninlil. The inscription itself appears to have been commissioned by Iddin-Nergal, the governor of Kish, and it was presumably he who actually had the work carried out.

B.6.21.4 line 2 For another possible writing of the name Iakīn with the signs ^{m}*ia*$_4$-*kin*$_7$, see Roux, Sumer 16 (1960) p. 27 and pl. V after p. 30.

COMMENTARY

The brick was found at Kish, or more precisely Hursagkalama (Tell Ingharra), at a depth of 6 metres in trench C.3 (Moorey, Kish pp. 81 and 84, against Langdon, Kish 3 p. 17) and is currently in the Ashmolean Museum (Ashmolean 1929.136). The brick has V 882 marked on it. It was cut down in size by the excavator for transport and currently measures 24.8×7×7.5 cm. Walker estimates that approximately one-quarter of the inscription is missing on the right side. The inscription is inscribed on the edge of the brick and has been collated.

The mention of a temple in line 4 and the fact that the brick was found on Tell Ingharra could indicate that the bridge was located near both that mound and the temple to the goddess Ninlil.

BIBLIOGRAPHY

1930 Langdon, Kish 3 pp. 17–19 and pl. XI (copy, edition)
1932 Albright, JAOS 52 p. 54 (study)
1964 Brinkman, Studies Oppenheim p. 42 no. 44.2.3 (study)
1972 Gibson, Iraq 34 p. 120 (provenance)
1978 Moorey, Kish pp. 81 and 84 (study)
1980 Dalley, RA 74 pp. 189–90 (study)
1981 Walker, CBI no. 75 (transliteration)

TEXT

1) *ana* ^{d}*nin-líl* GAŠAN GAL-*ti* GAŠAN *ṣir-ti* AMA *reme-ni-ti a-ši-bat é-kur-ní-*⸢*zu*⸣ *šá qé-reb ḫur-sag-*[*kalam-ma* (...) *bēltīšu*(?)]

2) ^{d}AMAR.UTU-A-MU <LUGAL> TIN.TIR.KI LUGAL KUR.EME.GI$_7$ *ù* URI.KI *ti-túr-ri* ÍD ^{d}*ba-ni-ti šá ul-tu* [...]

3) SIG$_4$.AL.ÙR.RA *ú-šal-bi-in-ma ana* TIN ZI.ME-*šú ù ba-*⸢*la*⸣*-ṭi-šú ú-še-piš-ma* BA-*eš ana šat-ti* [...]

4) É-*a šú-a-ti ḫa-diš ina nap*(?)*-lu-si-šú šá* ^{m}SUM.NA-^{d}U.GUR LÚ.GAR-*nu šá kiš*.KI *re-e-šú pa-liḫ-*⸢*ki*⸣ *ina ki*[*š*.KI ...]

5) *šal-meš i-tal-lu-ka ana* TIN u_4*-me* SÙ.ME MU.ME ḪÉ.NUN *ù* ḪÉ.GÁL *a-na* LUGAL EN-*šú šá-a-šú* [...]

6) *a-na* NÍG.BA *li-qis-su a-na* IGI ⸢LUGAL⸣-*ti* [...]

1) For the goddess Ninlil, great lady, august lady, compassionate mother, who dwells in Ekurnizu ("House, Fearsome Mountain"), which is inside Hursag[kalama (...), *his lady*]:

2–3a) Marduk-apla-iddina (II), <king> of Babylon, king of the land of Sumer and Akkad, had baked bricks made (for) the bridge over the Nār-Bānītu canal, which from [...]. He had (the bridge) built in order to ensure his good health and his life, and he presented (it to her).

3b–6) On account of this, when [*the goddess Ninlil* (...)] looks at this temple with pleasure, [...] of/which Iddin-Nergal, governor of Kish, the servant who reveres you, in Ki[sh ...] to live in safety, to have a long life (and) years of plenty and abundance, for the king, his lord, to that man [...] may she give him as a present! For kingship [...]!

2 There is no *šá* between *ti-túr-ri* and ÍD ^{d}*ba-ni-ti* (against Dalley, RA 74 [1980] p. 190, followed by Zadok, Rép. Géogr. 8 p. 366). For the name of a river immediately following the word "bridge," see also Rost, Tigl. p. 14 line 68.

Sargon II

B.6.22

When Sargon II (Šarru-kēnu), king of Assyria 721–705 BC, had seized the throne of Assyria upon the death of Shalmaneser V, Marduk-apla-iddina II had managed to win Babylonia's independence from Assyrian control and to maintain it for twelve years. In 710 BC, however, Sargon expelled Marduk-apla-iddina from Babylon and ruled Babylonia for the last five years of his life (709–705 BC). In his Assyrian inscriptions, Sargon claims that the citizens and temple personnel of Babylon and Borsippa had welcomed his victory over Marduk-apla-iddina and had invited him to enter Babylon. He took part in the New Year's ceremonies in Babylon in 709 BC, made offerings to the gods of the various cult centres of the land, and assumed Babylonian royal titulary. After driving Marduk-apla-iddina from Dūr-Iakīn, Sargon II reinstituted the ancient privileges of various Babylonian cities and reorganized the administration of the land, dividing it in two parts and putting one under the supervision of the governor of Babylon and the other under that of the governor of the Gambūlu, an Aramean tribe centred in eastern Babylonia. Troops were sent to deal with bandits who had been plundering caravans in the vicinity of Sippar, and the canal from Borsippa to Babylon was redug. Marduk-apla-iddina's tribal stronghold, Dūr-Iakīn, was destroyed in 707 BC and in order to prevent trouble in the future, Sargon claims to have deported over 108,000 Arameans and Chaldeans to other parts of his empire and to have settled people from Kummuḫu (Commagene) in southern Babylonia. For information on Sargon's relations with Babylonia, see Brinkman, Prelude pp. 45–55.

Royal inscriptions of Sargon II from Babylonia record the restoration of the city walls of Babylon (B.6.22.1–2) and work on the Eanna temple at Uruk (B.6.22.3–6). Inscriptions B.6.22.1 and B.6.22.3–4 are in Akkadian and B.6.22.2 and B.6.22.5–6 are in Sumerian; B.6.22.1–2 and B.6.22.4–6 are on bricks and B.6.22.3 is on a clay cylinder. Six Babylonian economic texts are dated by the regnal years of Sargon, of these one uses his regnal years as king of Assyria and at least four as ruler of Babylonia. The date formula of one text refers to him as "king of Assyria," three as "king of the world," and one as "king of Baby[lon]." (For the Babylonian economic texts from the reign of Sargon II, see Brinkman and Kennedy, JCS 35 [1983] p. 13 no. B and Kessler, Bagh. Mitt. 23 [1992] pp. 465–67).

1

Numerous bricks from Babylon and Kish are inscribed with an Akkadian inscription describing the restoration of the Imgur-Enlil ("The God Enlil Showed Favour") and Nēmet-Enlil ("Bulwark of the God Enlil") — the city walls of Babylon — by Sargon II for the god Marduk. In this and several other Babylonian inscriptions, Sargon takes the traditional Babylonian titles "viceroy of Babylon" and "king of the land of Sumer and Akkad."

CATALOGUE

Ex.	Museum number	Excavation number	Babylon photo number	Provenance	Dimensions (cm)	Lines preserved	cpn
1	EŞ number unknown	—	—	Kish, trench to SE corner of ziqqurat	9×34.2×12	1–25	c
2	Ash 1924.640	—	—	Kish	11.5×4.9×5	7–14	c
3	Ash 1932.652	—	—	Kish	6.5×8.2×8.5	14, 17, 19–20, 22–23, 25	c
4	Ash 1932.977	—	—	Kish	10×9.5×7.5	1–5, 7–8, 10	c
5	BM 90599 + 90629 (81-7-1,3406)	—	—	—	18.5×9×7	19–25	n
6	—	—	—	Kish	35×9.5	1–25	p
7	—	BE 30680	869	Babylon, NW corner of southern palace, Sargon's wall	30	1–25	p
8	—	BE 30681	868	As ex. 7	30	1–25	n
9	—	BE 30682	—	As ex. 7	30	1–25 ?	n
10	—	BE 30683	867	As ex. 7	—	1–25	p
11	—	BE 30684	868	As ex. 7	30	1–25	n
12	—	BE 30698	868	As ex. 7	—	1–25	n
13	—	BE 30700	—	As ex. 7	30	1–25 ?	n
14	—	BE 30706	868	As ex. 7	—	1–25	n
15	—	BE 30707	869	As ex. 7	—	1–25	n
16	YBC 13510	BE 30708	867	As ex. 7	30.5×7.5 ×2.8–3.9	1–25	c
17	—	BE 30709	869	As ex. 7	30	1–25	p
18	—	BE 30710	868	As ex. 7	30	1–25	n
19	—	BE 31080	—	As ex. 7	—	19–25	n
20	—	BE 32062	—	As ex. 7	—	1–25 ?	n

COMMENTARY

The inscription is inscribed (not stamped) on the edge of the brick and, in all cases where information is available, it is in contemporary Babylonian script. The number and arrangement of lines varies greatly among the exemplars. Some bricks have the inscription written down the edge (exs. 1–2, 7, 13, 15–17, and 19) in 24–28 lines, while others have it across the edge, in either one (exs. 8–12, 14, 18, and 20) or more columns (exs. 3–6) of 5–7 lines each. The line arrangement and the master line follow ex. 1, with help from ex. 10 in lines 9–12.

Exs. 1 and 6 were found during during H. de Genouillac's excavations at Kish in 1912. It is uncertain from Genouillac's publications whether ex. 6 was sent to Paris or to Istanbul since it was both catalogued among pieces in Paris (Kich 2 p. 29 P.208) and given a reference number indicating that it was in Istanbul (Kich 2 pl. 1 O.5). Exs. 2–4 were found during the excavations of the Oxford-Field Museum, Chicago, expedition to Kish 1923–1933. Ex. 5 comes from Rassam's excavations in Babylonia (probably from Babylon, according to Walker, CBI p. 65).

Exs. 7–20 were found during excavations by the Deutsche Orient-Gesellschaft at Babylon. No details are available about several exemplars and the inscriptions on several others are known only by excavation photographs. Babylon photos 868 and 869 show five and four exemplars respectively. Excavation records give the excavation numbers of four pieces for each photo, but do not indicate which bricks shown have which excavation numbers. The variants from all but two of these nine bricks will be cited by the photo number followed by A, B, C, etc. (e.g., 689D), with A indicating the brick on the photo which is separated from the others by the ruler. It is possible to be reasonably certain about the identification of two bricks on photo 689 — nos. B and C, exs. 17 and 7 respectively — and they are cited by exemplar number. The bricks are not all in good condition and the inscriptions are often difficult to read, particularly from photographs. Thus, readings must often be considered tentative. As is the customary practice in the RIM volumes, no score is provided in the microfiche for this brick inscription.

Gibson suggests that the bricks found at Kish with this inscription may have been brought to that city from Babylon for reuse in the Neo-Babylonian temple (Iraq 34 [1972] p. 120).

BIBLIOGRAPHY

1913 de Genouillac, RA 10 pp. 83–87 (ex. 1, copy, edition [translation by Thureau-Dangin]; variants from ex. 6)
1924 de Genouillac, Kich 1 pp. 18 and 45, and pl. 2 no. O.4 (ex. 1, provenance, copy, study)
1924–25 Unger, AfK 2 p. 21 no. 2 (ex. 10, study)
1925 de Genouillac, Kich 2 p. 29 no. P.208, pl. XXII no. 2, and pl. 1 no. O.5 (ex. 6, photo, copy, study)
1925 Koldewey, WEB[4] pp. 135–36 and fig. 86 (ex. 10, photo, translation [by Delitzsch])
1930 Unger in Wetzel, Stadtmauern p. 79 (exs. 7–20, study)
1930 Wetzel, Stadtmauern pp. 64–65 and pl. 12 (exs. 7–20, provenance)
1981 Walker, CBI no. 76 (exs. 2–5, transliteration)
1987 Beckman, ARRIM 5 pp. 2–3 no. 3 (ex. 16, copy, edition)
1988 Beckman, ARRIM 6 p. 2 (ex. 16, study)
1992 George, Topographical Texts pp. 344–45 (partial edition)

TEXT

1) *ana* ^{d}AMAR.UTU EN GAL-*i*
2) DINGIR *reme-ni-i*
3) *a-šib é-sag-gíl* EN TIN.TIR.KI UMUN-*šú*
4) LUGAL-GIN LUGAL *dan-nu*
5) LUGAL KUR *aš-šur*.KI LUGAL ŠÚ
6) GÌR.NÍTA TIN.TIR.KI
7) LUGAL KUR *šu-me-ru u* URI.KI
8) *za-nin é-sag-íl*
9) *ù é-zi-da*
10) *ana* DÙ-*eš* BÀD *im-gur-*^{d}*en-líl*
11) GEŠTU-*šú* GÁL-*ma ú-šal-bi-in-ma*
12) *a-gur-ru ki-ru* KÙ-*tim*
13) *ina kup-ru ù* ESIR
14) *ina* GÚ ÍD *pu-rat-ti*
15) *ina qé-reb an-za-nun-ze-e*
16) KAR *ib-ni-ma*
17) BÀD *im-gur-*^{d}50
18) *ù* BÀD *né-met-*^{d}50
19) *ki-ma ši-pik* KUR-*i*
20) *ú-šar-šid ṣe-ru-uš-šú*
21) *šip-ri šá-a-šú* ^{d}AMAR.UTU EN GAL-*ú*
22) *lip-pa-lis-ma a-na* LUGAL-GIN
23) NUN *za-nin-šú liš-ruk* TIN
24) *ki-ma te-me-en* TIN.TIR.KI
25) *li-ku-nu* BALA.MEŠ-*šú*

1–3) For the god Marduk, great lord, compassionate god who dwells in Esagila, lord of Babylon, his lord:

4–11a) Sargon (II), mighty king, king of Assyria, king of the world, viceroy of Babylon, king of the land of Sumer and Akkad, the one who provides for Esagila and Ezida, thought of (re)building the (city) wall Imgur-Enlil.

11b–20) He had bricks made and constructed a quay-wall of baked bricks fired in a (ritually) pure kiln, (laid) in (both) refined and crude bitumen, along the bank of the Euphrates River, (15) in deep water. He founded the (city) wall Imgur-Enlil and the (city) wall Nēmet-Enlil (as secure) upon it as a mountain range.

21–25) May the god Marduk, great lord, look upon this work (with pleasure) and may he bestow a (long) life on Sargon, the prince who provides for him! May his reign be as firm as the foundation of Babylon!

2

The renovation of the two city walls of Babylon — Imgur-Enlil and Nēmet-Enlil — by Sargon II is also commemorated in a Sumerian inscription found on a few bricks from Babylon.

14.10, 16, and 868D insert *i-te-e* KÁ.GAL ^{d}15 after *ina*, "beside the gate of the goddess Ištar, on the bank of the Euphrates River" for "along the bank of the Euphrates River." Exs. 7, 17, 868E, 869A, and 869D are all damaged but likely have the same insertion; they have ⸢*i-te-e* KÁ.GAL⸣ [...], [x x]-*e* KÁ.GAL ^{d}15, ⸢*i*(?)⸣-*te-*⸢*e*⸣ [...], *i-*⸢*te*⸣-[*e*] KÁ.GAL ^{d}1[5], and ⸢*i*(?)⸣-*te-e* ⸢KÁ⸣.GAL x x respectively.

CATALOGUE

Ex.	Museum number	Excavation number	Babylon photo number	Babylon provenance	Lines preserved	cpn
1	—	BE 38583	2007, 2305	Merkes g$_1$ 26 +5.00 m	10–18	p
2	—	BE 41861	2194, 2305, 2330	In debris in the bridge gate; Sachn y 40 +2.80 m	2–7	p
3	—	BE 42335 + 42417	2305, 2320, 3458	Sachn aa 40, c. -1.50 m	1–14	p
4	EŞ number unknown	BE 58377	3458	Southeast corner of inner city wall in debris at edge of mud-brick outer wall	1–14, 16–18	p

COMMENTARY

All exemplars come from the excavations of the Deutsche Orient-Gesellschaft at Babylon. The inscription is found inscribed (not stamped) down the edge of each brick in Babylonian script. Lines 1–2 and 8 are a conflation of exs. 3 and 4; lines 3–7 and 9–10 follow ex. 3; and lines 11–18 follow ex. 1. Ex. 4 may omit line 15 or have had it on the same line as 14 (the end of which is not preserved). No other variants are attested and no score for this inscription is presented in the microfiche.

BIBLIOGRAPHY

1930 Unger in Wetzel, Stadtmauern p. 79 (exs. 1–4, provenance, study)

1930 Wetzel, Stadtmauern pp. 61 and 65 (exs. 1–4, provenance), and pls. 37–38 and 51 (exs. 2, 4, provenance)

TEXT

1) x x x (x) [x]
2) ù-mu-un g[al]
3) lugal-a-ni-ir
4) LUGAL-GI.NA
5) lugal ma-da
6) *aš-šur*.KI-ke$_4$
7) lugal ki-šár-ra
8) GÌR.NÍTA
9) KÁ.DINGIR.RA.KI
10) lugal ki-in-gi
11) uri.KI-ke$_4$
12) bàd *im-gur-*^{d}*en-líl*
13) bàd *né-met-*^{d}*en-líl*
14) nam-ti-la-a-ni-šè
15) gibil-bi
16) ù-mu-un-na-dím
17) u$_4$-gin$_7$
18) ba-an-zálag

1–18) For *the god Marduk*, the gr[eat] lord, his lord: Sargon (II), king of the land of Assyria, king of the world, viceroy of Babylon, (10) king of Sumer (and) Akkad, constructed anew the (city) wall Imgur-Enlil (and) the (city) wall Nēmet-Enlil for the sake of his life (and) made (them) shine like daylight.

3

This inscription, written in Akkadian, describes the restoration of the Eanna temple by Sargon II for the goddess Ištar. It is known from a cylinder which has a colophon on it stating that it was a copy of the original inscription. The inscription is modelled upon one of Marduk-apla-iddina II's (B.6.21.1) and may have been intended to replace it.

COMMENTARY

The clay cylinder (YBC 2181) is reported to have been found at Uruk and was presented to the Yale Babylonian Collection (New Haven) by Dr. and Mrs. J.B. Nies. It measures 13.2×6.5 cm. The inscription is written in contemporary Babylonian script and is in two columns (40+41 lines). There are line rulings after every two or three lines, including one before the colophon. The inscription has been collated.

The use of -mu for the enclitic particle -ma (lines i 19, 20, 22, and ii 23, and 34) is noteworthy; see Röllig, ZA 56 (1964) p. 231.

BIBLIOGRAPHY

1915 Clay, YOS 1 no. 38 (photo, copy, edition)
1930 Jordan, UVB 1 p. 8 (study)
1933 von Soden, OLZ 36 424 (i 3, study)
1953 Gadd, Iraq 15 pp. 125–32 (study)
1954 Follet, Biblica 35 pp. 413–28 (partial transliteration, study)

TEXT

Col. i

1) [*ana*] ⸢^{d}INANNA⸣ *be-let* KUR.KUR *ti-iz-qar-ti* DINGIR.MEŠ
2) [*qaritti*(?)] *i-la-a-ti*
3) [x x x (x x)] ⸢*a*⸣-*bu-bu ez-zu šug-lu-tu*
4) [x x x (x x)] x *za-ʾ-na-át*
5) [x x x (x x)] QAR TI *šag-ga-pur-tu*
6) [x x x (x x)] *pul-ḫa-a-ti*
7) [x x x (x x)] x Ú ŠAT *bu-ru-mu*
8) [x x x (x x) A]Ḫ(?) ZU-*šu-un* ⸢ŠI(?) DA(?) AT(?)⸣
9) [x x x x (x)] *šá aš-rum*
10) [x x (x) *ga-mi-r*]*a*(?)-*át šip-ṭu u* EŠ.BAR
11) [x x x (x x)] *šu-luḫ-ḫu*
12) [x x x x (x)] x KÙ *šá qé-reb* UNUG.KI
13) [x x x (x x)-*t*]u_4 GAŠAN-*i-šu*
14) [*šarru-ukīn šar* (*māt*) *aš-š*]*ur* LUGAL ŠÚ GÌR.NÍTA KÁ.DINGIR.MEŠ.KI
15) [*šar* (*māt*) *šu-me*]-⸢*ru*⸣ *u* URI.KI NUN *za-a-nin-šá*
16) [*ana balāṭ*(?) ZI.M]E(?)-*šú* GÍD.DA u_4-*me-šú la-bar* BALA-*šú*
17) [x x x] x-*šú sa-kap* LÚ.KÚR-*i-šu*
18) [*é-an*]-⸢*na*⸣ *šá* ^{d}*šul-gi* LUGAL *maḫ-ru*
19) ⸢*ú-še*⸣-*pi-šu-mu il-li-ku la-ba-riš*
20) É *šu-a-tu*$_4$ É.GAR$_8$.MEŠ-*šú i-qu-pú-mu*
21) *up-ta-aṭ-ṭi-ru rik-su-ú-šu*$_{14}$
22) *sa-mit-su us-sar-ri-ḫu-ú-mu*
23) ⸢*iḫ*⸣-*ḫar*(*)-*mi-mu tì-mé-en-šú*
24) *ina lib-bi* LUGAL.MEŠ *a-lik maḫ-ru*
25) *la ib-bal-ki-tu* DÙ-*eš šip-ri-šu*
26) *i-nu-šú* LUGAL-*ú-kin* LUGAL KUR *aš-šur* LUGAL KIŠ
27) GÌR.NÍTA TIN.TIR.KI *ni-bit* ^{d}*asar-ri*
28) EN GAL-*ú* ^{d}AMAR.UTU GEŠTU.II *ṣir-ti iš-ruk-šum-ma*
29) ⸢*ú*⸣-*rap-pi-iš ḫa-si-is-su*

i 1–13) [For] the goddess Ištar, mistress of the lands, (most) eminent of the gods, [(*most*) *valiant*] of the goddesses, [...] fierce, terrifying flood, [(...) who] is endowed with [...] (i 5) [...] ... majestic, [...] awe, [...] ... the firmament (of the heavens), [...] ... [...] humble, (i 10) [... *who give*]*s* judgment and decision, [...] purification rites, [...] which is inside Uruk, [...], his lady:

i 14–15) [Sargon (II), king of Assy]ria, king of the world, viceroy of Babylon, [king of (the land of) Sume]r and Akkad, prince who provides for her,

i 16–17) [In order to ensure] his [*good health*], to prolong his days, to lengthen his reign, [to ...] his [...], (and) to overthrow his enemy,

i 18–25) [(With regard to) Ean]na, which Šulgi, a previous king, had had built and which had become old, (i 20) (with regard to) this temple, whose walls had buckled, whose bondings had disintegrated, whose parapet had become ruined, whose foundation had collapsed, (and) whose reconstruction had not occurred to (any of) the kings, (his) predecessors —

i 26–29) At that time, the great lord, the god Marduk, gave excellent judgment to Sargon (II), king of Assyria, king of the world, viceroy of Babylon, one who was chosen by the god Asari, and increased his understanding.

---

i 2 The restoration is based upon 5 R pl. 33 i 9–10 and cf. B.6.31.15 line 1 (*qa-rit-ti* DINGIR.MEŠ).
i 5 Possibly [... *tiz*]-*qar-ti*, "[emi]nent."
i 10 Or [... *na-di-n*]*a-át* instead of [... *ga-mi-r*]*a-át*.
i 23 *ḫar*(*): text has TAM.

30) *[ana u]d-du-šu ma-ḫa-zu u eš-re-e-ti*
31) *kal* DINGIR.MEŠ *na-du-tu šá* KUR.URI.KI GEŠTU.II-*šú* GÁL-⸢*ši*⸣-*ma*
32) *áš-rat é-an-na šu-bat* ^{d}INANNA GAŠAN KUR.KUR GAŠAN-*i-šú*
33) *iš-te-ʾ-e-ma*
34) É.GAR$_8$ *é-an-na ki-da-a-nu*
35) *šá ki-sal-li šap-li-i*
36) *sa-mit-su is-suḫ-ma* ZÁLAG-*ir te-mé-en-šú*
37) URU$_4$.MEŠ-*šú ina te-mi-qí ik-ri-bu*
38) *ù la-ba-a-nu ap-pi id-di-i-mi*
39) *tì-mé-en-šú ina i-rat ki-gal-la*
40) *ú-šar-ši-id šá-du-ú-ú-a-iš*
Col. ii
1) *ina ši-pir* ^{d}*kulla* LÚ.ŠITIM.GAL-*la*
2) *ù* UM.ME.A ⸢*mu*⸣-*de-e šip-ri*
3) *ina* SIG$_4$.ḪI.A KÙ-*tim* SAG.ME-*šú ul-li-mi*
4) *ú-šak-li-il ši-pi-ir-šú*
5) UGU *šá pa-an ú-šá-tir-ma*
6) *uš-te-ši-ra ú-ṣu-ra-a-ti*
7) *ana šat-ti šip-ru šá-a-šú* ^{d}INANNA GAŠAN KUR.KUR
8) ḪÚL-*iš lip-pa-lis-ma*
9) *a-na* LUGAL-GI.NA LUGAL KUR *aš-šur*.KI
10) LUGAL ŠÁR GÌR.NÍTA KÁ.DINGIR.RA.KI
11) LUGAL *za-a-nin-šá liš-ruk* TI.LA
12) *ma-ḫar* ^{d}AMAR.UTU LUGAL DINGIR.MEŠ
13) MUNUS.SIG$_5$-*šú lit-tas-qar*
14) *ina šá-áš-mu ù ta-ḫa-zu*
15) *lil-lik re-ṣu-ú-šu*
16) GIŠ.TUKUL.MEŠ ⸢*lem*⸣-*nu-ti-šú li-šab-bir-ma*
17) *li-im-ṣa-a ma-la lìb-bu-uš*
18) *gi-mir ma-al-ku la kan-šú-<<nu>>-ti-šú*
19) *li-šak-ni-šá še-pu-uš-šu*
20) *ina qí-bit* ^{d}INANNA *na-ram-ti* EN DINGIR.MEŠ
21) *li-iṣ-ṣi-ib bu-ʾ-a-ru*
22) TIN UD.MEŠ GÍD.DA.MEŠ *ṭu-ub lìb-bu*
23) *na-mar ka-bat-ti liš-šá-rik-šum-mu*
24) *li-ri-ik pa-lu-ú-šum*
25) SUḪUŠ GIŠ.GU.ZA-*šú ana u*$_4$*-mi ṣa-a-ti*
26) *li-šar-šid-ma li-ma-ʾ-ir*
27) *kib-ra-a-ti*
28) *šá* ÉRIN.MEŠ UBARA *šu-bar-e* DINGIR.MEŠ GAL.MEŠ
29) *ma-al-ku-ut-su-nu li-tep-pu-uš*
30) *šá šu-ba-re-e šu-nu-ú-tu ina* BALA-*šú*
31) *a-a ib-ba-ši e-šit-su-un*
32) *e-gi-it-su-nu li-šat-bil-ma*
33) *li-pa-as-si-is ḫi-ṭè-et-su-u[n]*
34) *saḫ*$_4$*-maš-tu*$_4$ *lu-ú ik-kib-šu-nu-mu*
35) *li-šá-li-iṣ kab-ta-at-su-un*
36) *ki-ma t[ì(?)]-⸢mé⸣-na* UNUG.KI
37) *ù é-an-na*
38) *li-ku-ú-na iš-da-šu-un*

i 30–36) He (Sargon) directed his attention [to] renovating the abandoned cult centres and sanctuaries of all the gods of the land of Akkad. He was assiduous toward the sanctuaries of Eanna, the abode of the goddess Ištar, mistress of the lands, his lady. (With regard to) the outer enclosure wall of Eanna in the lower courtyard, he tore down its parapet and laid bare its foundation.

i 37–ii 6) With fervent entreaties, prayers, and expressions of humility he (Sargon) laid its foundations (anew) and he fixed its foundation on the breast of the netherworld (as secure) as a mountain. (ii 1) With the work of the god Kulla, the chief builder, and (with the help of) artisans who know (their) craft, he raised its top with (ritually) pure bricks and completed its construction. He made (it) superior to what had been there before and carried out the plans correctly.

ii 7–15) On account of this, may the goddess Ištar, mistress of the lands, look upon this work with pleasure and may she bestow a (long) life on Sargon, king of Assyria, (ii 10) king of the world, viceroy of Babylon, the king who provides for her! May she say good things about him before the god Marduk, king of the gods! May she go (with him) as his helper in strife and battle!

ii 16–27) May he smash the weapons of his enemies and may he achieve whatever he wants! May he subjugate at his feet all rulers who are not submissive to him! (ii 20) By the command of the goddess Ištar, beloved of the lord of the gods, may he increase (his) good fortune! May long life, happiness, and gladness be bestowed on him and may his reign be long! May he make the foundation of his throne secure for future days and may he control (all) regions (of the world)!

ii 28–38) May he exercise the rule over the people who are of privileged status (and) freed from taxation by the great gods! (ii 30) During his reign may those ones freed from taxation not be in disorder! May he take away their negligence and may he remove their sin! Let turmoil be unknown to them (ii 35) (and) may he make their heart(s) rejoice! Like the foundations of Uruk and Eanna, may their foundations be firm!

ii 1 Kulla was the god of bricks (see Lambert, RLA 6/3–4 [1981] p. 305) and his "work" could refer either to the skill of that god or to (new) brickwork. Similar passages appear frequently in inscriptions of Esarhaddon and Ashurbanipal (e.g., B.6.31.11 line 16 and B.6.32.1 line 21).

ii 16 and **19** It is possible that the subject of the verbs "smash" and "subjugate" is the goddess Ištar rather than the king.

Colophon
39) GABA.RI MU.SAR-*e*
40) *šu-bul-tì* É.GAL KUR *aš-šur*.KI
41) *šá-ṭir-ma* IGI.KÁR

Colophon
ii 39–41) Copy of the inscription, dispatch *to/of* the palace of Assyria; copied and collated.

4

Numerous bricks from Uruk have an Akkadian inscription stamped upon them which states that Sargon had reconstructed various parts of the Eanna temple.

CATALOGUE

Ex.	Museum number	Excavation number	Warka provenance	Dimensions (cm)	Lines preserved	FuB 27	cpn
1	VA 14664m, edge	W 1635a	Od XVI 4, debris	7.5×17×17	1–8	31A	n
2	—	W 1831a	Oc XVI 3, highest debris	34×18×7	1–8	—	n
3	VA 14664a	W 1831b	As ex. 2	18×25×8	1–8	20	n
4	—	W 2589	Qb XIV 2	34×18×7	1–12	—	n
5	VA 14664b	W 2703	Oc XVI 2, at the door's pivot box in room 39 of Sargon's enclosure	18×34.5×8	1–12	21	n
6	—	W 2704	Od XVI 4, room 43	34×18×7	1–12	—	n
7	VA 14664c	W 2705	City area	7×20×21.5	5–12	22	n
8	VA 14664d	W 3200a	Oc XVI 2, Per. room 2 in the door's pivot box	18×34.5×8.5	1–12	23	n
9	VA 14664e	W 5753	Eanna, SE enclosure wall	17.5×35×8.5	1–12	24	n
10	VA 14664f	W 6420a	As ex. 7	18×35×8	1–12	25	n
11	VA 14664g	W 6420b/c	As ex. 7	18×35×8.5	1–12	26	n
12	VA 14664h	W 13393	Oe XVI 4	18×34×8	1–12	27	n
13	VA 14664i	—	—	17×34.5×8.5	1–12	28	n
14	VA 14664k	—	—	18×26.5×8.5	1–12	29	n
15	VA 14664l	—	—	18×21.5×7.5	1–8	30	n
16	—	—	G 22 b1 (from surface survey)	—	—	—	n

COMMENTARY

All exemplars were found by the German excavations at Uruk. The provenances given for exs. 1 and 8 come from the excavation's registry of finds rather than from the statements in UVB 1 (see Marzahn, FuB 27 [1989] pp. 60–61 and 64 nn. 17 and 21). Findspots for exs. 1, 5, and 8 are marked on pl. 3 of UVB 1 and these would suggest that ex. 1 was found in Od XVI 3 (as stated in UVB 1) and that ex. 5 was found in Ob XVI 1 rather than Oc XVI 2. The registry refers to three exemplars with the excavation number W 6420 (W6420a–c). Ex. 10 is W 6420a and ex. 11 is either W 6420b or c (the letter is no longer recognizable); one of exs. 13–15 may be the third brick originally given this excavation number. (See Marzahn, FuB 27 [1989] p. 64 n. 19.)

Exs. 1 and 7 are stamped on an edge of the brick, while exs. 2–6 and 8–15 are stamped on the face. Ex. 1 has inscription B.6.22.5 stamped on its face. The text is in three columns, each column having four lines. No variants are attested and no score for this brick inscription is presented in the microfiche. The edition is based upon the published composite copy and Marzahn's work in FuB 27.

BIBLIOGRAPHY

1930 Jordan, UVB 1 pp. 6–7 (provenance)
1930 Schott, UVB 1 p. 56 and pl. 28 no. 20 (exs. 1–8, provenance, composite copy, edition)
1989 Marzahn, FuB 27 pp. 59–61 no. X, nos. 20–31A (transliteration; exs. 1, 3, 5, 7–15, study)
1991 Kessler in Finkbeiner, AUWE 4 p. 183 no. 26 (ex. 16, study)

TEXT

Col. i
1) ᵈLUGAL-*ú-kin*
2) LUGAL GAL-*ú*
3) LUGAL *kiš-šat*
4) LUGAL TIN.TIR.KI
Col. ii
5) LUGAL KUR *šu-me-rú u* URI.KI
6) *mu-ir-rú* KUR ᵈ*aš-šur*
7) *u gi-mir* MAR.TU-*i*
8) *kir-ḫu ki-da-a-nu*
Col. iii
9) KISAL *é-an-na*
10) KÁ *qá-tan*
11) *u* KÁ *ki-i-nu*
12) *ú-še-pi-iš*

1–12) Sargon (II), great king, king of the world, king of Babylon, (5) king of the land of Sumer and Akkad, commander of Assyria and of all Amurru, had the outer enclosure wall, the courtyard of Eanna, (10) the narrow gate, and the regular gate built.

5

Several bricks found at Uruk bear a stamped inscription, written in Sumerian, which records the paving of the processional way in the Eanna temple with baked bricks by Sargon II for the goddess Inanna (Ištar). It is worthy of note that the king's name is preceded by the divine determinative in line 6.

CATALOGUE

Ex.	Museum number	Excavation number	Warka photo number	Warka provenance	Dimensions (cm)	Lines preserved	FuB 27	cpn
1	EŞ number unknown	W 2	8	Eanna area, surface of mound	34.5×34.5×7.5	1–14	—	p
2	VA 14664m, face	W 1635a	824	Od XVI 4, debris	7.5×17×17	1–6	31B	p
3	VA 14663a	W 1635c	823	As ex. 2	34×33.5×8	1–14	32	p
4	VA 14663b	W 1635d	823	As ex. 2	34.5×34×8	1–14	33	p
5	—	W 1635e	824	As ex. 2	33×33×7.5	1–14	—	p
6	VA 14663c	W 4663	821	Ziqqurat, north	22.5×29.5×8	1–9	34	p
7	VA 14663d	W 11747	—	Oe XVI 4, 5 m NW of the door in the SW wall of temple III, from debris under pavement of Cyrus	22.5×20×7.5	1–9	35	n
8	VA 14663e	W 13182	—	—	34.5×24×8	1–14	36	n

COMMENTARY

All exemplars were found by the excavations sponsored by the Deutsche Orient-Gesellschaft at Uruk. According to the excavator, J. Jordan, numerous bricks with this inscription and measuring 34×34×7 cm were found at one spot north of the ziqqurat within Eanna (Jordan, Uruk-Warka p. 48). The provenances given for exs. 2–5 come from the excavation's registry of finds rather than from the statements in UVB 1 (see Marzahn, FuB 27 [1989] pp. 61–62 and 64 n. 21). With regard to the findspot of ex. 2, see the commentary to B.6.22.4. The inscription is found stamped on the face of the brick. Ex. 2 also has inscription B.6.22.4 stamped on one edge. No variants are attested and no score of this brick inscription is provided in the microfiche.

The a(*) sign at the end of line 8 is made up of three vertical wedges. The reading of line 14 remains problematic. While the published copies and the transliteration by Marzahn suggest ki-bi bí-in-túm ("he brought to its place," i.e., "he restored"), in comparison with other inscriptions, including one of Sargon's brick inscriptions from Babylon (B.6.22.2) and one of Esarhaddon's from Babylon (B.6.31.13, Akkadian), we might expect u_4-gin_7 bí-in-zálag ("made shine like daylight"). From the photos examined, u_4, gin_7, and zálag appear to be as good or better than ki, bi, and túm respectively (in particular, the second sign appears to have a vertical wedge at the end, as noted on the copy in UVB 1). The final sign is more elongated than the first one and this might suggest túm rather than zálag, but the two vertical wedges appear to be angled, narrowing toward the left.

BIBLIOGRAPHY

1913 Jordan, MDOG 51 pp. 52–53 (ex. 1?, study [by Delitzsch])

1928 Jordan, Uruk-Warka pp. 42–43, 48, and 50–51 no. 6, and pl. 105c–d (ex. 1, provenance, photo, copy, edition [by Schroeder])

1930 Schott, UVB 1 pp. 55–56 and pl. 28 no. 19 (exs. 1–6, provenance, composite copy, edition)

1989 Marzahn, FuB 27 pp. 61–62 no. XI, nos. 32–36 and 31B (transliteration; exs. 2–4, 6–8, study)

TEXT

1) ^{d}inanna
2) nin unu.KI-ga-ta
3) dúr-mar é-an-na
4) gašan maḫ bùlug-gá
5) nin-a-ni-ir
6) ^{d}LUGAL-GI.NA
7) lugal ki-šár-ra
8) GÌR.NÍTA KÁ.DINGIR.RA.KI-a(*)
9) lugal ki-in-gi uri.KI
10) sipa ma-da *aš-šur*.KI-ke_4
11) sig_4-al-ùr-ra
12) ù-me-ni-dù-dù
13) gìr-gin é-an-na
14) u_4(?)-gin_7(?) bí-in-zálag(?)

1–14) For the goddess Inanna, lady of Uruk, who dwells in Eanna, the august, supreme lady, (5) his lady: Sargon (II), king of the world, viceroy of Babylon, king of Sumer (and) Akkad, (10) shepherd of the land of Assyria, had baked bricks made (and) *made* the processional way of Eanna *shine like daylight.*

6

A Sumerian inscription is found stamped upon two bricks discovered at Uruk by the expedition sponsored by the Deutsche Orient-Gesellschaft. The inscription records work on the Eanna temple by Sargon II for the goddess Inanna (Ištar). The edition is based upon the copy and information published by Marzahn in FuB 27.

CATALOGUE

Ex.	Museum number	Excavation number	Warka provenance	Dimensions (cm)	Lines preserved	Fub 27	cpn
1	VA 14663f	W 5452	Qd XVI, between highest pavements	34.5×35.5×8	1–12	37	n
2	VA 14663g	—	—	34.5×34.5×8	1–7	38	n

BIBLIOGRAPHY

1989 Marzahn, FuB 27 pp. 62–63 no. XII, nos. 37–38 (transliteration; ex. 1, copy; exs. 1–2, study)

TEXT

1) nin ^{d}⸢inanna⸣
2) nin ⸢kur-kur-ra⸣
3) nin-a-ni-ir
4) ^{d}LUGAL-*ú-kin*
5) lugal k[ala(?)]-ga
6) lugal KÁ.DINGIR.RA.⸢KI⸣
7) lugal ki-šár-⸢ra⸣
8) ⸢lugal(?)⸣ [x x x]
9) ⸢lugal(?)⸣ [x x] x
10) ⸢é-an-na⸣
11) ⸢é ki-ág-gá-ni⸣
12) ⸢mu-un-na-dím⸣

1–12) For the lady, the goddess Inanna, mistress of the lands, his lady: Sargon (II), (5) *m*[*ight*]*y* king, king of Babylon, king of the world, *king* [...], *king* [...], (re)constructed (10) Eanna, her beloved temple.

5 Marzahn notes that the traces of the sign after lugal could be those of either unu or kala. Since no other inscription from this period accords a ruler the title "king of Uruk" while several use the epithet "mighty king" (e.g., B.6.32.16 line 6), the latter restoration is preferred here.

Sennacherib

B.6.23

Sargon II was killed in battle and was succeeded by his son Sennacherib (Sîn-aḫḫē-erība), who ruled Assyria for twenty-four years (704–681 BC). During this time, Sennacherib controlled Babylonia directly for two periods: 704–703 BC and 688–681 BC. His first reign over Babylonia (B.6.23) was ended by a rebellion in that land which brought about the brief reigns of Marduk-zākir-šumi II (B.6.24) and Marduk-apla-iddina II (B.6.25), who ruled for a total of ten months in 703 BC. After putting down this rebellion, Sennacherib installed a Babylonian by the name of Bēl-ibni (B.6.26) on the throne of Babylon. This vassal ruler reigned for three years (702–700 BC) before he was removed by the Assyrian king and replaced by Aššur-nādin-šumi (B.6.27), one of Sennacherib's sons, who reigned for six years (699–694 BC). In 694 BC, the Elamite king Ḫallušu-Inšušinak invaded Babylonia, deposed Aššur-nādin-šumi, and put the Babylonian Nergal-ušēzib (B.6.28) on the throne of Babylon. After a reign of six months (693 BC), Nergal-ušēzib was defeated in battle near Nippur by the Assyrian army and carried off to Assyria. A Chaldean by the name of Mušēzib-Marduk (B.6.29) seized the throne of Babylon and carried on the rebellion for four more years (692–689 BC) until the Assyrians managed to capture Babylon and end the resistance to Assyrian domination. Sennacherib ruled Babylonia directly for the remaining eight years of his life, 688–681 BC (B.6.30), but he did not assume the titles "king of Babylon," "viceroy of Babylon," or "king of the land Sumer and Akkad." While Babylonian King List A and apparently the Assyrian Synchronistic King Lists included Sennacherib twice in their lists of rulers of Babylonia, the Ptolemaic Canon considered both periods when he directly controlled Babylonia to be "kingless." One Babylonian chronicle also considered the eight years of Sennacherib's second "reign" to be "kingless"; the section dealing with his first reign is not preserved on this chronicle. (See Grayson, Chronicles p. 81 no. 1 iii 28 and RLA 6/1–2 [1980] pp. 93, 101, 120, and 122.)

Only one royal inscription of Sennacherib can be considered Babylonian and included here. It is found on paving stones from Babylon and merely gives the king's name and the title "king of Assyria" (B.6.23.1). Since Sennacherib had Babylon destroyed and abandoned after he captured it in 689 BC, this inscription should come from his first reign over Babylonia (704–703 BC); it is not impossible, however, that the paving stones were made and engraved while either his vassal Bēl-ibni or his son Aššur-nādin-šumi sat on the throne of Babylon. Three Babylonian economic texts are dated by the regnal years of Sennacherib. Each refers to him as "king of Assyria" and each comes from his second "reign" over Babylonia (see Brinkman and Kennedy, JCS 35 [1983] p. 14 no. C, and Frame, Babylonia pp. 284–85).

For details on Babylonia during the time of Sennacherib, see Brinkman, Prelude pp. 54–70, and Frame, Babylonia pp. 52–63.

1

Some paving stones of breccia from Babylon have a short Akkadian inscription recording "Sennacherib, king of Assyria."

COMMENTARY

Some or all of these paving stones were later reused by Nebuchadnezzar II and have an inscription of that king on their other surface. Koldewey refers to one exemplar found on July 28, 1900, in Amran, and he and Unger refer to paving stones from the processional way in the entry court leading to the main eastern gate in the enclosure wall of the ziqqurat precinct. No museum or excavation numbers are known for any of these exemplars and the inscription is edited from the published copy.

BIBLIOGRAPHY

1900 Koldewey, MDOG 6 p. 11 (provenance, translation)
1901 Koldewey, Pflastersteine p. 10 and pl. 4 no. v (provenance, copy, translation)
1924–25 Unger, AfK 2 p. 21 no. 3 (study)
1925 Koldewey, WEB^{4} pp. 52–53 and 187, and fig. 36 (provenance, study)
1931 Unger, Babylon pp. 109 and 279 no. 19 (translation)

TEXT

1) ⌈^{d}⌉30-PAP.MEŠ-⌈SU⌉
2) MAN KUR AŠ

1–2) Sennacherib, king of Assyria.

Marduk-zākir-šumi II

B.6.24

In the early part of 703 BC, an individual by the name of Marduk-zākir-šumi led a rebellion against Assyria. King List A acknowledged him to have been king for one month, before he was ousted by Marduk-apla-iddina II. The king list also states that Marduk-zākir-šumi was the son (or descendant) of one Arad (Grayson, RLA 6/1–2 [1980] p. 93 iv 13′). It is likely that he should be identified with a provincial governor by this name who is said to have been the son (or descendant) of Arad-Ea and who appeared as a witness in a kudurru composed at Babylon in 715 (Messerschmidt and Ungnad, VAS 1 no. 37 v 2–3). The only royal inscription which might come from this king's reign is more probably to be assigned to the earlier king by this name and is edited there (B.6.7.1). No economic texts composed during this king's brief reign have been preserved. With regard to the reign of Marduk-zākir-šumi II, see Brinkman in Studies Oppenheim pp. 24–25 n. 137 and in RLA 7/5–6 (1989) p. 379.

Marduk-apla-iddina II

B.6.25

In 703 BC Marduk-apla-iddina II (Merodach-baladan) deposed Marduk-zākir-šumi II and occupied the throne of Babylon for a second time. King List A credits him with a reign of nine months (Grayson, RLA 6/1–2 [1980] p. 93 iv 14′) before Sennacherib regained control of Babylonia. The one royal inscription which appears to date to this time has been edited under his first reign (B.6.21.3).

Bēl-ibni

B.6.26

After defeating the forces of Marduk-apla-iddina II, Sennacherib installed as king of Babylonia Bēl-ibni, whom the Assyrian king describes as being "a member of the Rab-bānî class, a native of Babylon, who had grown up in my palace like a young dog." His reign lasted only three years (702–700 BC) and he appears to have lost jurisdiction of southern Babylonia toward its end. At that time, we hear of Assyrian officials in the south, and the Chaldeans may have been in effective control of that area. Sennacherib conducted another campaign into Babylonia in 700 BC; Bēl-ibni and his officials were taken to Assyria; and Sennacherib's son, Aššur-nādin-šumi, was made king (B.6.27). It is not known if Bēl-ibni was removed from office because of incompetence, disloyalty, or some other reason. One text records the grant of tax-exempt status to the town of Ša-uṣur-Adad by Bēl-ibni (B.6.26.1), and seven Babylonian economic texts are dated by his reign. With regard to the reign of Bēl-ibni, see Brinkman, Prelude pp. 58–60 and RA 77 (1983) pp. 175–76; Brinkman and Kennedy, JCS 35 (1983) pp. 14–15 no. E and 38 (1986) p. 99 no. E.

1

A copy of an inscription recording the granting of privileges to the town of Ša-uṣur-Adad by Bēl-ibni is found on a clay tablet in the Binning collection. Unlike other royal decrees of the period (such as Messerschmidt and Ungnad, VAS 1 no. 37, from the reign of Marduk-apla-iddina II), this inscription does not include a list of witnesses and (as a copy) is not in the form of a kudurru. It has thus been decided to include the inscription in this volume even though it is somewhat different in nature than the other inscriptions presented.

COMMENTARY

The clay tablet was published by C.B.F. Walker as no. 1 in the collection of Lord Binning of Mellerstain, Berwickshire. The tablet measures 12.3×6.4×2.8 cm and its curvature would suggest that only two or three lines are missing at the beginning. Line rulings are found after each of lines 1′–34′ and 40′. This Akkadian inscription is written in Late Babylonian script; it is edited from the published copy.

Walker (Iraq 44 [1982] p. 72) suggests that lines 1′–3′ may describe a state of turmoil in southern Babylonia for which the king (Marduk-apla-iddina II) was held responsible and that lines 4′–5′ may indicate that Marduk and the gods became angry and decided to depose him (Marduk-apla-iddina II) and appoint a new ruler (Bēl-ibni).

The reading of the name of the goddess ^{d}*ba*-KUR (lines 8′, 10′, and 15′) is not known. Walker reasonably suggests that since line 15′ indicates that the goddess shared a temple with the god Ninurta, she may have been regarded locally as his wife. He then notes that a hymn refers to the goddess Ba'u (Baba/Bawa), who is known to have been a wife of Ninurta, as the giver of omens and that ^{d}*ba*-KUR is described in our text in connection with omens (line 8′). (See Walker in Iraq 44 [1982] p. 74 commentary to line 8′.) As noted by Walker (ibid. p. 76), the reading of the name Bēl-ibni in line 19′ (and thus the understanding of the historical context of the inscription) is not completely certain. One would expect there to be a divine determinative with the first part of the name (i.e., ^{d}EN-) and not expect to have the title "king" written before the name of the ruler. Walker states that collation has shown that the name cannot be LUGAL-GI.NA.

The town of Ša-uṣur-Adad is presumably to be identified with the towns Ša-iṣṣur-Adad (a fortified city in the territory of the Chaldean tribe of Bīt-Amukāni) and Ša-ṣur(u)-Adad; see Zadok, Rép. Géogr. 8 p. 12 sub Ālu-ša-Iṣṣur-Adad.

Colophon 1 was probably the original colophon on the copy of the decree presented to Nabû-gamil and colophon 2 was added by the scribe who copied the present tablet.

BIBLIOGRAPHY

1982 Walker, Iraq 44 pp. 70–76 (copy, edition)
1983 Brinkman and Kennedy, JCS 35 p. 15 no. En.1 (study)

TEXT

Lacuna

1′) [...] x ⸢KA⸣ LI [x x x]
2′) [...] x *šá e-liš ana šap-liš* ⸢GAR-*un*(?)⸣ x [x]
3′) [... *ú*]-⸢*šá*⸣-*an-na-a šu-bat-su*-[*nu*]
4′) [*inūšu marduk* E]N GAL-*ú ez*-⸢*zi*⸣-<*iš*> ⸢*ka*⸣-*šad*-⸢*su*⸣ D[UG$_4$(?).GA-*ma*]
5′) [*ilānu šá* URU/KUR]-*šú i-gu-gu-ma šá*-⸢*a*⸣-*šú* x [x (x)] x [x x]
6′) x x *ra*-⸢*biš*⸣ *ú-ma-'e-r*[*u-ni*]*m* ⸢IŠ KU⸣ x [x x] x
7′) BÁRA.MEŠ DINGIR.MEŠ-*šú-nu iq-qur šá-a-šú-nu iḫ-bu-ut*-⸢*ma*⸣ DIN[GIR.MEŠ-*šú-n*]*u ú-dáp*-⸢*pír*⸣
8′) ^{d}*nin-urta* IBILA *a-šá-re-du* KIN-*tú* ^{d}*ba*-KUR ⸢GAŠAN⸣ *t*[*er*(?)-*t*]*i*(?)
9′) ⸢*ú*⸣-*šab-ri-šum-ma ú-šaḫ*(*)-*sis lìb-bu-uš-šú*
10′) ⸢*ina šil*⸣-*lat* URU *šá-pi-ia* ^{d}*ba*-KUR *i-mur-ru-ma*
11′) ⸢*ip*⸣-*laḫ ik-kud-ma sur*-⸢*qin*⸣-*nu ú-kin*
12′) DINGIR.MEŠ *šá* <*šá*>-URU.ÙRU-^{d}[IŠKU]R *ḫab-tu-tu a-na* ^{d}PA EN-*šú ú-za*[*k*]-⸢*ki*⸣
13′) ⸢*a-lak il*⸣-*ki u* ⸢*tup-šik*⸣-*ku is*-⸢*suḫ*⸣-*šú-nu-ti-ma* ⸢*šu*⸣-*bar*-<*re*>-*šú-nu iš-kun*

1′–13′) [...] ... [...] *he turned* upside down [... He] changed the[ir] abode. [At that time, the god Marduk], the great lord, angrily *or*[*dered*] his defeat. (5′) [The gods of] his [city/country] became angry and [...] him. ... they gave a magnificent commission ... He tore down the sanctuaries of their (the Babylonians') gods, plundered them, and removed (the statues of) [their] gods. The god Ninurta, foremost son (of the god Enlil), revealed to him (in a vision) an omen concerning the goddess Ba-KUR, lady *of omens*, and caused (him) to remember (this) in his heart. (10′) They saw the goddess Ba-KUR during the sacking of the town Šapīia; he became afraid (and) concerned. He (re-)established their offerings (and) released to the god Nabû, his lord, the plundered gods of Ša-uṣur-[Ada]d. He abolished their performance of feudal obligations and corvée-labour and established their freedom from taxation.

14′) [*ina u*$_4$]-⸢*mi*⸣-*šú-ma* ^{md}AG-⸢*ga-mil* DUMU⸣-*šú šá* ^{m}*ta-ri-bi*
15′) ⸢LÚ.KU$_4$⸣ É ^{d}MAŠ *u* ^{d}*ba*-KUR ŠU.II ^{d}*ba*-KUR *iṣ-bat-ma*
16′) *a-na šá*-URU.ÙRU-^{d}IŠKUR URU KÙ.GA *ú-šá-aṣ-bít*
17′) ⸢*i*⸣-*ru-um-ma a-na é-te-en-te-en pa-paḫ* <<*paḫ*>> *šu-bat-su*
18′) ⸢IM.DUB⸣ *ši-pir-e-tú šá za-ku-ti* <*šá*>-URU.ÙRU-^{d}IŠKUR
19′) LUGAL ⸢EN-DÙ(?) *iš*⸣-*ṭur-ma a-na* ^{md}AG-*ga-mil* ⸢*id*⸣-*din*
20′) *ù šá*-URU.ÙRU-^{d}IŠKUR *a-na* ^{d}PA EN-*šú ul-lil*

14′–20′) [At] that time Nabû-gamil, son of Tarībi, one privileged to enter the temple of the god Ninurta and the goddess Ba-KUR, grasped the hand of the goddess Ba-KUR and caused (her) to take (the road) to Ša-uṣur-Adad, the holy city. She entered the shrine Etenten ("House which Soothes"), her abode. The king *Bēl-ibni* wrote an official document (granting) exemption to Ša-uṣur-Adad and gave it to Nabû-gamil. Moreover, he made Ša-uṣur-Adad free of all claims for the god Nabû, his lord.

21′) *man-nu ár-ku-ú lu-ú* LUGAL *lu-ú* ⸢DUMU⸣ LUGAL *lu-ú* LÚ *ru-bu-u*
22′) *lu-ú šá-pi-ru* ⸢*lu*⸣-*ú* LÚ.DI.KUD *lu*-⸢*ú a*⸣-*a-um-ma*
23′) *šá* ^{d}AMAR.UTU EN GAL-*ú ú-ma-'a-ru-šú-ma ina* KUR *ip-pu-uš be-lu-tú*

21′–34′) With regard to anyone in the future — whether a king, or a son of a king, or a prince, or a governor, or a judge, or anyone else who is appointed by the god Marduk, the great lord, and (who) exercises lordship over the land — (who)

24′) *mim-ma ši-pir ni-kil-ti a-na* <*šá*>-URU.[Ù]RU-^{d}IŠKUR
25′) *ù* DINGIR.MEŠ *a-šib lìb-bi-šú ip-*⌈*pu*⌉*-uš*
26′) *lu-ú* UN.MEŠ *a-na il-ki ù til-lu-ti i-de-ek-ku-u*
27′) ⌈*lu-ú*⌉ A.ŠÀ.⌈MEŠ⌉-*šú-nu tu-šá-an-nu-ú-ma a-na pi-ḫa*(*)*-ta ta-man-nu-ú*
28′) [^{d}AMA]R.UTU EN GAL-*ú šá qí-bit-su ina ma-ḫar il-la-ku*
29′) [(x) *šim-t*]u_4 *da-mì-iq-ti li-lam-mìn-ma*
30′) [x x x *li*]*š-*⌈*ṭur*⌉ *ár-ḫiš* GIŠ.GU.⌈ZA⌉-*šú a-na a-a-bi-šú liš-ruk-*⌈*ma*⌉
31′) [*ina bu-bu*]-⌈*ti*⌉ *ḫu-šaḫ-ḫu li-šam-qit* UN.MEŠ-*šú*
32′) [*nabû* DUB.SA]R *é-*⌈*sag*⌉*-íl mu-ma*(*)-ʾ-⌈*ir*⌉ *kib-ra-a-ti*
33′) [*mu*]-⌈*deš-šu*⌉*-ú eš-*⌈*re*⌉*-e-ti* ⌈UD⌉.MEŠ-*šú* ⌈EGIR⌉.MEŠ *li-kar-ri-ma*
34′) [U]D [1]-⌈*en*⌉ <*la*> *ba-lat-*⌈*su liš*⌉*-ṭur*

does anything deceitful against Ša-uṣur-Adad (25′) and the gods who dwell there — whether they summon the people to (perform their) feudal obligations and *tillūtu*-service, or you alter (the status of) their fields and reckon them under (your own) jurisdiction — may [the god Mar]duk, the great lord whose command takes precedence, turn his favourable [desti]ny to evil and (30′) decree in writing [...]! May he promptly give his throne to his enemy and destroy his people [by hung]er (and) famine! May [the god Nabû, the scrib]e of Esagila, who directs (all) regions (of the world) and provides abundantly for the sanctuaries, cut short his future and decree in writing that his life (last) <not> one day (more)!

Colophon 1
35′) [IM.DU]B ⌈*ši*⌉*-pir-e-*[*t*]*i šá* LUGAL ⌈*im-te*(?)*-si*⌉
36′) [x x x] x *šá* [L]Ú.DUB.SAR É.GAL ⌈*šá*⌉ *ṭup-pi an-na-a*
37′) [x x] x-*ma* [GA]Z-*ú ú-ḫal-la-*[*a*]*q*
38′) [*l*]*u-*⌈*ú a*⌉*-šar la a-ma-ru i-*⌈*šak*⌉*-ka-*[*n*]*a*
39′) *a-ma-ti* N[A_4.RÚ].A *ú-šá-an-nu-*⌈*ú*⌉
40′) ^{d}AMAR.U[T]U E[N GAL]-*ú* ⌈ÍD⌉.MEŠ-*šú* ⌈*li*⌉*-pah-hi*

Colophon
35′–40′) Official [document] which the king *cleared* [...] of the palace scribe. With regard to anyone who [...] this tablet and [smas]hes (it or) destroys (it) or puts (it) in a place where it cannot be seen, (or) alters the wording of (this) [stel]a, may the god Mard[uk, the great] lo[rd], stop up his canals.

Space
Colophon 2
41′) GABA.RI KU-x.⌈KI⌉ GIM SUMUN-*šú* SAR IGI.KÁR ŠU.II
42′) ^{m}*mu-še-zib*-^{d}EN DUMU LÚ.SANGA ^{d}UTU
43′) LÚ.⌈ŠAGAN LÚ⌉.ḪAL BÀN.DA

Colophon 2
41′–43′) Copy (from) ..., written (and) collated according to its original. (By) the hand of Mušēzib-Bēl, son of the *šangû*-priest of the god Šamaš, an apprentice, a junior diviner.

34′ For the reading of this line (which follows Walker, Iraq 44 [1982] p. 74), see B.6.33.2001 line 20.

Aššur-nādin-šumi

B.6.27

After Sennacherib removed Bēl-ibni from the throne of Babylon, he installed his own son, Aššur-nādin-šumi, as ruler. Aššur-nādin-šumi's reign lasted for six years (699–694 BC). In 694 BC, an Elamite army invaded northern Babylonia and captured Sippar. Aššur-nādin-šumi was captured and taken away to Elam. No more is heard of him, although a letter written somewhat later refers to the fact that he had been betrayed to the Elamites by some Babylonians. No royal inscriptions of Aššur-nādin-šumi are attested, but at least four economic texts and one kudurru come from his reign. In addition, a text from the time of Šamaš-šuma-ukīn refers to a prebend which had originally been granted by Aššur-nādin-šumi. With regard to the reign of Aššur-nādin-šumi, see Brinkman, Prelude pp. 60–61 and NABU 1992 pp. 68–69 no. 88; Brinkman and Kennedy, JCS 35 (1983) pp. 15–16 no. F and 38 (1986) p. 99 no. F; and Brinkman and Dalley, ZA 78 (1988) pp. 76–98.

Nergal-ušēzib

B.6.28

The Elamite king Ḫallušu-Inšušinak installed Nergal-ušēzib on the throne of Babylon in place of Bēl-ibni. Nergal-ušēzib was a Babylonian, a member of the important Gaḫal family, and he is credited with a reign of one year (693 BC). An Assyrian army was sent to expel the Elamites and deal with the Babylonian rebels, but it was repulsed. In the fourth month of 693 BC, Nergal-ušēzib captured and plundered Nippur, which had presumably supported Assyria. In the seventh month, an Assyrian army entered Uruk and took the gods of that city as booty. Later in that same month, the Assyrians won a military victory in the province of Nippur, captured Nergal-ušēzib, and carried him off to Assyria. No inscriptions of Nergal-ušēzib are attested. One economic text dated by his reign was composed at Targibātu, but it was actually written after he had lost control of that town ("year one, after Nergal-ušēzib, king of Bab[ylon]"). With regard to the reign of Nergal-ušēzib, see Brinkman, Prelude pp. 61–62; and Brinkman and Kennedy, JCS 35 (1983) p. 16 no. G.

Mušēzib-Marduk

B.6.29

Although the Assyrians defeated the Babylonians and carried off Nergal-ušēzib in 693 BC, they did not gain control of all of the country. Mušēzib-Marduk, a Chaldean of the Bīt-Dakkūri tribe, succeeded to the throne of Babylon and held it for four years (692–689 BC). Previously, he had been an official of the governor of Laḫīru, an outlaw living in the marshes, and a fugitive in Elam. Mušēzib-Marduk took gold and silver belonging to the Esagila temple in Babylon and sent it to a new king of Elam, Ḫumban-nimena, in order to win his support against Assyria. With military support from Elam and the aid of Chaldeans, Arameans, and groups from western Iran, the Babylonian forces met the Assyrians in battle at Ḫalulê (located on the Tigris, possibly near Samarra), probably in the year 691 BC. Both sides claimed victory, but the following year the Assyrians besieged Babylon. The city held out for at least fifteen months, before falling on the first day of the ninth month of 689 BC. The Assyrian king, Sennacherib, had his men slaughter those Babylonians who had fought against him. Mušēzib-Marduk and his family were carried off to Assyria. Babylon was looted and then razed to the ground.

No royal inscriptions of Mušēzib-Marduk are preserved and only three economic texts are dated by his regnal years. With regard to the reign of Mušēzib-Marduk, see Brinkman, Prelude pp. 62–68; and Brinkman and Kennedy, JCS 35 (1983) p. 17 no. H.

Sennacherib

B.6.30

The Assyrian king Sennacherib controlled Babylonia directly during the years 688-681 BC. Having ordered the abandonment and destruction of Babylon and either the demolishment or removal of the statue of its tutelary god, Marduk, he did not pretend to be a true "king of Babylonia." He assumed neither the title "king of Babylon" nor "king of the land of Sumer and Akkad." Thus, one Babylonian chronicle and the Ptolemaic Canon stated there was no king of Babylonia during these eight years. No Babylonian royal inscriptions are attested from this period. For economic texts from this time, see the introduction to Sennacherib's first reign over Babylonia (B.6.23). For the history of Babylonia during this time, see Frame, Babylonia pp. 52–63.

Esarhaddon

B.6.31

Sennacherib was killed by one or more of his sons on the twentieth day of the tenth month of 681 BC. Dispute over the succession ensued for several weeks before Esarhaddon (Aššur-aḫa-iddin), who claims to have been Sennacherib's designated successor, gained the upper hand and ascended the throne of Assyria in the twelfth month of 681 BC. Unlike his father, Esarhaddon claimed to be king of both Assyria and Babylonia and he ruled over these two lands for twelve years (680–669 BC). Although he was included in the king lists as a ruler of Babylonia and although he took the titles "king of Babylon," "viceroy of Babylon," and "king of the land of Sumer and Akkad" in his royal inscriptions, it is worthy of note that only one economic text from Babylonia clearly gives him the title "king of Babylon" in its date formula. In other economic texts, he was called "king," "king of Assyria," "king of the world," or "king of the lands."

A great deal is known about Babylonia during the time of Esarhaddon, with information coming from royal inscriptions, chronicles, official correspondence, economic texts, and other types of inscriptions. Esarhaddon attempted to rule Babylonia as a true king of Babylonia and to erase any anti-Assyrian sentiment caused by the actions of his father. Babylon was rebuilt, repopulated, and honoured. The ancient city of Agade was restored; temples were built or renovated throughout the land; divine statues were repaired and adorned with costly accoutrements; and special privileges were granted to the old important cult centres. However, the statue of the god Marduk which had been carried off (or destroyed) in 689 BC and without which the important New Year's festival could not take place was not returned or replaced. Despite Esarhaddon's desire to be accepted by the Babylonians, his authority over that land did not go unchallenged. In 680 BC, soon after Esarhaddon ascended the throne, Nabû-zēr-kitti-līšir, the governor of the Sealand, attempted to capture the city of Ur. He fled to Elam when Assyrian troops moved south, but was put to death by the Elamite king. In 678 BC Assyrian troops fought with the Bīt-Dakkūri tribe and their leader Šamaš-ibni, who had taken control of land belonging to the people of Babylon and Borsippa. Esarhaddon's troops were victorious; he returned the land to its original owners and had Šamaš-ibni executed. An Elamite army invaded Babylonia in 675 BC and entered Sippar. The Elamites do not appear to have attempted to hold on to the city and the king of Elam died that same year back in Elam. In order to alleviate Assyrian anger at his predecessor's actions, the new Elamite king returned the statues of the gods of the city of Agade to Agade; these had probably been taken to Elam after a successful raid on that city. Nippur, or its governors, gave Assyria trouble on at least two occasions and an individual by the name of Ṣillāia carried out actions unacceptable to Assyria. In addition, at one point Elam supported an unsuccessful attempt by Nabû-ušallim, a brother of Nabû-zēr-kitti-līšir, to gain control of the Sealand from another brother, Na᾿id-Marduk, whom Esarhaddon had made governor following the death of Nabû-zēr-kitti-līšir. For details of the reign of Esarhaddon, see Frame, Babylonia pp. 64–101.

Only votive and building accounts of Esarhaddon dealing with Babylonia and/or coming from Babylonia will be presented here. The main inscription dealing with the rebuilding of Babylon (see, currently, Borger, Asarh. pp. 10–29 §11) will also not be included since some recensions of that text are only known from Assyria and since it may be compared more profitably with the Assyrian inscriptions of the king. Thus, this inscription and the Assyrian inscriptions of Esarhaddon will appear in the series of Assyrian royal inscriptions edited by E. Leichty (RIMA 7). Babylonian inscriptions of the king record the dedication of a seal to the god Marduk (B.6.31.1) and the dedication or rededication of individuals and animals to the goddess Ištar at Uruk (B.6.31.1001). The restoration of various Babylonian temples is the subject of several inscriptions: Esagila, the temple of the god Marduk at Babylon, including its ziqqurat and processional avenue (B.6.31.2–9); the temple of the goddess Gula at Borsippa (B.6.31.10); temples of the god Enlil and the goddess Ištar at Nippur (B.6.31.11–14); and Eanna, the temple of the goddess Ištar at Uruk, including the cellas Enirgalana and Eḫiliana (B.6.31.15–21). The inscriptions are found upon a lapis lazuli cylinder seal (B.6.31.1), clay cylinders (B.6.31.10–12 and B.6.31.15–18), bricks (B.6.31.2–9, B.6.31.13–14, and B.6.31.19–21), and clay tablets (B.6.31.9 ex. 8 [a later copy] and B.6.31.1001). With the exception of one brick inscription from Babylon written in Sumerian (B.6.31.9), all the inscriptions are written in the Akkadian language.

A bilingual inscription of the earlier Babylonian king Adad-apla-iddina which records the dedication of a gold belt for the statue of the god Nabû at Borsippa was copied during the reign of Esarhaddon and a colophon was appended to the copy. This inscription and colophon are presented as B.2.8.5. Approximately thirty Babylonian economic texts were dated by the regnal years of Esarhaddon; see Brinkman and Kennedy, JCS 35 (1983) pp. 17–20 no. I and JCS 38 (1986) pp. 99–100 no. I.

1

A monumental lapis lazuli cylinder seal from Babylon has inscribed upon it two, or more likely three, inscriptions written in Akkadian. The longest records the dedication of the object to the god Marduk by Esarhaddon.

COMMENTARY

The seal is in the collection of the Vorderasiatiches Museum, Berlin (VA Bab 647), and is depicted on Babylon excavation photo 701. It was found in a basket filled with various kinds of stones in room E of a Parthian building in Amran-ibn-Ali on April 18, 1900 and was given the excavation number BE 6403. See Wetzel, Spätzeit pl. 14 Dd8IV and pl. 15 for the location of the room. The piece measures 12.5 cm in length and 3.2 cm in diameter. The inscriptions have been collated from photographs. The two inscriptions are written in opposite directions on the seal; inscription A begins at the bottom of the seal, while inscription B begins at the top of the seal.

Watanabe (Bagh. Mitt. 16 [1985] pp. 390–91) has argued plausibly that inscription A may well be composed of two separate inscriptions. Since the god depicted on the seal is Adad, line 3 ("seal of the god Adad") may have been the original inscription on the piece. At some later point, an engraver was ordered to add the phrase "Property of the god Marduk of Esagila." He added "Property of the god Marduk" (line 1) and then began to put "of Esagila" immediately below it. However, after adding the first wedge (line 2) he realized that there was not quite enough room between line 1 and line 3 to put the new line. He thus put "of Esagila" (line 4) after the original inscription mentioning Adad. Still later, the inscription of Esarhaddon (inscription B) rededicating the piece to the god Marduk was added.

BIBLIOGRAPHY

1900 Delitzsch, MDOG 5 pp. 11–13 and fig. 2 (drawing of figure, translation)
1900 Koldewey, MDOG 5 pp. 4–6 (provenance, study)
1903 Weissbach, Miscellen no. 7 (copy, drawing of figure, edition)
1911 Koldewey, Tempel pp. 46–48 and pl. 8 fig. 75 (provenance, photo [inscription not visible], partial translation)
1924–25 Unger, AfK 2 p. 22 no. 6 (study)
1925 Koldewey, WEB^{4} pp. 215–16 and 217 fig. 134 (provenance, drawing of figure, partial translation)
1956 Borger, Asarh. p. 29 §12 (Bab. H) (edition)
1962 Meyer, Jahrtausende p. 104 (translation, study)
1957 Schmidt, Persepolis 2 p. 57 (translation of inscription A)
1957 Wetzel, Spätzeit pp. 32, 36–37 no. 14 and pls. 43a–d and 44a (provenance, photo, copy, study)
1971 Opificius, RLA 3/8 pp. 579–80 (study)
1975 Boehmer in Orthmann, Der alte Orient pp. 343, 362, and fig. 108b (copy, translation, study)
1975 Borger, WAO^{2} no. 170 (photo [inscription not visible], study)
1977 Gelb in Gibson and Biggs, Seals pp. 109–10, 112, 121, and 125 sub nos. XX and XXX (study)
1985 Watanabe, Bagh. Mitt. 16 pp. 390–91 (copy, edition, study)
1987 Collon, First Impressions no. 563 (copy, translation, study)
1987 Galter, ARRIM 5 pp. 13, 15, and 30 no. 82 (edition, study)
1987 Rost, Vorderasiatisches Museum p. 100 fig. 114 (photo [inscription not visible])
1992 Wittmann, Bagh. Mitt. 23 pp. 270–71 no. 121 (edition, study)
1994 Watanabe, ASJ 16 p. 242 no. 2.2 (edition)

TEXT

Inscription A

1) NÍG.GA ^{d}AMAR.UTU
2) <<DIŠ>>
3) NA$_{4}$.KIŠIB *šá* ^{d}IŠKUR
4) *šá é-sag-gíl*

1–4) Property of the god Marduk, <<...>> seal of the god Adad of Esagila ("House Whose Top Is High").

Inscription B

1) *ana* ^{d}ŠÚ EN GAL UMUN-*šú* ^{m}AN.ŠÁR-PAP-AŠ
2) MAN ŠÚ MAN KUR AŠ *a-na* TI-*šú* BA-*eš*

1–2) To the god Marduk, great lord, his lord: Esarhaddon, king of the world (and) king of Assyria, presented (this object) for the sake of his life.

2

A few bricks from Babylon have an Akkadian inscription stamped upon them which states that Esarhaddon had paved the processional way of Esagila and Babylon for the god Marduk.

CATALOGUE

Ex.	Museum number	Excavation number	Babylon photo number	Babylon provenance	Dimensions (cm)	Lines preserved	FuB 27	cpn
1	—	BE 8084	871	Esagila, avenue, 4th pavement	39×39	1–10	—	p
2	VA Bab 4052a	BE 41183	—	Sachn, South ai 34	30×30×9	1–10	1	n
3	VA Bab 4052b	—	—	—	39.5×28.5×8	1–10	2	n
4	—	BE 41472	3283	Kaṣr North	—	1–3	—	p

COMMENTARY

Exs. 1–3 have the inscription stamped on the face of the brick, while ex. 4 has it stamped on the edge. The stamped area of ex. 2 measures 15×7.2 cm and that of ex. 3 15.3×7.2 cm. Only the ends of the first three lines are preserved on ex. 4 and thus it is possible that this exemplar preserves some other inscription. There are no known variants and no score for this brick inscription is provided in the microfiche.

Wetzel and Weissbach, Hauptheiligtum p. 86 states that BE 8050 bears an inscription of Esarhaddon and had the same provenance as BE 8084 (ex. 1); however, BE 8050 is reported to be a terracotta plaque.

BIBLIOGRAPHY

1900–01 Koldewey, MDOG 7 pp. 22–23 and 23 n. ** (ex. 1, provenance, study)
1911 Koldewey, Tempel pp. 49 and 72 no. 9 (ex. 1, edition by Weissbach)
1924–25 Unger, AfK 2 p. 21 no. 5 (ex. 1, study)
1925 Koldewey, WEB[4] pp. 202–203 and 204 fig. 126 (ex. 1, provenance, photo)
1938 Wetzel and Weissbach, Hauptheiligtum p. 38 no. A.I.a and pp. 86–87 (exs. 1–2, 4, provenance, edition)
1956 Borger, Asarh. p. 30 §13 (Bab. I) (exs. 1–2, edition)
1985 Trenkwalder, Sumer 41 p. 38 (edition)
1989 Marzahn, FuB 27 p. 54 no. I, nos. 1–2 and fig. 1 (transliteration; ex. 3, copy; exs. 2–3, study)

TEXT

1) *ana* ^{d}AMAR.UTU UMUN-*šú*
2) ^{m}AN.ŠÁR-PAP-AŠ
3) MAN ŠÚ MAN KUR *aš-šur*
4) MAN KÁ.DIŠ.DIŠ
5) *ina a-gur-ri*
6) UDUN KÙ-*tim*
7) *tal-lak-ti*
8) *é-sag-gíl*
9) *ù*(*) KÁ.DINGIR.MEŠ
10) ZÁLAG-*ir*

1–10) For the god Marduk, his lord: Esarhaddon, king of the world, king of Assyria, (and) king of Babylon, made the processional way of Esagila *and* Babylon shine with baked bricks from a (ritually) pure kiln.

3

This Akkadian inscription is dedicated to the god Marduk by Esarhaddon and records the making of baked bricks for work on the Esagila temple and Babylon.

CATALOGUE

Ex.	Museum number	Excavation number	Babylon photo number	Babylon provenance	Dimensions (cm)	Lines preserved	FuB 27	cpn
1	—	BE 39840	1813	Sachn East as 20 (gate IV of ziqqurat enclosure wall)	30×30	1–9	—	p
2	VA Bab 4052g	BE 41099	—	Sachn, South ad 38	31.5×27.5×7	1–9	8	n
3	—	BE 46408	—	Merkes, brick pillar in "Ziqqurat Street"	32×32	—	—	n

COMMENTARY

The inscription is stamped on the face of the brick. The stamped area of ex. 2 measures 15.6×7.2 cm. The provenance of ex. 1 given above comes from Wetzel and Weissbach, Hauptheiligtum p. 86; excavation records state that it comes from "Sahn op (Tor) aS20 [or a520]." For the pillar in which ex. 3 was found, see

9 *ù*(*), sign indistinct on the photo of ex. 1; copy of ex. 3 in FuB 27 suggests KI; sign is not preserved on either ex. 2 or ex. 4.

Reuther, Merkes pp. 70–71. There are no known variants and no score for this brick inscription is provided in the microfiche.

BIBLIOGRAPHY

1924–25 Unger, AfK 2 p. 21 no. 4 (ex. 1, study)
1925 Koldewey, WEB[4] pp. 86 [correct 38940 to 39840], 203, and 205 fig. 127 (ex. 1, photo, study)
1931 Unger, Babylon pp. 167 and 280 no. 21 (ex. 1, translation)
1938 Wetzel and Weissbach, Hauptheiligtum p. 38 no. A.I.b and pp. 86–87 (exs. 1–3, provenance, edition)
1956 Borger, Asarh. p. 30 §14 (Bab. J) (exs. 1–3, edition)
1989 Marzahn, FuB 27 p. 56 no. IV, no. 8 and fig. 4 (transliteration; ex. 2, copy, study)

TEXT

1) *ana* [d]AMAR.UTU UMUN-*šú*
2) [m]AN.ŠÁR-PAP-AŠ
3) MAN KUR *aš-šur*
4) MAN KÁ.DIŠ.DIŠ
5) *a-gur-ri*
6) *é-sag-gíl*
7) *u* KÁ.DIŠ.DIŠ
8) *eš-šiš*
9) *ú-šal-bi-in*

1–9) For the god Marduk, his lord: Esarhaddon, king of Assyria (and) king of Babylon, had baked bricks made anew for Esagila and Babylon.

4

An Akkadian inscription which is stamped on numerous bricks from Babylon and which is dedicated to the god Marduk states that Esarhaddon had had baked bricks made for the Esagila temple and its ziqqurat Etemenanki ("House, Foundation of Heaven and Netherworld"). The inscription comes in three versions (B.6.31.4–6), which are distinguished by their varying line arrangement and orthography.

CATALOGUE

Ex.	Museum number	Excavation number	Babylon photo number	Babylon provenance	Dimensions (cm)	Lines preserved	FuB 27	cpn
1	VA Bab 4074	BE 44638	3283	Kasr, surface	7×23×17	1–3	7	p
2	—	BE 41230	—	Sachn South at 33	—	—	—	n
3	—	BE 41054	2008	Sachn South ad 38	33×33	1–3	—	p
4	—	BE 32167	—	Kasr k 21	—	—	—	n

COMMENTARY

The inscription on ex. 1 was in an almost perfect state of preservation when found (see the excavation photo), but is now damaged at a number of spots (see copy in FuB 27). The exact findspot of ex. 2 is indicated upon Hauptheiligtum pl. 9 (Schnitt 15, lower middle). Exs. 1, 2, and probably 4 are stamped along the edge of the brick; ex. 3 is stamped on the face of the brick. The area stamped on ex. 1 measures 5.0×20.5 cm. According to Wetzel and Weissbach, there were two different stamps with this inscription and exs. 3–4 were stamped with a different stamp than exs. 1–2. There are no known variants and no score for this brick inscription is provided in the microfiche.

BIBLIOGRAPHY

1938 Wetzel and Weissbach, Hauptheiligtum p. 38 no. A.I.c and pp. 86–87 (exs. 1–4, provenance, edition)
1956 Borger, Asarh. p. 30 §15 (Bab. K) (exs. 1–4, edition)
1989 Marzahn, FuB 27 pp. 55–56 no. III, no. 7 and fig. 3 (transliteration; ex. 1, copy, study)

TEXT

1) *ana* ᵈAMAR.UTU UMUN-*šú* ᵐ*aš-šur*-PAP-AŠ MAN KUR AŠ
2) MAN KÁ.DIŠ.DIŠ *a-gur-ri é-sag-gíl*
3) *u é-temen-an-ki eš-šiš ú-šal-bi-in*

1–3) For the god Marduk, his lord: Esarhaddon, king of Assyria (and) king of Babylon, had baked bricks made anew for Esagila and Etemenanki.

5

What is basically a duplicate of the previous inscription is found stamped on several other bricks from Babylon.

CATALOGUE

Ex.	Museum number	Excavation number	Babylon photo number	Babylon provenance	Dimensions (cm)	Lines preserved	FuB 27	cpn
1	VA Bab 4052c	BE 46402	2679	Merkes, baked brick pillar in "Ziqqurat Street," layer 31	31×31×8	1–9	3	p
2	—	BE 46403	2680	As ex. 1, layer 37	31×31	1–9	—	p
3	VA Bab 4052d	BE 46405	2681	As ex. 2	30.5×30.5×7	1–9	4	p
4	—	BE 46406	2681	As ex. 2	31.5×31.5	1–9	—	p
5	VA Bab 4052e	—	—	—	19×8×14	1–9	5	n
6	VA Bab 4052f	—	—	—	31.5×31.5×7.5	1–9	6	n
7	—	—	—	Amran	—	1–9	—	n

COMMENTARY

The inscriptions on exs. 1 and 2 have suffered some damage since the time the excavation photographs were made. A paper squeeze in the British Museum (squeeze 197) may have this inscription and may be connected to ex. 7, which cannot currently be located (see Wetzel and Weissbach, Hauptheiligtum p. 38). For the pillar in which exs. 1–4 were found, see Reuther, Merkes pp. 70–71. Exs. 1–4 and 6–7 are stamped on the face of the brick; ex. 5 is stamped down the edge. The area stamped on exs. 1 and 3 measures 15.8×7.3 cm, that on ex. 5 15×7 cm, and that on ex. 6 16.5×7.3 cm. There are no known variants and no score for this brick inscription is provided in the microfiche.

BIBLIOGRAPHY

1861 1 R pl. 48 no. 9 (ex. 7, copy in type)
1863 Oppert, EM 1 pp. 180–81 (ex. 7, translation; erroneously referred to as no. 6 on 1 R pl. 48)
1874 Ménant, Annales p. 247 (ex. 7, translation)
1875 Ménant, Babylone p. 167 (ex. 7, translation)
1886 Bezold, Literatur p. 107 §61.4.i (ex. 7, study)
1898 Meissner and Rost, BA 3 pp. 260–61 (ex. 7, edition)
1924–25 Unger, AfK 2 p. 22 no. 8 (ex. 7, study)
1927 Luckenbill, ARAB 2 §760 (ex. 7, translation)
1931 Unger, Babylon p. 280 no. 21 (ex. 7, translation)
1938 Wetzel and Weissbach, Hauptheiligtum p. 38 no. A.I.d and pp. 86–87 (exs. 1–4, provenance, edition)
1956 Borger, Asarh. p. 30 §15 (Bab. K) (exs. 1–4, 7, edition)
1989 Marzahn, FuB 27 pp. 54–55 no. II, nos. 3–6 and fig. 2 (transliteration; ex. 1, copy; exs. 1, 3, 5–6, study)

TEXT

1) *ana* ^{d}AMAR.UTU UMUN-*šú*
2) ^{m}AN.ŠÁR-PAP-AŠ
3) MAN KUR *aš-šur*
4) MAN KÁ.DIŠ.DIŠ
5) *a-gur-ri*
6) *é-sag-gíl*
7) *é-temen-an-ki*
8) *eš-šiš*
9) *ú-šal-bi-in*

1–9) For the god Marduk, his lord: Esarhaddon, king of Assyria (and) king of Babylon, had baked bricks made anew for Esagila (and) Etemenanki.

6

This Akkadian inscription stamped on a brick from Babylon is basically a duplicate of the two previous inscriptions.

COMMENTARY

The brick is located in the Archaeological Museum in Istanbul (EŞ number unknown). It is to be identified with the brick which was found on July 5, 1912 and given the Babylon excavation number BE 46404. It is shown on Babylon excavation photo 2679 and comes from the baked brick pillar in "Ziqqurat Street" (layer 34). For information on the pillar, see Reuther, Merkes pp. 70–71. The brick measures 32×32 cm. The inscription is stamped on the face of the brick and has been collated from photographs. The available photos of the brick suggest that the sign *ú* in line 10 may have been written upside down.

BIBLIOGRAPHY

1938 Wetzel and Weissbach, Hauptheiligtum p. 39 no. A.I.e and pp. 86–87 (provenance, edition)

1956 Borger, Asarh. p. 30 §15 (Bab. K) (edition)

TEXT

1) *ana* ^{d}AMAR.UTU
2) EN-*šú*
3) *aš-šur*-PAP-AŠ
4) MAN KUR AŠ
5) MAN KÁ.DIŠ
6) *a-gur-ri*
7) *é-sag-gíl*
8) *u é-temen-an-ki*
9) *eš-šiš*
10) *ú-šal-bi-in*

1–10) For the god Marduk, his lord: Esarhaddon, king of Assyria (5) (and) king of Babylon, had baked bricks made anew for Esagila and Etemenanki.

7

A brick from Babylon bears a stamped Akkadian inscription stating that Esarhaddon had had Etemenanki (the ziqqurat at Babylon) restored.

COMMENTARY

The brick was found at Babylon on July 5, 1912 in the baked brick pillar in "Ziqqurat Street" (layer 37). (For information on the pillar, see Reuther, Merkes pp. 70–71.) The brick was given the Babylon excavation number BE 46407 and measures 30.5×30.5 cm. The inscription is stamped on the face of the brick. The present location of the brick is not known and the edition follows that published by Weissbach which he made from a "copy" ("Abschrift") by Wetzel.

BIBLIOGRAPHY

1938 Wetzel and Weissbach, Hauptheiligtum p. 39 A.I.f and p. 86 (provenance, edition)

1956 Borger, Asarh. p. 30 §16 (Bab. L) (edition)

TEXT

1) *ana* dAMAR.UTU
2) EN-*šú*
3) m*aš-šur*-PAP-AŠ
4) MAN KUR AŠ
5) MAN KÁ.DIŠ
6) *é-temen-an-ki*
7) *eš-šiš*
8) *ú-še-piš*

1–8) For the god Marduk, his lord: Esarhaddon, king of Assyria (and) king of Babylon, had Etemenanki built anew.

8

A text written in Akkadian and inscribed upon a brick from Babylon records the fact that Esarhaddon had baked bricks made for the ziqqurat Etemenanki (name not fully preserved).

COMMENTARY

The brick was found at Babylon on July 5, 1912 in the baked brick pillar in "Ziqqurat Street" (layer 37). (For information on the pillar, see Reuther, Merkes pp. 70–71.) The brick was given the Babylon excavation number BE 46374, is shown on Babylon excavation photo 3220, and measures 33 cm in length. The brick has not been located. The text is inscribed along the edge of the brick. The inscription has been edited from the excavation photograph, but the inscription is faint and some readings must be considered tentative. There may be traces of a few signs after the *-me-* in line 2.

BIBLIOGRAPHY

1938 Wetzel and Weissbach, Hauptheiligtum p. 39 A.I.g and pp. 86–87 (provenance, edition)

1956 Borger, Asarh. p. 30 §17 (Bab. M) (edition)

TEXT

1) *ana* ⌈ᵈAMAR.UTU EN⌉-*šú* AN.ŠÁR-⌈PAP⌉-AŠ MAN ⌈KUR(?) *aš*(?)-*šur*(?)⌉
2) MAN ⌈KÁ⌉.DIŠ.DIŠ ⌈*a-gur*(?)-*ri é*(?)-*te-me*⌉-[*en-an-ki*]
3) *eš*-⌈*šiš ú*⌉-x (x) [(x)] x

1–3) For the god Marduk, his lord: Esarhaddon, king of *Assyria* (and) king of Babylon, *had* baked bricks *made* anew for Eteme[nanki].

9

A Sumerian inscription which is inscribed upon several bricks from Babylon states that Esarhaddon had (re)built Etemenanki for the god Asari (Marduk). This inscription was later seen and copied onto a clay tablet by one Šamaš-nāṣir, who then added a colophon in Akkadian recording this action.

CATALOGUE

Ex.	Museum number	Excavation number	Babylon photo number	Babylon provenance	Object	Dimensions (cm)	Lines preserved	cpn
1	—	BE 15316	502, 1146	Ninurta temple, South gate, courtyard door	Brick	—	2–11	p
2	—	BE 41419	2121	Sachn North aq 15	Brick	—	1–11	p
3	—	BE 46410	—	Merkes, baked brick pillar in "Ziqqurat Street," layer 37	Brick	—	—	n
4	—	BE 46435	—	As ex. 3	Brick	—	—	n
5	—	BE 46436	—	As ex. 3	Brick	—	1–11	n
6	CBS 14	—	—	—	Brick	19.4×7.3×8	1–11	c
7	VA Bab 4053	—	—	—	Brick	19×7.5×7.5	1–10	n
8	AO 5470	—	—	—	Tablet	3.2×5×2	1–11	c

COMMENTARY

For the pillar in which exs. 3–5 were found, see Reuther, Merkes pp. 70–71. Ex. 6 was part of the Joseph Shemtob collection which was purchased for the University Museum, Philadelphia, on July 21, 1888; the brick was given the registration number JS 7-21-88-6. Additional information on ex. 7 was kindly provided by J. Marzahn.

The inscription is inscribed, not stamped. Exs. 1–2 and 7 are written in contemporary Babylonian script, ex. 6 in an archaizing script, and ex. 8 in contemporary Babylonian script, but with a few signs showing archaizing characteristics; the script of exs. 3–5 is not known. The inscription appears on the face of ex. 1, down the edge of exs. 2, 4, and 7, and along the edge of ex. 5. Its location on ex. 3 is not known; ex. 6 appears to have been cut down in size in modern times and it is thus uncertain whether the inscription was on the face or on the edge of the brick. The area inscribed on ex. 7 measures 13.7×4.7 cm. The line numbering and master line follow ex. 6. Ex. 5 has the inscription on five lines and ex. 8 on twelve lines (7 on the obverse of the tablet and 5 on the reverse, plus a two-line colophon). No score for this inscription is provided in the microfiche.

---

3 Assuming that *agurrī* (line 2) is the object of the verb, one expects to find either *ú-šal-bi-in* (see B.6.31.3–6, B.6.32.7, and B.6.32.11) or *ú-še-piš* (see B.6.32.8) at the end of this line.

BIBLIOGRAPHY

1888–89 Harper, Hebraica 5 p. 75 (ex. 6, study)
1896 Hilprecht, BE 1/2 no. 151 (ex. 6, copy)
1910 Wetzel, MDOG 44 pp. 20–21 (ex. 2, provenance, translation)
1911 Koldewey, Tempel pp. 31 and 71 no. 8 (ex. 1, provenance, edition by Weissbach)
1922 Thureau-Dangin, RA 19 pp. 84–85 no. 38 (ex. 8, copy, study)
1924–25 Unger, AfK 2 p. 22 no. 7 (exs. 1–2, 8, study)
1925 Koldewey, WEB[4] pp. 182–83 and fig. 116 (ex. 2, photo, study)
1931 Unger, Babylon pp. 194 and 280 no. 20 (ex. 1, translation, study)
1938 Wetzel and Weissbach, Hauptheiligtum p. 16 and pl. 6 (ex. 2, provenance), p. 39 A.I.h and pp. 86–87 (exs. 1–5, provenance, edition)
1956 Borger, Asarh. p. 30 §18 (Bab. N) (exs. 1–6, 8, edition)
1985 Behrens, JCS 37 p. 244 no. 81 (ex. 6, study)
1989 Marzahn, FuB 27 pp. 56–57 no. V, no. 9 (ex. 7, transliteration, study)

TEXT

1) ^{d}asar-ri
2) lugal-a-ni-ir
3) AN.ŠÁR-ŠEŠ-MU
4) lugal ma-da *aš-šur*.KI-ke$_4$
5) lugal ki-šár-ra
6) lugal ub-da límmu-ba
7) GÌR.NÍTA TIN.TIR.KI
8) lugal ki-in-gi uri.KI
9) nam-ti-bi-šè
10) é-te-me-en-an-ki
11) mu-na-dím

1–11) For the god Asari, his lord: Esarhaddon, king of Assyria, (5) king of the world, king of the four quarters (of the world), viceroy of Babylon, (and) king of Sumer (and) Akkad, (re)constructed Etemenanki for the sake of his life.

Colophon on ex. 8 (lines 13–14 of exemplar)
1) GABA.RI TIN.TIR.KI *šá-ṭir-ma* IGI.KÁR
2) IM.GÍD.DA ^{md}UTU-PAB A LÚ *a-ri-ri*

Colophon on ex. 8
1) Copy of (a text from) Babylon; copied and collated.
2) Tablet of Šamaš-nāṣir, descendant of the Miller.

10

A cylinder fragment in the British Museum preserves part of an Akkadian inscription which may be assigned to Esarhaddon. The inscription appears to commemorate work on the temple of the goddess Gula at Borsippa and to mention the king's victorious campaign against the Chaldean tribe of Bīt-Dakkūri and its leader Šamaš-ibni.

COMMENTARY

The fragment BM 38345 (80-11-12,227) comes from Rassam's excavations in Babylonia and is part of a shipment of pieces which were mostly found at Babylon and Borsippa in 1880 (see Reade in Leichty, Sippar 1 p. xxx). Since the inscription describes a project of restoration at Borsippa, it seems likely that the piece came from that city. The fragment is the right end of an apparently solid cylinder and measures 9.2×6.5×4.3 cm. If the cylinder was completely inscribed, portions of not quite half of the total number of lines are preserved. The inscription is written in contemporary Babylonian script and has been collated.

The inscription was ascribed to Shalmaneser V by Luckenbill, but Meissner has shown that it must belong to Esarhaddon. The matter described in the historical section of the text appears to be the campaign directed against the Bīt-Dakkūri and their leader Šamaš-ibni, who had seized land belonging to the inhabitants of Babylon and Borsippa. On this action, see Frame, Babylonia pp. 79–81.

4.8 inserts a line lugal ma-da, "king of the land" before line 4 (presumably dittography for first part of line 4).

Inscriptions of Nebuchadnezzar II refer to the temple(s) of the goddess Gula at Borsippa by several names: é-gu-la, é-ti-la, é-zi-ba-ti-la. See George, House Most High nos. 424, 1095, and 1234.

BIBLIOGRAPHY

1923 S. Smith, CT 37 pl. 23 (copy)
1924–25 Luckenbill, AJSL 41 pp. 162–64 (edition)
1926 Luckenbill, ARAB 1 §§828–30 (translation)
1926 Meissner, AfO 3 pp. 13–14 (edition)
1956 Borger, Asarh. p. 32 §20 (Brs. A) (edition)

TEXT

Lacuna
1′) [...] x x [...] x x x x (x) [...]
2′) [... *š*]*á*(?) *a-na* (x) x.⸢MEŠ⸣-*šú la* IG x [x x x x]
3′) [...] x-*ti zi-kir* MU-*šú it-ú-du qí-bit-*⸢*su*⸣ [x x x x]
4′) [...] ⸢*ú*⸣-*šaḫ-ma-ṭu ma-ḫar* [...]
5′) [... *lā m*]*a-gi-ru qí-bi-t*[*i*]
6′) [... *šu*]-⸢*a*(?)-*ti*⸣ *ú-šal-pít ú-reb-bu da-ad-m*[*u* (x)]
7′) [... D]INGIR *ti-ik-li-šú*
8′) [... *i*(?)]-*na tukul-ti-šú kit-mu-su ú-sap-pu-ú be*(*)-*lut-su*
9′) [...] x *la* ⸢*i*⸣-*šu-ṭu ab-šá-ni*
10′) [*ša*(?) *eqlēt*(?) *mārī*(?) *bābili*(?) *u*(?) *barsipa*(?) *it-b*]*a-lu-ma ú-tar-ru ra-ma-nu-uš*
11′) [... *q*]*í-bit-su u zi-kir* MU-*šú la iš-ḫu-ṭu-ma la i-du-ru be-lut-su*
12′) [...] *ir-ḫi-iṣ-ma a-bu-ba-niš is-pu-un*
13′) [... *ḫattu r*]*am-ni-šú im-qut-su-ma na-piš-ta-šú ib-li*
14′) [... *iš-l*]*u-lam-ma ú-ra-a a-na* KUR *aš-šur*.KI
15′) [*aššur-aḫa-iddina šarru* GAL]-⸢*ú*⸣ LUGAL *dan-nu* LUGAL *kiš-šá-ti* LUGAL KUR *aš-šur*.KI
16′) [*šar kibrāt erbetti*] GÌR.NÍTA KÁ.DINGIR.RA.KI LUGAL KUR *šu-me-ri ù* URI.K[I]
17′) [*liplippi dārû ša bēl-bāni mār adasi*] LUGAL KUR *aš-šur*.KI *pir-ʾ bal-til*.KI *šu-qu-ru* NUMUN LUGAL-*ti ki-sit-ti ṣa-*⸢*a*⸣-[*ti*]
18′) [... *bīt* ᵈ*g*]*u-la bár-sipa*.KI *šá ina du-un-nu a-gi-i ez-zu-tu i-ni-šú m*[*u*(?)-*šab*(?)-*šu*(?)]
19′) [...] *ma-qit-ta-šú uš-ziz-ma ú-dan-nin rik-si-*[*šu*]
20′) [... *šip*(?)]-⸢*ri*⸣ *šu-a-*⸢*ti*⸣ *ḫa-diš lip-pa-*[*lis-ma*]
21′) [...] x x [...] x x x MI UR [x x x]
22′) [...] x RI[K x x x]
23′) [...] x [...]
Lacuna

Lacuna
1′) [...] ... [...] ... [...]
2′) [... *w*]*ho* to his ... not ... [...]
3′) [...] paid attention to the mention of this name, his command [...]
4′) [...] brings quickly before [...]
5′) [... unsub]missive to the comma[nd]
6′) [...] destroyed [*that*] *one*, making the inhabited world shake
7′) [...] the god, his helper
8′) [... wi]th this help, they knelt, beseeching his lordship
9′) [...] did *not* bear my yoke (lit. "pull my yoke-rope")
10′) [*who* took] away [*the fields of the citizens of Babylon and Borsippa*], appropriating (them) for himself
11′) [...] did not fear his command or the mention of his name, and was not afraid of his lordship
12′) [...] inundated and levelled like a flood.
13′) [...] his own [fear] overwhelmed him and his life ended.
14′) [... he to]ok as booty and brought to Assyria.
15′–17′) [Esarhaddon, gre]at [king], mighty king, king of the world, king of Assyria, [king of the four quarters (of the world)], viceroy of Babylon, king of the land of Sumer and Akkad, [descendant of the eternal line of Bēl-bāni, son of Adasi], king of Assyria, precious scion of Baltil (Aššur), (one of) royal lineage (and) anci[ent] stock —
18′–19′) [At that time ... the temple of the goddess G]ula of Borsippa, the *s*[*ite* of] which had become weak due to the strength of the (*river's*) destructive flooding, [...] I (re-)erected its dilapidated parts and reinforced [its] structure.
20′) May [*the goddess Gula, ...*], look upon this [*wo*]*rk* of mine with pleasure [and]
21′–23′) No translation possible.
Lacuna

8′ *be*(*), the sign appears to have been written over another sign (possibly ŠÀ).
10′ The restoration of the line is based upon Borger, Asarh. p. 52 §27 A iii 64–65.
13′ The restoration of *ḫattu* follows Borger, Asarh. p. 32 and is based upon such passages as ibid., p. 52 §27 A iii 74.
15′–17′ The restoration is based upon B.6.31.11 lines 4 and 14.

11

This Akkadian inscription of Esarhaddon is found on numerous barrel cylinders from Nippur. It describes the king's renovation of the Ebaradurgara ("House, Dias of the Throne") temple for the goddess "Queen-of-Nippur" (^{d}UN.GAL NIBRU.KI).

CATALOGUE

Ex.	Museum number	Excavation number	Nippur provenance	Dimensions (cm)	Lines preserved	cpn
1	Chicago A 31310	6 NT 1046	Inanna temple 141 fill	16×7.2	1–22	c
2	IM 61711	6 NT 1045	Inanna temple 141 fill	—	1–21	(c)
3	IM 66885	8 NT 2a–e	Sounding B, fill below level II	—	1–22	(c)
4	IM 61715	6 NT 1043	Sounding B 76	—	1–22	(c)
5	IM 59721	5 NT 476	Inanna temple 23, 45 cm above floor 1	—	1–21	(c)
6	Chicago A 32262	8 NT 3	Sounding L VI/VII	7.7×6	1, 17–21	c
7	Chicago A 33619	4 NT 76	Inanna temple, dump	8.2×5.7	1–5, 18–21	c
8	UM L-29-634 = PMA F29-6-387c	—	—	4.6×6.3	1–7, 17–22	c
9	Chicago A 33618	4 NT 75	Inanna temple, above Parthian floor and roughly above horizontal brick drain	6.5×6	1–13, 22	c
10	NBC 11323	5 NT 564	Inanna temple, NE corner of temple, fill	6×6.3	2–10	c
11	—	1 NT 142	Tablet hill, in debris near a well dug during the Assyrian period	8×5	10–17	n
12	UM L-29-637 = PMA F29-6-387f	—	—	8.7×6	13–21	c
13	NBC 10653	6 NT 1044	Sounding B 75 and 76	14.2×6.5	13–21	c
14	UM L-29-635 = PMA F29-6-387d	—	—	4.3×4.7	13–19	c
15	IM 70310	9 NT 9	Surface	5.8×11.4×3	4–12	(c)

COMMENTARY

Unpublished information on provenances and current museum numbers was provided by McG. Gibson. Exs. 2–5 and 15 were collated from casts in the Oriental Institute, Chicago. The casts of exs. 2–5 are not always clear and sometimes show a little more or less at the edges and adjacent to breaks than do the copies made by Goetze. In the latter circumstances, the transliteration in the score follows the copies by Goetze. The present location of ex. 11 is not known. It is not impossible that exs. 14–15 should be taken as exemplars of B.6.31.12 rather than of this inscription.

The inscription is written in both contemporary Babylonian script (exs. 1–7 and 9–14) and contemporary Assyrian script (exs. 8 and 15). The master exemplar is a conflation of the various exemplars, but mainly relies upon exs. 1 and 2.

A number of tiny fragments are stored with ex. 1 in the Oriental Institute. A few have traces of signs, but none were used in Goetze's copy. The largest of these fragments joins the main piece and adds parts of lines 10–13. This fragment is included in the score for ex. 1 but the remaining fragments are not because it is not absolutely certain that they do indeed come from ex. 1 and because it is uncertain where some of them would fit in the score. One in particular, however, may have parts of lines 1–3:

Lacuna
1′ [...] x [...],
2′ [...-*a*]*s*-*ḫa*-[... *l*]*i*-⌜*i*⌝-[...]
3′ [... GAŠA]N GA[L-...]
Lacuna

A lengthy hymn to the goddess "Queen-of-Nippur" has been published by W.G. Lambert in Kraus Festschrift pp. 173–218. Her exact character and identification are not clear. Lambert describes her as a "form of Ištar" (ibid., p. 173) which would seem likely since many of the exemplars were found on the site of the earlier temple of Inanna. Level 1 of the Inanna temple has been identified as Esarhaddon's restoration. For information on that level, see Zettler, Inanna Temple pp. 49–50.

BIBLIOGRAPHY

1950 Steele, JAOS 70 pp. 69–72 (exs. 8, 11, 12, copy; exs. 8, 11, 12, 14, edition [combined with text from Uruk])
1952 Falkenstein, BiOr 9 p. 88 and n. 7 (study)
1956 Borger, Asarh. p. 70 §39 (Npr. A) and pp. 73–75 sub §47, variants (exs. 8, 11, 12, 14, partial transliteration)
1959 Crawford, Archaeology 12/2 p. 83 (ex. 2, photo)
1963 Goetze, JCS 17 pp. 119–31 (exs. 1–7, 9–10, 13, copy; exs. 1–14, edition)
1969 Buccellati and Biggs, AS 17 no. 30 (ex. 15, copy, study)
1992 Zettler, Inanna Temple p. 240 no. 6 (study)

TEXT

1) *a-na* ^{d}UN.GAL NIBRU.KI *ma-al-kát uzu-mú-a*.KI *ṣir-ti ti-iz-qar-ti šá-ru-uḫ-tu* DINGIR.MEŠ ^{d}*in-nin-ni*

2) GAŠAN *šur-bu-tu šá a-na* LUGAL *mi-ig-ri-šá ba-an-ti-iš it-ta-na-as-ḫa-ru* BALA-*šú ú-šal-ba-ru i-šar-ra-ku-uš da-na-nu ù li-i-ti*

3) *šar-rat* NIBRU.KI *a-ši-bat é-bára-dúr-gar-ra* É *mu-kin šu-bat* LUGAL-*ú-tu* GAŠAN GAL-*ti* GAŠAN-*šú*

4) ^{m}AN.ŠÁR-ŠEŠ-SUM.NA LUGAL GAL-*ú* LUGAL *dan-nu* LUGAL ŠÚ LUGAL KUR *aš-šur*.KI LUGAL *kib-rat er-bet-ti* GÌR.NÍTA TIN.TIR.KI LUGAL KUR *šu-me-ri u* URI.KI *i-tu-ut kun lìb-bi* ^{d}*en-líl*

5) *šá ul-tu ṣe-ḫe-ri-šú ana* AN.ŠÁR ^{d}*en-líl* ^{d}30 ^{d}UTU ^{d}IŠKUR ^{d}AMAR.UTU ^{d}AG ^{d}U.GUR *u* DINGIR.MEŠ GAL.MEŠ EN.MEŠ-*šú it-tak-lu-ú-ma ni-is-mat-su ú-šak-šid-uš i-mu-ru da-na-an-šú-un*

6) *a-na nu-uḫ-ḫu lìb-bi* DINGIR-*ti-šú-nu u nu-up-pu-uš ka-bat-ti-šú-nu* GIŠ.MI-*šú-nu da-ru-ú it-ru-ṣu* UGU-*šú*

7) *ina e-muq* AN.ŠÁR ^{d}*en-líl* ^{d}EN *u* DUMU ^{d}EN DINGIR.MEŠ *ti-ik-li-šú kul-lat* KUR.KUR *i-bé-lu-ma gi-mir ma-li-ku ú-šak-ni-šu še-pu-uš-šu*

8) *ba-nu-ú* É AN.ŠÁR *mu-ud-diš é-kur e-piš é-sag-íl u* TIN.TIR.KI *mu-šak-lil eš-re-e-ti u ma-ḫa-zu mu-kin sat-tuk-ku*

9) LUGAL *šá i-na* UD.MEŠ BALA-*šú* EN GAL-*ú* ^{d}AMAR.UTU *ana* TIN.TIR.KI *sa-li-mu ir-šu-ú ina é-sag-íl* É.GAL-*šú ir-mu-ú šu-*[*bat*]*-su*

10) ^{d}*a-num* GAL-*ú ana* URU-*šú* BÀD.AN.KI *u* É-*šú é-dim-gal-kalam-ma ú-še-ri-bu-ma ú-še-ši-bu pa-rak da-ra-a-ti*

11) DINGIR.MEŠ KUR.KUR *šal-lu-tu šu-kut-ta-šú-nu ud-di-šu ul-tu qé-reb* KUR *aš-šur*.KI *a-na áš-ri-šú-nu ú-tir-šú-nu-ti-ma ú-ki-nu is-qu-uš-šú-un*

12) NUN *en-qu it-pe-šu ḫa-sis kal šip-ri šá ina ma-ḫa-zu* GAL.MEŠ *si-ma-a-ti iš-tak-ka-nu uš-te-ši-ru šu-luḫ-ḫu*

13) DUMU ^{md}30-ŠEŠ.MEŠ-*eri-ba* LUGAL ŠÚ LUGAL KUR *aš-šur*.KI DUMU ^{m}LUGAL-GIN LUGAL KUR *aš-šur*.KI GÌR.NÍTA TIN.TIR.KI LUGAL KUR *šu-me-ri u* URI.KI-*i*

1–3) For the goddess Queen-of-Nippur, ruler of Uzu-mú-a, august, eminent, most splendid of the gods, the goddess Innini, supreme lady who always cares like a mother for the king, her favourite, who makes his reign lengthy (and) bestows on him power and might, queen of Nippur, who dwells in Ebaradurgara, the temple which makes firm the royal abode, the great lady, his lady:

4–14) Esarhaddon, great king, mighty king, king of the world, king of Assyria, king of the four quarters (of the world), viceroy of Babylon, king of the land of Sumer and Akkad, selected by the steadfast heart of the god Enlil; (5) who from his childhood trusted in the gods Aššur, Enlil, Sîn, Šamaš, Adad, Marduk, Nabû, Nergal, and the (other) great gods, his lords, (who) allowed him to attain his desire; (the one who) recognized their power, (the one) over whom (the gods) extended their eternal protection in order to appease their divine heart(s) and set their mind(s) at rest; (the one who) by the might of the gods Aššur, Enlil, Bēl (Marduk), and the Son-of-Bēl (Nabû), the gods, his helpers, ruled over all lands and made all rulers submissive to him; the one who (re)constructed the temple of the god Aššur, renovated Ekur, (re)built Esagila and Babylon, completed the sanctuaries and cult centres, (and) (re)confirmed (their) regular offerings; the king during the days of whose reign the great lord, the god Marduk, became reconciled to Babylon (and again) took up his residence in Esagila, his palace; (10) (the one who) made the god Great-Anu enter into his city Dēr and his temple Edimgalkalama ("House, Great Mast of the Land") and had (him) sit upon (his) eternal dais; (the one who) restored the splendid appearance of the captive gods of the lands, returned them from Assyria to their (proper) places, and (re)confirmed their income; wise prince, expert who knows every craft, who constantly established appropriate procedures in the great cult centres (and) has purification rites performed correctly; son of Sennacherib, king of the world (and) king of Assyria; son of Sargon (II), king of Assyria, viceroy of Babylon, (and) king of the land of Sumer and

11 The term *šukuttu* (AHw p. 1267a "Schmuckausstattung"), loosely translated here "splendid appearance," refers to the richly decorated statues of the gods; see Lambert, AfO 18 (1957–58) p. 399 and Lipinski, UF 5 (1973) pp. 203–204.

14) *li-ip-li-pi da-ru-ú šá* ^{md}EN-*ba-ni* DUMU ^{m}*a-da-si* LUGAL KUR *aš-šur*.KI NUNUZ *bal-til*.KI *šu-qu-ru* NUMUN LUGAL-*ú-tu ki-sit-ti ṣa-a-ti*

15) *i-nu-šu é-bára-dúr-gar-ra* É ^{d}UN.GAL NIBRU.KI GAŠAN GAL-*ti* GAŠAN-*ia šá* LUGAL *maḫ-ri i-pu-šu la-ba-riš il-lik-ma i-qu-ú-pu* É.GAR$_8$.MEŠ-*šú*

16) *áš-ra-ti-šú áš-te-ʾ-e ma-qit-ta-šú as-suḫ te-me-en-šú ú-ṣab-bi-ma* GIM *si-ma-ti-šú la-bi-ra-a-ti ina ši-pir* ^{d}*kulla ar-ṣip ú-šak-lil ki-ma* KUR-*i re-ši-šú ul-li*

17) ^{d}UN.GAL NIBRU.KI GAŠAN *šur-bu-tu* GAŠAN-*ia ši-pir šu-a-tu ḫa-diš lip-pa-lis-ma a-mat* SIG$_5$-*tì-ia liš-šá-kin šap-tuš-šá* TIN UD.MEŠ SÙ.MEŠ *še-bé-e lit-tu-ú-tu* DÙG-*ub* UZU *u ḫu-ud lìb-bi li-šim ši-ma-a-ti*

18) *ma-ti-ma i-na aḫ-rat* UD.MEŠ NUN EGIR-*ú šá i-na u*$_4$-*me* BALA-*šú* É *šu-a-tu in-na-ḫu-ma ma-qit-ti i-raš-šu-ú áš-ra-ti-šú liš-te-ʾ-e ma-qit-ta-šú lik-šìr*

19) MU.SAR-*ú ši-ṭir* MU-*ia* Ì.GIŠ *lip-šu-uš* UDU.SÍSKUR BAL-*qí ina áš-ri-šú liš-kun ik-ri-bi-šú* DINGIR.MEŠ *i-šem-mu-ú ur-rak* UD.MEŠ *ú-rap-pa-áš kim-ti*

20) *šá* MU.SAR-*ú ši-ṭir* MU-*ia ina ši-pir ni-kil-ti ib-ba-tu lu-ú a-šar-šú ú-nak-ka-ru*

21) ^{d}UN.GAL NIBRU.KI GAŠAN GAL-*ti ag-giš lik-kil-me-šú-ma* MU-*šú* NUMUN-*šú ina nap-ḫar* KUR.KUR *li-ḫal-liq*

Left End

22) *šá é-bára-dúr-gar-ra*

Akkad; descendant of the eternal line of Bēl-bāni, son of Adasi, king of Assyria; precious scion of Baltil (Aššur), (one of) royal lineage (and) ancient stock —

15–16) At that time Ebaradurgara, the temple of the goddess Queen-of-Nippur, the great lady, my lady, which a previous king had built, became old and its walls buckled. I sought its (original) emplacement, removed its dilapidated parts (and) surveyed its (entire) foundation. I completely (re)built (it) with the work of the god Kulla according to its ancient specifications (and) raised its top (as high) as a mountain.

17) May the goddess Queen-of-Nippur, supreme lady, my lady, look upon this work with pleasure and may a good word for me be set upon her lips! May she determine as my fate a long life, fullness of old age, good health, and happiness!

18–19) If at any time in the future, during the days of the reign of some future prince, this temple falls into disrepair and becomes dilapidated, may (that prince) seek out its (original) emplacement (and) repair its dilapidated parts! May he anoint my royal inscription with oil, offer a sacrifice, (and) set (it) back in its place! The gods will (then) hearken to his prayers. He will lengthen (his) days (and) enlarge (his) family.

20–21) (But) as for the one who by some crafty device destroys my royal inscription or changes its position, may the goddess Queen-of-Nippur, great lady, glare at him angrily and make his name (and) his descendant(s) disappear from every land!

22) (Property) of Ebaradurgara.

12

An Akkadian inscription found on four cylinder fragments records the restoration of the Ekur temple at Nippur by Esarhaddon.

CATALOGUE

Ex.	Museum number	Excavation number	Nippur provenance	Dimensions (cm)	Lines preserved	cpn
1	CBS 2350	—	—	7.3×6.2	11–31	c
2	HS 1956	—	—	5.3×6.2×2.6	26–38	c
3	IM number unknown	12 N 43	Outer enclosure wall beside NW corner of locus FI 65, in mud brick of Parthian fortress	15.5×15.5×7.5	1–4, 35–41	(c)
4	UM L-9-639 = PMA F29-6-397	—	—	9.7×6.2	1–24	n

COMMENTARY

Exs. 1 and 3 were found at Nippur on April 10, 1889 and in 1973 respectively. Ex. 2 is part of the Frau Professor Hilprecht collection at the Friedrich-Schiller-Universität (Jena) and thus likely comes from the work of H.V. Hilprecht at Nippur. Ex. 2 was collated by J. Oelsner. Ex. 3 was collated from a cast of the piece in the Oriental Institute, Chicago, with additional collations from a new cast and mould provided by J.A. Brinkman. Information on ex. 4 comes from the publication of J.A. Brinkman. Ex. 4 is broken immediately before its first line (our line 1). Thus it is not impossible that that was not the first line of the inscription and that this exemplar had a different inscription than the others. According to E. Leichty, who has examined both exs. 1 and 2, the two fragments cannot be parts of the same cylinder as has sometimes been suggested. It is possible that exs. 3 and 4 are parts of the same cylinder.

The inscription is written in contemporary Babylonian script on all exemplars. Line rulings frequently indicate that two of our lines might have been considered one line by the ancient scribes; however, since the beginnings of the lines are not preserved it is not possible to determine whether or not the "second halves" of these lines were indented.

The line arrangement follows ex. 4 for lines 1–22, ex. 1 for lines 23–31, ex. 2 for lines 32–37, and ex. 3 for lines 38–41. The master line is based upon ex. 4 for lines 5–20, ex. 1 for lines 21 and 23–25, ex. 2 for lines 32–35, and ex. 3 for lines 39–41. The remaining lines are a conflation of various exemplars. Restorations in lines 7–39 are based upon B.6.31.11 lines 4–20 and B.6.31.15 lines 8–40; where B.6.31.11 and B.6.31.15 diverge, preference is given to B.6.31.11. Restorations in lines 40–41 are based upon B.6.31.16 lines 24–25 and B.6.31.17 lines 24–25.

BIBLIOGRAPHY

1922 Legrain, PBS 13 no. 81 (ex. 1, copy, edition)
1924 Poebel, OLZ 27 266 (ex. 1, study)
1956 Borger, Asarh. pp. 70–71 §40 (Npr. B) (exs. 1–2, edition)
1963 Goetze, JCS 17 p. 119 (exs. 1–2, study)
1969 Oelsner, WZJ 18 p. 54 no. 32 (ex. 2, study)
1974 Civil, RA 68 p. 94 (ex. 3, transliteration)
1978 Civil in Gibson, OIC 23 p. 112 (ex. 3, study)
1994 Brinkman, NABU pp. 4–5 no. 3 (ex. 4, partial copy, transliteration, study)

TEXT

1) *[ana enlil bēl mātāti š]á la in-nen-nu-ú qí-b[it]-*⸢*su*⸣
2) [x x x *ša lā uš-tam-s]a*(?)*-ku ṣi-it pi-*⸢*i*⸣*-šú*
3) [...] x DINGIR.MEŠ *šu-*⸢*ta*⸣-x [(...)] x-*su*
4) [...] ⸢*šá*(?) *la*(?)⸣ [(...)] x *ma-al-ku*
5) [...] DU
6) [...] EN GAL-*i* EN-*šú*

1–6) [For the god Enlil, lord of the lands], whose comma[nd] cannot be revoked, [... who]se utterance [cannot be reject]ed, [...] gods ... [...] ... ruler [...] ... [...] the great lord, his lord:

7) [... *kib*]-⸢*rat*⸣ *er-bet-ti*
8) [... *lìb-b*]*i* ^{d}*en-líl*
9) [... ^{d}A]G ^{d}U.GUR *u* DINGIR.MEŠ GAL.MEŠ
10) [... *ú-šak-šid-u*]*š i-mu-ru da-na-an-šú-un*
11) [...] GIŠ.MI-*šú-nu da-ru-ú*
12) [...] (x) UGU-*šú*
13) [...] *ti-ik-li-šú kul-lat* KUR.KUR *i-bé-lu-ma*
14) [...] x *še-pu-uš-šú*
15) [... *é*]*-sag-íl u* TIN.TIR.KI
16) [... *ma-ḫa-z*]*u mu-kin sat-tuk-ku*
17) [... T]IN.TIR.KI *sa-li-mu ir-šu-ú*
18) [...] *ir-mu-ú šu-bat-su*
19) [... É]-*šú é-dim-gal-kalam-ma ú-še-rib-ú-ma*
20) [...] *da-ra-a-ti*
21) [... *ud-diš-m*]*a ul-tu qé-reb* KUR *aš-šur*.KI

7–28) [Esarhaddon, great king, mighty king, king of the world, king of Assyria, king of] the four [quar]ters (of the world), [viceroy of Babylon, king of the land of Sumer and Akkad, selected by the steadfast hea]rt of the god Enlil; [who from his childhood trusted in the gods Aššur, Enlil, Sîn, Šamaš, Adad, Marduk, Na]bû, Nergal, and the (other) great gods, (10) [his lords, (who) allowed] him [to attain his desire]; (the one who) recognized their power, [(the one)] over whom [(the gods) extended] their eternal protection [in order to appease their divine heart(s) and set their mind(s) at rest; (the one who) by the might of the gods Aššur, Enlil, Bēl (Marduk), and the Son-of-Bēl (Nabû), the gods], his helpers, ruled over all lands

---

17.1 *sa-li-me*.

21 Instead of restoring "[(the one who) restored the splendid appearance of the captive gods of the lands, returned them] from Assyria [to ...]" (following B.6.31.11 line 11) the passage may read [(the one who) restored the splendid appearance of the great gods who had rushed to Assyria, returned them] from Assyria [to ...]" (following B.6.31.15 lines 22–23); however, there does not appear to be sufficient room for the latter restoration.

22) [... *ú*]-⸢*kin*⸣-*nu is-qu-uš-šú-un*
23) [... *i*]*na ma-ḫa-zu* GAL.MEŠ
24) [... *uš-te*]-*ši-ru šu-luḫ-ḫu*
25) [... *aš-šur*].KI DUMU ^{m}LUGAL-GIN LUGAL KUR *aš-šur*.K[I]
26) [...] x [...] *ù* URI.KI-⸢*i*⸣
27) [*liplippi da*]-*ru-ú šá* [^{md}EN-*ba*]-*ni* DUMU ^{m}*a-da-si* [L]UGAL KUR *aš-šur*.K[I]
28) [*pir'u bal-til*.K]I *šu-qu-ru* ⸢NUMUN⸣ [LUGAL-*ú*]-*tu ki-sit-ti* ⸢*ṣa*⸣-*a*-[*ti*]

and [made all rulers submissive] to him; (15) [the one who (re)constructed the temple of the god Aššur, renovated Ekur, (re)built E]sagila and Babylon, [completed the sanctuaries and cult centr]es, (and) (re)confirmed (their) regular offerings; [the king during the days of whose reign the great lord, the god Marduk], became reconciled [to] Babylon [(and again)] took up his residence [in Esagila, his palace]; (the one who) made [the god Great-Anu] enter [into his city Dēr and] his [temple] Edimgalkalama and (20) [had (him) sit upon (his)] eternal [dais; (the one who) restored the splendid appearance of the captive gods of the lands, returned them] from Assyria [to their (proper) places, and] (re)confirmed their income; [wise prince, expert who knows every craft, who constantly established appropriate procedures] in the great cult centres [(and) has] purification rites [perform]ed correctly; (25) [son of Sennacherib, king of the world (and) king of Assyria]; son of Sargon (II), king of Assyria, [viceroy of Babylon, (and) king of the land of Sumer] and Akkad; [descendant of the eter]nal line [of Bēl-bā]ni, son of Adasi, [k]ing of Assyria; precious [scion of Baltil (Aššur)], (one of) [roya]l lineage (and) ancient stock —

29) [*i-nu*]-*šu šá é-kur* É ^{d}*en*-[*lí*]*l* EN KUR.KUR EN-*ia šá* LUGAL *ma-ḫar i-p*[*u-šu*]
30) [*la-b*]*a-riš*(?) *il-lik-ma i*-[*qu*-(*ú*)-*p*]*u* É.GAR$_{8}$.ME[Š-*šú*]
31) [*ašrātišu áš-t*]*e-'-e ma-qit-ta-šú a*[*s-s*]*uḫ te-me-*⸢*en-šú ú-ṣab-bi-ma ki-ma*(?) *si*(?)⸣-[*ma-ti-šú*]
32) [*la-bi-ra*-(*a*)]-*ti ina ši-pir* ^{d}*kulla a*[*r-ṣip* ...]

29–32) [At that] time, Ekur ("House, Mountain"), the temple of the god En[li]l, lord of the lands, my lord, which a previous king had [built], became [ol]d and [its] walls [buckl]ed. [I sou]ght [its (original) emplacement], removed its dilapidated parts, (and) surveyed its (entire) foundation. I [completely] (re)bu[ilt (it)] with the work of the god Kulla according to [its ol]d ap[pearance (and) raised its top (as high) as a mountain.]

33) [(*ana šatti*?) ^{d}*en-l*]*íl* DINGIR *tu-kul-ti-ia ep-š*[*e-ti-ia* ...]
34) [*balāṭ ūmē*] SÙ.MEŠ *še-bé-e lit-tu-t*[*u* ...]

33–34) [(*On account of this*), may the god Enl]il, the god who helps me, [look upon my] wo[rks with pleasure and may a good word for me be set upon his lips! May he determine as my fate a] long [life], fullness of old age, [good health, and happiness!]

35) [*matīma ina aḫ*]-*rat* UD.MEŠ NUN EGIR-*ú šá* x [...]
36) [(...) *ma-qit*]-*ti i-raš-šu-ú áš-ra*-[*ti-šú liš-te-'*]-*e ma-qit-t*[*a*]-⸢*šú*(?)⸣ *l*[*ik*(?)-*šìr*]
37) [MU.SAR]-⸢*ú*⸣ *ši*-⸢*ṭir* MU-*ia* Ì(?).GIŠ(?)⸣ [*lipšuš* UDU.SÍ]SKUR BAL-*qí ina áš-r*[*i-šú* ...]

35–38a) [If at any time in the] future, [during the days of the reign] of some future prince, [this *temple* falls into disrepair and] becomes [dilapidat]ed, [may (that prince) seek out its (original) emplacem[ent (and) repair] its dilapidated parts! [May he anoint] my [royal inscri]ption *with oil*, offer a [sacri]fice, (and) [set (it) back] in [its] place! [The gods will (then) hearken to his prayers. He will lengthen (his) day]s (and) enlarge (his) fam[ily].

38) [...] x [... UD].ME[Š] *ú-rap-pa-áš kim*-[*ti* ...]
39) [... *ni-kil-t*]*i ib-ba-tu lu-ú a-šar-šú ú-na*[*k-ka-ru*]
40) [... *lik-kil-m*]*e-šú-ma ši-mat* ḪUL-*tim li-šim*-[*šú*]
41) [*šumšu* (*u*) *zērašu ina māti li-ḫal-li*]*q*(?)-*ma a-a ir-ši-šú re-e*-[*me*/*mu*]

38b–41) [(But as for) the one who by some crafty devi]ce destroys [my royal inscription] or cha[nges] its position, [may the god Enlil (...) glare] at him [angrily] and determine a bad fate [for him! May he make his name (and) his descendant(s) disappear from the land] and have no pity on him!

29 Following Borger, Asarh. p. 71, commentary, it is possible that the beginning of the line should be restored to read [*inūšu pa-rak*]-*ku šá é-kur* ("[At that time, the sanctu]ary of Ekur") or [*inūšu šub-t*]*u šá é-kur* ("[At that time, the abo]de of Ekur").

13

This Akkadian brick inscription states that Esarhaddon had renovated the Ekur temple at Nippur for the god Enlil.

CATALOGUE

Ex.	Museum number	Excavation number	Nippur provenance	Dimensions (cm)	Lines preserved	cpn
1	CBS 9482 (cast)	—	—	18.8×7.5	1–15	(c)
2	—	5 NT 702	Entrance of Inanna temple, level I		—	p

COMMENTARY

According to Legrain (PBS 15 p. 50) the original of ex. 1 is in Istanbul. It was not possible to locate it for collation, but a cast of it in the University Museum, Philadelphia, was examined. The edition of ex. 2 is based upon the excavation photograph of the piece and on a preliminary copy prepared by Goetze. The inscription of both exemplars is stamped in contemporary Babylonian script; that of ex. 1 appears on the face of the brick. There are no known variants to the inscription and no score for this brick inscription is presented in the microfiche.

BIBLIOGRAPHY

1926 Legrain, PBS 15 no. 86 (ex. 1, copy, edition)
1956 Borger, Asarh. p. 71 §41 (Npr. C) (ex. 1, edition)
1963 Goetze, JCS 17 p. 119 (ex. 2, study)
1985 Behrens, JCS 37 p. 244 no. 79 (ex. 1, study)
1992 Zettler, Inanna Temple p. 50 n. 42 (ex. 2, study)

TEXT

1) *a-na* ^{d}50
2) EN KUR.KUR EN-*šú*
3) ^{m}AN.ŠÁR-PAP-AŠ
4) MAN ŠÚ MAN KUR *aš-šur*
5) MAN TIN.TIR.KI
6) MAN KUR *šu-me-ri*
7) *ù* URI.KI
8) A ^{m}30-PAP.ME-SU
9) MAN ŠÚ MAN KUR *aš-šur*
10) A ^{m}MAN-GIN MAN ŠÚ
11) MAN KUR *aš-šur-ma*
12) *é-kur* É ^{d}50
13) EN-*iá ud-diš-ma*
14) *tal-lak-ta-šú*
15) *ki-ma* *u*$_4$*-me* ZÁLAG-*ir*

1–15) For the god Enlil, lord of the lands, his lord: Esarhaddon, king of the world, king of Assyria, (5) king of Babylon, (and) king of the land of Sumer and Akkad, son of Sennacherib, king of the world (and) king of Assyria, (10) son of Sargon, (who was) also king of the world (and) king of Assyria, renovated Ekur, the temple of the god Enlil, my lord, and made its processional way shine like daylight.

14

Two bricks from Nippur bear an Akkadian inscription recording the fact that Esarhaddon used baked bricks to enlarge the well Pukudadaga ("Pure, Shining Well") in the courtyard of the god Enlil.

CATALOGUE

Ex.	Museum number	Dimensions (cm)	Lines preserved	cpn
1	CBS 8645	35×24×9	1–6	c
2	UM 84-26-7	33×16×8.5	1–6	c

COMMENTARY

Exs. 1 and 2 are both inscribed, not stamped. Ex. 1 is found on the face of the brick; ex. 2 is a well-head brick, with the inscription on the edge. The inscription is in contemporary Babylonian script. The master line is based upon ex. 1. The inscription of ex. 2 is on three lines, with the lines splitting after KÁ.DINGIR.RA.K[I] (line 3 of ex. 1) and *a-gur-ru* (end of line 5 of ex. 1).

According to Peters, the brick depicted on plate I of his work (Nippur 2) was found "in later débris on the Temple Hill." The inscription on the brick is not completely clear from the photograph but may well match that of ex. 1. If ex. 1 is the brick depicted there, the piece would have been broken since the photograph was made since its shape does not match that of the brick on the photograph. Thus, a third exemplar of this inscription may be depicted in Peters' work.

BIBLIOGRAPHY

1897 Peters, Nippur 2 pp. 375-76 and pl. I lower right (ex. 1?, provenance, photo)
1926 Legrain, PBS 15 no. 75 (ex. 1, copy, edition)
1928 Poebel, OLZ 31 698 (ex. 1, study)
1929 Landsberger, ZA 38 p. 114 (study)
1956 Borger, Asarh. p. 71 §42 (Npr. D) (ex. 1, edition)
1985 Behrens, JCS 37 p. 244 no. 80 (exs. 1–2, study)

TEXT

1) *a-na* ^{d}50 ^{d}EN KUR.KUR.RE
2) ^{m}AN.ŠÁR-ŠEŠ-AŠ MAN KUR *aš-šur*.KI
3) MAN KÁ.DINGIR.RA.KI MAN KUR *šu-me-ri*
4) *u* URI.KI *a-na* TI-*šú pú-*⌜*kù*⌝*-dadag-ga*
5) KISAL ^{d}EN.LÍL.LÁ.KE$_4$ *ina a-gur-ru*
6) UDUN KÙ-*tim ú-rab-bi*

1–6) For the god Enlil, divine lord of the lands: Esarhaddon, king of Assyria, king of Babylon, (and) king of the land of Sumer and Akkad, for the sake of his life enlarged Pukudadaga (5) in the courtyard of the god Enlil with baked bricks from a (ritually) pure kiln.

15

Several clay cylinders have an inscription written in Akkadian which describes the restoration of the Eanna temple at Uruk by Esarhaddon for the goddess Ištar.

CATALOGUE

Ex.	Museum number	Excavation number	Warka photo number	Warka provenance	Dimensions (cm)	Lines preserved	cpn
1	BM 45793 (81-7-6,210)	—	—	—	Length: 14; R. dia.: 5.5; L dia.: 5.6	1–41	c
2	K 6386	—	—	—	3.7×3.5	1–8	c
3	NBC 2510	—	—	—	14.3×6.7; dia. at ends: 5.5	1–41	c
4	NBC 6055	—	—	—	14.8×7; dia. at ends: 5.8	1–41	c
5	—	W 18419	6747, 6748	Oe XIV 5, in the upper debris	13×6.6	6–25	(p)
6	IM number unknown	W 23852	—	Railway embankment	4.4×4.2	15–22	n

COMMENTARY

Ex. 1 was erroneously referred to as 81-6-7,209 by Winckler and later scholars; it is in fact 81-7-6,210. It was acquired by the British Museum in 1878 and its provenance is not known. A section of ex. 4 appears to have become detached from the main body of the cylinder in recent times. The piece was attached when the cylinder was studied by Stephens (YOS 9 no. 137) and he notes three variants in lines 8 and 41 which can no longer be confirmed. The score gives what is now preserved of the exemplar, but the additional variants are included in the notes, where they are attributed to Stephens. Ex. 5 is reported to be in Heidelberg, but it cannot be located at present. The first three lines and the last line preserved on this exemplar (lines 6–8 and 25 of the inscription) are not readable on the excavation photographs and are not included in the score. The inscription is written in contemporary Babylonian script.

The number of lines and line arrangement differs markedly among the various exemplars. The arrangement used for the master line follows that used by Borger, which goes back to the copies of ex. 1 made by Strong and Meissner-Rost. It should be noted, however, that these copies do not indicate indented lines and are inconsistent with regard to the manner in which they number them. The copy by Pinches indicates the indented lines and line rulings found on the ex. 1. The master line follows ex. 1, with help from ex. 3 in lines 22, 30, 32, and 37.

A cast of an exemplar of this inscription with "a large number of variant readings" was once owned by the Haskell Museum, Chicago (Luckenbill, ARAB 2 p. 279 n. 1), but the piece cannot at present be located in the Oriental Institute. Borger saw an uncorrected carbon-copy of a manuscript of Luckenbill's which gave the variants (without diacritics) for this piece and noted them in his edition of the inscription. These variants are included with the variants from the other texts — being noted as ex. 7 and "(Luckenbill-Borger)" — but are not included in the score. According to Keiser (BIN 2 p. 46), there is an exemplar of this inscription in the Harvard Semitic Museum; however, a search for the piece by S. Cole has not located it.

In his edition of this inscription, Borger listed variants from an inscription of Esarhaddon from Nippur (our B.6.31.11) for purposes of comparison; thus, a number of the variants listed in his edition are not found here.

BIBLIOGRAPHY

1883–84 Pinches and Budge, PSBA 6 pp. 181–82 (ex. 1, study)
1890 Winckler in Schrader, KB 2 pp. 120–21 n. 1 (ex. 1, partial edition)
1891 Barton, PAOS [=JAOS 15 (1893)] pp. cxxx–cxxxii and pl. following p. cxxx (ex. 1, copy by Pinches, edition)
1891 Bezold, Cat. 2 p. 783 (ex. 2, study)
1891–92 Strong, Hebraica 8 pp. 113–23 (ex. 1, copy, edition)
1898 King, First Steps pp. 306–11 (ex. 1, copy in type)
1898 Meissner and Rost, BA 3 pp. 260–63, 351–53, and 360–61 (exs. 1–2, copy, edition)
1920 Keiser, BIN 2 no. 28 (ex. 3, copy, study)
1927 Luckenbill, ARAB 2 §§729–34 (ex. 1, translation)
1937 Stephens, YOS 9 nos. 137 and 138 (exs. 3–4, study)
1956 Borger, Asarh. pp. 73–75 §47 (Uruk A) (exs. 1–4, edition)
1979 Cavigneaux, Bagh. Mitt. 10 p. 124 no. 9 (ex. 6, copy)
1982 Kessler, Bagh. Mitt. 13 p. 13 no. 10 and pl. 1 b, c (ex. 5, photo, study)
1983 Cavigneaux, UVB 31–32 p. 56 (ex. 6, study)

TEXT

1) *a-na* ᵈ*iš-tar* GAŠAN *šur-bu-ti e-tel-let* AN-*e u* KI-*tim qa-rit-ti* DINGIR.MEŠ *šá-ru-uḫ-ti*

2) ᵈINANNA UNUG.KI *ru-ba-a-ti ṣir-ti le-qa-a-ti pa-ra-aṣ* ᵈ*a-nù-ú-tu*

1–7) For the goddess Ištar, supreme lady, sovereign of heaven and netherworld, most valiant of the gods, splendid, the goddess Ištar-of-Uruk, august princess who has taken (unto herself all) divine offices of

3) *šá ri-kis te-re-e-ti ḫa-am-mat*
4) *ru-um-ti ti-iz-qar-ti šá a-na* LUGAL *mi-ig-ri-šá ki-niš ip-pal-la-su*
5) BALA-*šú ú-šal-ba-ru i-šar-ra-ku-uš da-na-nu ù li-i-ti*
6) *šá-nun-ka-at ád-na-a-ti šá-qu-ti* DINGIR.MEŠ *a-ši-bat é-nir-gál-an-na*
7) *šá qé-reb é-an-na be-let* UNUG.KI GAŠAN GAL-*ti* GAŠAN-*šú*

highest rank (and) has gathered to herself (all) ordinances, beloved, eminent, who looks upon the king — her favourite — with steady favour, (5) makes his reign lengthy, (and) bestows on him power and victory, empress of the world, most exalted of the gods, who dwells in Enirgalana ("House, Prince of Heaven") — which is inside Eanna — lady of Uruk, great lady, his lady:

8) ^{m}AN.ŠÁR-ŠEŠ-SUM.NA LUGAL GAL-*ú* LUGAL *dan-nu* LUGAL ŠÚ LUGAL KUR *aš-šur*.KI LUGAL *kib-rat* 4-*ti* GÌR.NÍTA TIN.TIR.KI LUGAL KUR *šu-me-ri ù* URI.KI
9) *ti-ri-iṣ* ŠU.II AN.ŠÁR *i-tu-ut kun lìb-bi* ^{d}*en-líl ni-bit* ^{d}AMAR.UTU *mi-gir* ^{d}*ir-ni-ni*
10) *šá ul-tu ṣe-ḫe-ri-šú a-na* AN.ŠÁR ^{d}*a-nim* ^{d}*en-líl* ^{d}*é-a* ^{d}30 ^{d}UTU ^{d}IŠKUR ^{d}AMAR.UTU ^{d}AG ^{d}U.GUR *u* ^{d}15
11) DINGIR.ME GAL.ME EN.ME-*šú it-tak-lu-ma ni-iz-mat-su ú-šak-ši-du-uš i-mu-ru da-na-an-šú-un*
12) *a-na nu-uḫ-ḫu lìb-bi* DINGIR-*ú-ti-šú-nu u nu-up-pu-uš ka-bat-ti-šú-nu* GIŠ.MI-*šú-nu da-ru-ú*
13) *it-ru-ṣu* UGU-*šú*
14) *ina e-muq* AN.ŠÁR ^{d}EN DUMU ^{d}EN *u* ^{d}15 DINGIR.ME *ti-ik-li-šú kul-lat* KUR.KUR *i-be-lu-ma*
15) *gi-mir ma-li-ku ú-šak-ni-šu še-pu-uš-šu*
16) *ba-nu-ú* É AN.ŠÁR *e-piš é-sag-íl u* TIN.TIR.KI *mu-ud-diš é-an-na*
17) *mu-šak-lil eš-re-e-ti u ma-ḫa-zu mu-kin sat-tuk-ku*
18) LUGAL *šá ina* u_4*-me* BALA-*šú* EN GAL-*ú* ^{d}AMAR.UTU *a-na* TIN.TIR.KI *sa-li-mu ir-šu-ú*
19) *ina é-sag-íl* É.GAL-*šú ir-mu-ú šu-bat-su*
20) ^{d}*a-num* GAL-*ú ana* URU-*šú* BÀD.AN.KI *ù* É-*šú é-dim-gal-kalam-ma ú-še-ri-bu-ma*
21) *ú-še-ši-bu pa-rak-ka da-ra-a-ti*
22) DINGIR.MEŠ KUR.KUR *šá a-na* KUR *aš-šur*.KI *i-ḫi-šu-ni šu-kut-ta-šú-nu ud-diš-ma ul-tu qé-reb* KUR *aš-šur*.KI
23) *ana áš-ri-šú-nu ú-tir-šú-nu-ti-ma ú-kin is-qu-uš-šú-un*
24) NUN *en-qu it-pe-šu ḫa-sis kal šip-ri šá ina ma-ḫa-zu* GAL.MEŠ
25) *si-ma-a-ti iš-tak-ka-nu uš-te-ši-ru šu-luḫ-ḫa*
26) DUMU ^{md}30-ŠEŠ.MEŠ-*eri-ba* LUGAL ŠÚ LUGAL KUR *aš-šur*.KI DUMU ^{m}LUGAL-GIN LUGAL KUR *aš-šur*.KI
27) GÌR.NÍTA TIN.TIR.KI LUGAL KUR *šu-me-ru ù* URI.KI
28) *li-ip-li-pi da-ru-ú šá* ^{d}EN-*ba-ni* DUMU ^{m}*a-da-si* LUGAL KUR *aš-šur*.KI
29) NUNUZ *bal-til*.KI *šu-qu-ru* NUMUN LUGAL-*ú-tu ki-sit-ti ṣa-a-ti*

8–29) Esarhaddon, great king, mighty king, king of the world, king of Assyria, king of the four quarters (of the world), viceroy of Babylon, king of the land of Sumer and Akkad; the one to whom the god Aššur has stretched out his hand, permanently selected by the god Enlil, who was chosen by the god Marduk, favourite of the goddess Irnini; (10) who from his childhood trusted in the gods Aššur, Anu, Enlil, Ea, Sîn, Šamaš, Adad, Marduk, Nabû, Nergal, and Ištar, the great gods, his lords, (who) allowed him to attain his desire, (the one who) recognized their power, (the one) over whom (the gods) extended their eternal protection in order to appease their divine heart(s) and set their mind(s) at rest; (the one who) by the might of the gods Aššur, Bēl (Marduk), the Son-of-Bēl (Nabû), and Ištar, the gods, his helpers, ruled over all lands and (15) made all rulers submissive to him; the one who (re)constructed the temple of the god Aššur, (re)built Esagila and Babylon, renovated Eanna, completed the sanctuaries and cult centres, (and) (re)confirmed (their) regular offerings; the king during the days of whose reign, the great lord, the god Marduk, became reconciled to Babylon (and again) took up his residence in Esagila, his palace; (20) the one who made the god Great-Anu enter into his city Dēr and his temple Edimgalkalama ("House, Great Bond of the Land") and had (him) sit upon (his) eternal dais; (the one who) restored the splendid appearance of the great gods who had rushed to Assyria, returned them from Assyria to their (proper) places and (re)confirmed their income; wise prince, expert who knows every craft, who (25) constantly established appropriate procedures in the great cult centres (and) has purification rites performed correctly; son of Sennacherib, king of the world (and) king of Assyria; son of Sargon (II), king of Assyria, viceroy of Babylon, (and) king of the land of Sumer and Akkad; descendant of the eternal line of Bēl-bāni, son of Adasi, king of Assyria; precious scion of Baltil (Aššur), (one of) royal lineage (and) ancient stock —

30) *i-nu-ma é-an-na* É ^{d}*a-nu-ú-tu na-ram* ^{d}15 GAŠAN-*ia šá* LUGAL *ma-ḫar i-pu-šu*

30–33) *At that time* Eanna, the temple of highest rank, beloved of the goddess Ištar, my lady, which a

8.4 omits LUGAL *kib-rat* 4-*ti*, "king of the four quarters (of the world)" (Stephens).

31) *la-ba-riš il-lik-ma i-qu-pu* É.GAR$_8$.MEŠ-*šú*
32) *áš-ra-ti-šú áš-te-ʾ-e ma-qit-ta-šú as-suḫ te-me-en-šú ú-ṣab-bi-ma ki-ma si-ma-ti-šú*
33) *la-bi-ra-a-ti ina ši-pir* ^{d}*kulla ar-ṣip ú-šak-lil ki-ma* KUR-*i re-e-ši-šú ul-li*

34) ^{d}15 GAŠAN *šur-bu-ti ši-pir šu-a-tu ḫa-diš lip-pa-lis-ma a-mat* MUNUS.SIG$_5$-*ia liš-šá-kin šap-tuš-šá*
35) *muḫ-ḫi kul-lat na-ki-ri li-šam-ri-ir* GIŠ.TUKUL.MEŠ-*ia*
36) *ma-ti-ma ina aḫ-rat* UD.⌈MEŠ⌉ NUN EGIR-*ú šá ina* UD.MEŠ BALA-*šú ši-pir šu-a-tu*
37) *in-na-ḫu-ma ma-qit-ti i-raš-šu-ú áš-ra-ti-šú liš-te-ʾ-e ma-qit-ta-šú lik-šìr*
38) MU.SAR-*ú ši-ṭir* MU-*ia* Ì.GIŠ *lip-šu-uš* UDU.SÍSKUR BAL-*qí ina áš-ri-šú liš-kun*
39) *ik-ri-bi-šú* DINGIR.MEŠ *i-šem-mu-ú ur-rak* UD.MEŠ *ú-rap-pa-áš kim-ti*

40) *šá* MU.SAR-*ú ši-ṭir* MU-*ia ina ši-pir ni-kil-ti ib-ba-tu lu-ú a-šar-šú ú-nak-ka-ru*
41) ^{d}*iš-tar* GAŠAN GAL-*ti ag-giš lik-kil-me-šú-ma* MU-*šú* NUMUN-*šú ina nap-ḫar* KUR.KUR *li-ḫal-liq*

previous king had built, became old and its walls buckled. I sought its (original) emplacement, removed its dilapidated parts, (and) surveyed its (entire) foundation. I completely (re)built (it) with the work of the god Kulla according to its ancient specifications (and) raised its top (as high) as a mountain.

34–35) May the goddess Ištar, supreme lady, look upon this work with pleasure and may a good word for me be set upon her lips! May she make my weapons prevail over all (my) enemies!

36–39) If at any time in the future, during the days of the reign of some future prince, this work falls into disrepair and becomes dilapidated, may (that prince) seek out its (original) emplacement (and) repair its dilapidated parts! May he anoint my royal inscription with oil, offer a sacrifice, (and) set (it) back in its place! The gods will (then) hearken to his prayers. He will lengthen (his) days (and) enlarge (his) family.

40–41) (But) as for the one who by some crafty device destroys my royal inscription or changes its position, may the goddess Ištar, great lady, glare at him angrily and make his name (and) his descendant(s) disappear from every land!

16

A second cylinder inscription commemorates the renovation of Enirgalana, a cella located within the Eanna temple at Uruk, by Esarhaddon for the goddess Ištar. The inscription is written in Akkadian.

CATALOGUE

Ex.	Museum number	Excavation number	Warka photo number	Warka provenance	Dimensions (cm)	Lines preserved	cpn
1	YBC 2147	—	—	—	11.2×4.6	1–25	c
2	NBC 2509	—	—	—	13.4×11	1–15, 22–24	c
3	—	W 856	729, 730	Pa XV 3	—	1–3, 21–25	p

COMMENTARY

Ex. 1 is reported to have been found at Uruk (Clay, YOS 1 p. 56). Where the photos of ex. 3 are not readable, the transliteration of that exemplar follows the published copy. Ex. 1 is written in Assyrian script while exs. 2 and 3 are in contemporary Babylonian script. The line arrangement and master line follow ex. 1.

Parallels to many sections of the inscription can be found in other inscriptions of Esarhaddon, in particular B.6.31.17–18. In his edition of this inscription, Borger listed variants from these two inscriptions for purposes of comparison; thus, a number of the variants listed in his edition are not found here.

BIBLIOGRAPHY

1915 Clay, YOS 1 no. 41 (ex. 1, photo, copy, edition)
1920 Keiser, BIN 2 no. 27 (ex. 2, copy)
1927 Luckenbill, ARAB 2 §§735–41 (ex. 1, translation)
1930 Schott, UVB 1 pp. 57–58 and pl. 28 no. 23 (ex. 3, copy, edition)
1956 Borger, Asarh. pp. 75–76 §48 (Uruk B) (exs. 1–3, edition)
1957–58 Borger, AfO 18 p. 116 §48 (study to line 19)

TEXT

1) *a-na* ^{d}INANNA UNUG.KI *e-tel-let* AN-*e u* KI-*tim qa-rit-ti* DINGIR.MEŠ *ṣir-ti*
2) GAŠAN *šur-bu-tú ḫa-me-mat pa-ra-aṣ* ^{d}*a-nù-u-tú ša na-gab šu-luḫ-ḫu šu-up-qu-ud-du qa-tuš-šá*
3) *šá-nu-kàt i-la-a-te ša ina er-me a-nu ù ki-gal-li šur-ru-ḫu zik-ru-šá*
4) *i-lat* MURUB$_{4}$ *ù ta-ḫa-zi a-li-kàt i-di* LUGAL *mi-gir-i-šá mu-ra-áš-ši-bat ga-re-e-šú*
5) *a-ši-bat é-nir-gál-an-na ša qé-reb é-an-na* GAŠAN UNUG.KI GAŠAN GAL-*ti* GAŠAN-*šú*

6) ^{m}AN.ŠÁR-ŠEŠ-SUM.NA MAN ŠÚ MAN KUR *aš-šur*.KI GÌR.NÍTA KÁ.DINGIR.RA.KI MAN KUR *šu-me-ri ù* URI.KI
7) LUGAL *šáḫ-ṭu muš-te-ʾ-u áš-ra-a-ti* DINGIR.MEŠ GAL.MEŠ *pa-liḫ* EN EN.EN
8) *ba-nu-u* É AN.ŠÁR *e-piš é-sag-íl ù* KÁ.DINGIR.RA.KI *za-nin é-zi-da*
9) *mu-ud-diš é-an-na mu-šak-lil eš-re-e-ti ma-ḫa-zi ša ina qé-reb-ši-na iš-tak-ka-nu si-ma-a-ti*
10) DUMU ^{md}30-PAP.MEŠ-SU MAN ŠÚ MAN KUR *aš-šur*.KI DUMU ^{m}MAN-GIN MAN KUR *aš-šur*.KI GÌR.NÍTA KÁ.DIŠ.DIŠ.KI MAN KUR *šu-me-ri u* URI.KI
11) *é-nir-gál-an-na* É *pa-pa-ḫi* ^{d}*iš-tar* GAŠAN-*ia ša qé-reb é-an-na*
12) *ša* MAN *maḫ-ri i-pu-šu la-ba-riš il-lik-ma mi-qit-ti ir-ši*
13) *áš-ra-ti-šú áš-te-ʾ ina a-gur-ri* UDUN KÙ-*tim ma-qit-ta-šú ak-še-er*
14) ŠU.II ^{d}INANNA UNUG.KI GAŠAN GAL-*ti aṣ-bat-ma a-na qé-reb-šú ú-še-rib šu-bat da-ra-a-te ú-šar-me*
15) UDU.SISKUR.MEŠ *taš-ri-iḫ-ti aq-qí uš-par-zi-iḫ si-ga-ar-šá*

16) ^{d}INANNA UNUG.KI GAŠAN *ṣir-ti ina qé-reb* É *pa-pa-ḫi šu-a-te ḫa-di-iš ina a-šá-bi-ki*
17) *ia-a-ti* ^{m}AN.ŠÁR-ŠEŠ-SUM.NA MAN KUR *aš-šur*.KI *a-mat* MUNUS.SIG$_{5}$-*ia liš-šá-kin šap-tuk-ki*
18) TI.LA UD.MEŠ SÙ.MEŠ *še-bé-e lit-tu-tu ṭu-ub* UZU *ù ḫu-ud lìb-bi ši-i-me ši-ma-ti*
19) *ina qab-lu ù ta-ḫa-zi i-da-a-a i-tas-ḫar-ma kul-lat na-ki-ri-ia lu-mì-iš kul-ba-biš*

20) *ma-ti-ma ina aḫ-rat u*$_{4}$-*me* NUN EGIR-*u ša ina* BALA-*šú* É *pa-pa-ḫi šu-a-te in-na-ḫu an-ḫu-us-su lu-ud-diš*

1–5) For the goddess Ištar of Uruk, sovereign of heaven and netherworld, most valiant of the gods, august, supreme lady, who has gathered to herself (all) divine offices of highest rank, the one into whose hand all purification rites are appointed, empress of the goddesses, whose words are pre-eminent in heaven and netherworld, goddess of war and battle, who goes at the side of the king, her favourite, (and) slays his foes, who dwells in Enirgalana — which is inside Eanna — lady of Uruk, great lady, his lady:

6–10) Esarhaddon, king of the world, king of Assyria, viceroy of Babylon, king of the land of Sumer and Akkad; respectful king who is assiduous toward the sanctuaries of the great gods; who reveres the lord of lords; who (re)constructed the temple of the god Aššur, (re)built Esagila and Babylon, provided for Ezida, renovated Eanna, completed the sanctuaries of the cult centres, (and) constantly established appropriate procedures in them; son of Sennacherib, king of the world (and) king of Assyria; son of Sargon (II), king of Assyria, viceroy of Babylon, (and) king of the land of Sumer and Akkad —

11–15) Enirgalana ("House, Prince of Heaven"), the cella of the goddess Ištar, my lady, which is inside Eanna, which a previous king had built, became old and dilapidated. I sought its (original) emplacement (and) repaired its dilapidated parts with baked bricks from a (ritually) pure kiln. I grasped the hands of the goddess Istar of Uruk, the great lady, brought (her) inside, (and) caused (her) to take up residence (there) forever. I offered splendid sacrifices and made her doorbolt extremely fine.

16–19) O goddess Ištar of Uruk, august lady, when you are happily dwelling inside that cella, may a good word for me — Esarhaddon, king of Assyria — be set upon your lips! Determine as my fate a long life, fullness of old age, good health, and happiness! Come to my side in war and battle so that I may squash all my enemies like ants!

20–22a) If at any time in the future, during the reign of some future prince, this cella falls into disrepair, may (that prince) repair its dilapidated state! May

3 Possibly "whose names are splendid" instead of "whose words are pre-eminent."

21) *šu-mì it-ti šu-me-šú liš-ṭur* MU.SAR-*ru-u ši-ṭir* MU-*ia* Ì.GIŠ *lip-šu-uš* UDU.SISKUR BAL-*qí it-ti* MU.SAR-*e-šú liš-kun*

22) *ik-ri-bi-šú* DINGIR.MEŠ *i-šem-mu(-)u ša šu-mì šaṭ-ru ina ši-pir ni-kil-ti i-pa-áš-ši-ṭu*

23) MU.SAR-*ru-u-a i-ab-bat lu-u a-šar-šú ú-nak-ka-ru*

24) [d]INANNA UNUG.KI *ag-giš lik-kil-me-šu-ma ši-mat le-mut-tú li-šim-šú*

25) MU-*šú* NUMUN-*šú ina* KUR *li-ḫal-liq-ma a-a ir-ši-šú re-e-me*

he write my name with his name! May he anoint with oil my royal inscription, offer a sacrifice, (and) set (my royal inscription) with his royal inscription! The gods will (then) hearken to his prayers.

22b–25) (But) as for the one who erases my inscribed name by some crafty device, destroys my royal inscription, or changes its position, may the goddess Ištar of Uruk glare at him angrily and determine a bad fate for him! May she make his name (and) his descendant(s) disappear from the land and have no pity on him!

17

This Akkadian inscription is found upon three clay cylinders and records Esarhaddon's renovation of the cella Eḫiliana for the goddess Nanāia. This cella was located within the Eanna temple complex at Uruk.

CATALOGUE

Ex.	Museum number	Excavation number	Warka photo number	Warka provenance	Dimensions (cm)	Lines preserved	cpn
1	AO 6772	—	—	—	15.1×7.2	1–25	c
2	BM 113204 (1915-4-10,2)	—	—	—	Length: 12.8; L. dia.: 4.0	1–25	c
3	—	W 4098	728	Pe XIV 5, at the NW courtyard wall of Sargon, 1 m under the upper edge of the older wall	Length: 5.5; Dia.: 4.7–6.5	1–25	(p)

COMMENTARY

According to Thureau-Dangin (RA 11 [1914] p. 96), ex. 1 was found at Uruk. Ex. 2 was purchased by the British Museum from J.E. Gejou (Paris) and thus its provenance is not known. Exs. 1 and 3 are written in Babylonian script and ex. 2 in Assyrian script. Where the photo of ex. 3 is not legible (in particular, for lines 1–2 and 18–19), the transliteration of that exemplar follows the published copy. The line arrangement follows ex. 1; the master line follows ex. 1, with help from ex. 2 in lines 2, 4, 6, 8–10, and 18.

Parallels to many sections of the inscription can be found in other inscriptions of Esarhaddon from Nippur and Uruk, in particular B.6.31.16 from Uruk.

BIBLIOGRAPHY

1914 Thureau-Dangin, RA 11 pp. 96–101 (ex. 1, copy, edition)
1921 Gadd, CT 36 pls. 15–16 (ex. 2, copy)
1922 BM Guide p. 228 no. 27 (ex. 2, study)
1923 Jean, Milieu biblique 2 pp. 306–308 (ex. 1, translation)
1924 Jean, Littérature p. 255 (ex. 1, translation)
1927 Luckenbill, ARAB 2 §§746–51 (exs. 1–2, translation)
1930 Schott, UVB 1 pp. 58–60 and pl. 29 no. 24 (ex. 3, copy, edition [with restorations and variants from exs. 1–2])
1956 Borger, Asarh. pp. 75–76 sub §48, variants, and p. 77 §49 (Uruk C) (exs. 1–3, partial edition, study)

24.3 [... GAŠA]N ⸢*šur*⸣-*bu-ti*, "[...] supreme [lad]y," for [d]INANNA UNUG.KI, "the goddess Ištar of Uruk."

TEXT

1) *a-na* ^{d}*na-na-a pu-su-um-ti i-la-a-ti šá* ḪI.LI *u ul-ṣi za-ʾ-na-tu lu-le-e ma-la-tu*

2) *bu-kúr-ti* ^{d}*a-nim šit-ra-aḫ-ti šá ina nap-ḫar be-le-e-ti šur-ba-a-tu e-nu-us-sa*

3) *ḫi-rat* ^{d}*mu-zib-sa*$_4$*-a ti-iz-qar-ti sek-ra-ti na-ʾ-it-ti na-ram-ti* NUN-*ú-ti-šú*

4) *ìl-tu*$_4$ *re-me-ni-tu*$_4$ *a-li-kát re-ṣi* LUGAL *pa-li-ḫi-šá mu-šal-bi-rat pa-le-e-šú*

5) *a-ši-bat é-ḫi-li-an-na šá qé-reb é-an-na šar-rat* UNUG.KI GAŠAN GAL-*tu*$_4$ GAŠAN-*šú*

6) ^{m}AN.ŠÁR-ŠEŠ-SUM.NA LUGAL ŠÚ LUGAL KUR *aš-šur*.KI GÌR.NÍTA KÁ.DINGIR.RA.KI LUGAL KUR *šu-me-ru ù* URI.KI

7) LUGAL *šáḫ-ṭu muš-te-ʾ-ú áš-ra-a-ti* DINGIR.MEŠ GAL.MEŠ *pa-a-liḫ* EN EN.EN

8) *ba-a-nu-ú* É AN.ŠÁR *e-piš é-sag-íl u* KÁ.DINGIR.RA.KI *za-a-nin é-zi-da*

9) *mu-ud-diš é-an-na mu-šak-lil eš-re-e-ti ma-ḫa-zi šá ina qer-bi-ši-na iš-tak-kan si-ma-a-ti*

10) DUMU ^{md}30-ŠEŠ.MEŠ-SU LUGAL ŠÚ LUGAL KUR *aš-šur*.KI DUMU ^{m}LUGAL-GIN LUGAL KUR *aš-šur*.KI GÌR.NÍTA KÁ.DINGIR.RA.KI LUGAL KUR *šu-me-ru ù ak-ka-di-i*

11) *é-ḫi-li-an-na* É *pa-pa-ḫi* ^{d}*na-na-a* GAŠAN-*ia šá qé-reb é-an-na*

12) *šá* LUGAL *maḫ-ri i-pu-šu la-ba-riš il-lik-ma mi-qit-ti ir-ši*

13) *eṣ-re-ti-šú áš-te-ʾ-i ina* SIG$_4$.AL.ÙR.RA UDUN KÙ-*tim ma-qit-ta-šú ak-ši-ir*

14) ŠU.II ^{d}*na-na-a* GAŠAN GAL-*tu*$_4$ *aṣ-bat-ma a-na qer-bi-šú ú-še-rib-ma šu-bat da-ra-a-ti ú-šar-me*

15) UDU.SISKUR.MEŠ *taš-ri-iḫ-ti aq-qí uš-par-zi-iḫ* ŠI.GAR-*šá*

16) ^{d}*na-na-a* GAŠAN *ṣir-tu*$_4$ *ina qé-reb* É *pa-pa-ḫi šu-a-ti ḫa-di-iš ina a-šá-a-bi-ki*

17) *ia-a-ti* ^{m}AN.ŠÁR-ŠEŠ-SUM.NA NUN *pa-a-liḫ-ki ina ma-ḫar* ^{d}AG *ḫa-a-a-i-ri-ki ti-iz-qa-ri ba-ni-ti*

18) TI UD.MEŠ SÙ.MEŠ *še-bé-e lit-tu-tu ṭu-ú-bi* UZU *u ḫu-ud lìb-bi ši-i-mi ši-ma-ti*

19) SUḪUŠ GIŠ.GU.ZA LUGAL-*ú-ti-ia ú-ḫum-meš šur-ši-di it-ti* AN-*e u* KI-*tim kin-ni* BALA-*ú-a*

20) *ma-ti-ma ina aḫ-rat* UD.MEŠ NUN EGIR-*ú šá ina* BALA-*šú* É *pa-pa-ḫi šu-a-ti in-na-ḫu an-ḫu-us-su lu-ud-diš*

21) *šu-mi it-ti šu-mi-šú liš-ṭur* MU.SAR-*ru-ú ši-ṭir* MU-*ia* Ì.GIŠ *lip-šu-uš* UDU.SISKUR BAL-*qí it-ti* MU.SAR-*e-šú liš-kun*

1–5) For the goddess Nanāia, veiled one of the goddesses, who is adorned with attractiveness and joy and full of glamour, splendid daughter of the god Anu, whose lordship is supreme among all ladies, eminent spouse of the god Muzibsâ, praised *sekretu*, beloved of his majesty, compassionate goddess, who goes to the help of the king who reveres her, who prolongs his reign, who dwells in Eḫiliana — which is inside Eanna — queen of Uruk, the great lady, his lady:

6–10) Esarhaddon, king of the world, king of Assyria, viceroy of Babylon, king of the land of Sumer and Akkad; respectful king who is assiduous toward the sanctuaries of the great gods; who reveres the lord of lords; who (re)constructed the temple of the god Assur, (re)built Esagila and Babylon, provided for Ezida, renovated Eanna, completed the sanctuaries of the cult centres, (and) constantly established appropriate procedures in them; son of Sennacherib, king of the world (and) king of Assyria; son of Sargon (II), king of Assyria, viceroy of Babylon, (and) king of the land of Sumer and Akkad —

11–15) Eḫiliana ("House, Luxuriance of Heaven"), the cella of the goddess Nanāia, my lady, which is inside Eanna, which a previous king had built, became old and dilapidated. I sought its (original) ground-plan (and) repaired its dilapidated parts with baked bricks from a (ritually) pure kiln. I grasped the hands of the goddess Nanāia, great lady, brought (her) inside, and caused (her) to take up residence (there) forever. I offered splendid sacrifices and made her doorbolt extremely fine.

16–19) O goddess Nanāia, august lady, when you are happily dwelling inside that cella, speak well of me — Esarhaddon, the prince who reveres you — before the god Nabû, your husband! Determine as my fate a long life, fullness of old age, good health, and happiness! Make the foundation of my royal throne as secure as a rocky mountain! Establish my reign as firm as heaven and netherworld!

20–22a) If at any time in the future, during the reign of some future prince, this cella falls into disrepair, may (that prince) repair its dilapidated state! May he write my name with his name! May he anoint with oil my royal inscription, offer a sacrifice, (and) set (my royal inscription) with his royal inscription! The gods will (then) listen to his prayers.

---

2 *e-nu-us-sa*, "whose lordship," comes from ex. 2; ex. 1 has of *dan-nu-us-sa*, "whose power" (*dan-* probably erroneously for *e-*). See also B.6.32.13 line 5.

3 The term *sekretu*/*sekertu*/*sekratu*, which CAD 15 [S] p. 215 describes as "1. (a woman of high rank, possibly cloistered), 2. (a woman of the palace household, court lady)," is not normally used to describe goddesses, but is used elsewhere for the goddess Nanāia (e.g., Goetze, YOS 10 no. 46 iv 49, where the term is followed by the epithet "beloved of the king").

13.2–3 *áš-ra-ti-šú*, "its (original) emplacement," for *eṣ-re-ti-šú*, "its (original) ground-plan."

17.2 MAN KUR *aš-šur*.KI, "king of Assyria," for NUN *pa-a-liḫ-ki*, "the prince who reveres you."

22) *ik-ri-bi-šú* DINGIR.MEŠ *i-šem-mu-ú u šá šu-mi šaṭ-ru ina ši-pir ni-kil-ti i-pa-áš-ši-ṭu*
23) MU.SAR-*ru-ú-a ib-ba-tu lu-u a-šar-šú ú-nak-ka-ru*
24) ^{d}*na-na-a* GAŠAN *šur-bu-ti ag-giš lik-kil-me-šú-ma ši-mat le-mut-tim li-šim-šú*
25) MU-*šú* NUMUN-*šú ina* KUR *li-ḫal-liq-ma a-a ir-ši-iš re-e-mu*

22b–25) But as for the one who erases my inscribed name by some crafty device, destroys my royal inscription, or changes its position, may the goddess Nanāia, supreme lady, glare at him angrily and determine a bad fate for him! May she make his name (and) his descendant(s) disappear from the land and have no pity on him!

18

A second clay cylinder inscription of Esarhaddon describes the restoration of Eḫiliana, the cella of the goddess Nanāia at Uruk. This inscription, also written in Akkadian, mentions that Nazi-Maruttaš, a Kassite king of Babylonia (1307–1282 BC), had originally built the structure and that it had later been restored by Erība-Marduk (B.6.13).

COMMENTARY

The cylinder is presently in New Haven (YBC 2146) and is reported to have been found at Uruk (Clay, YOS 1 p. 56). The cylinder measures 11.3×6 cm; the diameters of the left and right ends are 4.7 and 4.5 cm respectively. The inscription is written in Neo-Assyrian script and has been collated.

BIBLIOGRAPHY

1915 Clay, YOS 1 no. 40 and pl. LIII middle [misnumbered no. 42] (photo, copy, edition)
1927 Luckenbill, ARAB 2 §§742–45 (translation)
1956 Borger, Asarh. pp. 75–76 sub §48, variants, and p. 77 §50 (Uruk D) (partial edition)

TEXT

1) *a-na* ^{d}*na-na-a šar-rat* UNUG.KI GAŠAN GAL-*ti* GAŠAN-*šú*
2) ^{m}AN.ŠÁR-ŠEŠ-SUM.NA MAN KUR *aš-šur* GÌR.NÍTA KÁ.DINGIR.RA.KI
3) MAN KUR *šu-me-ri u* URI.KI *muš-te-ʾ-u áš-rat* DINGIR.ME GAL.ME
4) *ba-nu-u* É AN.ŠÁR *e-piš é-sag-íl u* KÁ.DINGIR.RA.KI
5) *mu-ud-diš é-an-na mu-šak-lil eš-ret kul-lat ma-ḫa-zi*
6) *ša ina qer-bi-ši-na iš-tak-ka-nu si-ma-a-ti*
7) *ka-šid ul-tu tam-tim e-li-ti a-di tam-tim šap-li-ti*
8) *ša gi-mir ma-li-ki ú-šak-ni-šu še-pu-uš-šu*
9) DUMU ^{md}30-PAP.MEŠ-SU MAN KUR *aš-šur* DUMU ^{m}MAN-GIN MAN KUR *aš-šur*.KI

1) For the goddess Nanāia, queen of Uruk, great lady, his lady:
2–10) Esarhaddon, king of Assyria, viceroy of Babylon, king of the land of Sumer and Akkad; who is assiduous toward the sanctuaries of the great gods; who (re)constructed the temple of Aššur, (re)built Esagila and Babylon, (5) renovated Eanna, completed the sanctuaries of all the cult centres, (and) constantly established appropriate procedures in them; who conquered from the Upper Sea to the Lower Sea (and) who made all rulers submissive to him; son of Sennacherib, king of Assyria; son of Sargon (II), king of Assyria, viceroy of Babylon, (and) king of the land of Sumer and Akkad —

B.6.31.17 line 24.2 omits GAŠAN *šur-bu-ti*, "supreme lady."
B.6.31.17 line 25.3 [...] *ù* NUMUN-*šú*, "[...] and his descendant(s)."
B.6.31.18 line 7 The "Upper Sea" refers to the Mediterranean Sea and the "Lower Sea" to the Gulf.

10) GÌR.NÍTA KÁ.DINGIR.RA.KI MAN KUR *šu-me-ri u* URI.KI
11) *é-ḫi-li-an-na* É *pa-paḫ* ᵈ*na-na-a* GAŠAN-*ia*
12) *ša* ᵐ*na-zi-múru-taš* MAN KÁ.DINGIR.RA.KI *i-pu-šu*
13) ᵐ*eri-ba-mar-duk* MAN KÁ.DINGIR.RA.KI *ú-ke-eš-šu-u*
14) *la-ba-riš il-lik-ma ma-qit-ti ir-ši*
15) *áš-ra-ti-šú áš-te-ʾ ina a-gur-ri* UDUN KÙ-*tim*
16) *ma-qit-ta-šú ak-šìr* ŠU.II ᵈ*na-na-a* GAŠAN-*ia*
17) *aṣ-bat-ma a-na qer-bi-šú ú-še-rib šu-bat da-rat ú-šar-me*
18) *ši-pir šá-a-šú* ᵈ*na-na-a ḫa-diš ina nap-lu-si-šá*
19) *ia-a-ti* ᵐAN.ŠÁR-ŠEŠ-SUM.NA MAN KUR *aš-šur* MAN KÁ.DIŠ.KI
20) *a-mat* MUNUS.SIG$_5$-*ia ina ma-ḫar* ᵈPA EN-*iá liš-šá-kin šap-tuš-šá*
21) *ša šu-mì šaṭ-ru ina ši-pir ni-kil-ti i-pa-áš-ši-ṭu*
22) MU.SAR-*u-a i-ab-bat lu-u a-šar-šú ú-nak-ka-ru*
23) ᵈ*na-na-a ag-giš lik-kil-me-šú-ma* MU-*šú* NUMUN-*šú lu-ḫal-liq*

11–17) Eḫiliana ("House, Luxuriance of Heaven"), the cella of the goddess Nanāia, my lady, which Nazi-Maruttaš, king of Babylon, had built, (and which) Erība-Marduk, king of Babylon, had *shored up*, became old and dilapidated. (15) I sought its (original) emplacement (and) repaired its dilapidated parts with baked bricks from a (ritually) pure kiln. I grasped the hands of the goddess Nanāia, my lady, brought (her) inside, (and) caused (her) to take up residence (there) forever.

18–20) When the goddess Nanāia looks upon this work with pleasure, may a good word for me — Esarhaddon, king of Assyria (and) king of Babylon — be set upon her lips before the god Nabû, my lord!

21–23) (But) as for the one who erases my inscribed name by some crafty device, destroys my royal inscription, or changes its position, may the goddess Nanāia glare at him angrily and make his name (and) his descendant(s) disappear!

19

An Akkadian inscription stamped on several bricks from Uruk records the restoration of the Eanna temple by Esarhaddon for the goddess Ištar of Uruk. The inscription is similar to two other brick inscriptions commemorating the same action (B.6.31.20–21).

CATALOGUE

Ex.	Museum number	Excavation number	Warka photo number	Warka provenance	Dimensions (cm)	Lines preserved	FuB 27	cpn
1	VA 14668	W 942	822	Stone building, supposedly Qb XV 4	30.5×30.5×8	1–13	39	c
2	—	W 3764	822	Qd XV 4, debris	—	1–13	—	p
3	—	W 3885	821	Eanna area	—	2–8	—	p
4	—	W 4238	—	Temple of Karaindaš, debris	—	1–13	—	n

COMMENTARY

The inscription is stamped on the face of the brick. The stamped area on ex. 1 measures 16.2×8 cm. The excavation photographs are not always clear and it is not possible to confirm the reading of many signs on exs. 1–3 from them. In particular, the inscription on ex. 2 is so faint as to be basically illegible on the photo. The edition is based upon the published edition of ex. 1 by J. Marzahn (with additional collations kindly supplied by Marzahn), with some help from the photograph for ex. 3 in lines 4–7. No score for this brick inscription is provided in the microfiche.

Schott (UVB 1 p. 57 n. 1 to no. 21) states that W. von Soden informed him of an additional piece with this inscription. It is not known to which piece he refers since he notes the same thing for the next text (our B.6.31.20). IM 43036, a brick in the Iraq Museum, may have either this inscription, B.6.31.20 or B.6.31.21. According to Basmachi, Treasures p. 206 no. 17, it was found at Uruk, belongs to Esarhaddon, and has an inscription describing the reconstruction of the "Inanna Temple at Warka."

BIBLIOGRAPHY

1930 Schott, UVB 1 p. 57 and pl. 28 no. 21 (exs. 1–4, composite copy, edition)
1956 Borger, Asarh. pp. 77–78 §51 (Uruk E) (exs. 1–4, edition)
1989 Marzahn, FuB 27 p. 63 no. XIII, no. 39 (ex. 1, transliteration, study)

TEXT

1) *ana* ^{d}INANNA UNUG.⌈KI⌉
2) GAŠAN KUR.KUR.R[A]
3) ^{m}AN.ŠÁR-PAP-AŠ
4) MAN ŠÚ MAN KUR *aš-šur*.KI
5) GÌR.NÍTA KÁ.⌈DIŠ⌉.KI
6) MAN *kib-rat* 4-*ti*
7) A ^{m}30-⌈ŠEŠ(?)⌉.MEŠ-SU
8) MAN ŠÚ MAN ⌈KUR⌉ *aš-šur*.KI
9) A ^{m}MAN-⌈GIN⌉ MAN ŠÚ
10) MAN ⌈KUR⌉ *aš-*[*šur*.K]I
11) *ana* TI-*šú é-an-na*
12) ⌈É⌉ ^{d}⌈*a-nu-u-ti*⌉
13) *ud-diš-ma* GIM u_4*-me* ZÁLAG-*ir*

1–13) For the goddess Ištar of Uruk, mistress of the lands: Esarhaddon, king of the world, king of Assyria, (5) viceroy of Babylon, (and) king of the four quarters (of the world), son of Sennacherib, king of the world (and) king of Assyria, son of Sargon, king of the world (and) (10) king of Ass[yria], renovated Eanna ("House of Heaven"), the temple of highest rank, for the sake of his life, and made (it) shine like daylight.

20

This partially preserved Akkadian inscription is similar to B.6.31.19 and B.6.31.21. It is stamped on a brick from Uruk and appears to describe the restoration of the Eanna temple by Esarhaddon for the goddess Ištar.

COMMENTARY

The brick was found at Uruk in the Eanna area (Qd XIV 5) and was given the excavation number W 4496. The excavation photograph of the piece (Warka photo 825) shows an inscription so faint as to be illegible from the photograph except for perhaps half a dozen signs. The present location of the brick is not known and the inscription is edited from the copy by Schott.

Schott proposed to read in line 3 only an uncertain *é-an-na* É before ^{d}*a-nù-u-ti*; however, a note in his work stated that according to von Soden a new exemplar of the inscription had "*ana balāṭi-šú*" before *é-an-na*. Since the same comment is credited to von Soden for B.6.31.19, it is uncertain if he had actually found two bricks or one, and if only one, whether it had inscription B.6.31.19 or B.6.31.20.

BIBLIOGRAPHY

1930 Schott, UVB 1 p. 57 and pl. 28 no. 22 (copy, edition)
1956 Borger, Asarh. pp. 77–78 §51 (Uruk F) (edition)

---

7 The identification of the second element of the name is not certain. Although Schott copied a PAP sign (UVB 1 pl. 28 no. 21), Marzahn informs me that more can be seen than just the wedges for PAP. He notes that although these additional marks may be just scratches, he feels that ŠEŠ is more likely than PAP.

TEXT

1) *a-na* ^{d}[INANNA (UNUG.KI)] ⸢GAŠAN KUR⸣.KUR.RA
2) ⸢^{m}⸣AN.ŠÁR-PAP-[AŠ] ⸢MAN KUR⸣ *aš-šur* MAN KÁ.DIŠ.⸢KI⸣
3) *ana* T[I(?)-*šú*/*šu*(?)] ⸢*é*(?)⸣-[*an*(?)-*n*]*a*(?) ⸢É⸣ ^{d}*a-nù-u-ti*
4) *ud-diš-ma ki-ma* u_4*-me* ZÁLAG-*ir*(*)

1–4) For the goddess [Ištar (of Uruk)], mistress of the lands: Esarha[ddon], king of Assyria (and) king of Babylon, renovated *E*[*ann*]*a* ("House of Heaven"), the temple of highest rank, for the sake of [*his*] *life*, and made (it) shine like daylight.

21

A third Akkadian brick inscription from Uruk records the restoration of the Eanna temple by Esarhaddon for the goddess Ištar ("[Lady]-of-Uruk").

COMMENTARY

No excavation or museum number is known for the brick which was found in a terrace connected with the ziqqurat (apparently in or near Ke XVII 3/4) at Uruk in the 1935/36 season of excavations. For details of the provenance, see UVB 8 p. 54 and pl. 21. The brick was unbaked and the inscription was inscribed, not stamped. An examination of the excavation photographs of the 1935/36 season did not locate any photograph of a brick with this inscription. The inscription is known only from a mixed transliteration/transcription prepared by Falkenstein and this has been reproduced here with only a few technical modifications since it is not always certain which signs were meant.

BIBLIOGRAPHY

1937 Heinrich, UVB 8 p. 54 (provenance, edition by Falkenstein)
1956 Borger, Asarh. pp. 77–78 §51 (Uruk G) (edition)
1956 Lenzen, UVB 12–13 p. 11 (translation by Falkenstein)

TEXT

1) *ana* ^{d}[*bēlet*] *uruk*.K[I]
2) ⸢*bēlet*⸣ *é-an-na* ⸢*bēlti*⸣ *šurbūti bēlti*-[*šú*]
3) ^{md}*aššur-aḫ-iddina šar kiššati šar māt aš-š*[*ur*.KI]
4) *šakkannak bābili*.[KI]
5) *šar māt šumeri u a*[*k-ka-di-i*]
6) *apal* ^{md}*sīn-aḫḫē*.ME[Š-*eriba šar kiššati*]
7) [*šar mā*]*t aš-š*[*ur*.KI]
8) [*apal* ^{m}*šarru-kīnu*] *šar kiššati šar māt aš-sur*.KI
9) [*é-an*]-*na*
10) [*bīt* ^{d}*a*]-*nù-u-ti*
11) *ú*-[*ud-diš-ma k*]*i-m*[*a ūme*.M]E *una*[*mmir-i*]*r*

1–11) For the goddess [the Lady]-of-Uruk, mistress of Eanna, supreme lady, [his] lady: Esarhaddon, king of the world, king of Assyr[ia], viceroy of Babylon, (and) (5) king of the land of Sumer and A[kkad], son of Sennach[erib, king of the world (and) king of] Assyr[ia, son of Sargon], king of the world (and) king of Assyria, [renovated Ean]na ("House of Heaven"), (10) [the temple of high]est rank, and made (it) [shine] like [daylight].

B.6.31.20 line 4 -*ir*(*): copy has NI.
B.6.31.21 line 1 The reading ^{d}[*bēlet*], "the goddess [the Lady]," follows that proposed by Falkenstein, but in comparison with B.6.31.19 line 1, we might instead read ^{d}[INANNA], "the goddess [Ištar]."

1001

This poorly preserved inscription is found on a fragment of a tablet from Uruk. It is written in Akkadian and records the dedication or rededication of animals and individuals to the goddess Ištar. The author of the inscription is described as the grandson of Sargon, and this presumably refers to Esarhaddon.

COMMENTARY

The piece was found during the German excavations at Uruk in 1928–29 and currently bears the museum number VAT 14519 in the Vorderasiatisches Museum (Berlin). It measures 7.0×5.5 cm and as far as it is preserved is inscribed on only one side. There are line rulings after lines 1′, 2′, 3′, 4′, 5′, 6′, 7′, and 16′. The inscription is written in contemporary Babylonian script and has been collated.

Falkenstein thought that the Sargon mentioned in line 6′ was Sargon of Akkad, which would then point to Narām-Sîn as the author of the inscription. Borger, however, has pointed out that the inscription appears to be much later in date than the Old Akkadian period and that it probably comes from the time of Esarhaddon, the grandson of Sargon II of Assyria.

BIBLIOGRAPHY

1931 Falkenstein, LKU no. 46 (copy, study)
1957–58 Borger, AfO 18 pp. 116–17 §51a (partial translation, study)

TEXT

Lacuna

1′) [(x)] x [... UN(?).ME]Š UNUG.KI BIR.MEŠ ⸢*mu*⸣-*te*[*r*(?) ...]

2′) *ina u*$_4$-⸢*me*⸣-*šu*-⸢*ma bu*⸣-*ul* BIR.MEŠ *šá* ^{d}15 *u* ^{d}[*na-na-a*(?) (...)]

3′) *šá ina maš-qat*$_6$-*ši-na gul-lu-ta-ma pa-qí-du* [*lā īšû*(?) (...)]

4′) *ú-paḫ-ḫi-ir-ma* 60-*šu* LIM ⸢US$_5$(?)⸣.UDU.ḪÁ *a-ki-*[*i* ...]

5′) 6 LIM ÁB.[G]U$_4$.ḪÁ *a-ki-i* LÚ *na-*⸢*qi*⸣-*da-*[*ti-ši-na*(?) (...)]

6′) *ši-*⸢*rik-ti*⸣ *a-bi* <*a*>-*bi-ia* LUGAL-GI[N ...]

7′) *šá it-ti bu-ul is-pu-ḫu ú-tir áš-*[*ru-uš-šu-un* (...)]

8′) DUMU.⸢MEŠ ^{m}⸣*sa-mi-ku* DUMU.⸢MEŠ⸣ ^{m}›-x [...]

9′) [*mārī*(?) ^{m}]⸢^{d}EN⸣-*ram-me-ni* DUMU.MEŠ ⸢^{m}⸣[...]

10′) [*mārī*(?) ^{m}] x KUR-*su-nu u ia-a-ti* [...]

11′) [...] ⸢*ú*(?)⸣-*rad-di-ma ṭup-*⸢*pi*⸣ [(...) *aštur*(?) (...)]

12′) [...] x *ina ma-ḫar* ^{d}1[5 ...]

13′) ⸢*u ana*(?) *bu*(?)⸣-*ul* BIR(*).MEŠ *a-n*[*a* ...]

14′) *ina gi-mir* KUR.KUR x [...]

Lacuna

1′) [... the] scattered [*people*] of Uruk, who *caused to re*[*turn* ...]

2′–7′) At that time, the scattered herds of the goddesses Ištar and [*Nanāia* (...)], those scared away from their watering place and [*having no*] caretaker [(...)] I gathered and 60,000 sheep and goats *together with* [...], (5′) 6,000 cows *together with* [*their*] herdsm[en (...)], a present of my grandfather Sargon (II) [...] which he/they had scattered with the herds, I brought back to [their] pla[ces (...)].

8′–16′) The sons of Samiku, the sons of [..., the sons of] Bēl-rammēni, the sons of [..., (10′) *the sons of*] ..., and me, [*Esarhaddon*, (...)] ... and [*I inscribed* (*their freedom*) *on*] a tablet. [...] in the presence of the goddess Iš[tar ...] and the *scattered* herds to [...] in all lands [...] (15′) ... [...] I established [*their*] *pri*[*vileged status* (...)]

10′ Could it be [DUMU.MEŠ ^{m}*b*]*a-lat-su-nu*, "[sons of B]alāssunu," even though such a personal name is not otherwise attested?
13′ With regard to BIR(*), the form of the sign is different to that found in lines 1′ and 2′ and is closer to that of ḪAR in line 12′.

15′) LU(?) ⸢LÚ(?)⸣ Ú MU *a-na* x [...]
16′) ⸢*ak*⸣*-ṣur ki-*⸢*di*(?)⸣-[*nu-ut/us-su-un*(?) (...)]
17′) *a-*⸢*na*⸣ *šat-ti* ⸢^{d}(?)⸣[*ištar*(?) ...]
18′) ⸢*ep-še-ti*⸣*-i*[a_5(?) ...]

17′–18′) On account of this, [*may*] *the goddess* [*Ištar*, (...) *look upon*] *my* [*good*] deeds [*with pleasure and* ...]

Lacuna

Left Edge

1) [...] ⸢*ki*(?)*-ma*⸣ *šu-mì-ia-a-ma* LUGAL *e-piš é-an-na ni-bi-t*[*i* ...]

l.e. 1) [...] *like* my *very* name, the king who builds Eanna, *the one who was chosen* [*by the god/goddess* ...]

15′ Collation shows *a-na*, not *a*-UD of copy in LKU.
17′–18′ With regard to the possible restoration of these lines, compare B.6.32.5 lines 14–15.

Ashurbanipal

B.6.32

Esarhaddon, king of Assyria and Babylonia, died on the tenth day of the month of Araḫsamna (VIII) in 669 BC while on the way to Egypt. Esarhaddon had arranged that upon his death one of his sons, Ashurbanipal (Aššur-bāni-apli), would become king of Assyria, and another son, Šamaš-šuma-ukīn, would become king of Babylonia, and in the following month of Kislīmu (IX) Ashurbanipal ascended the throne of Assyria. His brother was not to ascend the throne of Babylonia until the following year, when he conducted the statue of the god Marduk back to Babylon from Assyria. As king of Assyria, Ashurbanipal was his brother's overlord and interested himself in matters in the southern kingdom. Only one source records the length of Ashurbanipal's reign. The Harran inscription of Adad-guppiʾ, the mother of the last Neo-Babylonian monarch Nabonidus states that she had been born in Ashurbanipal's twentieth year and lived through his forty-second year, and on through the reigns of several following monarchs. His reign would thus have lasted from 668–627 BC. The last regnal year attested for Ashurbanipal in a contemporary text is his thirty-eighth year (631 BC). Because of this fact and the fact that there is an error of two years in the total length of time that Nabonidus' mother claims to have lived as compared to the known regnal years of the various kings she states she lived under, it has sometimes been thought that Ashurbanipal died before 627 BC or that he had abdicated the throne in favour of his son Aššur-etel-ilāni before that time, or that he had ruled as co-regent with his son during the later years of his life. The matter has been much debated and no scholarly consensus has been reached. There is no proof to indicate that the error in the calculations of Adad-guppiʾ lay in her statement about the years of Ashurbanipal. On these matters, see most recently N. Naʾaman, ZA 81 (1991) pp. 243–67, which argues that Ashurbanipal died and was succeeded by Aššur-etel-ilāni in 631 BC.

Over forty economic documents from Babylonia were dated according to the reign of Ashurbanipal. Four come from Uruk during the period between his own accession to the throne of Assyria and that of his brother to the throne of Babylonia. Only one document from Babylonia was dated by Ashurbanipal's regnal years while Šamaš-šuma-ukīn sat on the throne of Babylon and before the beginning of the latter's rebellion in 652 BC. During that rebellion (652–648 BC), documents from cities held by the Assyrians or their supporters were dated by Ashurbanipal's regnal years. After the rebellion had been crushed the Assyrian king appointed one Kandalānu to be king of Babylonia; however, Ashurbanipal kept direct control of Nippur. The only economic texts from Babylonia after the beginning of 646 BC which are dated by the regnal years of Ashurbanipal come from Nippur. No Babylonian economic text gives Ashurbanipal the title "king of Babylon," instead, he is called "king of Assyria," "king of the lands," or "king of the world." (See Brinkman and Kennedy, JCS 35 [1983] pp. 21–25 no. J and 38 [1986] p. 100 no. J; and Roth, AfO 36–37 [1989–90] p. 50 no. 3.)

A large number of Ashurbanipal's royal inscriptions come from or mention Babylonia, but only those votive and building inscriptions specifically dealing with Babylonia are edited here. The remainder will be published in RIMA 8. Ashurbanipal is known to have carried out work at Babylon on the city wall (B.6.32.1), Ekarzagina, the shrine of the god Ea (B.6.32.2 and likely B.6.32.3), Eturkalama, the temple of the goddess Ištar-of-Babylon (B.6.32.4), Emaḫ, the temple of the goddess Ninmaḫ (B.6.32.5), Esagila, the temple of the god Marduk (B.6.32.6–7), and Etemenanki, the ziqqurat (B.6.32.7–11). At Sippar he restored Ebabbar, the temple of the god Šamaš (B.6.32.12) and at Borsippa he did work on the city wall (B.6.32.13) and on Ezida, the temple of the god Nabû (B.6.32.14). Work was carried out at Nippur on the ziqqurat (B.6.32.15 and B.6.32.17), Ekur, the temple of the god Enlil (B.6.32.16), and another structure (B.6.32.18). Eanna, the temple of the goddess Ištar at Uruk, was also restored (B.6.32.19). A cylinder fragment mentioning the goddess Ištar of Akkad and the temple of the goddess Ištar can probably be assigned to Ashurbanipal (B.6.32.20); it likely describes work on the temple of the goddess Ištar of Akkad either at the city of Akkad or at Babylon. A brick found in the ziqqurat at Dūr-Kurigalzu and several from Ešaḫula, the temple of the god Nergal at Sirara (Mê-Turran), attest to work at these two sites (B.6.32.21 and B.6.32.22 respectively). A poorly preserved copy of a further dedicatory inscription of Ashurbanipal is also attested (B.6.32.23).

Exactly when in his reign the various building programs carried out in his name took place is unknown. The following inscriptions, however, mention his brother Šamaš-šuma-ukīn in a friendly manner and thus must date before the beginning of the latter's rebellion in 652: B.6.32.1 (city wall of Babylon), B.6.32.2 (Ekarzagina), B.6.32.3 (probably a structure at Babylon associated with the god Ea), B.6.32.4 (Eturkalama), B.6.32.5 (Emaḫ), B.6.32.6 (Esagila), B.6.32.12 (Ebabbar), B.6.32.13 (city wall of Borsippa), B.6.32.14 (Ezida), and B.6.32.19 (Eanna). Inscriptions B.6.32.9 and B.6.32.16–18 are written in Sumerian; the remainder are written in Akkadian. Two of the inscriptions are on stone stelae (B.6.32.2 and 14), ten upon clay cylinders (B.6.32.1, 3–6, 12–13, 15, and 19–20), ten upon bricks (B.6.32.7–11, 16–18, and 21–22), and one upon a clay tablet (B.6.32.23).

Sîn-balāssu-iqbi, who is clearly attested as governor of Ur for only 658–657 BC but who undoubtedly held that position for a much longer period of time, has left a number of inscriptions describing his own work at Ur. None mention Šamaš-šuma-ukīn but three refer to Ashurbanipal (B.6.32.2003–2004 and B.6.32.2015). Thus the inscriptions of this governor have been placed with those of Ashurbanipal rather than those of Šamaš-šuma-ukīn. Sîn-balāssu-iqbi's inscriptions record work on Etemennigurru, the temple of the god Sîn (B.6.32.2001–2002), the Gipāru of the goddess Ningal (B.6.32.2014), various other shrines (B.6.32.2003–2013), and a well (B.6.32.2015). While work was being carried out on the temple Ekišnugal, an inscribed brick from the time of Amar-Suen was discovered. The Sumerian inscription of this ruler of the Third Dynasty of Ur was recopied and provided with a colophon (B.6.32.2016). All the inscriptions of Sîn-balāssu-iqbi are written in Sumerian except for B.6.32.2015 and B.6.32.2016 (colophon), which are in Akkadian. Eleven of Sîn-balāssu-iqbi's inscriptions are found upon bricks (B.6.32.2003–2013), one upon a door socket (B.6.32.2001), two on clay nails (B.6.32.2002 and 2014), one upon clay disks (B.6.32.2015), and one upon a clay drum-like object (B.6.32.2016).

For details of Ashurbanipal's involvement with Babylonia, see Frame, Babylonia, especially pp. 102–213.

1

Numerous clay cylinders from Babylon have an Akkadian inscription which records the restoration of Nēmet-Enlil, the outer city wall of Babylon, and its gates by Ashurbanipal. The inscription was composed before the outbreak of his brother Šamaš-šuma-ukīn's rebellion in 652 BC.

CATALOGUE

Ex.	Museum number	Excavation number	Babylon photo number	Babylon provenance	Dimensions (cm)	Lines preserved	cpn
1	BM 86918 (1900-3-10,2)	—	—	—	Length: 18.5; Dia. of ends: 5.9	1–30	c
2	Bibliothèque Nationale Inv. 65 no. 5929	—	—	—	15.8×7.4	1–29	c
3	—	BE 8763	554	Kasr n 24, in debris	—	22–29	(p)
4	—	BE 12131	—	Kasr o 23, in debris above the north wall of the great court	—	3–12	n
5	VA 4902	BE 29275	680–684	Eastern side of the inner city wall 40 cm under the surface in the vicinity of the western face of the mud brick outer wall in debris by tower 4 of the main wall	Length: 17.5; R dia.: 5.5; L dia.: 5.8	1–30	c
6	VA Bab 634	BE 29362	691	Kasr w 22	Length: 15	1–30	c
7	VA Bab 602	BE 30112	688–689	Eastern side of the inner city wall in the vicinity of the western face of the outer wall in debris by tower 10 of the main wall	Length: 17.3; R dia.: 5.1; L dia.: 5.2	1–30	c
8	VA Bab 604	BE 30130	690	In the vicinity of tower 8 of the main wall	Length: 15.8; R dia.: 5.5; L dia.: 5.2	1–30	c
9	VA Bab 603	BE 30160	706	As ex. 8	Length: 16.3; R dia.: 5.1; L dia.: 4.8	1–30	c
10	VA Bab 601	BE 30161	704	As ex. 8	Length: 16.5; Dia.: 7.3	1–30	c
11	VA Bab 632	BE 30164	705	As ex. 8	Length: 17.7; R dia.: 5.6; L dia.: 5.6	1–30	c
12	BM 47655 (81-11-3,360)	—	—	—	4.2×3.6	1–4, 27–28, 30	c
13	BM 47656 (81-11-3,361)	—	—	—	4.2×3.6	1, 23, 25–29	c
14	BM 50662 (82-3-23,1653)	—	—	—	9.1×6	1–10	c
15	BM 68613 (82-9-18,8612)	—	—	—	11×5.8	1–6, 8–11, 28–30	c
16	BM 77223 (83-6-30,3)		—	—	7.5×7	1–3, 25–30	c
17	A Babylon 55	—	—	In a clay box, inside the inner wall, about 9 m from the point where it meets the Ištar Gate, near the fifth tower from the southeast corner	16.6×6.45	1–30	p
18	A Babylon 9	—	—	In filling of vaulted building	—	—	n
19	IM 124171	81-B-3	—	In debris of the inner wall 150 m east of the Ištar Gate	11.5×6	1–8, 27–30	p

COMMENTARY

Ex. 1 was purchased by the British Museum from J.E. Gejou (Paris) and ex. 16 from J.M. Shemtob (London). Exs. 3–11 come from the excavations of the Deutsche Orient-Gesellschaft at Babylon, exs. 12–15 from H. Rassam's work in Babylonia (see Reade in Leichty, Sippar 1 pp. xxxii–xxxiii), and exs. 17–19 from work by the Iraqi State Organization for Antiquities and Heritage at Babylon between 1979 and 1981. It is possible that exs. 12 and 13 come from the same cylinder. The exact findspots of exs. 5, 7, and 8 are noted on Wetzel, Stadtmauern pls. 32–33. According to Unger (in Wetzel, Stadtmauern p. 80), ex. 3 has part of the first two and the last nine lines preserved; the original of the piece has not been located for collation and only parts of the last 7 lines of the text (lines 22–29 of the master exemplar) are visible on the excavation photograph; only these lines are included in the catalogue and in the score. Parts of lines 1–8 of ex. 6 which are no longer preserved in Berlin with the main section of the exemplar are visible on Babylon photo 691; the score uses the photo for those portions of these lines. Parts of lines 23–25 of ex. 8 are no longer preserved but appear on Babylon photo 690; the score also includes those portions visible only on the photo. Ex. 10 was kindly collated by J. Marzahn.

Exs. 2–17 and 19 are written in contemporary Babylonian script, while ex. 1 is in archaizing script; the script of ex. 18 is not known. The number and arrangement of lines varies a great deal between the exemplars. When complete, the inscription is found upon 26 lines (ex. 17), 27 lines (exs. 2, 6, 7, and 10), 28 lines (exs. 5, 8, and 9), 29 lines (ex. 11) or 30 lines (ex. 1). The line arrangement follows ex. 1, as does the master line (with help from ex. 17 for lines 4, 12–19, 22–23, and 28 and from ex. 7 for line 21), with the exception of *ap-qid* and *li-ḫal-liq* in lines 14 and 30 respectively.

Unger (in Wetzel, Stadtmauern p. 80) states that BE 30113 is an exemplar of this inscription, but it actually has an inscription of Nabonidus. The fragment BM 83001, which was cited as a duplicate of this inscription in Lambert, Cat. p. 75, probably comes from the same cylinder as the fragment BM 83000 and is presented with that fragment as B.6.32.13.2.

The mention of Šamaš-šuma-ukīn, Ashurbanipal's brother, in a positive light in lines 13–14 and 27 indicates that the inscription was composed before the commencement of his rebellion in 652 BC.

BIBLIOGRAPHY

1880 Pognon, Bavian p. 122 and n. 1 (ex. 2, study)
1886 Strassmaier, AV passim (ex. 2, study)
1892 Lehmann-Haupt, Šamaššumukîn 1 p. 27, and 2 p. 62 and pls. XXX–XXXI no. 11 (P^{2}) (ex. 2, copy, study)
1900 King, CT 9 pls. 6–7 (ex. 1, copy)
1901 Koldewey, MDOG 8 p. 4 (ex. 3, study)
1905 Koldewey, MDOG 26 pp. 17–18 (exs. 5, 7–8, provenance)
1905–6 Fossey, ZA 19 pp. 371–77 (ex. 1, edition)
1916 Streck, Asb. pp. XLIII, XCI, 234–39 no. 4 (L^{6} [P^{2}]), 412, and 835–36 (exs. 1–2, edition; exs. 3–11, study)
1922 BM Guide p. 230 no. 37 (ex. 1, study)
1924–25 Unger, AfK 2 p. 23 no. 17 (exs. 3–11, study)
1925 Koldewey, WEB^{4} p. 149–51 and fig. 96 (exs. 3–11, provenance, translation [by Delitzsch]; ex. 11, photo)
1927 Luckenbill, ARAB 2 §§963–64 (exs. 1–2, translation)
1930 Unger in Wetzel, Stadtmauern p. 80 (exs. 3–11, study)
1933 Bauer, Asb. 2 p. 50 (exs. 1–11, study)
1970 Klengel-Brandt, Reise p. 26 fig. 11 (ex. 10, photo)
1985 Al-Rawi, Sumer 41 p. 25 (exs. 17–18, study)
1991 Al-Rawi, ARRIM 9 pp. 1–3 nos. 1–2 (ex. 17, copy, transliteration; ex. 19, photo)
1992 George, Topographical Texts pp. 345–46 (ex. 1, partial edition)

TEXT

1) *a-na* ^{d}AMAR.UTU LUGAL ŠÁR ^{d}*í-gì-gì u* ^{d}*a-nun-na-ki ba-ni* AN-*e u* KI-*tim mu-kin giš-ḫur-ru*
2) *a-ši-ib é-sag-íl* EN KÁ.DINGIR.RA.KI EN GAL-*i be-li-ia*

1–2) For the god Marduk, king of all the Igīgū gods and Anunnakū gods, creator of heaven and netherworld, who establishes archetypes (and) dwells in Esagila, lord of Babylon, great lord, my lord:

3) *a-na-ku* ^{m}AN.ŠÁR-DÙ-A LUGAL GAL LUGAL *dan-nu* LUGAL ŠÁR LUGAL KUR *aš-šur* LUGAL *kib-rat* 4-*ti*
4) DUMU ^{m}AN.ŠÁR-ŠEŠ-SUM.NA LUGAL GAL LUGAL *dan-nu* LUGAL ŠÁR LUGAL KUR *aš-šur* GÌR.NÍTA TIN.TIR.KI
5) LUGAL KUR.EME.GI$_{7}$ *u* URI.KI *mu-še-šib* KÁ.DINGIR.RA.KI *e-piš é-sag-íl*
6) *mu-ud-diš eš-re-e-ti kul-lat ma-ḫa-zi šá i-na qer-bi-ši-na*

3–9) I, Ashurbanipal, great king, mighty king, king of the world, king of Assyria, king of the four quarters (of the world); son of Esarhaddon, great king, mighty king, king of the world, king of Assyria, viceroy of Babylon, king of the land of Sumer and Akkad, who (re)settled Babylon, (re)built Esagila, renovated the sanctuaries of all the cult centres, constantly established appropriate procedures in them, and (re)confirmed their interrupted regular offerings, (who) restored the rites

7) *iš-tak-ka-nu si-ma-a-ti ù sat-tuk-ki-ši-na baṭ-lu-tu ú-ki-nu*
8) *par-ṣi ki-du-de-e ki-ma la-bi-ri-im-ma ú-te-ru áš-ru-uš-šu-un*
9) DUMU DUMU ^{md}30-ŠEŠ.MEŠ-SU LUGAL GAL LUGAL *dan-nu* LUGAL ŠÁR LUGAL KUR *aš-šur a-na-ku-ma*
10) *ina* BALA-*e-a* EN GAL ^{d}AMAR.UTU *ina ri-šá-a-ti a-na* TIN.TIR.KI *i-ru-um-ma*
11) *ina é-sag-íl šá da-ra-a-ti šu-bat-su ir-me sat-tuk-ki é-sag-íl*
12) *ù* DINGIR.MEŠ TIN.TIR.KI *ú-ki-in ki-din-nu-ú-tu* TIN.TIR.KI *ak-ṣur*
13) *áš-šú dan-nu a-na* SIG *la ḫa-ba-li* ^{md}GIŠ.NU$_{11}$-MU-GI.NA ŠEŠ *ta-li-me*
14) *a-na* LUGAL-*ú-tu* KÁ.DINGIR.RA.KI *ap-qid ù i-na* KÙ.BABBAR KÙ.GI
15) *ni-siq-ti* NA$_{4}$.MEŠ *é-sag-íl az-nu-un-ma*
16) *ki-ma ši-ṭir bu-ru-mu ú-nam-mir é-umuš-a ina u$_{4}$-me-šú-ma*
17) *im-gur-^{d}en-líl* BÀD KÁ.DINGIR.RA.KI *né-met-^{d}en-líl šal-ḫu-ú-šú*
18) *ša la-ba-riš il-lik-ú-ma i-qu-pu in-na-ab-tu*
19) *áš-šú ma-aṣ-ṣar-ti é-sag-íl ù eš-re-e-ti* KÁ.DINGIR.RA.KI
20) *du-un-nu-nu ina e-muq um-ma-na-a-ti-ia sur-riš né-met-^{d}en-líl*
21) *šal-ḫu-ú-šú ina ši-pir ^{d}kulla eš-šiš ú-še-piš-ma* KÁ.GAL.MEŠ-*šú ú-rak-kis*
22) GIŠ.IG.MEŠ *ú-še-piš-ma ú-rat-ta-a ina* KÁ.MEŠ-*šú*
23) NUN *ar-ku-ú šá ina* BALA-*e-šú ši-pir šu-a-ti in-na-ḫu um-ma-ni en-qu-tu*
24) *ši-ta-ʾ-al im-gur-^{d}en-líl* BÀD *né-met-^{d}en-líl šal-ḫu-ú*
25) *ki-ma si-ma-ti-šú-nu la-bi-ra-a-ti e-pu-uš* MU.SAR-*u-a a-mur-ma*
26) Ì.GIŠ *pu-šu-uš* UDU.SISKUR BAL-*qí it-ti* MU.SAR-*e-ka šu-kun*
27) *ik-ri-bi-ka* ^{d}AMAR.UTU *i-šem-me šá šu-mì šaṭ-ru u* MU *ta-lim-ia*
28) *ina ši-pir ni-kil-ti i-ab-bat* MU.SAR-*u-a it-ti* MU.SAR-*e-šú la i-šak-ka-nu*
29) ^{d}AMAR.UTU LUGAL *gi-im-ri ag-giš lik-kil-me-šú-ma*
30) MU-*šú* NUMUN-*šú i-na* KUR.KUR *li-ḫal-liq*

(and) rituals according to the old pattern; grandson of Sennacherib, great king, mighty king, king of the world, king of Assyria, I —

10–16a) During my reign, the great lord, the god Marduk, entered Babylon amidst rejoicing and took up his residence in the eternal Esagila. I (re)confirmed the regular offerings for Esagila and the gods of Babylon. I (re-)established the privileged status of Babylon (and) appointed Šamaš-šuma-ukīn, my favourite brother, to the kingship of Babylon in order that the strong might not harm the weak. I *decorated* Esagila ("House whose Top is High") with silver, gold, (and) precious stones and made Eumuša ("House of Counsel") glisten like the stars (lit. "writing") of the firmament.

16b–22) At that time, (with regard to) Imgur-Enlil ("The God Enlil Showed Favour"), the (city) wall of Babylon, (and) Nēmet-Enlil ("Bulwark of the God Enlil"), its outer wall, which had become old and buckled (and) collapsed, in order to increase the security of Esagila and the (other) sanctuaries of Babylon, with the strength of my labour forces I had Nēmet-Enlil, its outer wall, built quickly anew with the work of the god Kulla and I refitted its gates. I had (new) doors made and hung (them) in its gateways.

23–27a) O (you) future prince, during whose reign this work falls into disrepair, question skilled craftsmen! (Re)build Imgur-Enlil, the (city) wall, (and) Nēmet-Enlil, the outer wall, according to their ancient specifications! Look at my royal inscription, anoint (it) with oil, offer a sacrifice, (and) place (my royal inscription) with your (own) royal inscription! The god Marduk will (then) listen to your prayers.

27b–30) (But) as for the one who destroys my inscribed name or the name of my favourite (brother) by some crafty device, (or) does not place my royal inscription with his (own) royal inscription, may the god Marduk, king of everything, glare at him angrily and make his name (and) his descendant(s) disappear from the lands!

---

16 For the reading of the name of Marduk's cella in Esagila as *é-umuš-a* and for information on this cella, see George, Topographical Texts pp. 273 and 389–91.

2

This Akkadian inscription of Ashurbanipal found on one or two stone stelae commemorates the restoration of Ekarzagina ("House, Quay of Lapis Lazuli" or "House, Pure Quay"), the shrine of the god Ea within the Esagila complex, at Babylon. The inscription dates to the first part of the reign of Ashurbanipal (before 652 BC).

CATALOGUE

Ex.	Museum number	Registration number	Dimensions (cm)	Lines preserved	cpn
1	BM 90864 (=BM 12110)	81-3-24,367	35.9×22.2×6.4	1–100	c
2	BM 22533	94-1-15,335	4×7.5	18–22	p

COMMENTARY

Ex. 1 is a stela of pink marble with a relief of Ashurbanipal on the front; the Assyrian king is depicted carrying a basket on his head (i.e., aiding personally in the restoration of the shrine). It was found in an area of the temple of the god Marduk at Babylon. Stelae with similar reliefs have been found in the temple of the god Nabû at Borsippa (B.6.32.14 and B.6.33.3). Ex. 2 is a small fragment of pink marble with a relief showing part of a garment similar to the one worn by Ashurbanipal on ex. 1; it was purchased in 1894 and is said to have come from Babylon (see Reade and Walker, AfO 28 [1981–82] p. 119). Very little of ex. 2 is preserved and none of the building section. Thus it is quite possible that this exemplar did not describe the restoration of Ekarzagina. Rather than present a score for this inscription in the microfiche, the edition below follows ex. 1 (with lines 30–41 and 68–88 restored following B.6.32.14 lines 21–26 and 38–70 respectively). Ex. 2 has the following:

Lacuna

1′) [...]-⌜*du*⌝-*lu*₄ *šá ep*-[...]

2′) [... U]GU *ṣal-mat* S[AG(?) ...]

3′) [... A]N.ŠÁR-Š[EŠ(?)-...]

4′) [... *da*]*n*(?)-*n*[*u*(?) ...]

Lacuna

Thus ex. 2 has the following variants to ex. 1: -*lu*₄ for -*lu* in line 18 and U]GU for *e-li* in line 19. With regard to ex. 1, lines 1–28, 29–55, 56–84, and 85–100 are on the front, right side, back, and left side of the stela respectively. The inscription is written in contemporary Babylonian script.

The favourable mention of Šamaš-šuma-ukīn (lines 50–55 and 74–76) indicates that the inscription was composed before the commencement of the latter's rebellion in 652 BC.

BIBLIOGRAPHY

1886 Bezold, Literatur pp. 113–14 §64.3.d (ex. 1, study)
1890–91 Evetts, PSBA 13 p. 158 (ex. 1, study)
1891 Strong, JRAS pp. 469–71 (ex. 1, partial copy in type, partial edition)
1892 Lehmann-Haupt, Šamaššumukîn 1 frontpiece and p. 25, and 2 pp. 14–19, 59–61 and pls. XVII–XXII no. 7 (S³) (ex. 1, photo, copy, edition)
1895 Quentin, RB 4 pp. 553–62 (ex. 1, copy in type, edition)
1906 Babelon, Manual p. 89 fig. 64 (ex. 1, photo)
1913 Curtius, Münchner Jahrbuch der bildenden Kunst 8 pp. 11–12 and fig. 6 (ex. 1, photo, study [of relief])
1915 King, History pl. following p. 272 (ex. 1, photo)
1915 Meissner, AO 15 p. 74 fig. 131 (ex. 1, photo)
1916 Streck, Asb. pp. XLV and 244–49 no. 7 (S³) (ex. 1, edition)
1920 Meissner, BuA 1 pl. 38 fig. 40 (ex. 1, photo)
1922 BM Guide p. 74 no. 300 and pl. XXVIII (ex. 1, photo, study)
1924–25 Unger, AfK 2 p. 23 no. 10 (ex. 1, study)
1926 Bezold, Ninive und Babylon⁴ fig. 126 (ex. 1, photo)
1926 Unger, RLV 4 /2 pl. 267c (ex. 1, photo)
1927 Luckenbill, ARAB 2 §§978–80 (ex. 1, partial translation)
1929 Jeremias, HAOG² p. 18 fig. 8 (ex. 1, photo)
1931 Contenau, Manuel 3 p. 1299 and fig. 822 (ex. 1, photo, study)
1931 Unger, Babylon p. 225 no. 12 (ex. 1, study)
1958 Champdor, Babylon p. 137 fig. 89 (ex. 1, photo)
1961 Parrot, Assyria p. 35 fig. 40A (ex. 1, photo)
1961 Potratz, Orientalia NS 30 pp. 14–15 and pl. I fig. 3 (ex. 1, photo, study [of relief])
1962 Beek, Atlas p. 28 fig. 39 (ex. 1, photo)

1962 Strommenger and Hirmer, Mesopotamien pl. 262 (ex. 1, photo)
1966 Ellis, Berytus 16 pp. 47–48 and pl. VIII fig. 3 (ex. 1, photo, study)
1967 Margueron, Mesopotamia fig. 58 (ex. 1, photo)
1967 Moortgat, Kunst p. 157 and pl. 282 (ex. 1, photo, study)
1968 Ellis, Foundation Deposits pp. 24–25 (ex. 1, study)
1969 Pritchard, ANEP^{2} no. 450 (ex. 1, photo)
1972 Salonen, Ziegeleien pl. XIII (ex. 1, photo)
1979 J. Oates, Babylon p. 122 (ex. 1, photo)
1981–82 Reade and Walker, AfO 28 p. 119 (ex. 2, photo, transliteration)
1982 Börker-Klähn, Bildstelen no. 224 (ex. 1, photo, study)
1983 Galter, Ea/Enki pp. 199–200 (ex. 1, study)
1988 Parpola and Watanabe, SAA 2 p. 60 fig. 19 (ex. 1, photo)
1992 Frame, Babylonia cover (ex. 1, photo)

TEXT

1) *a-na-ku*
2) ^{m}AN.ŠÁR-DÙ-A
3) MAN GAL MAN *dan-nu*
4) MAN ŠÚ MAN KUR *aš-šur*
5) MAN *kib-rat* 4-*ti*
6) LUGAL LUGAL.ME NUN *la šá-na-an*
7) *šá ina a-mat* AN.ŠÁR ^{d}UTU
8) *u* ^{d}AMAR.UTU
9) *ul-tú tam-tim*
10) *e-lit a-di tam-tim*
11) *šap-lit i-be-lu-ma*
12) *gi-mir ma-lik ú-šak-niš*
13) *še-pu-uš-šú za-nin é-sag-íl*
14) É.GAL DINGIR.MEŠ *šá ki-ma ši-ṭir bu-ru-mu*
15) *ú-nam-mir* SI.GAR-*šú*
16) *u šá eš-re-e-te ka-li-ši-na*
17) *ḫi-bil-ta-ši-na ú-šal-lim*
18) *e-li kul-lat ma-ḫa-zi ú-kin an-dul-lu*
19) *šá ep-še-tu-šú* UGU *kal* DINGIR.MEŠ DÙG.GA *e-li*
20) *ṣal-mat* SAG.DU *du-uš-šu-pat* SIPA-*us-su*
21) DUMU ^{m}AN.ŠÁR-ŠEŠ-SUM.NA MAN GAL
22) MAN *dan-nu* MAN ŠÚ MAN KUR *aš-šur* GÌR.NÍTA KÁ.DIŠ
23) MAN KUR *šu-me-ri u* URI.KI(*) *mu-še-šib* TIN.TIR.KI
24) *e-piš é-sag-íl mu-ud-diš*
25) *eš-re-e-te kul-lat ma-ḫa-zu*
26) *šá ina qé-reb-ši-na iš-tak-⸢kan⸣*
27) *si-ma-a-ti*
28) *u sat-tuk-ki-ši-na baṭ-lu-tú ú-ki-nu*
29) *par-ṣi ⸢ki-du-de-e⸣*
30) *ki-ma la-bi-⸢rim⸣-[ma]*
31) *ú-⸢ter⸣-r[u]*
32) *a-na áš-r[i(?)-šu-un]*
33) A A ^{md}30-Š[EŠ(?).MEŠ-SU]
34) MAN GAL MAN *⸢dan⸣-n[u]*
35) MAN ŠÚ MAN KUR *aš-[šur]*

1–36a) I, Ashurbanipal, great king, mighty king, king of the world, king of Assyria, king of the four quarters (of the world), king of kings, prince who has no rival, who at the command of the gods Aššur, Šamaš, and Marduk rules from the Upper Sea (10) to the Lower Sea and has subjugated all rulers, who provides for Esagila, the palace of the gods — whose doorbolt I made glisten like the stars (lit. "writing") of the firmament —, who repaired the damaged parts of all their sanctuaries, (who) established (my) protection over all cult centres, whose deeds are pleasing to all the gods (and) (20) whose shepherdship is sweet to the black-headed people; son of Esarhaddon, great king, mighty king, king of the world, king of Assyria, viceroy of Babylon, king of the land of Sumer and Akkad, who (re)settled Babylon, (re)built Esagila, renovated the sanctuaries of all the cult centres, constantly established appropriate procedures in them, and (re)confirmed their interrupted offerings, (who) restored the rites and rituals according (30) to the old pattern; grandson of Senna[cherib], great king, mighty king, king of the world, king of Ass[yria], I —

36) *a-na-ku-ma* EN [GAL]
37) ^{d}AMAR.UTU *šá ina* BA[LA-*e*]
38) LUGAL *maḫ-[ri]*
39) *ina ma-ḫar* AD *ba-ni-[i-šú]*
40) *ú-ši-bu ina qé-[reb]*
41) *bal-til*.KI *ina* u_4-*[me]*
42) BALA-*iá ina ri-šá-t[i]*
43) *a-na* TIN.TIR.KI

36b–65a) During my reign, the [great] lord, the god Marduk, who during the reign of a previous king (40) had resided in Baltil (Aššur) in the presence of the father who created [him], entered Babylon amidst rejoicing. I (re)confirmed the regular offerings for Esagila and the gods of Babylon. I (re-)established the privileged status of Babylon (and) (50) in order that the strong might not harm

23 KI(*): text has KU(?).

44) *i-ru-um-ma*
45) *sat-tu[k]-k[i]*
46) *é-s[a]g-íl*
47) *u* DINGIR.M[EŠ] KÁ.DINGIR
48) *ú-ki[n k]i-din-nu-ut*
49) TIN.TI[R.K]I *ak-⸢ṣur⸣*
50) *áš-šú d[an]-nu a-na*
51) SIG *l[a ḫ]a-ba-lu*
52) ^{md}GIŠ.⸢NU$_{11}$⸣-MU-GI.NA
53) ŠEŠ ⸢*ta*⸣*-li-me*
54) ⸢*a-na* LUGAL*-ú-tú*⸣
55) TIN.TI[R.KI *a]p-qid*
56) *u ši-pir é-⸢sag⸣-íl*
57) *[š]á za-ru-u-a la ú-qa-at-tu-u*
58) *a-na-ku ú-šak-lil* GIŠ.ÙR.MEŠ
59) GIŠ *ere-nu u* GIŠ.ŠUR.MÌN *ṣi-ru-tú tar-bi-ti*
60) KUR *ḫa-ma-nu u* KUR *lab-na-nu e-li-⸢šú⸣*
61) ⸢*ú*⸣*-šat-ri-ṣi* GIŠ.IG.MEŠ GIŠ.TÚG GIŠ.MES.M[Á].⸢KAN⸣
62) [GI]Š.LI GIŠ *ere-nu ú-še-piš-ma ú-rat-[t]a-[a]*
63) *[ina]* KÁ.MEŠ*-šú ú-na-a-te* KÙ.GI KÙ.BABBAR Z[A]BAR
64) [A]N.BAR GIŠ.ME[Š] *u* NA$_4$.MEŠ DÙ*-ma ú-kin*
65) *[ina q]é-reb-šú i[na]* ⸢*u*$_4$⸣*-me-šú-ma é-kar-za-gìn-na*
66) ⸢É⸣ ^{d}⸢*é*⸣*-[a] šá qé-reb é-sag-íl eš-šiš*
67) ⸢*ú*⸣*-še-pi[š]* ⸢^{d}⸣*é-a* LUGAL ABZU *ši-[p]ir*
68) *[š]u-a-t[i ḫa-di]š* IGI.BAR*-ma ia-a-ti* ^{m}A[N.ŠÁR-D]Ù-A
69) MAN KUR *aš-šu[r* NUN] *pa-liḫ-šú a-mat* MUNUS.SIG$_5$*-iá liš-⸢šá⸣-[k]in*
70) *šap-tuš-⸢šú⸣* TIN *u*$_4$ *me* SÙ.MEŠ *še-bé-e li[t]-t[u-t]ú*
71) *ṭu-ub* U[Z]U *u* ⸢*ḫu-ud*⸣ *lìb-bi li-šim ši-ma-ti*
72) ⸢SUḪUŠ⸣ G[IŠ.G]U.Z[A LUGAL*-u-t]i-iá ki-ma* KUR*-i*
73) ⸢*li*⸣*-[šar-šid]* ⸢*it*⸣*-ti* AN*-e u* K[I*-t]im*
74) *[l]u-kin* BA[LA]-⸢*u*⸣*-a u šá* ^{md}GIŠ.NU$_{11}$-MU-[GI].⸢NA⸣
75) LUGAL TIN.TI[R].KI ŠEŠ *ta-lim-ia u*$_4$*-me-šú*
76) *li-ri-ku liš-bi bu-ʾ-a-⸢ri⸣ ma-⸢ti⸣-ma*
77) *ina aḫ-rat u*$_4$*-me* ⸢NUN⸣ *ar-ku-u š[á] i[na u*$_4$*-m]e* ⸢BALA*-šú*⸣
78) ⸢*ši*⸣*-pir š[u]-a-ti in-na-ḫu an-ḫu-us-⸢su⸣*
79) ⸢*lu-ud*⸣*-diš ṣa-lam* LUG[AL]*-u-ti-iá li-⸢mur⸣-ma*
80) [Ì.GIŠ *lip]-šu-u[š]* UDU.SISKUR BAL*-qí it-ti*
81) ⸢*ṣa*⸣*-[l]am-⸢i⸣-šú* ⸢*liš*⸣*-kun ik-ri-bi-⸢šú⸣*
82) ⸢^{d}⸣*é-a* ⸢*i-šem-me*⸣ *šá šu-⸢mi⸣ šaṭ-r[u]*
83) *i-p[a-áš-š]i-⸢tu ṣa-lam* LUGAL⸣*-u-ti-i[á]*
84) *[i-ab-ba]-t[u]*
85) ⸢*lu*⸣*-u* ⸢*a*⸣*-šar-šú*
86) *[ú]-⸢na-kar⸣-[(u)-m]a*
87) *[it]-⸢ti⸣ ṣa-[lam-šú]*
88) *la i-šak-[kan]*
89) ^{d}*é-a* EN
90) *ṣi-i-ru*

the weak, I appointed Šamaš-šuma-ukīn, my favourite brother, to the kingship of Babylon. I completed the work on Esagila which my father had not finished. I roofed it with immense beams of cedar and cypress, the produce of (60) Mount Amanus and Mount Lebanon. I had doors made of boxwood, *musukkannu*-wood, juniper, and cedar and I hung (them) [in] its gates. I had vessels made of gold, silver, bronze, iron, wood, and (precious) stones and I placed (them) inside it.

65b–67a) At that [time], I had Ekarzagina, the shrine of the god E[a] which is inside Esagila, (re)built anew.

67b–76a) May the god Ea, king of the Watery Abyss (*apsû*), look upon this work with [pleasure] and may a good word for me — [Ashurba]nipal, king of Ass[yria, prince] who reveres him — be set (70) upon his lips! May he determine as my fate a long life, fullness of ol[d a]ge, good health, and happiness! May he [make] the foundation of my [royal th]ro[ne as secure] as a mountain! May he make my reign *as* firm *as* heaven and netherworld! Moreover, with regard to Šamaš-šuma-[uk]īn, king of Babylon, my favourite brother, may his days be long and may he be fully satisfied with (his) good fortune!

76b–82a) If at any time in the future, [during the days] of the reign of some future prince, this work falls into disrepair, [may (that prince) re]pair its dilapidated state! May he look at my royal statue, (80) [an]oint (it) [with oil], offer a sacrifice, (and) place (my statue) with his (own) statue! The god Ea will (then) listen to his prayers.

82b–100) (But) as for the one who e[ras]es my inscribed name, (or) [destroys] my royal statue, or [*ch*]*an*[*ges*] its position [and] does not pla[ce] (it) with [his] (own) sta[tue], may the god Ea, (90) august lord, glare at him angrily, overthrow his royal rule, and take away his sovereignty. May he (Ea) make his name (and) his descendant(s) disappear from the lands and have no pity on him!

61 Postgate has recently supported the identification of *musukkannu*-wood, a valuable hardwood, with *Dalbergia sissoo* (BSA 6 [1992] p. 183).

91) *ag-gi-iš*
92) *lik-kil-me-šú-ma*
93) GIŠ.GU.ZA LUGAL-*ti-šú*
94) *li-šá-bal-kit-ma*
95) *li-ṭi-ir*
96) *be-lut-su* MU-*šú*
97) NUMUN-*šú ina* KUR.KUR
98) *li-ḫal-liq-ma*
99) *a-a ir-ši-šú*
100) *re-e-mu*

3

A cylinder fragment from Babylon preserves part of an Akkadian inscription of Ashurbanipal which would appear to commemorate some action for the god Ea. The inscription was composed at some point before 652 BC.

COMMENTARY

The cylinder fragment bears the Babylon excavation number BE 28510 and is now located in the Museum of the Ancient Orient in Istanbul (EŞ 7893). It was found in the Southern Palace at Babylon in December 1903 and is shown on Babylon excavation photo 558. Approximately one-half of the original circumference of the left end is preserved; the piece measures 7.3×7.0 cm. The inscription is in Neo-Assyrian script and has been collated. The restorations in the translation are based upon B.6.32.5 lines 1–12 and 21–24; however, there does not appear to be sufficient space at the end of line 5 to restore all the titles usually accorded to Esarhaddon. Two cylinder fragments, VA Bab 614 and B. 65, which are presented under B.6.32.4 (exs. 3 and 4), could conceivably be duplicates of this inscription.

The inscription is quite similar to other inscriptions of Ashurbanipal, in particular ones describing the king's work on the temples of the goddesses Ištar and Ninmaḫ at Babylon (B.6.32.4–5). Ashurbanipal renovated Ekarzagina, the shrine of the god Ea located inside Esagila, and had his action recorded on at least one stela (B.6.32.2). Since this cylinder inscription probably deals with a structure associated with Ea and since it comes from Babylon, it is quite likely that it also commemorated work on Ekarzagina.

The fact that the inscription preserves part of a passage describing Ashurbanipal's appointment of Šamaš-šuma-ukīn as king of Babylonia (line 11) indicates that the inscription was composed before the latter's rebellion, which commenced in 652 BC.

BIBLIOGRAPHY

1904 Koldewey, MDOG 21 p. 7 (provenance; partial translation, study [by Delitzsch])
1916 Streck, Asb. pp. XC–XCI (partial translation, study [by Delitzsch])
1931 Unger, Babylon p. 225 no. 16 (study)
1938 Wetzel and Weissbach, Hauptheiligtum p. 77 n. 1 (study)

TEXT

1) ^{m}AN.ŠÁR-*ba-a-ni*-IBILA LUGAL x [...]
2) LUGAL KUR *aš-šur* LUGAL *kib-ra-a-t*[*i* ...]
3) NUN *la šá-na-an šá ul-t*[*u* ...]
4) *šap-lit i-be-lu-ma gi-m*[*ir* ...]
5) DUMU ^{m}AN.ŠÁR-ŠEŠ-SUM.NA LUGAL (x) [...]
6) LUGAL KUR.EME.GI$_{7}$ *u* URI.KI DUMU [...]

1–7a) Ashurbanipal, [great] king, [mighty king, king of the world], king of Assyria, king of the [four] quarters (of the world), [king of kings], prince who has no rival, who rules from [the Upper Sea to the] Lower [Sea] and [has subjugated] all [rulers]; (5) son of Esarhaddon, [great] king, [(mighty king), (king of the world), (king of Assyria), (viceroy of Babylon)], king of the land of Sumer and Akkad; [grand]son of

7) LUGAL ŠÁR LUGAL KUR *aš-šur a-na-ku-[ma* ...]	[Sennacherib, (great king), mighty king], king of the world, king of Assyria, I —
8) *šá* AD *ba-nu-ú-a la ú-[qa-at-tu-u* ...]	7b–11) [I completed the work on Esagila] which (my) father who had engendered me had not [finished. I (re)confirmed] the regular offerings for Esagila [and the gods of Babylon. I (re-)established] the privileged status of B[abylon (and) appointed Šamas-šuma-ukīn, my favourite brother, to the kingship of Babylon in order that the strong might not harm] the weak.
9) *sat-tuk-ki é-sag-íl* [...]	
10) ⌜*ki-din*⌝*-nu-ut* K[Á.DINGIR.RA.KI ...]	
11) [*a-n*]*a* SIG [...]	
Lacuna	Lacuna
1′) MU.SA[R-*u-a* ...]	1′–3′) [(But) as for the one who ... destroys my] royal ins[cription, or changes its position], may the god Ea, king of the Wat[ery Abyss (*apsû*), speak evil of him before the god Bēl (Marduk) (and) the goddess Bēltīia (Zarpanītu) and make] his name (and) his descendant(s) [disappear] from [the lands!]
2′) ^{d}*é-a* LUGAL *a*[*p-si-i* ...]	
3′) MU-*šú* NUMUN-*šú i-na* [...]	

4

An Akkadian inscription recording the renovation of Eturkalama ("House, Cattle-Pen of the Land"), the temple of the goddess Ištar at Babylon, by Ashurbanipal is found on two or more clay cylinders. The inscription was composed during the first half of the reign of Ashurbanipal (before 652 BC).

CATALOGUE

Ex.	Museum number	Excavation number	Babylon photo number	Babylon provenance	Dimensions (cm)	Lines preserved	cpn
1	BM 90935 (81-2-1,103) (=BM 12064)	—	—	—	Length: 17.6; Dia. of ends: 5.3	1–24	c
2	BM 40074 (81-2-1,38)	—	—	—	7.1×6.8	7–21	c
3	VA Bab 614	BE 29482	—	Kasr q 24, in debris	9.1×7.5	1–4, 19–24	c
4	B 65	BE 38119	2198, 2691	"Outside"	—	1–4, 23–24	p

COMMENTARY

According to Strong (JRAS 1891 p. 472), ex. 1 was brought from Babylon by H. Rassam. Exs. 3 and 4 do not preserve enough of the building account to be certain they are duplicates of this inscription and not of either B.6.32.3 or B.6.32.5; in view of the major variant in line 23 of ex. 3, that exemplar may well represent a new and different inscription. All exemplars are written in Neo-Assyrian script. The master line follows ex. 1, with help from ex. 3 in line 21. Restorations in lines 18–21 follow B.6.32.5 lines 18–21.

According to the excavation register, ex. 4 was found "außerhalb"; since the immediately preceding and following items in the register are said to have been found in "Merkes," the register may simply mean that the piece was not found in that quarter. (Information courtesy of J. Marzahn.)

The positive mention of Ashurbanipal's brother Šamaš-šuma-ukīn in lines 11–12 and 19–21 indicates that the inscription was composed before the rebellion of that individual, which took place from 652 to 648 BC.

BIBLIOGRAPHY

1885 Lehmann-[Haupt], ZK 2 pp. 360–61 (ex. 1, study)
1886 Bezold, Literatur p. 113 §64.3.b (ex. 1, study)
1891 Strong, JRAS pp. 471–75 (ex. 1, copy in type, edition)
1892 Lehmann-Haupt, Šamaššumukîn 1 p. 25 and 2 p. 61 and pls. XXIII–XXIV no. 8 (L[1]) (exs. 1–2, copy, study)
1916 Streck, Asb. pp. XLI and 226–29 no. 1 (L[1]) (exs. 1–2, edition)
1922 BM Guide p. 230 no. 35 (ex. 1, study)
1927 Luckenbill, ARAB 2 §§953–55 (exs. 1–2, translation)
1930 Unger in Wetzel, Stadtmauern p. 80 (ex. 3, study)

TEXT

1) ^{m}AN.ŠÁR-DÙ-IBILA LUGAL GAL LUGAL *dan-nu* LUGAL ŠÁR LUGAL KUR *aš-šur*
2) LUGAL *kib-rat* 4-*ti* LUGAL LUGAL.MEŠ NUN *la šá-na-an*
3) *ša ul-tu tam-tim e-lit a-di tam-tim šap-lit i-be-lu-ma*
4) *gi-mir ma-li-ki ú-šak-niš še-pu-uš-šú*
5) DUMU ^{m}AN.ŠÁR-ŠEŠ-SUM.NA LUGAL GAL LUGAL *dan-nu* LUGAL ŠÁR LUGAL KUR *aš-šur*
6) GÌR.NÍTA KÁ.DINGIR.RA.KI LUGAL KUR.EME.GI$_7$ *ù* URI.KI
7) DUMU DUMU ^{md}30-PAP.MEŠ-SU LUGAL *dan-nu* LUGAL ŠÁR LUGAL KUR *aš-šur a-na-ku-ma*

1–7) Ashurbanipal, great king, mighty king, king of the world, king of Assyria, king of the four quarters (of the world), king of kings, prince who has no rival, who rules from the Upper Sea to the Lower Sea and has subjugated all rulers; (5) son of Esarhaddon, great king, mighty king, king of the world, king of Assyria, viceroy of Babylon, king of the land of Sumer and Akkad; grandson of Sennacherib, mighty king, king of the world, king of Assyria —

8) *ši-pir é-sag-íl šá* AD *ba-nu-u-a la ú-qa-at-tu-u*
9) *a-na-ku ú-šak-lil sat-tuk-ki é-sag-íl u* DINGIR.MEŠ TIN.TIR.KI
10) *ú-ki-in ki-din-nu-tu* KÁ.DINGIR.RA.KI *ak-ṣur*
11) *áš-šú dan-nu a-na* SIG *la ḫa-ba-li* ^{md}GIŠ.NU$_{11}$-<MU>-GI.NA
12) ŠEŠ *ta-li-me a-na* LUGAL-*u-ti* KÁ.DINGIR.RA.KI *ap-qid*
13) *ina u$_4$-me-šú-ma é-tùr-kalam-ma* É ^{d}INANNA TIN.TIR.KI
14) *eš-šiš ú-še-piš* ^{d}INANNA TIN.TIR.KI ^{d}GAŠAN *ṣir-tu*
15) *ep-še-te-ia* MUNUS.SIG$_5$.MEŠ *ḫa-diš lip-pal-lis-ma*
16) *u$_4$-me-šam-ma ma-ḫar* ^{d}EN ^{d}GAŠAN-*iá lit-tas-qar da-mì-iq-ti*
17) TI *u$_4$-me* SÙ.MEŠ *li-šim ši-ma-ti*
18) [*it*]-*ti* AN-*e ù* KI-*tim lu-ki-in* BALA-*ú-a*
19) [*ù šá* ^{md}GI]Š.⌈NU$_{11}$⌉-<MU>-GI.NA LUGAL KÁ.DINGIR.RA.KI
20) [*aḫi talīmīia ūmēšu*] *li-ri-ku liš-bi lit-tu-tu*

8–12) I completed the work on Esagila which (my) father who had engendered me had not finished. I (re)confirmed the regular offerings for Esagila and the gods of Babylon. (10) I (re-)established the privileged status of Babylon (and) appointed Šamaš-<šuma>-ukīn, my favourite brother, to the kingship of Babylon in order that the strong might not harm the weak.

13–14a) At that time, I had Eturkalama, the temple of the goddess Ištar-of-Babylon, (re)built anew.

14b–20) May the goddess Ištar-of-Babylon, the august lady, look upon my good deeds with pleasure and may she say good things about me daily before the god Bēl (Marduk) and the goddess Bēltīia (Zarpanītu)! May she determine as my fate a long life (and) make my reign [as] firm as heaven and netherworld! [Moreover, with regard to] Šamaš-<šuma>-ukīn, king of Babylon, [my favourite brother], may [his days] be long and may he experience the fullness of old age!

21) [*ša šumī šaṭru u šum ta*]-*lim-ia ina ši-pir ni-kil-ti i-pa-áš-ši-ṭu*
22) MU.⌈SAR⌉-*u-a i-ab-ba-tu lu-u a-šar-šú ú-nak-ka-ru*
23) ^{d}INANNA TIN.TIR.KI *ina ma-*⌈*ḫar*⌉ ^{d}EN ^{d}GAŠAN-*iá* MUNUS.ḪUL-*šú*
24) *lit-tas-qar* MU-*šú* NUMUN-*šú ina* KUR.KUR *li-ḫal-liq*

21–24) [(But) as for the one who] erases [my inscribed name or the name of] my [fav]ourite (brother) by some crafty device, (or) destroys my royal inscription, or changes its position, may the goddess Ištar-of-Babylon speak evil of him before the god Bēl (and) the goddess Bēltīia (and) make his name (and) his descendant(s) disappear from the lands!

23.3 [... ^{d}]AMAR.UTU ^{d}EN-*iá* MUNUS.ḪUL-*šú*, "[...] evil of him [before (...) the god] Marduk, my lord," instead of "evil of him before the god Bēl (and) the goddess Bēltīia."

5

An Akkadian inscription on two clay cylinders records the restoration of Emaḫ ("Exalted House"), the temple of the goddess Ninmaḫ at Babylon, by Ashurbanipal. The inscription was composed before the year 652 BC and is similar to B.6.32.3–4.

CATALOGUE

Ex.	Museum number	Excavation number	Babylon photo number	Babylon provenance	Dimensions (cm)	Lines preserved	cpn
1	VA 8409	BE 5457	494, 495, 530	Southwestern cella (E) of Emah temple, 10 m below surface	Length: 14.8; Dia. of ends: 6.2	1–24	c
2	BM 33338 (Rm 3,11)	—	—	—	Length: 9.4; L. dia.: 5.1	1–24	c

COMMENTARY

The exact findspot of ex. 1 is marked on Koldewey, Tempel pl. III (noted as "CYL" in the room designated A.2). Ex. 2 was part of a shipment sent by H. Rassam to the British Museum in 1879 which included items from Babylon, Borsippa, and Telloh, as well as a brick from Assur; see Reade in Leichty, Sippar 1 p. xxix. In view of the contents of the inscription, like ex. 1, it was probably found at Babylon. Both exemplars are written in Neo-Assyrian script. Two further exemplars of this inscription may be VA Bab 614 and B 65; see B.6.32.4.3–4 and the commentary to that text. The master line follows ex. 1.

Lines 11–12 refer in a positive manner to the appointment of Šamaš-šuma-ukīn, the "favourite brother" of Ashurbanipal, to the kingship of Babylon and thus indicate that the inscription was composed before the outbreak of the Šamaš-šuma-ukīn Revolt in 652 BC.

BIBLIOGRAPHY

1900 Koldewey, MDOG 4 pp. 6–7 (ex. 1, provenance, translation [by Meissner])

1903 Weissbach, Miscellen no. 8 (ex. 1, copy, edition)

1905 Jastrow, Religion 1 pp. 418–19 (ex. 1, partial translation)

1911 Koldewey, Tempel pp. 4, 13, 14 fig. 17, and 67 (ex. 1, provenance, photo, edition [by Delitzsch])

1916 Streck, Asb. pp. XLIII–XLIV and 238–41 no. 5 (Ê-maḫ) (ex. 1, edition)

1924–25 Unger, AfK 2 p. 23 no. 16 (ex. 1, study)

1925 Koldewey, WEB^{4} pp. 59–60 and fig. 41 (ex. 1, copy)

1927 Luckenbill, ARAB 2 §§965–67 (ex. 1, partial translation)

1983 Rost and Marzahn, Babylon pp. 15 and 17 (ex. 1, translation)

TEXT

1) ^{m}AN.ŠÁR-DÙ-A LUGAL GAL LUGAL *dan-nu* LUGAL ŠÁR LUGAL KUR *aš-šur*

2) LUGAL *kib-rat* 4-*ti* LUGAL LUGAL.MEŠ NUN *la šá-na-an*

3) *ša ul-tu tam-tim e-lit a-di tam-tim šap-lit i-be-lu-ma*

4) *gi-mir ma-li-ki ú-šak-niš še-pu-uš-šú*

5) DUMU ^{m}AN.ŠÁR-ŠEŠ-SUM.NA LUGAL GAL LUGAL *dan-nu* LUGAL ŠÁR LUGAL KUR *aš-šur*

1–7) Ashurbanipal, great king, mighty king, king of the world, king of Assyria, king of the four quarters (of the world), king of kings, prince who has no rival, who rules from the Upper Sea to the Lower Sea and has subjugated all rulers; (5) son of Esarhaddon, great king, mighty king, king of the world, king of Assyria, viceroy of Babylon, king of the land of Sumer and Akkad; grandson of Sennacherib, mighty king, king of the world, king of Assyria, I —

6) GÌR.NÍTA KÁ.DINGIR.RA.KI LUGAL KUR.EME.GI$_{7}$ ù URI.KI
7) DUMU DUMU ^{md}30-PAP.MEŠ-SU LUGAL *dan-nu* LUGAL ŠÁR LUGAL KUR *aš-šur a-na-ku-ma*
8) *ši-pir é-sag-íl šá* AD *ba-nu-u-a la ú-qa-at-tu-u*
9) *a-na-ku ú-šak-lil sat-tuk-ki é-sag-íl u* DINGIR.MEŠ TIN.TIR.KI
10) *ú-kin ki-di-nu-tu* KÁ.DINGIR.RA.KI *ak-ṣur*
11) *áš-šú dan-nu a-na* SIG *la ḫa-ba-li* ^{md}GIŠ.NU$_{11}$-MU-GI.NA
12) ŠEŠ *ta-li-me a-na* LUGAL*-u-tu* KÁ.DINGIR.RA.KI *ap-qid*
13) *ina u$_{4}$-me-šú-ma é-maḫ* É ^{d}*nin-maḫ šá qé-reb* KÁ.DINGIR.RA.KI
14) *eš-šiš ú-še-piš a-na šat-ti* ^{d}*nin-maḫ* GAŠAN *ṣir-tu*
15) *ep-še-te-ia* MUNUS.SIG$_{5}$.MEŠ *ḫa-diš lip-pal-lis-ma*
16) *u$_{4}$-me-šam-ma ma-ḫar* ^{d}EN ^{d}GAŠAN*-iá lit-tas-qar da-mì-iq-ti*
17) TI *u$_{4}$-me* SÙ.MEŠ *li-šim ši-ma-ti*
18) *it-ti* AN*-e u* KI*-tim lu-ki-in* BALA*-ú-a*
19) *ù šá* ^{md}GIŠ.NU$_{11}$-MU-GI.NA LUGAL KÁ.DINGIR.RA.KI
20) ŠEŠ *ta-lim-iá u$_{4}$-me-šú li-ri-ku liš-bi lit-tu-tu*
21) *ša šu-mì šaṭ-ru ù* MU *ta-lim-ia ina ši-pir ni-kil-ti i-pa-áš-ši-tu*
22) MU.SAR*-u-a i-ab-ba-tu lu-u a-šar-šú ú-nak-ka-ru*
23) ^{d}*nin-maḫ ina ma-ḫar* ^{d}EN ^{d}GAŠAN*-iá* MUNUS.ḪUL*-šú lit-tas-qar*
24) MU*-šú* NUMUN*-šú ina* KUR.KUR *li-ḫal-liq*

8–12) I completed the work on Esagila which (my) father who had engendered me had not finished. I (re)confirmed the regular offerings for Esagila and the gods of Babylon. (10) I (re-)established the privileged status of Babylon (and) appointed Šamaš-šuma-ukīn, my favourite brother, to the kingship of Babylon in order that the strong might not harm the weak.

13–14a) At that time, I had Emaḫ, the temple of the goddess Ninmaḫ which is inside Babylon, (re)built anew.

14b–20) On account of this, may the goddess Ninmaḫ, the august lady, look upon my good deeds with pleasure and say good things about me daily before the god Bēl (Marduk) and the goddess Bēltīia (Zarpanītu)! May she determine as my fate a long life (and) make my reign as firm as heaven and netherworld! Moreover, with regard to Šamaš-šuma-ukīn, king of Babylon, my favourite brother, may his days be long and may he experience the fullness of old age!

21–24) (But) as for the one who erases my inscribed name or the name of my favourite (brother) by some crafty device, (or) destroys my royal inscription, or changes its position, may the goddess Ninmaḫ speak evil of him before the god Bēl (and) the goddess Bēltīia and make his name (and) his descendant(s) disappear from the lands!

6

An Akkadian inscription of Ashurbanipal describing work on the platforms and daises of the temple Esagila at Babylon is found on a clay cylinder; the inscription was composed at some point before the year 652 BC.

COMMENTARY

The cylinder was once in the collection de Clercq. Neither its original provenance nor present location are known. The piece is reported to measure 15.6 cm in length, 7.5 cm in diameter at the centre, and 5.9 cm in diameter at the ends. The inscription is in archaizing Babylonian script. The inscription has been edited from the published heliographic reproductions of the cylinder.

The favourable mention of Šamaš-šuma-ukīn in lines 13–15 and 24–25 indicates that the inscription was composed before the beginning of his rebellion against Ashurbanipal in 652 BC.

BIBLIOGRAPHY

1870 3 R pl. 16 no. 5 (copy in type)
1886 Bezold, Literatur p. 113 §64.3.a (study)
1890 Jensen in Schrader, KB 2 pp. 258–61 (edition)
1903 de Clercq, Collection 2 pp. 148–54, figs. A.I–III following p. 116, and pls. XXIV–XXV (photo [heliograph], copy in type, edition, study)
1892 Lehmann-Haupt, Šamaššumukîn 1 pp. 26–27 and 2 p. 62 and pls. XXVIII–XXIX no. 10 (P[1]) (copy, study)
1916 Streck, Asb. pp. XLII–XLIII and 232–35 no. 3 (P[1]) (edition)
1916 Weissbach, LZB 430 (study)
1927 Luckenbill, ARAB 2 §§960–62 (translation)
1938 Wetzel and Weissbach, Hauptheiligtum pp. 77–78 (study)

TEXT

1) ^{m}AN.ŠÁR-DÙ-A LUGAL GAL LUGAL *dan-nu* LUGAL ŠÁR
2) LUGAL KUR *aš-šur* LUGAL *kib-rat* 4-*ti* LUGAL LUGAL.MEŠ
3) NUN *la šá-na-an* DUMU ^{m}AN.ŠÁR-ŠEŠ-SUM.NA
4) LUGAL GAL LUGAL *dan-nu* LUGAL ŠÁR LUGAL KUR *aš-šur*
5) GÌR.NÍTA TIN.TIR.KI LUGAL KUR.EME.GI$_{7}$ *u* URI.KI
6) DUMU DUMU ^{md}30-ŠEŠ.MEŠ-SU LUGAL GAL LUGAL *dan-nu*
7) LUGAL ŠÁR LUGAL KUR *aš-šur a-na-ku-ma* EN GAL ^{d}AMAR.UTU

1–7a) Ashurbanipal, great king, mighty king, king of the world, king of Assyria, king of the four quarters (of the world), king of kings, prince who has no rival; son of Esarhaddon, great king, mighty king, king of the world, king of Assyria, (5) viceroy of Babylon, king of the land of Sumer and Akkad; grandson of Sennacherib, great king, mighty king, king of the world, king of Assyria, I —

8) *šá ina* BALA-*e* LUGAL *maḫ-ri ina ma-ḫar* AD *ba-ni-i-šú*
9) *ú-ši-bu ina qé-reb bal til*.KI *ina u$_{4}$-me* BALA-*ia*
10) *ina ri-šá-a-ti a-na* TIN.TIR.KI *i-ru-um-ma*
11) *sat-tuk-ki é-sag-íl u* DINGIR.MEŠ TIN.TIR.KI *ú-kin*
12) *ki-din-nu-ú-tu* TIN.TIR.KI *ak-*⸢*ṣur*⸣
13) ⸢*áš*⸣-*šú dan-nu a-na* SIG *la ḫa-ba-li*
14) ^{md}GIŠ.NU$_{11}$-MU-GI.NA ŠEŠ *ta-li-me*
15) *a-na* LUGAL-*ú-tu* TIN.TIR.KI *ap-qí-di*
16) *ù ši-pir é-sag-*⸢*íl šá*⸣ *za-ru-ú-a*
17) *la* ⸢*ú*⸣-*qa-at-tu-ú a-na-ku ú-*⸢*šak*⸣-*lil*

7b–17) During my reign, the great lord, the god Marduk, who during the reign of a previous king had resided in Baltil (Aššur) in the presence of the father who had created him, (10) entered Babylon amidst rejoicing. I (re)confirmed the regular offerings for Esagila and the gods of Babylon. I (re-)established the privileged status of Babylon (and) appointed Šamaš-šuma-ukīn, my favourite brother, (15) to the kingship of Babylon in order that the strong might not harm the weak. I completed the work on Esagila which my father had not finished.

18) *ina u$_{4}$-me-šú-*⸢*ma*⸣ *di-ʾ-a-ni u* ⸢BÁRA.MEŠ *šá*⸣ *si-*⸢*ḫir*⸣-*ti*
19) *é-sag-*⸢*íl*⸣ *ki-i* ⸢*si*⸣-*ma-a-ti-šú-nu la-bi-ra-a-ti*
20) *ina áš-ri-šú-nu lu-u ad-di a-na šat-*⸢*ti*⸣ ^{d}AMAR.UTU EN GAL
21) *ep-še-ti-ia dam-qa-a-*⸢*ti*⸣ *ḫa-di-iš* IGI.BAR-*ma*
22) TI *u$_{4}$-me* SÙ.MEŠ *še-bé-e lit-tu-tu ṭu-ub* UZU
23) *ù ḫu-ud lìb-bi li-šim ši-ma-ti*
24) *ù šá* ^{md}GIŠ.NU$_{11}$-MU-GI.NA LUGAL TIN.TIR.KI
25) ŠEŠ *ta-lim-ia u$_{4}$-me-šú li-ri-ku liš-bi bu-ʾ-a-ri*

18–20a) At that time, I (re-)erected the platforms and daises of all of Esagila in their (original) positions according to their ancient specifications.

20b–25) On account of this, may the god Marduk, the great lord, look upon my good deeds with pleasure and determine as my fate a long life, fullness of old age, good health, and happiness! Moreover, with regard to Šamaš-šuma-ukīn, king of Babylon, my favourite brother, may his days be long and may he be fully satisfied with (his) good fortune!

26) *ma-ti-ma ina aḫ-rat u$_{4}$-me* NUN *ar-ku-u šá ina u$_{4}$-me* BALA-*šú*
27) *ši-pir šu-a-ti in-na-ḫu an-ḫu-us-su lu-ud-diš*
28) *šu-mì it-ti* MU-*šú liš-ṭur* MU.SAR-*u-a li-mur-ma*
29) Ì.GIŠ *lip-šu-uš* UDU.SÍSKUR BAL-*qí ina áš-ri-šú liš-kun*

26–30a) If at any time in the future, during the days of the reign of some future prince, this work falls into disrepair, may (that prince) repair its dilapidated state! May he write my name with his (own) name! May he look at my royal inscription, anoint (it) with oil, offer a sacrifice, (and) set (my royal inscription back) in its place! The god Marduk will (then) hearken to his prayers.

30) *ik-ri-bi-i-šú* ^{d}AMAR.UTU *i-šem-me* [*šá*] *šu-mì šaṭ-ru*
31) *i-pa-áš-ši-ṭu* MU.SAR-*ú-a i-ab-ba-tu*
32) *lu-u a-šar-šú ú-nak-ka-ru* EN GAL ^{d}AMAR.UTU *ag-gi-iš*
33) *lik-kil-me-šú-ma* MU-*šú* NUMUN-*šú i-na* KUR.KUR ⸢*li*⸣-*ḫal-liq*

30b–33) [(But) as for the one who] erases my inscribed name, (or) destroys my royal inscription, or changes its position, may the great lord, the god Marduk, glare at him angrily and make his name (and) his descendant(s) disappear from the lands!

7

A large number of bricks from Babylon have an Akkadian inscription of Ashurbanipal stamped upon them which states that the Assyrian king had had bricks made for Esagila ("House Whose Top Is High") and for the ziqqurat Etemenanki ("House, Foundation of Heaven and Netherworld").

CATALOGUE

Ex.	Museum number	Excavation number	Babylon photo number	Babylon provenance	Dimensions (cm)	Lines preserved	FuB 27	cpn
1	—	BE 8086	872	Esagila, passage, 4th pavement	37×37	1–9	—	p
2	VA Bab 4052i	BE 8083?	—	Esagila, court, 4th pavement	37×37×10	1–9	14	n
3	VA Bab 4052k	—	—	—	37×37×7.5	1–9	15	n
4	VA Bab 4073a	—	—	—	37×37×7.5	1–9	16	n
5	—	BE 8072	—	As ex. 1	37×37	1–9	—	n
6	—	BE 8010	—	Esagila, court, 3rd pavement	—	—	—	n
7	—	BE 8044	—	As ex. 1	30×30	—	—	n
8	—	BE 8045	—	As ex. 1	30×30	—	—	n
9	—	BE 8046	—	As ex. 1	30×30	—	—	n
10	—	BE 8047	—	As ex. 1	30×30	—	—	n
11	—	BE 8048	—	As ex. 1	30×30	—	—	n
12	—	BE 8049	—	As ex. 1	30×30	—	—	n
13	—	BE 8051	—	Esagila, inner court-yard, 3rd pavement	—	—	—	n
14	—	BE 8052	—	As ex. 13	—	—	—	n
15	—	BE 8053	—	As ex. 13	—	—	—	n
16	—	BE 8054	—	As ex. 13	—	—	—	n
17	—	BE 8073	—	As ex. 1	37×37	—	—	n
18	—	BE 8074	—	As ex. 1	37×37	—	—	n
19	—	BE 8075	—	As ex. 1	37×37	—	—	n
20	—	BE 8076	—	As ex. 1	37×37	—	—	n
21	—	BE 8077	—	As ex. 1	37×37	—	—	n
22	—	BE 8078	—	As ex. 1	37×37	—	—	n
23	—	BE 8079	870	As ex. 1	37×37	1–9	—	p
24	—	BE 8080	—	As ex. 1	37×37	—	—	n
25	—	BE 8081	—	As ex. 1	37×37	—	—	n
26	—	BE 8082	—	As ex. 1	37×37	—	—	n
27	EŞ number unknown	—	—	—	—	1–9	—	p

COMMENTARY

All exemplars either certainly or probably come from the excavations of the Deutsche Orient-Gesellschaft at Babylon in November 1900. With regard to the provenance of ex. 2 (assuming that VA Bab 4052i and BE 8083 are identical), see Marzahn, FuB 27 (1989) pp. 58 and 64 n. 12, against Wetzel and Weissbach, Hauptheiligtum p. 86. Exs. 3–4 and 27 may also be listed under Babylon excavation numbers. Where known, the inscription is stamped on the face of the brick. The stamp used on ex. 2 measures 16.5×7.7 cm and 16.8×6.8 cm on exs. 3–4. The inscription is in Babylonian script. The only variant reported for the inscription is MEŠ for ME in line 4 (exs. 2–4; see Marzahn, FuB 27 [1989] p. 58). No score for this brick inscription is presented in the microfiche.

BIBLIOGRAPHY

1900–1901 Koldewey, MDOG 7 pp. 22–23 (ex. 5, provenance, translation)
1911 Koldewey, Tempel pp. 44 and 72 no. 10 (ex. 5, provenance, edition)
1916 Streck, Asb. pp. LXIII and 350–51 no. 3.a.β (ex. 5, edition)
1924–25 Unger, AfK 2 p. 23 no. 12 (exs. 1, 5, study)
1925 Koldewey, WEB[4] pp. 202 and 203 fig. 125 (ex. 1, photo, study)
1927 Luckenbill, ARAB 2 §§1119–20 (ex. 5, translation)
1931 Unger, Babylon p. 280 no. 22 (exs. 1, 5, translation)
1938 Wetzel and Weissbach, Hauptheiligtum p. 39 no. A.II.a and pp. 86–87 (exs. 1–2, 5–26, provenance, edition)
1989 Marzahn, FuB 27 p. 58 no. VIII, nos. 14–16 and fig. 7 (transliteration; ex. 2, copy; exs. 2–4, study)

TEXT

1) *ana* ^d^AMAR.UTU UMUN-*šú*
2) ^m^AN.ŠÁR-DÙ-A
3) MAN ŠÚ MAN KUR *aš-šur*
4) *ana* TIN ZI.ME-*šú*
5) *a-gur-ri*
6) *é-sag-gíl*
7) *u é-temen-an-ki*
8) *eš-šiš*
9) *ú-šal-bi-in*

1–9) For the god Marduk, his lord: Ashurbanipal, king of the world (and) king of Assyria, in order to ensure his good health (5) had baked bricks made anew for Esagila and Etemenanki.

8

Several bricks from Babylon have an Akkadian inscription stamped upon them which states that Ashurbanipal had had bricks made for the ziqqurat Etemenanki.

CATALOGUE

Ex.	Museum number	Excavation number	Babylon photo number	Babylon provenance	Dimensions (cm)	Lines preserved	FuB 27	cpn
1	BM 90285 (DT 381)	—	—	—	31.5×25×6.5	1–10	—	n
2	VA Bab 4073b	BE 40145	1892	Merkes g 2 22	32×32×8.5	1–10	17	p
3	—	BE 40855	1965	Sachn South ak 37	31×31	1–10	—	p
4	VA Bab 4073c	BE 41032	—	Sachn South af 37	16.5×23×7.5	6–10	18	n
5	VA Bab 4073d	BE 41232	—	Sachn South ab 36	24×31×9	1–10	19	n

COMMENTARY

Ex. 1 comes from the expedition to Nineveh led by G. Smith on behalf of the Daily Telegraph newspaper in 1873 and is reported to be from Babylon. Exs. 2–5 were discovered during excavations at Babylon by the Deutsche Orient-Gesellachaft. The exact findspot of ex. 3 is noted on pl. 12 of Wetzel and Weissbach, Hauptheiligtum (cited erroneously as 40856); ex. 4 was found in January 1910. For the provenance of ex. 5, see Marzahn, FuB 27 (1989) p. 59 and p. 64 n. 14 (contra Wetzel and Weissbach, Hauptheiligtum p. 86). Each brick is stamped on the face. The area stamped on ex. 1 measures 13.3×7.1 cm, on ex. 2 10.3×8.0 cm, on ex. 4 4.5×7.9 cm, and on ex. 5 11.2×7.8 cm. The inscription is in Babylonian script. The line arrangement follows ex.

1; exs. 2–5 have lines 9 and 10 of ex. 1 on a single line. George Smith refers to having found a nine-line exemplar, but this must refer to ex. 1 since it is registered as having come from his expedition to Iraq. According to C.B.F. Walker (CBI p. 67), a copy of this exemplar is found in Smith's notebook, Add. MS 30413 fol. 19, no. 36. Exs. 2–3 and 5 have *aš-šur* not AN.ŠÁR in line 2. No score for this brick inscription is presented in the microfiche.

BIBLIOGRAPHY

1875 G. Smith, Assyrian Disc. p. 380 (ex. 1, translation)
1886 Bezold, Literatur p. 116 §65.4.m (ex. 1, study)
1916 Streck, Asb. pp. LXIII and 350–51 no. 3.a.α (ex. 1, edition)
1922 BM Guide p. 74 no. 302 (ex. 1, study)
1924–25 Unger, AfK 2 p. 23 nos. 13–14 (ex. 1, study)
1927 Luckenbill, ARAB 2 §1118 (ex. 1, translation)
1938 Wetzel and Weissbach, Hauptheiligtum p. 40 no. A.II.d and pp. 86–87 (exs. 2–5, provenance, edition)
1981 Walker, CBI no. 78 (ex. 1, transliteration)
1989 Marzahn, FuB 27 p. 59 no. IX, nos. 17–19 and fig. 8 (transliteration; ex. 5, copy; exs. 2, 4, 5, study)

TEXT

1) *ana* ^{d}AMAR.UTU UMUN-*šú*
2) ^{m}AN.ŠÁR-DÙ-A
3) MAN ŠÚ MAN KUR AŠ
4) A ^{m}*aš-šur*-PAP-AŠ
5) MAN ŠÚ MAN KUR AŠ
6) MAN KÁ.DIŠ.KI
7) *a-gur-ri*
8) *é-temen-an-ki*
9) *eš-šiš*
10) *ú-še-piš*

1–10) For the god Marduk, his lord: Ashurbanipal, king of the world (and) king of Assyria, son of Esarhaddon, (5) king of the world, king of Assyria, (and) king of Babylon, had baked bricks made anew for Etemenanki.

9

A number of bricks from Babylon bear a stamped inscription in Sumerian which records the renovation of Etemenanki, the ziqqurat at Babylon, by Ashurbanipal.

CATALOGUE

Ex.	Museum number	Excavation number	Babylon photo number	Babylon provenance	Dimensions (cm)	Lines preserved	FuB 27	cpn
1	BM 130712 (1942-1-28,1)	—	—	—	23×9.5×3.5	1–4	—	c
2	—	BE 39849	1192	City area?	—	1–4	—	p
3	VA Bab 4054c	BE 41252	—	Sachn SW ab 36	30.5×30.5×8.5	1–4	13	n
4	VA Bab 4054a	BE 36072	1914, 1916	Merkes n 27 II, +8.50	25×18×8.5	1–4	11	p
5	VA Bab 4054b	BE 39436	1916	Merkes g 2 24, +8.00	21×19×8.5	1–4	12	p
6	—	BE 39807	1916	Sachn South am 37	—	1–4	—	p
7	—	BE 41171	—	Sachn West z 26	—	—	—	n
8	—	BE 46433	3283	Merkes, baked brick pillar, layer 37	—	2–4	—	p

COMMENTARY

Ex. 1 was presented to the British Museum by Mrs. B.A. Varty; exs. 2–8 come from the excavations at Babylon by the Deutsche Orient-Gesellschaft in 1908–1912. All exemplars are stamped on the face of the brick. The area stamped on ex. 1 measures 5.3×20.7 cm, on ex. 3 5.5×20.7 cm, and on exs. 4–5 5.5×9.5 cm. The script is a mixture of sign forms; for example, lugal is written five times with the Old Babylonian form and the sixth time with the Neo-Babylonian form. Ex. 1 was kindly collated by C.B.F. Walker. No variants are attested and no score of this inscription is presented in the microfiche.

The inscription appears to have been written in Sumerian but the writing *eš-šiš* in line 4 and *aš-šur*.KI in lines 2 and 3 would suggest that it was to have been read in Akkadian.

BIBLIOGRAPHY

1938 Wetzel and Weissbach, Hauptheiligtum p. 40 no. A.II.e and pp. 86–87 (exs. 2–8, provenance, edition)

1981 Walker, CBI no. 79 (ex. 1, transliteration)

1989 Marzahn, FuB 27 pp. 57–58 no. VII, nos. 11–13 and fig. 6 (transliteration; ex. 3, copy; exs. 3–5, study)

TEXT

1) ^{d}asar-ri umun gal lugal-a-ni-ir ^{m}AN.ŠÁR-DÙ-A
2) lugal imin lugal ma-da *aš-šur*.KI dumu ^{m}AN.ŠÁR-PAP-AŠ
3) lugal imin lugal ma-da *aš-šur*.KI lugal TIN.TIR.KI
4) nam-ti-la-bi-šè é-temen-an-ki *eš-šiš* mu-na-dím

1–4) For the god Asari, great lord, his lord: Ashurbanipal, king of the world (and) king of Assyria, son of Esarhaddon, king of the world, king of Assyria, (and) king of Babylon, for the sake of his life had Etemenanki constructed anew.

10

This Akkadian inscription of Ashurbanipal is stamped upon a brick fragment found at Babylon and records the making of bricks for Etemenanki.

COMMENTARY

The brick fragment (BE 41186) was found at Babylon in Sachn, south ai 34, on March 16, 1910. The present location of the brick is not known and no photograph of it appears to have been made. The edition of the inscription is based upon that by Weissbach. Weissbach states that there does not appear to have been room to restore more than the name of Ashurbanipal at the end of line 1 and suggests that the lack of any title for Ashurbanipal might indicate that the text dates to the period before Ashurbanipal became king (that is, during the reign of Esarhaddon, but after Ashurbanipal had been named heir to the throne). There is, however, no evidence to suggest that Ashurbanipal held any authority in Babylonia during the reign of Esarhaddon or was active there with regard to building projects at that time. Since it was not possible to verify the spacing on the original piece, such a suggested date must remain improbable.

BIBLIOGRAPHY

1938 Wetzel and Weissbach, Hauptheiligtum p. 40 no. A.II.b and p. 86 (provenance, edition)

2 imin, the number seven, is used here for Akkadian *kiššatu*; see AHw p. 492 and CAD 8 [K] p. 457.

TEXT

1) [*ana*] dAMAR.UTU UMUN-*šu* mAN.ŠÁR-[*bāni-apli*]
2) A mAN.ŠÁR-PAP-AŠ MAN ŠÚ [*šar māt aššur*]
3) *a-gur-ri é-temen-a*[*n-ki*]
4) *eš-šiš ú-*[*še-piš*]

1–4) [For] the god Marduk, his lord: Ashur[banipal], son of Esarhaddon, king of the world (and) [king of Assyria had] baked bricks [made] anew for Etemena[nki].

11

Another Akkadian inscription stamped on a brick from Babylon records the making of bricks for Etemenanki by Ashurbanipal.

COMMENTARY

The brick is at present in the Vorderasiatisches Museum in Berlin and has the museum number VA Bab 4052h. It has the Babylon excavation number BE 41143 and is shown on Babylon excavation photo 2030. The piece was found in Sachn, south ao 38 on March 3, 1910. It measures 31.5×31.5×8.5 cm; the stamped area of the inscription is 4.3×19 cm. The inscription is stamped on the face of the brick and is in contemporary Babylonian script. It has been edited from the published photograph, supplemented by the published collations by Marzahn.

BIBLIOGRAPHY

1910 Wetzel, MDOG 43 p. 23 (provenance)
1916 Streck, Asb. pp. LXIII and 837 no. 8 (edition)
1924–25 Unger, AfK 2 p. 23 no. 15 (study)
1925 Koldewey, WEB4 p. 183 fig. 117 (photo)
1938 Wetzel and Weissbach, Hauptheiligtum p. 40 no. A.II.c and pp. 86–87 (provenance, edition)
1989 Marzahn, FuB 27 p. 57 no. VI, no. 10 and fig. 5 (copy, transliteration, study)

TEXT

1) *ana* ⌈d⌉AMAR.UTU UMUN-*šú* mAN.ŠÁR-DÙ-A MAN ŠÚ
2) MAN [K]UR *aš-šur a-gur-ri é-temen-an-ki*
3) *a-*⌈*na*⌉ TIN-⌈*šú eš*⌉*-šis* ⌈*ú*⌉*-šal-bi-in*

1–3) For the god Marduk, his lord: Ashurbanipal, king of the world (and) king of Assyria, for the sake of his life had baked bricks made anew for Etemenanki.

12

This Akkadian inscription is found on several clay cylinders and deals with the restoration of Ebabbar ("Shining House"), the temple of the god Šamaš at Sippar, by Ashurbanipal. The inscription was composed at some point previous to the outbreak of the the Šamaš-šuma-ukīn Revolt in 652 BC.

B.6.32.10 line 4 Or *ú-*[*šal-bi-in*].

CATALOGUE

Ex.	Museum number	Registration number	Dimensions (cm)	Lines preserved	cpn
1	BM 91115	82-7-14,1043	Length: 14.5; R dia.: 4.5; L dia.: 4.6	1–29	c
2	BM 56639	82-7-14,1044	10.9×6.8×4.3	9–17	c
3	DT 272	—	7.1×5.1	24–26, 28–29	c
4	BM 56634	82-7-14,1032	10.7×8.7×6.5	10–27	c
5	BM 78264	Bu 88-5-12,120	Length: 2.75″; segmental arc: 2.25″; chord: 2″	—	n
6	MMA number unknown	—	—	11–12	n
7	BM 28384 + BM 50843	98-10-11,20 + 82-3-23,1837	Length: 7.5; L dia.: 4.3	1–29	c

COMMENTARY

Exs. 1, 2, and 4 were found at Sippar by H. Rassam. Ex. 3 comes from the expedition led by G. Smith to Kuyunjik, but probably was not found at that site. Ex. 5 was purchased by E.A.W. Budge and ex. 6 comes from the Wolfe expedition of 1885. Part of ex. 7 (BM 28384) was acquired by the British Museum from K. Minassian and part (BM 50843) comes from a shipment sent by H. Rassam, some of whose pieces came from Sippar. Exs. 1–3 and 7 are written in contemporary Babylonian script while ex. 4 is in archaizing script. Exs. 5–6 cannot be located for collation and their script is unknown. Ex. 5 is said to have (parts of) nine lines (Bezold, Cat. 4 p. 1916), but it is not known to which lines of the incription these correspond. Ex. 6 is said to have (parts of) lines 11–12; since similar, though not exactly duplicate, lines appear in other inscriptions of Ashurbanipal (e.g., B.6.32.6 lines 12b–17a), it is not impossible that this exemplar does not belong to this inscription. The line arrangement and master line follow ex. 1, with help from ex. 4 for the end of line 18, from ex. 7 for the ends of lines 21–26, and from B.6.32.19 lines 25–26 for the ends of lines 19–20.

Following a comment by Winckler (OLZ 1 [1898] 76), Streck included the fragment 81-2-4,174 among the exemplars of this inscription (Streck, Asb. p. XLII). For that fragment, see B.6.32.20.

Since the inscription refers to Šamaš-šuma-ukīn in a favourable light (lines 11–12, 21–22, and 26), it must have been composed before 652 BC, when he led a rebellion against Assyrian control over Babylonia.

BIBLIOGRAPHY

1884 5 R pl. 62 no. 1 (ex. 1, copy in type)
1885–86 Craig and Harper, Hebraica 2 pp. 87–89 (ex. 1, edition)
1886 Bezold, Literatur pp. 113 §64.3.c and 349 (ex. 1, study)
1886 Lyon, Manual pp. 23–24 and 74–75 (ex. 1, transliteration, study)
1890 Abel and Winckler, KGV p. 31 (ex. 1, copy)
1892 Lehmann-Haupt, Šamaššumukîn 1 pp. 25–26, and 2 pp. 18–21 and 61 and pls. XXV–XXVII no. 9 (L^{2}) (exs. 1–4, copy, edition; exs. 1–4, 6, study)
1898 Winckler, OLZ 1 75 and 77 (exs. 3, 5, study)
1904 Smith in Harper, Literature pp. 129–30 (ex. 1, translation)
1905 Jastrow, Religion 1 p. 418 (ex. 1, partial translation)
1916 Streck, Asb. pp. XLI–XLII and 228–33 no. 2 (L^{2}) (exs. 1–6, edition)
1922 BM Guide p. 230 no. 36 (ex. 1, study)
1927 Luckenbill, ARAB 2 §§956–59 (ex. 1, translation)

TEXT

1) ^{m}AN.ŠÁR-DÙ-A LUGAL GAL LUGAL *dan-nu* LUGAL ŠÁR LUGAL KUR *aš-šur* LUGAL *kib-rat* 4-*ti*

2) LUGAL LUGAL.MEŠ NUN *la šá-na-an šá ina a-mat* DINGIR.MEŠ *ti-ik-li-šú ul-tu tam-tim e-lit*

3) *a-di tam-tim šap-lit i-be-lu-ma gi-mir ma-lik ú-šak-niš še-pu-uš-šú*

4) DUMU ^{m}AN.ŠÁR-ŠEŠ-SUM.NA LUGAL GAL LUGAL *dan-nu* LUGAL ŠÁR LUGAL KUR *aš-šur* GÌR.NÍTA TIN.TIR.KI

1–8a) Ashurbanipal, great king, mighty king, king of the world, king of Assyria, king of the four quarters (of the world), king of kings, prince who has no rival, who at the command of the gods, his helpers, rules from the Upper Sea to the Lower Sea and has subjugated all rulers; son of Esarhaddon, great king, mighty king, king of the world, king of Assyria, viceroy of Babylon, (5) king of the land of Sumer and Akkad, who (re)settled Babylon, (re)built Esagila, renovated the sanctuaries of all the cult centres, constantly established appropriate

5) LUGAL KUR.EME.GI$_7$ *u* URI.KI *mu-še-šib* TIN.TIR.KI *e-piš é-sag-íl*
6) *mu-ud-diš eš-re-e-ti kul-lat ma-ḫa-zi šá ina qé-reb-ši-na iš-tak-kan si-ma-ti*
7) *ù sat-tuk-ki-ši-na baṭ-lu-tu ú-ki-nu* DUMU DUMU ^{md}30-ŠEŠ.MEŠ-SU LUGAL GAL
8) LUGAL *dan-nu* LUGAL ŠÁR LUGAL KUR *aš-šur a-na-ku-ma ina* BALA-*e-a* EN GAL ^{d}AMAR.UTU *ina ri-šá-a-t*[*i*]
9) *a-na* TIN.⸢TIR⸣.KI *i-ru-um-ma ina é-sag-íl šá da-ra-ti šu-bat-su ir-me*
10) *sat-*⸢*tuk*⸣*-ki é-sag-íl u* DINGIR.MEŠ TIN.TIR.KI *ú-kin ki-din-nu-tu* TIN.TIR.KI
11) *ak-ṣur áš-šú dan-nu a-na* SIG *la ḫa-ba-li* ^{md}GIŠ.NU$_{11}$-MU-GI.NA ŠEŠ *ta-li-me*
12) *a-na* LUGAL-*ú-tú* TIN.TIR.KI *ap-qid ù ši-pir é-sag-íl la qa-ta-a*
13) *ú-šak-lil ina* KÙ.BABBAR KÙ.GI *ni-siq-ti* NA$_4$.MEŠ *é-sag-íl az-nun-ma*
14) *ki-ma ši-ṭir bu-ru-mu ú-nam-mir é-umuš-a ù šá eš-re-e-ti ka-li-ši-na*
15) *ḫi-bil-ta-ši-na ú-šal-lim e-li kul-lat ma-ḫa-zi ú-šat-ri-ṣi an-dul-lu*$_4$
16) *ina u*$_4$*-me-šú-ma é-babbar-ra šá qé-reb* ZIMBIR.KI É ^{d}UTU EN GAL EN-*iá šá la-ba-riš*
17) *il-lik-u-ma i-qu-pu in-nab-tu áš-ra-ti-šú áš-te-ʾ ina ši-pir* ^{d}*kulla*
18) *eš-šiš ú-še-piš-ma ki-ma* KUR-*i re-e-ši-i-šú ul-li a-na šat-ti* ^{d}UTU
19) DI.KUD.GAL DINGIR.MEŠ EN GAL EN-*iá ep-še-ti-ia dam-qa-a-ti ḫa-diš lip-p*[*a-lis*]*-ma*
20) *a-na ia-a-ši* ^{m}AN.ŠÁR-DÙ-A LUGAL KUR *aš-šur* NUN *pa-liḫ-šú* TIN *u*$_4$*-me* SÙ.MEŠ *še-bé-e l*[*it-tu-tu*]
21) *ṭu-ub* UZU *u ḫu-ud lib-bi li-šim ši-ma-ti u šá* ^{md}GIŠ.NU$_{11}$-MU-GI.NA
22) LUGAL TIN.TIR.KI ŠEŠ *ta-lim-ia u*$_4$*-me-šú li-ri-ku liš-bi bu-ʾ-a-ri ma-ti-ma*
23) *ina aḫ-rat u*$_4$*-me* NUN *ar-ku-ú šá ina u*$_4$*-me* BALA-*šú ši-pir šu-a-ti in-na-ḫu*
24) *an-ḫu-us-su lu-ud-diš šu-mì it-ti* MU-*šú liš-ṭur* MU.SAR-*u-a li-mur-ma*
25) Ì.GIŠ *lip-šu-uš* UDU.SISKUR BAL-*qí it-ti* MU.SAR-*e-šú liš-kun ik-ri-bi-šú*
26) ^{d}UTU *i-šem-me šá šu-mì šaṭ-ru ù* MU *ta-lim-ia ina ši-pir ni-kil-ti*
27) *i-pa-áš-ši-ṭu šu-mì it-ti* MU-*šú la i-šaṭ-ṭa-ru* MU.SAR-*ú-a*
28) *i-ab-ba-tu-ma it-ti* MU.SAR-*e-šú la i-šak-ka-nu* ^{d}UTU EN *e-la-ti u šap-la-ti*
29) *ag-gi-iš lik-kil-me-šú-ma* MU-*šú* NUMUN-*šú ina* KUR.KUR *li-ḫal-liq*

procedures in them, and (re)confirmed their interrupted regular offerings; grandson of Sennacherib, great king, mighty king, king of the world, king of Assyria, I —

8b–15) During my reign, the great lord, the god Marduk, entered Babylon amidst rejoicing and took up his residence in the eternal Esagila. (10) I (re)confirmed the regular offerings for Esagila and the gods of Babylon. I (re-)established the privileged status of Babylon (and) appointed Šamaš-šuma-ukīn, my favourite brother, to the kingship of Babylon in order that the strong might not harm the weak. I completed the unfinished work on Esagila. I *decorated* Esagila with silver, gold, (and) precious stones and made Eumuša glisten like the stars (lit. "writing") of the firmament. I restored the damage done to all the sanctuaries. I extended (my) protection over all the cult centres.

16–18a) At that time, I sought the (original) emplacement of Ebabbar, which is inside Sippar, the temple of the god Šamaš, the great lord, my lord, which had become old, buckled, and collapsed. I had (it) (re)built anew with the work of the god Kulla and raised its top (as high) as a mountain.

18b–22a) On account of this, may the god Šamaš, great judge of the gods, great lord, my lord, look upon my good deeds with pleasure! May he determine (20) for me — Ashurbanipal, king of Assyria, the prince who reveres him — as my fate, a long life, fullness of [old age], good health, and happiness! Moreover, with regard to Šamaš-šuma-ukīn, the king of Babylon, my favourite (brother), may his days be long and may he be fully satisfied with (his) good fortune!

22b–26a) If at any time in the future, during the days of the reign of some future prince, this work falls into disrepair, may (that prince) renovate its dilapidated sections! May he write my name with his (own) name! May he look at my royal inscription, (25) anoint (it) with oil, offer a sacrifice, (and) place (my royal inscription) with his (own) royal inscription! The god Šamaš will (then) listen to his prayers.

26b–29) (But) as for the one who erases my inscribed name or the name of my favourite (brother) by some crafty device, (or) does not write my name with his (own) name, (or) destroys my royal inscription, (or) does not place (my royal inscription) with his (own) royal inscription, may the god Šamaš, lord of the upper world and and the netherworld, glare at him angrily and make his name (and) his descendant(s) disappear from the lands!

13

This partially preserved inscription is written in Akkadian upon fragments of two clay cylinders and records the restoration of the city wall of Borsippa, Ṭābi-supūršu ("Its Fold Is Pleasant"), and its gates by Ashurbanipal. The inscription was composed at some point before the commencement of his brother Šamaš-šuma-ukīn's rebellion in 652 BC.

CATALOGUE

Ex.	Museum number	Registration number	Dimensions (cm)	Lines preserved	cpn
1	VA 3587	—	12×5.7	1–28	c
2	BM 83000	83-1-21,163	5.6×6	18–27	c
	(+) BM 83001	(+) 83-1-21,164	5×4.5	20–22, 24–28	c

COMMENTARY

Ex. 1 was purchased by the Vorderasiatisches Museum and ex. 2 is thought to come from H. Rassam's work (see Leichty, Sippar 3 pp. xiii and 327; Lambert, Cat. p. 75 indicates that BM 83001 comes from Kuyunjik). Both exemplars are written in Neo-Assyrian script. The line arrangement follows ex. 1. The master line comes from ex. 1 for lines 1–18 and 28 and is a conflation of exs. 1 and 2 for lines 19–27. Line 6 is restored from B.6.33.4 line 10 and the restoration of lines 7–23 and 25–28 is based upon B.6.32.1 lines 3–23 and 25–29.

The mention of Ashurbanipal's appointment of his brother Šamaš-šuma-ukīn to the rulership of Babylonia in a positive manner (lines 16–17, partially restored) indicates that the inscription must date before 652 BC.

BIBLIOGRAPHY

1939–41 Weidner, AfO 13 pp. 217–18 and pl. XVI (ex. 1, copy, edition)

1991–93 Frame, JCS 43–45, pp. 119–20 (ex. 2, copy, edition)

TEXT

1) [*ana nabium* ...] (x) GAR-*ni* DINGIR.MEŠ *ti-iz-qar šá-qu-u muš-tar-ḫu*
2) [... *n*]*a-šu-u ṭup-pi* NAM.MEŠ DINGIR.MEŠ *šá gu-um-mur*(*u*) *te-re-e-ti*
3) [...] x x x KI *šá-kin ši-tul-tú a-na* DINGIR.MEŠ *šu-ut* AN KI
4) [...] ⸢*šá*⸣ *la iš-šá-an-na-nu* GIŠ.TUKUL.MEŠ-*šú*
5) [...] *šá šur-ba-a-ti e-nu-us-su*
6) [*āšib ezida bītu kīnu ina barsipa māḫāz r*]*a-*⸢*áš*⸣*-bu* EN GAL EN-*ia*

1–6) [To the god Nabû ...] *commander* of the gods, eminent, exalted, splendid, [...] who bears the tablet of the fates of the gods, who controls the omens [...] ... who gives advice to the gods of heaven and netherworld, [...] whose weapons cannot be equalled, (5) [...] whose lordship is supreme, [who dwells in Ezida — the proper temple, (located) in Borsippa, the] awesome [cult centre] — great lord, my lord:

7) [*anāku aššur-bāni-apli šarru rabû šarru dannu šar kiššati šar māt aš-š*]*ur* LUGAL *kib-rat* 4-*ti*

7–12) [I, Ashurbanipal, great king, mighty king, king of the world, king of Assy]ria, king of the four

1 The name of the god appears in line 26.

2 The translation "who controls the omens" assumes that *gu-um-mur*(*u*) is a D stem stative subjunctive (see also B.6.33.4 line 3, *gu-um-mu-ru*) rather than a D stem infinitive ("... tablet of the fates of the gods for the control of the omens").

8) [*mār aššur-aḫa-iddin šarru rabû šarru dannu šar kiššati šar māt aššur šakkanak* TIN.TI]R.KI LUGAL KUR.EME.GI$_7$ *u* URI.K[I]
9) [*mušēšib bābili ēpiš esagil muddiš eš-re-e-t*]*i kul-lat ma-ḫa-z*[*i*]
10) [*ša ina qerbīšina ištakkanu simāti u sattukkīšina ba*]*ṭ-lu-tú ú-ki-n*[*u*]
11) [*parṣī kidudê kīma labīrimma uterru áš-r*]*u-uš-šu-u*[*n*]
12) [*mār māri sîn-aḫḫē-erība šarru rabû šarru dannu šar kiššati šar māt aš-š*]*ur a-na-ku-*⸢*ma*⸣
13) [*ina palêa bēlu rabû marduk ina rīšāti ana bābili*] ⸢*i*⸣*-ru-um-m*[*a*]
14) [*ina esagil ša dārâti šubassu irme sat-tuk*]-⸢*ki*⸣ *é-sag-í*[*l*(?)]
15) [*u ilāni bābili ukīn kidinnūtu* TIN.TI]R(?).KI *ak-ṣu*[*r*]
16) [*aššu dannu ana enši lā ḫabāli šamaš-šuma-ukīn* Š]EŠ *ta-li-me*
17) [*ana šarrūtu bābili apqidi u ina kaspi ḫurāṣi*] *ni-siq-ti* NA$_4$.MEŠ
18) [*esagil aznunma kīma šiṭir burūmû ú-n*]*am-mir é-umuš-a*
19) *ina* [*ūmēšuma ṭābi-supūršu dūr barsipa ša la-ba-r*]*iš il-lik-ú-ma*
20) [*iqūpu innabtu aššu* EN.NU]N ⸢*é-zi-da ù*⸣ *eš-re-e-te bár-sipa*.KI *dun-nu-nu*
21) [*ina emūq um-m*]*a-na-ti-ia* [*surriš* DÙG].GA-*su-pur-šú* BÀ[D-*šú ina š*]*i-pir* ^{d}*kulla eš-šiš ú-še-piš-ma*
22) [*abullēšu*] ⸢*ú*⸣*-rak-ki-si* GIŠ.IG.MEŠ (x) [...] x-*ni-ma ú-rat-ta-a ina* KÁ.MEŠ-*šú*
23) [*rubû ar-k*]*u-ú ša ina* BALA-*e-šú ši-pir šu-a-ti in-na-ḫu* LÚ *um-ma-a-ni en-qu-tu*
24) ⸢*ši*⸣*-ta-ʾ-al* [DÙG.GA-*s*]*u-pur-šú* BÀD *bár-sipa*.KI *ki-ma si-ma-ti-šú la-bi-ra-a-te e-pu-uš*
25) [*mušarûa*] ⸢*a*⸣*-mur-ma* Ì.GIŠ *pu-šu-uš* UDU.SISKUR BAL-*qí it-ti* MU.SAR-*e-ka šu-kun*
26) [*ik-ri-bi-k*]*a* ^{d}*na-bi-u*[*m i-še*]*m-me ša šu-mì šaṭ-ru ù* MU *ta-lim-ia*
27) [*ina šipir nikilti*] *i-ab-*[*bat* MU.S]AR-*u-a it-ti* MU.SAR-*e-šú la i-šak-ka-nu*
28) [*nabium* (...) *aggiš lik*]*-kil-me-šú-ma* MU-*šú* NUMUN-*šú ina* KUR.KUR *li-ḫal-liq*

quarters (of the world); [son of Esarhaddon, great king, mighty king, king of the world, king of Assyria, viceroy of Babyl]on, king of the land of Sumer and Akkad, [who (re)settled Babylon, (re)built Esagila, renovated the sanctuaries] of all cult centres, (10) [constantly established appropriate procedures in them, and] (re)confirmed [their int]errupted [regular offerings, (who) rest]ored [the rites (and) rituals according to the old pattern; grandson of Sennacherib, great king, mighty king, king of the world, king of Assy]ria, I —

13–18) [During my reign, the great lord, the god Marduk], entered [Babylon amidst rejoicing] and [took up his residence in the eternal Esagila. I (re)confirmed the regular offer]ings for Esagila (15) [and the gods of Babylon]. I (re-)established [the privileged status of Babyl]on (and) [appointed Šamaš-šuma-ukīn], my favourite brother, [to the kingship of Babylon in order that the strong might not harm the weak. I *decorated* Esagila with silver, gold, (and)] precious stones [and made] Eumuša glisten [like the stars (lit. "writing") of the firmament].

19–22) At [that time, (with regard to) Ṭābi-supūršu, the (city) wall of Borsippa, which] had become [ol]d and (20) [buckled (and) collapsed, in order to] increase [the securi]ty of Ezida and the (other) sanctuaries of Borsippa, [with the strength of] my [labour] forces I had [Ṭā]bi-supūršu, [its] (city) wall, built [quickly] anew [with] the work of the god Kulla and refitted [its gates. I *had*] (new) doors *made* and hung (them) in its gateways.

23–26a) [O (you) futu]re [prince], during whose reign this work falls into disrepair, question skilled craftsmen! (Re)build [Ṭābi-s]upūršu, the (city) wall of Borsippa, according to its ancient specifications! (25) Look at [my royal inscription], anoint (it) with oil, offer a sacrifice, (and) place (my royal inscription) with your (own) royal inscription! The god Nabû will (then) [lis]ten [to you]r [prayers].

26b–28) (But) as for the one who des[troys] my inscribed name or the name of my favourite (brother) [by some crafty device], (or) does not place my royal inscription with his (own) royal inscription, [may the god Nabû, (...)], glare at him [angrily] and make his name (and) his descendant(s) disappear from the lands!

22 Possibly a form of the verb *banû*, "to build," before *urattâ*. In a similar position, B.6.32.1 line 22 has GIŠ.IG.MEŠ *ú-še-piš-ma ú-rat-ta-a*.

14

A stone stela bears an Akkadian inscription of Ashurbanipal recording his restoration of Ezida ("True House"), the temple of the god Nabû at Borsippa. On the front of the stela is a relief of the king carrying a basket on his head, thus depicting him aiding in the restoration of the temple personally. The object was found in the same room of the temple as a stela with a similar inscription of Šamaš-šuma-ukīn (B.6.33.3), which has a relief depicting that ruler with a basket on his head. Another stela of Ashurbanipal with a similar relief is B.6.32.2. The inscription was composed at some point before 652 BC.

COMMENTARY

The stela (BM 90865; 80-6-17,2) was found in the room southwest of room C2 in Ezida during excavations at Borsippa in 1880 under the general direction of H. Rassam. It was not found at Babylon as has sometimes been thought (e.g., Unger, AfK 2 [1924–25] p. 23 no. 11). The stela measures 39×15.5×13 cm. The inscription is for the most part in contemporary Babylonian script (with some Neo-Assyrian sign forms) and has been collated. Lines 1–49 are on the back of the stela and lines 50–81 on the side of the stela.

The friendly mention of Šamaš-šuma-ukīn (lines 30–32 and 46–48) indicates that the inscription must date before 652 BC. Edition T of Ashurbanipal's annals, which was composed in the eponymy of Nabû-šar-ahhēšu (646 or 645 BC), refers to the setting up of large silver bulls in the gate of Ezida at Borsippa and possibly to the restoration of that temple (Thompson, Esarh. pp. 30 and 32 and pls. 14–15 ii 1–6 and iii 15–17).

BIBLIOGRAPHY

1886 Bezold, Literatur pp. 113–14 §64.3.d and 347 (study)
1890–91 Evetts, PSBA 13 p. 158 (study)
1891 Strong, JRAS pp. 457–68 (copy in type, edition)
1892 Lehmann-Haupt, Šamaššumukîn 1 p. 25 and 2 pp. 59–61 and pls. XIII–XVI no. 6 (S[2]) (copy, study)
1904 Smith in Harper, Literature pp. 127–29 (translation)
1910 Delitzsch, AO 11/1 p. 36 fig. 17 (photo [inscription not visible])
1916 Streck, Asb. pp. XLIV–XLV and 240–45 no. 6 (S[2]) (edition)
1922 BM Guide p. 74 no. 301 (study)
1924–25 Unger, AfK 2 p. 23 no. 11 (study)
1926 Unger, RLV 4/2 pl. 267d (photo [inscription not visible])
1927 Luckenbill, ARAB 2 §§974–77 (translation)
1931 Unger, Babylon p. 225 no. 13 and pl. 37 fig. 57 (photo [inscription not visible], study)
1962 Potratz, Orientalia NS 31 p. 46 and pl. I fig. 2 (photo [inscription not visible])
1968 Ellis, Foundation Deposits pp. 24–25 and 179 no. 24 (partial edition, study)
1981 Reade in Fales, ARIN pl. II fig. 3 (photo [inscription not visible])
1982 Börker-Klähn, Bildstelen no. 225 (photo [inscription not visible], study)
1986 Reade, Iraq 48 p. 109 and pl. XIII (provenance)
1992 Frame, Babylonia p. 352 fig. 2 (photo [inscription not visible])

TEXT

1) *a-na-ku* ⌈AN⌉.ŠÁR-DÙ-A
2) [MA]N GAL MAN *dan-nu* MAN ŠÚ MAN KUR *aš-šur*
3) [M]AN *kib-rat* 4-*ti* LUGAL LUGAL.MEŠ
4) ⌈NUN⌉ *la šá-na-an šá ina a-mat* AN.ŠÁR ^{d}⌈UTU⌉
5) ⌈*ù*⌉ ^{d}AMAR.UTU *ul-tu tam-tim e-li*[*t*]
6) ⌈*a*⌉-*di* [(x)] *tam-tim šap-lit i-be-*⌈*lu-ma*⌉

1–23a) I, Ashurbanipal, great [kin]g, mighty king, king of the world, king of Assyria, king of the four quarters (of the world), king of kings, prince who has no rival, who at the command of the gods Aššur, Šamaš, (5) and Marduk rules from the Upper Sea to the Lower Sea and has subjugated all rulers, [who provi]des for Esagila, the palace of the gods — [who]se [doorbo]lt I made glisten like the stars (lit.

7) ⸢*gi*⸣*-mir ma-lik ú-šak-niš še-pu-uš-*⸢*šú*⸣
8) [*za-ni*]*n é-sag-íl* É.GAL DINGIR.MEŠ
9) [*šá ki*]*-ma ši-ṭir bu-ru-mu ú-nam-mir*
10) [S]I.[G]AR*-šú ù šá eš-re-e-ti ka-li-ši-na*
11) *ḫi-bil-ta-ši-na ú-šal-lim e-li kul-lat*
12) *ma-ḫa-zi ú-kin an-dul-lu*$_4$ *šá ep-še-e-tú-*[*šú*]
13) UGU *kal* DINGIR.MEŠ DÙG.GA UGU *ṣal-mat* SAG.DU
14) *du-šu-pat* SIPA*-us-su* DUMU ^{m}AN.ŠÁR-ŠEŠ-MU
15) MAN ŠÚ MAN KUR *aš-šur* GÌR.NÍTA KÁ.DINGIR.RA.KI
16) MAN KUR.EME.GI$_7$ *ù* URI.KI *mu-še-šib* TIN.TIR.KI
17) *e-piš é-sag-íl mu-ud-diš eš-re-e-ti*
18) *kul-lat ma-ḫa-zi šá ina qer-bi-ši-na*
19) *iš-tak-kan si-ma-te sat-tuk-ki-š*[*i-n*]*a*
20) [*ba*]*ṭ-lu-tú ú-ki-nu par-ṣi ki-du-d*[*e-e*]
21) [*k*]*i-ma la-bi-rim-ma ú-ter-ru a-n*[*a*]
22) *áš-ri-šu-un* DUMU DUMU ^{md}30-ŠEŠ.ME[Š]-S[U]
23) MAN ŠÚ MAN KUR *aš-šur a-na-ku-ma* EN GAL ^{d}AMAR.U[TU]
24) *šá ina* BALA*-e* LUGAL *maḫ-ri ina ma-ḫar*
25) AD *ba-ni-i-šú ú-ši-bu ina qé-reb*
26) [*b*]*al-til*.KI *ina u*$_4$*-me* BALA*-e-a ina ri-šá-a-*[*ti/te*]
27) ⸢*a*⸣*-na* TIN.TIR.KI *i-ru-um-ma sat-tuk-k*[*i*]
28) *é-sag-íl u* DINGIR.MEŠ TIN.TIR.KI *ú-kin*
29) *ki-din-nu-ti* KÁ.DINGIR.RA.KI *ak-ṣur*
30) *áš-šú dan-nu a-na* SIG *la ḫa-ba-li*
31) ^{md}GIŠ.NU$_{11}$-MU-GI.NA ŠEŠ *ta-lim*
32) *a-na* LUGAL*-ú-ti* TIN.TIR.KI *ap-qid*
33) *ina u*$_4$*-me-šú-ma* É.GAR$_8$ *é-zi-da*
34) *šá la-ba-riš il-lik-u-ma i-ni-*⸢*šú*⸣
35) *tim-me-en-šú ina* BALA*-e-a an-ḫu-us-*⸢*su*⸣
36) *lu-diš-ma ú-za-aq-qí-ir ḫur-sa-ni*[*š*]
37) *a-na šat-ti* ^{d}*na-bi-um* EN *ṣi-ru*
38) *ep-še-te-ia* MUNUS.SIG$_5$.MEŠ *ḫa-diš* IGI.BAR-*m*[*a*]
39) *ia-a-ti* ^{m}AN.ŠÁR-DÙ-A NUN *pa-liḫ-šú*
40) *a-mat da-mi-iq-ti-iá liš-šá-kin šap-tuš-šú*
41) TIN *u*$_4$*-me* SÙ.MEŠ *še-bé-e lit-tu-tu*
42) *ṭu-ub* UZU *ḫu-ud lìb-bi li-šim*
43) *ši-ma-ti* SUḪUŠ GIŠ.GU.ZA LUGAL*-u-ti-ia*
44) *ki-ma* KUR*-i li-šar-šid it-ti*
45) ⸢AN⸣*-e u* KI*-tim lu-kin* BALA*-u-a*
46) ⸢*ù*⸣ *šá* ^{md}GIŠ.NU$_{11}$-MU-GI.NA
47) [LUGAL] TIN.TIR.KI ŠEŠ *ta-lim-iá u*$_4$*-me-šú*
48) [*li*]*-ri-ku liš-bi bu-ʾ-a-ri*
49) [*ma-t*]*i-*⸢*ma*⸣ *ina aḫ-rat u*$_4$*-me* NUN EGI[R]-⸢*u*⸣
50) *šá ina u*$_4$*-me* BALA*-šú*
51) ⸢*ši*⸣*-pir šu-a-ti*
52) [*i*]*n-na-ḫu*
53) *an-ḫu-us-su*
54) ⸢*lu*⸣*-ud-diš ṣa-lam*
55) LUGAL*-ti-ia*
56) *li-mur-ma* Ì.GIŠ
57) ⸢*lip*⸣*-š*[*u-u*]*š* UDU.SISKUR

"writing") of the firmament — who repaired the damaged parts (10) of all their sanctuaries, (who) established (my) protection over all cult centres, the one who[se] deeds are pleasing to all the gods (and) whose shepherdship is sweet to the black-headed people; son of Esarhaddon, (15) king of the world, king of Assyria, viceroy of Babylon, king of the land of Sumer and Akkad, who (re)settled Babylon, (re)built Esagila, renovated the sanctuaries of all the cult centres, constantly established appropriate procedures in them, (and) (20) (re)confirmed [thei]r [inter]rupted regular offerings, (who) restored the rites and rituals according to the old pattern; grandson of Sennache[rib], king of the world, king of Assyria, I —

23b–32) During my reign, the great lord, the god Mard[uk], who during the reign of a previous king (25) had resided in Baltil (Aššur) in the presence of the father who created him, entered Babylon amidst rejoicing. I (re)confirmed the regular offerings for Esagila and the gods of Babylon. I (re-)established the privileged status of Babylon (and) (30) in order that the strong might not harm the weak I appointed Šamaš-šuma-ukīn, my favourite brother, to the kingship of Babylon.

33–36) At that time, (with regard to) the enclosure wall of Ezida ("True House") which had become old and whose foundation had become weak, during my reign I renovated its dilapidated sections and made (it) high as a mountain.

37–48) On account of this, may the god Nabû, the august lord, look upon my good deeds with pleasure and (40) may a good word for me — Ashurbanipal, prince who reveres him — be set upon his lips! May he determine as my fate a long life, fullness of old age, good health, and happiness! May he make the foundation of my royal throne as secure as a mountain! (45) May he make my reign as firm as heaven and netherworld! Moreover, with regard to Šamaš-šuma-ukīn, [king] of Babylon, my favourite brother, may his days be long and may he be fully satisfied with (his) good fortune!

49–62) [If at] any time in the future, during the days of the reign of some future prince, this work falls into disrepair, may (that prince) repair its dilapidated state! May he look at (55) my royal statue, anoint (it) with oil, offer a sacrifice, (and) place (my statue) with his (own) statue! The god Nabû will (then) listen to his prayers.

58) ⸢BAL-*qí it*⸣-*ti*
59) *ṣa*-⸢*lam-i*⸣-*šú*
60) *li*-⸢*iš*⸣-*kun*(*)
61) *ik-ri*-⸢*bi*⸣-*i-šú*
62) ᵈ⸢AG⸣ *i-šem-me*
63) *šá šu-*[*m*]*ì šaṭ-ru*
64) *i-p*[*a*]*-áš-ši-ṭu*
65) *ṣa-lam* ⸢LUGAL⸣-*ti-ia*
66) *i-ab-*[*b*]*a-tu*
67) ⸢*lu*⸣-*u a*-⸢*šar*⸣-*šú*
68) *ú*-⸢*nak*⸣-*ka-ru-ma*
69) *it-t*[*i*] *ṣa-lam-šú*
70) *la i-*[*š*]*ak-kan*
71) ᵈ*na-*[*b*]*i-um*
72) EN ⸢*šur*⸣-*bu-ú*
73) *ag-gi-iš*
74) *lik-kil-*[*m*]*e-šú-ma*
75) GIŠ.GU.ZA LU[G]AL-*ti-šú*
76) *li*-⸢*šá*⸣-*bal-kit-ma*
77) *li-ṭir be-lut-su*
78) [M]U-*šú* NUMUN-*šú ina* KUR.KUR
79) [*l*]*i-ḫal-liq-ma*
80) ⸢*a*⸣-*a ir-ši-šú*
81) *re-e-mu*

63–81) (But) as for the one who erases my inscribed name, (or) destroys my royal statue, or changes its position and (70) does not place (it) with his (own) statue, may the god Nabû, supreme lord, glare at him angrily, overthrow (75) his royal rule, and take away his sovereignty! May he (Nabû) make his name (and) his descendant(s) disappear from the lands and have no pity on him!

15

This inscription, written in Akkadian upon two partially preserved cylinders, describes the restoration of the ziqqurat (likely the temple on top of it) at Nippur by Ashurbanipal for the god Enlil. The restoration of the same structure is recorded on a brick inscription of Ashurbanipal (B.6.32.17).

CATALOGUE

Ex.	Museum number	Excavation number	Nippur provenance	Dimensions (cm)	Lines preserved	cpn
1	UM L-29-632+633+636 = PMA F29-6-387a+b+e		In debris covering pavement of Ashurbanipal near east corner of court of the ziqqurat	Length: 8.5; Dia. of left end: 5.2	1–6, 8–25	c
2	UM 55-21-384	3 NT 840	Sounding K 2, near virgin soil	7.5×4.7	4–15	c

COMMENTARY

Ex. 1 is on loan to the University Museum (Philadelphia) from the Philadelphia Museum of Art. The piece was found by the University of Pennsylvania expedition to Nippur at the turn of the century. It has "an unusual conical shape, rather like a cone with the tip cut off" (Gerardi, Studies Sjöberg p. 207). Ex. 2 was found by the Oriental Institute and the University Museum expedition to Nippur in 1951–52. It would originally have been of similar size and shape to ex. 1 (ibid.). Both exemplars are written in contemporary Babylonian script. The line arrangement follows ex. 1. The master line follows ex. 1, with help from ex. 2 for lines 6–8 and 15. The restoration at the end of line 2 follows B.6.15.2001 line 3.

Since the inscription does not mention Šamaš-šuma-ukīn and since Nippur was kept under direct Assyrian control after the rebellion of 652–648 BC (i.e., it was not placed under the authority of the new king of Babylonia Kandalānu), it is more likely that this inscription comes from the time after the beginning of the rebellion than before it. Only a few fragmentary Assyrian inscriptions give Ashurbanipal the title "king of the land of Sumer and Akkad," and this is the only Babylonian one (see Frame, Babylonia pp. 304–306). The attribution of this title to Ashurbanipal could suggest that the inscription dates to a time when there was no separate king of Babylonia, or at least none acknowledged by the scribes at Nippur. This could point to the time of the rebellion itself as the date of composition for the text, but one would not expect restoration work to have been carried out while the land was in turmoil.

BIBLIOGRAPHY

1903 Hilprecht, Explorations pp. 460–62 (ex. 1, provenance, photo, partial translation)

1904 Hilprecht, Excavations pp. 460–62 (ex. 1, provenance, photo, partial translation)

1916 Streck, Asb. pp. LXIV and 352–53 no. 4 (ex. 1, partial translation)

1927 Luckenbill, ARAB 2 §1019 (ex. 1, partial translation)

1989 Gerardi, Studies Sjöberg pp. 207–15 (exs. 1–2, copy, edition, study)

TEXT

1) *a-na* ^{d}*en-líl* LUGAL DINGIR.DINGIR ⸢EN⸣ AN-*e ù* KI-*tim* NUN x [...]
2) *pa-ri-is pu-ru-us-su-ú šá la in-nin-nu-*⸢*ú*⸣ [*qibīssu*(?)]
3) *a-šá-rid* ^{d}*í-gì-gì ma-am-lu*$_4$ ^{d}*a-nun-na-ki mu-ma-*[*ʾ-ir* ...]
4) *ta-mi-iḫ ṣer-ret gi-im-ri sa-ni-*[*iq mitḫurti*(?)]
5) EN KUR.KUR IGI.GÁL DINGIR.MEŠ *a-šib é-kur šá qé-re*[*b nippur* (*bēli rabî*) *bēlīšu*]
6) AN.ŠÁ[R]-D[Ù]-⸢IBILA⸣ [*šarru rabû* LUGA]L *dan-nu* LUGAL *ki*[*š-šat šar māt aššur*]
7) [... *šarru ša ina kullat*] KUR.KUR *ma-ḫi-r*[*u lā īšû*]
8) [*mār aššur-aḫa-iddin šarru rabû šarru d*]*an-nu* LUGAL *kiš-šat* LUGAL K[UR *aššur*]
9) [*mār mār*] ⸢^{d}⸣3[0]-⸢ŠEŠ.MEŠ-SU⸣ LUGAL GAL LUGAL *dan-nu* LUGAL *kiš-šat* LUGAL KUR *aš-šur*.KI-⸢*ma*⸣
10) ⸢LUGAL⸣ KUR.EME.<<UR>>.GI$_7$ *u* URI.KI GÌR.NÍTA AN.ŠÁR ^{d}*en-líl u* ^{d}*nin-urta*
11) *za-nin ma-ḫa-zi* E MA TAR DU DÙ *sì-ma-ak-ku*

1–5) For the god Enlil, king of the gods, lord of the heaven and netherworld, prince [...], one who renders decisions, who[se *order*] cannot be changed, foremost of the Igīgū gods, hero of the Anunnakū gods, who ru[les ...], one who holds the lead-rope of every(one), one who makes [*opposing forces*] agr[ee], lord of the lands, wisest of the gods, one who dwells in Ekur which is inside [Nippur, (the great lord), his lord]:
6–11) Ash[ur]b[ani]p[al, great king], mighty [kin]g, king of the wor[ld, king of Assyria, ... king who has no] equal [in all] the lands; [son of Esarhaddon, great king], mighty [king], king of the world, king [of Assyria; grandson of Sennacherib], (who was) also great king, mighty king, king of the world, king of Assyria; (10) king of the land of Sumer and Akkad, vice-regent for the gods Aššur, Enlil and Ninurta, one who provides for the cult centres, ... sanctuaries —

12) *a-na ba-laṭ* ZI-*šu ur-ruk u*$_4$*-me-šú šu-un-mur* SU-*šú šu-ul-lum* NUMUN-*šú*
13) *e-*⸢*li*⸣ *a-a-bi-šu ú-zu-uz-zu* BAL.MEŠ-*šú la-ba-ri* GIŠ.GIDRU-*šú šu-te-šu-ri*
14) EN-*us-s*[*u* UGU K]UR-*šú šu-ṭúb-bi* UN.MEŠ-*šú ina ṭuḫ-di u nu-uḫ-šú i-tar-ri-i*

12–14) In order to ensure his good health, to prolong his days, to make his appearance (lit. "body") radiant, to ensure the well-being of his offspring, so that he stand (victoriously) over his enemies, that his reign endure, that he lead (his people) aright with his staff, that his rule please his [land], (and) that he guide his people in abundant prosperity,

15) *é-gi-gu-nu-ú ziq-qur-rat* NIBRU.KI *šá ina i-rat* ZU.AB *šur-šu-du tim-me-en-šú*

15–19) (With regard to) Egigunû, the ziqqurat of Nippur, whose foundation is made secure on the

---

4 The epithet *sāniq mitḫurti* (if restored correctly) is not otherwise used for Enlil, though it is frequently applied to Nabû (see Tallqvist, Götterepitheta p. 149).

9 There is room at the beginning of the line to restore A A (as found in B.6.32.2 line 33), but probably not for DUMU DUMU (found in the other inscriptions of Ashurbanipal in similar circumstances).

11 As noted by Gerardi (Studies Sjöberg p. 210 n. 9), DÙ possibly for *bāni*, "builder" of the sanctuaries or *kal*, "all" of the sanctuaries.

15 Instead of taking *é-gi-gu-nu-ú* as a name, "Egigunû," one might translate "high temple." It is not certain that the *é* was pronounced (note George, House Most High p. 92 sub no. 373: ^{é}*gi-gu-nu-ú*). The word also appears in line 21 and note é-gi-gùn-n[a] in B.6.32.17 line 10 (Sumerian text).

16) *šá i-ga-ri-šú la-ba-ri*[*š i*]*l*-⸢*li*⸣-*ku-ma ib-ba-šu-ú si-ri-iḫ-šú*
17) *ina* SIG$_4$.AL.ÙR.RA UDUN KÙ-*tim ma-qit*-⸢*ta*⸣-*šú* ⸢*ak-šìr-ma*⸣ *ú-šak-lil bu-na-a-šú*
18) *ina ši-pir* ^{d}*kulla eš-šiš ú-še-piš-ma ú-nam-mir-šú ki-ma* u_4-*mu*
19) *re-ši-šu ki-ma šá-di-i ul-li-ma ú-šá-an-bi-iṭ zi*-⸢*mi*⸣-[*šú*]
20) *a-na šat-ti* ^{d}*en-líl* LUGAL DINGIR.MEŠ ^{d}*en-líl* DINGIR.MEŠ EN [*rabû*(?) (EN-*šú*)]
21) *é-gi-gu-nu-ú ṣa-ad-di ma-a-tim ḫa-diš ina nap-l*[*u-si-šú*]
22) *šá* AN.ŠÁR-DÙ-IBILA LUGAL KUR *aš-šur*.KI SIPA *ki-i-nu pa-liḫ* DINGIR-*u-ti-š*[*ú rabīti*(?)]
23) LUGAL-*us-su lik-tar-rab* BALA.MEŠ-*šú li-iṣ-ṣur ana* UD.ME[Š *rūqūti*]
24) GIŠ.GIDRU SIPA-*tú sa-ni-qat mit-ḫur-ti li-šat-m*[*i-iḫ-šú*(?)]
25) UGU KUR-*šú liš-ṭib re-é-ut-su* UGU *na-ki-r*[*i-šú lišziz*(?)]

breast of the Watery Abyss (*apsû*), whose enclosure wall had become old and *eroded*, I repaired its dilapidated section(s) with baked bricks from a (ritually) pure kiln, and completed its structure. I had it built anew with the work of the god Kulla and made it shine like daylight. I raised its top (as high) as a mountain and made [its] appearance resplendent.

20–25) On account of this, when the god Enlil, king of the gods, chief god of the gods, [*great*] lord, [(*his lord*)], loo[ks] upon Egigunû, the sign of the lands, with pleasure, may he (Enlil) constantly bless the kingship of Ashurbanipal — king of Assyria, true shepherd who reveres his [*great*] divinity — (and) keep his reign safe until [far-off] days! May he *cause* [*him to*] *gr*[*asp*] a staff of shepherdship which makes opposing forces agree! May he make his shepherdship pleasant to his land! [*May he make* (*him*) *stand* (*victoriously*)] over [his] enemy!

16

Numerous bricks bear a stamped Sumerian inscription which states that Ashurbanipal had (re)built the temple Ekur ("House, Mountain") for the god Enlil. Ekur was the temple of that god at Nippur.

CATALOGUE

Ex.	Museum number	Excavation number	Provenance	Dimensions (cm)	Lines preserved	cpn
1	BM 90807 (51-10-9,78R)	—	—	14×12×6	4–11	c
2	BM 114299 (1919-10-11,4743)	—	Nippur	28.5×19×7.5	1–11	c
3	Ash 1922.181	—	—	23×12.5×6.5	1–11	c
4	Ash 1924.627	—	Tal Laḥam	32×32×7	1–11	c
5	Bristol H 5097	—	—	16×11×7	1–6	n
6	CBS 1632a	—	Nippur	23×14.5×4.5	1–11	c
7	CBS 8632	—	Nippur III, inner wall of ziqqurat	30×29×7	1–11	c
8	CBS 8633	—	Nippur	18×12×5	1–11	c
9	CBS 8654	—	Nippur	30×30×8	1–11	c
10	UM 84-26-8	—	Nippur	32.5×28×8	1–11	c
11	UM 84-26-9	—	Nippur	30×28×7.5	1–11	c
12	UM 84-26-10	—	Nippur	29×29×8	1–11	c
13	UM 84-26-11, face	—	Nippur	28×14×7	1–11	c
14	UM 84-26-11, edge				1–11	c
15	EŞ number unknown	—	—	29×29.5×6.5	1–11	p
16	EŞ number unknown	—	—	15.5×30.5×7	1–11	p
17	EŞ number unknown	—	—	15.5×30.5×7	1–11	p
18	EŞ number unknown	—	—	29×29.5×7	1–11	p
19	EŞ number unknown	—	—	29×30×7.5	1–11	p

16 The meaning of the noun *sirḫu* in the phrase *ibbašû siriḫšu*, tentatively translated "*eroded*" (literally "its *sirḫu* has occurred"), is unclear. The word appears in only one other text; CAD 15 [S] p. 313 and AHw p. 1037 (s.v. *serḫu*) take it to mean "earthen wall(?)" and "Erosionsschutt" respectively.

17 Collation suggests that *ak-šìr* ("I repaired") is more likely than *ik-šìr* ("He repaired"). This results, however, in an awkward shift of person. The other verbs in lines 15–19 referring to Ashurbanipal can be in either the first person singular or the third person singular, while in the remainder of the text he is referred to in the third person.

Ex.	Museum number	Excavation number	Provenance	Dimensions (cm)	Lines preserved	cpn
20	EŞ number unknown	—	—	29×30×7.5	1–11	p
21	YBC 2372	—	—	19.1×11×3	1–11	c
22	R.F. Harper coll.	—	Nippur	—	1–11	n
23	—	5 NT 703	Nippur; entrance gate of Inanna temple, level I	—	—	(c)
24	HS 2981	—	Nippur	17.5×9×2.5	1–11	n
25	McGill Ethnological Collections ML 1.18	—	—	17.8×10.4	1–11	p

COMMENTARY

Ex. 1 was purchased by the British Museum from H.C. Rawlinson. Collations for it and ex. 2 were kindly supplied by C.B.F. Walker. Ex. 3 is from the H. Weld Blundell collection. In 1923–24, Langdon acquired a brick with this inscription (ex. 4) and was told that it came from "Tal Laḥam," which some located "a short distance north-east of Afaj, and some south-east of Duraihim." He suggested that the name had been distorted and stood for "Tal Dulaihim, eleven miles south-east of Afaj" (Kish 1 p. 108). Ex. 5 was presented to the Bristol museum by Sir Leonard Woolley. Hilprecht states that other bricks with this inscription were found in the same structure as ex. 7 (BE 1/1 p. 52). He also notes that Ashurbanipal's inscribed bricks were "sometimes green (originally blue) enamelled on the edges" (Hilprecht, Explorations p. 376). Some of the bricks found by him are likely to be identified with exs. 6 and 8–20. Photographs and measurements of exs. 15–20 were kindly supplied by H. Galter. A cast of ex. 23 in the Oriental Institute, Chicago, was examined.

The inscription is sometimes stamped on the face of the brick (e.g., exs. 1–5, 7, 9–10, and 16–17) and sometimes on the edge (e.g., exs. 11–12); one brick has the inscriptions in both places (exs. 13–14). In some cases it is uncertain where the inscription appears (e.g., if the piece is known only from a photograph or if the brick has been cut down in size in modern times). The stamped area measures 14.5–15.0×6.5–7.0 cm. The script is archaic. The last sign of line 10 (*-ta*) is placed at the very end of the line and as a result the final vertical wedge of the sign often appears either to be omitted because of a lack of space or to have been obscured by the edge of the stamp. No variants are attested and no score for this brick inscription is presented in the microfiche.

The writing of the ruler's name (line 4) is unusual and as a result the inscription was not assigned to Ashurbanipal by the first editors of the text. As noted by Streck (Asb. p. LXIV), this inscription was likely modelled upon one of Adad-šuma-uṣur (BE 1/1 no. 81, and duplicates). An inscription of Aššur-etel-ilāni (B.6.35.4) appears to have been modelled upon the same inscription of Adad-šuma-uṣur.

BIBLIOGRAPHY

1889–90 Pinches, Hebraica 6 pp. 55–58 (ex. 22, copy, edition)
1893 Hilprecht, BE 1/1 no. 82 and pp. 35–36 (ex. 7, copy, edition)
1893 Hilprecht, ZA 8 pp. 389–91 (study)
1903 Hilprecht, Explorations pp. 312, 371, 375, and 376 (provenance, translation)
1904 Hilprecht, Excavations pp. 312, 371, 375, and 376 (provenance, translation)
1916 Streck, Asb. pp. LXIII–LXIV and 352–53 no. 3.b (ex. 7, 22, edition)
1924 Langdon, Kish 1 pp. 108–109 (ex. 4, study)
1927 Luckenbill, ARAB 2 §1121 (ex. 7, 22, translation)
1981 Walker, CBI no. 80 (exs. 1–5, transliteration)
1985 Behrens, JCS 37 p. 239 no. 53 (exs. 6–14, study)
1988 Beckman, ARRIM 6 p. 2 (ex. 21, study)
1988 Oeslner in Šilwa, Cracow and Jena p. 19 (ex. 24 study)
1989 Frame, ARRIM 7 pp. 42 and 45 no. 40 (ex. 25, photo, study)
1992 Zettler, Inanna Temple p. 50 n. 42 (ex. 23, study)

TEXT

1) ^{d}en-líl-lá
2) lugal kur-kur-ra
3) lugal-a-ni-ir
4) AN.ŠÁR-*ba-an-ap-lu*
5) sipa še-ga-bi
6) lugal kala-ga
7) lugal ub-da límmu-ba
8) é-kur
9) é ki-ág-gá-a-ni
10) sig_4-al-ùr-ra-ta
11) mu-un-na-dù

1–11) For the god Enlil, lord of the lands, his lord: Ashurbanipal, (5) his obedient shepherd, mighty king, king of the four quarters (of the world), (re)built Ekur, his beloved temple, with baked bricks.

17

A brick from Nippur in the University Museum (CBS 8644) has a Sumerian inscription stating that Ashurbanipal rebuilt the high temple with baked bricks for the god Enlil. (The restoration of the same structure is recorded on a cylinder inscription of Ashurbanipal, B.6.32.15.) The brick measures 30×7.5×7.5 and is inscribed on the edge. The inscription has been collated.

BIBLIOGRAPHY

1926 Legrain, PBS 15 no. 74 (copy, edition)
1928 Poebel, OLZ 31 698 (study)
1985 Behrens, JCS 37 p. 240 no. 54 (study)
1993 George, House Most High p. 92 sub no. 373 (study to line 10)

TEXT

1) ^{d}en-líl-lá
2) lugal ⸢dingir-re⸣-e-ne-ke$_4$
3) nir-gál an-ki-a
4) nun nam-tar-tar-ra
5) lugal-a-ni-ir
6) AN.ŠÁR-*ba-an*-IBILA
7) sipa še-ga-bi
8) lugal kala-ga
9) lugal ki-šár(?)-ra(?) x
10) é-gi-gùn-n[a]
11) sig$_4$-al-ùr-ra
12) mu-un-na-dù

1–12) For the god Enlil, king of the gods, sovereign of heaven (and) netherworld, prince (who decides) the fates, (5) his lord: Ashurbanipal, his obedient shepherd, mighty king, king *of the world*, (re)built Egigunû with baked bricks.

18

Two bricks are inscribed with a Sumerian text stating that Ashurbanipal built something within the sanctuary Eḫursaggalama at Nippur for the god Enlil. Both bricks were intended to be used in a well.

CATALOGUE

Ex.	Museum number	Excavation number	Provenance	Dimensions (cm)	Lines preserved	cpn
1	UM 84-26-12	—	—	36/20×23.5×7.5	1–16	c
2	—	18 N unregistered	Nippur, WC-2, in the lining of the mouth of a well in a courtyard of Building C	—	—	n

9 The reading ki-šár(?)-ra(?), "*world*," is based upon B.6.32.18 line 9; except for the sections dealing with the structures being rebuilt and the writing of the royal name, the two texts are duplicates. The signs, however, seem to be closer to ki-ub-da(?), thus possibly "king of the *four quarters* (of the world)."

COMMENTARY

Ex. 1 is a "well-head" brick located among the University Museum's collection of bricks from Nippur and Ur. In view of its inscription, it probably comes from the former site. The inscription is found on the outer edge of the brick and is written in archaic script. Information on ex. 2 comes from J.A. Armstrong and R.D. Biggs. The precise provenance of this brick is described in Armstrong's unpublished doctoral dissertation "The Archaeology of Nippur from the Decline of the Kassite Kingdom until the Rise of the Neo-Babylonian Empire" (University of Chicago, 1989) p. 42, where it is described as an "Ashurbanipal Ekur brick." The edition presented below comes from ex. 1.

Line 10 should record the name of the structure being restored, but the identification of the final sign(s) is not certain. Ex. 1 has: A- Ex. 2 appears to have A-NE.UD.

Eḫursaggalama was the cella of the god Enlil on the ziqqurat at Nippur; see George, House Most High pp. 100–101 no. 480. The name means "House, Skilfully Built Mountain" (ibid.) or "House, Stepped/Storied Mountain" (see Sjöberg, Temple Hymns p. 50 and the references cited there).

BIBLIOGRAPHY

1985 Behrens, JCS 37 p. 240 no. 55 (ex. 1, study)
1986 Gerardi, ARRIM 4 p. 37 (ex. 1, copy, edition)

TEXT

1) ^{d}en-líl-lá
2) lugal dingir-re-e-ne-ke$_{4}$
3) nir-gál an-ki-a
4) nun nam-tar-tar-ra
5) lugal-a-ni-ir
6) AN.ŠÁR-DÙ-IBILA
7) sipa še-ga-bi
8) lugal kala-ga
9) lugal ki-šár-ra
10) A-x
11) šà é-ḫur-sag-galam-ma-ke$_{4}$
12) pa-pa-ḫi nam-lugal-a-ni
13) libir-ra-bi-ta(*)
14) galam-bi
15) sig$_{4}$-al-ùr-ra
16) mu-un-na-dù

1–16) For the god Enlil, king of the gods, sovereign of heaven (and) netherworld, prince (who decides) the fates, (5) his lord: Ashurbanipal, his obedient shepherd, mighty king, king of the world, skilfully (re)built (10) with baked bricks ... within Eḫursaggalama, his ancient royal cella.

19

A few clay cylinders have been found which bear an Akkadian inscription recording Ashurbanipal's restoration of the Eanna temple ("House of Heaven") at Uruk for the goddess Ištar-of-Uruk. The inscription comes from the first half of the king's reign (before the outbreak of hostilities with his brother Šamaš-šuma-ukīn in 652 BC).

---

13 *ta*(*): final vertical wedge omitted. Ex. 2 appears to have ⌜gin$_{7}$⌝, "his royal cella, as (it had been) of old" instead of "his ancient royal cella" (information courtesy R.D. Biggs).

CATALOGUE

Ex.	Museum/excavation number	Warka photo number	Warka provenance	Dimensions (cm)	Lines preserved	cpn
1	YBC 2180	—	—	20.4×9.4	1–32	c
2	UCLM 9-1793 (formerly UCBC 1206)	—	—	20.2×9.5; dia. of end: 5.5	1–32	c
3	NBC 2507 +? W 4444	828 (W 4444)	NE of building J in Qc XVI 5 (W 4444)	6.5×7 (NBC 2507)	24–32	c; p
4	W 20942 (Heidelberg)	10191–10192	Surface in the area of the archive ("im Archivgelände")	—	1–3, 20–32	p

COMMENTARY

Ex. 2 was purchased for the University of California at Berkeley in 1930 by H.F. Lutz. The copy of the piece published by Lutz is defective at a number of places. In addition to numerous simple errors by the modern copyist (e.g., *ša* for *kin*, *su* for *šu*, and *ta* for *ṭa* in line 10 [lines 10–11 of the exemplar]; omission of *-šú* after ŠÈG.MEŠ in line 11; omission of *si* in line 22 [line 23]; *gu* for *kám* in line 23 [line 24]; and addition of an *u* after UZU in line 26 [27]), the copy has *iš-tu* for ⌈*e-li*⌉ in line 9; for the start of line 28 (line 29 of the exemplar) the copy has *ina aḫ-rat* u_4*-me um-ma*, while the piece simply has ⌈*a-a*⌉*-um-ma*. As is the normal procedure in the RIM volumes, a transliteration of the piece is found in the score but such errors of the modern copyist are not specifically noted. Some additional collations for this exemplar were kindly provided by D.A. Foxvog. With regard to ex. 3, it is uncertain if W 4444 joins NBC 2507 or not, but the two are tentatively kept together here. NBC 2507 has been collated from the original and W 4444 from a photo (on which line 24 is not legible owing to the curvature of the piece). Ex. 4 was found during the 21st season of excavations at Uruk (1962–63). The script of all four exemplars is contemporary Babylonian. The line arrangement follows ex. 1; ex. 2 has the inscription on 33 lines. The master line follows ex. 1, with help from ex. 2 for lines 1–5.

According to Koldewey (WEB^{4} p. 164), a piece of a cylinder describing Ashurbanipal's work on Eanna was found at Babylon. Its inscription may be this one, but this cannot be determined since neither the excavation number nor the present location of the piece mentioned by Koldewey is known. With regard to this piece, see also Unger, AfK 2 (1924–25) p. 24, and Unger, Babylon p. 225 no. 15.

The mention of Ashurbanipal's appointment of his brother Šamaš-šuma-ukīn to the kingship of Babylon in a positive manner (lines 18–19) and the inclusion of his brother in the invocation to the goddess (line 27) indicate that the inscription must date before the commencement of the latter's rebellion in 652 BC.

BIBLIOGRAPHY

1915 Clay, YOS 1 no. 42 (ex. 1, copy)
1917–18 Ungnad, ZA 31 pp. 33–37 (ex. 1, edition)
1920 Keiser, BIN 2 no. 35 (ex. 3 [NBC 2507], copy)
1927 Luckenbill, ARAB 2 §§968–73 (ex. 1, translation)
1930 Schott, UVB 1 p. 60 and pl. 29 no. 25 (ex. 3 [W 4444], copy, edition)
1931 Lutz, UCP 9/8 pp. 385–90 and pls. 7–8 (ex. 2, photo, copy, edition)
1932 Bauer, OLZ 35 254–55 (ex. 2, study)
1932–33 Meissner, AfO 8 p. 51 (exs. 1–2, study)
1933 Bauer, Asb. 2 p. 48 (exs. 1–2, study)
1957 Borger, Orientalia NS 26 p. 2 (ex. 3, study)
1969 Oppenheim, ANET^{3} p. 297 (ex. 1–2, partial translation)
1970 Berger, ZA 60 pp. 128–29 (ex. 3, study)
1978 Foxvog, RA 72 p. 43 (ex. 2, study)
1982 Kessler, Bagh. Mitt. 13 pp. 14–15 no. 11 (ex. 4, copy, transliteration)

TEXT

1) ⌈*a*⌉*-na* ⌈^{d}INANNA⌉ UNUG.KI *e-tel-lat* AN*-e u* KI*-tim ga-šir-ti* DINGIR.MEŠ *ṣi-ir-ti*

2) ⌈*šá*⌉ *ina ṣi-tan u ši-la-an ur-tu ta-nam-di-nu ta-šak-kan ši-*⌈*ki-in-šá*⌉

3) *i-lat tam-ḫa-ri ez-zi-ti šá ina qé-reb te-še-e a-šam-šá-niš i-su-ur-ru*

4) *a-li-kát i-di* LUGAL *mi-gir-i-šá mu-ra-si-*⌈*bat*⌉ *ga-re-e-šú*

5) *be-let* KUR.KUR *ḫa-mi-mat par-ṣi muš-te-ši-rat gi-mir šu-luḫ-ḫu*

1–6) For the goddess Ištar-of-Uruk, sovereign of heaven and netherworld, most powerful of the gods, august one, who *executes* the command she gives in the east and in the west, the fierce goddess of battle who whirls around in the melee like a dust storm, who goes at the side of the king, her favourite, (and) slays his foes, (5) mistress of the lands, who has gathered to herself (all) divine offices (and) administers correctly all purification rites, who dwells in Enirgalanim — which is inside Eanna —

6) *a-ši-bat é-nir-gál-*^{d}*a-nim šá qé-reb é-an-na be-el-ti* GAL-*ti* GAŠAN-*šú*

7) ^{m}AN.ŠÁR-DÙ-A LUGAL GAL LUGAL *dan-nu* LUGAL ŠÚ LUGAL KUR *aš-šur* LUGAL *kib-rat* 4-*ti* LUGAL LUGAL.MEŠ NUN *la šá-na-an*

8) *šá ul-tu tam-tim e-lit a-di tam-tim šap-lit i-bé-lu-ma gi-mir ma-lik ú-šak-niš še-pu-uš-šú*

9) *šá e-li* URU *ṣur-ru šá qa-bal tam-tim e-lit u* NI.TUK.KI *šá qa-bal tam-tim šap-lit*

10) *ni-ri be-lu-ti-šú ú-kin-nu-ú-ma i-šu-ṭu ab-šá-an-šú šá ep-še-tu-ú-šú e-li kal* DINGIR.MEŠ *ṭa-a-ba*

11) *e-li ṣal-mat* SAG.DU *du-uš-šu-pa-tu* SIPA-*ú-su šá ina* BALA-*šú* ^{d}IŠKUR ŠÈG.MEŠ-*šú* ^{d}*é-a nag-bi-šú*

12) *a-na ma-ti-šú uš-tab-ru-ú ina ṭuḫ-du u meš-re-e iš-te-ni-ʾ-ú* UN.MEŠ-*šú*

13) *gi-mir um-ma-ni-šú ṭuḫ-ḫu-du i-ru-uš-šú da-ád-me-šú* DUMU ^{m}AN.ŠÁR-ŠEŠ-SUM.NA LUGAL GAL LUGAL *dan-nu*

14) LUGAL ŠÚ LUGAL KUR *aš-šur* GÌR.NÍTA TIN.TIR.KI LUGAL KUR.EME.GI$_{7}$ *u* URI.KI *mu-še-šib* TIN.TIR.KI *e-piš é-sag-íl*

15) *mu-ud-diš eš-re-e-te kul-lat ma-ḫa-zi šá ina qer-bi-ši-na iš-tak-ka-nu si-ma-a-ti*

16) DUMU DUMU ^{md}30-ŠEŠ.MEŠ-SU LUGAL GAL LUGAL *dan-nu* LUGAL ŠÚ LUGAL KUR *aš-šur-ma ina* BALA-*e-a* EN GAL ^{d}AMAR.UTU

17) *ina ri-šá-a-ti a-na* TIN.TIR.KI ⸢*i*⸣-*r*[*u-um-ma*] *sat-tuk-ku é-sag-íl u* DINGIR.MEŠ TIN.TIR.KI *ú-kin*

18) *ki-din-nu-tu* TIN.TIR.KI *ak-ṣur áš-šú dan-nu a-na* SIG *la ḫa-ba-lu* ^{md}GIŠ.NU$_{11}$-MU-GI.NA

19) ŠEŠ *ta-li-mì a-na* LUGAL-*ú-t*[*u*] KÁ.DINGIR.RA.KI *ap-qid u ši-pir é-sag-íl la qa-ta-*[*a*]

20) *ú-šak-lil ina* KÙ.BABBAR KÙ.GI *u ni-siq-ti* NA$_{4}$.MEŠ *é-sag-íl az-nun-ma ki-ma š*[*i-ṭir burūmû*]

21) *ú-nam-mir é-umuš-a ù šá eš-re-e-te ka-li-ši-na hi-bil-ta-ši-na ú-šal-lim*

22) *e-li kul-lat* ⸢*ma-ḫa-zi*⸣ *ú-šat-ri-ṣi an-dul-lu*$_{4}$ *ina u*$_{4}$*-me-šú-ma* É.GAR$_{8}$ *é-a*[*n*(?)-*n*]*a*(?) *si-ḫir-ti* [...]

23) *šá la-ba-riš il-lik-u-ma i-qu-pu ik-kám-ru áš-ra-ti-šú-nu áš-te-ʾ-*[*ma eššiš ušēpišma*]

24) [*ú-š*]*ak-lil-ma ki-ma šá-di-i ul-la-a re-ši-šu-un a-na šat-ti* ⸢^{d}INANNA⸣ UNUG.KI GAŠAN GAL-[*ti*]

25) [*š*]*i-pir šá-a-šú ḫa-diš lip-pa-lis-ma ia-a-ti* ^{m}AN.ŠÁR-DÙ-A LUGAL KUR *aš-šur* NUN *pa-liḫ-šú a-mat da-m*[*i-iq-ti-ia*]

great lady, his lady:

7–16a) Ashurbanipal, great king, mighty king, king of the world, king of Assyria, king of the four quarters (of the world), king of kings, prince who has no rival, who rules from the Upper Sea to the Lower Sea and has subjugated all rulers; who imposed the yoke of his rulership upon the city Tyre — which is in the midst of the Upper Sea — and Dilmun — which is in the midst of the Lower Sea — (10) so that they bore his yoke (lit. "pulled his yoke-rope"); whose deeds are pleasing to all the gods (and) whose shepherdship is sweet to the black-headed people; during whose reign the god Adad made his rain (and) the god Ea his springs last a long time for his land, (who) continually seeks after his people with prosperity and wealth, whose people are all in a state of prosperity, and whose settlements rejoice; son of Esarhaddon, great king, mighty king, king of the world, king of Assyria, viceroy of Babylon, king of the land of Sumer and Akkad, who (re)settled Babylon, (re)built Esagila, (15) renovated the sanctuaries of all the cult centres, and constantly established appropriate procedures in them; grandson of Sennacherib, (who was) also great king, mighty king, king of the world, (and) king of Assyria —

16b–22a) During my reign, the great lord, the god Marduk, [entered] Babylon amidst rejoicing. I (re)confirmed the regular offerings for Esagila and the gods of Babylon. I (re-)established the privileged status of Babylon (and) appointed Šamaš-šuma-ukīn, my favourite brother, to the kingship of Babylon in order that the strong might not harm the weak. I completed the work on Esagila which had not been finished. (20) I *decorated* Esagila with silver, gold, and precious stones and made Eumuša glisten like the [stars (lit. "writing") of the firmament]. I repaired the damaged parts of all their sanctuaries (and) extended (my) protection over all cult centres.

22b–24a) At that time, (with regard to) the enclosure wall of *Ea*[*nn*]*a*, the perimeter [...] which had become old, buckled, (and) a heap of ruin, I sought their (original) emplacement [and had (them) (re)built anew. I] completed (them), raising their tops (as high) as a mountain.

24b–27) On account of this, may the goddess Ištar-of-Uruk, the great lady, look upon this work with pleasure and may a go[od] word for me — Ashurbanipal, king of Assyria (and) prince who reveres her — be set upon her lips! [May she determine as my fate] a long life, fullness of old

6 *é-nir-gál-*^{d}*a-nim* is to be identified with *é-nir-gál-an-na*, "House, Prince of Heaven," which was restored by Esarhaddon (B.6.31.16).

22 *é-a*[*n*(?)-*n*]*a*(?) only found on ex. 2 which has: *é-* (collation D.A. Foxvog).

26) *liš-šá-kin šap-tu-uš-šá* TI UD.MEŠ SÙ.MEŠ *še-bé-e lit-tu-tu ṭu-ub* UZU *ḫu-*⌈*ud*⌉ [*lìbbi lišīm šīmāti*]
27) *ù šá* ^{md}GIŠ.NU$_{11}$-MU-GI.NA LUGAL KÁ.DINGIR.RA.KI ŠEŠ *ta-lim-ia* UD.MEŠ-*šú li-ri-ku liš-*[*bi buʾāri*]

age, good health, (and) happ[iness]! Moreover, with regard to Šamaš-šuma-ukīn, king of Babylon, my favourite brother, may his days be long (and) may he be fully [satisfied with (his) good fortune]!

28) ⌈*a*⌉*-a-um-ma* NUN EGIR-*ú šá ina u*$_4$*-me* BALA-*e-šú ši-pir šu-a-ti in-na-ḫu an-ḫu-us-*⌈*su*⌉ [*luddiš*]
29) ⌈*šu-mì*⌉ *it-ti* MU-*šú liš-ṭur* MU.SAR-*u-a li-mur-ma* Ì.GIŠ *lip-šu-uš* ⌈UDU.SISKUR⌉ BAL-*qí*

28–30a) May any future prince, during the days of whose reign this work falls into disrepair, [renovate its] dilapidated sections! May he write my name with his (own) name, look at my royal inscription, anoint (it) with oil, offer a sacrifice, (and) place (my royal inscription) with his (own) royal inscription! The goddess Ištar-of-Uruk will (then) listen to his prayers.

30) ⌈*it*⌉*-ti* MU.SAR-*e-šú liš-kun ik-ri-bi-šú* ^{d}INANNA UNUG.KI *i-šem-me šá šu-mì it-ti* MU-*šú la i-šaṭ-ṭa-ru*
31) MU.SAR-*u-a i-a-ab-ba-tu lu-u a-šar-šú ú-nak-ka-ru-ma it-ti* MU.SAR-*e-šú la i-šak-ka-nu*
32) ^{d}INANNA UNUG.KI GAŠAN GAL-*ti ag-giš lik-kil-me-šú-ma* MU-*šú* NUMUN-*šú ina* KUR.KUR *li-ḫal-liq-ma a-a ir-ši-šú re-e-mu*

30b–32) (But) as for the one who does not write my name with his name, (or) destroys my royal inscription, or changes its position and does not place (it) with his (own) royal inscription, may the goddess Ištar-of-Uruk, great lady, glare at him angrily, make his name (and) his descendant(s) disappear from the lands, and have no pity on him!

20

A cylinder fragment in the British Museum has an Akkadian inscription which refers to the temple of the goddess Ištar and to the goddess Ištar-of-Akkad. The name of the king is not preserved and the inscription is assigned to Ashurbanipal because the wording is similar to that found in other texts of that king.

COMMENTARY

The fragment (81-2-4,174) is part of the Kuyunjik collection of the British Museum. It thus probably comes from that site, although some pieces from other places (e.g., Borsippa) have been mistakenly placed in that collection. It measures 8.2×7.5 cm and is shown on British Museum photograph 230549. The inscription is in contemporary Babylonian script and has been edited from the original.

The wording of the inscription is similar to that found on several other clay cylinder inscriptions of Ashurbanipal from Babylonia, in particular his text recording work on the city wall of Babylon (B.6.32.1 lines 23–28; see also B.6.32.12 lines 23–28 and B.6.32.13 lines 23–27), although the placement of some phrases is different in 81-2-4,174. Streck (Asb. pp. XLI–XLII) included this fragment among his exemplars for the inscription of Ashurbanipal describing the restoration of the Ebabbar temple at Sippar (B.6.32.12), but it is clear that he had not actually seen the piece and that he placed it there because of a comment by Winckler (OLZ 1 [1898] 76).

Since the name of the deity whose temple was built or restored is normally the deity mentioned in the curse formula, it is likely that it was a temple of the goddess Ištar-of-Akkad which was of concern in the text. Nabonidus records that Ashurbanipal had carried out work on Eulmaš, the temple of Ištar-of-Akkad at Akkad (King, CT 34 pls. 30–31 ii 37–45), thus this fragment may well describe the restoration of that temple. (For the history of the Eulmaš temple at Akkad, see Frame, Mesopotamia 28 [1993] pp. 21–50.) However, there was also a temple of Ištar-of-Akkad at Babylon — the temple Emašdari — and in view of Ashurbanipal's other work at that city, it is perhaps more likely that this inscription refers to that temple.

BIBLIOGRAPHY

1896 Bezold, Cat. 4 p. 1768 (study)
1993 Frame, Mesopotamia 28 pp. 45–48 (copy, edition, study)

TEXT

Lacuna
1′) [*ši-pi*]*r*(?) ⸢*šu-a*⸣-*ti* ⸢*in*⸣-*n*[*a-ḫu* ...]
2′) *en-qu-ú-tu ši-ta-a*[*l* ...]
3′) ⸢É d15⸣ *ki-i si-m*[*a-ti-šu*(?) ...]
4′) *i*-⸢*šem*⸣-*me* MU.SAR-⸢*ú*(?)⸣-[*a* ...]
5′) *it-ti* MU.⸢SAR⸣-*e-ka š*[*u-kun* ...]
6′) *it-ti* MU-*šú la i-šaṭ-ṭa-r*[*u* ...]
7′) ⸢*la i-šak-ka-nu qí*(?)-*bit*(?)⸣ x [...]
8′) dINANNA *a-ga-d*[*è*.(KI) ...]

Lacuna
1′–5a′) this [*work*] falls into dis[repair ...], question skilled [craftsmen! ... Rebuild (...)], the temple of the goddess Ištar according to [*its* ancient] specifi[cations! ... *The goddess Ištar-*(*of-Akkad*)] will (then) listen to [your prayers. Look at my] royal inscription, [anoint (it) with oil, offer a sacrifice, (and)] s[et] (my royal inscription) with your (own) royal inscription!
5b′–8′) [(But) as for the one who erases my inscribed name by some crafty device], (or) does not write [my name] with his name, (or) [destroys my royal inscription], (or) does not set [my royal inscription with his (own) royal inscription] ... [...] the goddess Ištar-of-Akkad [will ...]

21

An inscribed brick found in the ziqqurat at Dūr-Kurigalzu bears an Akkadian inscription of Ashurbanipal which may mention the god Enlil.

COMMENTARY

The brick was found at Aqar Quf, built into the southwest façade of the ziqqurat, which is reported not to have been its original position. That part of the ziqqurat was excavated by Iraqi archaeologists in 1968–69. No excavation or museum number is known and the inscription is edited from the published photograph. The text is inscribed (not stamped) in contemporary Babylonian script.

The reading of the divine name in line 1 is uncertain, but is supported by the fact that most royal inscriptions from Dūr-Kurigalzu were dedicated to the god Enlil.

BIBLIOGRAPHY

1971 Al-Jumaily, Sumer 27 pp. 84 and 89, and pl. 14 fig. 30 following p. 98 [Arabic section] (provenance, photo)
1992 Frame, Babylonia p. 113 n. 60 (partial transliteration, study)

TEXT

1) ⸢*a*(?)-*na*(?) d*en*(?)-*líl*(?)⸣ [(...) *bēlīšu*(?)]
2) mAN.ŠÁR(?)-DÙ-A MAN ŠÚ MAN KU[R *aššur* (...)]
3) MAN *kib-r*[*at*] 4-⸢*tim*(?)⸣ [(...)]
4) *a-na* TI-*šú ú-še-*⸢*piš*(?)⸣ [(...)]

1–4) *For the god Enlil*, [(...) *his lord*]: Ashurbanipal, king of the world, king of [Assyria, (...)] king of the four quarters (of the world), had (this) [(...)] *built* for the sake of his life.

22

A large number of bricks found in a temple dedicated to the god Nergal, "lord of Sirara," at Tell Ḥaddād (ancient Mê-Turran/Mê-Turnat) bear an Akkadian inscription of Ashurbanipal which describes how the king enlarged the courtyard of the temple Ešaḫula ("House of the Happy Heart").

COMMENTARY

The bricks were found in the pavement of the temple in 1980 and are said to measure 40×40×8 cm. The texts are inscribed, not stamped, and the script is contemporary Babylonian. No excavation or museum numbers are known for any of the exemplars. According to Rashid, the numerous exemplars of the inscription differ from one another with regard to the particular signs used and with regard to the length of the titles accorded to the god. Copies and editions of two of the exemplars were published by him. These two bricks have not been seen, neither in the original nor in photograph, and are edited from the published copies.

The edition presented below follows ex. 1. Since the first two lines of ex. 2 diverge substantially from ex. 1, they are presented separately here:

1) *a-na* ^{d}U.GUR *dan-dan-nu*(*) DINGIR.[ME]Š *šur-*⸢*bu*⸣*-ú* ⸢*kaš*⸣-[*kaš* (DINGIR.MEŠ)]
2) *a-šib é-šà-ḫúl*(*)*-la* EN *si-ra-ra*.KI ...
1–2) For the god Nergal, mightiest of the gods, the supreme, most over[powering (of the gods)], the one who dwells in (the temple) Ešaḫula, the lord of Sirara,

Both exemplars are presented in full in the score, without any master line.

BIBLIOGRAPHY

1981 F. Rashid, Sumer 37 pp. 72–80 [Arabic section] (exs. 1–2, copy, edition, study)

1982 Hannoun, BSMS 2 p. 6 (study)

TEXT

1) *a-na* ^{d}U.GUR *dan-dan-nu*(*) DINGIR.MEŠ *kaš-kaš* DINGIR.MEŠ *šur-bu-ú gít-ma-la*
2) *mut-tal-la e-tel-lu* ŠEŠ*-šú a-šib é-šà-ḫúl*(*)*-la* EN *si-ra-ra*.KI
3) EN*-šú* ^{m}AN.ŠÁR-DÙ-IBILA MAN GAL MAN *dan-nu*(*) MAN ŠÚ MAN KUR *aš-šur*.KI
4) DUMU ^{m}AN.ŠÁR-ŠEŠ-SUM.NA MAN GAL MAN *dan-nu*(*) MAN ŠÚ MAN KUR *aš-šur*.KI
5) MAN TIN.TIR.KI MAN KUR *šu-me-ri ù* URI.KI
6) DUMU DUMU ^{md}30-ŠEŠ.MEŠ-SU MAN GAL MAN *dan-nu*(*) MAN ŠÚ
7) MAN KUR *aš-šur*.KI*-ma ana* TIN ZI.MEŠ*-šú*
8) *i-na a-gur-ru* UDUN KÙ(*)*-tim ki-sal-li*
9) *é-šà-ḫúl*(*)*-la ú-ra-bi-i-ma*
10) *tal-lak-ta-šú ki-ma* u_4*-me ú-nam-mir*

1–3a) For the god Nergal, mightiest of the gods, most overpowering of the gods, the supreme, perfect, (and) noble sovereign of his brother(s), the one who dwells in (the temple) Ešaḫula, the lord of Sirara, his lord:

3b–7a) Ashurbanipal, great king, mighty king, king of the world, king of Assyria; son of Esarhaddon, great king, mighty king, king of the world, king of Assyria, (5) king of Babylon, king of the land of Sumer and Akkad; grandson of Sennacherib, great king, mighty king, king of the world, king of Assyria —

7b–10) In order to ensure his good health, he enlarged the courtyard of (the temple) Ešaḫula with baked bricks from a (ritually) pure kiln and made its processional way shine like daylight.

23

A fragmentary tablet in the University Museum (Philadelphia) preserves copies of two dedicatory texts written in the Akkadian language. The first, much shorter inscription on the tablet only mentions Ashurbanipal in as far as it is preserved; it is edited here. The second, longer one mentions both Šamaš-šuma-ukīn and Ashurbanipal and is edited with the inscriptions of Šamaš-šuma-ukīn (B.6.33.5); however, it is not inconceivable that that inscription should also be assigned to Ashurbanipal.

COMMENTARY

The tablet is composed of two fragments (CBS 733 + 1757) which were joined by W.G. Lambert. It measures 9.3×5.7×2.7 cm. The inscription is written in contemporary Babylonian script and is separated from B.6.33.5 by a line ruling. The inscription has been collated.

It is uncertain with what object or structure the inscription was concerned. The name of the temple Esagila is found in line 2′ and the second inscription on the tablet likely deals with a piece of equipment for the sacred boat of the god Nabû at Borsippa. As Lambert points out, in view of these facts and the appearance of the phrase "that light" in line 3, it is possible that the inscription "commemorates the giving of a lamp or lampstand to Marduk or Nabû" (AfO 18 [1957–58] p. 386).

BIBLIOGRAPHY

1908 Clay, BE 8/1 no. 142 (copy of CBS 733)
1909 Ungnad, ZA 22 pp. 13–16 (edition of CBS 733)
1957–58 Lambert, AfO 18 pp. 385–86 and pl. XXV (copy, edition)

TEXT

1) [x (x)] x x x x [...]
2) [(x)] x *qé-reb é-sag-í*[*l* ...]
3) ⌈*e*⌉*-nu-ma nu-ú-ru šu-a-t*[*i* ...]
4) [M]UNUS.SIG$_5$ *-tim* AN.ŠÁR-DÙ-A LUGAL KUR.[KUR(?) ...]
5) *u*$_4$*-mi-šam lit-ta*[*s*]-x x x [(...)]

1–5) ... [...] in Esagi[la ...]. When that light [...] the good of Ashurbanipal, king of the land[s ...]. Let him daily ... [(...)].

2001

Sîn-balāssu-iqbi, a governor of Ur for at least part of the time Ashurbanipal and Šamaš-šuma-ukīn were on the thrones of Assyria and Babylonia respectively, has left several inscriptions which record the construction or restoration of various structures at that city (B.6.32.2001–2016). None of these mention Šamaš-šuma-ukīn, but three refer to Ashurbanipal (B.6.32.2003–2004 and 2015). Thus the inscriptions of this important Babylonian governor have been placed with those of Ashurbanipal instead of Šamaš-šuma-ukīn. Sîn-balāssu-iqbi was preceded in office by his father Ningal-iddin, who held that position in the time of Esarhaddon and undoubtedly already in the time of Sennacherib. Two Babylonian economic texts composed in 658 and 657 BC refer to Sîn-balāssu-iqbi as governor, but he may have already taken office in the reign of Esarhaddon. He was succeeded by two of his brothers, Sîn-šarra-uṣur (see B.6.33.2001) and Sîn-tabni-uṣur, the latter of whom is known to have held office in at least 650 and 649 BC. (See Frame, Babylonia pp. 278–79.)

A stone door socket from Ur has a Sumerian inscription of Sîn-balāssu-iqbi which is dedicated to the god Sîn, the patron deity of Ur, and which records the governor's restoration of Etemennigurru ("House, Foundation Clad in Awe-Inspiring Radiance") and in particular the construction of a new door for that structure.

COMMENTARY

The door socket (BM 119065, 1927-10-3,60) was found during C.L. Woolley's excavations at Ur in 1924–25. It was discovered in situ in a brick-lined cavity against the jamb of the southwestern doorway of the outer sanctuary chamber in the Edublalmaḫ. The piece was given the excavation number U 2674 and is shown on British Museum negative U 342. The door socket was made from half of a kudurru and according to museum records measures 8 inches in height and 12×10 inches at the base. The inscription is written in archaizing script and has been edited from the published photographs.

BIBLIOGRAPHY

1925 Woolley, AJ 5 pp. 384–85 and pl. XLI no. 1 (provenance, photo, translation)
1925 MJ 16 p. 294 (photo)
1928 Gadd, UET 1 no. 169 (photo, copy, edition)
1929 Langdon, JRAS p. 371 (study)
1962 Woolley, UE 9 p. 14 (provenance, partial translation)
1965 Woolley, UE 8 pp. 11, 15–16, 21, and 101 (provenance, partial translation, study)
1982 Woolley and Moorey, Ur p. 224 (partial translation)

TEXT

Col. i
1) ^{d}EN.ZU an-na
2) pirig dingir-re-e-ne
3) lugal ^{d}en-líl-e-ne
4) lugal-a-ni-ir
5) ^{md}EN.ZU-TI.LA.BI-DU$_{11}$.GA
6) GÌR.NÍTA úri.KI-ma
7) dumu $^{m\ulcorner d\urcorner}$nin-gal-SUM.MA
8) GÌR.NÍTA úri.KI-ma
9) ú-a é-kíš-nu$_{6}$-gal
10) é-temen-ní-gùr-ru
11) níg-u$_{4}$-ul-lí(*)-a-ta
12) é-gar$_{8}$ diri-ga-bi
13) te-me-en-bi a-ri-a
14) uš$_{8}$-bi bí-in-šú-šú
15) ká-bi ḫa-lam-me-e-ne
16) ki-bi bí-in-kin-kin
17) šà dub te-me-en-bi
18) u-me-ni-dù
19) sag-bi ba-ni-in-íl

1–4) For the god Sîn of heaven, lion of the gods (and) king of the Enlil (circle of) gods, his lord:

5–9) Sîn-balāssu-iqbi, viceroy of Ur, son of Ningal-iddin, (who was also) viceroy of Ur, who provides for Ekišnugal —

10–31) (With regard to) Etemennigurru, whose (enclosure) wall had collapsed in the distant past, whose foundation terrace had lain waste, (and) whose foundations were covered over, I sought the location of (15) its forgotten gate(s). I put its foundation inscription inside a box and raised its (the temple's) top. I inlaid with silver (20) a door of boxwood, wood of finest quality from a distant mountain, fixed with a copper peg, whose band(s) were strong, (whose) *bottom* was of gold, (25)

i 3 The "Enlil (circle of) gods" was a group of deities, generally of minor importance, who were associated with the god Enlil. Some of the deities in this group are mentioned in B.6.32.2005–2010.
i 11 lí(*): the sign has the form of DÙ.
i 12 With regard to the translation of diri-ga as "had collapsed," see B.2.6.1 note to line 10.

Col. ii
20) GIŠ.ig GIŠ.túg giš sag
21) kur-bi-ta sù-ud-da
22) gag urudu bí-in-dù-a
23) kéš-da-bi kala-ga
24) uš kù-GI-a-ke$_4$
25) si-gar kù-babbar zálag-zálag
26) aškud nu-kúš-ù
27) urudu kala-ga
28) kù-babbar u-me-ni-dab-dab
29) ká é-sag-AŠ
30) é-ḫal-la-ta dù-a
31) da-rí-šè gub-bu-dè
32) lú mu-sar-ra-mu
33) šu bí-íb-ùr-e-a
34) ḫa-ba ki-bi kúr-ru-da
35) ^{d}EN.ZU ^{d}nin-gal
36) dingir bàd-gal-mu
37) mu-bi
38) ḫé-en-ḫa-lam-e-ne

(whose) doorbolt was of shining silver, (and whose) bar and pivot were of strong copper, in order that it might stand forever *fixed in the doorway of the "secret house," the house of divination.*

32–38) May the god Sîn (and) the goddess Ningal, the god(s), my helpers, destroy the name of anyone who erases my inscription or changes its position!

2002

This inscription of Sîn-balāssu-iqbi is written in Sumerian upon a clay nail and describes the restoration of Etemennigurru, the same structure of concern in the previous inscription.

COMMENTARY

The nail (BM 116987; 1924-9-20,250) was found by the British expedition to Ur in the main gateway on the southwest of the Great Court and was given the excavation number U 1262. The piece measures 7.2 cm in height and 5.9 cm in diameter. The sign forms are Babylonian and display some archaizing features. The inscription is found running along the side of the piece and has been collated.

BIBLIOGRAPHY

1928 Gadd, UET 1 no. 183 (copy, edition)

TEXT

1) ^{d}EN.ZU an-na
2) pirig dingir-re-⌜e⌝-ne
3) lugal ^{d}en-líl-e-ne
4) lugal-a-ni-ir
5) ^{md}EN.ZU-TI.LA.BI-DU$_{11}$.GA
6) GÌR.NÍTA
7) úri.KI-ma
8) dumu ^{md}nin-gal-SUM.MA
9) GÌR.NÍTA
10) úri.KI-ma

1–4) For the god Sîn of heaven, lion of the gods (and) king of the Enlil (circle of) gods, his lord:

5–14) Sîn-balāssu-iqbi, viceroy of Ur, son of Ningal-iddin, (10) (who was also) viceroy of Ur, (re)built anew Etemennigurru, his beloved temple.

11) é-temen-ní-gùr-ru
12) é ki-ág-gá(*)-na
13) gibil-bi
14) in-na-dù

2003

Several bricks from Ur have a Sumerian inscription of Sîn-balāssu-iqbi which mentions Ashurbanipal and which records the renovation of Elugalgalgasisa ("House, King of Righteous Counsel"). The same structure is mentioned in the next inscription.

CATALOGUE

Ex.	Museum number	Excavation number	Registration number	Ur provenance	Dimensions (cm)	Lines preserved	cpn
1	BM 114277	—	1919-10-11,4708	—	27×19.5×8	1–12	n
2	BM 114278	—	1919-10-11,4709	—	13×7.5×3	7–12	n
3	BM 137345	U 1664	1935-1-13,5	In debris, top of main staircase of ziqqurat	14.5×13×6	1–5	n
4	BM 137349	U 3161	1935-1-13,9	—	27×25.5×7.5	1–12	n
5	BM 137381	—	1979-12-18,16	—	25.5×25.5×8	1–12	n
6	BM 137408	—	1979-12-18,43	—	13×9×7	1–2	n
7	CBS 15337	U 152?	—	—	24×25×8	1–12	c
8	CBS 16491	—	—	—	26×26×8	1–12	c
9	CBS 16555a	—	—	—	26×26×8	1–12	c
10	CBS 16555b	—	—	—	26×26×7.5	1–12	c
11	IM number unknown	U 3161	—	—	27×27×7.5	1–12	n

COMMENTARY

Exs. 1–2 come from H.R. Hall's excavations. Exs. 3–4 and 7–10 come from Woolley's work at Ur, as probably do exs. 5–6. Gadd states that U 3161 was found "loose in Nin-gal temple" and is in the Iraq Museum (ex. 11; see UET 1 p. xviii); Woolley says that it was "from the temple of Nin-gal" and also indicates that it is in the Iraq Museum (UE 8 p. 103). According to Walker (CBI p. 68), BM 137349 (ex. 4) is U 3161. The Ur registry in the British Museum does not indicate that more than one brick was given this number and simply says it was found "loose on top." Ex. 7 has the Ur excavation number 152 crossed out on it; according to the Ur registry U 152 is a "string of beads." Ex. 7 also has the notation T.T.B. 17 written upon it.

Two further exemplars of this inscription may be found on U 3136 and 7824 (present locations not known); see UE 6 pp. 50 and 99. The Ur registry states that U 3136 is a moulded brick fragment from the front of the Dublal. U 7824 was found loose in room 6 of the Enunmaḫ; the Ur registry indicates that it has the same inscription as U 3161, except for za-nam-til-la-šu in line 2.

Exs. 1–2 and 4–10 are stamped; ex. 3 is inscribed; it is not clear if ex. 11 was stamped or inscribed. The area stamped on exs. 1–2 and 4–6 measures 16.8/16.2×10.0/9.5 cm. Information for exs. 1–6 comes from C.B.F. Walker. No score for this brick inscription is presented in the microfiche.

BIBLIOGRAPHY

1928 Gadd, UET 1 no. 170 (ex. 11, copy, edition; ex. 3, study)
1965 Woolley, UE 8 p. 103 (ex. 11, study)
1981 Walker, CBI no. 82 (exs. 1–6, transliteration)
1985 Behrens, JCS 37 p. 240 no. 56 (exs. 7–10, study)

12 gá(*): text has: 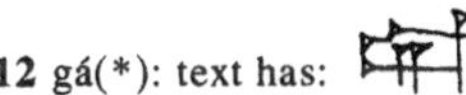

TEXT

1) ^{d}nanna lugal an-ki-a
2) zi nam-ti-la-šè
3) AN.ŠÁR-DÙ-IBILA-ke$_{4}$
4) lugal lugal-e-ne lugal-a-ni
5) ^{d}30-TIN-*su-iq-bi*
6) GÌR.NÍTA úri.KI-ma
7) eridu.KI-ga-ke$_{4}$
8) ú-a é-giš-nu$_{11}$-gal
9) èš abzu zálag-ga-ke$_{4}$
10) é-lugal-galga-si-sá
11) é ki-ág-gá-a-ni
12) gibil-bi mu-un-na-dù

1–12) (For) the god Nanna, king of heaven (and) netherworld: in order to ensure the good health of Ashurbanipal, king of kings, his lord, (5) Sîn-balāssu-iqbi, viceroy of Ur (and) Eridu, who provides for Ekišnugal, the shining shrine of the Watery Abyss (*apsû*), (re)built anew (10) Elugalgalgasisa, his beloved temple.

2004

This Sumerian inscription states that Sîn-balāssu-iqbi had rebuilt the shrine Elugalgalgasisa (the same structure mentioned in the previous inscription) and mentions Ashurbanipal. It is found stamped upon the edge of a fragmentary brick from Ur.

COMMENTARY

The brick (BM 119278; 1927-10-3,273) was found loose, south of the Egi(g)par, during Woolley's excavations at Ur, and was given the excavation number U 6341. It measures 21×10.5×7.5. The inscription is edited from the published copy, with collations from C.B.F. Walker, CBI no. 81 for lines 2 (⸢A⸣, not IB[I]LA of UET 1 copy) and 5 (úri, not uri$_{5}$ of UET 1 copy).

Gadd has suggested that a word for "god" or "protector" should be restored at the beginning of line 2 (i.e., "[god of As]hurbanipal" or "[protector of As]hurbanipal").

BIBLIOGRAPHY

1928 Gadd, UET 1 no. 168 (copy, edition)
1965 Brinkman, Orientalia NS 34 p. 251 (study)
1981 Walker, CBI no. 81 (transliteration)

TEXT

Col. i
1) [^{d}nanna lu]gal-a-ni
2) [x AN].ŠÁR-DÙ-⸢A⸣
3) [lugal] ki-šár-ra-ke$_{4}$
4) [^{md}3]0-TIN-*su-iq-bi*
Col. ii
5) GÌR.NÍTA úri.KI-ma
6) eridu.KI-ga ⸢zi⸣-ni-<<ki>>-šè
7) é-lugal-galga-si-sá
8) [gibi]l-bi mu-na-an-dù

1–8) [(For) the god Nanna], his [lo]rd, [... *of* As]hurbanipal, [king] of the world, [Sî]n-balāssu-iqbi, (5) viceroy of Ur (and) Eridu, for the sake of his life (re)built Elugalgalgasisa [an]ew.

B.6.32.2003 1.3 en gal ("great lord") for lugal ("king").
B.6.32.2003 5.3, 7–10 insert a masculine determinative before the name.

2005

This Sumerian inscription found upon a brick from Ur records the building of Eušumgalana ("House, Dragon of Heaven"), the dwelling of the deity Ninkasi, for the god Nanna (Sîn). It is the first of nine similar inscriptions from Ur which deal with shrines at that city (B.6.32.2005–2013). Two of these inscriptions mention only the god Nanna (B.6.32.2011-2012) and one assigns a shrine to the god Enlil (B.6.32.2013). The remaining six inscriptions for the most part ascribe shrines to relatively minor deities: Ninkasi, Šuzianna, Kusu, Nusku, Ninimma, and Ennugi (B.6.2005–2010). Each of these six deities was one of the "sons of Enmešarra," a god who was connected with the netherworld and viewed as an ancestor of Enlil (see Gadd, UET 1 p. 56, and Hibbert, OrAnt 21 [1982] pp. 256–57). Each is also known to have had a shrine at Enlil's city of Nippur (see Bernhardt and Kramer, Orientalia NS 44 [1975] p. 98, and George, House Most High pp. 12–13). All except Ninkasi are known to have been specifically associated with the god Enlil in some way (see An = *Anum* i 184, 252, 306, 318, and 324). It thus appears that in carrying out his renovations at Ur, Sîn-balāssu-iqbi was modelling his work upon the situation at Nippur. Since several of his inscriptions refer to Nanna/Sîn as "king of the Enlil (circle of) gods" (B.6.32.2001–2002 and 2005–2013) and since one refers to Nanna's Enlilship (nam-^{d}en-líl-lá-a-ni, B.6.32.2012 line 7), it seems that Sîn-balāssu-iqbi was attempting to promote a syncretism between Nanna (Sîn) and Enlil.

CATALOGUE

Ex.	Museum number	Excavation number	Ur provenance	Dimensions (cm)	Lines preserved	cpn
1	CBS 16483, face	U 3250	Wall, room left of sanctuary of Ningal temple	26×12.5×7.5	1-8	c
2	CBS 16483, edge	—	—	—	1-6, 8	c

COMMENTARY

CBS 16483 was found during the fourth season of excavations at Ur (1925–26). The inscriptions are inscribed, not stamped. Despite a statement in the Ur registry in the British Museum that U 3301 has the same inscription as U 3250 and one in JCS 37 that CBS 16490 (U 3301) and CBS 16483 (U 3250) both have this particular inscription, CBS 16490 has inscription B.6.32.2009, as previously noted by Gadd (UET 1 p. xviii) and Woolley (UE 8 p. 103).

Ex. 2, the inscription on the edge of CBS 16483, omits line 7. Gadd (UET 1 p. 55 sub no. 174) states that eight further brick inscriptions (UET 1 nos. 175–182 = B.6.32.2006–2013) show the same feature: the complete inscription on the face of the brick and a shorter version, omitting line 7, on the edge. However, none of the exemplars for B.6.32.2006–2013 which were examined has an inscription on the edge which omits line 7. However, in every case in which the inscription was collated, the edge inscription for B.6.32.2005–2013 had ^{d}50-e-ne in line 1, not ^{d}en-líl-e-ne as found on the face of the brick. No score for this brick inscription is presented in the microfiche.

Ninkasi is sometimes described as the goddess of beer (see Civil, Studies Oppenheim pp. 67–89).

BIBLIOGRAPHY

1925 Woolley, AJ 5 p. 368 (provenance)
1928 Gadd, UET 1 nos. 173–74 (exs. 1–2, copy, edition)
1939 Woolley, UE 5 pp. 32–33 and 60 (provenance)
1965 Woolley, UE 8 pp. 70 and 103 (provenance, study)
1985 Behrens, JCS 37 p. 240 no. 57 (exs. 1–2, study)

TEXT

1) ^{d}nanna lugal ^{d}en-líl-e-ne
2) lugal-a-ni
3) ^{md}EN.ZU-TI.LA.BI-DU_{11}.GA
4) GÌR.NÍTA úri.KI-ma
5) ú-a eridu.KI-ga
6) é-ušumgal-an-na
7) ⌜ki⌝-gub ^{d}nin-ka-si-ke_{4}
8) mu-na-dù

1–8) (For) the god Nanna, king of the Enlil (circle of) gods, his lord: Sîn-balāssu-iqbi, viceroy of Ur, (5) who provides for Eridu, built Eušumgalana, the station of the goddess Ninkasi.

2006

An inscribed brick from Ur has a Sumerian inscription of Sîn-balāssu-iqbi recording the fact that he had built Eešbanda (House, Little Chamber"), the abode of the goddess Šuzianna, for the god Nanna (Sîn). According to An = *Anum* i 184–84a, Šuzianna was a junior wife (dam bàn-da) of the god Enlil and the wet-nurse of the moon god Sîn. The inscription is similar to B.6.32.2005 and 2007–2013. The inscription is inscribed, not stamped. No score for this brick inscription is presented in the microfiche.

CATALOGUE

Ex.	Museum number	Excavation number	Ur provenance	Dimensions (cm)	Lines preserved	cpn
1	CBS 16484, face	U 3326	Well of Ningal temple	27×12×8	1–8	c
2	CBS 16484, edge	—	—	—	1–8	c

BIBLIOGRAPHY

1925 Woolley, AJ 5 p. 368 (provenance)
1928 Gadd, UET 1 no. 175 and sub no. 174 (exs. 1–2, copy, edition [as variant to UET 1 no. 173])
1939 Woolley, UE 5 pp. 32–33 and 60 (provenance)
1965 Woolley, UE 8 pp. 70 and 103 (provenance, study)
1985 Behrens, JCS 37 p. 240 no. 58 (study)

TEXT

1) ^{d}nanna lugal ^{d}en-líl-e-ne
2) lugal-a-ni
3) ^{md}EN.ZU-TI.LA.BI-DU_{11}.GA
4) GÌR.NÍTA úri.KI-ma
5) ú-a eridu.KI-ga
6) é-èš-bàn-da
7) ki-tuš ^{d}šu-zi-an-na
8) mu-na-dù

1–8) (For) the god Nanna, king of the Enlil (circle) of gods, his lord: Sîn-balāssu-iqbi, the viceroy of Ur, (5) who provides for Eridu, built Eešbanda, the abode of the goddess Šuzianna.

B.6.32.2005 1.2 ^{d}50-e-ne for ^{d}en-líl-e-ne.
B.6.32.2005 7.2 omits this line.
B.6.32.2006 1.2 ⌜^{d}50⌝-e-⌜ne⌝ for ^{d}en-líl-e-ne.
B.6.32.2006 6.1 é-èš-(x)-bàn-da; é-èš-bàn-da clear on ex. 2. With regard to the reading of the name, note George, House Most High p. 83 no. 265.
B.6.32.2006 7.2 Against Gadd, UET 1 p. 55 sub no. 174, line 7 not omitted; see commentary to B.6.32.2005.

2007

A brick from Ur has a Sumerian text inscribed upon it twice recording the building of the shrine Eankikuga ("House of the Pure Heaven and Netherworld"), the station of the goddess Kusu, by Sîn-balāssu-iqbi for the god Nanna (Sîn). The goddess Kusu was purification priest of the god Enlil and one of the children of Enmešarra. (With regard to this goddess, see Michalowski, Studies Hallo pp. 158–59.) The inscription is similar to B.6.32.2005–2006 and 2008–2013. The inscription is inscribed, not stamped. No score is provided for this brick inscription in the microfiche.

CATALOGUE

Ex.	Museum number	Excavation number	Ur provenance	Dimensions (cm)	Lines preserved	cpn
1	CBS 16485, face	U 3296	Well of Ningal temple	26x12x7	1–8	c
2	CBS 16485, edge	—	—	—	1–8	c

BIBLIOGRAPHY

1925 Woolley, AJ 5 p. 368 (provenance)
1928 Gadd, UET 1 no. 176 and sub no. 174 (exs. 1–2, copy, edition [as variant to UET 1 no. 173])
1939 Woolley, UE 5 pp. 32–33 and 60 (provenance)
1965 Woolley, UE 8 pp. 70 and 103 (provenance, study)
1985 Behrens, JCS 37 p. 240 no. 59 (study)

TEXT

1) ᵈnanna lugal ᵈen-líl-e-ne
2) lugal-a-ni
3) ᵐᵈEN.ZU-TI.LA.BI-DU$_{11}$.GA
4) GÌR.NÍTA úri.KI-ma
5) ú-a eridu.KI-ga
6) é-an-ki-kù-ga
7) ki-gub ᵈkù-sù-ke$_4$
8) mu-na-dù

1–8) (For) the god Nanna, king of the Enlil (circle of) gods, his lord: Sîn-balāssu-iqbi, viceroy of Ur, (5) who provides for Eridu, built Eankikuga, the station of the god Kusu.

2008

An inscribed brick from Ur bears two copies of a Sumerian inscription of Sîn-balāssu-iqbi which states that he had built Eadgigi ("House, Counsellor"), the abode of the god Nusku, for the god Nanna (Sîn). Nusku was a god of light and fire and the vizier of the god Enlil (see Tallqvist, Götterepitheta pp. 432–34). The inscription is similar to B.6.32.2005–2007 and 2009–2013 and is inscribed, not stamped. No score is presented in the microfiche.

1.2 ᵈ50-e-ne for ᵈen-líl-e-ne.
7.2 Against Gadd, UET 1 p. 55 sub no. 174, line 7 not omitted; see commentary to B.6.32.2005.

CATALOGUE

Ex.	Museum number	Excavation number	Ur provenance	Dimensions (cm)	Lines preserved	cpn
1	CBS 16489, face	U 3300	Well of Ningal temple	26×26×8	1–8	c
2	CBS 16489, edge	—	—	—	1–8	c

BIBLIOGRAPHY

1925 Woolley, AJ 5 p. 368 (provenance)
1928 Gadd, UET 1 no. 180 and sub no. 174 (exs. 1–2, copy, edition [as variant to UET 1 no. 173])
1939 Woolley, UE 5 pp. 32–33 and 60 (provenance)
1965 Woolley, UE 8 pp. 70 and 103 (provenance, study)
1985 Behrens, JCS 37 p. 241 no. 63 (study)

TEXT

1) dnanna lugal den-líl-e-ne
2) lugal-a-ni
3) mdEN.ZU-TI.LA.BI-DU11.GA
4) GÌR.NÍTA úri.KI-ma
5) ú-a eridu.KI-ga
6) é-ad-gi4-gi4
7) ki-tuš dnuska
8) mu-na-dù

1–8) (For) the god Nanna, king of the Enlil (circle of) gods, his lord: Sîn-balāssu-iqbi, viceroy of Ur, (5) who provides for Eridu, built Eadgigi, the abode of the god Nusku.

2009

This Sumerian inscription is found inscribed twice upon a brick from Ur and states that Sîn-balāssu-iqbi had built Ekišibgalekura (exact reading and interpretation not certain), the abode of the goddess Ninimma, for the god Nanna (Sîn). The inscription is similar to B.6.32.2005–2008 and 2010–13 and is inscribed, not stamped. No score for this brick inscription is provided in the microfiche.

CATALOGUE

Ex.	Museum number	Excavation number	Ur provenance	Dimensions (cm)	Lines preserved	cpn
1	CBS 16490, face	U 3301	Well of Ningal temple	25×27×7	1–8	c
2	CBS 16490, edge	—	—	—	1–8	c

COMMENTARY

Behrens (JCS 37 [1985] p. 240 sub no. 57) indicates that CBS 16490 (U 3301) has inscription B.6.32.2005 but the brick actually has this inscription.

The name of the temple may mean "House, Keeper of the Seal of the Ekur." A.R. George (House Most High p. 79 no. 202) has suggested that it might instead be é-dub-<sar>-gal-é-kur-ra ("House of the Great Scribe of the Ekur"). For the goddess Ninimma's position as a scribe and her connection with Enlil (whose temple was Ekur), see George, Topographical Texts p. 469.

1.2 d⌜50-e-ne⌝ for den-líl-e-ne.
7.2 Against Gadd, UET 1 p. 55 sub no. 174, line 7 not omitted; see commentary to B.6.32.2005.

BIBLIOGRAPHY

1925 Woolley, AJ 5 p. 368 (provenance)
1928 Gadd, UET 1 no. 181 and sub no. 174 (exs. 1–2, copy, edition [as variant to UET 1 no. 173])
1939 Woolley, UE 5 pp. 32–33 and 60 (provenance)
1965 Woolley, UE 8 pp. 70 and 103 (provenance, study)

TEXT

1) ^{d}nanna lugal ^{d}en-líl-e-ne
2) lugal-a-ni
3) ^{md}EN.ZU-TI.LA.BI-DU$_{11}$.GA
4) GÌR.NÍTA úri.KI-ma
5) ú-a eridu.KI-ga
6) é-kišib-gal-é-kur-ra
7) ki-tuš ^{d}nin-ìmma-ke$_{4}$
8) mu-na-dù

1–8) (For) the god Nanna, king of the Enlil (circle of) gods, his lord: Sîn-balāssu-iqbi, viceroy of Ur, (5) who provides for Eridu, built *Ekišibgalekura*, the abode of the god Ninimma.

2010

A poorly preserved Sumerian inscription of Sîn-balāssu-iqbi from Ur states that he had built the abode or station of the god Ennugi for the god Nanna (Sîn). The inscription is similar to B.6.32.2005–2009 and 2011–2013.

COMMENTARY

The inscription is found upon BM 119277 (1927-10-3,272), a fragment of a brick in the collections of the British Museum. The piece was given the Ur excavation number 3148 and is variously said to have been found northwest of the ziqqurat (Gadd, UET 1 p. xix) and in the great court of Nanna (Woolley, UE 8 p. 103). The inscription is found on the face of the brick and is inscribed, not stamped. The fragment measures 19×16×7.5 cm and is not sufficiently well preserved to determine if it also had an inscription on its edge or not. Woolley says that CBS 16559 also has this excavation number and inscription. A brick from the fourth season of excavations at Ur (1925–26) was accessioned in the University Museum on April 19, 1927, and given this museum number; however, no brick with this number or this inscription can currently be found in the University Museum. Thus the edition presented here represents only BM 119277, which was kindly collated by C.B.F. Walker.

The god Ennugi was associated both with looking after dikes and canals and with the netherworld; he was also the "throne-bearer" of the god Enlil. (See Tallqvist, Götterepitheta p. 305.) The reading of the name of the shrine in line 6 is not clear. Walker reads the sign before kù as ga, while George reads gú? (House Most High p. 161 no. 1255). The published copy has:

BIBLIOGRAPHY

1928 Gadd, UET 1 no. 182 (copy, edition [as variant to UET 1 no. 173])
1965 Woolley, UE 8 pp. 70 and 103 (provenance, study)
1981 Walker, CBI no. 86 (transliteration)

1.2 ^{d}50-e-[ne] for ^{d}en-líl-e-ne.
7.2 Against Gadd, UET 1 p. 55 sub no. 174, line 7 not omitted; see commentary to B.6.32.2005.

TEXT

1) [^{d}nanna lugal ^{d}en-líl-e-n]e
2) [lugal-a]-ni
3) [^{md}EN.ZU-TI.LA.BI-DU$_{11}$].GA
4) [GÌR.NÍTA úri].KI-ma
5) [ú-a eri]du.KI-ga
6) [é-x]-x-ga(?)-kù-ga
7) [ki-tuš/gub] ^{d}en-nu-gi-ke$_{4}$
8) [mu-na]-dù

1–8) [(For) the god Nanna, king of the Enlil (circle of) gods], his [lord: Sîn-balāssu-iq]bi, [viceroy of Ur, (5) who provides for Eri]du, built [E..].kuga, [the abode/station] of the god Ennugi.

2011

Several bricks from Ur bear a Sumerian inscription which states that Sîn-balāssu-iqbi built the shrine Eanšar ("House, All Heaven") for the god Nanna (Sîn). The inscription is similar to B.6.32.2005–2010 and 2012–2013.

CATALOGUE

Ex.	Museum number	Excavation number	Registration number	Ur provenance	Dimensions (cm)	Lines preserved	cpn
1	BM 119279, face	U 3297	1927-10-3,274	Well in temple of Ningal	25.5×25.5×7.5	1–8	c
2	BM 119279, edge	—	—	—	—	1–8	c
3	CBS 16486, face	U 3297a	—	As ex. 1	25.5×12.5×8	1–8	c
4	CBS 16486, edge	—	—	—	—	1–8	c
5	CBS 16556a, face	U 3297b	—	As ex. 1	26×26×8	1–8	c
6	CBS 16556a, edge	—	—	—	—	1–8	c
7	CBS 16556b, face	U 3297c	—	As ex. 1	25.5×25.5×6.5	1–8	c
8	CBS 16556b, edge	—	—	—	—	1–8	c
9	IM 1101	U 3297	—	As ex. 1	—	—	n
10	IM 1102	U 3297	—	As ex. 1	—	—	n

COMMENTARY

Collations for ex. 1–2 were kindly supplied by C.B.F. Walker. The designation a–c after the Ur excavation number for exs. 3–8 is one employed by the University Museum and is not part of the original excavation number. As for IM 1101 and 1102 (exs. 9–10), which have not been examined, it is possible that each has the inscription twice, once on the face and once on the edge. Woolley does not indicate whether they do or do not, but also does not do so for exs. 1–2, 3–4, 5–6, and 7–8 (see UE 8 p. 103). Gadd indicates that his copy and edition come from BM 119279, but the measurements he gives (25.5×12.0×7.0 cm) fit CBS 16486 better than BM 119279. All exemplars are inscribed, not stamped. No score is provided in the microfiche for this brick inscription.

BIBLIOGRAPHY

1925 Woolley, AJ 5 p. 368 (provenance)
1928 Gadd, UET 1 no. 177 and sub no. 174 (copy, edition [as variant to UET 1 no. 173])
1939 Woolley, UE 5 pp. 32–33 and 60 (provenance)
1965 Woolley, UE 8 pp. 70 and 103 (exs. 1–10, provenance, study)
1981 Walker, CBI no. 83 (exs. 1–2, transliteration)
1985 Behrens, JCS 37 p. 240 no. 60 (exs. 3–8, study)

TEXT

1) ^{d}nanna lugal ^{d}en-líl-e-ne
2) lugal-a-ni
3) ^{md}EN.ZU-TI.LA.BI-DU$_{11}$.GA
4) GÌR.NÍTA úri.KI-ma
5) ú-a eridu.KI-ga
6) é-an-šár
7) ki-tuš nam-lugal-la-ni
8) mu-na-dù

1–8) (For) the god Nanna, king of the Enlil (circle of) gods, his lord: Sîn-balāssu-iqbi, viceroy of Ur, (5) who provides for Eridu, built Eanšar, his royal abode.

2012

This Sumerian brick inscription from Ur records the building of the shrine Ešaduga ("House that Pleases the Heart") for the god Nanna (Sîn) by Sîn-balāssu-iqbi. The inscription is similar to B.6.32.2005–2011 and 2013.

CATALOGUE

Ex.	Museum number	Excavation number	Registration number	Ur provenance	Dimensions (cm)	Lines preserved	cpn
1	BM 119271, face	U 3298	1927-10-3,266	Well in temple of Ningal	25.5×25×7	1–8	c
2	BM 119271, edge	—	—	—	—	1–8	c
3	CBS 16487, face	U 3298a	—	As ex. 1	26×12×8	1–8	c
4	CBS 16487, edge	—	—	—	—	1–8	c
5	CBS 16557, face	U 3298b	—	As ex. 1	26×26×8	1–8	c
6	CBS 16557, edge	—	—	—	—	1–5	c
7	IM 1103	U 3298	—	As ex. 1	—	—	n

COMMENTARY

Collations for exs. 1–2 were kindly supplied by C.B.F. Walker. The designation a–b after the Ur excavation number for exs. 3–6 is one employed by the University Museum, Philadelphia, and is not part of the original excavation number. In view of the measurements given for the brick in UET 1 (25.5×12.0×7.0), it seems likely that Gadd used CBS 16487, or possibly IM 1103, for his model. It is possible that ex. 7 has the inscription twice, once on the face and once on the edge; however, it has not been possible to examine the brick. The inscription is inscribed, not stamped. No score for this brick inscription is presented in the microfiche.

BIBLIOGRAPHY

1925 Woolley, AJ 5 p. 368 (provenance)
1928 Gadd, UET 1 no. 178 and sub no. 174 (copy, edition [as variant to UET 1 no. 173])
1939 Woolley, UE 5 pp. 32–33 and 60 (provenance)
1965 Woolley, UE 8 pp. 70 and 103 (exs. 1–7, provenance, study)
1981 Walker, CBI no. 84 (exs. 1–2, transliteration)
1985 Behrens, JCS 37 p. 241 no. 61 (exs. 3–6, study)

1 2, 4, 6, 8 ^{d}50-e-ne for ^{d}en-líl-e-ne.
7 Against Gadd, UET 1 p. 55 sub no. 174, line 7 not omitted on those exemplars found on the side of a brick; see commentary to B.6.32.2005.

TEXT

1) ^{d}nanna lugal ^{d}en-líl-e-ne
2) lugal-a-ni
3) ^{md}EN.ZU-TI.LA.BI-DU$_{11}$.GA
4) GÌR.NÍTA úri.KI-ma
5) ú-a eridu.KI-ga
6) é-šà-du$_{10}$-ga
7) ki-tuš nam-^{d}en-líl-lá-a-ni
8) mu-na-dù

1–8) (For) the god Nanna, king of the Enlil (circle of) gods, his lord: Sîn-balāssu-iqbi, viceroy of Ur, (5) who provides for Eridu, built Ešaduga, the abode of his Enlilship.

2013

This inscription, written in Sumerian upon a few bricks from Ur, states that Sîn-balāssu-iqbi had built Eašanamar (exact reading and meaning uncertain), the abode of the god Enlil, for the god Nanna (Sîn). The inscription is similar to B.6.32.2005–2012.

CATALOGUE

Ex.	Museum number	Excavation number	Registration number	Ur provenance	Dimensions (cm)	Lines preserved	cpn
1	BM 119274, face	U 3299	1927-10-3,269	Well of Ningal temple	26×26×7	1–8	n
2	BM 119274, edge	—	—	—	—	3–8	n
3	CBS 16488, face	U 3299	—	As ex. 1	26×26×8	1–8	c
4	CBS 16488, edge	—	—	—	—	1–8	c
5	CBS 16558	U 3299	—	As ex. 1	—	—	n

COMMENTARY

Gadd (UET 1 p. 55 sub no. 174) indicates that the inscription on the edge of BM 119274 (ex. 2) omits line 7, but Walker does not indicate this in CBI. The brick cannot at present be located for collation, but in view of the same erroneous statement by Gadd about B.6.32.2006–2012, it seems likely that the line was not omitted. According to Woolley, UE 8 p. 103, CBS 16558 (ex. 5) has this inscription, but this brick cannot be located at present. All exemplars are inscribed, not stamped. No score is presented for this brick inscription in the microfiche.

The exact reading of the temple's name in line 6 is not certain. A.R. George tentatively suggests é-tilla$_{x}$-maḫ$^{!}$ ("House, Exalted Open Place"); see House Most High p. 69 no. 91 and p. 150 no. 1101.

BIBLIOGRAPHY

1925 Woolley, AJ 5 p. 368 (provenance)
1928 Gadd, UET 1 no. 179 and sub no. 174 (exs. 1–2, copy, edition [as variant to UET 1 no. 173])
1939 Woolley, UE 5 pp. 32–33 and 60 (provenance)
1965 Woolley, UE 8 pp. 70 and 103 (exs. 1–5, provenance, study)
1981 Walker, CBI no. 85 (exs. 1–2, transliteration)
1985 Behrens, JCS 37 p. 241 no. 62 (ex. 3, study)

---

1 2, 4, 6 ^{d}50-e-ne, ⌜^{d}50-e-ne⌝ and ^{d}⌜50-e⌝-n[e] respectively for ^{d}en-líl-e-ne.

7 Against Gadd, UET 1 p. 55 sub no. 174, line 7 not omitted on those exemplars found on the side of a brick; see commentary to B.6.32.2005.

TEXT

1) ^{d}nanna lugal ^{d}en-líl-e-ne
2) lugal-a-ni
3) ^{md}EN.ZU-TI.LA.BI-DU$_{11}$.GA
4) GÌR.NÍTA úri.KI-ma
5) ú-a eridu.KI-ga
6) é-AŠ-AN-AMAR
7) ki-tuš ^{d}en-líl-lá-ke$_{4}$
8) mu-na-dù

1–8) (For) the god Nanna, king of the Enlil (circle of) gods, his lord: Sîn-balāssu-iqbi, viceroy of Ur, (5) who provides for Eridu, built *Eašanamar*, the abode of the god Enlil.

2014

Thirteen clay nails from Ur bear a Sumerian inscription of Sîn-balāssu-iqbi which states that he had rebuilt the Gipāru and constructed a statue of the goddess Ningal.

CATALOGUE

Ex.	Museum number	Excavation number	Registration number	Ur provenance	Dimensions (cm)	Lines preserved	cpn
1	BM 119021	U 3249c	1927-10-3,16	Beneath pavement of the sanctuary of the Ningal temple	Length: 12.3; Dia.: 7	1–17	c
2	BM 119023	U 3249m	1927-10-3,18	As ex. 1	Length: 13; Dia.: 6.8	1–17	c
3	BM 119024	U 3249l	1927-10-3,19	As ex. 1	Length: 13.6; Dia.: 7.3	1–17	c
4	University Museum (Philadelphia)	U 3249i	—	As ex. 1	Length: 13.9; Dia.: 7.3	1–17	c
5	University Museum (Philadelphia)	U 3249g?	—	As ex. 1	Length: 13.8; Dia.: 7.2	1–17	c

COMMENTARY

Woolley found thirteen nails with this inscription "set upright, bedded in a little bitumen, in holes below the walls and pavement of the sanctuary" (AJ 5 [1925] p. 368). In addition to the three in the British Museum and the two in the University Museum listed above, six exemplars are reported to be in the Iraq Museum and to bear the museum number IM 1081 (see Edzard, Sumer 13 [1957] p. 178). The present locations of the remaining two exemplars are not known. Ex. 4 bears a faint museum number, CBS 1590x, where x stands for an illegible numeral; the identification of the letter at the end of the excavation number marked on ex. 5 is not certain. The inscription is written in archaizing Babylonian script. Ex 1 is the master exemplar.

The inscription literally states that Sîn-balāssu-iqbi rebuilt "the Gipāru, the house *of* the goddess Ninlil, beloved wife of the god Sîn" for the goddess Ningal. As Brinkman points out (Orientalia NS 38 [1969] pp. 337–38 n. 2), there are a number of problems with this: the gipāru was the residence of the *entu*-priestess, not of the goddess Ninlil; there is no reason for a temple of the goddess Ninlil to be erected "for the goddess Ningal"; Ninlil was not the wife of the god Sîn; and the structure in which the clay nails were found was the temple of Ningal, not the gipāru. He points out that the term *gipāru* could refer to the dwelling places of gods, as well as to the residence of the *entu*-priest or priestess, and suggests that it is likely that ^{d}nin-líl

---

1.4 ^{d}⌜50⌝-e-n[e] for ^{d}en-líl-e-ne; ex. 2 may also have had the same variant but it cannot be located for collation.
6.3 final sign more like ŠEŠ than AMAR; sign damaged on ex. 4.
7 Against Gadd, UET 1 p. 55 sub no. 174, ex. 4 and likely ex. 2 (latter not collated) do not omit line 7; see commentary to B.6.32.2005.
7.3 omits -ke$_{4}$.

should be taken "as an epithet referring to Ningal and connoting 'supreme goddess' or something similar." His suggestion is adopted here. It is possible that one should regard the inscription as indicating a syncretism between Ningal and Ninlil, just as previous texts appear to reflect a syncretism between Ningal's spouse Nanna (Sîn) and Ninlil's spouse Enlil (see introduction to B.6.32.2005).

BIBLIOGRAPHY

1925 Woolley, AJ 5 p. 368 and pl. XXXV no. 1 (provenance, photo [inscription illegible])

1925 Woolley, MJ 16 p. 47 (provenance)

1928 Gadd, UET 1 no. 171 (1–3, copy, edition)

1931 Van Buren, Found. p. 60 (provenance)

1939 Woolley, UE 5 pp. 63–64 and pl. 27b (provenance, photo [inscription illegible])

1965 Brinkman, Orientalia NS 34 p. 250 (study)

1968 Ellis, Foundation Deposits p. 83 (provenance)

1969 Brinkman, Orientalia NS 38 pp. 337–38 n. 2 (study)

1982 Woolley and Moorey, Ur pp. 226–27 (translation)

TEXT

1) ^{d}nin-gal un-gal
2) é-giš-nu$_{11}$-gal
3) ^{d}nin-men-na ki-ág-gá
4) úri.KI-ma nin-a-ni-ir
5) ^{md}EN.ZU-TIN-*su-iq-bi*
6) GÌR.NÍTA úri.KI-ma
7) gi$_{6}$-pàr é ^{d}nin-líl-le
8) nìta-dam ki-ág-gá
9) ^{d}EN.ZU
10) gibil-bi mu-na-dù
11) alam níg-dím-dím-ma
12) ^{d}nin-gal-ke$_{4}$ u-me-ni-dím
13) šà é dingir ḪU-dù-šè
14) u-mu-un-ku$_{4}$-ku$_{4}$
15) é-nun-ta
16) ki-tuš nam-en-na-ni dù
17) bí-in-ri-a

1–4) For the goddess Ningal, queen of Ekišnugal, divine Ninmenna ("Lady-of-the-Crown"), beloved of Ur, his lady:

5–17) Sîn-balāssu-iqbi, viceroy of Ur, built anew the Gipāru, the house *of the supreme goddess*, beloved wife of the god Sîn. After he constructed a statue, *a (re-)creation of* the goddess Ningal, (and) brought it into the house of the wise god, she took up residence in Enun, (*which was*) *built* (*to be*) her lordly abode.

2015

Eight clay disks from Ur bear an Akkadian inscription stating that Sîn-balāssu-iqbi, "viceroy of Ur, Eridu, and the Gurasimmu (tribe)," rebuilt a well named Puḫilituma ("Well That Brings Luxuriance") for the goddess Ningal. His action is stated to have been "in order to ensure the good health of Ashurbanipal, king of Assyria."

13 ḪU-dù (pa$_{7}$-dù or paq-dù) stands for Akkadian *mūdû* (AHw p. 666 and CAD 10/2 [M] p. 164).

CATALOGUE

Ex.	Museum number	Excavation number	Ur photo number	Ur provenance	Dimensions (cm)	Lines preserved	cpn
1	BM 124351 (1933-10-13,4)	U 18529c	—	Foundation deposit, bottom of Kurigalzu brickwork in well in Ningal temple	Dia.: 8.3	1–16	c
2	BM 124350 (1933-10-13,3)	U 18529g?	—	As ex. 1	Dia.: 7.5	1–16	c
3	IM 16429	U 18529h	—	As ex. 1	—	—	n
4	IM 48412	U 18529e	—	As ex. 1	—	1–16	n
5	IM 48413	U 18529f	—	As ex. 1	—	1–16	n
6	IM 48414	U 18529b	—	As ex. 1	—	1–16	n
7	UM 33-35-191a	U 18529a	—	As ex. 1	Dia.: 8	1–16	c
8	UM 33-35-191b	U 18529d	2178	As ex. 1	Dia.: 8	1–16	c

COMMENTARY

The disks were found during the eleventh season of excavations at Ur by Sir Leonard Woolley. Ex. 2 has U 18529b written on it, but as noted by Brinkman the "b" is probably an error for "g" (Orientalia NS 38 [1969] p. 340, n. 4 from p. 339). The disks are inscribed on both sides and the inscription is written in contemporary Babylonian script. The arrangement of lines can vary and the master line follows ex. 1. Exs. 2 and 6 have the inscription on 18 lines. For exs. 4–6, the score presents only the variants given by Brinkman (Orientalia NS 38 [1969] p. 340 n. 2) and nothing is given for ex. 3 since this exemplar was not available to him for examination and could not be collated by the author.

The reverse of ex. 7 has been cleaned since it was studied by Brinkman (Orientalia NS 38 [1969] p. 348) and it is now clear that it is not the disk whose reverse is shown on the right side of UE 5 pl. 22b. The disk on the photograph must be identified with one of exs. 3–5.

BIBLIOGRAPHY

1933 Woolley, AJ 13 p. 370 and pl. LVI no. 1 (provenance, photo [inscription illegible])
1939 Woolley, UE 5 p. 33 (provenance), pl. 22a (photo [inscription illegible]) and pl. 22b right (ex. unknown, photo) and left (ex. 8, photo)
1965 Brinkman, Orientalia NS 34 pp. 249–50 n. 5 (study)
1965 Sollberger, UET 8 no. 102 (exs. 1–2, copy [ex. 2 as variants to ex. 1]; exs. 1–8, study)
1968 Ellis, Foundation Deposits pp. 96, 104, and 194 no. 83 (study)
1969 Brinkman, Orientalia NS 38 pp. 339–42 and 348 (exs. 1–2, 4–8, edition; exs. 1–8, study)

TEXT

1) *a-na* ^{d}*nin-gal* GAŠAN *ṣir-ti*
2) *šar-rat i-la-a-ti qa-rit-ti*
3) DINGIR.MEŠ GAL.MEŠ

1–3) For the goddess Ningal, august lady, queen of the goddesses, (most) valiant of the great gods:

4) *ana* TIN ZI.MEŠ *šá* AN.ŠÁR-DÙ-IBILA
5) LUGAL KUR *aš-šur*.KI LUGAL *dan-nu* LUGAL *kiš-šat*
6) *be-lí-šú* ^{md}30-TIN-*su-iq-bi*
7) DUMU ^{md}*nin-gal*-MU
8) LÚ.GÌR.NÍTA ÚRI.KI
9) ERIDU.KI *u* LÚ *gu-ra-sim-mu*
10) *áš-ri ip-te-e-ma pú-ḫi-li-tùm-ma*
11) *ib-ni-ma ú-kin aḫ-ra-taš*
12) A.MEŠ *nag-bi da-ru-ti*
13) *ú-šab-ra-a qé-reb-šú*

4–13) In order to ensure the good health of Ashurbanipal, king of Assyria, mighty king, (and) king of the world, his lord, Sîn-balāssu-iqbi, son of Ningal-iddin, viceroy of Ur, Eridu and the Gurasimmu (tribe), (10) opened up (its) emplacement, (re)built (the well named) Puḫilituma, and established (it) for all time. He made inexhaustible spring water appear in it.

14) *šá* NUN *pe-tu-ú* PÚ *šu-a-ti*
15) *li-ri-ku* u_4-*mu-šú*
16) *liš-ta-an-dil* NUNUZ-*šú*

14–16) With regard to any (future) prince who (re)opens this well, may his days be long (and) his offspring extensive!

2.2, 6 add AMA, "mother" after *qa-rit-ti*, i.e., "the valiant, the mother of the great gods."

2016

While carrying out work on the Ekišnugal complex at Ur, Sîn-balāssu-iqbi found a brick with a Sumerian inscription of Amar-Suen (2046–2038 BC) recording the fashioning of a divine statue. A copy of the Sumerian text was made and a colophon written in Akkadian appended to it. The inscription is found on a clay drum-shaped object which, in view of a poorly preserved notation on the top of the object, may be a model for an altar or dais. Only the colophon and inscription on the top of the object are presented here; the inscription of Amar-Suen will be edited in RIME 3.

COMMENTARY

The clay object (BM 119014; 1927-10-3,9) was found in the "museum" of En-nigaldi-nanna in the gipāru of the time of Nabonidus and was given the Ur excavation number U 2757. Woolley indicates that the piece was found in room ES 2 of the building in AJ 5 [1925] p. 383 and in "room 5" (= ES 5?) in UE 9 p. 17; see UE 9 pl. 65 for a plan of the building. The object measures 10.8 cm in height and 6.8 cm in diameter. The colophon (col. iv) is written in contemporary Babylonian script, while the remainder of the inscription is written in an archaizing script. Since the passage on the top of the object is written in an archaizing script, it may well be a copy of an older inscription just like cols. i–iii; however, since it is not specifically a part of the Amar-Suen inscription it is presented here. The inscription has been collated.

The inscription of Amar-Suen appears to be based upon Amar-Suen inscription no. 3 (see Steible, NSBW 2 pp. 221–25); however, if so, the individual who copied the inscription for Sîn-balāssu-iqbi, Nabû-šuma-iddin, either made a bad job of copying the text or had a different or damaged version of it in front of him. The copy made by Nabû-šuma-iddin includes several errors and differs markedly from Amar-Suen no. 3.

BIBLIOGRAPHY

1925 Woolley, AJ 5 pp. 383–84 and pl. XL no. 1 (provenance, photo, translation)
1925 Woolley, MJ 16 p. 34 (photo)
1928 Gadd, UET 1 no. 172 (photo, copy, edition)
1962 Woolley, UE 9 pp. 14, 17, and 111 and pl. 29 (provenance, photo, study)
1965 Brinkman, Orientalia NS 34 p. 250 (study)
1965 Woolley, UE 8 pp. 4 and 102 (study)
1968 Hunger, Kolophone no. 73 (edition)
1971 Sollberger and Kupper, IRSA IIIA3e n. 1 (translation)
1980 Edzard, RLA 6/1–2 pp. 64–65 (translation)
1982 Woolley and Moorey, Ur p. 231 (photo)
1991 Steible, NSBW 2 pp. 221–25 Amarsuen 3 Text B (edition)

TEXT

Col. i–iii
1–28) (Inscription of Amar-Suen)
Col. iv
29) GABA.RI ⌜SIG$_4$⌝.AL.ÙR.RA
30) *nap-pal-ti* ÚRI.KI
31) *ep-šet amar-*^{d}EN.ZU LUGAL *ú-ri*
32) *ina ši-te-ʾ-ú ú-ṣu-ra-a-ti*
33) *é-giš-nu$_{11}$-gal* ^{md}EN.ZU-TIN-*su-*⌜*iq-bi*⌝
34) GÌR.NÍTA ⌜URI$_5$⌝.KI *iš-te-*⌜ʾ*-ú*⌝
35) ^{md}AG-MU-SUM.NA DUMU ^{m}MU-^{d}*pap-sukkal*
36) LÚ.GALA ^{d}EN.(erasure).ZU
37) *a-na ta-mar-*(erasure)*-ti*
38) *i-mur-ma iš-ṭur*

1–28) (Inscription of Amar-Suen)

29–38) Copy from a baked brick from the debris of Ur, the work of Amar-Suen, king of Ur, (which) Sîn-balāssu-iqbi, viceroy of Ur, had *discovered* while looking for the ground-plan of Ekišnugal. Nabû-šuma-iddin, son of Iddin-Papsukkal, the lamentation-priest of the god Sîn, saw (it) and wrote (it) down for display.

Top
39) [(x)] dBÁRA den-líl x
40) [...] ⌈AN⌉ ME
41) [...]-⌈ú(?)⌉
42 [...] x

Top
39–42) No translation warranted.

39 The sign at the end of the line cannot be *lá* (as tentatively proposed by Steible).

Šamaš-šuma-ukīn

B.6.33

Although Esarhaddon had died in the eighth month of 669 BC, it was not until the second month of the following year that Šamaš-šuma-ukīn escorted the statue of the god Marduk back to Babylonia from Assyria and ascended the throne of Babylon. Esarhaddon had appointed him heir to the crown of Babylonia four years earlier, at the same time that he had designated Ashurbanipal, another son, as heir to the throne of Assyria. Šamaš-šuma-ukīn reigned for twenty years (667–648 BC). The exact relationship between the two brothers is unclear, but Šamaš-šuma-ukīn seems in effect to have been a vassal of the Assyrian king, though an especially favoured vassal. Ashurbanipal claims to have been the one who installed his brother as king of Babyonia and he involved himself actively in Babylonian affairs while his brother sat on the throne of Babylon. It was probably this interference in Babylonia's affairs which eventually caused Šamaš-šuma-ukīn to rebel against Assyrian overlordship. The rebellion began early in 652 BC and lasted until Šamaš-šuma-ukīn died (or was killed) and Babylon fell to its Assyrian besiegers sometime after the fifth month of 648 BC.

Inscriptions of Šamaš-šuma-ukīn record the restoration of the city wall of Sippar (B.6.33.1) and of the Ebabbar temple at that city (B.6.33.2). At Borsippa, Šamaš-šuma-ukīn renovated the Ezida temple (B.6.33.3–4) and built something (perhaps a piece of equipment for a boat used in cultic ceremonies) for the god Nabû (B.6.33.5). A further inscription, whose original provenance is not known, simply preserves part of the genealogy of the ruler (B.6.33.6). A governor of Ur, Sîn-šarra-uṣur, has also left an inscription recording his dedication of a plot of land to two goddesses of the city of Uruk (Ištar and Nanāia) for the good health of the Šamaš-šuma-ukīn (B.6.33.2001). Of these inscriptions, one is bilingual, written in Akkadian and Sumerian (B.6.33.1); one is written in Sumerian (B.6.33.2), and the remainder are in Akkadian. One inscription is found upon a stone stela (B.6.33.3), three upon clay cylinders (B.6.33.1, B.6.33.4, and B.6.33.6), one upon bricks (B.6.33.2), and two upon clay tablets (B.6.33.5 and B.6.33.2001). It is not possible to be certain exactly when in the reign of the king these inscriptions were composed; however, the mention of the Assyrian king Ashurbanipal in a positive manner in B.6.33.2–4 and probably B.6.33.5 would indicate that these were written before relations between the two brothers became strained and rebellion broke out in 652 BC.

Two kudurrus date to the reign of Šamaš-šuma-ukīn; one records his confirmation of the ownership of a tract of land (King, BBSt no. 10) and the other his grant of a prebend in the Ebabbar temple at Sippar (Steinmetzer, Deimel Festschrift pp. 302–306). A fragmentary inscription also records his confirmation and augmentation of a prebend previously granted by Aššur-nādin-šumi (B.6.27); see Brinkman and Kennedy, JCS 35 [1983] p. 39 no. Kn.5. Approximately 180 economic texts are dated by the regnal years of Šamaš-šuma-ukīn (see Brinkman and Kennedy, JCS 35 [1983] pp. 25–39 no. K and 38 [1986] pp. 100–101 no. K) and numerous letters refer to events during his reign, in particular from the time around his rebellion. Šamaš-šuma-ukīn is also mentioned in a number of prayers, incantations, and rituals. For details of his reign, see Frame, Babylonia pp. 102–90.

1

A clay cylinder found at Sippar has a bilingual inscription of Šamaš-šuma-ukīn describing the renovation of the city wall of Sippar, which had been damaged by enemy disturbances.

COMMENTARY

The cylinder (BM 91112, AH 82-7-14,1038) was found at Sippar by H. Rassam. It measures 17.5 cm in length; the diameters of the left and right ends are 4.9 and 4.7 cm respectively. The piece is hollow, with a hole in the middle of each end. The text is written in two columns, with the Sumerian version in the left column and the Akkadian version in the right column; in the transliteration presented below, the Akkadian line is given below the Sumerian line. The inscription is written in pseudo-archaic Babylonian script; it has been collated. The translation follows the Akkadian version of the inscription.

Two or three lines are found on each section of the barrel cylinder's surface and each section is followed by a single line ruling. These rulings follow lines 3, 5, 8, 11, 13, 15, 18, 20, 22, 25, 27, 29, and 32. In addition, two line rulings separate the last line (35) from the first line.

The numerous grammatical peculiarities in the Sumerian version of the inscription have been pointed out and studied by Jacobsen (Studies Tadmor pp. 279–88).

BIBLIOGRAPHY

1884 5 R pl. 62 no. 2 (copy in type)
1886 Bezold, Literatur p. 125 §69.1 (study)
1892 Jensen in Schrader, KB 3/1 pp. 198–205 (edition)
1892 Lehmann-Haupt, Šamaššumukîn 1 p. 22 and 2 pp. 6–9 and 28–56 and pls. I–IV no. 1 (Bil.) (copy, edition, study)
1895 Lehmann-[Haupt], ZDMG 49 pp. 308–309 (study)
1916 Streck, Asb. p. CCLXI no. 1 (study)
1922 BM Guide p. 230 no. 38 (study)
1933–34 Poebel, AfO 9 p. 251 (study)
1953 Falkenstein, MDOG 85 pp. 4–5 (study)
1964–66 Landsberger, WO 3 p. 77 n. 116 (study)
1972 Borger, BiOr 29 p. 34 (study)
1991 Jacobsen, Studies Tadmor pp. 279–88 (edition, study)

TEXT

1) ^{d}GIŠ.NU$_{11}$-MU-GI.NA lugal kala-ga
^{d}GIŠ.NU$_{11}$-MU-GI.NA LUGAL *dan-nu*

2) lugal am-na-nu.KI lugal KÁ.DINGIR.RA.KI
LUGAL *am-na-nu* LUGAL *ba-bi-lu*

3) á-⸢gál⸣ šà-kúš-ù-e
le-é-um mu-un-tal-ku

4) sipa ^{d}en-líl-lá še-ga ^{d}utu ^{d}AMAR.UTU-bi-da
re-é-um mi-gir ^{d}*en-líl* ^{d}UTU

5) lugal ki-in-gi uri.KI-ra-me-en
ù ^{d}AMAR.UTU LUGAL KUR *šu-me-ri u ak-ka-di-i a-na-ku*

1–5) Šamaš-šuma-ukīn, mighty king, king of the Amnānu, king of Babylon, capable (and) judicious, shepherd, favourite of the gods Enlil, Šamaš, and Marduk, king of the land of Sumer and Akkad, I —

4 The Sumerian version has "shepherd of the god Enlil, favourite of the gods Šamaš and Marduk."

6) ki úlutim ama-ugu-mu nam-en-na lu-lu
a-šar nab-ni-it um-mi a-lit-ti-ia
7) un-gal dingir-e-ne ^{d}e$_{4}$-ru$_{6}$-u$_{8}$-a
a-na e-nu-ut UN.MEŠ *šu-mi ṭa-bi-iš*
8) mu du$_{10}$-ga ḫé-en-sa$_{4}$-a
lu-ú ta-am-bi šar-rat DINGIR.MEŠ ^{d}*e-ru-ú-a*

6–8) In the womb of (my) mother who bore me (lit. "in the place of creating of the mother who bore me"), the queen of the gods, the goddess Erua, gladly appointed me to be lord of the people.

9) un bir-bir-ra-a ba-ab-du$_{7}$-du$_{7}$ ḫúl-le-eš
a-na pu-uḫ-ḫur UN.MEŠ *sap-ḫa-a-ti*
10) ki-in-gi uri.KI-ke$_{4}$ dìm-me-er gal-gal-e-ne
šá KUR *ak-ka-di-i* DINGIR.MEŠ GAL.MEŠ
11) i-bí mu-un-ši-in-bar-àm-me-en
ḫa-diš lu-ú ip-pal-su-in-ni-ma
12) garza-bi silim-ma(*)-bi ki-du-du ḫa-lam-ma-bi
a-na šul-lum par-ṣi ù ki-du-de-e ma-šu-tu
13) ul-le-eš ḫu-mu-un-sa$_{4}$-a-bi ḫé-àm
ul-ṣi-iš lu-ú im-bu-in-ni-ma

9–13) The great gods looked with pleasure upon me to gather the scattered people of Akkad and they joyfully appointed me to carry out the forgotten rites and rituals.

14) lipiš bal-til.KI TIN.TIR.KI-ta zag-bi ḫúl ḫé-en-gá-gá
ul-tu qé-reb bal-<*til*>.KI *a-na šu-bat ba-la-ṭu*
15) lugal dingir-e-ne ^{da}asar-ri-ke$_{4}$
*it-ti-ia ḫa-diš lu-ú i*ʾ*-i-ra* LUGAL DINGIR.MEŠ ^{d}*a-sa-ri*

14–15) The king of the gods, the god Asari, came happily with me from Baltil (Aššur) unto "the Seat of Life."

16) umun gu-la ur-sag ^{d}asal-lú-ḫi
be-lum ra-bu-ú qar-ra-du ^{d}AMAR.UTU
17) é-sag-íl é-gal an-ki-a bára-a-ni
ina É.MIN É.GAL AN-*e ù er-ṣe-ti*
18) sikil-la zé-eb-bi-da-aš ḫu-mu-un-ni-in-ri
šu-bat-su el-le-ti ṭa-biš lu-ú ir-mi

16–18) The great lord (and) hero, the god Marduk, gladly took up his holy residence in Esagila, the palace of heaven and netherworld.

19) dìm-me-er gal-gal-e-ne bára ki-tuš-bi
šá DINGIR.MEŠ GAL.MEŠ *a-ši-ib pa-ra-ak-ka*
20) zag til-la é-kur-ra
šá gi-im-ri é-kur-ra
21) ⌈me⌉ kal-kal šu-luḫ-ḫa-e-ne billuda-bi SUḪ-ga-⌈e⌉-[n]e
par-ṣi-šú-nu šu-qu-ru-tu pil-lu-du-šu-nu
22) [k]i-⌈bi⌉-šè ḫé-en-gi$_{4}$-⌈gi$_{4}$⌉
nu-us-su-qu-tu a-na áš-ri-šú-nu lu-ú ú-tir

19–22) I restored the precious rites (and) choice cult practices of the great gods who sit upon dais(es) in the whole of Ekur.

23) ⌈u$_{4}$⌉-bi-a bàd-u$_{4}$-ul-lí-sa$_{4}$-⌈a⌉
i-nu-šu bàd-u$_{4}$*-ul-lí-sa*$_{4}$*-a*
24) [bà]d zimbir.KI-bi(*) lú-kúr-⌈ra⌉
du-ú-ru si-ip-par šá ina e-šá-a-ti nak-ri
25) [s]ùḫ-saḫ$_{4}$-e bí-in-sig-ga bi-diri-[ga]
i-ni-šu i-qu-pu
26) [r]i-ri-ga(*)-bi ḫe-ši-in-gub-bi-e[n]
[*m*]*i-qí-it-ta-šu lu-ú uš-ziz*
27) [níg]-sig-ga-bi kala-ga ḫé-à[m]
[*e*]*n-*⌈*šu*⌉*-us-su lu-ú ú-dan-ni-in*
28) [s]ag-bi saḫar-ta ḫur-sag-g[in$_{7}$]
re-ši-šu ki-ma šá-di-i

23–29) At that time, I (re-)erected the dilapidated parts of Badullisâ ("Wall Named in Ancient Times"), the (city) wall of Sippar, which had become weak and buckled because of enemy disturbances. I strengthened its weak sections (and) with earth raised its top (as high) as a mountain.

---

6 The phrase ki úlutim ama-ugu-mu / *a-šar nab-ni-it um-mi a-lit-ti-ia* is awkward, but the motif of an individual being chosen by a deity to be ruler while still in his mother's womb is well attested in ancient Mesopotamia. Some scholars, however, have argued that it refers to the place in which Šamaš-šuma-ukīn's mother was born — "In the place in which (my) mother who bore me was created" (see, for example, Borger, BiOr 29 [1972] p. 34 and Asarh. p. 88 commentary to §57 lines 13f.). On this matter, see most recently Jacobsen, Studies Tadmor p. 280 n. 3, and Frame, Babylonia p. 96.
10 The Sumerian version has "of Sumer and Akkad" for the Akkadian "of Akkad."
14 The Sumerian version has "Babylon," for the Akkadian "the Seat of Life."
16 The Sumerian version has "the god Asarluḫi" for the Akkadian "the god Marduk"; Asarluḫi was used as an alternate name for Marduk in Standard Babylonian incantations and prayers.
21 The Sumerian version has "the precious norms of lustration rites" for the Akkadian "the precious rites."

29) ḫé-ni-íb-íl
i-n[a] e-pe-ri lu-ú ul-li
30) e-ne-ra ur-sag šul ^{d}utu ^{d}šè-ri$_5$-da
a-⌈na šat⌉-ti qar-ra-du eṭ-lu ^{d}UTU
31) é-gi$_4$-a-bi-da-ke$_4$ níg-kì-kìd-da-mu
ù ^{d}*a-a kal-la-ti ep-še-ti-ia*
32) ḫúl-le-eš sa$_6$-sa$_6$ igi bar-ra-eš-àm
dam-qa-a-ti ḫa-diš <*nap*>*-li-sa-ma*
33) me-e-mu ^{d}GIŠ.NU$_{11}$-MU-GI.NA
šá ia-a-ti ^{d}GIŠ.NU$_{11}$-MU-GI.NA
34) ní-sun$_5$-en-zé-en
áš-ri pa-liḫ-ku-nu
35) du$_{11}$-du$_{11}$-ne-ne sa$_6$-ga-mu
at-ma-a du-um-qí-ia

30–35) On account of this, O god Šamaš, the manly hero, and goddess Aya, (his) bride, look upon my good deeds with pleasure and speak well of me — Šamaš-šuma-ukīn, the humble one who reveres you!

2

Two bricks have a Sumerian inscription upon them which records the restoration of the Ebabbar temple at Sippar for the god Utu (Šamaš) by Šamaš-šuma-ukīn.

CATALOGUE

Ex.	Museum number	Registration number	Dimensions (cm)	Lines preserved	cpn
1	BM 90281	1979-12-20,174	31×30.5×7	2–14	n
2	—	—	—	1–14	n

COMMENTARY

The provenance of ex. 1 is not known. Ex. 2 was found in 1894 north of the temple at Sippar; according to Scheil, the brick was sent to the museum in Istanbul. Ex. 1 has the inscription stamped on the face of the brick; the stamped area measures 16.2×9.8 cm. It is not known if ex. 2 was stamped or inscribed. The edition is based upon the published copies and Walker's transliteration (which was based upon an examination of ex. 1). No score is presented in the microfiche.

The fact that the inscription refers to Ashurbanipal as the favourite brother of Šamaš-šuma-ukīn indicates that the inscription dates from the time before the outbreak of hostilities between the two in 652 BC.

BIBLIOGRAPHY

1888 Bezold, ZA 3 pp. 415–17 (ex. 1, copy in type, translation)
1889 Winckler, Untersuchungen p. 89 (ex. 1, edition)
1892 Lehmann-Haupt, Šamaššumukîn 2 pl. XLII [a] (ex. 1, copy)
1894 Scheil, RT 16 pp. 91–92 (ex. 2, copy in type, translation)
1895 Lehmann-[Haupt], ZDMG 49 p. 309 (exs. 1–2, study)
1902 Scheil, Sippar pp. 71 and 140 (ex. 2, provenance, translation, study)
1916 Streck, Asb. pp. CCLXIII–CCLXIV no. 4 (exs. 1–2, study, translation)
1922 BM Guide p. 75 no. 312 (ex. 1, study)
1981 Walker, CBI no. 77 (exs. 1–2, transliteration)

TEXT

1) ^{d}utu
2) lugal zimbir.KI
3) lugal-a-ni-ir
4) ^{d}GIŠ.NU$_{11}$-MU-GI.NA
5) GÌR.NÍTA šu-an-na.KI
6) lugal ki-in-gi uri.KI
7) nam-ti-la-a-ni-šè
8) ti-la-bi-da
9) AN.ŠÁR-DÙ-IBILA
10) lugal ma-da *aš-šur*-ke$_{4}$
11) šeš tam-ma-bi
12) sig$_{4}$-al-ùr-ra
13) é-babbar-ra gibil-bi
14) mu-un-na-dím

1–14) For the god Šamaš, king of Sippar, his lord: Šamaš-šuma-ukīn, (5) viceroy of Šuanna (Babylon), king of Sumer (and) Akkad, (re)constructed Ebabbar ("Shining House") anew with baked bricks for the sake of his life and for the sake of the life of Ashurbanipal, (10) king of Assyria, his favourite brother.

3

A stone stela found in the Ezida temple at Borsippa has an Akkadian inscription of Šamaš-šuma-ukīn recording the restoration of the enclosure wall of that temple for the god Nabû.

COMMENTARY

The stela (BM 90866; 80-6-17,3) was found in the room southwest of room C2 of Ezida during excavations at Borsippa in 1880 under the general direction of H. Rassam. It was not found at Babylon as has sometimes been thought (e.g., Unger, AfK 2 [1924–25] p. 23). The king is depicted on the front of the stela holding a work-basket on his head (i.e., showing him aiding in the restoration). A similar stela of Ashurbanipal (B.6.32.14) was found in the same room. The relief of the Babylonian king has been defaced, likely by supporters of Ashurbanipal following the end of the rebellion of 652–648 BC. Since the inscription on the back of the piece is not damaged, Reade suggests that the stela "had originally been built into a wall, face outwards" (Iraq 48 [1986] p. 109). The piece is made of pink marble (Reade and Walker, AfO 28 [1981–82] p. 119) and measures 31.2×21.2×5.6–8 cm in size. The inscription is written in contemporary Babylonian script and has been collated.

The mention of Ashurbanipal in a friendly connection (line 12) indicates that the inscription is to be dated before the outbreak of rebellion early in 652 BC.

BIBLIOGRAPHY

1886 Bezold, Literatur p. 125 §69.2 (study)
1890–91 Evetts, PSBA 13 p. 158 (study)
1903 de Clercq, Collection 2 p. 151 (partial translation)
1892 Lehmann-Haupt, Šamaššumukîn 1 frontispiece and pp. 22–24 no. 2; 2 pp. 10–11, 56–57, and pls. V–VII no. 2 (S[1]) (photo [inscription not visible], copy, edition, study)
1895 Meissner, Chrestomathie pp. 35–36 (copy)
1916 Streck, Asb. pp. CCLXI–CCLXII no. 2 (study)
1922 BM Guide pp. 74–75 no. 311 (study)
1924–25 Unger, AfK 2 p. 23 no. 18 (study)
1926 Unger, RLV 4/2 pl. 267e (photo [inscription not visible])
1931 Unger, Babylon p. 225 no. 14 (study)
1968 Ellis, Foundation Deposits pp. 24–25 and 179 no. 25 (partial edition, study)
1975 Orthmann, Die alte Orient pl. 250 and p. 326 (photo [inscription not visible], study)
1981 Reade in Fales, ARIN pl. II fig. 3 (photo [inscription not visible])
1982 Börker-Klähn, Bildstelen no. 226 (photo [inscription not visible], study)
1986 Reade, Iraq 48 p. 109 and pl. XIII (provenance)
1990 Starr, SAA 4 p. 237 fig. 48 (photo [inscription not visible])
1992 Frame, Babylonia p. 353 fig. 3 (photo [inscription not visible])

5 Possibly ŠU.AN.NA.KI, read *bābili* ("Babylon" not "Šuanna").

TEXT

1) ⸢*a-na*⸣-[*ku*]
2) [^{d}]⸢GIŠ.NU$_{11}$⸣-MU-GI.NA MAN *d*[*an*(?)-*nu*]
3) [MAN] TIN.TIR.KI MAN KUR.EME.GI$_7$ *u* ⸢URI⸣.K[I]
4) [ÉN]SI *ṣi-ru* SIPA *ki-nu pa-liḫ* EN ⸢EN.EN⸣
5) [*šá*] *ina* BALA-*šú* ^{d}*en-líl* DINGIR.DINGIR <^{d}>AMAR.UTU ARḪUŠ *ir-šú-u*
6) ⸢*ina*⸣ *ri-šá-a-tú a-na* TIN.TIR.KI *i*-⸢*ru*⸣-*um-ma*
7) *ina é-sag-íl šá da-rat šu-bat-su ir*-⸢*me*(?)⸣
8) *sat-tuk-ku é-sag-gíl* DINGIR.ME KUR.EME.GI$_7$ *u* ⸢URI.KI *ú*⸣-*k*[*in*(?)]
9) ⸢DUMU⸣ AN.ŠÁR-PAP-AŠ MAN GAL MAN *dan-nu* MAN ŠÚ MAN KUR *aš*-⸢*šur*⸣
10) ⸢LUGAL⸣ KUR.EME.GI$_7$ *u* URI.KI A A ^{d}30-PAP.ME-SU MAN KUR ⸢*aš-šur*⸣
11) [Š]À.BAL.BAL LUGAL-GIN MAN KUR *aš-šur* MAN KUR.EME.GI$_7$ *u* ⸢URI⸣.KI
12) ⸢*ta*⸣-*lim* AN.ŠÁR-DÙ-A MAN ŠÚ MAN KUR *aš-šur* MAN *kib-rat* 4-*ti*
13) É.SIG$_4$ *é-zi-da šá* BALA-*e* LUGAL *maḫ-ri*
14) *la-ba-riš il-lik-ma i-ni-ši tim-me-en-šú*
15) *i-na* BALA-*e-a an-ḫu-us-su ud-diš-ma*
16) *ú-za-aq-qí-ir ḫur-sa-niš*
17) *man-nu ina* LUGAL.ME *ar-ku-tú* DUMU.ME-*e-a*
18) *šá* E$_{11}$-*ma ú-ma-ʾ-a-ru* KUR
19) *ṣa-lam-a li-mur ma* Ì.GIŠ *lip-šu-uš*
20) *ni-qa-a liq-qí* MU-*a it-ti* MU-*šú*
21) *liš-ṭur-ma ep-še-ti-iá lit-ta-ʾ-id*
22) ^{d}*na-bi-um* DUB.SAR *é-sag-íl*
23) *u$_4$-me* TIN-*šú* GÍD.MEŠ *ina ṭup-pi liš-ṭur*
24) *ši-mat la-ba-ri li-šim ši-mat-su*
25) *ina ma-ḫar* ^{d}AMAR.UTU LUGAL DINGIR.MEŠ MUNUS.SIG$_5$-*šú*
26) *lit-tas-qar* ⸢*ka*⸣-*a-a-an šá šu-mì šaṭ-ru*
27) *ù* MU *ta-lim-ia ina ši-pir ni-kil-tú*
28) *i-pa-áš-ši-ṭu-ma ṣa-lam-a ú-saḫ-ḫu-u*
29) *lu-ú a-šar-šú ú-nak-ka-ru-ma*
30) ⸢*it*⸣-*ti ṣa-lam-i-šú la i-šak-ka-nu*
31) ⸢^{d}AG⸣ EN *ṣi-ru ag-giš lik-kil-me-šú-m*[*a*]
32) [*šumšu* NUM]UN-⸢*šú pi-ir*⸣-*i-šú na-an-na*-⸢*ab*⸣-[*šú*]
33) [*ina pī nišē de-šá*]-⸢*a*(?)⸣-*ti li-ḫal-l*[*iq-ma*]
34) [*ai ir-ši*]-⸢*šú*⸣ *re*-⸢*e*(?)⸣-[*mu*]

1–12) I, Šamaš-šuma-ukīn, [*mighty*] king, [king] of Babylon, king of the land of Sumer and Akkad, august [vice]-regent, true shepherd, who reveres the lord of lords; (5) the one during [who]se reign the Enlil of the gods, the god Marduk, had pity, entered Babylon amidst rejoicing, and took up his residence in Esagila forevermore; [who (re)confirmed] the regular offerings (in) Esagila (for) the gods of the land of Sumer and Akkad; son of Esarhaddon, great king, mighty king, king of the world, king of Assyria, (and) king of the land of Sumer and Akkad; grandson of Sennacherib, king of Assyria; descendant of Sargon (II), king of Assyria (and) (10) king of the land of Sumer and Akkad; favourite (brother) of Ashurbanipal, king of the world, king of Assyria, (and) king of the four quarters (of the world) —

13–16) (With regard to) the enclosure wall of Ezida ("True House") which had become old during the reign of a previous king and whose foundation had become weak, during my reign, I renovated its dilapidated sections and made (them) high as a mountain.

17–26a) Whoever among the future kings, my descendants, appears and governs the land, may he read my statue, anoint (it) with oil, (and) (20) offer a sacrifice! May he write my name with his (own) name and praise my deeds! (Then), may the god Nabû, scribe of Esagila, inscribe a long life for him upon (his) tablet, determine (for him) longevity as his lot, (and) (25) constantly say good things about him in the presence of the god Marduk, king of the gods!

26b–34) (But), as for the one who erases my inscribed name or the name of my favourite brother by some crafty device and makes my statue unrecognizable, or changes its position and (30) does not put it with his (own) statue, may the god Nabû, august lord, glare at him angrily and make [his name], his descendants, his offspring, (and) [his] progeny disappear [from the mouths of the multi]tudes [of people, and may he have no] pi[ty] upon him!

4

An Akkadian inscription of Šamaš-šuma-ukīn found on two cylinders describes the renovation of the storehouses belonging to the Ezida temple at Borsippa for the god Nabû.

CATALOGUE

Ex.	Museum number	Registration number	Dimensions (cm)	Lines preserved	cpn
1	BM 91107	AH 82-7-14,1000	Length: 15.3 R. dia.: 5.5	1–33	c
2	BM 82598	93-10-14,50	7.5×6.2	1–15, 33	c

COMMENTARY

Ex. 1 is reported to come from H. Rassam's excavations at Sippar, but in view of the contents of the inscription, one might wonder if this supposed provenance is not erroneous. The published copy is defective at a number of points and omits several signs present on the cylinder (*mut-tal-*⸢*lu*$_4$⸣, the final *-mu*, *-šú*, GI$_7$, and GAL LUGAL in lines 1, 2, 5, 17, and 18 respectively). Ex. 2 was purchased by the British Museum from J.M. Shemtob. The two exemplars are written in contemporary Babylonian script. The master line follows ex. 1, with help from ex. 2 for lines 1–14.

With regard to the reading of, and restorations in, lines 2–4, see Pinckert, Nebo p. 32; for lines 1 and 3, see in particular Ebeling, KAR no. 25 ii 27–28 and 31. The restorations in lines 28–33 are based upon B.6.32.19 lines 28–32. The reading of the middle of line 14 (ex. 2) was confirmed by a collation by A.R. George (against the reading proposed in Seux, ERAS p. 365).

The favourable mention of Ashurbanipal (lines 20 and 24–25) indicates that the inscription is to be dated before 652 BC, when Šamaš-šuma-ukīn led a rebellion in Babylonia against Assyrian overlordship.

BIBLIOGRAPHY

1892 Jensen in Schrader, KB 3/1 pp. 194–99 (ex. 1, edition)

1892 Lehmann-Haupt, Šamaššumukîn 1 p. 24 and 2 pp. 12–13, 57–58, and pls. VIII–X no. 3 (L[5]) (ex. 1, copy, edition)

1893 Bezold, ZA 8 pp. 392–94 (ex. 2, copy in type; exs. 1–2, partial transcription)

1916 Streck, Asb. pp. CCLXII–CCLXIII no. 3 (exs. 1–2, study)

1920 Pinckert, Nebo no. 6 (exs. 1–2, edition)

1994 Watanabe, ASJ 16 pp. 251–54 no. 5.3.4 (exs. 1–2, edition [ex. 1 erroneously referred to as BM 90866])

TEXT

1) [*a-n*]*a* ^{d}*na-bi-um ga-*[*aš-ru*(?) *ti-iz-qa-r*]*u*(?) IGI.GÁL DINGIR.DINGIR *šá-qu-ú mut-tal-*⸢*lu*$_4$⸣

2) ⸢DUB.SAR⸣ *gim-ri pa-q*[*id*(?) *kiššat šamê u erṣeti*(?)] *sa-niq mit-ḫur-ti mu-du-ú ka-la-mu*

3) ⸢*šar*(?)*-ḫu gít*⸣*-ma-lu ḫa-*[*mi-im kul-lat*] *par-ṣi šá gu-um-mu-ru te-re-e-ti*

4) EN *nik-la-a-ti* [*ša ina puḫur ilāni*(?)] AD.MEŠ-*šú šur-ru-ḫa-at qí-bit-su*

5) *ṣur-ru šad-lu ša l*[*ìb*(?)]-⸢*bi*⸣*-šú la i-lam-ma-du* DINGIR.DINGIR *a-a-um-ma*

6) EN *šur-bu-ú na-šu-ú e-ni na-šu-ú zik-ri ma-al-*⸢*ki*(?)⸣

7) *na-din* GIŠ.GIDRU GIŠ.GU.ZA *ù* BALA.MEŠ *mu-ki-in-nu* LUGAL-⸢*ú*⸣-[*t*]*i*

8) *re-mi-nu-ú šá a-na* ⸢*ár*(?)⸣-[*k*]*at*(?) *u*$_4$-⸢*um*⸣ *i-šar-ra-ku da-na-nu ù* ⸢*li*⸣-[*i*]*-ti*

9) *bu-kúr* ^{d}*asar-ri* ⸢*reš-tu-ú i*⸣-[*lit-t*]*i* ^{d}*e*$_4$*-ru*$_6$ *šar-rat i-lat be-le-*⸢*e*⸣*-ti*

10) *a-ši-ib é-zi-da* É *ki-i-nu ina* [*bár*]*-sipa*.KI *ma-ḫaz ra-*⸢*áš-bu*⸣ EN GAL EN-*ia*

1–10) For the god Nabû, *po*[*werful, emine*]*nt*, wisest of the gods, exalted, noble, scribe of everything, *super*[*visor of the totality of heaven and netherworld*], who makes opposing forces agree, who knows everything, splendid, perfect, who has gat[hered to himself all] the (divine) offices, who controls the omens, lord of skilful works, whose command is pre-eminent [*in the assembly of the gods*], his fathers, (5) (one with) a far-reaching mind, whose *heart* none among the gods knows, supreme lord, who raises up lords (and) the fame of rulers, who gives sceptre, throne, and reign, who confirms kingship, compassionate one, who bestows for *future days* power and victory; most important son of the god Asari (Marduk), offspring of the goddess Erua — queen (and) goddess of ladies — who dwells in Ezida — the true house, (located) in [Bor]sippa, the cult centre which is worthy of honour — great lord, my lord:

---

3 The copy of ex. 2 by Bezold indicates *mu-se-ri-bu šu-lu-ḫa* for the first part of this line (section not preserved on ex. 1), but collation suggests the reading proposed.

8.2 E[GIR(?)] for ⸢*ár*(?)⸣-[*k*]*at*(?); possibly ⸢EGIR(?)⸣ also for ex. 1.

10.2 *a-šib*.

11) *a-na-ku* ^{d}GIŠ.NU$_{11}$-MU-GI.NA LUGAL *d*[*an*(?)-*nu* LUG]AL ⸢TIN.TIR⸣.KI LUGAL KUR *šu-me-ri ù* URI.KI
12) GÌR.NÍTA ⸢*it*⸣-*pe-šú* NUN *qar-du* x [...]-*ú-ti pa-lih* EN EN.EN
13) ⸢ÉNSI⸣ [*ṣ*]*i*-⸢*i*⸣-*ri* ⸢SIPA⸣ *ki-i-*[*nu muš-t*]*e-ʾ-ú áš-rat* DINGIR.DINGIR GAL.GAL
14) *mu-še-ši-*[*ib* KÁ.DINGIR.R]A.KI *e-pi*[*š*] ⸢*é-sag-íl*⸣ *za-nin é-zi-da*
15) *ša i-na* [*palê*]-⸢*šú* ^{d}*en-líl*⸣ DINGIR.DINGIR ^{d}AMAR.UTU *sa-li-mu ir-šu-ú*
16) *i-na ri-šá-a-tú* [*a-na* TI]N.TIR.KI *i-ru-um-ma i-na é-sag-íl šá da-rat šu-bat-su ir-me*
17) *sat-tuk-ki é-s*[*ag-í*]*l* DINGIR.DINGIR KUR.EME.GI$_{7}$ *ù* URI.KI *ú-kin-nu*
18) DUMU AN.ŠÁR-ŠEŠ-SUM.N[A L]UGAL GAL LUGAL *dan-nu* LUGAL KI.ŠÁR.RA LUGAL KUR *aš-šur*
19) GÌR.NÍTA TIN.TIR.KI LUGAL KUR *šu-me-ri ù ak-ka-di-i*
20) *ta-li-mu* AN.ŠÁR-*ba-a-ni*-IBILA LUGAL GAL LUGAL *dan-nu* LUGAL KI.ŠÁR.RA LUGAL KUR *aš-šur*
21) DUMU DUMU ^{d}30-ŠEŠ.MEŠ-SU LUGAL GAL LUGAL *dan-nu* LUGAL KI.ŠÁR.RA LUGAL KUR *aš-šur*
22) ŠÀ.BAL.BAL LUGAL-GI.NA LUGAL GAL LUGAL *dan-nu* LUGAL KI.ŠÁR.RA LUGAL KUR *aš-šur*
23) NUMUN LUGAL-*ú-ti da-ru-ú ša* ^{d}EN-*ba-ni* DUMU *a-da-si* NUNUZ *bal-til*.KI
24) *a-na* TI ZI.MEŠ GÍD.DA UD.MEŠ *šá-lam* NUMUN GIN BALA.MEŠ *sa*-⸢*kap*⸣ LÚ.KÚR
25) *ša* AN.ŠÁR-*ba-a-ni*-IBILA LUGAL KUR *aš-šur* ŠEŠ *ta-li-mi-ia ù ia-a-ti*
26) [*a-n*]*a* TI ZI.MEŠ-*ia* GÍD.DA ⸢*u*$_{4}$⸣-*me-ia šá-lam* NUMUN-*ia* GIN BALA.MEŠ-*ia la* GÁL-e GIG-*ia*
27) [...] x ⸢*bu*(?)⸣-*ru a-ha-meš* É.ŠUTUM$_{x}$(GI$_{6}$.NAM.AB.DU$_{7}$).MEŠ *é-zi-da eš-šiš ú-še-piš-ma ú-zaq-qìr hur-sa-niš*
28) [*aiumma* NU]N EGIR-*ú šá ina* BALA-*e-šú ši-pir šu-a-tú in-na-hu i-raš-šu-ú ni-kit-tú*
29) [*anhūssu l*]*u-ud-di-iš šu-mì it-ti* MU-*šú liš-ṭur* MU.SAR-*ú-a li-mur-ma*
30) [*šamni lipšuš* (UDU).S]ISKUR *liq-qí it-ti* MU.SAR-*e-šú liš-ku-un ik-ri-bi-šú* ^{d}*na-bi-um i-šem-me*
31) [*ša šumī šaṭru u šum*] ⸢*ta-li*⸣-*mi-ia i-na ši-pir ni-kil-ti i-pa-áš-ši-ṭu*
32) [*mušarûa iʾabbatu lū a*]-⸢*šar*⸣-*šú ú-nak-ka-ru-ma it-ti* MU.SAR-*e-šú la i-šak-ka-nu*
33) [*nabium bēlu ṣīru ag-g*]*iš lik-kil-mi-šú-ma* MU-*šú* NUMUN-*šú ina* KUR.KUR *li-hal-liq*

11–23) I, Šamaš-šuma-ukīn, [*mighty*] king, [ki]ng of Babylon, king of the land of Sumer and Akkad, wise viceroy, valiant prince, [...], who reveres the lord of lords, wise vice-regent, true shepherd, [who is assid]uous toward the sanctuaries of the great gods, who (re)settl[ed Babyl]on, (re)built Esagila, (and) provides for Ezida; (15) the one during whose [reign] the Enlil of the gods, the god Marduk, relented, entered Babylon amidst rejoicing, and took up his residence in Esagila forevermore; the one who (re)confirmed the regular offerings (in) Esagila (for) the gods of the land of Sumer and Akkad; son of Esarhaddon, great king, mighty king, king of the world, king of Assyria, viceroy of Babylon, (and) king of the land of Sumer and Akkad; (20) favourite (brother) of Ashurbanipal, great king, mighty king, king of the world, (and) king of Assyria; grandson of Sennacherib, great king, mighty king, king of the world, (and) king of Assyria; descendant of Sargon (II), great king, mighty king, king of the world, (and) king of Assyria; descendant of the enduring royal lineage of Bēl-bāni, son of Adasi, scion of Baltil (Aššur) —

24–27) In order to ensure the good health of Ashurbanipal, king of Assyria, my favourite brother, to prolong (his) life, to ensure the well-being of (his) descendant(s), to confirm (his) reign, and to defeat (his) enemy, and, with regard to me, to ensure my good health, to prolong my life, to ensure the well-being of my descendant(s), to confirm my reign, (and) to ensure that I might have no illness, [...] together, I had the storehouses of Ezida built anew and made (them) high as a mountain.

28–30) May [any] future [pr]ince, during whose reign this work falls into disrepair (and) sustains damage, repair [its dilapidated state]! May he write my name with his (own) name, look at my royal inscription, [anoint (it) with oil], offer a sacrifice, (and) place (my royal inscription) with his (own) royal inscription! The god Nabû will (then) listen to his prayers.

31–33) [(But) as for the one who] erases [my inscribed name or the name] of my favourite brother by some crafty device, [(or) destroys my royal inscription, or] changes its position and does not place (it) with his (own) royal inscription, may [the god Nabû, august lord], glare at him [ang]rily and make his name (and) his descendant(s) disappear from the lands!

---

27 É.ŠUTUM$_{x}$(GI$_{6}$.NAM.AB.DU$_{7}$).MEŠ is a fanciful writing for É.ŠUTUM(GI.NA.AB.DU$_{7}$).MEŠ; see George, House Most High p. 160 sub no. 1236.

5

A fragmentary tablet in the University Museum (Philadelphia) has two dedicatory texts inscribed upon it. As far as it is preserved, the first (lines 1–5) only mentions Ashurbanipal and it is edited with the inscriptions of that king (B.6.32.23). The second describes the building of an object — likely a piece of equipment for a boat — for the god Nabû either by Šamaš-šuma-ukīn alone or in collaboration with his brother Ashurbanipal. The inscription is written in Akkadian and was probably copied from the original text inscribed upon the object itself. Since the god is described as the "lord of Borsippa, who dwells in Ezida" (line 28), the object was undoubtedly dedicated to the god Nabû at that city.

COMMENTARY

The tablet is composed of two fragments (CBS 733+1757) which come from the Khabaza collections of the University Museum and which were joined by W.G. Lambert. It measures 9.3×5.7×2.7 cm. The inscription is written in contemporary Babylonian script and is separated from B.6.32.23 by a line ruling. The inscription has been collated.

Salonen thought that the inscription dealt with the making of a processional chariot for the journey from Borsippa to Babylon (Landfahrzeuge p. 59). Lambert, however, has argued that it more likely deals with a piece of equipment for the boat used by the god Nabû for the annual journey to Babylon for the New Year's festival. (The word for boat may actually appear in line 15, but the passage is damaged and thus this cannot be considered certain.) Since the object is described as being 18 1/2 cubits long and brought with difficulty, he suggests that it may be a mast or pole made of some exotic wood (AfO 18 [1957–58] p. 386).

Lambert notes that the names of Ashurbanipal and Šamaš-šuma-ukīn both appear on the tablet, "though always in broken lines so that it is uncertain if one or both were donors" (AfO 18 [1957–58] p. 385). In what is preserved of the first text, only the name Ashurbanipal appears; thus that text has been assigned to that king (B.6.32.23). In the second text only the name Šamaš-šuma-ukīn is preserved in the sections describing the making of the object and the verb used in these sections is in the singular (*ušēpišma*, lines 15 and 31). Thus the second text on the tablet is assigned to Šamaš-šuma-ukīn. The name of Ashurbanipal is preserved at one point in the second text (line 36), but at the end of the inscription in what might be an invocation to the god to bless the two brothers.

The mention of both Šamaš-šuma-ukīn and Ashurbanipal suggests that the inscription comes from the time before the outbreak of hostilities between the two brothers.

Nabû is called by the names Šiddukišarra and Mudugasâ (lines 18 and 21 respectively); for these names, see Pomponio, Nabû.

BIBLIOGRAPHY

1908 Clay, BE 8/1 no. 142 (copy of CBS 733)
1909 Ungnad, ZA 22 pp. 13–16 (edition of CBS 733)
1909–10 Kugler, SSB 2/1 pp. 78–81 (partial edition of CBS 733, study)
1951 Salonen, Landfahrzeuge p. 59 (study to line 17)
1957–58 Lambert, AfO 18 pp. 385–87 and pl. XXV (copy, edition)
1983 Brinkman and Kennedy, JCS 35 p. 39 no. Kn. 10 (study)

TEXT

Obverse
(For lines 1–5, see B.6.32.23)

6) *a-na* MUL ^{d}AMAR.UTU *mug-dáš-ru* x NE AŠ ŠU x (x) ḪA (erasure) *šá-qu-*⸢*ú*⸣ [*na*]*m-ru*

6–13) For the star of the god Marduk, mighty ... exalted, [br]ight, the god Šiḫṭu, lord of catchwater,

6 Marduk was usually associated with the "star" Jupiter, but at New Year's he was associated with Mercury (see Lambert, AfO 18 [1957–58] 387).

7) ^{d}GU$_{4}$.UD EN *kup-pu nag-b[i]* x *ta-ma-ti* DAGAL-*tim mu-*⸢*šab-šu-ú*⸣ ŠÈG *u* ILLU
8) ^{d}*im-du-du mut-t[al-l]i-ku šá* AN-*e u* KI-*tim*
9) EN *šib-ṭu šá-a-ru* x [x] *u*(?) *mi-ḫe-e šá-ki-nu* (erasure) *ri-*⸢*iḫ-ṣu*⸣
10) ⸢^{d}AG⸣ *ni-bu*(?)-⸢*ú*⸣ [*t*]*a*(?)-⸢*mi-iḫ*⸣ *ṣer-*⸢*ret er-ṣe*⸣-*t*[*im*] ⸢*ù*⸣ *ki-gal-l*[*i*]
11) MUL ^{d}UTU.È *ù* ^{d}UTU.ŠÚ.A ⸢ZA⸣ x [x] x Ú ŠU x [x]
12) *šá ana ta-mar-ti-šú* ^{d}*í-gì-gì u* ^{d}*a-nun-na-ki ḫ*[*a*(?)-*diš*(?)] x x ⸢MEŠ⸣ x [x (x)]
13) *a-šib é-zi-da šá qé-reb bár-sipa*.K[I ...]
14) ^{d}GIŠ.NU$_{11}$-MU-GI.NA GÌR.NÍTA TIN.TIR.KI x [...]

Lower Edge

15) ⸢*ú*⸣-*še-*⸢*piš-ma*⸣ GIŠ.⸢MÁ(?)⸣ x x x x [...]
16) [*ma*]*r-ṣi-iš ib-bab-la* x x (x) ⸢*iš*(?)-*di-iḫ*⸣ x x x [...]
17) [*a*]-*na ru-ku-bu be-lu-ti-šú* GAL-*tú a-la-*⸢*ku*⸣ *u ta-a-ru* x [...]
18) [^{d}*šid-d*]*ù-ki-šár-ra pa-qid kiš-šat* AN-*e u* KI-*tim* AŠ x x [...]
19) [x x] ⸢*a*⸣-*na* E$_{11}$-*šú e-ma mu-ú* ZI-*tì* KUR *ba-lat* ⸢ZI-*tì* É *kiš*⸣-x [...]

Reverse

20) [x (x)-*a*]*k-ku-uš ṣi-i-ru šit-ra-ḫu bu-*⸢*kúr*⸣ ^{d}⸢*asar*⸣-*ri ra*[*p-šú* ...]
21) ⸢^{d}⸣*mu-du*$_{10}$-*ga-sa*$_{4}$-*a šur-bu-ú ma-lik* x x x x ⸢AN⸣ x x [...]
22) EN *nik-la-a-ti da-pi-nu šá ina* ⸢*mil-ki*⸣ x [...] x ⸢MEŠ⸣ [...]
23) NUN.ME *kiš-šat* ⸢É⸣.[MEŠ(?)] x x x ⸢*ú*⸣ DUB [...] *mu*[*š*-...]
24) *sa-niq mit-*⸢*ḫur-ti*⸣ *pa-qí-du kul-*⸢*la*⸣-*t*[*i* x] DU x [...]
25) *rap-šá uz-ni ṭup-šar* ⸢*é*⸣-*sag-*⸢*íl*⸣ *ḫa-*[*a-a-i*]*ṭ* ^{d}*í-gì-gì u* [^{d}*a-nun-na-ki*]
26) *na-ši ṭup-pi* NAM.⸢MEŠ⸣ DINGIR.DINGIR GAL.GAL ⸢*a*⸣-*ši-ir ka-l*[*a-ma*]
27) ⸢*le*⸣-ʾ-⸢*ú* IGI.GÁL⸣-[*la*] DINGIR *šá šu-tu-*[*r*]*at be-lu-u*[*s-su*]
28) [E]N ⸢*bár*⸣-[*si*]*pa*.KI *a-šib* ⸢*é*⸣-*zi-*⸢*da* EN(?) GAL(?)⸣ E[N(?)-*šu*(?)]
29) ⸢^{d}GIŠ⸣.[N]U$_{11}$-MU-GI.NA ⸢GÌR.NÍTA⸣ [TIN.TIR.KI]
30) [L]UGAL KUR [*š*]*u-me-ri ù ak-k*[*a-di-i*]
31) ⸢*ú*⸣-[*še*]-⸢*piš*⸣-[*m*]*a šá* 18 1/2 ⸢KÙŠ⸣ [...]
32) [*a-na*] ⸢TIN ZI⸣.[ME(Š)]-⸢*šú* GÍD.DA⸣ UD.MEŠ-*šú* x [...]

Left Edge

33) [...] ⸢*li-šim*(?) *ši-mat-su*⸣
34) [...] x RI x [...]
35) [...] x ⸢DI AN⸣ x [...]
36) [...] x x *aš-šur*-DÙ-A [...]
37) [(x x) ^{d}GIŠ.N]U$_{11}$-MU-GI.NA LUG[AL x (x)]

spring ... (and) wide seas, who produces (both) rain and flood, the god Imdudu, who roams through heaven and netherworld, lord of the wind blast ... *and* storm, who establishes the inundation, (10) the god Nabû, the bright one who holds the lead-rope of earth and netherworld, star of East and West ..., at whose appearance the Igīgū gods and the Anunnakū gods *hap*[*pily*] ... who dwells in Ezida, which is inside Borsippa, [(...) *his lord*]:

14–31) Šamaš-šuma-ukīn, viceroy of Babylon [...] had (this) ... made and *a boat* ... it was brought with difficulty ... *procession* ... for the conveyance of his great lordship, (for his) going and returning [..., the god Šidd]ukišarra, who administers all of heaven and netherworld ... for his descent where water, the life of the land, the well-being of the house ...[...] (20) ... august, splendid, son of the god Asari (Marduk), *who has bro*[*ad understanding* ...], the god Mudugasâ, supreme, ruler ... lord of ingenious things, martial, who in counsel [...] expert of all the *temp*[*les*] ...[...] the one who makes opposing forces agree, who administers everything [...], (25) who has broad understanding, scribe of Esagila, who wa[tches ov]er the Igīgū gods and [the Anunnakū gods], who bears the tablet of the fates of the great gods, who supervises every[thing], capable, wise, god who[se] rule is pre-eminent, lord of Borsippa, who dwells in Ezida, *the great lord* [*his*] *l*[*ord*], Šamaš-šuma-ukīn, viceroy [of Babylon], (30) king of the land of Sumer and Akk[ad] had (this object) of 18 1/2 cubits made [...].

32–33) [In order] to ensure his good health, to prolong his days [...] may he *determine* as his fate!

34–37) [...] ... [...] ... [...] ... Ashurbanipal [... Šama]š-šuma-ukīn, kin[g ...]

7 Šiḫṭu was a name for the planet Mercury.

6

An Akkadian inscription on a cylinder fragment preserves part of the epithets and genealogy of Šamaš-šuma-ukīn.

COMMENTARY

The cylinder fragment, BM 41650 (81-6-25,266), was purchased by the British Museum from Mssrs. Spartali & Co; it measures 6.5×4.7 cm. The inscription is similar to, but is not an exact duplicate of, B.6.33.3 lines 5–11 and B.6.33.4 lines 15–19 and 21–22, from which the restorations come. The inscription is written in contemporary Babylonian script and is published here with the permission of the Trustees of the British Museum.

TEXT

Lacuna

1′) [...] x [...]

2′) [*ina*] *ri-šá-a-*⸢*ti a*⸣*-na* ⸢KÁ.DINGIR⸣.[RA.KI *īrumma*]

3′) [*ina*] *é-sag-íl ša da-ra-*[*ti šubassu irme*]

4′) [*sat-tuk-k*]*i é-sag-íl ù* DINGIR.MEŠ KUR [*šumeri u akkadî ukinnu*]

5′) [*mār* A]N.ŠÁR-ŠEŠ-SUM.NA LUGAL GAL LUGAL *da*[*n-nu šar kiššati šar māt aššur*]

6′) [GÌR.NÍT]A TIN.TIR.KI LUGAL KUR *šu-me-*[*ri u akkadî*]

7′) [DUMU DUM]U ^{d}30-ŠEŠ.MEŠ-SU LUGAL GAL L[UGAL *dannu šar kiššati šar māt aššur*]

8′) [ŠÀ.BAL.B]AL ⸢LUGAL-GI.NA LUGAL⸣ G[AL *šarru dannu šar kiššati šar māt aššur*]

Lacuna

Lacuna

1′–8′) [the one during whose reign, the Enlil of the gods, the god Marduk, relented, entered] Babylon [amidst] rejoicing [and took up his residence in] Esagila forever[more; the one who (re)confirmed the regular offer]ings for Esagila and the gods of the land of [Sumer and Akkad; (5′) son of] Esarhaddon, great king, mig[hty] king, [king of the world, king of Assyria, vicero]y of Babylon, (and) king of the land of Sume[r and Akkad; grandso]n of Sennacherib, great king, [mighty] k[ing, king of the world, (and) king of Assyria; descend]ant of Sargon (II), gr[eat] king, [mighty king, king of the world, (and) king of Assyria]

Lacuna

2001

Sîn-šarra-uṣur, a governor of Ur during the time of Šamaš-šuma-ukīn, has left an Akkadian inscription recording his gift of a tract of land to two goddesses of Uruk — Ištar and Nanāia. According to the inscription, he dedicated the land to the two deities for the good health of the king Šamaš-šuma-ukīn.

CATALOGUE

Ex.	Museum museum	Dimensions (cm)	Lines preserved	cpn
1	AO 6793	7.35×5.1×2.2	1–20	c
2	HE 144	5.7×7.7	1–20	(p)

COMMENTARY

The original provenance of the two tablets is not known, although in view of their contents it seems likely that they came from Uruk or possibly Ur. The published photo of ex. 2 shows only lines 1–13; thus, the published copy has been used to edit the remainder of this exemplar. The master line follows ex. 1, with help from ex. 2 in lines 1 and 20. Both exemplars are written in contemporary Babylonian script. Ex. 1 was collated by D.R. Frayne.

Sîn-šarra-uṣur was the son of Ningal-iddin, an individual who had held the governorship of Ur in the time of Esarhaddon, and the brother of two other governors of Ur (Sîn-balāssu-iqbi and Sîn-tabni-uṣur). Durand has argued cogently that Sîn-šarra-uṣur's tenure in office followed that of Sîn-balāssu-iqbi and preceded that of Sîn-tabni-uṣur, that he was appointed governor at some point before the outbreak of Šamaš-šuma-ukīn's rebellion in 652 BC, and that he was a supporter of Šamaš-šuma-ukīn rather than of Ashurbanipal. In Babylonian economic texts, Sîn-balāssu-iqbi is attested in office in 658 and 657 BC and Sîn-tabni-uṣur in 650 and 649 BC. With regard to the activities of Sîn-šarra-uṣur, see Frame, Babylonia, particularly pp. 126 and 162–67.

BIBLIOGRAPHY

1914 Scheil, RT 36 pp. 188–90 no. 24 (ex. 2, copy, edition)
1927 Contenau, TCL 12 no. 13 (ex. 1, copy)
1935 Moore, NBAD no. 13 (ex. 1, edition)
1981 Durand, RA 75 pp. 181–85 (exs. 1–2, photo, study)
1982 Durand, Doc. Cun. 1 no. 144 (ex. 2, copy)
1983 Brinkman and Kennedy, JCS 35 p. 39 no. Kn.11 (exs. 1–2, study)

TEXT

1) *a-na* ^{d}INANNA GAŠAN *šur-bu-tu* ^{md}30-LUGAL-ÙRU LÚ.⸢GÌR⸣.NÍTA ÚRI.KI
2) *a-na* TIN ZI.MEŠ *šá* ^{md}GIŠ.NU$_{11}$-MU-GI.NA LUGAL E.KI
3) 6 ME 60-*šu* SAG.KI AN.TA ÚS.SA.DU ^{m}*at-ra-a*
4) *a-di* É LÚ.U$_{4}$.SAKAR.ŠE.GA *i-šad-da-ad*
5) UŠ AN.TA *u* KI.TA *ul-tu* ZIMBIR.KI
6) *a-di* URU *su-ra-nu i-šad-da-ad*
7) *a-na* ^{d}*iš-tar u* ^{d}*na-na-a id-din*
8) *man-nu at-ta lu-ú* LUGAL *lu-ú* LÚ.UGULA
9) *šá te-el-lam-ma mi-ṣir ù* NÍG.DU
10) *tu-šá-an-nu-ú* ^{d}AMAR.UTU EN GAL-*ú*
11) ^{d}*en-líl* EN KUR.KUR *a-ga-nu-til-la-a*
12) *še-rit-su šá la pa-ṭa-ru lu-šar-šiš*
13) ^{d}INANNA UNUG.KI GAŠAN *ṣir-tim a-bi-ik-ti*
14) BAD$_{5}$.BAD$_{5}$ ÉRIN-*ni-šú liš-ku-un ina ma-ḫar* LÚ.KÚR-*šú*
15) *qab-li-šú lip-ṭur* ^{d}*na-na-a ra-ʾ-mat*
16) ^{d}AG *u* ^{d}AMAR.UTU *ina ma-ḫar* ^{d}AG *ra-ʾi-mi-šú*
17) *le-mut-ta-šú lit-taz-kar* ^{d}U.GUR *dan-nu-dan-nu* DINGIR.MEŠ
18) *kaš-kaš* DINGIR.MEŠ *zi-kìr qar-du ina šib-ṭu*
19) *u* BAD$_{5}$.BAD$_{5}$ *la i-gam-mil nap-šat-su*
20) NUMUN *u* MU *li-kim-šú-ma* 1-*en* UD *la ba-lat-su liq-bi*

1–7) For the goddess Ištar, supreme lady: Sîn-šarra-uṣur, viceroy of Ur, in order to ensure the good health of Šamaš-šuma-ukīn, king of Babylon, gave to the goddesses Ištar and Nanāia (a plot of land measuring) 660 (cubits along its) upper width, bordering (the property of) Atrāia (and) stretching to the estate of the *simmagir*-official; (5) its upper and lower lengths stretch from the Euphrates (River) to the town Sūrānu.

8–20) Whoever you are, whether king or overseer, who appears and changes the border or boundary line, may the god Marduk, the great lord, highest-ranking god (and) lord of the lands, afflict him with dropsy (as) his punishment which cannot be alleviated! May the goddess Ištar of Uruk, the august lady, inflict defeat and rout on his army! (15) May she ungird him (lit. "loosen his loins") in the presence of his enemy! May the goddess Nanāia, beloved of the gods Nabû and Marduk, continually speak evil of him in the presence of the god Nabû, the one who loves him (Sîn-šarra-uṣur)! May the god Nergal, the mightiest of the gods, most overpowering of the gods (and) valiant male, not spare his life in plague or bloody battle! May he take away his descendant(s) (and) his name, and decree that his life (last) not one day (more)!

Kandalānu

B.6.34

After the death of Šamaš-šuma-ukīn, the fall of Babylon to the Assyrians, and thus the end of the rebellion in 648 BC, the Assyrian king Ashurbanipal appointed an individual by the name of Kandalānu as king of Babylonia. It has sometimes been thought that Ashurbanipal and Kandalānu were the same person, with the Assyrian king ruling Babylonia under a separate "Babylonian throne name," but it seems more likely that they were separate individuals. Although Kandalānu reigned for twenty-one years (647–627 BC), nothing is known about him and he was probably a puppet ruler, one installed merely to keep up the pose of a separate kingship of Babylonia. More than two hundred economic documents are dated by the regnal years of Kandalānu, but no royal inscriptions of this king are attested and almost nothing is known of political events in Babylonia during this time. A few inscriptions of Ashurbanipal which were found in Babylonia, however, were probably composed during the time Kandalānu was ruler of that land (for example B.6.32.15). An inscription of the earlier Babylonian king Marduk-šāpik-zēri which records work on the Ezida temple at Borsippa was copied during the reign of Kandalānu and a colophon noting this was appended to the copy; this inscription and colophon are presented as B.2.7.2. With regard to the reign of Kandalānu, see Frame, Babylonia pp. 191–213 and 296–306; Brinkman, RLA 5/5–6 (1980) pp. 368–69; and Brinkman and Kennedy, JCS 35 (1983) pp. 39–52 no. L and 38 (1986) pp. 101–102 no. L.

Aššur-etel-ilāni

B.6.35

Ashurbanipal was succeeded as ruler of Assyria by his son Aššur-etel-ilāni (or Aššur-etelli-ilāni). No inscription ever calls Aššur-etel-ilāni "king of Babylon," "viceroy of Babylon," or "king of the land of Sumer and Akkad," nor is he included in the various lists of rulers of Babylonia, which put Sîn-šumu-līšir or Nabopolassar after Kandalānu. However, a number of royal inscriptions of Aššur-etel-ilāni do come from Babylonia and describe actions in that land and thus these have been included here. Over ten economic texts dated by his regnal years as "king of Assyria" or "king of the lands" come from Nippur and these attest to his accession, first, second, third, and fourth years (see Brinkman and Kennedy, JCS 35 [1983] pp. 52–53 and 38 [1986] p. 103 no. M). In her inscription from Harran, however, the mother of the Neo-Babylonian king Nabonidus refers to only three years for Aššur-etel-ilāni (though this number does not necessarily have to refer to his full reign). If Ashurbanipal did not die or relinquish the throne of Assyria until 627 BC (see above) and if Aššur-etel-ilāni did not ascend the throne of Assyria before that time (either as co-ruler or full ruler), then Aššur-etel-ilāni would have reigned over at least part of the Assyrian empire from 626 (first regnal year) until at least 623 BC (fourth regnal year). However, the dates of the successors to Ashurbanipal and Kandalānu and the events at that time present many difficulties; they have been much discussed and remain uncertain. N. Na'aman has recently supported the view that Ashurbanipal died and was succeeded by Aššur-etel-ilāni in 631 BC and that the latter reigned until sometime in 627 BC (ZA 81 [1991] pp. 243–67). For a discussion of previous attempts to deal with these matters, see Zawadzki, Fall of Assyria pp. 23–63. With regard to the reign of Aššur-etel-ilāni, see in particular J. Oates, CAH² 3/2 pp. 162–78, 184, and 186.

Royal inscriptions of Aššur-etel-ilāni record that he had an offering table made for use before the statue of the god Marduk in (presumably) Babylon (B.6.35.1) and gave a gold sceptre to the statue of that god in Sippar-Aruru (B.6.35.2). He also carried out work on the temple of the god Uraš at Dilbat (B.6.35.3) and on the Ekur temple of the god Enlil at Nippur (B.6.35.4). Another inscription records how he returned the body of a Chaldean from Assyria to the latter's home and laid it in a tomb (B.6.35.5). Inscription B.6.35.4 is written in Sumerian and the remainder are in Akkadian. The inscriptions are found upon clay tablets (B.6.35.1–2 and B.6.35.5 ex. 2), bricks (B.6.35.3–4), and clay cylinders (B.6.35.5 exs. 1 and 3).

1

This Akkadian inscription records the dedication of an offering table to the god Marduk by Aššur-etel-ilāni. A private note at the end of the text mentions food offerings, an individual's name, and a date (eleventh day of the sixth month of the third year).

COMMENTARY

The tablet (PTS 2253) is part of the Princeton Theological Seminary collection and is currently on loan to the University Museum, Philadelphia. The collection was purchased by the Princeton Theological Seminary from Yale University in 1915 and Yale had earlier acquired the items in the collection from various dealers. Thus, the original provenance of the text is not known. Since Marduk is described as "lord of Babylon, one who dwells in Esagila" (lines 8–9), it is likely that the table mentioned in the inscription was to be placed in the Esagila temple. This might suggest that the inscription comes from Babylon. The tablet is roughly oval in shape and has been flattened at the edges. Leichty states that it appears that a previously inscribed tablet had been moistened and flattened for reuse. The tablet measures 11.8×8.7 cm and the inscription has been collated.

Leichty suggests that lines 1–20 are the manuscript for the inscription to be carved or painted upon the offering table and that they were written by the individual who appears in line 22 — Nādin, son of Bēl-aḫḫē-iqīša — to serve as a model for the craftsmen. The offerings mentioned in line 21 were perhaps to have been presented to Marduk in the name of Nādin when the table was dedicated. Line 12 is unintelligible and appears to have been inserted in between lines 11 and 13; there is no contextual break between lines 11 and 12. In the left margin between lines 16 and 17 are traces of what may be two signs, possibly ŠÁ NU. Leichty suggests that "they, as well as the blank spaces on the tablet, have to do with the placing of the inscription on the table ... Perhaps these notes refer to decoration on the table in which case we should probably read NU as *ṣalam* 'relief, drawing.'"

The inscription is written in contemporary Babylonian script, although a few sign forms are in Neo-Assyrian script.

BIBLIOGRAPHY

1983 Leichty, JAOS 103 pp. 217–20 (photo, edition)
1986 Brinkman and Kennedy, JCS 38 p. 103 no. Mn.2 (study)

TEXT

Obverse

1) [*a-na* ^{d}AMAR.UT]U(?) ⌈*kab*⌉-*tu šit-ra-ḫu* ^{d}*en-líl* DINGIR.MEŠ *šá-qu-ú*
2) [*e-li* DINGIR].MEŠ *a*-⌈*šir*⌉ DINGIR.MEŠ *ka-la-me mu-kil mar-kas* ^{d}*í-gì-gì*
3) [*ù* ^{d}*a*]-⌈*nun*⌉-*na-ki mu-ma-ʾ-ir* DINGIR *ku-na* LUGAL ŠÚ AN-*e ù* KI-*tim*
4) ⌈*šá*(?) *a*(?)-*na*(?) *zik*⌉-*ri-šú* DINGIR.MEŠ GAL.MEŠ *pal-ḫiš ú-taq-qu-ú qí-bit-su*
(space)

1–4) [To the god Mardu]k, venerable, splendid, the Enlil of the gods, most exalted [of the god]s, one who directs all the gods (and) holds the link between the Igīgū gods [and the A]nunnakū [gods], commander, honoured god, king of the totality of heaven and netherworld, at whose mention the great gods fearfully attend his command,

---

5) *šaḫ-tú la-a-nu ši-i-ḫu šá ina* ZU.AB *ir-bu-ú bal-ti šùr-ru-ḫu*
6) *me-na-a-ta šu-tu-ru ṣu-ub-bu-ú nab-ni-ti le-ʾ-u*$_{16}$
7) *le-ʾ-ú-tu mu-du-ú ka-la-me la-mid ṭè-em* ZU.AB

5–9a) respectful, large of stature, one who grew up in the Watery Abyss (*apsû*), (whose) dignity is splendid, (whose) body is superior, (and whose) features are perfect, most capable of all (the gods),

---

3 The translation takes *ku-na* to be from *kunnû*, "honoured," although one would expect *ku-un-nu-ú*.

8) *a-ḫi-iz pi-riš-ti làl-gar* EN KÁ.DINGIR.RA.KI

one who knows everything, understands the will of the Watery Abyss, (and) comprehends the secret(s) of the *lalgar*, lord of Babylon, one who dwells in Esagila, great lord, lord of the world:

9) *a-šib é-sag-íl* EN GAL-*ú* EN ŠÚ ^{m}AN.ŠÁR-*e-tel-li*-DINGIR.MEŠ
10) LUGAL ŠÚ LUGAL KUR AN.ŠÁR.KI GIŠ.BANŠUR GIŠ.MES.MÁ.KAN.NA
11) *iṣ-ṣi da-ru-ú* ⸢*šá ṣa*⸣-*ri-ri* ḪUŠ.A *uḫ-ḫu-zu*
Reverse
12) ŠÁ NU KÁT MAŠ x
(space)
13) [*i*]-⸢*na*⸣ *ši-pir* DUMU.ME *um*-⸢*ma*⸣-*nu nak-liš šu-pu-šú a-na si-ma-a-ta*
14) ⸢*ma-ka-le*⸣-*e* KÙ.ME *šu-lu-ku a-na* TIN ZI.MEŠ-*šú še-me-e*
15) *su-pe-e-šú sa-kap* LÚ.KÚR.MEŠ-*šú* BA-*eš*

9b–15) Aššur-etel-ilāni, king of the world (and) king of Assyria, presented (this) table of *musukkannu*-wood — durable wood, which is mounted with red *ṣāriru*-gold ... artistically made by the skill of craftsmen, (and) suitable for the fitting things of the pure food offerings — in order to ensure his good health, so that his prayers be heard, and to overthrow his enemies.

16) ^{d}AMAR.UTU EN GAL-*ú* (erasure) GIŠ.BANŠUR *šu-a-ti*
17) *ḫa-diš ina nap-lu-si-ka* ^{d}*šul-pa-è-a* EN GIŠ.BANŠUR
18) *ina ra-kas* GIŠ.BANŠUR *šá-rak sur-qin-nu ka-a-a-an la na-par-ka-a*
19) *a-mat* MUNUS.SIG$_5$ ^{m}AN.ŠÁR-*e-tel-li*-DINGIR.ME LUGAL KUR AN.ŠÁR.KI
20) NUN *mi-gir lìb-bi-ka lit-tas-qar ma-ḫar-ka*
(erased line)
(space)

16–20) O god Marduk, great lord, when you look upon this table with pleasure, (and) when (this) table is set (and) the regular, ceaseless offerings are presented, may the god Šulpaea, the lord of the table, speak well of Aššur-etel-ilāni, king of Assyria (and) your favourite prince, before you!

21) 2 SÌLA 3 *šal-šú* NINDA SISKUR 1 (PI) 1 (BÁN) GIŠ.PÈŠ ḪÁD.A *ina maš-šar-ti šá* ITI.DU$_6$
22) ^{m}*na-din* A ^{md}EN-PAP.ME-BA-*šá* ITI.KIN UD 11.KÁM MU 3.KÁM

21–22a) Two *qû* (and) three and one-third *akalu* (as) offerings; one *pānu* (and) one *sūtu* of dried figs from the *maššartu*-deliveries of the month of Tašrītu. Nādin, son of Bēl-aḫḫē-iqīša.
22b) Month of Elūlu, eleventh day, third year.

2

An inscription of Aššur-etel-ilāni, written in Akkadian, describes how the king had had a gold sceptre made for the god Marduk and had placed it in the god's temple at Sippar-Aruru.

COMMENTARY

The clay tablet VAT 13142 was found at Babylon in the Merkes Temple (entry) in 1911. It bears the Babylon excavation number 42262 and is shown on Babylon excavation photograph 2329. VAT 13142 was identified by W.G. Lambert as the piece published in the Deimel Festschrift by Ebeling (who gave no museum or excavation number for the piece and stated that it was among the Assur texts of the Berlin museum). The piece measures 6.8×3.5×1.9 cm. The inscription is written in Neo-Assyrian script and shows evidence of several erasures. The tablet was collated by J. Marzahn.

---

8 CAD 9 [L] p. 47 describes *lalgar* as "cosmic subterranean water."
21 Two *qû* and three and one-third *akalu* are equivalent to approximately two and one-third litres. One *pānu* and one *sūtu* are equivalent to approximately forty-two litres (assuming a *sūtu* of 6 *qû*, see M. Powell, RLA 7/7–8 [1990] p. 498 §IV.7).

The name of the temple *é-èš-ér-ke*$_4$ means "House, Shrine of Weeping" and is not otherwise attested. A.R. George tentatively suggests that the name may be a corruption of *é-še-ri-ga* ("House Which Gleans Barley"), the temple of Šidada at Dūr-Šarrukīn (=Sippar-Aruru), which may well have contained a secondary cult of the god Marduk (George, House Most High p. 83 no. 269). W.G. Lambert has suggested to me that "weeping" may refer to that of the gods Tiāmat and Kingu, and their allies, whose defeat by Marduk is mentioned in lines 5–6.

BIBLIOGRAPHY

1935 Ebeling, Deimel Festschrift pp. 71–73 (edition)
1995 Marzahn and Frame, JCS 47 (copy, study) [in press]

TEXT

1) ⌈*a*⌉-*na* ^{d}MES EN *šur-bé-e* UR.⌈SAG⌉ MAḪ
2) EN EN.EN *šá-qu-u šá gat-tú šur-ru-ḫu*
3) UGU *kal* DINGIR.MEŠ *ma-ʾ-diš šur-bu-ú*
4) *na-ši* [*m*]*e*-⌈*lam*⌉-*me ez-zu-ti la-biš na-mur-ra-te*
5) *ṭa-r*[*id*] ⌈^{d}⌉*kin-gu ka-šid tam-tim gal-la-ti*
6) *ka*-⌈*mu lem-nu*⌉-*ti a-šib é-èš-ér-ke*$_4$
7) *šá qé-reb* ZIMBIR.KI-^{d}*a-ru-ru* EN GAL-*e* EN-*šú*

8) ⌈^{m}⌉[A]N.[ŠÁR]-⌈*e*⌉-*tel-li*-DINGIR.MEŠ MAN ŠÚ MAN KUR *aš-šur*.KI
9) ⌈DUMU ^{m}AN.ŠÁR-DÙ⌉-A MAN ŠÚ MAN KUR *aš-šur*.KI
10) *ú-še-piš-ma* GIŠ.NÍG.GIDRU KÙ.GI ḪUŠ.A
11) *šá a-na ṣi-bít* ŠU.II-*šú* KÙ-*tu*$_4$ *šar-ku*
12) *a-na* TI.LA ZI.MEŠ-*šú* GÍD.DA UD.MEŠ-*šú*
13) GIN BALA.MEŠ-*šú šá-lam* NUMUN-*šú šur-šú-du* GIŠ.GU.ZA MAN-*ti-šú*
14) *še-me-e su*(*)-*up-pi-šú ma-ḫa-ri taṣ-lit-i-šú*
15) *ina qé-reb é-èš-ér-ke*$_4$ *ú-kin da-riš*
16) *ù šá* LÚ.KU$_4$.É LÚ *ki-na-al-ti* UN.MEŠ *šú-a-te*
17) *mal ba-šú-u mu-šal-li-mu al-ka-ka-ti-šú*
18) *šu-bar-ra*-<*šú*>-*nu a-na u*$_4$-*me ṣa-a-ti iš-kun*

Colophon
19) (erasure) *šá ina* UGU GIŠ.NÍG.GIDRU KÙ.GI *šá* ^{d}MES

1–7) For the god Marduk, supreme lord, august hero, lord of lords, exalted, who(se) figure is splendid (and who) is vastly superior to all the (other) gods, bearer of awe-inspiring, terrible radiance, clothed in splendour, (5) who drove [off] the god Kingu, defeated the *angry* sea, (and) overcame the evil ones, who dwells in Eešerke — which is inside Sippar-Aruru — great lord, his lord:
8–15a) Aš[šur]-etel-ilāni, king of the world (and) king of Assyria, son of Ashurbanipal, king of the world (and) king of Assyria, (10) had a sceptre of red gold made which was (then) presented for his (Marduk's) pure hands to grasp. He (Aššur-etel-ilāni) set (it) up forever inside Eešerke in order to ensure his good health, to prolong his days, to confirm his reign, to ensure the well-being of his descendant(s), to make his royal throne secure, (and) to ensure that his prayers are heard (and) his supplication(s) granted.
15b–18) He established for (all) future days the freedom from taxation of those privileged to enter the temple, the collegium, *those* people, as many as there are, who look after his (Marduk's) ways.

Colophon
19) That which is (written) upon the gold sceptre of the god Marduk.

3

This Akkadian inscription of Aššur-etel-ilāni found upon a brick records his restoration of E-ibbi-Anum ("House the God Anum Named"), the temple of the god Uraš and the goddess Ninegal at Dilbat, and in particular his clearing of the well in that temple.

5 The "sea," *tam-tim*, is the goddess Tiāmat, who, like her son and supporter Kingu (or Qingu), was defeated by Marduk in the Babylonian creation epic *Enūma eliš*.
16 Instead of the singular form *šuāte*, one expects a plural form to modify UN.MEŠ, "people."

COMMENTARY

The brick (Ash 1922.190) is part of the Weld-Blundell collection in the Ashmolean Museum, Oxford, and measures 38×9.5×8 cm. According to Langdon the piece comes from Dilbat (Langdon, OECT 1 p. 37); however, it is unclear if this provenance was determined solely by means of the contents of the inscription or by some knowledge about where the piece was actually found. The inscription is inscribed along the edge of the brick in Babylonian script and has been collated.

With regard to the temple E-imbi-Anum/E-ibbi-Anum, see Unger in RLA 2/3 (1935) pp. 222–23 and George, House Most High p. 102 no. 493.

BIBLIOGRAPHY

1923 Langdon, OECT 1 pp. 37–38 and pl. 29 (copy, edition)

1927 Luckenbill, ARAB 2 §1135A (translation)

1957 Borger, Orientalia NS 26 p. 7 (study to line 3 ^{d}*báḫar*)

1981 Walker, CBI no. 87 (transliteration)

TEXT

1) *a-na* ^{d}*uraš* EN MAḪ SAG.KAL DINGIR.ME GAL.ME *é-i-bí-*^{d}*a-num* BÁRA *ra-aš-bu* EN GAL-*u* EN-*šú* ^{m}AN.ŠAR$_4$-NIR.GÁL-DINGIR.ME MAN KUR AN.ŠÁR.KI

2) *mu-ud-diš* BÁRA DINGIR.ME GAL.MEŠ <<GAL.ME>> DUMU ^{m}⸢AN⸣.ŠÁR-DÙ-A MAN KUR AN.ŠÁR.KI SIPA *ṣal-mat* SAG.DU *é-i-bí-*^{d}*a-num áš-ri el-lu*

3) *šá qé-reb dil-bat*.KI *šu-bat* ^{d}*uraš u* ^{d}*nin-é-ga*[*l*] *uš-šiš a-gur-ru pi-ti-iq* ^{d}*báḫar eš-šiš ib-ni-ma* SUḪUŠ PÚ KI-*šú*

4) *ki-i pi-i la-bi-ri-im-ma ú-kin* ⸢*u*⸣-[*n*]*a du-ur u*$_4$*-me zu-mur* PÚ MU.MEŠ GIM ÍD.IDIGNA *u* ÍD.<BURANUN> *ub-bi-ib-ma*

5) *ana nap-ta-nu* DINGIR.ME GAL.MEŠ *ú-kin* A.⸢MEŠ⸣-*šú* A.MEŠ *šu-nu-ti-e-ma a-na nap-ta-nu uš-taḫ-ma-ṭu u*$_4$*-mi-šam ana* ^{d}AG

6) ^{d}AMAR.UTU ^{d}*uraš u* ^{d}*nin-é-gal a-ši-bu q*[*é-r*]*eb* É MU(*).ME SIG$_5$*-tim* ^{m}AN.ŠÁR-NIR.GÁL-DINGIR.ME(*) MAN *mi-gir-šú-un li-iq-bu-u li-ri-ik* BALA-*šú*

1a) For the god Uraš, august lord, foremost of the great gods of E-ibbi-Anum — the shrine (which is) worthy of honour — great lord, his lord:

1b–6) Aššur-etel-ilāni, king of Assyria, who renovated the shrine(s) of the great gods, son of Ashurbanipal, king of Assyria, shepherd of the black-headed (people), renovated E-ibbi-Anum, the holy place which is inside Dilbat, the abode of the god Uraš and the goddess Ninegal. He (re)built (it) anew with baked bricks, the product of the god Baḫar and, with regard to the foundation of the well, he (re-)established its position as (it had been) in ancient times. For future days he cleaned this entire well (in order to make its water as pure) as (that of) the Tigris and <Euphrates> rivers, and (5) he established its water for the meals of the great gods. That water shall be brought every day in good time for (their) meals. May they say good things about Aššur-etel-ilāni, the king, their favourite, to the gods Nabû, Marduk, Uraš, and Ninegal, who dwell in that temple! May his reign be long!

4

A fragment of an inscribed brick has a Sumerian inscription stating that Aššur-etel-ilāni (re)built the Ekur temple at Nippur.

3 Baḫar was the god of potters.

5 The understanding of the passage follows a suggestion by J.N. Postgate.

COMMENTARY

Since the piece is part of the Hilprecht collection of the Friedrich-Schiller-Universität at Jena (HS 1958, formerly HS 42), it probably comes from the excavations of the University of Pennsylvania at Nippur between 1888 and 1900. The contents of the inscription would also support such a provenance. The fragment measures 15.2×9.6×6.6 cm, but was cut down to this size in modern times. The inscription is inscribed, not stamped, and is written in Babylonian script, with some of the sign forms having archaizing features. The inscription was collated by J. Oelsner.

As noted by Edzard, both this inscription and one of Ashurbanipal's (B.6.32.16) appear to be based upon an inscription of Adad-šuma-uṣur which has been found on several bricks from Nippur (Hilprecht, BE 1/1 no. 81 and duplicates).

BIBLIOGRAPHY

1959–60 Edzard, AfO 19 p. 143 (photo, edition)
1969 Oelsner, WZJ 18 p. 54 no. 33 (study)

TEXT

1) [^{d}en-líl]
2) [lugal kur]-⸢kur⸣-[ra]
3) [lugal-a]-ni-ir
4) [AN.ŠÁ]R-*e-tel-lu*$_4$-DINGIR.MEŠ
5) [sip]a še-ga-bi
6) ú-a nibru.KI(*)
7) sag-ús(*) é-kur-ra
8) lugal kala-ga
9) lugal ub-da límmu-ba
10) é-kur-ra
11) é ki-ág-gá-a-ni
12) sig$_4$-al-ùr-ra-ta
13) mu-un-na-dù

1–13) For [the god Enlil, lord of the la]nds, his [lord: Aššu]r-etel-ilāni, (5) his obedient [shephe]rd, who provides for Nippur, supporter of Ekur, mighty king, king of the four quarters (of the world), (re)built (10) Ekur, his beloved temple with baked bricks.

5

Three exemplars exist of an Akkadian inscription in which Aššur-etel-ilāni records how he moved the tomb of a Dakkurian by the name of Šamaš-ibni from Assyria to Bīt-Dakkūri. This Šamaš-ibni is probably to be identified with the leader of Bīt-Dakkūri who was taken to Assyria and executed in 678 BC. Aššur-etel-ilāni's action presumably reflects an attempt by him to win the support of this important Chaldean tribe.

CATALOGUE

Ex.	Museum number	Object	Dimensions (cm)	Lines preserved	cpn
1	YBC 2151	Cylinder	10.6×5.4	1–20	c
2	NBC 6069	Tablet	9.7×2.7	1–2, 19–20	c
3	NBC 6070	Cylinder	10.3×4.9; Dia. of end: 3.3	2–17	c

COMMENTARY

According to Clay (YOS 1 p. 60), the dealer from whom ex. 1 was purchased stated that it had been found at "Tel Khaled a few miles to the southeast of Hilla, near the present course of the Euphrates." This may be Tulūl al-Ḫālidija; see Zadok, WO 16 (1985) pp. 54–55 and n. 166. There is no information on the provenances of the other two exemplars, which passed through the antiquities market (Clay, YOS 1 p. 60 n. 1). Ex. 1 was collated both before and after it was baked. Several tiny fragments — at least some of which do not belong to this cylinder — had been attached to the piece in modern times and these were removed at the time of baking. These fragments are currently stored with YBC 2151 and preserve all or parts of one or more signs. These fragments are not taken into consideration in the score. All three exemplars are inscribed in contemporary Babylonian script. The line arrangement is the same for all three texts (as far as they are preserved) and the master line follows ex. 1, with help from exs. 2–3 in line 2 and ex. 3 in lines 3 and 7–12.

According to two chronicles, the governor of Nippur and Šamaš-ibni, "the Dakkurian" (i.e., ruler of the tribe of Bīt-Dakkūri), were taken to Assyria and executed in the third year of Esarhaddon (678 BC). While nothing more is known of the governor of Nippur, Esarhaddon's royal inscriptions tell us of Šamaš-ibni's crime. They record that this Chaldean sheikh had forcibly taken possession of fields belonging to the inhabitants of Babylon and Borsippa. Undoubtedly Šamaš-ibni had taken control of this land while Babylon lay abandoned after its destruction by Sennacherib in 689 BC and problems had probably arisen over ownership of the land when Esarhaddon began the restoration of Babylon. Esarhaddon sent Assyrian troops south, plundered Bīt-Dakkūri, returned the land to its original owners, and made Nabû-ušallim, son of Balāssu, head of the tribe instead of Šamaš-ibni. On this matter, see Frame, Babylonia pp. 79–80.

Dūru-ša-Ladīni, to which the tomb was transferred, was a fortified settlement in the area of the Bīt-Dakkūri tribe. See Unger, RLA 2/4 (1936) p. 247 sub Dûr-Ladinna.

BIBLIOGRAPHY

1915 Clay, YOS 1 no. 43 (ex. 1, copy, edition)
1918 Meissner, OLZ 21 223 (ex. 1, partial translation)
1922 Ungnad, OLZ 25 3 (ex. 1, study)
1927 Luckenbill, ARAB 2 §§1132–35 (ex. 1, translation)
1937 Stephens, YOS 9 no. 81 (ex. 2, copy) and no. 82 (ex. 3, copy)
1982 Bottéro in Gnoli and Vernant, La mort pp. 383–86 no. 6 and p. 403 (exs. 1–3, edition)
1988 Hecker, TUAT 2/4 p. 478 (exs. 1–3, translation)

TEXT

1) KI.MAḪ *šá* ^{md}UTU-*ib-ni* DUMU ^{m}*da-ku-*⸢*ru šá*⸣ ^{m}AN.ŠÁR-NIR.GÁL-DINGIR.MEŠ LUGAL KUR *aš-šur*
2) *re-e-mu ir-šá-áš-šum-ma ul-tu qé-reb* KUR *aš-šur a-na* É-^{m}*da-kur* KUR-*šú*
3) *ú-bil-la-áš-šum-ma ina* KI.MAḪ *ina qé-reb* É-*šú šá* BÀD-*šá-la-di-ni ú-šá-aṣ-li-lu-šú*

1–3) The tomb of Šamaš-ibni, the Dakkurian, upon whom Aššur-etel-ilāni, king of Assyria, had pity, brought from Assyria to Bīt-Dakkūri, his (own) country, and laid to rest in a tomb inside his home of Dūru-ša-Ladīni ("Fortess of Ladīnu").

4) *man-nu at-ta lu-ú* LÚ *šak-nu lu-ú* LÚ *šá-pi-ru lu-ú da-a-a-nu*
5) *lu-ú* NUN *šá ina* KUR *iš-šak-ka-nu a-na* KI.MAḪ *u e-ṣe-et-ti*
6) *šu-a-ti la ta-ḫa-aṭ-ṭu a-šar-šú ú-ṣur*
7) *ṣi-il-li ṭa-a-bi e-li-šú tu-ru-uṣ*
8) *a-na šu-a-ti* ^{d}AMAR.UTU EN GAL-*ú pa-le-e-ka lu-ur-ri*[*k*]
9) *ṣu-lul-šú ṭa-a-bu e-li-ka li-iš-k*[*un*]
10) ⸢MU⸣-*ka* NUMUN-⸢*ka ù ba-la-ṭu* u_4⸣-*me*-⸢*ka* GÍD.DA.MEŠ *a-na* u_4-*me ṣa-a-ta*⸣ *lik*-⸢*ru*(?)-*bu*(?)⸣

4–10) Whoever you are, whether governor or commander or judge or prince, who is appointed in the land, do not harm this tomb or (its) bone(s)! (But rather) look after its position (and) extend (your) good protection over it! For (doing) this, may the god Marduk, the great lord, lengthen your reign, establish his good protection over you, (and) *bless* your name, your descendant(s), and your long life for all time!

11) *šum-ma* NUN *šu-ú lu-ú* LÚ *šak-nu lu-ú* LÚ *šá-pi-ru lu-ú da-a-a-nu*
12) *lu-ú* GÌR.NÍTA *šá ina* KUR *ib-ba-áš-šu-ú*
13) *a-na* KI.MAḪ *u e-ṣe-et-ti šu-a-ti i-ḫa-aṭ-ṭu-ú*
14) *a-šar-šú ú-nak-ka-ri a-na a-šar šá-nam-ma i-leq-qu-ú*

11–20) (But) if that prince or governor or commandant or judge or viceroy who appears in the land harms this tomb or (its) bone(s), (or) changes its position, taking (it) to another place, (15) or (if) another person incites him to plan wicked things (against this tomb) and he listens (to him), may the

15) *ù man-ma a-na li-mut-tu*$_4$ *ú-šad-ba-bu-šú-ma i-šem-mu-ú*
16) ᵈAMAR.UTU EN GAL-*ú* MU-*šú* NUMUN-*šú* NUNUZ.MEŠ-*šú ù na-an-nab-šú*
17) *i-na pi-i* UN.MEŠ *li-ḫal-liq*
18) ᵈAG *sa-ni-iq mit-ḫur-ti mi-na-a-ta u*$_4$*-me-*⸢*šú* GÍD.DA⸣.MEŠ ⸢*li-kar-ri*⸣
19) ⸢ᵈU.GUR⸣ *ina di-ʾ šib-*⸢*ṭu*⸣ *u šag-*⸢*ga*⸣*-áš-ti*
20) *la i-gam-mi-il nap-šat-su*

god Marduk, the great lord, make his name, his descendant(s), his offspring, and his progeny disappear from (mention by) the mouth(s) of the people! May the god Nabû, who makes opposing forces agree, cut short the number of his days (lit. "the number of his long days")! May the god Nergal not spare his life from *malaria*, plague, or slaughter!

Sîn-šumu-līšir

B.6.36

According to the Uruk King List, there were two kings of Babylonia in the year following the reign of Kandalānu (626 BC): Sîn-šumu-līšir and Sîn-šarra-iškun. Babylonian King List A may also record Sîn-šumu-līšir as the successor of Kandalānu, but the reading of the name in the text is most uncertain. The Ptolemaic Canon, however, appears to assign this year to Kandalānu by crediting him with a reign of twenty-two years instead of the twenty-one known. Aššur-etel-ilāni states that upon the death of Ashurbanipal he was installed on the throne of Assyria by an official by the name of Sîn-šumu-līšir, who is presumably to be identified with the individual mentioned in the Uruk King List. Such an identification does, however, present some difficulty. Aššur-etel-ilāni was king of Assyria for at least four years and he seems to indicate that Sîn-šumu-līšir was a loyal supporter of his for some time after the death of Ashurbanipal. Unless we assume a date of death for Ashurbanipal before 627 BC (see introduction to B.6.32), the Uruk King List would indicate that he had rebelled soon after that death. It is clear that there was some uncertainty in Babylonia following the end of Kandalānu's reign and that the land was divided in its loyalties. One chronicle indicates that there had been no king in the land in 626 BC until Nabopolassar ascended the throne in the eighth month of that year and another chronicle refers to insurrections in Assyria and Babylonia at that time. In the eighth month of 627 and the eighth month of 626 BC economic texts were dated at Babylon in, respectively, year twenty-one and year twenty-two "after (the death of) Kandalānu," thereby indicating that the scribes did not know whom to acknowledge as the current authority. See Grayson, Chronicles p. 88 no. 2 lines 14–15 and p. 132 no. 16 lines 24–27; Grayson, RLA 6/1–2 (1980) p. 93 iv 23′, p. 97 obv. 4′, and p. 101; and Postgate, Royal Grants nos. 13–14.

No royal inscriptions of Sîn-šumu-līšir are attested from Babylonia. At least seven Babylonian economic texts (including four from Babylon and one from Nippur) are dated by his accession year. In these he is either given no title, or called "king of Assyria" or simply "king." With regard to the reign of Sîn-šumu-līšir, see J. Oates, CAH^2 3/2 pp. 163, 168–70 and 172–76; Brinkman and Kennedy, JCS 35 (1983) pp. 53–54 no. N and 38 (1986) p. 104 no. N; and Naʾaman, ZA 81 (1991) pp. 243–57.

Sîn-šarra-iškun

B.6.37

The last Assyrian king to exercise any control over at least part of Babylonia was Sîn-šarra-iškun, a son of Ashurbanipal. Exactly when he became ruler of Assyria and when he held authority in Babylonia is unclear, but his reign over Assyria ended in 612 BC. Only the Uruk King List includes him among the rulers of Babylonia, assigning the year following the reign of Kandalānu and preceding the reign of Nabopolassar (626 BC) to Sîn-šumu-līšir and Sîn-šarra-iškun jointly (Grayson, RLA 6/1–2 [1980] p. 97 obverse 4′–5′). No known inscription gives him the title "king of Babylon," "viceroy of Babylon," or "king of the land of Sumer and Akkad." Although he is mentioned in a Babylonian chronicle, he is given no title and it is not clear if the entry refers to the year 628, 627, or 626 BC. The passage in the chronicle is damaged but his name appears to be mentioned in connection with the hostilities between Assyria and Babylonia at that time (Grayson, Chronicles pp. 87–88 no. 2 lines 1–13). According to the Hellenistic writer Berossos, Sîn-šarra-iškun (Sarakos) sent Nabopolassar to Babylon as general to deal with a force invading from the Sealand; Nabopolassar then rebelled against him (see Scurlock, RA 77 [1983] pp. 95–96). If this is correct, Sîn-šarra-iškun must have made Nabopolassar general before the latter took the Babylonian throne toward the end of 626 BC.

No Babylonian royal inscriptions of Sîn-šarra-iškun are attested and his Assyrian inscriptions will be edited elsewhere in the RIM series (as A.0.116). Approximately sixty economic texts were dated by his regnal years in Babylonia. These indicate that at times he controlled Babylon, Nippur, Sippar, and Uruk; the earliest texts come from his accession year and the latest from his seventh year. None of these economic texts, however, gives him the title "king of Babylon"; he is called instead "king of Assyria," "king of the lands," and "king of the world." With regard to the reign of Sîn-šarra-iškun, see in particular J. Oates, CAH[2] 3/2 pp. 162–70 and 172–85; Borger, JCS 19 (1965) pp. 67–68; and Brinkman and Kennedy, JCS 35 (1983) pp. 54–59 no. O and 38 (1986) p. 104 no. O.

Unidentified

B.6.0

There are a few of inscriptions of officials whose exact date is not known but which may well come from the tenth to seventh centuries. These are presented here.

2001

A mace head bears an inscription stating that the object had been given to the god Nabû by Nabû-mukīn-apli, the governor of Babylon. A date for the inscription around the seventh century has been proposed by Brinkman (PKB p. 171 n. 1034). The family of Nūr-Sîn, to which Nabû-mukīn-apli belonged, is best attested during the time of the Neo-Babylonian kings, thus it is possible that the inscription comes from that period. The inscription is in the Akkadian language and written in Neo-Babylonian script.

COMMENTARY

The mace head is made of blue chalcedony and was once in the possession of C.J. Ball. Its present location is not known. The inscription is edited from a copy prepared by I.L. Finkel from a plaster cast of the inscription which was once in the possession of T.G. Pinches; the published photograph has also been consulted for those parts of the inscription visible upon it.

With regard to the family of Nūr-Sîn, see the unpublished doctoral dissertation of L.B. Shiff, "The Nūr-Sîn Archive: Private Entrepreneurship in Babylon (603–507 B.C.)" (University of Pennsylvania, 1987).

BIBLIOGRAPHY

1899 Ball, Light pp. 51 and 216–17 (photo, edition)

1926 Speleers, Les Arts de l'Asie Antérieure ancienne (Brussels) pl. 24 fig. 518 (photo [inscription illegible])

1951 Cocquerillat, RA 45 p. 22 no. 24 (study)

1968 Brinkman, PKB p. 171 n. 1034 (study)

1987 Finkel, RA 81 p. 189 (copy, edition)

TEXT

1) *ana* ᵈPA EN *ṣi-ri* UMUN-*šú* ᵐᵈPA-GIN-A A ᵐZÁLAG-ᵈ30

2) LÚ.BUR.GUL ᵈAMAR.UTU LÚ.GAR.UŠ$_8$ TIN.TIR.KI *ana* TIN ZI.ME-*šú* GÍD.DA *u$_4$-me-šú* SILIM NUMUN-*šú*

1-3) For the god Nabû, the august lord, his lord: Nabû-mukīn-apli, son of Nūr-Sîn, the seal-cutter of the god Marduk, governor of Babylon, had (this mace head) made and presented (it to him) forever in Babylon in order to ensure his good health, to

3) DÙG-*ub lìb-bi-šú* GIN SUḪUŠ.ME-*šú ina* TIN.TIR.KI *ana da-ra-a-ti ú-še-piš-ma* BA

prolong his days, to ensure the well-being of his offspring, to ensure his happiness, (and) to confirm his position.

2002

Three bronze situlae bear short inscriptions of officials (B.6.0.2002–2004). The date of these cannot be determined with any degree of precision; however, similar bronze situlae are generally thought to come from the tenth and ninth centuries. (With regard to the dating of bronze situlae, see Calmeyer, Reliefbronzen pp. 223–33.) Two other situlae with inscriptions have already been presented as B.6.1.2001–2002. The first of these three situlae is in Teheran and bears a possession inscription of a governor of Babylon and chief administrator of the Esagila temple by the name of Nabû-šumu-līšir.

COMMENTARY

The piece is said to come from the Māh-i-dasht plain and is currently no. 7409–1409 in the Iran Bastan Museum. Amiet states that the piece measures 7.2 cm in height, while Calmeyer says it measures 14.1 cm in height and the maximum diameter of the opening is 6.[illegible] cm. The relief on the situla depicts two bulls facing each other. The inscription has not been collated and is edited from the published copy, with some help from the published photograph which shows only a portion of the inscription.

Calmeyer (Reliefbronzen p. 148) notes that a palace of a Nabû-šumu-līšir of the Dakkūru tribe is mentioned on a stone weight (B.6.10.2001). While it is not impossible that both texts refer to one individual, it seems more likely that two different individuals are meant.

BIBLIOGRAPHY

1965 Calmeyer, BJVF 5 p. 38 no. L1 (provenance, study)
1966 Calmeyer, BJVF 6 p. 70 no. L1 (study)
1969 Calmeyer, Datierbare Bronzen p. 166 no. 83 (transliteration)
1971 Moorey, Catalogue Ashmolean p. 34 no. 5 (study)
1973 Calmeyer, Reliefbronzen pp. 74–75 and 148 no. L1 (provenance, drawing, edition by Edzard and Wilcke, study; additional bibliography)
1976 Amiet, Luristan p. 45 n. 10 and p. 46 fig. 31 (photo, copy, edition)

TEXT

1) ⸢*šá*⸣ [md]AG-MU-SI.SÁ DUMU [m]MU-*líb-ši*(?) EN NAM KÁ.DINGIR.RA.KI
2) ŠÀ.TAM *é-sag-íl*

1–2) (Property) of Nabû-šumu-līšir, son of Šumu-libši, provincial governor of Babylon (and) chief administrator of Esagila.

2003

A bronze situla in the collection of the Louvre Museum bears a possession inscription of a royal official (*ša rēš šarri*) by the name of Šamaš-mukīn-aḫi.

COMMENTARY

The situla (AO 25000) was once in the David-Weill collection; it entered the Louvre in 1931. The piece is similar to bronze situlae thought to come from Luristan. It measures 11.1 cm in height and 5.5 cm in diameter. The relief on the situla depicts a banquet. The inscription has been edited from the published photograph.

Instead of *mukīn*, the middle element of the individual's name could also be read *kīn*. The term *ša rēš šarri* is possibly to be translated "royal eunuch." For a bronze dagger with an inscription of another *ša rēš šarri*, see B.2.6.2001.

BIBLIOGRAPHY

1972 Amiet, Revue du Louvre 22 p. 430 and fig. 10 (photo, translation)
1973 Calmeyer, Reliefbronzen p. 32 and 148 no. A27 (study)
1976 Amiet, Luristan no. 79 (photo, copy, edition [by W.G. Lambert], study)

TEXT

1) *šá* ^{md}[UT]U-GIN-PAP DUMU ^{md}UTU-PAB LÚ.SAG LUGAL

1) (Property) of Šamaš-mukīn-aḫi, son of Šamaš-nāṣir, the *ša rēši* of the king.

2004

A bronze situla in the Foroughi collection bears an inscription of a royal official (*ša rēš šarri*). The piece is said to come from Luristan, but nothing about its actual provenance is known. The published photograph of the piece shows part of the inscription, but not a sufficient amount to warrant an edition here. See Calmeyer, Reliefbronzen pp. 72–73 no. K2 (photo, study).

2005

A bronze mace head in the Foroughi collection bears a short Akkadian possession inscription of a royal official (*ša rēš šarri*). Since a similar piece in the same collection bears an inscription mentioning the Assyrian king Adad-nārārī III (810–783 BC), it is quite possible that this inscription should be assigned to an Assyrian official as opposed to a Babylonian one. (For the inscription mentioning Adad-nārārī III, see Dossin, IrAnt 2 [1962] pp. 162–63 and pl. XXX no. 27.) The piece is said to come from Luristan, but nothing is known about its actual provenance.

COMMENTARY

The inscription has been edited from the published photograph of an impression of the inscription. The reading of the name of the individual is not clear and the proposed reading assumes that ^{d}EN is written with a ligature, as is commonly done in first millennium texts. Dossin suggested *Eri-šu*(?)-x-x and Calmeyer *eri-ba*$^{!?}$-x. If the final sign of the name is IGI, we may have some form of the verb *amāru* or *maḫāru*.

BIBLIOGRAPHY

1962 Dossin, IrAnt 2 p. 162 and pl. XXX no. 26 (photo, edition)
1968 Brinkman, PKB p. 11 no. 14 and p. 363 no. q (study)
1969 Calmeyer, Datierbare Bronzen p. 93 no. 43B and p. 167 no. 90 (transliteration, study)
1971 Moorey, Catalogue Ashmolean p. 34 no. 1 (study)

TEXT

1) *šá* ^{m}⌈^{d}(?)EN(?)-IGI(?)⌉ LÚ.SAG LUGAL	1) (Property) of *Bēl-...*, the *ša rēši* of the king.

SŪḪU

S.0

The land of Sūḫu was situated on the Middle Euphrates, from the northwestern border of Babylonia (probably located somewhere around modern Ramādī) as far as the small state of Ḫindānu (which was located in the region around modern Abū Kemal), and included such cities as Anat, Suru, and Ra'il. Salvage work in the Ḥadītha area recently uncovered a number of inscriptions and these have been published by Antoine Cavigneaux and Bahija Ismail. Those which can be assigned to a particular individual with any degree of certainty come from two governors of "the land of Sūḫu and the land of Mari": Šamaš-rēša-uṣur (S.0.1001) and his son and successor Ninurta-kudurrī-uṣur (S.0.1002). The ancient city of Mari was situated in the part of the Middle Euphrates which was called the land of Laqû, an area controlled by the Assyrians at this time. Thus, it is likely that neither Šamaš-rēša-uṣur nor Ninurta-kudurrī-uṣur actually controlled Mari and that the term "land of Mari" was employed in the title for historical reasons. Ninurta-kudurrī-uṣur was previously unknown, but Šamaš-rēša-uṣur has long been known from a stela of his found at Babylon (S.0.1001.1), though even the relative date of his governorship has been disputed. In connection with an Aramean incursion which occurred at the beginning of his tenure as governor, Ninurta-kudurrī-uṣur's inscriptions mention Sîn-šallimanni, the governor of Ruṣapu (Raṣappa); see S.0.1002.1 line 27 (partially restored) and S.0.1002.2 i 33. Sîn-šallimanni is included in the Assyrian eponym lists as governor of Raṣappa in 747 BC and is known to have been appointed to that post at some point after 775 BC and to have relinquished it before 737 BC (see RLA 2/5 [1938] pp. 424–25, 430–32, and 454). Thus, it is likely that Šamaš-reša-uṣur and Ninurta-kudurrī-uṣur ruled Sūḫu sometime in the first two-thirds of the eighth century, and in particular around the second quarter of that century. Sūḫu's independence was probably brought to an end by Tiglath-Pileser III (744–727 BC), who extended Assyrian control in the west and south.

The new inscriptions give the genealogies of Šamaš-rēša-uṣur and Ninurta-kudurrī-uṣur and provide information on previous governors of Sūḫu and Mari. The immediate ancestors of Šamaš-rēša-uṣur and Ninurta-kudurrī-uṣur were: Kudurru, Adad-nādin-zēri, an individual whose name is not preserved, Uaiiāmu (reading uncertain), and Iqīša-Marduk (the father of Šamaš-rēša-uṣur). Each is said to be the son of the preceding and all except Uaiiāmu, and possibly the individual whose name is not preserved, are stated to have been governors of the land of Sūḫu and the land of Mari. Ultimately, Šamaš-rēša-uṣur and Ninurta-kudurrī-uṣur traced their ancestry back to Ḫammu-rāpi, the king of Babylonia, via a descendant (literally "son," *māru*) of Ḫammu-rāpi's by the name of Tunamissaḫ; Tunamissaḫ is known to be a Kassite name. (See in particular S.0.1001.2–3 and S.0.1002.1.) The inscriptions of Ninurta-kudurrī-uṣur also inform us that immediately prior to the time of his father, Šamaš-rēša-uṣur, the city of Anat had been ruled by Assyria for fifty years (and also for the first three years of his father's governorship) and that during those fifty years the governors of the land of Sūḫu had been Tabnēa, Iqīša-Marduk, and Nasḫir-Adad (see for example S.0.1002.9). Nergal-ēriš (or Palil-ēriš), the Assyrian governor of Raṣappa who held the office of Assyrian eponym in 803 and 775 BC, claimed to be governor of numerous other places, including Anat, Sūḫu, Ḫindānu, and Laqû (see RLA 2/5 [1938] pp. 422–23, 429–30, and 457 sub Urigal-êriš, and RIMA 3 A.0.104.6 lines 23–25 and 7 lines 13–20). It would seem likely that he controlled Sūḫu during part of these fifty years; possibly one or more of the individuals mentioned by Ninurta-kudurrī-uṣur were subordinate to him. The inscriptions of Ninurta-kudurrī-uṣur also state that one Enamḫe-zēra-ibni had been a governor of the land of Sūḫu and the land of Mari at some point in the past (see, for example, S.0.1002.1 line 9 and S.0.1002.2 iv 9′–10′).

Šamaš-rēša-uṣur's and Ninurta-kudurrī-uṣur's ancestor Kudurru is mentioned as governor of the land of Sūḫu in Assyrian inscriptions from the time of Ashurnasirpal II (king of Assyria 883–859 BC). Ashurnasirpal II states that although Kudurru had received military support from the Babylonian king Nabû-apla-iddina (B.6.6), Kudurru and his allies were defeated in battle by the Assyrians; some time later the inhabitants of the Middle Euphrates again rebelled against Assyria and were defeated by Ashurnasirpal's troops for a second time (see RIMA 2 A.0.101.1 iii 15–38). Kudurru is also depicted upon one of the bronze bands from the gates at Balawat (see RIMA 2 A.0.101.97). Kudurru's son Adad-nādin-zēri may be the object of a complaint in a letter which was likely written by a ruler of Anat to a ruler of Hamath, but the name is only partially preserved (Adad-nādin-[zēri(?)]) and some other individual may be meant. That letter, however, was written by Marduk-apla-uṣur, who is probably to be identified with the individual by that name called "the man of Sūḫu" (KUR *s*[*u*]-*ḫu-a-a*), who presented tribute to Shalmaneser III (king of Assyria 858–824 BC). (See S. Parpola in Hama 2/2 pp. 257–65 and Michel, WO 2/2 [1955] pp. 142–43 no. D.) Tukultī-Ninurta II, who preceded Ashurnasirpal II on the throne of Assyria (890–884 BC), states that he had received tribute from Ilī-ibni, the governor of the land of Sūḫu; the latter had to flee to Assyria for safety three years later, in the time of Ashurnasirpal (RIMA 2 A.0.100.5 lines 67–73 and A.0.101.1 i 99–101). Moving back even further in time, an Assyrian economic text dating to the year 1133 refers to sheep given as a gift by Adad-šuma-iddina, the man of Sūḫu (KUR *su-ḫa-ia-e*); it is not inconceivable that he was ruler of that land (see Donbaz, NTA A. 1750 lines 2–3).

The texts recently found in the Ḥadītha region have been published by Antoine Cavigneaux and Bahija Ismail in Bagh. Mitt. 21 (1990) pp. 321–456 and pls. 35–38. They are to be thanked both for the quality and thoroughness of their work and for the speed with which they produced it. They were working under difficult conditions and yet produced a truly important work. Inevitably, some minor inconsistencies resulted in the publication which further work with the originals — which they were prevented from doing owing to the circumstances of the time — would undoubtedly have eliminated. Current conditions have prevented the author from collating these texts from the originals and thus it has not been possible to clear up most of these problems. Frequently, the copy indicates that a sign has a slightly anomalous form, is missing one or more wedges, or has one or more wedges in addition to those expected, while this is not noted in the published transliteration. Thus, it is often uncertain whether the copy accurately represents what is preserved on the original or whether unrecorded damage to the original obscures the signs in question. Where it has been thought advisable, references to these unusual sign forms have been made in the editions presented below. The published copies frequently indicate that the initial vertical wedge of KU, LU, and PÚ signs is omitted, yet it is most likely simply obscured by the heads of the horizontal wedges; these variations have not been noted. I am informed that the published transliterations occasionally rely upon collations made after the copies had been prepared; thus I have sometimes indicated divergences between the two in my notes. My thanks must be expressed to A. Cavigneaux who kindly put at my disposal his original transliterations of these inscriptions and photographs of three of them.

For details on the history of Sūḫu, see in particular Brinkman, PKB pp. 183–84 n. 1127; N. Háklár, OrAnt 22 (1983) pp. 25–36; Bahija Ismail, M.D. Roaf, and J.A. Black in Northedge, IAR 1 pp. 1–5; and Grayson, Studies Smith pp. 80–84. A study of the Arameans of the Middle Euphrates in the eighth century which is based on these texts is presented by P.-E. Dion in the proceedings of the XIVème Congrès de l'Organisation Internationale pour l'Étude de l'Ancien Testament (Supplements to Vetus Testamentum, in press).

Šamaš-rēša-uṣur

S.0.1001

Šamaš-rēša-uṣur has left a few inscriptions in which he calls himself "governor (*šaknu*) of the land of Sūḫu and the land of Mari" and one of these is dated in his thirteenth year as governor (S.0.1001.1), thus giving some indication as to the length of his tenure in office. Since he mentions no overlord in the inscriptions, it is likely that he ruled his section of the Middle Euphrates independently of Assyria.

The inscriptions of Šamaš-rēša-uṣur are written in the Babylonian dialect of the Akkadian language. Two were found at Sūr Jarʿā (Sur Jurʿeh) (S.0.1001.2–3), one at ʿĀnā (S.0.1001.4), and one at Babylon (S.0.1001.1); a fifth inscription which might belong to Šamaš-rēša-uṣur was also found at Sūr Jarʿā (S.0.1001.1001). The text from Babylon, a stone stela with a relief, had presumably been carried off to that city by some later ruler of Babylonia. Each of the inscriptions clearly assignable to Šamaš-rēša-uṣur either certainly or likely mentions the town Āl-gabbāri-bānî (exact reading uncertain), which Šamaš-rēša-uṣur claims to have founded. This town may well have been located at Sūr Jarʿā, as noted by Cavigneaux and Bahija Ismail, Bagh. Mitt. 21 (1990) pp. 330–31. Perhaps the most interesting statement by Šamaš-rēša-uṣur is his claim to have introduced honey-bees to the land of Sūḫu (S.0.1001.1 and 4).

1

This inscription, written in Akkadian on a stela and found at Babylon, describes campaigns fought by Šamaš-rēša-uṣur against the Tuʾmānu tribe and records how he dug canals, planted date palms, and built the town Āl-gabbāri-bānî (exact reading uncertain). Šamaš-rēša-uṣur took particular pride in his claim to have introduced apiculture into the region and this claim is stated in both this inscription and S.0.1001.4.

COMMENTARY

The white limestone stela is on display in the Archaeological Museum in Istanbul (EŞ 7815) and a cast of it is found in the Vorderasiatisches Museum (Berlin) with the number VAG 1023. The stela was found at Babylon on September 14, 1899, in Kasr q 8, near the monumental stone lion, but about 4 metres deeper in the rubble. Excavation records indicate that the piece was given the excavation number 3381, but that 3382 might be a fragment of the same stela; Koldewey, Königsburgen 2 p. 20 refers to 3381/82 as Istanbul 7815. The piece measures 118×132 cm. The inscription is edited from the copy published by Weissbach, with some help from published photographs and the cast in the Vorderasiatisches Museum.

The stela was found in what has been termed the "palace museum" of Nebuchadnezzar II. It had probably been taken to Babylon by a Neo-Babylonian king from some original location on the Middle Euphrates, and in this connection it may be noted that Nabopolassar, Nebuchadnezzar's predecessor, is said to have captured the city of Ra'il (Raḫi-ilu) and probably the city of Anat (Grayson, Chronicles pp. 93–94 no. 3 lines 31–36). Šamaš-rēša-uṣur certainly controlled the former city (see iv 1) and likely also the latter, since he has left an inscription there (S.0.1001.4) and since his son and successor Ninurta-kudurrī-uṣur clearly controlled that city (see for example S.0.1002.11). S.0.1001.4, a stone fragment which was found at ʿĀnā, duplicates iv 13 – v 6 (S.0.1001.4 side A 1–6); thus it is not inconceivable that this stela originally came from ʿĀnā as well.

The relief on the stela depicts Šamaš-rēša-uṣur standing before the goddess Ištar and the god Adad. A third deity stands behind Šamaš-rēša-uṣur. Cavigneaux and Bahija Ismail identify this deity with the goddess Anat and suggest there was an epigraph stating this. Their proposal has been followed here (epigraph no. 5).

The inscription appears to have been written in several stages. One expects the date to be at the very end of the text, immediately preceded by the curse formulae. In this inscription, however, the curse is at the end of column iii and the date part way through column iv. The inscription may have originally ended at iii 12 and then had two additions: iv 1–12 and iv 13 – v 6. The part after the date (iv 13 – v 6) is not really connected with the remainder of the inscription and it is clear that a passage was added to the end of iv 8. The text is very difficult in places because of unusual writings; some of these may perhaps represent the local dialect.

The reading of the name of the town in ii 18′, 38′, and 40′, URU *ri-ba-niš*, follows Zadok, Rép. Géogr. 8 p. 260, but it is possible that the first sign was read /*tal*/ or /*dal*/, rather than /*ri*/ (see also Cavigneaux and Bahija Ismail, Bagh. Mitt. 21 [1990] p. 330 n. 43 and the possibility of identifying a Talbaniš with Talbiš/Talmiš). This town is also mentioned in two inscriptions of Ninurta-kudurrī-uṣur (S.0.1002.3 iv 12′ and S.0.1002.9 ii 17).

The reading and interpretation of the name of the town in iii 1, 3, and iv 16 is uncertain and Āl-gabbāri-bānî is only one of several possibilities. Zadok (Rép. Géogr. 8 p. 135) proposed the reading Gabbarīni, thus emending the final sign DÙ to NI, even though this would mean three emendations, as Weissbach pointed out (Miscellen p. 11 n. 4). However, Zadok's proposal was made before the publication of the texts found during recent work in the Ḥadītha area. The town is mentioned in four of these texts (S.0.1001.2 obv. 5, 9 [mostly restored], and 10; S.0.1001.3 obv. 9 [mostly restored] and 11; S.0.1002.2 ii 26 and iv 21′; and S.0.1002.8 ii 11′); the final sign is written DÙ in every case but one (S.0.1001.2 obv. 5), when it is omitted entirely. On this matter, see Cavigneaux and Bahija Ismail, Bagh. Mitt. 21 (1990) pp. 355–56 sub ii 26.

BIBLIOGRAPHY

1899 [Koldewey], MDOG 3 pp. 2–3 (provenance, translation of epigraphs, study)
1900 Koldewey, MDOG 5 p. 5 n. * (study by Delitzsch)
1903 Weissbach, Miscellen no. 4 (photo, copy, edition)
1910 Meissner, MVAG 15/5 pp. 23–25 (partial edition, study)
1915 King, History p. 265–67 and fig. 64 (drawing of relief, partial translation)
1915 Meissner, AO 15 pp. 75–76 and fig. 132 (photo, study)
1925 Koldewey, WEB[4] pp. 159–62 and fig. 102 (photo, study)
1925 Meissner, BuA 2 pl. [3] fig. 8 (photo)
1926 Unger, RLV 4/2 pp. 416–17 and pl. 194a (photo, study)
1927 Gressmann, ABAT[2] p. 94 and pl. CXXXI fig. 330 (photo, study)
1929 Jeremias, HAOG[2] p. 369 fig. 199 (photo of relief)
1930 Meissner, Literatur p. 33 fig. 62 (photo)
1931 Contenau, Manuel 3 pp. 1302–1303 and fig. 823 (photo of relief, study)
1931 Unger, Babylon p. 225 no. 9 and pl. 40 fig. 63 (photo, study)
1932 Koldewey, Königsburgen 2 p. 20 no. 11 and pl. 20 (photo of relief, study)
1959 Levey, Chemistry pp. 94–95 (partial translation)
1962 Meyer, Jahrtausende pp. 105–106 (partial translation, study)
1968 Brinkman, PKB p. 219 (study)
1968 Herzfeld, Persian Empire pp. 47–48 (study)
1969 Pritchard, ANEP[2] no. 533 (photo of relief)
1970 Klengel-Brandt, Reise pp. 77–78 and fig. 33 (photo, partial translation)
1977 von Soden, Orientalia NS 46 p. 192 (iii 6, study)
1978 Neufeld, UF 10 pp. 238–39 and fig. 10 (photo, partial translation, study)
1979 J. Oates, Babylon p. 195 (photo, partial translation)
1982 Börker-Klähn, Bildstelen no. 231 (photo, study [erroneously given the excavation number 3108])
1984 Dalley, Mari and Karana pp. 201–203 (translation, study, drawing of relief)
1984 Saggs, Assyria p. 83 (partial translation)
1990 Cavigneaux and Bahija Ismail, Bagh. Mitt. 21 pp. 333 and 398–405 no. A (edition, drawing of relief)

TEXT

Col. i
Lacuna
1′) [...] x
2′) [...] x-*šú*
3′) [...] *ù* GIŠ.⸢GIGIR⸣.MEŠ
4′) [... GI]Š(?).⸢TUKUL(?)⸣.MEŠ
5′) [... ^{md}UTU-S]AG-PAB LÚ.GAR KUR
6′) [*su-ḫi u* KUR *ma*]-*ri*

Lacuna
i 1′–6′) [...] ... [...] his [...] and chariots [...] *weapons* [... Šamaš-r]ēša-uṣur, governor of the land [of Sūḫu and the land of Ma]ri

Col. ii

Lacuna

1′) [...] x
2′) [...] x GAR
3′) [...]-*ia*
4′) [...] x *u* URU.KAR-^{d}AG *ú-du-ul*
5′) [... *m*]*a*(?)*-du-ú ina* PÚ
6′) [...] LU *bal-ṭu-ti*
7′) [...] x-*ri-ḫu-in-nu*
8′) [...] KUN TE BU NE *a-na*
9′) [...] ⌜*a*⌝*-na na-gi-ti it-lu-ú*
10′) [... *manzaz*(?)] *pa-nu u* LÚ *ḫa-za-na-ti* (erasure)
11′) [...] GIŠ.MÁ.MEŠ *ki-i e-bi-ru*
12′) [...] (x) *ṣe-e-nu bu-ši*
13′) [x NA]M(?).RA *ka-bit-ti*
14′) [x (x)]-*ma ú-še-rib*
15′) [x *q*]*é*(?)*-reb* KUR *su-ḫi na-gi-ti*
16′) [(x)] x-*bu-ú a-di ik-kan-na*
17′) [*u*]*l ú-šib* 4 ME LÚ *tu-ʾ-ma-a-nu*
18′) *il-lik-nim-ma ina* URU *ri-ba-niš it-bu-ú*
19′) *ana-ku a-na i-sin-na a-na* URU *eš-ši*
20′) *al-lik-ma i-na* URU *ba-qa ki-i*
21′) *áš-mu-ú ina* ÉRIN.MEŠ É.GAL *šá it-ti-ia*
22′) *a-na* Á KUR *e-bir-ma ár-du-du-šú-nu-ti-ma*
23′) *e-nu e-bir-ma ina qaq-qa-ru a-ra-da-tu*
24′) *ak-šu-ud-šú-nu-ti-ma* 3 ME 50 ÉRIN.MEŠ
25′) *ina lìb-bi-šú-nu ad-duk šit-tu-tu-šú-nu*
26′) *a-na da-li-li un-dáš-šir*
27′) *ana-ku* ^{md}UTU-SAG-PAB LÚ.GAR KUR *su-ḫi* *u* KUR *ma-ri*
28′) *a-tap-pá* KUR *su-ḫi* DU-*ku la-ba-riš* ÉRIN.[M]EŠ
29′) *ma-at-tu* TA URU *ḫur-ze-e*
30′) *a-di* URU *ia-a-bi-ʾ ad*(*)*-kám-ma*
31′) 1 LIM GI.MEŠ *ina lìb-bi ú-sad-dir*
32′) *a-tap-pá šu-ma-tu*$_4$ 22 *ina* 1 KÙŠ *ur-tap-iš*
33′) *ti-tur-ru šá* KÁ *a-tap-pu ú-paṭ-ṭir-ma*
34′) GIŠ.MÁ.U$_5$ *šá* 25 *ina* 1 KÙŠ *a-na lìb-bi*
35′) *ul-te-rib ana-ku* LÚ.GAL.MEŠ-*ia*
36′) *ina lìb-bi ni-il-lik* GIŠ.MÁ *ina bit-qu*
37′) *šá* É.SAL.A KUR *ul-te-ṣi* GIŠ.GIŠIMMAR.MEŠ
38′) *šá* <*ina*> TÙR É.GAL *šá* URU *ri-ba-niš ana-ku*
39′) *az-qup-šú-nu-ti*
40′) GIŠ.GU.ZA *u* GIŠ.GÌR.GUB *šá ina* URU *ri-ba-niš*(*)

Lacuna

ii 1′–17a′) [...] ... [...] ... [...] my [...] and the town Kār-Nabû *was closed* (ii 5′) [...] ... [...] in the well [...] the living [...] ... [...]... to/for [...] *went up* to the *water-meadow* (ii 10′) [... *cour*]*tiers* and mayors [...] when they crossed over [*in*] boats [...] flocks (and) goods [...] weighty [*boo*]*ty* [...] I/he caused to enter. (ii 15′) [... in]side the land of Sūḫu, the *water-meadow* ... *until now* I/he did not *inhabit*.

ii 17b′–26′) Four hundred of the Tuʾmānu came and *rose up against* the town Ribaniš. I had gone to the New City for the festival (ii 20′) and when in the town Baqa I heard (of the uprising), I crossed over (the river) to *the landside with* the palace troops who were with me and I pursued them. When I crossed over (the river), I defeated them at Qaqqaru-aradātu. I killed three hundred and fifty soldiers among them (and) let the remainder go free to (spread the news of my) glory.

ii 27′–37a′) I, Šamaš-rēša-uṣur, governor of the land of Sūḫu and the land of Mari — (when) the canal of the land of Sūḫu became old, I called up numerous workmen from the town Ḫurzē (ii 30′) as far as the town Iābiʾ and I *realigned* (it over a distance of) one thousand reeds. I made that canal twenty-two cubits wide. I took down the bridge at the entrance to the canal so that I could send a boat of twenty-five cubits through it. (ii 35′) I (and) my nobles went inside (the boat). When the boat reached the opening of the canal at É.SAL.A, I brought (it) out (of the canal).

ii 37b′–41′) I planted the date palm trees which are <in> the courtyard of the palace of the town Ribaniš. I set up the throne and footstool which are in the town Ribaniš.

ii 9′ With regard to the meaning of *nagīti*, "*water-meadow*," see Cavigneaux, RA 76 (1982) p. 190. Following Cavigneaux and Bahija Ismail, Bagh. Mitt. 21 (1990) p. 340, *it-lu-ú* (also appearing in S.0.1002.2 ii 20 and cf. *it-la-a* in ibid. i 22) is taken to stand for *ītelû*.

ii 16′ *a-di ik-kan-na* for *adi akanni/a*, "until now" or "until here."

ii 17′ The Tuʾmānu may or may not be identical with the Aramean tribe by the name of Tuʾmuna mentioned in Neo-Assyrian inscriptions (see Brinkman, PKB p. 219 n. 1371, and Zadok, Rép. Géogr. 8 p. 314).

ii 22′ Compare for example S.0.1002.3 iv 11′, where one finds Á KUR *ù* ÁKUR-*i šá* URU *an-at*, "*the landside* and *the hillside* of the city Anat." The distinction may be between the right (west) and left (east) sides of the river (thus Cavigneaux and Bahija Ismail, Bagh. Mitt. 21 [1990] p. 387) or possibly the narrow river plain as opposed to the higher land on either side of it.

ii 23′ Or "in the district Aradātu" instead of "at Qaqqaru-aradātu." Cavigneaux and Bahija Ismail, Bagh. Mitt. 21 (1990) p. 404 suggest that Qaqqaru-aradātu may be connected with the town Ḫaradu (modern Khirbet ed-Dīniye).

ii 28′ Following Zadok, Rép. Géogr. 8 p. 347, possibly a proper name "Atap-Sūḫi" rather than "the canal of the land of Sūḫu" (also in iv 6).

ii 29′ Or URU *ḫar-ze-e*.

ii 31′ Literally "I lined (it) up in it (the canal bed)" for "I *realigned* (it)," *ina lìb-bi ú-sad-dir*.

ii 37′ Possibly Bīt-S/Šal(l)ê for É.SAL.A; compare É.SAL.LE.E in iv 7.

41′) *ana-ku ad-di*

Col. iii

1) URU DÙ-*ma* URU-*gab-ba-ri*-DÙ MU-*šú az-kur*
2) ᵈIŠKUR ᵈA-ᵈIŠKUR ᵈ*ša-la* ᵈDI.KUD *at-ru-ṣu*
3) *ina qé-reb* URU-*ia* URU-*gab-ba-ri*-DÙ
4) KI.TUŠ *ṭa-ab-tu ú-šar-mi-šú-nu-ti*
5) *man-nu ár-ku-ú šá* E$_{11}$-*ma a-na* NA$_4$.NA.RÚ.A
6) *an-na-a i-quṭ-ṭu-ú u šá* MU *šá-aṭ-ra*
7) LAL-*ṭu-ma* MU-*šú i-šaṭ-ṭa-ri* DINGIR.MEŠ GAL.MEŠ
8) *šá* AN-*e u* KI-*tim* MU-*šú* NUMUN-*šú* NUNUZ-*šú*
9) *na-an-nab-šú ina* KA (erasure) UN.MEŠ *lu-še-lu-ú*
10) *ma-la dul-la šá ana-ku* DÙ-*uš a-a* DÙ-*uš*
11) *e-ti-iq an-na-a-ti la a-dir*
12) *a-ma-ti ár-rat lik-šu-us-su*

Col. iv

1) GIŠ.GIŠIMMAR.MEŠ *šá ina* TÙR É.GAL *šá* URU *ra-ìl ana-ku* ⸢*az*⸣-*qup-šú-nu-ti*
2) GIŠ.GIŠIMMAR.MEŠ *šá ina* TÙR É.GAL *šá* URU KAR-⸢ᵈ⸣AG *ana-ku az-qup-šú-nu-ti*
3) 2 (GUR) 3 (PI) 2 (BÁN) ZÚ.LUM.MA KI-*tim* URU *ia-a-du-ru ina* URU *ú-ka-la-a-a*
4) GIŠ.GIŠIMMAR.⸢MEŠ⸣ *ana-ku az-qup-šú-nu-ti* 3 ME ⸢60-*šu*⸣ *ina* 1 KÙŠ *mi-iḫ-ru*
5) *eš-ši ana*-⸢*ku*⸣ *a-na* UGU *la-bi-ri ak-si-ir-ma*
6) *ina lìb-bi* A.MEŠ *ina a-tap-pu* KUR *su-ḫi im-i-du*
7) TA *mi-iḫ-ri a-di* É.SAL.LE.E *ma-la* GIŠ.KÌM *šá ina* UGU *a-tap-pu-i*
8) *ana-ku az-qup-šú-nu-ti úš-šú* GIŠ *ku-du-ra-a-nu šá a-tap-pu ina lìb-bi i-ḫar-ru-ú ù* GIŠ.ÙR.MEŠ-*šú-nu a-na*-⸢*ki*⸣-*is-am-ma a-na* GIŠ *a-ra-a-ti ep-pu-šú*
9) (erasure) GIŠ.KÌM *šá ina* UGU *a-tap-pu az-qup-šú-nu-ti gab-bi-šú-nu*
10) *šá* É.GAL LÚ *su-ḫa-a-a a-na* UGU *ul i-qar-ru-bu*
11) MU.AN.NA 13.MEŠ *šá* ᵐᵈUTU-SAG(*)-PAB LÚ.GAR KUR *su-ḫi u* KUR *má-rí*
12) NA$_4$.KIŠIB *ka-nik*
13) *ana-ku* ᵐᵈUTU-SAG-PAB LÚ.GAR KUR *su-ḫi u* KUR *ma-ri ḫa-bu-bé-e-ti šá* LÀL
14) *i-la-qa-ta-ni šá ul-tu* AD.M[EŠ]-*ú-a maḫ-ru-ta mam-ma la i-mu-ru*
15) *u a-na* KUR *su-ḫi la ú-še-ri-du-nu ana-ku* TA KUR-*i šá* LÚ *ḫa-ab-ḫa*
16) *ú-še-ríd*(RAD)-*am-ma ina* GIŠ.KIRI$_6$.MEŠ *šá* URU-*gab-ba-ri*-DÙ *ú-še-šib*

iii 1–4) I built a (new) town and named it Āl-gabbāri-bānî. I set up (statues of) the gods Adad, Apla-Adad, Šala, (and) Madānu; I settled them in a pleasant abode inside my town Āl-gabbāri-bānî.

iii 5–12) With regard to anyone in the future who comes forward, approaches this stela, effaces (my) inscribed name, and inscribes his (own) name, may the great gods of heaven and netherworld remove (the mention of) his name, his seed, his offspring, (and) his progeny from the mouth(s) of the people! (iii 10) May he not accomplish any task that I have done! May (this) curse reach the one who transgresses against these words (and) does not fear them!

iv 1–4a) I planted the date palm trees which are in the courtyard of the palace of the city Ra'il. I planted the date palm trees which are in the courtyard of the palace of the town Kār-Nabû. I planted (an area which could be seeded by) two *kurru*, three *pānu*, and two *sūtu* of dates in the district of the town Iāduru, in the town Ukalāia, (for the growing of) date palm trees.

iv 4b–10) I constructed a new weir along the old one over (a length of) three hundred and sixty cubits and thus the water in the canal of the land of Sūḫu was plentiful. From the weir as far as É.SAL.LE.E, I planted all the willows which are along *my* canal so that carrying baskets for (use in connection with) the canal could *be woven* with them and so that I could cut beams from them and make (them) into .... The willows which I planted along the canal all belong to the palace; the people of Sūḫu may not bring a claim about (them).

iv 11–12) (This) document was sealed in the thirteenth year of Šamaš-rēša-uṣur, governor of the land of Sūḫu and the land of Mari.

iv 13 – v 6) I, Šamaš-rēša-uṣur, governor of the land of Sūḫu and the land of Mari, brought down from the mountain of the people of Ḫabḫu the bees which gather honey — which none from among my forefathers had seen or brought down to the land of Sūḫu — and I established them in the gardens of the town Āl-gabbāri-bānî. (v 1) They (now) collect honey and wax (there). I know how (to separate)

iii 2 For the god Apla-Adad, see Lipinski, Orientalia NS 45 (1976) pp. 53–74.

iv 3 Assuming a *kurru* of 300 *qû* and a *sūtu* of 10 *qû* (see Powell, RLA 7/7–8 [1990] p. 498 §IV.6), two *kurru*, three *pānu*, and two *sūtu* are equivalent to approximately 800 litres.

iv 7 For É.SAL.LE.E, see the note to ii 37′.

iv 8 Following a suggestion of J.N. Postgate, it is assumed that the passage refers to the use of two different parts of the tree: the shoots (used to weave baskets) and the trunk (used to make *a-ra-a-ti*). The word *i-ḫar-ru-ú* is assumed to come from a verb meaning "to weave, plait, tie"; possibly compare AHw p. 329 *ḫarû* V and CAD 6 [Ḫ] p. 118 *ḫarû* F and *ḫarû* v.; note that a palm shoot is called *ḫarû* (AHw p. 329 *ḫarû* IV and CAD 6 [H] pp. 117–18 *ḫarû* B). See also Dalley, Mari and Karana p. 207 n. 51. The word *a-ra-a-ti* may come from *arītu*, "shield," or *erretu*, "bank reinforcements"; for the latter suggestion, see Dalley, Mari and Karana p. 207 n. 52.

iv 9 The signs erased are *i-ḫar-ru-ú*. These signs also appear in the middle of the previous line. This erasure and the unusual length of iv 8 presumably reflect some change of mind by the scribe as to what should appear at this point in the text.

Col. v

1) LÀL *u* DUḪ.LÀL *ú-paḫ-ḫa-ra šu-ub-šú-lu šá* LÀL
2) *u* DUḪ.LÀL *ana-ku a-le-ʾ-i u* LÚ.NU.GIŠ.KIRI$_6$.MEŠ
3) *i-le-ʾ-ú-ma man-nu ár-ku-ú šá* E$_{11}$*-ma*
4) *ši-bu-ut* KUR*-šú liš-al um-ma kit-tu-ú šá* ^{md}UTU-SAG-PAB
5) LÚ.GAR KUR *su-ḫi ḫa-bu-bé-e-ti šá* LÀL *ina* KUR *su-ḫi*
6) *ú-še-la-a*

honey and wax by melting (the combs) and (my) gardeners (also) know how (to do it). Anyone in the future who comes forward should ask the elders of his land: "Is it true that Šamaš-rēša-uṣur, the governor of the land of Sūḫu, introduced honey-bees into the land of Sūḫu?"

Epigraph 1 (next to the figure of the goddess Ištar)

1) [NU ^{d}]15

1) [Image of the goddess] Ištar.

Epigraph 2 (next to the figure of the god Adad)

1) NU ^{d}IŠKUR

1) Image of the god Adad.

Epigraph 3 (above the figure of Šamaš-rēša-uṣur)

1) NU ^{md}UTU-SAG-PAB
2) LÚ.GAR KUR *su-ḫi u* KUR *ma-rí*

1–2) Image of Šamaš-rēša-uṣur, governor of the land of Sūḫu and the land of Mari.

Epigraph 4 (between the figures of the god Adad and Šamaš-rēša-uṣur)

1) 1 SÌLA NINDA.ḪI.A 1 SÌLA KAŠ.SAG
2) *gi-né-e* NA$_4$.NA.RÚ.A
3) *an-na-a uk-tin*
4) *šá* É.GAL
5) *i-na-aṣ-ṣa-ri*
6) *li-kul*

1–3) I have established one *qû* of bread (and) one *qû* of fine beer as the regular offerings for this stela.

4–6) Anyone who protects the palace may eat (it).

Epigraph 5 (restored to right of figure of Šamaš-rēša-uṣur)

1) [NU *an-at*]

1) [Image of (the goddess) Anat.]

2

A partially preserved clay tablet (IM 124199) found at Sūr Jarʿā (located on the left bank of the Euphrates about thirty kilometres southeast of ʿĀnā) bears an Akkadian inscription recording that Šamaš-rēša-uṣur carried out various works of construction. In particular it states that he built the town Āl-gabbāri-bānî and settled the gods Madānu (or Mandānu) and Rammānu there. The inscription could not be collated and the edition presented here is based upon the copy in Bagh. Mitt. 21, with the help of the transliteration published by Cavigneaux and Bahija Ismail and with some additional information supplied by Cavigneaux.

COMMENTARY

According to Cavigneaux and Bahija Ismail (Bagh. Mitt. 21 [1990] p. 365) the obverse of the tablet is poorly preserved and their readings are often uncertain; however, little shading of signs is found on the copy or indicated in the published transliteration. It is thus possible that some of the readings presented below are not correct.

Restorations in obv. 1–15 are based upon S.0.1001.3 obv. 1–13 and S.0.1002.2 i 1–3; restorations in rev. 4′–7′ are based upon S.0.1001.3 rev. 8′–10′.

BIBLIOGRAPHY

1990 Cavigneaux and Bahija Ismail, Bagh. Mitt. 21 pp. 364–66 and 423–24 no. 5 (copy, edition)

TEXT

Obverse

1) [...] x-*a*-^{d}AMAR.UTU DUMU ^{m}Ú-A-A-MU(*) ^{m}Ú-A-A-MU(*)
2) [... ^{md}IŠKUR-SUM-NUM]UN MIN ^{md}IŠKUR-SUM-NUMUN DUMU ^{m}NÍG.DU MIN NUMUN *da-ru-ú*
3) [... ^{m}(*ḫa*)-*am-m*]*u-ra-pu* LUGAL TIN.TIR.KI *ma-ʾ-du* AD.MEŠ-*ú-a*
4) [... *u*]*l áš-ṭur ana-ku* ^{md}UTU-SAG-PAB LÚ.GAR KUR
5) [... U]RU *ab-ni-ma* URU-*gab-ba-ri*-<DÙ> MU-*šú az-kur*
6) [... *di*(?)]-*ma-ti-šú šá* ESIR.ḪI.A *u a-gur-ru*
7) [... *eli ša* A]D.MEŠ-*e-a maḫ-ru-ú-tu ú-šá-tir*$_{x}$(DIR)
8) [... ^{d}]DI.KUD ^{d}*ram-ma-nu* DINGIR.MEŠ GAL.MEŠ
9) [... URU-*gab-ba-r*]*i*-DÙ KI.TUŠ *ṭa*(*)-*ab-ti*
10) [*ušarmēšunūti* ... UR]U-⸢*gab*⸣-*ba-ri*-DÙ 1-*niš* ⸢*na*(?)⸣-*šú-u*
11) [...] x A DA KU *a-na ṭar-ṣu*
12) [... ÍD/KAR/BÀD(?)-^{md}UTU-S]AG-PAB MU-*šú az-kur* x-*ri-is-su*
13) [...] x *šá*/*a*(?) *ṭa*(*)-*ḫu* x x ^{md}UTU-SAG-PAB
14) [... *r*]*a*(?)-*a* AŠ x x ḪU x AN(?)
15) [... BÀ]D(?)-^{md}UTU-SAG-PAB MU-*šú az-kur*
16) [...]-*ṣir qa*(?)-*te-ia*
17) [... ÍD/KAR/BÀD(?)-^{md}UTU-S]AG-PAB MU-*šú* ⸢*az*⸣-*kur*
18) [...] x-*šú ina lìb-bi áš-kun*
19) [...] *i-ba-áš-šú-ú*
20) [...] x KUR *su-ḫi*
21) [...] x ⸢BÀD(?)⸣-^{md}UTU-SAG-PAB
22) [...] ŠÀ TI ⸢LA(?) I(?)⸣ KUR *ú-qa*(?)-*a*(*)-*a*
23) [...] x x GI TI
24) [...]-*ti-ia al*(?)-*si-ma*(?)
25) [...] x NU *a-ša*[*k*]-⸢*kan*(?)⸣
26) [...] x x [x x x]

Lacuna

1–4a) [I, Šamaš-rēša-uṣur, governor of the land of Sūḫu and the land of Mari, am the son of *Iqīša-Marduk, ditto* (*governor of the land of Sūḫu and the land of Mari*); *Iqīš*]*a*-Marduk was the son of *Uaiiāmu*; *Uaiiāmu* [was the son of ..., (ditto [governor of the land of Sūḫu and the land of Mari]); ... was the son of Adad-nādin-zēr]i, ditto (governor of the land of Sūḫu and the land of Mari); Adad-nādin-zēri was the son of Kudurru, ditto (governor of the land of Sūḫu and the land of Mari); one of an enduring lineage; [distant descendant of Tunamissaḫ, son of Ḫamm]u-rāpi, king of Babylon. My ancestors are numerous; [(...)] I have not written down [*their name*(*s*) *from* ... *to Kudurru*].

4b–26) I, Šamaš-rēša-uṣur, governor of the land [of Sūḫu and the land of Mari, ...] built a town and named it Āl-gabbāri-<bānî>. [...] its [*to*]*wer, which with* bitumen and baked bricks [...] I made greater [than] my forefathers. [...] the gods Madānu (and) Rammānu, the great gods, [(...) I settled them in] a pleasant abode [inside my town Āl-gabbār]i-bānî. (10) [... Ā]l-gabbāri-bānî *at the same time* ... [...] ... facing [...] I named it [*Nār*/*Kār*/*Dūr*-Šamaš-rē]ša-uṣur. ... [...] ... *near* ... Šamaš-rēša-uṣur [...] ... (15) [...] I named it [*Dū*]*r*-Šamaš-rēša-uṣur. [...] my *hands* [...] I named it [*Nār*/*Kār*/*Dūr*-Šamaš-rē]ša-uṣur. [...] I established there [... *which*] exists (20) [...] the land of Sūḫu [...] *Dūr*-Šamaš-rēša-uṣur [...] ... the land *Uqāia* [...] ... [...] my [...] *I surrounded and* (25) [...] ... *I est*[*abli*]*sh* [...] ...

Lacuna

obv. 1 One expects [... ^{m}*i-qi*]*š-a-* or possibly [... ^{m}BA-*š*]*á-a-*, but neither seems clear from the copy (see also Bagh. Mitt. 21 [1990] p. 365).

obv. 5, 9, 10 With regard to the reading of the town name, see S.0.1001.1, commentary.

obv. 12 According to Bagh. Mitt. 21 (1990) p. 366, repeated collation has shown that the final word cannot be *ḫi-ri-is-su*, "its canal."

obv. 13 Possibly ⸢BÀD⸣-^{md}UTU-SAG-PAB, "Dūr-Šamaš-rēša-uṣur"?

Reverse
Lacuna
1′) [...] x GAL(?) x [...]
2′) [...] *man-nu ár*(*)-*ku*-⸢*ú*⸣ [x x (x)]
3′) [...] ⸢*ina*(?)⸣ IGI-*šú lil-su*(*)-*ú* [(x x)]
4′) [... *ina*] IGI(*)-*šú la i-šá-as-su*(*)-[*ú*]
5′) [... *ši-bu*]-*ut* KUR-*šú liš-al um-ma kit-t*[*u-ú*]
6′) [... KUR] *ma-ri dul-la-a-ti*
7′) [*an-na-a-ti i-pu-u*]*š*

Lacuna
rev. 1′–7′) [...] ... [...] Anyone in the future [who comes forward ...] they should read [this inscription] out loud to him [... that (man), (if)] no [one] can read (this inscription) out loud to him (rev. 5′) [(...)] should ask [(...) the eld]ers of his land: "[Is it] true [that Šamaš-rēša-uṣur, governor of the land of Sūḫu and the land of] Mari, [accomplished these] tasks?"

3

This text, found on a clay tablet (IM 124193) from Sūr Jarʿā, bears a fragmentary inscription of Šamaš-rēša-uṣur written in Akkadian which mentions the town Āl-gabbāri-bānî and which appears to be similar to, though not an exact duplicate of, the previous inscription.

COMMENTARY

The tablet fragment was found by the British Archaeological Expedition to Iraq in 1982 while sectioning the middle city wall on the south side of Sūr Jarʿā. Only the upper right corner of tablet is preserved. The edition presented below is based upon the published copy made by J. Black, with occasional help from photographs kindly provided by A. Cavigneaux.

The restoration of obv. 1–13 is based upon S.0.1001.2 obv. 1–15 (with help from S.0.1001.1 iii 3–4 for obv. 9) and that of rev. 9′–10′ upon S.0.1001.2 rev. 5′–6′.

BIBLIOGRAPHY

1983 Killick and Roaf, Iraq 45 p. 221 (provenance)
1990 Cavigneaux and Bahija Ismail, Bagh. Mitt. 21 pp. 378–80 and 434 no. 16 (copy [by J. Black], edition)

TEXT

Obverse
1) [... DUM]U ^{m}BA-*šá*-^{d}AMAR.[U]TU MIN DUMU ^{m}Ú-A-⸢A⸣-[M]U(?)
2) [... ^{d}IŠ]KUR-SUM-NUMUN MIN ^{md}IŠKUR-⸢SUM⸣-NUMUN ⸢DUMU⸣ ^{m}NÍG.⸢DU⸣
3) [... ^{m}*ḫa*]-*am-mu-ra-pí* LUGAL TIN.TI[R.KI (x)]
4) [...] ^{m}NÍG.DU MU-*šú-nu ul* [*ašṭur*(?)]

1–4) [I, Šamaš-rēša-uṣur, governor of the land of Sūḫu and the land of Mari, (...) am the so]n of Iqīša-Marduk, ditto (governor of the land of Sūḫu and the land of Mari), son of *Uaiiāmu*, [... son of A]dad-nādin-zēri, ditto (governor of the land of Sūḫu and the land of Mari); Adad-nādin-zēri was the son of Kudurru, [... son of Ḫ]ammu-rāpi, king of Babylon. [*My ancestors are numerous*; (...) *I have*] not [*written down*] their name(s) [*from ... to*] Kudurru.

5) [... UR]U(?) *im-gur*-^{d}*en-líl* URU x [x (x)]
6) [... *ma*(?)-*t*]*i*(?)-*šú šá* NA$_4$.ZA.GÌN [(x)] x É x [x x (x)]
7) [... UG]U(?) ⸢*šá*⸣ AD.MEŠ-*e-a* ⸢*maḫ*⸣-*ru*-⸢*tu ú-šá*⸣-*tir*$_x$(DIR)
8) [... ^{d}D]I.KUD ^{d}*ra*[*m*]-*ma-an-nu* DINGIR.⸢MEŠ GAL⸣.MEŠ

5–13) [*I, Šamaš-rēša-uṣur, governor of the land of Sūḫu and the land of Mari, ... the to*]wn Imgur-Enlil, the town [...] *of* his [*land*] *which with* lapis lazuli ... [...] I made greater [*tha*]n my forefathers. [...] the gods [Ma]dānu (and) Rammānu, the great gods, [(...)] I settled them in a pleasant ab[ode inside my town Āl-gabbā]ri-bānî. (10) [...] ... house of the

9) [... *ina qereb ālīia* URU-*gab-ba*]-*ri*-DÙ K[I.TUŠ] *ṭa-ab-ta ú-šar-me-šú-nu-ti*
10) [...] x GIŠ(?) ME/[I]GI(?) [x] É DINGIR.MEŠ GAL.MEŠ
11) [...] ⸢*a*⸣-*na* URU-⸢*gab*⸣-*ba-ri*-DÙ *ina* EDIN URU DÙ-*ma*
12) [...] ⸢*a*⸣-*na* ^{d}IŠKUR *ina* UD.MEŠ-*ia* ^{d}[I]ŠKUR
13) [...] x URU.⸢BÀD⸣-^{md}UTU-⸢SAG⸣-P[AB MU(?)-*šú*(?) *az*(?)-*ku*]*r*(?)
14) [...] x-⸢*la*(?)-*a*(?)⸣ *ina ba*-⸢*la*⸣(?)-x [...]
15) [...] NA ⸢TA(?)/UŠ(?)⸣ x [...]
16) [... T]I(?) ⸢I(?)⸣ [...]
17) [...] x [...]

Lacuna

Reverse

Lacuna

1′) [...] x x [...]
2′) [...] x TA(?) KU DIŠ x [(x) x]
3′) [... ALA]M(?).MEŠ *ina* ⸢*áš*⸣-*ri-ši-na*
4′) [... *lil*(?)]-*ṭur u ki*-⸢*i*(?) MU⸣ *at-tu-ú-a*
5′) [... *nadê*(?) *aḫi*(?) *ilāni*(?)] x GAL.MEŠ-*a-a* <*a*>-*a* DÙ-⸢*uš*⸣ 10 SÌLA(?) ZÌ [(x)]
6′) [...] x *šá* KUR-*ia ana-ku* ⸢*mim*⸣-*ma a-qab-bu*-[*ú*]
7′) [*kittuma*(?) ...] x-*i a-na* ⸢*ia*⸣-*a-šú* 1 (BÁN) ZÌ.DA B[A-*eš*]
8′) [...] x-*ri šú-ú mam-ma ina* IGI-*šú la i-šá-s*[*i*]
9′) [...] x *um-ma kit-tu-ú* $^{m⸢d⸣}$UTU-SAG-PAB
10′) [... *dullāti an-n*]*a-ta i-pu-uš*

great gods [...] I built a town in the steppe *for* Āl-gabbāri-bānî and [...] for the god Adad, during my days the god Adad [... *I named it*] Dūr-Šamaš-rēša-u[ṣur].

14–17) No translation warranted.

Lacuna

Lacuna

rev. 1′–10′) [...] ... [...] ... [... the *stat*]*ues* in their places [... *may he insc*]*ribe* and *like* my own name (rev. 5′) [...] he should not be [*negligent about the gods in*] my [*pal*]*aces*. Ten *qû* of flour [...] of my land, I, whatever I say [*is true* ...] *he should* pres[ent] one *sūtu* of flour to me. [...] that (man), (if) no one can read (this inscription) out loud to him, [(...) should ask the elders of his land]: "Is it true that Šamaš-rēša-uṣur, [governor of the land of Sūḫu and the land of Mari], accomplished [the]se [tasks]?"

4

A fragment of diorite which was found at ʿĀnā preserves part of an Akkadian inscription of Šamaš-rēša-uṣur which describes the introduction of honey-bees into the land of Sūḫu, an action also described in S.0.1001.1.

COMMENTARY

Neither the museum number nor the excavation number of this stone fragment is cited in the original publication of the inscription. The inscription could not be collated and thus the edition presented here is based upon the copy by F. Al-Rawi, with notes to the transliteration published by Cavigneaux and Bahija Ismail.

Line rulings are found after line 7 of Side A; on Side B, line rulings are found before line 1 and following each of lines 1–5. The restoration of Side A lines 1–6 is based upon S.0.1001.1 iv 13–v 6. However, in S.0.1001.1 iv 15 we have TA KUR-*i šá* LÚ *ḫa-ab-ḫa*, "from the mountain of the people of Ḫabḫu," while in Side A 2b–3a of this text we have [...] *aš-šur*.KI, "[... *from*] Aššur."

---

obv. 9, 11 With regard to the reading of the town name, see S.0.1001.1, commentary.

obv. 11 Possibly ⸢*a*⸣-*na* <*tar-ṣi*>, "facing," instead of ⸢*a*⸣-*na*, "*for*," following Cavigneaux and Bahija Ismail, Bagh. Mitt. 21 (1990) p. 380.

obv. 14 As suggested by Cavigneaux and Bahija Ismail (Bagh. Mitt. 21 [1990] p. 380), one might read [... *t*]*am-la-a*, "terrace, filling"; cf. the use of this term in S.0.1002.3 iv 19′.

rev. 5′ Or "he should not be [*negligent about the*] great [*gods*]" (... GAL.MEŠ *a-a* <<*a*>> DÙ-⸢*uš*⸣); see Cavigneaux and Bahija Ismail, Bagh. Mitt. 21 (1990) pp. 379–80.

BIBLIOGRAPHY

1990 Cavigneaux and Bahija Ismail, Bagh. Mitt. 21 pp. 390 and 442 no. 20 (copy [by F. Al-Rawi], edition)

TEXT

Side A

1) *ana-ku* ^{md}UTU-SAG-PAB LÚ.GAR KUR *su-ḫi u*(?) [KUR *ma-ri* ...]
2) [*u*]*l-tu* LÚ.AD.MEŠ-*ú-a maḫ-ru-tu mam-ma* [...]
3) *aš-šur*.KI *ú-še-*⸢*ríd*(RAD)⸣*-am-mu ina* GIŠ.KIRI$_{6}$.M[EŠ(?) ...]
4) *ú-paḫ-ḫa*-[(x)]*-ra šu*(*)*-ub-šu-lu šá* LÀ[L ...]
5) *i-le-ʾ-ú-ma man-nu ár-ku-ú šá* E$_{11}$*-m*[*a* ...]
6) LÚ.GAR KUR *su-ḫi ḫa-bu-bé-e-*[*ti* ...]
7) *ana-ku* ^{md}UTU-S[AG-PAB ...]
8) [x (x)] ⸢RA⸣ [...]

Lacuna

Side B

1) [... N]IM(?) *i-na* ŠÈG *šá* ^{d}IŠKUR
2) [...] x *iz-nu-nu*
3) [...] ⸢*e*⸣*-te-riš ù i-na*
4) [... B]U *al-te-qu*
5) [... *ḫ*]*u*(?)*-ru-*⸢*ú*⸣ [(x)]
6) [...] x BA [(x x)]

Lacuna

Side A

1–6) I, Šamaš-rēša-uṣur, governor of the land of Sūḫu *and* [the land of Mari], brought down [*from*] Aššur [the bees which gather honey — which] none from among my forefathers [had seen or brought down to the land of Sūḫu] — and [I established them] in the gardens [of the town Āl-gabbāri-bānî]. They (now) collect [honey and wax (there). I know how (to separate)] honey [and wax by] melting (the combs) [and (my) gardeners] (5) (also) know how (to do it). Anyone in the future who comes forward [should ask the elders of his land: "Is it true that Šamaš-rēša-uṣur], the governor of the land of Sūḫu, [introduced honey]-bees [into the land of Sūḫu?]"

7–8) I, Šamaš-rē[ša-uṣur ...] ... [...]

Lacuna

Side B

1–6) [...] by the rain which the god Adad [...] rained [...] I planted and in [...] I took [...] ... [...] ...

Lacuna

1001

A fragment of a clay tablet from Sūr Jarʿā (IM 124885) preserves part of an Akkadian inscription which likely mentions Šamaš-rēša-uṣur (name partially preserved). It is possible, however, that the inscription was composed by his son Ninurta-kudurrī-uṣur and simply refers back to the time of his father. The inscription has not been collated and the edition presented here is based upon the publication of Cavigneaux and Bahija Ismail, with some additional information supplied by Cavigneaux.

BIBLIOGRAPHY

1990 Cavigneaux and Bahija Ismail, Bagh. Mitt. 21 pp. 377 and 433 no. 13 (copy, edition)

TEXT

Obverse
Lacuna
1′) [...] x [...]
2′) [...] x x [...]
3′) [...] x ŠI x [...]
4′) [...] x [...]
5′) [...] ⸢LÚ(?)⸣ [x x (x)] x [...]
6′) [...] x x x x (x) [...]
7′) [...] E(?) [x (x)] AL [...]
8′) [...] x x [...]
9′) [...] x x-*a-ti* [...]
10′) [...] x [x (x)] x x [...]
11′) [...] x [x x (x)] x [...]
12′) [...] x [...]
13′) [...] IS(?) x [...]
14′) [...] NU x [...]
Lacuna

Lacuna
1′–14′) Too poorly preserved to allow translation.
Lacuna

Reverse
Lacuna
1′) [...] x x [...]
2′) [... ^{d}]DI.KUD [...]
3′) [...] x ṢU *ina*(?) x [...]
4′) [...] *ú-še-*[...]
5′) [...] x *na-šú-ú* [...]
6′) [... ^{md}UTU-SA]G(?)-PAB LÚ.GAR K[UR ...]
7′) [...] x-*šú-nu* x [...]
8′) [...] EL? [...]
Lacuna

Lacuna
rev. 1′–8′) [...] ... [... the god] Madānu [...] ... [...] *I/he caused* [... (rev. 5′) ...] carry [... Šamaš-rē]ša-uṣur, governor of the l[and of ...] their [...] ... [...].
Lacuna

rev. 2′–3′ If these lines can be compared to S.0.1001.1 iii 2–3 (... ^{d}DI.KUD *at-ru-ṣu ina qé-reb* URU-*ia* URU-*gab-ba-ri*-DÙ, "I set up ... the god Madānu; inside my town Āl-gabbāri-bānî"), the inscription may have described the construction of the town Āl-gabbāri-bānî. One would then read in rev. 3′ [... *at-r*]*u-ṣu ina q*[*é*(?)*-reb* ...]. The published copy of rev. 3′ suggests BE x not *ina* x, but a preliminary copy of the signs by Cavigneaux has *ina* followed by traces which are not incompatible with the first part of a QÉ sign.

Ninurta-kudurrī-uṣur

S.0.1002

Ninurta-kudurrī-uṣur was the son of Šamaš-rēša-uṣur and his successor as governor of the land of Sūḫu. Ninurta-kudurrī-uṣur's inscriptions mention Sîn-šallimanni, the governor of Ruṣapu (Raṣappa) (S.0.1002.1 line 27 [partially restored] and S.0.1002.2 i 33), who is included in the Assyrian eponym lists as governor of that city in 747 (see RLA 2/5 [1938] pp. 424–25, 430, 432, and 454). Thus it is clear that Ninurta-kudurrī-uṣur governed this section of the Middle Euphrates around the middle of the eighth century. Ninurta-kudurrī-uṣur held the position of governor for at least seven years (see S.0.1002.2 iv 38′–39′) and although he never specifically took the title "king," one of his inscriptions states that the gods Šamaš, Marduk, Adad, and Apla-Adad had given him the "kingship over the land of Sūḫu" (S.0.1002.2 i 4–7).

A number of his inscriptions were found during salvage work in the Ḥadītha area and all are written in the Babylonian dialect of the Akkadian language, though both Assyrian and Aramaic influence can be noted. Most of these inscriptions were found at Sūr Jarʿā (S.0.1002.1–2, 4–5, 7–8, and 11–13), but some were discovered at ʿĀnā (S.0.1002.3 and 9–10), Dawālī (S.0.1002.6), and Jedīdē (S.0.1002.14). Two others which may well be assigned to him, S.0.1002.1001 and 1002, were found at Sūr Jarʿā and Zawiyyā respectively. Most of the inscriptions are poorly preserved, and in fact, only one is completely preserved (S.0.1002.11); however, the inscriptions frequently duplicate one another and thus allow restorations to be made with some degree of confidence.

The most prominent event mentioned in the inscriptions of Ninurta-kudurrī-uṣur is his victory over a band of marauding Aramean tribesmen. In brief, two thousand Ḫatallu tribesmen, from the Sarugu and Luḫuāiia (variant: Minuʾû) clans, under their leader Šamaʾgamni were plundering the land of Laqû (located upstream of Sūḫu), and the governor of that land, Adad-daʾʾānu, appealed to Ninurta-kudurrī-uṣur for help. Sin-šallimanni, the governor of Ruṣapu, went against the Arameans but did not attack them when he saw their numbers. Ninurta-kudurrī-uṣur assembled his forces, fell upon the Arameans in the steppe, and annihilated them. He proudly stated that not one of his ancestors had ever won such a decisive victory and credited his accomplishment to the support of the gods. A short account of this victory is found in S.0.1002.1, while a longer version is found in S.0.1002.2–8. None of the texts with the longer version preserves the whole description and more than one recension of the long version is clearly attested (e.g., while the end of column i of S.0.1002.4 and the start of column of i of S.0.1002.5 likely describe the same incident, the two accounts diverge considerably). The chart on the following page attempts to show the approximate relationship between the accounts found in the various texts and is adapted from the one presented by Cavigneaux and Bahija Ismail on Bagh. Mitt. 21 (1990) p. 336. For a study which includes a brief discussion of this Aramean incursion, see Liverani, SAAB 6 (1992) pp. 35–40.

Ninurta-kudurrī-uṣur claims to have been victorious over the city Raʾil, which had revolted against him (S.0.1002.1–3 and 6). He also states that at

Incursion by Arameans

S.0.1002.2 S.0.1002.3 S.0.1002.4 S.0.1002.5 S.0.1002.6 S.0.1002.7 S.0.1002.8

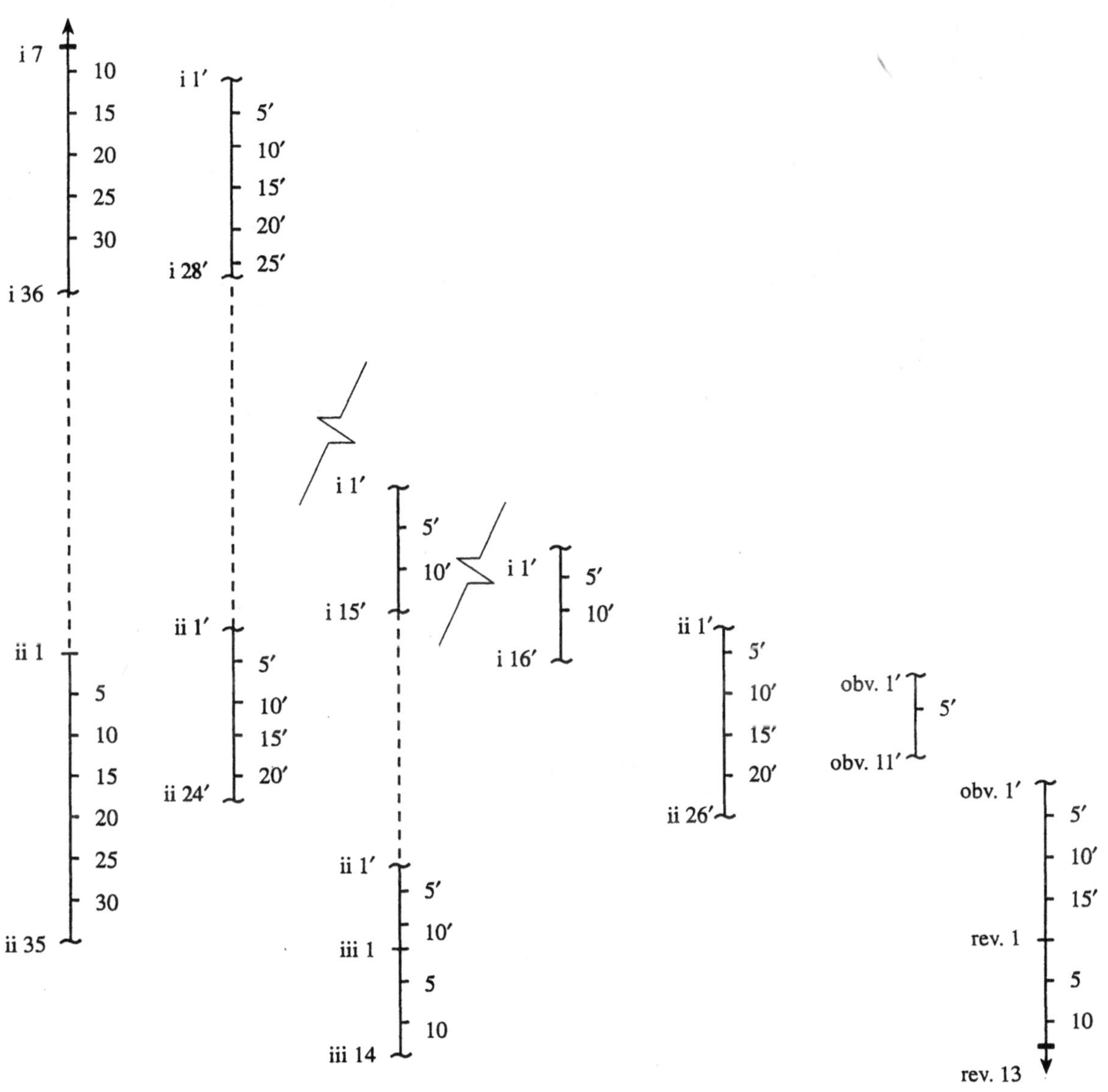

▬ Beginning/end of account

~ Text broken

⚡ Exact placement uncertain (S.0.1002.4)

some point in the past, Tabnēa, the governor of the land of Sūḫu, had gone to Assyria with tribute and had (apparently) been killed there. The city Anat is said to have revolted against the land of Sūḫu, given itself up to "the Assyrian" of its own free will, been ill-treated, and then, after approximately fifty years, turned to Ninurta-kudurrī-uṣur's father, Šamaš-rēša-uṣur (S.0.1002.4–5 and 9–10). Ninurta-kudurrī-uṣur claims to have resettled the city, returned its gods, which had fled to the town Ribaniš (exact reading uncertain) out of fear of "the Assyrian," re-established the cult of the goddess Anat, restored the Akītu temple for the gods Adad and Apla-Adad ("Heir of the God Adad"), and built two palaces (S.0.1002.3, 5, and 9–11). Exactly who "the Assyrian" was is unclear. It might refer to the Assyrian king or to an Assyrian governor.

The construction or restoration of various other cities and structures is also mentioned in the inscriptions of Ninurta-kudurrī-uṣur: an Akītu temple to the gods Adad and Mīšarum (Mešar) at the town Udada (S.0.1002.1–3, 6, 8, and 12), two palaces in the district of the city Raʾil (S.0.1002.1–3, 6–7, 12, and likely 8), the town Dūr-Ninurta-kudurrī-uṣur ("Fort Ninurta-kudurrī-uṣur") and/or its well (S.0.1002.2–4 and 13), the town Kār-Apla-Adad ("Quay of the God Apla-Adad") (S.0.1002.2), and the town Āl-gabbāri-bānî (S.0.1002.2). The capture of a caravan from Tema and Šaba is also reported in one inscription (S.0.1002.2 iv 26′–38′). An overview of the texts of Ninurta-kudurrī-uṣur is presented by Bahija Ismail in Sumer 42 (1986) pp. 87–88 [Arabic section].

1

Two damaged clay tablets from the Iraqi excavations at Sūr Jarʿā bear an Akkadian inscription which describes Ninurta-kudurrī-uṣur's restoration of the Akītu temple at the town Udada, construction of two palaces in the district of Raʾil, victory over the people of Raʾil, and decisive defeat of the Ḫatallu tribe and their leader Šamaʾgamni.

CATALOGUE

Ex.	Museum no.	Provenance	Lines preserved	Bagh. Mitt. 21	cpn
1	IM 95915	Sūr Jarʿā	1–50	4	n
2	IM 124196	Sūr Jarʿā	1–51	3	n

COMMENTARY

The edition is based upon the published copies, with notes to the transliteration by Cavigneaux and Bahija Ismail. The line arrangement follows ex. 1 for lines 1–50; line 51 is found only on ex. 2 (where it is line 53 of the exemplar). The master line is a conflation of exs. 1 and 2; ex. 2 is followed where the two diverge.

With regard to restorations and parallel/similar passages, note the following:

For lines 1–4a, see S.0.1002.2 i 1–4, S.0.1002.9 i 1–5, S.0.1002.10 lines 9–14, S.0.1002.11 lines 11–14, and S.0.1002.14 lines 1–6.

For lines 4b–9a, see S.0.1002.2 iv 2′–9′, S.0.1002.3 iii 1′–4′, S.0.1002.6 iii 4′–12′, S.0.1002.8 rev. 13–20, S.0.1002.11 lines 17–20, and S.0.1002.12 lines 4′–8′.

For lines 9b–14, see S.0.1002.2 iv 9′–15′, S.0.1002.3 iii 5′–14′, S.0.1002.6 iii 12′–21′, S.0.1002.7 rev. 1′–8′, S.0.1002.8 rev. 21–22, and S.0.1002.12 lines 8′–12′.

For lines 15–19a, see S.0.1002.2 iv 15′–21′, S.0.1002.3 iii 14′–21′, and S.0.1002.6 iii 21′–27′.

For lines 19b–24a, see S.0.1002.2 i 8–13 and 28–30, and S.0.1002.3 i 1′–4′ and 20′–22′.

For lines 24b–26, see S.0.1002.2 i 30–32 and S.0.1002.3 i 22′–25′.

For lines 27–28, see S.0.1002.2 i 33–35 and S.0.1002.3 i 26′–28′.

For lines 29–43a, see S.0.1002.2 i 36, ii 6–11, 15–16, 20, 23–25, and 27–29; S.0.1002.3 ii 9′–15′ and 20′–21′; S.0.1002.4 i 2′–3′ and 7′–13′; S.0.1002.6 ii 10′–15′ and 20′–21′; S.0.1002.7 obv. 4′–9′; and S.0.1002.8 lines 5′, 8′–10′, and 12′–15′.

For lines 43b–50, see S.0.1002.2 ii 29–34, S.0.1002.4 ii 10′–iii 4, and S.0.1002.8 lines 15′–rev. 4.

The description of Ninurta-kudurrī-uṣur's actual conflict with the Ḫatallu tribe and their leader Šama'gamni (lines 29–43a) is an abbreviated account of the one presented in the following inscriptions (S.0.1002.2–8). For an attempt to reconcile the various figures cited in these texts for the numbers of the enemy who were killed and who got away alive, see Cavigneaux and Bahija Ismail, Bagh. Mitt. 21 (1990) pp. 352–53.

Various unusual phrases appear in the inscriptions of Ninurta-kudurrī-uṣur and may reflect local dialect; see Cavigneaux and Bahija Ismail, Bagh. Mitt. 21 (1990) p. 340 on the style and language of these texts. One phrase which appears in several of them is: *ina libbi pānū'a ana muḫḫi ul aškunma uṣurta ul ēṣirši*, which is tentatively translated "*With regard to this matter, I did not pay (great) attention to it and did not make a relief (commemorating) it.*" Several variants to the phrase are found (e.g., *ù* for *ina libbi*, *pānīia* for *pānū'a*, and *ēṣiršu* for *ēṣirši*). The phrase is found in connection with the building of palaces at Ra'il (S.0.1002.1 line 14, S.0.1002.3 iii 13′–14′, and S.0.1002.6 iii 20′–21′; in at least one, if not all, of these cases, the text has *ù*, "*Moreover*," rather than *ina libbi*, "*With regard to this matter*") and in connection with a rebellion at Ra'il (S.0.1002.1 line 16, S.0.1002.2 iv 19′–20′, S.0.1002.3 iii 16′–17′, and S.0.1002.6 iii 23′–24′). In addition, we once have simply GIŠ.ḪUR *e-ṣir-šú* (S.0.1002.3 iv 18′); this is in connection with the building of palaces at Anat. While the meaning "plan" or "outline" for *uṣurtu* might be permissible when the passage deals with the construction of buildings, such a meaning would not fit well with the passages describing the revolt at Ra'il. Assuming a meaning "relief" here, one would think of a pictorial relief accompanied by an inscription, such as S.0.1002.10 and S.0.0.1007. See also Cavigneaux and Bahija Ismail, Bagh. Mitt. 21 (1990) p. 332.

BIBLIOGRAPHY

1990 Cavigneaux and Bahija Ismail, Bagh. Mitt. 21 pp. 358–63 and 418–22 nos. 3–4 (exs. 1–2, copy, edition)

TEXT

1) *a-na-ku* ^{md}MAŠ-NÍG.DU-ÙRU LÚ.GAR KUR *su-ḫi u* KUR *má-rí* DUMU ^{md}UTU-SAG-PAB LÚ.GAR KUR *su-ḫi u* KUR *ma-ri*
2) DUMU ^{m}BA-*šá*-^{d}AMAR.UTU MIN Š[À].BAL.BAL ^{md}IŠKUR-SUM-NUMUN LÚ.GAR KUR *su-ḫi u* KUR *má-rí*
3) [(...)] NUMUN *da-ru-ú li-pu ru-qu šá* ^{m}*tu-na-mis-saḫ* DUMU ^{m}(*)*ḫa-am-mu-ra-pu*
4) [*šar bābili* (...)] É *a-ki-*tu_4 *šá* ^{d}IŠKUR *u* ^{d}*mi-šar-rum* DINGIR.MEŠ GAL.MEŠ *a-ši-bu-tu*
5) [*udada*] EN.MEŠ-*e-a la-ba-riš il-lik-ma muš-šu-rat a-a-*⸢*um*⸣*-ma ina lìb-bi*
6) [*abbēa*] SAG-*su ul iš-ši-ma ul i-pu-uš ana-ku* É *a-ki-t*[u_4 UR_5-*t*]*ú* ⸢*ú*⸣*-šak-lil-ma*
7) *a-na* ^{d}IŠKUR *ù* ^{d}*mi-ša-rum* DINGIR.MEŠ GAL.MEŠ EN.MEŠ-*e-a a-na ba-laṭ* ZI.MEŠ-*ia*
8) *šá-lam* NUMUN-*ia* GÍD.DA UD.MEŠ-*ia ku-un* BALA.MEŠ-*e-a sa-kap* KUR LÚ.KÚR-*ia ú-še-piš-ma*

1–4a) I, Ninurta-kudurrī-uṣur, governor of the land of Sūḫu and the land of Mari, son of Šamaš-rēša-uṣur, governor of the land of Sūḫu and the land of Mari, son of Iqīša-Marduk, ditto (governor of the land of Sūḫu and the land of Mari), descendant of Adad-nādin-zēri, governor of the land of Sūḫu and the land of Mari, [(...)] one of an enduring lineage, distant descendant of Tunamissaḫ, son of Ḫammu-rāpi, [king of Babylon (...)] —

4b–9a) The Akītu temple of the gods Adad and Mīšarum — the great gods who dwell in [the town Udada], my lords — had become old and been abandoned. None among [my ancestors] had paid attention (to it) and (re)built (it). I completely (re)built [this] Akītu temple. I had (this temple) (re)built and dedicated (it) to the gods Adad and Mīšarum, the great gods, my lords, in order to ensure my good health (and) the well-being of my offspring, to prolong my days, to confirm my reign, (and) to defeat the land of my enemy.

3–4 It is unlikely that anything is to be restored before NUMUN in line 3 and in addition to *šar bābili* in line 4.

4 In the texts of Ninurta-kudurrī-uṣur, the word *akītu* is sometimes preceded by É and sometimes not (cf. S.0.1002.1 lines 4 and 6 [present] with S.0.1002.2 iv 5′ and S.0.1002.11 lines 14 and 17 [omitted]). Cavigneaux and Bahija Ismail (Bagh. Mitt. 21 [1990] pp. 342–43) suggest that the term *akītu* simply means "temple" in these texts, and not specifially a temple for the *akītu* festival. The gods Adad and Mīšarum had an "*akītu*" temple at Udada (e.g., S.0.1002.1 lines 4–5 and S.0.1002.6 iii 4′–5′) and the gods Adad and Apla-Adad had one at Anat (S.0.1002.11 lines 14–15).

5 Cavigneaux and Bahija Ismail (Bagh. Mitt. 21 [1990] p. 357) suggest that Udada (URU *ú-da-da* in S.0.1002.2 iv 3′ and S.0.1002.6 iii 5′) may be identical to the town Ḫudada appearing in the Adad-šuma-uṣur Epic (Grayson, BHLT pp. 63 and 76 iv 15′ and 20′).

9) BA-*eš* É.GAL ^{m}[*é-nam-ḫ*]*é*-NUMUN-*ib-ni* LÚ.GAR KUR *su-ḫi u* KUR *ma-ri* KI-*tim* URU *ra-ìl*
10) *šá qab-lat* ÍD.[BURANUN.KI] *la-ba-riš il-lik-ma un-dáš-šìr-šú* É.GAL *šá-ni-tu*$_4$
11) AN.TA-*šú e-pu-uš-m*[*a* 60-*šu*] ⸢4⸣ *ina* 1 KÙŠ GÍD.DA-*šú* 12 *ina* 1 KÙŠ *ù ma-la ú-ṭu ru-pu-us-su*
12) *a-na la* É.GAL *šá* ^{m}⸢*é*(*)⸣-[*nam*]-*ḫé*-NUMUN-DÙ 20 *ina* 1 KÙŠ *ú-šá-rik-šú* 4 *ina* 1 KÙŠ *ur-tap-pis-su*
13) *šá-ni-tu*$_4$ É.GAL AN.T[A-*šú ina* U]GU *ki-iṣ-ri e-pu-uš-ma* 45 *ina* 1 KÙŠ *ú-šá-rik-šú*
14) 9 *ina* 1 KÙŠ *ur-tap-pis-*[*su ù*] *pa-nu-ú-a a-na muḫ-ḫi ul áš-kun-ma* GIŠ.ḪUR *ul e-ṣir-ši*

9b–14) The palace of [Enamḫ]e-zēra-ibni, governor of the land of Sūḫu and the land of Mari, (which is located in) the district of the city Ra᾿il, which is in the middle of the [Euphrates] River, had become old and I abandoned it. I built another palace above it: [6]4 cubits is its length (and) 12 1/2 cubits is its width. I made it 20 cubits longer (and) 4 cubits wider than the palace of E[nam]ḫe-zēra-ibni. I built (even) another palace above [it on] top of an *embankment*; I made it 45 cubits long (and) 9 cubits wide. [*Moreover*], *I did not pay* (*great*) *attention to this matter and did not make a relief* (*commemorating*) *it.*

15) LÚ *ra-ìl-a-a* LÚ.ḪI.GAR.M[EŠ(?)-*šú-nu* ḪI.GA]R(?) *a-na* UGU AD-*ia i-pu-šú-ma* AD-*ú-a id-duk-šú-nu-ti*
16) *i-na lìb-bi pa-nu-*⸢*ú*⸣-[*a ana mu*]*ḫ-ḫi ul áš-kun-ma* GIŠ.ḪUR *ul e-ṣir-ši i-na re-eš*
17) LÚ.GAR.KUR-*ú-ti-ia* [*šá ina* GIŠ.G]U.ZA *šá* AD-*ia ú-ši-bu* LÚ *ra-ìl-a-a a-na muḫ-ḫi-ia*
18) *ib-bal-kit-ú-m*[*a a-duk*]-⸢*šú*⸣-*nu-ti man-ni ár-ku-ú šá* E$_{11}$-*ma a-na* LÚ *ra-ìl-a-a*

15–19a) With regard to the people of Ra᾿il (*and*) [their] rebels, they had [rebell]ed against my father, but my father had defeated them. *With regard to this matter, I did not pay* (*great*) *attention* [*to*] *it and did not make a relief* (*commemorating*) *it.* At the beginning of my governorship, [when] I ascended [the th]rone of my father, the people of Ra᾿il revolted against me, but [I defeated] them. No one in the future who comes forward should neg[lect] the people of Ra᾿il!

19) *na-de-e a-ḫi la* [*i-raš-ši*]-⸢*šú*⸣-*nu-ti ina re-eš* LÚ.GAR.KUR-*ú-ti-ia šá i-na* GIŠ.GU.ZA
20) *šá* AD-*ia ú-ši-b*[*u* 2 LIM LÚ *ḫa-ta*]*l-li ul-tu* LÚ *sa-ru-gu a-di* LÚ *mi-nu-*᾿*-i*
21) *ip-ḫu-ru-ú-m*[*a* ^{m}*šá-ma-*᾿*-ga-a*]*m-ni* LÚ.NIMGIR LÚ *sa-ru-gu a-lik pa-ni-šu-nu*
22) *a-na ḫu-ub-tu* [*ana* KUR *la-qé*]-⸢*e*⸣ *il-li-ku-ma* <<KUR>> 1 ME É.DURU$_5$.MEŠ *šá* KUR *la-qé-e*
23) *iṣ-bat-ú-ma ḫ*[*u-ub-tu lā mīni iḫ-b*]*u-tu-nim-ma* KUR *la-qé-e a-na* DU$_6$ *ù kar-mi*
24) *ut-tir-ru* ^{md}[IŠKUR-*da-*᾿*a-nu šaknu māt l*]*a-qé-e*

19b–24a) At the beginning of my governorship, when I ascended the throne of my father, [two thousand Ḫata]llu (tribesmen) — from the Sarugu (clan) to the Minu᾿û (clan) — gathered and [Šama᾿ga]mni, the *herald* of the Sarugu (clan), was their leader. They went to plunder [the land of Laq]û. They seized one hundred villages of the land of Laqû, [to]ok [countless] bo[oty], and turned the land of Laqû into a heap of ruins.

ina lìb-bi 4 GIŠ.GIGIR.MEŠ 2 ME ÉRIN.MEŠ
25) *a-na pa-ni-i*[*a illikamma qaqqari*] *i-na pa-ni-ia iš-šiq-ma ù ú-sap-pa-an-ni-ma*
26) *šum-ma ki-i* [x x x x x x] *at-ta ù ki-i tu-un-dáš-šìr-an-ni at-ta-a-ma*

24b–26) [Adad-da᾿᾿ānu, the governor of the land of L]aqû, [came] before me with four chariots (and) two hundred soldiers. He kissed [the ground] before me and then implored me (for aid), (saying): “*If you* [...] *or if you abandon me,* (*you will surely die*)!”

27) *ù* ^{md}30-[SILIM-*im-an-ni*] LÚ.EN.NAM KUR *ru-ṣa-pu* ⸢*a*⸣-[*d*]*i e-mu-qu gab-bi šá* KUR *ru-ṣa-pu*
28) *a-na mu*[*ḫ-ḫi-šú-nu illikamma*] *i-mur-šu-nu-ti-ma*

27–28) Moreover, Sîn-[šallimanni], the provincial governor of the land of Ruṣapu [went] against [them (the Arameans) wi]th all the troops of the land of

12 As noted by Cavigneaux and Bahija Ismail (Bagh. Mitt. 21 [1990] p. 357 sub iv 12ff.), the original palace had then been 44×8.5 cubits (ca. 22×4 m) in size.

14 The parallel passage in S.0.1002.3 iii 13′ has *ru-pu-us-su*, “its width,” for *ur-tap-pis-su*, “I made it wide.” Thus, it is better to assume that the passage tells us that the second palace measured 45×9 cubits rather than that it was 45 cubits longer and 9 cubits wider than the old palace of Enamḫe-zēra-ibni (that is 85×17.5 cubits in size). Possibly restore *ina libbi* instead of *ù* before *pānū᾿a* (see commmentary to this text), but the one occasion where this passage is fully preserved in this location has *ù pa-ni-ia* (S.0.1002.6 iii 20′).

15 Or less likely LÚ.ḪI.GAR-*š*[*ú-nu* ḪI.GA]R. For the restoration, see S.0.1002.2 iv 15′–16′, S.0.1002.3 iii 15′, and S.0.1002.6 iii 21′. S.0.1002.2 iv 15′ has ḪI.GAR-*šú-nu*, “their rebellion,” not LÚ.ḪI.GAR.MEŠ-*šú-nu*. See Cavigneaux and Bahija Ismail, Bagh. Mitt. 21 (1990) p. 357.

20 The parallel passage in S.0.1002.2 i 10 has *a-di* LÚ *lu-ḫu-ú-a-a* TA ÉRIN.MEŠ GIŠ.BAN *ù* LÚ.SAG KAL×BAD.MEŠ-*šú-nu*, “to the Luḫuāiia (clan) — with archers and their *military commanders*,” instead of *a-di* LÚ *mi-nu-*᾿*-i*, “to the Minu᾿û (clan).”

21 The term LÚ.NIMGIR, Akkadian *nāgiru*, is usually translated “herald” but can also refer to other high officials; see CAD 11/1 [N] pp. 115–18.

26 S.0.1002.2 i 32 and S.0.1002.3 i 25′ have *su-pe-šú am-ḫur*, “I accepted his supplication,” for this line.

a-na muḫ-ḫi-šú-nu ul im-qut

29) *a-na-ku* ^{md}M[AŠ-*kudurrī-uṣur šaknu māt sūḫi*] *u* KUR *ma-ri am-ri šá* ^{d}UTU *u* ^{d}AMAR.UTU ^{d}IŠKUR *u* ^{d}A-^{d}IŠKUR

30) *ù* ^{d}*iš-tar* [x x x x x (x x)] *ù* ^{d}AMAR.UTU *i-pu-šú-ma* UGU LUGAL.MEŠ *dan-nu-ú-tu*

31) *ù* UGU LÚ.GAR.[KUR.MEŠ x x x x (x x)] *ú-šaq-qu-ú* ^{d}A-^{d}IŠKUR EN GAL-*ú* EN-*ia áš-al-ma*

32) *ina a-mat* ^{d}A-^{d}IŠ[KUR] EN GAL-*ú* EN-*ia ina lìb-bi* 1 ME 5 GIŠ.GIGIR.MEŠ 2 ME 20 *pít-ḫal-lu* 3 LIM *zu*(*)-*uk* GÌR.II

33) *ù* KUR *su-ḫi gab-bi ul ip-ḫu-ru a-na muḫ-ḫi-šú-nu a-na* EDIN *e-li-ma* 1-*en* u$_4$-*mi*

34) *i-na* UGU PÚ *ṣu-mu-ú-a ú-šib-ma šu-nu* 2 LIM-*šú-nu* ÉRIN.MEŠ GIŠ.BAN *a-na* UGU PÚ *ma-ki-ri*

35) *ik-šu-du-nim-ma a-na lìb-bi-šú-nu am-qu-ut-ma* 1 LIM 7 ME 11[+5(?)] ÉRIN.MEŠ *ina lìb-bi-šú-nu ad-duk*

36) *ul-tu* PÚ *ma-ki-ri a-di* PÚ *gal-la-bu ù a-di* UGU PÚ ⸢*su*⸣-*ri*-⸢*bu*⸣ BAD$_5$.BAD$_5$-*šú-nu*

37) *áš-kun gul-gul-la-ti-šu-nu* KUR.MEŠ *ù na-ḫal* ⸢*um*⸣-*dal-li* ⸢*ù šá*⸣ 80 ⸢ÉRIN⸣.MEŠ *ina lìb-bi-šú-nu*

38) *kap-pi-šú-nu sa-ap-sa-pi-šú-nu áš-ši-ma a-na da-li-li un-dáš-šìr-šu-nu-ti*

39) *ù* 2 ME ÉRIN.MEŠ *bal-ṭu-ú-tu ina lìb-bi-šú-nu it-ta-par-ši-du*(*) *ù* ^{m}*šá-ma-ʾ-ga-am-ni*

40) LÚ.NIMGIR LÚ *sa-ru-gu a-lik pa-ni-šú-nu* LÚ.ÌR *la tar-ṣu šá* KUR *su-ḫi* KUR *aš-šur*.KI *u* AD.MEŠ-*e-a*

41) *ú-šá-an-si*(*)-<*ku*(?)>-*šu ik-šu-ud* ŠU.II-*a-a a*-⸢*duk*⸣-*šú-ma i-nu-uḫ lìb-bi šá mam-ma ina lìb-bi* AD.MEŠ-*e-a*

42) *la i-du-ku ana-ku ad-duk* ⸢AD⸣.MEŠ-*ú-a* 10-*šú* LÚ.KÚR GAZ-*ma ma-lu-ú-a ul ú-šam-ṣu-ú*

43) *ana-ku* 1-*et di-ik-ti a-duk-ma a-na la* AD.MEŠ-*e-a ú-šá-tir*$_x$(DIR) *man-ni ár-ku-ú šá* E$_{11}$-*ma*

44) *i-qab-bu-ú um-ma ki-i-ki-i* ^{md}MAŠ-NÍG.DU-PAB LÚ.GAR KUR *su-ḫi u* KUR *ma-ri di-ik-ti*

45) *an-ni-tu*$_4$ *id-duk ul i-na e-muq-ia a-duk ina e-muq* ^{d}UTU *u* ^{d}AM[AR].UTU ^{d}IŠKUR *u* ^{d}A-^{d}IŠKUR

46) DINGIR.MEŠ GAL.MEŠ EN.MEŠ-*e-a di-ik-ti an-ni*-⸢*tu*$_4$⸣ *ad-duk man-ni ár-ku-ú šá* E$_{11}$-*ma*

47) *ši-bu-ut* KUR-*šú ù ši-b*[*u*]-⸢*tu*⸣ *šá* KUR *la-qé-e liš*-⸢*al*⸣-*ma um-ma* ⸢*kit*⸣-*tu-ú*

48) *šá* ^{md}MAŠ-NÍG.DU-PAB LÚ.GAR KUR *su-ḫi u* KUR *má-rí ina a-mat* ^{d}A-^{d}IŠKUR EN GAL-*ú* EN-*šú*

49) [*dīktu*] *an-ni-ti i-du-ku a-ga-a ši-kin qa-ti šá* ^{d}A-^{d}IŠKUR DINGIR EN-*ia*

Ruṣapu, [but] (when) he saw them, he did not fall upon them.

29–43a) I, Ni[nurta-kudurrī-uṣur, governor of the land of Sūḫu] and the land of Mari, the chosen one, whom the gods Šamaš and Marduk, Adad and Apla-Adad, and Ištar made [... *for* ...] and the god Marduk and [...] exalted over mighty kings and over [(...)] gover[nors] — I questioned the god Apla-Adad, the great lord, my lord. At the command of the god Apla-Ad[ad], the great lord, my lord, I went up to the steppe against them with 105 chariots, 220 mounted soldiers, (and) 3,000 foot soldiers — and (thereby) not even all of the land of Sūḫu was gathered! I waited at the well Ṣumūa for one (whole) day and (then) they — two thousand of them, (*all/including*) archers — arrived at the well Makiru. (35) I fell upon them and killed one thousand seven hundred and *sixteen* of their men. From the well Makiru as far as the well Gallabu and the well Suribu, I defeated them. I filled the mountains and wadis with their skulls. Moreover, I removed the arms (and) lower lips of eighty of their men and let them go to (spread the news of my) glory. Two hundred soldiers from among them got away alive. Moreover, with regard to Šamaʾgamni, (40) the *herald* of the Sarugu (clan), their leader, the dishonest servant whom the land of Sūḫu, Assyria, and my fathers *rejected*, I got hold (of him and) killed him, (thereby) easing my heart. I inflicted such a defeat as none among my ancestors had inflicted. My ancestors had defeated the enemy ten times, but they did not achieve as much as I. I inflicted a single defeat (of such an extent that) I surpassed my ancestors.

43b–50) Anyone in the future who comes forward and says: "How did Ninurta-kudurrī-uṣur, the governor of the land of Sūḫu and the land of Mari, (45) inflict this defeat?" (should be told that) I did not inflict (this) by my own power, (but rather) I inflicted this defeat by the power of the gods Šamaš and Marduk, Adad and Apla-Adad, the great gods, my lords. Anyone in the future who comes forward and *should* ask the elders of his land and the elders of the land of Laqû: "Is it true that Ninurta-kudurrī-uṣur, the governor of the land of Sūḫu and the land of Mari inflicted this [defeat] at the command of the god Apla-Adad, the great lord, his lord?" (should be told that) this was the handiwork of the god Apla-Adad, my divine lord [...] he loves me and set my hands to this task.

---

28 S.0.1002.2 i 35 has *ip-làḫ*-⸢*ma*⸣ "he became afraid and" after *īmuršunūtima* "he saw them."

41.1 *si*(*): copy has KID, while Bagh. Mitt. 21 transliteration has *si*; not preserved on ex. 2. Or *ú-šá-an-si-ku*(Text: ŠU)? Assuming that the initial word is a form of *nasāku* (suggested by von Soden, apud Cavigneaux) and that the proposed reading *ušansikūšu* is correct, S.0.1002.2 ii 25 would also omit the KU sign. Cavigneaux has pointed out to me that this would suggest that both inscriptions were copied from a third source. Cf. Cavigneaux and Bahija Ismail, Bagh. Mitt. 21 (1990) p. 355 sub ii 25.

43 The phrase *ana lā abbēa ušātir* ("I surpassed my ancestors") is awkward and may reflect local dialect.

50) [x x x x] *i-ra-man-ni-ma dul-la an-na-a a-na* ŠU.II-*ia iš-kun*

51) *ba-⌈a⌉-[ri]*

51) Collated.

2

A four-column clay tablet found at Sūr Jarʿā (IM 95917) has a lengthy Akkadian inscription of Ninurta-kudurrī-uṣur, which was composed in the seventh year of his governorship (see iv 38b′–40′). The largest part of the inscription describes his defeat of the Ḫatallu tribe and their leader Šamaʾgamni, who had attacked the nearby land of Laqû, plundered it, and turned it into "a heap of ruins" (cols. i–ii). A victory over rebels from the city Raʾil and the capture of a caravan from Tema and Šaba, which had gone to Ḫindānu, are also mentioned (col. iv). In addition, the inscription records his construction of the towns Dūr-Ninurta-kudurrī-uṣur ("Fort Ninurta-kudurrī-uṣur") and Kār-Apla-Adad ("Quay of the God Apla-Adad"), an Akītu temple for the gods Adad and Mīšarum (Mešar) at the town Udada, two palaces in the district of the city Raʾil, and fortification works for the town Āl-gabbāri-bānî (cols. iii–iv).

COMMENTARY

The inscription has not been collated and the edition presented here is based upon the published copy, with notes to the transliteration by Cavigneaux and Bahija Ismail.

With regard to restorations and parallel/similar passages, note the following:

For i 1–4, see S.0.1002.1 lines 1–4 and 29–30, S.0.1005 i 9′, S.0.1002.9 i 1–5, S.0.1002.10 lines 9–14, S.0.1002.11 lines 11–14, and S.0.1002.14 lines 1–6.

For i 8b–16a, see S.0.1002.1 lines 19–22 and S.0.1002.3 i 1′–6′.

For i 16b–27a, see S.0.1002.3 i 7′–19′.

For i 27b–30a, see S.0.1002.1 lines 22–24 and S.0.1002.3 i 19′–22′.

For i 30b–32, see S.0.1002.1 lines 24–25 and S.0.1002.3 i 22′–25′.

For i 33–35, see S.0.1002.1 lines 27–28 and S.0.1002.3 i 26′–28′.

For i 36, see S.0.1002.1 line 29.

For ii 1–29a, see S.0.1002.3 ii 3′–24′, S.0.1002.5 i 14′–16′, S.0.1002.6 ii 3′–26′, S.0.1002.7 obv. 1′–11′, and S.0.1002.8 obv. 3′–15′; see also S.0.1002.1 lines 35–43.

For ii 29b–35, see S.0.1002.1 lines 43–47, S.0.1002.4 ii 10′–12′, and S.0.1002.8 obv. 15′–20′.

For iii 16b′-22a′, see S.0.1002.4 iv 1–5 and S.0.1002.13 rev. 1–8.

For iv 2′–9a′, see S.0.1002.1 lines 4–9, S.0.1002.3 iii 1′–4′, S.0.1002.6 iii 3′–12′, S.0.1002.8 rev. 13–20, S.0.1002.11 lines 17–20, and S.0.1002.12 lines 3′–8′.

For iv 9b′–15a′, see S.0.1002.1 lines 9–14, S.0.1002.3 iii 5′–14′, S.0.1002.6 iii 12′–21′, S.0.1002.7 rev. 1′–8′, S.0.1002.8 rev. 21–22, and S.0.1002.12 lines 8′–12′.

For iv 15b′–21a′, see S.0.1002.1 lines 15–19, S.0.1002.3 iii 14′–21′, and S.0.1002.6 iii 21′–27′.

BIBLIOGRAPHY

1986 Bahija Ismail, Sumer 42 pp. 87–88 [Arabic section] (study)

1990 Cavigneaux and Bahija Ismail, Bagh. Mitt. 21 pp. 334–37, 343–57, and 412–17 no. 2 (copy, edition, study)

50 S.0.1002.8 rev. 3–4 has a variant passage at this point: [...]-RI-*ka-a ú-ma-ʾ-ir* [...] x LÚ.KÚR-*a a-n*[*a qa-ti*] *-ia im-ni*, "He ordered *my* [...; ...]. He delivered my enemy into my [hands]."

51 Ex. 1 may omit this line. The notation "collated" is also found at the end of S.0.1002.2.

TEXT

Col. i

1) *ana-ku* ^{md}MAŠ-NÍG.DU-PAB LÚ.GAR KUR *su-ḫi u* KUR *ma-ri* DUMU ^{md}UTU-SAG-PAB MIN
2) DUMU ^{m}BA-*šá*-^{d}AMAR.UTU MIN ŠÀ.BAL ^{md}IŠKUR-SUM-NUMUN MIN NUMUN *da-ru-ú*
3) *li-pu ru-qu šá* ^{m}*tu-na-mis-saḫ* DUMU ^{m}*ḫa-am-mu-ra-pu*
4) LUGAL TIN.TIR.KI *am*(*)-*ri šá* ^{d}UTU *u* ^{d}AMAR.UTU ^{d}IŠKUR *u* ^{d}A-^{d}IŠKUR *ḫa-diš*(*)
5) *nam-riš ina* KAL *pa-ni-šú-nu nam-ru-ti ip-pal-su-in*(*)-*ni-ma*
6) *e-mu-qu gaš-ra-a-tu_4 da-na-nu ù* LUGAL-*ú-tu šá* KUR *su-ḫi*
7) *id-di-nu-nim-ma ù kit-ti a-na* NAM-*ia iš-ru-ku* 3 ITI.MEŠ
8) *ina muḫ-ḫi ṭup-pi-šú ina* SAG LÚ.GAR.KUR-*ú-tu-ia šá i-na* GIŠ.GU.ZA
9) *šá* AD-*ia ú-ši-bu* 2 LIM LÚ *ḫa-tal-lu ul-tu* LÚ *sa-ru-gu*
10) *a-di* LÚ *lu-ḫu-ú-a-a* TA ÉRIN.MEŠ GIŠ.BAN *ù* LÚ.SAG KAL×BAD.MEŠ-*šú-nu*
11) *ip-ḫu-ru-ú-ma ṭè-e-mi a-na a-ḫa-meš iš-kun-ú-ma*
12) ^{m}*šá-ma-ʾ-ga-am-ni* LÚ.NIMGIR LÚ *sa-ru-gu šá ina la kit-ti bal-lu*
13) *a-lik pa-ni-šú-nu a-na ḫu-ub-tu a-na* KUR *la-qé-e* E_{11}-*nim-ma*
14) *ina* EDIN *in-dal-ku-ú-ma um-ma* LÚ.GAR KUR *su-ḫi it-ti-ni*
15) *na-kir-ma um-ma ki-ki-ma ni-it-ti-iq-ma ḫu-ub-ti*
16) *ul-tu* KUR *la-qé-e ni-ḫab-bat* ^{m}*šá-ma-ʾ-ga-am-ni* LÚ.NIMGIR
17) LÚ *sa-ru-gu ù* ^{m}*ia-a-ʾ-e* DUMU ^{m}*ba-la-am-mu* LÚ *a-mat-a-a*
18) LÚ.SAG KAL×BAD.MEŠ-*šú-nu ki-a-ma iq-bu-niš-šú-nu-tim-ma um-ma*
19) LÚ.GAR.KUR.MEŠ *šá* KUR *su-ḫi* AD.MEŠ-*šú mam-ma ina lìb-bi-šú-nu a-na lìb-bi* 1 LIM
20) LÚ *a-ra-mu a-na ṣal-ta ul il-lik um-ma en-na šu-ú*
21) *a-na lìb-bi* 2 LIM LÚ *a-ra*(*)-*mu a-na ṣal-ta il-la-ku um-ma ki-i*
22) *a-na pa-ni-ni it-la-a a-na ṣal-ta a-na lìb-bi-šú ni-lak-ma*
23) *ù* KUR *su-ḫi a-na šá ram-ni-ni nu-tar-ru ù ki-i la it-la-a*
24) *ḫu-ub-tu nu-še-rid-ma ù* ÉRIN.MEŠ *a-na muḫ-ḫi-ni nu-rad-dam-ma*

i 1–7a) I, Ninurta-kudurrī-uṣur, governor of the land of Sūḫu and the land of Mari, son of Šamaš-rēša-uṣur, ditto (governor of the land of Sūḫu and the land of Mari), son of Iqīša-Marduk, ditto (governor of the land of Sūḫu and the land of Mari), descendant of Adad-nādin-zēri, ditto (governor of the land of Sūḫu and the land of Mari), one of an enduring lineage, distant descendant of Tunamissaḫ, son of Ḫammu-rāpi, king of Babylon; the chosen one, upon whom the gods Šamaš and Marduk, Adad and Apla-Adad, happily (and) (i 5) radiantly looked with their *full* shining faces, to whom they gave mighty power, strength, and the kingship over the land of Sūḫu, and for whose lot they bestowed (a sense of) justice —

i 7b–16a) Three months had hardly passed, at the beginning of my governorship, when I ascended the throne of my father, (when) two thousand Ḫatallu (tribesmen) — from the Sarugu (clan) (i 10) to the Luḫuāiia (clan) — with archers and their *military commanders* gathered and came to an agreement. Šamaʾgamni, the *herald* of the Sarugu (clan), who is thoroughly pervaded with falsehood, was their leader. They came up to plunder the land of Laqû, but while in the steppe they deliberated, saying: "The governor of the land of Sūḫu (i 15) is hostile to us. How shall we pass by (him) in order to plunder the land of Laqû?"

i 16b–27a) Šamaʾgamni, the *herald* of the Sarugu (clan), and Iâʾe, the son of Balammu, a member of the Amatu (tribe), their *military commanders*, said the following to them: "Not one among the governors of the land of Sūḫu, his ancestors, (i 20) (ever dared to) go to fight against one thousand Arameans. Now then, this one will (have to) go to fight against two thousand Arameans! If he *comes up* against us, we will go to fight him and take the land of Sūḫu for our own. However, if he does not come up (against us), we will take away booty and draw (more) men to us. (i 25) Then we will go and attack the houses of the land of Sūḫu. We will seize his towns which are (located) in the steppe and cut down their fruit trees."

---

i 8 With regard to the phrase *ina muḫḫi ṭuppīšu*, which is translated here as "had hardly passed," see Cavigneaux and Bahija Ismail, Bagh. Mitt. 21 (1990) pp. 351–52.

i 10 For *a-di* LÚ *lu-ḫu-ú-a-a* TA ÉRIN.MEŠ GIŠ.BAN *ù* LÚ.SAG KAL×BAD.MEŠ-*šú-nu*, "to the Luḫuāiia (clan) — with archers and their *military commanders*," S.0.1002.1 line 20 has *a-di* LÚ *mi-nu-ʾ-i*, "to the Minuʾû (clan)."

i 17 S.0.1002.3 i 8′ writes the individual's name ^{m}*ia-a-a-e* DUMU ^{m}*ba-li-am-mu*. P.-E. Dion connects the paternal name to the biblical form Balaam, and Amatu with Hamath (in press).

i 22 *it-la-a* (also in line 23 and S.0.1002.3 i 13′ and 15′) and *it-lu-ú* (ii 20) are taken to be for *ītelâ* and *ītelû* respectively, following Cavigneaux and Bahija Ismail, Bagh. Mitt. 21 (1990) p. 340.

25) *ù ni-il-la-kám-ma a-na* UGU É.MEŠ *šá* KUR *su-ḫi*
26) *ni-teb-bé-e-ma* URU.MEŠ-*šú šá ina* EDIN *ni-ṣab*(*)-*bat-ma ù* GIŠ *gáp-ni-šú-nu*
27) *ni-nék-kis a-na e-mu-qí-šú-nu it-kal-ú-ma a-na* KUR *la-qé-e*
28) *i-ti-qu* 1 ME É.DURU$_5$.MEŠ *šá* KUR *la-qé-e iṣ-bat-ú-ma ḫúb-tu*
29) *la mi-ni iḫ-bu-tu-nim-ma* KUR *la-qé-e a-*<*na*> DU$_6$ *u kar-mi*
30) *ut-tir-ru* ^{md}IŠKUR-*da-*ʾ*a-nu* LÚ *šak-nu* KUR *la-qé-e ina lìb-bi* 4
31) GIŠ.GIGIR.MEŠ 2 ME ÉRIN.MEŠ *a-na pa-ni-ia il-li-kám-ma qaq-qa-ri*
32) *ina pa-ni-ia iš-šiq-ma ù ú-sap-pa-an-ni-ma su-pe-šú am-ḫur*
33) *ù* ^{md}30-SILIM-*im-an-ni* LÚ.EN.NAM KUR *ru-ṣa-pu a-di e-muq* [(x)]
34) *gab-bi šá* KUR *ru-ṣa-pu a-na muḫ-ḫi-šú-nu il-li-kám-m*[*a* (x x)]]
35) *i-mur-šú-nu-ti-ma ip-làḫ-*⸢*ma a*(?)⸣-[*na*(?) *muḫḫišunu*(?) *ul*(?) *imqut*(?)]
36) *ana-ku* ^{md}M[AŠ-NÍG.DU-PAB ...]

Lacuna (20-30 lines)

Col. ii

1) *ri-iḫ-ṣi*(*) UGU(*)-*šú-nu* ⸢GAR⸣-*un*(*)-⸢*ma*⸣ *ina lìb-bi* GIŠ.GIGIR-*ia ki-ma ḫa-*[*mi* ŠE.BAR]
2) *ár-ḫi-is-su-nu-ti šil-ta-ḫu ki-ma e-re-bu* UGU KARAŠ-[*ia*/*ia*$_5$]
3) *i-šub-bu a-a-um-ma ina lìb-bi* KARAŠ.MEŠ-*ia*$_5$ *ul im-qut*
4) 38(*) ÉRIN.MEŠ *šá ina lìb-bi* LÚ.KARAŠ.MEŠ-*ia ú-maḫ-ḫi-ṣu a-a-u*[*m-ma*]
5) *ina lìb-bi-šú-nu* LÚ.ÚŠ-*šú ina* EDIN *ul im-qut ki-ma* ^{d}GIBIL$_6$
6) *mut-tan-pi-ḫu a-na lìb-bi-šú-nu am-qut-ma* 1 LIM 6 ME 16 ÉRIN.MEŠ
7) *ina lìb-bi-šú-nu a-na pi-i* GÍR.AN.BAR GAR-*un ù šá* 80 ÉRIN.MEŠ
8) *ina lìb-bi-šú-nu kap-pi-šú-nu sa-ap-sa-pi-šú-nu áš-ši-ma a-na*
9) *da-li-li un-dáš-šìr*(*)-*šú-nu-ti* TA *muḫ-ḫi* PÚ *ma-ki-ri* <*a-di*>
10) PÚ *gal-la-bu u a-di* UGU PÚ *su-ri*(*)-*bu ina* UGU(*) 3 PÚ.MEŠ
11) BAD$_5$.BAD$_5$-*šú-nu áš-kun ka-mar-šú-nu* SÌG-*aṣ* ILLAT-*su*(*)-*nu ka-bit-ti*
12) *ap-ṭur-ma ú-par-ri-ir ki-iṣ-ri-šu-un šá* È-*u*(*) *ki-šit-ti*
13) *qa-ti* UGU-*šú-nu* GAR-*un* ÚŠ.MEŠ-*šú-nu ki-ma* A.MEŠ ÍD

i 27b–30a) Trusting in their (own) forces, they proceeded on to the land of Laqû (and) seized one hundred villages of the land of Laqû. They took countless booty and turned the land of Laqû into a heap of ruins.

i 30b–32) Adad-daʾʾānu, the governor of the land of Laqû, came before me with four chariots (and) two hundred soldiers. He kissed the ground before me and then implored me (for aid). I accepted his supplication.

i 33–35) Moreover, Sîn-šallimanni, the provincial governor of the land of Ruṣapu, went against them (the Arameans) with all the troops of the land of Ruṣapu, but (when) he saw them, he became afraid and [*did not fall upon them*].

36) I, Ni[nurta-kudurrī-uṣur ...]

Lacuna

ii 1–29a) I brought about a [cloud]-burst over them and from inside my chariot I blew them away (lit. "washed them away") like ch[aff]. Arrows quivered like locusts over [my] forces, (but) not one person among my forces fell. (Although) they wounded thirty-eight men from among my forces, not one person (ii 5) among them (my forces) fell dead in the steppe. I fell upon them (the enemy) like a blazing fire and put one thousand six hundred and sixteen of their men to the sword. Moreover, I removed the arms (and) lower lips of eighty of their men and let them go free to (spread the news of my) glory. From the well Makiru <as far as> (ii 10) the well Gallabu and the well Suribu, at (these) three wells, I defeated (and) annihilated them. I broke up their *numerous* auxiliary troops and split up their military contingents. I captured those who tried to get away; I made their blood run like the water of a river. Eagles and vultures *hovered* over their corpses. (ii 15) I filled the mountains and wadis with their skulls like mountain-stones; birds made (their) nests in their skulls. Three hundred and four of their men had quickly retreated before me. (Because) my horses and my men had become thirsty for water due to the fighting, I did not pursue them. Forty of these (three hundred and four) men perished due to thirst

i 25 The word "houses" (É.MEŠ) in the phrase "houses of the land of Sūḫu" may refer to "households," "families," or "tribes" rather than to physical structures. The parallel passage in S.0.1002.3 i 17′–18′ appears to omit "of the land of Sūḫu."
i 35 Bagh. Mitt. 21 transliteration has for the end of the line *ip-làḫ-ma* x x x x [...]. The restoration is based upon S.0.1002.1 line 28 (which omits *iplaḫma*, "he became afraid and").
ii 4 38(*): copy has 38, while Bagh. Mitt. 21 transliteration has 39; the number is not preserved in any of the other texts.
ii 6 S.0.1002.1 line 35 has 1 LIM 7 ME 11[(+5(?)], "one thousand seven hundred and *sixteen*."
ii 10 The passage *ina muḫḫi* 3 *būrāti*, "at (these) three wells," is also found in S.0.1002.3 ii 15′, but is omitted in the other parallels to this passage (S.0.1002.1 line 36, S.0.1002.6 ii 15′, and S.0.1002.7 obv. 9′).

14) *ú-šá-aṣ-bit ḫar-ra-nu ina* LÚ.ÚŠ.MEŠ-*šú-nu a-ru-ú u zi-bu*
15) *in-na-aṭ-ṭal gul-gul-la-ti-šú-nu ki-ma* NA$_4$.MEŠ KUR-*i* KUR.MEŠ
16) *u na-ḫal um-dal-lu ina* GUL.GUL.MEŠ-*šú-nu* MUŠEN.ḪI.A *qin-na iq-nun*
17) 3 ME 4 ÉRIN.MEŠ *ina lìb-bi-šú-nu iḫ-ru-pu-ú*(*)*-ma la-pa-ni-ia ib-bal-kit*
18) ANŠE.KUR.⸢RA⸣.MEŠ-*ia la-pa-an ṣal-ta ù* ÉRIN.MEŠ-*ia*$_5$ A.MEŠ *iṣ-mu-ú*
19) *ul ar-du-ud-šú-nu-ti* 40 ÉRIN.MEŠ *ina lìb-bi-šú-nu ina ṣu-um* A.MEŠ
20) *in-*⸢*nab*⸣*-tu* 2 ME 54 ÉRIN.MEŠ *ina lìb-bi-šú-nu it-lu-ú* 1 LIM 8 ME 46
21) ÉRIN.MEŠ *ina lìb-bi-šú-nu ad-duk a-ga-a* 1-*et*(*) *di-ik-ti*
22) *šá* ^{md}MAŠ-NÍG.DU-PAB LÚ.GAR KUR *su-ḫi u* KUR *ma-ri ina lìb-bi* LÚ *ḫa-tal-lu*
23) *i-du-ku* ^{m}*šá-ma-ʾ-ga-am-ni* LÚ.NIMGIR LÚ *sa-ru-gu a-lik*
24) *pa-ni-šú-nu* ÌR *la tar-ṣu*(*) *šá* KUR *su-ḫi* KUR *aš-šur*.KI *u* AD.MEŠ-*ú-a*
25) *ú-šá-an-si*(*)-<*ku*(?)>-*šu ik-šu-ud* ŠU.II-*a-a a-duk-šú-ma i-nu-uḫ lìb-bi*
26) KUŠ-*šú ki-ma* KUŠ UDU.NÍTA *aṣ-ṣi-ma ina pa-an* KÁ.GAL *šá* URU-*gab*(*)*-ba-ri*-DÙ
27) *áš-kun šá mam-ma ina lìb-bi* <AD.MEŠ-*e-a*> *la* GAZ *ana-ku a-duk* AD.MEŠ-*ú-a*
28) 10-*šú* LÚ.KÚR GAZ-*ma ma-lu-ú-a ul ú-šam-ṣu-ú ana-ku* 1-*et*
29) *di-ik-ti a-duk-ma a-na la* AD.MEŠ-*e-a ú-šá-tir*$_x$(DIR) *man-ni ár-ku-ú*
30) *šá* E$_{11}$-*ma i-qab-bu-ú um-ma ki-ki-i* ^{md}MAŠ-NÍG.DU-⸢PAB⸣
31) LÚ.GAR KUR *su-ḫi u* KUR *ma-ri di*(*)*-ik-ti an-ni-ti i*[*d*(?)*-duk ul ina emūqīia*]
32) *a-duk ina e-muq* ^{d}UTU *u* ^{d}AMAR.UTU ⸢^{d}⸣I[ŠKUR *u apla-adad ilāni rabûti*]
33) EN.MEŠ-*e-a di-ik-ti* [*annītu addūk manni arkû*]
34) *šá* E$_{11}$-*ma ši-bu-ut* K[UR-*šú u šībūtu ša māt laqê*]
35) x [...] x [...]

Lacuna (20–30 lines)

Col. iii

Lacuna (20–30 lines)

1′) Trace(s) [...]
2′) SA KIB x x [... *šaknu māt sūḫi u māt mari* ...]
3′) PÚ *bu-uk-re-e a-mur-ma qa*[*q-qa-ri ul ba-ni* ...]
4′) *ul*(*) *e-pu-uš* AN.TA PÚ *bu-uk-*[*re-e* ...]
5′) *a-mur-ma ḫu-up-pat ši-i ap-pa-ri* x x [...]
6′) *ap-te-ši-ma* A.MEŠ-*šú ma-ʾ-du* 3 KASKAL.II.MEŠ *šá* x [...]

for water; (ii 20) (the remaining) two hundred and fifty-four men of them *got away*. I (thus) killed one thousand eight hundred and forty-six of their men. This is a single defeat which Ninurta-kudurrī-uṣur, governor of the land of Sūḫu and the land of Mari, inflicted upon the Ḫatallu (tribesmen). With regard to Šamaʾgamni, the *herald* of the Sarugu (clan), their leader, the dishonest servant whom the land of Sūḫu, Assyria, and my fathers (ii 25) *rejected*, I got hold (of him and) killed him, (thereby) easing my heart. I *stripped off* his skin like the skin of a sheep and set (it) in front of the gate of Āl-gabbāri-bānî. I inflicted such a defeat as none among <my ancestors> had inflicted. My ancestors had defeated the enemy ten times, but they did not achieve as much as I. I inflicted a single defeat (of such an extent that) I surpassed my ancestors.

ii 29b–35) Anyone in the future who comes forward and says: "How [did] Ninurta-kudurrī-uṣur, the governor of the land of Sūḫu and the land of Mari [inflict] this defeat?" (should be told that) I did [not] inflict (this) [by my own power, (but rather) I inflicted this] defeat by the power of the gods Šamaš and Marduk, A[dad and Apla-Adad, the great gods], my lords. [Anyone in the future] who comes forward and [*should* ask] the elders of [his] l[and and the elders of the land of Laqû: ...]"

Lacuna

Lacuna

iii 1′–22a′) [...] ... [... governor of the land of Sūḫu and the land of Mari ...] I saw [(...) *in the vicinity of*] the well Bukrê, but [(its) location was not good ...] had not been built. Above the well Buk[rê ...] (iii 5′) I discovered. *It consisted of depressions*; a reed marsh ... [...] I opened it up and its water was abundant. Three routes [...] which go to the land of

ii 15 For the tentative translation "hover" for *innaṭṭal*, see Cavigneaux and Bahija Ismail, Bagh. Mitt. 21 (1990) p. 355.

ii 25 *si*(*): copy indicates GIŠ, while Bagh. Mitt. 21 transliteration has *si*. With regard to the tentative reading *ušansikūšu*, see the note to S.0.1002.1 line 41.

ii 26 *gab*(*): copy has GA, while Bagh. Mitt. 21 transliteration has *gab*; the duplicate passage in S.0.1002.8 obv. 11′ and all other occurrences of the city name have *gab*. With regard to the reading of the city name, see the commentary to S.0.1001.1.

ii 27 For the insertion of AD.MEŠ-*e-a*, see S.0.1002.1 line 41 and S.0.1002.8 obv. 12′ (mostly restored).

iii 4′ *e-pu-uš* (also in iii 12′) and *ep-pu-uš* of iii 14′ are tentatively taken to be irregular forms of the G stative of *epēšu*. They might be Assyrian forms of the D stative, but in which case they should be *uppuš* (see Postgate, BSOAS 34 [1971] pp. 503–504 n. 26).

7′) *šá a-na* KUR *la-qé-e* URU *ḫi-in-da-a-nu u* KUR *su-ḫi il-l*[*a-k*]*u*

8′) *šá ina lìb-bi* UD.MEŠ *šá* LÚ.GAR.KUR.MEŠ AD.MEŠ-*ú-a šá pit-ḫal-lu ina lìb-bi*

9′) *la ú-še*(*)-*zi-bu man-ni ár-ku-ú šá* E$_{11}$-*ma i-qab-bu-ú*

10′) *um-ma* LÚ.KÚR *šá it-ti-qu ina mi-nim-ma* A.MEŠ *i-šat-ti*

11′) *ina* PÚ *ni-iq-bu-ú-nu i-šat-ti ina maḫ-ri-ia* URU *ina muḫ-ḫi*

12′) *ul e-pu-uš e-pe-šú* URU UR$_5$-*tú ina lìb-bi-ia ib-ši-ma ul-tu*

13′) SIG$_4$ LÚ *ki-na-al-ta ina* UGU *i-lab-bi-ni a-di la* URU *i-na*

14′) UGU *ep-pu-uš* 20 LÚ *gu-du-du šá* LÚ *a-ra-mu* DU-*ku-nim-ma*

15′) 1-*en* LÚ.U$_5$ *šá pít-ḫal-lu šá* EN.NUN *ina lìb-bi ú-šá-az-zi-zu*

16′) *iṣ-ṣab-ta-áš-šú-nu-ti* URU *ina muḫ-ḫi* DÙ(*)-*ma* URU.BÀD-^{md}MAŠ-NÍG.DU-PAB

17′) MU-*šú az-kur* LÚ *áš-bu-tú ina lìb-bi-šú ul-te-šib pít-ḫal-lu ina lìb-bi-šú ú-šá-az-ziz*

18′) *áš-šú* EN.NUN *ana* KUR *su-ḫi* IGI.II *pe-ti-ti šá* KUR *su-ḫi ši-i man-ni ár-ku-ú*

19′) *šá* E$_{11}$(*)-*ma na-de-e a-ḫi a-na* URU UR$_5$-*tú la i-raš-ši áš-bu-tú šá ina lìb-bi*

20′) URU UR$_5$-*tú ú-še-šib a-a ú-nak-kìr*(*)-*šú-nu-ti áš-šú* EN.NUN *šá* KUR *su-ḫi la-pa-an*

21′) LÚ.KÚR *li-iṣ-ṣu-ru ki-ma ia-a-ti-ma* SAG URU UR$_5$-*tú liš-ši*

Laqû, the city Ḫindānu, and the land of Sūḫu, which in the days of the governors, my ancestors, who had left no mounted soldiers there, <...> Anyone in the future who comes forward and says: (iii 10′) "How is it that (any) stranger who passes by may drink (this) water?" (should be told that) he may drink from the well which we *formed.* No town had been built there before my time. I conceived the idea of building this town. While the workforce was making bricks for it, before the town had (yet) been (completely) built there, twenty Aramean marauders came (there), but (iii 15′) one mounted *officer* whom I had stationed there on guard seized them. I built a town there and named it Dūr-Ninurta-kudurrī-uṣur ("Fort Ninurta-kudurrī-uṣur"). I settled people in it (and) stationed mounted soldiers in it. This (town) is the open eyes of the land of Sūḫu for the sake of the security of the land of Sūḫu. No one in the future who comes forward should neglect this town (or) expel the inhabitants whom (iii 20′) I settled in this town. They should (continue to) guard (this town) against the enemy for the sake of the security of the land of Sūḫu. Just as I (did), he should pay attention to this town (and) not neglect this town.

22′) *na-de-e a-ḫi a-na* URU UR$_5$-*tú la i-raš-ši ana-ku* ^{md}MAŠ-NÍG.DU-PAB

23′) LÚ.GAR KUR *su-ḫi u* KUR *ma-ri qaq-qa-ri mi-ri-ši ina* SAG *ka-pu a-mur-ma*

24′) *e-pe-šú* URU *lìb-bi ub-la-an-ni-ma tem-mé-en-nu* NA$_4$.MEŠ *ad-di-ma*

25′) *ú-dan-nin* URU *ina* UGU DÙ-*ma* URU *kar-*^{d}A-^{d}IŠKUR MU-*šú az-kur* 50 LÚ x-ŠUK

26′) DUMU KUR *su-ḫi šá* ^{md}MAŠ-NÍG.DU-PAB LÚ.GAR KUR *su-ḫi u* KUR *ma-ri šá áš-šú a-šá-b*[*u*(*)]

27′) *šá* URU *im-ḫu-ru-ma um-ma ina* URU-*ka šu-šib-an-na-ši ina lìb-bi-šú u*[*l-te-šib*]

28′) GIŠ.KIRI$_6$ *ina ṭa-ḫi az-qup* É.KUR *a-na* ^{d}A-^{d}IŠKUR DÙ-*uš-ma ḫu*-x [...]

29′) *šá* ^{d}A-^{d}IŠKUR *a-šib* URU *an-at ina lìb-bi ul-te-šib* 1 (BÁN) NINDA.ḪI.A *u* KAŠ.SA[G ...]

30′) *a-na gi-ni-šú uk-tin a-na* LÚ.KU$_4$ É *ù* LÚ *ḫa-za-an-ni* BA-[*eš*]

31′) É.GAL *šá* LÚ.GAR.KUR *ina lìb-bi e-pu-uš ki-iṣ-ri* TA *pu-rat-t*[*u*$_4$]

32′) *ak-šìr-ma ú-še-la-a e-li-ti* <*ina*> *muḫ-ḫi* DÙ-*uš da-l*[*i*(?) ...]

iii 22b′–32′) I, Ninurta-kudurrī-uṣur, governor of the land of Sūḫu and the land of Mari, discovered land (capable of being) cultivated on the top of a cliff and conceived the idea of building a town (there). I laid a stone foundation, (iii 25′) reinforced (it), built a town upon (it), and named it Kār-Apla-Adad ("Quay of the God Apla-Adad"). I [settled] there fifty ..., citizens of the land of Sūḫu, who had approached (me) — Ninurta-kudurrī-uṣur, governor of the land of Sūḫu and the land of Mari — about settling in (this) town, saying: "Settle us in your town!" I planted orchard(s) near it. I built a temple to the god Apla-Adad and [(...)] I settled inside (it) [...] of the god Apla-Adad, who had (previously) dwelt in the city Anat. I established one *sūtu* of bread and fine beer [...] (iii 30′) as regular offerings for him (and) presen[ted] (them) to those privileged to enter the temple and to the mayor. I built a palace for the governor there. I constructed an *embankment* from the Euphrates, made it high, (and) built a ... upon (it). [...]

---

iii 11′ Following Cavigneaux and Bahija Ismail (Bagh. Mitt. 21 [1990] p. 356), the verb *niqbûnu*, which is tentatively translated here "we *formed,*" might be connected with the Syriac root q^{e}bā, "collect (water)."

iii 13′ The term *kinaltu*/*kiništu*, which is translated here as "the workforce" is normally used in connection with temple personnel.

iii 14′ Following Cavigneaux and Bahija Ismail (Bagh. Mitt. 21 [1990] p. 356), LÚ *gu-du-du* is connected with the Hebrew/Aramaic g^{e}dūd.

Col. iv
Lacuna (20–30 lines)
1′) x [...]
2′) *ana-ku* ^{md}MA[Š]-N[ÍG.DU-PAB *šaknu māt sūḫi u māt mari akītu ša adad*]
3′) *u* ^{d}*me-šár* DINGIR.MEŠ GAL.MEŠ *a-šib-ú-tu* URU *ú-da-d*[*a*]
4′) *la-ba-riš il-lik-ma muš-šu-rat a-a-um-ma ina l*[*ìb-bi*]
5′) AD.MEŠ-*e-a* SAG *ul iš-ši-ma ul* DÙ-*uš ana-ku a-ki-t*[u_4]
6′) UR$_5$-*tú ú-šak-lil-ma a-na* ^{d}IŠKUR *u* ^{d}*me-šár* DINGIR.MEŠ GAL.[MEŠ]
7′) EN.MEŠ-*e-a a-na ba-laṭ* ZI.MEŠ-*iá šá-lam*(*) NUMUN-*ia* GÍD.D[A]
8′) UD.MEŠ-*ia ku-un* BALA.MEŠ-*e-a sa-kap* KUR LÚ.KÚR-*ia*(*) DÙ-*ma*
9′) BA-*eš* É.GAL ^{m}*é-nam-ḫé*-NUMUN-DÙ LÚ.GAR KUR *su-ḫi* KI-*tim*
10′) URU *ra*(*)-*ìl šá qab-lat pu-rat-ti la-ba-riš* DU-*ku-ma*
11′) *un-dáš-šìr-šú* É.GAL *šá-ni-tu*$_4$ AN.TA-*šú* DÙ-*uš-ma*
12′) 60(*)-*šu*(*) 4 *ina* 1 KÙŠ GÍD.DA-*šú* 12 *ina* 1 KÙŠ *u ma-la ú-ṭu* DAGAL-*su*
13′) *a-na la* É.GAL *šá* ^{m}*é-nam-ḫé*-NUMUN-DÙ 20 *ina* 1 KÙŠ *ú-šá-rik-šú*
14′) 4 *ina* 1 KÙŠ *ur-tap-pis-su šá-ni-ti* É.GAL AN.TA-*šú* DÙ-*ma*
15′) 45 *ina* 1 KÙŠ GÍD.DA-*šú* 9 *ina* 1 KÙŠ DAGAL-*su* LÚ *ra-il-a-a* <LÚ>.ḪI.GAR-*šú-nu*
16′) ḪI.GAR *a-na* UGU AD-*ia i-pu-šú-ma* AD-*ú-a id-duk-šú-nu-ti*
17′) *ina* SAG LÚ.GAR.KUR-*ú-ti-ia šá ina* GIŠ.GU.ZA *šá* AD-*ia ú-ši-bu*
18′) LÚ *ra-il-a-a a-na* UGU-*ia ib-bal-kit-ma a-na-ku*
19′) *a-duk-šú-nu-ti ina lìb-bi pa-ni-ia a-na* UGU *ul áš-kun-ma*
20′) GIŠ.ḪUR <<*ul e*>> *ul e-ṣir-šú man-ni ár-ku-ú šá* E$_{11}$-*ma a-na*
21′) LÚ *ra-ìl-a-a na-de-e a-ḫi la i-raš*^{áš}-*šú-nu-ti* URU-*gab-ba-ri*-DÙ
22′) URU *šá* ^{md}UTU-SAG-PAB LÚ.GAR KUR *su-ḫi u* KUR *ma-ri* AD-*ia i-pu-šú*
23′) *ana-ku a-di-ri a-ḫu-na-ḫi* DÙ-*ma* URU *ú-šá-rik ur-tap-pi-iš*

Lacuna
iv 1′) ... [...]
iv 2′–9a′) I, Ninurta-ku[durrī-uṣur, governor of the land of Sūḫu and the land of Mari: the Akītu (temple) of the gods Adad] and Mešar (Mīšarum) — the great gods who dwell in the town Udada — had become old and been abandoned. None am[ong] (iv 5′) my ancestors had paid attention (to it) and (re)built (it). I completely (re)built this Akītu (temple). I had (this temple) (re)built and dedicated (it) to the gods Adad and Mešar (Mīšarum), the great gods, my lords, in order to ensure my good health (and) the well-being of my offspring, to prolong my days, to confirm my reign, (and) to defeat the land of my enemy.

iv 9b′–15a′) The palace of Enamḫe-zēra-ibni, governor of the land of Sūḫu, (which is located in) the district of the city Ra᾽il, which is in the middle of the Euphrates (River), had become old and I abandoned it. I built another palace above it: 64 cubits is its length (and) 12 1/2 cubits is its width. I made it 20 cubits longer (and) 4 cubits wider than the palace of Enamḫe-zēra-ibni. I built (even) another palace above it: I made it 45 cubits long (and) 9 cubits wide.

iv 15b′–21a′) With regard to the people of Ra᾽il (*and*) their *rebels*, they had rebelled against my father, but my father had defeated them. At the beginning of my governorship, when I ascended the throne of my father, the people of Ra᾽il revolted against me, but I defeated them. *With regard to this matter, I did not pay (great) attention to it and did not make a relief (commemorating) it.* No one in the future who comes forward should neglect the people of Ra᾽il!

iv 21b′–26a′) With regard to Āl-gabbāri-bānî, the town which Šamaš-rēša-uṣur, governor of the land of Sūḫu and the land of Mari, my father, had built, I built *an enclosure* around it. I made the town longer and wider, and I strengthened (it). The wall of *the enclosure* which I built is thirteen cubits thick. I dug

iv 9′ S.0.1002.1 line 9, S.0.1002.6 iii 13′, S.0.1002.8 rev. 21, and S.0.1002.12 line 9′ add "and of the land of Mari" after "governor of the land of Sūḫu."
iv 14′ S.0.1002.1 line 13, S.0.1002.3 iii 11′–12′, and S.0.1002.6 iii 18′–19′, add *ina muḫḫi kiṣri*, "on top of an *embankment*," after AN.TA-*šú*, "above it."
iv 15′ S.0.1002.1 line 14, S.0.1002.3 iii 13′–14′, and S.0.1002.6 iii 20′–21′ add the passage "*Moreover* (or *With regard to this matter*), *I did not pay* (*great*) *attention to this matter and did not make a relief* (*commemorating*) *it*" after "9 cubits wide."
iv 19′–20′ The passage "*With regard to ... (commemorating) it*" is found after "my father had defeated them" in S.0.1002.1 line 16, S.0.1002.3 iii 16′–17′, and S.0.1002.6 iii 23′–24′.
iv 23′ The word written *a-di-ri*, which appears here and in iv 24′, is not otherwise attested in Akkadian literature; the tentative translation "*enclosure*" is based upon the context and a possible connection to the verb *edēru*, "to hug, embrace," and to the Hebrew root ᾽ZR. See Cavigneaux and Bahija Ismail, Bagh. Mitt. 21 (1990) p. 357. *a-ḫu-na-ḫi* is for *aḫu ana aḫi*, literally "side to side" (also in iv 25′ and 26′).

24′) *u ud-dan-nin* 13 *ina* 1 KÙŠ *ku-ub-bur-ri i-ga-ru šá a-di-ri*
25′) *šá ana-ku e-pu-šú ḫa-ri-ṣi a-ḫu-na-ḫi šá* URU *aḫ-ru-uṣ-ma*
26′) A.MEŠ *a-ḫu-na-ḫi šá* URU *ul-te-el-ma-a ana-ku* ^{md}MAŠ-NÍG.DU-PAB
27′) LÚ.GAR KUR *su-ḫi u* KUR *ma-ri* LÚ *te-ma-ʾ-a-a* LÚ *šá-ba-ʾ-a-a*
28′) *šá a-šar-šú-nu ru-qu* LÚ.A.KIN-*šú-nu a-na muḫ-ḫi-ia ul* DU-*ku*
29′) *ù a-na muḫ-ḫi-ia ul it-ti-qu-ú-nu a-na muḫ-ḫi*(*) *ma*(*)*-mu*
30′) PÚ *mar-tu u* PÚ *ḫa-la-tu*$_4$ *a-lak-ta-šú-nu* TE *u it-ti-iq-ma*
31′) *u a-na* URU *ḫi-in-da-a-nu ir-ru-bu-nu*(*) *ina* URU.KAR-^{d}A-^{d}IŠKUR *i-na*
32′) AN.BAR$_7$ *ši-mu-su-nu áš-mé-e-ma ni-ri aṣ-mid ina* GE$_6$ ÍD
33′) *e-bir-ma ina šá-ni-i u*$_4$*-me a-di la* AN.BAR$_7$ *a-na* URU *az-la-a-a-nu*
34′) *ak-šu-ud-ma* 3 *u*$_4$*-mi ina* URU *az-la-a-a-nu ú-šib-ma ina* 3-*šú u*$_4$*-me*
35′) *ik-šu-du-nim-ma* 1 ME-*šú-nu bal-ṭu-su*(*)*-nu* ŠU.II *ik-šu-ud* 2 ME *gam-ma-lu-šú-nu*
36′) *a*(*)*-di* GUN-*šú-nu* SÍK *ta-kil*(*)*-tu*$_4$ SÍK KASKAL(*) AN.BAR NA$_4$.<BABBAR>.DILI.MEŠ *mim-ma mi-reš-ti* DÙ.A.BI(*)
37′) *ik-šu-ud* ŠU.II-*a-a* NAM.RI-*su-nu ka-bit-ti áš-lu-lam*(*)*-ma*
38′) *ú-še*(*)*-rib a-na qé-reb* KUR *su-ḫi* MU 7.KÁM
39′) ^{md}MAŠ-NÍG.DU-PAB LÚ.GAR KUR *su-ḫi u* KUR *ma-ri da-ba-ba*
40′) *an-na-a da-bi-ib*
41′) *ba-a-ri*

a moat around the town and (thereby) completely surrounded the town with water.

iv 26b′–38a′) I, Ninurta-kudurrī-uṣur, governor of the land of Sūḫu and the land of Mari: with regard to the people of Tema and Šaba, whose own country is far away, (whose) messenger(s) had never come to me, and (who) had never travelled to (meet) me, their caravan came near to the water (iv 30′) of the well Martu and the well Ḫalatu, but passed by and then entered into the city Ḫindānu. I heard a report about them at midday, (while I was) in the town Kār-Apla-Adad and (immediately) harnessed (the horses of) my chariot. I crossed the river during the night and reached the town Azlāiiānu before midday of the next day. I waited in the town Azlāiiānu for three days and on the third day (iv 35′) they approached. I captured one hundred of them alive. I captured their two hundred camels, together with their loads — blue-purple wool, ... wool, iron, <*pappar*>*dilû*-stones, every kind of merchandise. I took abundant booty from them and brought it into the land of Sūḫu.

iv 38b′–40′) This report was made in the seventh year of Ninurta-kudurrī-uṣur, governor of the land of Sūḫu and the land of Mari.

iv 41′) Collated.

3

Part of a four-column tablet found at ʿĀnā (IM 124202) preserves part of an inscription of Ninurta-kudurrī-uṣur which describes his actions against the Ḫatallu tribesmen and their leader Šamaʾgamni. In addition, the inscription describes the rebellion of the people of the city Raʾil, the restoration of an Akītu temple for the gods Adad and Mīšarum in the town Udada, and the construction of two palaces in the district of the city Raʾil, a well in the steppe (and presumably the related town Dūr-Ninurta-kudurrī-uṣur), and a palace in the city Anat.

iv 24′ Cavigneaux and Bahija Ismail, Bagh. Mitt. 21 (1990) p. 357, note that thirteen cubits (ca. 6.5 m) is approximately the width of the wall of Sūr Jarʿā.
iv 30′ Possibly *te-<<u>>-et-ti-iq-ma* ("their caravan passed by ... the well Martu and the well Ḫalatu and then entered ...")? We might read PÚ MAR.TU, "the well Amurru" or "the western well," instead of PÚ *mar-tu*, "the well Martu."
iv 36′ Cavigneaux and Bahija Ismail, Bagh. Mitt. 21 (1990) p. 357, point out that the reading might be NA$_4$.NU.MEŠ ("statues"?) or possibly NA$_4$.BAD.MEŠ (meaning unknown) instead of NA$_4$.<BABBAR>.DILI.MEŠ, "<*pappar*>*dilû*-stones."
iv 41′ The notation "collated" is also found at the end of S.0.1002.1 ex. 2.

COMMENTARY

The piece measures 11.8×10.8×2.7 cm. The edition is based upon the published copy, with some help from photographs kindly loaned to the author by A. Cavigneaux and with notes to the transliteration published by Cavigneaux and Bahija Ismail.

With regard to restorations and parallel/similar passages, note the following:

For i 1′–6′, see S.0.1002.2 i 11–16; see also S.0.1002.1 lines 21–22.

For i 7′–19a′, see S.0.1002.2 i 16–27.

For i 19b′–28′, see S.0.1002.1 lines 22–28 and S.0.1002.2 i 27–34.

For ii 1′–24′, see S.0.1002.2 ii 1–18, S.0.1002.5 i 12′–16′, S.0.1002.6 ii 1′–24′, and S.0.1002.7 obv. 2′–10′; see also S.0.1002.1 lines 35–38.

For iii 1′–4′, see S.0.1002.1 lines 6–9, S.0.1002.2 iv 6′–9′, S.0.1002.6 iii 8′–12′, S.0.1002.8 rev. 17–20, S.0.1002.11 lines 17–20, and S.0.1002.12 lines 5′–8′.

For iii 5′–14a′, see S.0.1002.1 lines 9–14, S.0.1002.2 iv 9′–15′, S.0.1002.6 iii 12′–21′, S.0.1002.7 rev. 1′–8′, S.0.1002.8 rev. 21–22, and S.0.1002.12 lines 8′–12′.

For iii 14b′–21a′, see S.0.1002.1 lines 15–19, S.0.1002.2 iv 15′–21′, and S.0.1002.6 iii 21′–27′.

For iii 21b′–29′, see S.0.1002.2 iii 1′–9′.

For iv 2′–14a′, see S.0.1002.5 iv 12–16, S.0.1002.9 ii 4–19, and S.0.1002.10 lines 30–32.

For iv 14b–17 and 26′–30′, see S.0.1002.9 ii 19–25 and iii 8?–12.

BIBLIOGRAPHY

1990 Cavigneaux and Bahija Ismail, Bagh. Mitt. 21 pp. 391–95 and 443–45 no. 21 (copy, edition)

TEXT

Col. i

Lacuna

1′) [*ṭēmi a-n*]*a* ⸢*a-ḫa*⸣-[*m*]*eš* ⸢*iš*⸣-[*ku*]*n*-⸢*ú*⸣-*m*[*a šama*ʾ*gamni*]

2′) [LÚ.NIMGIR LÚ] *sa-ru-gu šá ina la kit-ti b*[*al-lu*]

3′) [*ālik pa*]-*ni-šú-nu a-na ḫu-ub-ti a-na* KUR *la-q*[*é*(*)-*e*]

4′) ⸢E_{11}⸣([DU_6.D]U)-*nim-ma ina* EDIN *in-dal-ku-ma um-ma* LÚ.GAR KUR *su-ḫ*[*i*]

5′) *it-ti-ni na-kir-ma um-ma ki-ki-ma ni-it-ti-iq-*[(*ma*)]

6′) *ḫu-ub-tu ul-tu* KUR *la-qé-e ni-ḫab-*[(x)]*-bat*

7′) ᵐ*šá-ma-*ʾ*-ga-am-ni* LÚ.NIMGIR LÚ *sa-ru-g*[*u*(*)*] *ù*

8′) ᵐ*ia-a-a-e* DUMU ᵐ*ba-li-am-mu* LÚ *a-mat-a-a* [LÚ.SA]G ⸢KAL×BAD(*)⸣.MEŠ-*šú-nu*

9′) [*k*]*i-a-am iq-bu-niš-šú-nu-tim-ma um-ma* L[Ú.GAR KUR.M]EŠ

10′) [*ša māt*] *su-ḫi* AD.MEŠ-*šú mam-ma ina lìb-bi-šú-nu a-na lìb-bi* 1 LIM

11′) [LÚ *a-r*]*a-me a-na ṣal-ti ul il-lik um-ma en-na*

12′) [*šū*] ⸢*a*⸣*-na lìb-bi* 2 LIM LÚ *a-ra-me a-na ṣal-ta*

13′) [*il-l*]*a-ku um-ma ki-i a-na pa-ni-ni it-la-a a-na*

14′) [*ṣalta*] ⸢*a*(?)⸣*-na lìb-bi-šú ni-il-lak-ma ù* KUR *su-ḫi a-na*

15′) [*ša ram*]*-ni-ni nu-tar-ru ù ki-i la it-la-a*

16′) [*ḫu-ub-t*]*i nu-še-rid-ma ù* ÉRIN.MEŠ *a-na muḫ-ḫi-ni*

Lacuna

i 1′–6′) they came to [an agreement. Šamaʾgamni, the *herald* of the] Sarugu (clan), who is th[oroughly pervaded with] falsehood, was their [lead]er. [They came] up to plunder the land of Laq[û], but while in the steppe deliberated, saying: "The governor of the land of Sūḫu (i 5′) is hostile to us. How shall we pass by (him) in order to plunder the land of Laqû?"

i 7′–19a′) Šamaʾgamni, the *herald* of the Sarugu (clan), and Iâʾe, the son of Balammu (Baliʾammu), a member of the Amatu (tribe), their *military* [*command*]*ers*, said the following to them: "Not one among the [governor]s (i 10′) [of the land of] Sūḫu, his ancestors, (ever dared to) go to fight against one thousand [Ar]ameans. Now then, [this one will (have to) g]o to fight against two thousand Arameans! If he comes up against us, we will go to [fight] him and we will take the land of Sūḫu for (i 15′) our [ow]n. However, if he does not come up (against us), we will take away [booty] and [draw] (more) men to us. Then we will go and [at]tack the houses [(of the land of Sūḫu)]. We will seize his towns which are (located) in the steppe and cut down their fruit trees."

i 1′–3′ The copy suggests that there is not sufficient room at the beginning of these lines for the proposed restorations, but a photograph of the tablet indicates that there is.

i 8′ S.0.1002.2 i 17 writes the individual's name as ᵐ*ia-a-*ʾ*-e* DUMU ᵐ*ba-la-am-mu*.

i 13′ and **15′** *it-la-a*, see note to S.0.1002.2 i 22.

17′) [*nu-rad-d*]*am-ma ù ni-il-lak-am-ma a-na muḫ-ḫi* É.MEŠ
18′) [(x) *ni-t*]*e-eb*(*)-*bé-e-ma* URU.MEŠ-*šú šá ina* EDIN *ni-ṣab-bat-ma*
19′) [*ù* GIŠ *gá*]*p-ni-šú-nu ni-nék-kis a-na* LÚ *e-mu-qí-šú-nu*
20′) [*itkalūma*] ⌈*ana*⌉ KUR *la-qé-e i-*<*ti*>-*qu* 1 ME É.[DURU$_5$].MEŠ
21′) [*ša māt laqê iṣ*]-*bat-ú-ma ḫu-ub-ti l*[*a mi*]-*ni iḫ-bu-tu-nim-ma*
22′) [*māt laqê ana*] DU$_6$ *ù kar-mi ut-*[*tir-r*]*u* ^{md}IŠKUR-*da-*ʾ*a-nu*
23′) [*šaknu māt laqê i-n*]*a*(?) *lìb-bi* 4 GIŠ.GIGIR.MEŠ 2 [M]E ÉRIN.MEŠ
24′) [*ana pānīia il-li-kám-m*]*a*(*) *qaq-qa-ri ina pa-ni-ia*
25′) [*iššiqma u ú-sap-pa-a*]*n*(?)-⌈*ni*(?)-*ma*(?)⌉ *su-pe-šú am-ḫur*
26′) [*u sîn-šallimanni bēl pīḫat māt ru-ṣa*]-*pu a-di*
27′) [*emūq gabbi ša māt ruṣapu ana muḫ-ḫi*]-*šú-nu*
28′) [*illikamma* ...] x-*ti*
Lacuna

i 19b′–22a′) [Trusting] in their (own) troops, they proceeded on to the land of Laqû. They [se]ized one hundred vill[age]s [of the land of Laqû], took count[less] booty, and turned [the land of Laqû into] a heap of ruins.

i 22b′–25′) Adad-daʾʾānu, [the governor of the land of Laqû, came before me] with four chariots (and) two hundred soldiers. [He kissed] the ground before me [and then implored] *me* (for aid). I accepted his supplication.

i 26′–28′) [Moreover, Sîn-šallimanni, the provincial governor of the land of Ruṣa]pu, [went against] them (the Arameans) with [all the troops of the land of Ruṣapu, but ...]
Lacuna

Col. ii
Lacuna
1′) x [... UGU(?) LÚ(?) ...]
2′) *e-ziz-ma* [(...) *āgugma kīma nēši danni* (...)]
3′) UGU LÚ.GAL [... *ašgugma erpet riḫṣi*]
4′) UGU-*šú-nu áš-k*[*un-ma* (*ina libbi*) *narkabtīia kīma ḫāmī*]
5′) ŠE.BAR *ár-ḫi-is-s*[*u-nu-ti šiltāḫū kīma erebū*]
6′) UGU LÚ.KARAŠ.MEŠ-[*ia išubbū aiiumma ina libbi*]
7′) LÚ.KARAṢ.MEŠ-*ia u*[*l imqut* 38 *ṣābē ša ina libbi karāšīia*]
8′) *ú-maḫ-ḫi-ṣu* ⌈*a*⌉-[*a-um-ma ina libbīšunu* LÚ.ÚŠ-*šú ina ṣēri*]
9′) *ul im-qut ki-ma* [*girra muttanpiḫu ana*]
10′) *lìb-bi-šú-nu an-qu-u*[*t-ma* 1616 *ṣābē ina libbīšunu*]
11′) *a-na pi-i* GÍR.AN.BAR [*aškun u ša* 80 *ṣābē ina libbīšunu*]
12′) *kap-pi-šú-nu sa-ap-s*[*a-pi-šú-nu aššīma ana dalīli*]
13′) *un-dáš-šìr-šú-nu-ti u*[*l-tu muḫḫi būrti makiri*]
14′) *a-di* PÚ *gal-la-bu* ⌈*ù*⌉ [*adi muḫḫi būrti suribu*]
15′) *i-na muḫ-ḫi* 3 PÚ.MEŠ BAD$_5$.BAD$_5$-[*šú-nu aškun kamāršunu*]
16′) SÌG-*aṣ* ILLAT-*su-nu ka-bi*[*t-ti apṭurma uparrir*]
17′) *ki-iṣ-ri-šu-un šá* ⌈È⌉-[*u kišitti qāti muḫḫīšunu aškun*]
18′) ÚŠ.MEŠ-*šú-nu ki-ma* A.MEŠ Í[D *ušaṣbit ḫarrānu*]

Lacuna
ii 1′–24′) [...] I became furious [*with the*...] and [(...) I became angry. Like a mighty lion (...) I roared] against the chief [...]. I brought [about a cloud-burst] over them [and from (inside) my chariot] I blew [them] away (lit. "washed [them] away") [like cha]ff. (ii 5′) Arrows quivered like locusts] over [my] forces, (but) not [one person among] my forces [fell]. (Although) they wounded [thirty-eight men from among my forces], not one [person among them (my forces)] fell [dead in the steppe]. I fell [up]on them (the enemy) like [a blazing fire (ii 10′) and put one thousand six hundred and sixteen of their men] to the sword. [Moreover, I removed] the arms (and) lower [lips of eighty of their men and] let them go free [to (spread the news of my) glory. From the well Makiru] as far as the well Gallabu and [the well Suribu], (ii 15′) at (these) three wells, [I] defeat[ed (and) annih]ilated [them. I broke up] their *num*[*erous*] auxiliary troops [and split up] their military contingents. [I captured] those who tried to get away; [I made] their blood [run] like the water of a river. Eagles and [vultures *hovered*] over their corpses. (ii 20′) I filled [the mountains] and wadis with their skulls like [mountain-stones]; birds made (their) nests in [their skulls. Three hundred and four of their men] had quickly [retreated before me. (Because) my] horses [...]
Lacuna

i 17′–18′ S.0.1002.2 i 25–26 has É.MEŠ *šá* KUR *su-ḫi ni-teb-bé-e-ma* ("we will attack the houses of the land of Sūḫu"). [(x) *ni-t*]*e-eb*(*)-*bé-e-ma*: the copy suggests [x x] DIŠ ZU-*bé-e-ma* and Bagh. Mitt. 21 transliteration has [*šá* KUR *su-ḫi ni-te*]-*eb-bi-e-ma*. The photo is not clear, but might allow [x x (x) *n*]*i-teb-bé-e-ma*.
ii 2′ Or *e-mid-ma*, "I imposed [*upon the* ...]."
ii 15′ The passage *ina muḫḫi* 3 *būrāti*, "at (these) three wells," is also found in S.0.1002.2 ii 10, but is omitted in the other parallels to this passage (S.0.1002.1 line 36, S.0.1002.6 ii 15′, and S.0.1002.7 obv. 9′).

19′) *ina* LÚ.ÚŠ.MEŠ-*šú-nu a-ru-ú* ⸢*ù*⸣ [*zību innaṭṭal*]
20′) *gul-gul-la-ti-šú-nu ki-ma* [*abnē šadî šadê*]
21′) *ù na-ḫal um-dal-lu ina* [*gulgullātīšunu*]
22′) MUŠEN.ḪI.A *qin-ni iq-nun* [304 *ṣābē ina libbīšunu*]
23′) *iḫ-ru-pu-ú-ma l*[*a-pa-ni-ia ibbalkit*]
24′) ⸢ANŠE⸣.KUR.RA.M[EŠ-*ia* ...]
Lacuna

Col. iii

Lacuna
1′) x x x x [...]
2′) ^{d}*me-šár* DINGIR.MEŠ [...]
3′) ZI.MEŠ-*ia šá-l*[*am*(?) ...]
4′) BALA.MEŠ-*e-a sa-*[*kap* ...]

5′) É.GAL ^{m}*é-nam-*[*ḫé-zēra-ibni* ...]
6′) KI-*tim* URU *ra-i*[*l*(?) ...]
7′) *la-ba-riš il-l*[*i*(?)-*ku-ma* ...]
8′) AN.TA-*šú* DÙ-*uš-ma* ⸢60(*)⸣-*š*[*u*(*) ...]
9′) *ma-la ú-ṭu r*[*u-pu-us-su* ...]
10′) *šá* ^{m}*é-nam-ḫé-*[*zēra-ibni* ...]
11′) *ur-tap-pis-su šá-n*[*i*(?)-*ti* ...]
12′) *ki-iṣ-ri* DÙ-*u*[*š* ...]
13′) *ru-pu-us-su* ⸢*ù*(?)⸣ [...]

14′) GIŠ.ḪUR *ul e-ṣir*(*)-[*ši* ...]
15′) ḪI.GAR *a-na muḫ-ḫi* A[D-*ia* ...]
16′) *id-duk-šú-nu-ti ina l*[*ìb*(?)-*bi* ...]
17′) *ul áš-kun-ma* GIŠ.ḪUR *u*[*l* ...]
18′) *šá ina* GIŠ.GU.ZA *šá* AD-*i*[*a* ...]
19′) *a-na muḫ-ḫi-ia ib-*[*bal-kit-ú-ma* ...]
20′) *man-ni ár-ku-ú šá* ⸢E_{11}⸣(DU_6.D[U])-[*ma* ...]

21′) *a-ḫu la i-rašší*(*)$^{-áš}$-*š*[*i*(*)-*šú-nu-ti* ...]
22′) LÚ.GAR KUR *su-ḫi u* KUR *ma-*[*ri* ...]
23′) *qaq-qa-ri ul ba-ni* [...]
24′) PÚ *bu-uk-re-*⸢*e*⸣ [...]
25′) *ši-i ap-pa-r*[*i* ...]
26′) A.MEŠ-*šú ma-*⸢ʾ⸣-[*du* ...]
27′) KUR *la-qé-*[*e* ...]
28′) *šá ina lìb-b*[*i*(?)...]
29′) *ina lìb-bi* [...]
30′) x [...]
Lacuna

Col. iv

Lacuna
1′) [...] x KI
2′) [...] x AD-ia_5 *it-tu-ru*

Lacuna

iii 1′–4′) [(...) I had (this temple) (re)built and dedicated (it) to the gods Adad and] Mešar (Mīšarum), the [great] gods, [my lords, in order to ensure my good] health (and) the well-be[ing of my offspring, to prolong my days, to confirm] my reign, (and) to def[eat the land of my enemy].

iii 5′–14a′) The palace of Enam[ḫe-zēra-ibni, governor of the land of Sūḫu and the land of Mari], (which is located in) the district of the city Raʾi[l, which is in the middle of the Euphrates River], had be[come] old [and I abandoned it]. I built [another palace] above it: *6*[*4* cubits is its length (and) 12] 1/2 [cubits is its] w[idth]. I made it [20 cubits longer (and) 4 cubits] wider [than the palace] (iii 10′) of Enamḫe-[zēra-ibni]. I built (even) ano[ther palace above it on top of] an *embankment*: [45 cubits is its length (and) 9 cubits] is its width. *Mo*[*reover, I did not pay* (*great*) *attention to this matter and*] *did not make a relief* (*commemorating*) [*it*].

iii 14b′–21a′) [With regard to the people of Raʾil (*and*) their rebels, they had] rebel[led] against [my] fat[her, but my father] had defeated them. *With re*[*gard to this matter*], *I did not pay* [(*great*) *attention to it*] *and* [*did*] *not* [*make*] *a relief* (*commemorating*) [*it*]. At the beginning of my governorship], when [I ascended] the throne of my father, [the people of Raʾil] re[volted] against me, [but I defeated them]. (iii 20′) No one in the future who comes [forward] should [ne]glect [the people of Raʾil]!

iii 21b′–30′) [...] governor of the land of Sūḫu and the land of Ma[ri ... I saw (...) *in the vicinity of* the well Bukrê, but] (its) location was not good. [... had not been built. Above] the well Bukrê [... I discovered]. *It* [*consisted of depressions*]; (iii 25′) a reed marsh [... I opened it up and] its water was abund[ant. Three routes ... which go to] the land of Laqû, [the city Ḫindānu, and the land of Sūḫu], which in [the days of the governors, my ancestors, who had left no mounted soldiers] there [...]
Lacuna

Lacuna

iv 1′–14a′) [...] ... [... the city Anat] returned (its allegiance) [to] my father. [*After* four years, during

---

iii 13′ Bagh. Mitt. 21 transliteration has ⸢x⸣ [...] at the end of the line, while the published copy would suggest *in*[*a libbi* ...], "*With* [*regard to this matter* ...]" (see commentary to S.0.1002.1). However, the photograph and a copy of the traces made by Cavigneaux would suggest *u* [...], or ⸢*ù*⸣ [...] as in S.0.1002.6 iii 20′.

iii 30′ Possibly ⸢*i*⸣-[*qab-bu-ú* ...], "s[ays ...]"; see S.0.1002.2 iii 9′.

3′) [*ina* 4 *šanāti ša* URU *an-a*]*t i-ša-ru* AD-*ia*
4′) [*ana šīmātīšu kî i*]*l-li-ku a-na-ku i-na*
5′) [...] MA(?) [(x x x)] *gi-na-né-e*
6′) [... *i*]*-sin-na-a-ti* [(x x)] *šá* ^{d}IŠKUR
7′) [*kī p*]*i-i* ^{m}*ḫa-am-mu-ra-pi* LUGAL TIN.TIR.KI
8′) [*a-na-k*]*u uk-tin* LÚ *áš-bu-ti ina* URU *an-at*
9′) [Á KUR *u*] Á KUR-*i ú-še-šib* URU URU *an-at*
10′) [*kī pa-na*]*-a-ma* Á KUR *ù* Á KUR-*i* <<ḪI>> *ú-se-šib*
11′) [*ilāni*] *šá* Á KUR *ù* Á KUR-*i šá* URU *an-at*
12′) [*ša l*]*a-pa-an* LÚ *aš-šur*.KI-*a-a a-na* URU *ri-ba-niš* DU-*ku-ú-nu*
13′) [*anāku*] ⸢*ú*⸣*-še-ṣa-áš-šú-nu-ti-ma ki-i pa-na-a-ma i-na*
14′) [KI.TUŠ-*š*]*ú-nu ú-še-šib-šú-nu-ti* É.GAL *ina* URU *an-at*
15′) [*e-pu-uš-m*]*a* 1 ME *ina* 1 KÙŠ GÍD.DA-*šú* 16 *ina* 1 KÙŠ *ru-pu-us-su*
16′) [*ekal p*]*a*(?)*-ni ina ṭa-ḫi* DÙ-*uš-ma* 47 *ina* 1 KÙŠ GÍD.DA-*šú*
17′) [8 *ina* 1 *ammati r*]*u-pu-us-su* É.GAL.MEŠ *ḫi-da-a-tu*$_4$ *ù*
18′) [*rīšātu*] DÙ-*uš-ma* GIŠ.ḪUR *e-ṣir*(*)*-šú* GIŠ.KAK KAR.RA
19′) [*ḫurāṣi*(?) (x)] x ⸢*ù*⸣ NA$_4$.ZA.GÌN *tam-la-a ú-mál-li-ma*
20′) [...] *ḫi-da-a-ti ù ri-šá-a-tu*$_4$ *al-mi*
21′) [...] KI.LÁ KÙ.GI *šá ina muḫ-ḫi* GIŠ.KAK KAR.RA
22′) [...] x KÁ AN.ZA.GÀR.MEŠ *ki-li-li šá* NA$_4$.ZA.GÌN
23′) [...] UR$_5$*-tú al-me* GIŠ.IG.MEŠ *šá* EREN DÙ-*uš-ma*
24′) [*ina bāb*] ⸢É⸣.GAL UR$_5$*-tú az-qup* GIŠ *tal-li* KÁ.MEŠ-*šú ana* UGU(*)
25′) [...-*m*]*i*(?) *tam-la-a ú-mal-li-ma ina* KÁ É.GAL
26′) [... *m*]*an-ni ár-ku-ú šá* E$_{11}$*-ma* É.GAL UR$_5$*-tú* GIŠ.ḪU[R-*šú*]
27′) [... É].GAL UR$_5$*-tú ina muḫ-ḫi tem-mé-en-nu šá* DIŠ x [(...)]
28′) [... *e*(?)]*-pu-uš* 10 *ina* 1 KÙŠ *tem-mé-en-n*[*a*] ⸢*an-na*⸣*-*[*a*]
29′) [*ušappil*(?) x (x)] x NA$_4$.MEŠ KUR.MEŠ GAL.MEŠ *aḫ-pe-*⸢*e*⸣*-*[*ma* (x x)]
30′) [*temmennu ad-d*]*i-ma ú-dan-*⸢*nin*⸣ x [x x]
Lacuna

which the city Ana]t prospered, [when] my father [di]ed (lit. "went [to his fate]"), I (iv 5′) [ascended the throne of my father]. I (re-)established the regular offerings, [*offerings, and*] festivals of the god Adad [according to the word]ing (of the commands) of Ḫammu-rāpi, king of Babylon. I settled people in the city Anat [on (both) *the landside* and] *the hillside.* I settled the *city* of Anat (iv 10′) [as (it had been) bef]ore, on (both) *the landside* and *the hillside.* I brought out [the gods] of (both) *the landside* and *the hillside* of the city Anat [who] had gone to the town Ribaniš on account of the Assyrian and I settled them in their [dwelling(s)], (just) as (they had been) before.

iv 14b′–30′) [I built] a palace in the city Anat: 100 cubits is its length (and) 16 cubits is its width. I built a ... [palace] beside (it): 47 cubits is its length (and) [8 cubits is] its width. I built palaces of gladness and [rejoicing] and *made a relief* (*commemorating*) *it.* I *inlaid* knobbed nail(s) [with *gold*, ...], and lapis lazuli, and (iv 20′) surrounded [*the palace*] of gladness and rejoicing (*with them*). [...] (is) the weight of the gold which is on the knobbed nail(s). [...] the towered gate *with* battlements of lapis lazuli [(...)] this [...] I surrounded. I made doors of cedar and erected (them) [in the gate] of this palace. The transoms of its gates *against/upon* (iv 25′) [...] I built up the terrace and in the gate of the palace [...]. Anyone in the future who comes forward [*should not change*] *the des*[*ign*] of this palace. [*I*] built this [pal]ace upon a foundation of [...; *I made*] this foundation 10 cubits [*deep*]. I *dressed* large mountain-stones, [laid a foundation], and made (it) fast. [...]
Lacuna

iv 9′ The reason for the presence of two URU signs before *an-at* (also in S.0.1002.9 ii 14 and S.0.1002.10 line 19) is uncertain; see Cavigneaux and Bahija Ismail, Bagh. Mitt. 21 (1990) pp. 382–83.
iv 11′ With regard to Á KUR *ù* Á KUR-*i*, "*the landside and the hillside*," see the note to S.0.1001.1 ii 22′.
iv 12′ With regard to the identity of "the Assyrian," see the introduction to the inscriptions of Ninurta-kudurrī-uṣur. With regard to the reading of the city name Ribaniš, see the commentary to S.0.1001.1.
iv 14′–15′ The same(?) structure is described as an *akītu* temple in S.0.1002.9 ii 19–21; see Cavigneaux and Bahija Ismail, Bagh. Mitt. 21 (1990) p. 387, commentary to ii 19.
iv 16′ *ekal pāni* (?), "*forepalace*" (also in S.0.1002.9 ii 22).

4

The inscription, written in Akkadian on a fragmentary four-column clay tablet which was found at Sūr Jarʿā (IM 124201), preserves portions of the description of Ninurta-kudurrī-uṣur's victory over the Ḫatallu tribesmen. It also preserves the end of a passage describing the foundation of the town Dūr-Ninurta-kudurrī-uṣur and records how the people of the city Anat had earlier revolted against the land of Sūḫu and joined with the Assyrians.

COMMENTARY

The fragment has not been collated and the edition presented here is based upon the published copy, with notes to the transliteration by Cavigneaux and Bahija Ismail.

With regard to restorations and parallel/similar passages, note the following:

For i 2′–13′, see S.0.1002.1 lines 29–34.

For ii 9′–iii 4a, see S.0.1002.1 lines 45–50, S.0.1002.2 ii 32–34, and S.0.1002.8 17′–rev. 3.

For iii 4b–11, see S.0.1002.8 rev. 4–10.

For iv 1–5a, see S.0.1002.2 iii 19′–22′ and S.0.1002.13 rev. 6–8.

For iv 5b–15, see S.0.1002.5 iv 1–5, S.0.1002.9 i 6–19, and S.0.1002.10 lines 15–19.

BIBLIOGRAPHY

1990 Cavigneaux and Bahija Ismail, Bagh. Mitt. 21 pp. 373–76 and 430–31 no. 10 (copy, edition)

TEXT

Col. i

Lacuna

1′) [...] Traces

2′) [...] x NA x [x] ^{d}UTU *u* ^{d}AMAR.[UTU]

3′) [... *dan*(?)-*n*]*u*(?)-*ti ù*(?) x-*li* <LÚ>.GAR.KUR.ME[Š]

4′) [... *a-ma-a*]*t*(?) ^{d}A-^{d}IŠKUR *u* ^{d}TAR.DI.NI

5′) [...] x-*ma a-la-ku šá* ÉRIN.MEŠ *šú-nu-ti*

6′) [...] x *ṭè-e-me iš-kun-an-ni-ma a-na-ku a-ḫi*

7′) [*ul ad-d*]*i-ma a-na a-mat* ^{d}A-^{d}IŠKUR EN GAL DINGIR EN-*ia*$_{5}$

8′) [*at-k*]*al-ma ina lìb-bi* 1 ME 5 GIŠ.GIGIR.MEŠ 2 ME 20 *pít-ḫal-lu*

9′) [*t*]*e*(?)-*li-tu* ANŠE.KUR.RA.MEŠ *na-as-qu-tu*$_{4}$ *ba-nu-ti*

10′) 3 LIM *zu*-<*uk*> GÌR.II *ù* ÉRIN.MEŠ É.GAL *ad-ke*(*)-*e-ma*

11′) *ni-ri aṣ-mid-ma* KASKAL.II *šá-áš-mu u* ⌜MÈ⌝ *al-lik-šú-nu-ti-*[*m*]*a*

Lacuna

i 1′–15′) [*I, Ninurta-kudurrī-uṣur, governor of the land of Sūḫu and the land of Mari, the chosen one, whom*] the gods Šamaš and Mar[duk ... *elevated over migh*]*ty* [*kings*] *and over* [(...)] governors, [... *the comma*]*nd* of the gods Apla-Adad and TAR.DI.NI (i 5′) [...] the marching of these soldiers [...] he instructed me. I [was not negli]gent, but (rather) [trus]ted the command(s) of the god Apla-Adad, the great lord, my divine lord. I therefore mobilized 105 chariots, 220 *experienced* mounted soldiers, good, choice horses, (i 10′) 3,000 foot soldiers, and the palace guard. I harnessed (the horses of) my chariot and went out on campaign to do battle with them. I waited at the well Ṣumūa, which (is located) between the well Makiru and the well Gallabu, for one (whole) day in the month Duʾūzu. Opposite the well Ṣumūa were *four* pens which *did* not *hold* (any)

i 2′–3′ The passage may have a parallel in S.0.1002.1 lines 30–31: ... [...] *ù* AMAR.UTU *i-pu-šú-ma* UGU LUGAL.MEŠ *dan-nu-ú-tu ù* UGU LÚ.GAR.[KUR.MEŠ ...]; however, Cavigneaux and Bahija Ismail (Bagh. Mitt. 21 [1990] p. 375) note that a reading *e-li* in line 3 is unlikely.

i 4′ The reading of the divine name written ^{d}TAR.DI.NI is uncertain; Brinkman (apud Cavigneaux and Bahija Ismail, Bagh. Mitt. 21 [1990] p. 375) suggests *Tardennu* rather than *Purus-dīni*.

i 11′ Cavigneaux and Bahija Ismail (Bagh. Mitt. 21 [1990] p. 375) state that to a certain extent there are only traces present after *šá-áš-mu*.

12′) *ina muḫ-ḫi* PÚ *ṣu-mu-ú-a šá ina bi-rit* PÚ *ma-ki*(*)-*ri ù*
13′) PÚ *gal-la-bu i-na* ITI.ŠU 1-*en* *u*$_4$-*mi ú-šib-ma* ⸢*i*(?)-*na*(?)⸣
14′) *pa-an* PÚ *ṣu-mu-ú-a* 4(*) *ḫa-aṭ-ra-a-nu šá* U$_8$.UDU.ḪI.A
15′) *la ú-kal-lu*$_4$ *ù a-na-ku*(*) *i-de*(*)-*e-ma šá* PÚ *ṣu-mu-ú-a*

Col. ii

Lacuna

1′) x [...]
2′) UD [...]
3′) *áš-k*[*un* ...]
4′) x x [...]
5′) *a-na-k*[*u* ...]
6′) *ú*-x x [...]
7′) *um-ma k*[*i*(?)-*i*(?) ...]
8′) x x x [...]
9′) x x x [...]
10′) DINGIR.MEŠ GAL.MEŠ EN.[MEŠ-*e-a* ...]
11′) x x [x] x [...]
12′) *šá* KUR *la-qé*-⸢*e*(?)⸣ [*liš*ʾ*alma umma kittû*]
13′) *šá* ^{md}MAŠ-<NÍG>.DU-PAB [*šaknu māt sūḫi u māt mari*]

Col. iii

1) *i*(?)-[*na a-mat* ^{d}]A(?)-^{d}IŠKUR EN G[AL(?)-*ú*(?) *bēlīšu* (...)]
2) *d*[*i*(?)-*ik-tu*$_4$] *an-ni-tu*$_4$ *i-du-*[*ku agâ šikin qātī*]
3) *šá* ⸢^{d}(?)⸣[A-^{d}]IŠKUR DINGIR EN-*ia* x [... *irammannima*(?)]
4) *du*[*l-l*]*a an-na-a a-na q*[*a-ti-ia iškun*(?) *mannu arkû*]
5) *šá* E$_{11}$-*ma ki-ma i*[*a*(?)-*ti-ma ana amat ilānī litkalma*/*liqūlma*(?)]
6) LÚ.KAL GAL LÚ.KÚR(*)-*šú* x [... *ul*(?) *ibbašši*(?) *agâ*(?)]
7) *a-ma-ru ù* x [(...) *apla-adad*(?) *bēlīia*(?) *u*(?) *ilāni*(?) (...)]
8) DUMU.MEŠ ID D[I ... LÚ.KÚR-*a ina šupal šēpēia*]
9) *ú-šak-bi-s*[*u*(?) *mannu arkû ša illâmma lā iqabbi*]
10) *um-ma k*[*i-i-ki-i ninurta-kudurrī-uṣur dīkta annīta idduk ana*(?)]
11) ^{d}IŠKUR *u* [*apla-adad* ...]
12) *man-ni ár-k*[*u*(?)-*ú* ...]
13) *kit*(*)-*t*[*u*$_4$(?)-*ú*(?) ...]
14) x [...]

Lacuna

Col. iv

1) [... *i-n*]*a*(?) URU *šu-a-tu*$_4$ *ú-še-ši-bu*
2) [*ai ú-nak-kìr-šú-nu-t*]*i áš-šú* EN.NUN *šá* KUR *su-ḫi*

sheep. I knew, however, that the well Ṣumūa

Lacuna

ii 1′–9a′) No translation warranted.

ii 9′– iii 4a) [*I inflicted this defeat by the power of the gods Šamaš and Marduk, Adad and Apla-Adad*], the great gods, [my] lord[s. Anyone in the future who comes forward and *should* ask the elders of his land and the elders] of the land of Laqû: ["Is it true] that Ninurta-<kudu>rrī-uṣur, [governor of the land of Sūḫu and the land of Mari], infl[icted] this de[feat] a[t the command of the god] Apla-Adad, the g[reat] lord, [his lord?" (...) (should be told that) this was the handiwork] of the god [Apla]-Adad, my divine lord [... *he loves me and set* my] h[ands to] this task.

iii 4b–14) [Anyone in the future] who comes forward [*should*] like m[e *pay attention* to the command(s) of the gods]. (*Then*) ... his enemy [... *will not exist. This is*] *the experience* and [(...) *the god Apla-Adad, my lord, and the gods* (...)] sons ... [...] they *allowed* (*me*) *to* trample [my enemy under my feet. No one in the future who comes forward should say]: (iii 10) "H[ow did Ninurta-kudurrī-uṣur inflict this defeat?" *By*] the gods Adad and [Apla-Adad ...]. Anyone in the fut[ure who comes forward and *should* ask *the elders of his land and the elders of the land of Laqû*: "*Is it*] *true* [*that* ...]

Lacuna

iv 1–5a) [No one in the future who comes forward should neglect this town (or) expel the inhabitants whom] I settled *in* this town. [They should (continue

---

ii 1′–9′ The passage may duplicate S.0.1002.2 ii 25–32 (approximately); for example, the *aš-k*[*un*, *a-na-k*[*u*, and *um-ma* of ii 3′, 5′, and 7′ may match S.0.1002.2 ii 27 (*aš-kun*), 28 (*ana-ku*), and ii 30 (*um-ma*) respectively.

iii 6 Cavigneaux and Bahija Ismail (Bagh. Mitt. 21 [1990] pp. 374 and 376) suggest that one might correct the text to read É (i.e., LÚ.É.GAL, "man of the palace").

iv 1 The parallel passage S.0.1002.2 iii 19′ has *ina lib-bi* before URU.

3) [*lapān nakri li-iṣ-ṣ*]*u-ru ki-ma ia-a-ti-ma*
4) [*rēš āli šu'ātu liššii n*]*a-de-e a-ḫi a-na* URU UR$_5$(*)-*tú*
5) [*lā iraššii tabnēa* LÚ].GAR KUR *su-ḫi it-ti*
6) [*biltīšu ša tāmarti ana māt aš*]-*šur*.KI E$_{11}$-*ma*
7) [*ina māt aššur iddūkšu u*] LÚ *áš-bu-tu šá* URU *an-at*
8) [*lapān māt sūḫi ib-ba*]*l-kit-ú-ma* ŠU.II-*su-nu*
9) [*ana aššurāiia it-ta*]*n-nu ù* LÚ *aš-šur*.KI-*a-a*
10) [*ana anat ul-te-lu*]-⌈*ú*⌉-*nu* LÚ *aš-šur*.KI-*a-a*
11) [*ul ina danāni ul ina ṣa*]*l-ta* URU *an-at iṣ-bat*
12) [*ṣabū mārū āli ramānšunu a-n*]*a* LÚ *aš-šur*.KI-*a-a*
13) [*ittannū arkānu* LÚ *aš-šu*]*r*.KI-*a-a ú-šag-li-šu-nu-ti-m*[*a*]
14) [*pirik mātāti ú-sap-pi-iḫ-šú-nu*]-*ti* É.MEŠ
15) [...] x x
Lacuna

to) gu]ard (this town) [against the enemy] for the sake of the security of the land of Sūḫu. Just as I (did), [he should pay attention to this town (and) not ne]glect this town.
iv 5b–15) [Tabnēa, the governor of the land of Sūḫu, went up [to Ass]yria with [his tribute for an audience], but [he killed him in Assyria. Then] the inhabitants of the city Anat [rev]olted [against the land of Sūḫu. They jo]ined hands [with the Assyrian] and [broug]ht the Assyrian up (iv 10) [to the city Anat]. The Assyrian took the city Anat [neither by force nor by ba]ttle; [(rather) the men — the citizens of the city themselves — gave (it) t]o the Assyrian. [Afterwards, the Ass]yrian exiled them and [scattered th]em [over (all) the lands. He turned] the houses [...] ...
Lacuna

5

A fragment of a tablet which once probably had four columns (IM 124200) was found by Iraqi archaeologists at Sūr Jarʿā. The Akkadian inscription preserves part of the campaign against the Ḫatallu tribesmen and part of the description of the city Anat's earlier defection to the Assyrians and of Ninurta-kudurrī-uṣur's later restoration of that city.

COMMENTARY

Only the lower left corner of the tablet is preserved. The fragment has not been collated and the edition is based upon the published copy, with notes to the transliteration published by Cavigneaux and Bahija Ismail. With regard to restorations and parallel/similar passages, note the following:

For i 8b′–9′, see S.0.1002.1 line 29 and S.0.1002.2 i 4.

For i 12′–16′, see S.0.1002.2 ii 1–3, S.0.1002.3 ii 2′-6′, and S.0.1002.6 ii 1′–6′.

For iv 1–7a, see S.0.1002.4 iv 10–14, S.0.1002.9 i 13–22, and S.0.1002.10 line 19.

For iv 7b–17, see S.0.1002.3 iv 2′–6′, S.0.1002.9 i 22–ii 10, and S.0.1002.10 line 30.

This text (iv 7b–10) and S.0.1002.9 (i 22b–ii 1) state that Anat had been controlled by Assyria for the fifty years preceding the governorship of Ninurta-kudurrī-uṣur's father Šamaš-rēša-uṣur and for the first three years of his father's governorship. During at least part of that time, Anat must have been under the control of Nergal-ēriš, Assyrian governor of Raṣappa. Nergal-ēriš was an Assyrian eponym in 803 and 775 BC and claimed to be governor of numerous places in addition to Raṣappa; these additional places included Anat, Sūḫu, Ḫindānu, and Laqû.

BIBLIOGRAPHY

1990 Cavigneaux and Bahija Ismail, Bagh. Mitt. 21 pp. 368–69 and 426 no. 7 (copy, edition)

iv 9 With regard to the identity of "the Assyrian," see the introduction to the inscriptions of Ninurta-kudurrī-uṣur.

TEXT

Col. i

Lacuna

1′) *ki-i ki-nim* x [...]

2′) *mul-li-šú-nu-t*[*i* ...]

3′) ^{d}A-^{d}IŠKUR EN GAL [...]

4′) *u a-na* ^{d}AMAR.UTU EN G[AL ...]

5′) *ù* KI-*tim il-la-k*[*u*(?) ...]

6′) *a-*[*n*]*a* PÚ *ma-ki-ri* x [...]

7′) [*im*]-*ḫur-in-ni-ma* ⸢*ina*⸣ UGU PÚ *m*[*a-ki-ri* ...]

8′) [*i*]*s*(?)-*di-ru-ma ana-ku* ^{md}MAŠ-NÍG.D[U-PAB ...]

9′) [*šá*(?)] ^{d}UTU *u* ^{d}AMAR.UTU ^{d}IŠKUR(*) *u* ^{d}A-⸢^{d}⸣[IŠKUR ...]

10′) [x (x)] ⸢*ḫa*⸣-*di-tim a-na re-ṣi-šú a*[*l-lik* ...]

11′) *a-*[*n*]*a ár-ki-ia áš-kun-ma ù ina* x [...]

12′) *a-na pa-ni-šú-nu ú-ṣi-ma* UGU LÚ x [... *ēzizma* (...)]

13′) *a-gu-ug-ma ki-ma* UR.MAḪ *dan-nu* U[GU(?) ...]

14′) *áš-gu-ug-ma* IM.DIRI *ri-iḫ-ṣi muḫ-ḫi-*[*šú-nu aškunma*]

15′) *ina* GIŠ.GIGIR-*ia ki-ma ḫa-mi* ŠE.BAR *ar-ḫ*[*i-is-su-nu-ti*]

16′) *šil-ta-ḫu ki-ma e-re-bu*(*) UGU LÚ.KARAŠ(*)-[*ia išubbū*]

Col. ii

Not preserved

Col. iii

Not preserved

Col. iv

1) *ul-te-lu-ú-nu* LÚ *aš-šur*.KI-*a-a u*[*l ina danāni ul ina ṣalti*]

2) URU *an-at iṣ-bat* ÉRIN.MEŠ DUMU.MEŠ U[RU *ramānšunu ana aššurāiia*]

3) *it-tan-nu ár-ka-a-nu* LÚ *aš-šur*.KI-*a-*[*a ušaglīšunūtima*]

4) *pi-rik* KUR.KUR.MEŠ *ú-sap-pi-iḫ-š*[*ú*(?)-*nu-ti bītāti*]

5) *šá* Á KUR *u* Á KUR-*i šá* URU *an-at* [*ana tilli u karmi*]

6) *ut-tir ù* LÚ *aš-šur*.KI-*a-a* ÉRIN.MEŠ *šá* [*ramnīšu ina anat*]

7) *ul-te-še-bu* ⸢*ul-tu*(?)⸣ *muḫ-ḫi* ^{m}*t*[*ab-né-e-a iqīša-marduk*]

8) *ù* ^{m}NIGIN-*ir*-^{d}IŠKUR 3 LÚ.GAR.KU[R.MEŠ 50 *šanāti anat*]

9) *šá* LÚ *aš-šur*.KI-*a-a* 3 MU.A[N.NA.MEŠ *ina ūmē šá šamaš-rēša-uṣur*]

10) LÚ.GAR KUR *su-ḫi u* KUR *ma-ri* A[D-*ia adi ina kussî*]

11) AD-*ia la uš-šá-bu* ^{d}IŠK[UR *u apla-adad* ...]

Lacuna

i 1′–16′) *as an honest man* [... *into my hands*] deliver them up! [...] The god Apla-Adad, the great lord [...] and to the god Marduk, the gr[eat] lord [... *of heaven*] (i 5′) and earth *they will go* [...] to the well Makiru [... he ap]proached me and at the well M[akiru ... *they de*]*ployed*, but I, Ninurta-kudurrī-[uṣur, (governor of the land of Sūḫu and the land of Mari) (the chosen one) *whom*] the gods Šamaš and Marduk, Adad and Apla-[Adad ...] (i 10′) ... I [went] to his aid [...] I set behind me and in [...] I went out before them. [I became furious] with the [... *and* (...)] I became angry. Like a mighty lion I roared *a*[*gainst* ... I brought about] a cloud-burst over [them and] (i 15′) from my chariot I blew [them away] (lit. "washed [them away]") like chaff. Arrows [quivered] like locusts over [my] forces.

ii (Not preserved)

iii (Not preserved)

iv 1–7a) they brought up. The Assyrian took the city Anat neit[her by force nor by battle]; (rather) the men — the citizens of the ci[ty themselves] — gave (it) [to the Assyrian]. Afterwards, the Assyrian [exiled them and] scattered t[hem] over (all) the lands. He turned [the houses] (iv 5) on (both) *the landside* and *the hillside* of the city Anat [into heaps of ruins]. Then the Assyrian settled [his own] men [in the city Anat].

iv 7b–17) From (the time of) T[abnēa, Iqīša-Marduk], and Nasḫir-Adad — three governors (in all) — [for fifty years, the city Anat] was (under the control) of the Assyrian, (and also) for three yea[rs, in the days of Šamaš-rēša-uṣur], (iv 10) the governor of the land of Sūḫu and the land of Mari, [my] fat[her, bef]ore I ascended [the throne] of my father. When the gods Ad[ad and Apla-Adad] set [...], the city Anat [returned (its allegiance) to my father].

---

i 5′ Or *il-la-m*[*a* ...], "will go up," instead of "*they will go*."

i 12′ S.0.1002.3 ii 3′ has UGU LÚ.GAL [...], but the traces copied after LÚ in this text do not seem to fit GAL.

i 14′ *ašgug* stands for *ašgum*.

iv 1 With regard to the identity of "the Assyrian," see the introduction to the inscriptions of Ninurta-kudurrī-uṣur.

iv 11–12 As suggested by Cavigneaux and Bahija Ismail (Bagh. Mitt. 21 [1990] p. 387, commentary to ii 3 [for our text S.0.1002.9]), one might restore at the end of the iv 11 *rēmu*, *gimillu*, or *andurāru*, thus: "When the gods Ad[ad and Apla-Adad] had [mercy]/established [(its) freedom]."

12) *ki-i iš-ku-nu* URU *an-a[t ana abīia ittūru]*
13) *ina* 4 MU.AN.NA(*).MEŠ *šá* UR[U *anat īšaru*(?) *abīia*]
14) *a-na* NAM.MEŠ-*šú ki-i [il-li-ku anāku ina kussî]*
15) [A]D(?)-*ia ú-šib [ginānê u*(?) *nīqê* (...)]
16) [*u i-sin*]-*na-a-ti šá [adad* ...]
17) [x x x (x x)] x [...]
Lacuna

After four years, during which the city [Anat prospered], when [my father di]ed (lit. "[went] to his fate"), I ascended [the throne (iv 15) of] my [*fat*]*her*. [The regular offerings, offerings (...) and fe]stivals of [the god Adad ...]
Lacuna

6

The right side of a clay tablet (IM 124195) found in 1981 by Sd. Nadhir ar-Rawi at Dawālī (on the left bank of the Euphrates, about 2 km south of the island of ʿĀnā) preserves part of an Akkadian inscription of Ninurta-kudurrī-uṣur which describes the campaign against the Ḫatallu tribesmen and their leader Šamaʾgamni, the restoration of the Akītu temple of the gods Adad and Mīšarum in the town Udada, the construction of two palaces in the district of the city Raʾil, and the rebellion of the people of that city.

COMMENTARY

The tablet has not been collated and the edition is based upon the published copy, with notes to the transliteration by Cavigneaux and Bahija Ismail. According to Cavigneaux and Bahija Ismail, the tablet would have had originally four columns (two on each side) and we thus have preserved only parts of columns ii and iii. The copy suggests that the beginning and end of each column is missing, while the Bagh. Mitt. 21 transliteration only indicates that the end of each column is missing. Thus, it is possible that ii 1′ and iii 1′ were actually the first lines of the respective columns.

With regard to restorations and parallel/similar passages, note the following:

For ii, see S.0.1002.2 ii 1–20, S.0.1002.3 ii 2′–24′, S.0.1002.5 i 12′–16′, S.0.1002.7 obv. 2′–10′, and S.0.1002.8 obv. 1′ 5′; see also S.0.1002.1 lines 35–38.

For iii 3b′–12a′, see S.0.1002.1 lines 4–9, S.0.1002.2 iv 2′–9′, S.0.1002.3 iii 2′–4′, S.0.1002.8 rev. 13–20, S.0.1002.11 lines 17–20, and S.0.1002.12 lines 4′–8′.

For iii 12b′–21a′, see S.0.1002.1 lines 9–14, S.0.1002.2 iv 9′–15′, S.0.1002.3 iii 5′–14′, S.0.1002.7 rev. 1′–8′, S.0.1002.8 rev. 21–22, and S.0.1002.12 lines 8′–12′.

For iii 21b′–27′, see S.0.1002.1 lines 15–19, S.0.1002.2 iv 15′–21′, and S.0.1002.3 iii 14′–21′.

BIBLIOGRAPHY

1983 Killick and Roaf, Iraq 45 p. 209 (study)
1990 Cavigneaux and Bahija Ismail, Bagh. Mitt. 21 pp. 388–89 and 440–41 no. 19 (copy, edition)

TEXT

Col. i
Not preserved.
Col. ii
Lacuna(?)
1′) [...] UGU [(x x)]
2′) [...] ⌜*a*⌝-*gu-ug-ma ki-ma* U[R(?).MAḪ]

i (Not preserved)

Lacuna(?)
ii 1′–26′) [... I became furious] with [the ... *and* (...)] I became angry. Like a [mighty] l[ion] I roared

ii 2′–4′ Bagh. Mitt. 21 transliteration restores *dan-nu* and *ri-iḫ-ṣi* at the ends of lines 2′ and 3′ respectively, but the spacing of the copy would suggest that they belong at the beginning of 3′ and 4′ respectively.

3′) [*dannu* ... Z]U(?) *áš-gu-ug-ma* IM.DIR[I]
4′) [*riḫṣi muḫḫi-š*]*ú-nu áš-kun-ma ina lìb-bi* GIŠ.GIGIR-*i*[*a*]
5′) [*kīma ḫāmī*] ŠE.BAR *ar-ḫi-is-su-nu-ti-ma šil-ta-*⌜*ḫu*⌝
6′) [*kīma e-r*]*e-bu* UGU LÚ.KARAŠ.MEŠ-*ia i-šu-ub-bu*
7′) [*a-a-um-m*]*a ina lìb-bi* LÚ.KARAŠ.MEŠ-*ia ul im-qut*
8′) [38 (x)] ÉRIN.MEŠ *šá ina lìb-bi* LÚ.KARAŠ.MEŠ-*ia ú-maḫ-ḫi-ṣu*
9′) [*a-a*]*-um-ma ina lìb-bi-šú-nu* LÚ.ÚŠ-*šú ina* EDIN *ul im-qut ki-ma*
10′) [^{d}G]IBIL$_{6}$ *mut-tan-pi-ḫu a-na lìb-bi-šú-nu an-qu-ut-ma*
11′) [1000] 6 ME 16 ÉRIN.MEŠ *ina lìb-bi-šú-nu a-na pi-i* GÍR.AN.BAR GAR-*un*
12′) [*ù š*]*á* 80 [É]RIN.MEŠ *ina lìb-bi-šú-nu kap-pi-šú-nu sa-ap-sa-pi-šú-nu*
13′) [*aššīma a-n*]*a da-li-li un-dáš-šìr-šú-nu-ti ul-tu*
14′) [*muḫḫi būrti ma*]*-ki-ri a-di* PÚ(*) *gal-la-bu ù a-di*
15′) [*muḫḫi būrti su*]*-ri*(*)*-bu* BAD$_{5}$.BAD$_{5}$-*šú-nu áš-kun ka-mar-šú-nu*
16′) [*amḫaṣ* ILLAT]-*su*(*)*-nu ka-bit-ti ap-ṭur-ma*
17′) [*uparrir k*]*i-iṣ-ri-šu-un šá* È-*ù ki-šit-ti*
18′) [*qāti muḫḫīšunu*] GAR-*un da-mi-šú-nu ki-ma* A.MEŠ ÍD
19′) [*ušaṣbit ḫar-ra*]-⌜*a*⌝*-ni i-na* LÚ.ÚŠ.MEŠ-*šú-nu* TI$_{8}$.MUŠEN
20′) [*u zību in-na-a*]*ṭ-ṭal gul-gul-la-ti-šú-nu*
21′) [*kīma abnē šadî šadê*] *ù na-ḫal um-dal-lu*
22′) [*ina gulgullātīšunu i*]*ṣ-ṣu-ru qin-na iq-nun*
23′) [304 *ṣābē ina libbīšunu iḫ*]*-ru-pu-ú-ma la-pa-ni-ia*
24′) [*ibbalkit sīsêia l*]*a-pa-an ṣal-ta*
25′) [*u ṣābēia mê iṣmû ul a*]*r-du-ud-šú-nu-ti*
26′) [40 *ṣābū ina libbīšunu ina ṣūm mê in-na*]*b-*⌜*tu*⌝

Lacuna

[*against* ...]. I brought about a cloud-[burst over] them and from inside my chariot (ii 5′) I blew them away (lit. "washed them away") [like cha]ff. Arrows quivered [like loc]usts over my forces, (but) not [one] person among my forces fell. (Although) they wounded [thirty-eight] men from among my forces, not one person among them (my forces) fell dead in the steppe. (ii 10′) I fell upon them (the enemy) like a blazing fire and put [one thousand] six hundred and sixteen of their men to the sword. [Moreover, I removed] the arms (and) lower lips of eighty of their men [and] let them go free [to] (spread the news of my) glory. [From the well Ma]kiru as far as the well Gallabu and (ii 15′) [the well Su]ribu, I defeated (and) [annihil]ated them. I broke up their *numerous* [auxiliary troops] and [split up] their military contingents. I captu[red those] who tried to get away; [I made their blood ru]n like the water of a river. Eagle(s) (ii 20′) [and vulture(s) *hov*]*ered* over their corpses. I filled [the mountains] and wadis with their skulls [like mountain-stones]; birds made (their) nests [in their skulls. Three hundred and four of their men had qu]ickly [retreated] before me. [(Because) my horses (ii 25′) and my men had become thirsty for water] due to the fighting, I did [not] pursue them. [Forty of (these three hundred and four) men peris]hed [due to thirst for water].

Lacuna

Col. iii

Lacuna(?)

1′) [...] x (x)
2′) [... *a*]-⌜*bi*⌝*-ia*
3′) [...] ⌜*a*⌝*-na-ku* ^{md}MAŠ-NÍG.DU-PAB
4′) [*šaknu māt sūḫi u māt mari* (*bīt*)] *a-ki-tu*$_{4}$ *šá* ^{d}IŠKUR *u* ^{d}*me-šár*
5′) [*ilāni rabûti a-ši-bu-u*]*t* URU *ú-da-da* EN.MEŠ-*e-a*
6′) [*labāriš il*]*-lik-ma muš-šu-rat a-a-um-ma*
7′) [*ina libbi* AD].MEŠ-*e-a* SAG-*su ul iš-ši-ma ul* DÙ-*uš*
8′) [*anāku* (*bīt*)] ⌜*á*⌝*-ki-it šu-a-tu*$_{4}$ *ú-šak-lil-ma a-na* ^{d}IŠKUR
9′) [*u* ^{d}*m*]*i-šar-rum* DINGIR.MEŠ GAL.MEŠ EN.MEŠ-*e-a a-na ba-laṭ*
10′) [ZI.MEŠ]-*ia šá-lam* NUMUN-*ia* GÍD.DA UD.MEŠ-*ia ku-un*

Lacuna(?)

iii 1′–3a′) [...] my [fat]her [...]

iii 3b′–12a′) I, Ninurta-kudurrī-uṣur, [governor of the land of Sūḫu and the land of Mari]: the Akītu [(temple)] of the gods Adad and Mešar (Mīšarum) — (iii 5′) [the great gods who dwell] in the town Udada, my lords — [had] become [old] and been abandoned. None [among] my [ancestor]s had paid attention (to it) and (re)built (it). I completely (re)built this Akītu [(temple)]. I had (this temple) (re)built and [dedicated] (it) to the gods Adad [and M]īšarum, the great gods, my lords, in order to ensure my good (iii 10′) [health] (and) the well-being of my offspring, to prolong my days, to confirm my [reign], (and) to defeat the land of my [enemy].

---

ii 3′ See S.0.1002.5 note to i 14′.

11′) [BALA].MEŠ-*e-a sa-kap* KUR LÚ.KÚR-*ia ú-še-piš-ma*
12′) [BA-*e*]*š* É.GAL ^{m}*é-nam-ḫé*-NUMUN-DÙ LÚ.GAR KUR *su-ḫi*
13′) [*u* KU]R *má-rí* KI-*tim* URU *ra-il šá qab-lat* ÍD.BURANUN.KI
14′) [*la-ba*]-*riš il-lik-ma un-dáš-šìr-šú* É.GAL *šá-ni-tu*$_{4}$
15′) [AN.TA-*š*]*ú* DÙ-*uš-ma* 60-*šu* 4(*) *ina* 1 KÙŠ GÍD.DA-*šú* 12 *ina* 1 KÙŠ
16′) [*u m*]*a-la ú-ṭu ru-pu-us-su a-na la* É.GAL
17′) [*ša* ^{m}]⸢*é*⸣-*nam-ḫé*-NUMUN-DÙ 20 *ina* 1 KÙŠ *ú-šá-rik-šú* 4 *ina* 1 KÙŠ
18′) [*ur-t*]*ap-pis-su šá-ni-ti* É.GAL AN.TA-*šú ina muḫ-ḫi*
19′) [*ki-i*]*ṣ-ri e-pu-uš-ma* 45 *ina* 1 KÙŠ GÍD.DA-*šú* 9(*) *ina* 1 KÙŠ
20′) [*ur-t*]*ap-pis-su ù pa-ni-ia a-na muḫ-ḫi ul áš-kun-ma*
21′) [*uṣurta u*]*l e-ṣir-ši* LÚ *ra-il-a-a* LÚ.ḪI.GAR.MEŠ-*šú-nu*
22′) [*bārta ana m*]*uḫ-ḫi* AD(*)-*ia i-pu-šú-ma* AD-*ia*
23′) [*iddūkšunūti ina libbi pa-n*]*i-ia a-na muḫ-ḫi ul áš-kun-ma*(*)
24′) [*uṣurta ul ēṣirši ina rēš*] LÚ.GAR.KUR-*ú-ti-ia šá ina* GIŠ.G[U(?)].⸢ZA⸣
25′) [*ša abīia ūšibu* LÚ *ra-i*]*l-a-a a-na muḫ-ḫi-ia* [(...)]
26′) [*ibbalkitūma a-duk-šú-n*]*u-ti man-ni ár-ku-ú* [(...)]
27′) [*ša illâmma ana ra*ʾ*ilāiia na-d*]*e*(?)-⸢*e*⸣ *a-ḫi la* [*iraššī*]

Lacuna

Col. iv

Not preserved.

iii 12b′–21a′) The palace of Enamḫe-zēra-ibni, governor of the land of Sūḫu [and the lan]d of Mari, (which is located in) the district of the city Raʾil, which is in the middle of the Euphrates River, had become [old] and I abandoned it. I built another palace (iii 15′) [above] it: 64 cubits is its length (and) 12 1/2 cubits is its width. I made it 20 cubits longer (and) 4 cubits wider than the palace of Enamḫe-zēra-ibni. I built (even) another palace above it on top of [an *emba*]*nkment*; I made it 45 cubits long (and) 9 cubits (iii 20′) wide. *Moreover, I did not pay* (*great*) *attention to this matter and did not make* [*a relief*] (*commemorating*) *it.*

iii 21b–27′) With regard to the people of Raʾil (*and*) their rebels, they had [rebelled ag]ainst my father, but my father [had defeated them. *With regard to this matter*], *I did not pay* (*great*) [*attent*]*ion to it and* [*did not make a relief* (*commemorating*) *it.* At the beginning] of my governorship, (when) [I ascended] the throne (iii 25′) [of my father, the people of Raʾi]l [revolted] against me, [but I defeated th]em. No one in the future [who comes forward should neg]lect [the people of Raʾil!]

Lacuna

iv (Not preserved)

7

This Akkadian inscription of Ninurta-kudurrī-uṣur is inscribed upon a fragment of the right side of a clay tablet (IM 124880) which was found at Sūr Jarʿā. The inscription records part of the campaign against the Ḫatallu tribesmen and the construction of palaces in the district of the city Raʾil. The fragment has not been collated and the edition presented here is based upon the published copy, with notes to the transliteration published by Cavigneaux and Bahija Ismail.

iii 15′ 4(*): copy has 6, while the transliteration has 4; in the parallel passages where the number is reasonably clear, it is 4 (S.0.1002.2 iv 12′ and S.0.1002.7 rev. 3′).
iii 19′ 9(*): copy has 4; in the parallel passages where the number is preserved, it is 9 (S.0.1002.1 line 14 and S.0.1002.2 iv 15′). Bagh. Mitt. 21 transliteration has GÍD.DA-[*šú* 9 *ina* 1] KÙŠ.

COMMENTARY

Cavigneaux and Bahija Ismail (Bagh. Mitt. 21 [1990] p. 376) suggest that the tablet may have had originally four columns.

With regard to restorations and parallel/similar passages, note the following:

For obverse, see S.0.1002.2 ii 4–12, S.0.1002.3 ii 7′–17′, and S.0.1002.6 ii 8′–17′; see also S.0.1002.1 lines 35–38.

For reverse, see S.0.1002.1 lines 9–14, S.0.1002.2 iv 9′–15′, S.0.1002.3 iii 5′–13′, S.0.1002.6 iii 12′–20′, S.0.1002.8 rev. 21–22, and S.0.1002.12 lines 8′–13′.

BIBLIOGRAPHY

1990 Cavigneaux and Bahija Ismail, Bagh. Mitt. 21 pp. 376 and 432 no. 11 (copy, edition)

TEXT

Obverse

Lacuna

1′) [...] x [...] x x

2′) [... *ú*(?)-*maḫ*(?)-*ḫ*]*i*(?)-⸢*ṣu*(?)⸣ *a-a-u*[*m*(?)-*ma(?) ina*(?) *lìb*(?)-*bi*(?)]-*šú-nu*

3′) [LÚ.ÚŠ-*šú ina ṣēri*] *ul i*[*m-q*]*ut* GIM ^{d}GIBI[L$_{6}$ *mut-ta*]*n-pi-ḫu*

4′) [*ana lìb-b*]*i-šú-nu an-qu-ut-ma* 1 LIM 6 ME [16 ÉRIN].MEŠ

5′) [*ina lìb-b*]*i-šú-nu a-na pi-i* GÍR.AN.BAR *áš-kun* ⸢*ù*⸣ [*šá* 80] ÉRIN.MEŠ

6′) [*ina lìb-b*]*i-šú-nu kap-pi-šú-nu sa-ap-sa-pi-šú-nu áš-ši-ma*

7′) [*ana d*]*a-li-li un-dáš-šìr-šú-nu-ti ul-tu muḫ-ḫi*

8′) [*būrti ma*]-*ki-ri a-di* PÚ *gal-la-bu ù a-di muḫ-ḫi*

9′) [*būrti su-r*]*i*-⸢*bu*⸣ BAD$_{5}$.BAD$_{5}$-*šú-nu* GAR-*un ka-mar-šú-nu* ⸢SÌG-*aṣ*⸣

10′) [*tillassunu k*]*a-bit-ti a*[*p-ṭ*]*ur*-<*ma*>⸢*ú*⸣-[*par-ri-ir*]

11′) [...] x x [...]

Lacuna

Lacuna

obv. 1′–11′) [...] ... [(*Although*) *they wou*]*nded* [*thirty-eight men from among my forces*], not *one* [*person among*] them (my forces) fell [dead in the steppe]. I fell [upon] them (the enemy) like a [bla]zing fire and put one thousand six hundred [and sixteen of] their [men] (obv. 5′) to the sword. Moreover, I removed the arms (and) lower lips [of eighty of] their men and let them go free [to] (spread the news of my) glory. From [the well Ma]kiru as far as the well Gallabu and [the well Sur]ibu, I defeated (and) annihilated them. (obv. 10′) I b[ro]ke up [their] *numerous* [auxiliary troops] <and> [split up their military contingents (...)] ... [...]

Lacuna

Reverse

Lacuna

1′) [...] x x [(x)]

2′) [... *la-ba-r*]*iš*(?) DU [x] x

3′) [...] x x 64 *ina* 1 KÙŠ

4′) [... *ru-pu*]-⸢*us*⸣-*su*

5′) [... ^{m}*é-nam-ḫé*-NUMUN]-DÙ(*) 20 *ina* 1 KÙŠ(*)

6′) [... *šá-ni*]-*tu*$_{4}$ ⸢É.GAL⸣

7′) [... *ēpuš-m*]*a*(?) ⸢45(*)⸣ *ina* 1 KÙŠ

8′) [...] x NA [(x)]

Lacuna

Lacuna

rev. 1′–8′) [The palace of Enamḫe-zēra-ibni, governor of the land of Sūḫu (and the land of Mari), (which is located in) the district of the city Raʾil, which is in the middle of the Euphrates River], had become [old and I abandoned it. I built another palace above it]: 64 cubits [is its length (and) 12 1/2 cubits is] its [wid]th. (rev. 5′) [I made it] 20 cubits [longer and 4 cubits wider than the palace of Enamḫe-zēra]-ibni. [I built (even) anoth]er palace [above it on top of an *embankment*; I made it] 45 cubits [long (and) 9 cubits wide. ...] ...

Lacuna

obv. 2′ The tentative restoration is based upon parallel passages (S.0.1002.2 ii 4–5, S.0.1002.3 ii 8′, and S.0.1002.6 ii 8′–9′); the copy would suggest [...] x [(x)] IA A x [x]-*šú-nu*.

obv. 3′ The reading *ul i*[*m-q*]*ut* is based upon a preliminary copy of the signs by Cavigneaux and parallel passages (S.0.1002.2 ii 5, S.0.1002.3 ii 9′, and S.0.1002.6 ii 9′); the copy would suggest N]E x x. Based upon what is missing at the beginning of the following lines, the copy would suggest that there is not sufficient room to restore both LÚ.ÚŠ-*šú* and *ina* EDIN.

obv. 5′ Bagh. Mitt. 21 transliteration indicates that part of the number 80 is preserved.

rev. 2′ In comparing parallel passages (e.g., S.0.1002.2 iv 10′), one expects -*ri*]*š* DU-*ku-ma* at the end of the line; the copy suggests -*ri*]*š*(?) DU [x] x, while Bagh. Mitt. 21 transliteration has -*r*]*iš* DU ⸢x x⸣.

rev. 7′ ⸢45(*)⸣: copy indicates 30[(+)] + 4; Bagh. Mitt. 21 transliteration has 45; parallel passages have 45 (e.g., S.0.1002.1 line 13).

8

A fragment of a clay tablet has a poorly preserved Akkadian inscription describing Ninurta-kudurrī-uṣur's defeat of the Ḫatallu tribe and their leader Šamaʾgamni. In addition, the inscription records his construction of an Akītu temple for the gods Adad and Mīšarum at the town Udada and likely work on palaces in the district of the city Raʾil. The fragment was found at Sūr Jarʿā and is the lower right part of what probably would have been a four-column clay tablet. Thus we likely have the end of column ii and the beginning of column iii of the inscription. The fragment has not been collated and the edition presented here is based upon the published copy, with notes to the transliteration published by Cavigneaux and Bahija Ismail.

COMMENTARY

The tablet fragment is in the Iraq Museum in Baghdad, but the museum number is uncertain. Both this piece and S.0.0.1002 are stated to be IM 124881. It is possible that this piece is IM 124194 (information from A. Cavigneaux). The copy indicates that there is a gap for about one line after obv. 15′ and after rev. 8, although this is not noted in the Bagh. Mitt. 21 transliteration. With regard to restorations and similar/parallel passages, note in particular the following:

For obv. 1′–15a′, see S.0.1002.2 ii 18–29 and S.0.1002.6 ii 24′–26′; see also S.0.1002.1 lines 39–43.

For obv. 15b′–rev. 4a, see S.0.1002.1 lines 43–50, S.0.1002.2 ii 29–34, and S.0.1002.4 ii 9′–iii 4.

For rev. 4b–10, see S.0.1002.4 iii 4–11.

For rev. 13b–20, see S.0.1002.1 lines 4–9, S.0.1002.2 iv 2′–9′, S.0.1002.3 iii 1′–4′, S.0.1002.6 iii 3′–12′, S.0.1002.11 lines 17–20, and S.0.1002.12 lines 4′–8′.

For rev. 21–22, see S.0.1002.1 lines 9–10, S.0.1002.2 iv 9′–10′, S.0.1002.3 iii 5′–6′, S.0.1002.6 iii 12′–13′, and S.0.1002.12 lines 9′–10′.

BIBLIOGRAPHY

1990 Cavigneaux and Bahija Ismail, Bagh. Mitt. 21 pp. 371–73 and 428–29 no. 9 (copy, edition)

TEXT

Obverse
Lacuna
1′) [...] x
2′) [...] x x x
3′) [... *iṣ*]-*mu-ú*
4′) [... *lib-bi-šú-n*]*u*(?) *ina ṣu*(*)-*um*(*) *me-e*
5′) [... *lìb-b*]*i-šú-nu it-lu-ú*
6′) [... *di-i*]*k-ti šá* ᵐᵈMAŠ-NÍG.DU-PAB
7′) [... L]Ú *ḫa-tal-la i-du-ku*
8′) [... LÚ] *sa-ru-gu a-lik pa-ni-šú-nu*
9′) [... *a*]*š-šur*.KI *ù* AD.MEŠ-*e-a*
10′) [... ŠU.II-*a*]-*a a-duk-šú-ma i-nu-uḫ lìb-bi*
11′) [... *aṣ-ṣi-m*]*a ina pa-an* KÁ.GAL *šá* URU-*gab-ba-ri*-DÙ
12′) [... AD.MEŠ-*e*]-*a la i-du-ku ana-ku ad-duk*
13′) [... *m*]*a*(*)-*lu-ú-a ul ú-šam-ṣu*(*)-*ú*
14′) [... *a*]-*na la* AD.MEŠ-*e-a*

Lacuna
obv. 1′–15a′) [...] ... [(Because) my horses and my men had become th]irsty [for water due to the fighting, I did not pursue them. Forty of (these three hundred and four) men perished] due to thirst for water; (obv. 5′) [(the remaining) two hundred and fifty-four men of] them got away. [I (thus) killed one thousand eight hundred and forty-six of their men. This is a single def]eat which Ninurta-kudurrī-uṣur, [governor of the land of Sūḫu and the land of Mari], inflicted [upon] the Ḫatallu (tribesmen). [With regard to Šamaʾgamni, the *herald* of the] Sarugu (clan), their leader, [the dishonest servant whom the land of Sūḫu], Assyria, and my fathers (obv. 10′) [*rejected*], I [got hold (of him and)] killed him, (thereby) easing my heart. [I *stripped off* his skin like the skin of a sheep] and [set (it)] in front of the

gate of Āl-gabbāri-bānî. I inflicted [such] a defeat [as] none [among] my [ancestors] had inflicted. [My ancestors had defeated the enemy ten times, but] they did not achieve as much as I. [I inflicted a single defeat (of such an extent that) I surpassed] my ancestors.

15′) [...] *i-qab-bu-ú um-ma*
16′) [...] *su-ḫi u* KUR *ma-ri di-ik-ti*
17′) [...] *u* ^{d}AMAR.UTU ^{d}IŠKUR
18′) [... EN.MEŠ-*e*]-⸢*a*(?)⸣ *di-ik-ti*
19′) [...] *ši-bu-ut* KUR-*šú*
20′) [...] *kit*(*)-⸢*tu*⸣-*ú*
Reverse
1) [...] *a-mat* ^{d}A-^{d}IŠKUR
2) [... *i-d*]*u-ku a-ga-a*
3) [...]-RI-*ka-a ú-ma-ʾ-ir*

obv. 15b′ – rev. 4a) [Anyone in the future who comes forward and] says: "[How did Ninurta-kudurrī-uṣur, the governor of the land of] Sūḫu and the land of Mari, [inflict this] defeat?" (should be told that) [I did not inflict (this) by my own power, (but rather) I inflicted this] defeat [by the power of the gods Šamaš] and Marduk, Adad [and Apla-Adad, the great gods], my [lords. Anyone in the future who comes forward and *should* ask] the elders of his land (obv. 20′) [and the elders of the land of Laqû:] "Is it true [that Ninurta-kudurrī-uṣur, the governor of the land of Sūḫu and the land of Mari] inflicted [this defeat at] the command of the god Apla-Adad, [the great god, his lord?"] (should be told that) this [was the handiwork of the god Apla-Adad, my divine lord]. He ordered *my* [...; ...]. He delivered my enemy into my [hands].

4) [...] x LÚ.KÚR-*a a-n*[*a qa-ti*]-*ia im-ni man-ni*
5) [... *ki-m*]*a*(*) *ia-a-ti-ma a-na a-mat* DINGIR.MEŠ
6) [... *u*]*l ib-ba-áš-ši a-ga-a a-ma-ru*
7) [...] ^{d}A-^{d}IŠKUR EN-*ia ù* DINGIR.MEŠ
8) [...] LÚ.KÚR-*a ina šu-pal* GÌR.II-*ia ú-šak-bi-su*
9) [...] *la i-qab-bi um-ma ki-i-ki-i*
10) [...] *id-duk a-na* ^{d}IŠKUR *u* ^{d}A-^{d}IŠKUR
11) [...] x *ana-ku* ^{d}IŠKUR *ù* ^{d}A-^{d}IŠKUR *ú-kal-lam-šú*
12) [... ^{d}A-^{d}I]ŠKUR DINGIR <GAL(?)> EN-*ia*$_{5}$ *al-lik-ma* ÉRIN.MEŠ *an-nu-tu*
13) [... ^{m}]⸢^{d}⸣MAŠ-NÍG.DU-PAB LÚ.GAR KUR *su-ḫi u* KUR *ma-ri*
14) [... ^{d}]*mi-šar-rum* DINGIR.MEŠ GAL.MEŠ *a-ši-bu-ut*
15) [... EN.MEŠ]-⸢*e*⸣-*a la-ba-riš il-lik-ma*
16) [... *ina lìb*]-⸢*bi*⸣ AD.MEŠ-*e-a* SAG-*su ul iš-ši-ma*
17) [... *ú-š*]*ak-lil-ma a-na* ^{d}IŠKUR
18) [... EN].MEŠ-*e-a a-na ba-laṭ*
19) [...] UD.MEŠ-*ia ku-un*
20) [...] ⸢*ú*⸣-*še-piš-ma* BA-*eš*

rev. 4b–13a) Anyone [in the future who comes forward should li]ke me [*pay attention*] to the command(s) of the gods. (*Then*) [... *his enemy* ...] will not exist. This is *the experience* [and ...] the god Apla-Adad, my lord, and the gods [...] they *allowed* (*me*) *to* trample my enemy under my feet. No [one in the future who comes forward] should say: "How (rev. 10) [did Ninurta-kudurrī-uṣur] inflict [this defeat]?" *By* the gods Adad and Apla-Adad [...] I. I shall show him the gods Adad and Apla-Adad. [... *at the command of* the god Apla]-Adad, the <*great*> god, my lord, I went and [*defeated*] these soldiers.

rev. 13b–20) [I], Ninurta-kudurrī-uṣur, governor of the land of Sūḫu and the land of Mari: [the Akītu (temple) of the gods Adad and] Mīšarum — the great gods who dwell (rev. 15) [in the town Udada], my [lords] — had became old and [been abandoned. None amo]ng my ancestors had paid attention (to it) and [(re)built (it). I com]pletely (re)built [this Akītu (temple)]. I had (this temple) (re)built and dedicated (it) to the gods Adad [and Mīšarum, the great gods], my [lord]s, in order to ensure my good [health (and) the well-being of my offspring, to prolong] my days, to confirm [my reign], (and) [to defeat the land of my enemy].

21) [...] *u* KUR *ma-ri* KI-*tim*
22) [...] x x x x x x
Lacuna

rev. 21–22) [The palace of Enamḫe-zēra-ibni, governor of the land of Sūḫu] and the land of Mari, (which is located in) the district [of the city Raʾil, ...] ...
Lacuna

9

A stone stela (IM 132897) found by Iraqi archaeologists on the island of ʿĀnā preserves part of an Akkadian inscription of Ninurta-kudurrī-uṣur which describes the earlier revolt of the city Anat against the land of Sūḫu, that city's alliance with "the Assyrian," and "the Assyrian's" actions at Anat. Ninurta-kudurrī-uṣur records that he restored the city and constructed an Akītu temple and a palace there.

COMMENTARY

The inscription has not been collated from the original and the edition presented below is based upon the published copy, with some help from photographs, and with notes to the transliteration published by Cavigneaux and Bahija Ismail. Cavigneaux kindly loaned me his original photograph of columns i and ii of the inscription; however, the photograph is not always clear. Columns i–ii are on the face of the stela and column iii is on the right side of the stela.

With regard to restorations and parallel/similar passages, note the following:

For i 1–5, see S.0.1002.1 lines 1–4, S.0.1002.2 i 1–4, S.0.1002.10 lines 9–14, S.0.1002.11 lines 11–14, and S.0.1002.14 lines 1–6.

For i 6–22a, see S.0.1002.4 iv 5–14, S.0.1002.5 iv 1–7, and S.0.1002.10 lines 15–19.

For i 22b–ii 19a, see S.0.1002.3 iv 2′–14′, S.0.1002.5 iv 7–16, and S.0.1002.10 lines 30–32.

For ii 19b–25, see S.0.1002.3 iv 14′–17′.

For iii 8–12a, see S.0.1002.3 iv 26′–30′.

BIBLIOGRAPHY

1990 Cavigneaux and Bahija Ismail, Bagh. Mitt. 21 pp. 383–88, 437–39, and pl. 36 no. 18 (photo, copy, edition)

TEXT

Col. i

1) *ana-ku* ^{md}MAŠ-NÍG.DU-ÙRU LÚ.GAR KUR
2) *su-ḫi u* KUR *ma-ri* A ^{md}UTU-SAG-PAB MIN
3) ŠÀ.BAL.BAL ^{md}IŠKUR-SUM-NUMUN MIN
4) NUMUN *da-ru-ú šá* ^{m}*tu-na-mis-saḫ*
5) DUMU ^{m}*ḫa-am-mu-ra-pí* LUGAL TIN.TIR.KI

6) ^{m}*tab-né-e-a* LÚ.GAR KUR *su-ḫi it-ti*
7) GUN-*šú šá* IGI.DU *a-na* KUR *aš-šur*.KI
8) *i-li-ma ina* KUR *aš-šur*.KI *id-duk-šú*
9) *ù* LÚ *áš-bu-tu šá* URU *an-at*
10) *la-pa-an* KUR *su-ḫi ib-bal-kit-ú-ma*
11) ŠU.II-*su-nu a-na* LÚ *aš-šur*.KI-*a-a it-ta*[*n*(?)-*nu*]
12) *ù* LÚ *aš-šur*.KI-*a-a a-na* URU *an-at*
13) *ul-te-lu-ú-nu* LÚ *aš-šur*.KI-*a-a*
14) *ul ina da-na-nu ul ina ṣal-ta* URU *an-at*

i 1–5) I, Ninurta-kudurrī-uṣur, governor of the land of Sūḫu and the land of Mari, son of Šamaš-rēša-uṣur, ditto (governor of the land of Sūḫu and the land of Mari), descendant of Adad-nādin-zēri, ditto (governor of the land of Sūḫu and the land of Mari), one of the enduring lineage of Tunamissaḫ, son of Ḫammu-rāpi, king of Babylon —

i 6–22a) Tabnēa, the governor of the land of Sūḫu, went up to Assyria with his tribute for an audience, but he killed him in Assyria. Then the inhabitants of the city Anat (i 10) revolted against the land of Sūḫu. They joi[ned] hands with the Assyrian and brought the Assyrian up to the city Anat. The Assyrian [to]ok the city Anat neither by force nor by battle; (i 15) (rather) the men — the citizens of the city themselves — gave (it) [to] the Assyrian.

---

i 7 The translation "audience" assumes that IGI.DU stands for IGI.DU$_8$.(A), *tāmartu*.
i 8 It is unclear who is the subject of the phrase "he killed him"; Cavigneaux and Bahija Ismail (Bagh. Mitt. 21 [1990] p. 386) plausibly suggest "he" is "the Assyrian" who appears in i 11ff.
i 11 With regard to the identity of "the Assyrian," see the introduction to the inscriptions of Ninurta-kudurrī-uṣur.

15) [*iṣ*]-*bat* ÉRIN.MEŠ DUMU.MEŠ URU *ra-man-šú-nu*
16) [*ana* L]Ú *aš-šur*.KI-*a-a it-tan-nu ár-ka-a-ni*(*)
17) LÚ *aš-šur*.KI-*a-a ú-šag-li-šú-nu-ti-ma*
18) *pi-rik* KUR.KUR.MEŠ *ú-sap-pi-iḫ-šu-nu-ti*
19) É.MEŠ *šá* Á KUR *ù* Á KUR-*i šá* URU *an-at*
20) *a-na* DU$_6$ *ù kar-mi ut-tir* ⸢*ù*⸣
21) LÚ *aš-šur*.KI-*a-a* ÉRIN.MEŠ *šá ram-ni-šú* ⸢*ina*⸣ URU *an-at*

Afterwards, the Assyrian exiled them and scattered them over (all) the lands. He turned the houses on (both) *the landside* and *the hillside* of the city Anat (i 20) into heaps of ruins. Then the Assyrian settled his own men in the city Anat.

22) *ul-te-še-bu ul-tu* UGU ^{m}*tab-né-e-a*
23) ^{m}BA-*šá*-^{d}AMAR.UTU *ù* ^{m}(*)NIGIN-*ir*-^{d}IŠKUR
24) 3 LÚ.GAR.KUR.MEŠ 50 MU.AN.NA.MEŠ URU *an-at*
25) *šá* LÚ *aš-šur*.KI-*a-a* 3 MU.AN.NA.MEŠ
26) [(x)] *i-na* UD.MEŠ *šá* ^{md}UTU-SAG-PAB MIN

Col. ii
1) AD-*ia a-d*[*i*] MAN ME [...]
2) *ina* GIŠ.GU.ZA AD-[*ia lā uššabu*]
3) ^{d}IŠKUR *u* ^{d}A-^{d}[IŠKUR ...]
4) *ki-i iš-ku-nu* URU *a*[*n-at ana abīia*]
5) *it-tu-ru i-na* ⸢4⸣[(+) *šanāti*]
6) *šá* URU *an-at i*(?)-*š*[*a*(?)]-*r*[*u*(?) AD-*ia*]
7) *a-na* NAM.MEŠ-*šú ki-i i*[*l*(*)-*li-ku*]
8) *a-na-ku ina* GIŠ.GU.ZA AD-*i*[*a ūšib*(*ma*)]
9) *gi-na-né-e ù* SISKUR.[(SISKUR).MEŠ (...)]
10) *ù i-sin-na-a-ti šá* ^{d}[IŠ]KUR [(...)]
11) [*k*]*i*(?)-*i pi-i* ^{m}*ḫ*[*a*(?)]-*am*-[*mu*]-*ra-p*[*í šar bābili u*(?)]
12) *a-bi a-li-di-ia a-na-ku* ⸢*uk-tin*⸣ [(...)]
13) *u áš-bu-ti ina* URU *an-at* Á KUR *u* Á KU[R-*i*]
14) *ul-te-šib* URU [UR]U *an-at ki pa-na-a-m*[*a*(*)]
15) Á KUR *u* Á KUR-*i ú-še-šib* DINGIR.MEŠ *šá* Á KUR(*) [(*u id šadî*) *ša*(?)]
16) URU *an-at šá la-pa-an* LÚ *aš-šur*.KI-*a-a*
17) [*a-n*]*a* URU *ri-ba-niš* DU-*ku* x x [x (x) *ana*(?)]-*ku*
18) *ú-te-ri-šú-nu-ti-ma ki-i pa-na-a-ma*
19) *ina* KI.TUŠ-*šú-nu ú-še-šib-šú-nu-ti á-ki-ti*

i 22b– ii 19a) From (the time of) Tabnēa, Iqīša-Marduk, and Nasḫir-Adad — three governors (in all) — for fifty years, the city Anat (i 25) was (under the control) of the Assyrian, (and also) for three years, in the days of Šamaš-rēša-uṣur, ditto (governor of the land of Sūḫu and the land of Mari), my father, bef[ore] ... [... I ascended] the throne of [my] father. When the gods Adad and Apla-[Adad] set [...], the city A[nat] returned (its allegiance) [to my father]. (ii 5) *After four* [years], during which the city Anat *pros*[*pered*], when [my father di]ed (lit. "[went] to his fate"), I [ascended] the throne of my father. I (re-)established the regular offerings, offe[rings, (...)] (ii 10) and festivals of the god Adad [(...)] according to the wording (of the commands) of Ḫam[mu]-rāp[i, king of Babylon, *and*] the father who begot me. [(...)] Moreover, I settled people in the city Anat on (both) *the landside* and on *the h*[*ill*]*side*. I settled the *city* of Anat as (it had been) before, (ii 15) on (both) *the landside* and *the hillside*. I returned the gods of (both) the *landside* [(*and the hillside*) *of*] the city Anat who had gone [t]o the town Ribaniš on account of the Assyrian ... and I settled them in their dwelling(s), (just) as (they had been) before.

20) *ina* URU *an-at e-pu-uš-ma*(*) 1 [ME] *ina* 1 KÙŠ GÍD.DA-*šú*
21) 16 *ina* 1 KÙŠ *ru-pu-us-su*
22) É.GAL *pa*-[*n*]*i*(?) *i*-⸢*na*⸣ *ṭa-ḫi e-pu-uš-ma*
23) 47(*) *ina* [1] KÙŠ GÍD.DA-*šú*
24) 8 *ina* 1 KÙŠ *ru-pu-us*-[*s*]*u*
25) É.GAL *ḫi-da-a-tu*$_4$ [...]

(ii 19b–25) I built an Akītu (temple) in the city Anat: 1[00] cubits is its length (and) 16 cubits is its width. I built a ... palace beside (it): *47* cubits is its length (and) 8 cubits is its width. A palace of gladness [...]

Col. iii
1-6) Traces of only a few traces are preserved.
7) [...] x [...] x [...] x

iii 1–7) No translation possible.

8) [...] E$_{11}$-*ma*(*) [...] x x [x] x
9) [... *t*]*im-mé-en*-[*na*(?) (x)] *a*[*n*(?)-*n*]*a*(?)-*a*
10) [*ú-š*]*ap-pil* NA$_4$.MEŠ KUR.M[E]Š GA[L.ME]Š

iii 8–18) [*Anyone in the future who*] comes forward [... I made] *this* foundation [10 cubits] deep. [I *qua*]*rried* (iii 10) large mountain-stones, laid the

i 19 With regard to Á KUR *ù* Á KUR-*i*, "*the landside* and *the hillside*," see the note to S.0.1001.1 ii 22′.
ii 3–4 For a possible restoration, see the note to S.0.1002.5 iv 11–12.
ii 15 KUR(*): copy has BA/MA, while Bagh. Mitt. 21 transliteration indicates that there is nothing preserved after Á. Possibly Á [KUR *u*] ⸢Á⸣ [KUR-*i šá*]?
ii 17 With regard to the reading of the city name, see the commentary to S.0.1001.1.
ii 19–21 The construction of the same structure may be mentioned in S.0.1002.11 lines 14–20 and possibly in S.0.1002.3 iv 14′–15′ (where it is called a palace, not an *akītu*).
ii 22 See S.0.1002.3, note to iv 16′.
ii 23 The copy has 66, while Bagh. Mitt. 21 transliteration has 46/47?. S.0.1002.3 iv 16 has the number 47.

11) [*aḫ*]-*pe-e-ma tim-mé-en-nu ad-d*[*i-ma*]
12) [*ú*]-*dan-nin* MU *at-tu-ú-a i*[*t*(?)-*ti*]
13) [M]U *at-tu-šú* [*áš*]-⸢*kun*⸣ *man-ni*(*) *ár-ku-*[*ú*]
14) [*šá*] E$_{11}$-*ma* ^{d}IŠKUR *u* ^{d}A-^{d}[IŠKUR]
15) *líp-làḫ-ma ù na-de-e a-ḫi*
16) LÚ *šal-mu ù* LÚ.KÚR *a-na* URU *an-at*
17) *la i-raš-ši* ⸢*ki-ma*⸣ [*i*]*a*(?)-*tu* [(x)]
18) *ḫu-ud lìb-*⸢*bi*⸣ *li*(*)-*pu-*⸢*uš*⸣

foundation, [and] made (it) fast. [I s]et my own name [*with*] his own [na]me. Anyone in the future [who] comes forward should revere the gods Adad and Apla-[Adad] (iii 15) and not neglect those who are favourable and those who are hostile to the city Anat. Like me, may he (then) enjoy happiness!

10

A stone stela found by Iraqi archaeologists on the island of ʿĀnā bears a relief and an accompanying inscription written in Akkadian. Ninurta-kudurrī-uṣur describes his restoration of the statue and cult of the goddess Anat which had earlier been desecrated by "the Assyrian" after the people of Anat had revolted against the land of Sūḫu and joined with "the Assyrian."

COMMENTARY

The stela (IM 132899) has been collated for lines 1–27 from photographs kindly supplied by A. Cavigneaux. Lines 28ff. are poorly preserved and not clear from the photographs. The published copy has been followed for lines 28–30 and the Bagh. Mitt. 21 transliteration for lines 31–34. The inscription is written in an archaizing script and the signs are not always written in the same way (e.g., the two RU signs in line 3).

For lines 9b–14, see S.0.1002.1 lines 1–4, S.0.1002.2 i 1–4, S.0.1002.9 i 1–5, S.0.1002.11 lines 11–14, and S.0.1002.14 lines 1–6.

For lines 15–19a, compare S.0.1002.4 iv 7–10, S.0.1002.5 iv 1, and S.0.1002.9 i 9–13.

For lines 30–32, compare S.0.1002.3 iv 5′–8′, S.0.1002.5 iv 15–16, and S.0.1002.9 ii 9–12.

The relief depicts an individual (likely Ninurta-kudurrī-uṣur) with his hand raised before a deity (likely the goddess Anat); above the inscription appear what are probably symbols of various deities.

BIBLIOGRAPHY

1983 Killick and Roaf, Iraq 45 p. 204 (study)
1990 Cavigneaux and Bahija Ismail, Bagh. Mitt. 21 pp. 380–83, 435–36 and pl. 35 no. 17 (photo, copy, edition)

TEXT

1) *a-na an-at* GAŠAN *gít-mu-ul-tu šá-qa-a-at i-la-a-ti*
2) *gaš-rat* ^{d}IŠ$_{8}$.TÁR.MEŠ GAL-*at* ^{d}*i-gi$_{4}$-ge$_{4}$-e be-let ṣir-tú*
3) *ša šur-ru-ḫas* DINGIR-*us-su* GAŠAN *šá-ru-uḫ-tu$_{4}$ šá i-na*
4) ^{d}IŠ$_{8}$.TÁR.MEŠ *la iš-šá-an-na-nu qur-di-šu*
5) *ṣa-bi-ta-at qa-ti en-šú qa-i-šat ba-la-ṭu*
6) *ù a-na* LUGAL *pa-liḫ-šú ta-nam-din ur-tu$_{4}$*
7) *a-na* UN.MEŠ *da-ad-mi-šu ta-šar-ra-ku* ḪÉ.NUN

1–9a) For (the goddess) Anat, the perfect lady, most exalted of the goddesses, most powerful of the goddesses, greatest of the Igīgū gods, august lady whose godhead is splendid, splendid lady whose valour is not equalled by (that of any of) the (other) goddesses, (5) one who grasps the hand of the weak, grants life, and gives instruction(s) to the king who reveres her, (one who) presents plenty and abundance to the people of her settlements, who dwells in Ešuziana ("House, True Hand of Heaven") — the holy cella, the august shrine — the great

S.0.1002.10 line 3 As noted by Cavigneaux and Bahija Ismail, Bagh. Mitt. 21 (1990) p. 382, *šurruḫas* for *šurruḫat*.

8) *ù* NÍG.TUKU *a-ši-bat é-šu-zi-an-na ku-um-mu* KÙ *at-ma-nu*
9) *ṣi-ri* GAŠAN GAL-*ti* GAŠAN-*šu* ^{md}*nin-urta*-NÍG.DU-ÙRU LÚ.GAR KUR
10) *su-ḫi u* KUR *ma-ri* DUMU ^{md}UTU-SAG-[Ù]RU LÚ.GAR KUR *su-ḫ*[*i*]
11) *u* KUR *ma-ri* ŠÀ.BAL.BAL ^{md}IŠKUR-SUM-NUMUN
12) LÚ.GAR KUR *su-ḫi u* KUR *ma-ri* ⸢*li*⸣-*pu*
13) *ru-qu šá* ^{m}*tu-un-mis-saḫ*
14) DUMU ^{m}*ḫa-am-mu-ra-pi* LUGAL KÁ.DINGIR.RA.KI
15) ÉRIN.MEŠ LÚ *an-at-a-a a-šib* URU *a-na-at*
16) *la-pa-an* KUR *su-ḫi ib-bal-kit-ú-ma*
17) ŠU-*su-nu a-na* LÚ *aš-šur*.KI-*a-a it-tan-nu*
18) *ù* LÚ *aš-šur*.KI-*a-a a-na* URU *an-at*
19) *ul-te-lu-ni* URU URU *an-at ù* DINGIR.MEŠ-*šu*
20) *ú-šal-pit* TÚG SIG$_{5}$ *an-at* KÙ.GI *ṣa-ri-ri*
21) NA$_{4}$.MEŠ *ni-siq-tim ù mim-ma si-mat*
22) DINGIR-*ti-šu ú-šal-pit-ma ù a-na šá-a-ši*
23) *ú-še-šib-šú i-na pu-uz-ru a-na-ku*
24) ^{md}*nin-urta*-NÍG.DU-ÙRU LÚ.GAR KUR ⸢*su*⸣-*ḫi u* KUR *ma-ri*
25) ÌR *pa-liḫ* DINGIR-*ti-šu* GAL-*ti an-at ul*-⸢*tu*⸣
26) *pu-uz-ru ú-še-ṣa-am-ma* TÚG SIG$_{5}$ ⸢KÙ.GI⸣
27) [*ṣa-r*]*i-ri* ⸢*ù* NA$_{4}$⸣.MEŠ ⸢*ni-siq-tim*⸣ [x]-x-⸢*tú*⸣
28) [x x x x *ú*]-*šak-lil* DINGIR-*us*-⸢*su*⸣ *ù*
29) *i-na* [...] *ú-še-šib-šú*
30) *gi-na*-[*né-e* (x)] x [x x (x)]-*šú ki-i*
31) *pi-i* ^{m}*ḫa-am-mu-ra-pu* LUGAL
32) [KÁ.DINGIR].RA.KI LUGAL *maḫ*(?)-*ri-ia ú-kin*
33) DI/KI(?) x GAL(?) x KI IB(?) RI x x x x x
34) *pu-uz*(?)-*ri*(?) x x x x x x x x

Traces of about five more lines.
Lacuna

lady, his lady:

9b–14) Ninurta-kudurrī-uṣur, governor of the land of Sūḫu and the land of Mari, son of Šamaš-rēša-uṣur, governor of the land of Sūḫu and the land of Mari, descendant of Adad-nādin-zēri, governor of the land of Sūḫu and the land of Mari, distant descendant of Tunamissaḫ, the son of Ḫammu-rāpi, king of Babylon —

15–23a) The people of Anat who live in the city Anat (itself) revolted against the land of Sūḫu. They joined hands with the Assyrian and brought the Assyrian up to the city Anat. (However) he desecrated the *city of* Anat and its gods. He desecrated (20) the fine garment of (the goddess) Anat, the *ṣāriru*-gold, the precious stones, and all the (other) things befitting her godhead. Then he cached her (statue) *by itself* in a hidden place.
23b–32) I, Ninurta-kudurrī-uṣur, governor of the land of Sūḫu and the land of Mari, (25) the servant who reveres her great godhead, brought Anat out from (that) hidden place and [*returned*] (her) fine garment, [*ṣār*]*iru*-gold, and ... precious stones. [I] made her godhead complete (again) and caused her to reside in [...]. I (re-)established (30) the regular [offerings (...) *and*] her [...] according to the wording (of the commands) of Ḫammu-rāpi, king of [Baby]lon, a king who preceded me.

33–34) No translation warranted.
Lacuna

11

This Akkadian inscription is written upon a small clay tablet (IM 95916) found at Sūr Jarʿā by Iraqi archaeologists. It describes the restoration of an Akītu temple at Anat by Ninurta-kudurrī-uṣur for the gods Adad and Apla-Adad; this temple may be identical with the one mentioned in S.0.1002.9 ii 19–20.

22 Cavigneaux and Bahija Ismail suggest that *abnī nisiqtim* should be translated "necklaces" or "ornamental stones" (Bagh. Mitt. 21 [1990] p. 383).
27 Cavigneaux and Bahija Ismail suggest [*an-n*]*u*?-*tú*, "(*all*) [*th*]*ese*" (Bagh. Mitt. 21 [1990] pp. 381–82).
29 Cavigneaux and Bahija Ismail note that a reading KI.TUŠ, "abode," in the damaged section is possible (Bagh. Mitt. 21 [1990] p. 383).
30 Bagh. Mitt. 21 transliteration has: *gi-na-né*?-*e*? *ù* x x -*šu ki-i*; Cavigneaux and Bahija Ismail note that the traces do not fit a reading *isinnu*, *nīqu*, or *ilūtu* (Bagh. Mitt. 21 [1990] p. 383).

COMMENTARY

Cavigneaux and Bahija Ismail suggest that the inscription may have been copied from an original upon stone which was set up at Anat, possibly even S.0.1002.1001. The inscription has not been collated and the edition presented here is based upon the published copy.

With regard to parallel/similar passages, note the following:

For lines 11b–14a, see S.0.1002.1 lines 1–4, S.0.1002.2 i 1–4, S.0.1002.9 i 1–5, S.0.1002.10 lines 9–14, and S.0.1002.14 lines 1–6.

For lines 17b–20, see S.0.1002.1 lines 7–9, S.0.1002.2 iv 7′–9′, S.0.1002.3 iii 3′–4′, S.0.1002.6 iii 9′–12′, S.0.1002.8 rev. 18–20, S.0.1002.12 lines 6′–8′, and S.0.1002.1001 lines 1′–4′.

BIBLIOGRAPHY

1990 Cavigneaux and Bahija Ismail, Bagh. Mitt. 21 pp. 341–43 and 411 no. 1 (copy, edition)

TEXT

1) *a-na* ^{d}IŠKUR *u* ^{d}A-^{d}IŠKUR EN.MEŠ GAL.MEŠ *ti-iz-qa-ri*
2) *mut-tal-lu šá-ga-pi-ri mug-dáš-ri dan-dan* DINGIR.MEŠ
3) *šá i-na nap-ḫar* AN-*e u* KI-*tim šu-tu-rat be-lut-su*
4) *ma-al-ku šit-ra-ḫu šá i-na* DINGIR.MEŠ ŠEŠ.MEŠ-*šú*
5) *la iš-ša-an-na-nu e-mu-qa-šú* GÚ.GAL AN-*e*
6) DAGAL-*tim* DUMU ^{d}*a-nim el-lu*$_{4}$ *mar-ma-ru šá ina uz-zi-šu*
7) *dan-nu* DINGIR *mam-ma la i-par-ra-ku pa-nu-uš-šú a-šib*
8) *é-nam-ḫé* EN URU *an-at ki-iṣ-ṣu* KÙ
9) *at-ma-nu* LUGAL-*ú-tu ki-sal-la ra-áš-bu*
10) *šá qab-lat* ÍD.BURANUN.KI *šá* KUR *su-ḫi u* KUR *ma-r*[*i*]
11) *be-lí-šú* ^{md}MAŠ-NÍG.DU-PAB LÚ.GAR KUR *su-ḫi u* KUR *má-r*[*í*]
12) [DUMU] ⸢^{m}⸣^{d}UTU-SAG-ÙRU MIN ŠÀ.BAL.BAL ^{md}IŠKUR-SUM-NUMUN
13) [NUMUN] *da-ru-ú li-pu ru-qu šá* ^{m}*tu-na-mis-sa*[*ḫ*]
14) [DUM]U ^{m}*am-mu-ra-pu* LUGAL TIN.TIR.KI *a-ki-tu*$_{4}$
15) *šá* ^{d}IŠKUR *ù* ^{d}A-^{d}IŠKUR *u* DINGIR.MEŠ *a-šib* URU *an-at*
16) EN.MEŠ-*e-a la-ba-riš il-lik-ma up-te-eṭ-*⸢*ṭir*⸣ x
17) *a-ki-tu*$_{4}$ UR$_{5}$-*tú ú-dan-nin-ma a-na ba-laṭ*
18) ZI.MEŠ-*ia šá-lam* NUMUN-*ia* GÍD.DA UD.MEŠ-*ia*
19) *ku-un* BALA.MEŠ-*e-a sa-kap* KUR LÚ.KÚR-*ia*
20) DÙ-*ma a-na* ^{d}IŠKUR *u* ^{d}A-^{d}IŠKUR EN.MEŠ-*e-a* BA-*eš*

1–11a) For the gods Adad and Apla-Adad, the great lords; (to the god Adad), the eminent, noble, majestic, powerful, mightiest of the gods, whose rule is pre-eminent in all of heaven and earth, the splendid ruler, whose (5) strength cannot be rivalled by any of his brother gods, the canal inspector of the extensive heavens, the holy son of the god Anu, the strong one, whose mighty anger no god can face, the one who dwells in (the temple) Enamḫe ("House of Plenty"), lord of the city Anat — (Anat), the holy sanctuary, royal shrine, awe-inspiring court, which is situated in the middle of the Euphrates River, in the land of Sūḫu and the land of Mari — his lord:

11b–14a) Ninurta-kudurrī-uṣur, governor of the land of Sūḫu and the land of Mari, [son] of Šamaš-rēša-uṣur, ditto (governor of the land of Sūḫu and the land of Mari), descendant of Adad-nādin-zēri, one of an enduring [lineage], distant descendant of Tunamissaḫ, [so]n of Ḫammu-rāpi, king of Babylon —

14b–20) The Akītu (temple) of the gods Adad and Apla-Adad, and of the gods who dwell in the city Anat, my lords, had become old and ruined (...) I strengthened this Akītu (temple); I (re)built (it) in order to ensure my good health (and) the well-being of my offspring, to prolong my days, to confirm my reign, (and) to defeat the land of my enemy; and I dedicated (it) to the gods Adad and Apla-Adad, my lords.

---

8 Enamḫe was also the name of the temple of the god Adad at Babylon; see George, House Most High pp. 129–30 no. 839.

14 With regard to the possibility that the term *akītu* refers simply to a temple here, and not specifically to a temple for the *akītu*-festival, see S.0.1002.1, note to line 4.

16 Bagh. Mitt. 21 transliteration has for the end of the line *up-te-eṭ-ṭir* ⸢x x⸣ [(x x)].

12

A fragment of a clay tablet from Sūr Jarʿā (IM 124883) preserves part of Ninurta-kudurrī-uṣur's description of his rebuilding of an Akītu temple for the gods Adad and Mīšarum at the town Udada and of his construction of a new palace in the district of the city Raʾil. The inscription is written in Akkadian. The fragment has not been collated and the edition presented here is based upon the published copy, with notes to the transliteration published by Cavigneaux and Bahija Ismail.

COMMENTARY

With regard to restorations and parallel/similar passages, note the following:

For 4′–8a′, see S.0.1002.1 lines 5–9, S.0.1002.2 iv 4′–9′, S.0.1002.3 iii 2′–4′, S.0.1002.6 iii 6′–12′, S.0.1002.8 rev. 16–20, and S.0.1002.11 lines 17–20.

For 8b′–12′, see S.0.1002.1 line 9–11, S.0.1002.2 iv 9′–12′, S.0.1002.3 iii 5′–9′, S.0.1002.6 iii 12′–16′, S.0.1002.7 rev. 2′–4′, and S.0.1002.8 rev. 21.

This inscription could be treated simply as a duplicate of one of the above texts (in particular S.0.1002.1, 2, 7, or 8, which are inscriptions also found on clay tablets from Sūr Jarʿā).

BIBLIOGRAPHY

1990 Cavigneaux and Bahija Ismail, Bagh. Mitt. 21 pp. 377 and 433 no. 12 (copy, edition)

TEXT

Lacuna
1′) [...] x [...]
2′) [...] x [...]
3′) [...] x RAD x x [...]
4′) [... *iš-š*]*i-ma ul* DÙ [...]
5′) [... *ú-šak-lil-m*]*a a-na* ^{d}IŠKUR [...]
6′) [... EN].MEŠ(*)-*e-a a-na* [...]
7′) [... GÍD.D]A(*) UD.MEŠ-*ia k*[*u*(*)-*un* ...]
8′) [...] ⌈*ú*⌉-*še-piš-ma* B[A-*eš* ...]
9′) [... LÚ].GAR KUR *su-ḫi u* KUR *m*[*a-ri* ...]
10′) [... Í]D *pu-rat-tu*$_{4}$ *la-*[*ba-riš* ...]
11′) [...] É(*).GAL *šá-ni-tu*$_{4}$ [...]
12′) [... G]ÍD.DA-*šú* 12 *ina* 1 KÙŠ *u* [*ma-la* ...]
13′) [...] x x x x x (x) [...]
Lacuna

Lacuna
1′–8a′) [...] ... [(...) None among my ancestors had paid attenti]on (to it) and (re)built (it). [I completely (re)built this Akītu (temple)]. I had (this temple) (re)built and dedi[cated] (it) to the gods Adad [and Mīšarum, the great gods], my [lord]s, in order to [ensure my good health (and) the well-being of my offspring, to prolo]ng my days, to con[firm my reign, (and) to defeat the land of my enemy].
8b′–13′) [The palace of Enamḫe-zēra-ibni], governor of the land of Sūḫu and the land of M[ari, (which is located in) the district of the city Raʾil, which is in the middle of the ri]ver Euphrates, [had become] o[ld and I abandoned it. I built] another palace [above it: 64 cubits is] its length (and) 12 [1/2] cubits [is its width. ...] ... [...]
Lacuna

3′ Based upon parallel passages (e.g., S.0.1002.1 line 5) and the spacing, one might read [... *muš-š*]*u*(?)-*rat* ⌈*a*(?)-*a*(?)⌉-*u*[*m-ma* ...], ("[... *aband*]*oned. No*[*ne* ...]"), but the copy would suggest ⌈ŠI⌉ rather than *a-a* and possibly ŠÚ rather than *š*]*u*.
13′ Based upon parallel passages (e.g., S.0.1002.1 line 12) and the spacing, one might read [... É.GA]L(?) *šá*(?) ^{m}⌈*é*(?)⌉-*n*[*am*(?)-*ḫé*-NUMUN-DÙ ...], "[... *The palac*]*e of En*[*amḫe-zēra-ibni* ...]."

13

A fragment of the lower left corner of a clay tablet which was found at Sūr Jarʿā by Iraqi archaeologists preserves part of an Akkadian inscription of Ninurta-kudurrī-uṣur. Only the reverse of the fragment is legible and it contains part of Ninurta-kudurrī-uṣur's description of the building of the town Dūr-Ninurta-kudurrī-uṣur ("Fort-Ninurta-kudurrī-uṣur") in the steppe.

COMMENTARY

The original publication of the fragment refers to it as IM 1244882, but it is actually IM 124882 (information courtesy A. Cavigneaux). The text has not been collated and the edition presented here is based upon the copy, with notes to the transliteration published by Cavigneaux and Bahija Ismail. Restorations in rev. 1–8 are based upon S.0.1002.2 iii 16′–21′ and S.0.1002.4 iv 1–3; it is possible that this inscription should be treated as a duplicate of one of these two texts (both of which are also found on clay tablets from Sūr Jarʿā).

Cavigneaux and Bahija Ismail suggest that the tablet may have had originally four columns, in which case we would have the end of col. i and the beginning of col. iv.

BIBLIOGRAPHY

1990 Cavigneaux and Bahija Ismail, Bagh. Mitt. 21 pp. 378 and 434 no. 15 (copy, edition)

TEXT

Obverse
Lacuna
1′) [...] x [...]
2′) x x x x x x ME [...]
3′) x x (x) [(x)] x x KUR [...]
4′) DIN x [U]L(?) BI x x [...]
5′) x x x x BE [...]
6′) x x BA KUR [*m*]*a-r*[*i*(?) ...]
7′) x x RI ⸢ŠI⸣ x [...]
8′) x [(x)] x [(x)] x [...]
9′) x x BE x x [...]
10′) x x x (x) [x (x)] x [...]
Reverse
1) [(x)] x *ina muḫ-ḫi* DÙ-*m*[*a* ...]
2) ⸢*az*⸣-[*ku*]*r* LÚ *áš-bu-ti* [...]
3) *ina lìb-bi ú-šá-az-ziz* [...]
4) *pe-ti-ti šá* KUR *su-*[*ḫi* ...]
5) *šá* ⸢E$_{11}$⸣-*ma* ⸢*a*⸣-*na* ⸢*na*(?)⸣-[*de-e* ...]
6) [*l*]*a* ⸢*i*(?)-*raš*(?)⸣-*ši* L[Ú(?) *á*]*š*-[*bu-tu* ...]
7) *ú-še-šib a-a ú-na*[*k-kìr-šú-nu-ti* ...]
8) *šá* KUR *su-*[*ḫi*] *la-pa-an* LÚ.[KÚR ...]
9) x x x x x x x [...]
Lacuna

Lacuna
obv. 1′–10′) Not sufficiently preserved to allow translation.

rev. 1–9) I built [a town] there and named [it Dūr-Ninurta-kudurrī-uṣur. I settled] people [in it (and)] stationed [mounted soldiers] in it. [This (town) is the] open [eyes] of the land of Sū[ḫu for the sake of the security of the land of Sūḫu]. No [one in the future] (rev. 5) who comes forward *should ne*[*glect* this town] (or) ex[pel] the in[habitants whom] I settled [in this town. They should (continue to) guard (this town)] against the [enemy for the sake of the security] of the land of Sū[ḫu]. ... [...]
Lacuna

rev. 9 Possibly [*k*]*i*(?)-⸢*ma*(?)⸣ *i*[*a*(?)-*a-t*]*i*(?)-⸢*ma*(?) SAG⸣ UR[U(?) UR$_5$-*tú liš-ši* ...], "Just as I (did) [he should pay att]ention to [this] town [...]" (see S.0.1002.2 iii 21′ and S.0.1002.4 iv 3–4 [mostly restored]), but the spacing would suggest that the first part of this should be at the end of the previous line.

14

A fragment from the upper left corner of a clay tablet (IM 97871) was found at Jedīdē (Judaide, Judeideh), located on the left bank of the Euphrates about ten kilometres south of ʿĀnā. The fragment preserves part of an Akkadian inscription of a son (or possibly descendant) of Šamaš-rēsa-[uṣur], thus probably of Ninurta-kudurrī-uṣur.

COMMENTARY

The fragment has not been collated and the edition presented below is based upon the copy, with notes to the transliteration published by Cavigneaux and Bahija Ismail. There are line rulings between the lines of cuneiform, and Cavigneaux and Bahija Ismail suggest that the inscription is probably a copy of an inscription upon stone.

The Bagh. Mitt. 21 transliteration indicates that there is only one line before what is given here as line 3; however, the traces of that line in the published copy would not seem to fit what one expects to find in the first line of the inscription. Thus, it is tentatively assumed here that there were two lines before the line mentioning Šamaš-rēša-uṣur. It has not been possible to examine the original in order to see if the shape of the piece precludes restoring this additional line.

With regard to the possible restoration of lines 1–6, see S.0.1002.1 lines 1–4, S.0.1002.2 i 1–4, S.0.1002.9 i 1–5, S.0.1002.10 lines 9–14, and S.0.1002.11 lines 11–14.

BIBLIOGRAPHY

1990 Cavigneaux and Bahija Ismail, Bagh. Mitt. 21 pp. 396 and 446 no. 22 (copy, edition)

TEXT

1) [(*anāku*) *ninurta-kudurrī-uṣur*(?) ...]
2) x x [...]
3) DUMU ᵐᵈUTU-SAG-[PAB ...]
4) ŠÀ.BAL.BAL [...]
5) *li-pu-*[*ú*...]
6) ⌜A⌝ [...]
Lacuna

1–6) [(I), *Ninurta-kudurrī-uṣur* ...] son of Šamaš-rēša-[uṣur ...] descendant [...] descendant [...] *son* [...]
Lacuna

1001

A fragment of a stone stela found at Sūr Jarʿā (IM 96748A) preserves part of an Akkadian inscription which is similar (though not necessarily identical) to a passage found in several inscriptions of Ninurta-kudurrī-uṣur, in particular S.0.1002.11 lines 18–20. Cavigneaux and Bahija Ismail suggest that it is possible that this is the original inscription from which S.0.1002.11 was copied (Bagh. Mitt. 21 [1990] pp. 342 and 396). The inscription has not been collated and the edition presented here is based upon the copy in Bagh. Mitt. 21, with the help of additional information supplied by A. Cavigneaux.

---

6 Possibly *a-*[*ki-tu₄* ...], "the A[kītu (temple) ...]"? See S.0.1002.1 line 4 and the note to that line.

BIBLIOGRAPHY

1990 Cavigneaux and Bahija Ismail, Bagh. Mitt. 21 pp. 396 and 446 no. 23 (copy, edition)

TEXT

Lacuna
1′) [... *š*]*á-la*[*m*]
2′) [*zērīia arāk ūmēia kūn* BALA.(MEŠ)]-⸢*e*⸣-*a*
3′) [... *sakāp*] KUR LÚ KÚR-[*ia ēpušma*(?)] *a-na*
4′) [... EN.MEŠ]-⸢*e*(?)⸣-*a* BA-*eš*

Lacuna
1′–4′) [I (re)built (it) in order to ensure ... the we]ll-being [of my offspring, to prolong my days, to confirm] my [reign, ... (and) to defeat] the land of [my] enemy, [and] I dedicated (it) to [the gods ...], my [lords].

1002

Excavations at the site of Zawiyyā (Zawiyeh), located on the left bank of the Euphrates about five kilometres southwest of Sūr Jarʿa, conducted by the Iraqi State Antiquities Organization in 1978 uncovered a number of bricks with coloured decoration (see Iraq 41 [1979] p. 159). At least one of these preserves part of an inscription which might belong to Ninurta-kudurrī-uṣur.

COMMENTARY

Immediately to the left of the first preserved signs are a depiction of a flower and a vertical line, both in yellow glaze. Thus, it is quite possible that there is nothing missing on either line before the first signs preserved. Information on the inscription was provided by A.K. Grayson, who saw it in the museum at Ramādī.

TEXT

Lacuna
1′) [(...) *ninurta*(?)]-NÍG.DU-ÙRU [(...)]
2′) [(...)] ⸢d⸣IŠKUR [(...)]
Lacuna

Lacuna
1′–2′) [(... *Ninurta*)]-kudurrī-uṣur [(...)] the god Adad [(...)]
Lacuna

S.0.1002.1001 line 3′ The copy would suggest that there is not sufficient room to restore [*ia ēpušma*].

Unidentified

S.0.0

There are a number of miscellaneous inscriptions which were either found in the Ḥadītha area or are reported to have been found there. The dates of most these are not known and some may have been composed for Assyrian rulers or not be royal inscriptions at all. Nevertheless, it has been thought useful to present all of them here.

1001

A fragment of a tablet from Sūr Jarʿā preserves part of an Akkadian inscription which mentions the city of Ālu-eššu ("New City") several times and which may belong to Šamaš-rēša-uṣur, Ninurta-kudurrī-uṣur, or possibly some other individual.

COMMENTARY

IM 124198 is the lower right corner of a clay tablet found during Iraqi excavations at Sūr Jarʿā. The tablet may have had originally two columns of inscription per side; thus we may have the end of column ii and the start of column iii. The inscription has not been collated and the edition presented here is based upon the copy, with notes to the transliteration published by Cavigneaux and Bahija Ismail.

Cavigneaux and Bahija Ismail note that the *ītedel* of obverse 9′ and the *ana šadî ītelû* of obverse 8′ are reminiscent of S.0.1001.1 ii 4′ *uddul* and ii 9′ *ana nagīti itlû* respectively.

BIBLIOGRAPHY

1990 Cavigneaux and Bahija Ismail, Bagh. Mitt. 21 pp. 366–67 and 425 no. 6 (copy, edition)

TEXT

Obverse

Lacuna

1′) [... *mu*]*ḫ-ḫi-*⌈*ia it-ta-bal-kit*⌉

2′) [...] x-*ti* LÚ.URU-*eš-šá-a-a*

3′) [... L]Ú *ḫa-an-za-nu-ú-a*

Lacuna

obv. 1′– rev. 11) [...] revolted [aga]inst me [...] the people of Ālu-eššu [...] the *Ḫanzanūa* (tribe) [... ga]thered and the people of Raʾil (obv. 5′) [...] of

obv. 3′ Cavigneaux and Bahija Ismail argue that *ḫa-an-za-nu-ú-a* cannot be a by-form of *ḫazannūa*, "my mayors" (Bagh. Mitt. 21 [1990] p. 367).

4′) [... *ip*]-*ḫu-ru-ma* LÚ *ra-ìl-a-a*
5′) [... K]I-*pi šá* URU-*eš-ši šá ana-ku*
6′) [... *e-l*]*i ia-a-ti it-tal-ku-nu*
7′) [... K]I(?) 80(?) *pít-ḫal-lu ul-tu*
8′) [... *im-ḫ*]*ur-in-ni a-na* KUR-*i i-te-lu-ú*
9′) [...] x *i-te-de-el šá ni-ia-ʾ-i*
10′) [...]-*a-ti ak-šú-ud-ma* LÚ.URU-*eš-šá-a-a*
Reverse
1) [... B]ÀD AM *a-na* KI.TA
2) [... *š*]*ú*(?)-*nu* GIŠ.BAN.MEŠ-*šú-nu*
3) [... *e-l*]*i ia-a-ti*
4) [...] x ḪU MA SU-*ú-šú-nu*
5) [... *a*]*z-kur ina u₄-mi-šú-ma*
6) [... *a*(?)-*d*]*i-ri* URU-*eš-ši*
7) [...] Á KUR-*i*
8) [... *a*]*d-di*
9) [...] x-*nu-nu*
10) [...] x-*la* ÉRIN.MEŠ
11) [...] x-⌈*nu*⌉-*nu*
Lacuna

Ālu-eššu, which I [...] marched [aga]inst me [...] *eighty* mounted soldiers from [... ap]proached me and (then) went up to the mountain(s) [...] he closed; *of ours* [...] (obv. 10′) I reached and the people of Ālu-eššu [... the w]all ... below [...] *their* [...] their archers [... again]st me [...] their ... (rev. 5) [... I n]amed. At that time [... *the encl*]*osure of* Ālu-eššu [...] *hillside* [... *I t*]*hrew* [...] ... (rev. 10) [...] soldiers [...] ...
Lacuna

1002

A fragment from the surface of a clay tablet which was found at Sūr Jarʿā preserves part of an Akkadian inscription that may refer to a rebellion by the people of Raʾil against the governor of Sūḫu. Such rebellions are known to have occurred in both the time of Šamaš-rēša-uṣur and that of Ninurta-kudurrī-uṣur (see for example S.0.1002.1 lines 15–19). Both this fragment and S.0.1002.8 are published as being IM 124881; it is possible that the latter is IM 124194 (see commentary to S.0.1002.8). The inscription has not been collated and the edition presented here is based upon the published copy, with notes to the transliteration by Cavigneaux and Bahija Ismail.

BIBLIOGRAPHY

1990 Cavigneaux and Bahija Ismail, Bagh. Mitt. 21 pp. 370–71 and 427 no. 8 (copy, edition)

TEXT

Lacuna
1′) [...] x ŠI [...]
2′) [...] A *ki-ki-i* ⌈*ma-ti*(?)⌉ [...]
3′) [...]-*šú ú-ši-ba* 7 ITI.MEŠ LÚ [...]
4′) [...] x x-*ḫi-šú gul-lul-ta-šu-nu man-nu a*[*r*(?)-*ku*(?)-*u*(?) ...]
5′) [... LÚ *r*]*a-ìl-a-a ina il-ki man-da-at-tu la ú-zak-ki-šú-nu*-[*ti* ...]

Lacuna
1′–12′) [...] ... [...] how *my land* [...] his [...] he/I dwelt; *for* seven months the [...] his [...] their crime(s). Anyone *in the fu*[*ture who comes forward* ... (5′) ...] he/I exempted [(...) the] people of Raʾil from *ilku*-duty (and) tribute. [...] he revolted [*agai*]*nst* the land of Sūḫu. Nabû-šumu-līšir [*came*] *from* the land [*of* ...]. *They* made [(...) *a peace*

S.0.0.1001 obv. 7′ The number could also be 610; Bagh. Mitt. 21 transliteration has 120?.
S.0.0.1001 rev. 4 Bagh. Mitt. 21 transliteration has *zu-ú-šú-nu*, which Cavigneaux and Bahija Ismail tentatively translate as "their excrement" (Bagh. Mitt. 21 [1990] p. 367).
S.0.0.1001 rev. 6 With regard to the word *adīru*, see the note to S.0.1002.2 iv 23.

6′) [... *a-n*]*a*(?) ⸢KUR⸣ *su-ḫi it-ta*(*)-*bal-kit* ᵐᵈAG-MU-SI.SÁ *ina* KUR [...]
7′) [... *salīma*(?) *ina*(?) URU.K]AR(?)-ᵈAG *a-na lìb-bi a-ḫa-meš* DÙ-*uš-ma* ᵐᵈA[G-MU(?)-SI.SÁ(?) ...]
8′) [...] x-ᵈIŠKUR LÚ.GAR KUR *su-ḫi ib-bal-kit-ú* [...]
9′) [...] x-*šú-nu ina* NA₄.NA.RÚ.A *iš-ṭur-ma* [...]
10′) [... *a-n*]*a muḫ-ḫi-ia ib-bal-k*[*it* ...]
11′) [...] ⸢30(?)⸣ ÉRIN.MEŠ MI x [...]
12′) [...] x TU x [...]
Lacuna

agreement] with one another [*in the town*] *Kār*-Nabû and Na[bû-*šuma-līšir* ...] they revolted [against ...]-Adad, governor of the land of Sūḫu [...] he recorded [(...)] their [*defeat*] on a stela and [... (10′) ...] he revolted [ag]ainst me [...] *thirty* soldiers [...] ... [...]
Lacuna

1003

A tiny surface fragment of a clay tablet (IM 124884) which was found at Sūr Jarʿā bears an inscription. So little of it is preserved that it is not certain that it is part of a royal inscription. The inscription has not been collated and the edition presented here is based upon the published copy, with notes to the transliteration by Cavigneaux and Bahija Ismail.

BIBLIOGRAPHY

1990 Cavigneaux and Bahija Ismail, Bagh. Mitt. 21 pp. 378 and 433 no. 14 (copy, edition)

TEXT

Lacuna
1′) [...] ⸢TU(?)⸣ [...]
2′) [...] NI IS x x x [...]
3′) [...] x x RI ŠI [...]
4′) [...] DUMU LÚ.GAL *ḫu-ṣa-b*[*u* ...]
Space
(Lacuna)

Lacuna
1′–4′) No translation warranted.
(Lacuna)

1004

A fragment of a stone stela found at Sūr Jarʿā (IM 96749) preserves part of an inscription whose contents cannot be determined. Cavigneaux and Bahija Ismail state that the fragment may be from the same stela as S.0.0.1005.

S.0.0.1002 line 6′ A Chaldean of the Bīt-Dakkūri tribe by the name of Nabû-šumu-līšir is known from about this time (see B.6.10.2001), but there is no reason to assume he is the individual mentioned in this text.
S.0.0.1002 line 8′ A Nasḫir-Adad was governor of Sūḫu before the time of Šamaš-rēša-uṣur, but the traces before ᵈIŠKUR do not fit the writing ᵐNIGIN-*ir*, which is found in S.0.1002.5 iv 8 and S.0.1002.9 i 23 (as noted by Cavigneaux and Bahija Ismail, Bagh. Mitt. 21 [1990] p. 370 n. 72). They might, however, fit a reading [... ᵐ*na-as*]-⸢*ḫír*⸣.
S.0.0.1002 line 12′ Bagh. Mitt. 21 transliteration has [... *u*]*l*?-*tu* U[RU? ...] ("[....*f*]*rom the c*[*ity* ...]").

The original has not been collated and the edition is based upon the published copy.

BIBLIOGRAPHY

1990 Cavigneaux and Bahija Ismail, Bagh. Mitt. 21 pp. 396 and 446 no. 24 (copy, study)

TEXT

Lacuna	Lacuna
1′) [...] x A [...]	1′–8′) No translation warranted.
2′) [...] KA [...]	Lacuna
3′) [...] *iṣ-ṣ*[*i*(?) ...]	
4′) [...] ⌜Á(?)⌝.MEŠ(?)–*šú* [...]	
5′) [...] EŠ x AŠ [...]	
6′) [...] x ÉRIN.MEŠ [...]	
7′) [...] x RI x [...]	
8′) [...] UZ [...]	
Lacuna	

1005

A second fragment of a stone stela found at Sūr Jarʿā (IM 96748B) preserves part of an inscription whose contents cannot be determined. Cavigneaux and Bahija Ismail indicate that the fragment may be from the same stela as S.0.0.1004. Parts of two lines are preserved: (1′) x [...] (2′) A x [...]. The original has not been collated and the transliteration is based upon the published copy. See Cavigneaux and Bahija Ismail, Bagh. Mitt. 21 (1990) pp. 396 and 446 no. 25 (copy, study).

1006

A tiny fragment of a stone stela (IM 96751) which was found at Glaiʿā (Gleiʿeh), a site located on the right bank of the Euphrates opposite Sūr Jarʿā, preserves parts of two lines of an inscription: (1′) [...] MA ŠE x [...] (2′) [...] x [...]. The original has not been collated and the transliteration is based upon the published copy and additional information kindly supplied by A. Cavigneaux. See Cavigneaux and Bahija Ismail, Bagh. Mitt. 21 (1990) pp. 396 and 446 no. 26 (copy, study). For a second inscription from Glaiʿā, see S.0.0.1009.

1007

A stone stela (IM 132177) with a relief depicting a battle scene, involving two riders, two fallen individuals, and a scribe, was found on the island of ʿĀnā. It has a poorly preserved epigraph which cannot be understood at present.

COMMENTARY

The transliteration presented below is based upon the published copy since the published photograph is indistinct. Cavigneaux and Bahija Ismail suggest that the first word might be *ṣalmē* (i.e., *ṣa-al-*[*me*]), "figures," and that it is unlikely to be *ṣaltu* (i.e., *ṣa-al-*[*t*]*u*/[*t*]*ú*), "battle." Thus it is not clear that the relief depicts the decisive victory of Ninurta-kudurrī-uṣur over the Ḫatallu.

BIBLIOGRAPHY

1990 Cavigneaux and Bahija Ismail, Bagh. Mitt. 21 pp. 397, 447, and pl. 37 no. 27 (photo, copy, edition)

TEXT

1) ZA AL [(x)] x Ú(?) ZA BA(?)
2) LÚ AŠ [x x] ⸢ZA⸣ x
Lacuna (3 or 4 lines completely effaced)

1–2) No translation warranted.
Lacuna

1008

In connection with their publication of the texts of the governors of Sūḫu and Mari found in the Ḥadītha area, Cavigneaux and Bahija Ismail published a fragment of a baked brick (IM 121928) which is stated to come from Tell Razzuq and which preserves traces from two lines: (1′) x [...] (2′) A x [...]. Too little of the text is preserved to determine its nature, but bricks usually bear official inscriptions. Cavigneaux and Bahija Ismail were informed that the text came from the Ḥadītha area, but were not provided with any further information on the site or the provenance of the piece. M. Roaf kindly informs me that the only tell by the name Tell Razzuq known to him is in the Ḥamrīn area. The fragment has not been collated and the transliteration is based upon the published copy. See Cavigneaux and Bahija Ismail, Bagh. Mitt. 21 (1990) pp. 405 and 456 no. B (copy, study).

1009

A fragment of a jar rim (excavation number Glaiʿa 79) which was found at Glaiʿā (Gleiʿeh), a site located on the right bank of the Euphrates opposite Sūr Jarʿā, preserves part of an inscription: [... SU]KKAL(?) ⌜É(?)⌝ [...]. The inscription has not been collated and the transliteration is based upon the published copy. See Cavigneaux and Bahija Ismail, Bagh. Mitt. 21 (1990) pp. 405 and 456 no. C (copy, transliteration).

1010

A badly eroded inscription is found on a large stone slab which was reused to cover a well in the courtyard of the mosque on the island at ʿĀnā. The text is reported to be written in several columns and in Babylonian script, but no transliteration is available. It remains uncertain if the inscription is to be assigned to one of the independent rulers of the area in the eighth century BC or if the inscription comes from some other period entirely. See Roaf, Iraq 43 (1981) p. 194, and Cavigneaux and Bahija Ismail, Bagh. Mitt. 21 (1990) p. 322 n. 3.

1011

Gertrude Bell reports in Geographical Journal 36 (1910) p. 536 that "From two informants in ʾAna [*sic*] I heard that there had been big stone slabs at the northern end of the island 'with figures of men upon them, and a writing like nails;' but they had fallen into the water within the memory of the older inhabitants, and had been washed away or covered by the stream. This tale of cuneiform inscriptions would not in itself be worth much; but while I was examining the minaret, a villager brought me a fragment of stone covered with carvings in relief which were unmistakably Assyrian. I asked him whence it came, and he replied that it had formed part of a big stone picture which had fallen into the river." Nothing further is known about the inscriptions, but a drawing of the fragment seen by Bell is published by Viollet (MAIB 12/2 [1913] p. 575 fig. 4). (See also Horn, ZA 34 [1922] p. 136.) It is not inconceivable that the inscriptions date to the time of Šamaš-rēša-uṣur or Ninurta-kudurrī-uṣur since these individuals left stone stelae at ʿĀnā (S.0.1001.4 and S.0.1002.9–10) or even that the inscriptions are connected in some way with the known stelae. However, they could well belong to some other governor of the region or to an Assyrian king; Ashurnasirpal II, for example, claims to have left an image of himself with an accompanying inscription in the city of Sūru, another city of the land of Sūḫu (see RIMA 2 A.0.101.1 iii 24–26). Another stone stela with a relief found at ʿĀnā is S.0.0.1007 and the famous relief of Šamaš-rēša-uṣur (S.0.1001.1) may also have originally come from that location.

1012

A fragment of a lapis lazuli cylinder found at Persepolis bears an inscription which mentions a sceptre and the land of Sūḫu and which may record a dedicatory inscription from that region. The script is Babylonian. G.G. Cameron says that it is possible that the inscription belongs to Šamaš-rēša-uṣur (see Schmidt, Persepolis 2 p. 60) and J.A. Brinkman suggests that the inscription comes from the first half of the first millennium BC and may be that of an independent ruler of the Middle Euphrates (PKB p. 184 n. 1127). It is not impossible that the text was composed in the Neo-Babylonian period.

COMMENTARY

The fragment of bluish gray (scorched) lapis lazuli was found in the Treasury at Persepolis (room 33, NE corner, floor) and given the excavation number PT4 942. (For information on the items found in the same room, see Schmidt, Persepolis 1 pp. 174–75.) The piece is found in the museum of the Oriental Institute in Chicago (A 23364) and depicted on photos P–227a (object) and P–227c (cast). The fragment measures 8.4 cm in length and 1.9 cm in diameter; it is polished and pierced lengthwise. If the object originally comes from the middle Euphrates region, it may have been taken to Babylon as booty by some Neo-Babylonian monarch, perhaps Nabopolassar (see the commentary to S.0.1001.1), and then later sent to Persepolis.

Cameron notes that "not only has the engraver carelessly fashioned certain signs, but on different occasions has written quite differently one and the same sign" (in Schmidt, Persepolis 2 p. 59). The inscription is faint and not always clear (particularly at the edges), even though it has been collated from the original, photographs, and a cast kindly supplied by R.D. Tindel of the Oriental Institute. R.D. Biggs kindly re-collated a few problem spots.

There is nothing on the piece to indicate which is the first line to be read, but the context would suggest that we begin with the line numbered 1 here (following Cameron). B. Landsberger suggested that what is preserved may be part of the second column of the inscription (acccording to Schmidt, Persepolis 2 p. 59); the name of the author would then have been at the start of the first column. It is unclear how much is missing at the beginning and end of each line; it is not impossible that only two or three words separate NUMUN-*šú*, "his seed," of line 10 and MU-*šú*, "his name," of line 11.

BIBLIOGRAPHY

1957 Schmidt, Persepolis 2 pp. 59–60 and pl. 25 no. 10 (photo, edition, study by Cameron)

TEXT

1)	[...] x MEŠ-*šú* *u* x x-⸢*šú*⸣ TA É ^{d}x ⸢*ú-na-kir*(?)⸣ [...]	1) [...] its/his [...] and its/his ... I *appropriated* from the temple of the god ... [...]
2)	[... A]LAM *šá* ^{d}15 NÁ-*ma* ⸢^{d}⸣GAŠAN [...]	2) [...] I laid [*before*] the statue of the goddess Ištar, and the Lady [...]
3)	[...] KUR *su-ḫi* MU GIŠ.NÍG.GIDRU UR$_5$-*tú* *ina* URU *ḫa-zi-i*(-)[...]	3) [...] the land of Sūḫu I named. That sceptre in the town Ḫazī [...]
4)	[...]-*šú* GIŠ.NÍG.GIDRU UR$_5$-*tú* GIŠ.ŠU x-*su* *u* BAD$_4$-*su* *ra-ma-a* x [...]	4) [...] ... with regard to that sceptre, its ... and its *base* were loose [...]
5)	[...] x x x ^{m}x-x-*su* LÚ(*).GAR.UŠ$_4$ *u* ^{m}*ab-di*-DINGIR [...]	5) [...] ..., the governor, and Abdi-ili [...]

---

1 The sign following the divine determinative is: [cuneiform sign] (collation by R.D. Biggs).
5 LÚ(*): text has ^{m}20.

6) [... *ip*]-*la-ḫu-ma* DUMU.MUNUS.MEŠ-*šú-nu ù man-da-at-tú* ⸢SUM⸣.MEŠ (x) [...]

7) [... *si*(?)-*i*]*m-mu* ⸢GAL⸣ SA$_5$ *man-nu ar-ku-ú šá* GIŠ.NÍG.GIDRU(*) UR$_5$-*tú ina* UGU [...]

8) [... Í]L-*ma ana* LUGAL KALA.GA SUM-*nu* TI.SI *liz-ku-ur* M[U ...]

9) [... *ša šumī*] ⸢*ú-pa-aš*⸣-*ši-ṭu-ma* MU-*šú* SAR ^{d}UTU ⸢^{d}⸣[...]

10) [... *ezziš*] *lik-kil-mu-šú-ma* SUḪUŠ-*su* ZI-*ḫu* NUMUN-*šú* [...]

11) [... *zikir*] MU-*šú u* NAG A.MEŠ-*šú ina* KUR *su-ḫi* ZÁḪ.M[EŠ (...)]

6) [... became af]raid and gave their daughters and tribute [*to me* ...]

7) [...] *afflicted with a serious* [*di*]*sease*. ... Anyone in the future who [...] that sceptre upon [...]

8) [... car]ries and gives (it) to a mighty king, ... may he name [...]

9) [... (But with regard to anyone) who] erases [my name] and inscribes his own name, the god Šamaš, the god [...]

10) [...] may they look upon him [angrily] and tear out his foundation! His seed [...]

11) [... the mention of] his name and one who would libate water for him may they make disappear from the land of Sūḫu! [(...)].

6 The piece has been damaged since the published photo was made. Currently all that is preserved at the end of the line is ⸢SUM⸣.M[EŠ ...].

7 GIDRU(*): the sign has two vertical wedges instead of one.

Minor Variants and Comments

Nebuchadnezzar I

B.2.4.8

Sumerian version:
3.3 Omits ì-. **8**.1 ba-an-ág for na-an-na-ke$_{4}$; ṇa-an-na-ke$_{4}$ on ex. 3. **10**.2 [...] x-uš-bi for [ba-a]b-su-uš-me. **18**.4 al-mu-un-da-ab-ba. **19**.2 al-gub-ba. **21**.4 è-ra for é-ra. **21**.4 nam-m[u-...] for nam-BAD-e-ne. **21**.2 <<⌈la⌉>> found only on this exemplar; possibly ⌈úru⌉? **23**.2 [...] x BAD AŠ before nu-mu-un-... **24**.4 [ir-r]a-a-šè. **28**.4 á-tuš for á-šu-uš.

Akkadian version:
4.3 Spacing suggests likely omission of divine determinative before MIN ([x] *š*[*ar-*...]). **6**.2 *-šu* for *-šú*. **7**.3 omits divine determinative before MIN. **8**.3 *ru-ú-qu*. **10**.3 *ù* for *u*. **11**.3 *šar mi-šá-ri re-*⌈*é*⌉-[...]. **11**.2 *ki-ni*. **12**.3 ⌈*pi*⌉-[*ir-ʾi*]. **13**.3–4 *an-gub-bu-ú*. **13**.1, 3 [...]-⌈*ú*⌉ and *reš-tu-ú* respectively. **14**.4 *u* for *ù*. **15**.3 *i-nu-šu i-na*. **15**.3–4 LUGAL and L[UGAL] for *šar-ri* respectively. **16**.3–4 [*d*]*a-mi-iq-ti* and *da-mi-iq-tu* respectively. **16**.4 *is-se-*⌈*e*⌉-[...]. **16**.3 *sad-*[*rat le-mut-tu*] or possibly *l*[*e*(?)*-mut-tu sad-rat*]. **17**.1, 3–4 [...] ⌈*e*(?)⌉*-gug-ma*, ⌈*i*⌉*-gu-ug-*(x) [...], and *i-gu-*⌈*ug*(?)⌉*-m*[*a*] respectively; *i-gug-ma* clear on ex. 2. **18**.4 *id-du-šá*. **20**.2 *gim-rat-si-im*. **21**.4 *im-lu-ú*. **21**.4 *nam-tar*. **22**.4 *ma-a-ti*. **23**.4 *e-la-mu-ú*. **24**.4 *na-mu-u$_{8}$-i*[*š* ...]. **27**.4 *ina* for *a-na*. **28**.4 *ki-gal-la*. **29**.4 *ú-ḫu-m*[*u* ...]. **30**.4 ⌈*mim*⌉*-ma* MU-*šú qa-tu*[*š-*...].

B.2.4.9

1 For the start of the line, ex. 1 has [...]-⌈e-šè⌉ and ex. 4 has [...] (x) in-šub-bé-e-ne-še; not preserved on the other two exs. **1** The copy for ex. 1 (4 R^{2} pl. 20 no. 1) has ug$_{5}$-ga-gin$_{7}$ šèg-šèg; the tablet may have sustained damage since the time the copy was prepared since all one can read now is ug$_{5}$-⌈ga⌉-x x-šèg. Ex. 4 has [...-gi]n$_{7}$(?) im-šèg. **1**.4 á-ba lal-⌈e⌉. **2**.4 *uk-ta-si-i uṣ-ṣ*[*u*(?)-...]. **3**.4 á-gùb-⌈bì⌉. **3**.4 a-⌈má⌉-ru$_{10}$-ra. **3**.4 [...]-sìg-ga bí-íb-si. **4**.4 *im-ni u šu-me-lu*. **4**.4 *u ár-ku*. **4**.4 *a-lu ṣe-e-ri u ba-ma-a-tú*. **5**.4 [...-gu]l-⌈gá-gá⌉-bi. **5**.4 omits -bi on igi-du$_{8}$-a-bi. **8**.3 x ⌈*ad*⌉*-di* at start of line. **10**.3 *šu-um-ru-ṣu-ti*. **12**.3 -a-rá for -a-ra. **13** *lu*(*): text has KU; only found on ex. 1. **20**.2 [...]*-tu$_{4}$* for *ri-šá-a-ti*. **23** CAD 10/1 [M] p. 52 reads min-na rather than a-na, but both exemplars preserving this passage clearly have a-na. **28** Ex. 1 has bí-in-d[u$_{10}$-x]; ex. 2 has bí-in-du$_{10}$(text: ZIB)-[x].

Marduk-nādin-aḫḫē

B.2.6.4

1.1 Moorey states that "Langdon incorrectly restores *ša* at beginning of inscription" (Ancient Bronzes p. 29) but collation by B. Cifola confirms Langdon's copy, which has *šá* at the beginning of the line. **2**.3 omits ŠÁR, "world." **3**.3 omits KI. **4**.3 omits URI.KI, "Akkad."

Marduk-šāpik-zēri

B.2.7.2

11 am(*): form somewhat anomalous (see King's copy). **15** ne(*): sign appears to be GIBIL. **18** *šú*(*): form anomalous (see King's copy). **23** *an*(*): omits one diagonal wedge (see King's copy).

Adad-apla-iddina

B.2.8.5

Sumerian version:
3.1 lú(*): text has NIR. **6**.2 ^{m}(*): text has AŠ. **7** Ex. 1 has [K]A-sì-s[ì, while ex. 2 has KA-sa$_{6}$-sa$_{6}$-k[e. **9**.1 kù(*): text has AD.

Akkadian version:
1.1 *mut-le-*⌈*li*⌉*-i* ⌈*e*⌉-[x x (x)] x [(x)], not *mut-le-*<*li*>*-i e-*[...] SAR of copy in StOr 1. The final sign may have been damaged since Smith copied it.

Simbar-Šipak

B.3.1.1

2.2 [NIR.G]ÁL for *e-tel*. **2**.2 *u* over erasure. **3**.2 [*gi*]-⌈*mir*⌉ for ⌈*gim*⌉*-ri*. **4**.2 *ina* for *a-na*. **26**.2 [*a*]-⌈*šá*⌉*-bi-*⌈*iš*⌉. **26**.2 ^{m}*sim-bar-ši-i-*[x (...)]. **27**.2 *a-na* SIG$_{5}$*-tim* for *ana* MUNUS.SIG$_{5}$.

Nabû-mukīn-apli

B.6.1.1

1.1, 13, and possibly 12 ^{d}AG- for ^{d}PA-. **1**.3, 8–9, 13 GI.NA for GIN. **1**.1–4 The edition of exs. 1–4 in IrAnt 2 (1962) p. 161 has DUMU.UŠ for the last element of the name, but all exemplars known appear to have A.

Marduk-zākir-šumi I

B.6.7.2

obv. 9′ *ša*(*): text has LA. **obv. 10′** *din*(*): text has two small winkelhakens instead of three. **obv. 16′** KUD(*): text has NUMUN.

Nabû-nāṣir

B.6.15.2001

5.1 *šu-uš-šu*(*): the second ŠU has an extraneous winkelhaken in front of it. **6**.2 *uš-šá-šu-un*, not *uš-šá*-BA-*un* of Stephens' YOS 9 copy. **11**.3 *u* for *ù*. **12**.3 *lìb-bi-šú*(*)-*nu*: the vertical wedge of the ŠU is obscured by the head of the horizontal wedge of NU.

Sargon II

B.6.22.1

1.16 omits *ana*. **1**.17 ⸢*a*(?)-*na*(?)⸣. **1**.16 omits -*i*. **2**.868E *re-*[*me*]-⸢*ni-i*⸣. **2**.16 *reme-nu-u*. **3**.17 *é-sag-í*[*l*(?)]. **3**.16 KÁ.DÙG.⸢KI⸣. **3**.17 ⸢KÁ.DINGIR⸣.RA.KI. **3**.10, 16, 868E EN-*šú*; ex. 17 E[N(?)-*šú*]. **3**.869A ⸢*be*⸣-*lí-šú*. **4**.10 LUGAL-⸢GIN⸣ squeezed in between lines, below -*šú* ⸢LUGAL *dan*⸣-. **5**.868D omits KI. **5–6**.7 traces after *aš-šur* and before start of line 7 unreadable; likely part omitted. **6**.17, 868D *šak*-⸢*ka-nak-ka*⸣ and ⸢*šak-ka-nak-ka*⸣ respectively. **6**.10, 16 KÁ.DINGIR.RA.KI. **7**.7, 869A ⸢EME(?).GI$_{7}$(?)⸣ and ⸢EME⸣.GI$_{7}$ respectively. **7**.4, 6, 10, 16, 17, 868 E -*ri* for -*ru*; only ex. 1 clearly has -*ru*. **7**.6 *ù*. **8**.2, 6, 7, 16, 17 -*gíl*. **9**.6, 7, 10, 16, 17 *u* for *ù*. **10**.869A ⸢*a-na*⸣. **10**.7 *e-peš*. **10**.10, 16 *e-pe-šú* (against *e*-BE-*šú* of published copy of ex. 16). **10**.17, 869A *e-pe-ši*. **10**.868C, D, E *e*-⸢*pe*⸣-x, ⸢*e*⸣-*pe*-[...], and *e*-x-x respectively. **10**.7, 10, 16, 17, 869D omit BÀD. **10**.2, 7, 16 -^{d}50. **11**.6, 10, 16, 17, 868D *ú-zu-un-šú*. **11**.6, 7, 10, 16, 868D *ib-ši-ma* for GÁL-*ma*. **11**.2, 17 [*i*]*b-ši-ma* and *ib-ši*(?)-*ma* respectively. **12**.2, 6, 17, 868D, 869D -*ri* for first -*ru*. **12**.6, 16, 17, 868D, 869D -*ri* for second -*ru*. **12**.7, 10, and likely 868C GIR$_{4}$ for *ki-ru*. **12**.17 ⸢*el*(?)-*li*(?)-*ti*(?)⸣ for KÙ-*tim*. **13**.869A *i-na*. **13**.6, 7, 16, 17, 868C–E, 869D, and possibly 10 -*ri* for -*ru*. **13**.7, 10, 16, 17, 868C–E, 869D *u* for *ù*. **13**.10, 16, 868C *it-te-e* for ESIR. **13**.17, 868D *it*(?)-*te*-⸢*e*⸣ and *it*(?)-*te-e*(?) respectively. **14**.869A *i-na*. **16**.869A *ka-a*-⸢*ru*(?)⸣. **16**.6 ⸢DÙ(?)-*ma*(?)⸣. **16**.16 *ib*-⸢*ni*/*nu*⸣-*ma*. **17**.7, 10, 16, 17, 868D–E omit BÀD. **17**.17, 868D–E -^{d}*en-líl*; ex. 3 ^{d}*en-l*[*íl*]. **18**.6 omits *ù*. **18**.7, 10, 16, 868D–E, 869A *u* for *ù*. **18**.7, 10, 16, 17, 868D–E omit BÀD. **18**.7, 10, 17, 868D–E *né-met-ti*-. **18**.16 *né-met-tú*. **18**.17, 868D–E -^{d}*en-líl*. **19**.7, 10, 868E and likely 17 GIM for *ki-ma*. **21**.5 -*ši* for -*šú*. **21**.16 -*u* for -*ú* (-*u* omitted on published copy, but present). **21**.7, 868E omit -*ú*. **22**.7, 10, 16, 868C, 868E IGI.BAR-*ma*. **22**.6, 10, 16, 868C–E, 869A *ana*. **22**.5 -*ú-kin* for -GIN. **23**.5, 16 *ba-la-ṭu* for TIN. **23**.17, 868D *ba-la-ṭi* for TIN. **23**.868E ⸢TI⸣.LA for TIN. **24**.7, 10, 868E GIM for *ki-ma*. **24**.10 KÁ.DIŠ.KI. **24**.16, 868D URU.DÙG.K[I] and URU.⸢DÙG⸣.KI respectively. **24**.17 [KÁ.DI]NGIR.RA.KI. **25**.10 GIN-*un*. **25**.17, 868D ME for MEŠ.

Bēl-ibni

B.6.26.1

9′ *šaḫ*(*): text has SIK. **14′** ^{m}*ta-ri-bi* written over an erasure. **27′** *ḫa*(*): text has KUD. **32′** *ma*(*): text has LU.

Esarhaddon

B.6.31.9

3.1 and possibly 2 PAP for ŠEŠ. **3**.1 -AŠ for -MU. **4**.1 and possibly 2 omit -ke$_{4}$. **7**.1 KÁ.DIŠ.DIŠ for TIN.TIR.KI. **9**.1 nam-ti-la-bi-šè.

B.6.31.11

1.3 *šá-ru-uḫ-tú*. **1**.3 DINGIR.ME. **2**.8 *š*[*a*] for *šá*. **2**.7 ⸢*ù*⸣ or *u*. **3**.3 *a-ši*(text: ME)-*bat é-bára-*<*dúr*>-*gar-ra*. **4**.8 ^{m}AN.ŠÁR-PAP-AŠ. **4**.8, 15 KÁ.[DINGIR.RA.KI] and KÁ.⸢DINGIR⸣.[RA.KI] for TIN.TIR.KI respectively. **5**.5, 8 DINGIR.ME GAL.ME. **5**.15 [E]N.ME-*šú*. **5**.9–10 *it-tak-lu-ma*. **5**.15 [...-*ša*]*k-ši-du-šú*. **6**.10 [... DINGI]R(?)-*ú-ti-šú-nu*; possibly insufficient room to restore [*a-na nu-uḫ-ḫu lìb-bi* DINGI]R-. **7**.15 ^{d}50 for ^{d}*en-líl*. **7**.3 despite copy in JCS 17, third ^{d}EN seems all right. **7**.10 DINGIR.ME. **7**.9 despite copy in JCS 17, *ma-li-ku*, not ŠU-*li-ku*. **7**.15 *ma-li-ki*. **7**.1 despite copy in JCS 17, original has -*ni*- not -DÙ- in second last word. **7**.10 *ú-šak-ni-šú*. **8**.15 KÁ.D[INGIR.RA.KI] for TIN.TIR.KI. **8**.15 *ma-ḫa-zi*. **9**.15 GAL-*u*. **9**.15 *a-na* KÁ.DINGIR.RA.KI *sa-li-me*. **9**.15 *ir-mu-u*. **10**.4, 9, 15 *a-na* (exs. 1, 9) and [*a-n*]*a* (ex. 15) for *ana*. **10**.5 ⸢*ú*⸣-*še-rib-ú-ma*. **11**.2 [*ul-t*]*u*, not [*ul-t*]*u*$_{4}$ of JCS 17 copy. **11**.11 *ú-kin*(?)-*nu*; the copy in JAOS 70 appears to have an extraneous winkelhaken at the beginning of the sign. **12**.3 *it-pe-šu*, not *it-pa-šu* of copy in JCS 17. **12**.15 *ša* for *šá*. **12**.11 *i-na* for *ina*. **13**.11 *ù* for *u*. **13**.14 ⸢URI.KI⸣-<*i*>. **14**.2 -⸢DÙ⸣ for -*ba-ni*. **14**.13 -*ba-na* for -*ba-ni*. **15**.1, 5, 14 *ma-ḫar* for *maḫ-ri*. **16**.4 *áš-te-*<ʾ>*-e*. **16**.11 [*a*]*s*(*)-*suḫ*(*): copy has] *ma-ḫa-su*. **16**.11, 14 *ki-ma* for GIM. **16**.2, 4 *la-bi-ra-a-tú*. **16**.13 GIM for *ki-ma*. **16**.2 *re-ši-i-šú*. **16**.12–13 *re-ši-i-ši*. **16**.5, 14 *ul-lu*. **17**.12 SIG$_{5}$-*tì-ia*, not SIG$_{5}$-*ti-ia* of copy in JAOS 70. **17**.2, 4 TIN.ME. **17**.2 UD.ME SÙ.ME. **17**.12–13 *lit-tu-tu*. **17**.12 DÙG-*ub* UZU *u* not ZIB -*ub* GAB TI of copy in JAOS 70. **17**.5 *ši-mat*. **17**.12, 14 *ši-ma-ti*. **18**.2, 3, 13 *ina* for *i-na* (second occurrence). **18**.12 UD.MEŠ for *u*$_{4}$*-me*. **18**.13 omits *u*$_{4}$*-me*. **19**.8 MU.SAR-*u*. **19**.1 <UD>.MEŠ. **19**.13 <BAL>-*q*[*í* ...]. **19**.12 *ina* omitted on copy in JAOS 70 but present on exemplar. **20**.8 *ša* MU.SAR-*u*. **20**.6 copy in JCS 17 has SAL-*ṭir* for *ši-ṭir*, but cast suggests a form closer to *ši* than SAL. **20**.2 *ib-ba*-⸢*tu*⸣, not *ib*-ŠU-⸢*tu*⸣ of JCS 17 copy. **20**.3 *lu-u*. **21**.6 *i-na* for *ina*. **21**.7 omits *ina*.

B.6.31.14

1.2 ^{d}*en-líl* EN for ^{d}50 ^{d}EN. **1**.1 erasure between ^{d}50 and ^{d}EN. **1**.1 RE written over an erasure. **2**.2 omits masculine determinative. **2**.2 -PAP-MU for -ŠEŠ-AŠ. **2**.2 LU[GAL KU]R for MAN KUR. **3**.2 LUGAL for MAN on both occurrences. **4**.2 URI.KI.<<KI>>. **4**.2 *pú-*<*kù*>*-dadag-ga*. **6**.2 *ú-rab-ba*(*): the final sign appears to have four horizontal wedges.

B.6.31.15

1.3 *šur-bu*-⸢*tu*⸣. **1**.3 *šá-ru-uḫ-tu*. **2**.4 ^{d}*a-nu-ú-tu*. **2**.7 -*ti* for -*tu* (Luckenbill-Borger). **4**.3 *ru-um-tu* (against *ru-um-ti* of copy [BIN 2 no. 28]). **4**.7 *ana* for *a-na* (Luckenbill-Borger). **8**.3 *kiš-šat* for ŠÚ. **8**.3 ⸢*kib*⸣*-ra-a-ti er-bit-ti*. **8**.3 *u* for *ù*. **8**.3–4 *ak-ka-di-i* and *ak*-⸢*ka*(?)-*ad*(?)⸣ respectively for URI.KI. **10**.7 *ana* for *a-na* (Luckenbill-Borger). **10**.7 ^{d}IDIM for ^{d}*é-a* (Luckenbill-Borger). **10**.3 inserts an *u* after ^{d}AG. **10**.5 omits *u*. **10**.3, 5 ^{d}*iš-tar* for ^{d}15. **11**.3, 5 DINGIR.MEŠ GAL.MEŠ. **11**.5 EN.MEŠ-*šú*. **11**.4 *ú-šak-šid-uš*. **12**.3, 5 -*ḫi for -ḫu*. **12**.5 *ù* for *u*. **12**.3–4 -*šú* for -*uš*. **12**.4 *da-ru-u*. **13**.3–4 *e-li-šú* for UGU-*šú*. **14**.3, 5 DINGIR.MEŠ. **14**.4 *i-bé-lu-ma*. **15**.3, 5 *ú-šak-ni-šú*. **15**.3–5 *še-pu-uš-šú*. **16**.3 *ba-a-nu-ú*. **17**.7 adds -*nu* to end of *mu-kin* (Luckenbill-Borger). **17**.3 -*ka* for -*ku*. **17**.7 -*šin* for -*ku* (Luckenbill-Borger). **18**.3 ⸢*u*$_{4}$⸣-*mu*. **18**.3 *ana* for *a-na*. **18**.3 *ir*-⸢*šu*⸣-*ú sa-li-mu*. **20**.3 *a-na* for *ana*. **20**.3, 5 *u* for *ù*. **21**.4 *pa-rak-ku*. **21**.5–7 omit -*ka* (for ex. 7: Luckenbill-Borger). **21**.4 *da-ra-a-tu*. **21**.5 *da-ra-a-a*(?)-*t*[*i*]. **22**.1 ⸢*a*⸣-<*na*>. **22**.7 *ana* for *a-na* (Luckenbill-Borger). **22**.7 omits -*ma* of *ud-diš-ma* (Luckenbill-Borger). **23**.3, 5 *a-na* and [*a*]-*na* respectively for *ana*. **23**.5 *áš-ri-šu-nu*. **23**.5 *ú-tir-šu-nu-ti-ma*. **23**.3 *ú-kin-nu*. **24**.3 *it-pe-šú ḫa-a-sis*. **24**.3, 5 *ši-pir* and *ši*(?)-*pir* respectively. **26**.3 omits KI at end of line. **27**.3 KUR *šu-me-ri*. **27**.7 *ak-ka-di-i* for URI.KI (Luckenbill-Borger). **28**.3 ^{md}EN-*ba-ni*. **28**.4 ⸢A⸣ for DUMU. **29**.7 -*ti* for -*tu* of LUGAL-*ú-tu* (Luckenbill-Borger). **30**.3 *i-nu-šú* for *i-nu-ma*; ex. 7 has -*šu* for the -*ma* (Luckenbill-Borger). **30**.1 *a-n*[*u*(?)]-⸢*ú*⸣-*tu*; the second sign is damaged, but seems more likely to be *nu* than *nù*. *nu* clear on ex. 3. **31**.7 -*ri-iš* for -*riš* (Luckenbill-Borger). **32**.1 *ṣab*(*): text has UD. **34**.3 BIN 2 no. 28 copy has ^{d}5, but the piece actually has ^{d}15. **34**.3 *šu-a-ti*. **35**.3 UGU for *muḫ-ḫi*. **36**.3 *u*$_{4}$-*mu* for first UD.MEŠ. **36**.3–4 *u*$_{4}$-*me* and [*u*$_{4}$-*m*]*e* respectively for second

UD.MEŠ. **36**.7 u_4*-mu* for second UD.MEŠ (Luckenbill-Borger). **36**.3–4 *šu-a-ti*. **37**.1 *qit*(*): text has TA. **39**.3 *ur-ra-ak*. **39**.4 [UD].ME for UD.MEŠ. **41**.4 ^{d}15 for ^{d}*iš-tar* (Stephens). **41**.4 *lik-kil-me-šu-ma* (Stephens).

B.6.31.16

1.3 ⸢*ù*⸣ for *u*. 2.1 ^{d}*a-nù-u-tú*, not ^{d}*a-nù-tú* of YOS 1 copy. 2.3 ^{d}*a-nù-ú-ti*. 3.2 [...*-l*]*a*-⸢*a-ti šá*⸣. 3.2 *u* for *ù*. 4.2 [(*u*) M]È(?) for *ù ta-ḫa-zi*. 4.2 *a-li-kát*. 4.2 *mu-ra-a*[*s-*...]. 5.2 *šá* for *ša*. 6.2 -MU for -SUM.NA. 6.2 LUGAL for MAN on all three occasions. 6.2 KUR.EME.(x) [...] for KUR *šu-me-ri*. 7.2 *-ú* for *-u*. 7.2 *pa-a-liḫ*. 8.2 *-ú* for *-u*. 8.2 *u* ⸢KÁ⸣.DIŠ.DIŠ.KI *za-a-ni*[*n*] for *ù* KÁ.DINGIR.RA.KI *za-nin*. 9.2 K[I.ŠU.PEŠ$_5$] *šá ina qer-bi-ši-na* for *ma-ḫa-zi ša ina qé-reb-ši-na*. 10.2 -ŠEŠ.MEŠ- for -PAP.MEŠ-. 10.2 LUGAL for MAN on all five occasions. 11.2 *šá* for *ša*. 12.2 *šá* LUGAL for *ša* MAN. 13.2 *áš-te-ʾ-i*. 22.3 [*šu-m*]*i*(?) for *šu-mì*. 23.2 -⸢*ú-a*⸣ for *-u-a*. 23.2, 3 [...]-⸢*tu*⸣ [*l*]*u-ú* and ⸢*ib*⸣*-ba-*⸢*tu*⸣ *lu-ú* respectively.

B.6.31.17

1.3 *pu-su-um-tú*. 1.2 *i-la-a-te ša ku-uz-bu ù ul-ṣu za-ʾ-na-at*. 1.2 *ma-la-ti*. 2.2 *ša* for *šá*. 2.2 *be-le-e-te šur-ba-at*. 3.2 *sek-ra-at*. 3.2 *na-ra-mat ru-bu-ti-*⸢*šú*⸣. 4.2 *-ti* for *-tu*$_4$. 4.2 *-kàt* for *-kát*. 4.1 *pa-e-le-šú*. 5.2 *ša* for *šá*. 5.2 GAL*-ti*. 6.2 MAN for LUGAL on all three occasions. 6.2 KUR *šu-me-ri*. 7.2 *-u* for *-ú*. 7.2 *pa-liḫ*. 8.2 *ba-nu-u*. 8.2 *ù* for *u*. 8.2 *za-nin*. 9.2 *-e-te* for *-e-ti*. 9.1 *ma-ḫa*(Text: ZA)*-zi*. 9.2 *ša* for *šá*. 9.2 *qé-reb-ši-na iš-tak-ka-nu*. 9.1 *qer-bi-ši-*<*na*>. 10.2 -PAP.MEŠ- for -ŠEŠ.MEŠ-. 10.2 MAN for LUGAL on all five occasions. 10.2 KÁ.DIŠ.DIŠ.KI for KÁ.DINGIR.RA.KI. 10.2 KUR *šu-me-ri u* URI.KI. 11.2 *ša* for *šá*. 12.2 *ša* MAN. 12.3 *ma-ḫar* for *maḫ-ri*. 13.2 omits *-i*. 13.2 *a-gur-ri* for SIG$_4$.AL.ÙR.RA. 13.2 *ak-še-er*. 14.2 GAL*-ti*. 14.2 *qé-reb-šú*. 14.2 omits *-ma*. 14.2 *da-ra-a-te*. 15.2 *si-ga-ar-šá*. 16.2 *ṣir-ti*. 16.2 *a-šá-bi-ki*. 17.3 -MU for -SUM.NA. 17.2 ^{d}PA for ^{d}AG. 17.2 omits *-i-*. 17.2 *da mi iq ti* for *ba ni-ti*. 18.2 TI.LA. 18.2 *ṭu-ub*. 18.1 UZU(*): text has AM-TI. 18.2 *ù* for *u*. 18.2 *ši-i-me*. 19.2 LUGAL*-ti-ia*. 20.2 u_4*-me*. 20.2 EGIR*-u ša*. 21.2–3 *šu-mì* and MU respectively. 21.2–3 *šu-mì-šú* and MU*-šú* respectively. 21.2 *-ru-u* for *-ru-ú*. 22.2 *i-šem-mu*(*-*)*u ša šu-mì* for *i-šem-mu-ú u šá šu-mi*. 23.2 *-u-a* for *-ú-a*. 23.2 *i-ab-bat*. 24.2 *ag-gi-iš*. 24.2 *-šu-ma* for *-šú-ma*. 24.2 *-tú* for *-tim*. 25.2 *ir-ši-šú*.

Ashurbanipal

B.6.32.1

1.2 MAN for LUGAL. 2.1 ib(*): form anomalous or over erasure. 2.2, 15 TIN.TIR.KI. 2.6, 16 *ra-bi-*[...] and *ra-bi-*⸢*ti*⸣ respectively. 2.8 EN*-ia* for *be-li-ia*. 3.10, 14, 17 *-ba-ni-* for DÙ-. 3.5, 10, 14, 17 IBILA for A. 3.2, 5–6, 8–11, 14–17, 19 MAN for LUGAL on all occurrences preserved; only exs. 1 and 7 have LUGAL. 3.2, 5–6, 8–11, 14–15, 17, 19 ŠÚ for ŠÁR; only ex. 1 has ŠÁR. 3.8, 19 *kib-ra-ti*. 3.9, 17 *kib-ra-a-ti*. 3.11 *kib-*⸢*ra*⸣-[...]. 4.2, 5–6, 8–11, 14–15, 17, 19 MAN for LUGAL on all occurrences preserved; only exs. 1 and 7 have LUGAL. 4.2, 5–6, 8–11, 14–15, 17, 19 ŠÚ for ŠÁR; only ex. 1 has ŠÁR. 4.5 KÁ.DINGIR.RA.KI. 5.2, 5, 9–11, 17, 19 MAN for LUGAL; only 1, 7–8 have LUGAL. 5.2, 8–9, 11, 15 KUR *šu-me-ri* for KUR.EME.GI$_7$; ex. 10 has ÉME.RI. 5.2, 8–10, 15, 17 TIN.TIR.KI. 5.10 *íl*(*): text has a form which appears to be a mixture of IL and ÍL. 6.2 *eš-re-e-te*. 6.5–11, 17 *ša*. 6.2, 5–6, 17 *ina*. 7.2, 5–8, 11, 14 *si-ma-a-te*. 7.2 *u*. 7.2 *baṭ-lu-te*. 7.8–11, 17, 19 *baṭ-lu-tú*. 7.2 *ú-kin-*[*nu*]. 7.15 Possibly insufficient room to restore all of this line. 8.2, 5–6, 8–9, 11, 14 *-rim-* for *-ri-im-*. 8.2, 10 *-šú-*[*un*] and *-šú-un* for *-šu-un* respectively. 9.17 SU(*): copy has ŠA (not visible on photograph). 9.2, 5, 8–11, 14–15, 17 MAN for LUGAL on all occurrences preserved; only exs. 1 and 6–7 have LUGAL. 9.2, 5, 8–11, 17 ŠÚ for ŠÁR; only ex. 1 and 6–7 have ŠÁR. 10.2, 5, 8, 11 *-te* for *-ti*. 10.6 [K]Á.DINGIR.RA.KI. 11.10, 17 *ša* for *šá*. 11.2, 5, 8–9, 11 *-te* for *-ti*. 11.2 *sat-tuk-ku*. 12.7, 10, 17 KÁ.DINGIR.RA.KI on both occurrences. 12.5 KÁ.DINGIR.RA.KI on first occurrence only. 12.2, 5–8, 10–11 *ú-kin*; ex. 9 has *ú-k*[*in*]; only exs. 1 and 17 have *ú-ki-in*. 12.2 *ki-din-ú-te*. 12.6 K[Á].DINGIR.RA.KI on second occurrence (first occurrence not preserved). 13.2 omits masculine determinative. 14.2 *-te* for *-tu*. 14.2, 9 TIN.TIR.KI; ex. 8 has [TI]N.⸢TIR⸣.KI; ex. 11 has TIN.[T]IR.KI. 14.1 *ap-qí-di*. 14.2 *u* for *ù*. 14.2, 5–11, 17 *ina* for *i-na*; only ex. 1 has *i-na*. 15.2 *-tú* for *-ti*. 15.2, 9, 11 *-nun-* for *-nu-un-*; ex. 8 has *-n*]*un-*. 16.11 <*ú*>*-nam-mir*. 17.2, 8–11, 17 TIN.TIR.KI. 17.5, 8–9 *-u-* for *-ú-*. 18.5, 7 *šá* for *ša*. 18.2, 7, 11 *-u-* for *-ú-*. 18.9 [*in-n*]*ab-*⸢*tu*⸣. 19.2, 5–8, 10, 17 EN.NUN; only exs. 1 and 9 have *ma-aṣ-ṣar-ti*. 19.2 *u* for *ù*. 19.2, 8, 11 *-e-te* for *-e-ti*. 19.7–8, 10–11 TIN.TIR.KI. 20.9 *dun-nu-n*[*u*]. 20.9 *i-na*. 20.2, 9, 17 *e-mu-qu*. 20.2, 8, 9 omit *-a-*. 20.11 *-iá* for *-ia*. 21.9 *-u-šú* for *-ú-šú*. 21.9 *i-na* for *ina*. 21.5, 10, 17 *ú-rak-ki-si*. 22.8–9, 11 *i-na* for *ina*. 23.2, 5, 9–10, 17 EGIR*-ú*; ex. 7 [EGI]R-⸢*ú*⸣; only exs. 1 and 8 have *ar-ku-ú*. 23.7–9, 11 *ša* for *šá*. 23.8–9, 11 *i-na* for *ina*. 23.5, 7–8, 11 omit *-e-*. 23.3, 10 *šu-a-tú*(?) and *šú-a-ti* respectively. 23.5–7, 10, 17 LÚ *um-ma-a-ni*; ex. 3 ⸢*um*⸣*-ma-a-ni*. 23.8–9 *-tú* and *-t*[*ú*] for *-tu* respectively; ex. 1 *-t*[*u*]/*t*[*ú*]/*t*[*e*]. 24.3, 8–9, 11, 17 *-u* for *-ú*; ex. 10 has -⸢*šú*⸣ for *-ú*. 25.10 *-šu-nu* for *-šú-nu*. 25.17 *-ú-a* for *-u-a*. 27.5, 7–11, 16–17 *ù* for *u*; only ex. 1 has *u*. 27.10, 17, 19 *ta-li-mi-* for *ta-lim-*. 28.6 *i-ab-ba-tu*. 28.17 *-ú-a* for *-u-a*. 29.2, 3, 5–6, 8–10, 15, 17 *gim-* for *gi-im-*; only exs. 1 and 11 have *gi-im-*. 29.11 *ag-gi-iš*. 30.5, 8–10, 17, 19 *ina* for *i-na*. 30.11 *ma-ta-a-ti* for KUR.KUR. 30.1 *li-ḫal-li-qi*.

B.6.32.4

10.2 *-tú* for *-tu*. 11.1 omits -MU; other exemplars not preserved at this point. 15.2 IGI.[BAR*-ma*] for *lip-pal-lis-ma*. 19.1 omits -MU; other exemplars not preserved at this point. 22.3 *i-ab-bat lu* for *i-ab-ba-tu lu-u*.

B.6.32.5

1.2 -IBILA for -A. 10.2 *ú-ki-in ki-di*[*n-*...]. 20.2 *-ia* for *-iá*.

B.6.32.12

1.7 -IBILA for -A. 12.2 *-tu* for *-tú*. 14.2, 4 *u* for *ù*. 14.4 *-te* for *-ti*. 15.4 UGU for *e-li*. 18.4 DÙ*-ma* for *ú-še-piš-ma*. 19.4 [...]-⸢*a*⸣*-te* for *dam-qa-a-ti*. 19.4 IGI.BAR*-ma* for *lip-p*[*a-lis*]*-ma*. 25.3 ⸢*lip-šú-uš*⸣. 26.3 *ta-li-*<*mi*>*-ia*. 27.7 *-u-a* for *-ú-a*. 28.7 *e-la-a-ti*. 29.7 *i-n*[*a* ...].

B.6.32.13

19.2 *il-lik-u-m*[*a*]. 20.2 [...]*-ti* for *ù eš-re-e-te*. 24.2 [...*-r*]*a-ti* for *la-bi-ra-a-te*.

B.6.32.15

10.1 KUR.EME.<<UR>>.GI$_7$; ex. 2 not preserved at this point. 10.2 *ù* for *u* (second occasion; first occasion not preserved). 12.2 UD.MEŠ for u_4*-me-šú*.

B.6.32.19

1.2 Although none of the writings of the divine name in this exemplar (lines 2, 24, 30, and 32) is entirely clear, the sign ^{d}INANNA appears to be written with the ligature: AŠ+MÙŠ rather than AN+MÙŠ (information D.A. Foxvog). 4.2 *bat*(*): text has MU. 7.2 -IBILA for -A. 9.2 *e-li-ti*. 10.1 *ba*(*): text has ŠU. 12.2 MEŠ(*): anomalous form. 14.2 KÁ.DI[NGIR.RA.KI] for TIN.TIR.KI (second occurrence only). 15.2 *eš-re-e-ti*. 23.2 *il-lik-ú-ma*. 25.3 *lip-pa-l*[*i*(?)-...]. 27.2–3 TIN.TIR.KI and TIN.TIR respectively. 29.2–3 *-ú-a* for *-u-a*. 31.3 *lu-ú*.

B.6.32.22

1.1–2 *-nu*(*): texts have PAP. **1**.2 *šur-*⸢*bu*⸣*-ú* ⸢*kaš*⸣*-*[*kaš* (DINGIR.MEŠ)] for *kaš-kaš* DINGIR.MEŠ *šur-bu-ú gít-ma-la*. **2**.2 Omits *mut-tal-la e-tel-lu* ŠEŠ-*šú*. **3**.2 -A for -IBILA.

2.1–2 *ḫúl*(*): copies have **3**.1–2 *-nu*(*): texts have PAP. **4**.1–2 *-nu*(*): texts have PAP. **6**.1–2 *-nu*(*): texts have PAP.

8.2 *ina* for *i-na*. **8**.1–2 KÙ(*): copies have **9** *ḫúl*(*): as in line 2. **10**.2 *ki-ma* <<*ki-ma*>>.

B.6.32.2015

1.4 *ṣir-ta*. **1**.5, 8 *ṣir-tú*. **3**.4–5, 7–8 DINGIR.ME. **3**.5, 7–8 GAL.ME. **3**.2 GAL.MEŠ-*te*. **4**.2, 6 *a-na*. **5**.4 *kiš-šá-ti*. **7**.2, 8 -SUM.NA for -MU. **9**.5–8 *-ma* for *-mu*. **12**.2 *nag-bu*. **12**.2, 6–7 *da-ru-tu*. **15**.2 UD.MEŠ-*šú*. **15**.6 u_4*-mi-šú*. **16**.2, 6 *liš-ta-an-di-il*.

Šamaš-šuma-ukīn

B.6.33.1

12 ma(*): the sign has two vertical wedges at the end rather than one. **24** bi(*): text has TA. **26** ga(*): there is a vertical wedge at the end of the sign.

Aššur-etil-ilāni

B.6.35.2

6 *-ti* written over an erasure. **10** KÙ written over an erasure. **14** *su*(*): text has ŠU. **15** *ina*, *-reb*, and *é* written over erasures. **16** *šá*, KU_4, and MEŠ *šú-a-te* written over erasures.

B.6.35.3

6 MU(*): the form of the sign is different from that of the MU in line 2 and may be an attempt to present the archaic form of the sign. **6** ME(*): copy has DIŠ. On the brick, one can see a trace of a horizontal line passing through the middle of the sign, but this appears to be a continuation of the final wedge of the preceding sign rather than a new horizontal wedge.

B.6.35.4

6 KI(*): the sign has no horizontal wedges and is somewhat similar to the A in lines 6 and 11. **7** ús(*): text has DÙ.

B.6.35.5

1.2 A ^{m}*da-ku-*<*ru šá*>. **2**.3 ⸢É-^{m}*da-ku-ri*⸣. **3**.1 *qé-reb* É(Text: RIB)-<*šú*> *šá*, not *qé-reb* <É-*šú*> *šá* of YOS 1 copy. **10** For the end of the line, ex. 1 has ⸢*lik*⸣*-r*[*u*(?)-x] and ex. 3 has *lik-*⸢*ru*(?)*-bu*(?)⸣.

Ex. 1: Ex. 3: This passage is not preserved on ex. 2. **14**.3 *ú-nak-ka-ru-ma*.

Šamaš-rēša-uṣur

S.0.1001.1

ii 30' *ad*(*): copy has ṢI. **ii 40'** *niš*(*): text has EŠ. **iv 11** SAG(*): copy has U+SAG.

S.0.1001.2

obv. 1 MU(*): Bagh. Mitt. 21 transliteration has MU on both occurrences, but the copy has only two small slanted wedges at the very end of the sign, not three. The sign is, however, distinct from the NUMUN as copied in the following line. **obv. 6** Bagh. Mitt. 21 transliteration indicates that there is part of a sign before *ma-ti-šú*. **obv. 9** *ṭa*(*): copy has ŠA, while Bagh. Mitt. 21 transliteration has *ṭa*. **obv. 13** *ṭa*(*): copy has ŠA, while Bagh. Mitt. 21 transliteration has *ṭa*. **obv. 14** According to Bagh. Mitt. 21 (1990) p. 366, the first sign could be *m*]*a* rather than *r*]*a*; the copy would suggest] RA(?). **obv. 22** Copy has LA I, while Bagh. Mitt. 21 transliteration has ⸢LA⸣ *i*?; ⸢LA(?) I(?)⸣ from information supplied by A. Cavigneaux. *a*(*): copy has MIN, while Bagh. Mitt. 21 transliteration has *a*. **obv. 23** Copy has] x AŠ, but I am informed that the passage is damaged. **obv. 24** Transliteration follows copy; Bagh. Mitt. 21 transliteration has] ⸢x⸣*-ti*?*-ia al-si*?*-ma*. **rev. 2´** *ár*(*): Bagh. Mitt. 21 transliteration has *ár*, while the copy omits the lower horizontal wedge of the sign. **rev. 3´** *su*(*): Bagh. Mitt. 21 transliteration has *su*, while the copy has IS. **rev. 4´** IGI(*) and *su*(*): copy has U-DIŠ and *sú* respectively, while Bagh. Mitt. 21 transliteration has IGI and *su*; *sú* does not occur elsewhere in these royal inscriptions from the middle Euphrates.

S.0.1001.4

Side A 4 *šu*(*): copy has *su*, while Bagh. Mitt. 21 transliteration has *šu*. **5** Bagh. Mitt. 21 transliteration indicates that the first sign, *i-*, is not preserved. **7** Bagh. Mitt. 21 transliteration indicates that the *-ti* of *ha-bu-bé-e-ti* is fully preserved. **8** Bagh. Mitt. 21 transliteration has [x] ⸢x⸣ *ma* ⸢x⸣ [...].

Ninurta-kudurrī-uṣur

S.0.1002.1

3 ^{m}(*): the personal determinative is not shown on the copy of ex. 1, but is given in Bagh. Mitt. 21 transliteration; ex. 2 is not preserved at this point. **4**.2 ^{d}*mi-ša*[*r*(?)*-rum* ...]; Bagh. Mitt. 21 transliteration has ^{d}*mi-ša*[*r* ...], but copy would suggest ^{d}*mi-š*[*a-rum* ...] also possible (cf. copy of ŠA in line 7). **9**.2 Trace of sign after personal determinative preserved; copy suggests LÁ [...] for ^{m}x [...] of Bagh. Mitt. 21 transliteration. **12**.1 ^{m}⸢*é*(*)⸣-[...]: copy suggests ^{m}AŠ [...], while Bagh. Mitt. 21 transliteration indicates ^{m}⸢*é*⸣-[...]; not preserved on ex. 2. **21**.2 *pa-ni-šú-nu*. **22**.2 *u*[*b*(*): copy has AŠ [...], while Bagh. Mitt. 21 transliteration has *u*[*b-*. **22**.1 Bagh. Mitt. 21 transliteration does not note the presence of the extraneous KUR after *il-li-ku-ma*, which is found on the copy. Possibly an error of the modern copyist based upon following line where KUR does follow MA? Passage not preserved on ex. 2. **32**.1 *zu*(*): copy has SU, while Bagh. Mitt. 21 transliteration has *zu*; sign not preserved on ex. 2. **33**.1 *b*[*i*(*): copy has AŠ [...], while Bagh. Mitt. 21 transliteration has *b*[*i*. **37**.2 *gul-gul-la*(*)*-ti-šú-nu*; *la*(*): copy has QA(?), while Bagh. Mitt. 21 transliteration has *la*. **38**.2 *a*[*p*(*): copy suggests AŠ [...], while Bagh. Mitt. 21 transliteration has -[*ap-* ...]. **38**.2 *un-dáš-šìr*(*)*-šú-nu-ti*; copy omits one wedge of *šìr*. **39**.1 *du*(*): copy omits one wedge; sign not preserved on ex. 2. **40**.1 NIMGIR(*): copy indicates anomalous form. **40**.1 *su*(*): copy has GÁN(?), while Bagh. Mitt. 21 transliteration has *su*. **40**.2 *ù* for *u*. **42**.2 Copy has *i-du-ku-ma* <*ma*>*-lu-ú-a*, while Bagh. Mitt. 21 transliteration has *i-du-ku-ma ma-lu-ú-a*. **43**.2 AD.MEŠ-*ú-a*. **43**.2 *t*[*ir*$_x$(*): copy has AŠ [...], while Bagh. Mitt. 21 transliteration has *t*[*ir*$_x$. **45**.2 *e*(copy: KAL)*-mu-q*[*í-*...]. **45**.2 *ù* for *u* (second occurrence; first occurrence not preserved). **46**.2 The copy indicates that there is a gap for about one line before *šá* E_{11}*-ma* (which starts a new line in this exemplar). **48**.2 Bagh. Mitt. 21 transliteration has *u* K[UR, but the copy does not have any trace of a sign after *u*. **49**.1 [... *an-ni-t*]u_4.

S.0.1002.2

i 4 *am*(*): copy indicates that the lower horizontal wedge is missing. *diš*(*): copy suggests ŠÚ, while Bagh. Mitt. 21 transliteration has *diš*. **i 5** *in*(*): copy indicates I(?), while Bagh. Mitt. 21 transliteration has *in*. **i 21** *ra*(*): copy has UM, while Bagh. Mitt. 21 transliteration has *ra*. **i 26** *ṣab*(*): copy and Bagh. Mitt. 21 transliteration have IṢ. **ii 1** *ṣi*(*), UGU(*), and *un*(*): copy indicates that each sign is missing one horizontal wedge. **ii 4** The copy suggests *a-a-*TAB for the end of the line, while Bagh. Mitt. 21 transliteration has *a-a-u*[*m-ma*]. **ii 9** *šir*(*): copy indicates sign missing one horizontal wedge. **ii 10** *ri*(*): copy and Bagh. Mitt. 21 transliteration indicate ḪU. UGU(*): copy indicates that one horizontal wedge is missing. **ii 11** *su*(*): copy indicates form anomalous. **ii 12** *u*(*): sign not present on copy, but found in Bagh. Mitt. 21 transliteration. **ii 17** *ú*(*): copy indicates form anomalous and Bagh. Mitt. 21 transliteration has *ú*$^!$. **ii 21** *et*(*): copy indicates form anomalous. **ii 24** *ṣu*(*): copy indicates form closer to GU than ṢU. **ii 31** *di*(*): copy has KI, while Bagh. Mitt. 21 transliteration has *di*. Bagh. Mitt. 21 transliteration indicates *an-ni-ti* x [...] x x x for the end of the line. **iii 1´** The copy does not indicate any trace(s) for this line, but the transliteration has "..." **iii 4´** *ul*(*): copy indicates form anomalous. **iii 7´** Bagh. Mitt. 21 transliteration has *il-l*[*a-k*]*u*, while copy indicates *il-l*[*a-ku*]. **iii 8´** According to Cavigneaux, there is an erased sign, (x), at the end of line. **iii 9´** *še*(*): copy has only three wedges instead of four. **iii 16´** DÙ(*): copy has NI, while Bagh. Mitt. 21 transliteration has DÙ. **iii 19´** E$_{11}$(*): copy has RIM-DU, while Bagh. Mitt. 21 transliteration has E$_{11}$. **iii 20´** *kìr*(*): copy has GIŠ, while Bagh. Mitt. 21 transliteration has *kìr*. **iii 26´** *b*[*u*(*)]: copy has ŠE, while Bagh. Mitt. 21 transliteration has *b*[*u*]. **iv 1´** Bagh. Mitt. 21 transliteration indicates for this line NIM(?) x [...]. **iv 7´** *lam*(*): copy indicates the sign is missing a winkelhaken, while Bagh. Mitt. 21 transliteration has *lam*. **iv 8´** *ia*(*): copy and Bagh. Mitt. 21 transliteration have MA. **iv 10´** *ra*(*): copy suggests UM(?), while Bagh. Mitt. 21 transliteration has *ra*. **iv 12´** 60(*)-*šu*(*) 4: copy suggests ŠÚ-GIŠ 4, while Bagh. Mitt. 21 transliteration has 64. **iv 29´** *ḫi*(*): copy suggests ḪI-U, while Bagh. Mitt. 21 copy simply has *ḫi*. *ma*(*): copy indicates omission of final vertical wedge; the reading was suggested by W.G. Lambert. **iv 31´** *nu*(*): sign not present on copy but given in Bagh. Mitt. 21 transliteration. **iv 34´** Bagh. Mitt. 21 transliteration erroneously omits one A sign in city name (information courtesy Cavigneaux). **iv 35´** *su*(*): Bagh. Mitt. 21 transliteration has *su*$^!$. **iv 36´** *a*(*) and KASKAL(*): Bagh. Mitt. 21 transliteration has *a*$^!$ and KASKAL$^?$ respectively. *kil*(*): copy indicates PÚ, while Bagh. Mitt. 21 transliteration has *kil*. BI(*): copy indicates that BI is followed by the word divider sign, while this is not mentioned in the Bagh. Mitt. 21 transliteration. **iv 37´** *lam*(*): copy and Bagh. Mitt. 21 transliteration have EL. **iv 38´** *še*(*): copy has only three wedges not four; Bagh. Mitt. 21 transliteration has *še*.

S.0.1002.3

i 3´ *q*[*é*(*)-*e*]: copy has BE [x (x)], while photograph and Bagh. Mitt. 21 transliteration indicate *q*[*é-e*]. **i 7´** *g*[*u*(*)]: copy suggests BE [x]; Bagh. Mitt. 21 transliteration has *gu*, while photograph suggests *g*[*u*]. **i□8´** ⸢KAL×BAD(*)⸣: copy has KAL and Bagh. Mitt. 21 transliteration ⸢KAL$^?$⸣. **i 14´** Bagh. Mitt. 21 transliteration has at the beginning of the line [*ṣal-ti a-n*]*a*. **i 20´** The copy indicates É [x] x MEŠ, while Bagh. Mitt. 21 transliteration indicates É.[DURU$_5$].MEŠ. **i 24´** *m*]*a*(*): copy suggests G]IŠ, while Bagh. Mitt. 21 transliteration has *m*]*a*. **ii 3´** Bagh. Mitt. 21 transliteration indicates that there is the trace of a sign after GAL. **iii 8´** 60(*)-*š*[*u*(*)]: copy has x, while Bagh. Mitt. 21 transliteration has *u*[*n*; for the desired 60-*šu*, see S.0.1002.2 iv 12´ and S.0.1002.6 iii 15´. **iii 14´** *ṣir*(*): the copy has UZ, while Bagh. Mitt. 21 transliteration has *ṣir*. **iii 16´** The photo and arrangement of the lines would suggest that *l*[*ib* is more likely than the S[AG of Bagh. Mitt. 21 transliteration; compare S.0.1002.1 line 16 to S.0.1002.2 iv 17´. **iii 21´** *šá*(*): Bagh. Mitt. 21 transliteration omits this sign. *š*[*i*(*): the copy suggests *šú* [, while Bagh. Mitt. 21 transliteration has *š*[*i*. **iv 18´** *ṣir*(*): copy has UZ, while Bagh. Mitt. 21 transliteration has *ṣir*. **iv 21´** Bagh. Mitt. 21 transliteration indicates that there are traces of a sign before KI. **iv□24´** UGU(*): the copy and Bagh. Mitt. 21 transliteration both have KA; the emendation is tentative.

S.0.1002.4

i 1´ No traces of the line are depicted on the copy, but Bagh. Mitt. 21 transliteration indicates that there are some. **i 2´** Bagh. Mitt. 21 transliteration indicates that there are traces of four signs before ^{d}UTU. **i 10´** *ke*(*): copy has only one horizontal wedge in the middle of the sign, while Bagh. Mitt. 21 transliteration has DI. **i 12´** *ki*(*): copy has only one horizontal wedge in the middle of the sign, while Bagh. Mitt. 21 transliteration has *ki*. **i 14´** Although the copy has 4, Bagh. Mitt. 21 transliteration indicates that the number is not certain. **i 15´** Bagh. Mitt. 21 transliteration indicates that the forms of the KU and DE signs are not normal. **ii 7´** Bagh. Mitt. 21 transliteration has *um* (x) *ma* [...]. **i 11´** Bagh. Mitt. 21 transliteration indicates the presence of the traces of six signs. **iii 1** Bagh. Mitt. 21 transliteration indicates *ṣ*[*u*(?) x x x] ^{d}A-^{d}IŠKUR EN [...]. **iii 6** KÚR(*): copy has KUR, while Bagh. Mitt. 21 transliteration has KÚR. **iii 13** *kit*(*): copy has SI, while Bagh. Mitt. 21 transliteration has *kit*. **iv 4** UR$_5$(*): copy has ḪI-DIŠ; Bagh. Mitt. 21 transliteration has UR$_5$. **iv 14** Bagh. Mitt. 21 transliteration indicates that part of the NU sign is preserved. **iv 15** Bagh. Mitt. 21 transliteration indicates that traces of four signs are preserved.

S.0.1002.5

i 8´ The copy does not show any traces before DI, but Cavigneaux informs me that a vertical wedge is preserved. **i 9´** IŠKUR(*): copy has two parallel horizontal wedges rather than one; Bagh. Mitt. 21 transliteration has IM. **i 14´** Copy has *muḫ-ḫi-*[...], while Bagh. Mitt. 21 transliteration has *muḫ-ḫi-š*[*ú-nu* ...]. **i 16´** *bu*(*): form anomalous. KARAŠ(*): copy has KI.KID×BAD, while Bagh. Mitt. 21 transliteration has KI$^!$.KAL×BAD. **iv 8** Copy has LÚ.GAR.KU[R.MEŠ ...; Bagh. Mitt. 21 transliteration has LÚ.GAR.KUR.M[EŠ ...]. **iv 13** NA(*): copy has NU, while Bagh. Mitt. 21 transliteration has NA. **iv 15** Bagh. Mitt. 21 transliteration indicates that there is an erasure between IA and Ú. **iv 16** Bagh. Mitt. 21 transliteration has [*ù i*]-*sin-na-a-ti* ...

S.0.1002.6

ii 1´ Bagh. Mitt. 21 transliteration has [...] ⸢x⸣ [x x x] UGU [...]. **ii 2´** Bagh. Mitt. 21 transliteration indicates that there is the trace of a sign before *āgugma*. **ii 8´** Bagh. Mitt. 21 transliteration indicates that there are traces of a sign before ÉRIN.MEŠ. **ii 14´** PÚ(*): copy and Bagh. Mitt. 21 transliteration have LÚ. **ii 15´** *ri*(*): copy and Bagh. Mitt. 21 transliteration have ḪU. **ii 16´** *su*(*): copy has three horizontal wedges followed by three vertical wedges instead of four and two respectively. **ii 18´** Bagh. Mitt. 21 transliteration indicates that part of a NU sign is preserved before GAR-*un*. **iii 1´** Bagh. Mitt. 21 transliteration indicates traces of several more signs than are indicated on the copy: [...] x x [x x] x x x x. **iii 3´** Bagh. Mitt. 21 transliteration has *a*$^?$-*na*$^?$-*ku*$^?$. **iii 11´** Bagh. Mitt. 21 transliteration indicates LÚ.[KÚR]-*ia*. **iii 13´** Bagh. Mitt. 21 transliteration indicates that the KUR is fully preserved. **iii 18´** Bagh. Mitt. 21 transliteration has AN.TA-[*šú ina m*]*uḫ-ḫi*. **iii 22´** AD(*): copy has ṢI, while Bagh. Mitt. 21 transliteration has AD. **iii 23´** *ma*(*): copy has ŠU(?), while Bagh. Mitt. 21 transliteration has MA. **iii 24´** Bagh. Mitt. 21 transliteration indicates *i-na* GIŠ.GU.ZA.

S.0.1002.7

obv. 4´ Bagh. Mitt. 21 transliteration indicates ... 6 M[E] ⸢x⸣ [x x x].MEŠ. **obv. 9´** Bagh. Mitt. 21 transliteration indicates for the end of the line *ka-mar-*[*šú-nu*] SÌG-*aṣ*. **obv. 10´** Bagh. Mitt. 21 transliteration has [... *k*]*a-bit-ti* [*ap-ṭu*]*r-ma*$^?$ *ú-*[...]. **rev. 3´** Bagh.

Mitt. 21 transliteration has [...] 64 *ina* 1 KÙŠ, while the copy would suggest [...] x x 64 *ina* 1 KÙŠ or possibly [...] x 60-⸢*šu*⸣ 4 *ina* 1 KÙŠ. **rev. 5′** DÙ(*): copy suggests GIŠ, while Bagh. Mitt. 21 transliteration has x. KÙŠ(*): copy has only one horizontal wedge.

S.0.1002.8

obv. 4′ *ṣu*(*)-*um*(*): copy indicates GU AB, while Bagh. Mitt. 21 transliteration has *ṣu-um*. **obv. 13′** *m*]*a*(*): copy suggests G]IŠ, while Bagh. Mitt. 21 transliteration has] *ma*-. *ṣu*(*): copy indicates GU, while Bagh. Mitt. 21 transliteration has *ṣu*. **obv. 19′** Bagh. Mitt. 21 transliteration indicates that there is part of a MA sign before ŠI (i.e., [... E$_{11}$-*m*]*a*). **obv. 20′** *kit*(*): copy indicates Ú; Bagh. Mitt. 21 transliteration indicates for this line [...] x *kit-tu-ú*. **rev. 5** *m*]*a*(*): copy suggests G]IŠ, while Bagh. Mitt. 21 transliteration has *m*]*a*.

S.0.1002.9

i 11 Bagh. Mitt. 21 transliteration for the end of the line has ⸢*it-tan*⸣-[*nu*]. **i 16** *ni*(*): the copy has DÙ, while Bagh. Mitt. 21 transliteration has *nu*; the photograph suggests *ni*. **i 23** ᵐ(*): copy has MAŠ, while the photograph and Bagh. Mitt. 21 transliteration suggest the form is correct. **ii 1** Bagh. Mitt. 21 transliteration has AD-*ia a*$^{?}$-*di*$^{?}$ ⸢x x⸣ [...]. **ii 6** Bagh. Mitt. 21 transliteration has for the end of the line ⸢*i*$^{?}$⸣-*š*[*a*$^{??}$-*ru* A]D-[*ia*]. **ii 7** *i*[*l*(*): copy has AL, Bagh. Mitt. 21 transliteration has *i*[*l*. **ii 8** Bagh. Mitt. 21 transliteration indicates GIŠ.[GU.ZA], while photograph suggests only traces preserved. **ii□11** Bagh. Mitt. 21 transliteration indicates nothing of either *ḫa* or *pí* preserved. **ii 14** *m*[*a* (*)]: copy suggests GI[Š], while Bagh. Mitt. 21 transliteration has *m*[*a*]. **ii 15** Copy has MAN DIŠ for *še-šib*, but photograph and Bagh. Mitt. 21 transliteration indicate *še-šib*. **ii 20** *ma*(*): copy has ŠU, while Bagh. Mitt. 21 transliteration has *ma*. **ii 24** Bagh. Mitt. 21 transliteration has for the end of the line *ru-pu-us-s*[*u* x] ⸢x⸣ [...]; the photograph suggests that there may be traces after *rupussu*. **iii 8** *ma*(*): copy has GIŠ, while Bagh. Mitt. 21 transliteration has ⸢x⸣. **iii 9** Bagh. Mitt. 21 transliteration has for the end of the line [...] *na*$^{?}$-*a*. **iii 10** Bagh. Mitt. 21 transliteration indicates KUR.[MEŠ GA]L.M[EŠ]. **iii 13** *ni*(*): copy has DÙ, while Bagh. Mitt. 21 transliteration has *ni*. **iii 17** Bagh. Mitt. 21 transliteration has *ki?-m*[*a i*]*a-tu*. **iii 18** *li*(*): copy has ŠE ḪU, while Bagh. Mitt. 21 transliteration has ⸢*li*⸣.

S.0.1002.10

18 Although the copy indicates that there are only two A signs, the photograph shows that three are present (as indicated in the Bagh. Mitt. 21 transliteration) **29** Bagh. Mitt. 21 transliteration has: *i-na* x *el*$^{?}$ x x *tum ú-še-šib-šú*.

S.0.1002.12

6′ MEŠ(*): copy has ME-U, while Bagh. Mitt. 21 transliteration indicates MEŠ. **7′** D]A(*): copy suggests G]IŠ, while Bagh. Mitt. 21 transliteration has] ⸢x⸣. **7′** *k*[*u*(*): copy suggests M[A, while Bagh. Mitt. 21 transliteration has *k*[*u*. **11′** É(*): copy suggests GÁN, while Bagh. Mitt. 21 transliteration has É.

S.0.1002.13

rev. 2 Bagh. Mitt. 21 transliteration has *az-kur*. **rev. 6** Bagh. Mitt. 21 transliteration indicates *la*$^{!}$ *i*$^{!}$-*raš-ši* LÚ *áš-b*[*u-tu* ...].

S.0.1002.14

4 Bagh. Mitt. 21 transliteration indicates that there are traces of two signs preserved after ŠÀ.BAL.BAL. **5** The copy has *li-pu*-[...], while Bagh. Mitt. 21 transliteration has *li-pu-ú* [...].

Unidentified Fragments

S.0.0.1002

2′ Bagh. Mitt. 21 transliteration has for the end of the line *ma*$^{?}$-*ti*$^{?}$ ⸢x⸣ [...]. **3′** Bagh. Mitt. 21 transliteration indicates that there is a trace of a sign before *šú* and the trace of another after LÚ. **4′** Bagh. Mitt. 21 transliteration tentatively suggests L]Ú at the beginning of the line. **6′** *ta*(*): copy has UŠ, but Bagh. Mitt. 21 transliteration has *ta*.

S.0.0.1003

1′ Bagh. Mitt. 21 transliteration has [...] ⸢x⸣-*tu* [...]. **2′** Bagh. Mitt. 21 transliteration has [...] ⸢x⸣ NI IS ⸢xxxx[...]. **3′** Bagh. Mitt. 21 transliteration indicates that there is a trace of a sign after ŠI.

Index of Museum Numbers

Baghdad, Iraq Museum

Berlin, Vorderasiatisches Museum

London, British Museum

No.	RIM
BM 12064	B.6.32.4.1
BM 12110	B.6.32.2.1
BM 22533	B.6.32.2.2
BM 26295	B.2.7.2
BM 28384+	B.6.32.12.7
BM 33338	B.6.32.5.2
BM 33428	B.6.14.2001
BM 34637	B.2.4.1001
BM 35000	B.2.4.9.4
BM 38345	B.6.31.10
BM 40074	B.6.32.4.2
BM 41650	B.6.33.6
BM 45793	B.6.31.15.1
BM 47655	B.6.32.1.12
BM 47656	B.6.32.1.13
BM 47805+	B.2.4.8.4
BM 48032+	B.2.4.8.4
BM 48035+	B.2.4.8.4
BM 48037+	B.2.4.8.4
BM 48046+	B.2.4.8.4
BM 50662	B.6.32.1.14
BM 50843+	B.6.32.12.7
BM 51255	B.2.4.10
BM 56634	B.6.32.12.4
BM 56639	B.6.32.12.2
BM 62908	B.6.7.2
BM 68613	B.6.32.1.15
BM 77223	B.6.32.1.16
BM 78264	B.6.32.12.5
BM 79503	B.2.8.5.1
BM 82598	B.6.33.4.2
BM 82953	B.3.1.1.2
BM 83000(+)	B.6.32.13.2
BM 83001(+)	B.6.32.13.2
BM 86918	B.6.32.1.1
BM 90269	B.6.21.2.7
BM 90270+	B.6.21.2.8
BM 90271	B.6.21.2.9
BM 90281	B.6.33.2.1
BM 90285	B.6.32.8.1
BM 90286	B.2.8.4.1
BM 90599+	B.6.22.1.5
BM 90629+	B.6.22.1.5
BM 90740+	B.6.21.2.8
BM 90807	B.6.32.16.1
BM 90858	B.2.4.11
BM 90864	B.6.32.2.1
BM 90865	B.6.32.14
BM 90866	B.6.33.3
BM 90935	B.6.32.4.1
BM 91107	B.6.33.4.1
BM 91112	B.6.33.1
BM 91115	B.6.32.12.1
BM 91432	B.2.11.1
BM 91433	B.6.13.1
BM 99067+	B.2.4.9.1
BM 113204	B.6.31.17.2
BM 113205	B.6.15.2001.3
BM 114277	B.6.32.2003.1
BM 114278	B.6.32.2003.2
BM 114299	B.6.32.16.2
BM 116987	B.6.32.2002
BM 116989	B.2.8.10.1
BM 119014	B.6.32.2016
BM 119021	B.6.32.2014.1

No.	RIM
BM 119023	B.6.32.2014.2
BM 119024	B.6.32.2014.3
BM 119065	B.6.32.2001
BM 119271	B.6.32.2012.1–2
BM 119274	B.6.32.2013.1–2
BM 119277	B.6.32.2010
BM 119278	B.6.32.2004
BM 119279	B.6.32.2011.1–2
BM 120518	B.2.6.1.2
BM 123060	B.2.6.2001
BM 123061	B.2.6.4.2
BM 123124	B.2.6.2
BM 124350	B.6.32.2015.2
BM 124351	B.6.32.2015.1
BM 129532	B.6.10.2002
BM 130712	B.6.32.9.1
BM 137345	B.6.32.2003.3
BM 137349	B.6.32.2003.4
BM 137381	B.6.32.2003.5
BM 137408	B.6.32.2003.6
40-4-4,4	B.6.13.1
48-11-4,128	B.2.11.1
51-1-1,276	B.6.21.2.8
51-1-1,277	B.6.21.2.9
51-1-1,282	B.6.21.2.7
51-10-9,78R	B.6.32.16.1
80-6-17,2	B.6.32.14
80-6-17,3	B.6.33.3
80-11-12,227	B.6.31.10
81-2-1,38	B.6.32.4.2
81-2-1,103	B.6.32.4.1
81-2-4,174	B.6.32.20
81-3-24,367	B.6.32.2.1
81-6-7,209	see B.6.31.15.1
81-6-25,266	B.6.33.6
81-7-1,3406	B.6.22.1.5
81-7-6,210	B.6.31.15.1
81-11-3,360	B.6.32.1.12
81-11-3,361	B.6.32.1.13
81-11-3,512+	B.2.4.8.4
81-11-3,741+	B.2.4.8.4
81-11-3,744+	B.2.4.8.4
81-11-3,746+	B.2.4.8.4
81-11-3,755+	B.2.4.8.4
82-3-23,1653	B.6.32.1.14
82-3-23,1837+	B.6.32.12.7
82-3-23,2251	B.2.4.10
82-5-22,1800	B.2.4.11
82-7-14,1000	B.6.33.4.1
82-7-14,1032	B.6.32.12.4
82-7-14,1038	B.6.33.1
82-7-14,1043	B.6.32.12.1
82-7-14,1044	B.6.32.12.2
82-9-18,2877	B.6.7.2
82-9-18,8612	B.6.32.1.15
83-1-21,116	B.3.1.1.2
83-1-21,163(+)	B.6.32.13.2
83-1-21,164(+)	B.6.32.13.2
83-6-30,3	B.6.32.1.16
89-10-14,51	B.2.8.5.1
93-10-14,50	B.6.33.4.2
94-1-15,335	B.6.32.2.2
98-5-14,113	B.2.7.2
98-10-11,20+	B.6.32.12.7

No.	RIM
1821-1-20,13	B.2.8.4.1
1900-3-10,2	B.6.32.1.1
1915-4-10,2	B.6.31.17.2
1915-4-10,3	B.6.15.2001.3
1919-10-11,4708	B.6.32.2003.1
1919-10-11,4709	B.6.32.2003.2
1919-10-11,4743	B.6.32.16.2
1924-9-20,250	B.6.32.2002
1924-9-20,252	B.2.8.10.1
1927-10-3,9	B.6.32.2016
1927-10-3,16	B.6.32.2014.1
1927-10-3,18	B.6.32.2014.2
1927-10-3,19	B.6.32.2014.3
1927-10-3,60	B.6.32.2001
1927-10-3,266	B.6.32.2012.1–2
1927-10-3,269	B.6.32.2013.1–2
1927-10-3,272	B.6.32.2010
1927-10-3,273	B.6.32.2004
1927-10-3,274	B.6.32.2011.1–2
1928-10-9,1	B.2.6.1.2
1932-5-14,1	B.2.6.2001
1932-5-14,2	B.2.6.4.2
1932-10-8,8	B.2.6.2
1933-10-13,3	B.6.32.2015.2
1933-10-13,4	B.6.32.2015.1
1935-1-13,5	B.6.32.2003.3
1935-1-13,9	B.6.32.2003.4
1942-1-28,1	B.6.32.9.1
1945-10-13,76	B.6.10.2002
1979-12-18,16	B.6.32.2003.5
1979-12-18,43	B.6.32.2003.6
1979-12-20,174	B.6.33.2.1
Bu 88-5-12,120	B.6.32.12.5
Ki 1904-10-9,96+	B.2.4.9.1
K 2211+	B.2.4.8.2
K 2660	B.2.4.6
K 3317+	B.2.4.9.2
K 3319+	B.2.4.9.2
K 3426	B.2.4.5
K 3444+	B.2.4.9.1
K 3649+	B.2.4.8.2
K 4874(+)	B.2.4.8.1
K 5191	B.2.4.9.3
K 6088(+)	B.2.4.8.1
K 6189+	B.2.4.8.2
K 6386	B.6.31.15.2
K 8636+	B.2.4.8.2
K 9168+	B.2.4.8.2
K 10739(+)	B.2.4.8.2
K 18603	B.2.0.1001
DT 272	B.6.32.12.3
DT 381	B.6.32.8.1
Rm 255(+)	B.2.4.8.1
Rm 3,11	B.6.32.5.2
Rm 3,105	B.6.14.2001
Sm 397	B.2.8.5.2
Sp 2,120	B.2.4.1001
Sp 2,524	B.2.4.9.4

Philadelphia, University Museum

No.	RIM	No.	RIM	No.	RIM
CBS 14	B.6.31.9.6	CBS 16487	B.6.32.2012.3–4	UM 84-26-7	B.6.31.14.2
CBS 733+	B.6.32.23; B.6.33.5	CBS 16488	B.6.32.2013.3–4	UM 84-26-8	B.6.32.16.10
		CBS 16489	B.6.32.2008.1–2	UM 84-26-9	B.6.32.16.11
CBS 1632a	B.6.32.16.6	CBS 16490	B.6.32.2009.1–2	UM 84-26-10	B.6.32.16.12
CBS 1757+	B.6.32.23; B.6.33.5	CBS 16491	B.6.32.2003.8	UM 84-26-11	B.6.32.16.13–14
		CBS 16555a	B.6.32.2003.9	UM 84-26-12	B.6.32.18.1
CBS 2350	B.6.31.12.1	CBS 16555b	B.6.32.2003.10		
CBS 8632	B.6.32.16.7	CBS 16556a	B.6.32.2011.5–6	UM L-29-632+	B.6.32.15.1
CBS 8633	B.6.32.16.8	CBS 16556b	B.6.32.2011.7–8	UM L-29-633+	B.6.32.15.1
CBS 8644	B.6.32.17	CBS 16557	B.6.32.2012.5–6	UM L-29-634	B.6.31.11.8
CBS 8645	B.6.31.14.1	CBS 16558	B.6.32.2013.5	UM L-29-635	B.6.31.11.14
CBS 8654	B.6.32.16.9	CBS 16559	see B.6.32.2010	UM L-29-636+	B.6.32.15.1
CBS 9482	B.6.31.13.1	CBS 17244	B.2.6.1.1	UM L-29-637	B.6.31.11.12
CBS 15337	B.6.32.2003.7			UM L-29-639	B.6.31.12.4
CBS 16482	B.2.8.11	JS 7-21-88-6	B.6.31.9.6		
CBS 16483	B.6.32.2005.1–2			—	B.2.4.2
CBS 16484	B.6.32.2006.1–2	UM 33-35-191a	B.6.32.2015.7	—	B.6.32.2014.5
CBS 16485	B.6.32.2007.1–2	UM 33-35-191b	B.6.32.2015.8		
CBS 16486	B.6.32.2011.3–4	UM 55-21-384	B.6.32.15.2		

MISCELLANEOUS

Babylon, Nebuchadnezzar Museum

No.	RIM
A Babylon 9	B.6.32.1.18
A Babylon 55	B.6.32.1.17

Berkeley, R.H. Lowie Museum of Anthropology

No.	RIM
UCLM 9-1793 (=UCBC 1206)	B.6.32.19.2

Bristol, City of Bristol Museum and Art Gallery

No.	RIM
H 5097	B.6.32.16.5

Chicago, Field Museum of Natural History

No.	RIM
FMNH 156011	B.2.8.4.4

Chicago, Oriental Institute

No.	RIM	No.	RIM
A 3647	B.2.4.1.2	A 32262	B.6.31.11.6
A 23364	S.0.0.1012	A 33618	B.6.31.11.9
A 31310	B.6.31.11.1	A 33619	B.6.31.11.7

Heidelberg, Seminar für Assyriologie, Universität Heidelberg

No.	RIM
—	B.6.32.19.4

Istanbul, Archaeological Museum

No.	RIM	No.	RIM
B 65	B.6.32.4.4	EŞ—	B.6.22.2.4
B 230a	B.2.8.2	EŞ—	B.6.22.5.1
		EŞ—	B.6.31.6
EŞ 7815	S.0.1001.1	EŞ—	B.6.32.7.27
EŞ 7893	B.6.32.3	EŞ—	B.6.32.16.15–20
EŞ—	B.6.22.1.1		

Jena, Fr. Schiller University

No.	RIM	No.	RIM
HS 42	B.6.35.4	HS 1958	B.6.35.4
HS 1956	B.6.31.12.2	HS 2981	B.6.32.16.24

Leiden, Nederlands Instituut voor het Nabije Oosten

No.	RIM
LB 1530	B.2.4.1.1

Los Angeles, Los Angeles County Museum of Art

No.	RIM
LA M.76.97.361	B.6.7.2001
LA M.76.97.498	B.2.6.4.1

Montreal, McGill University Ethnological Collections

No.	RIM
ML 1.18	B.6.32.16.25

New Haven, Yale Babylonian Collection

No.	RIM	No.	RIM
NBC 2502	B.6.15.2001.1	YBC 2146	B.6.31.18
NBC 2507+?	B.6.32.19.3	YBC 2147	B.6.31.16.1
NBC 2509	B.6.31.16.2	YBC 2151	B.6.35.5.1
NBC 2510	B.6.31.15.3	YBC 2170	B.6.15.2001.2
NBC 6055	B.6.31.15.4	YBC 2180	B.6.32.19.1
NBC 6069	B.6.35.5.2	YBC 2181	B.6.22.3
NBC 6070	B.6.35.5.3	YBC 2372	B.6.32.16.21
NBC 10653	B.6.31.11.13	YBC 13510	B.6.22.1.16
NBC 11323	B.6.31.11.10		

New York, Metropolitan Museum of Art

No.	RIM
MMA 74.51.4426	B.6.10.2001
MMA —	B.6.32.12.6

Oxford, Ashmolean Museum

No.	RIM	No.	RIM
Ash 1922.181	B.6.32.16.3	Ash 1929.136	B.6.21.2001
Ash 1922.190	B.6.35.3	Ash 1930.39	B.2.8.4.3
Ash 1924.627	B.6.32.16.4	Ash 1932.652	B.6.22.1.3
Ash 1924.634	B.2.8.4.2	Ash 1932.977	B.6.22.1.4
Ash 1924.640	B.6.22.1.2		

Paris, Bibliothèque Nationale

No.	RIM
Inv. 65 no. 5929	B.6.32.1.2

Paris, École Pratique des Hautes Études, IVe Section

No.	RIM
HE 144	B.6.33.2001.2

Paris, Louvre

No.	RIM	No.	RIM
AO 5470	B.6.31.9.8	AO 25276	B.5.1.1.6
AO 6772	B.6.31.17.1	AO 25552	B.6.1.2003.2
AO 6793	B.6.33.2001.1	AO 26245	B.4.1.1.17
AO 7038	B.4.0.2001	AO 26246	B.6.1.1.9
AO 14055	B.2.6.3	AO 26247	B.5.1.1.7
AO 25000	B.6.0.2003	AO 26248	B.6.1.1.12
AO 25212	B.4.1.1.16	AO 26249	B.6.1.1.10
AO 25213	B.5.1.1.5	AO 26250	B.6.1.1.11
AO 25214	B.6.1.1.8		

Philadelphia, Philadelphia Musem of Art
(pieces on loan to the University Museum, Philadelphia)

No.	RIM
PMA F29-6-387a+	B.6.32.15.1
PMA F29-6-387b+	B.6.32.15.1
PMA F29-6-387c	B.6.31.11.8
PMA F29-6-387d	B.6.31.11.14
PMA F29-6-387e+	B.6.32.15.1
PMA F29-6-387f	B.6.31.11.12
PMA F29-6-397	B.6.31.12.4

Princeton, Princeton Theological Seminary
(collection on loan to the University Museum, Philadelphia)

No.	RIM
PTS 2253	B.6.35.1

Saint Louis, Saint Louis Art Museum

No.	RIM
11:64	B.2.8.12

Teheran, Muse Iran Bastan

No.	RIM
7409-1409	B.6.0.2002
—	B.2.4.3.4

Toronto, Royal Ontario Museum

No.	RIM
ROM 938.35 (=D 1513)	B.2.7.3

Urbana, World Heritage Museum

No.	RIM
WHM 13.14.1729 (= UIOM 2499)	B.3.1.1.1

PRIVATE COLLECTIONS

Index of Excavation Numbers

Babylon

No.	RIM	No.	RIM	No.	RIM	No.	RIM
79-B-13	B.2.8.1001	BE 8078	B.6.32.7.22	BE 30698	B.6.22.1.12	BE 41186	B.6.32.10
81-B-3	B.6.32.1.19	BE 8079	B.6.32.7.23	BE 30700	B.6.22.1.13	BE 41230	B.6.31.4.2
		BE 8080	B.6.32.7.24	BE 30706	B.6.22.1.14	BE 41232	B.6.32.8.5
BE 3381	S.0.1001.1	BE 8081	B.6.32.7.25	BE 30707	B.6.22.1.15	BE 41252	B.6.32.9.3
BE 3382	see S.0.1001.1	BE 8082	B.6.32.7.26	BE 30708	B.6.22.1.16	BE 41419	B.6.31.9.2
BE 5457	B.6.32.5.1	BE 8083	B.6.32.7.2	BE 30709	B.6.22.1.17	BE 41472	B.6.31.2.4
BE 6403	B.6.31.1	BE 8084	B.6.31.2.1	BE 30710	B.6.22.1.18	BE 41861	B.6.22.2.2
BE 6404	B.6.7.1	BE 8086	B.6.32.7.1	BE 31080	B.6.22.1.19	BE 42262	B.6.35.2
BE 8010	B.6.32.7.6	BE 8763	B.6.32.1.3	BE 32062	B.6.22.1.20	BE 42335+	B.6.22.2.3
BE 8044	B.6.32.7.7	BE 12131	B.6.32.1.4	BE 32167	B.6.31.4.4	BE 42417+	B.6.22.2.3
BE 8045	B.6.32.7.8	BE 15316	B.6.31.9.1	BE 33135	B.2.4.8.3	BE 44638	B.6.31.4.1
BE 8046	B.6.32.7.9	BE 28510	B.6.32.3	BE 36072	B.6.32.9.4	BE 46154	B.2.4.7
BE 8047	B.6.32.7.10	BE 29275	B.6.32.1.5	BE 38119	B.6.32.4.4	BE 46374	B.6.31.8
BE 8048	B.6.32.7.11	BE 29362	B.6.32.1.6	BE 38583	B.6.22.2.1	BE 46402	B.6.31.5.1
BE 8049	B.6.32.7.12	BE 29482	B.6.32.4.3	BE 39436	B.6.32.9.5	BE 46403	B.6.31.5.2
BE 8050	see B.6.31.2	BE 30112	B.6.32.1.7	BE 39807	B.6.32.9.6	BE 46404	B.6.31.6
BE 8051	B.6.32.7.13	BE 30113	see B.6.32.1	BE 39840	B.6.31.3.1	BE 46405	B.6.31.5.3
BE 8052	B.6.32.7.14	BE 30130	B.6.32.1.8	BE 39849	B.6.32.9.2	BE 46406	B.6.31.5.4
BE 8053	B.6.32.7.15	BE 30160	B.6.32.1.9	BE 40145	B.6.32.8.2	BE 46407	B.6.31.7
BE 8054	B.6.32.7.16	BE 30161	B.6.32.1.10	BE 40855	B.6.32.8.3	BE 46408	B.6.31.3.3
BE 8072	B.6.32.7.5	BE 30164	B.6.32.1.11	BE 41032	B.6.32.8.4	BE 46410	B.6.31.9.3
BE 8073	B.6.32.7.17	BE 30680	B.6.22.1.7	BE 41054	B.6.31.4.3	BE 46433	B.6.32.9.8
BE 8074	B.6.32.7.18	BE 30681	B.6.22.1.8	BE 41099	B.6.31.3.2	BE 46435	B.6.31.9.4
BE 8075	B.6.32.7.19	BE 30682	B.6.22.1.9	BE 41143	B.6.32.11	BE 46436	B.6.31.9.5
BE 8076	B.6.32.7.20	BE 30683	B.6.22.1.10	BE 41171	B.6.32.9.7	BE 58377	B.6.22.2.4
BE 8077	B.6.32.7.21	BE 30684	B.6.22.1.11	BE 41183	B.6.31.2.2	BE 59431	B.2.8.1

Nippur

No.	RIM	No.	RIM	No.	RIM	No.	RIM
9 N 99	B.2.7.2001	2 NT 483	B.2.4.2	5 NT 564	B.6.31.11.10	6 NT 1045	B.6.31.11.2
12 N 43	B.6.31.12.3	3 NT 840	B.6.32.15.2	5 NT 702	B.6.31.13.2	6 NT 1046	B.6.31.11.1
18 N —	B.6.32.18.2	4 NT 75	B.6.31.11.9	5 NT 703	B.6.32.16.23	8 NT 2a–e	B.6.31.11.3
		4 NT 76	B.6.31.11.7	6 NT 1043	B.6.31.11.4	8 NT 3	B.6.31.11.6
1 NT 142	B.6.31.11.11	5 NT 476	B.6.31.11.5	6 NT 1044	B.6.31.11.13	9 NT 9	B.6.31.11.15

Ur

No.	RIM	No.	RIM	No.	RIM	No.	RIM
U 152	see B.6.32.2003.7	U 2757	B.6.32.2016	U 3148	B.6.32.2010	U 3249g?	B.6.32.2014.5
U 1262	B.6.32.2002	U 2877	B.2.8.11	U 3161	B.6.32.2003	U 3249i	B.6.32.2014.4
U 1664	B.6.32.2003.3	U 3130	B.2.8.10.1–2	U 3249	see B.6.32.2014	U 3249l	B.6.32.2014.3
U 2674	B.6.32.2001	U 3136	see B.6.32.2003	U 3249c	B.6.32.2014.1	U 3249m	B.6.32.2014.2

No.	RIM	No.	RIM	No.	RIM	No.	RIM
U 3250	B.6.32.2005	U 3298a	B.6.32.2012.3–4	U 7818	B.2.6.1.1–4	U 18529e	B.6.32.2015.4
U 3296	B.6.32.2007	U 3298b	B.6.32.2012.5–6	U 7824	see B.6.32.2003	U 18529f	B.6.32.2015.5
U 3297	B.6.32.2011	U 3299	B.6.32.2013	U 17627a	B.2.6.2	U 18529g?	B.6.32.2015.2
U 3297a	B.6.32.2011.3	U 3300	B.6.32.2008	U 18529a	B.6.32.2015.7	U 18529h	B.6.32.2015.3
U 3297b	B.6.32.2011.5	U 3301	B.6.32.2009	U 18529b	B.6.32.2015.6		
U 3297c	B.6.32.2011.7	U 3326	B.6.32.2006	U 18529c	B.6.32.2015.1		
U 3298	B.6.32.2012	U 6341	B.6.32.2004	U 18529d	B.6.32.2015.8		

Uruk

No.	RIM	No.	RIM	No.	RIM	No.	RIM
W 2	B.6.22.5.1	W 1701a	B.6.21.2.3	W 4098	B.6.31.17.3	W 6420b/c	B.6.22.4.11
W 69	B.6.21.2.4	W 1831a	B.6.22.4.2	W 4238	B.6.31.19.4	W 11747	B.6.22.5.7
W 856	B.6.31.16.3	W 1831b	B.6.22.4.3	W 4382	B.6.21.3.3	W 13182	B.6.22.5.8
W 942	B.6.31.19.1	W 2589	B.6.22.4.4	W 4431	B.6.21.3.4	W 13393	B.6.22.4.12
W 1253d	B.6.21.2.5	W 2703	B.6.22.4.5	W 4444+?	B.6.32.19.3	W 18419	B.6.31.15.5
W 1635a	B.6.22.4.1; B.6.22.5.2	W 2704	B.6.22.4.6	W 4496	B.6.31.20	W 20942	B.6.32.19.4
		W 2705	B.6.22.4.7	W 4556	B.6.21.3.5	W 22660/0	B.6.14.1
W 1635c	B.6.22.5.3	W 3200a	B.6.22.4.8	W 4663	B.6.22.5.6	W 23428	B.6.13.2
W 1635d	B.6.22.5.4	W 3283	B.6.21.3.1	W 4767	B.6.21.2.6	W 23556	B.2.8.8
W 1635e	B.6.22.5.5	W 3764	B.6.31.19.2	W 5452	B.6.22.6.1	W 23852	B.6.31.15.6
W 1700a	B.6.21.2.1	W 3885	B.6.31.19.3	W 5753	B.6.22.4.9	W —	B.6.21.2.10
W 1700b	B.6.21.2.2	W 4089	B.6.21.3.2	W 6420a	B.6.22.4.10	W —	B.6.21.3.6

MISCELLANEOUS

Glaiʿa

No.	RIM
79	S.0.0.1009

Kish

No.	RIM
HMR 342	B.2.8.4.2

Nimrud

No.	RIM
ND 2090	B.6.21.1

Isin

No.	RIM
IB 148a	B.2.8.7.1
IB 148b	B.2.8.7.2

Larsa

No.	RIM
L 7084	B.2.8.9

Persepolis

No.	RIM
PT4 942	S.0.0.1012

Concordances of Selected Publications

Behrens, JCS 37 (1985) pp. 229–48

No.	RIM	No.	RIM	No.	RIM	No.	RIM
51	B.2.4.2	56	B.6.32.2003.7–10	60	B.6.32.2011.3–8	80	B.6.31.14.1–2
52	B.2.8.11	57	B.6.32.2005;	61	B.6.32.2012.3–6	81	B.6.31.9.6
53	B.6.32.16.6–14		B.6.32.2009	62	B.6.32.2013.3		
54	B.6.32.17	58	B.6.32.2006	63	B.6.32.2008		
55	B.6.32.18	59	B.6.32.2007	79	B.6.31.13.1		

Borger, Asarh.

P.	RIM	P.	RIM	P.	RIM
29 §12 (Bab. H)	B.6.31.1	30 §18 (Bab. N)	B.6.31.9.1–6, 8	75–76 §48 (Uruk B)	B.6.31.16.1–3
30 §13 (Bab. I)	B.6.31.2.1–2	32 §20 (Brs. A)	B.6.31.10	77 §49 (Uruk C)	B.6.31.17.1–3
30 §14 (Bab. J)	B.6.31.3.1–3	70 §39 (Npr. A)	B.6.31.11.8, 11–12,	77 §50 (Uruk D)	B.6.31.18
30 §15 (Bab. K)	B.6.31.4.1–4;		14	77–78 §51 (Uruk E)	B.6.31.19.1–4
	B.6.31.5.1–4, 7;	70–71 §40 (Npr. B)	B.6.31.12.1–2	77–78 §51 (Uruk F)	B.6.31.20
	B.6.31.6	71 §41 (Npr. C)	B.6.31.13.1	77–78 §51 (Uruk G)	B.6.31.21
30 §16 (Bab. L)	B.6.31.7	71 §42 (Npr. D)	B.6.31.14.1	117 §87a	B.2.4.8.1
30 §17 (Bab. M)	B.6.31.8	73–75 §47 (Uruk A)	B.6.31.15.1–4		

Brinkman, PKB pp. 323–64, Chronological Catalogue of Written Sources

P.	No.	RIM	P.	No.	RIM
324	2.2.1	B.2.2.1	336–37	8.2.5	B.2.8.10.1–2
325	3.2.1	B.2.3.1.1–2	337	8.2.6	B.2.8.11
325–26	4.2.1	B.2.4.1.1–2	337	8.2.7	B.2.8.12
326	4.2.2	B.2.4.3.4	339–40	11.2.1	B.2.11.1
326	4.2.3	B.2.4.2	340	12.2.1	B.3.1.1.1
326	4.2.4	B.2.4.4	342	15.2.1	B.4.1.1.1–14
326	4.2.5	B.2.4.3.1–3	342–43	16.2.1	B.4.2.1001.1–2
327	4.2.9	B.2.4.11	344	18.2.1	B.5.1.1.1–4
328	4.3.8	B.2.4.5	344	19.2.1	B.6.1.1.1–4
328	4.3.9	B.2.4.6	344–45	19.2.4	B.6.1.2001
329	4.3.10	B.2.4.9.1–4	345	19.2.5	B.6.1.2002
329	5.2.1	B.2.5.1	345	19.2.6	B.6.1.2004
330	6.2.1	B.2.6.1	349–50	25.2.1	B.6.7.1
330–31	6.2.2	B.2.6.4.1–2	351	26.2.1	see B.6.8
331	6.2.3	B.2.6.3	354	31.2.1	B.6.13.1
331	6.2.4	B.2.6.4.3	356	32.2.3	B.6.14.2001
331	6.2.5	B.2.6.2	356–57	33.2.3	B.6.15.2001.1–3
334	7.2.1	B.2.7.2	362	i	B.2.6.2001
334	7.2.2	B.2.7.1	363	m	B.4.0.2002
334	7.2.3	B.2.7.3	363	n	B.4.0.2003
335	7.2.7	B.2.7.2001	363	p	B.6.7.2001
336	8.2.1	B.2.8.1	363	q	B.6.0.2005
336	8.2.2	B.2.8.5.1	363–64	s	B.6.10.2001
336	8.2.3	B.2.8.4.1, 4	364	t	B.6.10.2002
336	8.2.4	B.2.8.6			

Brinkman, Studies Oppenheim pp. 41–49, Catalogue of Documents

P.	No.	RIM	P.	No.	RIM
41	44.2.1	B.6.21.1	42	44.2.2b	B.6.21.3.1–4
42	44.2.2a	B.6.21.2.1–5, 7, 9–10	42	44.2.3	B.6.21.2001

Calmeyer, Datierbare Bronzen pp. 161–67, Katalog

No.	RIM	No.	RIM	No.	RIM	No.	RIM
25–26	B.2.3.1.1–2	38	B.2.6.4.3	66–69	B.5.1.1.1–4	81	B.6.1.2003.1
28–29	B.2.4.4	39	B.2.7.3	70–73	B.6.1.1.1–4	82	B.6.1.2005
30	B.2.4.3.4	40	B.2.8.12	74	B.6.1.2004	83	B.6.0.2002
31–33	B.2.4.3.1–3	41	B.2.6.2001	77	B.4.0.2002	87	B.6.7.2001
34	B.2.5.1	49	B.3.3.1	78	B.4.0.2003	90	B.6.0.2005
35–36	B.2.6.4.1–2	50–63	B.4.1.1.1–14	79	B.6.1.2001		
37	B.2.6.3	64–65	B.4.2.1001.1–2	80	B.6.1.2002		

Cavigneaux and Bahija Ismail, Bagh. Mitt. 21 (1990) pp. 321–456

No.	RIM	No.	RIM	No.	RIM	No.	RIM
1	S.0.1002.11	9	S.0.1002.8	17	S.0.1002.10	25	S.0.0.1005
2	S.0.1002.2	10	S.0.1002.4	18	S.0.1002.9	26	S.0.0.1006
3	S.0.1002.1.2	11	S.0.1002.7	19	S.0.1002.6	27	S.0.0.1007
4	S.0.1002.1.1	12	S.0.1002.12	20	S.0.1001.4	A	S.0.1001.1
5	S.0.1001.2	13	S.0.1001.1001	21	S.0.1002.3	B	S.0.0.1008
6	S.0.0.1001	14	S.0.0.1003	22	S.0.1002.14	C	S.0.0.1009
7	S.0.1002.5	15	S.0.1002.13	23	S.0.1002.1001		
8	S.0.0.1002	16	S.0.1001.3	24	S.0.0.1004		

Dossin, IrAnt 2 (1962) pp. 149–64 and pls. XIII–XXXIV

No.	RIM	No.	RIM	No.	RIM	No.	RIM
3	B.2.3.1.1–2	6	B.2.5.1	19	B.5.1.1.1–4	25	B.4.0.2003
4	B.2.4.3.1–3;	14	B.2.4.4	20	B.6.1.2004	26	B.6.0.2005
	B.2.0.1002	17	B.4.1.1.2–14	21	B.6.1.1.1–4		
5	B.2.6.4.3	18	B.4.2.1001.1–2	24	B.4.0.2002		

Gadd, UET 1

No.	RIM	No.	RIM	No.	RIM	No.	RIM
166	B.2.8.10.1	171	B.6.32.2014.1–3	176	B.6.32.2007	181	B.6.32.2009
167	B.2.8.11	172	B.6.32.2016	177	B.6.32.2011	182	B.6.32.2010
168	B.6.32.2004	173	B.6.32.2005.1	178	B.6.32.2012	183	B.6.32.2002
169	B.6.32.2001	174	B.6.32.2005.2	179	B.6.32.2013.1–2	306	B.2.6.1
170	B.6.32.2003.3, 11	175	B.6.32.2006	180	B.6.32.2008		

Lehmann-Haupt, Šamaššumukîn pls. I–XLVII

Pl.	RIM	Pl.	RIM	Pl.	RIM
I–IV no. 1 (Bil.)	B.6.33.1	XXIII–XXIV no. 8[a] (L[1])	B.6.32.4.1	XXVII no. 9d	B.6.32.12.4
V–VII no. 2 (S[1])	B.6.33.3	XXIV no. 8[b]	B.6.32.4.2	XXVIII–XXIX no. 10 (P[1])	B.6.32.6
VIII–X no. 3 (L[5])	B.6.33.4.1	XXV–XXVI no. 9[a] (L[2])	B.6.32.12.1	XXX–XXXI no. 11 (P[2])	B.6.32.1.2
XIII–XVI no. 6 (S[2])	B.6.32.14	XXVI no. 9b	B.6.32.12.2	XLII [a]	B.6.33.2.1
XVII–XXII no. 7 (S[3])	B.6.32.2.1	XXVI no. 9c	B.6.32.12.3		

Marzahn, FuB 27 (1989) pp. 53–64

No.	RIM	No.	RIM	No.	RIM	No.	RIM
I	B.6.31.2	2	B.6.31.2.3	16	B.6.32.7.4	30	B.6.22.4.15
II	B.6.31.5	3	B.6.31.5.1	17	B.6.32.8.2	31A	B.6.22.4.1
III	B.6.31.4	4	B.6.31.5.3	18	B.6.32.8.4	31B	B.6.22.5.2
IV	B.6.31.3	5	B.6.31.5.5	19	B.6.32.8.5	32	B.6.22.5.3
V	B.6.31.9	6	B.6.31.5.6	20	B.6.22.4.3	33	B.6.22.5.4
VI	B.6.32.11	7	B.6.31.4.1	21	B.6.22.4.5	34	B.6.22.5.6
VII	B.6.32.9	8	B.6.31.3.2	22	B.6.22.4.7	35	B.6.22.5.7
VIII	B.6.32.7	9	B.6.31.9.7	23	B.6.22.4.8	36	B.6.22.5.8
IX	B.6.32.8	10	B.6.32.11	24	B.6.22.4.9	37	B.6.22.6.1
X	B.6.22.4	11	B.6.32.9.4	25	B.6.22.4.10	38	B.6.22.6.2
XI	B.6.22.5	12	B.6.32.9.5	26	B.6.22.4.11	39	B.6.31.19.1
XII	B.6.22.6	13	B.6.32.9.3	27	B.6.22.4.12		
XIII	B.6.31.19	14	B.6.32.7.2	28	B.6.22.4.13		
1	B.6.31.2.2	15	B.6.32.7.3	29	B.6.22.4.14		

Schott, UVB 1 pp. 45–67 and pls. 24–31

No.	RIM	No.	RIM	No.	RIM	No.	RIM
16	B.6.21.3.1–4	19	B.6.22.5.1–6	22	B.6.31.20	25	B.6.32.19.3
17	B.6.21.3.6	20	B.6.22.4.1–8	23	B.6.31.16.3		
18	B.6.21.2.1–5	21	B.6.31.19.1–4	24	B.6.31.17.3		

Streck, Asb. pp. 1–397

P.	RIM	P.	RIM	P.	RIM
226–29 no. 1 (L[1])	B.6.32.4.1–2	238–41 no. 5 (Ê-maḫ)	B.6.32.5.1	350–51 no. 3.a.β	B.6.32.7.5
228–33 no. 2 (L[2])	B.6.32.12.1–6	240–45 no. 6 (S[2])	B.6.32.14	352–53 no. 3.b	B.6.32.16.7, 22
232–35 no. 3 (P[1])	B.6.32.6	244–49 no. 7 (S[3])	B.6.32.2.1	352–53 no. 4	B.6.32.15.1
234–39 no. 4 (L[6] [P[2]])	B.6.32.1.1–2	350–51 no. 3.a.α	B.6.32.8.1		

Walker, CBI

No.	RIM	No.	RIM	No.	RIM	No.	RIM
72	B.2.8.4.1–3	76	B.6.22.1.2–5	80	B.6.32.16.1–5	84	B.6.32.2012.1–2
73	B.2.8.10.1	77	B.6.33.2.1–2	81	B.6.32.2004	85	B.6.32.2013.1–2
74	B.6.21.2.7–9	78	B.6.32.8.1	82	B.6.32.2003.1–6	86	B.6.32.2010
75	B.6.21.2001	79	B.6.32.9.1	83	B.6.32.2011.1–2	87	B.6.35.3

Wetzel and Weissbach, Hauptheiligtum pp. 38–56

No.	RIM	No.	RIM	No.	RIM	No.	RIM
A.I.a	B.6.31.2.1–2, 4	A.I.e	B.6.31.6	A.II.a	B.6.32.7.1–2, 5–26	A.II.e	B.6.32.9.2–8
A.I.b	B.6.31.3.1–3	A.I.f	B.6.31.7	A.II.b	B.6.32.10		
A.I.c	B.6.31.4.1–4	A.I.g	B.6.31.8	A.II.c	B.6.32.11		
A.I.d	B.6.31.5.1–4	A.I.h	B.6.31.9.1–5	A.II.d	B.6.32.8.2–5		

Scores of Inscriptions

1 0 zà-mí x [...] nam-kala ki-šár-ra u$_{4}$-ul-dù-a-a-ni-šè
1 1 zà-mí x [...] nam-kala ki-šár-ra u$_{4}$-ul-dù-a-a-ni-šè
1 2 [...] u$_{4}$-ul-dù-a-a-n[i-x]
1 3 [...-u]l(?)-[...]
1 4 [...]

1 0 *ta-nit-[ti ... dan-n]u-us-su šá kiš-šá-ti ana u$_{4}$-mi ṣa-a-ti*
1 1 *ta-nit-[...-n]u-us-su šá kiš-šá-ti ana u$_{4}$-mi ṣa-a-ti*
1 2 [...] ⸢*šá kiš*⸣*-šá-ti ana u$_{4}$-mi ṣa-a-*[x]
1 3–4 [...]

2 0 KÁM(?)-ri-a-bi [...]-⸢bi(?)⸣ lá-lá ka-tar zi du$_{11}$-ga
2 1 KÁM(?)-ri-a-bi [...-l]á ka-tar zi du$_{11}$-ga
2 2 [...]-⸢bi(?)⸣ lá-lá ka-tar zi du$_{11}$-g[a(?)]
2 3 [...-ta]r zi x [...]
2 4 [...]

2 0 *uz-zu-u[š(?) ...]-*ḪAR*-šú ṭa-a-bu šu-pa-a a-na da-la-li*
2 1 *uz-zu-u[š(?) ...-š]ú ṭa-a-bu šu-pa-a a-na da-la-li*
2 2 [...]-ḪAR-*šú ṭa-a-bu šu-pa-a a-na da-la-l[i]*
2 3–4 [...]

3 0 ki dúru ki šub [...] ba-ab-lá-e giskim-bi ì-ma-al-la
3 1 ki dúru ki šub [...] ba-ab-lá-e giskim-bi ì-ma-al-la
3 2 [...]
3 3 [... g]iskim-bi ma-a[l(?)-x]
3 4 [...]

3 0 *šá šu-ud-d[u]-u šu-šu-bu ba-šu-ú it-ti-šú aḫ-ra-taš* UN.MEŠ *kul-lu-mu na-ṣa-ar it-ti-šú*
3 1 *šá šu-ud-d[u-...-ta]š* UN.MEŠ *kul-lu-mu na-ṣa-ar it-ti-šú*
3 2 [...]*-u-šu-šu-bu ba-šu-ú it-ti-šú aḫ-ra-taš* UN.MEŠ *kul-lu-mu na-ṣa-ar i[t-...]*
3 3–4 [...]

4 0 [d]*na-bi-um-k[u$_{7}$-dur-ri-ú-ṣur* lugal KÁ.DINGIR.RA.KI a]l-si-sá ki-šu-peš$_{6}$ da-gan-bi sá-dug$_{4}$ bí-in-gi$_{4}$-gi$_{4}$
4 1 [d]*na-bi-um-k[u$_{7}$-...* a]l-si-sá ki-šu-peš$_{6}$ da-gan-bi sá-dug$_{4}$ bí-in-gi$_{4}$-gi$_{4}$
4 2 [... a]l-si-sá ki-šu-peš$_{6}$ da-gan-bi sá-dug$_{4}$ bí-in-gi$_{4}$-g[i$_{4}$]
4 3 [... s]á-dug$_{4}$ bí-in-gi$_{4}$-g[i$_{4}$]
4 4 [...]

4 0 ^{d}MIN *ša[r ba-ab-ì-lí muš-te-ší]r kul-lat ma-ḫa-zi mu-kin sat-tuk-ki*
4 1 ^{d}MIN *ša[r ...-ší]r kul-lat ma-ḫa-zi mu-kin sat-tuk-ki*
4 2 [...*-ší]r kul-lat ma-ḫa-zi mu-kin sat-tuk-k[i]*
4 3 [x] *š[ar* ...]
4 4 [...]

5 0 nam-kù-zu x [...] x á-na ár mu-un-da-i-i sag-bi-šè íb-ta-an-è
5 1 nam-kù-zu x [...] ⸢á⸣-na ár mu-un-da-i-i sag-bi-šè íb-ta-an-è
5 2 [...] x á-na ár mu-un-da-i-i sag-bi-šè íb-ta-an-è
5 3 [... sa]g-bi-šè íb-ta-an-è
5 4 [...]

5 0 *ú-šar-ri-[ḫa* ...] *is-su ú-še-ṣa-a a-na re-še-e-ti*
5 1 *ú-šar-ri-*[...] *is-su ú-še-ṣa-a a-na re-še-e-ti*
5 2 [...*-s]u ú-še-ṣa-a* [x*-n]a re-še-e-ti*
5 3 *ú-šar-*x [...]
5 4 [...]

6 0 maḫ-bi íl-l[a ... nam-gu-l]a-bi
6 1 maḫ-bi íl-l[a ...]
6 2 [...]
6 3 [...-l]a-bi
6 4 [...]

6 0 *ú-šar-ba-a* [...] *ul-la-a pa-ra-aṣ nar-bi-šú*
6 1 [...] *ul-la-a pa-ra-aṣ nar-bi-šú*
6 2 [...*-l]a-a pa-ra-[a]ṣ nar-bi-šu*
6 3 *ú-šar-ba-a* [...]
6 4 [...]

7 0 ^{d}*na-bi-um-ku$_{7}$-d[ur(?)-ri-ú-ṣur* lugal KÁ.DINGIR.RA.KI al-s]i-sá ki-šu-peš$_{6}$ da-gan-bi sá-dug$_{4}$ bí-in-gi$_{4}$-gi$_{4}$
7 1 ^{d}*na-bi-um-ku$_{7}$-d[ur(?)-*...-s]i-sá ki-šu-peš$_{6}$ da-gan-bi sá-dug$_{4}$ bí-in-gi$_{4}$-gi$_{4}$
7 2 [...-s]á ki-šu-peš$_{6}$ da-[x]-bi sá-dug$_{4}$ bí-in-gi$_{4}$-g[i$_{4}$]
7 3 [...-ga]n-bi sá-dug$_{4}$ bí-in-gi$_{4}$-gi$_{4}$
7 4 [...]

7 0 ^{d}MIN *šar ba-ab-ì-⸢lí⸣ mu[š-te-šír ku]l-lat ma-ḫa-zi mu-kin sat-tuk-ki*
7 1 ^{d}MIN *šar b[a-... ku]l-lat ma-ḫa-zi mu-kin sat-tuk-ki*
7 2 [... *ku]l-lat ma-ḫa-zi m[u-ki]n sat-⸢tuk⸣-k[i]*
7 3 MIN *šar ba-ab-ì-⸢lí⸣ mu[š-*...]
7 4 [...]

8 0 nu-nus(NUNUZ) bala sù [...] a-má-ru$_{10}$ na-an-na-ke$_{4}$
8 1 nu-nus(NUNUZ) bala sù [...] a-má-ru$_{10}$ ba-an-ág
8 2 [...]
8 3 [...-m]á(?)-ru$_{10}$ na-an-na-ke$_{4}$
8 4 [...]

8 0 *li-i-pu ru-u-qu šá šar-ru-ú-⸢ti ze⸣-ru na-aṣ-ru šá la-am a-bu-bi*
8 1 *li-i-pu ru-*[...]*-ru šá la-am a-bu-bi*
8 2 [*l*]*i-*⸢*i*⸣*-pu ru-u-qu šá šar-ru-ú-*⸢*ti ze*⸣*-ru na-aṣ-r*[*u* ...]
8 3 *li-i-pu ru-ú-qu* ⸢*šá*⸣ *š*[*ar-*...]
8 4 [...]

9 0 ⸢^{d}en⸣-me-dur-a[n-ki lugal zimbir.KI-r]a-ta è DUG.bur-zi-gal kù-ga al-gub-ba GIŠ.erin-na-ta gùr-ru
9 1 ⸢^{d}en⸣-me-dur-a[n-...b]ur-zi-gal kù-ga al-gub-ba GIŠ.erin-na-ta gùr-ru
9 2 [...-r]a-ta è DUG.bur-zi-gal kù-ga ⸢al⸣-gub-ba GIŠ.eri[n-...]
9 3 [... G]IŠ.erin-na-ta gùr-ru
9 4 [...]

9 0 *ṣi-it* ^{d}*en-*[*me-dur-an-ki*] *šar si-ip-par mu-kin ma-k*[*al*]*-ti* KÙ*-ti na-šu-ú e-ri-ni*
9 1 [x-*i*]*t* ^{d}*en-*[... K]Ù*-ti na-šu-ú e-ri-ni*
9 2 [...] *mu-kin ma-k*[*al*]*-ti* KÙ*-ti na-šu-ú* [...]
9 3 *ṣi-it* MIN *šar si-ip-par mu-k*[*in* ...]
9 4 [...]

10 0 [x x (x)] x (x) [... ba-a]b-su-uš-me
10 1 [x x (x)] x (x) [...]
10 2 [...] x-uš-bi
10 3 [...-a]b-su-uš-me
10 4 [...]

10 0 *a-šib ma-ḫar* ^{d}UTU *u* ^{d}IŠKUR DINGIR.MEŠ *da-a-a-ni*
10 1 [...] ^{d}UTU *u* ^{d}IŠKUR DINGIR.MEŠ *da-a-a-ni*
10 2 *a-šib ma-ḫar* ^{d}⸢UTU⸣ *u* ^{d}IŠKUR DINGIR.MEŠ ⸢*da*⸣-[...]
10 3 *a-šib ma-ḫar* ^{d}UTU *ù* ⸢^{d}⸣[...]
10 4 [...]

11 0 [... lugalníg-si-s]á sipa zi-da suḫuš kalam-ma bí-in-gi-na-ta
11 1 [...-d]a(?) suḫuš kalam-ma bí-in-gi-na-ta
11 2 [...-s]á sipa zi-da suḫuš kalam-ma bí-in-g[i-...]
11 3 [... b]í-in-gi-na-ta
11 4 [...]

11 0 *ap-lu a-šá-ri-du* [*šá* ^{d}*nin-urta-na-din*]-⸢*šu*⸣-*me* LUGAL *mì-šá-ri re-ʾ-u ki-i-nu mu-kin iš-di ma-a-ti*
11 1 [... *r*]*e-ʾ-u ki-i-nu mu-kin iš-di ma-a-ti*
11 2 [...]-⸢*šu*⸣-*me* LUGAL *mì-šá-ri re-ʾ-u ki-ni mu-kin iš-di m*[*a-*...]
11 3 *ap-lu a-šá-ri-du* MIN *šar mi-šá-ri re-*⸢*é*⸣-[...]
11 4 [...]

12 0 [...] x-bi bíl dur-an-ki-ke$_4$ u$_4$-ul-dù-a u$_4$-ul-dù-a-ke
12 1 [...-k]e$_4$(?) u$_4$-ul-dù-a u$_4$-ul-dù-a-ke$_4$
12 2 [...] x-bi bíl dur-an-ki-ke$_4$ u$_4$-ul-dù-a u$_4$-ul-dù-[...]
12 3 [...] ⸢u$_4$(?)⸣-ul-dù-a-ke$_4$
12 4 [...]

12 0 *um-mat* ^{d}IŠKUR *u* ^{d}*gu-la* DINGIR.MEŠ *šur-bu-ti pir-ʾi ni-ip-pu-ru ki-si-it-ti ṣa-a-ti*
12 1 [...]-⸢*la*⸣ DIN[GIR...] x *ki-si-it-ti ṣa-a-ti*
12 2 [...-*t*]*i pir-ʾi ni-ip-pu-ru ki-si-it-ti ṣa-*⸢*a*⸣-[x]
12 3 *um-mat* ^{d}IŠKUR *u* ^{d}*gu-la* DINGIR.MEŠ *šur-bu-ti* ⸢*pi*⸣-[...]
12 4 [...]

13 0 [...] x ⸢^{d}šu-zi⸣-an-na-ke$_4$ na[m-... a]n-šár gal-la
13 1 [...-a]n-na-ke$_4$ na[m-...]
13 2 [... a]n-šár gal-la
13 3 [...] (x)-la
13 4 [...] x ⸢^{d}šu-zi⸣-an-na-ke$_4$ [...]

13 0 *an-gub-bu-u reš-tu-u šá* ^{d}*šu-zi-an-na ta-li-mat an-šár*
13 1 [...]-⸢*ú*⸣ *šá* ^{d}*šu-zi-an-na ta-li-mat an-šár*
13 2 *an-gub-bu-u reš-tu-u šá* ^{d}*šu-zi-an-n*[*a ta-l*]*i*(?)-*mat an-*⸢*šár*⸣
13 3 *an-gub-bu-ú reš-tu-ú šá* ^{d}M[IN ...]
13 4 *an-gub-bu-ú* [...]

14 0 [an ^{d}en-líl]l-⸢bi⸣-da mu-ni-in-sa$_4$-a dingir gal-gal-e-ne šà-ge-pà-da-me-en
14 1 [...-d]a mu-⸢ni⸣-[...]-ne šà-ge-pà-da-me-en
14 2 [...-s]a$_4$-a dingir gal-gal-e-ne [...]-me-en
14 3 [...-e]n
14 4 [...-líl]l-⸢bi⸣-da mu-ni-in-sa$_4$-a [...]

14 0 *ni-bit* ^{d}*a-nim ù* ^{d}*da-gan i-tu-ut ku-un lib-bi* DINGIR.[MEŠ G]AL.MEŠ *a-na-ku-ma*
14 1 [... *d*]*a-gan* ⸢*i*⸣-[... G]AL.MEŠ *a-na-ku-ma*
14 2 [...-*u*]*t ku-un lìb-bi* DINGIR.[...-*n*]*a-*⸢*ku*⸣-*ma*
14 3 *ni-bit* ^{d}*a-nim ù* ^{d}*da-gan i-tu-u*[*t* ...]
14 4 *ni-bit* ^{d}*a-nim u* ^{d}*d*[*a-*...]

15 0 ⸢u$_4$⸣-bi-a bala lugal sag̃-gá-ke$_4$ giskim-bi a[b-...]
15 1 [...-g]á-ke$_4$ giskim-bi a[b-...]
15 2–3 [...]
15 4 ⸢u$_4$⸣-bi-a bala lugal sag-gá-ke$_4$ [...]

15 0 *i-nu-šú ina pa-le-e šar-ri maḫ-ri-i iš-na-a i-da-a-tu*
15 1 [...]-*e šar-ri maḫ-ri-i iš-na-a i-da-a-tu*
15 2 *i-nu-šú ina pa-le-*⸢*e*⸣ *š*[*ar-...-t*]*u*(?)
15 3 *i-nu-šu i-na pa-le-e* LUGAL *maḫ-r*[*i-*...]
15 4 *i-nu-šú ina pa-le-e* L[UGAL ...]

16 0 níg-sig$_5$-ga ab-te-ri-a [n]am-ḫul-la ba-ab-x [...]
16 1 [... n]am-ḫul-la ba-ab-x [...]
16 2–3 [...]
16 4 níg-sig$_5$-ga ab-te-ri-a [...]

16 0 *da-mì-iq-tu is-si-ma le-mut-tu sad-rat*
16 1 [...-*t*]*u*(?) *is-si-ma le-mut-tu sad-rat*
16 2 *da-mì-iq-tu is-si-ma* [...]-*rat*
16 3 [*d*]*a-mi-iq-ti is-si-ma sad-*[...]
16 4 *da-mi-iq-tu is-se-*⸢*e*⸣-[...]

17 0 en-e lipiš-bi na-an-bal-la [šà]-dib-ba in-[...]
17 1 [...]-dib-ba in-[...]
17 2 [...] (x) [...]
17 3 [...]
17 4 en-e lipiš-bi na-an-bal-la [...]

17 0 *be-lu$_4$ i-gug-ma ki-mil-ta ir-ši*
17 1 [...] ⸢*e*(?)⸣-*gug-ma ki-mil-ta ir-ši*
17 2 *be-lu$_4$ i-gug-ma* [...-*š*]*i*
17 3 [...] ⸢*i*⸣-*gu-ug*-(x) [...]
17 4 *be-lu$_4$ i-gu-*⸢*ug*(?)⸣-*m*[*a*(?) ...]

18 0 kur-ra al-mu-un-da-ab-bé dingir-re-e-ne m[u-un-š]ub-ba al-bal šu sag-gá-na níg-lul-la ab-zi-zi-e-a
18 1 [...-a]b-bé dingir-re-e-ne m[u-... sa]g-gá-na níg-lul-la ab-zi-zi-e-a
18 2 [...-š]ub-ba al-bal šu sag-⸢gá⸣-n[a(?) ...]-⸢e⸣-a
18 3 [...]
18 4 kur-ra al-mu-un-da-ab-ba dingir-re-⸢e-ne⸣ [...]

18 0 *iq-bi-⌈ma ma-a⌉-ta id-du-ši* DINGIR.MEŠ-*š[á] iš-ni ṭè-em* UN.MEŠ-*šá šu-ḫu-za sur-ra-a-ti*
18 1 [...] *id-du-ši* DINGIR.MEŠ-*š[á*(?) ... U]N.MEŠ-*šá šu-ḫu-za sur-ra-a-ti*
18 2 [...] *iš-ni tè-em* UN.MEŠ-[(x)] x x [...]-⌈*a*⌉-*ti*
18 3 [...].⌈MEŠ⌉-[...]
18 4 *iq-bi-⌈ma ma-a⌉-ta id-du-šá* DINGIR.MEŠ-*š[á* ...]

19 0 sag-é/líl x [x] x (x) ⌈gú⌉-šub-ba-meš ul-ḫé ⌈ši-in⌉-[e$_{11}$ (...)] x ^{d}lamma níg-si-sá ki-bar-ra al-gub-bu
19 1 [...]-šub-ba-meš u[l-...] x ^{d}lamma níg-si-sá ki-bar-ra al-gub-bu
19 2 [... la]mma níg-si-sá ki-bar-ra al-gub-ba
19 3 [...]
19 4 sag-é/líl x [x] x (x) ⌈gú-šub-ba-meš⌉ ul-ḫé ⌈ši-in⌉-[...]

19 0 ⌈*iz*⌉-*nu*-⌈*ú ra-bi*⌉-[*ṣu*] *šul-me e-lu*-⌈*u*⌉ [*ana šu-puk* AN-*e la-mas-si*] *mi-šá-ri it-ta-ziz a-ḫi-ta*
19 1 [...] *šul-me e-lu*-⌈*u*⌉ [...] *mi-šá-ri it-ta-ziz a-ḫi-ta*
19 2 [...]-⌈*šá*⌉-*ri it-ta-ziz a-ḫi-ta*
19 3 [...]
19 4 ⌈*iz*⌉-*nu*-⌈*ú ra-bi*⌉-[...]

20 0 ^{d}x [x zi-a]l-la-aš nam-lú-u$_{18}$-lu ba-an-šub-ba dingir ma-ra-ab-tuku-a gú-sag-KAL-ir sì-ga
20 1 [... n]am-lú-u$_{18}$-lu b[a-...-r]a(?)-ab-tuku-a gú-sag-KAL-ir sì-ga
20 2 [...]-⌈šub⌉-ba dingir ma-ra-ab-t[uku-a g]ú(?)-[...-i]r sì-ga
20 3 [...]
20 4 ^{d}x [x x-a]l-la-aš ⌈nam-lú⌉-u$_{18}$-lu ba-an-šub-ba [...]

20 0 [^{d}x] x *na-ṣir nap-šá-a-ti ni-ši i-te-ez-ba ki-ma* [*la r*]*aš*(?) DINGIR-*ma e-ma-a gim-rat-si-in*
20 1 [... *na*]*p*(?)-*šá-a-ti ni-ši* ⌈*i*(?)⌉-[... *r*]*aš*(?) DINGIR-*ma e-ma-a gim-rat-si-in*
20 2 [...] *ni-ši i-te-ez-ba ki-ma* [...] ⌈*e-ma-a*⌉ *gim-rat-si-im*
20 3 [...]
20 4 [x x] x *na-ṣir nap-šá-a-ti ni-ši i-t*[*e*-...]

21 0 udug-ḫul-didli šà-ba kalam-ma e-ra nam-tar sag nam-BAD-e-ne <<⌈la⌉>> [ú]ru-šu-peš$_{6}$ al-sun$_{5}$-ne-eš
21 1 [...]-ma e-ra nam-tar s[ag ... ú]ru-šu-peš$_{6}$ al-sun$_{5}$-ne-eš
21 2 [...] nam-tar sag nam-BAD-e-ne <<⌈la⌉>> [...] al-sun$_{5}$-ne-eš
21 3 [...]
21 4 udug-ḫul-didli šà-ba kalam-ma è-ra nam-tar sag nam-m[u-...]

21 0 *ú-tuk-[k]u lem-nu-ti im-lu-u qé-reb ma-a-ti nam-ta-ru la [p]a-du-u ma-ḫa-zi-iš i-ter-bu*
21 1 *[... i]m-lu-u qé-reb ma-a-t[i ... p]a-du-u ma-ḫa-zi-iš i-ter-bu*
21 2 *[...-r]eb ma-a-ti nam-ta-ru la [...] ma-ḫa-zi-iš i-ter-bu*
21 3 [...]
21 4 *ú-tuk-[k]u lem-nu-ti im-lu-ú qé-reb ma-a-ti nam-tar l[a ...]*

22 0 ma-da ab-tur-ra-àm [m]a-al-gi-bi ši-in-kúr-ru-da
22 1 [...-g]i-bi ši-in-kúr-r[u-(x)]
22 2 [... m]a-al-gi-bi ši-in-kúr-ru-da
22 3 [...]
22 4 ma-da ab-tur-ra-àm [...]

22 0 *iṣ-ḫir-ma ma-a-tu$_4$ mi-lik-šá iš-ni*
22 1 *[...]-a-tu$_4$ mi-lik-šá iš-ni*
22 2 *[...] iš-ni*
22 3 [...]
22 4 *iṣ-ḫir-mã ma-a-ti mi-lik-šá i[š(?)-x]*

23 0 níg-zi elam-ma.KI ḫé-⌈li⌉-bi nu-mu-un-da-ab-kal-la [... m]è gìr-íl-la-a-ni ši-in-sar-re
23 1 [...-m]u-un-da-ab-k[al-... m]è gìr-íl-la-a-ni ši-in-sar-re
23 2 [...] x BAD AŠ nu-mu-un-da-ab-kal-l[a ...-n]i ši-in-sar-re
23 3 [...]
23 4 níg-zi elam-ma.KI ḫé-⌈li⌉-bi nu-mu-un-da-ab-kal-la [...]

23 0 *ṣe-e-nu e-la-mu-u la mu-šá-qir* AN *[... ta]-ḫa-za-šú ti-bu-šú iḫ-tam-ṭù*
23 1 *[...] mu-šá-qir* AN *[...]-ḫa-za-šú ti-bu-šú iḫ-tam-ṭù*
23 2 *[...] ⌈e⌉-la-mu-u la mu-šá-qir* AN *[...-b]u-šú iḫ-tam-ṭù*
23 3 [...]
23 4 *se-e-nu e-la-mu-ú l[a ...]*

24 0 úru-didli íb-ta-an-gi ir-ra-šè ba-an-si dingir-re-e-ne ši-in-bi-ra-ka zag líl-lá ba-ni-in-ri
24 1 [...] x-šè ba-an-[...-n]e(?) ši-in-bi-ra-ka zag líl-lá ba-ni-in-ri
24 2 [...-t]a(?)-an-gi ir-ra-šè ba-a[n-... b]a-ni-in-ri
24 3 [...]
24 4 úru-didli íb-ta-an-g[i ir-r]a-a-šè ba-an-si dingir-re-e-ne [...]

24 0 *ú-šá-aḫ-rib da-ád-me na-mu-iš um-me* [DINGIR.MEŠ *iš-t]a-lal ú-nam-me eš-re-e-ti*
24 1 *[...]-iš um-me [...-t]a-lal ú-nam-me eš-re-e-ti*
24 2 *[... d]a-ád-me ⌈na-mu⌉-iš [...-r]e-e-ti*
24 3 [...]
24 4 *ú-šá-aḫ-rib da-ád-me na-mu-u$_8$-i[š ...]*

Line	MS	Text
25	0	^{d}⸢šà⸣-zu lugal dingir-re-⸢e⸣-[ne n]am tar-tar-e-dè [...] x ši-in-zi gi$_4$-gi$_4$ ba-an-è
25	1	[... na]m tar-tar-e-d[è(?) ...] x ši-in-zi gi$_4$-gi$_4$ ba-an-è
25	2	[...] ⸢dingir(?)⸣-[...-a]n-è
25	3	[...]
25	4	^{d}⸢šà⸣-zu lugal dingir-re-⸢e⸣-[ne n]am tar-tar-e-dè [...]
25	0	^{d}AMAR.UTU *šár-ri* DINGIR.⸢MEŠ *mu*⸣*-šim ši-ma-a-t*[*i* ...] x KUR.KUR *i-ḫaṭ gim-re-e-ti*
25	1	[...]*-šim ši-ma-a-*[...] x KUR.KUR *i-ḫaṭ gim-re-e-ti*
25	2	[...*-r*]*e-e-ti*
25	3	[...]
25	4	^{d}AMAR.UTU *šár-ri* DINGIR.⸢MEŠ *mu-šim ši-ma*⸣*-a-t*[*i* ...]
26	0	[x-šà-í]b-bi-me-a ^{d}nu[n]-gal-e-ne an-na-ke$_4$ [...] x nu-mu-un-da-ab-íl-íl
26	1	[...-g]al-e-ne an-[...] x nu-mu-un-da-ab-íl-íl
26	2	[...]-íl
26	3	[...]
26	4	[x-x-í]b-bi-me-a ^{d}nu[n]-gal-e-ne an-na-ke$_4$ [...]
26	0	*ag-ga-gi-ma be-lu*$_4$ ^{d}*í-gì-gì ina* [AN-*e la*] ⸢*i*⸣*-na-áš-šu-ú ka-dàr-šu*
26	1	[...*-l*]*u*$_4$(?) ^{d}*í-gì-gì ina* [...] ⸢*i*⸣*-na-áš-šu-ú ka-dàr-šu*
26	2	[...]-⸢*dàr*⸣*-šu*
26	3	[...]
26	4	*ag-ga-gi-ma be-lu*$_4$ ^{d}*í-*[...]
27	0	[su-zi-bi ḫ]u-[l]uḫ-ḫa igi-túl-bi šúr-ra [(x)] lú na-me nu-gub-ba
27	1	[...] igi-túl-bi š[úr-...] lú na-me nu-gub-ba
27	2–3	[...]
27	4	[x x x ḫ]u-[l]uḫ-ḫa i[gi-t]úl-bi šúr-ra [...]
27	0	*gal-ta-at-ma na-mur-rat-su a-na né-kel-*[*mi-šu a-me-l*]*u ma-na-ma ul iz-ziz*
27	1	[...*-ra*]*t-su a-na né-kel-*[...*-l*]*u ma-na-ma ul iz-ziz*
27	2	[... *u*]*l iz-ziz*
27	3	[...]
27	4	*gal-ta-at-ma na-mur-rat-su ina* [...]
28	0	[ki-gal(?)] gìr-ús-bi á-šu-uš nu-un-gál-la [(x x) dum-d]am-a-ni-ta ab-didli ur$_4$-ur$_4$-re-e-dè
28	1	[... g]ìr-ús-bi á-šu-uš nu-u[n]-g[ál-...-d]am-a-ni-ta ab-didli ur$_4$-ur$_4$-re-e-dè
28	2	[...]-dè
28	3	[...]
28	4	[...] g[ìr(?)-ú]s-bi á-tuš nu-un-gál-la [...]

28 0 *ul ip-tin ki-gal-lu ki-bi-is-su ul i-*x [... *a-na ú-t*]*a-zu-me-šú i-ár-ru-ra ta-ma-a-ti*
28 1 [...]*-gal-lu ki-bi-is-su ul i-*x [...*-t*]*a-zu-me-šú i-ár-ru-ra ta-ma-a-ti*
28 2–3 [...]
28 4 *ul ip-tin ki-gal-la k*[*i-*...]

29 0 [... nu-mu-u]n-da-ab-ḫa-za gá-gá-bi dingir-ki-šár-ra-e-ne [e]-ne-šè bí-in-gúr-ru-uš
29 1 [...-u]n-da-ab-ḫa-za gá-gá-bi di[ngir-...]-ne-šè bí-in-gúr-ru-uš
29 2–3 [...]
29 4 [...-g]á-bi dingir-ki-šár-ra-e-ne [...]

29 0 *ul uk-til ú-ḫu-me ši-kin še-pi-*[*šu* DINGIR.MEŠ *šá k*]*iš-šá-ti šá-a-šú kan-šu-uš*
29 1 [...*-ti*]*l ú-ḫu-me ši-kin še-pi-*[... *k*]*iš-šá-ti šá-a-šú kan-šu-uš*
29 2–3 [...]
29 4 *ul uk-til ú-ḫu-m*[*u* ...]

30 0 [... n]am-gu-la šu-bé ši-⌈in-šid-da⌉ [(...) mir-r]a a-ba ši-in-šed$_7$-dè
30 1 [... n]am-gu-la šu-bé ši-i[n-...-r]a a-ba ši-in-šed$_7$-dè
30 2–3 [...]
30 4 [...-i]n-⌈šid-da⌉.[...]

30 0 ⌈*bu-uš kul-lat*⌉ *mim-ma-ma qa-tu*[*š-šu pa-qid* ...] x *i-gu-gu li-ni-iḫ-šú man-nu*
30 1 [...*-la*]*t mim-ma-ma qa-t*[*uš-*...] x *i-gu-gu li-ni-iḫ-šú man-nu*
30 2–3 [...]
30 4 ⌈*bu-uš kul-lat mim*⌉*-ma* MU*-šú qa-tu*[*š-*...]

31 0 [... a]l-zu-zu-e-d[è ...] x-biníg-galam-ma-bi igi in-è
31 1 [... a]l-zu-zu-e-d[è ...] x-bi níg-galam-ma-bi igi in-è
31 2–4 [...]

31 0 [...] x *šá il-ma-du* [...] x*-šu-ma i-bar-ru-u ník-lat-su*
31 1 [...] x *šá il-ma-du* [...] x*-šu-ma i-bar-ru-u ník-lat-su*
31 2–3 [...]
31 4 [...] x [...]

32 0 [... n]í-te-a-ni [... k]ur-kur-ra mu-lu ḪI-du$_{11}$-ga
32 1 [... n]í-te-a-ni [... k]ur-kur-ra mu-lu ḪI-du$_{11}$-ga
32 2–4 [...]

32 0 [...] x *ra-ma-*[*an-šu* ...] ^{d}*en-líl* DINGIR.MEŠ *te-le-'u*
32 1 [...] x *ra-ma-*[...] ^{d}*en-líl* DINGIR.MEŠ *te-le-'u*
32 2–4 [...]

33 0 [... ^{d}nun-gal]-e-n[e ... id]im bí-tar-ri-in
33 1 [...]-e-n[e ... id]im bí-tar-ri-in
33 2–4 [...]

33 0 [...] ^{d}⸢í⸣-[*gì-gì* ...] *ru-bu-u muš-tal-lu*$_4$
33 1 [...] ^{d}⸢í⸣-[...] *ru-bu-u muš-tal-lu*$_4$
33 2–4 [...]

34 0 [...] tar-r[a(?) ...] x da-ra-aḫ ní-te bí-íb-ri-a
34 1 [...] tạr-r[a(?) ...] x da-ra-aḫ ní-te bí-íb-ri-a
34 2–4 [...]

34 0 x [...] *šá ina* x [...] *me-lam-me zu-'u-nu ra-mu-u pul-ḫa-a-ti*
34 1 x [...] *šá ina* x [...] *me-lam-me zu-'u-nu ra-mu-u pul-ḫa-a-ti*
34 2–4 [...]

35 0 kala-g[a(?) ...] x [...] nam-en-bi sag-rib-bé
35 1 kala-g[a(?) ...] x [...] nam-en-bi sag-rib-bé
35 2–4 [...]

35 0 *dan-n*[*u*(?) ...] *šu-tu-qat be-lu-us-su*
35 1 *dan-n*[*u*(? ...] *šu-tu-qat be-lu-us-su*
35 2–4 [...]

Catch-line on ex. 1 (line 64 of exemplar)

1) ní-galam [... ár mu-u]n-da-i-i gír-gal-nin-ma-ke$_4$

Colophon on ex. 1 (lines 65–68 of exemplar)

1) DUB 1.KÁM [(...) *ekal aššur-bāni-apli šar kiššati šar māt aššur ša* ^{d}*na-bi-u*]*m*(?) *u* ^{d}*taš-me-tu*$_4$ *uz-nu ra-pa-áš-tu iš-ru-ku-uš*
2) *i-ḫu-u*[*z-zu īna namirtu nisiq ṭupšarrūti ša ina šarrāni ālik maḫ*]*-ri-ia mám-ma šip-ru šu-a-tu la i-ḫu-uz-zu*
3) *né-me-e*[*q nabû tikip santakki mala bašmu ina* DUB.ME]Š(?) *áš-ṭur as-niq ab-re-e-ma*
4) *a-na t*[*a-mar-ti šitassīia q*]*é-reb* É.GAL*-ia ú-kin*

1	0	[...] (x) in-šub-bé-e-ne-⸢šè⸣ ní-bi-⸢ta⸣ nam-kur-re-e-ne ug$_5$-⸢ga-gin$_7$(?)⸣ im-šèg GIŠ.tukul á-bi lál-e adda-a-ni sal-la-ke$_4$
1	1	[...]-⸢e-šè ní-bi-ta⸣ nam-kur-re-e-ne ug$_5$-⸢ga⸣-x x-šèg GIŠ.tukul á-bi lál-e adda-a-ni sal-la-ke$_4$
1	2–3	[...]
1	4	[...] (x) in-šub-bé-e-ne-še ní-b[i-...-gi]n$_7$(?) im-šèg GIŠ.tukul á-ba lal-⸢e⸣ [...]
2	0	[x x *i*]*p*(?)*-par-ši-du ma-la ik-šu-du-uš kak-ku ina ra-ma-ni-šú-nu* ⸢*ki*⸣*-ma mi-*⸢*tu-ut ḫal-pe*⸣*-e i-di-šú-nu uk-tas-sa-ma mu-uṣ-ṣu-u šal-mat-su-un*
2	1	[...] x *ma-la ik-šu-du-uš kak-ku ina ra-ma-ni-šú-nu* ⸢*ki*⸣*-ma mi-*⸢*tu-ut ḫal-pe*⸣*-e i-di-šú-nu uk-tas-sa-ma mu-uṣ-*⸢*ṣu*⸣*-u šal-mat-su-un*
2	2	[...]
2	3	[...] x x [...]
2	4	[x x *i*]*p*(?)*-par-ši-du ma-la ik-šu-du-uš* ⸢*kak*⸣-[...](x)*-pe-e i-di-šú-nu uk-ta-si-i us-s*[*u*(?)-...]
3	0	[x x] an-ta ki-ta á-zi-da á-gùb-bu igi egir a-má-ru$_{10}$ mu-un-dib-eš-àm uru šà-ba uru bar-ra edin edin-na sìg-sìg bí-in-si a-ri-a mu-un-DU-DU
3	1	[...-t]a á-zi-da á-gùb-bu igi egir a-má-ru$_{10}$ mu-un-dib-eš-àm uru šà-ba uru bar-ra edin edin-na sìg-sìg bí-in-si a-ri-a mu-un-DU-DU
3	2	[...]
3	3	[x x] an-ta ki-ta ⸢á⸣-[...]
3	4	[...-d]a á-gùb-⸢bi⸣ igi egir a-⸢má⸣-ru$_{10}$-ra mu-un-d[ib(?)-...]-sìg-ga bí-íb-si a-ri-a mu-un-D[U-DU]
4	0	[x] x AN *e-liš u šap-liš im-na ù šu-me-la pa-ni ù ar-ku uš-bi-ʾ a-bu-ba-niš-ma* ŠÀ URU *a-ḫat* URU *ṣi-i-ru ba-ma-a-ti šá-qu-um-ma-tu ú-šam-li-ma ú-šá-li-ka na-mu-iš*
4	1	[... *i*]*m-na ù šu-me-la pa-ni ù ar-ku uš-bi-ʾ a-bu-ba-niš-ma* ŠÀ URU *a-ḫat* URU *ṣi-i-ru ba-ma-a-ti šá-qu-um-ma-tu ú-šam-li-ma ú-šá-li-ka na-mu-iš*
4	2	[...]
4	3	[x] x AN *e-liš u šap-li*[*š* ...]
4	4	[... *š*]*ap-liš im-ni u šu-me-lu pa-ni u ár-ku uš-bi-*⸢ʾ⸣ [...] x *a-ḫat a-lu ṣe-e-ri u ba-ma-a-tú šá-*[...]
5	0	[(x) lú(?)-s]ag ní-te-a-ni ù-⸢gul⸣-gá-gá še-še-ga lú igi-du$_8$-a-bi sag-ús ab-ta-bu-bu-lu en-e šà-ba-a-ni na-me mu-un-BU-i šà-ne-ša$_4$ nam-mi-in-gub
5	1	[...-g]á-gá še-še-ga lú igi-du$_8$-a-bi sag-ús ab-ta-bu-bu-lu en-e šà-ba-a-ni na-me mu-un-BU-i šà-ne-ša$_4$ nam-mi-in-gub
5	2	[...]
5	3	[(x) x s]ag ní-te-a-ni ù-⸢gul-gá⸣-[...]
5	4	[...-gu]l-⸢gá-gá⸣-bi še-še-ga lú igi-du$_8$-a sag-ús ab-t[a-...] na-me m[u(?)-...]

6 0 *[(x) r]e-e-ši pa-li-iḫ-šu mut-nen-nu-ú mu-un-dag-ri šá ana ta-mar-ti-šú kak-da-a pu-tuq-qu-ma a-di ú-šam-ṣu-šú ma-la lib-bu-uš la ik-la-a un-nen-ni*
6 1 *[(x) r]e-⌈e-ši pa-li-iḫ-šu mut-nen⌉-nu-ú mu-un-dag-ri šá ana ta-mar-ti-šú kak-da-a pu-tuq-qu-ma a-di ú-šam-ṣu-šú ma-la lib-bu-uš la ik-la-a un-nen-ni*
6 2 [...]
6 3 *[(x) r]e-e-ši pa-li-iḫ-šu mut-nen-nu-⌈ú⌉* [...]
6 4 [...-*r*]*i*(?) ⌈*šá ana ta-mar-ti*⌉-x x [...]

7 0 [en]-⌈e⌉ i-bí-bar-ra alam sukud-da-a-ni u$_4$-šú-uš-e múš nu-túm-ma su-GAM-ma su-mu nu-ku$_5$-da úr-ra-a-ni gi$_6$ du$_{10}$-ga-bi nu-til-la-e-da-ni ù-sá na-nam
7 1 [en]-⌈e⌉ i-bí-bar-ra alam sukud-da-a-ni u$_4$-šú-uš-e múš nu-túm-ma su-GAM-ma su-mu nu-ku$_5$-da úr-ra-a-ni gi$_6$ du$_{10}$-ga-bi nu-til-la-e-da-ni ù-sá na-nam
7 2 [...]
7 3 [en]-⌈e⌉ i-bí-bar-ra alam sukud-da-a-ni u$_4$-šú-uš-e m[úš ...]
7 4 [...]

8 0 [(x)] ⌈*a*⌉-*di at-tap-la-su la-an-šu e-la-a u*$_4$*-mi-šam la na-par-ka-a ṣur-ri qid-da-a-ti ina zu-um-ri-ia la ip-par-su-ú-ma ina ut-lu mu-ši ṭa-a-bu la ú-qat-ta-a šit-ti*
8 1 [(x)] ⌈*a*⌉-*di at-tap-la-su la-an-šu* ⌈*e*⌉-*la-a u*$_4$*-mi-šam la na-par-ka-a ṣur-ri qid-da-a-ti ina zu-um-ri-ia la ip-par-su-ú-ma ina ut-lu mu-ši ṭa-a-bu la ú-qat-ta-a šit-ti*
8 2 [...]
8 3 x ⌈*ad*⌉-*di at-tap-la-su la-an-šu e-la-a u*$_4$*-mi-ša*[*m* ...]
8 4 [...]

9 0 [šà (x)] mu-un-gig-ga-mu šùd-dè kúš-ù-mu šu-íl-la-mu u$_4$-šú-uš-e kir$_4$ šu mar-ra-mu sískur-ra-a-ni ù-gul-gá-gá šà-bi dagal-la arḫuš tuk-a gú-bi nigin šà-bi-ta uru kù-ga
9 1 [x (x)] mu-un-gig-ga-mu šùd-dè kúš-ù-mu šu-íl-la-mu u$_4$-šú-uš-e kir$_4$ šu mar-ra-mu sískur-ra-a-ni ù-gul-gá-gá šà-bi dagal-la arḫuš tuk-a gú-bi nigin šà-bi-ta uru kù-ga
9 2 [...]
9 3 [...-u]n-gig-ga-mu šùd-dè kúš-ù-mu šu-í[l-...]
9 4 [...]

10 0 [*ina u*]*n-nen-ni-ia šum-ru-ṣu-ti ik-ri-bi-ia šu-nu-ḫu-ti ni-iš qa-ti-ia ù la-ban ap-pi-ia šá u*$_4$*-mi-šam a-bal-lu-uš ut-nen-nu-šú*
10 1 [x *u*]*n-nen-ni-ia šum-ru-ṣu-ti ik-ri-bi-ia šu-nu-ḫu-ti ni-iš qa-ti-ia ù la-ban ap-pi-ia šá u*$_4$*-mi-šam a-bal-lu-uš ut-nen-nu-šú*
10 2 [...]
10 3 [...-*n*]*i-ia šu-um-ru-ṣu-ti ik-ri-bi-ia š*[*u-*...]
10 4 [...]

11 0 [*ṣu*]*r-ru-uš šad-lim re-e-mu ir-ši-ma ki-šad-su ú-saḫ-ḫi-ra ana qé-reb* URU KÙ.GA

11 1 [*ṣu*]*r-ru-uš šad-lim re-e-mu ir-ši-ma ki-šad-su ú-saḫ-ḫi-ra ana qé-reb* URU KÙ.GA

11 2–4 [...]

12 0 [x (x) š]à-bi túm-ma-a-ra uru edin mu-un-DU-a-ni šà-bi-ta níg-ḫul elam-ma.KI-ke$_4$ kaskal a-li-ri ḫar-ra-an asila$_4$ ḫé-en-da-še-še-ga šà šu-an-na-ta mu-un-dib

12 1 [x (x) š]à-bi túm-ma-a-ra uru edin mu-un-[D]U-a-ni šà-bi-ta níg-ḫul elam-ma.KI-ke$_4$ kaskal a-li-ri ḫar-ra-an asila$_4$ ḫé-en-da-še-še-ga šà šu-an-na-ta mu-un-dib

12 2 [...]

12 3 [...] x-ma-a-rá uru edin mu-un-DU-a-n[i ...]

12 4 [...]

13 0 [x] *šá ub-la lìb-ba-šú a-lak* URU EDIN *ki i-ku-šam-ma iš-tu qé-reb lem-né-ti e-lam-ti ḫar-ra-an šu-lu-lu*(*) *ú-ru-uḫ ri-šá-a-ti*

13 1 [x] *šá ub-la lìb-ba-šú a-lak* URU EDIN ⸢*ki*⸣ *i-ku-šam-ma iš-tu qé-reb lem-né-ti e-lam-ti ḫar-ra-an šu-lu-lu*(*) *ú-ru-uḫ ri-šá-a-ti*

13 2 [...]

13 3 [... *lì*]*b*(?)-⸢*ba*⸣-*šú a-lak* URU EDIN *ki i-k*[*u-*...]

13 4 [...]

14 0 [*ṭ*]*u-da-at taš-me-e ù ma-ga-ri iṣ-ba-ta ana qé-reb šu-an-na*.KI

14 1 [*ṭ*]*u-da-at taš-me-e ù ma-ga-ri iṣ-ba-ta ana qé-reb šu-an-na*.KI

14 2–4 [...]

15 0 un ma-da igi-kár-kár-ra-ab é-gar$_8$-bi ⸢sukud⸣-da ḫé-du$_7$ še-er-ma-al šu-li-li-eš bar-dagal-la da-gan-bi ir$_5$-ra-ag-a-e-dè

15 1 [un m]a-da igi-kár-kár-ra-ab é-gar$_8$-bi ⸢sukud⸣-da ḫé-du$_7$ še-er-ma-al šu-li-li-eš bar-dagal-la da-gan-bi ir$_5$-ra-ag-a-e-dè

15 2 un ⸢ma-da⸣ x x [...]

15 3–4 [...]

16 0 *ib-tar-ra-a ni-iš ma-a-ti la-an-šú e-la-a šu-su-mu e-tel-la na-par-da-a šu-lu-la kul-lat-si-na pu-tuq-qa-šu*

16 1 [*i*]*b-tar-ra-a ni-iš ma-a-ti la-an-šú e-la-a šu-su-mu e-tel-la na-par-da-a šu-lu-la kul-lat-si-na pu-tuq-qa-šu*

16 2 *ib-tar-ra-a ni-ši ma-*⸢*a-ti la-an*⸣-[...]

16 3–4 [...]

17 0 nam-ba-ni-íb-sun$_5$-na ù-mu-un ba-ni-in-ri dul-mar-ra-bi ní-dúb-dúb-bu

17 1 [n]am-ba-ni-íb-sun$_5$-na ù-mu-⸢un⸣ ba-ni-in-ri dul-mar-ra-bi ní-dúb-dúb-bu

17 2 nam-ba-ni-íb-sun$_5$-na ù-mu-u[n ...]

17 3–4 [...]

18 0 *i-ru-um-ma be-lu$_4$ ir-⸢ta⸣-me šu-bat-su ni-iḫ-ta*
18 1 *i-ru-um-ma be-lu$_4$ ir-⸢ta⸣-me šu-bat-su ni-iḫ-ta*
18 2 *i-ru-um-ma* [...]
18 3–4 [...]

19 0 ká-su-lim nam-lugal-la-bi-šè é-šà-sìg-ga pirig-gá ba-ni-íb-si-sá-e me-li ár-i-i
19 1 ká-su-lim nam-lugal-la-bi-šè é-šà-sìg-ga pirig-gá ba-ni-íb-si-sá-e me-li ár-i-i
19 2 ká-su-lim nam-lugal-la-bi-šè [...] (x x)
19 3–4 [...]

20 0 *ká-su-lim pa-paḫ be-lu-ti-šú im-me-ra ma-li ri-šá-a-ti*
20 1 *ká-su-lim pa-paḫ be-lu-ti-šú im-me-ra ma-li ri-šá-a-ti*
20 2 *ká-su-lim pa-paḫ be-lu-ti-šú ⸢im⸣-m[e-...]-tu$_4$*
20 3–4 [...]

21 0 an-ki-bi-ta du$_8$-du$_8$-bé-e-ne a-ab-ba za-ba-lam-a-ni si ba-ni-íb-sá ḫur-sag máš mu-un-da-ri-bi
21 1 an-ki-bi-ta du$_8$-du$_8$-bé-e-ne a-ab-ba za-ba-lam-a-ni si ba-ni-íb-sá ḫur-sag máš mu-un-da-ri-bi
21 2 an-ki-bi-ta du$_8$-du$_8$-bé-e-ne a-ab-ba ⸢za⸣-ba-lam-⸢a⸣-[...-r]i-bi
21 3–4 [...]

22 0 *šá-mu-ú ḫé-en-gál-la-šú-nu er-ṣe-tu$_4$ ḫi-ṣib-šá tam-tu$_4$ mi-šir-ta-šá šá-du-ú i-rib-šú*
22 1 *[šá-m]u-ú ḫé-en-gál-la-šú-nu er-ṣe-tu$_4$ ḫi-ṣib-šá tam-tu$_4$ mi-šir-ta-šá šá-du-ú i-rib-šú*
22 2 *šá-mu-ú ḫé-en-gál-la-šú-nu er-ṣe-tu$_4$ ḫi-sib-⸢šá⸣ tam-t[u$_4$ ...]-rib-šú*
22 3–4 [...]

23 0 sískur-bi-ne-ne èm i-bí nu-mu-un-bar-ra níg a-na eme gù-bal-bal-e
23 1 [sísku]r-bi-ne-ne èm i-bí nu-mu-un-bar-ra níg a-na eme gù-bal-bal-e
23 2 ⸢sískur⸣-bi-ne-ne èm i-bí nu-mu-un-bar-ra níg a-⸢na eme gù⸣-[bal]-bal-e
23 3–4 [...]

24 0 *kit-ru-ba-áš-šú šu-ut la maḫ-ra ma-la šu-un-na-a li-šá-a-nu*
24 1 *[...]-⸢ba⸣-áš-šú šu-ut la ⸢maḫ⸣-ra ma-la šu-un-na-a li-šá-a-nu*
24 2 *kit-ru-ba-áš-šú šu-ut la maḫ-⸢ra⸣ ma-la ⸢šu⸣-un-na-a li-šá-a-nu*
24 3–4 [...]

25 0 mu-un-dugud-da-bi mu-un-ši-in-íl-íl-eš ù-mu-un lugal-la-šè : *ka-bit-ti bi-lat-su-nu na-šu-ú a-na be-el be-lu$_4$*
25 1 [...] ⸢mu-un-ši-in-íl⸣-í[l-eš] ⸢ù⸣-mu-un lugal-la-šè : *ka-bit-ti bi-lat-su-nu na-šu-ú a-na be-el be-lu$_4$*
25 2 mu-un-dugud-da-bi mu-un-ši-in-íl-íl-eš ù-mu-un lugal-la-šè *ka-bit-ti bi-lat-su-nu na-šu-ú a-na be-el be-lu$_4$*
25 3–4 [...]

26 0 ^{e}UDU bí-in-šum-mu-dè-eš gud-gal-⸢gal⸣-la bí-in-šár-šár-ra níg-KU-DU ul mu-un-ši-in-gál-le-eš na-NE bí-in-si-si
26 1 [... gu]d(?)-g[al(?)-gal]-la bí-in-šár-šár-ra níg-KU-DU ul mu-un-ši-in-gál-le-eš na-NE bí-in-si-si
26 2 ^{e}UDU bí-in-šum-mu-dè-eš gud-gal-⸢gal⸣-la bí-in-šár-šár-ra níg-KU-DU ul mu-un-ši-in-gál-le-eš na-NE bí-in-si-si
26 3–4 [...]

27 0 *as-lu ṭu-ub-bu-ḫu du-⸢uš⸣-šu-ú* GU$_4$.MAḪ*-e zi-i-bu šur-ru-ḫu ṣe-e-lí qut-rin-na*
27 1 [...] x x ⸢*zi-i-bu šur*⸣*-r*[*u-ḫu*] *ṣe-e-lí qut-rin-na*
27 2 *as-lu ṭu-ub-bu-ḫu du-⸢uš⸣-šu-ú* GU$_4$.MAḪ*-e zi-i-bu šur-ru-ḫu ṣe-e-lí qut-rin-na*
27 3–4 [...]

28 0 ir-si-im mi-ni-in-⸢è⸣ ir-sim bí-in-du$_{10}$(*)-[ga]
28 1 [...] bí-in-d[u$_{10}$-x]
28 2 ir-si-im mi-ni-in-⸢è⸣ ir-sim bí-in-du$_{10}$(*)-[x]
28 3–4 [...]

29 0 *ar-man-nu uš-te-eṣ-⸢ṣa⸣-*[*ni*]*m*(?) *i-ri-⸢še⸣ ṭa-bu-⸢ú*(?)⸣
29 1 [...] *ṭa-bu-⸢ú*(?)⸣
29 2 *ar-man-nu uš-te-eṣ-⸢ṣa⸣-*[*ni*]*m*(?) *i-ri-⸢še⸣ ṭa-bu-*[x]
29 3–4 [...]

30 0 sískur-didli [...]-in-du$_8$-du$_8$ me-⸢li⸣-gal si ba-ni-íb-si
30 1 [... s]i ba-ni-íb-si
30 2 sískur-didli [...]-in-du$_8$-du$_8$ me-⸢li⸣-gal si ba-ni-íb-[x]
30 3–4 [...]

31 0 *ni-qé-e* [...] x*-ti na-qí* [*m*]*a*(?)*-li ri-šá-a-ti*
31 1 [...] *ri-šá-a-ti*
31 2 *ni-qé-e* [...] x*-ti na-qí* [*m*]*a*(?)*-li ri-šá-*[x x]
31 3–4 [...]

32 0 x [(x)] x [...] x dag gir$_{17}$-zal nam-mu-un-ši-in-gá-gá
32 1 [...-i]n-gá-gá
32 2 x [(x)] x [...] x dag gir$_{17}$-zal nam-mu-un-ši-in-[x x]
32 3–4 [...]

33 0 [...] x DU U *ta-⸢šil⸣-ta šak-na-at*
33 1 [... *ša*]*k-na-at*
33 2 [...] x DU U *ta-⸢šil⸣-ta šak-*[...]
33 3–4 [...]

34 0 [...] x zú-NE-NE-ra-bi igi-⸢du$_8$ gu$_4$⸣-ud ^{d}asar-ri-ke$_4$
34 1 [... ^{d}a]sar-ri-ke$_4$
34 2 [...] x zú-NE-NE-ra-bi igi-⸢du$_8$ gu$_4$⸣-ud ^{d}asar-r[i-x]
34 3–4 [...]

35 0 [DINGIR.MEŠ *ša-m*]*a-me u qaq-qa-ri ṣi-ḫi-*⸢*iš i*⸣-[*n*]*a*(?)-*ṭa-lu* ^{d}AMAR.UTU *qar-du*
35 1 [... .UT]U *qar-du*
35 2 [...-*m*]*a-me u qaq-qa-ri ṣi-ḫi-*⸢*iš i*⸣-[*n*]*a*(?)-*ṭa-lu* ^{d}AMAR.UTU [...]
35 3–4 [...]

36 0 [...] x z[à]-mí an-ti
36 1 [... a]n-ti
36 2 [...] x z[à]-mí an-[x]
36 3–4 [...]

37 0 [...] *t*[*a*]-*nit-tu$_4$ qur-di*
37 1 [...] *qur-di*
37 2 [...] *t*[*a*]-*nit-tu$_4$* [...]
37 3–4 [...]

38 0 [... še]n(?)-šen-na ⸢šen-(erasure)-ḫur⸣-[s]ag-gá a-lá-e
38 1 [...]-lá-e
38 2 [... še]n(?)-šen-na ⸢šen-(erasure)-ḫur⸣-[s]ag-gá a-[...]
38 3–4 [...]

39 0 [...] *ú-nam-ma-ru a-*⸢*lu*⸣*-ú* ⸢*u*⸣ [*l*]*i-li-si*
39 1 [... *l*]*i-li-si*
39 2 [...] *ú-nam-ma-ru a-*⸢*lu*⸣*-ú* ⸢*u*⸣ [x x (x)]
39 3–4 [...]

Colophon on ex. 1

40) [(DUB x.KÁM ...) *ekal aššur-bāni-apli šar kiššati* LUGA]L KUR *aš-šur*.KI
41) [*ša nabû u tašmētu uznu rapaštu išrukūš īḫuzu īna namirtu nisiq*] *ṭup-šar-ru-ti*
42) [*ša ina šarrāni ālik maḫrīia mamma šipru šu ʾātu lā īḫuzu nēmeq nabû tikip sa-an-tak-k*]*i*(?) *ma-la ba-áš-mu*
43) [*ina ṭuppāni ašṭur asniq abrēma ana tāmarti šitassīia qereb* É.GAL]-*ia ú-kin*

Colophon on ex. 2 (rev. 17–18 of exemplar)

1) [...] I x x [...]
2) [(*ekal*) *aššur-bāni-apli*] MAN ŠÚ MAN KUR [*aš-šur*.KI]

1	0	^{d}nanna lugal-a-ni-ir
1	1	^{d}nanna lugal-⸢a⸣-ni-ir
1	2	^{d}⸢nanna⸣ lug[al]-a-ni-ir
1	3–4	—
2	0	^{d}AMAR.UTU-SUM-ŠEŠ.MEŠ
2	1	^{d}AMAR.UTU-SUM-ŠEŠ.MEŠ
2	2	^{d}AMAR.UTU-SUM-⸢ŠEŠ⸣.MEŠ
2	3–4	—
3	0	lugal kiš
3	1	lugal kiš
3	2	lugal ⸢kiš⸣
3	3–4	—
4	0	lugal úri.KI-ma
4	1	lugal úri.KI-ma
4	2	lugal ⸢úri.KI-ma⸣
4	3–4	—
5	0	lugal KÁ.DINGIR.RA
5	1	lugal KÁ.DINGIR.RA
5	2	⸢lugal KÁ.DINGIR.RA⸣
5	3–4	—
6	0	lugal ki-in-gi uri.KI
6	1	lugal ki-in-gi uri.KI
6	2	lugal ki-in-⸢gi⸣ x.⸢KI⸣
6	3–4	—
7	0	ú-a úri.KI-ma
7	1	ú-a úri.KI-ma
7	2	⸢ú-a úri.KI-ma⸣
7	3–4	—
8	0	mú-mú é-kiš-nu-gál
8	1	mú-mú é-kiš-nu-gál
8	2	⸢mú⸣-x ⸢é-kiš-nu-gál⸣
8	3–4	—

9 0 é-gá-nun-maḫ
9 1 é-gá-nun-maḫ
9 2 ⸢é⸣-x-(x)-x-⸢maḫ⸣
9 3–4 —

10 0 é libir-ra diri-ga
10 1 é libir-ra diri-ga
10 2 é ⸢libir-ra⸣ [x]-ga
10 3–4 —

11 0 mu-na-an-dù
11 1 mu-na-an-dù
11 2 ⸢mu⸣-x-⸢an⸣-dù
11 3–4 —

12 0 ki-bi-šè bí-in-gi$_4$-a
12 1 ki-bi-šè bí-in-gi$_4$-a
12 2 x-⸢bi⸣-x bí-in-gi$_4$-a
12 3–4 —

13 0 KU GIŠ.ig
13 1 KU GIŠ.ig
13 2 KU GIŠ.ig
13 3–4 —

14 0 na$_4$ mu-bi inanna-a
14 1 na$_4$ mu-bi inanna-a
14 2 na$_4$ mu-bi inanna-a
14 3–4 —

15 0 a mu-un-na-ru
15 1 a mu-un-na-ru
15 2 a mu-un-na-ru
15 3–4 —

Obverse

1 0 *šá* ^{d}AMAR.UTU-SUM-ŠEŠ.MEŠ

1 1 *šá* ^{d}AMAR.UTU-SUM-ŠEŠ.MEŠ

1 2 *šá* ^{d}AMAR.UTU-SUM-ŠEŠ.ME[Š]

1 3 *šá* ^{d}AMAR.UTU-SUM-ŠEŠ.MEŠ

2 0 LUGAL ŠÁR

2 1 LUGAL ŠÁR

2 2 LUGAL ŠÁR

2 3 LUGAL <ŠÁR>

Reverse

3 0 LUGAL KÁ.DINGIR.RA.KI

3 1 LUGAL KÁ.DINGIR.RA.KI

3 2 LUGAL KÁ.DINGIR.RA.KI

3 3 LUGAL KÁ.DINGIR.RA.<KI>

4 0 LUGAL KI.IN.GI URI.KI

4 1 LUGAL KI.IN.GI URI.KI

4 2 LUGAL KI.IN.GI URI.KI

4 3 ⌈LUGAL KI.IN.GI⌉ <URI.KI>

1 0 *a-na* ^{d}*en-líl* EN *šur-bi-i šá-qí-i* LUGAL *gim-r[i]*
1 1 *a-na* ^{d}*en-líl* EN *šur-bi-i šá-qí-i* LUGAL *gim-r[i]*
1 2 [...] ⸢*šá-qí*⸣-*i* LUGAL *gim*-[x]

2 0 MAS.SÙ-*ú ṣi-i-ri e-tel* AN-*e u* KI-*tim mu-šim* NAM.MEŠ
2 1 MAS.SÙ-*ú ṣi-i-ri e-tel* AN-*e u* KI-*tim mu-šim* NAM.MEŠ
2 2 [... NIR.G]ÁL AN-*e u* KI-*tim mu-šim* N[AM.MEŠ]

3 0 *kab-ti šit-ra-ḫu šá i-na* ⸢*gim*⸣-*ri* DINGIR.MEŠ *la iš-šá-an-na-nu* EN-*us-su*
3 1 *kab-ti šit-ra-ḫu šá i-na* ⸢*gim*⸣-*ri* DINGIR.MEŠ *la iš-šá-an-na-nu* EN-*us-su*
3 2 [... *gi*]-⸢*mir*⸣ DINGIR.MEŠ *la iš-šá-an-na-n*[*u* ...]

4 0 LUGAL DINGIR.MEŠ EN *si-ḫi-ip* ⸢*šá*⸣-*ma-mi šá a-na ṣi-it* KA-*šú* ^{d}*í-gì-gì kul-lat-su-nu i-nu-qu pal-ḫiš*
4 1 LUGAL DINGIR.MEŠ EN *si-ḫi-ip* ⸢*šá*⸣-*ma-mi šá a-na ṣi-it* KA-*šú* ^{d}*í-gì-gì kul-lat-su-nu i-nu-qu pal-ḫiš*
4 2 [...]-⸢*ma*⸣-*mi šá ina ṣi-it* KA-*šú* ⸢^{d}(?)*í*(?)⸣-[...]

5 0 *ù a-na na-da-nu ur-*⸢*ti*⸣-*šú* ^{d}*a-nun-na-ki kiš-šat-su-nu i-šu-bu a-*⸢*pi*⸣-*šam*
5 1 *ù a-na na-da-nu ur-*⸢*ti*⸣-*šú* ^{d}*a-nun-na-ki kiš-šat-su-nu i-šu-bu a-*⸢*pi*⸣-*šam*
5 2 [...] x [...]

6 0 EN *é-kur u* NIBRU.KI *a-šib é-kur-igi-gál* EN-*šú*
6 1 EN *é-kur u* NIBRU.KI *a-šib é-kur-igi-gál* EN-*šú*
6 2 [...]

7 0 ^{m}*sim-bar-*^{d}*ši-i-pak* LUGAL *mi-šá-ru re-e-šú šaḫ-ṭi*
7 1 ^{m}*sim-bar-*^{d}*ši-i-pak* LUGAL *mi-šá-ru re-e-šú šaḫ-ṭi*
7 2 [...]

8 0 *muš-te-šir al-ka-ka-a-ti* ^{d}*a-nim ù* ^{d}*da-gan mu-šal-li-mu me-si-šú-un*
8 1 *muš-te-šir al-ka-ka-a-ti* ^{d}*a-nim ù* ^{d}*da-gan mu-šal-li-mu me-si-šú-un*
8 2 [...]

9 0 GIŠ.GU.ZA ^{d}*en-líl šá é-kur-igi-gál šá* ^{md}AG-NÍG.DU-ÙRU LUGAL *maḫ-ri i-pu-uš*
9 1 GIŠ.GU.ZA ^{d}*en-líl šá é-kur-igi-gál šá* ^{md}AG-NÍG.DU-ÙRU LUGAL *maḫ-ri i-pu-uš*
9 2 [...]

10 0 *i-na* BALA-*e* ^{md}IŠKUR-IBILA-MU LUGAL TIN.TIR.KI LÚ.KÚR *a-ra-mu ù su-tu-ú*
10 1 *i-na* BALA-*e* ^{md}IŠKUR-IBILA-MU LUGAL TIN.TIR.KI LÚ.KÚR *a-ra-mu ù su-tu-ú*
10 2 [...]

11	0	*a-a-bi é-kur ù* NIBRU.KI *mu-šal-pít dur-an-ki*
11	1	*a-a-bi é-kur ù* NIBRU.KI *mu-šal-pít dur-an-ki*
11	2	[...]
12	0	*šá* ZIMBIR.KI URU *ṣa-a-ti šu-bat* DI.KUD.GAL.LA DINGIR.MEŠ *ú-šaḫ-bit me-si-šú-un*
12	1	*šá* ZIMBIR.KI URU *ṣa-a-ti šu-bat* DI.KUD.GAL.LA DINGIR.MEŠ *ú-šaḫ-bit me-si-šú-un*
12	2	[...]
13	0	*iš-lul-ú-ma* KUR *šu-me-ri u ak-ka-di-i ú-šam-qí-tu gi-mir* É.KUR.MEŠ
13	1	*iš-lul-ú-ma* KUR *šu-me-ri u ak-ka-di-i ú-šam-qí-tu gi-mir* É.KUR.MEŠ
13	2	[...]
14	0	*bu-šá-a* NÍG.GA ^{d}*en-líl šá a-ra-mu it-ba-lu-ma i-ki-⸢mu⸣ su-bar-ti*
14	1	*bu-šá-a* NÍG.GA ^{d}*en-líl šá a-ra-mu it-ba-lu-ma i-ki-⸢mu⸣ su-bar-ti*
14	2	[...]
15	0	*ina qí-bit* ^{d}*en-líl ma-lik* DINGIR.MEŠ *šá-qí-i* E[N] EN.EN
15	1	*ina qí-bit* ^{d}*en-líl ma-lik* DINGIR.MEŠ *šá-qí-i* E[N] EN.EN
15	2	[...]
16	0	^{d}AMAR.UTU LUGAL *gim-ri šá šu-ud-du-ú ù šu-šu-⸢bu⸣ ba-šu-ú* KI-*šú*
16	1	^{d}AMAR.UTU LUGAL *gim-ri šá šu-ud-du-ú ù šu-šu-⸢bu⸣ ba-šu-ú* KI-*šú*
16	2	[...]
17	0	^{d}*ut-u$_{18}$-lu ḫur-ba-šú a-a-bi ⸢sa-ʾ-i⸣-di ga-re-⸢e⸣*
17	1	^{d}*ut-u$_{18}$-lu ḫur-ba-šú a-a-bi ⸢sa-ʾ-i⸣-di ga-re-⸢e⸣*
17	2	[...]
18	0	*bu-šá-a* NÍG.GA ^{d}*en-líl aš-šur*.KI-*ú i-du-ú-ma ú-še-ri-ib qé-reb bal-til*.[KI]
18	1	*bu-šá-a* NÍG.GA ^{d}*en-líl aš-šur*.KI-*ú i-du-ú-ma ú-še-ri-ib qé-reb bal-til*.[KI]
18	2	[...]
19	0	*ul-tu qé-reb bal-til*.KI *a-na dur-an-ki i-tu-ru áš-ru-uš-š[ú(?)]*
19	1	*ul-tu qé-reb bal-til*.KI *a-na dur-an-ki i-tu-ru áš-ru-uš-š[ú(?)]*
19	2	[...]
20	0	^{m}*sim-bar-*^{d}*ši-i-pak* GÌR.NÍTA ^{d}*en-líl ⸢it-pe-šú⸣ na-ram* ^{d}[x]
20	1	^{m}*sim-bar-*^{d}*ši-i-pak* GÌR.NÍTA ^{d}*en-líl ⸢it-pe-šú⸣ na-ram* ^{d}[x]
20	2	[...]

21 0 *re-ʾ pal-ḫu šá áš-rat* ^{d}*en-líl ši-te-*⸢ʾ⸣*-a mu-du-*[*ú*]
21 1 *re-ʾ pal-ḫu šá áš-rat* ^{d}*en-líl ši-te-*⸢ʾ⸣*-a mu-du-*[*ú*]
21 2 [... ^{d}*e*]*n-*⸢*líl*⸣ [...]

22 0 *a-na ud-du-uš é-kur ù* NIBRU.KI *ik-kud it-*⸢*ta*⸣*-ʾ-id* [x]
22 1 *a-na ud-du-uš é-kur ù* NIBRU.KI *ik-kud it-*⸢*ta*⸣*-ʾ-id* [x]
22 2 [... N]IBRU.KI [...]

23 0 GIŠ.GU.ZA GIŠ.MES GIŠ *da-ru-ú šá iḫ-zi-šú ṣa-ri-ri-um-ma šu-tu-ru nab-nit-*[*su*]
23 1 GIŠ.GU.ZA GIŠ.MES GIŠ *da-ru-ú šá iḫ-zi-šú ṣa-ri-ri-um-ma šu-tu-ru nab-nit-*[*su*]
23 2 [...] x *iḫ-zi-šú* ⸢*ṣa*⸣*-r*[*i-*...]

24 0 *a-na si-ma-a-ti* ^{d}EN.LÍL*-ú-ti-šú ṣir-ti ú-še-piš-ma iš-*[*kun*]
24 1 *a-na si-ma-a-ti* ^{d}EN.LÍL*-ú-ti-šú sir-ti ú-še-piš-ma iš-*[*kun*]
24 2 [...*-t*]*i-šú ṣir-ti ú-še-*[...]

25 0 *a-na šat-ti* ^{d}AMAR.UTU EN GAL*-ú* ^{d}*en-líl* DINGIR.MEŠ *š*[*ur*(?)]*-b*[*u*(?)*-ú*(?)]
25 1 *a-na šat-ti* ^{d}AMAR.UTU EN GAL*-ú* ^{d}*en-líl* DINGIR.MEŠ [*šur*(?)]*-b*[*u*(?)*-ú*(?)]
25 2 [...] GAL*-ú* ^{d}⸢*en*⸣*-líl* DINGIR.MEŠ *š*[*ur*(?)-...]

26 0 *i-na* GIŠ.GU.ZA *šu-*⸢*a-šú*⸣ *ina a-šá-bi-šú ši-mat* ^{m}*sim-bar-*⸢^{d}⸣*ši-i-p*[*ak*]
26 1 *i-na* GIŠ.GU.ZA *šu-*⸢*a-šú*⸣ *ina a-šá-bi-šú ši-mat* ^{m}*si*[*m-bar*]*-*⸢^{d}*ši-i*(?)⸣*-p*[*ak*]
26 2 [... *a*]*-*⸢*šá*⸣*-bi-*⸢*iš ši*⸣*-mat* ^{m}*sim-bar-ši-i-*[x (...)]

27 0 LUGAL *mi-šá-ru re-ʾ bi-bil lìb-bi-šú ana* MUNUS.SIG$_5$ ⸢*li-iš*⸣*-ša-k*[*ín*(?)]
27 1 LUGAL *mi-šá-ru re-ʾ bi-bil lìb-bi-šú ana* MUNUS.SIG$_5$ ⸢*li-iš*⸣*-ša-k*[*ín*(?)]
27 2 [...] *lìb-bi-ka a-na* SIG$_5$*-tim* [...]

Colophon on ex. 1

28) *ki-ma* SUMUN*-šú šá-ṭir-ma* IGI.TAB ŠU.II ^{md}AMAR.UTU-LUGAL-⸢*a*⸣*-ni* A*-šú šá* ^{m}*ri-mu-ut-*^{d}AG
29) A ^{m}*lu-*È*-a-na-*ZÁLAG*-*^{d}*ìr-ra* ŠÀ.BAL.⸢BAL ^{m}⸣^{d}EN.ZU-TI-⸢A.RA⸣.ZU LÚ.⸢GALA⸣
30) ^{d}INANNA UNUG.KI *u* ^{d}*na-na-a* LÚ.KU$_4$.É ^{d}⸢*ka*⸣*-ni-sur-*⸢*ra*⸣ [DUB.SA]R(?) *é-an-na*
31) *ṭup-pi* (erasure) ^{m}*ri-mu-ut-*^{d}AG ŠÀ.BAL.BAL ^{md}EN.ZU-TI-A.RA.ZU
32) LÚ.GALA ^{d}INANNA UNUG.KI *u* ^{d}*na-na-a* LÚ.KU$_4$ É ^{d}*ka-ni-šur-ra* (erasure)
33) ITI.GAN.GAN.NA UD 1.KÁM *šá-ṭir*

Colophon on ex. 2 (rev. 8′ of exemplar)

1) [*ša ina muḫḫi* GIŠ.G]U.ZA *šá* NIBRU.KI [(...)]

Obverse

1 0 *šá* ^{d}PA-GIN-A
1 1 *šá* ^{d}AG-GIN-A
1 2 *šá* ^{d}PA-GIN-A
1 3 *šá* ^{d}PA-GI.NA-A
1 4 —
1 5 *šá* ^{d}PA-⸢GIN-A⸣
1 6 *šá* ⸢^{d}⸣PA-GIN-A
1 7 [...](x)-GIN-A
1 8 ⸢*šá*⸣ ^{d}PA-GI.NA-A
1 9 *šá* ^{d}PA-GI.NA-A
1 10 *šá* ^{d}PA-GIN-A
1 11 *šá* ^{d}PA-GIN-A
1 12 ⸢*šá*⸣ ^{d}⸢AG(?)⸣-[...]
1 13 *šá* ^{d}AG-GI.NA-A

Reverse

2 0 LUGAL ŠÁR
2 1 LUGAL ŠÁR
2 2 LUGAL ŠÁR
2 3 LUGAL ŠÁR
2 4 —
2 5 LUGAL ŠÁR
2 6 LUGAL ŠÁR
2 7 [LUGA]L ŠÁR
2 8 LUGAL ŠÁR
2 9 LUGAL ŠÁR
2 10 LUGAL ŠÁR
2 11 LUGAL ŠÁR
2 12 LUGAL ŠÁR
2 13 LUGAL ŠÁR

Obverse

1	0	^{m}*ri-mut*-DINGIR.MEŠ
1	1	^{m}*ri-mut*-DINGIR.MEŠ
1	2	^{m}*ri-mut*-DINGIR.MEŠ
1	3	^{m}*ri-mut*(?)-DINGIR.MEŠ

Reverse

2	0	A LUGAL
2	1	A LUGAL
2	2	A LUGAL
2	3	A LUGAL(?)

1 0 *a-na* ^{d}ÙRU-*a-mat-su* GAŠAN *ṣir-ti da-i-na-at di-ni ma-a-ti*
1 1 *a-na* ^{d}ÙRU-*a-mat-su* GA[ŠAN ...]-⸢*a*⸣-*ti*
1 2 *a-na* ^{d}ÙRU-*a-mat-su* GAŠAN *ṣir-ti da-i-na-at di-ni ma-a-ti*
1 3 *a-na* ^{d}ÙRU-*a-mat-*⸢*su*⸣ GAŠAN *sir-ti da-i-na-*⸢*at*⸣ *di-ni ma-a-ti*

2 0 *pa-ri-sa-at* EŠ.BAR AN-*e ù er-ṣe-ti bu-uk-rat* ^{d}IŠKUR
2 1 *pa-ri-sa-at* EŠ.⸢BAR⸣ [...-*r*]*at* ^{d}IŠKUR
2 2 *pa-ri-sa-at* EŠ.BAR AN-*e ù er-ṣe-ti bu-uk-rat* ^{d}IŠKUR
2 3 *pa-ri-sa-at* EŠ.BAR AN-*e ù er-*⸢*ṣe*⸣-*ti bu-uk-rat* ^{d}IŠKUR

3 0 *na-ár-mat* ^{d}AMAR.UTU *šá la in*$_{5}$(NIN)-*né-nu-ú qí-bi-is-su*
3 1 *na-ár-mat* ^{d}AMAR.UTU *šá l*[*a* ...]-*is-su*
3 2 *na-ár-mat* ^{d}AMAR.UTU *šá la in*$_{5}$(NIN)-*né-nu-ú qí-bi-is-su*
3 3 *na-ár-mat* ^{d}AMAR.UTU *šá* ⸢*la*⸣ *in*$_{5}$(NIN)-*né-nu-ú qí-bi-is-su*

4 0 *a-ki-ti šá ul-tu u*$_{4}$-*mu ru-qu-tu la-ba-riš il-lik-ma*
4 1 *a-ki-ti šá ul-tu u*$_{4}$-*m*[*u* ...-*ri*]*ṣ̌*(?) *il-lik-ma*
4 2 *a-ki-ti šá ul-tu u*$_{4}$-*mu ru-qu-tu la-ba-riš il-lik-ma*
4 3 *a-ki-ti šá ul-tu u*$_{4}$-*mu ru-qu-tu la-ba-riš il-lik-ma*

5 0 *šu-uš-šu im-ma-šu-ma sa-ra-ḫi-iš uš-bu*
5 1 *šu-uš-šu*(*) *im-ma-šu-ma* ⸢*sa*⸣-[...]-*bu*
5 2 ⸢*šu-uš*⸣-*šu im-ma-šu-ma sa-ra-ḫi-iš uš-bu*
5 3 *šu-uš-šu im-ma-šu-ma sa-ra-ḫi-iš uš-bu*

6 0 *i-ga-ru-šú i-qu-pu-ma qup-pu-ʾ uš-šá-šu-un*
6 1 *i-ga-ru-šú i-qu-pu-ma* ⸢*qup*⸣-*pu-ʾ u*[*š*-x-x]-*un*
6 2 [...] ⸢*i*(?)-*qu*⸣-*pu-ma* ⸢*qup*⸣-*pu-ʾ uš-šá-šu-un*
6 3 *i-ga-ru-šú i-qu-pu-ma* ⸢*qup*⸣-*pu-ʾ uš-šá-šu-un*

7 0 *ú-ṣu-ra-tu-šú im-ma-šá-a-ma iš-nu-ú ši-kin-ši-in*
7 1 *ú-ṣu-ra-tu-šú im-ma-šá-a-ma iš-nu-ú š*[*i-ki*]*n-*⸢*ši-in*⸣
7 2 [...] x-⸢*nu-ú ši-kin*⸣-*ši-*⸢*in*⸣
7 3 *ú-ṣu-ra-tu-šú im-ma-šá-a-ma iš-nu-ú ši-kin-ši-in*

8 0 LUGAL LÚ *qí-pu* LÚ *ru-bu-ú ù* LÚ.EN URU
8 1 LUGAL LÚ *qí-pu* LÚ *ru-bu-ú ù* LÚ.E[N URU]
8 2 [...] x [(x)] URU
8 3 LUGAL LÚ *qí-pu* LÚ *ru-bu-ú ù* LÚ.EN URU

9 0 *a-na e-peš šip-ru šu-a-ti ù ud-dúš a-ki-ti ú-zu-šú la iš-kun-nu-ma*
9 1 *a-na e-peš šip-ru šu-a-ti ù ud-dúš a-ki-ti ú-zu-šú l*[*a* ...]
9 2 [...]
9 3 *a-na e-peš šip-ru šu-a-ti ù ud-dúš a-ki-ti ú-zu-šú la iš-kun-nu-ma*

10 0 *ár-ka-na* ^{md}EN-*ib-ni ù* ^{md}AG-NUMUN-GÁL-*ši* DUMU.MEŠ *šá* ^{m}*bul-lu-ṭu* UNU[G].⌜KI-*ú*⌝
10 1 *ár-ka-na* ^{md}EN-*ib-ni ù* ^{md}AG-NUMUN-GÁL-*ši* DUMU.MEŠ *šá* ^{m}*bul-l*[*u-*...]
10 2 [...]
10 3 *ár-ka-na* ^{md}EN-*ib-ni ù* ^{md}⌜AG⌝-NUMUN-GÁL-*ši* DUMU.MEŠ *šá* ^{m}*bul-lu-ṭu* UNU[G].⌜KI-*ú*⌝

11 0 *a-na e-peš šip-ru šu-a-ti ù ud-dúš a-ki-ti ú-zu-šú-nu iš-kun-nu-ma*
11 1 *a-na e-peš šip-ru šu-a-ti ù ud-dúš a-ki-ti ú-zu-šú-nu iš-*⌜*kun*⌝*-nu-ma*
11 2 [...]
11 3 *a-na e-peš šip-ru šu-a-ti u ud-dúš a-ki-ti ú-zu-šú-nu iš-kun-nu-ma*

12 0 *al-la ù tup-šik-ki ina gi-mir lìb-bi-šú-nu in-na-šu-ma*
12 1 *al-la ù tup-šik-ki ina gi-mir lìb-bi-šú-nu in-na-šu-ma*
12 2 x [...]
12 3 *al-la ù tup-šik-ki ina gi-mir lìb-bi-šú*(*)*-nu in-na-šu-ma*

13 0 *maš-tak la-le-e el-lu-tu a-na* ^{d}*iš-tar ú-še-pi-iš*
13 1 *maš-tak la-le-e el-lu-tu a-na* ^{d}*iš-tar ú-še-pi-iš*
13 2 *maš-*⌜*tak*⌝ x [...-*t*]*u a-na* ^{d}*iš-tar ú-*[...]
13 3 *maš-tak la-le-e el-*⌜*lu*⌝*-tu a-na* ^{d}*iš-tar ú-še-pi-iš*

14 0 *ina šat-ti* ^{d}ÙRU-*a-mat-su* GAŠAN *ṣir-ti a-na a-ki-ti* É-*šá ḫa-diš ina e-re-bi-šá*
14 1 *ina šat-ti* ^{d}ÙRU-*a-mat-su* GAŠAN *ṣir-ti a-na a-ki-ti* É-*šá ḫa-diš ina e-re-bi-šá*
14 2 *ina šat-ti* ^{d}ÙR[U]-⌜*a-mat-su*⌝ GA[ŠAN] *ṣ*[*ir*]*-ti a-na a-ki-ti* É-⌜*šá*⌝ [...]
14 3 *ina šat-ti* ^{d}ÙRU-*a-mat-su* GAŠAN *ṣir-ti a-na a-ki-ti* É-*šá ḫa-diš ina e-re-bi-š*[*á*]

15 0 *ù ina šu-bat* DINGIR-*ti-šá* GAL-*ti šá-qí-iš i-na a-šá-bi-šá*
15 1 *ù ina šu-bat* DINGIR-*ti-šá* GAL-*ti šá-qí-iš i-na a-šá-bi-šá*
15 2 *ù ina šu-bat* DINGIR-*ti-šá* GAL-*ti šá-qí-iš i-na a-šá-bi-*[*šá*]
15 3 *ù ina šu-bat* DINGIR-*ti-šá* GAL-*ti šá-qí-iš i-na a-šá-bi-šá*

16 0 UGU ^{md}EN-*ib-ni ù* ^{md}AG-NUMUN-GÁL-*ši bu-ni-šá nam-ru-tú ki-niš lit-ru-uṣ-ma*
16 1 UGU ^{md}EN-*ib-ni ù* ^{md}AG-NUMUN-GÁL-*ši bu-ni-šá nam-ru-tú ki-niš lit-ru-uṣ-ma*
16 2 UGU ^{md}EN-*ib-ni ù* ^{md}AG-NUMUN-GÁL-*ši bu-ni-šá nam-ru-tú ki-niš lit-ru-*[...]
16 3 UGU ^{md}EN-*ib-ni ù* ^{md}AG-NUMUN-GÁL-*ši bu-ni-šá nam-ru-tú ki-niš lit-ru-*[*u*]*ṣ*(?)*-ma*

17 0 *li-ir-ri-ki* u_4*-mi-šú-nu a-na* GÍD.DA u_4*-mi-šú-nu* TI.LA *nap-šá-ti-šú-nu*
17 1 *li-ir-ri-ki* u_4*-mi-šú-nu a-na* GÍD.DA u_4*-mi-šú-nu* TI.LA *nap-šá-ti-šú-nu*
17 2 *li-ir-ri-ki* u_4*-mi-šú-nu a-na* GÍD.DA u_4*-mi-šú-nu* TI.LA *nap-šá-ti-šú-n[u]*
17 3 *li-ir-ri-ki* u_4*-mi-šú-nu a-*⸢*na*⸣ GÍD.DA u_4*-mi-šú-nu* TI.LA *nap-šá-ti-šú-nu*

18 0 *šá-la-ma* NUMUN-*šú-nu la ba-še-e* GIG-*šú-nu a-ki-ti eš-šiš ú-še-piš*
18 1 *šá-la-ma* NUMUN-*šú-nu la ba-še-e* GIG-*šú-nu a-ki-ti eš-šiš ú-še-piš*
18 2 *šá-la-ma* NUMUN-*šú-nu la ba-še-e* ⸢GIG⸣-*šú-nu a-ki-ti eš-šiš ú-še-*⸢*piš*⸣
18 3 *šá-la-ma* NUMUN-*šú-nu la ba-*⸢*še*⸣*-e* GIG-*šú-nu a-ki-ti eš-šiš ú-še-piš*

19 0 MU 5.KAM ^{d}AG-ÙRU-*ir* LUGAL KÁ.DINGIR.RA.KI
19 1 MU 5.KAM ^{d}AG-ÙRU-*ir* LUGAL KÁ.DINGIR.RA.KI
19 2 MU 5.KAM ^{d}AG-ÙRU-*ir* LUGAL KÁ.DINGIR.RA.KI
19 3 MU 5.KAM ^{d}AG-ÙRU-*ir* LUGAL KÁ.DINGIR.RA.KI

20 0 *ina* GUB *šá* ^{md}AG-GIN-NUMUN DUMU ^{md}AG-NUN.ME-DINGIR.MEŠ GÌR.NÍTA KUR.UG.UD.KI
20 1 *ina* GUB *šá* ^{md}AG-GIN-NUMUN DUMU ^{md}AG-⸢NUN⸣.ME-DINGIR.[...] x [(x)]-x.⸢KI⸣
20 2 *ina* ⸢GUB⸣ *šá* ^{md}AG-GIN-NUMUN DUMU ^{md}AG-NUN.ME-DINGIR.MEŠ GÌR.NÍTA KUR.UG.UD.KI
20 3 *ina* GUB *šá* ^{md}AG-GIN-NUMUN DUMU ^{md}AG-NUN.ME-DINGIR.MEŠ GÌR.NÍTA KUR.UG.⸢UD.KI⸣

21 0 GIŠ ^{md}AG-*na-ʾ-id*
21 1 GIŠ ^{md}AG-*na-ʾ-*⸢*id*⸣
21 2 GIŠ ^{md}AG-*na-ʾ-id*
21 3 *šá* ^{m}ÌR-^{d}*na-na-a*

22 0 DUMU ^{m}*nad-na-a*
22 1 DUMU ^{m}*nad-na-a*
22 2 DUMU ^{m}*nad-na-a*
22 3 DUMU ^{m}AN.NAM(?) *ú-a*

23 0 LÚ.GALA
23 1 LÚ.GALA
23 2 LÚ.GALA
23 3 LÚ.É.BAR UNUG.KI

24 0 ^{d}INANNA UNUG.KI
24 1 ^{d}INANNA UNUG.KI
24 2 ^{d}INANNA UNUG.⸢KI⸣
24 3 *ú-šá-pu-ú*

25 0 *ú-šá-bal-kit*
25 1 *ú-šá-bal-kit*
25 2 ⸢*ú*⸣-[...]
25 3 —

1	0	*a-na* ^{d}UN.GAL NIBRU.KI *ma-al-kát uzu-mú-a*.KI *ṣir-ti ti-iz-qar-ti šá-ru-uḫ-tu* DINGIR.MEŠ ^{d}*in-nin-ni*
1	1	*a-na* ^{d}⸢UN⸣.[G]AL NIBRU.KI *ma-al-*⸢*kát*⸣ *uzu-mú-a*.⸢KI⸣ *ṣ*[*ir*]-⸢*ti ti*⸣-*iz-q*[*ar-*...]
1	2	*a-na* ^{d}UN.GAL NIBRU.KI *ma-al-kát uzu-mú-a*.KI *ṣir-ti ti-iz-qar-ti šá-ru-uḫ-tu* DINGIR.MEŠ ^{d}*in-nin-ni*
1	3	[... ^{d}U]N.⸢GAL⸣ NIBRU.KI *ma-al-kát uzu-mú-a*.KI *ṣir-ti ti-iz-qar-ti šá-ru-uḫ-tú* DINGIR.ME ^{d}⸢*in-nin-ni*⸣
1	4	*a-na* ^{d}UN.GAL NIBRU.K[I ...]
1	5	[...]-*ti ti-iz-qar-ti šá-ru-uḫ-tu* [...] ^{d}*in-nin-ni*
1	6	[... N]IBRU.KI *ma-al-*⸢*kát*⸣ x x x x [...]
1	7	[... .K]I(?) [*ṣi*]*r-ti ti-iz-*⸢*qar*⸣*-ti šá-ru-u*[*ḫ*(?)-...]
1	8	*a-na* ^{d}UN.GAL NIB[RU.KI ...]
1	9	[*a-n*]*a* [...]
1	10–15	[...]
2	0	GAŠAN *šur-bu-tu šá a-na* LUGAL *mi-ig-ri-šá ba-an-ti-iš it-ta-na-as-ḫa-ru* BALA-*šú ú-šal-ba-ru i-šar-ra-ku-uš da-na-nu ù li-i-ti*
2	1	GAŠAN *šur-bu-tu šá* ⸢*a*⸣-[*n*]*a* LUGAL *mi-ig-ri-š*[*á b*]*a-an-ti-iš i*[*t-t*]*a-na-*[...] BALA-*šú ú-šal-*[*ba-r*]*u* ⸢*i-šar-ra*⸣*-ku-uš da-na-nu* [...]
2	2	GAŠAN *šur-bu-tu šá a-na* LUGAL *mi-ig-ri-šá ba-an-ti-iš it-ta-na-as-ḫa-ru* BALA-*šú ú-šal-ba-ru i-šar-ra-ku-uš da-na-nu ù li-i-ti*
2	3	⸢GAŠAN *šur*⸣*-bu-tu šá a-na* LUGAL *mi-ig-ri-šá ba-an-ti-iš it-ta-na-as-ḫa-ru* BALA-*šú ú-šal ba-ru i-šar-ra-ku-uš da-na-nu ù li-i-ti*
2	4	GAŠAN *šur-bu-tu šá a-na* LUGAL *mi-i*[*g-*...] BALA-*šú ú-šal-ba-ru i-*[...]
2	5	[...-*i*]*š it-ta-na-as-ḫa-ru* [...-*n*]*a-nu ù li-i-ti*
2	6	[...]
2	7	[...-*a*]*n-ti-iš i*[*t-*... *d*]*a-*⸢*na*⸣*-nu u/*⸢*ù*⸣ [...]
2	8	GAŠAN *šur-bu-tu š*[*a* ...] BALA-*šú ú-*[...]
2	9	[... *š*]*ur-b*[*u-*...] BALA-*š*[*ú* ...]
2	10	[...] x [...-*b*]*a-ru* ⸢*i*⸣-[...]
2	11–15	[...]
3	0	*šar-rat* NIBRU.KI *a-ši-bat é-bára-dúr-gar-ra* É *mu-kin šu-bat* LUGAL-*ú-tu* GAŠAN GAL-*ti* GAŠAN-*šú*
3	1	*šar-rat* NIBRU.KI *a-š*[*i-bat*] ⸢*é*⸣*-bára-dúr-gar-ra* É *mu-kin š*[*u-*...]
3	2	*šar-rat* NIBRU.KI ⸢*a*⸣*-ši-bat é-bára-dúr-gar-ra* É *mu-kin šu-bat* LUGAL-*ú-tu* GAŠAN GAL-*ti* GAŠAN-*šú*
3	3	*šar-rat* NIBRU.KI *a-ši*(*)*-bat é-bára-*<*dúr*>*-gar-ra* É *mu-kin šu-bat* LUGAL-*ú-tu* GAŠAN GAL-*ti* GAŠAN-*šú*
3	4	*šar-rat* NIBRU.KI *a-ši-bat* ⸢*é*⸣-[...]
3	5	[... *m*]*u-*⸢*kin*⸣ *šu-bat* LUGAL-*ú-tu* GAŠAN GAL-*ti* GAŠAN-*šú*
3	6	[...]
3	7	[...] ⸢É⸣ *mu-kin šu-bat* LUGAL-*ú-tu* GAŠAN [...]

3 8 *šar-rat* NIBRU.[KI ...]

3 9 [*ša*]*r-rat* N[IBRU.KI ...]

3 10 [....K]I *a-ši-bat* ⸢*é*⸣-[...]

3 11–15 [...]

4 0 ^{m}AN.ŠÁR-ŠEŠ-SUM.NA LUGAL GAL-*ú* LUGAL *dan-nu* LUGAL ŠÚ LUGAL KUR *aš-šur*.KI LUGAL *kib-rat er-bet-ti* GÌR.NÍTA TIN.TIR.KI LUGAL KUR *šu-me-ri u* URI.KI *i-tu-ut kun lìb-bi* ^{d}*en-líl*

4 1 ^{m}AN.ŠÁR-ŠEŠ-SUM.NA LUGAL G[AL-*ú*] ⸢LUGAL *dan*⸣-[*nu*] ⸢LUGAL⸣ [ŠÚ] ⸢LUGAL⸣ [...] GÌR.NÍTA TIN.TIR.KI LU[GAL ...]

4 2 ^{m}AN.ŠÁR-ŠEŠ-SUM.NA ⸢LUGAL⸣ GAL-*ú* LUGAL *dan-nu* LUGAL ŠÚ LUGAL KUR *aš-šur*.KI LUGAL *kib-rat er-bet-ti* GÌR.NÍTA TIN.TIR.KI [LU]GAL KUR *šu-me-ri u* URI.KI *i-tu-ut kun lìb-bi* ^{d}*en-líl*

4 3 ^{m}AN.ŠÁR-ŠEŠ-SUM.NA LUGAL GAL-*ú* LUGAL *dan-nu* LUGAL ŠÚ LUGAL KUR *aš-šur*.KI LUGAL *kib-rat er-bet-ti* GÌR.NÍTA TIN.TIR.KI LUGAL KUR *šu-me-ri u* URI.KI *i-tu-ut kun lìb-bi* ^{d}*en-lí*[*l*]

4 4 ^{m}AN.ŠÁR-ŠEŠ-SUM.NA LUGAL GAL-*ú* LU[GAL ...] GÌR.NÍTA TIN.TIR.KI LUGAL KUR *šu-m*[*e-*...]

4 5 [... L]UGAL KUR *aš-šur*.KI LUGAL *kib-rat er-bet-ti* [... U]RI.KI *i-tu-ut kun lìb-bi* ^{d}*en-líl*

4 6 [...]

4 7 [...]-*nu* LUGAL ŠÚ LUGAL KUR *aš-šur*.KI LU[GAL ...-*r*]*i u* URI.KI *i-tu-ut* ⸢*kun lìb*⸣-[...]

4 8 ^{m}AN.ŠÁR-PAP-AŠ [...] GÌR.NÍTA KÁ.[...]

4 9 [^{m}A]N.ŠÁR-ŠEŠ-SUM.N[A ...] GÌR.NÍTA TIN.TIR.K[I ...]

4 10 [... .N]A LUGAL GAL-*ú* LU[GAL ... TIN.TI]R.KI LUGAL KUR *šu*-[...]

4 11–14 [...]

4 15 [...] x [... GÌR.N]ÍTA KÁ.⸢DINGIR⸣.[...]

5 0 *šá ul-tu ṣe-ḫe-ri-šú ana* AN.ŠÁR ^{d}*en-líl* ^{d}30 ^{d}UTU ^{d}IŠKUR ^{d}AMAR.UTU ^{d}AG ^{d}U.GUR *u* DINGIR.MEŠ GAL.MEŠ EN.MEŠ-*šú it-tak-lu-ú-ma ni-is-mat-su ú-šak-šid-uš i-mu-ru da-na-an-šú-un*

5 1 *šá ul-tu ṣe-ḫe-ri-šú* [...] ⸢^{d}U.GUR *u*⸣ [...] *it-tak-lu-ú-ma* (x) [...-*r*]*u da-*(x) [...]

5 2 *šá ul-tu ṣe-ḫe-ri-*[... A]N.ŠÁR ^{d}*en-líl* ^{d}30 ^{d}UTU ^{d}IŠKUR ^{d}AMAR.UTU ^{d}AG ^{d}U.GUR *u* DINGIR.MEŠ GAL.MEŠ EN.MEŠ-*šú it-tak-lu-ú-ma ni-i*[*s-mat-s*]*u ú-šak-šid-uš i-mu-ru da-na-an-šú-un*

5 3 *šá ul-tu ṣe-ḫe-ri-šú ana* AN.ŠÁR ^{d}*en-líl* ^{d}30 ^{d}UTU ^{d}IŠKUR ^{d}AMAR.UTU ^{d}AG ^{d}U.GUR *u* DINGIR.ME[Š G]AL.MEŠ E[N ...] *it-tak-lu-ú-ma ni-is-mat-su ú-šak-šid-uš i-mu-ru* ⸢*da-na*⸣-[*a*]*n*-[...]

5 4 *šá ul-tu ṣe-ḫe-ri-šú ana* AN.ŠÁR ^{d}*en-lí*[*l* ...] *it-tak-lu-ú-ma ni-is-mat-s*[*u* ...]

5 5 [...] ⸢^{d}⸣UTU ^{d}IŠKUR ^{d}AMAR.UTU ^{d}AG ^{d}U.GUR *u* DINGIR.ME GAL.ME [...] *ú-šak-šid-uš i-mu-ru da-na-an-šú-un*

5 6 [...]

5 7 [... ^{d}]⸢UTU ^{d}IŠKUR ^{d}⸣[...]

5 8 *šá ul-tu ṣ*[*e-*...] *u* DINGIR.ME GAL.ME E[N ...]

5 9 ⸢šá⸣ ul-tu ṣe-ḫe-ri-šú ana AN.ŠÁR [...] it-tak-lu-ma ni-is-mat-s[u ...]

5 10 [... ṣ]e-ḫe-ri-šú ana AN.ŠÁR ^{d}en-⸢líl ^{d}⸣[... E]N(?).MEŠ-šú it-tak-lu-ma ni-[...]

5 11–14 [...]

5 15 [...]-tu ṣe-ḫe-r[i-...] ⸢^{d}⸣[I]ŠKUR ^{d}[... E]N.ME-šú it-tak-(x) [...-ša]k-ši-du-šú ⸢i(?)⸣-[...]

6 0 a-na nu-uḫ-ḫu lìb-bi DINGIR-ti-šú-nu u nu-up-pu-uš ka-bat-ti-šú-nu GIŠ.MI-šú-nu da-ru-ú it-ru-ṣu UGU-šú

6 1 a-na nu-uḫ-ḫu lìb-bi DINGI[R-...-u]š ⸢ka-bat-ti-šú-nu GIŠ⸣.MI-šú-nu [...]

6 2 ⸢a⸣-na nu-uḫ-ḫu lìb-bi DINGIR-t[i-...] ⸢u nu⸣-up-pu-uš ka-bat-ti-šú-nu GIŠ.MI-šú-nu da-ru-ú it-ru-ṣu UGU-šú

6 3 a-na nu-uḫ-ḫu lìb-bi DINGIR-ti-šú-nu u nu-up-pu-uš ka-bat-ti-šú-nu (x) [...] it-ru-ṣu [...]

6 4 a-na nu-uḫ-ḫu lìb-bi DINGIR-ti-šú-nu u [...]

6 5 [... k]a-bat-ti-šú-nu GIŠ.MI-šú-nu da-ru-ú [...] UGU-šú

6 6–7 [...]

6 8 a-na nu-u[ḫ-...] GIŠ.[...]

6 9 a-na nu-uḫ-ḫu lìb-bi DINGIR-ti-šú-nu u [...]

6 10 [... DINGI]R(?)-ú-ti-šú-nu u nu-up-pu-[...]

6 11–14 [...]

6 15 [...] nu-uḫ-ḫu lìb-bi DINGIR-t[i]-x [x (x)] u nu-up-pu-uš ka-bat-[... d]a-ru-ú it-ru-ṣu [...]

7 0 ina e-muq AN.ŠÁR ^{d}en-líl ^{d}EN u DUMU ^{d}EN DINGIR.MEŠ ti-ik-li-šú kul-lat KUR.KUR i-bé-lu-ma gi-mir ma-li-ku ú-šak-ni-šu še-pu-uš-šu

7 1 ina e-muq AN.ŠÁR ^{d}en-líl ⸢^{d}⸣[EN] u ⸢DUMU⸣ x [... t]i-ik-li-šú kul-lat KUR.KUR [...] gi-mir ma-⸢li⸣-ku ú-⸢šak⸣-ni-⸢šu⸣ [...]

7 2 [...] ⸢e-muq⸣ AN.ŠÁR ^{d}⸢en-líl⸣ [...].⸢MEŠ ti⸣-i[k]-⸢li-šú kul⸣-lat KUR.KUR i-bé-⸢lu-ma⸣ [...]-⸢pu-uš⸣-[x]

7 3 ina e-muq AN.ŠÁR ^{d}en-líl ^{d}EN u DUMU ^{d}EN DINGIR.⸢MEŠ⸣ [...] gi-mir ma-li-ku ú-šak-⸢ni⸣-[...]

7 4 ina e-muq AN.ŠÁR ^{d}en-líl ^{d}EN u DUMU ⸢^{d}⸣E[N ...] gi-mir ma-li-ku ú-šak-ni-[...]

7 5 [...-l]i-šú kul-lat KUR.KUR i-bé-lu-ma [...] še-pu-uš-šu

7 6–7 [...]

7 8 [ina] ⸢e⸣-[...]

7 9 ina e-muq AN.ŠÁR ^{d}en-líl ^{d}EN u DU[MU ...] gi-mir ma-li-ku ú-[...]

7 10 [...] ⸢^{d}EN⸣ u DUMU ^{d}EN DINGIR.MEŠ ti-⸢ik⸣-l[i-...-k]u ú-šak-ni-šú š[e(?)-...]

7 11–14 [...]

7 15 [...] (x) AN.ŠÁR ^{d}50 ^{d}EN u DUMU ^{d}EN DINGIR.⸢MEŠ⸣ ti-ik-li-šú ku[l-l]at [... g]i-mir ma-li-ki ú-šak-ni-šu [š]e-[...]

8 0 ba-nu-ú É AN.ŠÁR mu-ud-diš é-kur e-piš é-sag-íl u TIN.TIR.KI mu-šak-lil eš-re-e-ti u ma-ḫa-zu mu-kin sat-tuk-ku

8 1 ba-nu-ú É AN.ŠÁR mu-ud-diš é-kur e-piš é-⸢sag-íl u⸣ [...] mu-šak-⸢lil⸣ eš-re-e-ti u ma-ḫa-zu mu-⸢kin⸣ sat-tu[k-ku]

8 2 [... m]u-⸢šak-lil eš⸣-[...]

8	3	*ba-nu-ú* É AN.ŠÁR *mu-ud-diš* [...] *mu-šak-lil eš-re-*⌈*e*⌉-[...]
8	4	*ba-nu-ú* É AN.ŠÁR *mu-ud-diš é-kur* ⌈*e*⌉-[...] *mu-šak-lil eš-re-e-ti* ⌈*u*⌉ [...]
8	5	[...] *u* TIN.TIR.KI [...] *sat-*⌈*tuk*⌉*-ku*
8	6–8	[...]
8	9	*ba-nu-ú* É AN.ŠÁR *mu-ud-diš* ⌈*é*⌉-[...] *mu-šak-lil eš-re-e-t*[*i* ...]
8	10	[... *m*]*u-ud-diš é-kur e-piš* ⌈*é*⌉-[...*-r*]*e-e-ti u ma-ḫ*[*a-*...]
8	11–14	[...]
8	15	[...]-*ú* É AN.ŠÁR *mu-ud-diš é-kur e-piš é-sag-*⌈*íl*⌉ *u* KÁ.D[INGIR...*-š*]*ak-lil eš-re-e-ti u ma-ḫa-zi mu-*⌈*kin*⌉ *sat-*[...]
9	0	LUGAL *šá i-na* UD.MEŠ BALA-*šú* EN GAL-*ú* ^{d}AMAR.UTU *ana* TIN.TIR.KI *sa-li-mu ir-šu-ú ina é-sag-íl* É.GAL-*šú ir-mu-ú šu-*[*bat*]*-su*
9	1	LUGAL *šá i-na* UD.⌈MEŠ⌉ BALA-*šú* EN GAL-*ú* ^{d}⌈AMAR⌉.UTU *ana* TIN.TIR.⌈KI⌉ *sa-li-mu ir-š*[*u-ú*] *ina é-*[*s*]*ag-íl* É.GAL-*šú* ⌈*ir*⌉*-mu-ú šu-*[...]
9	2	⌈LUGAL⌉ *šá i-na* UD.MEŠ BAL[A-...] *ina é-sag-íl* ⌈É.GAL-*šú ir*⌉-[...]
9	3	LUGAL *šá i-na* UD.MEŠ BAL[A-...] *ina é-*⌈*sag*⌉*-íl* [...]
9	4	LUGAL *šá ina* UD.M[E]Š BALA-*šú* EN GAL-*ú* ^{d}AMAR.UTU [...] *ina é-*⌈*sag*⌉-[*í*]*l* É.GAL-*šú ir-mu-*⌈*ú*⌉ [...]
9	5	[...]-⌈*li*⌉*-mu ir-šu-ú* [...]-*su*
9	6–8	[...]
9	9	LUGAL *šá i-na* UD.MEŠ BALA-*šú* EN GAL-⌈*ú*(?)⌉ [...] *ina* ⌈*é*⌉*-sag-íl* É.GAL-*šú ir-m*[*u-*...]
9	10	[... E]N GAL-*ú* ^{d}⌈AMAR.UTU⌉ [... É.G]AL-*šú* ⌈*ir*⌉*-m*[*u-*...]
9	11–14	[...]
9	15	[...] x BALA-*šú* EN GAL-*u* ^{d}AMAR.UTU *a-na* KÁ.DINGIR.RA.KI *sa-li-me i*[*r-*...]-*íl* É.GAL-*šú ir-mu-u šu-*[...]
10	0	^{d}*a-num* GAL-*ú ana* URU-*šú* BÀD.AN.KI *u* É-*šú é-dim-gal-kalam-ma ú-še-ri-bu-ma ú-še-ši-bu pa-rak da-ra-a-ti*
10	1	^{d}*a-num* G[AL]-⌈*ú*⌉ *ana* URU-*šú* BÀD.AN.⌈KI *u*⌉ [...*-m*]*a* ⌈*ú-še-ri*⌉*-bu-*⌈*ma ú-še-ši*⌉-[...]
10	2	^{d}*a-num* GAL-*ú ana* URU-*šú* BÀD.AN.KI *u* ⌈É⌉-[...*-di*]*m-gal-*⌈*kalam-ma*⌉ *ú-*⌈*še-ri*⌉-[...] *ú-še-ši-bu pa-rak da-r*[*a-*...]
10	3	^{d}*a-num* GAL-*ú ana* URU-*šú* [...] *ú-še-ši-bu pa-rak* [...]
10	4	^{d}*a-num* GAL-*ú a-na* URU-*šú* BÀD.AN.KI ⌈*u*⌉ [...] *ú-še-ši-bu pa-rak* [...]
10	5	[...] ⌈*ú*⌉*-še-rib-ú-ma* [... *d*]*a-ra-a-ti*
10	6–8	[...]
10	9	^{d}*a-num* GAL-*ú a-na* URU-*šú* BÀD.[...] *ú-še-ši-bu* [...]
10	10	[...] BÀD.AN.KI *u* É-⌈*šú*⌉ [...]
10	11	[...] ⌈*da-ra-a-ti*⌉
10	12–14	[...]
10	15	[... *a-n*]*a* URU-*šú* BÀD.AN.KI *u* É-*šú é-dim-gal-kalam-ma ú-še-r*[*i-*...*-b*]*u pa-rak da-ra-*[...]

11 0 DINGIR.MEŠ KUR.KUR *šal-lu-tu šu-kut-ta-šú-nu ud-di-šu ul-tu qé-reb* KUR *aš-šur*.KI *a-na áš-ri-šú-nu ú-tir-šú-nu-ti-ma ú-ki-nu is-qu-uš-šú-un*

11 1 DINGIR.MEŠ KUR.KUR [*šal-l*]*u-tu šu-kut-ta-š*[*ú-...-t*]*u qé-reb* [...] *a-na* ⸢*áš*⸣-[*ri-š*]*ú-nu ú-tir-šú-nu-*[...] *is-q*[*u-*...]

11 2 DINGIR.MEŠ KUR.KUR *šal-lu-tu šu-kut-ta-šú-nu ud-d*[*i-...-t*]*u qé-reb* KUR [...] *a-na áš-ri-šú-nu ú-tir-šú-nu-ti-ma* ⸢*ú*⸣-[...] *is-qu-uš-*(x x) [x]

11 3 [DING]IR.⸢MEŠ⸣ KUR.KUR *šal-lu-tu šu-k*[*ut-*...] *a-na áš-ri-šú-nu ú-tir-šú-nu-*[...]

11 4 DINGIR.MEŠ KUR.KUR *šal-lu-tu šu-kut-ta-šú-nu ud-di-*x [...] *a-na áš-ri-šú-nu ú-tir-šú-nu-ti-m*[*a* ...]

11 5 [...*-re*]*b* KUR *aš-šur*.KI [...*-q*]*u-uš-šú-un*

11 6–8 [...]

11 9 DINGIR.MEŠ KUR.KUR *šal-lu-tu šu-kut-t*[*a-*...] *a-na áš-ri-šú-nu ú-ti*[*r-*...]

11 10 [...]

11 11 [...] *ul-tu qé-reb* KUR *aš-šur*.KI [...*-t*]*i-ma ú-kin*(?)*-nu is-qu-uš-šú-un*

11 12–14 [...]

11 15 [... *š*]*u-kut-ta-šú-nu ud-di-šu ul-tu qé-reb* [...] ⸢*ú*⸣*-tir-šú-nu-ti-ma ú-ki-nu* [...]

12 0 NUN *en-qu it-pe-šu ḫa-sis kal šip-ri šá ina ma-ḫa-zu* GAL.MEŠ *si-ma-a-ti iš-tak-ka-nu uš-te-ši-ru šu-luḫ-ḫu*

12 1 NUN *en-q*[*u i*]*t-pe-šu ḫa-sis kal šip-r*[*i* ...] *si-ma-*⸢*a*⸣-[...] *uš-te-ši-r*[*u* ...]

12 2 NUN *en-qu it-pe-*⸢*šu*⸣ *ḫa-sis kal šip-r*[*i š*]*á ina ma-ḫa-zu* GAL.[...] *si-ma-a-*⸢*ti*⸣ [...] *uš-te-ši-ru šu-luḫ-ḫu*

12 3 NUN *en-qu it-pe-šu ḫa-sis k*[*al*(?) ...] *si-ma-a-ti iš-tak-ka-nu* [...]

12 4 NUN *en-qu it-pe-šu ḫa-sis kal šip-ri* [...] *si-ma-a-ti iš-tak-ka-nu uš-*[...]

12 5 [... G]AL.MEŠ [...] *šu-luḫ-ḫu*

12 6–8 [...]

12 9 ⸢NUN⸣ *en-qu it-pe-šu ḫa-s*[*is* ... *u*]*š-*⸢*te-ši-ru*⸣ [...]

12 10 [...]

12 11 [... *ka*]*l šip-ri šá i-na ma-ḫa-zu* GAL.MEŠ [...*-k*]*a-nu uš-te-ši-ru šu-luḫ-ḫu*

12 12–14 [...]

12 15 [...] ⸢*kal*⸣ *šip-ri ša ina ma-*⸢*ḫa-zu* GAL⸣.[... *u*]*š-*⸢*te*⸣*-ši-*[...]

13 0 DUMU ^{md}30-ŠEŠ.MEŠ-*eri-ba* LUGAL ŠÚ LUGAL KUR *aš-šur*.KI DUMU ^{m}LUGAL-GIN LUGAL KUR *aš-šur*.KI GÌR.NÍTA TIN.TIR.KI LUGAL KUR *šu-me-ri u* URI.KI-*i*

13 1 DUMU ^{md}[...].⸢MEŠ-*eri*⸣*-ba* LUGAL ŠÚ ⸢LUGAL⸣ [...] x (x) [...] G[ÌR.NÍ]TA TIN.TI[R.K]I ⸢LUGAL⸣ KUR *šu-*⸢*me*⸣-[...]

13 2 DUMU ^{md}30-⸢ŠEŠ.MEŠ⸣-[...*-š*]*ur*.⸢KI DUMU⸣ ^{m}LUGAL-GIN LUGAL KUR *aš-*⸢*šur*⸣.KI GÌR.N[ÍTA ...] *u* ⸢URI.KI⸣-*i*

13 3 DUMU ^{md}30-ŠEŠ.MEŠ-⸢*eri-ba* LUGAL ŠÚ LUGAL⸣ [...] GÌR.NÍTA TI[N].⸢TIR⸣.[KI LUGA]L(?) [KUR *š*]*u-*⸢*me*⸣-[...]

13 4 DUMU ^{md}30-ŠEŠ.MEŠ-*eri-ba* LUGAL ŠÚ LUGAL KUR [...] GÌR.NÍTA TIN.TIR.KI LUGAL KUR *šu-me-r*[*i* ...]

13 5 [...] LUGAL KUR *aš-šur*.KI [...] URI.KI-*i*

13 6–8 [...]

13 9 [...] (x) [...]

13 10 [...]

13 11 [...] LUGAL ŠÚ LUGAL KUR *aš-šur*.KI DUMU ^{m}LUGAL-GIN LUGAL KUR *aš-šur*.KI [...] *šu-me-ri ù* URI.KI-*i*

13 12 [...] KUR ⸢*aš*⸣-*š*[*ur*.KI ... UR]I.KI-*i*

13 13 [...] x [...] x [...]-*ri u* [...]

13 14 [...] ⸢URI.KI⸣-<*i*>

13 15 [...]

14 0 *li-ip-li-pi da-ru-ú šá* ^{md}EN-*ba-ni* DUMU ^{m}*a-da-si* LUGAL KUR *aš-šur*.KI NUNUZ *bal-til*.KI *šu-qu-ru* NUMUN LUGAL-*ú-tu ki-sit-ti ṣa-a-ti*

14 1 *li-ip-*[... *d*]*a-*⸢*ru*⸣*-ú šá* ^{md}EN-*ba-ni* [...] ^{m}*a-da-si* LUGAL K[UR ...] NUNUZ [...-*r*]*u* NUMUN LUGAL-[*ú-t*]*u ki-sit-ti* ⸢*ṣa*⸣-[...]

14 2 *li-i*[*p-l*]*i-*⸢*pi da-ru-ú šá* ^{md}⸢E[N]-⸢DÙ⸣ [D]UMU ^{m}*a-da-si* LUGAL KUR *aš-šur*.KI ⸢NUNUZ⸣ *bal-til*.KI *šu-qu-ru* NUMUN LUGAL-⸢*ú-tu*⸣ *ki-sit-ti ṣa-a-ti*

14 3 *li-ip-l*[*i-pi d*]*a-ru-ú šá* ^{m}⸢^{d}⸣[... *ba*]*l-til*.KI *šu-qu-ru* NUMUN LUGAL-[...]

14 4 *li-ip-li-pi da-ru-ú šá* ^{md}E[N-...] NUNUZ *bal-til*.KI *šu-qu-ru* N[UMUN ...]

14 5 [...] LUGAL KUR *aš-šur*.KI [...] *ṣa-a-ti*

14 6–10 [...]

14 11 [... ^{m}]⸢^{d}⸣EN-*ba-ni* DUMU ^{m}*a-da-si* LUGAL KUR *aš-šur*.KI [... NUMU]N LUGAL-*ú-tu ki-sit-ti ṣa-a-ti*

14 12 [...-*d*]*a-si* LUGAL KUR *aš-šur*.KI [...]-*sit-ti ṣa-a-ti*

14 13 [... *š*]*á* ^{md}EN-*ba-na* DUMU ^{m}*a-da-si* LUGAL [...-*r*]*u* NUMUN LUGAL-*ú-tu ki-sit-ti* [...]

14 14 [...] LUGAL KUR *aš-šur*.KI [...]-*a-ti*

14 15 [...]

15 0 *i-nu-šu é-bára-dúr-gar-ra* É ^{d}UN.GAL NIBRU.KI GAŠAN GAL-*ti* GAŠAN-*ia šá* LUGAL *maḫ-ri i-pu-šu la-ba-riš il-lik-ma i-qu-ú-pu* É.GAR$_{8}$.MEŠ-*šú*

15 1 *i-nu-šu* ⸢*é*⸣-*bá*[*ra-*... ^{d}U]N.GAL [N]IBRU.KI GAŠAN GAL-*ti* GAŠAN-*ia šá* LUGAL *ma-ḫar* ⸢*i*⸣-[...] *la-ba-riš i*[*l-*...-*p*]*u* É.GAR$_{8}$.MEŠ-[x]

15 2 [*i-n*]*u-šu é-bára-dúr-gar-ra* É ^{d}UN.GAL NIBRU.⸢KI⸣ GAŠAN GAL-*ti* GAŠAN-*ia šá* LUGAL *maḫ-ri i-pu-šu* [*l*]*a-ba-riš il-lik-ma i-qu-ú-pu* É.GAR$_{8}$.MEŠ-*šú*

15 3 [*i-nu-š*]*u é-bára-dúr-gar-ra* É ^{d}U[N.GAL .. *la-ba-r*]*iš il-lik-ma i-q*[*u-*...]

15 4 *i-nu-šu é-bára-dúr-gar-ra* É ^{d}UN.GA[L ...] *la-ba-riš il-lik-ma i-q*[*u-*...]

15 5 [...-*i*]*a šá* LUGAL *ma-ḫar i-pu-šu* [...]-*šú*

15 6–10 [...]

15 11 [... ^{d}U]N.GAL NIBRU.KI GAŠAN GAL-*ti* GAŠAN-*ia šá* LUGAL *maḫ-ri i-pu-šu* [...]-*pu* É.GAR$_{8}$.MEŠ-*šú*

15 12 [... GA]L-*ti* GAŠAN-*ia šá* LUGAL *maḫ-ri i-pu-šu* [...] É.GAR$_{8}$.MEŠ-*šú*

15 13 [...] ⸢É(?)⸣ ^{d}UN.GAL NIBRU.KI GAŠAN GAL-*ti* GAŠAN-*ia šá* LUGAL *m*[*aḫ-*...] *la-*⸢*ba*⸣-[...] *i-qu-ú-pu* É.GAR$_{8}$.[...]

15 14 [... LUGA]L *ma-ḫar i-pu-šu* [... ME]Š-*šú*
15 15 [...]

16 0 *áš-ra-ti-šú áš-te-ʾ-e ma-qit-ta-šú as-suḫ te-me-en-šú ú-ṣab-bi-ma* GIM *si-ma-ti-šú la-bi-ra-a-ti ina ši-pir* ^{d}*kulla ar-ṣip ú-šak-lil ki-ma* KUR-*i re-ši-šú ul-li*
16 1 *áš-ra-ti-šú áš-te-ʾ-e* ⸢*ma*⸣-*qi*[*t-... a*]*s-suḫ te-me-en-šú ú-ṣab-bi-ma* GIM *si-ma-t*[*i*-x] *la-bi-ra-a-ti ina ši-pir* ^{d}*kull*[*a*] ⸢*ar-ṣip*⸣ *ú-šak-lil ki-ma* KUR-*i re-ši-šú u*[*l*-x]
16 2 [*áš*]-*ra-ti-šú áš-te-ʾ-e ma-qit-ta-šú as-suḫ te-me*-⸢*en*⸣-*šú ú-ṣab-bi-ma* GIM *si-ma-ti-šú la-bi-ra-a-tú* [x *š*]*i-pir* ^{d}*kulla ar-ṣip ú-šak-lil ki-ma* KUR-*i re-ši-i-šú ul-li*
16 3 [...-*t*]*i-šú áš-te-ʾ-e ma-qit*-⸢*ta*⸣-[... *la-bi-r*]*a-a-ti ina ši-pir* ^{d}*kulla ar-ṣip* [...]
16 4 *áš-ra-ti-šú áš-te*-<ʾ>-*e ma-qit-t*[*a*(?)-...] *la-bi-ra-a-tú ina ši-pir* ^{d}[...]
16 5 [...-*ṣa*]*b-bi-ma* GIM *si-ma-ti-šú* [...-*m*]*a* KUR-*i re-ši-šú ul-lu*
16 6–10 [...]
16 11 [... *a*]*s*(*)-*suḫ*(*) *te-me-en-šú ú-ṣab-bi-ma ki-ma si-ma-t*[*i-šú* ...-*ṣ*]*ip ú-šak-lil ki*-⸢*ma* KUR-*i*(?)⸣ [x (x)] x [...]
16 12 [...]-*en-šú ú-ṣab-bi-ma* GIM *si-ma-ti-šú la-bi-ra-a-ti* [...-*li*]*l ki-ma* KUR-*i re-ši*-⸢*i*⸣-*ši ul-li*
16 13 *áš-ra-ti-šú áš-te*-⸢ʾ⸣-[*e ma*]-*qit-ta-šú as-suḫ te-me-en-šú ú-ṣab-bi-ma* GIM *si-ma-ti*-[...] *ina ši-pir* ^{d}*kulla a*[*r-ṣip*] *ú-šak-lil* GIM KUR-*i re-ši-i-ši* ⸢*ul-li*⸣
16 14 [...]-*ṣab-bi-ma ki-ma* [...-*m*]*a* KUR-*i re-ši-šú ul-lu*
16 15 [...]

17 0 ^{d}UN.GAL NIBRU.KI GAŠAN *šur-bu-tu* GAŠAN-*ia ši-pir šu-a-tu ḫa-diš lip-pa-lis-ma a-mat* SIG$_5$-*tì-ia liš-šá-kin šap-tuš-šá* TIN UD.MEŠ SÙ.MEŠ *še-bé-e lit-tu-ú-tu* DÙG-*ub* UZU *u ḫu-ud lìb-bi li-šim ši-ma-a-ti*
17 1 ^{d}UN.GAL NIBRU.KI GAŠAN *šur-bu-tu* GAŠAN-*i*[*a ši*]-⸢*pir*⸣ *šu-a-tu ḫa-diš lip-pa-lis*-[*ma*] *a-mat* SIG$_5$-*tì-ia liš-šá-kin šap-t*[*uš*(?)-*šá*] ⸢TIN⸣ UD.⸢MEŠ SÙ.MEŠ⸣ *še*-⸢*bé-e*⸣ *lit-tu-ú-tu* DÙG-⸢*ub* UZU⸣ [...] *li-ši*[*m*] ⸢*ši*⸣-[...]
17 2 [^{d}U]N.GAL ⸢NIBRU⸣.KI GAŠAN *šur-bu-tu* GAŠAN-*ia ši-pir šu-a-tu ḫa-diš lip-pa-lis-ma* [*a-m*]*at* SIG$_5$-*tì-ia liš-šá-kin šap-tuš-šá* TIN.ME UD.ME SÙ.ME *še-bé-e lit-tu-ú-tu* DÙG-*ub* UZU *u ḫu-ud lìb-bi* [*l*]*i-šim ši-ma-a-ti*
17 3 [... N]IBRU.KI GAŠAN *šur-bu-tu* GAŠAN-*ia ši-pir šu-a*-[... S]Ù.MEŠ *še-bé-e lit-tu-ú-tu* [...]
17 4 ^{d}UN.GAL NIBRU.KI GAŠAN *šu*[*r*-...] *liš-šá-kin šap-tuš-šá* TIN.ME [...]
17 5 [... *ḫ*]*a-diš lip-pa-lis-ma* [...-*b*]*é-e lit-tu-ú-tu* DÙG-*ub* UZU [...] *ši-mat*
17 6 [...*š*]*ap-tuš-šá* TIN UD.M[EŠ(?) ... *lì*]*b-bi li-šim* [...]
17 7 [...]
17 8 ⸢^{d}⸣U[N ...] *a-mat* [...]
17 9–10 [...]
17 11 [... *ši*]-*pir šu-a*-⸢*tu*⸣ [...]
17 12 [...-*i*]*a ši-pir šu-a-tu ḫa-diš lip-pa-lis-ma a-mat* SIG -*tì-ia* [...-*b*]*é-e lit-tu-tu* DÙG-*ub* UZU *u ḫu-ud lìb-bi li-šim ši-ma-ti*
17 13 ^{d}UN.GAL NIBRU.KI ⸢GAŠAN *šur-bu-tu*⸣ GAŠAN-*ia ši-pir šu-a-tu ḫa-diš* [...] *a-mat* SIG$_5$-*tì-ia liš-šá-kin šá*[*p*]-*tuš-šá* TIN UD.MEŠ ⸢SÙ⸣.MEŠ *še-bé-e lit-tu-tu* ⸢DÙG⸣-*u*[*b* ...]

17 14 [...-p]a-lis-ma [...] ⸢ši-ma⸣-ti

17 15 [...]

18 0 ma-ti-ma i-na aḫ-rat UD.MEŠ NUN EGIR-ú šá i-na u_4-me BALA-šú É šu-a-tu in-na-ḫu-ma ma-qit-ti i-raš-šu-ú áš-ra-ti-šú liš-te-ʾ-e ma-qit-ta-šú lik-šìr

18 1 ma-ti-ma i-na aḫ-rat UD.MEŠ NUN EGI[R]-ú šá i-n[a ... BA]L[A]-⸢šú É⸣ šu-a-tu in-na-ḫ[u-ma] ma-qit-ti i-raš-šu-ú áš-ra-⸢ti-šú liš-te-ʾ⸣-e ma-q[it-t]a-šú lik-š[ìr]

18 2 [... a]ḫ-rat UD.MEŠ NUN EGIR-ú šá ina u_4-me BAL[A-x] ⸢É⸣ šu-a-tu in-na-ḫu-ma [...-t]i i-raš-⸢šu⸣-ú áš-ra-t[i-x] l[iš]-⸢te⸣-ʾ-e ⸢ma⸣-[... li]k-šìr

18 3 [... a]ḫ-rat UD.MEŠ NUN EGIR-ú šá ina u_4-⸢me BALA-šú⸣ [...-r]aš-šu-ú áš-ra-ti-šú liš-te-ʾ-e m[a-...]

18 4 [m]a-ti-ma i-na a[ḫ-...] ma-qit-ti ⸢i⸣-[...]

18 5 [... BAL]A-šú É šu-a-tu in-na-ḫu-ma [...] ma-qit-ta-šú lik-šìr

18 6 [...-r]at UD.MEŠ NUN EGIR-ú šá i-na ⸢u_4⸣-[...] ma-qit-ti i-raš-šu-ú áš-ra-ti-⸢šú⸣ liš-[...]

18 7 [... i]n-n[a-... m]a-q[it-ta]-šú li[k-šìr]

18 8 ma-t[i-...] i-raš-[... á]š(?)-r[a(?)-...]

18 9–11 [...]

18 12 [... E]GIR-ú šá i-na UD.MEŠ BALA-šú É šu-a-tu in-na-ḫu-ma [...-r]a-ti-šú liš-te-ʾ-e ma-qit-ta-šú lik-šìr

18 13 ma-ti-ma i-na aḫ-rat UD.MEŠ NUN EGIR-ú šá ina <u_4-me> BALA-šú É šu-a-t[u ...] ma-qit-ti i-raš-šu-ú ⸢áš⸣-ra-ti-šú liš-te-ʾ-⸢e⸣ m[a-...]

18 14 [...-ḫ]u-ma [...-šì]r

18 15 [...]

19 0 MU.SAR-ú ši-ṭir MU-ia Ì.GIŠ lip-šu-uš UDU.SÍSKUR BAL-qí ina áš-ri-šú liš-kun ik-ri-bi-šú DINGIR.MEŠ i-šem-mu-ú ur-rak UD.MEŠ ú-rap-pa-áš kim-ti

19 1 MU.SAR-ú ši-ṭir MU-ia Ì.GIŠ lip-šu-uš UDU.SÍS[K]UR BAL-qí ina áš-ri-šú liš-[kun] ik-ri-bi-šú ⸢DINGIR⸣.MEŠ i-šem-mu-ú ur-rak <UD>.MEŠ ú-rap-pa-áš kim-[ti]

19 2 [...] ⸢MU-ia Ì.GIŠ⸣ [x x]-⸢uš⸣ UDU.SÍSKUR BAL-⸢qí⸣ ina áš-ri-⸢šú liš⸣-ku[n ...]-rak UD.MEŠ ú-rap-pa-áš kim-ti

19 3 [...-ṭi]r MU-ia Ì.⸢GIŠ⸣ lip-šu-uš UDU.SÍSKUR [... M]EŠ i-šem-mu-ú ur-rak UD.MEŠ ú-rap-p[a-...]

19 4 MU.SAR-ú ši-ṭ[ir ...] ik-ri-bi-šú DING[IR ...]

19 5 [...-q]í ina áš-ri-šú liš-kun [...] ú-rap-pa-áš kim-ti

19 6 [... š]i-ṭir MU-ia Ì.GIŠ lip-šu-uš UDU.SÍS[KUR ...-b]i-šú DINGIR.MEŠ i-šem-mu-ú ur-rak UD.MEŠ ⸢ú⸣-[...]

19 7 [... BA]L-qí ⸢ina⸣ [áš]-⸢ri-šú liš⸣-[...-ra]p(?)-pa-áš [...]

19 8 MU.SAR-u ⸢ši-ṭir⸣ MU-i[a ...] ik-ri-bi-šú DINGIR.M[EŠ ...]

19 9–11 [...]

19 12 [...]-⸢uš⸣ UDU.SÍSKUR BAL-qí ina áš-ri-šú liš-kun [...-ra]k UD.MEŠ ú-rap-pa-áš kim-ti

19 13 MU.SAR-ú ši-ṭir MU-ia Ì.GI[Š li]p-⸢šu⸣-uš UDU.SÍSKUR <BAL>-q[í ...] ik-ri-bi-šú DINGIR.MEŠ i-še[m-...]-rak UD.MEŠ ⸢ú⸣-[...]

19 14 [...-*ku*]*n*(?) [...]
19 15 [...]

20 0 *šá* MU.SAR-*ú ši-ṭir* MU-*ia ina ši-pir ni-kil-ti ib-ba-tu lu-ú a-šar-šú ú-nak-ka-ru*
20 1 *šá* MU.SAR-*ú* ⸢*ši*⸣-*ṭir* MU-*ia ina ši-pir ni-kil-ti* ⸢*ib*⸣-*ba-tu lu-ú a-šar-šú ú-n*[*ak-*...]
20 2 [...]-*kil-ti ib-ba-*⸢*tu*⸣ [*lu*]-*ú a-šar-šú ú-nak-ka-ru*
20 3 [... M]U-*ia ina ši-pir ṇi-kil-ti ib-ba-tu lu-u* ⸢*a*⸣-[...]
20 4 *šá* MU.SAR-*ú ši-ṭi*[*r* ...]
20 5 [... *l*]*u-ú a-šar-šú ú-nak-ka-ru*
20 6 [...]-⸢*ú*⸣ *ši*(*)-*ṭir* MU-*ia ina ši-pir ni-kil-ti i*[*b-*...] ⸢*a*⸣-*šar-šú* ⸢*ú*⸣-[...]
20 7 [...-*t*]*u lu-ú* ⸢*a*⸣-[*šar*]-*šú* ⸢*ú*⸣-[...]
20 8 *ša* MU.SAR-*u ši-ṭir* MU-*i*[*a* ...]
20 9–11 [...]
20 12 [...]-⸢*ba-tu*⸣ *lu-ú a-šar-šú ú-nak-ka-ru*
20 13 *šá* MU.SAR-*ú ši-ṭir* MU-'[*a* ...]
20 14–15 [...]

21 0 ᵈUN.GAL NIBRU.KI GAŠAN GAL-*ti ag-giš lik-kil-me-šú-ma* MU-*šú* NUMUN-*šú ina nap-ḫar* KUR.KUR *li-ḫal-liq*
21 1 ᵈUN.GAL NIBRU.KI GAŠAN GAL-*ti* ⸢*ag-giš*⸣ *lik-kil-me-šú-ma* MU-*šú* NUMUN-*šú ina nap-ḫar* KUR.KUR *l*[*i-*...]
21 2 ⸢ᵈUN⸣.[GAL] ⸢NIBRU.KI⸣ GAŠAN GA[L-...-*ki*]*l*-⸢*me*⸣-*šú*-⸢*ma* MU⸣-*šú* NUMUN-*šú* ⸢*ina nap*⸣-*ḫar* KUR.KUR *li-ḫal-liq*
21 3 [... G]AL-*ti ag-giš lik-kil-me-šú-ma* MU-*šú* x x (x) [...]
21 4 ᵈUN.GAL NIBRU.K[I ...]
21 5 [... M]U-*šú* NUMUN-*šú ina nap-ḫar* KUR.KUR *li-ḫal-liq*
21 6 [... N]IBRU.KI GAŠAN GAL-*ti ag-giš lik-kil-me-*[... NU]MUN-*šú i-na nap-ḫar* KUR.KUR [...]
21 7 [...-*m*]*a* ⸢MU⸣-*šú* NUMUN-*šú* <*ina*> *nap-*⸢*ḫar*⸣ KUR.KUR [...]
21 8 ᵈUN.GAL NIBRU.KI GAŠAN GAL-[...]
21 9–11 [...]
21 12 [... NUM]UN-⸢*šú ina nap-ḫar*⸣ K[UR ...]
21 13 ⸢ᵈUN.GAL⸣ NIBRU.⸢KI GAŠAN⸣ G[AL-...]
21 14–15 [...]

Left end
22 0 *šá é-bára-dúr-gar-ra*
22 1 *šá é-bára-dúr-gar-ra*
22 2 [(...)]
22 3 *šá é-bára-dúr-*⸢*gar-ra*⸣
22 4 *šá é-bára-dúr-gar-ra*
22 5–7 [(...)]
22 8 [...]-*gar-ra*
22 9 *šá é-bára-d*[*úr-*...]
22 10–15 [(...)]

1	0	[*ana enlil bēl mātāti š*]*á la in-nen-nu-ú qí-b*[*it*]-⸢*su*⸣
1	1–2	[...]
1	3	[... *š*]*á la in-nen-nu-ú qí-b*[*it*-x]
1	4	[...]-⸢*su*⸣
2	0	[x x x *ša lā uš-tam-s*]*a*(?)-*ku ṣi-it pi*-⸢*i*⸣-*šú*
2	1–2	[...]
2	3	[x x x x x x x-*s*]*a*(?)-*ku ṣi-it pi*-⸢*i*⸣-[x]
2	4	[...]-*šú*
3	0	[...] x DINGIR.MEŠ *šu*-⸢*ta*⸣-x [(...)] x-*su*
3	1–2	[...]
3	3	[...] x DINGIR.MEŠ *šu*-⸢*ta*⸣-x [...]
3	4	[...] x-*su*
4	0	[...] ⸢*šá*(?) *la*(?)⸣ [(...)] x *ma-al-ku*
4	1–2	[...]
4	3	[...] ⸢*šá*(?) *la*(?)⸣ [...]
4	4	[...] x *ma-al-ku*
5	0	[...] DU
5	1–3	[...]
5	4	[...] DU
6	0	[...] EN GAL-*i* EN-*šú*
6	1–3	[...]
6	4	[...] EN GAL-*i* EN-*šú*
7	0	[... *kib*]-⸢*rat*⸣ *er-bet-ti*
7	1–3	[...]
7	4	[...]-⸢*rat*⸣ *er-bet-ti*
8	0	[... *lìb-b*]*i* ^{d}*en-líl*
8	1–3	[...]
8	4	[...-*b*]*i* ^{d}*en-líl*
9	0	[... ^{d}A]G ^{d}U.GUR *u* DINGIR.MEŠ GAL.MFŠ
9	1–3	[...]
9	4	[... ^{d}A]G ^{d}U.GUR *u* DINGIR.MEŠ GAL.MEŠ
10	0	[... *ú-šak-šid-u*]*š i-mu-ru da-na-an-šú-un*
10	1–3	[...]
10	4	[...-*u*]*š i-mu-ru da-na-an-šú-un*

11 0 [...] GIŠ.MI-*šú-nu da-ru-ú*
11 1 [...] x x [(x)⸣
11 2–3 [...]
11 4 [...] GIŠ.MI-*šú-nu da-ru-ú*

12 0 [...] (x) UGU-*šú*
12 1 [...] UGU-[x]
12 2–3 [...]
12 4 [...] (x) UGU-*šú*

13 0 [...] *ti-ik-li-šú kul-lat* KUR.KUR *i-bé-lu-ma*
13 1 [...]-⸢*li-šú*⸣ *kul-lat* KUR.KUR *i-bé-lu-m*[*a*]
13 2–3 [...]
13 4 [...] *ti-ik-li-šú kul-lat* KUR.KUR *i-bé-lu-ma*

14 0 [....] x *še-pu-uš-šú*
14 1 [...] *še-pu-uš-šú*
14 2–3 [...]
14 4 [...] x *še-pu-uš-šú*

15 0 [... *é*]-*sag-íl u* TIN.TIR.KI
15 1 [...-*sa*]*g-íl u* TIN.TIR.KI
15 2–3 [...]
15 4 [... *é*]-*sag-íl u* TIN.TIR.KI

16 0 [... *ma-ḫa-z*]*u mu-kin sat-tuk-ku*
16 1 [...] *mu-kin sat-tuk-ku*
16 2–3 [...]
16 4 [...-*z*]*u mu-kin sat-tuk-ku*

17 0 [... T]IN.TIR.KI *sa-li-mu ir-šu-ú*
17 1 [... TI]N.TIR.KI *sa-li-me ir-šu-ú*
17 2–3 [...]
17 4 [... T]IN.TIR.KI *sa-li-mu ir-šu-ú*

18 0 [...] *ir-mu-ú šu-bat-su*
18 1 [...-*m*]*u-ú šu-bat-su*
18 2–3 [...]
18 4 [...] *ir-mu-ú šu-bat-su*

19	0	[... É]-*šú é-dim-gal-kalam-ma ú-še-rib-ú-ma*
19	1	[...-*d*]*im-gal-kalam-ma ú-še-rib-ú-ma*
19	2–3	[...]
19	4	[...]-*šú é-dim-gal-kalam-ma ú-še-rib-ú-ma*
20	0	[...] *da-ra-a-ti*
20	1	[...] *da-řa-a-ti*
20	2–3	[...]
21	4	[...] *da-ra-a-ti*
21	0	[... *ud-diš-m*]*a ul-tu qé-reb* KUR *aš-šur*.KI
21	1	[...-*m*]*a ul-tu qé-reb* KUR *aš-šur*.KI
21	2–3	[...]
21	4	[... *u*]*l*-⸢*tu*⸣ *qé-reb* KUR *aš-šur*.K[I]
22	0	[... *ú*]-⸢*kin*⸣-*nu is-qu-uš-šú-un*
22	1	[... -*ki*]*n-nu is-qu-uš-šú-un*
22	2–3	[...]
22	4	[...]-⸢*kin-nu is-qu*⸣-*uš-šú* x [(x)]
23	0	[... *i*]*na ma-ḫa-zu* GAL.MEŠ
23	1	[... *i*]*na ma-ḫa-zu* GAL.MEŠ
23	2–3	[...]
23	4	[...] x (x) [...]
24	0	[... *uš-te*]-*ši-ru šu-luḫ-ḫu*
24	1	[...]-*ši-ru šu-luḫ-ḫu*
24	2–3	[...]
24	4	[...] (x) x [...]
25	0	[... *aš-šur*].KI DUMU ^{m}LUGAL-GIN LUGAL KUR *aš-šur*.K[I]
25	1	[...].KI DUMU ^{m}LUGAL-GIN LUGAL KUR *aš-šur*.K[I]
25	2–4	[...]
26	0	[...] x [...] *ù* URI.KI-⸢*i*⸣
26	1	[...] *ù* URI.KI-⸢*i*⸣
26	2	[...] x [...]
26	3–4	[...]
27	0	[*liplippi da*]-*ru-ú šá* [^{md}EN-*ba*]-*ni* DUMU ^{m}*a-da-si* [L]UGAL KUR *aš-šur*.K[I]
27	1	[...]-*ni* DUMU ^{m}*a-da-si* [L]UGAL KUR *aš-šur*.K[I]
27	2	[...]-*ru-ú šá* [...]
27	3–4	[...]

28	0	[*pir'u bal-til*.K]I *šu-qu-ru* ⸢NUMUN⸣ [LUGAL-*ú*]-*tu ki-sit-ti* ⸢*ṣa*⸣-*a*-[*ti*]
28	1	[...]-*tu ki-sit-ti* ⸢*ṣa*⸣-*a*-[*ti*]
28	2	[... .K]I *šu-qu-ru* ⸢NUMUN⸣ [...]
28	3–4	[...]
29	0	[*i-nu*]-*šu šá é-kur* É ^{d}*en*-[*lí*]*l* EN KUR.KUR EN-*ia šá* LUGAL *ma-ḫar i-p*[*u-šu*]
29	1	[...-*lí*]*l* EN KUR.KUR EN-*ia šá* LUGAL *ma-ḫar i-p*[*u*-x]
29	2	[...]-*šu šá é-kur* É ^{d}*en*-[...]
29	3–4	[...]
30	0	[*la-b*]*a-riš*(?) *il-lik-ma i*-[*qu*-(*ú*)-*p*]*u* É.GAR$_{8}$.ME[Š-*šú*]
30	1	[...-*p*]*u* É.GAR$_{8}$.ME[Š-x]
30	2	[x-*b*]*a-riš*(?) *il-lik-ma i*-[...]
30	3–4	[...]
31	0	[*ašrātišu áš-t*]*e-'-e ma-qit-ta-šú a*[*s-s*]*uḫ te-me*-⸢*en-šú ú-ṣab-bi-ma ki-ma*(?) *si*(?)⸣-[*ma-ti-šú*]
31	1	[...-*s*]*uḫ te-me*-⸢*en-šú ú-ṣab-bi-ma ki-ma*(?) *si*(?)⸣-[...]
31	2	[... -*t*]*e-'-e ma-qit-ta-šú a*[*s*-...]
31	3–4	[...]
32	0	[*la-bi-ra*-(*a*)]-*ti ina ši-pir* ^{d}*kulla a*[*r-ṣip* ...]
32	1	[...]
32	2	[...]-*ti ina ši-pir* ^{d}*kulla a*[*r*-...]
32	3–4	[...]
33	0	[(*ana šatti*?) ^{d}*en-l*]*íl* DINGIR *tu-kul-ti-ia ep-š*[*e-ti-ia* ...]
33	1	[...]
33	2	[(...) ^{d}*en-l*]*íl* DINGIR *tu-kul-ti-ia ep-š*[*e*-...]
33	3–4	[...]
34	0	[*balāṭ ūmē*] SÙ.MEŠ *še-bé-e lit-tu-t*[*u* ...]
34	1	[...]
34	2	[...] SÙ.MEŠ *še-bé-e lit-tu-t*[*u* ...]
34	3–4	[...]
35	0	[*matīma ina aḫ*]-*rat* UD.MEŠ NUN EGIR-*ú šá* x [...]
35	1	[...]
35	2	[...]-*rat* UD.MEŠ NUN EGIR-*ú ša* x [...]
35	3	[...] x x [...]
35	4	[...]

36 0 [(...) *ma-qit*]-*ti i-raš-šu-ú áš-ra*-[*ti-šú liš-te-'*]-*e ma-qit-t*[*a*]-⸢*šú*(?)⸣ *l*[*ik*(?)-*šìr*]
36 1 [...]
36 2 [...]-*ti i-raš-šu-ú áš-ra*-[...]
36 3 [...]-*e ma-qit-t*[*a*]-⸢*šú*(?)⸣ *l*[*ik*(?)-x]
36 4 [...]

37 0 [MU.SAR]-⸢*ú*⸣ *ši*-⸢*ṭir* MU-*ia* Ì(?).GIŠ(?)⸣ [*lipšuš* UDU.ṢÍ]SKUR BAL-*qí ina áš-r*[*i-šú* ...]
37 1 [...]
37 2 [...]- ⸢*ú*⸣ *ši*-⸢*ṭir* MU-*ia* Ì(?).GIŠ(?)⸣ [...]
37 3 [... SÍ]SKUR BAL-*qí ina áš-r*[*i*-...]
38 4 [...]

38 0 [...] x [... UD].ME[Š] *ú-rap-pa-áš kim*-[*ti* ...]
38 1 [...]
38 2 [...] x [...]
38 3 [...].ME[Š] *ú-rap-pa-áš kim*-[...]
38 4 [...]

39 0 [... *ni-kil-t*]*i ib-ba-tu lu-ú a-šar-šú ú-na*[*k-ka ru*]
39 1–2 [...]
39 3 [...-*t*]*i ib-ba-tu lu-ú a-šar-šú ú-na*[*k*-x x]
39 4 [...]

40 0 [... *lik-kil-m*]*e-šú-ma ši-mat* ḪUL-*tim li-šim*-[*šú*]
40 1–2 [...]
40 3 [...-*m*]*e-šú-ma ši-mat* ḪUL-*tim li-šim*-[x]
40 4 [...]

41 0 [*šumšu* (*u*) *zērašu ina māti li-ḫal-li*]*q*(?)-*ma a-a ir-ši-šú re-e*-[*me*/*mu*]
41 1–2 [...]
41 3 [...-*li*]*q*(?)-*ma a-a ir-ši-šú re-e*-[x]
41 4 [...]

1 0 *a-na* ^{d}*iš-tar* GAŠAN *šur-bu-ti e-tel-let* AN-*e u* KI-*tim qa-rit-ti* DINGIR.MEŠ *šá-ru-uḫ-ti*
1 1 *a-na* ^{d}*iš-tar* GAŠAN *šur-bu-ti e-tel-let* AN-*e u* KI-*tim qa-rit-ti* DINGIR.MEŠ *šá-ru-uḫ-ti*
1 2 [*a-n*]*a* ^{d}⸢*iš*⸣-[...]
1 3 *a-na* ^{d}*iš-tar* GAŠAN *šur-bu-*⸢*tu*⸣ *e-tel-*⸢*let* AN⸣-*e u* KI-*tim qa-*⸢*rit-ti*⸣ DINGIR.MEŠ *šá-ru-uḫ-tu*
1 4 [... *q*]*a-rit-ti* DINGIR.MEŠ *šá-ru-uḫ-ti*
1 5–6 [...]

2 0 ^{d}INANNA UNUG.KI *ru-ba-a-ti ṣir-ti le-qa-a-ti pa-ra-aṣ* ^{d}*a-nù-ú-tu*
2 1 ^{d}INANNA UNUG.KI *ru-ba-a-ti ṣir-ti le-qa-a-ti pa-ra-aṣ* ^{d}*a-nù-ú-tu*
2 2 ^{d}INANNA UNUG.KI [...]
2 3 ^{d}INANNA UNUG.KI *ru-ba-a-ti ṣir-ti le-qa-a-ti pa-ra-aṣ* ^{d}*a-nù-ú-tu*
2 4 [...]-*ra-aṣ* ^{d}*a!-nu-ú-tu*
2 5–6 [...]

3 0 *šá ri-kis te-re-e-ti ḫa-am-mat*
3 1 *šá ri-kis te-re-e-ti ḫa-am-mat*
3 2 *šá ri-kis* [...]
3 3 *šá ri-kis te-re-e-ti ḫa-am-mat*
3 4 [...] *ḫa-am-mat*
3 5–6 [...]

4 0 *ru-um-ti ti-iz-qar-ti šá a-na* LUGAL *mi-ig-ri-šá ki-niš ip-pal-la-su*
4 1 *ru-um-ti ti-iz-qar-ti šá a-na* LUGAL *mi-ig-ri-šá ki-niš ip-pal-la-su*
4 2 *ru-um-t*[*i* ...]
4 3 *ru-um-tu ti-iz-qar-ti šá a-na* LUGAL *mi-ig-ri-šá ki-niš ip-pal-la-su*
4 4 [...] *ki-niš ip-pal-la-*⸢*su*⸣
4 5–6 [...]

5 0 BALA-*šú ú-šal-ba-ru i-šar-ra-ku-uš da-na-nu ù li-i-ti*
5 1 BALA-*šú ú-šal-ba-ru i-šar-ra-*⸢*ku-uš*⸣ *da-na-nu ù li-i-ti*
5 2 BALA-*šú* ⸢*ú*⸣-[...]
5 3 BALA-*šú ú-šal-ba-ru i-šar-ra-ku-uš da-na-nu ù li-i-ti*
5 4 [...-*n*]*a*(?)-*nu ù li-i-ti*
5 5–6 [...]

6 0 *šá-nun-ka-at ád-na-a-ti šá-qu-ti* DINGIR.MEŠ *a-ši-bat é-nir-gál-an-na*
6 1 *šá-nun-ka-at ád-na-a-ti šá-qu-ti* DINGIR.MEŠ *a-ši-bat é-nir-gál-an-na*
6 2 *šá-nun-ka-a*[*t* ...]
6 3 *šá-nun-ka-at ád-na-a-ti šá-qu-ti* DINGIR.MEŠ *a-ši-bat é-nir-gál-an-na*
6 4 [...] ⸢*a*⸣-*ši-bat é-nir-gál-an-na*
6 5 (Not visible on excavation photographs)
6 6 [...]

7	0	*šá qé-reb é-an-na be-let* UNUG.KI GAŠAN GAL-ti GAŠAN-*šú*
7	1	*šá qé-reb é-an-na be-let* UNUG.KI GAŠAN GAL-*ti* GAŠAN-*šú*
7	2	*šá qé-reb* (x) [...]
7	3	*šá qé-reb é-an-na be-let* UNUG.KI GAŠAN GAL-*ti* GAŠAN-*šú*
7	4	[... GA]L-*ti* GAŠAN-*šú*
7	5	(Not visible on excavation photographs)
7	6	[...]
8	0	^{m}AN.ŠÁR-ŠEŠ-SUM.NA LUGAL GAL-*ú* LUGAL *dan-nu* LUGAL ŠÚ LUGAL KUR *aš-šur*.KI LUGAL *kib-rat* 4-*ti* GÌR.NÍTA TIN.TIR.KI LUGAL KUR *šu-me-ri ù* URI.KI
8	1	^{m}AN.ŠÁR-ŠEŠ-SUM.NA LUGAL GAL-*ú* LUGAL *dan-nu* LUGAL ŠÚ LUGAL KUR *aš-šur*.KI LUGAL *kib-rat* 4-*ti* GÌR.NÍTA TIN.TIR.KI LUGAL KUR *šu-me-ri ù* URI.KI
8	2	^{m}AN.ŠÁR-ŠEŠ-[...] ⸢GÌR⸣.NÍTA (x) [...]
8	3	^{m}AN.ŠÁR-ŠEŠ-SUM.NA LUGAL GAL-*ú* LUGAL *dan-nu* LUGAL *kiš-šat* LUGAL KUR *aš-šur*.KI LUGAL ⸢*kib*⸣-*ra-a-ti er-bit-ti* GÌR.NÍTA TIN.TIR.⸢KI⸣ LUGAL KUR *šu-me-ri u ak-ka-di-i*
8	4	[... G]ÌR.NÍTA TIN.TIR.KI (erasure) [...-*r*]*i ù ak-*⸢*ka*(?)-*ad*(?)⸣
8	5	(Not visible on excavation photographs)
8	6	[...]
9	0	*ti-ri-iṣ* ŠU.II AN.ŠÁR *i-tu-ut kun lìb-bi* ^{d}*en-líl ni-bit* ^{d}AMAR.UTU *mi-gir* ^{d}*ir-ni-ni*
9	1	*ti-ri-iṣ* ŠU.II AN.ŠÁR *i-tu-ut kun lìb-bi* ^{d}*en-líl ni-bit* ^{d}AMAR.UTU *mi-gir* ^{d}*ir-ni-ni*
9	2	[...]
9	3	*ti-ri-iṣ* ŠU.II AN.ŠÁR *i-tu-ut kun lìb-bi* ^{d}*en-líl ni-bit* ^{d}AMAR.UTU *mi-gir* ^{d}*ir-ni-ni*
9	4	[... UT]U(?) *mi-gir* ^{d}*ir-ni-ni*
9	5	[...-*ku*]*n* ⸢*lìb*⸣-*bi* ^{d}*en-líl ni-bit* ⸢^{d}AMAR⸣.UTU traces [...]
9	6	[...]
10	0	*šá ul-tu ṣe-ḫe-ri-šú a-na* AN.ŠÁR ^{d}*a-nim* ^{d}*en-líl* ^{d}*é-a* ^{d}30 ^{d}UTU ^{d}IŠKUR ^{d}AMAR.UTU ^{d}AG ^{d}U.GUR *u* ^{d}15
10	1	*šá ul-tu ṣe-ḫe-ri-šú a-na* AN.ŠÁR ^{d}*a-nim* ^{d}*en-líl* ^{d}*é-a* ^{d}30 ^{d}UTU ^{d}IŠKUR ^{d}AMAR.UTU ^{d}AG ^{d}U.GUR *u* ^{d}15
10	2	[...]
10	3	*šá ul-tu ṣe-ḫe-ri-šú a-na* AN.ŠÁR ^{d}*a-nim* ^{d}*en-líl* ^{d}*é-a* ^{d}30 ^{d}UTU ^{d}IŠKUR ^{d}AMAR.UTU ^{d}AG <<*u*>> ^{d}U.GUR *u* ^{d}*iš-tar*
10	4	[...-*lí*]*l*̀ ⸢^{d}*é-a* ^{d}30⸣ ^{d}UTU ^{d}IŠKUR ^{d}AMAR.UTU ^{d}AG ^{d}U.GUR [...]
10	5	[...-*ḫ*]*e-ri-šú a-na* AN.ŠÁR ^{d}*a-nim* ^{d}*en-líl* ^{d}⸢*é*⸣-*a* ^{d}30 ^{d}UTU ^{d}IŠKUR [...] x ^{d}U.GUR ^{d}*iš-tar*
10	6	[...]

11 0 DINGIR.ME GAL.ME EN.ME-*šú it-tak-lu-ma ni-iz-mat-su ú-šak-ši-du-uš i-mu-ru da-na-an-šú-un*

11 1 DINGIR.ME GAL.ME EN.ME-*šú it-tak-lu-ma ni-iz-mat-su ú-šak-ši-du-uš i-mu-ru da-na-an-šú-un*

11 2 [...]

11 3 DINGIR.MEŠ GAL.MEŠ EN.ME-*šú it-tak-lu-ma ni-iz-mat-su* ⸢*ú*⸣-*šak-ši-du-uš i-mu-ru da-na-an-šú-un*

11 4 [... *i*]*t-tak-lu-ma ni-iz-mat-su ú-šak-šid-uš i-mu-ru da-na-an-šú-un*

11 5 DINGIR.MEŠ GAL.MEŠ EN.MEŠ-*šú* [...]-⸢*lu-ma*⸣ *ni-iz-mat-su ú-šak-ši-du-uš i-mu-ru da-na-an-šú-un*

11 6 [...]

12 0 *a-na nu-uḫ-ḫu lìb-bi* DINGIR-*ú-ti-šú-nu u nu-up-pu-uš ka-bat-ti-šú-nu* GIŠ.MI-*šú-nu da-ru-ú*

12 1 *a-na nu-uḫ-ḫu lìb-bi* DINGIR-*ú-ti-šú-nu u nu-up-pu-uš ka-bat-ti-šú-nu* GIŠ.MI-*šú-nu da-ru-ú*

12 2 [...]

12 3 *a-na nu-uḫ-ḫi lìb-bi* DINGIR-*ú-ti-šú-nu u nu-up-pu-šú ka-bat-ti-šú-nu* GIŠ.MI-*šú-nu da-ru-ú*

12 4 [...-*p*]*u-šú ka-bat-ti-šú-nu* GIŠ.MI-*šú-nu da-ru-u*

12 5 [...]-⸢*uḫ*⸣-*ḫi lib-bi* DINGIR-*ú-ti-šú-nu ù nu-up-pu-uš ka-bat-ti-šú-nu* [...]-⸢*šú-nu da*⸣-*ru-ú*

12 6 [...]

13 0 *it-ru-ṣu* UGU-*šú*

13 1 *it-ru-ṣu* UGU-*šú*

13 2 [...]

13 3 *it-ru-ṣu e-li-šú*

13 4 *it-ru-ṣu e-li-šú*

13 5 *it-ru-ṣu* UGU-*šú*

13 6 [...]

14 0 *ina e-muq* AN.ŠÁR ^{d}EN DUMU ^{d}EN *u* ^{d}15 DINGIR.ME *ti-ik-li-šú kul-lat* KUR.KUR *i-be-lu-ma*

14 1 *ina e-muq* AN.ŠÁR ^{d}EN DUMU ^{d}EN *u* ^{d}15 DINGIR.ME *ti-ik-li-šú kul-lat* KUR.KUR *i-be-lu-ma*

14 2 [...]

14 3 *ina e-muq* AN.ŠÁR ^{d}EN DUMU ^{d}EN *u* ^{d}15 DINGIR.MEŠ *ti-ik-li-šú kul-lat* KUR.KUR *i-be-lu-ma*

14 4 [...-*i*]*k-li-šú kul-lat* KUR.KUR *i-bé-lu-ma*

14 5 [...] x ⸢^{d}EN⸣ *u* ^{d}15 DINGIR.MEŠ *ti-ik-li-šú* [...]

14 6 [...]

15 0 *gi-mir ma-li-ku ú-šak-ni-šu še-pu-uš-šu*

15 1 *gi-mir ma-li-ku ú-šak-ni-šu še-pu-uš-šu*

15 2 [...]

15 3 *gi-mir ma-li-ku ú-šak-ni-šú še-pu-uš-šú*
15 4 [...] x *še-pu-uš-šú*
15 5 ⸢*gi*⸣*-mir ma-li-ku ú-šak-ni-šú še-pu-uš-šú*
15 6 [...] *še-*[...]

16 0 *ba-nu-ú* É AN.ŠÁR *e-piš é-sag-íl u* TIN.TIR.KI *mu-ud-diš é-an-na*
16 1 *ba-nu-ú* É AN.ŠÁR *e-piš é-sag-íl u* TIN.TIR.KI *mu-ud-diš é-an-na*
16 2 [...]
16 3 *ba-a-nu-ú* É AN.ŠÁR *e-piš é-sag-íl u* TIN.TIR.KI *mu-ud-diš é-an-na*
16 4 [...-*í*]*l u* TIN.TIR.KI *mu-ud-diš é-an-na*
16 5 [...-*pi*]*š é-sag-íl u* TIN.TIR.KI *mu-ud-diš é-an-na*
16 6 [... .TI]R.KI *mu-ud-diš* ⸢*é*⸣-[...]

17 0 *mu-šak-lil eš-re-e-ti u ma-ḫa-zu mu-kin sat-tuk-ku*
17 1 *mu-šak-lil eš-re-e-ti u ma-ḫa-zu mu-kin sat-tuk-ku*
17 2 [...]
17 3 *mu-šak-lil eš-re-e-ti u ma-ḫa-zu mu-kin sat-tuk-ka*
17 4 [...-*ḫ*]*a-zu mu-kin sat-tuk-ku*
17 5 [...] x-*ti u ma-ḫa-zu mu-*⸢*kin*⸣ *sat-tuk-ku*
17 6 [...] *mu-kin sat-*[...]

18 0 LUGAL *šá ina* u_4*-me* BALA-*šú* EN GAL-*ú* ^{d}AMAR.UTU *a-na* TIN.TIR.KI *sa-li-mu ir-šu-ú*
18 1 LUGAL *šá ina* u_4*-me* BALA-*šú* EN GAL-*ú* ^{d}AMAR.UTU *a-na* TIN.TIR.KI *sa-li-mu ir-šu-ú*
18 2 [...]
18 3 LUGAL *šá ina* ⸢u_4⸣*-mu* BALA-*šú* EN GAL-*ú* ^{d}AMAR.UTU *ana* TIN.TIR.KI *ir-*⸢*šu*⸣*-ú sa-li-mu*
18 4 [...] x TIN.TIR.KI *sa-li-mu ir-šu-ú*
18 5 [...] x ^{d}AMAR.UTU *a-na* TIN.TIR.KI *sa-*⸢*li*⸣*-mu ir-šu-ú*
18 6 [... .TI]R(?).KI *sa-li-mu i*[*r-*...]

19 0 *ina é-sag-íl* É.GAL-*šú ir-mu-ú šu-bat-su*
19 1 *ina é-sag-íl* É.GAL-*šú ir-mu-ú šu-bat-su*
19 2 [...]
19 3 *ina é-sag-íl* ⸢É⸣.GAL-*šú ir-*⸢*mu-ú*⸣ *šu-bat-su*
19 4 [... *i*]*r-mu-ú šu-bat-su*
19 5 [...] x *ir-mu-ú šu-bat-su*
19 6 [...] *ir-mu-*[...]

20 0 ^{d}*a-num* GAL-*ú ana* URU-*šú* BÀD.AN.KI *ù* É-*šú é-dim-gal-kalam-ma ú-še-ri-bu-ma*
20 1 ^{d}*a-num* GAL-*ú ana* URU-*šú* BÀD.AN.KI *ù* É-*šú é-dim-gal-kalam-ma ú-še-ri-bu-ma*
20 2 [...]
20 3 ^{d}*a-num* GAL-*ú* (x) *a-na* URU-*šú* ⸢BÀD⸣.A[N].⸢KI⸣ *u* É-*šú é-dim-gal-*⸢*kalam*⸣*-ma ú-še-ri-bu-ma*
20 4 [...-*di*]*m-gal-kalam-ma ú-še-ri-bu-ma*

20 5 [... BÀ]D.AN.KI *u* É-*šú é-dim-gal-kalam-m*[*a* ...]
20 6 [...] ⸢*ù*(?)⸣ É-*šú é-dim-gal-kalam-ma* [...]

21 0 *ú-še-ši-bu pa-rak-ka da-ra-a-ti*
21 1 *ú-še-ši-bu pa-rak-ka da-ra-a-ti*
21 2 [...]
21 3 *ú-še-ši-bu pa-rak-ka da-ra-a-ti*
21 4 *ú-še-ši-bu pa-rak-ku da-ra-a-tu*
21 5 [...-*š*]*i-bu pa-rak da-ra-a-a*(?)-*t*[*i*]
21 6 [...]-*rak da-r*[*a*-...]

22 0 DINGIR.MEŠ KUR.KUR *šá a-na* KUR *aš-šur*.KI *i-ḫi-šu-ni šu-kut-ta-šú-nu ud-diš-ma ul-tu qé-reb* KUR *aš-šur*.KI
22 1 DINGIR.MEŠ KUR.KUR *šá* ⸢*a*⸣-<*na*> KUR *aš*-⸢*šur*⸣.KI *i-ḫi-šu-ni šu-kut-ta-šú-nu ud-diš-ma ul-tu qé-reb* KUR *aš-šur*.KI
22 2 [...]
22 3 DINGIR.MEŠ KUR.KUR *šá a-na* KUR *aš-šur*.KI *i-ḫi-šu-ni šu-kut-ta-šú-nu ud-diš-ma ul-tu qé-reb* KUR *aš-šur*.KI
22 4 [...-*t*]*a*(?)-⸢*šú*⸣-*nu ud-diš-ma ul-tu qé-reb* KUR *aš-šur*.KI
22 5 [...].⸢KI⸣ *i-ḫi-šu-ni šu-kut-ta-šú-nu ud*-⸢*diš*⸣-[...]
22 6 [...-*t*]*a*(?)-[x x] ⸢*ud*⸣-*diš*-⸢*ma ul*⸣-[...]

23 0 *ana áš-ri-šú-nu ú-tir-šú-nu-ti-ma ú-kin is-qu-uš-šú-un*
23 1 *ana áš-ri-šú-nu ú-tir-šú-nu-ti-ma ú-kin is-qu-uš-šú-un*
23 2 [...]
23 3 *a-na áš-ri-šú-nu ú*-⸢*tir*⸣-*šú-nu-ti-ma ú-kin-nu is-qu-uš-šú-un*
23 4 [...-*m*]*a*(?) *ú-kin is-qu-uš-šú-un*
23 5 [*a*]-*na áš-ri-šu-nu ú-tir-šu-nu-ti-ma* ⸢*ú*⸣-(x) [...]
23 6 [...]

24 0 NUN *en-qu it-pe-šu ḫa-sis kal šip-ri šá ina ma-ḫa-zu* GAL.MEŠ
24 1 NUN *en-qu it-pe-šu ḫa-sis kal šip-ri šá ina ma-ḫa-zu* GAL.MEŠ
24 2 [...]
24 3 NUN *en-qu it-pe-šú ḫa-a-sis* ⸢*kal*⸣ *ši-pir šá ina ma-ḫa-zu* GAL.MEŠ
24 4 [...] *ma-ḫa-zu* GAL.MEŠ
24 5 [...] ⸢*kal*(?) *ši*(?)-*pir šá ina*(?) *ma*(?)-*ḫa*(?)-*zu*(?)⸣ [...]
24 6 [...]

25 0 *si-ma-a-ti iš-tak-ka-nu uš-te-ši-ru šu-luḫ-ḫa*
25 1 *si-ma-a-ti iš-tak-ka-nu uš-te-ši-ru šu-luḫ-ḫa*
25 2 [...]
25 3 *si-ma-a-ti iš-tak-ka-nu uš-te-ši-ru šu-luḫ-ḫa*

25 4 *si-ma-a-ti iš-tak-ka-nu* [...] *šu-luḫ-ḫa*
25 5 (Only traces visible on photo)
25 6 [...]

26 0 DUMU ^{md}30-ŠEŠ.MEŠ-*eri-ba* LUGAL ŠÚ LUGAL KUR *aš-šur*.KI DUMU ^{m}LUGAL-GIN LUGAL KUR *aš-šur*.KI
26 1 DUMU ^{md}30-ŠEŠ.MEŠ-*eri-ba* LUGAL ŠÚ LUGAL KUR *aš-šur*.KI DUMU ^{m}LUGAL-GIN LUGAL KUR *aš-šur*.KI
26 2 [...]
26 3 DUMU ^{md}30-ŠEŠ.MEŠ-*eri-ba* LUGAL ŠÚ LUGAL KUR *aš-šur*.KI DUMU ^{m}LUGAL-GIN LUGAL KUR *aš-šur*
26 4 [...].KI ⸢DUMU⸣ ^{m}LUGAL-GIN LUGAL KUR *aš-šur*.KI
26 5–6 [...]

27 0 GÌR.NÍTA TIN.TIR.KI LUGAL KUR *šu-me-ru ù* URI.KI
27 1 GÌR.NÍTA TIN.TIR.KI LUGAL KUR *šu-me-ru ù* URI.KI
27 2 [...]
27 3 GÌR.NÍTA TIN.TIR.KI LUGAL KUR *šu-me-ri ù* URI.KI
27 4 [...] x *ù* URI.KI
27 5–6 [...]

28 0 *li-ip-li-pi da-ru-ú šá* ^{d}EN-*ba-ni* DUMU ^{m}*a-da-si* LUGAL KUR *aš-šur*.KI
28 1 *li-ip-li-pi da-ru-ú šá* ^{d}⸢EN-*ba*⸣-*ni* DUMU ^{m}*a-da-si* LUGAL KUR *aš-šur*.KI
28 2 [...]
28 3 *li-ip-li-pi da-ru-ú šá* ^{md}EN-*ba-ni* DUMU ^{m}*a-da-si* LUGAL KUR *aš-šur*.KI
28 4 [...] ⸢A ^{m}*a-da*⸣-*si* LUGAL KUR *aš-šur*.KI
28 5–6 [...]

29 0 NUNUZ *bal-til*.KI *šu-qu-ru* NUMUN LUGAL-*ú-tu ki-sit-ti ṣa-a-ti*
29 1 NUNUZ *bal-til*.KI *šu-qu-ru* ⸢NUMUN LUGAL⸣-*ú-tu ki-sit-ti ṣa-a-ti*
29 2 [...]
29 3 NUNUZ *bal-til*.KI *šu-qu-ru* NUMUN LUGAL-*ú-tu ki-sit-ti ṣa-a-ti*
29 4 [...-*t*]*u* ⸢*ki*⸣-*sit-ti ṣa-a-ti*
29 5–6 [...]

30 0 *i-nu-ma é-an-na* É ^{d}*a-nu-ú-tu na-ram* ^{d}15 GAŠAN-*ia šá* LUGAL *ma-ḫar i-pu-šu*
30 1 *i-nu-ma é-an-na* É *a-n*[*u*(?)]-⸢*ú*⸣-*tu na-ram* ^{d}15 GAŠAN-*ia šá* LUGAL *ma-ḫar i-pu-šu*
30 2 [...]
30 3 *i-nu-šú* ⸢*é*⸣-*an-na* É ^{d}*a-nu-ú-tu na-ram* ^{d}15 GAŠAN-*ia šá* LUGAL *ma-ḫar i-pu*-⸢*šu*⸣
30 4 [...-*r*]*am* ^{d}15 GAŠAN-*ia šá* LUGAL *ma-ḫar i-pu-šu*
30 5–6 [...]

31 0 *la-ba-riš il-lik-ma i-qu-pu* É.GAR$_8$.MEŠ-*šú*
31 1 *la-ba-riš il-lik-ma i-qu-pu* É.GAR$_8$.MEŠ-*šú*
31 2 [...]
31 3 *la-ba-riš il-lik-ma i-qu-pu* É.GAR$_8$.MEŠ-*šú*
31 4 [...-*p*]*u* É.GAR$_8$.MEŠ-*šú*
31 5–6 [...]

32 0 *áš-ra-ti-šú áš-te-ʾ-e ma-qit-ta-šú as-suḫ te-me-en-šú ú-ṣab-bi-ma ki-ma si-ma-ti-šú*
32 1 *áš-ra-ti-šú áš-te-ʾ-e ma-qit-ta-šú as-suḫ te-me-en-šú ú-ṣab*(*)*-bi-ma ki-ma si-ma-ti-šú*
32 2 [...]
32 3 *áš-ra-ti-šú áš-te-ʾ-e ma-qit-ta-šú* ⌈*as-suḫ*⌉ *te-me-en-šú ú-ṣab-bi-ma* ⌈*ki*⌉*-ma si-ma-ti-šú*
32 4 [...-*su*]*ḫ*(?) *te-me-en-šú ú-ṣab-bi-ma* [...]
32 5–6 [...]

33 0 *la-bi-ra-a-ti ina ši-pir* ^{d}*kulla ar-ṣip ú-šak-lil ki-ma* KUR-*i re-e-ši-šú ul-li*
33 1 *la-bi-ra-a-ti ina ši-pir* ^{d}*kulla ar-ṣip ú-šak-lil ki-ma* KUR-*i re-e-ši-šú ul-li*
33 2 [...]
33 3 *la-bi-ra-a-ti ina ši-pir* ^{d}*kulla ar-ṣip ú-šak-lil ki-ma KUR-i re-e-ši-šú* ⌈*ul*⌉*-li*
33 4 [...] ⌈^{d}⌉*kulla ar-ṣip ú-šak-lil ki-ma* KUR-*i re-e-ši-šú ul-li*
33 5–6 [...]

34 0 ^{d}15 GAŠAN *šur-bu-ti ši-pir šu-a-tu ḫa-diš lip-pa-lis-ma a-mat* MUNUS.SIG$_5$-*ia liš-šá-kin šap-tuš-šá*
34 1 ^{d}15 GAŠAN *šur-bu-ti ši-pir šu-a-tu ḫa-diš lip-pa-lis-ma a-mat* MUNUS.SIG$_5$-*ia liš-šá-kin šap-tuš-šá*
34 2 [...]
34 3 ^{d}15 GAŠAN *šur-bu-ti ši-pir šu-a-ti ḫa-diš lip-pa-lis-ma a-mat* MUNUS.SIG$_5$-*ia liš-šá-kin šap-tuš-šá*
34 4 [...-*l*]*is-ma a-mat* MUNUS.SIG$_5$-*ia liš-šá-kin šap-tuš-šá*
34 5–6 [...]

35 0 *muḫ-ḫi kul-lat na-ki-ri li-šam-ri-ir* GIŠ.TUKUL.MEŠ-*ia*
35 1 *muḫ-*⌈*ḫi*⌉ *kul-lat na-ki-ri li-šam-ri-ir* GIŠ.TUKUL.MEŠ-*ia*
35 2 [...]
35 3 UGU *kul-lat na-ki-ri li-šam-ri-ir* GIŠ.TUKUL.MEŠ-*ia*
35 4 [...] GIŠ.TUKUL.MEŠ-*ia*
35 5–6 [...]

36 0 *ma-ti-ma ina aḫ-rat* UD.⌈MEŠ⌉ NUN EGIR-*ú šá ina* UD.MEŠ BALA-*šú ši-pir šu-a-tu*
36 1 *ma-ti-ma ina aḫ-rat* UD.⌈MEŠ⌉ NUN EGIR-*ú šá ina* UD.MEŠ BALA-*šú ši-pir šu-a-tu*
36 2 [...]
36 3 *ma-ti-ma ina* ⌈*aḫ*⌉*-rat u$_4$-mu* NUN EGIR-*ú šá ina u$_4$-me* BALA-*šú ši-pir šu-a-ti*

36 4 [...-*m*]*e* BALA-*šú ši-pir šu-a-ti*
36 5–6 [...]

37 0 *in-na-ḫu-ma ma-qit-ti i-raš-šu-ú áš-ra-ti-šú liš-te-ʾ-e ma-qit-ta-šú lik-šir*
37 1 *in-na-ḫu-ma ma-qit-ti i-raš-šu-ú* ⸢*áš*⸣*-ra-ti-šú liš-te-ʾ-e ma-qit(*)-ta-šú lik-šir*
37 2 [...]
37 3 *in-na-ḫu-ma ma-qit-ti i-raš-*⸢*šu-ú áš*⸣*-ra-ti-šú liš-te-*⸢*ʾ*⸣*-e ma-*⸢*qit-ta*⸣*-šú lik-šir*
37 4 [...]*-ra-ti-šú liš-te-ʾ-e ma-qit-ta-šú lik-šir*
37 5–6 [...]

38 0 MU.SAR-*ú ši-ṭir* MU-*ia* Ì.GIŠ *lip-šu-uš* UDU.SÍSKUR BAL-*qí ina áš-ri-šú liš-kun*
38 1 MU.SAR-*ú ši-ṭir* MU-*ia* Ì.⸢GIŠ⸣ *lip-šu-uš* UDU.SÍSKUR BAL-*qí ina áš-ri-šú liš-kun*
38 2 [...]
38 3 MU.⸢SAR-*ú*⸣ *ši-ṭir* MU-⸢*ia*⸣ Ì.GIŠ ⸢*lip-šu-uš* UDU.SÍSKUR⸣ BAL-*qí ina* ⸢*áš-ri*⸣*-šú liš-*⸢*kun*⸣
38 4 [...].SÍSKUR BAL-*qí ina áš-ri-šú liš-kun*
38 5–6 [...]

39 0 *ik-ri-bi-šú* DINGIR.MEŠ *i-šem-mu-ú ur-rak* UD.MEŠ *ú-rap-pa-áš kim-ti*
39 1 *ik-ri-bi-šú* DINGIR.MEŠ *i-šem-mu-ú ur-rak* UD.MEŠ *ú-rap-pa-áš kim-ti*
39 2 [...]
39 3 *ik-ri-bi-šú* DINGIR.MEŠ *i-*⸢*šem*⸣*-mu-ú ur-ra-ak* UD.MEŠ *ú-rap-pa-áš kim-ti*
39 4 [...].ME *ú-rap-pa-áš kim-ti*
39 5–6 [...]

40 0 *šá* MU.SAR-*ú ši-ṭir* MU-*ia ina ši-pir ni-kil-ti ib-ba-tu lu-ú a-šar-šú ú-nak-ka-ru*
40 1 *šá* MU.SAR-*ú ši-ṭir* MU-*ia ina ši-pir ni-kil-ti ib-ba-tu lu-ú a-šar-šú ú-nak-ka-ru*
40 2 [...]
40 3 *šá* MU.SAR-*ú ši-ṭir* MU-⸢*ia*⸣ *ina ši-pir ni-kil-ti ib-ba-tu* ⸢*lu*⸣*-ú a-šar-šú ú-nak-ka-ru*
40 4 [... *i*]*b-ba-tu lu-ú a-šar-šú ú-nak-ka-ru*
40 5–6 [...]

41 0 ^{d}*iš-tar* GAŠAN GAL-*ti ag-giš lik-kil-me-šú-ma* MU-*šú* NUMUN-*šú ina nap-ḫar* KUR.KUR *li-ḫal-liq*
41 1 ^{d}*iš-tar* GAŠAN GAL-*ti ag-giš lik-kil-me-šú-ma* MU-*šú* NUMUN-*šú ina nap-ḫar* KUR.KUR *li-ḫal-liq*
41 2 [...]
41 3 ^{d}⸢*iš*⸣*-tar* GAŠAN GAL-*ti ag-giš lik-kil-me-šú-ma* MU-*šú* NUMUN-*šú ina nap-*⸢*ḫar*⸣ KUR.KUR *li-ḫal-liq*
41 4 [...]-⸢*šú*⸣ NUMUN-*šú ina nap-ḫar* KUR.KUR *li-ḫal-liq*
41 5–6 [...]

1 0 *a-na* ^{d}INANNA UNUG.KI *e-tel-let* AN-*e u* KI-*tim qa-rit-ti* DINGIR.MEŠ *ṣir-ti*
1 1 *a-na* ^{d}INANNA UNUG.KI *e-tel-let* AN-*e u* KI-*tim qa-rit-ti* DINGIR.MEŠ *ṣir-ti*
1 2 [...] traces [...]
1 3 [... UNU]G.⸢KI *e*⸣-*tel-let* AN-*e* ⸢*ù* KI⸣-*ti*[*m* ...]

2 0 GAŠAN *šur-bu-tú ḫa-me-mat pa-ra-aṣ* ^{d}*a-nù-u-tú ša na-gab šu-luḫ-ḫu šu-up-qu-ud-du qa-tuš-šá*
2 1 GAŠAN *šur-bu-tú ḫa-me-mat pa-ra-aṣ* ^{d}*a-nù-u-tú ša na-gab šu-luḫ-ḫu šu-up-qu-ud-du qa-tuš-šá*
2 2 [...] x [...]
2 3 [...-*r*]*a*-⸢*aṣ*⸣ ^{d}*a-nù-ú-ti* [...]

3 0 *šá-nu-kàt i-la-a-te ša ina er-me a-nu ù ki-gal-li šur-ru-ḫu zik-ru-šá*
3 1 *šá-nu-kàt i-la-a-te ša ina er-me a-nu ù ki-gal-li šur-ru-ḫu zik-ru-šá*
3 2 (x) [... -*l*]*a*-⸢*a-ti šá*⸣ *ina* ⸢*er*⸣-*me a-nu u* ⸢*ki*⸣-*gal*-⸢*li šur-ru*⸣-[...]
3 3 [...] x (x) [...]

4 0 *i-lat* MURUB$_4$ *ù ta-ḫa-zi a-li-kàt i-di* LUGAL *mi-gir-i-šá mu-ra-áš-ši-bat ga-re-e-šú*
4 1 *i-lat* MURUB$_4$ *ù ta-ḫa-zi a-li-kàt i-di* LUGAL *mi-gir-i-šá mu-ra-áš-ši-bat ga-re-e-šú*
4 2 ⸢*i-lat* MURUB$_4$⸣ [(*u*) M]È(?) *a-li-kát i*-⸢*di*⸣ LUGAL ⸢*mi*⸣-*gir-i-šá mu-ra-a*[*s*-...]
4 3 [...]

5 0 *a-ši-bat é-nir-gál-an-na ša qé-reb é-an-na* GAŠAN UNUG.KI GAŠAN GAL-*ti* GAŠAN-*šú*
5 1 *a-ši-bat é-nir-gál-an-na ša qé-reb é-an-na* GAŠAN UNUG.KI GAŠAN GAL-*ti* GAŠAN-*šú*
5 2 *a-ši-bat é-nir-gál-an-na šá qé-reb é-an-na* GAŠAN UNUG.KI GAŠAN GA[L...]
5 3 [...]

6 0 ^{m}AN.ŠÁR-ŠEŠ-SUM.NA MAN ŠÚ MAN KUR *aš-šur*.KI GÌR.NÍTA KÁ.DINGIR.RA.KI MAN KUR *šu-me-ri ù* URI.KI
6 1 ^{m}AN.ŠÁR-ŠEŠ-SUM.NA MAN ŠÚ MAN KUR *aš-šur*.KI GÌR.NÍTA KÁ.DINGIR.RA.KI MAN KUR *šu-me-ri ù* URI.KI
6 2 ^{m}AN.ŠÁR-ŠEŠ-MU LUGAL ŠÚ LUGAL KUR *aš-šur*.KI GÌR.NÍTA KÁ.DINGIR.RA.KI LUGAL KUR EME.(x) [...]
6 3 [...]

7 0 LUGAL *šáḫ-ṭu muš-te-ʾ-u áš-ra-a-ti* DINGIR.MEŠ GAL.MEŠ *pa-liḫ* EN EN.EN
7 1 LUGAL *šáḫ-ṭu muš-te-ʾ-u áš-ra-a-ti* DINGIR.MEŠ GAL.MEŠ *pa-liḫ* EN EN.EN
7 2 ⸢LUGAL *šáḫ*⸣-*ṭu muš-te-ʾ-ú áš-ra-a-ti* DINGIR.MEŠ GAL.MEŠ *pa-a-liḫ* [...]
7 3 [...]

8 0 *ba-nu-u* É AN.ŠÁR *e-piš é-sag-íl ù* KÁ.DINGIR.RA.KI *za-nin é-zi-da*
8 1 *ba-nu-u* É AN.ŠÁR *e-piš é-sag-íl ù* KÁ.DINGIR.RA.KI *za-nin é-zi-da*
8 2 *ba-nu-ú* É AN.ŠÁR *e-piš é-*⸢*sag*⸣*-íl u* ⸢KÁ⸣.DIŠ.DIŠ.KI *za-a-ni*[*n* ...]
8 3 [...]

9 0 *mu-ud-diš é-an-na mu-šak-lil eš-re-e-ti ma-ḫa-zi ša ina qé-reb-ši-na iš-tak-ka-nu si-ma-a-ti*
9 1 *mu-ud-diš é-an-na mu-šak-lil eš-re-e-ti ma-ḫa-zi ša ina qé-reb-ši-na iš-tak-ka-nu si-ma-a-ti*
9 2 *mu-ud-diš é-an-na mu-šak-lil eš-re-e-ti* K[I.ŠU.PEŠ₅] *šá ina qer-bi-ši-na iš-tak-ka-nu ṣ*[*i*-...]
9 3 [...]

10 0 DUMU ^{md}30-PAP.MEŠ-SU MAN ŠÚ MAN KUR *aš-šur*.KI DUMU ^{m}MAN-GIN MAN KUR *aš-šur*.KI GÌR.NÍTA KÁ.DIŠ.DIŠ.KI MAN KUR *šu-me-ri u* URI.KI
10 1 DUMU ^{md}30-PAP.MEŠ-SU MAN ŠÚ MAN KUR *aš-šur*.KI DUMU ^{m}MAN-GIN MAN KUR *aš-šur*.KI GÌR.NÍTA KÁ.DIŠ.DIŠ.KI MAN KUR *šu-me-ri u* URI.KI
10 2 DUMU ^{md}30-ŠEŠ.MEŠ-SU LUGAL ŠÚ LUGAL KUR *aš-šur*.KI DUMU ^{m}LUGAL-GIN ⸢LUGAL⸣ [...] GÌR.NÍTA KÁ.DIŠ.DIŠ.KI LUGAL KUR (x) [...]
10 3 [...]

11 0 *é-nir-gál-an-na* É *pa-pa-ḫi* ^{d}*iš-tar* GAŠAN-*ia ša qé-reb é-an-na*
11 1 *é-nir-gál-an-na* É *pa-pa-ḫi* ^{d}*iš-tar* GAŠAN-*ia ša qé-reb é-an-na*
11 2 *é-nir-gál-an-na* É *pa-pa-ḫi* ^{d}*iš-tar* GAŠAN-*ia šá* [...]
11 3 [...]

12 0 *ša* MAN *maḫ-ri i-pu-šu la-ba-riš il-lik-ma mi-qit-ti ir-ši*
12 1 *ša* MAN *maḫ-ri i-pu-šu la-ba-riš il-lik-ma mi-qit-ti ir-ši*
12 2 *šá* LUGAL *maḫ-ri i-pu-šu la-ba-riš il-lik-m*[*a*] *m*[*i*- ...]
12 3 [...]

13 0 *áš-ra-ti-šú áš-te-ʾ ina a-gur-ri* UDUN KÙ-*tim ma-qit-ta-šú ak-še-er*
13 1 *áš-ra-ti-šú áš-te-ʾ ina a-gur-ri* UDUN KÙ-*tim ma-qit-ta-šú ak-še-er*
13 2 *áš-ra-ti-šú áš-te-ʾ-i ina a-gur-ri* UDUN ⸢KÙ-*tim*⸣ [...]
13 3 [...]

14 0 ŠU.II ^{d}INANNA UNUG.KI GAŠAN GAL-*ti aṣ-bat-ma a-na qé-reb-šú ú-še-rib šu-bat da-ra-a-te ú-šar-me*
14 1 ŠU.II ^{d}INANNA UNUG.KI GAŠAN GAL-*ti aṣ-bat-ma a-na qé-reb-šú ú-še-rib šu-bat da-ra-a-te ú-šar-me*
14 2 ŠU.II ^{d}INANNA UNUG.KI GAŠAN GAL-*t*[*i*] ⸢*aṣ*⸣-[...]
14 3 [...]

15 0 UDU.SISKUR.MEŠ *taš-ri-iḫ-ti aq-qí uš-par-zi-iḫ si-ga-ar-šá*

15 1 UDU.SISKUR.MEŠ *taš-ri-iḫ-ti aq-qí uš-par-zi-iḫ si-ga-ar-šá*

15 2 UDU.SISKUR.MEŠ *taš-*[...]

15 3 [...]

16 0 ^{d}INANNA UNUG.KI GAŠAN *ṣir-ti ina qé-reb* É *pa-pa-ḫi šu-a-te ḫa-di-iš ina a-šá-bi-ki*

16 1 ^{d}INANNA UNUG.KI GAŠAN *ṣir-ti ina qé-reb* É *pa-pa-ḫi šu-a-te ḫa-di-iš ina a-šá-bi-ki*

16 2–3 [...]

17 0 *ia-a-ti* ^{m}AN.ŠÁR-ŠEŠ-SUM.NA MAN KUR *aš-šur*.KI *a-mat* MUNUS.SIG$_5$*-ia liš-šá-kin šap-tuk-ki*

17 1 *ia-a-ti* ^{m}AN.ŠÁR-ŠEŠ-SUM.NA MAN KUR *aš-šur*.KI *a-mat* MUNUS.SIG$_5$*-ia liš-šá-kin šap-tuk-ki*

17 2–3 [...]

18 0 TI.LA UD.MEŠ SÙ.MEŠ *še-bé-e lit-tu-tu ṭu-ub* UZU *ù ḫu-ud lìb-bi ši-i-me ši-ma-ti*

18 1 TI.LA UD.MEŠ SÙ.MEŠ *še-bé-e lit-tu-tu ṭu-ub* UZU *ù ḫu-ud lìb-bi ši-i-me ši-ma-ti*

18 2–3 [...]

19 0 *ina qab-lu ù ta-ḫa-zi i-da-a-a i-tas-ḫar-ma kul-lat na-ki-ri-ia lu-mì-iš kul-ba-biš*

19 1 *ina qab-lu ù ta-ḫa-zi i-da-a-a i-tas-ḫar-ma kul-lat na-ki-ri-ia lu-mì-iš kul-ba-biš*

19 2–3 [...]

20 0 *ma-ti-ma ina aḫ-rat u$_4$-me* NUN EGIR*-u ša ina* BALA*-šú* É *pa-pa-ḫi šu-a-te in-na-ḫu an-ḫu-us-su lu-ud-diš*

20 1 *ma-ti-ma ina aḫ-rat u$_4$-me* NUN EGIR*-u ša ina* BALA*-šú* É *pa-pa-ḫi šu-a-te in-na-ḫu an-ḫu-us-su lu-ud-diš*

20 2–3 [...]

21 0 *šu-mì it-ti šu-me-šú liš-ṭur* MU.SAR*-ru-u ši-ṭir* MU*-ia* Ì.GIŠ *lip-šu-uš* UDU.SISKUR BAL*-qí it-ti* MU.SAR*-e-šú liš-kun*

21 1 *šu-mì it-ti šu-me-šú liš-ṭur* MU.SAR*-ru-u ši-ṭir* MU*-ia* Ì.GIŠ *lip-šu-uš* UDU.SISKUR BAL*-qí it-ti* MU.SAR*-e-šú liš-kun*

21 2 [...]

21 3 [... *š*]*i*(?)-⌜*ṭir*(?)⌝ M[U(?)-...]-⌜*e*⌝*-šú liš-kun*

22 0 *ik-ri-bi-šú* DINGIR.MEŠ *i-šem-mu-u ša šu-mì šaṭ-ru ina ši-pir ni-kil-ti i-pa-áš-ši-ṭu*

22 1 *ik-ri-bi-šú* DINGIR.MEŠ *i-šem-mu-u ša šu-mì šaṭ-ru ina ši-pir ni-kil-ti i-pa-áš-ši-ṭu*

22 2 [...] traces [...]

22 3 *i*[*k*(?)- ... *-m*]*i*(?) *šaṭ-ru ina ši-pir ni-kil-t*[*i*(?) ...]

23	0	MU.ŠAR-*ru-u-a i-ab-bat lu-u a-šar-šú ú-nak-ka-ru*
23	1	MU.SAR-*ru-u-a i-ab-bat lu-u a-šar-šú ú-nak-ka-ru*
23	2	[...]-⸢*ú-a*⸣ (x) [...]-⸢*tu*⸣ [*l*]*u-ú* [...]
23	3	[...]-*a* ⸢*ib*⸣-*ba*-⸢*tu*⸣ *lu-ú a*-[...]
24	0	^{d}INANNA UNUG.KI *ag-giš lik-kil-me-šu-ma ši-mat le-mut-tú li-šim-šú*
24	1	^{d}INANNA UNUG.KI *ag-giš lik-kil-me-šu-ma ši-mat le-mut-tú li-šim-šú*
24	2	[...] traces [...]
24	3	[... GAŠA]N ⸢*šur*⸣-*bu-ti* ⸢*ag*⸣-*giš lik-kil-me*-[...]
25	0	MU-*šú* NUMUN-*šú ina* KUR *li-ḫal-liq-ma a-a ir-ši-šú re-e-me*
25	1	MU-*šú* NUMUN-*šú ina* KUR *li-ḫal-liq-ma a-a ir-ši-šú re-e-me*
25	2	[...]
25	3	[...] NUMUN-⸢*šú*⸣ *ina* KUR *li-ḫal-liq-ma a*-[...]

1 0 *a-na* ^{d}*na-na-a pu-su-um-ti i-la-a-ti šá* ḪI.LI *u ul-ṣi za-ʾ-na-tu lu-le-e ma-la-tu*
1 1 *a-na* ^{d}*na-na-a pu-su-um-ti i-la-a-ti šá* ḪI.LI *u ul-ṣi za-ʾ-na-tu lu-le-e ma-la-tu*
1 2 *a-na* ^{d}*na-ṇa-a pu-su-um-ti i-la-a-te ša ku-uz-bu ù ul-ṣu za-ʾ-na-at lu-le-e ma-la-ti*
1 3 [x x x x]*-na-a pu-su-um-tú i-*[...]

2 0 *bu-kúr-ti* ^{d}*a-nim šit-ra-aḫ-ti šá ina nap-ḫar be-le-e-ti šur-ba-a-tu e-nu-us-sa*
2 1 *bu-kúr-ti* ^{d}*a-ni̦m šit-ra-aḫ-ti šá ina nap-ḫar be-le-e-ti šur-ba-a-tu e*(Text: *dan*)*-nu-us-sa*
2 2 *bu-kúr-ti* ^{d}*a-nim šit-ra-aḫ-ti ša ina nap-ḫar be-le-e-te šur-ba-at e-nu-us-sa*
2 3 [x x x] ⸢^{d}⸣*a-nim šit*(?)*-ra*(?)*-aḫ-*[...]

3 0 *ḫi-rat* ^{d}*mu-zib-sa*$_{4}$*-a ti-iz-qar-ti sek-ra-ti na-ʾ-it-ti na-ram-ti* NUN*-ú-ti-šú*
3 1 *ḫi-rat* ^{d}*mu-zib-sa*$_{4}$*-a ti-iz-qar-ti* ⸢*sek*⸣*-ra-ti na-ʾ-it-ti na-ram-ti* NUN*-ú-ti-šú*
3 2 *ḫi-rat* ^{d}*mu-zib-sa*$_{4}$*-a ti-iz-qar-ti sek-ra-at na-ʾ-it-ti na-ra-mat ru-bu-ti-*⸢*šú*⸣
3 3 [...]*-sa*$_{4}$*-*⸢*a ti*⸣*-iz-*[...]

4 0 AN*-tu*$_{4}$ *re-me-ni-tu*$_{4}$ *a-li-kát re-ṣi* LUGAL *pa-li-ḫi-šá mu-šal-bi-rat pa-le-e-šú*
4 1 AN*-tu*$_{4}$ *re-me-ni-tu*$_{4}$ *a-li-kát re-ṣi* LUGAL *pa-li-ḫi-šá mu-šal-bi-rat pa-e-le-šú*
4 2 AN*-tu*$_{4}$ *re-me-ni-ti a-li-kàt re-ṣi* LUGAL *pa-li-ḫi-šá mu-šal-bi-rat pa-le-e-*⸢*šú*⸣
4 3 [...]*-tu*$_{4}$ *a-li-kát r*[*e-* ...]

5 0 *a-ši-bat é-ḫi-li-an-na šá qé-reb é-an-na šar-rat* UNUG.KI GAŠAN GAL*-tu*$_{4}$ GAŠAN*-šú*
5 1 *a-ši-bat é-ḫi-li-an-na šá qé-reb é-an-na šar-rat* UNUG.KI GAŠAN GAL*-tu*$_{4}$ GAŠAN*-šú*
5 2 *a-ši-bat é-ḫi-li-an-na ša qé-reb é-an-na šar-rat* UNUG.KI GAŠAN GAL*-ti* GAŠAN*-šú*
5 3 [...]*-li-an-na šá* [...]

6 0 ^{m}AN.ŠÁR-ŠEŠ-SUM.NA LUGAL ŠÚ LUGAL KUR *aš-šur*.KI GÌR.NÍTA KÁ.DINGIR.RA.KI LUGAL KUR *šu-me-ru ù* URI.KI
6 1 ^{m}AN.ŠÁR-ŠEŠ-SUM.NA LUGAL ŠÚ LUGAL KUR *aš-šur*.KI GÌR.NÍTA KÁ.DINGIR.RA.KI LUGAL KUR *šu-me-ru ù* U[RI.KI]
6 2 ^{m}AN.ŠÁR-ŠEŠ-SUM.NA MAN ŠÚ MAN KUR *aš-šur*.KI GÌR.NÍTA KÁ.DINGIR.RA.KI MAN KUR *šu-me-ri ù* URI.KI
6 3 [...] LUGAL ŠÚ LUGAL [K]UR [...]

7 0 LUGAL *šáḫ-ṭu muš-te-ʾ-ú áš-ra-a-ti* DINGIR.MEŠ GAL.MEŠ *pa-a-liḫ* EN EN.EN
7 1 LUGAL *šáḫ-ṭu muš-te-ʾ-ú áš-ra-a-ti* DINGIR.MEŠ GAL.MEŠ *pa-a-liḫ* EN EN.EN
7 2 LUGAL *šáḫ-ṭu muš-te-ʾ-u áš-ra-a-ti* DINGIR.MEŠ GAL.MEŠ *pa-liḫ* EN EN.EN
7 3 [...] *muš-te-ʾ-*⸢*ú*⸣ [...]

8 0 *ba-a-nu-ú* É AN.ŠÁR *e-piš é-sag-íl u* KÁ.DINGIR.RA.KI *za-a-nin é-zi-da*
8 1 [*b*]*a-a-nu-ú* É AN.ŠÁR *e-piš é-sag-íl u* KÁ.DINGIR.RA.KI *za-a-nin é-zi-d*[*a*]
8 2 *ba-nu-u* É AN.ŠÁR *e-piš é-sag-íl ù* KÁ.DINGIR.RA.KI *ẓa-nin é-zi-da*
8 3 [...] ⸢É⸣ AN.ŠÁR *e-p*[*iš* ...]

9 0 *mu-ud-diš é-an-na mu-šak-lil eš-re-e-ti ma-ḫa-zi šá ina qer-bi-ši-na iš-tak-kan si-ma-a-ti*
9 1 [*m*]*u-ud-diš é-an-na mu-šak-lil eš-re-e-ti ma-ḫa*(*)-*zi šá ina qer-bi-ši-*<*na*> *iš-tak-kan si-ma-*⸢*a*⸣-[x]
9 2 *mu-ud-diš é-an-na mu-šak-lil eš-re-e-te ma-ḫa-zi ša ina qé-reb-ši-na iš-tak-ka-nu si-ma-a-ti*
9 3 [...]-*an-na m*[*u*(?)- ...] *šá ina q*[*er*(?)-...]

10 0 DUMU ^{md}30-ŠEŠ.MEŠ-SU LUGAL ŠÚ LUGAL KUR *aš-šur*.KI DUMU ^{m}LUGAL-GIN LUGAL KUR *aš-šur*.KI GÌR.NÍTA KÁ.DINGIR.RA.KI LUGAL KUR *šu-me-ru ù ak-ka-di-i*
10 1 [D]UMU ^{md}30-ŠEŠ.MEŠ-SU LUGAL ŠÚ LUGAL KUR *aš-šur*.KI DUMU ^{m}LUGAL-GIN LUGAL KUR *aš-šur*.KI GÌR.NÍTA KÁ.DINGIR.RA.KI LUGAL KUR *šu-me-ru ù ak-ka-dì-i*
10 2 DUMU ^{md}30-PAP.MEŠ-SU MAN ŠÚ MAN KUR *aš-šur*.KI DUMU ^{m}MAN-GIN MAN KUR *aš-šur*.KI GÌR.NÍTA KÁ.DIŠ.DIŠ.KI MAN KUR *šu-me-ri u* URI.KI
10 3 [x x (x)-ŠE]Š.MEŠ-SU [...]

11 0 *é-ḫi-li-an-na* É *pa-pa-ḫi* ^{d}*na-na-a* GAŠAN-*ia šá qé-reb é-an-na*
11 1 *é-ḫi-li-an-na* É *pa-pa-ḫi* ^{d}*na-na-a* GAŠAN-*ia šá qé-reb é-an-na*
11 2 *é-ḫi-li-an-na* É *pa-pa-ḫi* ^{d}*na-na-a* GAŠAN-*ia ša qé-reb é-an-na*
11 3 [x x-*l*]*i-an-na* É [...]

12 0 *šá* LUGAL *maḫ-ri i-pu-šu la-ba-riš il-lik-ma mi-qit-ti ir-ši*
12 1 *šá* LUGAL *maḫ-ri i-pu-šu la-ba-riš il-lik-ma mi-qit-ti ir-ši*
12 2 *ša* MAN *maḫ-ri i-pu-šu la-ba-riš il-lik-ma mi-qit-ti ir-ši*
12 3 ⸢*šá*⸣ LUGAL *ma-ḫar i-pu-šu* [...]

13 0 *eṣ-re-ti-šú áš-te-ʾ-i ina* SIG$_4$.AL.ÙR.RA UDUN KÙ-*tim ma-qit-ta-šú ak-ši-ir*
13 1 *eṣ-re-ti-šú áš-te-ʾ-i ina* SIG$_4$.AL.ÙR.RA UDUN KÙ-*tim ma-qit-ta-šú ak-ši-ir*
13 2 *áš-ra-ti-šú áš-te-ʾ ina a-gur-ri* UDUN KÙ-*tim ma-qit-ta-šú ak-še-er*
13 3 *áš-ra-ti-šú áš-te-*⸢*ʾ*⸣-[...]

14 0 ŠU.II ^{d}*na-na-a* GAŠAN GAL-*tu*$_4$ *aṣ-bat-ma a-na qer-bi-šú ú-še-rib-ma šu-bat da-ra-a-ti ú-šar-me*
14 1 ŠU.II ^{d}*na-na-a* GAŠAN GAL-*tu*$_4$ *aṣ-bat-ma a-na qer-bi-šú ú-še-rib-ma šu-bat da-ra-a-ti ú-šar-me*
14 2 ŠU.II ^{d}*na-na-a* GAŠAN GAL-*ti aṣ-bat-ma a-na qé-reb-šú ú-še-rib šu-bat da-ra-a-te ú-šar-me*
14 3 ŠU.II ^{d}*na-na-a* GAŠAN GA[L-...]

15 0 UDU.SISKUR.MEŠ *taš-ri-iḫ-ti aq-qí uš-par-zi-iḫ* ŠI.GAR-*šá*
15 1 UDU.SISKUR.MEŠ *taš-ri-iḫ-ti aq-qí uš-par-zi-iḫ* ŠI.GAR-*šá*
15 2 UDU.SISKUR.MEŠ *taš-ri-iḫ-ti aq-qí uš-par-zi-iḫ si-ga-ar-šá*
15 3 UDU.SISKUR.MEŠ *taš-ri-i*[*ḫ*(?)-...]

16 0 ^{d}*na-na-a* GAŠAN *ṣir-tu*$_{4}$ *ina qé-reb* É *pa-pa-ḫi šu-a-ti ḫa-di-iš ina a-šá-a-bi-ki*
16 1 ^{d}*na-na-a* ⸢GAŠAN⸣ *ṣir-tu*$_{4}$ *ina qé-reb* É *pa-pa-ḫi šu-a-ti ḫa-di-iš ina a-šá-a-bi-ki*
16 2 ^{d}*na-na-a* GAŠAN *ṣir-ti ina qé-reb* É *pa-pa-ḫi šu-a-ti ḫa-di-iš ina a-šá-bi-ki*
16 3 ^{d}*na-na-a* GAŠAN *ṣir-*[...]

17 0 *ia-a-ti* ^{m}AN.ŠÁR-ŠEŠ-SUM.NA NUN *pa-a-liḫ-ki ina ma-ḫar* ^{d}AG *ḫa-a-a-i-ri-ki ti-iz-qa-ri ba-ni-ti*
17 1 *ia-a-ti* ^{m}AN.ŠÁR-ŠEŠ-SUM.NA NUN *pa-a-liḫ-ki ina ma-ḫar* ^{d}AG *ḫa-a-a-i-ri-ki ti-iz-qa-ri ba-ni-ti*
17 2 *ia-a-ti* ^{m}AN.ŠÁR-ŠEŠ-SUM.NA MAN KUR *aš-šur*.KI *ina ma-ḫar* ^{d}PA *ḫa-a-a-ri-ki ti-iz-qa-ri da-mi-iq-ti*
17 3 *ia-a-ti* ^{m}AN.ŠÁR-ŠEŠ-MU [...]

18 0 TI UD.MEŠ SÙ.MEŠ *še-bé-e lit-tu-tu ṭu-ú-bi* UZU *u ḫu-ud lìb-bi ši-i-mi ši-ma-ti*
18 1 TI UD.MEŠ SÙ.MEŠ *še-bé-e lit-tu-tu ṭu-ú-bi* UZU(*) *u ḫu-ud lìb-bi ši-i-mi ši-ma-ti*
18 2 TI.LA UD.MEŠ SÙ.MEŠ *še-bé-e lit-tu-tu ṭu-ub* UZU *ù ḫu-ud lìb-bi ši-i-me ši-ma-t*[*i*]
18 3 TI UD.MEŠ SÙ.MEŠ *še-bé-*⸢*e*⸣ [...]

19 0 SUḪUŠ GIŠ.GU.ZA LUGAL-*ú-ti-ia ú-ḫum-meš šur-ši-di it-ti* AN-*e u* KI-*tim kin-ni* BALA-*ú-a*
19 1 SUḪUŠ GIŠ.GU.ZA LUGAL-*ú-ti-ia ú-ḫum-meš šur-ši-di it-ti* AN-*e u* KI-*tim kin-ni* BALA-*ú-*⸢*a*⸣
19 2 SUḪUŠ GIŠ.GU.ZA LUGAL-*ti-ia ú-ḫum-meš šur-ši-di it-ti* AN-*e u* KI-*tim* ⸢*kin*⸣-x x [x x]
19 3 SUḪUŠ GIŠ.GU.ZA LUGAL-*ú-ti-ia ú-*[...]

20 0 *ma-ti-ma ina aḫ-rat* UD.MEŠ NUN EGIR-*ú šá ina* BALA-*šú* É *pa-pa-ḫi šu-a-ti in-na-ḫu an-ḫu-us-su lu-ud-diš*
20 1 *ma-ti-ma ina aḫ-rat* UD.MEŠ NUN EGIR-*ú šá ina* BALA-*šú* É *pa-pa-ḫi šu-a-ti in-na-ḫu an-ḫu-us-su lu-ud-diš*
20 2 *ma-ti-ma ina aḫ-rat u*$_{4}$*-me* NUN EGIR-*u ša ina* BALA-*šú* É *pa-pa-ḫi šu-a-ti in-na-ḫu* ⸢*an-ḫu-us-su*⸣ [...]
20 3 *ma-ti-ma ina aḫ-rat* UD.MEŠ [...]

21 0 *šu-mi it-ti šu-mi-šú liš-ṭur* MU.SAR-*ru-ú ši-ṭir* MU-*ia* Ì.GIŠ *lip-šu-uš* UDU.SISKUR BAL-*qí it-ti* MU.SAR-*e-šú liš-kun*
21 1 *šu-mi it-ti šu-mi-šú liš-ṭur* MU.SAR-*ru-ú ši-ṭir* MU-*ia* Ì.GIŠ *lip-šu-uš* UDU.SISKUR ⸢BAL⸣-*qí it-ti* MU.SAR-*e-šú liš-kun*
21 2 *šu-mì it-ti šu-mì-šú liš-ṭur* MU.SAR-*ru-u ši-*⸢*ṭir* MU-*ia*⸣ Ì.GIŠ *lip-šu-uš* UDU.SISKUR BAL-*qí it-ti* MU.SAR-*e-šú liš-kun*
21 3 MU *it-ti* MU-*šú liš-ṭur* ⸢MU⸣.[...]

22 0 ik-ri-bi-šú DINGIR.MEŠ i-šem-mu-ú u šá šu-mi šaṭ-ru ina ši-pir ni-kil-ti i-pa-áš-ši-ṭu
22 1 ik-ri-bi-šú DINGIR.MEŠ i-šem-mu-ú u šá šu-mi šaṭ-ru ina ši-pir ni-kil-ti i-pa-áš-ši-ṭu
22 2 ik-ri-bi-šú DINGIR.MEŠ i-šem-mu(-)u ša šu-mì šaṭ-ru ina ši-pir ni-kil-ti i-pa-áš-ši-ṭ[u]
22 3 ik-ri-bi-šú DINGIR.⌈MEŠ⌉ i-šem-m[u-...]

23 0 MU.SAR-ru-ú-a ib-ba-tu lu-u a-šar-šú ú-nak-ka-ru
23 1 MU.SAR-ru-ú-a ib-ba-tu lu-u a-šar-šú ú-nak-ka-ru
23 2 MU.SAR-ru-u-a i-ab-bat lu-u a-šar-šú ú-nak-ka-r[u(?)]
23 3 MU.SAR-ru-ú-a ib-ba-t[u ...]

24 0 ^{d}na-na-a GAŠAN šur-bu-ti ag-giš lik-kil-me-šú-ma ši-mat le-mut-tim li-šim-šú
24 1 ^{d}na-na-a GAŠAN šur-bu-ti ag-giš lik-kil-me-šú-ma ši-mat le-mut-tim li-šim-šú
24 2 ^{d}na-na-a ag-gi-iš lik-kil-me-šu-ma ši-mat le-mut-tú li-šim-[x]
24 3 ⌈^{d}⌉na-na-a GAŠAN šur-bu-ti ag-[...]

25 0 MU-šú NUMUN-šú ina KUR li-ḫal-liq-ma a-a ir-ši-iš re-e-mu
25 1 MU-šú NUMUN-šú ina KUR li-ḫal-liq-ma a-a ir-ši-iš re-e-mu
25 2 MU-šú NUMUN-šú ina KUR li-ḫal-liq-ma a-a ir-ši-šú re-e-[x]
25 3 [x x] ù NUMUN-šú ina KUR l[i-...]

1 0 *a-na* ^{d}AMAR.UTU LUGAL ŠÁR ^{d}*í-gì-gì u* ^{d}*a-nun-na-ki ba-ni* AN-*e u* KI-*tim mu-kin giš-ḫur-ru*

1 1 *a-na* ^{d}AMAR.UTU LUGAL ŠÁR ^{d}*í-gì-gì u* ^{d}*a-nun-na-ki ba-ni* AN-*e u* KI-*tim mu-kin giš-ḫur-ru*

1 2 *a-na* ^{d}AMAR.UTU MAN ŠÁR ^{d}*í-gì-gì u* ⸢^{d}*a*⸣-[...]

1 3 (Not visible on photo)

1 4 [...]

1 5 *a-na* ^{d}AMAR.UTU LUGAL ŠÁR ^{d}*í-gì-gì u* ^{d}*a-nun-na-ki ba-ni* AN-*e u* KI-*tim mu-kin giš-ḫur-ru*

1 6 [...] ŠÁR ^{d}*í-gì-gì u* ^{d}*a-nun-na-ki ba-ni* AN-*e* x x[...]

1 7 (x) [...]-⸢*gì-gì u* ^{d}*a*⸣-[*nun-na*]-⸢*ki ba*⸣-*ni* AN-⸢*e*(?)⸣ [*u*] K[I(?)-... *gi*]*š*(?)-⸢*ḫur*⸣-*r*[*u*(?)]

1 8 *a-na* ^{d}AMAR.UTU LUGAL ŠÁR ^{d}*í-gì-gì u* ^{d}*a*-⸢*nun*⸣-*na-ki ba-ni* AN-*e u* KI-*tim mu-kin giš-ḫur-ru*

1 9 *a-na* ^{d}AMAR.UTU LUGAL ŠÁR ^{d}*í-gì-gì u* ^{d}*a-nun-na-ki ba-ni* AN-*e u* KI-*tim mu-kin giš-ḫur-ru*

1 10 *a-na* ^{d}AMAR.UTU LUGAL ŠÁR ^{d}*í-gì-gì u* ^{d}*a-nun-na-ki ba-ni* AN-*e u* KI-*tim mu-kin giš-ḫur-ru*

1 11 *a-na* ^{d}AMAR.UTU LUGAL ŠÁR ^{d}*í-gì-gì u* ^{d}*a-nun-na-ki ba-ni* AN-*e u* KI-*tim mu-kin giš*-[...]

1 12 [... *m*]*u-kin giš-ḫur-ru*

1 13 x x [...]

1 14 [...] ⸢AMAR.UTU⸣ LUGAL ŠÁR ^{d}*í-gì-gì u* ^{d}⸢*a*⸣-[...]

1 15 *a-na* ^{d}AMAR.UTU LUGAL ⸢ŠÁR⸣ ^{d}*í-gì-gì u* ^{d}*a-nun-na-ki ba-ni* AN-⸢*e*⸣ [...]

1 16 [...] AN-*e u* KI-*tim* [...]

1 17 *a-na* ^{d}AMAR.UTU LUGAL ŠÁR ^{d}*í-gì-gì u* ^{d}*a-nun-na-ki ba-ni* AN-*e u* KI-*tim mu-kin giš-ḫur-ru*

1 18 —

1 19 [...]-*gì-gì u* ^{d}*a-nun-na-ki ba-ni* AN-*e u* KI-*tim mu-kin giš-ḫur*-⸢*ru*⸣

2 0 *a-ši-ib é-sag-íl* EN KÁ.DINGIR.RA.KI EN GAL-*i be-li-ia*

2 1 *a-ši-ib*(*) *é-sag-íl* EN KÁ.DINGIR.RA.KI EN GAL-*i be-li-ia*

2 2 *a-ši-ib é-sag-íl* EN TIN.TIR.KI (x) [...]

2 3 (Not visible on photo)

2 4 [...]

2 5 *a-ši-ib é-sag-íl* EN KÁ.DINGIR.RA.KI EN GAL-*i be-li-ia*

2 6 [...]-*sag-íl* EN KÁ.DINGIR.RA.KI EN *ra-bi*-[...]

2 7 ⸢*a*⸣-*š*[*i-ib* ... E]N K[Á.DINGIR.RA.K]I EN ⸢GAL⸣-[...] (x)

2 8 *a-ši-ib é-sag-íl* E[N K]Á.DINGIR.RA.KI EN GAL-*i* EN-*ia*

2 9 *a-ši-ib é-sag-íl* EN KÁ.DINGIR.RA.KI EN GAL-*i be-li-ia*

2 10 *a-ši-ib é-sag-íl* EN KÁ.DINGIR.RA.KI EN GAL-*i be-li-ia*

2 11 *a-ši-ib é-sag-íl* EN KÁ.DINGIR.RA.KI EN GAL-*i be*-[*l*]*i*-[*ia*]

2 12 [...]-*li-ia*

2 13 [...]

2 14 [*a-ši-i*]*b é-sag-íl* EN ⸢KÁ⸣.DINGIR.⸢RA.KI⸣ [...]

2	15	*a-ši-ib* ⸢*é-sag-íl*⸣ EN TIN.TIR.⸢KI⸣ EN GAL-⸢*i*⸣ [...]
2	16	[... K]I EN *ra-bi*-⸢*i*⸣ [...]
2	17	*a-ši-ib é-sag-íl* EN KÁ.DINGIR.RA.KI EN GAL-*i be-li-ia*
2	18	—
2	19	[...] KÁ.DINGIR.RA.KI ⸢EN GAL-*i*⸣ *be-li-ia*
3	0	*a-na-ku* ^{m}AN.ŠÁR-DÙ-A LUGAL GAL LUGAL *dan-nu* LUGAL ŠÁR LUGAL KUR *aš-šur* LUGAL *kib-rat* 4-*ti*
3	1	*a-na-ku* ^{m}AN.ŠÁR-DÙ-A LUGAL GAL LUGAL *dan-nu* LUGAL ŠÁR LUGAL KUR *aš-šur* LUGAL *kib-rat* 4-*ti*
3	2	[*a*]-⸢*na*⸣-*ku* ^{m}AN.ŠÁR-DÙ-A MAN GAL MAN *dan-nu* MAN ŠÚ MAN KUR *aš*-⸢*šur* MAN *kib-rat* 4-*ti*(?)⸣
3	3	[...]
3	4	...
3	5	*a-na-ku* ^{m}AN.ŠÁR-DÙ-IBILA MAN GAL MAN *dan-nu* MAN ŠÚ MAN KUR *aš-šur* MAN *kib-rat* 4-*ti*
3	6	[... A]N.ŠÁR-DÙ-A MAN GAL MAN *dan-nu* MAN ŠÚ MAN KUR *aš-šur* MAN *ki*[*b*-...]
3	7	⸢*a*⸣-*n*[*a-ku* ... GA]L(?) ⸢LUGAL⸣ *da*[*n-nu* ...] x [...]-*ti*
3	8	*a-na-ku* ^{m}AN.ŠÁR-DÙ-A MAN GAL [...] MAN ŠÚ MAN KUR *aš-šur* MAN *kib-ra*-⸢*ti* 4⸣-[*ti*]
3	9	*a-na-ku* ^{m}AN.ŠÁR-DÙ-A MAN GAL MAN *dan-nu* MAN ŠÚ MAN KUR *aš-šur* MAN *kib-ra-a-ti* 4-*ti*
3	10	*a-na-ku* ^{m}AN.ŠÁR-*ba-ni*-IBILA MAN GAL MAN *dan-nu* MAN ŠÚ MAN KUR *aš-šur* MAN *kib-rat* 4-*ti*
3	11	*a-na-ku* ^{m}AN.ŠÁR-DÙ-A MAN GAL MAN *dan-nu* MAN ŠÚ MAN KUR *aš-šur* MAN *kib*-⸢*ra*⸣-[...]
3	12	[...] x 4-*ti*
3	13	[...]
3	14	[... ^{m}]AN.ŠÁR-*ba-ni*-IBILA MAN GAL MAN *dan-nu* MAN ŠÚ M[AN ...]
3	15	*a-na-ku* ^{m}AN.ŠÁR-DÙ-A MAN GAL MAN ⸢*dan*⸣-*nu* MAN ŠÚ MAN KUR *aš-šur* [...]
3	16	[... M]AN KUR *aš-šur* MAN ⸢*kib*⸣-x [...]
3	17	*a-na-ku* ^{m}AN.ŠÁR-*ba-ni*-IBILA MAN GAL MAN *dan-nu* MAN ŠÚ MAN KUR *aš-šur* MAN *kib-ra-a-ti* 4-*ti*
3	18	—
3	19	[... G]AL MAN *dan-nu* MAN ŠÚ MAN KUR *aš-šur* MAN *kib-ra-ti* 4-*ti*
4	0	DUMU ^{m}AN.ŠÁR-ŠEŠ-SUM.NA LUGAL GAL LUGAL *dan-nu* LUGAL ŠÁR LUGAL KUR *aš-šur* GÌR.NÍTA TIN.TIR.KI
4	1	DUMU ^{m}AN.ŠÁR-ŠEŠ-SUM.NA LUGAL GAL ⸢LUGAL *dan*⸣-*nu* LUGAL ⸢ŠÁR LUGAL⸣ KUR *aš-šur* GÌR.NÍTA TIN.TI[R.KI]
4	2	⸢DUMU⸣ ^{m}AN.ŠÁR-ŠEŠ-SUM.NA MAN GAL MAN *dan-nu* MAN ŠÚ MAN KUR *aš-šur* GÌR.NÍTA TIN.T[IR.KI]
4	3	[...]
4	4	...

4	5	DUMU ^{m}AN.ŠÁR-ŠEŠ-SUM.NA MAN GAL MAN *dan-nu* MAN ŠÚ MAN KUR *aš-šur* GÌR.NÍTA KÁ.DINGIR.RA.KI
4	6	[...-ŠE]Š-SUM.NA MAN GAL MAN *dan-nu* MAN ŠÚ MAN KUR *aš-šur* GÌR.NÍ[TA ...]
4	7	⸢DUMU ^{m}⸣[AN].⸢ŠÁR⸣-Š[EŠ-... G]AL ⸢LUGAL *dan-nu*⸣ [...] x [...].⸢KI⸣
4	8	DUMU ^{m}AN.ŠÁR-ŠEŠ-SUM.NA ⸢MAN⸣ G[AL MA]N ⸢*dan-nu* MAN⸣ ŠÚ MAN KUR *aš-šur* GÌR.NÍTA TIN.[TIR.KI]
4	9	DUMU ^{m}AN.ŠÁR-ŠEŠ-SUM.NA MAN GAL MAN *dan-nu* MAN ŠÚ MAN KUR *aš-šur* GÌR.NÍTA TIN.TIR.KI
4	10	DUMU ^{m}AN.ŠÁR-ŠEŠ-SUM.NA MAN GAL MAN *dan-nu* MAN ŠÚ MAN KUR *aš-šur* GÌR.NÍTA TIN.TIR.KI
4	11	DUMU ^{m}AN.ŠÁR-ŠEŠ-SUM.NA MAN GAL MAN *dan-nu* MAN ŠÚ MAN [K]UR *aš-šur* [...] x [...]
4	12	[....NÍT]A(?) TIN.TIR.K[I]
4	13	[...]
4	14	[...-Š]EŠ-SUM.NA MAN ⸢GAL MAN⸣ *dan-nu* MAN ŠÚ MAN KUR *aš-*[...]
4	15	⸢DUMU⸣ ^{m}AN.ŠÁR-ŠEŠ-SUM.NA MAN GAL MAN ⸢*dan*⸣*-nu* MAN ŠÚ MAN KUR *aš-*⸢*šur*⸣ [...]
4	16	[...]
4	17	[D]UMU ^{m}AN.ŠÁR-ŠEŠ-SUM.NA MAN GAL MAN *dan-nu* MAN ŠÚ MAN KUR *aš-šur* GÌR.NÍTA TIN.TIR.KI
4	18	—
4	19	[...] GAL MAN *dan-nu* MAN ŠÚ MAN KUR *aš-šur* GÌR.NÍTA TIN.TIR.KI
5	0	LUGAL KUR.EME.GI₇ *u* URI.KI *mu-še-šib* KÁ.DINGIR.RA.KI *e-piš é-sag-íl*
5	1	LUGAL KUR.EME.GI₇ *u* URI.KI *mu-še-šib* ⸢KÁ.DINGIR⸣.RA.KI *e-piš é-sag-í*[*l*]
5	2	MAN KUR *šu-me-ri u* URI.KI *mu-še-šib* TIN.TIR.KI *e-piš é-sag-í*[*l*]
5	3	[...]
5	4	...
5	5	MAN KUR.EME.GI₇ *u* URI.KI *mu-še-šib* KÁ.DINGIR.RA.KI *e-piš é-sag-íl*
5	6	[...] x *u* URI.KI *mu-še-šib* KÁ.DINGIR.RA.KI *e-piš é-s*[*ag*-x]
5	7	LUGAL KUR.EME.⸢GI₇ *u* URI(?).KI(?) *mu-še*⸣-[...] x x [...-*í*]*l*
5	8	LUGAL KUR *šu-me-ri u* ⸢URI⸣.KI *mu-še-šib* TIN.TIR.KI *e-piš é-*[...]
5	9	MAN KUR *šu-me-ri u* URI.KI *mu-še-šib* TIN.TIR.KI *e-*⸢*piš*⸣ *é-sag-íl*
5	10	MAN KUR.ÉME.RI *u* URI.KI *mu-še-šib* TIN.TIR.KI *e-piš é-sag-íl*(*)
5	11	MAN KUR *šu-me-ri u* URI.KI *mu-še-šib* ⸢KÁ⸣.DINGIR.⸢RA.KI⸣ *e-p*[*iš ...-í*]*l*
5	12–13	[...]
5	14	[...] x URI.KI *mu-še-šib* KÁ.DINGIR.RA.KI [...]
5	15	[x] ⸢KUR⸣ *šu-me-ri u* ⸢URI⸣.KI ⸢*mu-še*⸣*-šib* TIN.⸢TIR.KI *e*⸣-[...]
5	16	[...]
5	17	MAN KUR.EME.GI₇ *u* URI.KI *mu-še-šib* TIN.TIR.KI *e-piš é-sag-íl*
5	18	—
5	19	MAN KUR.EME.GI₇ *u* URI.KI [...] *e-piš é-sag-íl*

6 0 mu-ud-diš eš-re-e-ti kul-lat ma-ḫa-zi šá i-na qer-bi-ši-na
6 1 mu-ud-diš eš-re-e-ti kul-lat ma-ḫa-zi šá i-na qer-bi-ši-n[a]
6 2 mu-ud-diš eš-re-e-te kul-lat ma-ḫa-zi šá ina qer-bi-ši-n[a]
6 3 [...]
6 4 ...
6 5 mu-ud-diš eš-re-e-ti kul-lat ma-ḫa-zi ša ina qer-bi-ši-na
6 6 [...] eš-re-e-ti kul-lat ma-ḫa-zi ša ina qer-bi-š[i-na]
6 7 mu-ud-diš eš-re-e-ti kul-lat ma-⸢ḫa-zi ša⸣ i-na qer-⸢bi⸣-ši-na
6 8 mu-ud-diš eš-re-e-ti kul-lat ma-ḫa-zi ša i-na qer-[...]
6 9 mu-ud-diš eš-re-e-ti kul-lat ma-ḫa-zi ša i-na ⸢qer⸣-bi-ši-na
6 10 mu-ud-diš eš-re-e-ti kul-lat ma-ḫa-zi ša i-na qer-bi-ši-na
6 11 [m]u-ud-diš ⸢eš-re-e-ti kul-lat ma-ḫa⸣-zi ša i-na qer-bi-ši-n[a]
6 12–13 [...]
6 14 [... -r]e(?)-e-ti kul-lat ma-ḫa-zi [...]
6 15 [mu]-⸢ud⸣-diš eš-re-e-ti kul-lat ma-ḫa-zi x [...]
6 16 [...]
6 17 mu-ud-diš eš-re-e-ti kul-lat ma-ḫa-zi ša ina qer-bi-ši-na
6 18 —
6 19 mu-ud-diš eš-re-e-ti kul-lat ma-ḫa-zi [...]

7 0 iš-tak-ka-nu si-ma-a-ti ù sat-tuk-ki-ši-na baṭ-lu-tu ú-ki-nu
7 1 iš-tak-ka-nu si-ma-a-ti ù sat-tuk-ki-ši-na baṭ-lu-tu ú-ki-⸢nu⸣
7 2 iš-tak-ka-nu si-ma-a-te u sat-tuk-ki-ši-na baṭ-lu-te ú-kin-[nu]
7 3 [...]
7 4 ...
7 5 iš-tak-ka-nu si-ma-a-te ù sat-tuk-ki-ši-na baṭ-lu-tu ú-ki-nu
7 6 [...]-nu si-ma-a-te ù sat-tuk-ki-ši-na baṭ-lu-tu ú-ki-[nu]
7 7 iš-tak-ka-nu si-ma-a-te ù sat-tuk-ki-ši-na baṭ-lu-tu ú-ki-nu
7 8 (x) [...-n]u si-ma-a-te ù sat-tuk-ki-⸢ši⸣-na baṭ-lu-tú [...]
7 9 iš-tak-ka-nu si-ma-a-ti ù sat-tuk-ki-ši-na ⸢baṭ⸣-lu-tú ú-ki-nu
7 10 iš-tak-ka-nu si-ma-a-ti ù sat-tuk-ki-ši-na baṭ-lu-tú ú-ki-nu
7 11 [i]š-[ta]k-ka-nu si-ma-a-te ù sat-tuk-ki-ši-na baṭ-lu-tú ú-ki-nu
7 12–13 [...]
7 14 [...] si-ma-a-te ù sat-tu[k-...]
7 15 [... <...>(?)]
7 16 [...]
7 17 iš-tak-ka-nu si-ma-a-ti ù sat-tuk-ki-ši-na baṭ-lu-tú ú-ki-nu
7 18 —
7 19 [i]š-tak-ka-nu si-ma-a-ti ù sat-tuk-ki-ši-na baṭ-lu-tú ú-ki-nu

8 0 par-ṣi ki-du-de-e ki-ma la-bi-ri-im-ma ú-te-ru áš-ru-uš-šu-un
8 1 par-ṣi ki-du-de-e ki-ma la-bi-ri-im-ma ú-te-ru áš-ru-uš-šu-u[n]
8 2 par-ṣi ki-du-de-e ki-ma la-bi-rim-ma ú-te-ru áš-ru-uš-šú-[un]

8 3 [...]

8 4 ...

8 5 *par-ṣi ki-du-de-e ki-ma la-bi-rim-ma ú-te-ru* ⸢*áš*⸣*-ru-uš-šu-un*

8 6 [... *-d*]*u-de-e ki-ma la-bi-rim-ma ú-te-ru áš-ru-uš-šu-*[*un*]

8 7 *par-ṣi ki-du-de-e ki-ma la-bi-ri-im-ma ú-te-ru áš-ru-uš-šu-un*

8 8 [...*-d*]*u-de-e ki-ma la-bi-rim-ma ú-te-ru áš-*⸢*ru*⸣-[...]

8 9 *par-ṣi ki-du-de-e ki-ma la-bi-rim-ma ú-te-*⸢*ru*⸣ *áš-ru-uš-šu-un*

8 10 *par-ṣi ki-du-de-e ki-ma la-bi-ri-im-ma ú-te-ru áš-ru-uš-šú-un*

8 11 [*p*]*ar-ṣi ki-du-de-e ki-ma la-bi-rim-ma ú-te-ru áš-ru-uš-šu-un*

8 12–13 [...]

8 14 [...]-⸢*e*(?) *ki*⸣*-ma la-bi-ri*[*m-*...]

8 15 [*par-ṣ*]*i ki-du-de-e ki-ma la-b*[*i-*...]

8 16 [...]

8 17 *par-ṣi ki-du-de-e ki-ma la-bi-ri-im-ma ú-te-ru áš-ru-uš-šu-un*

8 18 —

8 19 [...*-m*]*a* ⸢*la-bi*⸣*-ri-im-ma ú-te-ru áš-ru-uš-šu-*⸢*un*⸣

9 0 DUMU DUMU ^{md}30-ŠEŠ.MEŠ-SU LUGAL GAL LUGAL *dan-nu* LUGAL ŠÁR LUGAL KUR *aš-šur a-na-ku-ma*

9 1 DUMU DUMU ^{md}30-ŠEŠ.MEŠ-SU LUGAL GAL LUGAL *dan-nu* LUGAL ŠÁR LUGAL KUR *aš-šur a-na-ku-m*[*a*]

9 2 DUMU DUMU ^{md}30-ŠEŠ.MEŠ-SU MAN GAL MAN *dan-nu* MAN ŠÚ MAN KUR *aš-šur a-na-ku-*[*ma*]

9 3 [...]

9 4 ...

9 5 DUMU DUMU ^{md}30-ŠEŠ.MEŠ-SU MAN GAL MAN *dan-*⸢*nu*⸣ MAN ŠÚ MAN KUR *aš-šur a-na-ku-ma*

9 6 [...].⸢MEŠ⸣-SU LUGAL GAL LUGAL *dan-nu* LUGA[L] ⸢ŠÁR⸣ LUGAL KUR *aš-šur a-na-ku-*[*ma*]

9 7 DUMU DUMU ^{md}30-ŠEŠ.MEŠ-SU LUGAL GAL LUGAL *dan-nu* LUGAL ŠÁR LUGAL KUR *aš-šur a-na-ku-ma*

9 8 [... 3]0-ŠEŠ.MEŠ-SU MAN GAL MAN *dan-nu* MAN ŠÚ MAN KUR [...]

9 9 DUMU DUMU ^{md}30-ŠEŠ.MEŠ-SU MAN GAL MAN *dan-nu* MAN ŠÚ M[AN K]UR *aš-šur a-na-ku-ma*

9 10 DUMU DUMU ^{md}30-ŠEŠ.MEŠ-SU MAN GAL MAN *dan-nu* MAN ŠÚ MAN KUR *aš-šur a-na-ku-ma*

9 11 DUMU DUMU ^{md}30-ŠEŠ.MEŠ-SU MAN GAL MAN *dan-nu* MAN ŠÚ MAN KUR *aš-šur a-na-ku-ma*

9 12–13 [...]

9 14 [...-S]U MAN ⸢GAL⸣ [...]

9 15 [D]UMU DUMU ^{md}30-ŠEŠ.MEŠ-SU MA[N ...]

9 16 [...]

9	17	DUMU DUMU ^{md}30-ŠEŠ.MEŠ-SU(*) MAN GAL MAN *dan-nu* MAN ŠÚ MAN KUR *aš-šur a-na-ku-ma*
9	18	—
9	19	traces
10	0	*ina* BALA-*e-a* EN GAL ^{d}AMAR.UTU *ina ri-šá-a-ti a-na* TIN.TIR.KI *i-ru-um-ma*
10	1	*ina* BALA-*e-a* EN GAL ^{d}AMAR.UTU *ina ri-šá-a-ti a-na* TIN.TIR.KI *i-ru-um-m*[*a*]
10	2	*ina* BALA-*e-a* EN GAL ^{d}AMAR.UTU *ina ri-šá-a-te* ⸢*a*⸣-*na* TIN.TIR.KI *i-ru-um-*[*ma*]
10	3	[...]
10	4	...
10	5	*ina* BALA-*e-a* EN GAL ^{d}AMAR.UTU *ina ri-šá-a-te a-na* TIN.TIR.KI *i-ru-um-ma*
10	6	[...] ^{d}AMAR.UTU *ina ri-šá-a-ti a-*[*na* K]Á.DINGIR.RA.KI *i-ru-um-*[*ma*]
10	7	*ina* BALA-*e-a* EN GAL ^{d}AMAR.UTU *ina ri-šá-a-ti a-na* TIN.TIR.KI *i-*⸢*ru*⸣-*um-ma*
10	8	[... E]N GAL ^{d}AMAR.UTU *ina ri-šá-a-te a-na* TI[N].⸢TIR.KI⸣ [...]
10	9	*ina* BALA-*e-a* EN GAL ⸢^{d}⸣AMAR.UTU *ina ri-šá-a-t*[*i a*]-*na* TIN.TIR.KI *i-ru-um-ma*
10	10	*ina* BALA-*e-a* EN GAL ^{d}AMAR.UTU *ina ri-šá-a-ti a-na* TIN.TIR.KI *i-ru-um-ma*
10	11	*ina* BALA-*e-a* EN GAL ^{d}AMAR.UTU *ina ri-šá-a-te a-na* TIN.TIR.KI *i-ru-um-ma*
10	12–13	[...]
10	14	[... ^{d}]UTU *ina* [...]
10	15	[*ina* BA]LA-*e-a* EN GAL ^{d}AMAR.UTU *i*[*na*(?) ...]
10	16	[...]
10	17	*ina* BALA-*e-a* EN GAL ^{d}AMAR.UTU *ina ri-šá-a-ti a-na* TIN.TIR.KI *i-ru-um-ma*
10	18	—
10	19	[...]
11	0	*ina é-sag-íl šá da-ra-a-ti šu-bat-su ir-me sat-tuk-ki é-sag-íl*
11	1	*ina é-sag-íl šá da-ra-a-ti šu-bat-su ir-me sat-tuk-ki é-sag-í*[*l*]
11	2	*ina é-sag-íl šá da-ra-a-*⸢*te*⸣ *šu-bat-su* ⸢*ir*⸣-*me sat-tuk-ku é-sag-í*[*l*]
11	3	[...]
11	4	...
11	5	*ina é-sag-íl šá da-ra-a-te šu-bat-su ir-me sat-tuk-ki é-sag-íl*
11	6	[...-*r*]*a-a-ti* ⸢*šu*⸣-[*bat-su*] ⸢*ir-me sat-tuk-ki*⸣ *é-sag-í*[*l*]
11	7	*ina é-sag-íl šá da-ra-a-ti šu-bat-su ir-me sat-tuk-ki é-sag-íl*
11	8	[...] x ⸢*da-ra-a-te šu-bat*(?)-*su*(?)⸣ [...]
11	9	*ina é-sag-íl š*[*á d*]*a-ra-a-te šu-bat-*⸢*su*⸣ *ir-me sat-tuk-ki é-sag-íl*
11	10	*ina é-sag-íl ša da-ra-a-ti šu-bat-su ir-me sat-tuk-ki é-sag-íl*
11	11	*ina é-sag-íl šá da-ra-a-te šu-bat-su ir-me sat-tuk-ki é-sag-íl*
11	12–14	[...]
11	15	[*ina é-sag*]-⸢*íl šá da*⸣-*r*[*a-*...]
11	16	[...]
11	17	*ina é-sag-íl ša da-ra-a-ti šu-bat-su ir-me sat-tuk-ki é-sag-íl*
11	18	—
11	19	[...]

12 0 *ù* DINGIR.MEŠ TIN.TIR.KI *ú-ki-in ki-din-nu-ú-tu* TIN.TIR.KI *ak-ṣur*
12 1 ⸢*ù*⸣ DINGIR.MEŠ TIN.TIR.KI *ú-ki-in ki-din-nu-ú-tu* TIN.TIR.KI *a*[*k-ṣur*]
12 2 *ù* DINGIR.MEŠ TIN.TIR.KI *ú-kin ki-din-ú-te* TIN.TIR.KI *ak-ṣ*[*ur*]
12 3 [...]
12 4 ...
12 5 *ù* DINGIR.MEŠ KÁ.DINGIR.RA.KI *ú-kin ki-din-nu-ú-tu* TIN.TIR.KI *ak-ṣur*
12 6 [...].⸢KI *ú-kin ki*⸣*-din-nu-ú-tu* K[Á].DINGIR.RA.KI *ak-ṣur*
12 7 *ù* DINGIR.MEŠ KÁ.DINGIR.RA.KI *ú-kin ki-din-nu-ú-tu* KÁ.DINGIR.RA.KI *ak-ṣur*
12 8 ⸢*ù*⸣ [... TIN.TI]R(?).KI *ú-kin ki-din-nu-*⸢*ú*⸣*-t*[*u* ...]
12 9 *ù* DINGIR.⸢MEŠ TIN⸣.TIR.KI *ú-k*[*in k*]*i-din-nu-ú-t*[*u* TIN].TIR.KI *ak-ṣur*
12 10 *ù* DINGIR.MEŠ KÁ.DINGIR.RA.KI *ú-kin ki-din-nu-ú-tu* KÁ.DINGIR.RA.KI *ak-ṣu*
12 11 *ù* DINGIR.MEŠ TIN.TIR.KI *ú-kin ki-din-nu-ú-tu* TIN.TIR.KI *ak-ṣur*
12 12–16 [...]
12 17 *ù* DINGIR.MEŠ KÁ.DINGIR.RA.KI *ú-ki-in ki-din-nu-ú-tu* KÁ.DINGIR.RA.KI *ak-ṣur*
12 18 —
12 19 [...]

13 0 *áš-šú dan-nu a-na* SIG *la ḫa-ba-li* ^{md}GIŠ.NU$_{11}$-MU-GI.NA ŠEŠ *ta-li-me*
13 1 [*áš-š*]*ú*(?) *dan-nu a-na* SIG *la ḫa-ba-li* ^{md}GIŠ.NU$_{11}$-MU-GI.NA ŠEŠ *t*[*a-li-me*]
13 2 *áš-šú dan-nu a-na* SIG *la ḫa-ba-*⸢*li*⸣ ^{d}⸢GIŠ⸣.NU$_{11}$-MU-GI.NA ŠEŠ *ta-li-*[*me*]
13 3–4 [...]
13 5 *áš-šú dan-nu a-na* SIG *la ḫa-ba-li* ^{md}GIŠ.NU$_{11}$-MU-GI.NA ŠEŠ *ta-li-me*
13 6 [... *l*]*a ḫa-ba-li* ^{md}GIŠ.NU$_{11}$-MU-⸢GI⸣.NA ŠEŠ *ta-li-me*
13 7 *áš-šú dan-nu a-na* SIG *la ḫa-ba-li* ^{md}GIŠ.NU$_{11}$-MU-GI.NA ŠEŠ *ta-li-me*
13 8 *áš-š*[*ú* ...] *la ḫa-ba-li* ^{md}GIŠ.NU$_{11}$-M[U-G]I.⸢NA⸣ Š[EŠ ...]
13 9 *áš-šú da*[*n-n*]*u* ⸢*a*⸣*-na* SIG *la ḫa-*[*ba*]*-*⸢*li* ^{m}⸣[^{d}GIŠ.N]U$_{11}$-MU-GI.NA Š[EŠ *t*]*a-li-me*
13 10 *áš-šú dan-nu a-na* SIG *la ḫa-ba-li* ^{md}GIŠ.NU$_{11}$-MU-GI.NA ŠEŠ *ta-li-me*
13 11 *áš-šú dan-nu a-na* SIG *là ḫa-ba-li* ^{md}GIŠ.NU$_{11}$-MU-GI.NA ŠEŠ *ta-li-me*
13 12–16 [...]
13 17 *áš-šú dan-nu a-na* SIG *la ḫa-ba-li* ^{md}GIŠ.NU$_{11}$-MU-GI.NA ŠEŠ *ta-li-me*
13 18 —
13 19 [...]

14 0 *a-na* LUGAL-*ú-tu* KÁ.DINGIR.RA.KI *ap-qid ù i-na* KÙ.BABBAR KÙ.GI
14 1 [*a-na* L]UGAL-*ú-tu* KÁ.DINGIR.RA.KI *ap-qí-di ù i-na* KÙ.BABBAR KÙ.[GI]
14 2 *a-na* LUGAL-*ú-te* TIN.TIR.KI *ap-qid u ina* KÙ.BABBAR KÙ.GI
14 3–4 [...]
14 5 *a-na* LUGAL-*ú-tu* KÁ.DINGIR.RA.KI *ap-qid ù ina* KÙ.BABBAR KÙ.GI
14 6 [...].⸢DINGIR.RA.KI⸣ *ap-qid ù ina* KÙ.BABBAR KÙ.GI
14 7 *a-na* LUGAL-*ú-tu* KÁ.DINGIR.RA.KI *ap-qid ù ina* KÙ.BABBAR KÙ.GI
14 8 *a-na* ⸢LUGAL⸣-[*ú-tu* TI]N.⸢TIR⸣.KI ⸢*ap-qid ù*⸣ *ina* [KÙ.BABB]AR KÙ.GI
14 9 *a-na* LUGAL-*ú-tu* TIN.TIR.KI *ap-qid ù ina* K[Ù. ... .G]I(?)
14 10 *a-na* LUGAL-*ú-tu* KÁ.DINGIR.RA.KI *ap-qid ù ina* KÙ.BABBAR KÙ.GI

14 11 *a-na* LUGAL-*ú-tu* TIN.[T]IR.KI *ap-qid ù ina* KÙ.BABBAR KÙ.GI
14 12–16 [...]
14 17 *a-na* LUGAL-*ú-tu* KÁ.DINGIR.RA.KI *ap-qid ù ina* KÙ.BABBAR KÙ.GI
14 18 —
14 19 [...]

15 0 *ni-siq-ti* NA$_4$.MEŠ *é-sag-íl az-nu-un-ma*
15 1 [*ni-s*]*iq-ti* NA$_4$.MEŠ *é-sag-íl az-nu-un-*[*ma*]
15 2 *ni-siq-tú* NA$_4$.[MEŠ] *é-sag-íl az-nun-ma*
15 3–4 [...]
15 5 *ni-siq-ti* NA$_4$.MEŠ *é-sag-íl az-nu-un-ma*
15 6 *ni-siq-ti* NA$_4$.MEŠ [...]
15 7 *ni-siq-ti* NA$_4$.MEŠ *é-sag-íl az-nu-un-ma*
15 8 *ni-siq-t*[*i* ...] *é-sag-íl a*[*z*(?)-*n*]*un-ma*
15 9 ⸢*ni-siq-ti*⸣ [N]A$_4$.MEŠ *é-*⸢*sag*⸣*-íl az-nun-ma*
15 10 *ni-siq-ti* NA$_4$.MEŠ *é-sag-íl az-nu-un-m*
15 11 *ni-siq-ti* NA$_4$.MEŠ *é-sag-íl az-nun-*⸢*ma*⸣
15 12–16 [...]
15 17 *ni-siq-ti* NA$_4$.MEŠ *é-sag-íl az-nu-un-ma*
15 18 —
15 19 [...]

16 0 *ki-ma ši-ṭir bu-ru-mu ú-nam-mir é-umuš-a ina u$_4$-me-šú-ma*
16 1 [*ki-m*]*a ši-ṭir bu-ru-mu ú-nam-mir é-umuš-a ina u$_4$-me-šú-*[*ma*]
16 2 *ki-ma ši-ṭir bu-ru-*⸢*mu*⸣ *ú-nam-mir* ⸢*é*⸣-[*umuš-a*] *ina u$_4$-me-šú-ma*
16 3–4 [...]
16 5 *ki-ma ši-ṭir bu-ru-mu ú-nam-mir é-umuš-a ina u$_4$-me-šú-ma*
16 6 [*k*]*i-ma ši-ṭir b*[*u-ru*]*-mu ú-nam-mir é-umuš-a* [...]
16 7 *ki-ma ši-ṭir bu-ru-mu ú-nam-mir é-umuš-a ina u$_4$-me-šú-ma*
16 8 *ki-ma ši-*⸢*ṭir*⸣ *bu-ru-m*[*u*] *ú-nam-mir* (x) [...] *ina u$_4$-me-šú-ma*
16 9 *ki-ma ši-tir bu-*⸢*ru*⸣*-m*[*u*(?)] *ú-n*[*am-mi*]*r é-umuš-a ina u$_4$-me-*⸢*šú*⸣*-ma*
16 10 ...
16 11 *ki-ma ši-ṭir bu-ru-mu* <*ú*>*-nam-mir é-umuš-a ina* ⸢*u$_4$-me*⸣*-šú-ma*
16 12–16 [...]
16 17 *ki-ma ši-ṭir bu-ru-mu ú-nam-mir é-umuš-a ina u$_4$-me-šú-ma*
16 18 —
16 19 [...]

17 0 *im-gur-*^{d}*en-líl* BÀD KÁ.DINGIR.RA.KI *né-met-*^{d}*en-líl šal-ḫu-ú-šú*
17 1 [*im*]*-gur-*^{d}*en-líl* BÀD KÁ.DINGIR.RA.KI *né-met-*^{d}*en-líl šal-ḫu-ú-*[*šú*]
17 2 *im-gur-*^{d}*en-líl* BÀD TIN.TIR.KI *né-met-*^{d}*en-líl šal-*[...]
17 3–4 [...]
17 5 *im-gur-*^{d}*en-líl* BÀD KÁ.DINGIR.RA.KI *né-met-*^{d}*en-líl šal-ḫu-u-šú*

17	6	[...] ⸢KÁ.DINGIR⸣.R[A.KI *né*]-⸢*met*⸣-^{d}*en-líl šal-ḫu-ú-šú*
17	7	*im-gur-*^{d}*en-líl* BÀD KÁ.DINGIR.R[A.K]I *né-met-*^{d}*en-líl šal-ḫu-ú-šú*
17	8	*i*[*m-g*]*ur-*^{d}*en-líl* BÀD TIN.TIR.KI *né-*⸢*met*⸣-^{d}*en-líl šal-ḫu-u-š*[*ú*]
17	9	*im-gur-*^{d}*en-líl* BÀD TIN.TIR.KI *né-*[...-*ḫ*]*u-u-šú*
17	10	*im-gur-*^{d}*en-líl* BÀD TIN.TIR.KI ⸢*né-met-*^{d}*en-líl*⸣ *šal-*[*ḫu*]-⸢*ú*⸣-*šú*
17	11	⸢*im*⸣-*gur-*⸢^{d}*en*⸣-*líl* BÀD TIN.TIR.KI *né-met-*^{d}*en-líl šal-ḫu-ú-šú*
17	12–16	[...]
17	17	*im-gur-*^{d}*en-líl* BÀD TIN.TIR.KI *né-met-*^{d}*en-líl šal-ḫu-ú-šú*
17	18	—
17	19	[...]
18	0	*ša la-ba-riš il-lik-ú-ma i-qu-pu in-na-ab-tu*
18	1	[*š*]*a la-ba-riš il-lik-ú-ma i-qu-pu in-na-ab-*[*tu*]
18	2	*ša la-ba-riš i*[*l*]-*lik-u-ma i-qu-pu in-*[...]
18	3–4	[...]
18	5	*šá la-ba-riš il-lik-ú-ma i-qu-pu in-na-ab-tu*
18	6	[...-*a*]*b-tu*
18	7	*šá la-ba-riš il-lik-u-ma i-qu-pu in-na-ab-tu*
18	8	*ša la-ba-r*[*i*]*š il-lik-ú-ma i-qu-pu in-na-ab-tu*
18	9	*ša* ⸢*la*⸣-*ba-riš il-lik-ú-ma i-qu-*[*pu in-n*]*ab-*⸢*tu*⸣
18	10	*ša la-ba-riš il-lik-ú-ma i-qu-pu in-na-ab-tu*
18	11	[...]-⸢*riš il-lik-u*⸣-[*m*]*a i-qu-pu in-na-*⸢*ab*⸣-*tu*
18	12–16	[...]
18	17	*ša la-ba-riš il-lik-ú-ma i-qu-pu in-na-ab-tu*
18	18	—
18	19	[...]
19	0	*áš-šú ma-aṣ-ṣar-ti é-sag-íl ù eš-re-e-ti* KÁ.DINGIR.RA.KI
19	1	*áš-šú ma-aṣ-ṣar-ti é-sag-íl ù eš-re-e-ti* KÁ.DINGIR.R[A.KI]
19	2	*áš-šú* EN.NUN *é-sag-*⸢*íl*⸣ *u eš-re-e-*⸢*te*⸣ x [...]
19	3–4	[...]
19	5	*áš-šú* EN.NUN *é-sag-íl ù eš-re-e-ti* KÁ.DINGIR.RA.KI
19	6	*áš-šú* EN.NUN *é-sag-íl* [...]
19	7	*áš-šú* EN.NUN *é-sag-íl ù eš-re-e-ti* TIN.TIR.KI
19	8	*áš-šú* EN.NUN *é-s*[*a*]*g-íl ù eš-re-e-te* TIN.TIR.KI
19	9	*áš-šú* ⸢*ma*⸣-*aṣ-ṣar-ti é-sag-íl* ⸢*ù*⸣ [... .K]I
19	10	*áš-šú* EN.NUN *é-sag-íl ù eš-re-e-ti* TIN.TIR.KI
19	11	*á*[*š-*...-*í*]*l ù eš-re-e-te* TIN.TIR.KI
19	12–16	[...]
19	17	*áš-šú* EN.NUN *é-sag-íl ù eš-re-e-ti* KÁ.DINGIR.RA.KI
19	18	—
19	19	[...]

20 0 *du-un-nu-nu ina e-muq um-ma-na-a-ti-ia sur-riš né-met-^{d}en-líl*
20 1 [*d*]*u-un-nu-nu ina e-muq um-ma-na-a-ti-ia sur-riš né-met-^{d}en-lí*[*l*]
20 2 [...] *ina e-mu-qu um-ma-na-ti-ia* [...]
20 3 (Not visible on photo)
20 4 [...]
20 5 *du-un-nu-nu ina e-muq um-ma-na-a-ti-ia sur-riš né-met-^{d}en-líl*
20 6 [...-*n*]*u ina e-muq um-ma-na-a-ti-ia* [...]
20 7 *du-un-nu-nu ina e-muq um-ma-na-a-ti-ia sur-riš né-met-^{d}en-líl*
20 8 *du-un-nu-nu ina e-muq um-ma-na-ti-ia sur-riš né-met-^{d}en-líl*
20 9 *dun-nu-n*[*u*] *i-na e-mu-*⸢*qu um*⸣*-ma-na-ti-i*[*a* ...-^{d}*e*]*n-*⸢*líl*⸣
20 10 *du-un-nu-nu ina e-muq um-ma-na-a-ti-ia sur-riš né-met-^{d}en-líl*
20 11 *du-un-nu-nu ina* ⸢*e*⸣-[...]-*ti-iá sur̂-riš né-met-^{d}en-líl*
20 12–16 [...]
20 17 *du-un-nu-nu ina e-mu-qu um-ma-na-a-ti-ia sur-riš né-met-^{d}en-líl*
20 18 —
20 19 [...]

21 0 *šal-ḫu-ú-šú ina ši-pir ^{d}kulla eš-šiš ú-še-piš-ma* KÁ.GAL.MEŠ-*šú ú-rak-kis*
21 1 *šal-ḫu-ú-šú ina ši-pir ^{d}kulla eš-šiš ú-še-piš-ma* KÁ.GAL.MEŠ-*šú* ⸢*ú*⸣-[...]
21 2 [...] *ina ši-pir ^{d}kulla eš-*⸢*šiš*⸣ [...]
21 3 (Not visible on photo)
21 4 [...]
21 5 *šal-ḫu-ú-šú ina ši-pir ^{d}kulla eš-šiš ú-še-piš-ma* KÁ.GAL.MEŠ-*šú ú-rak-ki-si*
21 6 [... *k*]*ulla eš-šiš ú-še-piš-ma* [...]
21 7 *šal-ḫu-ú-šú ina ši-pir ^{d}kulla eš-šiš ú-še-piš-ma* ⸢KÁ⸣.GAL.MEŠ-*šú ú-rak-kis*
21 8 *šal-ḫu-ú-šú ina ši-pir ^{d}kulla eš-šiš ú-še-piš-ma* KÁ.GAL.MEŠ-*šú ú-rak-kis*
21 9 *šal-ḫu-u-šú i-na ši-pir* ^{d}⸢*kulla*⸣ *eš-šiš ú-š*[*e*-... .ME]Š-*šú ú-rak-kis*
21 10 *šal-ḫu-ú-šú ina ši-pir ^{d}kulla eš-*[*šiš*] *ú-š*[*e-p*]*iš-ma* KÁ.GAL.MEŠ-*šú ú-rak-ki-si*
21 11 *šal-ḫu-ú-šú ina ši-pi*[*r* ...] *ú-še-piš-ma* KÁ.GAL.MEŠ-*šú ú-rak-*⸢*kis*⸣
21 12–16 [...]
21 17 *šal-ḫu-ú-šú ina ši-pir ^{d}kulla eš-šiš ú-še-piš-ma* KÁ.GAL.MEŠ-*šú ú-rak-ki-si*
21 18 —
21 19 [...]

22 0 GIŠ.IG.MEŠ *ú-še-piš-ma ú-rat-ta-a ina* KÁ.MEŠ-*šú*
22 1 GIŠ.IG.MEŠ *ú-še-piš-ma ú-rat-ta-a ina* KÁ.ME[Š-x]
22 2 GIŠ.IG.MEŠ *ú-še-piš-m*[*a* ...]
22 3 (Photo indicates preserved in part)
22 4 [...]
22 5 GIŠ.IG.MEŠ *ú-še-piš-ma ú-rat-ta-a ina* KÁ.MEŠ-*šú*
22 6 [...]-*piš-ma ú-rat-ta-a ina* KÁ.MEŠ-*šú*
22 7 GIŠ.IG.MEŠ *ú-še-piš-ma ú-rat-ta-a ina* KÁ.MEŠ-*šú*
22 8 GIŠ.IG.MEŠ *ú-še-piš-ma ú-rat-ta-a i-na* KÁ.MEŠ-*šú*

22	9	GIŠ.IG.MEŠ *ú-še-piš-ma ú-rat-⸢ta-a i⸣-na* KÁ.MEŠ-*šú*
22	10	GIŠ.IG.MEŠ *ú-še-p*[*iš-ma*] *ú*-[*ra*]*t-ta-a ina* KÁ.MEŠ-*šú*
22	11	⸢GIŠ.IG⸣.[MEŠ *ú-š*]*e*-⸢*piš*⸣-*ma ú-rat-ta-a i-na* KÁ.MEŠ-[*šú*]
22	12–16	[...]
22	17	GIŠ.IG.MEŠ *ú-še-piš-ma ú-rat-ta-a ina* KÁ.MEŠ-*šú*
22	18	—
22	19	[...]
23	0	NUN *ar-ku-ú šá ina* BALA-*e-šú ši-pir šu-a-ti in-na-ḫu um-ma-ni en-qu-tu*
23	1	NUN *ar-ku-ú šá ina* ⸢BALA⸣-*e-šú ši-pir šu-a-ti in-na-ḫu um-ma-ni en-qu-t*[*u*]/*t*[*ú*]/*t*[*e*]
23	2	NUN EGIR-*ú šá ina* BALA-*e*-[...]
23	3	[...] ⸢*ši*⸣-*pir šu-a-tú*(?) *in-na-ḫu* ⸢*um*⸣-*ma-a-ni e*[*n*-...]
23	4	[...]
23	5	NUN EGIR-*ú šá ina* BALA-*šú ši-pir šu-a-ti in-na-ḫu* LÚ *um-ma-a-ni en-qu-tu*
23	6	[...]-*na-ḫu* LÚ *um-ma-a-ni en-qu-tu*
23	7	[NUN EGI]R-⸢*ú*⸣ *ša ina* BALA-*šú ši*-⸢*pir šu*⸣-*a-ti* ⸢*in*⸣-*na-ḫu* LÚ *um*-⸢*ma*⸣-*a-ni e*[*n-q*]*u-tu*
23	8	NUN *ar-ku-ú ša i-na* BALA-*šú ši-pir šu-a-ti in-na-ḫu um-ma-ni en-qu-tú*
23	9	NUN EGIR-*ú ša i-na* BALA-*e-šú ši-pir šu-a-ti in-na-ḫu um-ma-ni* ⸢*en*⸣-*qu-t*[*ú*]
23	10	NUN EGIR-*ú šá ina* BALA-*e-šú ši-pir šú-a-ti in-na*-[*ḫ*]*u* LÚ *um-ma-a-ni en-qu-tú*
23	11	[...] ⸢*ša*⸣ *i-na* BALA-*šú ši-pir šu-a-ti in-na*-[...]
23	12	[...]
23	13	[...] *u*[*m*(?)-...]
23	14–16	[...]
23	17	NUN EGIR-*ú šá ina* BALA-*e-šú ši-pir šu-a-ti in-na-ḫu* LÚ *um-ma-a-ni en-qu-tu*
23	18	—
23	19	[...]
24	0	*ši-ta-ʾ-al im-gur-*^{d}*en-líl* BÀD *né-met-*^{d}*en-líl šal-ḫu-ú*
24	1	*ši-ta-ʾ-al im-gur-*^{d}*en-líl* BÀD *né-met-*^{d}*en-líl šal-ḫu-ú*
24	2	[...] BÀD *né-met-*^{d}*en-líl šal*-⸢*ḫu*⸣-[...]
24	3	[...] BÀD *né-met-*^{d}*en-líl šal-ḫu-u*
24	4	[...]
24	5	*ši-ta-ʾ-al im-gur-*^{d}*en-líl* BÀD *né-met-*^{d}*en-líl šal-ḫu-ú*
24	6	[... *n*]*é-met-*^{d}*en-líl šal-ḫu-ú*
24	7	[...] ⸢*im-gur*⸣-[^{d}*e*]*n*-[...] (x) *šal*-⸢*ḫu*⸣-*ú*
24	8	*ši-ta-ʾ-al im-gur-*^{d}*en-líl* BÀD *né-met-*^{d}*en-líl šal-ḫu-u*
24	9	*ši-ta-ʾ-al im-gur-*^{d}*en-líl* BÀD *né-met-*^{d}*en-líl šal-ḫu-u*
24	10	*ši-ta-ʾ-al im-gur-*^{d}*en-líl* BÀD *né-met-*^{d}*en-líl* [*š*]*al*-⸢*ḫu-šú*⸣
24	11	[*ši-t*]*a*-⸢*ʾ-al im*⸣-*gur-*^{d}*en-líl* BÀD *né-met-*^{d}*en-líl šal*-⸢*ḫu*⸣-*u*
24	12–16	[...]
24	17	*ši-ta-ʾ-al im-gur-*^{d}*en-líl* BÀD *né-met-*^{d}*en-líl šal-ḫu-u*
24	18	—
24	19	[...]

25 0 *ki-ma si-ma-ti-šú-nu la-bi-ra-a-ti e-pu-uš* MU.SAR-*u-a a-mur-ma*
25 1 *ki-ma si-ma-ti-šú-nu la-bi-ra-a-ti e-pu-uš* MU.SAR-*u-a a-mur-ma*
25 2 [...] *a-mur-ma*
25 3 *ki-ma s*[*i*-...] MU.SAR-*u-a a-mur-ma*
25 4 [...]
25 5 *ki-ma si-ma-ti-šú-nu la-bi-ra-a-ti e-pu-uš* MU.SAR-*u-a a-mur-ma*
25 6 *ki-ma si-ma-ti-šú-nu* [...].SAR-*u-a a-mur-ma*
25 7 [...] x [...-*u*]*š*(?) MU.SAR-*u-a* [*a*]-*mur-ma*
25 8 *ki-ma si-ma-ti-šú-nu la-bi-*⸢*ra*⸣*-a-ti e-pu-uš* MU.SAR-*u-a a-mur-ma*
25 9 *ki-ma si-ma-ti-šú-nu la-bi-ra-a-ti e-pu-uš* MU.SAR-*u-a a-mur-ma*
25 10 *ki-ma si-ma-ti-šu-nu la-bi-ra-a-ti e-pu-uš* MU.SAR-*u-a a-mur-ma*
25 11 ⸢*ki-ma si-ma-ti-šú*⸣*-nu la-*⸢*bi-ra-a-ti e-pu-uš*⸣ MU.SAR-*u-a a-mur-ma*
25 12 [...]
25 13 *ki-m*[*a* ...]
25 14–15 [...]
25 16 [...]-*ti-šú-nu* ⸢*la-bi*⸣*-ra-*⸢*a*⸣-x [...]
25 17 *ki-ma si-ma-ti-šú-nu la-bi-ra-a-ti e-pu-uš* MU.SAR-*ú-a a-mur-ma*
25 18 —
25 19 [...]

26 0 Ì.GIŠ *pu-šu-uš* UDU.SISKUR BAL-*qí it-ti* MU.SAR-*e-ka šu-kun*
26 1 Ì.GIŠ *pu-šu-uš* UDU.SISKUR BAL-*qí it-ti* MU.SAR-*e-ka šu-kun*
26 2 Ì.GIŠ *pu-šu-u*[*š* ...]
26 3 Ì.GIŠ *pu-šu-uš* UDU.[...] *šu-kun*
26 4 [...]
26 5 Ì.GIŠ *pu-šu-uš* UDU.SISKUR BAL-*qí it-ti* MU.SAR-*e-ka šu-kun*
26 6 Ì.GIŠ *pu-šu-uš* UDU.SISKUR BAL-⸢*qí*⸣ [...]
26 7 [... BA]L-*qí it-ti* MU.SAR-*e-ka* ⸢*šu*⸣*-kun*
26 8 Ì.GIŠ *pu-šu-uš* ⸢UDU.SISKUR⸣ BAL-*qí it-ti* MU.SAR-*e-ka šu-kun*
26 9 Ì.GIŠ *pu-*⸢*šu*⸣*-uš* UDU.SISKUR BAL-*qí it-ti* MU.SAR-*e-ka šu-kun*
26 10 Ì.GIŠ *pu-šu-u*[*š* UDU.SISK]UR BAL-*qí it-ti* MU.SAR-*e-ka šu-kun*
26 11 Ì.GIŠ *pu-šu-uš* UDU.SISKUR BAL-*qí it-ti* MU.SAR-⸢*e*⸣*-ka šu-kun*
26 12 [...]
26 13 Ì.GI[Š ...]
26 14–15 [...]
26 16 [...] UDU.SISKUR BAL-*qí it-ti* MU.[...]
26 17 Ì.GIŠ *pu-šu-uš* UDU.SISKUR BAL-*qí it-ti* MU.SAR-*e-ka šu-kun*
26 18 —
26 19 [...]

27 0 *ik-ri-bi-ka* ^{d}AMAR.UTU *i-šem-me šá šu-mì šaṭ-ru u* MU *ta-lim-ia*
27 1 *ik-ri-bi-ka* ^{d}AMAR.UTU *i-šem-me šá* ⸢*šu*⸣*-mì šaṭ-ru u* MU *ta-lim-i*[*a*]
27 2 *ik-ri-bi-ka* ^{d}AMAR.UTU [...]

27 3 *ik-ri-bi-ka* ^{d}AMAR.UTU ⸢*i*⸣-[...]
27 4 [...]
27 5 *ik-ri-bi-ka* ^{d}AMAR.UTU *i-šem-me šá šu-mì šaṭ-ru ù* MU *ta-lim-ia*
27 6 *ik-ri-bi-ka* ^{d}AMAR.UTU *i-šem-me* [...*-l*]*im-ia*
27 7 *i*[*k-*...]*-šem-me šá šu-mì šaṭ-ru* ⸢*ù* MU *ta*⸣*-lim-ia*
27 8 *ik-ri-bi-ka* ^{d}AMAR.UTU *i-šem-me šá šu-mì šaṭ-ru ù* MU *ta-lim-ia*
27 9 *ik-ri-bi-ka* ⸢^{d}AMAR⸣.UTU *i-šem-me šá šu-mì šaṭ-ru ù* MU *ta-lim-ia*
27 10 *ik-ri-bi-ka* ^{d}AMAR.UTU *i-šem-me š*[*á šu*]*-mì šaṭ-ru ù* MU *ta-li-mi-ia*
27 11 *ik-ri-bi-ka* ^{d}AMAR.UTU *i-šem-me šá šu-mì šaṭ-ru ù* MU ⸢*ta-lim*⸣*-ia*
27 12 [...] ⸢*ta*⸣*-lim-i*[*a*]
27 13 *ik-ri-*[...]
27 14–15 [...]
27 16 [... *š*]*á šu-mì šaṭ-ru ù* MU *t*[*a-*...]
27 17 *ik-ri-bi-ka* ^{d}AMAR.UTU *i-šem-me šá šu-mì šaṭ-ru ù* MU *ta-li-mi-ia*
27 18 —
27 19 [...] MU ⸢*ta-li-mi*⸣*-*[*ia*]

28 0 *ina ši-pir ni-kil-ti i-ab-bat* MU.SAR*-u-a it-ti* MU.SAR*-e-šú la i-šak-ka-nu*
28 1 *ina ši-pir ni-kil-ti i-ab-bat* MU.SAR*-u-a it-*⸢*ti*⸣ MU.SAR*-e-šú la i-šak-k*[*a-nu*]
28 2 *ina ši-pir ni-kil-ti i-a*[*b-*...]
28 3 *ina ši-pir ni-kil-ti i-ab-bat* MU.SAR*-u-*(x) [...]
28 4 [...]
28 5 *ina ši-pir ni-kil-ti i-ab-bat* MU.SAR*-u-a it-ti* MU.SAR*-e-šú la i-šak-ka-nu*
28 6 *ina ši-pir ni-kil-ti i-ab-ba-tu* [...*-t*]*i* MU.⸢SAR⸣*-e-šú la i-šak-ka-nu*
28 7 (x) [...]*-u-*⸢*a it*⸣*-ti* MU.⸢SAR*-e*⸣*-*[*šú l*]*a i-š*[*a*]*k-*⸢*ka-nu*⸣
28 8 *ina ši-pir ni-kil-ti i-ab-bat* MU.SAR*-u-a it-ti* MU.SAR*-e-šú la i-šak-ka-nu*
28 9 *ina ši-pir ni-kil-ti i-*⸣*ab-bat* MU⸣.SAR*-u-a it-ti* MU.SAR*-e-šú la i-šak-ka-nu*
28 10 *ina ši-pir ni-kil-ti i-ab-bat* MU.SAR*-u-a it-ti* MU.SAR*-e-šú la i-šak-ka-nu*
28 11 *ina ši-pir ni-kil-ti i-ab-bat* MU.SAR*-u-a it-ti* MU.SAR*-e-šú la i-šak-ka-nu*
28 12 [... *l*]*a i-šak-ka-nu*
28 13 *ina ši-pi*[*r* ...]
28 14 [...]
28 15 [...] (x)*-*⸢*kil-ti i-ab-bat* MU.SAR*-u-a it*⸣*-t*[*i* ...]
28 16 [... *i*]*t-ti* MU.SAR*-e-šú la* [...]
28 17 *ina ši-pir ni-kil-ti i-ab-bat* MU.SAR*-ú-a it-ti* MU.SAR*-e-šú la i-šak-ka-nu*
28 18 —
28 19 [...]*-*⸢*ú*⸣*-a it-ti* MU.SAR*-e-šú la i-ša*[*k-*...]

29 0 ^{d}AMAR.UTU LUGAL *gi-im-ri ag-giš lik-kil-me-šú-ma*
29 1 ^{d}AMAR.UTU LUGAL *gi-im-ri ag-giš lik-kil-me-šú-m*[*a*]
29 2 ^{d}AMAR.UTU LUGAL *gim-ri ag-gi*[*š* ...]
29 3 ^{d}AMAR.UTU LUGAL *gim-ri ag-giš lik-kil-*[...]
29 4 [...]

29	5	{d}AMAR.UTU LUGAL *gim-ri ag-giš lik-kil-me-šú-ma*
29	6	{d}AMAR.UTU LUGAL *gim-r*[*i* ...]*-šú-ma*
29	7	⸢{d}⸣[...]-⸢*lik-kil-me-šú*⸣-[*ma*]
29	8	{d}AMAR.UTU LUGAL *gim-ri ag-giš lik-kil-me-šú-ma*
29	9	{d}AMAR.UTU LUGAL *gim-ri ag-giš lik-*⸢*kil*⸣*-me-šú-ma*
29	10	{d}AMAR.UTU LUGAL *gim-ri ag-giš lik-kil-me-šú-ma*
29	11	{d}AMAR.UTU LUGAL *gi-im-ri ag-gi-iš lik-kil-me-šú-ma*
29	12	[...]
29	13	{d}AMAR.UTU L[UGAL ...]
29	14	[...]
29	15	[{d}AMAR.UT]U LUGAL *gim-ri ag-giš lik-kil-me-šú-ma*
29	16	[...*-m*]*e*(?)*-šú-*⸢*ma*⸣
29	17	{d}AMAR.UTU LUGAL *gim-ri ag-giš lik-kil-me-šú-ma*
29	18	—
29	19	[...]-⸢*giš*⸣ *lik-kil-me-šú-ma*
30	0	MU-*šú* NUMUN-*šú i-na* KUR.KUR *li-ḫal-liq*
30	1	MU-*šú* NUMUN-*šú i-na* KUR.KUR *li-ḫal-li-qi*
30	2–4	[...]
30	5	MU-*šú* NUMUN-*šú ina* KUR.KUR *li-ḫal-liq*
30	6	MU-*šú* NUMUN-*šú i-na* KUR.KUR *li-ḫal-*[x]
30	7	MU-*šú* NUMUN-*šú* (x) [...] (x) [...]-⸢*liq*⸣ (x)
30	8	MU-*šú* NUMUN-*šú ina* KUR.KUR *li-ḫal-liq*
30	9	MU-⸢*šú* NUMUN-*šú*⸣ *ina* KUR.KUR *li-ḫal-liq*
30	10	MU-*šú* NUMUN-*šú ina* KUR.KUR *li-ḫal-liq*
30	11	MU-*šú* NUMUN-*šú i-na ma-ta-a-ti li-ḫal-liq*
30	12	[... KU]R *li-ḫal-liq*
30	13–14	[...]
30	15	MU-*šú* NUMU[N-...]
30	16	MU-*šú* NUMUN-*šú* ⸢*i*⸣*-n*[*a* ...]
30	17	MU-*šú* NUMUN-*šú ina* KUR.KUR *li-ḫal-liq*
30	18	—
30	19	MU-*šú* NUMUN-*šú ina* KUR.KUR *li-*[...]

1	0	^{m}AN.ŠÁR-DÙ-IBILA LUGAL GAL LUGAL *dan-nu* LUGAL ŠÁR LUGAL KUR *aš-šur*
1	1	^{m}AN.ŠÁR-DÙ-IBILA LUGAL GAL LUGAL *dan-nu* LUGAL ŠÁR LUGAL KUR *aš-šur*
1	2	[...]
1	3	[... LU]GAL *dan-nu* LUGAL ŠÁR LUGAL KUR *aš-šur*
1	4	[...*-n*]*u* LUGAL ŠÁR LUGAL KUR *aš-šur*
2	0	LUGAL *kib-rat* 4-*ti* LUGAL LUGAL.MEŠ NUN *la šá-na-an*
2	1	LUGAL *kib-rat* 4-*ti* LUGAL LUGAL.MEŠ NUN *la šá-na-an*
2	2	[...]
2	3	[...] ⸢LUGAL⸣.MEŠ NUN *la šá-na-an*
2	4	[...] NUN *la šá-na-an*
3	0	*ša ul-tu tam-tim e-lit a-di tam-tim šap-lit i-be-lu-ma*
3	1	*ša ul-tu tam-tim e-lit a-di tam-tim šap-lit i-be-lu-ma*
3	2	[...]
3	3	[...*-d*]*i tam-tim šap-lit i-*⸢*be*⸣*-l*[*u-*x]
3	4	[... *ša*]*p-*⸢*lit*⸣ *i-*⸢*be*⸣*-lu-m*[*a*]
4	0	*gi-mir ma-li-ki ú-šak-niš še-pu-uš-šú*
4	1	*gi-mir ma-li-ki ú-šak-niš še-pu-uš-šú*
4	2	[...]
4	3	[...]-⸢*niš še*⸣*-p*[*u-*...]
4	4	[...] x x (x) [...]
5	0	DUMU ^{m}AN.ŠÁR-ŠEŠ-SUM.NA LUGAL GAL LUGAL *dan-nu* LUGAL ŠÁR LUGAL KUR *aš-šur*
5	1	DUMU ^{m}AN.ŠÁR-ŠEŠ-SUM.NA LUGAL GAL LUGAL *dan-nu* LUGAL ŠÁR LUGAL KUR *aš-šur*
5	2–4	[...]
6	0	GÌR.NÍTA KÁ.DINGIR.RA.KI LUGAL KUR.EME.GI, ù URI.KI
6	1	GÌR.NÍTA KÁ.DINGIR.RA.KI LUGAL KUR.EME.GI, ù URI.KI
6	2–4	[...]
7	0	DUMU DUMU ^{md}30-PAP.MEŠ-SU LUGAL *dan-nu* LUGAL ŠÁR LUGAL KUR *aš-šur a-na-ku-ma*
7	1	DUMU DUMU ^{md}30-PAP.MEŠ-SU LUGAL *dan-nu* LUGAL ŠÁR LUGAL KUR *aš-šur a-na-ku-ma*
7	2	[...-S]U(?) ⸢LUGAL *dan*⸣-[...]
7	3–4	[...]

8	0	*ši-pir é-sag-íl šá* AD *ba-nu-u-a la ú-qa-at-tu-u*
8	1	*ši-pir é-sag-íl šá* AD *ba-nu-u-a la ú-qa-at-tu-u*
8	2	[...*-í*]*l šá* AD *ba-nu-u-*⸢*a*⸣ *l*[*a* ...]
8	3–4	[...]
9	0	*a-na-ku ú-šak-lil sat-tuk-ki é-sag-íl u* DINGIR.MEŠ TIN.TIR.KI
9	1	*a-na-ku ú-šak-lil sat-tuk-ki é-sag-íl u* DINGIR.MEŠ TIN.TIR.KI
9	2	[...*-li*]*l sat-tuk-ki é-sag-í*[*l* ...]
9	3–4	[...]
10	0	*ú-ki-in ki-din-nu-tu* KÁ.DINGIR.RA.KI *ak-ṣur*
10	1	*ú-ki-in ki-din-nu-tu* KÁ.DINGIR.⸢RA.KI⸣ *ak-ṣur*
10	2	[...*-d*]*in-nu-tú* KÁ.DINGIR.RA.KI x [...]
10	3–4	[...]
11	0	*áš-šú dan-nu a-na* SIG *la ḫa-ba-li* ^{md}GIŠ.NU$_{11}$-<MU>-GI.NA
11	1	*áš-šú dan-nu a-na* SIG *la ḫa-ba-li* ^{md}GIŠ.NU$_{11}$-<MU>-GI.NA
11	2	[...] x *la ḫa-ba-li* ^{md}GIŠ.N[U$_{11}$-...]
11	3–4	[...]
12	0	ŠEŠ *ta-li-me a-na* LUGAL*-u-ti* KÁ.DINGIR.RA.KI *ap-qid*
12	1	ŠEŠ *ta-li-me a-na* LUGAL*-u-ti* KÁ.⸢DINGIR⸣.RA.KI *ap-qid*
12	2	[...*-n*]*a* LUGAL*-u-ti* KÁ.DINGIR.R[A....]
12	3–4	[...]
13	0	*ina u$_4$-me-šú-ma é-tùr-kalam-ma* É ^{d}INANNA TIN.TIR.KI
13	1	*ina u$_4$-me-šú-ma é-tùr-kalam-ma* É ^{d}INANNA TIN.TIR.KI
13	2	[...*-tù*]*r-kalam-ma* É ^{d}INANNA TIN.[...]
13	3–4	[...]
14	0	*eš-šiš ú-še-piš* ^{d}INANNA TIN.TIR.KI ^{d}GAŠAN *ṣir-tu*
14	1	*eš-šiš ú-še-piš* ^{d}INANNA TIN.TIR.KI ^{d}GAŠAN *ṣir-tu*
14	2	[...] ^{d}IINANNA TIN.TIR.KI ^{d}G[AŠAN ...]
14	3–4	[...]
15	0	*ep-še-te-ia* MUNUS.SIG$_5$.MEŠ *ḫa-diš lip-pal-lis-ma*
15	1	*ep-še-te-ia* MUNUS.SIG$_5$.MEŠ *ḫa-diš lip-pal-lis-ma*
15	2	[... SI]G$_5$.MEŠ *ḫa-diš* IGI.[BAR*-ma*]
15	3–4	[...]

16 0 u_4-*me-šam-ma ma-ḫar* ^{d}EN ^{d}GAŠAN-*iá lit-tas-qar da-mì-iq-ti*
16 1 u_4-*me-šam-ma ma-ḫar* ^{d}EN ^{d}GAŠAN-*iá lit-tas-qar da-mì-iq-ti*
16 2 [... E]N ^{d}GAŠAN-*iá lit-tas-qar d*[*a*-...]
16 3–4 [...]

17 0 TI u_4-*me* SÙ.MEŠ *li-šim ši-ma-ti*
17 1 TI u_4-*me* SÙ.MEŠ *li-šim ši-ma-ti*
17 2 [... M]EŠ *li-šim š*[*i*-...]
17 3–4 [...]

18 0 [*it*]-*ti* AN-*e ù* KI-*tim lu-ki-in* BALA-*ú-a*
18 1 [*it*]-*ti* AN-*e ù* KI-*tim lu-ki-in* BALA-*ú-a*
18 2 [... K]I-*tim lu-ki-i*[*n* ...]
18 3–4 [...]

19 0 [*ù šá* ^{md}GI]Š.⸢NU_{11}⸣-<MU>-GI.NA LUGAL KÁ.DINGIR.RA.KI
19 1 [...GI]Š.⸢NU_{11}⸣-<MU>-⸢GI⸣.NA LUGAL KÁ.DINGIR.RA.KI
19 2 [...-G]I.NA LUGAL KÁ.[...]
19 3 [...-GI.N]A ⸢LUGAL⸣ [... .K]I
19. 4 [...]

20 0 [*aḫi talīmīia ūmēšu*] *li-ri-ku liš-bi lit-tu-tu*
20 1 [...] (x) *li-ri-ku* ⸢*liš*⸣-*bi lit-tu-tu*
20 2 [... *l*]*i-ri-ku liš*-[...]
20 3 [... *l*]*i*(?)-*ri-ku liš-bi l*[*it-t*]*u-tu*
20 4 [...]

21 0 [*ša šumī šaṭru u šum ta*]-*lim-ia ina ši-pir ni-kil-ti i-pa-áš-ši-ṭu*
21 1 [...] *š*[*i-pi*]*r* ⸢*ni-kil-ti i*⸣-*pa-áš-ši-ṭu*
21 2 [...] (x) ⸢*i*⸣-[...]
21 3 [...]-*lim-ia ina ši-pir ni-kil-ti* [...]
21 4 [...]

22 0 MU.⸢SAR⸣-*u-a i-ab-ba-tu lu-u a-šar-šú ú-nak-ka-ru*
22 1 MU.⸢SAR⸣-*u*-⸢*a i*⸣-*ab-ba-tu lu-u a-šar-šú ú-nak-ka-ru*
22 2 [...]
22 3 [...]-⸢*a*⸣ *i-qb-bat lu a-šar-šú ú-nak-ka-ru*
22 4 [...]

23 0 ^{d}INANNA TIN.TIR.KI *ina ma-⸢har⸣* ^{d}EN ^{d}GAŠAN-*iá* MUNUS.ḪUL-*šú*
23 1 ^{d}INANNA TIN.TIR.KI *ina ma-⸢har⸣* ^{d}EN ^{d}GAŠAN-*iá* MUNUS.ḪUL-*šú*
23 2 [...]
23 3 [... ^{d}]AMAR.UTU ^{d}EN-*iá* MUNUS.ḪUL-*šú*
23 4 traces

24 0 *lit-tas-qar* MU-*šú* NUMUN-*šú ina* KUR.KUR *li-ḫal-liq*
24 1 *lit-tas-qar* MU-*šú* NUMUN-*šú ina* KUR.KUR *li-ḫal-liq*
24 2 [...]
24 3 [...] *ina* KUR.KUR *li-ḫal-liq*
24 4 [...] *li-ḫal-liq*

1	0	^{m}AN.ŠÁR-DÙ-A LUGAL GAL LUGAL *dan-nu* LUGAL ŠÁR LUGAL KUR *aš-šur*
1	1	^{m}AN.ŠÁR-DÙ-A LUGAL GAL LUGAL *dan-nu* LUGAL ŠÁR LUGAL KUR *aš-šur*
1	2	[^{m}]AN.ŠÁR-DÙ-IBILA LUGAL GAL LUGA[L ...]
2	0	LUGAL *kib-rat* 4-*ti* LUGAL LUGAL.MEŠ NUN *la šá-na-an*
2	1	LUGAL *kib-rat* 4-*ti* LUGAL LUGAL.MEŠ NUN *la šá-na-an*
2	2	[LU]GAL *kib-rat* 4-*ti* LUGAL L[UGAL(?) ...]
3	0	*ša ul-tu tam-tim e-lit a-di tam-tim šap-lit i-be-lu-ma*
3	1	*ša ul-tu tam-tim e-lit a-di tam-tim šap-lit i-be-lu-ma*
3	2	[x] ⸢*ul*⸣-*tu tam-tim e*-⸢*lit a*⸣-[...]
4	0	*gi-mir ma-li-ki ú-šak-niš še-pu-uš-šú*
4	1	*gi-mir ma-li-ki ú-šak-niš še-pu-uš-šú*
4	2	⸢*gi-mir ma-li*⸣-*ki* ⸢*ú*⸣-[...]
5	0	DUMU ^{m}AN.ŠÁR-ŠEŠ-SUM.NA LUGAL GAL LUGAL *dan-nu* LUGAL ŠÁR LUGAL KUR *aš-šur*
5	1	DUMU ^{m}AN.ŠÁR-ŠEŠ-SUM.NA LUGAL GAL LUGAL *dan-nu* LUGAL ŠÁR LUGAL KUR *aš-šur*
5	2	DUMU ^{m}AN.ŠÁR-ŠEŠ-SUM.N[A ...]
6	0	GÌR.NÍTA KÁ.DINGIR.RA.KI LUGAL KUR.EME.GI$_7$ *ù* URI.KI
6	1	GÌR.NÍTA KÁ.DINGIR.RA.KI LUGAL KUR.EME.GI$_7$ *ù* URI.KI
6	2	GÌR.NÍTA KÁ.DINGIR.R[A ...]
7	0	DUMU DUMU ^{md}30-PAP.MEŠ-SU LUGAL *dan-nu* LUGAL ŠÁR LUGAL KUR *aš-šur a-na-ku-ma*
7	1	DUMU DUMU ^{md}30-PAP.MEŠ-SU LUGAL *dan-nu* LUGAL ŠÁR LUGAL KUR *aš-šur a-na-ku-ma*
7	2	DUMU DUMU ^{md}30-PAP.M[EŠ-...]
8	0	*ši-pir é-sag-íl šá* AD *ba-nu-u-a la ú-qa-at-tu-u*
8	1	*ši-pir é-sag-íl šá* AD *ba-nu-u-a la ú-qa-at-tu-u*
8	2	*ši-pir é-sag-íl* [...]
9	0	*a-na-ku ú-šak-lil sat-tuk-ki é-sag-íl u* DINGIR.MEŠ TIN.TIR.KI
9	1	*a-na-ku ú-šak-lil sat-tuk-ki é-sag-íl u* DINGIR.MEŠ TIN.TIR.KI
9	2	*a-na-ku ú-šak-lil* [...]

10 0 *ú-kin ki-di-nu-tu* KÁ.DINGIR.RA.KI *ak-ṣur*
10 1 *ú-kin ki-di-nu-tu* KÁ.DINGIR.RA.KI *ak-ṣur*
10 2 *ú-ki-in ki-di*[*n-*...]

11 0 *áš-šú dan-nu a-na* SIG *la ḫa-ba-li* ^{md}GIŠ.NU$_{11}$-MU-GI.NA
11 1 *áš-šú dan-nu a-na* SIG *la ḫa-ba-li* ^{md}GIŠ.NU$_{11}$-MU-GI.NA
11 2 *áš-šú dan-nu a-na* SIG *l*[*a* ...]

12 0 ŠEŠ *ta-li-me a-na* LUGAL-*u-tu* KÁ.DINGIR.RA.KI *ap-qid*
12 1 ŠEŠ *ta-li-me a-na* LUGAL-*u-tu* KÁ.DINGIR.RA.KI *ap-qid*
12 2 ŠEŠ *ta-li-me a-na* [...]

13 0 *ina* *u*$_4$-*me-šú-ma é-maḫ* É ^{d}*nin-maḫ šá qé-reb* KÁ.DINGIR.RA.KI
13 1 *ina* *u*$_4$-*me-šú-ma é-maḫ* É ^{d}*nin-maḫ šá qé-reb* KÁ.DINGIR.RA.KI
13 2 *ina* *u*$_4$-*me-šú-ma é-maḫ* x [...]

14 0 *eš-šiš ú-še-piš a-na šat-ti* ^{d}*nin-maḫ* GAŠAN *ṣir-tu*
14 1 *eš-šiš ú-še-piš a-na šat-ti* ^{d}*nin-maḫ* GAŠAN *ṣir-tu*
14 2 *eš-*⸢*šiš*⸣ *ú-še-pi*[*š* ...]

15 0 *ep-še-te-ia* MUNUS.SIG$_5$.MEŠ *ḫa-diš lip-pal-lis-ma*
15 1 *ep-še-te-ia* MUNUS.SIG$_5$.MEŠ *ḫa-diš lip-pal-lis-ma*
15 2 *ep-še-*⸢*te*⸣*-ia* ⸢MUNUS⸣.[...]

16 0 *u*$_4$-*me-šam-ma ma-ḫar* ^{d}EN ^{d}GAŠAN-*iá lit-tas-qar da-mì-iq-ti*
16 1 *u*$_4$-*me-šam-ma ma-ḫar* ^{d}EN ^{d}GAŠAN-*iá lit-tas-qar da-mì-iq-ti*
16 2 ⸢*u*$_4$-*me*⸣-*šam-ma ma-ḫar* ⸢^{d}⸣E[N ...]

17 0 TI *u*$_4$-*me* SÙ.MEŠ *li-šim ši-ma-ti*
17 1 TI *u*$_4$-*me* SÙ.MEŠ *li-šim ši-ma-ti*
17 2 [x] ⸢*u*$_4$-*me* SÙ⸣.M[EŠ ...]

18 0 *it-ti* AN-*e u* KI-*tim lu-ki-in* BALA-*ú-a*
18 1 *it-ti* AN-*e u* KI-*tim lu-ki-in* BALA-*ú-a*
18 2 [...] x x [...]

19 0 *ù šá* ^{md}GIŠ.NU$_{11}$-MU-GI.NA LUGAL KÁ.DINGIR.RA.KI
19 1 *ù šá* ^{md}GIŠ.NU$_{11}$-MU-GI.NA LUGAL KÁ.DINGIR.RA.KI
19 2 ⸢*ù*⸣ *šá* ^{md}GIŠ.N[U$_{11}$-...]

20 0 ŠEŠ *ta-lim-iá u_4-me-šú li-ri-ku liš-bi lit-tu-tu*
20 1 ŠEŠ *ta-lim-iá u_4-me-šú li-ri-ku liš-bi lit-tu-tu*
20 2 [Š]EŠ *ta-lim-ia u_4*-[...]

21 0 *ša šu-mì šaṭ-ru ù* MU *ta-lim-ia ina ši-pir ni-kil-ti i-pa-áš-ši-ṭu*
21 1 *ša šu-mì šaṭ-ru ù* MU *ta-lim-ia ina ši-pir ni-kil-ti i-pa-áš-ši-ṭu*
21 2 [x] *šu-mì šaṭ-ru* ⌈*ù*⌉ [...]

22 0 MU.SAR-*u-a i-ab-ba-tu lu-u a-šar-šú ú-nak-ka-ru*
22 1 MU.SAR-*u-a i-ab-ba-tu lu-u a-šar-šú ú-nak-ka-ru*
22 2 [MU.S]AR-*u-a i-ab-ba-t*[*u*(?) ...]

23 0 ^{d}*nin-maḫ ina ma-ḫar* ^{d}EN ^{d}GAŠAN-*iá* MUNUS.ḪUL-*šú lit-tas-qar*
23 1 ^{d}*nin-maḫ ina ma-ḫar* ^{d}EN ^{d}GAŠAN-*iá* MUNUS.ḪUL-*šú lit-tas-qar*
23 2 ⌈^{d}⌉*nin-maḫ ina ma-ḫar* ⌈^{d}(?)⌉[...]

24 0 MU-*šú* NUMUN-*šú ina* KUR.KUR *li-ḫal-liq*
24 1 MU-*šú* NUMUN-*šú ina* KUR.KUR *li-ḫal-liq*
24 2 MU-*šú* NUMUN-*šú ina* KU[R....]

1	0	^{m}AN.ŠÁR-DÙ-A LUGAL GAL LUGAL *dan-nu* LUGAL ŠÁR LUGAL KUR *aš-šur* LUGAL *kib-rat* 4-*ti*
1	1	^{m}AN.ŠÁR-DÙ-A LUGAL GAL LUGAL *dan-nu* LUGAL ŠÁR LUGAL KUR *aš-šur* LUGAL *kib-rat* 4-*ti*
1	2–4	[...]
1	5	—
1	6	[...]
1	7	⌈^{m}⌉AN.ŠÁR-DÙ-IBILA LUGAL GA[L ...]
2	0	LUGAL LUGAL.MEŠ NUN *la šá-na-an šá ina a-mat* DINGIR.MEŠ *ti-ik-li-šú ul-tu tam-tim e-lit*
2	1	LUGAL LUGAL.MEŠ NUN *la šá-na-an šá ina a-mat* DINGIR.MEŠ *ti-ik-li-šú ul-tu tam-tim e-lit*
2	2–4	[...]
2	5	—
2	6	[...]
2	7	[LU]G[AL] LUGAL.MEŠ NUN *la šá-na-an* [...]
3	0	*a-di tam-tim šap-lit i-be-lu-ma gi-mir ma-lik ú-šak-niš še-pu-uš-šú*
3	1	*a-di tam-tim šap-lit i-be-lu-ma gi-mir ma-lik ú-šak-niš še-pu-uš-šú*
3	2–4	[...]
3	5	—
3	6	[...]
3	7	[...] *tam-tim šap-lit i-be-lu-m*[*a* ...]
4	0	DUMU ^{m}AN.ŠÁR-ŠEŠ-SUM.NA LUGAL GAL LUGAL *dan-nu* LUGAL ŠÁR LUGAL KUR *aš-šur* GÌR.NÍTA TIN.TIR.KI
4	1	DUMU ^{m}AN.ŠÁR-ŠEŠ-SUM.NA LUGAL GAL LUGAL *dan-nu* LUGAL ŠÁR LUGAL KUR *aš-šur* GÌR.NÍTA TIN.TIR.KI
4	2–4	[...]
4	5	—
4	6	[...]
4	7	[... ^{m}]AN.ŠÁR-ŠEŠ-SUM.NA LUGAL GAL LU[GAL ...]
5	0	LUGAL KUR.EME.GI$_7$ *u* URI.KI *mu-še-šib* TIN.TIR.KI *e-piš é-sag-íl*
5	1	LUGAL KUR.EME.GI$_7$ *u* URI.KI *mu-še-šib* TIN.TIR.KI *e-piš é-sag-íl*
5	2–4	[...]
5	5	—
5	6	[...]
5	7	[... KU]R.EME.GI$_7$ *u* URI.KI *mu-*[...]

6	0	*mu-ud-diš eš-re-e-ti kul-lat ma-ḫa-zi šá ina qé-reb-ši-na iš-tak-kan si-ma-ti*
6	1	*mu-ud-diš eš-re-e-ti kul-lat ma-ḫa-zi šá ina qé-reb-ši-na iš-tak-kan si-ma-ti*
6	2–4	[...]
6	5	—
6	6	[...]
6	7	[...-*u*]*d-diš eš-re-e-ti ku*[*l-lat* ...]
7	0	*ù sat-tuk-ki-ši-na baṭ-lu-tu ú-ki-nu* DUMU DUMU ^{md}30-ŠEŠ.MEŠ-SU LUGAL GAL
7	1	*ù sat-*⸢*tuk-ki*⸣*-ši-na baṭ-lu-tu ú-ki-nu* DUMU DUMU ^{md}30-ŠEŠ.MEŠ-SU LUGAL GAL
7	2–4	[...]
7	5	—
7	6	[...]
7	7	[x *sa*]*t-*⸢*tuk-ki-ši-na*⸣ *baṭ-l*[*u-tu* ...]
8	0	LUGAL *dan-nu* LUGAL ŠÁR LUGAL KUR *aš-šur a-na-ku-ma ina* BALA-*e-a* EN GAL ^{d}AMAR.UTU *ina ri-šá-a-t*[*i*]
8	1	LUGAL *dan-nu* LUGAL ŠÁR LUGAL KUR *aš-šur a-na-ku-ma ina* BALA-*e-a* EN GAL ^{d}AMAR.UTU *ina ri-šá-a-t*[*i*]
8	2–4	[...]
8	5	—
8	6	[...]
8	7	[... ŠÁ]R ⸢LUGAL KUR *aš-šur a*⸣*-n*[*a-*...]
9	0	*a-na* TIN.⸢TIR⸣.KI *i-ru-um-ma ina é-sag-íl šá da-ra-ti šu-bat-su ir-me*
9	1	*a-na* TIN.⸢TIR⸣.KI *i-ru-um-ma ina é-sag-íl šá da-ra-ti šu-bat-su ir-me*
9	2	[...-*í*]*l*(?) ⸢*šá da-ra-ti*⸣ [...]
9	3–4	[...]
9	5	—
9	6	[...]
9	7	[...] ⸢*i*⸣*-ru-um-ma ina é-*[...]
10	0	*sat-*⸢*tuk*⸣*-ki é-sag-íl u* DINGIR.MEŠ TIN.TIR.KI *ú-kin ki-din-nu-tu* TIN.TIR.KI
10	1	*sat-*⸢*tuk*⸣*-ki é-sag-íl u* DINGIR.MEŠ TIN.TIR.KI *ú-kin ki-din-nu-tu* TIN.TIR.KI
10	2	[... DINGIR.ME]Š ⸢TIN.TIR⸣.KI *ú-kin ki-din-nu-tu* ⸢TIN.TIR⸣.[KI]
10	3	[...]
10	4	[...]-x-⸢*ki é-sag*⸣*-í*[*l* ... TIN.T]IR.KI
10	5	—
10	6	[...]
10	7	[...] ⸢*u*⸣ DINGIR.MEŠ TIN.TIR.KI ⸢*ú*⸣-[...]

11 0 *ak-ṣur áš-šú dan-nu a-na* SIG *la ḫa-ba-li* ^{md}GIŠ.NU$_{11}$-MU-GI.NA ŠEŠ *ta-li-me*
11 1 *ak-ṣur áš-šú dan-nu a-na* SIG *la ḫa-ba-li* ^{md}GIŠ.NU$_{11}$-MU-GI.NA ŠEŠ *ta-li-me*
11 2 [... SI]G ⌈*la*⌉ *ḫa-ba-li* ^{md}GIŠ.NU$_{11}$-MU-GI.N[A ...]
11 3 [...]
11 4 *ak-ṣur áš-šú dan-nu* [...-G]I.NA ŠEŠ *ta-li-me*
11 5 —
11 6 ...
11 7 [...] *la ḫa-ba-li* ^{md}GIŠ.[...]

12 0 *a-na* LUGAL-*ú-tú* TIN.TIR.KI *ap-qid ù ši-pir é-sag-íl la qa-ta-a*
12 1 *a-na* LUGAL-*ú-tú* TIN.TIR.KI *ap-qid ù ši-pir é-sag-íl la qa-ta-a*
12 2 [... LU]GAL-*ú-tu* TIN.TIR.KI *ap-qid ù ši-pir é-sag-íl* [...]
12 3 [...]
12 4 [...] x *ši-pir é-sag-*⌈*íl*⌉ *la qa-ta-a*
12 5 —
12 6 ...
12 7 [...] *ù ši-pir é-sag-íl l*[*a*(?) ...]

13 0 *ú-šak-lil ina* KÙ.BABBAR KÙ.GI *ni-siq-ti* NA$_4$.MEŠ *é-sag-íl az-nun-ma*
13 1 *ú-šak-lil ina* KÙ.BABBAR KÙ.GI *ni-siq-ti* NA$_4$.MEŠ *é-sag-íl az-nun-ma*
13 2 [...-*l*]*il ina* KÙ.BABBAR KÙ.GI *ni-siq-ti* NA$_4$.MEŠ *é-sag-íl* [...]
13 3 [...]
13 4 [... NA$_4$.M]EŠ *é-sag-íl az-nun-ma*
13 5 —
13 6 [...]
13 7 [...] ⌈*é*⌉*-sag-íl az-nun-ma*

14 0 *ki-ma ši-ṭir bu-ru-mu ú-nam-mir é-umuš-a ù šá eš-re-e-ti ka-li-ši-na*
14 1 *ki-ma ši-ṭir bu-ru-mu ú-nam-mir é-umuš-a ù šá eš-re-e-ti ka-li-ši-na*
14 2 [...] ⌈*bu-ru-mu*⌉ *ú-nam-mir é-umuš-a u šá eš-re-e-ti* [...]
14 3 [...]
14 4 [...-*na*]*m-mir é-umuš-a u šá eš-re-e-te* [...]
14 5 —
14 6 [...]
14 7 *k*[*i-*...] *ù šá eš-re-e-ti ka-li-š*[*i-na*]

15 0 *ḫi-bil-ta-ši-na ú-šal-lim e-li kul-lat ma-ḫa-zi ú-šat-ri-ṣi an-dul-lu$_4$*
15 1 *ḫi-bil-ta-ši-na ú-šal-lim e-li kul-lat ma-ḫa-zi ú-šat-ri-ṣi an-dul-lu$_4$*
15 2 [...-*š*]*al-lim e-li kul-lat ma-ḫa-zi* [...]
15 3 [...]
15 4 [...-*š*]*i-na ú-šal-lim* UGU *kul-lat ma-ḫa-zi* [...]
15 5 —

15	6	[...]
15	7	[...] ⸢ú⸣-šat-ri-ṣi an-dul-lu$_4$
16	0	ina u$_4$-me-šú-ma é-babbar-ra šá qé-reb ZIMBIR.KI É ^{d}UTU EN GAL EN-iá šá la-ba-riš
16	1	ina u$_4$-me-šú-ma é-babbar-ra šá qé-reb ZIMBIR.KI É ^{d}UTU EN GAL EN-iá šá la-ba-riš
16	2	[...] ⸢é(?)-babbar⸣-ra šá qé-reb ZIMBIR.KI [...]
16	3	[...]
16	4	[...] ⸢é⸣-babbar-ra šá qé-reb ⸢ZIMBIR⸣.KI [...-ri]š
16	5	—
16	6	[...]
16	7	ina u$_4$-[... GA]L EN-iá šá la-ba-riš
17	0	il-lik-u-ma i-qu-pu in-nab-tu áš-ra-ti-šú áš-te-ʾ ina ši-pir ^{d}kulla
17	1	il-lik-u-ma i-qu-pu in-nab-tu áš-ra-ti-šú áš-te-ʾ ina ši-pir ^{d}⸢kulla⸣
17	2	[...]-⸢qu-pu in⸣-[na]b-tu [...]
17	3	[...]
17	4	il-lik-u-ma i-qu-pu [... i]na ši-pir ^{d}⸢kulla⸣
17	5	—
17	6	[...]
17	7	il-l[ik-...] ⸢^{d}⸣kulla
18	0	eš-šiš ú-še-piš-ma ki-ma KUR-i re-e-ši-i-šú ul-li a-na šat-ti ^{d}UTU
18	1	eš-šiš ú-še-piš-ma ki-ma KUR-i re-e-ši-i-šú ul-li a-na šat-ti ⸢^{d}⸣[x]
18	2–3	[...]
18	4	eš-šiš DÙ-ma [...]-⸢li⸣ a-na šat-⸢ti ^{d}⸣UTU
18	5	—
18	6	[...]
18	7	eš-šiš ú-še-piš-[...]⸢UTU⸣
19	0	DI.KUD.GAL DINGIR.MEŠ EN GAL EN-iá ep-še-ti-ia dam-qa-a-ti ḫa-diš lip-p[a-lis]-ma
19	1	DI.KUD.GAL DINGIR.MEŠ EN GAL EN-iá ep-še-ti-ia dam-qa-a-ti ḫa-diš lip-p[a-...]
19	2–3	[...]
19	4	DI.KUD.GAL DINGIR.MEŠ [...]-⸢a⸣-te ḫa-diš IGI.BAR-ma
19	5	—
19	6	[...]
19	7	⸢DI⸣.KUD.GAL DINGIR.MEŠ EN GA[L ...]
20	0	a-na ia-a-ši ^{m}AN.ŠÁR-DÙ-A LUGAL KUR aš-šur NUN pa-liḫ-šú TIN u$_4$-me SÙ.MEŠ še-bé-e l[it-tu-tu]
20	1	a-na ia-a-ši ^{m}AN.ŠÁR-DÙ-A LUGAL KUR aš-šur NUN pa-liḫ-šú TIN u$_4$-me SÙ.MEŠ še-bé-e l[it-...]
20	2–3	[...]

20	4	[... *aš-šu*]*r* NUN *pa-liḫ-šú* [...]
20	5	—
20	6	[...]
20	7	[*a-n*]*a ia-a-ši* ^{m}AN.ŠÁR-DÙ-⸢A⸣ [...-*t*]*u*(?)
21	0	*ṭu-ub* UZU *u ḫu-ud lìb-bi li-šim ši-ma-ti u šá* ^{md}GIŠ.NU_{11}-MU-GI.NA
21	1	*ṭu-ub* UZU *u ḫu-ud lìb-bi li-šim ši-ma-ti u šá* ^{md}GIŠ.NU_{11}-MU-G[I.NA]
21	2–3	[...]
21	4	[*ṭ*]*u-ub* UZU *u ḫu-ud lìb-bi* [...-G]I.NA
21	5	—
21	6	[...]
21	7	*ṭu-ub* UZU *u ḫu-u*[*d* ...] ⸢^{md}GIŠ⸣.NU_{11}-MU-GI.NA
22	0	LUGAL TIN.TIR.KI ŠEŠ *ta-lim-ia* u_4*-me-šú li-ri-ku liš-bi bu-ʾ-a-ri ma-ti-ma*
22	1	LUGAL TIN.TIR.KI ŠEŠ *ta-lim-ia* u_4*-me-šú li-ri-ku liš-bi bu-ʾ-a-ri ma-t*[*i-ma*]
22	2–3	[...]
22	4	LUGAL TIN.TIR.KI [... *bu*]-⸢ʾ(?)⸣*-a-ri ma-ti*-⸢*ma*⸣
22	5	—
22	6	[...]
22	7	LUGAL TIN.TI[R.KI ... *b*]*u-ʾ-a-ri ma-ti-ma*
23	0	*ina aḫ-rat* u_4*-me* NUN *ar-ku-ú šá ina* u_4*-me* BALA-*šú ši-pir šu-a-ti in-na-ḫu*
23	1	*ina aḫ-rat* u_4*-me* NUN *ar-ku-ú šá ina* u_4*-me* BALA-*šú ši-pir šu-a-ti in-na-ḫ*[*u*]
23	2–3	[...]
23	4	[... *š*]*i-pir šu-a-*⸢*ti*⸣ [...]
23	5	—
23	6	[...]
23	7	*ina aḫ-rat* u_4*-m*[*e* ...*-p*]*ir šu-a-ti in-na-ḫu*
24	0	*an-ḫu-us-su lu-ud-diš šu-mì it-ti* MU-*šú liš-ṭur* MU.SAR-*u-a li-mur-ma*
24	1	*an-ḫu-us-su lu-ud-diš šu-mì it-ti* MU-*šú liš-ṭur* MU.SAR-*u-a li-mur-m*[*a*]
24	2	[...]
24	3	[...]-*ma*
24	4	[...]-*šú liš-ṭu*[*r* ...]
24	5	—
24	6	[...]
24	7	*an*-⸢*ḫu*⸣-[... MU.S]AR-*u-a li-mur-ma*
25	0	Ì.GIŠ *lip-šu-uš* UDU.SISKUR BAL-*qí it-ti* MU.SAR-*e-šú liš-kun ik-ri-bi-šú*
25	1	Ì.GIŠ *lip-šu-uš* UDU.SISKUR BAL-*qí it-ti* MU.SAR-*e-šú liš-kun ik-ri-bi-*[...]
25	2	[...]
25	3	⸢Ì.GIŠ *lip-šú-uš*⸣ [UDU.SISKU]R(?) [...]

25 4 [... BA]L(?)-*qí it-t*[*i* ...]
25 5 —
25 6 [...]
25 7 [...] ⸢*ik-ri-bi*⸣-*šú*

26 0 ^{d}UTU *i-šem-me šá šu-mì šaṭ-ru ù* MU *ta-lim-ia ina ši-pir ni-kil-ti*
26 1 ^{d}UTU *i-šem-me šá šu-mì šaṭ-ru ù* MU *ta-lim-ia ina ši-pir ni-kil-t*[*i*]
26 2 [...]
26 3 [...] ⸢*ù*⸣ MU *ta-li-*<*mi*>*-ia ina ši-p*[*ir* ...]
26 4 [... *š*]*u-mì šaṭ-ru* [...]
26 5 —
26 6 [...]
26 7 ⸢^{d}⸣[...]-*p*[*ir*(?) x-x]-*ti*

27 0 *i-pa-áš-ši-ṭu šu-mì it-ti* MU-*šú la i-šaṭ-ṭa-ru* MU.SAR-*ú-a*
27 1 *i-pa-áš-ši-ṭu šu-mì it-ti* MU-*šú la i-šaṭ-ṭa-ru* MU.SAR-*ú-a*
27 2–3 [...]
27 4 [... *i*]*t*-⸢*ti* MU-*šú*⸣ [...]
27 5 —
27 6 [...]
27 7 *i-p*[*a*-...] MU.SAR-*u-a*

28 0 *i-ab-ba-tu-ma it-ti* MU.SAR-*e-šú la i-šak-ka-nu* ^{d}UTU EN *e-la-ti u šap-la-ti*
28 1 *i-ab-ba-tu-ma it-ti* MU.SAR-*e-šú la i-šak-ka-nu* ^{d}UTU EN *e-la-ti u šap-la-ti*
28 2 [...]
28 3 [... M]U.SAR-*e-šú la i-šak*-[...]
28 4 [...]
28 5 —
28 6 [...]
28 7 *i-ab-ba-t*[*u*(?)-...] ^{d}UTU EN *e-la-a-ti* (x) [...]

29 0 *ag-gi-iš lik-kil-me-šú-ma* MU-*šú* NUMUN-*šú ina* KUR.KUR *li-ḫal-liq*
29 1 *ag-gi-iš lik-kil-me-šú-ma* MU-*šú* NUMUN-*šú ina* KUR.KUR *li-ḫal-liq*
29 2 [...]
29 3 [... M]U-*šú* NUMUN-*šú ina* KUR.KUR *li-ḫ*[*al*-x]
29 4 [...]
29 5 —
29 6 [...]
29 7 [...] MU-*šú* NUMUN-*šú i-n*[*a* ...]

1 0 [*ana nabium* ...] (x) GAR-*ni* DINGIR.MEŠ *ti-iz-qar šá-qu-u muš-tar-ḫu*
1 1 [...] (x) GAR-*ni* DINGIR.MEŠ *ti-iz-qar šá-qu-u muš-tar-ḫu*
1 2 [...]

2 0 [... *n*]*a-šu-u ṭup-pi* NAM.MEŠ DINGIR.MEŠ *šá gu-um-mur te-re-e-ti*
2 1 [... *n*]*a-šu-u ṭup-pi* NAM.MEŠ DINGIR.MEŠ *šá gu-um-mur te-re-e-ti*
2 2 [...]

3 0 [...] x x x KI *šá-kin ši-tul-tú a-na* DINGIR.MEŠ *šu-ut* AN KI
3 1 [...] x x x KI *šá-kin ši-tul-tú a-na* DINGIR.MEŠ *šu-ut* AN KI
3 2 [...]

4 0 [...] ⸢*šá*⸣ *la iš-šá-an-na-nu* GIŠ.TUKUL.MEŠ-*šú*
4 1 [...] ⸢*šá*⸣ *la iš-šá-an-na-nu* GIŠ.TUKUL.MEŠ-*šú*
4 2 [...]

5 0 [...] *šá šur-ba-a-ti e-nu-us-su*
5 1 [...] *šá šur-ba-a-ti e-nu-us-su*
5 2 [...]

6 0 [*āšib ezida bītu kīnu ina barsipa māḫāz r*]*a-*⸢*áš*⸣*-bu* EN GAL EN-*ia*
6 1 [... *r*]*a-*⸢*áš*⸣*-bu* EN GAL EN-*ia*
6 2 [...]

7 0 [*anāku aššur-bāni-apli šarru rabû šarru dannu šar kiššati šar māt aš-š*]*ur* LUGAL *kib-rat* 4-*ti*
7 1 [...-*š*]*ur* LUGAL *kib-rat* 4-*ti*
7 2 [...]

8 0 [*mār aššur-aḫa-iddin šarru rabû šarru dannu šar kiššati šar māt aššur šakkanak* TIN.TI]R.KI LUGAL KUR.EME.GI₇ *u* URI.K[I]
8 1 [...TI]R.KI LUGAL KUR.EME.GI₇ *u* URI.K[I]
8 2 [...]

9 0 [*mušēšib bābili ēpiš esagil muddiš eš-re-e-t*]*i kul-lat ma-ḫa-z*[*i*]
9 1 [...-*t*]*i kul-lat ma-ḫa-z*[*i*]
9 2 [...]

10 0 [*ša ina qerbīšina ištakkanu simāti u sattukkīšina ba*]*ṭ-lu-tú ú-ki-n*[*u*]
10 1 [... *ba*]*ṭ-lu-tú ú-ki-n*[*u*]
10 2 [...]

11	0	[*parṣī kidudê kīma labīrimma uterru áš-r*]*u-uš-šu-u*[*n*]
11	1	[...-*r*]*u-uš-šu-u*[*n*]
11	2	[...]
12	0	[*mār māri sîn-aḫḫē-erība šarru rabû šarru dannu šar kiššati šar māt aš-š*]*ur a-na-ku-*⸢*ma*⸣
12	1	[...-*š*]*ur a-na-ku-*⸢*ma*⸣
12	2	[...]
13	0	[*ina palêa bēlu rabû marduk ina rīšāti ana bābili*] ⸢*i*⸣*-ru-um-m*[*a*]
13	1	[...] ⸢*i*⸣*-ru-um-m*[*a*]
13	2	[...]
14	0	[*ina esagil ša dārâti šubassu irme sat-tuk*]-⸢*ki*⸣ *é-sag-í*[*l*(?)]
14	1	[...]-⸢*ki*⸣ *é-sag-í*[*l*(?)]
14	2	[...]
15	0	[*u ilāni bābili ukīn kidinnūtu* TIN.TI]R(?).KI *ak-ṣu*[*r*]
15	1	[....TI]R(?).KI *ak-ṣu*[*r*]
15	2	[...]
16	0	[*aššu dannu ana enši lā ḫabāli šamaš-šuma-ukīn* Š]EŠ *ta-li-me*
16	1	[... Š]EŠ *ta-li-me*
16	2	[...]
17	0	[*ana šarrūtu bābili apqidi u ina kaspi ḫurāṣi*] *ni-siq-ti* NA_4.MEŠ
17	1	[...] *ni-siq-ti* NA_4.MEŠ
17	2	[...]
18	0	[*esagil aznunma kīma šiṭir burūmû ú-n*]*am-mir é-umuš-a*
18	1	[...-*n*]*am-mir é-umuš-a*
18	2	[...-*umu*]*š-*⸢*a*⸣
19	0	*ina* [*ūmēšuma ṭābi-supūršu dūr barsipa ša la-ba-r*]*iš il-lik-ú-ma*
19	1	[...-*r*]*iš il-lik-ú-ma*
19	2	*ina* [...-*ri*]*š*(?) *il-lik-u-m*[*a*]
20	0	[*iqūpu innabtu aššu* EN.NU]N ⸢*é-zi-da ù*⸣ *eš-re-e-te bár-sipa*.KI *dun-nu-nu*
20	1	[...] ⸢*ù*⸣ *eš-re-e-te bár-sipa*.KI *dun-nu-nu*
20	2	[...EN.NU]N ⸢*é-zi-da*⸣ [...]-*ti bár-sipa*.K[I ...]

21 0 [ina emūq um-m]a-na-ti-ia [surriš DÙG].GA-su-pur-šú BÀ[D-šú ina š]i-pir ^{d}kulla eš-šiš ú-še-piš-ma
21 1 [... š]i-pir ^{d}kulla eš-šiš ú-še-piš-ma
21 2 [...-m]a-na-ti-ia [...].GA-su-pur-šú BÀ[D-...] ⸢ú⸣-še-piš-ma

22 0 [abullēšu] ⸢ú⸣-rak-ki-si GIŠ.IG.MEŠ (x) [...] x-ni-ma ú-rat-ta-a ina KÁ.MEŠ-šú
22 1 [...] x-ni-ma ú-rat-ta-a ina KÁ.MEŠ-šú
22 2 [...] ⸢ú⸣-rak-ki-si GIŠ.IG.MEŠ (x) [...] ina KÁ.MEŠ-šú

23 0 [rubû ar-k]u-ú ša ina BALA-e-šú ši-pir šu-a-ti in-na-ḫu LÚ um-ma-a-ni en-qu-tu
23 1 [... š]u-a-ti in-na-ḫu LÚ um-ma-a-ni en-qu-tu
23 2 [...-k]u-ú ša ina BALA-e-šú ši-pir ⸢šu-a⸣-[...]

24 0 ⸢ši⸣-ta-ʾ-al [DÙG.GA-s]u-pur-šú BÀD bár-sipa.KI ki-ma si-ma-ti-šú la-bi-ra-a-te e-pu-uš
24 1 [... b]ár-sipa.KI ki-ma si-ma-ti-šú la-bi-ra-a-te e-pu-uš
24 2 ⸢ši⸣-ta-ʾ-al [...s]u-pur-šú BÀD bár-⸢sipa.KI⸣ [...-r]a-ti e-pu-uš

25 0 [mušarûa] ⸢a⸣-mur-ma Ì.GIŠ pu-šu-uš UDU.SISKUR BAL-qí it-ti MU.SAR-e-ka šu-kun
25 1 [...-š]u-uš UDU.SISKUR BAL-qí it-ti MU.SAR-e-ka šu-kun
25 2 [...] ⸢a⸣-mur-ma Ì.GIŠ pu-šu-u[š ...]-e-ka šu-kun

26 0 [ik-ri-bi-k]a ^{d}na-bi-u[m i-še]m-me ša šu-mì šaṭ-ru ù MU ta-lim-ia
26 1 [...-še]m-me ša šu-mì šaṭ-ru ù MU ta-lim-ia
26 2 [...-k]a ^{d}na-bi-u[m ... M]U ta-lim-ia

27 0 [ina šipir nikilti] i-ab-[bat MU.S]AR-u-a it-ti MU.SAR-e-šú la i-šak-ka-nu
27 1 [...S]AR-u-a it-ti MU.SAR-e-šú la i-šak-ka-nu
27 2 [...] i-ab-[...-š]ak-ka-nu

28 0 [nabium (...) aggiš lik]-kil-me-šú-ma MU-šú NUMUN-šú ina KUR.KUR li-ḫal-liq
28 1 [...] (x)-kil-me-šú-ma MU-šú NUMUN-šú ina KUR.KUR li-ḫal-liq
28 2 [... l]i-ḫal-liq

1 0 *a-na* ^{d}*en-líl* LUGAL DINGIR.DINGIR ⸢EN⸣ AN-*e ù* KI-*tim* NUN x [...]
1 1 *a-na* ^{d}*en-líl* LUGAL DINGIR.DINGIR ⸢EN⸣ AN-*e ù* KI-*tim* NUN x [...]
1 2 [...]

2 0 *pa-ri-is pu-ru-us-su-ú šá la in-nin-nu-*⸢*ú*⸣ [*qibīssu*(?)]
2 1 *pa-ri-is pu-ru-us-su-ú šá la in-nin-nu-*⸢*ú*⸣ [...]
2 2 [...]

3 0 *a-šá-rid* ^{d}*í-gì-gì ma-am-lu*$_4$ ^{d}*a-nun-na-ki mu-ma-*[ʾ*-ir* ...]
3 1 *a-šá-rid* ^{d}*í-gì-gì ma-am-lu*$_4$ ^{d}*a-nun-na-ki mu-ma-*[...]
3 2 [...]

4 0 *ta-mi-iḫ ṣer-ret gi-im-ri sa-ni-*[*iq mitḫurti*(?)]
4 1 *ta-mi-iḫ ṣer-ret gi-im-ri sa-ni-*[...]
4 2 [...] ⸢*sa-ni*⸣-[...]

5 0 EN KUR.KUR IGI.GÁL DINGIR.MEŠ *a-šib é-kur šá qé-re*[*b nippur* (*bēli rabî*) *bēlīšu*]
5 1 EN KUR.KUR IGI.GÁL DINGIR.MEŠ *a-šib é-kur šá qé-re*[*b* ...]
5 2 [...] ⸢*é*⸣-[*ku*]*r* ⸢*šá*⸣ *qé-re*[*b* ...]

6 0 AN.ŠÁ[R]-D[Ù]-⸢IBILA⸣ [*šarru rabû* LUGA]L *dan-nu* LUGAL *ki*[*š-šat šar māt aššur*]
6 1 AN.ŠÁ[R]-D[Ù]-⸢IBILA⸣ (x) [...]
6 2 [... LUGA]L *dan-nu* LUGAL *ki*[*š-*...]

7 0 [... *šarru ša ina kullat*] KUR.KUR *ma-ḫi-r*[*u lā īšû*]
7 1 [...]
7 2 [...] KUR.KUR *ma-ḫi-r*[*u* ...]

8 0 [*mār aššur-aḫa-iddin šarru rabû šarru d*]*an-nu* LUGAL *kiš-šat* LUGAL K[UR *aššur*]
8 1 [...-*š*]*at* ⸢LUGAL⸣ K[UR ...]
8 2 [... *d*]*an-nu* LUGAL *kiš-šat* LUGAL [...]

9 0 [*mār mār*] ⸢^{d}⸣3[0]-⸢ŠEŠ.MEŠ-SU⸣ LUGAL GAL LUGAL *dan-nu* LUGAL *kiš-šat* LUGAL KUR *aš-šur*.KI-⸢*ma*⸣
9 1 [x x] ⸢^{d}⸣3[0]-⸢ŠEŠ.MEŠ-SU LUGAL GAL LUGAL *dan-nu*⸣ LUGAL *kiš-šat* LUGAL KUR *aš-šur*.KI-⸢*ma*⸣
9 2 [...-S]U(?) LUGAL GAL LUGAL *dan-nu* LUGAL *kiš-šat* LUGAL KUR [...]

10 0 ⸢LUGAL⸣ KUR.EME.<<UR>>.GI$_7$ *u* URI.KI GÌR.NÍTA AN.ŠÁR ^{d}*en-líl u* ^{d}*nin-urta*
10 1 ⸢LUGAL⸣ KUR.EME.<<UR>>.GI$_7$ *u* URI.KI GÌR.NÍTA AN.ŠÁR ^{d}*en-líl u* ^{d}*nin-urta*
10 2 [...].KI GÌR.NÍTA AN.ŠÁR ^{d}*en-líl ù* ⸢^{d}⸣[...]

11 0 *za-nin ma-ḫa-zi* E MA TAR DU DÙ *sì-ma-ak-ku*
11 1 *za-nin ma-ḫa-zi* E MA TAR DU DÙ *sì-ma-ak-ku*
11 2 [...-*z*]*i* E MA TAR DU DÙ *sì-ma-*[...]

12 0 *a-na ba-laṭ* ZI-*šu ur-ruk* u_4*-me-šú šu-un-mur* SU-*šú šu-ul-lum* NUMUN-*šú*
12 1 *a-na ba-laṭ* ZI-*šu ur-ruk* u_4*-me-šú šu-un-mur* SU-*šú šu-ul-lum* NUMUN-*šú*
12 2 [...] *ur-ruk* UD.MEŠ *šu-un-mur* ⸢SU⸣-*šú šu-u*[*l-*...]

13 0 *e-*⸢*li*⸣ *a-a-bi-šu ú-zu-uz-zu* BAL.MEŠ-*šú la-ba-ri* GIŠ.GIDRU-*šú šu-te-šu-ri*
13 1 *e-*⸢*li*⸣ *a-a-bi-šu ú-zu-uz-zu* BAL.MEŠ-*šú la-ba-ri* GIŠ.GIDRU-*šú šu-te-šu-ri*
13 2 [...-*š*]*u ú-zu-uz-zu* BAL.⸢MEŠ⸣ [...]

14 0 EN-*us-s*[*u* UGU K]UR-*šú šu-ṭúb-bi* UN.MEŠ-*šú ina ṭuḫ-di u nu-uḫ-šú i-tar-ri-i*
14 1 EN-*us-s*[*u* UGU K]UR-*šú šu-ṭúb-bi* UN.MEŠ-*šú ina ṭuḫ-di u nu-uḫ-šú i-tar-ri-i*
14 2 [...]-*šú šu-ṭúb-bi* UN.ME[Š-...]

15 0 *é-gi-gu-nu-ú ziq-qur-rat* NIBRU.KI *šá ina i-rat* ZU.AB *šur-šu-du tim-me-en-šú*
15 1 *é-gi-gu-nu-ú z*[*iq-qur-r*]*at* NIBRU.KI *šá ina i-rat* ZU.AB *šur-šu-du tim-me-en-šú*
15 2 [... *z*]*iq-qur-rat* N[IBR]U.K[I ...]

16 0 *šá i-ga-ri-šú la-ba-ri*[*š i*]*l-*⸢*li*⸣*-ku-ma ib-ba-šu-ú si-ri-iḫ-šú*
16 1 *šá i-ga-ri-šú la-ba-ri*[*š i*]*l-*⸢*li*⸣*-ku-ma ib-ba-šu-ú si-ri-iḫ-šú*
16 2 [...]

17 0 *ina* SIG$_4$.AL.ÙR.RA UDUN KÙ-*tim ma-qit-*⸢*ta*⸣*-šú* ⸢*ak-šìr-ma*⸣ *ú-šak-lil bu-na-a-šú*
17 1 *ina* SIG$_4$.AL.ÙR.RA UDUN KÙ-*tim ma-qit-*⸢*ta*⸣*-šú* ⸢*ak-šìr-ma*⸣ *ú-šak-lil bu-na-a-šú*
17 2 [...]

18 0 *ina ši-pir* ^{d}*kulla eš-šiš ú-še-piš-ma ú-nam-mir-šú ki-ma* u_4*-mu*
18 1 *ina ši-pir* ^{d}*kulla eš-šiš ú-še-piš-ma ú-nam-mir-šú ki-ma* u_4*-mu*
18 2 [...]

19 0 *re-ši-šu ki-ma šá-di-i ul-li-ma ú-šá-an-bi-iṭ zi-*⸢*mi*⸣*-*[*šú*]
19 1 *re-ši-šu ki-ma šá-di-i ul-li-ma ú-šá-an-bi-iṭ zi-*⸢*mi*⸣*-*[*šú*]
19 2 [...]

20 0 *a-na šat-ti* ^{d}*en-líl* LUGAL DINGIR.MEŠ ^{d}*en-líl* DINGIR.MEŠ EN [*rabû*(?) (EN-*šú*)]
20 1 *a-na šat-ti* ^{d}*en-líl* LUGAL DINGIR.MEŠ ^{d}*en-líl* DINGIR.MEŠ EN [...]
20 2 [...]

21	0	*é-gi-gu-nu-ú ṣa-ad-di ma-a-tim ḫa-diš ina nap-l[u-si-šú]*
21	1	*é-gi-gu-nu-ú ṣa-ad-di ma-a-tim ḫa-diš ina nap-l[u-...]*
21	2	[...]
22	0	*šá* AN.ŠÁR-DÙ-IBILA LUGAL KUR *aš-šur*.KI SIPA *ki-i-nu pa-liḫ* DINGIR-*u-ti-š[u rabīti*(?)]
22	1	*šá* AN.ŠÁR-DÙ-IBILA LUGAL KUR *aš-šur*.KI SIPA *ki-i-nu pa-liḫ* DINGIR-*u-ti-š[ú* ...]
22	2	[...]
23	0	LUGAL-*us-su lik-tar-rab* BALA.MEŠ-*šú li-iṣ-ṣur ana* UD.ME[Š *rūqūti*]
23	1	LUGAL-*us-su lik-tar-rab* BALA.MEŠ-*šú li-iṣ-ṣur ana* UD.ME[Š ...]
23	2	[...]
24	0	GIŠ.GIDRU SIPA-*tú sa-ni-qat mit-ḫur-ti li-šat-m[i-iḫ-šú*(?)]
24	1	GIŠ.GIDRU SIPA-*tú sa-ni-qat mit-ḫur-ti li-šat-m[i-*...]
24	2	[...]
25	0	UGU KUR-*šú liš-ṭib re-é-ut-su* UGU *na-ki-r[i-šú lišziz*(?)]
25	1	UGU KUR-*šú liš-ṭib re-é-ut-su* UGU *na-ki-r[i-*...]
25	2	[...]

1	0	⸢*a*⸣-*na* ⸢^{d}INANNA⸣ UNUG.KI *e-tel-lat* AN-*e u* KI-*tim ga-šir-ti* DINGIR.MEŠ *ṣi-ir-ti*
1	1	[... U]NUG.KI *e-tel-lat* AN-*e u* KI-*tim* ⸢*ga-šir-ti*⸣ DINGIR.MEŠ *ṣ*[*i*-x x]
1	2	⸢*a*⸣-*na* ⸢^{d}INANNA⸣ UNUG.KI *e-tel-lat* AN-*e u* KI-*tim ga-šir-ti* DINGIR.MEŠ *ṣi-ir-ti*
1	3	[...]
1	4	[... U]NUG.KI *e-tel-lat* [...]
2	0	⸢*šá*⸣ *ina ṣi-tan u ši-la-an ur-tu ta-nam-di-nu ta-šak-kan ši*-⸢*ki-in-šá*⸣
2	1	[...-*ta*]*n u ši-la*-⸢*an ur-tu ta-nam-di-nu*⸣ [*ta-š*]*ak-kan ši*-⸢*ki*⸣-[x x]
2	2	⸢*šá*⸣ *ina ṣi-tan* ⸢*u*⸣ *ši-la-an ur-tu ta-nam-di-nu ta-šak-kan* (erasure) *ši*-⸢*ki-in-šá*⸣
2	3	[...]
2	4	[...] (x) ⸢*u*⸣ *ši-la-an ur*-[...]
3	0	*i-lat tam-ḫa-ri ez-zi-ti šá ina qé-reb te-še-e a-šam-šá-niš i-su-ur-ru*
3	1	[...-*ḫ*]*a-ri ez-zi-ti šá ina qé-reb* ⸢*te-še*⸣-*e a-šam-šá-niš i-su-u*[*r*(?)-x]
3	2	*i-lat tam-ḫa-ri ez-zi-ti šá ina qé-reb te-še-e a-šam-šá-niš i-su-ur-ru*
3	3	[...]
3	4	[...-z]*i*(?)-⸢*ti*(?)⸣ [...]
4	0	*a-li-kát i-di* LUGAL *mi-gir-i-šá mu-ra-si*-⸢*bat*⸣ *ga-re-e-šú*
4	1	[x x-*k*]*át i-di* LUGAL *mi-gir-i-šá mu-ra-si*-⸢*bat*⸣ *ga-re*-[x x]
4	2	*a-li-kát i-di* LUGAL (erasure) *mi-gir-i-šá mu-ra-si-bat*(*) *ga-re-e-šú*
4	3–4	[...]
5	0	*be-let* KUR.KUR *ḫa-mi-mat par-ṣi muš-te-ši-rat gi-mir šu-luḫ-ḫu*
5	1	[*be-le*]*t*(?) KUR.KUR *ḫa-mi-mat par-ṣi muš-te-ši-rat gi-mir šu-luḫ*-(x)-⸢*ḫu*⸣
5	2	*be-let* KUR.KUR *ḫa-mi*-⸢*mat*⸣ *par-ṣi muš-te ši-rat gi-mir šu-luḫ-ḫu*
5	3–4	[...]
6	0	*a-ši-bat é-nir-gál-*^{d}*a-nim šá qé-reb é-an-na be-el-ti* GAL-*ti* GAŠAN-*šú*
6	1	⸢*a*⸣-*ši-bat é-nir-gál-*^{d}*a-nim šá qé-reb é-an-na be-el-ti* GAL-*ti* GAŠAN-*šú*
6	2	*a-ši-bat é-nir-gál-*^{d}*a-nim šá qé-reb é-an-na be-el-ti* GAL-*ti* ⸢GAŠAN⸣-*šú*
6	3–4	[...]
7	0	^{m}AN.ŠÁR-DÙ-A LUGAL GAL LUGAL *dan-nu* LUGAL ŠÚ LUGAL KUR *aš-šur* LUGAL *kib-rat* 4-*ti* LUGAL LUGAL.MEŠ NUN *la šá-na-an*
7	1	^{m}AN.ŠÁR-DÙ-A LUGAL GAL LUGAL *dan-nu* LUGAL ŠÚ LUGAL KUR *aš-šur* LUGAL *kib-rat* 4-*ti* LUGAL LUGAL.MEŠ NUN *la šá-na-an*
7	2	^{m}AN.ŠÁR-DÙ-IBILA LUGAL GAL LUGAL *dan-nu* LUGAL ŠÚ LUGAL KUR *aš-šur* LUGAL *kib-rat* 4-*ti* LUGAL LUGAL.MEŠ NUN *la šá-na-an*
7	3–4	[...]

8 0 *šá ul-tu tam-tim e-lit a-di tam-tim šap-lit i-bé-lu-ma gi-mir ma-lik ú-šak-niš še-pu-uš-šú*
8 1 *šá ul-tu tam-tim e-lit a-di tam-tim šap-lit i-bé-lu-ma gi-mir ma-⸢lik⸣ ú-šak-niš še-pu-uš-šú*
8 2 *šá ⸢ul⸣-tu tam-tim e-lit a-di tam-tim šap-lit i-bé-lu-ma gi-mir ma-lik ú-šak-niš še-pu-uš-⸢šú⸣*
8 3–4 [...]

9 0 *šá e-li* URU *ṣur-ru šá qa-bal tam-tim e-lit u* NI.TUK.KI *šá qa-bal tam-tim šap-lit*
9 1 *šá e-li* URU *ṣur-ru šá qa-bal tam-tim e-lit u* NI.TUK.KI *šá qa-bal tam-tim šap-lit*
9 2 *šá ⸢e-li⸣* URU *ṣur-ru šá qa-bal tam-tim e-li-ti u* NI.TUK.KI *šá qa-bal tam-tim šap-lit*
9 3–4 [...]

10 0 *ni-ri be-lu-ti-šú ú-kin-nu-ú-ma i-šu-ṭu ab-šá-an-šú šá ep-še-tu-ú-šú e-li kal* DINGIR.MEŠ *ṭa-a-ba*
10 1 *ni-ri be-lu-ti-šú ú-kin-nu-ú-ma i-šu-ṭu ab-šá-an-šú šá ep-še-tu-ú-šú e-li kal* DINGIR.MEŠ *ṭa-a-ba*(*)
10 2 *⸢ni⸣-ri be-lu-ti-šú ú-kin-nu-ú-ma i-šu-ṭu ab-šá-an-šú šá ep-še-tu-ú-šú e-li kal* DINGIR.MEŠ *ṭa-a-ba*
10 3–4 [...]

11 0 *e-li ṣal-mat* SAG.DU *du-uš-šu-pa-tu* SIPA-*ú-su šá ina* BALA-*šú* ^{d}IŠKUR ŠÈG.MEŠ-*šú* ^{d}*é-a nag-bi-šú*
11 1 *e-li ṣal-mat* SAG.DU *du-uš-šu-pa-tu* SIPA-*ú-⸢su⸣ šá ina* BALA-*šú* ^{d}IŠKUR ŠÈG.MEŠ-*šú* ^{d}*é-a nag-bi-šú*
11 2 *e-li ṣal-mat* SAG.DU *du-uš-šu-pa-tu* SIPA-*ú-su šá ina* BALA-*šú* ^{d}IŠKUR ŠÈG.MEŠ-*šú* ^{d}*é-a nag-bi-šú*
11 3–4 [...]

12 0 *a-na ma-ti-šú uš-tab-ru-ú ina ṭuḫ-du u meš-re-e iš-te-ni-ʾ-ú* UN.MEŠ-*šú*
12 1 *a-na ma-ti-šú uš-tab-ru-ú ina ṭuḫ-du u meš-re-e iš-te-ni-ʾ-ú* UN.MEŠ-*šú*
12 2 *a-na ma-ti-šú uš-tab-ru-ú ina ṭuḫ-du u meš-re-e iš-te-ni-ʾ-ú* UN.MEŠ(*)-*⸢šú⸣*
12 3–4 [...]

13 0 *gi-mir um-ma-ni-šú ṭuḫ-ḫu-du i-ru-uš-šú da-ád-me-šú* DUMU ^{m}AN.ŠÁR-ŠEŠ-SUM.NA LUGAL GAL LUGAL *dan-nu*
13 1 *gi-mir um-ma-⸢ni⸣-šú ⸢ṭuḫ⸣-ḫu-du i-ru-uš-šú da-⸢ád⸣-me-šú* DUMU ^{m}AN.ŠÁR-ŠEŠ-SUM.NA LUGAL GAL LUGAL *dan-nu*
13 2 *gi-mir um-ma-ni-šú ṭuḫ-ḫu-⸢du⸣ i-ru-uš-šú da-ád-me-šú* DUMU ^{m}AN.ŠÁR-ŠEŠ-SUM.NA ⸢LUGAL GAL⸣ L[UGAL ...]
13 3–4 [...]

14 0 LUGAL ŠÚ LUGAL KUR *aš-šur* GÌR.NÍTA TIN.TIR.KI LUGAL KUR.EME.GI₇ *u* URI.KI *mu-še-šib* TIN.TIR.KI *e-piš é-sag-íl*
14 1 LUGAL ŠÚ LUGAL KUR *aš-šur* ⌈GÌR⌉.NÍTA TIN.TIR.KI LUGAL KUR.EME.GI₇ *u* URI.KI *mu-še-šib* TIN.TIR.KI *e-piš é-sag-íl*
14 2 LUGAL ŠÚ LUGAL KUR *aš-šur* GÌR.NÍTA TIN.TIR.KI LUGAL ⌈KUR⌉.EME.GI₇ *u* URI.KI *mu-še-šib* KÁ.DI[NGIR.RA.KI] *e-piš é-sag-íl*
14 3–4 [...]

15 0 *mu-ud-diš eš-re-e-te kul-lat ma-ḫa-zi šá ina qer-bi-ši-na iš-tak-ka-nu si-ma-a-ti*
15 1 *mu-ud-diš eš-re-e-te kul-lat ma-ḫa-zi šá ina qer-bi-ši-na iš-tak-ka-nu si-ma-a-ti*
15 2 *mu-ud-diš eš-re-e-ti kul-lat ma-ḫa-zi šá* ⌈*ina*⌉ *q*[*er-*...] *si-ma-a-ti*
15 3–4 [...]

16 0 DUMU DUMU ^{md}30-ŠEŠ.MEŠ-SU LUGAL GAL LUGAL *dan-nu* LUGAL ŠÚ LUGAL KUR *aš-šur-ma ina* BALA-*e-a* EN GAL ^{d}AMAR.UTU
16 1 DUMU DUMU ^{md}30-ŠEŠ.MEŠ-⌈SU LUGAL GAL⌉ LUGAL *dan-nu* ⌈LUGAL⌉ ŠÚ LUGAL KUR *aš-šur-ma ina* BALA-*e-a* EN GAL ^{d}AMAR.UTU
16 2 DUMU DUMU ^{md}30-ŠEŠ.MEŠ-SU LUGAL GAL LUGAL *dan-nu* LUGA[L ...] *ina* BALA-*e-a* EN GAL ^{d}AMAR.UTU
16 3–4 [...]

17 0 *ina ri-šá-a-ti a-na* TIN.TIR.KI ⌈*i*⌉-*r*[*u-um-ma*] *sat-tuk-ku é-sag-íl u* DINGIR.MEŠ TIN.TIR.KI *ú-kin*
17 1 *ina ri-šá-a-ti a-na* TIN.TIR.KI ⌈*i*⌉-*r*[*u-...-í*]*l*(?) ⌈*u* DINGIR.MEŠ TIN.TIR.KI *ú-kin*⌉
17 2 *ina* ⌈*ri*⌉-*šá-a-ti a-na* TIN.TIR.KI [...] *sat-tuk-ku é-sag-íl u* DINGIR.MEŠ TIN.TIR.KI *ú-*⌈*kin*⌉
17 3–4 [...]

18 0 *ki-din-nu-tu* TIN.TIR.KI *ak-ṣur áš-šú dan-nu a-na* SIG *la ḫa-ba-lu* ^{md}GIŠ.NU$_{11}$-MU-GI.NA
18 1 *ki-din-nu-tu* TIN.TIR.KI *ak-ṣur á*[*š-*...]
18 2 *ki-din̩-*[...] *áš-šú dan-nu a-na* SIG *la ḫa-ba-lu* ^{md}GIŠ.NU$_{11}$-MU-GI.NA
18 3–4 [...]

19 0 ŠEŠ *ta-li-mì a-na* LUGAL-*ú-t*[*u*] KÁ.DINGIR.RA.KI *ap-qid u ši-pir é-sag-íl la qa-ta-*[*a*]
19 1 ŠEŠ *ta-li-mì a-na* LUGAL-*ú-t*[*u* ...]-⌈*qid*(?)⌉ [...]
19 2 ⌈ŠEŠ⌉ [...] KÁ.DINGIR.RA.KI *ap-qid u ši-pir é-sag-íl la qa-ta-*[*a*]
19 3–4 [...]

20 0 *ú-šak-lil ina* KÙ.BABBAR KÙ.GI *u ni-siq-ti* NA$_4$.MEŠ *é-sag-íl az-nun-ma ki-ma š*[*i-ṭir burūmû*]
20 1 *ú-šak-lil ina* KÙ.BABBAR KÙ.GI *u ni-si*[*q-ti* NA$_4$].MEŠ ⌈*é*⌉-*sag-í*[*l* ...]
20 2 [...] *ina* KÙ.BABBAR KÙ.GI *u ni-siq-ti* NA$_4$.MEŠ *é-sag-íl az-nun-ma ki-ma š*[*i-*...]
20 3 [...]
20 4 [...] x [...]

21	0	*ú-nam-mir é-umuš-a ù šá eš-re-e-te ka-li-ši-na ḫi-bil-ta-ši-na ú-šal-lim*
21	1	*ú-nam-mir é-umuš-a* ⌈*ù šá eš*⌉*-re-e-te ka-li-š*[*i-*...]
21	2	[...] *ù šá eš-re-e-te ka-li-ši-na ḫi-bil-ta-ši-na ú-šal-lim*
21	3	[...]
21	4	[...-*r*]*e*(?)*-e-t*[*e*(?) ...]
22	0	*e-li kul-lat* ⌈*ma-ḫa-zi*⌉ *ú-šat-ri-ṣi an-dul-lu*$_4$ *ina u*$_4$*-me-šú-ma* É.GAR$_8$ *é-a*[*n*(?)*-n*]*a*(?) *si-ḫir-ti* [...]
22	1	*e-li kul-lat* ⌈*ma-ḫa-zi*⌉ *ú-šat-ri-ṣi an-dul-lu*$_4$ *ina u*$_4$-[...]
22	2	*e-l*[*i* ...] *ú-šat-ri-ṣi an-dul-lu*$_4$ *ina u*$_4$*-me-šú-ma* É.GAR$_8$ *é-a*[*n*(?)*-n*]*a*(?) *si-ḫir-ti* [...]
22	3	[...]
22	4	[...-*ṣ*]*i an-du*[*l-*...]
23	0	*šá la-ba-riš il-lik-u-ma i-qu-pu ik-kám-ru áš-ra-ti-šú-nu áš-te-ʾ-*[*ma eššiš ušēpišma*]
23	1	⌈*šá la-ba*⌉*-riš* ⌈*il*⌉*-lik-u-ma i-qu-pu ik-kám-ru áš-ra-t*[*i-*...]
23	2	*šá la-ba-riš il-lik-ú-ma i-qu-pu ik-kám-ru áš-ra-ti-šú-nu áš-te-ʾ-*[...]
23	3	[...]
23	4	[...-*ri*]*š il-li*[*k-*...]
24	0	[*ú-š*]*ak-lil-ma ki-ma šá-di-i ul-la-a re-ši-šu-un a-na šat-ti* ⌈^{d}INANNA⌉ UNUG.KI GAŠAN GAL-[*ti*]
24	1	[*ú-š*]*ak-lil-ma ki-ma šá-di-i ul-la-a re-ši-šu-un a-n*[*a* ...]
24	2	[...] *ki-ma šá-di-i ul-la-a re-ši-šu-un a-na šat-ti* ⌈^{d}INANNA⌉ UNUG.KI GAŠAN GAL-[x]
24	3	[...-*li*]*l-*⌈*ma*⌉ *k*[*i-*...]
24	4	[...-*d*]*i-i ul-l*[*a-*...]
25	0	[*š*]*i-pir šá-a-šú ḫa-diš lip-pa-lis-ma ia-a-ti* ^{m}AN.ŠÁR-DÙ-A LUGAL KUR *aš-šur* NUN *pa-liḫ-šú a-mat da-m*[*i-iq-ti-ia*]
25	1	[*š*]*i-pir šá-a-šú ḫa-diš* ⌈*lip*⌉*-pa-lis-ma ia-a-ti* ^{m}AN.ŠÁR-DÙ-A LUGAL KUR *aš-š*[*ur* ...]
25	2	[...] *ḫa-diš* ⌈*lip*⌉*-pa-lis-ma ia-a-ti* ^{m}AN.ŠÁR-DÙ-A LUGAL KUR *aš-šur* NUN *pa-liḫ-šú a-mat da-m*[*i-*...]
25	3	[...]*-a-šú ḫa-diš lip-pa-l*[*i*(?)-...]
25	4	[... *l*]*ip-pa-lis-ma i*[*a-*...]
26	0	*liš-šá-kin šap-tu-uš-šá* TI UD.MEŠ SÙ.MEŠ *še-bé-e lit-tu-tu ṭu-ub* UZU *ḫu-*⌈*ud*⌉ [*libbi lišīm šīmāti*]
26	1	*liš-šá-kin šap-tu-uš-šá* TI UD.MEŠ SÙ.MEŠ *še-bé-e lit-tu-*[...]
26	2	*liš-šá-kin šap-tu-uš-šá* TI UD.MEŠ SÙ.MEŠ *še-bé-e lit-tu-tu ṭu-ub* UZU *ḫu-*⌈*ud*⌉ [...]
26	3	[...]*-kin šap-tu-uš-š*[*á*(?) TI] ⌈UD.MEŠ SÙ⌉.MEŠ *še-b*[*é-*...]
26	4	[...] (x) *šap-tu-uš-*[...]

27 0 *ù šá* ^{md}GIŠ.NU$_{11}$-MU-GI.NA LUGAL KÁ.DINGIR.RA.KI ŠEŠ *ta-lim-ia* UD.MEŠ-*šú li-ri-ku liš-*[*bi bu'āri*]
27 1 *ù šá* ^{md}GIŠ.NU$_{11}$-MU-GI.NA LUGAL KÁ.DINGIR.RA.KI ŠEŠ *ta-lim-i*[*a* ...]
27 2 *ù šá* ^{md}GIŠ.NU$_{11}$-MU-GI.NA LUGAL TIN.TIR.KI ŠEŠ *ta-lim-ia* UD.MEŠ-*šú li-ri-ku liš-*[...]
27 3 [... *š*]*á* ^{md}GIŠ.NU$_{11}$-MU-⸢GI⸣.NA LUGAL TIN.TIR ŠEŠ *ta-lim*(over erasure)-*i*[*a* ...]
27 4 [... ^{md}]GIŠ.NU$_{11}$-⸢MU⸣-[...]

28 0 ⸢*a*⸣-*a-um-ma* NUN EGIR-*ú šá ina u*$_{4}$*-me* BALA-*e-šú ši-pir šu-a-ti in-na-ḫu an-ḫu-us-*⸢*su*⸣ [*luddiš*]
28 1 ⸢*a*⸣-*a-um-ma* NUN EGIR-*ú šá ina u*$_{4}$*-me* BALA-*e-šú ši-pir šu-a-ti in-n*[*a-*...]
28 2 ⸢*a-a*⸣-*um-ma* NUN EGIR-*ú šá ina u*$_{4}$*-me* BALA-*e-šú ši-pir šu-a-ti in-na-ḫu an-ḫu-us-*⸢*su*⸣ [...]
28 3 [...-*m*]*a* NUN EGIR-⸢*ú*⸣ *šá ina u*$_{4}$*-me* BALA-*e-šú ši-pir šu-*⸢*a*⸣-[...]
28 4 [...] ⸢NUN⸣ EGIR-⸢*ú*⸣ [...]

29 0 ⸢*šu-mì*⸣ *it-ti* MU-*šú liš-ṭur* MU.SAR-*u-a li-mur-ma* Ì.GIŠ *lip-šu-uš* ⸢UDU.SISKUR⸣ BAL-*qí*
29 1 [x-*m*]*ì*(?) *it-ti* MU-*šú liš-ṭur* MU.SAR-*u-a li-mur-ma* Ì.GIŠ *lip-šu-*[...]
29 2 ⸢*šu-mì*⸣ *it-ti* MU-*šú liš-ṭur* MU.SAR-*ú-a li-mur-ma* Ì.GIŠ *lip-šu-uš* ⸢UDU.SISKUR⸣ BAL-*qí*
29 3 [... M]U-*šú liš-ṭ*[*ur*] ⸢MU⸣.SAR-*ú-a li-*⸢*mur*⸣*-ma* Ì.G[IŠ ...]
29 4 [...-*t*]*i* MU-*šú liš-ṭur* [...]

30 0 ⸢*it*⸣-*ti* MU.SAR-*e-šú liš-kun ik-ri-bi-šú* ^{d}INANNA UNUG.KI *i-šem-me šá šu-mì it-ti* MU-*šú la i-šaṭ-ṭa-ru*
30 1 [x-*t*]*i* MU.SAR-*e-šú liš-kun ik-ri-bi-šú* ^{d}INANNA UNUG.KI *i-šem-me šá šu-m*[*ì* ...]
30 2 ⸢*it*⸣-*ti* MU.SAR-*e-šú liš-kun ik-ri-bi-šú* ⸢^{d}INANNA⸣ UNUG.KI ⸢*i-šem*⸣*-me šá šu-mì it-ti* MU-*šú la i-šaṭ-ṭa-ru*
30 3 [... *i*]*k*(?)-*ri-bi-šú* ^{d}INANNA UNUG.KI *i-š*[*em*(?)-...]
30 4 [...] MU.SAR-*e-šú liš-kun ik-r*[*i-*...]

31 0 MU.SAR-*u-a i-a-ab-ba-tu lu-u a-šar-šú ú-nak-ka-ru-ma it-ti* MU.SAR-*e-šú la i-šak-ka-nu*
31 1 [...] x-*a i-a-ab-ba-*⸢*tu*⸣ *lu-u a-*⸢*šar*⸣*-šú ú-nak-ka-ru-ma it-ti* MU.S[AR-...]
31 2 MU.SAR-*u-a i-a-ab-ba-tu lu-u a-šar-šú ú-*⸢*nak*⸣*-ka-ru-ma* ⸢*it*⸣*-ti* MU.SAR-*e-šú la i-šak-ka-nu*
31 3 [...]-*ab-ba-tu lu-ú* [...-*n*]*u*
31 4 [...]-*u-a i-a-ab-ba-tu lu-*[...]

32 0 ^{d}INANNA UNUG.KI GAŠAN GAL-*ti ag-giš lik-kil-me-šú-ma* MU-*šú* NUMUN-*šú ina* KUR.KUR *li-ḫal-liq-ma a-a ir-ši-šú re-e-mu*
32 1 [... UNU]G.KI GAŠAN GAL-*ti ag-giš lik-kil-me-šú-ma* MU-*šú* NUMUN-*šú ina* KUR.KUR *li-ḫal-li*[*q* ...]
32 2 ⸢^{d}INANNA⸣ UNUG.KI GAŠAN GAL-*ti ag-giš lik-kil-me-šú-*⸢*ma* MU⸣-*šú* NUMUN-*šú ina* KUR.KUR *li-ḫal-liq-ma a-a ir-ši-šú re-e-mu*
32 3 ^{d}INANNA UNUG.K[I ... KU]R.⸢KUR⸣ *li-ḫ*[*al-*...]
32 4 [... UNU]G.KI GAŠAN GAL-*ti a*[*g-*...]

1 1 *a-na* ^{d}U.GUR *dan-dan-nu*(*) DINGIR.MEŠ *kaš-kaš* DINGIR.MEŠ *šur-bu-ú gít-ma-la*
1 2 *a-na* ^{d}U.GUR *dan-dan-nu*(*) DINGIR.[ME]Š *šur-⸢bu⸣-ú ⸢kaš⸣-[kaš* (DINGIR.MEŠ)]

2 1 *mut-tal-la e-tel-lu* ŠEŠ-*šú a-šib é-šà-ḫúl-la* EN *si-ra-ra*.KI
2 2 *a-šib é-šà-ḫúl-la* EN *si-ra-ra*.KI

3 1 EN-*šú* ^{m}AN.ŠÁR-DÙ-IBILA MAN GAL MAN *dan-nu*(*) MAN ŠÚ MAN KUR *aš-šur*.KI
3 2 EN-[*šú*] ^{m}AN.ŠÁR-DÙ-A MAN GAL MAN *dan-nu*(*) MAN ŠÚ MAN KUR *aš-šur*.⸢KI⸣

4 1 DUMU ^{m}AN.ŠÁR-ŠEŠ-SUM.NA MAN GAL MAN *dan-nu*(*) MAN ŠÚ MAN KUR *aš-šur*.KI
4 2 DUMU ^{m}AN.ŠÁR-ŠEŠ-SUM.NA MAN GAL MAN *dan-nu*(*) MAN ŠÚ MAN KUR *aš-šur*.KI

5 1 MAN TIN.TIR.KI MAN KUR *šu-me-ri ù* URI.KI
5 2 MAN TIN.TIR.KI MAN KUR *šu-me-ri ù* URI.KI

6 1 DUMU DUMU ^{md}30-ŠEŠ.MEŠ-SU MAN GAL MAN *dan-nu*(*) MAN ŠÚ
6 2 DUMU DUMU ^{md}30-ŠEŠ.MEŠ-SU MAN GAL MAN *dan-nu*(*) MAN ŠÚ

7 1 MAN KUR *aš-šur*.KI-*ma ana* TIN ZI.MEŠ-*šú*
7 2 MAN KUR *aš-šur*.KI-*ma ana* TIN ZI.M[E]Š-*šú*

8 1 *i-na a-gur-ru* UDUN KÙ(*)-*tim ki-sal-li*
8 2 *ina a-gur-ri* UDUN KÙ(*)-⸢*tim ki*⸣-*sal-li*

9 1 *é-šà-ḫúl-la ú-ra-bi-i-ma*
9 2 *é-šà-ḫúl-la ú-⸢ra-bi⸣-i-ma*

10 1 *tal-lak-ta-šú ki-ma* u_4*-me ú-nam-mir*
10 2 ⸢*tal*⸣-*lak-ta-šú ki-ma* <<*ki-ma*>> ⸢u_4⸣-*me ú-nam-mir*

1 0 ^{d}nin-gal un-gal
1 1 ^{d}nin-gal un-gal
1 2 ^{d}nin-gal un-gal
1 3 ^{d}nin-gal un-gal
1 4 ^{d}nin-gal un-gal
1 5 [^{d}nin]-⸢gal un⸣-gal

2 0 é-giš-nu$_{11}$-gal
2 1 é-giš-nu$_{11}$-gal
2 2 é-giš-nu$_{11}$-gal
2 3 é-giš-nu$_{11}$-gal
2 4 é-giš-nu$_{11}$-gal
2 5 ⸢é-giš⸣-nu$_{11}$-gal

3 0 ^{d}nin-men-na ki-ág-gá
3 1 ^{d}nin-men-na ki-ág-gá
3 2 ^{d}nin-men-na ki-ág-gá
3 3 ^{d}nin-men-na ki-ág-gá
3 4 ^{d}nin-men-na ki-ág-gá
3 5 ⸢^{d}⸣nin-men-na ki-ág-gá

4 0 úri.KI-ma nin-a-ni-ir
4 1 úri.KI-ma nin-a-ni-ir
4 2 úri.KI-ma nin-a-ni-ir
4 3 úri.KI-ma nin-a-ni-ir
4 4 úri.KI-ma nin-a-ni-ir
4 5 úri.KI-ma nin-a-ni-ir

5 0 ^{md}EN.ZU-TIN-*su-iq-bi*
5 1 ^{md}EN.ZU-TIN-*su-iq-bi*
5 2 ^{md}EN.ZU-TIN-*su-iq-bi*
5 3 ^{md}EN.ZU-TIN-*su-iq-bi*
5 4 ^{md}EN.ZU-TIN-*su-iq-bi*
5 5 ^{md}EN.ZU-TIN-*su-iq-bi*

6 0 GÌR.NÍTA úri.KI-ma
6 1 GÌR.NÍTA úri.KI-ma
6 2 GÌR.NÍTA úri.KI-ma
6 3 GÌR.NÍTA úri.KI-ma
6 4 GÌR.NÍTA úri.KI-ma
6 5 GÌR.NÍTA úri.⸢KI⸣-ma

7	0	gi$_6$-pàr é ^{d}nin-líl-le
7	1	gi$_6$-pàr é ^{d}nin-líl-le
7	2	gi$_6$-pàr é ^{d}nin-líl-le
7	3	gi$_6$-pàr é ^{d}nin-líl-le
7	4	gi$_6$-pàr é ^{d}nin-líl-le
7	5	gi$_6$-pàr é ^{d}nin-líl-le
8	0	nìta-dam ki-ág-gá
8	1	nìta-dam ki-ág-gá
8	2	nìta-dam ki-ág-gá
8	3	nìta-dam ki-ág-gá
8	4	nìta-dam ki-ág-gá
8	5	nìta-dam ki-ág-gá
9	0	^{d}EN.ZU
9	1	^{d}EN.ZU
9	2	^{d}EN.ZU
9	3	^{d}EN.ZU
9	4	^{d}EN.ZU
9	5	^{d}EN.ZU
10	0	gibil-bi mu-na-dù
10	1	gibil-bi mu-na-dù
10	2	gibil-bi mu-na-dù
10	3	gibil-bi mu-na-dù
10	4	gibil-bi mu-na-dù
10	5	⸢gibil⸣-bi mu-na-dù
11	0	alam níg-dím-dím-ma
11	1	alam níg-dím-dím-ma
11	2	alam níg-dím-dím-ma
11	3	alam níg-dím-dím-ma
11	4	alam níg-dím-dím-ma
11	5	alam níg-dím-dím-ma
12	0	^{d}nin-gal-ke$_4$ u-me-ni-dím
12	1	^{d}nin-gal-ke$_4$ u-me-ni-dím
12	2	^{d}nin-gal-ke$_4$ u-me-ni-dím
12	3	^{d}nin-gal-ke$_4$ u-me-ni-dím
12	4	^{d}nin-gal-ke$_4$ u-me-ni-dím
12	5	^{d}nin-gal-ke$_4$ u-me-ni-dím

13	0	šà é dingir Ḫ̮U-dù-šè
13	1	šà é dingir ḪU-dù-šè
13	2	šà é dingir ḪU-dù-šè
13	3	šà é dingir ḪU-dù-šè
13	4	šà é dingir ḪU-dù-šè
13	5	šà é dingir ḪU-dù-šè
14	0	u-mu-un-ku$_4$-ku$_4$
14	1	u-mu-un-ku$_4$-ku$_4$
14	2	u-mu-un-ku$_4$-ku$_4$
14	3	u-mu-un-ku$_4$-ku$_4$
14	4	u-mu-un-ku$_4$-ku$_4$
14	5	u-mu-un-ku$_4$-ku$_4$
15	0	é-nun-ta
15	1	é-nun-ta
15	2	é-nun-ta
15	3	é-nun-ta
15	4	é-nun-ta
15	5	[é]-nun-ta
16	0	ki-tuš nam-en-na-ni dù
16	1	ki-tuš nam-en-na-ni dù
16	2	ki-tuš nam-en-na-ni dù
16	3	ki-tuš nam-en-na-ni ⸢dù⸣
16	4	ki-tuš nam-en-na-ni dù
16	5	[...]-en-na-ni dù
17	0	bí-in-ri-a
17	1	bí-in-ri-a
17	2	bí-in-ri-a
17	3	bí-in-ri-⸢a⸣
17	4	bí-in-ri-a
17	5	[bí-i]n-ri-a

1 0 *a-na* ^{d}*nin-gal* GAŠAN *ṣir-ti*
1 1 *a-na* ^{d}*nin-gal* GAŠAN *ṣir-ti*
1 2 *a-na* ^{d}*nin-gal* GAŠAN *ṣir-ti*
1 3 —
1 4 ... *ṣir-ta*
1 5 ... *ṣir-tú*
1 6 ...
1 7 *a-na* ^{d}*nin-gal* GAŠAN *ṣir-ti*
1 8 *a-na* ^{d}*nin-gal* GAŠAN *ṣir-tú*

2 0 *šar-rat i-la-a-ti qa-rit-ti*
2 1 *šar-rat i-la-a-ti qa-rit-ti*
2 2 *šar-rat i-la-a-ti qa-rit-ti* AMA
2 3 —
2 4–5 ...
2 6 ... *qa-rit-ti* AMA
2 7 *šar-rat i-la-a-ti qa-rit-ti*
2 8 *šar-rat i-la-a-ti qa-rit-ti*

3 0 DINGIR.MEŠ GAL.MEŠ
3 1 DINGIR.MEŠ GAL.MEŠ
3 2 DINGIR.MEŠ GAL.MEŠ-*te*
3 3 —
3 4 DINGIR.ME ...
3 5 DINGIR.ME GAL.ME
3 6 ...
3 7 DINGIR.ME GAL.ME
3 8 DINGIR.ME GAL.ME

4 0 *ana* TIN ZI.MEŠ *šá* AN.ŠÁR-DÙ-IBILA
4 1 *ana* TIN ZI.MEŠ *šá* AN.ŠÁR-DÙ-IBILA
4 2 *a-na* TIN ZI.MEŠ *šá* AN.ŠÁR-DÙ-IBILA
4 3 —
4 4–5 ...
4 6 *a-na* ...
4 7 *ana* TIN ZI.MEŠ *šá* AN.ŠÁR-DÙ-IBILA
4 8 *ana* TIN ZI.MEŠ *šá* AN.ŠÁR-DÙ-IBILA

5 0 LUGAL KUR *aš-šur*.KI LUGAL *dan-nu* LUGAL *kiš-šat*
5 1 LUGAL KUR *aš-šur*.KI LUGAL *dan-nu* LUGAL *kiš-šat*
5 2 LUGAL KUR *aš-šur*.KI LUGAL *dan-nu* LUGAL *kiš-šat*
5 3 —
5 4 ... *kiš-šá-ti*
5 5–6 ...
5 7 LUGAL KUR *aš-šur*.KI LUGAL *dan-nu* LUGAL *kiš-šat*
5 8 LUGAL KUR *aš-šur*.KI LUGAL *dan-nu* LUGAL *kiš-šat*

6 0 *be-lí-šú* ^{md}30-TIN-*su-iq-bi*
6 1 *be-lí-šú* ^{md}30-TIN-*su-iq-bi*
6 2 *be-lí-šú* ^{md}30-TIN-*su-iq-bi*
6 3 —
6 4–6 ...
6 7 *be-lí-šú* ^{md}30-TIN-*su-iq-bi*
6 8 *be-lí-šú* ^{md}30-TIN-*su-iq-bi*

7 0 DUMU ^{md}*nin-gal*-MU
7 1 DUMU ^{md}*nin-gal*-MU
7 2 DUMU ^{md}*nin-gal*-SUM.NA
7 3 —
7 4–6 ...
7 7 DUMU ^{md}*nin-gal*-MU
7 8 DUMU ^{md}*nin-gal*-SUM.NA

8 0 LÚ.GÌR.NÍTA ÚRI.KI
8 1 LÚ.GÌR.NÍTA ÚRI.KI
8 2 LÚ.GÌR.NÍTA ÚRI.KI
8 3 —
8 4–6 ...
8 7 LÚ.GÌR.NÍTA ÚRI.KI
8 8 LÚ.GÌR.NÍTA ÚRI.KI

9 0 ERIDU.KI *u* LÚ *gu-ra-sim-mu*
9 1 ERIDU.KI *u* LÚ *gu-ra-sim-mu*
9 2 ERIDU.KI *u* LÚ *gu-ra-sim-mu*
9 3 —
9 4 ...
9 5 ... *gu-ra-sim-ma*
9 6 ... *gu-ra-sim-ma*
9 7 ERIDU.KI *u* LÚ *gu-ra-sim-ma*
9 8 ERIDU.KI *u* LÚ *gu-ra-sim-ma*

10 0 *áš-ri ip-te-e-ma pú-ḫi-li-tùm-ma*
10 1 *áš-ri ip-te-e-ma pú-ḫi-li-tùm-ma*
10 2 *áš-ri ip-te-e-ma pú-ḫi-li-tùm-ma*
10 3 —
10 4–6 …
10 7 *áš-ri ip-te-e-ma pú-ḫi-li-tùm-ma*
10 8 *áš-ri ip-te-e-ma pú-ḫi-li-tùm-ma*

11 0 *ib-ni-ma ú-kin aḫ-ra-taš*
11 1 *ib-ni-ma ú-kin aḫ-ra-taš*
11 2 *ib-ni-ma ú-kin aḫ-ra-taš*
11 3 —
11 4–6 …
11 7 *ib-ni-ma ú-kin aḫ-ra-taš*
11 8 *ib-ni-ma ú-kin aḫ-ra-taš*

12 0 A.MEŠ *nag-bi da-ru-ti*
12 1 A.MEŠ *nag-bi da-ru-ti*
12 2 A.MEŠ *nag-bu da-ru-tu*
12 3 —
12 4–5 …
12 6 … *da-ru-tu*
12 7 A.MEŠ *nag-bi da-ru-tu*
12 8 A.MEŠ *nag-bi da-ru-ti*

13 0 *ú-šab-ra-a qé-reb-šú*
13 1 *ú-šab-ra-a qé-reb-šú*
13 2 *ú-šab-ra-a qé-reb-šú*
13 3 —
13 4–6 …
13 7 *ú-šab-ra-a qé-reb-šú*
13 8 *ú-šab-ra-a qé-reb-šú*

14 0 *šá* NUN *pe-tu-ú* PÚ *šu-a-ti*
14 1 *šá* NUN *pe-tu-ú* PÚ *šu-a-ti*
14 2 *šá* NUN *pe-tu-ú* PÚ *šu-a-ti*
14 3 —
14 4–6 …
14 7 *šá* NUN *pe-tu-ú* PÚ *šu-a-ti*
14 8 *šá* NUN *pe-tu-ú* PÚ *šu-a-ti*

15 0 *li-ri-ku* u_4*-mu-šú*
15 1 *li-ri-ku* u_4*-mu-šú*
15 2 *li-ri-ku* UD.MEŠ-*šú*
15 3 —
15 4–5 …
15 6 … u_4*-mi-šú*
15 7 *li-ri-ku* u_4*-mu-šú*
15 8 *li-ri-ku* u_4*-mu-šú*

16 0 *liš-ta-an-dil* NUNUZ-*šú*
16 1 *liš-ta-an-dil* NUNUZ-*šú*
16 2 *liš-ta-an-di-il* NUNUZ-*šú*
16 3 —
16 4–5 …
16 6 *liš-ta-an-di-il* …
16 7 *liš-ta-an-dil* NUNUZ-*šú*
16 8 *liš-ta-an-dil* NUNUZ-*šú*

1 0 [a-n]a ^{d}na-bi-um ga-[aš-ru(?) ti-iz-qa-r]u(?) IGI.GÁL DINGIR.DINGIR šá-qu-ú mut-tal-⸢lu$_4$⸣
1 1 [...-r]u(?) IGI.GÁL DINGIR.DINGIR šá-qu-ú mut-tal-⸢lu$_4$⸣
1 2 [x-n]a ^{d}na-bi-um ga-[...]

2 0 ⸢DUB.SAR⸣ gim-ri pa-q[id(?) kiššat šamê u erṣeti(?)] sa-niq mit-ḫur-ti mu-du-ú ka-la-mu
2 1 [...] sa-niq mit-ḫur-ti mu-du-ú ka-la-mu
2 2 ⸢DUB.SAR⸣ gim-ri pa-q[id(?) ...]

3 0 ⸢šar(?)-ḫu gít⸣-ma-lu ḫa-[mi-im kul-lat] par-ṣi šá gu-um-mu-ru te-re-e-ti
3 1 [...] par-ṣi šá gu-um-mu-ru te-re-e-ti
3 2 ⸢šar(?)-ḫu gít⸣-ma-lu ḫa-[...]

4 0 EN nik-la-a-ti [ša ina puḫur ilāni(?)] AD.MEŠ-šú šur-ru-ḫa-at qí-bit-su
4 1 [...] AD.MEŠ-šú šur-ru-ḫa-at qí-bit-su
4 2 EN nik-la-a-ti [...]

5 0 ṣur-ru šad-lu ša l[ib(?)]-⸢bi⸣-šú la i-lam-ma-du DINGIR.DINGIR a-a-um-ma
5 1 [...] (x)-⸢bi⸣-šú la i-lam-ma-du DINGIR.DINGIR a-a-um-ma
5 2 ṣur-ru šad-lu ša l[ib(?)-...]

6 0 EN šur-bu-ú na-šu-ú e-ni na-šu-ú zik-ri ma-al-⸢ki(?)⸣
6 1 [... n]a-šu-ú e-ni na-šu-ú zik-ri ma-al-⸢ki(?)⸣
6 2 EN šur-bu-ú na-šu-(x) [...]

7 0 na-din GIŠ.GIDRU GIŠ.GU.ZA ù BALA.MEŠ mu-ki-in-nu LUGAL-⸢ú⸣-[t]i
7 1 [... GI]Š.GU.ZA ù BALA.MEŠ mu-ki-in-nu LUGAL-⸢ú⸣-[t]i
7 2 na-din GIŠ.GIDRU GIŠ.GU.[...]

8 0 re-mi-nu-ú šá a-na ⸢ár(?)⸣-[k]at(?) u$_4$-⸢um⸣ i-šar-ra-ku da-na-nu ù ⸢li⸣-[i]-ti
8 1 [...] ⸢a⸣-na ⸢ár(?)⸣-[k]at(?) u$_4$-⸢um⸣ i-šar-ra-ku da-na-nu ù ⸢li⸣-[i]-ti
8 2 re-mi-nu-ú šá a-na E[GIR(?) ...]

9 0 bu-kúr ^{d}asar-ri ⸢reš-tu-ú i⸣-[lit-t]i ^{d}e$_4$-ru$_6$ šar-rat i-lat be-le-⸢e⸣-ti
9 1 [...-t]i ^{d}e$_4$-ru$_6$ šar-rat i-lat be-le-⸢e⸣-ti
9 2 bu-kúr ^{d}asar-ri ⸢reš-tu-ú i⸣-[...]

10 0 a-ši-ib é-zi-da É ki-i-nu ina [bár]-sipa.KI ma-ḫaz ra-⸢áš-bu⸣ EN GAL EN-ia
10 1 ⸢a⸣-ši-ib ⸢é⸣-[...]-sipa.KI ma-ḫaz ra-⸢áš-bu⸣ EN GAL EN-ia
10 2 a-šib é-zi-da É ki-i-nu ina [...]

11	0	*a-na-ku* ^{d}GIŠ.NU$_{11}$-MU-GI.NA LUGAL *d[an(?)-nu* LUG]AL ⸢TIN.TIR⸣.KI LUGAL KUR *šu-me-ri ù* URI.KI
11	1	*a-na-ku* ^{d}G[IŠ.... LUG]AL ⸢TIN.TIR⸣.KI LUGAL KUR *šu-me-ri ù* URI.KI
11	2	⸢*a-na*⸣*-ku* ^{d}GIŠ.NU$_{11}$-MU-GI.NA LUGAL *d[an(?)-...]*
12	0	GÌR.NÍTA ⸢*it*⸣*-pe-šú* NUN *qar-du* x [...]-*ú-ti pa-liḫ* EN EN.EN
12	1	GÌR.NÍTA [...]-*ú-ti pa-liḫ* EN EN.EN
12	2	[x NÍ]T[A] ⸢*it*⸣*-pe-šú* NUN *qar-du* x [...]
13	0	⸢ÉNSI⸣ [*ṣ*]*i*-⸢*i*⸣*-ri* ⸢SIPA⸣ *ki-i-[nu muš-t]e-ʾ-ú áš-rat* DINGIR.DINGIR GAL.GAL
13	1	⸢ÉNSI⸣ [*...-t*]*e-ʾ-ú áš-rat* DINGIR.DINGIR GAL.GAL
13	2	[x x x (x) *ṣ*]*i*-⸢*i*⸣*-ri* ⸢SIPA⸣ *ki-i-[...]*
14	0	*mu-še-ši-[ib* KÁ.DINGIR.R]A.KI *e-pi[š]* ⸢*é-sag-íl*⸣ *za-nin é-zi-da*
14	1	*mu-še-ši-[...]* ⸢*é-sag-íl*⸣ *za-nin é-zi-da*
14	2	[....R]A.KI *e-pi[š ...]*
15	0	*ša i-na [palê]*-⸢*šú* ^{d}*en-líl*⸣ DINGIR.DINGIR ^{d}AMAR.UTU *sa-li-mu ir-šu-ú*
15	1	*ša i-na [...]*-⸢*šú* ^{d}*en-líl*⸣ DINGIR.DINGIR ^{d}AMAR.UTU *sa-li-mu ir-šu-ú*
15	2	[...] x x [...]
16	0	*i-na ri-šá-a-tú [a-na* TI]N.TIR.KI *i-ru-um-ma i-na é-sag-íl šá da-rat šu-bat-su ir-me*
16	1	*i-na ri-šá-a-tú* [x x TI]N.TIR.KI *i-ru-um-ma i-na é-sag-íl šá da-rat šu-bat-su ir-me*
16	2	[...]
17	0	*sat-tuk-ki é-s[ag-í]l* DINGIR.DINGIR KUR.EME.GI, ù URI.KI *ú-kin-nu*
17	1	*sat-tuk-ki é-s[ag-í]l* DINGIR.DINGIR KUR.EME.GI, *ù* URI.KI *ú-kin-nu*
17	2	[...]
18	0	DUMU AN.ŠÁR-ŠEŠ-SUM.N[A L]UGAL GAL LUGAL *dan-nu* LUGAL KI.ŠÁR.RA LUGAL KUR *aš-šur*
18	1	DUMU AN.ŠÁR-ŠEŠ-SUM.N[A L]UGAL GAL LUGAL *dan-nu* LUGAL KI.ŠÁR.RA LUGAL KUR *aš-šur*
18	2	[...]
19	0	GÌR.NÍTA TIN.TIR.KI LUGAL KUR *šu-me-ri ù ak-ka-di-i*
19	1	GÌR.NÍTA TIN.TIR.KI LUGAL KUR *šu-me-ri ù ak-ka-di-i*
19	2	[...]

20 0 *ta-li-mu* AN.ŠÁR-*ba-a-ni*-IBILA LUGAL GAL LUGAL *dan-nu* LUGAL KI.ŠÁR.RA LUGAL KUR *aš-šur*

20 1 *ta-li-mu* AN.ŠÁR-*ba-a-ni*-IBILA LUGAL GAL LUGAL *dan-nu* LUGAL KI.ŠÁR.RA LUGAL KUR *aš-šur*

20 2 [...]

21 0 DUMU.DUMU.ᵈ30-ŠEŠ.MEŠ-SU LUGAL GAL LUGAL *dan-nu* LUGAL KI.ŠÁR.RA LUGAL KUR *aš-šur*

21 1 DUMU.DUMU ᵈ30-ŠEŠ.MEŠ-SU LUGAL GAL LUGAL *dan-nu* LUGAL KI.ŠÁR.RA LUGAL KUR *aš-šur*

21 2 [...]

22 0 ŠÀ.BAL.BAL LUGAL-GI.NA LUGAL GAL LUGAL *dan-nu* LUGAL KI.ŠÁR.RA LUGAL KUR *aš-šur*

22 1 ŠÀ.BAL.BAL LUGAL-GI.NA LUGAL GAL LUGAL *dan-nu* LUGAL KI.ŠÁR.RA LUGAL KUR *aš-šur*

22 2 [...]

23 0 NUMUN LUGAL-*ú-ti da-ru-ú ša* ᵈEN-*ba-ni* DUMU *a-da-si* NUNUZ *bal-til*.KI

23 1 NUMUN LUGAL-*ú-ti da-ru-ú ša* ᵈEN-*ba-ni* DUMU *a-da-si* NUNUZ *bal-til*.KI

23 2 [...]

24 0 *a-na* TI ZI.MEŠ GÍD.DA UD.MEŠ *šá-lam* NUMUN GIN BALA.MEŠ *sa*-⌈*kap*⌉ LÚ.KÚR

24 1 *a-na* TI ZI.MEŠ GÍD.DA UD.MEŠ *šá-lam* NUMUN GIN BALA.MEŠ *sa*-⌈*kap*⌉ LÚ.KÚR

24 2 [...]

25 0 *ša* AN.ŠÁR-*ba-a-ni*-IBILA LUGAL KUR *aš-šur* ŠEŠ *ta-li-mi-ia ù ia-a-ti*

25 1 *ša* AN.ŠÁR-*ba-a-ni*-IBILA LUGAL KUR *aš-šur* ŠEŠ *ta-li-mi-ia ù ia-a-ti*

25 2 [...]

26 0 [*a-n*]*a* TI ZI.MEŠ-*ia* GÍD.DA ⌈*u*$_4$⌉-*me-ia šá-lam* NUMUN-*ia* GIN BALA.MEŠ-*ia la* GÁL-*e* GIG-*ia*

26 1 [*a-n*]*a* TI ZI.MEŠ-*ia* GÍD.DA ⌈*u*$_4$⌉-*me-ia šá-lam* NUMUN-*ia* GIN BALA.MEŠ-*ia la* GÁL-*e* GIG-*ia*

26 2 [...]

27 0 [...] x ⌈*bu*(?)⌉-*ru a-ḫa-meš* É.ŠUTUM$_x$(GI$_4$.NAM.AB.DU$_7$).MEŠ *é-zi-da eš-šiš ú-še-piš ma ú-zaq-qìr ḫur-sa-niš*

27 1 [...] x ⌈*bu*(?)⌉-*ru a-ḫa-meš* É.ŠUTUM$_x$(GI$_4$.NAM.AB.DU$_7$).MEŠ *é-zi-da eš-šiš ú-še-piš-ma ú-zaq-qìr ḫur-sa-niš*

27 2 [...]

28 0 [*aiiumma* NU]N EGIR-*ú šá ina* BALA-*e-šú ši-pir šu-a-tú in-na-ḫu i-raš-šu-ú ni-kit-tú*
28 1 [... NU]N EGIR-*ú šá ina* BALA-*e-šú ši-pir šu-a-tú in-na-ḫu i-raš-šu-ú ni-kit-tú*
28 2 [...]

29 0 [*anḫūssu l*]*u-ud-di-iš šu-mì it-ti* MU-*šú liš-ṭur* MU.SAR-*ú-a li-mur-ma*
29 1 [... *l*]*u-ud-di-iš šu-mì it-ti* MU-*šú liš-ṭur* MU.SAR-*ú-a li-mur-ma*
29 2 [...]

30 0 [*šamni lipšuš* (UDU).S]ISKUR *liq-qí it-ti* MU.SAR-*e-šú liš-ku-un ik-ri-bi-šú* ^{d}*na-bi-um i-šem-me*
30 1 [... S]ISKUR *liq-qí it-ti* MU.SAR-*e-šú liš-ku-un ik-ri-bi-šú* ^{d}*na-bi-um i-šem-me*
30 2 [...]

31 0 [*ša šumī šaṭru u šum*] ⸢*ta-li*⸣-*mi-ia i-na ši-pir ni-kil-ti i-pa-áš-ši-ṭu*
31 1 [...] ⸢*ta-li*⸣-*mi-ia i-na ši-pir ni-kil-ti i-pa-áš-ši-ṭu*
31 2 [...]

32 0 [*mušarûa iʾabbatu lū a*]-⸢*šar*⸣-*šú ú-nak-ka-ru-ma it-ti* MU.SAR-*e-šú la i-šak-ka-nu*
32 1 [...]-⸢*šar*⸣-*šú ú-nak-ka-ru-ma it-ti* MU.SAR-*e-šú la i-šak-ka-nu*.
32 2 [...]

33 0 [*nabium bēlu ṣīru ag-g*]*iš lik-kil-mi-šú-ma* MU-*šú* NUMUN-*šú ina* KUR.KUR *li-ḫal-liq*
33 1 [...-*g*]*iš lik-kil-mi-šú-ma* MU-*šú* NUMUN-*šú ina* KUR.KUR *li-ḫal-liq*
33 2 [...] x [...]

1	0	*a-na* ^{d}INANNA GAŠAN *šur-bu-tu* ^{md}30-LUGAL-ÙRU LÚ.⸢GÌR⸣.NÍTA ÚRI.KI
1	1	*a-na* ^{d}INANNA GAŠAN ⸢*šur-bu-tu* ^{m}⸣^{d}30-L[UGAL-ÙR]U ⸢LÚ.GÌR⸣.NÍTA ÚRI.KI
1	2	*a-na* ^{d}INANNA GAŠAN *šur-bu-tu* ^{md}30-LUGAL-ÙRU LÚ.⸢GÌR⸣.N[ÍTA(?) ...]
2	0	*a-na* TIN ZI.MEŠ *šá* ^{md}GIŠ.NU$_{11}$-MU-GI.NA LUGAL E.KI
2	1	*a-na* TIN ZI.MEŠ *šá* ^{md}GIŠ.NU$_{11}$-MU-GI.NA LUGAL E.KI
2	2	⸢*a*⸣*-na* TIN ⸢ZI⸣.MEŠ *šá* ^{md}GIŠ.NU$_{11}$-MU-GI.NA LUGAL ⸢E⸣.K[I]
3	0	6 ME 60-*šu* SAG.KI AN.TA ÚS.SA.DU ^{m}*at-ra-a*
3	1	6 ME 60-*šu* SAG.KI AN.TA ÚS.SA.DU ^{m}*at-ra-a*
3	2	6 ME 60-*šu* SAG.KI AN.TA ÚS.SA.DU ^{m}*at-ra-*[*a*]
4	0	*a-di* É LÚ.U$_{4}$.SAKAR.ŠE.GA *i-šad-da-ad*
4	1	*a-di* É LÚ.U$_{4}$.SAKAR.ŠE.GA *i-šad-da-ad*
4	2	*a-di* É LÚ.U$_{4}$.SAKAR.ŠE.GA *i-šad-da-a*[*d*]
5	0	UŠ AN.TA *u* KI.TA *ul-tu* ZIMBIR.KI
5	1	UŠ AN.TA *u* KI.TA *ul-tu* ZIMBIR.KI
5	2	UŠ AN.TA *u* KI.TA *ul-tu* ZIMBIR.[KI]
6	0	*a-di* URU *su-ra-nu i-šad-da-ad*
6	1	*a-di* URU *su-ra-nu i-šad-da-ad*
6	2	*a-di* URU *su-ra-nu i-šad-da-a*[*d*]
7	0	*a-na* ^{d}*iš-tar u* ^{d}*na-na-a id-din*
7	1	*a-na* ^{d}*iš-tar u* ^{d}*na-na-a id-din*
7	2	*a-na* ^{d}*iš-tar u* ^{d}*na-na-a id-*[*din*]
8	0	*man-nu at-ta lu-ú* LUGAL *lu-ú* LÚ.UGULA
8	1	*man-nu at-ta lu-ú* LUGAL *lu-ú* LÚ.UGULA
8	2	*man-nu at-ta lu-ú* LUGAL *lu-ú* LÚ.[UGULA]
9	0	*šá te-el-lam-ma mi-ṣir ù* NÍG.DU
9	1	*šá te-el-lam-ma mi-ṣir ù* NÍG.DU
9	2	*šá te-el-lam-ma mi-ṣir ù* NÍG.D[U]
10	0	*tu-šá-an-nu-ú* ^{d}AMAR.UTU EN GAL-*ú*
10	1	*tu-šá-an-nu-ú* ^{d}AMAR.UTU EN GAL-*ú*
10	2	*tu-šá-an-nu-ú* ^{d}AMAR.UTU EN GAL-⸢*ú*⸣

11 0 ^{d}*en-líl* EN KUR.KUR *a-ga-nu-til-la-a*
11 1 ^{d}*en-líl* EN KUR.KUR *a-ga-nu-til-la-a*
11 2 ^{d}*en-líl* EN KUR.KUR *a-ga-nu-til-la-*[*a*]

12 0 *še-rit-su šá la pa-ṭa-ru lu-šar-šiš*
12 1 *še-rit-su šá la pa-ṭa-ru lu-šar-šiš*
12 2 *še-rit-su šá la pa-ṭa-ru lu-šar-ši*[*š*]

13 0 ^{d}INANNA UNUG.KI GAŠAN *ṣir-tim a-bi-ik-ti*
13 1 ^{d}INANNA UNUG.KI GAŠAN *ṣir-tim a-bi-ik-ti*
13 2 ^{d}INANNA UNUG.KI GAŠAN *ṣir-tim a-bi-ik-ti*

14 0 BAD$_5$.BAD$_5$ ÉRIN-*ni-šú liš-ku-un ina ma-ḫar* LÚ.KÚR-*šú*
14 1 BAD$_5$.BAD$_5$ ÉRIN-*ni-šú liš-*⸢*ku*⸣*-un ina ma-ḫar* LÚ.KÚR-*šú*
14 2 BAD$_5$.BAD$_5$ ÉRIN-*ni-šú liš-ku-un ina ma-ḫar* LÚ.KÚR-⸢*šú*⸣

15 0 *qab-li-šú lip-ṭur* ^{d}*na-na-a ra-*ʾ*-mat*
15 1 *qab-li-šú lip-ṭur* ^{d}*na-na-a ra-*ʾ*-mat*
15 2 *qab-li-šú lip-ṭur* ^{d}*na-na-a ra-*ʾ*-m*[*at*]

16 0 ^{d}AG *u* ^{d}AMAR.UTU *ina ma-ḫar* ^{d}AG *ra-*ʾ*i-mi-šú*
16 1 ^{d}AG *u* ^{d}AMAR.UTU *ina ma-ḫar* ^{d}AG *ra-*ʾ*i-mi-šú*
16 2 ^{d}AG *u* ^{d}AMAR.UTU *ina ma-ḫar* ^{d}AG *ra-*ʾ*i-mi-š*[*ú*]

17 0 *le-mut-ta-šú lit-taz-kar* ^{d}U.GUR *dan-nu-dan-nu* DINGIR.MEŠ
17 1 *le-mut-ta-šú lit-taz-kar* ^{d}U.GUR *dan-nu-dan-nu* DINGIR.MEŠ
17 2 *le-mut-ta-šú lit-tàz-kar* ^{d}U.GUR *dan-nu-dan-nu* DINGIR.ME[Š]

18 0 *kaš-kaš* DINGIR.MEŠ *zi-kir qar-du ina šib-ṭu*
18 1 *kaš-kaš* DINGIR.MEŠ *zi-kir qar-du ina šib-ṭu*
18 2 *kaš-kaš* DINGIR.MEŠ *zi-kir qar-du ina šib-ṭu*

19 0 *u* BAD$_5$.BAD$_5$ *la i-gam-mil nap-šat-su*
19 1 *u* BAD$_5$.BAD$_5$ *la i-gam-mil nap-šat-su*
19 2 *u* BAD$_5$.BAD$_5$ *la i-gam-mil nap-šat-s*[*u*]

20 0 NUMUN *u* MU *li-kim-šú-ma* 1-*en* UD *la ba-lat-su liq-bi*
20 1 NUMUN *u* M[U ...] ⸢1-*en*⸣ UD *la ba-lat-su liq-*⸢*bi*⸣
20 2 NUMUN *u* MU *li-kim-šú-ma* 1-*en* UD *la ba-lat-su liq-b*[*i*]

1 0 KI.MAḪ *šá* ^{md}UTU-*ib-ni* DUMU ^{m}*da-ku-⸢ru šá⸣* ^{m}AN.ŠÁR-NIR.GÁL-DINGIR.MEŠ LUGAL KUR *aš-šur*
1 1 KI.MAḪ *šá* ^{md}UTU-*ib-ni* DUMU ^{m}*da-ku-⸢ru šá⸣* ^{m}AN.ŠÁR-NIR.GÁL-DINGIR.MEŠ LUGAL KUR *aš-šur*
1 2 KI.MAḪ *šá* ^{md}UTU-*ib-ni* A ^{m}*da-ku-<ru šá>* ^{m}AN.ŠÁR-NIR.GÁL-DINGIR.MEŠ LUGAL KUR *aš-šur*
1 3 [...]

2 0 *re-e-mu ir-šá-áš-šum-ma ul-tu qé-reb* KUR *aš-šur a-na* É-^{m}*da-kur* KUR-*šú*
2 1 *re-e-mu ir-šá-áš-šum-ma ul-tu qé-re*[*b* KU]R *a*[*š*]-⸢*šur*⸣ *a-na* É-^{m}*da-kur* KUR-*šú*
2 2 ⸢*re-e-mu ir-šá-áš-šum-ma ul-tu qé-reb* KUR⸣ [*aš-šu*]*r* ⸢*a-na* É ^{m}*da-kur* KUR⸣-[*šú*]
2 3 *re-e-mu* ⸢*ir-šá-áš*⸣-[*šum*]-⸢*ma ul-tu qé-reb* KUR *aš-šur a-na* É-^{m}*da-ku-ri*⸣ [...]

3 0 *ú-bil-la-áš-šum-ma ina* KI.MAḪ *ina qé-reb* É-*šú šá* BÀD-*šá-la-di-ni ú-šá-aṣ-li-lu-šú*
3 1 *ú-bil-la-áš-šum-ma ina* KI.MAḪ *ina qé-reb* É(*)-<*šú*> *šá* BÀD-*šá-la-d*[*i-ni*] ⸢*ú*⸣-*šá-aṣ-li-lu-šú*
3 2 [...]
3 3 *ú-bil-la-áš-*⸢*šum*⸣-*ma ina* KI.MAḪ *ina qé-reb* É-*šú šá* BÀD-*šá-la-di-ni ú-šá-aṣ-li-lu-šú*

4 0 *man-nu at-ta lu-ú* LÚ *šak-nu lu-ú* LÚ *šá-pi-ru lu-ú da-a-a-nu*
4 1 *man-nu at-ta lu-ú* LÚ *šak-nu lu-ú* LÚ *šá-pi-ru lu-*⸢*ú da*⸣-*a-a-nu*
4 2 [...]
4 3 *man-nu at-ta lu-ú* LÚ *šak-nu lu-ú* LÚ *šá-pi-ru lu-ú da-a-a-*⸢*nu*⸣

5 0 *lu-ú* NUN *šá ina* KUR *iš-šak-ka-nu a-na* KI.MAḪ *u e-ṣe-et-ti*
5 1 *lu-ú* NUN *šá ina* KUR *iš-šak-ka-nu a-na* KI.MAḪ *u* ⸢*e*⸣-*ṣe-et-ti*
5 2 [...]
5 3 *lu-ú* NUN *šá ina* KUR *iš-šak-ka-nu a-na* KI.MAḪ *u e-ṣe-et-ti*

6 0 *šu-a-ti la ta-ḫa-aṭ-ṭu a-šar-šú ú-ṣur*
6 1 *šu-a-ti la ta-ḫa-aṭ-ṭu a-šar-šú* ⸢*ú*⸣-*ṣur*
6 2 [...]
6 3 *šu-a-ti la ta-ḫa-aṭ-ṭu a-šar-šú ú-ṣur*

7 0 *ṣi-il-li ṭa-a-bi e-li-šú tu-ru-uṣ*
7 1 *ṣi-il-li ṭa-a-bi e-li-šú t*[*u*]-*ru-uṣ*
7 2 [...]
7 3 *ṣi-il-li ṭa-a-bi e-*⸢*li-šú*⸣ *tu-ru-*⸢*uṣ*⸣

8 0 *a-na šu-a-ti* ^{d}AMAR.UTU EN GAL-*ú pa-le-e-ka lu-ur-ri*[*k*]
8 1 *a-na šu-a-ti* ^{d}AMAR.UTU EN GAL-*ú pa-le-e-ka* [*lu-u*]*r-ri*[*k*]
8 2 [...]
8 3 *a-na šu-a-ti* ^{d}AMAR.UTU EN GAL-*ú pa-le-e-ka lu-ur-r*[*ik*]

9 0 *ṣu-lul-šú ṭa-a-bu e-li-ka li-iš-k*[*un*]
9 1 *ṣu-lul-šú ṭa-a-bu e-li-ka* [*l*]*i-iš-k*[*un*]
9 2 [...]
9 3 *ṣu-lul-šú ṭa-a-bu e-li-ka li*-⸢*iš*⸣-[*kun*]

10 0 ⸢MU⸣-*ka* NUMUN-⸢*ka ù ba-la-ṭu u*$_4$⸣-*me*-⸢*ka* GÍD.DA.MEŠ *a-na u*$_4$*-me ṣa-a-ta*⸣ *lik*-⸢*ru*(?)-*bu*(?)⸣
10 1 [M]U-*ka* NUMUN-⸢*ka ù ba-la-ṭu u*$_4$*-me-ka* GÍD.DA⸣.M[EŠ] ⸢*a-na u*$_4$*-me ṣa-a-ta lik*⸣-*r*[*u*(?)-x]
10 2 [...]
10 3 ⸢MU-*ka* NUMUN-*ka ù ba-la-ṭu u*$_4$⸣-*me*-⸢*ka* GÍD.DA.MEŠ *a-na u*$_4$*-me ṣa-a-ta*⸣ *lik*-⸢*ru*(?)-*bu*(?)⸣

11 0 *šum-ma* NUN *šu-ú lu-ú* LÚ *šak-nu lu-ú* LÚ *šá-pi-ru lu-ú da-a-a-nu*
11 1 [*šu*]*m-ma* NUN *šu-ú lu-ú* LÚ *šak-nu lu-ú* LÚ *šá-pi-ru lu-ú da-a-a-nu*
11 2 [...]
11 3 *šum-ma* NUN *šu-ú lu-ú* LÚ *šak-nu lu-ú* LÚ *šá-pi-ru lu-ú da-a-a*-⸢*nu*⸣

12 0 *lu-ú* GÌR.NÍTA *šá ina* KUR *ib-ba-áš-šu-ú*
12 1 [*l*]*u-ú* GÌR.NÍTA *šá ina* KUR *ib-ba-áš-šu-ú*
12 2 [...]
12 3 *lu-ú* GÌR.NÍTA *šá ina* KUR *ib-ba-áš-šu-ú*

13 0 *a-na* KI.MAḪ *u e-ṣe-et-ti šu-a-ti i-ḫa-aṭ-ṭu-ú*
13 1 *a-na* KI.MAḪ *u e-ṣe-et-ti šu-a-ti i-ḫa-aṭ-ṭu-ú*
13 2 [...]
13 3 *a-na* KI.MAḪ *u e-ṣe-et-ti šu-a-ti i-ḫa-aṭ-ṭu-ú*

14 0 *a-šar-šú ú-nak-ka-ri a-na a-šar šá-nam-ma i-leq-qu-ú*
14 1 *a-šar-šú ú-nak-ka-ri a-na a-šar šá-nam-ma i-leq-qu-ú*
14 2 [...]
14 3 *a-šar-šú ú-nak-ka-ru-ma a-na a-šar šá-nam-ma i-leq-qu-ú*

15 0 *ù man-ma a-na li-mut-tu*$_4$ *ú-šad-ba-bu-šú-ma i-šem-mu-ú*
15 1 *ù man-ma a-na li-mut-tu*$_4$ *ú-šad-ba-bu-šú-ma i-šem-mu-ú*
15 2 [...]
15 3 *ù man-ma a-na li-mut-tu*$_4$ *ú-šad-ba-bu-šú-ma i-šem-mu-ú*

16 0 ^{d}AMAR.UTU EN GAL-*ú* MU-*šú* NUMUN-*šú* NUNUZ.MEŠ-*šú ù na-an-nab-šú*
16 1 ^{d}AMAR.UTU EN GAL-*ú* MU-*šú* NUMUN-*šú* NUNUZ.MEŠ-*šú ù na-an-nab-šú*
16 2 [...]
16 3 ⸢^{d}AMAR.UTU EN GAL-*ú* MU-*šú* NUMUN-*šú* NUNUZ.MEŠ⸣-*šú ù na-an-nab-šú*

17 0 *i-na pi-i* UN.MEŠ *li-ḫal-liq*
17 1 *i-na pi-i* UN.MEŠ *li-ḫal-liq*
17 2 [...]
17 3 [... *l*]*i-ḫal-liq*

18 0 ^{d}AG *sa-ni-iq mit-ḫur-ti mi-na-a-ta* u_4*-me-*⸢*šú* GÍD.DA⸣.MEŠ ⸢*li-kar-ri*⸣
18 1 ^{d}AG *sa-ni-iq mit-ḫur-ti mi-na-a-ta* u_4*-me-*⸢*šú* GÍD.DA⸣.MEŠ ⸢*li-kar-ri*⸣
18 2 [...]
18 3 [...]

19 0 ⸢^{d}U.GUR⸣ *ina di-ʾ šib-*⸢*ṭu*⸣ *u šag-*⸢*ga*⸣*-áš-ti*
19 1 ⸢^{d}U.GUR⸣ *ina di-ʾ šib-*⸢*ṭu*⸣ *u šag-*⸢*ga*⸣*-áš-ti*
19 2 ⸢^{d}U.GUR *ina di-ʾ*⸣ *š*[*ib-*...]
19 3 [...]

20 0 *la i-gam-mi-il nap-šat-su*
20 1 *la i-gam-*⸢*mi*⸣*-il nap-šat-su*
20 2 *la i-gam-mi-il nap-*[...]
20 3 [...]

1 0 a-na-ku ^{md}MAŠ-NÍG.DU-ÙRU LÚ.GAR KUR su-ḫi u KUR má-rí DUMU ^{md}UTU-SAG-PAB LÚ.GAR KUR su-ḫi u KUR ma-ri
1 1 [....GA]R KUR su-ḫi u KUR má-rí DUMU ^{md}UTU-SAG-PAB LÚ.GAR KUR su-ḫi u KUR ma-ri
1 2 a-na-ku ^{md}MAŠ-NÍG.DU-ÙRU LÚ.GAR KUR [...] u KUR ma-ri

2 0 DUMU ^{m}BA-šá-^{d}AMAR.UTU MIN Š[À].BAL.BAL ^{md}IŠKUR-SUM-NUMUN LÚ.GAR KUR su-ḫi u KUR má-rí
2 1 [...].BAL.BAL ^{md}IŠKUR-SUM-NUMUN LÚ.GAR KUR su-ḫi u KUR má-rí
2 2 DUMU ^{m}BA-šá-^{d}AMAR.UTU MIN Š[À....]

3 0 [(...)] NUMUN da-ru-ú li-pu ru-qu šá ^{m}tu-na-mis-saḫ DUMU ^{m}(*)ḫa-am-mu-ra-pu
3 1 [... -p]u ru-qu šá ^{m}tu-na-mis-saḫ DUMU ^{m}(*)ḫa-am-mu-ra-pu
3 2 [(...)] NUMUN da-ru-ú li-pu ru-q[u ...]

4 0 [šar bābili (...)] É a-ki-tu$_4$ šá ^{d}IŠKUR u ^{d}mi-šar-rum DINGIR.MEŠ GAL.MEŠ a-ši-bu-tu
4 1 [...-t]u$_4$ šá ^{d}IŠKUR u ^{d}mi-šar-rum DINGIR.MEŠ GAL.MEŠ a-ši-bu-tu
4 2 [...] É a-ki-tu$_4$ šá ^{d}IŠKUR u ^{d}mi-ša[r(?)-...]

5 0 [udada] EN.MEŠ-e-a la-ba-riš il-lik-ma muš-šu-rat a-a-⸢um⸣-ma ina lìb-bi
5 1 [...]-⸢e⸣-a la-ba-riš il-lik-ma muš-šu-rat a-a-⸢um⸣-ma ina lìb-bi
5 2 [...] EN.MEŠ-e-a la-ba-riš il-lik-[...]

6 0 [abbēa] SAG-su ul iš-ši-ma ul i-pu-uš ana-ku É a-ki-t[u$_4$ UR$_5$-t]ú ⸢ú⸣-šak-lil-ma
6 1 [...] iš-ši-ma ul i-pu-uš ana-ku É a-ki-t[u$_4$ UR$_5$-t]ú ⸢ú⸣-šak-lil-ma
6 2 [...] SAG-su ul iš-ši-ma ul i-p[u-...]

7 0 a-na ^{d}IŠKUR ù ^{d}mi-ša-rum DINGIR.MEŠ GAL.MEŠ EN.MEŠ-e-a a-na ba-laṭ ZI.MEŠ-ia
7 1 [...-ru]m DINGIR.MEŠ GAL.MEŠ EN.MEŠ-e-a a-na ba-laṭ ZI.MEŠ-ia
7 2 a-na ^{d}IŠKUR ù ^{d}mi-ša-rum DIN[GIR ...]

8 0 šá-lam NUMUN-ia GÍD.DA UD.MEŠ-ia ku-un BALA.MEŠ-e-a sa-kap KUR LÚ.KÚR-ia ú-še-piš-ma
8 1 [...-i]a ku-un BALA.MEŠ-e-a sa-kap KUR LÚ.KÚR-ia ú-še-piš-ma
8 2 šá-lam NUMUN-ia GÍD.DA UD.MEŠ-ia [...] ú-še-piš-ma

9 0 BA-eš É.GAL ^{m}[é-nam-ḫ]é-NUMUN-ib-ni LÚ.GAR KUR su-ḫi u KUR ma-ri KI-tim URU ra-il
9 1 [...-ḫ]é-NUMUN-ib-ni LÚ.GAR KUR su-ḫi u KUR ma-ri KI-tim URU ra-il
9 2 BA-eš É.GAL ^{m}x [...] KI-tim URU ra-il

10 0 *šá qab-lat* ÍD.[BURANUN.KI] *la-ba-riš il-lik-ma un-dáš-šìr-šú* É.GAL *šá-ni-tu*$_4$

10 1 [...] *la-ba-riš il-lik-ma un-dáš-šìr-šú* É.GAL *šá-ni-tu*$_4$

10 2 *šá qab-lat* ÍD [...] É.GAL *šá-ni-tu*$_4$

11 0 AN.TA-*šú e-pu-uš-m*[*a* 60-*šu*] ⸢4⸣ *ina* 1 KÙŠ GÍD.DA-*šú* 12 *ina* 1 KÙŠ *ù ma-la ú-ṭu ru-pu-us-su*

11 1 [...]-*uš-m*[*a* ...] ⸢4⸣ *ina* 1 KÙŠ GÍD.DA-*šú* 12 *ina* 1 KÙŠ *ù ma-la ú-ṭu ru-pu-us-su*

11 2 AN.TA-*šú e-pu*-[...] *ú-ṭu ru-pu-us-su*

12 0 *a-na la* É.GAL *šá* ᵐ⸢*é*(*)⸣-[*nam*]-*ḫé*-NUMUN-DÙ 20 *ina* 1 KÙŠ *ú-šá-rik-šú* 4 *ina* 1 KÙŠ *ur-tap-pis-su*

12 1 [... *l*]*a* É.GAL *šá* ᵐ⸢*é*(*)⸣-[*nam*]-*ḫé*-NUMUN-DÙ 20 *ina* 1 KÙŠ *ú-šá-rik-šú* 4 *ina* 1 KÙŠ *ur-tap-pis-su*

12 2 *a-na l*[*a* ...] 4 *ina* 1 KÙŠ *ur-tap-pis-su*

13 0 *šá-ni-tu*$_4$ É.GAL AN.T[A-*šú ina* U]GU *ki-iṣ-ri e-pu-uš-ma* 45 *ina* 1 KÙŠ *ú-šá-rik-šú*

13 1 ⸢*šá-ni*⸣-*tu*$_4$ É.GAL AN.T[A-... U]GU *ki-iṣ-ri e-pu-uš-ma* 45 *ina* 1 KÙŠ *ú-šá-rik-šú*

13 2 *šá-ni-tu*$_4$ [...] 45 *ina* 1 KÙŠ *ú-šá-rik-šú*

14 0 9 *ina* 1 KÙŠ *ur-tap-pis*-[*su ù*] *pa-nu-ú-a a-na muḫ-ḫi ul áš-kun-ma* GIŠ.ḪUR *ul e-ṣir-ši*

14 1 9 *ina* 1 KÙŠ *ur-tap-pis*-[...] *pa-nu-ú-a a-na muḫ-ḫi ul áš-kun-ma* GIŠ.ḪUR *ul e-ṣir-ši*

14 2 9 *ina* 1 KÙŠ [...] *ul áš-kun-ma* GIŠ.ḪUR *ul* ⸢*e*⸣-[...]

15 0 LÚ *ra-ìl-a-a* LÚ.ḪI.GAR.M[EŠ(?)-*šú-nu* ḪI.GA]R(?) *a-na* UGU AD-*ia i-pu-šú-ma* AD-*ú-a id-duk-šú-nu-ti*

15 1 LÚ *ra-ìl-a-a* LÚ.ḪI.GAR.M[EŠ(?)-*šú-nu* ḪI.GA]R(?) *a-na* UGU AD-*ia i-pu-šú-ma* AD-*ú-a id-duk-šú-nu-ti*

15 2 [...] AD-*ia i-pu-šú-ma* AD-*ú-a* [...]

16 0 *i-na lìb-bi pa-nu*-⸢*ú*⸣-[*a ana mu*]*ḫ-ḫi ul áš-kun-ma* GIŠ.ḪUR *ul e-ṣir-ši i-na re-eš*

16 1 *i-na lìb-bi pa-nu*-⸢*ú*⸣-[... *mu*]*ḫ-ḫi ul áš-kun-ma* GIŠ.ḪUR *ul e-ṣir-ši i-na re-eš*

16 2 [...] *ul áš-kun-ma* GIŠ.ḪUR *ul* [...]

17 0 LÚ.GAR.KUR-*ú-ti-ia* [*šá ina* GIŠ.G]U.ZA *šá* AD-*ia ú-ši-bu* LÚ *ra-ìl-a-a a-na muḫ-ḫi-ia*

17 1 LÚ.GAR.KUR-*ú-ti-ia* [... G]U.ZA *šá* AD-*ia ú-ši-bu* LÚ *ra-ìl-a-a a-na muḫ-ḫi-ia*

17 2 [...] *ú-ši-bu* LÚ *ra-ìl-a-a a-n*[*a* ...]

18 0 *ib-bal-kit-ú-m*[*a a-duk*]-⸢*šú*⸣-*nu-ti man-ni ár-ku-ú šá* E$_{11}$-*ma a-na* LÚ *ra-ìl-a-a*

18 1 *ib-bal-kit-ú-m*[*a* ...]-⸢*šú*⸣-*nu-ti man-ni ár-ku-ú šá* E$_{11}$-*ma a-na* LÚ *ra-ìl-a-a*

18 2 [...] *man-ni ár-ku-ú šá* E$_{11}$-*ma a*-[...]

19 0 na-de-e a-ḫi la [i-raš-ši]-⸢šú⸣-nu-ti ina re-eš LÚ.GAR.KUR-ú-ti-ia šá i-na GIŠ.GU.ZA
19 1 na-de-e a-ḫi la [...]-⸢šú⸣-nu-ti ina re-eš LÚ.GAR.KUR-ú-ti-ia šá i-na GIŠ.GU.ZA
19 2 [...] LÚ.GAR.KUR-ú-ti-ia šá i-na GIŠ.GU.[ZA]

20 0 šá AD-ia ú-ši-b[u 2 LIM LÚ ḫa-ta]l-li ul-tu LÚ sa-ru-gu a-di LÚ mi-nu-ʾ-i
20 1 šá AD-ia ú-ši-b[u ...-ta]l-li ul-tu LÚ sa-ru-gu a-di LÚ mi-nu-ʾ-i
20 2 [...] a-di LÚ mi-nu-ʾ-i

21 0 ip-ḫu-ru-ú-m[a ^{m}šá-ma-ʾ-ga-a]m-ni LÚ.NIMGIR LÚ sa-ru-gu a-lik pa-ni-šu-nu
21 1 ip-ḫu-ru-ú-m[a ...-a]m-ni LÚ.NIMGIR LÚ sa-ru-gu a-lik pa-ni-šu-nu
21 2 [...] a-lik pa-ni-šú-nu

22 0 a-na ḫu-ub-tu [ana KUR la-qé]-⸢e⸣ il-li-ku-ma <<KUR>> 1 ME É.DURU$_5$.MEŠ šá KUR la-qé-e
22 1 a-na ḫu-ub-tu [...]-⸢e⸣ il-li-ku-ma <<KUR>> 1 ME É.DURU$_5$.MEŠ šá KUR la-qé-e
22 2 a-na ḫu-u[b(*)-...] šá KUR la-qé-e

23 0 iṣ-bat-ú-ma ḫ[u-ub-tu lā mīni iḫ-b]u-tu-nim-ma KUR la-qé-e a-na DU$_6$ ù kar-mi
23 1 iṣ-bat-ú-ma ḫ[u-...-b]u-tu-nim-ma KUR la-qé-e a-na DU$_6$ ù kar-mi
23 2 iṣ-bat-ú-m[a(?) ...] a-na DU$_6$ ù kar-mi

24 0 ut-tir-ru ^{md}[IŠKUR-da-ʾa-nu saknu māt l]a-qé-e ina lìb-bi 4 GIŠ.GIGIR.MEŠ 2 ME ÉRIN.MEŠ
24 1 ut-tir-ru ^{md}[... l]a-qé-e ina lìb-bi 4 GIŠ.GIGIR.MEŠ 2 ME ÉRIN.MEŠ
24 2 u[t-...] ina lìb-bi 4 GIŠ.GIGIR.MEŠ 2 ME [...]

25 0 a-na pa-ni-i[a illikamma qaqqari] i-na pa-ni-ia iš-šiq-ma ù ú-sap-pa-an-ni-ma
25 1 a-na pa-ni-i[a ...-n]a pa-ni-ia iš-šiq-ma ù ú-sap-pa-an-ni-ma
25 2 [...] i-na pa-ni-ia iš-šiq-[...]

26 0 šum-ma ki-i [x x x x x x] at-ta ù ki-i tu-un-dáš-šìr-an-ni at-ta-a-ma
26 1 šum-ma ki-i [x x x x x x x x x x]-i tu-un-dáš-šìr-an-ni at-ta-a-ma
26 2 [...] at-ta ù ki-i t[u(?)-...]

27 0 ù ^{md}30-[SILIM-im-an-ni] LÚ.EN.NAM KUR ru-ṣa-pu ⸢a⸣-[d]i e-mu-qu gab-bi šá KUR ru-ṣa-pu
27 1 ù ^{md}30-[...-d]i e-mu-qu gab-bi šá KUR ru-ṣa-pu
27 2 [...] LÚ.EN.NAM KUR ru-ṣa-pu ⸢a⸣-[...]

28 0 a-na mu[ḫ-ḫi-šú-nu illikamma] i-mur-šu-nu-ti-ma a-na muḫ-ḫi-šú-nu ul im-qut
28 1 a-na mu[ḫ-...-t]i-ma a-na muḫ-ḫi-šú-nu ul im-qut
28 2 [...] i-mur-šu-nu-ti-ma a-na m[uḫ-...]

29 0 *a-na-ku* ^{md}M[AŠ-*kudurrī-uṣur šaknu māt sūḫi*] *u* KUR *ma-ri am-ri šá* ^{d}UTU *u* ^{d}AMAR.UTU ^{d}IŠKUR *u* ^{d}A-^{d}IŠKUR
29 1 *a-na-ku* ^{md}M[AŠ-... *a*]*m*(?)-*ri šá* ^{d}UTU *u* ^{d}AMAR.UTU ^{d}IŠKUR *u* ^{d}A-^{d}IŠKUR
29 2 [...] *u* KUR *ma-ri am-ri šá* ^{d}UTU [...]

30 0 *ù* ^{d}*iš-tar* [x x x x x (x x)] *ù* ^{d}AMAR.UTU *i-pu-šú-ma* UGU LUGAL.MEŠ *dan-nu-ú-tu*
30 1 *ù* ^{d}*iš-tar* [x x x x x x x x x (x x)] ⸢*i*⸣-*pu-šú-ma* UGU LUGAL.MEŠ *dan-nu-ú-tu*
30 2 [...] *ù* ^{d}AMAR.UTU *i-pu-šú-ma* UGU [...]

31 0 *ù* UGU LÚ.GAR.[KUR.MEŠ x x x x (x x)] *ú-šaq-qu-ú* ^{d}A-^{d}IŠKUR EN GAL-*ú* EN-*ia áš-al-ma*
31 1 *ù* UGU LÚ.GAR.[...-*q*]*u-ú* ^{d}A-^{d}IŠKUR EN GAL-*ú* EN-*ia áš-al-ma*
31 2 [...] *ú-šaq-qu-ú* ^{d}A-^{d}IŠKUR [...]

32 0 *ina a-mat* ^{d}A-^{d}IŠ[KUR] EN GAL-*ú* EN-*ia ina lìb-bi* 1 ME 5 GIŠ.GIGIR.MEŠ 2 ME 20 *pít-ḫal-lu* 3 LIM *zu*(*)-*uk* GÌR.II
32 1 *ina a-mat* ^{d}A-^{d}IŠ[KUR ...-*b*]*i* 1 ME 5 GIŠ.GIGIR.MEŠ 2 ME 20 *pít-ḫal-lu* 3 LIM *zu*(*)-*uk* GÌR.II
32 2 [...] EN GAL-*ú* EN-*ia ina lìb-bi* 1 ME 5 [...]

33 0 *ù* KUR *su-ḫi gab-bi ul ip-ḫu-ru a-na muḫ-ḫi-šú-nu a-na* EDIN *e-li-ma* 1-*en* u_4-*mi*
33 1 *ù* KUR *su-ḫi gab-b*[*i*(*) ...-*n*]*a muḫ-ḫi-šú-nu a-na* EDIN *e-li-ma* 1-*en* u_4-*mi*
33 2 [...] *gab-bi ul ip-ḫu-ru a-na m*[*uḫ*-...]

34 0 *i-na* UGU PÚ *ṣu-mu-ú-a ú-šib-ma šu-nu* 2 LIM-*šú-nu* ÉRIN.MEŠ GIŠ.BAN *a-na* UGU PÚ *ma-ki-ri*
34 1 *i-na* UGU PÚ *ṣu-mu*-⸢*ú*⸣-[...-*m*]*a šu-nu* 2 LIM-*šú-nu* ÉRIN.MEŠ GIŠ.BAN *a-na* UGU PÚ *ma-ki-ri*
34 2 [...] PÚ *ṣu-mu-ú-a ú-šib-ma šu*-[...]

35 0 *ik-šu-du-nim-ma a-na lìb-bi-šú-nu am-qu-ut-ma* 1 LIM 7 ME 11[+5(?)] ÉRIN.MEŠ *ina lìb-bi-šú-nu ad-duk*
35 1 *ik-šu-du-nim-ma a-na* ⸢*lìb-bi-šú*⸣-*nu am-qu-ut-ma* 1 LIM 7 ME 11[+5(?)] ÉRIN.MEŠ *ina lìb-bi-šú-nu ad-duk*
35 2 *ik-šu-du-nim-ma a-na lìb-bi-šú*-[...]

36 0 *ul-tu* PÚ *ma-ki-ri a-di* PÚ *gal-la-bu ù a-di* UGU PÚ ⸢*su*⸣-*ri*-⸢*bu*⸣ BAD_5.BAD_5-*šú-nu*
36 1 *ul-tu* PÚ *ma-ki-ri a-di* PÚ *gal-la-bu ù a-di* UGU PÚ ⸢*su*⸣-*ri*-⸢*bu*⸣ BAD_5.BAD_5-*šú-nu*
36 2 *ul-tu* PÚ *ma-ki-ri a-di* PÚ [...]

37 0 áš-kun gul-gul-la-ti-šu-nu KUR.MEŠ ù na-ḫal ⸢um⸣-dal-li ⸢ù šá⸣ 80 ⸢ÉRIN⸣.MEŠ ina lìb-bi-šú-nu
37 1 áš-kun gul-gul-la-ti-šu-nu KUR.MEŠ ù na-ḫal ⸢um⸣-dal-li ⸢ù šá⸣ 80 ⸢ÉRIN⸣.MEŠ ina lìb-bi-šú-nu
37 2 áš-kun gul-gul-la(*)-ti-šú-nu [...] ina lìb-bi-šú-nu

38 0 kap-pi-šú-nu sa-ap-sa-pi-šú-nu áš-ši-ma a-na da-li-li un-dáš-šìr-šu-nu-ti
38 1 kap-pi-šú-nu sa-ap-sa-pi-šú-nu áš-ši-ma a-na da-li-li-un-dáš-šìr-šu-nu-ti
38 2 kap-pi-šú-nu sa-a[p(*)-...] un-dáš-šìr(*)-šú-nu-ti

39 0 ù 2 ME ÉRIN.MEŠ bal-ṭu-ú-tu ina lìb-bi-šú-nu it-ta-par-ši-du(*) ù ^{m}šá-ma-ʾ-ga-am-ni
39 1 ù 2 ME ÉRIN.MEŠ bal-ṭu-ú-tu ina lìb-bi-šú-nu it-ta-par-ši-du(*) ù ^{m}šá-ma-ʾ-ga-am-ni
39 2 ù 2 ME ÉRIN.[...] ù ^{m}šá-ma-ʾ-ga-am-ni

40 0 LÚ.NIMGIR LÚ sa-ru-gu a-lik pa-ni-šú-nu LÚ.ÌR la tar-ṣu šá KUR su-ḫi KUR aš-šur.KI u AD.MEŠ-e-a
40 1 LÚ.NIMGIR(*) LÚ sa-ru-gu a-lik pa-ni-šú-nu LÚ.ÌR la tar-ṣu šá KUR su(*)-ḫi KUR aš-šur.KI u AD.MEŠ-e-a
40 2 LÚ.NIMGI[R ...] šá KUR su-ḫi KUR aš-šur.KI ù ⸢AD⸣ [...]

41 0 ú-šá-an-si(*)-<ku(?)>-šu ik-šu-ud ŠU.II-a-a a-⸢duk⸣-šú-ma i-nu-uḫ lìb-bi šá mam-ma ina lìb-bi AD.MEŠ-e-a
41 1 ú-šá-an-si(*)-<ku(?)>-šu ik-šu-ud ŠU.II-a-a a-⸢duk⸣-šú-ma i-nu-uḫ lìb-bi šá mam-ma ina lìb-bi AD.MEŠ-e-a
41 2 [...] i-nu-uḫ lìb-bi šá mam-ma ina lìb-[...]

42 0 la i-du-ku ana-ku ad-duk ⸢AD⸣.MEŠ-ú-a 10-šú LÚ.KÚR GAZ-ma ma-lu-ú-a ul ú-šam-ṣu-ú
42 1 la i-du-ku ana-ku ad-duk ⸢AD⸣.MEŠ-ú-a 10-šú LÚ.KÚR GAZ-ma ma-lu-ú-a ul ú-šam-ṣu-ú
42 2 [...] LÚ.KÚR i-du-ku-ma <ma>-lu-ú-a u[l ...]

43 0 ana-ku 1-et di-ik-ti a-duk-ma a-na la AD.MEŠ-e-a ú-šá-tir$_{X}$(DIR) man-ni ár-ku-ú šá E$_{11}$-ma
43 1 ana-ku 1-et di-ik-ti a-duk-ma a-na la AD.MEŠ-e-a ú-šá-tir$_{X}$(DIR) man-ni ár-ku-ú šá E$_{11}$-ma
43 2 [...] a-na la AD.MEŠ-ú-a ú-šá-t[ir$_{X}$(DIR)(*) ...]

44 0 i-qab-bu-ú um-ma ki-i-ki-i ^{md}MAŠ-NÍG.DU-PAB LÚ.GAR KUR su-ḫi u KUR ma-ri di-ik-ti
44 1 i-qab-bu-ú um-ma ki-i-ki-i ^{md}MAŠ-NÍG.DU-PAB LÚ.GAR KUR su-ḫi u KUR ma-ri di-ik-ti
44 2 [...] um-ma ki-i-ki-i ^{md}MAŠ-N[ÍG....]

45 0 *an-ni-tu*$_4$ *id-duk ul i-na e-muq-ia a-duk ina e-muq* ^{d}UTU *u* ^{d}AM[AR].UTU ^{d}IŠKUR *u* ^{d}A-^{d}IŠKUR
45 1 *an-ni-tu*$_4$ *id-duk ul i-*⸢*na*⸣ *e-muq-ia a-duk ina e-muq* ^{d}UTU *u* ^{d}AM[AR].UTU ^{d}IŠKUR *u* ^{d}A-^{d}IŠKUR
45 2 [...] *id-duk ul i-na e*(*)-*mu-q*[*í-*...] *ù* ^{d}A-^{d}IŠKUR

46 0 DINGIR.MEŠ GAL.MEŠ EN.MEŠ-*e-a di-ik-ti an-ni-*⸢*tu*$_4$⸣ *ad-duk man-ni ár-ku-ú šá* E$_{11}$*-ma*
46 1 [DIN]GIR.MEŠ GAL.MEŠ EN.MEŠ-*e-a di-ik-ti an-ni-*⸢*tu*$_4$⸣ *ad-duk man-ni ár-ku-ú šá* E$_{11}$*-ma*
46 2 DINGIR.MEŠ GAL.MEŠ [...] *šá* E$_{11}$*-ma*

47 0 *ši-bu-ut* KUR-*šú ù ši-b*[*u*]-⸢*tu*⸣ *šá* KUR *la-qé-e liš-*⸢*al*⸣*-ma um-ma* ⸢*kit*⸣*-tu-ú*
47 1 [*ši-bu-u*]*t* KUR-*šú ù ši-b*[*u*]-⸢*tu*⸣ *šá* KUR *la-qé-e liš-*⸢*al*⸣*-ma um-ma* ⸢*kit*⸣*-tu-ú*
47 2 *ši-bu-ut* KUR-*šú* ⸢*ù*⸣ [...]

48 0 *šá* ^{md}MAŠ-NÍG.DU-PAB LÚ.GAR KUR *su-ḫi u* KUR *má-rí ina a-mat* ^{d}A-^{d}IŠKUR EN GAL-*ú* EN-*šú*
48 1 [....D]U-PAB LÚ.GAR KUR *su-ḫi u* KUR *má-rí ina a-mat* ^{d}A-^{d}IŠKUR EN GAL-*ú* EN-*šú*
48 2 *šá* ^{md}MAŠ-NÍG.DU-PAB LÚ.GAR KUR *su-ḫi u* [...]

49 0 [*dīktu*] *an-ni-ti i-du-ku a-ga-a ši-kin qa-ti šá* ^{d}A-^{d}IŠKUR DINGIR EN-*ia*
49 1 [...-*t*]*u*$_4$ *i-du-ku a-ga-a ši-kin qa-ti šá* ^{d}A-^{d}IŠKUR DINGIR EN-*ia*
49 2 [...] *an-ni-ti i-du-ku a-ga-a ši-*[...]

50 0 [x x x x] *i-ra-man-ni-ma dul-la an-na-a a-na* ŠU.II-*ia iš-kun*
50 1 [x x x x x x-*m*]*an-ni-ma dul-la an-na-a a-na* ŠU.II-*ia iš-kun*
50 2 [...] *i-ra-man-ni-ma dul-la an-na-*⸢*a*⸣ [...]

51 0 *ba-*⸢*a*⸣*-*[*ri*]
51 1 [(...)]
51 2 *ba-*⸢*a*⸣*-*[*ri*]

www.ingramcontent.com/pod-product-compliance
Lightning Source LLC
LaVergne TN
LVHW082158080826
844660LV00046B/1280
9781442623743